DICTIONARY OF PUKHTO/ PUSHTO LANGUAGE OF THE AFGHANS

DICTIONARY OF PUKHTO/ PUSHTO LANGUAGE OF THE AFGHANS

H. G. RAVERTY

GYAN

Published by

Gyan Publishing House
5, Ansari Road
Daryaganj, New Delhi-110002
Phone: 011-47034999, 9811692060
E-mail: books@gyanbooks.com

Distribution Network
gyanbooks.com
India, USA, Canada, UK, Australia, France

ISBN : 978-81-212-4291-2 (PB)

2nd Impression 2020

Printed at: Gyan Press, Delhi.

Dictionary of Pukhto/ Pushto Language of The Afghans
Author: H. G. Raverty

A

DICTIONARY

OF THE

PUḰHTO, PUŚHTO,

OR

LANGUAGE OF THE AFGHĀNS;

WITH

REMARKS ON THE ORIGINALITY OF THE LANGUAGE,

AND ITS AFFINITY TO OTHER ORIENTAL TONGUES,

ETC., ETC.:

BY

MAJOR H. G. RAVERTY,

BOMBAY ARMY, RETIRED LIST.

AUTHOR OF A GRAMMAR OF THE PUŚHTO LANGUAGE; THE GULSHAN-I-ROH, OR PROSE AND POETICAL SELECTIONS IN THE PUŚHTO OR AFGHAN LANGUAGE; THE POETRY OF THE AFGHĀNS, TRANSLATED FROM THE ORIGINALS IN THE PUŚHTO LANGUAGE; THE GOSPEL FOR THE AFGHĀNS; A THESAURUS OF ENGLISH AND HINDŪSTĀNĪ TECHNICAL TERMS, ETC. ETC.

خوشحال خان او دولتا مي غلامان دي   زه رحمان په پښتو ژنه عالم گير يم

SECOND EDITION, WITH CONSIDERABLE ADDITIONS.

LONDON:

WILLIAMS AND NORGATE,

HENRIETTA STREET, COVENT GARDEN, AND 20, SOUTH FREDERICK STREET, EDINBURGH.

CALCUTTA:

W. NEWMAN AND CO.

MDCCCLXVII.

STEPHEN AUSTIN,

PRINTER, HERTFORD.

TO THE RIGHT HONORABLE

SIR STAFFORD HENRY NORTHCOTE, BART., M.P., C.B.,

SECRETARY OF STATE FOR INDIA,

AND

PRESIDENT OF THE INDIAN COUNCIL,

THIS DICTIONARY OF THE PUS'HTO LANGUAGE,

IS,

BY SPECIAL PERMISSION,

RESPECTFULLY DEDICATED

BY HIS MOST OBEDIENT SERVANT,

H. G. RAVERTY, MAJOR
BOMBAY ARMY, RETIRED LIST.

LIST OF SUBSCRIBERS TO THE THREE WORKS.

The Royal Library, Windsor Castle.
His Royal Highness the Prince Consort.
His Grace the Duke of Manchester.
The Right Honorable the Earl of Derby, K.G.
The Right Honorable Lord Viscount Palmerston, K.G.
The Right Honorable John, Baron Elphinstone, G.C.B., K.C.H., etc. etc , late Governor of Bombay.
The Right Rev. The Lord Bishop of St. David's.
Lord A. Vane Tempest, M.P.
His Excellency M. Kowalewski, Minister of Public Instruction, for the Imperial Government of Russia.
His Excellency Count Keilmansegge, for the Government of Hanover.
His Excelleney Count D'Apponyi, for the Imperial Government of Austria.
His Excellency Count Bernstorf, for the Government of Prussia.
His Excellency Count Platen, for the Government of Sweden.
His Excellency the Marquis D'Azeglio, for the Government of Sardinia.
His Excellency Baron de Cetto, for the Government of Bavaria.
His Excellency le Ministre de la Maison de l'Empereur.
The Government of Spain.
His Excellency M. Rogier, Belgian Minister of the Interior.
The Royal Library, Copenhagen.
The Honorable the Court of Directors of the East India Company.
The (late) Honorable Mountstuart Elphinstone (formerly Envoy at the Court of Caubul).
Bibliotheque Imperial, Paris.
Major General Sir Henry Rawlinson, K.C.B., late Envoy to the Shāh of Persia.
Major General Sir Proby Thomas Cautley, K.C.B., Member of the Council of India.
His Highness the Rājā of Travancore.
Lieutenant General W. Cullen, Madras Artillery, Resident in Travancore.
The Nawwāb Sālār Jang, Minister of His Highness the Nizām of the Dahkan.
The Right Honorable Sir Erskine Perry, Knt., M.P.
The Honorable A. Murray, late Ambassador at the Court of Persia.
The Royal Society of Literature.
The Royal Geographical Society.
The Library of the London Institution.
University Library, Edinburgh.
The Church Missionary Society.
The Society for the Propagation of the Gospel in Foreign Parts.
The London Missionary Society.
The Wesleyan Missionary Society.
The Library, Presbyterian Missionary Society, New York.
The Imperial Academy of Sciences, St. Petersburgh, through M. Bernhard Dorn, Phil. Doct.

University Library, Glasgow.
The Rev. Dr. Bandinel, Bodleian Library, Oxford.
J. Stuart Dalton, Esq., Librarian Free Public Library, Liverpool.
Professor Monier Williams (late Professor of Sanskrit, East India College, Haileybury), Cheltenham.
Professor Max Müller, All Souls' College, Oxford.
Dr. Reinhold Rost, LL.D., Professor of Oriental Languages, St. Augustine's College, Canterbury.
Rev. Peter Daly, P.P., Galway.
Messrs. Longman and Co., Paternoster Row, London.
Messrs. J. H. and J. Parker, Oxford.
Messrs. Trübner and Co., American Literary Agency, London.
Messrs. Williams and Norgate, London, Edinburgh, and Leipzig.
Messrs. A. Asher and Co., Berlin.
Stephen Austin, Oriental Printer and Bookseller, Hertford.

BOMBAY PRESIDENCY.

The Honorable the Government of Bombay.
Colonel Walter Scott, Chief Engineer, Bombay Engineers.
Colonel Haughton James, Commandant of Fortress of Aseergurh.
Major W. H. R. Green, C.B., 19th Regt. Bombay N.I., Political Agent in Balūchistān.
James Christie, Esq., Assistant Military Accountant General, Bombay.
Commodore Ethersey (the late), Indian Navy.
Assistant Surgeon J. P. Stratton, Esq., M.D., Civil Employ.
The Bombay Branch Royal Asiatic Society.
Arthur St. John Richardson, Esq., Bombay Civil Service.
Captain P. A. Elphinstone, 18th Regt. Bombay N.I.
Lieutenant J. Havelock, 6th Regt. Bombay N.I.
Captain T. M. Baumgartner, H.M. 83rd Regt. Foot.
Lieutenant E. J. Checkley (the late), 19th Regt. Bombay N.I.

MADRAS PRESIDENCY.

The Honorable the Government of Madras.
The Madras Literary Society.
E. Story, Esq., Madras Civil Service.
Lieutenant M. W. Carr, Quarter Master and Interpreter, 9th Regt. Madras N.I.

PANJĀB AND ITS DEPENDENCIES.

The Government of the Panjāb.
Lieutenant Colonel A. Cunningham, Secretary to the Government of the North-west Provinces
Captain Stuart Graham, Deputy Commissioner of Peshāwar, for the District Courts.
Lieutenant P. W. Powlett, Assistant Commissioner, Peshāwar.
Rev. Isidor Lowenthal, for the Afghān Mission.
Rev. R. Clark, for the Church Mission, Peshāwar.
Rev. Dr. Ernest Trumpp, Peshāwar.
Lieutenant G. Short, Assistant Commissioner, Hotī Mardān, Peshāwar.
Colonel H. B. Lumsden, C.B., Commandant Panjāb Guide Corps.

Lieutenant T. G. Kennedy, Adjutant Panjāb Guide Corps, Peshāwar.
George D. Westropp, Esq., Extra Assistant Commissioner, Rawul Pandee.
Lieutenant Colonel W. T. Martin, Retired List, Peshāwar.
Mīr Akbar Æālī, Director of Canals Office, Mahdūpūr, Gordāspūr.
A. K. Blackall, Esq., Extra Assistant Commissioner, Mooltan.
Lieutenant-Colonel G. W. Hamilton, Commissioner Mooltan Division.
P. O'Brien, Esq., Canal Department, Mooltan.
William Lloyd, Esq., Gordāspūr.
D. W. McLeod, Esq., B.C.S., C.B., Financial Commissioner for the Panjāb.
Captain N. W. Elphinstone, Deputy Commissioner.
Captain J. E. Cracroft, Deputy Commissioner.
Frederick Cooper, Esq., B.C.S., C.B., Deputy Commissioner.
Major J. R. Becher, C.B., Deputy Commissioner, Hazārah.
Lieutenant W. F. Leicester, 3rd Regt. Sikh Infantry.
Carapit Stephen, Esq., Extra Assistant Commissioner, Pānīpatt.
G. Barnes, Esq., B.C.S., C.B., Commissioner Cis-Sutlej States.
Major J. Wale, Brigade Major (the late), Peshāwar.
C. J. Luckstedt, Esq.
Major W. A. Crommelin, C.B., Bengal Engineers.
Major J. A. Wilson, Executive Engineer, Hazārah.
Captain F. J. Davies, 58th Regt. Bengal N.I.
Captain W. S. Oliphant, Bengal Engineers.
Captain A. W. Garnett, Bengal Engineers, Kohatt.
Captain J. Pulladio Basevi, Bengal Engineers, Derajāt.
Captain Sir W. Hamilton, Bart., Bengal Artillery.
Major-General John Nicholson (the late), Bengal Army, Deputy Commissioner, Derah Ismāæil Khān.
Captain C. J. Curtis, Commandant 6th Regt. Bengal Irregular Cavalry.
Arthur Brandreth, Esq., B.C.S., Settlement Officer, Panjāb.
Lieutenant-Colonel Alexander Taylor, C.B., Bengal Engineers.

BENGAL PRESIDENCY.

The Asiatic Society of Bengal.
Captain W. Nassau Lees, LL.D., for the College of Fort William.
Captain W. Nassau Lees, LL.D., for the Calcutta Madrasa.
R. Gamble, Esq., M.D., H.M. 24th Regt. Foot.
Lieutenant F. B. Norman, 14th Regt. Bengal N.I.
Captain F. E. Smallpage, Bengal Artillery.
Major C. Pattenson, 4th Regt. Bengal N.I.
Captain H. A. Browne, 10th Regt. Bengal N.I.
Lieutenant R. H. Price, 31st Regt. Bengal N.I.
Ensign E. A. Phillips (the late) 11th Regt. Bengal N.I.
Professor Gryffith, Benares College.
Captain G. W. McBarnet (the late), 55th Regt. Bengal N.I.
Major George O. Jacob (the late) 1st Bengal Fusiliers.

ERRATA.

PAGE	LINE	FOR	READ
18	last	bandy-legged, etc.	bandy-legs, etc.
22	14	آريري	آريري
37	36	كروه	كدوه
47	9	comp. of s etc.	corrup. of s etc.
53	43	انخير	انخر
61	32	ارو	اره
63	33	ړاود	اوړد
69	23	ninety-eight,	ninety-nine.
79	2	*bājawarrey,*	*bājawarraey.*
82	11	s.f. (2nd),	s.m. (2nd).
85	11	*bālikhta-kān,*	*bālikhtak-ān*
87, 88	44, 2	بتان *batān*, etc.	*battān*, etc.
89	21	re-instalment,	re-installment.
92	38	*bud-ra'ī,*	*bud-rī.*
106	6	cerclew,	curlew.
112	19	*blārbejzey,*	*blārbejzī.*
113	21	to-morrow,	day after to-morrow
116	9	tuft of gorse,	tuft of reed, or long grass.
118	3	fem.	fut.
120	25	s.m. (6th)	s.m. (5th) Pl. بوران *bawrān.*
121	17	cerclew,	curlew.
126	31	prosperity,	prosperous.
132	37	ecstacy,	ecstasy.
135	7	طالع بي	بي طالع
140	28	s.m. (5th)	s.m. (6th)
153	33	fermenter	fomenter.
167	31	*jaley,*	*jalaey.*
168	16	verb intrans.	verb trans.
,,	26	پري ربه دي	پري به ړدي
185	30-34	پلوند *palwand, etc.*	پلوند *palwandd*, etc.
188	2	پمبن	پمنه
195	6	پورونكي and پوروني	پورونكي and پورونيَ
208	19	ؤ پيژانده	ؤ پيژانده
,,	21	پيژندنكي	پيژندونكي
214	9	to fasten, tie, etc.	to become fastened, tied, etc.
225	4	act. past.	act. part.
238	40	*trott khwarral,* or *rasedal*, etc.	*trott khwarral*, verb trans. or *rasedal*, etc.
239	33	ترهكيي	ترهيكي
268	33	*tor-bakhtey,*	*tor-bakhtaey.*
275	10	s.f. (2nd),	s.f. (3rd).
283	11	ناق وهل verb intrans.	verb trans.
285	25	*wajzey* or *wagey,*	*wajzaey* or *wagaey*
287	28	s.m. (1st),	s.f. Pl. (3rd).
291	13	*ttak-sarey-shaey,*	*ttak-saraey-shaey.*
296	35	to truss, to stack, etc.	the meanings have been transposed for the two meanings "to assemble, to muster," and *vice versa* in last line.
308	26	*tsrapwūnkaey,*	*tsrapawūnkaey.*
310	17	*tsar-masha'ī*, etc.	*tsar-mashka'ī*. etc.
315	3	cohesion,	cohesiveness.
378	25	April-May,	March-April.
504	22	past part.	act. part.
564	7	s.m. (1st)	s.f. (3rd) Pl.
609	28	Agency,	Agony.
723	41	See تنرا	See تنر
736	9	s.m. (4th)	s.m. (2nd)
740	18	Scarbæus,	Scarabæus.
825	31	pres.	pl.
881	34	gorse, reed, long grass	reed, or long grass
888	24	ايوت	لويت
954	37	s.m. (4th)	s.m. (4th) (E.) s.m. (2nd) (W.)

PREFACE.

It will generally be allowed, I imagine, that the position of the British with regard to the Afghāns and their country, since the annexation of the Panjāb—by which a large portion of Afghānistān Proper, containing nearly two millions of inhabitants, came under our rule—demands that due attention should be paid by the government officials to the language of the people over whom they are appointed as rulers and administrators.

The late state of affairs in Persia and Central Asia, and the visit of our old antagonist, the Amīr, Dost Muḥammad Khān, Bārakzī, to Peshāwer, appear like "coming events" that "cast their shadows before," and indicate the desire of the British Indian Government with regard to our future connection with the Afghān tribes, who look upon an alliance with their former enemies with much less aversion than formerly. Indeed, they appear unquestionably inclined to become our friends; and it will depend entirely on the temper and tact of the agents of the Government to bring about this most politic and desirable result. It is necessary, too, that we should not lose sight of the important events which must arise in Afghānistān on the death of the Dost, now a very aged man, and the influence of those events upon our relations with Central Asia and its little known tribes.

On all future occasions, however, if we desire to avoid the disasters that followed the failures and blunderings of Burnes and others, we must take care to avoid the mistake of employing any native go-betweens, in the shape of Hindū "Knights of the Lion and Sun," or Multānī or Hindūstānī Afghāns, who are a very different and far inferior race to the Afghāns proper, who, indeed, hold them in the greatest contempt. The persons I refer to are never to be depended upon: they constantly intrigue for the purpose of making themselves necessary to us, and end in deceiving both sides—English and Afghāns. But we can only free ourselves from dependence upon them, by sending as agents into the country men practically acquainted with the language spoken by the people, or, at least, with the language in general use at the Court of the ruler to which they may be accredited. This policy is so indispensable, that there are no circumstances under which a departure from it should be permitted.

The deplorable events of the last few years have shown, that we must, in future, draw largely on the Hill tribes of the north-west frontier of India to fill the ranks of the Indian army. When no dependence whatever could be placed on the Native Regular or Irregular troops of Hindūstān, and when regiment after regiment was mutinying or being disarmed, the Irregular Corps of the Derājāt, the majority of which were chiefly, and some of them exclusively,—composed of Afghāns, were staunch and faithful, and aided in disarming and destroying the mutineers. At Peshāwer, one corps, standing side by side with the European troops, attacked the mutinous Sepoys of the late 55th N. I.; and on the flight of the latter to the mountains of Suwāt, it was detached, alone, to complete their destruction. The 1st Bombay Baluch Battalion, consisting chiefly of Afghāns, proved equally reliable, and formed a portion of the storming columns at Delhī, along with the Panjāb Guides and other Afghān corps.

It has, therefore, been proved, that dependence may be placed on Afghān soldiers, especially when opposed to other races, or to different tribes of their own countrymen. And who that has ever seen the hardy and sturdy Afghāns on their native hills, can, for a moment doubt that these men—who have on more than one occasion been themselves the conquerors of Hindūstān, and who have ever been the best troops in the armies of other invaders—would, if organised and trained like the regular Native Regiments, and led by an equal number of European officers, be second to none but European troops, and more than a match for the soldiers of every other Asiatic nation?

The Afghān country, in many places, is poor; and the people—too proud to follow any other callings than those of arms, agriculture, or trade, and wanting land to cultivate, or a commerce large enough for their employment, have frequently found it difficult to procure a subsistence. Hence, for centuries past, great numbers of Afghāns, Pattāns, or Rohilahs, as they are variously termed, have entered into the military service of other native States. The re-organization of the Bengal Army, therefore, affords an opportunity, which should by no means be lost, of availing ourselves of the services of this race. Henceforth we should enlist Afghāns, as well as Sikhs and Gūrkahs, into every regiment; or what would be better still, as tending to secure a praiseworthy emulation and rivalry, and, in case of accident, enabling us to employ one race against the other, and prevent combination—we should form them into distinct corps, according to their nationality. Surely, in future, no dependence will be placed on the bloodthirsty and fanatical Musalmān of India, or the mild-seeming but merciless and bigoted Brāhmin and other Pūrbīah castes. The atrocities they have so lately perpetrated make it impossible for us to trust in them; but the Afghāns are a different race.*

* To give the Afghāns their due, although they did act treacherously towards us on the retreat from Kābul in 1842, yet we were invaders of their country; and, treating us as such, they attacked and destroyed our force: but the prisoners they took were safe, and the women and children were respected. This offers a very favorable contrast, on the part of an uncivilized race, to the demoniacal doings, at Delhī and Khānpūr, of those who for more than a century had been eating our salt, and were considered to have advanced a good way in the scale of civilization.

From the intercourse with the Afghān people, to which my researches into their language and literature during the last twelve or fourteen years have naturally led, I know that the Western Afghāns are desirous of cultivating our friendship, and would be glad to see a British force again located at Kandahār, were it only to deliver them from the grinding tyranny of Dost Muḥammad Khān, or rather of his sons; or, at least, to restrain their oppression. The people look back with not a little regret to the time of our sojourn, when money flowed freely, and when, as they say, "a man could enjoy in security the fruits of his own industry."

The fault will have been entirely on our own part if the late golden opportunity has not been taken advantage of, and the foundation of friendly intercourse laid upon a firm basis. But one great fact should be remembered in all our intercourse with the Afghāns—that they are, in disposition and temper, not at all unlike Irishmen and Scottish Highlanders of a century or two ago: they may be led but are not to be driven; and a bearish, overbearing manner, on the part of those who come into contact with them, whatever their rank or position may be, and however well it may answer with a tyranny-worshipping Panjābī and Hindūstānī idiosyncrasy, will produce quite a contrary effect upon the free and independent sons of the mountains.

The Afghāns, being Sunnīs, or orthodox Muḥammadans, are held in high esteem among the people of Islām; but for the same reason they are the bitter and natural enemies of their Shīææ neighbours, the Persians, who, with equally rancorous feeling, hate the Afghāns, and have occasion to remember the conquest of their country by the Ghalzī tribe in the former half of the last century. And, as we all know that no enmity burns so fiercely as that of religious fanatics and schismatics, we may be certain there will be no danger of the Afghān people throwing themselves into the arms of the Mughal, on any occasion, without very pressing reasons for taking such a course. Hatred on the part of the Afghāns towards the Farangīs, or rather towards the English, is of comparatively recent growth: Englishmen, or any other Europeans, could visit any part of Afghānistān, unattended and unmolested, as in the case of Vinge and Masson, before the fatal *faux pas* of the Burnes's, the Mohan Lāls, and others; whilst at present, in the twelfth year of the Panjāb annexation, Europeans, if they venture to take an evening ride outside the bounds of the cantonments at Peshāwer and other border stations, unarmed and unattended, do so at the risk of their lives.

The death of Dost Muḥammad Khān, who has long since passed his seventieth year, is an event which cannot be far off. It will be the signal for dissensions that will, I fear, deluge Afghānistān with blood; and in which, for the sake of our own safety, we may be compelled, as in the case of the Sikhs, to interfere. Therefore, in whatever light the question be viewed, the cultivation of the Pus͟hto language is necessary. As a means of present intercommunication, and as a preparation for the future, it should be insisted upon by the British Government—"a monarchy of many kings, whose sceptre sways over the entire length and breadth of India, and the ægis of whose power casts its broad shadow over the whole East."*

But there is another incentive to the cultivation of Pus͟hto. The Russians have, for some time past, paid great attention to, and made great progress in, the study of the Afg͟hān language; the Imperial Government having, as usual, been most liberal with its aid for that especial purpose,† and the Pus͟hto is now taught, as well as other Oriental tongues, at St. Petersburgh, although the Russians do not hold an inch of land where it is spoken. The Russian capital is, indeed, the only city in the world where the Afg͟hān language is made a branch of study. The British authorities in the Panjāb, though ruling over a large portion of Afg͟hānistān Proper, containing nearly two millions of people, to whom Puś͟hto is the mother tongue, have hitherto wholly neglected it.

Let us turn, however, to the Bombay province of Sindh, with about half the number of inhabitants, and not yielding so great an amount of revenue as our Afg͟hān districts. There the Sindhīān dialect is used in all the Civil Courts; liberal premiums are given to officers and others, as an inducement to qualify themselves and pass an examination in the language; and officers in civil employ must pass before they are confirmed in their appointments, or considered eligible for promotion. Yet the Sindhīān language has no literature in comparison with the Pus͟hto, and no aids beyond a short grammar by Wathen, published many years since, and another by Stack, who also prepared a vocabulary; but who, surprising to state, instead of using the Nask͟h character of the Arabic, in which Sindhīān books are written, has adopted the Nāgrī character of the Sanskrit for both his works, probably because unacquainted with the Nask͟h.‡ If so much can be done in Sindh with such few appliances, surely much more may be effected beyond the Indus, now that the necessary aids for the acquirement of the Puś͟hto language are available, and its study and cultivation merely require to be enforced by the authorities.

A mission has for some time past been established at Pes͟hāwer to evangelize the Afg͟hāns, and may probably, in time—but very slowly, if we are to judge from the progress hitherto made,—do something to advance the study of the language; but any great success cannot be expected until schools (which would be attended, I

* "The Kings of the East, and Exposition of the Prophecies," p. 155.

† The present works have also shared in this liberality; and I take this opportunity of respectfully acknowledging the support of His Excellency M. Kowalewski, Minister of Public Instruction at St. Petersburg, and of Professor Bernhard Dorn, of the Imperial Academy of Sciences.

‡ For a number of years past, a German missionary, who considers himself learned in Oriental lore (and himself only), has been employed upon a Sindhīān Dictionary, which is not likely to be completed, I am told, the greater portion of the time having been devoted to disputes and discussions about determining the character to be used. One would have fancied that the character in which its literature is written would be the one to follow.

have no doubt, even by persons beyond our frontier) are established for the express study of Pushto. Little real progress, however, will in any case be effected until the example is set on the part of Government, by the issue and enforcement of a general order, making it incumbent on all officers, whether civil or military, staff or regimental, holding appointments beyond the Indus, to qualify in the language of the people. A year's perseverance, to the extent of a few hours' study daily, with the helps now obtainable, ought to enable any person of ordinary abilities to acquire a decent knowledge of the Afghān tongue.

The plea for not enforcing the study of the Pushto language hitherto, has been the want of guide books, without which the acquirement of such a language is certainly up-hill work; and, undoubtedly, requires more patience and persevering industry than the generality of people in India are endowed with. To remove this difficulty, I now submit the fruit of the labours of every spare moment—often snatched from the necessary hours of rest and repose—of my life during the last twelve years, in the shape of the present work; together with a Text Book entitled "Gulshan-i-Roh," or "The Flower-garden of Roh"—as the Afghān country is termed by ancient writers—containing selections, in poetry and prose, from the writings of all the standard native authors, and from many rare MSS. not to be met with in the present day; and a copious Grammar, the second edition of which, considerably improved and extended, is published with this Dictionary. These works will, I hope, prove useful to Officers in India, to the Orientalists of Europe and Asia, and to the Public generally to whom Oriental subjects are attractive, or who may feel interested in the *Ban-i-Isrāīl*, as the Afghāns term themselves—THE LOST TRIBES OF THE HOUSE OF ISRAEL. The translation of the New Testament into Pushto, just completed previous to leaving India a few months back, and translations into English of a great number of the poems of celebrated authors, will probably close my studies; for, after having devoted seventeen of the best years of my life, and expended much money in acquiring, more or less, a knowledge of nine Oriental languages, I find that the pursuit has never brought me advantage or advancement—in fact, nothing but the satisfaction which one derives from the habit of patient labour and the fact of knowing.

As regards natives of India, and the Afghāns themselves, no grammar exists in the Pushto itself that could be available for them; but this obstacle can be remedied. I have already offered to compile one from the Grammar I have just published, if such encouragement, as I might naturally expect to receive from the Indian or the British Government, be extended to me.

Having thus set forth, and, I trust, proved, the imperative necessity of cultivating and encouraging the study of the Afghān language, it will be, doubtless, expected that I should offer some remarks on the Pushto, and the family to which it belongs.

INTRODUCTORY REMARKS.

"The gross errors of European writers on Asiatic literature have long convinced me that no satisfactory account can be given of any nation with whose language we are not perfectly acquainted."—Sir William Jones.

Some Orientalists of the present day have endeavoured to make out that the Pu<u>sh</u>to language belongs to the Indian or Indū-Teutonic family of tongues, because it contains some Sanskrit words, and because the Urdū or Hindūstānī dialect bears, as it is affirmed, some resemblance in point of idiom. Some persons have even gone to such lengths as to assert that the Pu<u>sh</u>to is not a written language. They, however, are not to be recognized as authorities on such a subject. One of these assertions, contained in a note to a work entitled, "Caravan Journeys, and Wanderings in Persia, Afghanistan, etc.," by J. P. Ferrier, is worth quoting,—"There is some excuse for this irregularity in spelling Afghan words, *the Pushto being merely a colloquial language*." * So much for Sir J. Login's authority on the matter, for the note in question is said to be from his pen. It, however, seems to have been entirely overlooked by those who would prove the former theory, that the Pu<u>sh</u>to contains a far greater number of Semitic, Zand, Pehlavī, Persian, and Turkish words, and bears much more similarity to the modern Persian and the Semitic languages than to the hybrid dialect called *Urdū*, the meaning of which Turkish word, signifying a *camp* or *army*, in itself shows that it was formed in the camps of the Mu<u>gh</u>al invaders and their successors, whose legions, drawn from almost every country of the Asiatic continent, and some even from Africa, contained Mu<u>gh</u>als, Persians, Af<u>gh</u>āns, Balū<u>ch</u>īs, Arabs, Georgians, Kūrds, Tūrkomāns, Kalmāks, and other Tārtar tribes; Abyssiniāns, Ethiopians, and Negroes; together with Brāhmans, Rājpūts, Marā<u>tt</u>as, and other races of the peninsula of India. It was, consequently, a sort of *olla-podrida*, containing words of each language, so as to meet the wants of the parties composing the motley and heterogeneous armies of those who swayed the sceptre of India. In fact, the Urdū was formed much in the same manner as the *lingua franca* spoken on the shores of the Mediterranean.

It is certainly true that the Pu<u>sh</u>to dialect has many words which are also to be met with in the Urdū; but the whole of these, when not clearly traceable to the

* Page 185.

Sanskrit, I am inclined to consider—at least until they can be satisfactorily proved to belong to some other original language—pure Pushto terms that have, in the same manner as Sanskrit, Arabic, Persian, etc., and even Portuguese and Malāyam words, been appropriated and adopted into the *rekhtah* or 'scattered,' another term applied to the camp language of Hindūstān.

That this should be the case is by no means astonishing, when we take into consideration the prominent part which, since the invasions of Maḥmūd of Ghaznī, in the twelfth century of our era, the Afghāns have played upon the theatre of the Indian peninsula; their constant and continual influx; their conquests and permanent settlements therein; and the fact that their descendants, by intermarriage with the natives, are known as Hindūstānī Pattāns, who still constitute a large portion of the Muḥammadans of India, and who, almost exclusively, speak the Urdū language. To such an extent did these immigrations extend, that some tribes have long since totally disappeared from Afghānistān, and their descendants now are only to be found in India itself.

In some localities in India, however, the offspring of the Afghān settlers have preserved the Pushto language almost in its purity up to the present day, having, from the outset, continued to intermarry amongst themselves; and in some parts of Bandalkand and in the territory of the Rāmpūr Nawwāb, whole towns and villages may be found in which the Afghān language is still almost exclusively spoken, and is the vehicle of general communication.*

It does not appear, also, to have been taken into consideration that the Urdū is, comparatively, a very modern language, formed, so far as we can discover, as recently as the period of the foundation of the kingdom of Delhī—where it has ever been, and still continues to be, most pure and cultivated—in the reign of the Emperor Akbar, at which time attention began to be paid to Indian literature; and after whose accession, purely Muḥammadan learning, derived from the Arabs, which had flourished in the preceding reigns, began to decline. I have in my possession Pushto works which were composed very many years before and during Akbar's reign (from A.D. 1555 to 1604); whilst the earliest author who wrote in the Urdū dialect is the poet Wālī, who flourished so recently as the middle of the seventeenth century—two hundred and thirty-seven years after Shaykh Malī, Yūsufzī, in A.D. 1417, wrote the "History of his tribe and their conquests in the Peshāwer Valley, and in the Sama'h or Plain, on the northern bank of the Landdaey Sind or Kābul River." This is the earliest work I have been able to discover; but, of course, it must not for a moment be inferred that previous to this there was no Pushto literature. On the contrary, Ākhūnd Darwezah mentions in his work entitled "Taẕkirāt-ul-Abarār," written in Persian, that in his time there was a celebrated book entitled صراح "The Pure," which had been in the possession of the Yūsufzīs for some cen-

* Elphinstone's "Caubul."

turies past, and was ever held in great veneration by the tribe. Another history in Pushto was written by Khān Kajū, Rārrnīzī, in the year 1494 A.D.; and a hundred years before we meet with a single work in Urdū, Ākhūnd Darwezah, wrote his "Makhzan Pushto," in refutation of the tenets of the Roshānīān sect of schismatics, promulgated by its founder Bāyazīd Anṣārī, and contained in a work entitled "Khair-ul-By-ān." In this very work the Ākhūnd refers to the Pushto authors who had preceded him; and, therefore, it is plain that the Pushto had been in existence as a written language several centuries before the Urdū dialect was formed. That the Pushto is a very ancient tongue cannot be doubted.

Other dialects sprung up about the same time as the Urdū—the Guzarāttī, and the languages of the Dakhan—which have largely drawn on Persian and Arabic, but without forming a new language.

What has been chiefly urged with regard to the similarity of idiom between the two languages is, that the past tenses of transitive verbs, both Pushto and Urdū, are governed by the objective case; but in the latter, together with the Marāttī, Guzarāttī, and other cognate dialects of the Sanskrit family, the particle نے (*ne*)—in Sanskrit ना or ना—proving their Indian origin, immediately follows, or is affixed to the nominative or noun denoting the *agent*, which, if not the first or second personal pronoun, is inflected, if capable of inflection. The verb, however, is made to agree with the object in gender and number—*quite contrary to the foregoing rule*—provided the object be, as is most usual, in the nominative case. When, however, the *object* is placed in the oblique case, or is not a word but a member of the sentence, *the verb must then be used invariably in the third person masculine singular.** There is, likewise, but one form of personal pronoun in the Urdū.

Pushto, on the other hand, has no such particle whatever as نے; and it has no less than four classes of pronouns—the two first, prefixed personal, that may or may not be used with the verbs; and affixed personal, which have no meanings apart from the verbs, and correspond to the Semitic dialects, the Pehlavī, and modern Persian, and in which respect the Sindhīān language also agrees. With regard to the two other classes of pronouns, one is used with the past tenses of transitive verbs in the active voice, to denote the *agent*, and has no signification separate from the verbs. With any other than transitives, the construction entirely changes, and the pronouns then point out the *object* or the *possessive* case. The other class is a mere pronominal affix, and is alone used, both with transitives and intransitives, to denote the *object* in a sentence, and in the formation of the compound infinitives, of which there are several in Pushto.

The past tenses of Pushto transitives, contrary to Urdū, *must* invariably agree with the *object* both in gender, number, and person, the agent being in the instrumental case; and to this rule there is no exception whatever. These rules again

* See Shakespear's Hindūstānī Grammar," p. 44.

hold good in regard to the imperfect tense in Puśhto, which, according to the canons of the Semitic dialects, is a *past* tense, whilst in Urdū and the Hindū languages of its class, it is precisely contrary, for with it the particle ڀي cannot be used. In all other instances than those mentioned, the verb, in Puśhto, whether transitive or intransitive, is governed by the *agent* in the nominative.

Puśhto, like the Arabic, Hebrew, and other dialects of the Semitic, together with the Pehlavī, Persian, Turkish, and Sindhīān, has but two genders—the masculine and feminine. In the Puśhto and Semitic languages the purely feminine nouns have a different termination, and others are formed from masculines by adding peculiar terminations. In this matter Urdū agrees in a measure; but, save in the case of Arabic nouns adopted into Urdū, those affixes do not assimilate. The Pehlavī, Persian, and Turkish languages, again, have no difference in termination whatever for gender; whilst, on the other hand, the Sanskrit family of languages, as well as the Zand, have a neuter gender as well. The Semitic, Sanskrit, and Zand have three numbers—singular, dual, and plural; whilst Puśhto, Pehlavī, Persian, Turkish, Sindhīān, and Urdū or Hindūstānī have no dual. The feminine terminations in Puśhto are four: first—ه (*hā-i-khafī*) *a'h* (the same as the Arabic *tānīs*, and the Hebrew and Chaldaik ה · *h*), which becomes ې (*hā-i-maj-hūl*) or *ey* in the plural, and which may also be written in Puśhto with simple (َ) *fat-ḥa'h* or *i*; second—ي *ī*, which becomes ۍ *a'ī* in the plural; third—ۍ *a'ī*, which is both singular and plural; and fourth—ا *ā*, also singular and plural in the Eastern dialect, but takes وي, *wī* in the Western. These, in their construction, have no connection with Urdū.

The Puśhto pronouns bear no similarity whatever with those of the Sanskrit family of languages, but they have a great affinity to those of the Semitic dialects, and to the Pehlavī, Persian, and Sindhīān, which are all applied and used in such a manner as to show a decided and undoubted affiliation between them.

The Puśhto verbs are exceedingly irregular, and the infinitives, without exception, terminate in either ل, يدل, or ول, which exhibit no similarity whatever to Sanskrit and its cognates, and are as wide apart from the Urdū infinitive termination نا as the West is from the East.

I have only mentioned here the most glaring differences. A glance at my Grammar will show that, although Puśhto bears a great and remarkable similarity to the Semitic and Irānīān languages on numerous points, it is totally different in construction, and in idiom also, from any of the Indū-Sanskrit dialects. With the Sclāvonic and Tārtārīān tongues I have no acquaintance, and therefore am unable to state whether any affinity exists between them. The Circassian, in the matter of words, shows not the most remote resemblance.

After mature consideration, I am inclined to conclude—from the great affinity I have shown to exist between the Puśhto and the Semitic and Irānīān dialects;

from the numerous traditions on the subject; from the Levitical customs still prevalent amongst the Afghāns, after the lapse of twenty-five centuries from the Jewish captivity; from their great and decided difference in feature from any other people; from their stubbornness and treachery, even towards each other; from their acuteness in matters of trade and their love of gain; and from the numerous proofs we possess of their having gradually advanced from the west of Asia,—that the Afghāns are a remnant of the lost tribes of Israel. They have, as was inevitable, adopted numerous words and idioms from the languages spoken in the countries into which their wanderings and sojournings led them; and the fact that these countries are, for the most part, mountainous, and inhabited by a variety of tribes continually separating into smaller clans, none of them, however, possessing facilities of communication with foreigners, will at once account for the peculiarities noticeable in the language. One link is, however, wanting to prove satisfactorily their Israelitish descent, and that is—the proof that the Afghāns bore Jewish names before they became converts to Islām.

On the other hand again, the peculiarities of the Pushto verbs and pronouns, together with some other characteristics, would seem to indicate that it is a peculiar and very ancient original language, different from any other known tongue. But it must be considered that, even in these days of steam and electricity, Europeans—with the exception of the Russians, who are far in advance of all others, and foster instead of treating coldly such researches—are quite in the dark with regard to many countries, peoples, and languages of Central Asia, particularly with respect to those immediately north and east of the Panjāb, on the slopes and in the valleys of the stupendous range of Hindū Kush,* and the more central parts of Afghānistān. When these shall have been explored by Europeans, additional light may be thrown on the subject. It is highly probable, that many of the Jewish tribes, particularly those dwelling in the eastern parts of Judea, after their return from the land of the Pharoahs, by degrees, engrafted on and mixed up with their own,† many words and idioms of the dialects spoken in Palestine amongst the Ammonites, Moabites, and other aboriginals of the Promised Land, and which, probably, are the basis of the Pushto, mixed up with the dialects of the countries the Afghāns passed through, and in which they tarried, in their wanderings, before they reached their present country.‡

My humble opinion and convictions I have stated unreservedly: the decision

* See my "NOTES ON KĀFIRISTĀN, and Account of the SĪ'ĀH-POSH TRIBES," "Journal of the Asiatic Society of Bengal," for 1859, p. 317.

† In the same manner the Hindūstānī and Multānī Afghāns of the present day speak the language of their adopted country, and have lost their mother tongue.

‡ When Cyrus gave them (the Jews) their liberty, with leave to go back into Judæa and rebuild the temple, they did not *all* return, nor at *one time*. There was a great number that stayed at Babylon and in all places where they were settled; and they that came back were not all Jews: some few of the ten tribes joined themselves to them, and yet they made but a small number altogether."—ABBE FLEURY'S "ANCIENT ISRAELITES."

of the point may be left for the learned of Europe, who will be able to bring to bear on it a profound knowledge of Hebrew and of other dead languages of Western Asia, necessary for the solution of such a question.*

The difficulties that have hitherto existed, in the want of books available to all, both in India and in Europe, have now, I trust, been removed through my humble labours, the result of which I submit, with due deference, to the learned Orientalist and to the Public generally. I would fain believe that I have rescued from oblivion, and thrown considerable light upon, an ancient and unique language, which has not hitherto received the attention it deserves from Oriental scholars, and which has been also greatly neglected by the Afghāns themselves, owing to the never-ceasing civil dissensions of which their country has been the theatre during the last eighty years; but whose cultivation and study it is incumbent on the British Government, and on those interested in the preaching of the Gospel, to foster and promote by every means in their power. To the English Government I would say, that there is only one course open to them, if they desire not to leave a clear field to the Russians in Central Asia, as they have hitherto done.

It appears most astonishing that persons who have had no opportunity of becoming practically, and, too often, not even theoretically, acquainted with a language—who do not even know the correct pronunciation of its letters; and who are altogether ignorant whether it be a written or a colloquial tongue,—should venture to put forth their opinions—often very decidedly—with regard to its origin and its affinity to other tongues, of which they may be equally ignorant. Yet we often find such presumption (I can call it by no milder term), as in the case of a traveller, who, whatever his acquirements in Hebrew, was not, that I can discover, acquainted with Pus̲h̲to, or had ever seen a book in that language. I refer more particularly to the following extract from a little work entitled "The Afg̲h̲āns the Kings of the East," in which the author very pertinently remarks: "Dr. Wolff does not tell us that he understood Pus̲h̲to, and we presume he did not, as we learn from Sir Alexander Burnes that 'the language of the Afg̲h̲āns is Persian, (!) but not the smooth and elegant tongue of Irān.'† It is on this language that Dr. Wolff is so decisive. A residence of *thirty-four days* in Afg̲h̲ānistān would not appear to afford time sufficient to make much acquaintance with a language, strange to all other nations, and confined to the most illiterate portion of a rude population."‡

* For other information respecting the Afg̲h̲āns and the tradition of their descent, see the INTRODUCTION TO THE GRAMMAR.

† By which absurd and incorrect statement, Burnes proved himself to have been acquainted with neither the one nor the other of these languages.

‡ I must, however, correct this last very erroneous statement by the author of "The Afg̲h̲āns the Kings of the East." Pus̲h̲to is no more "confined to the most illiterate portion of a rude population" than English itself. All Afg̲h̲āns speak Pus̲h̲to, which is their mother tongue; and even in the families of the Sadozī kings, and in the dwelling of the Amīr, Dost Muḥammad K̲h̲ān, at the present day, Pus̲h̲to is always spoken. Persian is only the official language of the country, as regards correspondence, as it was in India, until very recently.

Dr. Wolff then proceeds to give specimens of Afghān words, taken partly from the Afghāns themselves, and partly from Elphinstone's "Caubul." In a foot-note he says, "اور 'light,'* is the only Hebrew word I found in the Afghān tongue"—every word of which we must presume he had heard without exception. Again he says: "The construction of the Pushto Grammar (of which none then existed in any European language, and never did in Pushto itself) differs entirely from that of the Hebrew." These words would imply a complete acquaintance with Pushto (acquired without books or teachers, by instinct or by miracle, in the space of *thirty-four days!*). This is more than we would infer as to the former, since the specimens were, it seems, picked up in conversation with the Afghāns themselves, or from Mr. Elphinstone's Vocabulary!

The above is ridiculous enough in all conscience; but another instance, to which I must also refer, beats even this in absurdity. There is a work lately published, under the name of 'Barnes' Philological Grammar,'† as a help (?) to the grammars of all languages, in which Hindūstānī or Urdū is quoted as Persian, and Persian as Hindūstānī and Arabic, and *vice versâ*; and totally incorrect as to pronunciation in the most painful degree. I quote a few specimens at random. For example: pp. 68-69, referring to patronymics, the author states—

> "These compounds are found also in Celtic languages and in Persian, Hindoostanee, etc.
> Irish—*lâim-dia*, hand-god, *i.e.*, teraph or household-god.
> Persian—*jinistan*, fairy-land; *gulzar*, rose-bed.
> Hindoostanee—*nishan-burdar*, standard-bearer; *ghorasal*, horse-place, *i.e.*, a stable."

Now *nishān-bardār* is not Hindūstānī, it is pure and unadulterated Persian; *nishān* being the active participle of نشانيدن 'to mark, delineate, to fix in the ground,' etc., and *bardār* the active participle of برداشتن 'to take up, to carry, to bear.' The other word put forth as Hindūstānī is pure Sanskrit, from घोटक 'a horse,' and शाला 'a place.'

Again at p. 79 we find—

> "Hindoostanee—*beetaio*, son; *beetai*, daughter."

How it must affect the risible faculties of any one who has resided in India, to see the state to which the author of 'A Help to the Grammars of all Languages' has brought these unfortunate words! A glance at any dictionary of the Hindūstānī language would have shown him that the pronunciation of بيٹا, 'a son,' is *bê-tā* or *bey-tā* (I give two systems of orthography), and بيٹي, 'a daughter,' *bê-tī* or *bey-tee*.

Again at page 80—

> "Persian—*sheer-i-nur*, lion, a he-lion.
> Hindoostanee—*nur-gaoo*, bull, he-bullock; *madah-gaoo*, cow, she-bullock."

* اور *aor* is FIRE, not *light*, in the Pushto language. خيل *khel*, too, applied to the subdivisions of a clan, is a Hebrew word (חיל); and many others could be named.

† SMITH, Soho Square, London, 1854.

The Persian for lion is *shêr* (with *yā-i-maj-hūl*), not *sheer*, as in the work in question, which gives the sound of *yā-i-maæ-rūf*, equivalent to *shīr*, which is the Persian for *milk.* نر with the vowel point ـَ (short *a*) *nar*, not with ـُ (short *u*) *nur*, signifies 'male,' 'masculine.' As regards the so-called Hindūstānī *nur-gaoo*, *nar* is Persian and Sanskrit also, and گاو *gāw* (with *wāw-i-maj-hūl*), not *gaoo* (equivalent to *gā-ū* with *wāw-i-maæ-rūf*) is Persian, and गौ: in Sanskrit.

The foregoing will be sufficient, I should imagine, to show that persons should be sure they are right, before publishing their opinions, and will add force to the words of Baron William Humboldt with regard to researches into the affinity of languages—"If we would make ourselves acquainted with the relation between two languages, we ought to possess a thorough and profound knowledge of each of them. This is the principle dictated alike by common sense and by that precision acquired by the habit of scientific research. . . . I only insist on it that we should not prescribe to ourselves arbitrary limits, and imagine that we are forming our judgment on a firm basis while in reality it is insufficient." *

These specimens will serve to show the utter folly and loss of precious time in attempting to study Oriental languages, beyond the mere elements, at home, unless the teachers and professors employed have qualified themselves by study and residence in the countries where the languages they profess to teach are spoken.

I must now mention the sources from whence the materials of the present work have been derived, and the assistants who have aided me in my labours.

This work includes the result of my own researches during the last twelve years, together with the whole of the words contained in the very rare, though not extensive, lexicographical works existing on the Pus̲h̲to language—the Æajā'ib-ul-Lug̲h̲at ('Curiosities of Language') of Nawwāb Allah Yār K̲h̲ān, of the Barec̲h̲ tribe, and the Rī'az-ul-Maḥabbat ('Gardens of Friendship') by Nawwāb Ḥāfiẓ Maḥabbat K̲h̲ān,—both explained in Persian; the whole of which have, whenever the slightest doubt or variation existed, been tested and compared, and submitted to learned Afg̲h̲āns, both in the eastern and western parts of Afg̲h̲ānistān, as well as to other persons of various tribes; in fact, to all whose assistance I could command, and they have not been a few.

During the whole time I had the valuable assistance of a Molawī of the G̲h̲alzī tribe, located in central Afg̲h̲ānistān in the district around K̲h̲elāt-i-G̲h̲alzī, and whose father was for some time Ḳāẓī of the city of Ḳandahār, in which office the Molawī, who is better acquainted with Pus̲h̲to, both theoretically and practically, than any other man I ever saw or heard of, assisted. His profound knowledge of Arabic—the foundation of all Muḥammadan languages—and without which the situation of Ḳāẓī in the western capital of Afg̲h̲ānistān could not have been held, together

* "An Essay on the best means of ascertaining the Affinities of Oriental Languages."

with the fact of his possessing no mean poetical powers, rendered him peculiarly fitted for a task of this kind, in which many works had to be examined and collated. I also had for many years the valuable aid of a very clever old Ākhūndzādah of the Muḥammadzī tribe, resident in the Peshāwer district, who is well acquainted with Arabic and with his mother tongue, and has resided at various times amongst almost every Afghān tribe, particularly those of Bājawṛṛ, Panjkorah, Suwāt, and Buner—the most northern portions of Afghānistān—the population of which, at the present day, speak Pushto in its greatest purity, and display the peculiarities of their nation in more perfection than others of their race. The greater number of authors who have written in the Pushto language, indeed all who have obtained any celebrity, have belonged almost exclusively to the tribes inhabiting the districts round about the Peshāwer valley.

I have thus, with the native assistance referred to, been able to render all three works—the Dictionary, the Text-Book, and the Grammar—equally subservient to the study of both the Eastern and Western dialects, which differ only with regard to a few minor peculiarities, and certainly not more than the difference of locality might lead us to expect—the Eastern containing several pure Sanskrit terms, but generally used in poetry as a play on some other word—whilst the Western has more Persian in proportion, and differs in the pronunciation of four letters, which in the latter have been softened down. These are: ښ *khīn* (E.), *shey* (W.); ګ *gāf* (E.), ږ *jzay* (W.); ز *zey* (E.), ځ *dzey* (W.); and ج *jīm* (E.), ژ *jzey* (W.)

The derivations of all words, which have been adopted from, or can be traced to, the Semitic, Irānīān, or Sanskrit family of languages, have been generally shown. Another peculiar feature of this Dictionary—which the experience I have gained from the study of a number of Oriental languages has led me to adopt—is, that the plural form of each noun is given, together with the Class or Declension to which it belongs, as arranged in my Grammar of the Pushto language—a second and improved edition* of which has been issued, uniform in size and style with the present work, and with the Selections Prose and Poetical, before referred to, which forms a complete Text-Book of the Afghān language and literature.

The greatest difficulty in the path of the student in this language, is the conjugations of the verbs, which are complex from their great irregularities, and the number of classes they resolve themselves into. To obviate this intricacy, the third persons masculine singular of the present, past, and future tenses; the imperative mood; the active and past participles, also used as nouns and adjectives; and the verbal nouns, which are of constant use, have been given under each infinitive, both according to the Eastern and Western pronunciation, where

* The first edition was unfortunately published at Calcutta, and consequently allowance should be made for numerous typographical errors (although revised three times) of Indian presses, for everything Indian is just one century behind that which is European, in every respect.

difference exists, except in a few instances of those verbs which are derived from adjectives, and whose conjugations are according to the same rules, one model serving for all. With this aid, and reference to the Grammar and the rules therein laid down, the conjugations will be found simple enough.

The Arabic and Persian words of common use in the language at present, and those of constant occurrence in religious writings, and for which there are often no equivalents in Puṣhto, have been included in this work—indeed they could not well have been left out; but, as the extent of the use of Arabic and Persian, depends on the taste and learning of the different authors, I should have greatly increased the bulk of the work without giving a corresponding advantage, if I had included all the words which may be used, in poetry in particular. The student, however, will be able to refer, if necessary, to the Dictionary of those languages for words of more rare occurrence. I have not alluded generally to the Hebrew and Chaldaik words, because the whole of their roots, so used, are common to the Arabic and other cognate dialects of the Semitic, from whence they have, in all probability, crept into Puṣhto, as in the languages of all Muḥammadans, through the Muḥammadan religion.

The system of orthography adopted, and also used by Richardson and Shakspear in their Persian and Arabic, and Hindūstānī Dictionaries, is that of Sir William Jones,*—than which there is no other nearly so capable of giving the correct sound of Oriental words,—together with other combinations according to the same rules, to suit the letters and sounds peculiar to the Puṣhto, the whole of which will be found explained in the body of the work at the commencement of each letter, and which, with regard to و, ه, and ي, should be particularly attended to, on account of the number of uses to which they are applicable.

The short vowels are written as simple *a*, *i*, and *u*, which are equivalent in sound to short *a* in *marine*, or the initial vowel in the word *America*; short *i* in *pin*; and short *u* in *bull*. The letters ا, و, and ي, used as the long vowels, denominated معروف (*maœ-rūf*), or 'known,' are distinguished by a dash over them; as *ā* in the word *fāther*; *ī* in *machīne*; and *ū* in *rūle*. The two latter letters, when not preceded by either of the short vowels, are termed مجهول (*maj-hūl*), or 'unknown,' and may then be considered consonants, and will be found written, the و as *o* in the word *no* or *rose*, or *ow* in *flow* and *blow*; and the ي as *e* in *bell*, in French *le*, or *ey* in *they* or *obey*. The other modifications of the latter letter, peculiar to Puṣhto, will be found in the body of the work under its proper head.

When the initial letter ا has the mark ~ (*madd*) over it, it then conveys the sound of long *ā* in *āll*. Another vowel peculiar to Puṣhto—and not to be found in any other Eastern language, that I am aware of—partaking of the sounds of short *a*

* With the exception of the sound of Arabic ع, which I have written *œ* with the vowels used with it, as giving a more correct definition of its sound.

and *i* combined, but somewhat shortened, has been written *æ*, as being the nearest possible approach to its true sound, which can only be perfectly acquired from an Afg͟hān mouth.

The initial capital letters before words, refer to the languages to which they belong; thus, A Arabic, P Persian, H Hebrew, C Chaldaik, PLV Pehlavī, S Sanskrit, G Greek, T Turkish. Words which are found in Urdū as well as in Puḱhto, and probably taken from the latter, have, for the reasons mentioned at page xv, been marked by way of distinction HI. Pure Puḱhto words are unmarked.

The abbreviations for parts of speech and grammatical terms are those common to all Dictionaries. The letters W. and E., inserted in parentheses after words, refer respectively to the Western and Eastern pronunciation, and sometimes indicate that they are used exclusively in those two divisions of Afg͟hānistān.

The types peculiar to the Puḱhto alphabet have been cut expressly for this and the other works.

H. G. R.

LONDON, 16TH JULY, 1860.

A

DICTIONARY;

PUS͟HTO AND ENGLISH.

آب

ا

ا *alif* is the first letter of the Pus͟hto, as also of the Arabic, Hebrew, Persian, and other oriental alphabets; and its powers are precisely the same as in those languages, with which the student of Pus͟hto is supposed to be in some measure acquainted. The Afg͟hān authors do not make much difference between ا and (ـَ), and they are often interchanged one for the other, particularly in the vocative case. According to the Arabian system of substituting letters for figures, known as the *abjad*, the letter ا stands for 'one.' Placed between two nouns, as in the Persian, it denotes continuity, conjunction, or proximity; as, مخامخ *mak͟hā-mak͟h*, Face to face; ورځا ورځ *wrad͟zā-wrad͟z*, Every day.

A اب *ab*, s.m. (9th) Father, master, possessor. Sing. and Pl. See پلار

P آب *āb*, s.m. (9th) Water; character, honor, reputation, lustre, etc. Sing. and Pl. It is only used in composition; as, آب و ادب *āb-o-adab*, Courtesy, politeness; آب حيوان *āb-i-ḥaiwān*, or آب حيات *āb-i-ḥaiyāt*, The water of life or immortality; آب رو *āb-rū*, or آب روي *āb-rū-e*, The water of the face; reputation, renown, honor, lustre; or دَ مخ آب *da mak͟h āb*; بي آبَ کول *be āba kawul*, verb trans. To dishonor, to disgrace, to lower in the estimation of another; بي آبَ کيدل *be āba kedal*, verb intrans. To become dishonored or disgraced.

ابا

ابا *abā*, A word of endearment to a father.

A ابا *ibā*, s.f. (6th) Denial, refusal. (E.) Sing. and Pl. (W.) Pl. اباوي *ibāwī*. ابا کول *ibā kawul*, verb trans. To refuse, to deny; or ابا راوړل *ibā rā-w'ṟṟal*.

A ابابکر *abā-bakr*, or ابوبکر *abū-bakr*, s. prop. The name of the first K͟halīfah.

A ابابيل *abā-bīl*, s.m. (2nd) The swallow. Pl. ابابيلونه *abā-bīlūnah*.

A اباحتي *abā-ḥatī*, s.m. (5th) The name of a sect of Muhammadans who maintain that the law and good works are of no avail. Pl. اباحتيان *abāḥatī-ān*. اباحتۍ *abāḥata'ī*, s.f. (6th) A female of the above sect. Sing. and Pl. Also called اباحتيه *abā-ḥatia'h*.

اباخيل *abā-khel*, s.m. (6th) The name of a tribe of Afghāns. Sing. and Pl. اباخيله *abā-khela'h*, s.f. (3rd) A female of the above. Pl. ې *ey*.

P آباد *ābād*, adj. Cultivated, populous, inhabited, prosperous, thriving; (Fem.) آباده *ābāda'h*. آباد کيدل *ābād kedal*, verb intrans. To become cultivated, inhabited, prosperous; آباد کول *ābād kawul*, verb trans. To cultivate, to people, to make or render prosperous.

P آبادي *ābādī*, s.f. (3rd) or آباداني *ābādānī*, s.f. (3rd) Population, cultivation, abundance, prosperity. Pl. ئ *a'ī*. See ودان and وداني

ابازي *abā-zī*, s.m. (1st) Pl. The name of a tribe of Afghāns. ابازی *abā-zaey*, Sing. A male of the Abā-zī tribe. ابازئ *abā-za'ī*, s.f. (6th) A female of the above. Sing. and Pl.

اباسين *abā-sīn*, or ابا سيند *abā-sīnd*, s. prop. The Father of Rivers—the Afghān name for the Indus (from A ابا 'father', and S سين or سيند 'a river').

A ابتدا *ibtidā*, s.f. (6th) Beginning, commencement. (E.) Sing. and Pl. (W.) Pl. ابتداوي *ibtidā-wī*. ابتدا کول *ibtidā kawul*, verb trans. To begin, to commence.

A ابتر *abtar*, adj. Ruined, spoiled, worthless; dissolute, wanton (from بتر destitute of a tail; H בתר cut short); (Fem.) ابتره *abtara'h*; ابتر کول *abtar kawul*, verb trans. To spoil, to ruin. See اوتر

ابتري *abtarī*, s.f. (3rd) Worthlessness, wantonness. Pl. ئ *a'ī*.

A ابد *abad*, s.m. (9th) Eternity, without end. Sing. and Pl. ته ابدَ *tah abada*, تر ابدَ *tar abada*, تر ابدَ پورِ *tah abada pori*, or پوري *porī*, For ever and ever, to all eternity.

P آبدار *ābdār*, adj. Watery, moist. 2. Glancing as a gem or sword. 3. Sharp, dazzling; (Fem.) آبداره *ābdāra'h*.

A ابدال *abdāl*, s.m. (5th) A saint, a devotee. Pl. ابدالان *abdālān*.

ابدالي *abdālī*, s.m. (1st) Pl. The name of one of the great divisions or septs of the Afghāns, of which Aḥmad Shāh, the first king of Afghānistān, was the hereditary chieftain.

ابدالی *abdālaey*, Sing. A male of the above. ابدالئ *abdāla'ī*, s.f. (6th) A female of the tribe. Sing. and Pl. Also written اودالي and اودل, which see.

A ابدي *abadī* or ابداً *abadan*, adj. Eternal, without end.

P ابر *abr*, s.m. (9th) Clouds. Sing. and Pl. See اوريځ

A ابرار *abrār*, adj. (s. Pl. A) Holy, just, pious.

A ابراهيم *ibrāhīm*, s. prop. The patriarch Abraham. 2. A man's name.

P ابرو *ab-rū*, s.m. (5th) The eyebrow. Pl. ابروان *ab-rū-ān*. See ورځه

P آبرو *āb-rū*, s.m. (9th) Honour, reputation, character, renown, good name. Sing. and Pl. آبرو تويول *āb-rū to-yawul*, verb trans. To disgrace, to dishonor, to take away one's character or reputation. آبرو ورکول *āb-rū war-kawul*, verb trans. To honor, to treat with respect or distinction.

P ابره *abra'h*, s.f. (3rd) The outer cloth of a double garment. 2. A small shawl worn round the waist. Pl. ې *ey*.

ابړئ *ub-ṛṛa'ī*, s.f. (6th) Green vegetation at the bottom of pools or cisterns. Sing. and Pl.

P آبشار *āb-shār*, s.m. (2nd) A cascade, a cataract, a waterfall. Pl. آبشارونه *āb-shārūnah*.

A آبق *ābiḳ*, s.m. (5th) A runaway slave. Pl. آبقان *ābiḳān*. آبقه *ābiḳa'h*, s.f. (3rd) The feminine of the above. Pl. ې *ey*.

A ابلاغ *ib-lāgh*, s.m. (2nd) Informing, converging, aiming at, obtaining an end, causing to arrive, sending. Pl. ابلاغونه *ib-lāghūnah*. ابلاغ کول *ib-lāgh kawul*, verb trans. To inform, to make aware of, to acquaint.

ابل *abl*, adj. Bare, barefooted, unshod; (Fem.) ابله *abla'h*. ابلې خپې *ab-ley khpey* (E.), or ابلې پښې *abley pshey* (W.), Barefooted. See يبله

A ابلق *ab-laḳ*, adj. Piebald, black and white, party-coloured; (Fem.) ابلقه *ablaḳa'h*.

ابلک *ablak*, adj. (Fem.) ابلکه *ablaka'h*, Corruption of preceding.

A ابله *ablah*, adj. Foolish, silly, a fool; (Fem.)

ابلهه *ab-laha'h.* ابلهي *ab-lahī*, s.f. (3rd) Foolishness, silliness, simplicity. Pl. ئ *a'ī.*

A ابليس *ib-līs*, s. prop. The devil.

A ابن *ibn*, s.m. (9th) A son. Sing. and Pl.

P آبنوس *āb-nūs*, s.m. (6th) Ebony. Sing. and Pl. آبنوسي *āb-nūsī*, adj. Made of ebony.

A ابو *abū*, s.m. (9th) Father. Sing. and Pl. Used as a prefix to proper names; as ابوبكر *abū-bakr*, The father-in-law of Muḥammad, and his successor.

P آبوتاب *āb-o-tāb*, or آبتاب *āb-tāb*, s.m. (2nd) Splendor, lustre, honor. Pl. آبوتابونه *āb-o-tābūnah*, or آبتابونه *āb-tābūnah.* بي آبوتابَ كول *bey āb-o-tāba kawul*, verb trans. To disgrace, to dishonor, to lower.

P آبي *ā-bī*, or ابي *abī*, adj. Watery, blue-coloured. 2. Moist, aqueous.

ابئي *aba'ī*, A title of endearment for a mother. See ادي

A ابيات *ab-yāt*, s. (Pl. of بيت) Houses. 2. Verses.

ابير *abīr*, s.m. (6th) corrup. of عبير) Ambergris. Sing. and Pl.

آپرين *ā-prīn*, interj. Bravo! well done! 2. s.m. (2nd) Praise, applause, approbation. Pl. آپرينونه *ā-prīnūnah.* آپرين ويل *ā-prīn wa-yal*, verb trans. To praise, to applaud. See آفرين

اپريدي *aprī-dī*, s.m. (1st) Pl. The name of a tribe of Afghāns who are the pest of the Peshāwer district. اپريدئ *aprī-daey*, Sing. A male of the above tribe. اپريدئ *aprī-da'ī*, s.f. (6th) A female of the above. Sing. and Pl. Also written افريدي

اپس ډنډئ *a-pas ḏḏanḏḏa'ī*, s.f. (6th) The game of cat and dog, tip-cat. Sing. and Pl.

اپلاس *ip-lās*, s.m. (2nd) (corrup. of A افلاس) Poverty, penury, indigence, bankruptcy. Pl. اپلاسونه *ip-lāsūnah.*

اپلت *ap-lat*, adj. Low, obscene, dirty, filthy; (Fem.) اپلته *ap-lata'h.* اپلتي خبري *ap-latey khabarey*, s.f. (3rd) Pl. Low or obscene language.

اپوټه *a-pūṯṯæh*, adj. Disturbed, troubled; (Fem.) اپوټه *a-pūṯṯa'h.*

اتبار *it-bār*, s.m. (9th) Sunday. Sing. and Pl. (s اتوار)

اترنګ *at-rang*, s.m. (6th) The name of a plant used in dyeing. Sing. and Pl.

P آتش *ā-tash*, s.m. (9th) Fire. Sing. and Pl. Used only in composition, as آتش بازي *ā-tash bāzī*, s.f. (3rd) Fire-works. Pl. ئ *a'ī.* آتش پرست *ā-tash parast*, s.m. (5th) A worshipper of fire, a Gabr, one of the Māgī, a Pārsī. Pl. آتش پرستان *ā-tash-parastān.* آتش پرسته *ā-tash-parasta'h*, s.f. (3rd) A female Gabr. Pl. ئ *ey.* آتش پرستي *ā-tash-parastī*, s.f. (3rd) The worship of fire. Pl. ئ *a'ī.* آتش خانه *ā-tash khāna'h*, s.f. (3rd) A fireplace; the part of a matchlock where the charge is placed. Pl. ئ *ey.* آتش كده *ā-tash kada'h*, s.f. (3rd) A grate, a fireplace; a temple of fire-worshippers. Pl. ئ *ey.* See اور

P آتشک *ā-tashak*, s.m. (9th) The venereal disease. Sing. and Pl.

P آتش ګير *ā-tash gīr*, s.m. (6th) Tinder. Sing. and Pl.

P آتشي *ā-tashī*, adj. Fiery, hot, irascible; sensual.

آتشي ښيښه *ā-tashī shīsha'h* (W.) or *khīkha'h* (E.) s.f. (3rd) A burning glass. Pl. ئ *ey.* (P شيشه)

A اتعاظ *iti-æāẓ*, s.m. (9th) Admonition, advice, admonishing, receiving admonition. Sing. and Pl. اتعاظ كول *iti-æāẓ kawul*, verb trans. To admonish, to advise.

A اتفاق *itta-fāḳ*, s.m. (2nd) Concord, agreement, agreeing, consenting. Pl. اتفاقونه *itta-fāḳūnah.* په اتفاق سره *pah itta-fāḳ sarah*, By chance, accidentally; or اتفاقاً *itta-fāḳan.* اتفاق كيدل *itta-fāḳ kedal*, verb intrans. To happen, to befal; to be agreed. اتفاق كول *itta-fāḳ kawul*, verb trans. To agree, to consent, to concur; to conspire; to happen.

A اتفاقي *itta-fāḳī*, adj. Accidental, casual, fortuitous. 2. Agreeing, concurring.

A اتقي *at-ḳā*, adj. More, or most pious.

A اتكا *itti-kā*, s.f. (6th) Leaning against, reclining upon, trusting to, confiding in. (E.) Sing. and Pl. (W.) Pl. اتکاوي *itti-kāwī.* اتکا کول *itti-kā kawul*, verb trans. To trust to, to confide in.

اتلس *at-las*, s.m. (2nd) (corrup. of A اطلس), Satin. Pl. اتلسونه *at-lasūnah.*

اتم *atam*, adj. (from اته eight) The eighth; (Fem.) اتمه *atama'h.*

A اتمام *it-mām*, s.m. (9th) Completing, perfecting, accomplishing. Sing. and Pl. اتمام کيدل *it-mām kedal*, verb intrans. To become perfected, completed. اتمام کول *it-mām kawul*, verb trans. To complete, to perfect, to accomplish.

اتمان خيل *ut-mān-khel*, s.m. (6th) The name of a tribe of Afghāns. Sing. and Pl. اتمان خيله *ut-mān khela'h*, s.f. (3rd) A female of the above. Pl. ي *ey.*

اتمان خي *ut-mān-dzī*, s.m. (1st) Pl. The name also given to the preceding Afghān tribe. اتمان خيَ *ut-mān-dzaey*, Sing. A male of the tribe. اتمان خي *ut-mān-dza'ī*, s.f. (6th) A female of the above. Sing. and Pl.

اتنړ *a-tarrn*, s.m. (2nd) A kind of dance. Pl. اتنړونه *a-tarrnūnah.* Also written اتڼ. اتنړ وهل *a-tarrn wahal*, or اتنړ آچول *a-tarrn āchawul*, verb trans. To dance the *a-tarrn.*

S اتوار *it-wār*, s.m. (9th) Sunday. Sing. and Pl.

اتوب *a-tūb*, s.m. (2nd) A dish made from flour, sugar, and butter. Pl. اتوبونه *a-tūbūnah.*

اتوزي *ato-zī*, s.m. (1st) Pl. The name of an Afghān tribe. اتوزيَ *ato-zaey*, Sing. A male of the tribe. اتوزي *ato-za'ī*, s.f. (6th) A female of the above. Sing. and Pl.

اته *a-tah*, adj. Eight; اتم *atam*, The eighth; (Fem.) اتمه *atama'h.* اته لس *a-tah-las*, Eighteen; اته ويشت *a-tah-wisht*, Twenty-eight; اته ديرش *a-tah-dersh*, Thirty-eight; اته څلويښت *a-tah-tsal-wesht* (W.) or *tsal-wekht* (E.) Forty-eight; اته پنځوس *a-tah-pīn-dzos*, Fifty-eight; اته شپيته *a-tah-shpe-tah*, Sixty-eight; اته اويا *a-tah-aw-yā*, Seventy-eight; اته اتيا *a-tah at-yā*, Eighty-eight; اته نوي *a-tah nawī*, Ninety-eight.

اتيا *at-yā*, adj. Eighty; اتيايم *at-yāyam*, The eightieth; (Fem.) اتيايمه *at-yāyama'h.*

اټال *a-ṭṭāl*, adj. Unemployed, out of place; (Fem.) اټاله *a-ṭṭāla'h.*

اټک *aṭṭak*, s. prop. The name of a town on the Indus, the river Indus. (From HI اټک hinderance, bar, obstruction.)

HI اټکل *aṭṭ-kal*, s.m. (2nd) Guess, conjecture, judgment. Pl. اټکلونه *aṭṭ-kalūnah* اټکلول *aṭṭ-kalawul*, verb trans. To guess, to conjecture, to judge, to think, to estimate. Pres. اټکلوي *aṭṭ-kalawī*; past و اټکلاوه *wu-aṭṭ-kalāwuh* or و اټکلاوو *wu-aṭṭ-kalāwo*; fut. و به اټکلوي *wu bah aṭṭ-kalawī*; imp. و اټکلوه *wu-aṭṭ-kalawah*; act. part. اټکلونکيَ *aṭṭ-kalawūnkaey* or اټکلونيَ *aṭṭ-kalawūnaey*; past part. اټکوليَ *aṭṭ-kala-wulaey*; verb. n. اټکلونه *aṭṭ-kalawuna'h.*

اټه *aṭṭa'h*, s.f. (3rd) A ball or reel of thread or cotton; a hank or skein of thread or silk. Pl. ي *ey.* Also written اټيه *aṭṭe-a'h* and اټيهه *aṭṭeh-a'h*, which see.

اټيران *aṭṭe-rān*, s.m. (2nd) A reel for winding silk, thread, cotton, etc. Pl. اټيرانونه *aṭṭe-rānūnah.*

اټيرل *aṭṭe-ral*, verb intrans. To trouble with indigestion; to make dyspeptic. Pres. اټيري *aṭṭe-rī*; past و اټيره *wu aṭṭe-rah*; fut. و به اټيري *wu bah aṭṭe-rī*; imp. و اټيره *wu-aṭṭe-rah*; act. part. اټيرونکيَ *aṭṭe-rūnkaey* or اټيرونيَ *aṭṭe-rūnaey*; past part. اټيرليَ *aṭṭe-ralaey*; verb. n. اټيرنه *aṭṭe-rana'h.* See اغيرل

اټيرليَ *aṭṭe-ralaey*, adj. (past part.) Undigested, crude, dyspeptic. 2. A person troubled with dyspepsia; (Fem.) اټيرلِ *aṭṭe-rali.* Pl. (Masc. and Fem.) ي *ī.* See اغيرليَ

اټيرنه *aṭṭe-rana'h*, s.f. (3rd) Indigestion, dyspepsia. Pl. ي *ey.* See اغير

اټيه *aṭṭe-a'h*, s.f. (3rd) A ball or reel of thread or cotton, a hank or skein of thread or silk. Pl. ي *ey.*

اټيهه *aṭṭeh-a'h*, s.f. (3rd) A ball or reel of thread, etc. See preceding. Pl. ي *ey.*

A اثبات *is-bāt*, s.m. (2nd) Confirming, corroborating. 2. Confirmation, proof, affirmation.

Pl. اثباتونه *iṣ-bātūnah.* اثبات کيدل *iṣ-bāt kedal* or په اثبات رسيدل *pah iṣ-bāt rasedal,* verb intrans. To become corroborated, confirmed, proved. اثبات کول *iṣ-bāt kawul* or په اثبات رسول *pah iṣ-bāt rasawul,* verb trans. To confirm, to corroborate, to prove. See زباد etc.

A اثر *aṣar,* s.m. (2nd) A mark, sign, trace, impression, effect. Pl. اثرونه *aṣarūnah.* اثر کول *aṣar kawul,* verb trans. To operate, to take effect, to make impression.

آثره *āṣ-ra'h,* s.f. (3rd) (corrup. of s آسرا), Asylum, defence, hope, trust, reliance, refuge, shelter, means of defence. Pl. ۍ *ey.*

اڅکه *uts-ka'h,* s.f. (3rd) Dried grapes, raisins. Pl. ۍ *ey.* See وڅکه

اڅرړل *atsarrnal,* verb trans. To level, to make level, to trim, to make even, to reduce or remove inequalities in anything, to reduce to an even surface, to arrange, to place in order, to classify, to regulate, to assign places to. 2. To long stitch, to baste. 3. To tune, to harmonise, to attune, to arrange, to make even. Pres. اڅرړي *atsarrnī*; past و اڅاړه *wu-atsārrnah*; fut. و به اڅرړي *wu bah atsarrnī*; imp. و اڅرړه *wu atsarrnah*; act. part. اڅرړونکي *atsarrnūnkaey* or اڅرړونى *atsarrnūnaey*; past part. اڅرړلى *atsarrnalaey*; verb. n. اڅرړنه *atsarrnana'h.*

اڅرړلى *atsarrnalaey,* adj. (past part.) Basted, stitched. 2. Tuned, arranged, made even; (Fem.) اڅرړلِ *atsarrnali.* Pl. (Masc. and Fem.) ي *ī.*

A اجابت *ijā-bat,* s.m. (2nd) Consenting, answering, complying, compliance, consent. Pl. اجابتونه *ijā-batūnah.* اجابت کول *ijā-bat kawul,* verb trans. To answer, to comply, to consent to.

A اجاره *ijā-ra'h,* s.f. (3rd) Hire, rent; income or privilege sold or let for a fixed sum. 2. A farm, a contract. Pl. ۍ *ey.* اجاره دار *ijā-ra'h-dār,* s.m. (5th) A farmer of land revenue, the holder of a monopoly or contract. Pl. اجاره داران *ijā-ra'h-dārān.* اجاره کول *ijā-ra'h kawul,* verb trans. To hire, to rent. اجاره آخستل *ijā-ra'h ākhistal,* verb trans. To take a contract or monopoly.

A اجازت *ijā-zat,* s.m. (2nd) (inf. IV of جوز) Permission, leave, dispensation, sanction, order. Pl. اجازتونه *ijā-zatūnah.* اجازت آخستل *ijā-zat ākhistal,* verb trans. To take leave, to take permission. اجازت غوښتل *ijā-zat-ghokhtal* (E.), or *ghoshtal* (W.). verb trans. To ask leave, to request sanction or permission. اجازت ورکول *ijā-zat war-kawul,* verb trans. To grant permission, to give sanction or dispensation.

A اجر *ajar,* s.m. (2nd) Retribution, reward of good or bad actions; hire, fare, fee. Pl. اجرونه *ajarūnah.* اجر ورکول *ajar war-kawul,* verb trans. To recompense, to reward.

A اجرت *uj-rat,* s.m. (2nd) Wages, hire, reward. Pl. اجرتونه *uj-ratūnah.*

A اجل *ajal,* s.m. (2nd) The term of life, the hour of death; fate, death. 2. A stated time, delay, respite. Pl. اجلونه *ajalūnah.* اجل رسيده *ajāl rasīdah,* adj. Overtaken by fate. اجل نيولى *ajal nī-walaey,* adj. Seized by fate, in the jaws of death. د اجل پياله *da ajal pī-ā'a'h,* The cup of fate or destiny.

A اجماع *ijmāœ,* s.f. (1st) (inf. IV of جمع) An assembly, senate, council, a crowd, collection; amount, whole. Pl. اجماعِ *ijmāœi.*

A اجمال *ij-māl,* s.m. (9th) (inf IV of جمل) An abstract, synopsis. Sing. and Pl.

A اجمالي *ij-mālī,* adj. Abridged, compendious.

A اجناس *aj-nās,* s. pl. of جنس, which see.

A اجنبي *aj-nabī,* adj. Foreign, strange, unknown (person). See پردي

اجوبه *ajū-ba'h,* s.f. (3rd) Wonder, astonishment, miracle, prodigy. Pl. ۍ *ey.* See اعجوبه

P آچار *āchār,* s.m. (6th) Pickles. Sing. and Pl.

اچت *uchat,* adj. Raised, lifted, high, lofty; (Fem.) اچته *uchata'h.* اچت والي *uchat-wālaey,* s.m. (1st) Height, altitude, elevation, loftiness. Pl. والي *wālī.* اچت کيدل *uchat kedal,* verb intrans. To become raised or elevated, to become or grow high or lofty. اچت کول *uchat kawul,* verb trans. To raise, to elevate, to render high or lofty. اچت اوچت uchat nī-wal, verb trans. To hold up, to raise on high. See اوچت

اچرلي ucharlaey, s.m. (1st) The forehead, the brow. Pl. ي ī. See وچولي and تندي

اچکزي achak-zī or اڅکزي atsakzī, s.m. (1st) The name of an Afghān tribe. اچکزي achak-zaey or اڅکزي atsakzaey, Sing. A male of the above tribe. اچکزئي achakza'ī or اڅکزئي atsakza'ī, s.f. (6th) A female of the above. Sing. and Pl.

آچول āchawul, verb trans. To throw, to cast, to fling, to impel, to chuck, to fire off, to launch, to let fly, to discharge, to let off, etc. Pres. آچوي āchawī; past واچاوه wāchāwuh or واچاوو wāchāwo; fut. وا به چوي wā bah chawī; imp. واچوه wāchawah; act. part. آچوونکي āchawūnkaey or آچووني āchawūnaey; past part. آچولي āchawulaey; verb. n. آچونه āchawuna'h.

آچولي āchawulaey, adj. (past part.) Thrown, cast, impelled, let off, discharged, etc.; (Fem.) آچولې āchawuli. Pl. (Masc. and Fem.) ي ī.

اچولي uch-wulaey, s.m. (1st) The forehead, the brow. Pl. ي ī. See وچولي

آچوني āchawunaey, adj. A child brought forth before its time; fœtus, embryo; (Fem.) آچونې āchawuni. Pl. (Masc. and Fem.) ي ī.

A احد ahad, s.m. (6th) Unity; an unit, one. Sing. and Pl.

احاديث ahādīs, s.m. (6th) (Pl. of حديث) Traditions, (particularly) the sayings of Muhammad. Sing. and Pl.

A احاطه ihā-ta'h, s.f. (3rd) (inf. IV of حوط) An enclosure, a fence, a surrounding; compass, circuit, etc. Pl. ئ ey. احاطه کول ihā-ta'h kawul, verb trans. To enclose, to fence, to surround, to besiege, to blockade, to invest. 2. To comprehend.

A احباب ah-bāb, s.m. (Pl. of حبيب) Lovers, beloved friends.

A احتراز ih-tirāz, s.m. (9th) Taking care, abstaining, abstinence, keeping from improper actions, forbearance, regimen, controlling one's passions. Sing. and Pl. احتراز کول ih-tirāz kawul, verb trans. To abstain, to forbear, to control one's passions.

A احتلام ih-tilām, s.m. (9th) (inf. VIII of حلم) Dreaming; nocturnal pollution. Sing. and Pl. See اودس اوبهتل and شيطان خطا کول

A احتمال ih-timāl, s.m. (2nd) (inf. VIII of حمل) Laying on a burden; bearing, patience. 2. Possibility, probability. Pl. احتمالونه ih-timālūnah.

A احتياج ih-tiyāj, s.m. (2nd) Necessity, want, need, indigence, exigence, occasion. Pl. احتياجونه ih-tiyājūnah.

A احتياط ih-tiyāt, s.m. (2nd) Care, caution, circumspection, foresight. Pl. احتياطونه ih-tiyāt-ūnah.

A احرام ih-rām, s.m. (2nd) (inf. IV of حرم) Act of forbidding; putting on a pilgrim's habit at a certain distance from Makka; the cloak or mantle alluded to. Pl. احرامونه ih-rāmūnah.

A احسان ih-sān, s.m. (2nd) Beneficence, benevolence, favour, kindness, courtesy. Pl. احسانونه ih-sānūnah. احسان کول ih-sān kawul, verb trans. To confer favor or benefit, to oblige, to gratify.

A احکام ah-kām, s.m. (6th) (Pl. of حکم) Orders, commands, decrees. Sing. and Pl.

A احمق ah-mak, adj. Foolish, very ignorant; a blockhead, a dunce; (Fem.) احمقه ah-maka'h. احمقي ah-makī, s.f. (3rd). Pl. ئ a'ī; or احمق والي ah-mak wālaey, s.m. (1st) Stupidity, ignorance, doltishness. Pl وا wā-lī, and احمق توب ah-mak-tob, s.m. (2nd). Pl. توبونه tob-ūnah.

A احوال ah-wāl, s.m. (6th) Pl. of حال) Events, occurrences, state, account, condition, circumstances. Sing. and Pl.

A احول ah-wal, adj. Squinting, one who squints or sees objects double; (Fem.) احوله ah-wala'h.

A آخ ākh, interj. An exclamation of joy or pleasure. Ah! How good! 2. An imitative sound of coughing. آخ آخ ākh ākh, Well done! bravo! آخښ آخښ ākhkh or آخښ آخښ

ā*khkh-ākhkh*, and آخ سخ *ākh sakh*, Oh! alas! sorrow!

اخاړه *akhā-ṛrah*, s.m. (6th) Plastering, bedaubing; plaster, the plastering of a wall, etc. Sing. and Pl. See اخيړل

آخاړئي *ākhāṛrna'ī*, 2nd pers. pl. of imp. of آخستل, 'Take you up,' 'seize you,' etc. It is not common.

A اخبار *akh-bār*, s.m. (2nd) (Pl. of خبر) News, intelligence, a newspaper. Pl. اخبارونه *akh-bārūnah*.

P اختر *akh-tar*, s.m. (2nd) A star, a constellation. 2. Good fortune, good omen, horoscope. Pl. اخترونه *akh-tarūnah*. See page 1093.

A اختصار *ikh-tiṣār*, s.m. (9th) Abridgment, abbreviation, brevity, contraction, cutting short. Sing. and Pl. اختصار كول *ikh-tiṣār kawul*, verb trans. To abridge, to contract, to abbreviate.

A اختلاط *ikh-tilāṭ*, s.m. (2nd) The act of mixing, mixture, confusion; commerce, intercourse, friendship. Pl. اختلاطونه *ikh-tilāṭūnah*. اختلاط كول *ikh-tilāṭ kawul*, verb trans. To hold intercourse.

A اختلاف *ikh-tilāf*, s.m. (2nd) Difference of opinion, opposition, discord, misunderstanding, breach, coolness. Pl. اختلافونه *ikh-tilāf-ūnah*. اختلاف كول *ikh-tilāf kawul*, verb trans. To quarrel, to differ in opinion.

P آخته *ākh-tah*, adj. Caught, imprisoned, confined, involved (in calamity). 2. Castrated, آخته كول *ākh-tah kawul*, verb trans. To involve, to confine, to imprison. 2. To castrate. آخته كيدل *ākh-tah kedal*, verb intrans. To become involved (in calamity, etc.), to be caught, imprisoned, confined. 2. To be castrated.

A اختيار *ikh-tiyār*, s.m. (2nd) Choice, approbation, authority, power, free-will, option. Pl. اختيارونه *ikh-tiyārūnah*. اختيار لرل *ikh-tiyār laral*, verb trans. To have the option, to possess authority, power, free-will, etc. اختيارول *ikh-tiyārawul*, verb trans. To choose, to adopt, to approve of.

A آخر *ākhir*, adj. Last, latter. 2. s.m. (9th) The end, issue, termination. Sing. and Pl. (Fem.) آخره *ākhira'h*. آخراً *ākhiran*, adv. Lastly, finally. آخر كيدل *ākhir kedal*, verb intrans. To finish, to terminate, to end. آخر كول *ākhir kawul*, verb trans. To bring to an end, to terminate, to conclude.

A اخراج *ikh-rāj*, s.m. (9th) Drawing forth, derivation; expulsion, evacuation. Sing. and Pl. اخراج كول *ikh-rāj kawul*, verb trans. To expel, to evacuate, to draw forth. See يستل

A آخرت *ākhirat*, s.m. (9th) Futurity, a future state, the world to come. Sing. and Pl. دَ آخرت روځ or ورځ *da ākhirat rwadz* or *wradz*, The last, or judgment day.

A آخري *ākhirī*, adj. Last, final, latter, extreme.

A آخرين *ākhirīn*, adv. The last. See آخراً

آخستل *ākhistal*, verb trans. To take, to seize, to lay hold of, to gripe, to capture, to apprehend, etc. Pres. آخلي *ākhlī*; past واخست *wa-khist*; fut. وا به خلي *wā bah khlī*; imp. واخله *wākh-lah*; act. part. آخستونكي *ākhist-ūnkaey* or آخستونَي *ākhistūnaey*; past part. آخستلَي *ākhistalaey* or آخستي *ākhistaey*; verb. n. آخستنه *ākhistana'h* or آخسته *ākhis-tah*.

آخستنه *ākhistana'h*, s.f. (3rd) (verb. n.) Seizing, taking, grasping, laying hold of, apprehending. Pl. ي *ey*. آخسته *ākhistah*, s.m. (6th) (verb. n.) Sing. and Pl.

آخښ *ākhkh*, interj. Alas! sorrow! well-a-day! also آخښ آخښ *ākhkh-ākhkh* and آخ سخ *ākh-sakh*.

آخښي *ākh-shaey* (W.) or *ākh-khaey* (E.) s.m. (1st) A wife's brother, a sister's husband, a brother-in-law. Pl. ي *ey*. See اوښَي

P اخگر *akh-gar*, s.m. (2nd) A firebrand, a spark of fire. Pl. اخگرونه *akh-garūnah*. See سكروټه

A اخلاص *ikh-lāṣ*, s.m. (2nd) Sincerity, friendship, affection, love. Pl. اخلاصونه *ikh-lāṣūnah*. له اخلاصه *lah ikh-lāṣah* or له اخلاصَ *lah ikh-lāṣa* or په اخلاص سره *pah ikh-lāṣ sarah*, adv. Sincerely, lovingly, affectionately.

A اخلاق *akh-lāk*, s.m. (6th) (Pl. of خلق) Manners, disposition, virtues, morality. Sing. and Pl.

P آخور *ā<u>kh</u>or*, s.m. (2nd) or (5th) A manger, a trough. 3. A stable, a stall. Pl. آخورونه *ā<u>kh</u>orūnah* or آخوران *ā<u>kh</u>orān*.

P آخون *ā<u>kh</u>ūn*, or آخوند *ā<u>kh</u>ūnd*, s.m. (5th) An instructor, a teacher, a preceptor, a learned man. Pl. آخونان *ā<u>kh</u>ūnān* or آخوندان *ā<u>kh</u>ūndān*. آخونزاده *ā<u>kh</u>ūnzādah*, s.m. (5th) A tutor, a doctor, a master, a learned man. Pl. آخونزادگان *ā<u>kh</u>ūnzādagān*.

اخيرل *a<u>kh</u>erral*, verb trans. To plaster, to besmear, to overlay with plaster, to mend, etc. Pres. اخيري *a<u>kh</u>errī*; past وُ اخيره *wu-a<u>kh</u>errah*; fut. وُ به اخيري *wu bah a<u>kh</u>errī*; imp. وُ اخيره *wu-a<u>kh</u>errah*; act. part. اخيرونكَي *a<u>kh</u>errūnkaey* or اخيرونَي *a<u>kh</u>errūnaey*; past part. اخيرلَي *a<u>kh</u>erralaey*; verb. n. اخيرنه *a<u>kh</u>errana'h* or اخاره *a<u>kh</u>ārrah*.

اخيرنه *a<u>kh</u>errana'h*, s.f. (3rd) Plastering, bedaubing; plaster or plastering of a wall. Pl. يْ *ey*. See اخاره

A ادا *adā*, s.f. (6th) Performance, payment, discharge, execution. 2. Blandishment, coquetry, (E.) Sing. and Pl. (W.) Pl. اداوي *adāwī*. ادا كيدل *adā kedal*, verb intrans. To be performed, fulfilled, executed. ادا كول *adā kawul*, verb trans. To perform, to fulfil, to discharge.

A ادب *adab*, s.m. (2nd) Politeness, courtesy, good-breeding, respect. Pl. ادبونه *adabūnah*. ادب كول *adab kawul*, verb trans. To respect, to behave politely. په ادب *pah adab* or په ادب سره *pah adab sarah*, adv. Politely, with respect, courteously, becomingly.

A ادرار *id-rār*, s.m. (2nd) Flowing of milk. 2. Involuntary discharge of urine. 3. Munificence, liberality. Pl. ادرارونه *id-rārūnah*.

A ادراك *id-rāk*, s.m. (9th) Capacity, genius, understanding, comprehension. Sing. and Pl. ادراك كول *id-rāk kawul*, verb trans. To comprehend, to understand.

S ادرك *adrak*, s.m. (6th) Ginger in the undried state. Sing. and Pl.

HI ادل بدل *adal-badal*, s.m. (2nd) Exchange, barter, chopping and changing; confusion. Pl. ادل بدلونه *adal-badalūnah*. ادل بدل كول *adal-badal kawul*, verb trans. To barter, to exchange, to swop.

A آدم *ādam*, s. prop. Adam, the first man. 2. A man's name. آدم خور *ādam-<u>kh</u>or*, adj. Man-eater, man-devouring, cannibal; (Fem.) آدم خوره *ādam-<u>kh</u>ora'h*. آدم زاد *ādam-zād* or آدم زات *ādam-zāt*, Man, mankind; (Fem.) آدم زاده *ādam-zāda'h* or زاته *zāta'h*.

P آدمي *ādamaey*, s.m. (1st) A man, a human being, an individual. Pl. ي *ī*. s.f. (6th) آدمئي *ādama'ī*, A woman, a female. Sing. and Pl. See سړي and ښځه

A آدميت *ādmī-yat*, s.m. (2nd) Humanity, civility. Pl. آدميتونه *ādmī-yatūnah*. See سړيتوب

آدم خيل *ādam-<u>kh</u>el*, s.m. (6th) The name of an Afghān tribe. 2. A man of the tribe. Sing. and Pl. آدم خيله *ādam-<u>kh</u>ela'h*, s.f. (3rd) A female of the above. Pl. يْ *ey*.

A ادنا *ad-nā*, adj. Inferior, mean, little, trivial, small, unimportant. (Masc. and Fem.)

ادو بدو *adū-badū*, adj. Much swollen, very fat. (Masc. and Fem.)

ادي *adey*, A term of address or endearment to a mother; mother! See ابي

P آدينه *ādīna'h*, s.f. (3rd) Friday, the sabbath of the Muḥammadans. Pl. يْ *ey*. See اتبار

ادئي *ada'ī*, s.f. (6th) A division of the lands of a village. Sing. and Pl.

A اذان *azān*, s.m. (2nd) The summons to prayer (usually proclaimed from the minaret of a mosque). Pl. اذانونه *azānūnah*. اذان ويل *azān wa-yal*, verb trans. To repeat the call to prayer, to summon to prayer.

A اذن *izn*, s.m. (2nd) Permission; dismissal, dismission. Pl. اذنونه *izn-ūnah*. اذن آخستل *iznā<u>kh</u>istal*, verb trans. To take leave or permission. اذن وركول *izn war-kawul*, verb trans. To permit, to dismiss, to order, to give permission.

اذوقه *azū-ḳa'h* or ازوقه *azū-ḳa'h*, s.f. (3rd)

(corrup. of A ذوق), Food, provisions. Pl. ئي *ey*.

ار *ar*, s.m. (2nd) A fetter. Pl. ارونه *arūnah*. See پاي بند and ام.

P. ارابه *arā-ba'h*, s.f. (3rd) A wheeled-carriage, a gun-carriage, a cart, a tumbril. Pl. ئي *ey*.

اراخ *arā<u>kh</u>*, s.m. (2nd) A rivulet, a brook, a linn, a sluice, a gush or rush of water. Pl. اراخونه *arā<u>kh</u>-ūnah*.

A. ارادت *irā-dat*, s.m. (2nd) Wish, desire, inclination. Pl. ارادتونه *irādatūnah*. See following.

A. اراده *irā-da'h*, s.f. (3rd) Wish, desire, inclination, purpose, design, plan. Pl. ئي *ey*. اراده لرل *irāda'h laral*, verb trans. To have or possess wish, desire, inclination, etc. اراده كول *irāda'h kawul*, verb trans. To form a design, to make an attempt, to design, to plan.

آراستگي *ārās-tagī*, s.f. (3rd) Preparation, decoration, ornament, arrangement, refinement. Pl. ئي *a'ī*.

آراسته *ārās-tah*, adj. Adorned, dressed, prepared, embellished, improved. آراسته كول *ārās-tah kawul*, verb trans. To adorn, to decorate, to embellish.

A اراك *a-rāk*, s.m. (6th) The name of a tree from which tooth-pickers are made. Sing. and Pl.

P آرام *ārām*, s.m. (2nd) Ease, rest, comfort, repose. Pl. آرامونه *ārāmūnah*. بي آرام *be ārām*, adj. Indisposed, ill at ease; (Fem.) بي آرامه *be ārāma'h*. دل آرام *dil-ārām*, A beloved object, as a son, etc. دل آرامه *dil-ārāma'h*, A sweetheart, a mistress. آرام مندل *ārām mundal*, verb trans. To recover, to obtain ease, rest, quiet, repose, etc. آراميدل *ārāmedal*, verb intrans. To be at ease, to become tranquil, quiet; to become comforted. آرامول *ārāmawul*, verb trans. To rest, to repose, to take rest. آرام وركول *ārām war-kawul*, verb trans. To ease, to appease, to assuage, to relieve.

P آرامگاه *ārām-gāh*, s.m. (2nd) A resting-place, a bed-chamber. Pl. آرامگاهونه *ārām-gāhūnah*.

آرامي *ārāmī*, adj. Slothful, idle; a lover of ease. (Masc. and fem.)

P آرايش *ārā-ī<u>sh</u>*, s.m. (2nd) Ornament, embellishment, dressing, preparation; equipage. Pl. آرايشونه *ārā-ī<u>sh</u>ūnah*.

P آرائي *ārā-'ī*, s.f. (3rd) Adorning, embellishing. Pl. ئي *a'ī*.

A ارباب *ar-bāb*. s.m. (5th) Lords, possessors, masters (pl. of رب). 2. The chief, or head man of a village or <u>kh</u>el amongst the Eastern Af<u>gh</u>āns. Pl. اربابان *arbābān*.

اربوز *ur-būz*, s.m. (2nd) A muzzle of wood or leather for a dog, calf, etc., to prevent biting or drinking. 2. The muzzle. Pl. اربوزونه *ur-būzūnah*. See تربوزك and تمبوزك.

ارت *art*, or *arat*, adj. Loose, open, wide, apart, free, unconfined; (Fem.) ارته *arta'h*, or *arata'h*. ارت والي *arat-wālaey*, s.m. (1st) Looseness, openness, width, freedom. Pl. والي *wālī*. ارتيدل *arte-dal*, or *arate-dal*, verb intrans. To become loosened, loose, open, relaxed, freed. Pres. ارتيږي *aratejzī* (W.), or ارتيگي *arategī* (E.); past ارت شه *arat <u>sh</u>ah*, or وُ شه *wu-<u>sh</u>ah*; fut. ارت به شي *arat bah <u>sh</u>ī*, or به وُ شي *bah wu-<u>sh</u>ī*; imp. ارت شه *arat <u>sh</u>ah*, or وُ شه *wu-<u>sh</u>ah*; act. part. ارتيدونكي *arate-dūnkaey*, or ارتيدوني *arate-dūnaey*; past part. ارت *arat*, or ارت شوي *arat <u>sh</u>awaey*; verb. n. ارتيدنه *aratedana'h*, or ارتيده *aratedah*.

ارتول *aratawul*, verb trans. To disengage, to unloose, to relax, to untie, to open, to unbind, to render unconfined, to free, to set free. Pres. ارتوي *aratawī*; past. ارت كم *arat ka<u>rr</u>*, or وُ كم *wu-ka<u>rr</u>*; fut. ارت به كړي *arat bah k<u>rr</u>ī*, or به وُ كړي *bah wu-k<u>rr</u>ī*; imp. ارت كړه *arat k<u>rr</u>ah*, or وُ كړه *wu-k<u>rr</u>ah*; act. part. ارتوونكي *aratawūnkaey*, or ارتووني *aratawū-naey*; past part. ارت كړي *arat ka<u>rr</u>aey*; verb. n. ارتونه *aratawuna'h*.

ښپه ارته *<u>Kh</u>pa'h arta'h*, The first visit of a lover to the house of his betrothed (*lit.* 'foot-relaxed'); or پښه ارته *p<u>sh</u>a'h arata'h* (W.). ښپه or پښه ارته كول *<u>Kh</u>pa'h*, or *p<u>sh</u>a'h artah*, or *arata'h kawul*, verb trans. To visit a betrothed female (the lover). ارتي ښپي *artey <u>Kh</u>pey*, or ارتي پښي *aratey p<u>sh</u>ey*; adj. Bow or bandy-legged, knock-kneed.

ارتل *aratal*, verb trans. To break wind, to fart. Pres. ارتي *aratī*, or ارزي *arazī*; past وارت *wā-rat*; fut. وُ به ارتي *wu bah aratī*, or ارزي *arazī*; imp. وارزه *wā-razah*; act. part. ارتونکي *aratūnkaey*, or ارتوني *aratūnaey*; past part. ارتلي *aratalaey*; verb. n. ارتنه *aratana'h*.

ارتنه *artina'h*, s.f. (3rd) A wife, a woman, a female. Pl. ې *ey*.

ارتينه *ar-tīna'h*, s.f. (3rd) Pl. ې *ey*. Same as preceding. See ښځه and ماندينه.

ارجل برجل *ar-jal-barjal*, adj. Entangled, entrapped (as a bird in a net), noosed; (Fem.) ارجل برجله *ar-jal-bar-jala'h*.

آرخښ *ārkhakh* (E.), s.m. (2nd) A gasping or guggling noise produced in the throat when crying violently or sobbing, a paroxysm or outburst of grief, convulsive weeping or sobbing. Pl. آرخښونه *ārkhakh-ūnah*. آرخښ کول *ārkhakh kawul*, verb trans., or آرخښ ښکل *ārkhakh kk'kul*, verb trans. To sob or cry convulsively or with violence.

P ارزان *ar-zān*, adj. Cheap, not dear, inexpensive; (Fem.) ارزانه *ar-zāna'h*. ارزان کيدل *ar-zān kedal*, verb intrans. To become cheap, to lessen or grow less or low in price. ارزان کول *ar-zān kawul*, verb trans. To cheapen, to make or render cheap or inexpensive. See لوله, وله, and ول or ويل.

P ارزاني *ar-zānī*, s.f. (3rd) Cheapness, lowness of price. Pl. ئي *a'ī*. See ويل.

P آرزو *ār-zū*, s.m. (9th) Wish, desire, hope, distress, want. Sing. and Pl. آرزومند *ār-zū-mand*, or من *man*; adj. Desirous, longing, wanting; (Fem.) آرزومنده *ār-zū-manda'h*, or منه *mana'h*. آرزو لرل *ār-zū laral*, verb trans. To have a wish, want, or hope, to require, to want.

P آرزومندي *ār-zū-mandī*, s.f. (3rd) Desire, longing, hankering. Pl. ئي *a'ī*.

ارزيدل *ar-zedal*, verb intrans. To be worth, to fetch, to bring. Pres. ارزيږي *ar-zejzī* (W.), or ارزيګي *ar-zegī* (E.); past وُ ارزيده *wu-ar-zedah*, or وُ ارزيدَ *wu-ar-zeda*; fut. وُ به ارزيږي *wu bah ar-zejzī*, or ارزيګي *ar-zegī*; imp. وُ ارزيږه *wu-ar-zejzah*, or وُ ارزيګه *wu-ar-zegah*; act. part. ارزيدونکي *ar-zedūnkaey*, or ارزيدوني *ar-zedūnaey*; past part. ارزيدلي *ar-zedalaey*; verb. n. ارزيدنه *ar-zedana'h*, or ارزيده *ar-zedah*.

اروړمي *ar-jzamaey*, s.m. (1st) (W.), A gape, a yawn; (E.) A belch, eructation. Pl. ي *ī*. اروړمي کول *ar-jzamaey kawul*, verb trans. To yawn, to gape. See ارګمي.

اروړي *ar-jzaey*, s.m. (1st) (W.), A belch, eructation. Pl. ي *ī*. اروړي يستل *ar-jzaey yas-tal*, or کول *kawul*, verb trans. To belch. See ارګي and تيغ.

A ارسال *ir-sāl*, s.m. (9th) The act of sending, mission, remittance. Sing. and Pl. ارسال کول *ir-sāl kawul*, verb trans. To send, to transmit, to remit.

A ارسطو *aristū*, s. prop. Aristotle.

آرسي *ār-sa'ī*, s.f. (6th) (HI. ارسي) A mirror, a small mirror for the thumb worn by women. Sing. and Pl.

A ارشاد *ir-shād*, s.m. (2nd) Direction, command, order. Pl. ارشادونه *ir-shādūnah*. ارشاد کول *ir-shād kawul*, verb trans. To command, to order, to direct.

A ارض *arz*, s.m. (9th) The earth, a portion of land. Sing. and Pl.

ارغند *ar-ghund*, s.m. (5th) A large knuckle-bone used in a game. Pl. ارغندان *ar-ghundān*. See بجل and تکه ارغند.

P ارغوان *ar-ghawān*, s.m. (6th) The name of a plant whose flowers are of a beautiful red colour. Sing. and Pl. Also written ارغون *arghwan*.

P ارغواني *ar-ghawānī*, adj. Of a red or purple colour.

ارغومي *ur-ghūmaey*, s.m. (1st) A male kid. Pl. ي *ī*; ارغومۍ *ur-ghūma'ī*, s.f. (6th) A female kid. Sing. and Pl. See ورغومي.

A ارکان *ar-kān*, s.pl. (of رکن) Pillars, props, supports. ارکان دولت *ar-kān-i-daw-lat*, Nobles, grandees, ministers of state.

ارګمي *ar-gamaey*, s.m. (1st) A gape, a yawn. Pl. ي *ī*. See اروړمي.

ارګي *ar-gaey*, s.m. (1st) (E.) A belch, eructation. Pl. ي *ī*. ارګي يستل *ar-gaey yastal*, or کول *kawul*, verb trans. To belch. See اروي.

P ارمان *ar-mān*, s.m. (2nd) Sorrow, regret, longing. 2. Desire, wish, inclination. 3. Also used as an interjection, Alas! sorrow! Pl. ارمانونه *ar-mānūnah*. ارمان کول *ar-mān kawul*, verb trans. To regret, to sorrow. 2. To desire, to long after.

A ارواح *ar-wāḥ*, s.pl. (of روح) Spirits, souls.

ارونه *ar-wata'h*, s.f. (3rd) A female, a woman, a wife. Pl. ې *ey*. (T اروت).

آرويدل *ār-wedal*, verb trans. To hear, to listen, to hearken. Pres. آروي *ār-wī*; past وارويده *wār-wedah*, or واروېد *wār-weda*; fut. وا به روي *wā bah rwī*; imp. واروه *wār-wah*; act. part. آرويدونکي *ār-wedūnkaey*, or آرويدوني *ār-wedūnaey*; past part. آرويدلي *ār-wedalaey*; verb. n. آرويدنه *ār-wedana'h*, or آرويده *ār-wedah*. آروول *ār-wawul*, verb trans. (caus.) To cause to hear, to make hear. Pres. آرووي *ār-wawī*; past وارواوه *wār-wāwuh*, or وارواوو *wār-wāwo*; fut. وا به رووي *wā bah rawawī*, or وُ به آرووي *wu bah ār-wawī*; imp. وارووه *wār-wawah*; act. part. آرووونکي *ār-wawūnkaey*, or آرووونې *ār-wawūnaey*; past part. آروولي *ār-wawulaey*; verb. n. آروونه *ār-wawuna'h*.

S اره *ara'h*, s.f. (3rd) A saw. Pl. ې *ey*. P (آره).

اره *urah*, s.m. (6th) Clouds. Sing. and Pl. See اوره.

آره *ārah*, s.f. (3rd) Foundation, basis. Pl. ې *ey*.

ارهټ *ar-haṯṯ*, s.m. (2nd) A well with a Persian wheel for drawing water. Pl. ارهټونه *arhaṯṯūnah*. Also رهټ, which see. (HI. ارهٹ).

S ارهر *ar-har*, s.m. (6th) A species of pulse (Cytisus cajan). Sing. and Pl.

ارهرو *ar-harū*, s.m. (6th) Same as preceding. Sing and Pl.

ارهنډ *ar-handd*, s.m. (6th) The Palma Christi, or castor-oil tree. Sing. and Pl.; or ارهنډه *ar-handda'h*, s.f. (3rd). Pl. ې *ey*. (S ارنڈ).

اريځه *ur-yadza'h*, s.f. (3rd) A cloud. Pl. ې *ey*. See اوريځه.

آړ *ārr*, or اړ *arr*, s.m. (2nd) Hinderance, stoppage, prevention. 2. Difficulty, embarrassment, perplexity, dilemma. 3. A screen, shelter, concealment, protection. 4. A fetter, a manacle. Pl. آړونه *ārrūnah*, or اړونه *arrūnah*. 5. adj. Obstructed, hindered, stopped, clogged, embarrassed, perplexed. (Fem.) آړه *ārra'h*, or اړه *arra'h*. آړ آخستل *ārr ākhistal*, verb trans. To lie in wait, to lie in ambush or concealment (*lit.* 'to take concealment.')

آړيدل *ārredal*, verb intrans. To become obstructed, hindered, stopped, checked, clogged, impeded. 2. To become embarrassed, perplexed, to fall into a dilemma. 3. To be screened, protected, etc. Pres. آړيږي *ārrejzī* (W.), or آړيګي *ārregī* (E.); past آړ شه *ārr shah*, or وُ شه *wu-shah*; fut. آړ به شي *ārr bah shī*, or به وُ شي *bah wu-shī*; imp. آړ شه *ārr shah*, or وُ شه *wu-shah*; act. part. آړيدونکي *ārredūnkaey*, or آړيدوني *ārredūnaey*; past part. آړ شوي *ārr shawaey*; verb. n. آړيدنه *ārredana'h*, or آړيده *ārredah*. آړول *ārrawul*, verb trans. To impede, to hinder, to obstruct, to clog, check, retard, to oppose. 2. To embarrass, to perplex, to place in a dilemma. Pres. آړوي *ārrawī*; past آړ کړ *ārr karr*, or وُ کړ *wu-karr*; fut. آړ به کړي *ārr bah krrī*, or به وُ کړي *bah wu-krrī*; imp. آړ کړه *ārr krrah*, or وُ کړه *wu-krrah*; act. part. آړوونکي *ārrawūnkaey*, or آړووني *ārrawūnaey*; past part. آړ کړي *ārr karraey*; verb. n. آړونه *ārrawuna'h*. (HI. آڑ). See اړه.

اړخ *arrkh*, or *arrakh*, s.m. (2nd) The side, the armpit. Pl. اړخونه *arrkhūnah*, or *arrakhūnah*. See څنګ. اړخ په اړخ *arrkh pah arrkh*, or *arrakh pah arrakh*, Side by side, close to each other (as soldiers in their ranks, etc.)

اړم *arram*, s.m. (2nd) A prop, a bar of wood placed against a door, a support, a pillar. Pl. اړمونه *arramūnah*. اړم کول *arram kawul*, verb trans. To prop, to support. See ټمبه.

اړمي *arramaey*, s.m. (1st) (dim. of above) A small prop, a small bar of wood placed against a door or shutter. Pl. ي *ī*.

اړول *aṟṟawul*, verb trans. To turn, to turn over, to capsize, to tilt over, to overturn or overset, to pervert. Pres. اړوي *aṟṟawī*; past واړاوه *wāṟṟāwuh*, or واړاوو *wāṟṟāwo*; fut. وا به ړوي *wā bah ṟṟwī*; imp. واړوه *wāṟṟawah*; act. part. اړوونکي *aṟṟawūnkaey*, or اړووني *aṟṟawūnaey*; past. part. اړولي *aṟṟawulaey*; verb. n. اړونه *aṟṟawuna'h*.

اړولي *aṟṟawulaey*, adj. (past part.) Inverted, overturned, capsized, upside down, tilted over, perverted, turned; (Fem.) اړولِ *aṟṟawuli*. Pl. (masc. and fem.) ي *ī*; اړولي بخت *aṟṟawulaey ba<u>kh</u>t*, Inverted fortune, misfortune, bad luck. اړولي چارې *aṟṟawūlī <u>ch</u>ārey*, Confused or unsettled actions. 2. Improper or fruitless actions. اړولي خبرې *aṟṟawulī <u>kh</u>abarey*, Confused or incoherent words, or words spoken in anger. ښپه اړول *<u>Kh</u>pa'h aṟṟawul* (E.), or پښه اړول *p<u>sh</u>a'h aṟṟawul* (W.) To sit cross-legged, to mount on horseback.

اړه *aṟṟa'h*, s.f. (3rd) Obstacle, hindrance, impediment, stop, prevention. 2. A screen, shelter, concealment. 2. Adj. (fem. of اړ), Impeded, obstructed, stopped, clogged, hindered. Pl. ې *ey*.

اړيړۍ *aṟṟeṟṟa'ī*, s.f. (6th) The small pieces of wood inserted between the ropes over a Persian wheel, and to which the earthen waterpots are fastened. Sing. and Pl.

اړيکي *aṟṟekaey*, s.m. (1st) A bar of wood for a door or gate, a pole, a prop, a support. 2. (W.) Perplexity, plague, difficulty, embarrassment. Pl. ي *ī*.

P آز *āz*, s.m. (2nd) Desire, love, passion, lust, avidity, avarice, covetousness. Pl. آزونه *āzūnah*.

P آزاد *āzād*, adj. Free, liberated. 2. Lonely, solitary; (Fem.) آزاده *āzāda'h*. آزاديدل *āzādedal*, verb intrans. To be set free, manumitted, liberated, emancipated. 2. To become lonely. آزادول *āzādawul*, verb trans. To free, to liberate, to deliver, to set at liberty, to emancipate, to manumit.

P آزاده *āzādah*, adj. Free, noble, independent. (Masc. and Fem.); Pl. آزادګان *āzādahgān*; (Fem.) pl. آزادګانِ *āzādah-gāni*.

P آزادګي *āzādagī*, or آزادي *azādī*, s.f. (3rd) Freedom, independence, manumission, deliverance, freedom, emancipation. Pl. ئ *a'ī*.

P آزار *āzār*, s.m. (2nd) Sickness, disorder, disease; trouble, affliction, injury. Pl. آزارونه *āzārūnah*. آزار رسول *āzār rasawul*, verb trans. To injure, to afflict, to torture. آزاريدل *āzāredal*, or آزار کيدل *āzār kedal*, verb intrans. To be injured, troubled, afflicted. آزار کول *āzār kawul*, or آزارول *āzārawul*, verb trans. To afflict, to injure, to torture, to trouble.

P آزاري *āzārī*, adj. Sick, diseased, afflicted, troubled. 2. A sick person.

ازبک *uz-bak*, s.m. (5th) The name of a tribe inhabiting the countries about Bal<u>kh</u>. 2. A male of the tribe. Pl. ازبکان *uz-bakān*. ازبکه *az-baka'h*, s.f. (3rd) A female of the above tribe. Pl. ې *ey*.

P آزرده *āzur-dah*, adj. Afflicted, sad, vexed, dispirited, displeased, weary. آزرده کيدل *āzur-dah kedal*, verb trans. To become sad, dispirited, uneasy. آزرده کول *āzur-dah kawul*, verb trans. To vex, to displease, to afflict. آزرده خاطر *āzur-dah <u>kh</u>āṭir*, or آزرده دل *āzur-dah dil*, adj. Troubled in mind, disgusted, vexed; (Fem.) آزرده خاطره *āzur-da'h <u>kh</u>āṭira'h*, or آزرده دله *āzurda'h dila'h*.

ازغي *az-<u>gh</u>aey*, s.m. (1st) A thorn. Pl. ي *ī*. See اغزي.

ازغن *az-<u>gh</u>an*, adj. Thorny, prickly; (Fem.) ازغنه *az-<u>gh</u>ana'h*. See اغزن.

A ازل *azal*, s.m. (9th) Eternity, without beginning. Sing. and Pl. ازل و ابد *azal-o-abad*, Without beginning and without end. له ازل نه *lah azal nah*, or له ازلَ *lah azala*, From all eternity. تر ازلَ پورِ or پوري *tar azala pori* or *porī*, Eternally, to all eternity, everlastingly.

P آزمايش *āz-mā'ī<u>sh</u>*, s.m. (2nd) Trial, proof, essay, examination, experiment. 2. Temptation. Pl. آزمايشونه *az-mā'ī<u>sh</u>ūnah*. آرمايش

کول *āz-mā'ī<u>sh</u> kawul*, verb trans. To try, to prove, to essay, to examine.

آزمایښت *āz-mā'ī<u>kh</u>t* (E.), or *āzmā'ī<u>sh</u>t* (W.) Trial, essay, etc. Pl. آزمایښتونه *āz-mā'ī<u>kh</u>t-ūnah*, or *āzmā'ī<u>sh</u>tūnah*. آزمایښت کول *āz-mā'ī<u>kh</u>t*, or *āz-mā'ī<u>sh</u>t kawul*, verb trans. To try, to prove. See preceding.

آزمایل *āz-mā-yil*, verb trans. To prove, to examine, to try, to investigate, to essay. 2. To tempt. Pres. آزمایي *āz-mā-yī*; past وُ آزمایه *wu-āz-mā-yah*; fut. وُ به آزمایي *wu bah āz-mā-yī*; imp. وُ آزمایه *wu-āz-mā-yah*; act. part. آزمایونکي *āz-māyūnkaey*, or آزمایوني *āz-māyūnaey*; past part. آزمایلي *āz-mā-yalaey*; verb n. آزماینه *āz-māyana'h*.

P آزموده *āz-mūdah*, adj. Tried, proved, examined; experienced, veteran. آزموده کول *āz-mūdah kawul*, verb trans. To try, to prove, to examine. آزموده کار *āz-mūdah-kār*, adj. Experienced in business; (Fem.) آزموده کاره *āz-mūdah-kāra'h*.

آزمویل *āz-mo-yal*, verb trans. (W.) To try, to prove, to examine, to essay. See آزمایل and change ا for و for inflexions.

آزمیل *āz-mayil*, verb trans. See آزمایل.

P اژدها *aj<u>z</u>dahā*, s.m. (6th) A large snake, a dragon, a sea-serpent. Sing. and Pl.

S اژدهات *aj<u>z</u>dahāt*, s.m. (6th) The name of a mixed metal, bell-metal or brass. Sing. and Pl. See هژدات.

اږد *uj<u>z</u>d*, adj. Long, elongated, extended, stretched out, prolonged; (Fem.) اږده *uj<u>z</u>da'h*. See اګد and اوږد or اوږده.

آږیل *āj<u>z</u>i-yil*, verb trans. To incite, to stimulate, to instigate, to set on, to provoke, to urge, to rouse, to pat on the back. Pres. آږيي *āj<u>z</u>i-yī*; past وُ آږيه *wu-āj<u>z</u>i-yah*; fut. وُ به آږيي *wu bah āj<u>z</u>i-yī*; imp. وُ آږيه *wu āj<u>z</u>i-yah*; act. part. آږيونکي *aj<u>z</u>i-yūnkaey*, or آږيوني *āj<u>z</u>i-yūnaey*; past. part. آږيلي *āj<u>z</u>i-yalaey*; verb. n. آږينه *āj<u>z</u>i-yana'h*. See اګئیل.

آس *ās*, s.m. (2nd) A horse. Pl. آسونه *ās-ūnah*; (W.) s.m. (5th) Pl. آسان *ās-ān*; له آسَ کوزیدل *lah āsa kūzedal*, verb intrans. To dismount from a horse. په آس سپریدل *pah ās sparedal*, verb intrans. To mount or get on horseback.

A اساس *as-ās*, s.m. (9th) Foundation, basis; a pedestal. Sing. and Pl.

P آسان *āsān*, adj. Easy, convenient, facile, commodious, not difficult; (Fem.) آسانه *āsāna'h*; آسان کیدل *āsān kedal*, verb intrans. To become easy, facile, or convenient. آسان کول *āsān kawul*, verb. trans. To facilitate, to expedite, to render easy or smooth.

P آسایش *āsā-īsh*, s.m. (2nd) Rest, ease, repose, tranquillity, quiet. Pl. آسایشونه *āsā-ī<u>sh</u>ūnah*. آسایش کول *āsā-ī<u>sh</u> kawul*, verb trans. To rest, to repose.

A اسباب *as-bāb*, s.m. (2nd) (Pl. of سبب) Causes, motives, means. 2. Goods and chattels, furniture, stores, baggage. Pl. اسبابونه *asbābūnah*.

P اسپغول *is-pa<u>gh</u>ol*, s.m. (6th) The name of a plant—the flea-wort, a plant of the plantain family. Sing. and Pl.

آسپه *ās-pa'h*, s.f. (3rd) A mare. Pl. ې *ey*.

اسپه *as-pa'h*, s.f. (3rd) The quinsy, suffocation, strangulation. 2. A kind of cutaneous disease, in which spots appear on the body, and the remedy for which is indigo. (W.) Pl. ې *ey*. See خناق and هسپه.

P استاد *us-tād*, s.m. (5th) A teacher, preceptor, master, artist. Pl. استادان *ustādān*. استاده *us-tāda'h*, s.f. (3rd) A preceptress, a schoolmistress. Pl. ې *ey*.

P استادي *us-tādī*, s.f. (1st) Teaching, instruction, mastership, skill, art. Pl. ۍ *a'ī*.

استاذ *us-tā<u>z</u>*, s.m. (5th) A teacher, a master (corrup. of P استاد). Pl. استاذان *ustā<u>z</u>-ān*. استاذه *us-tā<u>z</u>a'h*, s.f. (3rd) A mistress, a preceptress. Pl. ې *ey*.

استازی *as-tāzaey*, s.m. (1st) A messenger, a legate, a delegate, an apostle, an umpire, a peace-maker. Pl. ي *ī*. See استیځه and ګواښ.

استاځي *as-tā<u>dz</u>aey*, s.m. (1st) A messenger, etc. See preceding. Pl. ي *ī*. See استوځي.

P آستان *āstān*, s.m. (2nd) A threshold, an entrance. Pl. آستانونه *āstānūnah*; or آستانه *āstānah*, s.f. (3rd). Pl. ي *ey*.

P استخوان *ustukhwān*, s.m. (2nd) A bone, a stone or kernel in fruit. Pl. استخوانونه *ustukhwānūnah*. See هد and هدوكي.

A استدعا *is-tidæā*, s.f. (6th) (inf. x of دعوت) Request, desire, application, invitation (E.) Sing. and Pl. (W.) Pl. استدعاوي *is-tidæāwī*.

A استعداد *is-tiædād*, s.m. (2nd) (inf. x of عد) Readiness, proficiency, capacity, means, ability. Pl. استعدادونه *is-tiædādūnah*.

A استعفا *is-tiæfā*, s.f. (6th) (inf. x of عفو) Asking forgiveness, deprecating. 2. Giving in one's resignation from office or duty. (E.) Sing. and Pl.; (W.) Pl. استعفاوي *is-tiæfāwī*.

A استعمال *is-tiæmāl*, s.m. (2nd) (inf. x of عمل) Custom, daily practice, exercise, use. Pl. استعمالونه *is-tiæmālūnah*. استعمال كول *is-tiæmāl kawul*, verb trans. To use, to exercise.

A استعمالي *is-tiæmālī*, adj. Used, usual.

A استغاثه *is-tighāsa'h*, s.f. (3rd) (inf. x of غوث) Asking for help, demanding justice, complaining. Pl. ي *ey*. استغاثه كول *is-tighāsa'h kawul*, verb trans. To complain, to demand justice.

A استغفار *is-tigh-fār*, s.m. (2nd) (inf. x of غفران) Begging mercy, craving grace, asking forgiveness. Pl. استغفارونه *is-tigh-fārūnah*. استغفار كول *is-tigh-fār kawul*, verb trans. To deprecate, to crave mercy.

A استغفر الله *as-tagh-firu-llah*, interj. I entreat forgiveness of God! God forbid!

A استغنا *is-tighnā*, s.f. (6th) (inf. x of غنا) Content, independence, exemption. 2. Adj. Contented, independent. (E.) Sing. and Pl.; (W.) Pl. استغناوي *is-tighnāwī*.

A استفسار *is-tifsār*, s.m. (2nd) (inf. x of فسر) Inquiry, asking an explanation, interrogating. Pl. استفسارونه *is-tifsārūnah*. استفسار كول *is-tifsār kawul*, verb trans. To enquire, to ask, to interrogate.

A استقامت *is-tikāmat*, s.m. (2nd) (inf. x of قيام) Standing erect. 2. Rectitude, stability, integrity, constancy. Pl. استقامتونه *is-tikāmatūnah*.

A استقبال *is-tikbāl*, s.m. (2nd) (inf. x of قبل) Meeting, encountering. 2. The ceremony of meeting and receiving a visitor. 3. Futurity. Pl. استقبالونه *is-tikbālūnah*.

A استقلال *is-tiklāl*, s.m. (2nd) (inf. x of قلت) Absolute power, authority, sovereignty, independence, absoluteness, etc. Pl. استقلالونه *is-tiklālūnah*.

A استماع *is-timāæ*, s.f. (1st) (inf. VIII of سمع) Hearing, listening, giving ear to. Pl. استماعِ *is-timāæi*.

A استمرار *is-timrār*, s.m. (2nd) (inf. x of مرور) Continuation, perseverance, perpetuity. 2. The name of the continuative tense in grammar. Pl. استمرارونه *is-timrārūnah*.

A استمراري *is-timrārī*, adj. Continuative, perpetual.

P استوار *us-tuwār*, adj. Strong, firm, stable, powerful, brave, resolute; (Fem.) استواره *us-tuwāra'h*.

استوزه *as-toza'h*, s.f. (3rd) Residence, dwelling, habitation. Pl. ي *ey*. استوزه كول *as-toza'h kawul*, verb trans. To dwell, to reside.

استوځي *as-todzaey*, adj. (past part. from استول) Sent, dispatched. 2. A messenger, a legate, a party sent in place of another, a courier; (Fem.) استوځ *as-todzi*. Pl. (Masc. and Fem.) ي *ī*. See استاځي.

استوژه *as-tojza'h*, s.f. (3rd) Residence, etc. Pl. ي *ey*. See استوزه and استوګه.

استوکه *as-toka'h*, s.f. (3rd) Pl. ي *ey*. See following.

استوګنه *as-tognah*, s.f. (3rd) Residence, dwelling, abode. 2. Tranquillity. Pl. ي *ey*. استوګنه كول *as-togna'h kawul*, verb trans. To dwell, to reside, to take up residence.

استوګه *as-toga'h*, s.f. (3rd) Residence, etc. Pl. ي *ey*. استوګه كول *as-toga'h kawul*, verb trans. To dwell, to reside. See preceding words.

آستول *āstawul*, verb trans. To send, to depute, to dispatch, to forward, to transmit. Pres. آستوي *āstawī*; past واستاوه *wās-tāwuh*, or واستاوو *wās-tāwo*; fut. وا به ستوي *wā bah stawī*; imp. واستوه *wās-tawah*; act. part. آستوونکي *ās-tawūnkaey*, or آستووني *as-*

tawūnaey; past part. آستولي *ās-tawulaey*, and آستوځي *ās-todzaey*; verb n. آستونه *ās-tawuna'h*.

آستيدل *ās-tedal*, verb intrans. To dwell, to inhabit, to reside, to abide, to stay, to sojourn, to halt, etc. Pres. آستيږي *ās-tejzī* (W.) or آستيګي *ās-tegī* (E.); past وُ آستيده *wu-āstedah*, or وُ آستيده *wu-āsteda*; fut. وُ به آستيږي *wu bah astejzī*, or آستيګي *āstegī*; imp. وُ آستيږه *wu-āstejzah*, or وُ آستيګه *wu-astegah*; act. part. آستيدونکي *āstedūnkaey*, or آستيدوني *āstedūnaey*; past part. آستيدلي *āstedalaey*; verb. n. آستيدنه *āstedana'h*, or آستيده *āstedah*.

آستول *ās-tawul*, verb trans. (caus.), To make or cause to dwell or reside, to station, to locate, to halt, to cause or make to sojourn or stay. Pres. آستوي *āstawī*; past وُ آستاوه *wu-āstāwuh*, or وُ آستاوو *wu-āstāwo*; fut. وُ به آستوي *wu bah āstawī*; imp. وُ آستوه *wu-āstawah*; act. part. آستوونکي *āstawūnkaey*, or آستووني *āstawūnaey*; past part. آستولي *āstawulaey*; verb. n. آستونه *āstawuna'h*. See استيدل.

A اسحاق *is-ḥāḳ*, s. prop. The patriarch Isaac.

اسحاقزي *is-ḥāḳzī*, s.m. (1st) Pl. The name of an Afghān tribe; اسحاقزي *is-ḥāḳzaey*, Sing. A male of the above tribe; اسحاقزۍ *is-ḥāḳza'ī*, s.f. (6th) A female of the tribe. Sing. and Pl.

A اسرار *is-rār*, s.m. (2nd) (inf. IV of سر) Concealment, keeping secret. 2. Disclosure, revealing of a secret. Pl. اسرارونه *is-rārūnah*. اسرار ساتل *is-rār sātal*, verb trans. To keep a secret. اسرار ويل *is-rār wa-yal*, verb trans. To reveal a secret.

A اسراف *is-rāf*, s.m. (2nd) (inf. IV of سرف), Prodigality, abuse of wealth, dissipation, extravagance. Pl اسرافونه *is-rāfūnah*. اسراف کول *is-rāf kawul*, verb trans. To dissipate, to act extravagantly, to abuse wealth.

A اسرافيل *is-rāfīl*, s. prop. The name of the angel who, it is said, will sound the last trump at the resurrection. 2. A seraph.

G اسطرلاب *us-ṭurlāb*, s.m. (2nd) An astrolabe. Pl. اسطرلابونه *us-ṭurlābūnah*.

A اسقاط *is-ḳāṭ*, s.m. (2nd) (inf. IV of سقط), Causing to fall, procuring abortion, miscarriage. Pl. اسقاطونه *is-ḳāṭūnah*. اسقاط کول *is-ḳāṭ kawul*, verb trans. To produce miscarriage, to cause abortion. See امغلن آچول.

A اسکندر *is-kandar*, s. prop. Alexander the Great.

A اسکندريه *is-kandriā*, s. prop. Alexandria.

A اسلام *is-lām*, s.m. (9th) (inf. IV. of سلم), The Muḥammadan religion, orthodoxy. Sing. and Pl.

A اسم *ism*. s.m. A name, a noun. Pl. اسماء *as-mā'a*. اسم جامد *ism-i-jāmid*, A primitive noun. اسم جنس *ism-i-jins*, A generic noun. اسم حاليه *ism-i-ḥāliya'h*, The present participle. اسم صفت *ism-i-ṣifat*, A concrete noun, an adjective. اسم عدد *ism-i-æadad*, A cardinal number. اسم مشتق *ism-i-mushtaḳ*, An ordinal number. اسم فاعل *ism-i-fā'æil*, The agent, actor, or active participle. اسم مفعول *ism-i-mafæūl*, The past participle. اسم مصدر *ism-i-maṣdar*, A verbal noun, etc.

اسماعيلزي *is-mā-æīlzī*, s.m. (1st) Pl. The name of an Afghān tribe; اسماعيلزي *is-mā-æīlzaey*, Sing. A male of the above tribe; اسماعيلزۍ *is-mā-æīlza'ī*, s.f. (6th) A female of the above. Sing. and Pl. (A اسماعيل *is-mā-æīl*, Ishmael the son of Abraham).

P آسمان *ās-mān*, s.m. (2nd) The sky, the heavens, the firmament. Pl. آسمانونه *ās-mān-ūnah*.

P آسماني *āsmānī*, adj. Heavenly, celestial, cerulean, azure.

A اسمي *is-mī*, adj. Nominal, titular. See نوماندي.

آسو *asū*, s.m. (9th) The sixth month of the Hindū year. The last month of the rainy season. (s آسن). The Afghāns in the vicinity of Peshāwer use the names of the Hindū months when speaking of, or referring to, agriculture. Sing. and Pl.

P آسودګي *āsūdagī*, or آسوده ګي *āsūdah-gī*, s.f. (3rd) Quiet, rest, content, tranquility. Pl. ۍ *a'ī*.

P آسوده *āsūdah*, adj. At rest, quiet, tranquil, satisfied, contented. آسوده حال *āsūdah ḥāl*, adj. Affluent, in easy circumstances.

اسويلي *as-welaey*, s.m. (1st) A deep-drawn sigh, a cold sigh, a sob. 2. The sound uttered by

a person when shivering from cold. Pl. ي *ī*.
اسويلئ كول *as-welaey kawul*, verb trans. To sigh, to sob; to tremble through cold, to utter a shivering sound when cold. Also اسويلكئ *as-welkaey*, s.m. (1st). Pl. ي *ī*.

اسي *asī*, adj. Unlucky, bad, inauspicious. 2. An unfortunate person. Pl. اسيان *asī-ān*. (Fem.) اسئ *asa'ī*, Sing. and Pl. (6th).

اسئ *asa'ī*, s.f. (6th) Hoar-frost. Sing. and Pl.

P آسيا *ā-siyā*, s.f. (6th) A water-mill. Pl. (W.) آسياوي *ā-siyāwī*; (E.) Sing. and Pl. See ژرنده.

P آسيانه *ā-siyāna'h*, s.f. (3rd) A whetstone. Pl. ئ *ey*.

P آسيب *ā-seb*, s.m. (2nd) Misfortune (the consequence of a demon's shadow having fallen on one), trouble, calamity, damage. Pl. آسيبونه *ā-sebūnah*.

A اسير *a-sīr*, s.m. (5th) A prisoner, a captive. Pl. اسيران *a-sīrān*. اسيره *a-sīra'h*, s.f. (3rd) A female captive or prisoner. Pl. ئ *ey*. اسيركيدل *a-sīr kedal*, verb intrans. To become captive. اسير كول *a-sīr kawul*, verb trans. To take captive.

P آسياوان *ā-siyā-wān*, or آسيوان *ā-sewān*, s.m. (5th) A miller. Pl. آسياوانان *ā-siyā-wānān*, or آسيوانان *ā-sewānān*.

P آش *āsh*, s.m. (6th) Meat, victuals, viands, soup, broth, gruel, pottage, a kind of dish made from barley. Sing. and Pl.

A اشارت *ishā-rat*, s.m. (2nd) Sign, wink, hint, signal, allusion. Pl. اشارتونه *ishā-ratūnah* or اشاره *ishā-ra'h*, s.f. (3rd). Pl. ئ *ey*. اشاره كول *ishā-ra'h kawul*, verb trans. To give a hint, to make a sign, signal, or allusion.

A اشتباه *ish-tibā'h*, s.f. (3rd) Doubt, scruple, ambiguity. Pl. ئ *ey*. اشتباهي *ish-tibāhī*, adj. Suspicious, doubtful.

اشتراني *ash-tarānī*, s.m. (1st) Pl. The name of a tribe of Afghāns; اشترانئ *ash-tarānaey*, Sing. A man or male of the tribe; اشترانئ *ash-tarāna'ī*, s.f. (6th) A female of the above. Sing. and Pl.

اشتغال *ish-tighāl*, s.m. (2nd) (inf. VIII of شغل), Occupation, employment, study, business. Pl. اشتغالونه *ish-tighālūnah*.

اشتوكه *ash-toka'h*, s.f. (3rd) Peace, concord, reconciliation. Pl. ئ *ey*. See آشتي.

A اشتها *ish-tihā*, s.f. (6th) Appetite, desire. (E.) Sing. and Pl.; (W.) Pl. اشتهاوي *ish-tihāwī*. See also ليوال.

A اشتهار *ish-tihār*, s.m. (2nd) Publication, report, fame, divulging. Pl. اشتهارونه *ish-tihārūnah*. اشتهار كول *ish-tihār kawul*, verb trans. To publish, to divulge, to report, to spread abroad.

P آشتي *āshtī*, s.f. (3rd) Peace, concord. 2. Amour, intrigue. Pl. ئ *a'ī*. آشتي كول *āshtī kawul*, verb trans. To make peace, to live in concord with.

اشتياق *ish-tiyāḳ*, s.m. (2nd) (inf. VIII of شوق), Wish, desire, strong inclination. Pl. اشتياقونه *ish-tiyāḳūnah*. اشتياق لرل *ish-tiyāḳ laral*, verb trans. To have a strong inclination, to desire, to wish.

اشرپئ *ash-rapa'ī*, s.f. (6th) (E.) The name of a gold coin in value from 17 to 20 rupees. Sing. and Pl.; (W.) اشرپي *ash-rapī*, s.f. (3rd). Pl. ئ *a'ī* (P اشرفي).

P آشفتگي *āshuftagī*, s.f. (3rd) Distraction, uneasiness, perturbation, misery. Pl. ئ *a'ī*.

P آشفته *āshuf-tah*, adj. Distracted, distressed, miserable, uneasy, disturbed. آشفته حال *āshuftah-ḥāl*, Distressed in circumstances, in adversity.

P اشك *ashk*, s.m. (2nd) A tear. Pl. اشكونه *ashkūnah*. See اوښي.

آشناي *āsh-nā'e*, s.m. (5th) Anacquaintance, a lover, a friend. Pl. آشنايان *āsh-nā'e-ān*; آشنايه *āsh-nāya'h*, s.f. (3rd) A mistress, a sweetheart, a female friend. Pl. ئ *ey*. Also (P) آشنا *āsh-nā*, s.m. (5th) Pl. آشنايان *āsh-nāyān*.

P آشنائي *āsh-nā'ī*, s.f. (3rd) Acquaintanceship, intimacy, friendship. Pl. ئ *a'ī*. آشنائي لرل *āsh-nā'ī laral*, verb trans. To have or hold acquaintanceship; (Eng. verb intrans.) To be intimate, or on terms of intimacy. آشنائي كول

āsh-nā'ī kawul, verb trans. To make acquaintance, to form intimacy.

اشنغر *ash-naghar*, s. prop, The name of a town, consisting of three separate villages, in the Do-ābah of Peshāwer, properly هشت نگر *hasht-nagar*, Or the eight towns.

P آشوب *āshūb*, s.m. (2nd) Clamour, tumult. 2. Storm, tempest. 3. Terror. 4. Misfortune. Pl. آشوبونه *āshūbūnah*. Also written *āshob*.

اشوره *ash-ūra'h*, s.f. (3rd) (corrup. of A عاشوره), The first ten days of the month Muharram. Pl. ې *ey*.

آشول *ā-shol*, s.m. (2nd) Noise, tumult, disturbance, outcry, clamour, bustle. Pl. آشولونه *ā-sholūnah*. آشول کول *ā-shol kawul*, verb trans. To raise or create a tumult, disturbance, outcry, etc.

A اشيا *ash-yā*, s.m. (A Pl. of شي) Things, effects.

P آشيانه *āshiyāna'h*, s.f. (3rd) A bird's nest. Pl. ې *ey*. See جاله.

آښل *ākhal*, verb trans. (E.) To mix, to mingle (as flour and water for bread), to knead, to leaven, to excite fermentation. Pres. آغکي *āgh-gī*; past واښل *wā-khal*; fut. وا به غکي *wā bah gh'gī*; imp. واغکه *wā-gh'gah*; act. part. آښونکَي *ākhūnkaey*, or آښونَي *ākhūnaey*; past part. آښلَي *ākhalaey*; verb. n. آښنه *ākhana'h*. See آغزل.

آښلي *ākhalī*, s.m. (1st) Pl. (past part. of آښل) Dough.

A اصحاب *aṣ-ḥāb*, s.pl. (of صاحب) Lords, masters, companions, friends, apostles.

A اصراف *iṣ-rāf*, s.m. (2nd) (inf. IV of صرف) Expenditure, waste, prodigality. Pl. اصرافونه *iṣ-rāfūnah*. اصراف کول *iṣ-rāf kawul*, verb trans. To expend, to waste.

A اصل *aṣl*, s.m. (2nd) Root, origin, original, foundation, lineage. 2. Capital. Pl. اصلونه *aṣl-ūnah*. بد اصل *bad aṣl*, Of mean or bad lineage; نيک اصل *nek aṣl*, Of good family or lineage.

A اصلي *aṣl-ī*, adj. Original, radical, essential, genuine, noble.

A اصيل *aṣīl*, adj. Well-born, noble, genuine; (Fem.) اصيله *aṣīla'h*.

A اضطراب *iẓ-ṭirāb*, s.m. (2nd) (inf. VIII of ضرب) Agitation, perturbation, restlessness, distraction, anguish, trouble, chagrin. Pl. اضطرابونه *iẓ-ṭirābūnah*.

A اطاعت *iṭā-æat*, s.m. (2nd) (inf. IV of طوع), Obeying, submission, reverence, observance. اطاعت کول *iṭā-æat kawul*, verb trans. To obey, to reverence.

A اطراف *aṭ-rāf*, s.m. (Pl. of طرف) Sides, skirts, districts, environs, confines.

A اطفال *aṭ-fāl*, s. pl. (of طفل) Children. عيال و اطفال *æiyāl-o-aṭ-fāl*, Wife and children, family.

A اطلاع *iṭṭilāæ*, s.f. (1st) (inf. VIII of طلوع) Notice, manifesting, declaring, information, knowledge. اطلاع کول *iṭṭilāæ kawul*, verb trans. To acquaint, to inform, to apprize.

A اطلس *aṭ-las*, s.m. (2nd) Satin. Pl. اطلسونه *aṭ-lasūnah*.

A اطوار *aṭ-wār*, s.m. (Pl. of طور) Manners, behaviours, ways, habits.

A اظهار *iẓ-hār*, s.m. (2nd) (inf. IV of ظهور) Manifestation, revelation, disclosure, publication, display, declaration. Pl. اظهارونه *iẓ-hārūnah*. اظهار کول *iẓ-hār kawul*, verb trans. To disclose, to reveal, to notify, to declare.

اعتبار *iæ-tibār*, s.m. (2nd) (inf. VIII of عبر) Confidence, trust, faith, belief, credit, reliance. 2. Taking as an example, reasoning by comparison. Pl اعتبارونه *iæ-tibārūnah*. اعتبار کول *iæ-tibār kawul*, verb trans. To give credit to, to believe, to trust.

A اعتقاد *iæ-tiḳād*, s.m. (2nd) (inf. VIII of عقد) Confidence, faith, trust. Pl. اعتقادونه *iæ-tiḳādūnah*. بي اعتقادَ *be iæ-tiḳāda*, Faithless.

A اعتمادي *iæ-timādī*, adj. Trustworthy.

A اعجب *aæ-jab*, adj. More, or most wonderful. 2. Wondering, being astonished, causing surprise or admiration; (Fem.) اعجبه *aæ-jaba'h*.

A اعجوبه *aæ-jūbah*, s.m. (6th) Wonder, astonishment, miracle, prodigy. Sing. and Pl. See اجوبه.

A اعراب *aæ-rāb*, s.m. (6th) Wild wandering Arabs; the Arabians who live in cities being called عرب. Sing. and Pl.

A اعرابي *aæ-rābī*, s.m. (5th) A wanderer, a vagabond. Pl. اعرابيان *aæ-rābīān*; (Fem.) (6th) ۍ *a'ī*. Sing. and Pl.

A اعراض *iæ-rāz̤*, s.m. (2nd) (inf. IV of عرض) Aversion, avoiding, dislike, averseness. Pl. اعراضونه *iæ-rāz̤ūnah*.

A اعراف *iæ-rāf*, s.m. (9th) Purgatory, a wall intervening between heaven and hell. Sing. and Pl.

A اعزاز *iæ-zāz*, s.m. (2nd) (inf. IV of عزت) Honouring, magnifying; respect, honour, attention, esteem. Pl. اعزازونه *iæ-zāzūnah*.

A اعظم *aæ-z̤am*, adj. (compar. of عظيم) Greater, greatest; (Fem.) اعظمه *aæ-z̤ama'h*.

A اعلا *aæ-lā*, or اعلي, adj. Most high, supreme, high, sublime.

P آغاز *ā-ghāz*, s.m. (9th) Beginning, commencement. Sing. and Pl. آغاز کول *ā-ghāz kawul*, verb trans. To begin, to commence.

اغ دغ *agh-dugh*, s.m. (6th) Deception, deceit, craft, duplicity, cheat, trick, double dealing, cunning. Sing. and Pl. Also written اغ دوغ *agh-dūgh*.

اغر *aghar*, s.m. (9th) Fitting an arrow to the bow-string ready to shoot. Sing. and Pl. اغر کول *a-ghar kawul*, verb trans. To fit or place an arrow to the bow preparatory to shooting.

آغزکي *āgh-zakaey*, s.m. (1st) A species of thorny plant. Pl. ي *ī*.

آغزن *āgh-zan*, adj. Thorny, prickly (as a thorn-tree, etc.); (Fem.) آغزنه *āgh-zana'h*. آغزنه ونه *āgh-zana'h wana'h*, s.f. (3rd) A thorn-tree. Pl. ۍ *ey*. See آزغن.

آغزي *āgh-zaey*, s.m. (1st) A thorn, a prickle. Pl. ي *ī*. See آزغي.

اغږل *agha-jzal*, verb trans. (W.) To mix, to mingle (as flour and water in making bread), to knead, to leaven, to excite fermentation. Pres. اغږي *agha-jzī*; past وا غږل *wā-ghajzal*; fut. وا به غږي *wā bah ghajzī*; imp. واغږه *wā-ghajzah*; act. part. اغږونکي *aghajzūnkaey*, or اغږوني *aghajzūnaey*; past part. اغږلي *aghajzalī* (Pl.); verb. n. اغږنه *aghajzana'h*. See آهل.

آغستل *āghustal*, verb trans. To dress, to clothe, to array, to attire, to apparel, to accoutre, to wrap up, to envelope. Pres. آغندي *āghundī*; past واغست *wā-ghust*; fut. وا به غندي *wā bah ghundī*; imp. واغنده *wā-ghundah*; act. part. آغستونکي *āghustūnkaey*, or آغستوني *āghustūnaey*; past part. آغستلي *āghustalaey*; verb. n. آغستنه *āghustana'h*, or آغستن *āghustan*.

آغستلي *āghustalaey*, adj. (past part.) Dressed, attired, clothed, arrayed, accoutred, enveloped; (Fem.) آغستلِ *āghustali*. Pl. (Masc. and Fem.) ي *ī*.

آغستول *āghustawul*, verb trans. (caus.) To cause to dress, attire, array, etc.; to dress out, to decorate. Pres. آغندوي *āghundawī*; past واغستاوه *wā-ghustāwuh*, or واغستاوو *wā-ghustāwo*; fut. وا به غندوي *wā bah ghundawī*; imp. واغندوه *wā-ghundawah*; act. part. آغستوونکي *āghustawūnkaey*, or آغستووني *āghustawūnaey*; past part. آغستولي *āghustawulaey*; verb. n. اغستونه *aghustawuna'h*.

A اغلب *aghlab*, adj. (compar. of غالب) Superior, stronger; adv. Most likely; (Fem.) اغلبه *aghlaba'h*.

آغله *āghalah*, adj. Pleasing, handsome, good-looking, agreeable. 2. s.f. (3rd) (W.) Assisting by one's prayers (particularly a devotee). Pl. ۍ *ey*. See بهاغل.

آغلي *āghalaey*, adj. Pleasing, agreeable, gratifying. 2. Good, excellent, prime; (Fem.) اغلِ *aghali*. Pl. (Masc. and Fem.) ي *ī*.

آغوستل *āghostal*, verb trans. To dress, to clothe, to array, to accoutre, etc. آغوستول *āghostawul*, verb trans. (caus.) To cause to dress, to deck out, etc. See آغستل and آغستول.

آغوستنه *āghostana'h*, or آغستن *āghustan*, s.f. (3rd) (verb. n.), Pl. ۍ *ey*; s.m. (9th) Dress, clothing, raiment, apparel, costume, habiliment, uniform, etc. Sing. and Pl.

P آغوش *āghosh*, s.m. (2nd) The embrace, the side, the space between the bosom and the arms. 2. An armful. Pl. آغوشونه *āghoshūnah* ; آغوش كول *āghosh kawul*, or په آغوش كښې نيول *pah āghosh k'khey*, or *kshey nīwal*, verb trans. To take in the arms, to embrace.

A اغيار *agh-yār*, s.m. (5th) (Pl. of غير) Stranger, foreigner, a rival, an unknown person. Pl. اغياران *agh-yārān*. اغياره *agh-yār'ah*, s.f. (3rd). Pl. ې *ey*.

اغير *a-gherr*, s.m. (2nd) Indigestion, flatulence, dyspepsia. Pl. اغيرونه *a-gherrūnah*.

اغيرل *a-gherral*, verb trans. To trouble or afflict with indigestion or dyspepsia. Pres. اغيري *agherrī* ; past و اغيره *wu-agherrah* ; fut. و به اغيري *wu bah agherrī* ; imp. و اغيره *wu-agherrah* ; act. part. اغيرونكې *agherrūnkaey*, or اغيرونې *agherrūnaey* ; past part. اغيرلي *agherralaey* ; verb. n. اغيرنه *agherrana'h*.

اغيرلې *agherralaey*, adj. Troubled with dyspepsia, dyspeptic ; (Fem.) اغيرلِ *agherrali*. Pl. (Masc. and Fem.) ي *ī*.

اغيري *agherraey*, adj. Dyspeptic ; (Fem.) اغير *agherri*. Pl. (Masc. and Fem.) ي *ī*. See preceding.

A آفت *āfat*, s.m. (2nd) Calamity, misfortune, wretchedness. Pl. آفتونه *āfatūnah*. آفت وهلې *āfat wahalaey*, Unfortunate, overtaken with calamity, wretched ; (Fem.) آفت وهلِ *āfat wahali*. Pl. (Masc. and Fem.) ي *ī*.

P آفتاب *āf-tāb*, s.m. (9th) The sun, sunshine. Sing. and Pl. آفتاب پرست *āf-tāb parast*, A worshipper of the sun ; (Fem.) آفتاب پرسته *āf-tāb parasta'h*.

P آفتابه *āf-tāba'h*, s.f. (3rd) An ewer, a kind of pitcher. Pl. ې *ey*. See گروه.

P آفتابي *āf-tābī*, adj. Solar, of the sun. 2. Faded, yellow.

P افتاده *uf-tādah*, adj. (P. fallen, descended) Humble, meek.

P افروز *afroz*, act. part. of افروختن, Illuminating, enlightening, kindling. Used only in composition ; as, جهان افروز *jahān-afroz*, Enlightening the world.

افرا *af-rā*, s.m. (9th) The name of a demon. Sing. and Pl.

A افراط *if-rāṭ*, s.m. (2nd) (inf. IV of فرط) Excess, superfluity, abundance. Pl. افراطونه *if-rāṭūnah*.

P آفريدگار *āfrīd-gār*, s.m. (9th) The creator, Sing. and Pl.

P آفريده *āf-rīdah*, adj. Created, creature.

آفريدي *āf-rīdī*, s.m. (1st) Pl. The name of a tribe of Afghāns, notorious robbers, the bugbear of the Peshāwerīs. آفريدې *af-rīdaey*, Sing. A male of the tribe. آفريدۍ *āf-rīda'ī*, s.f. (6th) A female of the above. Sing. and Pl. See آپريدي.

P آفرين *āf-rīn*, or *āfa-rīn*, s.m. (2nd) Praise, applause, acclamation. Pl. آفرينونه *āf-rīnūnah* or *āfarīnūnah*. 2. interj. Bravo ! well done ! آفرين ويل *af-rīn wa-yal*, To praise, to applaud.

P افسانه *af-sāna'h*, s.f. (3rd) A tale, story, romance, fiction. Pl. ې *ey*.

P افسر *af-sar*, s.m. (5th) A crown, a diadem. Pl. افسران *af-sarān*.

P افسرده *af-surdah*, adj. Frozen, withered, faded ; dispirited, dejected, melancholy, low-spirited. افسرده دل *af-surdah-dil*, adj. Faint-hearted, low-spirited, dejected.

P افسوس *af-sos*, s.m. (2nd) Sorrow, concern, regret, vexation. Pl. افسوسونه *af-sosūnah*. 2. interj. Alas ! ah ! افسوس كول *af-sos kawul*, verb trans. To sigh, to regret, to mourn, to grieve, to lament, to bewail, to moan. Also written اپسوس *ap-sos*, etc.

P افسون *af-sūn*, s.m. (2nd) Incantation, a spell, enchantment, sorcery, fascination. Pl. افسونونه *af-sūnūnah*. افسون كول *af-sūn kawul*, To enchant, to fascinate, to cast a spell over one. افسون گر *af-sūngar*, s.m. (5th) An enchanter, a sorcerer. Pl. گران *garān*. افسون گره *afsūngara'h*, s.f. (3rd) A sorceress, an enchantress. Pl. ې *ey*.

P افشان *af-shān*, pres. part. of افشاندن (used in comp.) Scattering, shedding, dispersing ; as, گل افشان *gul-afshān*, Strewing roses ; زر افشان *zar-afshān*, Scattering gold.

A افضل *af-ẓal*, adj. (compar. of فاضل) More or most eminent, pre-eminent. 2. A proper name; (Fem.) افضله *afẓala'h*.

افغان *af-ghān*, s.m. (5th) The name of a powerful nation inhabiting Afghānistān, supposed to be the descendants of the Lost Tribes. 2. An Afghān. 3. The name of the grandson of Malik Tālūt (Saul), king of Israel, from whom the Afghāns, called also Afghānah, claim descent. According to the Taẕkirat-ul-Mulūk, "the original meaning of the word Afghānah is *fighān*, a Persian word, which means complaint or lamentation, because Malik Afghān, the ancestor of the Afghāns, was a cause of lamentation to the devil, the jinns, and mankind. From the constant use of the word, the vowel-point (ـِ) *kasrah* was dropped, after which the other letters could not be sounded without the aid of a vowel, and *alif-i-waṣl* was placed before the *gh*, and thus made *afghānah*." See "Remarks on the Afghān people and language:" Journal of Bengal Asiatic Society, vol. xxiii, page 560, and the Introduction to my Pushto Grammar. Pl. افغانان *afghānān*. افغانه *afghāna'h*, s.f. (3rd) An Afghān female. Pl. يْ *ey*. افغاني *afghānī*, s.f. (3rd) The language of the Afghāns, the Pushto (W.), or Pukhto (E.). Pl. يْ *a'ī*. 2. adj. Of the Afghāns, relating to the Afghāns.

A افق *ufuḳ*, s.m. (2nd) The horizon. 2. A tract or region of the earth. Pl. افقونه *ufuḳūnah*, or, A Pl. آفاق *āfāḳ*.

P افگار *af-gār*, adj. Wounded; (Fem.) افگاره *afgāra'h*. دل افگار *dil-afgār*, Heart-broken.

A افلاس *if-lās*, s.m. (2nd) (inf. IV of فلس) Penury, poverty, indigence, bankruptcy. Pl. افلاسونه *if-lāsūnah*.

A افلاطون *af-lāṭūn*, s. prop. Plato.

A افلاک *af-lāk*, s.m. (6th) (Pl. of فلک) The heavens, celestial orbs or spheres. Sing. and Pl.

A افليج *if-līj*, s.m. (9th) Paralysis. Sing. and Pl. See گزن.

A افيون *af-yūn*, s.m. (6th) Opium. Sing. and Pl. See ترياك.

P افيوني *af-yūnī*, adj. An opium-eater, a sot. See افيم چي and ترياكي.

A اقامت *iḳā-mat*, s.m. (2nd) (inf. IV of قيام) Resting, staying, abode, residence, dwelling. 2. Being earnest in prayer or supplication, rising up and sitting down in prayer. Pl. اقامتونه *iḳā-matūnah*. اقامت كول *iḳā-mat kawul*, verb trans. To rest, to stay, to abide, to dwell. 2. To rise up and sit down at prayer, to repeat prayers with earnestness; or اقامت ويل *iḳā-mat wayal*.

A اقبال *iḳ-bāl*, s.m. (2nd) (inf. IV of قبل) Prosperity, good fortune, auspices. Pl. اقبالونه *iḳ-bālūnah*. اقبال مند *iḳ-bāl-mand*, adj. Prosperous, fortunate; (Fem.) اقبال منده *iḳ-bāl-manda'h*.

A اقتدا *iḳ-tidā*, s.f. (inf. VIII of قدوت) Imitation, following (E.) Sing. and Pl.; (W.) Pl. اقتداوي *iḳ-tidāwī*. اقتدا كول *iḳ-tidā kawul*, verb trans. To follow, to imitate.

A اقدس *aḳ-das*, adj. (comp. of قدس) Very or most holy, most sacred; (Fem.) اقدسه *aḳ-dasa'h*.

A اقرار *iḳ-rār*, s.m. (2nd) (inf. IV of قرار) Confession, avowal, affirmation, confirmation, agreement, attestation, assertion. Pl. اقرارونه *iḳ-rārūnah*. اقرار كول *iḳ-rār kawul*, verb trans. To confess, to avow, to agree. اقرار نامه *iḳ-rār nāma'h*, s.f. (3rd) A bond, a contract, a written agreement. اقراريدل *iḳ-rāredal*, verb intrans. To become confessed, avowed, asserted, affirmed. اقراوول *iḳ-rārawul*, verb trans. To confess, to avow, to agree to.

A اقران *aḳ-rān*, s.m. (6th) (Pl. of قرين) Equals, cotemporaries. Sing. and Pl.

A اقرب *aḳ-rab*, adj. (comp. of قريب) More or most near, nearer, nearest. 2. (Pushto) Wretched, unfortunate, wicked, miserable; (Fem.) اقربه *aḳ-raba'h*.

A اقربا *aḳ-ribā*, s.m (6th) (pl. of قريب) Kindred, relations, friends, allies. Sing. and Pl.

A اقليم *iḳ-līm*, s.m. (2nd) Clime, region, country, climate. Pl. اقليمونه *iḳ-līmūnah*. (A Pl. اقاليم *aḳā-līm*.)

A اقوام *aḳ-wām*, s.m. (6th) (Pl. of قوم) Tribes, people, nations, castes. Sing. and Pl.

اکا *a-kā*, s.m. (5th) An uncle, a paternal uncle. Pl. اکاگان *a-kāgān*. See تره, ماما, and نوي.

A اکبر *ak-bar*, adj. (comp. of کبير) Greater, very great, greatest; (Fem.) اکبره *ak-bara'h*.

A اکثر *ak-ṣar*, adj. (comp. of کثير) Most, very much, many, much, frequent. 2. adv. Generally, for the most part, frequently, mostly; (Fem.) اکثره *ak-ṣara'h*.

اکر *ak-ar*, s.m. (2nd) Giddiness, swimming of the head. Pl. اکرونه *ak-arūnah*.

A اکرام *ik-rām*, s.m. (2nd) (inf. IV of کرم) Honouring, complimenting, treating with attention; ceremony, veneration, respect. Pl. اکرامونه *ik-rāmūnah*. اکرام کول *ik-rām kawul*, verb trans. To honour, to venerate, to respect.

A اکراه *ik-rāh*, s.m. (2nd) (inf. IV of کره) Aversion, abhorrence, detestation, horror, forcing against one's will. Pl. اکراهونه *ik-rāhūnah*. See کرکه.

A اکرم *ak-ram*, adj. (comp. of کريم) Merciful, very kind, bountiful, generous; (Fem.) اکرمه *ak-rama'h*.

P اکنون *ak-nūn*, adv. Now, at this time.

اکو بکو *akū-bakū*, s.m. (6th) The name of a bird whose voice is imitated by these words: hence the name. 2. A play amongst children. Sing. and Pl.

اکو خيل *ako-khel*, s.m. (6th) The name of an Afghān tribe, a male of the tribe. Sing. and Pl. اکو خيله *ako-khela'h*, s.f. (3rd) A female of the above. Pl. ې *ey*.

اکوړ *akoṛr*, s.m. (6th) A walnut. Sing. and Pl. See اوغز.

اکوړه *ako-ṛra'h*, s. prop. The name of a town about half way between Attak and Peshāwer, the chief place of the Khattak tribe.

اکوړی *ako-ṛraey*, s.m. (1st) Red leather or morocco. Pl. ي *ī*.

اکوزي *ako-zī*, s.m. (1st) Pl. The name of an Afghān tribe. اکوزی *ako-zaey*, Sing. A male of the above. اکوزۍ *ako-za'ī*, s.f. (6th) A female of the above. Sing. and Pl.

P آگاه *ā-gāh*, adj. Informed of, acquainted with, apprized; intelligent, aware, vigilant; or آگاه مند *ā-gāh-mand*; (Fem.) آگاه منده *ā-gāh-manda'h*. آگاه کيدل *ā-gāh kedal*, verb intrans. To become aware of, to become apprized of. آگاه کول *ā-gāh kawul*, verb trans. To apprize of, to make aware of.

آگر *ā-gar*, s.m. (2nd) A kind of perfume, aloewood (s. اگر). Pl. آگرونه *ā-gar-ūnah*.

P اگر *agar*, conj. If. See که.

اگر *agar*, s.m. (5th) A slave, a captive. Pl. اگران *agarān*. اگره *agar-a'h*, s.f. (3rd) A female slave or captive. Pl. ې *ey*. See مريي and مينځه or وينځه.

P اگرچه *agar-chih*, conj. Although, though, notwithstanding.

اگرمی *ag-ramaey*, s.m. (1st) A yawn, a gape. 2. A belch, eructation. Pl. ي *ī*. اگرمی کول *ag-ramaey kawul*, verb trans. To belch, to yawn, to gape. See اربمی.

اگن *a-gan*, s.m. (5th) The name of a kind of lark (Alauda aggia. Buch.) Pl. اگنان *a-ganān*. (HI. اگن).

اگواړۍ *ag-wāṛra'ī*, s.f. (6th) The head ropes for picketing a horse. Sing and Pl. (HI.)

P آگه *ā-gah*, adj. Informed. See آگاه.

اگۍ *a-ga'ī*, s.f. (6th) The egg of any bird. Sing. and Pl. See ها and هگي.

اگئيل *age-yil*, verb trans. To chafe, to taunt, to irritate, to excite, to rouse, to twit, to play upon. 2. To sew up, to stop up (as the mouth of a sack) (W.) Pres. اگيي *age-yī*; past وُ اگيه *wu-age-yah*; fut. وُ به اگيي *wu bah age-yī*; imp. وُ اگيه *wu-age-yah*; act. part. اگيونکی *age-yūnkaey*, or اگيونی *age-yūnaey*; past part. اگيلی *age-yalaey*; verb. n. اگينه *age-yana'h*.

A آل *āl*, s.m. (6th) Children, family, race, progeny, offspring, dynasty. Sing. and Pl. د آدم آل *da ādam āl*, The race of Adam. آل اولاد *āl aw-lād*, Offspring, progeny, race.

A الا *illā*, adv. If not, if, besides, except, otherwise, else, but, unless; or و الا *wo-illā*.

A آلات *ā-lāt*, s.m. (6th) (Pl. of آلت) Tools, instruments, utensils.

الاج *a-lāj,* s.m. (5th) A comber or carder of cotton (corrup. of A. حلاج). Pl. الاجان *a-lājān.* الاجه *a-lāja'h,* s.f. (3rd) A female who cards cotton. Pl. ئ *ey.*

الاجي *a-lājī,* s.f. (3rd) An instrument for separating the cotton from the seed. Pl. ئ *a'ī.* الاجي كول *a-lājī kawul,* verb trans. To card or comb cotton.

S الاچي *ilā-chī,* s.f. (3rd) Cardamoms. Pl. ئ *a'ī.* See هيل.

الستي *a-lāstī,* adj. Absent, invisible, the invisible world.

HI الاو *alā-o,* s.m. (2nd) A bonfire. Pl. الاوونه *alā-o-ūnah.* See دوهه.

A الاهي *ilā-hī,* adj. Divine. 2. interj. Oh my God!

A البته *al-battah,* adv. Certainly, indeed, positively, really, absolutely. See بي شكه.

A آلت *ā-lat,* s.m. (2nd) A tool, an instrument, apparatus, membrum virile, veretrum animalium. Pl. آلتونه *ā-latūnah,* or آلات *ā-lāt* (A). See غيتر.

A التجا *il-tijā,* s.f. (6th) (inf. VIII of لجأ) Fleeing to any one for protection, refuge, protection; petition, entreaty. (E.) Sing. and Pl. (W.) Pl. التجاوي *il-tijāwī.*

A التفات *il-tifāt,* s.m. (2nd) (inf. VIII of لفت) Friendship, kindness, respect, regard, attention, courtesy. Pl. التفاتونه *il-tifātūnah.* التفات كول *il-tifāt kawul,* verb trans. To have regard or respect, to attend to, to show kindness, etc.

A التماس *il-timās,* s.m. (2nd) (inf. VIII of لمس) Beseeching, petitioning, supplication, prayer, request. Pl. التماسونه *il-timāsūnah.* التماس كول *il-timās kawul,* verb trans. To beseech, to petition. التماس لرل *il-timās laral,* verb trans. To have a desire, wish, request, etc.

الجه *ul-ja'h,* s.f. (3rd) Plunder, spoil, prey, booty, pillage. Pl. ئ *ey.* الجه كول *ul-jah kawul,* verb trans. To plunder, to rob, to pillage. See اوار.

T الچي *il-chī,* s.m. (5th) An ambassador, an envoy, a legate. Pl. الچيان *il-chīān.* الچي گري *il-chī garī,* s.f. (3rd) The employment of an envoy or ambassador. Pl. ئ *a'ī.*

A الحال *il-ḥāl,* adv. Now, at present, just now.

الس *u'las,* s.m. (2nd) A large family, a clan, a tribe, a sept, a crowd. Pl. السونه *u'lasūnah.* السي سپاهي *u'lasī spā-hī,* A militia-man. السي لښكر *u'lasī lashkar* (W.), or *lakhkar* (E.), A militia force. (T. الوس).

السي *u'lasī,* adj. Clannish, of or belonging to a tribe or family. 2. Militia.

A الغياث *al-ghiyāṣ,* s.m. (9th) Complaint, complaining, demanding justice. 2. interj. Alas! Sorrow! Sing. and Pl.

A الفاظ *al-fāẓ,* s.m. (6th) Pl. of لفظ) Words, sounds, terms.

P الف بي *alif be,* s.f. (9th) The a, b, c; the alphabet. Sing. and Pl.

A الفت *ul-fat,* s.m. (2nd) Friendship, affection, attachment, kindness, intimacy, familiarity. Pl. الفتونه *ul-fatūnah.* الفت كول *ul-fat kawul,* verb trans. To show affection towards or attachment. الفت لرل *ul-fat laral,* verb trans. To have friendship for, to have or hold intimacy with.

آلفته *ā-luftah,* adj. Distracted, distressed, uneasy, disturbed, wretched, miserable, divided (corrup. ? of P آشفته). آلفته كيدل *ā-luftah kedal,* verb intrans. To become or grow distracted, wretched, miserable, etc. آلفته كول *ā-luftah kawul,* verb trans. To make or render miserable, distracted, wretched, etc.

الك *al-ak,* s.m. (5th) A boy, a youth to the period of puberty. Pl. الكان *al-akān.* 2. adj. Small, young, youthful, juvenile; (Fem.) الكه *al-aka'h;* and s.f. (3rd) A young girl. Pl. ئ *ey.* الك والي *al-ak wālaey,* s.m. (1st) Childhood, youth, smallness, etc. Pl. والي *wālī.* See هلك.

A الله *allah,* s. prop. God, the Almighty. الله اكبر *allahu akbar,* God is great. الله الله *allah-allah,* An interjection expressive of surprise and approbation. الله ري *allah re,* Oh my God! My God! Good God!

الله باش *allah-bāsh,* s.m. (2nd) Salutation on meeting, greeting, shaking hands. Pl. الله باشونه *allah-bāsh-ūnah.* الله باش كول *allah-*

bāsh kawul, verb trans. To greet, to salute, to shake hands on meeting.

P الماس *al-mās*, s.m. (2nd) A diamond, adamant. Pl. الماسونه *al-māsūnah.* الماسي *al-māsī*, adj. Of diamond, of the colour of a diamond.

T الم غلم *allam ghallam*, s.m. (6th) Trifling talk or business, toying, wickedness. Sing. and Pl.

الو *a-lū*, s.m. (6th) A kind of plum. Sing. and Pl. الوبالو *a-lū-bālū*, A cherry. الوبخارا *alū bokhārā*, A kind of plum.

الوان *al-wān*, s.m. (2nd) A kind of cloth of a fine texture. Pl. الوانونه *al-wānūnah.*

آلوتل *āl-watal*, or *āl-wutal* (W.) verb intrans. To fly, to pass through the air as a bird; Pres. آلوزي *āl-wazī*; past والوت *wāl-wat*; fut. وا به لوزي *wā bah lwazī*; imp. والوزه *wāl-wazah*; act. part. آلوتونكي *āl-watūnkaey*, or آلوتوني *āl-watūnaey*; past part. آلوتلي *āl-watalaey*, or آلوتي *āl-wataey*; verb. n. آلوتنه *āl-watana'h*, or آلواته *āl-wātah.* See آلوزول.

الوجه *alū-ja'h*, s.m. (6th) A kind of plum very plentiful at Peshāwer.

الوچه *alūchah*, s.m. (6th) A kind of plum. Sing. and Pl. See preceding.

P آلوده *ālūdah*, adj. (past part. of آلودن) Stained, soiled, besmeared, polluted, covered, etc. خون آلوده *khūn ālūdah*, Smeared or covered with blood.

آلودهگي *ālūdah-gī*, s.f. (3rd) Contamination, defilement, pollution, stain, foulness. Pl. ئ *a'ī.*

آلوزول *āl-wazawul* (E.) or *al-wuzawul* (W.) verb trans. (caus.) To cause or make to fly, to put to flight. Pres. آلوزوي *āl-wazawī*; past والوزاوه *wāl-wazāwuh*, or والوزاوو *wāl-wazāwo*; fut. وا به لوزوي *wā bah lwazawī*; imp. والوزوه *wāl-wazawah*; act. part. آلوزوونكي *āl-wazawūnkaey*, or آلوزووني *āl-wazawūnaey*; past part. آلوزولي *āl-wazawulaey*; verb. n. آلوزونه *āl-wazawuna'h.*

T الوس *u-lūs*, s.m. (2nd) A large family, a clan, a tribe, a sept. Pl. الوسونه *ulūs-ūnah.* الوسي *u-lūsī*, adj. Clannish, relating to a tribe or family. 2. Militia troops. See الس.

الوگردگو *a-lū garda-gao*, s.m. (6th) A very large kind of plum, a nectarine. Sing and Pl.

الول *alu-wal*, adj. All of a heap, head over heels, by the run, plump (as in falling); (Fem.) الوله *alu-walah.* الول پريوتل *alu-wal pre-watal*, verb intrans. To fall suddenly, to come down plump or by the run, to fall head over heels, or all of a heap, to topple.

الوويل *al-wo-yal*, verb trans. To scorch, to roast, to parch with heat, etc.; (met.) to perplex with grief, to aggrieve, to distress. Pres. الووي *al-wo-yī*; past وُ الوويه *wu-al-wo-yah*; fut. وُ به الووي *wu bah al-wo-yī*; imp. وُ الوويه *wu-al-wo-yah*; act. part. الوويونكي *al-wo-yūnkaey*, or الوويوني *al-wo-yūnaey*; past part. الوويلي *al-wo-yalaey*; verb. n. الووينه *al-wo-yana'h.*

الوويلي *al-wo-yalaey*, adj. (past part.) Scorched, much burned, parched; afflicted, distressed, heart-scorched; (Fem.) الوويل *al-wo-yali.* Pl. (Masc. and Fem.) ي *ī.* See اولوي and الوي.

الوي *alawaey*, adj. Roasted, burnt (particularly through grief, etc.); (Fem.) الوِ *alawi.* Pl. (Masc. and Fem.) ي *ī.*

A اله *ilah*, s.prop. God. الها *ilāh-ā*, Oh God! لا اله الا الله *lā ilahā illallah*, There is no other god than God.

A الهام *il-hām*, s.m. (2nd) (inf. IV of لهم) Inspiration, revelation. Pl. الهامونه *il-hāmūnah.* الهاميدل *il-hāmedal*, verb intrans. To become inspired. الهامول *il-hāmawul*, or الهام كول *il-hām kawul*, verb trans. To inspire, to make inspired.

A الهاميه *il-hāmiyah*, s m. (6th) The name of an antinomian sect. Sing. and Pl.

الهنگ *al-hang*, s.m. (2nd) Ebullition or burst of grief, convulsive sobbing or weeping (generally applied to males rather than females). Pl. الهنگونه *al-hang-ūnah.* الهنگ كول *al-hang kawul*, verb trans. To weep or sob with violence.

A الهي *ilahī*, adj. Divine. 2. interj. Oh God!

A الي *ila*, prep. Up to, until.

A الياس *ilyās*, s. prop. The prophet Elias, said to be the grandson of Shem, son of Noah. الياس‌زي *ilyās-zī*, s.m. (1st) Pl. The name of an Afghān clan. الياس‌زي *ilyās-zaey*, Sing. A male of the above. الياس زئي *ilyās-za'ī*, s.f. (6th) A female of the above. Sing. and Pl.

اليت پليت *alīt-palīt*, adj. Higgledy-piggledy, topsy-turvy. 2. s.m. (9th) Confusion, subversion, transposition. Sing. and Pl.

اليټ پليټ *alīṯṯ-palīṯṯ*, adj. and s.m. (9th). Sing. and Pl. See preceding word. (HI. الٹ پلٹ).

ام *am*, s.m. (6th) (comp. of s. آم) The mango tree and its fruit. Sing. and Pl.

A اما *ammā*, conj. But, moreover, however, nevertheless. See ولي.

A امارت *imārat*, s.m. (2nd) Government, office, dignity of امير, which see. Pl. امارتونه *imāratūnah*.

A اماره *ammārah*, adj. Imperious, headstrong, obstinate. نفس اماره *nafs-i-ammārah*, Concupiscence, cupidity, lust.

P اماس *amās*, s.m. (2nd) Swelling, a swelling. Pl. اماسونه *amāsūnah*. See پاړسوب.

ام الولده *um-ul-walada'h*, s.f. (3rd) (in law sense) A female slave who has borne a child to her master (*lit.* Mother of children). Pl. ئي *ey*. See سوريته.

A امام *imām*, s.m. (5th) A leader in religious matters, a prelate, a patriarch, a priest. 2. The large bead in a rosary, which remains fixed in the hand and not turned over in telling the beads. Pl. امامان *imāmān*.

A امامت *imām-at*, s.m. (2nd) The office or dignity of an Imām. Pl. امامتونه *imām-atūnah*.

A اماميه *imāmiyah*, s.m. (6th) Followers of the Imām Æalī, who consider him the rightful Imām immediately after Muḥammad. Sing. and Pl.

A امان *amān*, s.m. (2nd) Quarter, protection, safety, mercy, grace. Pl. امانونه *amānūnah*. امان غوښتل *amān ghoshtal* (W.), or *ghokhtal* (E.), verb trans. To demand quarter or protection. امان ور كول *amān war-kawul*, verb trans. To give quarter, to grant mercy or protection.

A امان *imān*. See ايمان.

A امانت *amā-nat*, s.m. (2nd) Deposit, charge, anything given in trust. 2. Faith, religion. Pl. امانتونه *amā-natūnah*. امانت دار *amā-nat-dār*, s.m. (5th) A trustee, a guardian. 2. adj. Trusty, honest. Pl. امانت داران *amā-nat-dārān*; (Fem.) امانت داره *amā-nat-dāra'h*. Pl. ئي *ey*. امانت داري *amā-nat-dārī*, s.f. (3rd) Guardianship, agency, faithfulness, trust. Pl. ئي *a'ī*. امانت ييښول *amā-nat yeshawul* (W.), or *yekhawul* (E.), verb trans. To deposit, to leave in charge or trust, to intrust. امانت خيانت كول *amā-nat khiyānat kawul*, verb trans. To embezzle anything left in one's charge, to be guilty of breach of trust.

اماني *amānī*, adj. All, the whole, entire. 2. adv. Entirely, wholly.

A آماني *amānī*. s.f. (3rd) Security. 2. Charge, trust, deposit. Pl. ئي *a'ī*.

P امبار *am-bār*, s.m. (2nd) A stack or rick of corn, a granary, a grain store. Pl. امبارونه *am-bārūnah*.

P امبور *am-būr*, s.m. (2nd) Pincers, forceps, tweezers. Pl. امبورونه *am-būrūnah*.

A امت *ummat*, s.m. (2nd) People, sect, a people of the same religion. Pl. امتونه *ummatūnah*.

A امتحان *im-tiḥān*, s.m. (2nd) (inf. VIII of محن) Proof, trial, examination, experiment, temptation. Pl. امتحانونه *im-tiḥānūnah*. امتحان آخستل *im-tiḥān ākhistal*, verb trans. To examine, to try, to prove. امتحان كول *im-tiḥān kawul*, verb trans. To make experiment, to prove, to examine.

A امتياز *im-tiyāz*, s.m. (2nd) (inf. VIII of ميز) Discrimination, distinction, discretion, separation. 2. Pre-eminence. 3. Good breeding, ceremony. Pl. امتيازونه *im-tiyāzūnah*. امتياز كول *im-tiyāz kawul*, verb trans. To discriminate, to discern, to distinguish.

P آمدني *āmadanī*, s.f. (3rd) (from آمدن) Import, income, revenue, ways. Pl. ئي *a'ī*.

A امر *amr*, s.m. (9th) An order, a command. 2. The imperative mood in grammar. 3. Affair, transaction. Sing. and Pl. امر معروف *amr-i-maærūf*, A lawful or known order or command, a self-evident duty. امر و نهي *amr-o-nahī*, Command and prohibition. امر كول *amr kawul*, or ور كول *war-kawul*, verb trans. To order, to command.

A امرا *um-rā*, s.m. (5th) (Pl. of امير) Nobles, grandees (generally), a noble; also امرايان *um-rāyān*, or امراگان *um-rāgān*.

S امرت *am-rat*, s.m. (6th) The guava. Sing. and Pl.

A امرد *am-rad*, adj. Beardless, a handsome youth. امرد پرست *am-rad parast*, A sodomite.

S امروت *am-rūt*, s.m. (6th) A guava. Sing. and Pl.

امړي *um-ṟṟaey*, adj. Prior, former, previous, preceding, foremost; (Fem.) امړئ *um-ṟṟa'ī*. See اولني, اوړنبي, ړنبي and وړنبي.

امسا *am-sā*, s.f. (6th) A staff, a stick, a bludgeon, a club. (E.) Sing. and Pl.; (W.) Pl. امساوي *am-sāwī*. See همسا.

امغلن *um-ghalan*, adj. Immature, crude, unready, uncooked, raw, unripe, embryonic; (Fem.) امغلنه *um-ghalana'h*. امغلن آچول or غورزول *um-ghalan āchawul*, or *ghor-zawul*, verb trans. To miscarry.

A امكان *im-kān* (inf. IV of مكن) s.m. (9th) Possibility; contingent existence. Sing. and Pl. امكان لرل *im-kān laral*, verb trans. To have or possess possibility, (Eng. verb intrans.) to be possible.

A امن *amn*, s.m. (6th) Security, safety. Sing. and Pl. په امن كول *pah amn kawul*, verb trans. To bring into safety or security.

P آموخته *āmokhtah*, past part. Learned, taught. آموخته كول *āmokhtah kawul*, verb trans. To teach, to make learned. آموخته كيدل *āmokhtah kedal*, verb trans. To become taught.

A امي *ummī*, or (W.) *ammī*, adj. Illiterate, unlearned, uneducated.

P اميد *umīd*, s.m. (2nd) Hope, expectation, trust, dependence. Pl. اميدونه *umīdūnah*. اميد لرل *umīd laral*, verb trans. To have or possess hope, trust, or expectation. اميد كول *umīd kawul*, verb trans. To hope, to trust, to place reliance on, or dependence in. اميد ور كول *umīd warkawul*, verb trans. To give hope or expectation.

P اميدوار *umīd-wār*, adj. Hopeful, hoping, expecting. 2. s.m. (5th) An expectant, a dependant, a candidate. Pl. اميدواران *umīd-wārān*; (Fem.) اميدواره *umīd-wāra'h*. 2. s.f. (3rd) A pregnant woman. Pl. ئ *ey*.

P اميدواري *umīd-wārī*, s.f. (3rd) Expectation, hope, hopefulness, dependence. Pl. ئ *a'ī*.

A امير *a-mīr*, s.m. (5th) A commander, a grandee, a nobleman, a lord. Pl. اميران *a-mīrān*. See امرا.

A P اميرانه *a-mīrānah*, adj. Princely, lordly, befitting or worthy of a noble.

اميرزاده *a-mīr-zādah*, s.m. (5th) (Masc. and Fem.) Nobly-born, the son of a noble or lord. Pl. اميرزادهگان *a-mīr-zādah-gān*; (Fem.) اميرزادهگانې *a-mīr-zādah-gāni*.

A اميري *a-mīrī*, s.f. (3rd) Lordship, sway, the dignity of a noble. Pl. ئ *a'ī*.

A آمين *ā-mīn*, adv. Amen, so be it.

A امين *a-mīn*, adj. Constant, faithful, safe, guarded. 2. s.m. (5th) A trustee, a guardian, an umpire, an arbitrator, an inspector, an investigator. Pl. امينان *a-mīnān*; (Fem.) امينه *a-mīna'h*, s.f. (3rd). Pl. ئ *ey*.

امين توب *a-mīn-tob*, s.m. (2nd) Guardianship, trusteeship, the office of an arbitrator or umpire. Pl. توبونه *tob-ūnah*.

انا *a-nā*, s.f. (6th) A grandmother, paternal or maternal. (E.) Sing. and Pl.; (W.) Pl. اناوي *a-nā-wī*, or s.f. (5th). Pl. اناگانې *a-nā-gāni*. ورله انا *warlah-a-nā*, A great-grandmother. لا ورله انا *lā warlah-a-nā*, A great-great-grandmother. See نيا.

P انار *a-nār*, s.m. (2nd) A pomegranate. Pl. انارونه *a-nārūnah*.

P امبار *am-bār*, s.m. (2nd) A heap, a stack, a barn, a granary. Pl. امبارونه *am-bārūnah*.

P امباز *am-bāz*, s.m. (5th) A partner, an associate. Pl. امبازان *am-bāzān*. امبازه *am-bāza'h*, s.f. (3rd). Pl. ئ *ey*.

P امبازي *am-bāzī*, s.f. (3rd) Partnership, association. Pl. ئ *a'ī*.

انبالئ *an-bāla'ī*, s.f. (6th) A howdah or seat placed on the back of an elephant or camel. Sing. and Pl.

انبور *an-bor*, s.m. (2nd) Pincers, forceps, pliers, tongs. Pl. انبورونه *an-bor-ūnah.*

P انبوه *an-boh*, s.m. (9th) A crowd, concourse, mob, multitude, throng. 2. Great quantity, abundance. Sing. and Pl.

انبوهي *an-bohī*, s.f. (3rd) A crowd, etc. Pl. ئي *a'ī*. See preceding, and تولي.

A انبيا *an-biyā*, s.m. (6th) (Pl. of نبي) Prophets.

A انتخاب *in-tikhāb*, s.m. (2nd) (inf. VIII of نخب) Selection, drawing out, election, choice. Pl. انتخابونه *in-tikhābūnah.* انتخاب کول *in-tikhāb kawul*, verb trans. To select, to choose.

A انتظار *in-tiẓār*, s.m. (2nd) (inf. VIII of نظر) Expectation, looking out for, awaiting. Pl. انتظارونه *in-tiẓārūnah.* انتظار لرل *in-tiẓār laral*, verb trans. To have or possess expectation. انتظار کول *in-tiẓār kawul*, verb trans. To expect, to await.

A انتظام *in-tiẓām*, s.m. (2nd) (inf. VIII of نظم) Arrangement, disposition, order, management, administration, regularity. Pl. انتظامونه *in-tiẓāmūnah.* انتظام کول *in-tiẓām kawul*, verb trans. To arrange, to regulate, to dispose.

A انتقال *in-tiḳāl*, s.m. (2nd) (inf. VIII of نقل) Migration, transporting, transferring, passing from one to another, translation, conveyance, travelling ; departure, decease, dying. Pl. انتقالونه *in-tiḳālūnah.*

A انتقام *in-tiḳām*, s.m. (2nd) (inf. VIII of نقم) Revenge, retaliation. Pl. انتقامونه *in-tiḳāmūnah.* انتقام آخستل *in-tiḳām ākhistal*, verb trans. To take revenge, to revenge.

A انتها *in-tihā*, s.f. (6th) (inf. VIII of نهي) Termination, end, extremity, summit. (E.) Sing. and Pl. ; (W.) Pl. انتهاوي *in-tihāwī*. 2. adj. Finished, completed, terminated.

انڅئي *an-tsa'ī*, s.f. (6th) Yarn made of wool or *pashm*, worsted. Sing. and Pl. See نڅئي.

P انجام *an-jām*, s.m. (2nd) End, termination, accomplishment. 2. Accident, vexation. Pl. انجامونه *an-jāmūnah.* انجام کول *anjām kawul*, or په انجام رسول *pah anjām rasawul*, verb trans. To accomplish, to terminate, to bring to an end.

P انجمن *an-juman*, s.m. (2nd) An assembly, a meeting, a company. Pl. انجمنونه *an-jumanūnah.* See مجلس.

G انجيل *in-jīl*, s. prop. The New Testament, the Gospel.

اند *and*, s.m. (2nd) A period of 500 years, an age. 2. Idea, thought, fancy, imagination. 3. (s) A testicle. 4. An egg. Pl. اندونه *andūnah.*

P انداز *an-dāz*, s.m. (9th) Measure, measurement, valuation, weighing, conjecture, guess. Sing. and Pl. 2. s.m. (5th) (act. part. of انداختن) Throwing, casting, a thrower, a caster. Pl. اندازان *an-dāzān.* تير انداز *tīr-andāz*, An archer. تير اندازي *tīr-andāzī*, s.f. (3rd) Archery. Pl. ئي *a'ī*.

P اندازه *an-dāza'h*, s.f. (3rd) Measure, measurement, dimension, weighing, valuation, guess ; manner, propriety ; time in music. Pl. ئي *ey*. اندازه کول *an-dāza'h kawul*, verb trans. To measure, to weigh, to guess, to value. اندازه نيول *an-dāza'h nī-wal*, verb trans. To take measurement, to compute.

P اندام *an-dām*, s.m. (2nd) Body, stature, figure. Pl. اندامونه *an-dāmūnah.* اندام نهاني *an-dām ni-hānī*, The private parts.

اندر پايه *andar-pā-ya'h*, s.f. (3rd) A ladder, steps, a staircase. Pl. ئي *ey*. See پوري and پارچنګ.

اندرور *an-dror*, or *an-drūr*, s.f. (5th) A husband's sister. Pl. اندرندِ *an-drandi*, or اندرندئي *an-drandey*. See ندرور.

اندرکه *an-darka'h*, s.f. (3rd) A quilted coat, a vest, a doublet. Pl. ئي *ey*. (HI. انگرکها).

P اندک *an-dak*, adj. Little, few, small ; (Fem.) اندکه *an-daka'h.*

P اندوه *an-doh*, s.m. (2nd) Grief, anxiety, trouble. Pl. اندوهونه *an-dohūnah.* اندوه کول *an-doh kawul*, verb trans. To grieve. اندوه وهلي *an-doh wahalaey*, adj. (past part.) Distressed, grieved ; (Fem.) اندوه وهلِ *an-doh wahali.* Pl. (Masc. and Fem.) ي *ī*. اندوه ګين *an-doh-gīn*, adj. Full of grief, sad, afflicted ; (Fem.) اندوه ګينه *an-doh-gīna'h.*

انده *in-dah*, s.f. (3rd) A mouthful or sip of

drink of any kind. 2. (W.) A gulph. Pl. ئ *ey*.

HI اندهير *and-her*, s.m. (2nd) Misfortune, calamity, injustice, violence, tumult, outrage. Pl. اندهيرونه *and-herūnah*.

انديښ *an-dekh* (E.) or *an-desh* (W.), act. part. in compos. (from P انديشيدن) Thinking, considering, meditating. دور انديښ *dūr-andekh*, or (W.) دور انديش *dūr-andesh*, Provident, foreseeing, circumspect, wise, prudent; (Fem.) دور انديښه *dūr-andekha'h*, or دور انديشه *dūr-andesha'h*; or انديښمن *an-dekhman*, or انديشمن *an-deshman*; (Fem.) انديښمنه *an-dekhmana'h*, or انديشمنه *an-deshmana'h*.

انديښنه *an-deshna'h* (W.), or *an-dekhna'h* (E.), s.f. (3rd) Thought, meditation, concern, care, dread, fear, anxiety, suspicion. Pl. ئ *ey*.

اندو خر *an-ddo-kharr*, s.m. (5th) Name of a child's game. Pl. اندو خُر *an-ddo-khærr*.

اندئ *an-ddaey*, s.m. (1st) A package, a bundle, the half of a horse or camel load. Pl. ي *ī*. See كوار, كاره, كاري, سته and غندي.

اندريَ *an-dderacy*, s.m. (1st) A mat made from a peculiar kind of cane called ميزري, which see. Pl. ي *ī*.

انذور *an-zor*, s.m. (2nd) Ornament, embellishment, impression, figure, flowers worked on anything, etc. Pl. انذورونه *an-zorūnah*. انذوريدل *an-zoredal*, verb intrans. To become marked, impressed, embellished, etc. انذورول *an-zorawul*, verb trans. To embellish, to ornament, to mark.

A انزال *in-zāl*, s.m. (2nd) (inf. IV of نزول) Causing to descend, emission, emissio seminis. Pl. انزالونه *in-zālūnah*.

انزوروئ *an-zorwaey*, s.m. (1st) Ornament, embellishment, decoration, impression, mark, etc. Pl. ي *ī*. See انذور.

انځور *an-dzor*, s.m. (2nd) Ornament, embellishment, impression, mark. Pl. انځورونه *an-dzorūnah*. انځور كول *an-dzor kawul*, verb trans. To ornament, to embellish, to mark. See انذور.

انځير *an-dzīr*, s.m. (6th) A fig. Sing. and Pl. See انجير.

A انساب *an-sāb*, s.m. (6th) (Pl. of نسب) Races, genealogies, lineages. Sing. and Pl.

A انسان *in-sān*, s.m. (5th) Man, mankind, a human being. Pl. انسانان *insānān*. انسانه *in-sāna'h*, s.f. (3rd) Woman kind. Pl. ئ *ey*.

A انسانيت *in-sānīyat*, s.m. (2nd) Humanity, human kindness, affability, politeness, civility. Pl. انسانيتونه *in-sānīyatūnah*. See سري توب.

انسټ *an-sitt*, s.m. (6th) The name of a plant used in medicine. Sing. and Pl.

A انشا *in-shā*, s.f. (6th) (inf. IV of نشأ) Writing, composition, the belles lettres. (E.) Sing. and Pl.; (W.) Pl. انشاوي *inshāwī*.

A ان شأ الله تعالي *in shā allahu taæālā*, God willing, please God.

A انصار *an-ṣār*, s.m. (6th) (Pl. of ناصر) Assistants, aiders, auxiliaries, companions, etc. Sing. and Pl.

A انصاري *an-ṣārī*, s.m. (5th) The name of a tribe of Arabs, a number of whom are to be found in Afghānistān and the Panjāb. 2. The founder of the Roshānīān sect—Bāyazīd, was of the Anṣārī tribe. Pl. انصاريان *an-ṣārīān*. انصارئ *an-ṣāra'ī*, s.f. (6th) A female of the above. Sing. and Pl.

A انصاف *in-ṣāf*, s.m. (2nd) (inf. IV of نصف) Justice, equity, decision. Pl. انصافونه *in-ṣāfūnah*. انصاف طلب *in-ṣāf ṭalab*, Seeking justice. انصاف كول *in-ṣāf kawul*, verb trans. To judge, to administer justice, to decide. بي انصاف *be-inṣāf*, adj. Unjust, iniquitous; (Fem.) بي انصافه *be-inṣāfa'h*. بي انصافي *be-inṣāfī*, s.f. (3rd) Injustice, iniquity. Pl. ئ *a'ī*.

A انعام *in-æām*, s.m. (2nd) (inf. IV of نعمت) Benefaction, a present, a gift, a favour, a benefit. Pl. انعامونه *in-æāmūnah*. انعام ور كول *in-æām war-kawul*, verb trans. To confer a benefit or favour, to bestow a gift or present.

A انفصال *in-fiṣāl*, s.m. (2nd) (inf. VII of فصل) Separation, division, settling, the decision of a case. Pl. انفصالونه *in-fiṣālūnah*. انفصال كول *in-fiṣāl kawul*, verb trans. To decide, to settle.

A انكار *in-kār*, s.m. (2nd) (inf. IV of نكر) Denial,

refusal, negation. Pl. انکارونه *in-kārūnah*. انکار کول *in-kār kawul*, verb trans. To deny, to refuse, to disallow.

s انګار *an-gār*, s.m. (2nd) Embers, lighted coals. Pl. انګارونه *an-gārūnah*.

انګازه *an-gāza'h*, s.f. (3rd) Echo, reverberation, symphony. Pl. ې *ey*. انګازه ختل *an-gāzah khatal*, verb intrans. To echo, to resound, to be sounded back. See انګۍ.

P انګبين *an-gabīn*, s.m. (6th) Honey. Sing. and Pl. See شهد.

P انګشت *an-gusht*, s.m. (2nd) A finger. Pl. انګشتونه *an-gushtūnah*. انګشت نما *an-gusht-numā*, One who is pointed at, famous, notorious.

P انګشتانه *an-gushtāna'h*, s.f. (3rd) A ring (particularly the one worn on the thumb), a thimble. Pl. ې *ey*.

انګړ *an-garr*, s.m. (2nd) A building, a house containing many stories. Pl. انګړونه *an-garrūnah*.

انګڼ or انګن *an-garrn*, s.m. (2nd) A court, an area, a yard, an enclosed space close to a house. Pl. انګڼونه *an-garrnūnah*. (s. انګن).

P انګور *an-gūr*, s.m. (5th) A grape, grapes. Sing. and Pl. See کور.

انګوړی *an-gorraey*, sm. (1st) A small pomegranate. Pl. ي *ī*. See انګوړي and انګک.

انګولا *an-golā*, s.f. (6th) A howl (as of a dog at night, or of a jackal). Pl. (W.) انګولاوي *an-golāwī*; (E.) Sing. and Pl.. انګولا کول *an-golā kawul*, verb trans. To howl. See غپا.

انګه *inga'h*, s.f. (3rd) A female who accompanies and waits on a bride for a few days after marriage, generally a female relation. Pl. ې *ey*; also written اينګه *īn-ga'h*.

انګهار *an-gahār*, s.m. (5th) Pl. Groaning, sighing, moaning, crying out through pain; groans, moans. انګهار کول *an-gahār kawul*, verb trans. To groan, to moan, to cry out. See هنګهار and زګيروي.

انګی *an-gaey*, s.m. (1st) The cheek. Pl. ي *ī*. See انګي.

انګۍ *an-ga'ī*, s.f. (6th) A game played by children —hide and seek—in which, one player, being "out," as the term is, seeks the others on their giving the word, which is termed انګازه ختل *an-gāzah khatal*, verb intrans., which see.

انګيرل *an-geral*, verb trans. To think, to imagine, to fancy, to suppose, to conceive, to apprehend. Pres. انګيري *an-gerī*; past وانګيره *wān-gerah*; fut. وا به نګيري *wā bah 'ngerī*; imp. وانګيره *wān-gerah*; act. part. انګيرونکی *an-gerūnkaey* or انګيرونی *an-gerūnaey*; past part. انګيرلی *an-geralaey*; verb. n. انګيرنه *an-gera-na'h*.

P انګيز *an-gez*, (act. part. of انګيختن, used in comp.) Exciting, rousing, causing; an exciter; (Fem.) انګيزه *an-geza'h*. فتنه انګيز *fit-na'h angez*, A mischief maker, an insurgent, a fomenter of disturbances, an incendiary; (Fem.) فتنه انګيزه *fit-na'h angeza'h*. فتنه انګيزي *fit-na'h angezī*, s.f. (3rd) Seditiousness, disturbance, sedition, mischievousness. Pl. ئ *a'ī*.

s انند *an-nand*, s.m. (2nd) Happiness, joy, delight, felicity, pleasure. Pl. انندونه *an-nand-ūnah*.

اننګ *an-nang*, s.m. (6th) A pomegranate. Sing. and Pl.

انګوړی *an-nangorraey*, s.m. (1st) (dimin. of preceding) A small pomegranate. Pl. ي *ī*. See انګوړي.

اننګی *an-nangaey*, s.m. (1st) The cheek, the side of the face. Pl. ي *ī*.

اني *aney*, s. prop. The name borne by two women, the wives of Kamāl-bin-Oṣmān, an Afghān chief, the one old, and the other young. They each bore him a son, whose descendants are known as Kashranzīs and Mashranzīs from their respective mothers,—*kashra'h* being the Pushto for an old woman, and *mashra'h* for a young one.

G انيسون *anī-sūn*, s.m. (6th) The seed of the anise, aniseed (Pimpinella anisum). Sing. and Pl.

انړل *arrnal*, verb trans. (W) To grind, to triturate, to powder, to bruise. Pres. انړي *arrnī*; past وُ انړل *wu-arrnal*; fut. وُ به انړي *wu bah arrnī*;

imp. وُ انړه *wu-arrnah*; act. part. انړونکيَ *arrnūnkaey*, or انړونيَ *arrnūnaey*; past part. انړليَ *arrnalaey*; verb. n. انړنه *arrnana'h*. See اوړول.

انړول *arrn-awul*, verb trans. To pick, to gather, to collect, to reap, to glean; to choose, to select, to pick out, to cull, etc. Pres. انړوي *arrn-awī*; past. وُ انړول *wu-arrn-awul*; fut. وُ به انړوي *wu bah arrn-awī*; imp. وُ انړوه *wu-arrnawah*; act. part. انړوونکيَ *arrnawūnkaey*, or انړوونيَ *arrnawūnaey*; past part. انړوليَ *arrnawulaey*; verb. n. انړونه *arrnawuna'h*.

او *ao*, adv. Yes. 2. interj. Oh! hallo! used in calling or addressing a person. See هو and و.

او *aw*, or *o*, conj. And, also.

P آوار *ā-wār*, or اوار *a-wār*, s.m. (2nd) Injustice, tyranny. Pl. آوارونه *ā-wārūnah*, or اوارونه *a-wārūnah*.

اوار *a-wār*, s.m. (2nd) Plunder, spoil, prey, booty, pillage. Pl. اوارونه *a-wārūnah*. اوار کول *a-wār kawul*, verb trans. To plunder, to pillage, to sack, to rob. See الجه.

P آواره *ā-wārah*, adj. Vagabond, wanderer, dissolute. آواره کيدل *ā-wārah kedal*, verb trans. To wander, to be distressed or miserable. آواره کول *ā-wārah kawul*, verb trans. To make a wanderer or vagabond, to expel, to harass.

P آوارهگي *āwārah-gī*, s.f. (3rd) Wandering, the state of a wanderer, vagabondism, vagrancy. Pl. ئي *a'ī*.

P آواز *ā-wāz*, s.m. (2nd) Voice, sound, echo. Pl. آوازونه *ā-wāzūnah*. آواز لرل *ā-wāz laral*, verb trans. To have or possess a sound (generally pleasant), to resound, to echo. آواز کول *ā-wāz kawul*, verb trans. To raise the voice, to call out.

P آوازه *ā-wāza'h*, s.f. (3rd) Fame, report, rumour. Pl. ئ *ey*.

A آوان *ā-wān*, s.m. (2nd) Time, period, moment. Pl. آوانونه *ā-wān-ūnah*.

P اواه *a-wāh*, s.m. (2nd) Echo, voice, sound, clamour. Pl. اواهونه *a-wāh-ūnah*; or اوا *a-wā*, s.f. (6th) Sing. and Pl. See انگازه.

P اوباش *au-bāsh*, s.m. (5th) A rake, a libertine, a debaucheé, a vagabond. 2. The mob, the canaille, the common, the meanest people. Pl. اوباشان *au-bāshān*. اوباشه *au-bāsha'h*, s.f. (3rd) A vagabond woman, a quean, a whore. Pl. ئ *ey*.

P اوباشي *au-bāshī*, s.f. (3rd) Dissipation, debauchery, dissoluteness, attending games and spectacles. Pl. ئي *a'ī*.

اوبال *ao-bāl*, s.m. (2nd) A crime, a fault. 2. Punishment for a crime. Pl. اوبالونه *ao-bāl-ūnah*. (A وبال). اوبال گټل *ao-bāl gattal*, verb trans. To commit a crime or fault (*lit.* to win, or gain a crime). اوبال گټليَ *ao-bāl gattalaey*, adj. (past part.) A criminal, one who has committed a fault; (Fem.) گټلِ *gattali*. Pl. (Masc. and Fem.) ي *ī*.

H I اوبچي *aob-chī*, or اوپچي *aop-chī*, s.m. (5th) A man clothed in mail, an armed man. Pl. اوبچيان *aob-chīān*, or اوپچيان *aop-chīān*.

اوبړئ *ao-brra'ī*, s.f. (6th) The green plant which grows at the bottom of pools (Valisneria spiralis octandra). Sing. and Pl. See ابړئ.

اوبه *ao-bah*, s.f. (6th) Water. Sing. and Pl.

اوبه *ao-ba'h*, s.f. (3rd) A splint in the leg of a horse. Pl. ئ *ey*.

اوپره *aop-rah*, adj. Foreign, strange, unacquainted. 2. s.m. (6th) A stranger, a foreigner. Sing. and Pl.

اوتر *aw-tar*, adj. Ruined, spoiled, worthless, destitute of good qualities, disordered, wanton; (Fem.) اوتره *aw-tara'h*. اوتر کول *aw-tar kawul*, verb trans. To ruin, to spoil, to render worthless. See ابتر.

اوڅار *au-tsār*, adj. Apparent, manifest, clear, evident, open; (Fem.) اوڅاره *aw-tsāra'h*.

A اوج *auj*, s.m. (2nd) Height, summit, the top. 2. Dignity, preferment, promotion. 3. The higher apsis of a planet. Pl. اوجونه *auj-ūnah*.

اوجاړ *ū-jārr*, adj. Desolate, waste, ruinous, deserted; (Fem.) اوجاړه *ū-jārra'h*. اوجاړيدل *ū-jārredal*, verb intrans. To become desolated, waste, or deserted. Pres. اوجاړيږي *ū-jārrejzī* (W.), or اوجاړيگي *ū-jārregī* (E.); past اوجاړ

شه *ū-jārr shah*, or وُ شه *wu-shah*; fut. اوجاړ به شي *ū-jārr bah shī*, or به وُ شي *bah wu-shī*; imp. اوجاړ شه *ū-jārr shah*, or وُ شه *wu-shah*; act. part. اوجاړيدونکي *ū-jārredūnkaey*, or اوجاړيدوني *ū-jārredūnaey*; past part. اوجاړ *ū-jārr*, or اوجاړ شوي *ū-jārr shawaey*; verb.n. اوجاړيدنه *ū-jārredana'h*.

اوجاړول *ū-jārrawul*, verb trans. To desolate, to ruin, to lay waste, to depopulate. Pres. اوجاړوي *ū-jārrawī*; past اوجاړ کړ *ū-jārr karr*, or وُ کړ *wu-karr*; fut. اوجاړ به کړي *ū-jārr bah krrī*, or به وُ کړي *bah wu-krrī*; imp. اوجاړ کړه *ū-jārr krrah*, or وُ کړه *wu-krrah*; act. part. اوجاړوونکي *ū-jārrawūnkaey*, or اوجاړووني *ū-jārrawūnaey*; past part. اوجاړ کړي *ū-jārr karrey*; verb. n. اوجاړونه *ū-jārrawuna'h*.

اوجاړ والي *ū-jārr-wālaey*, s.m. (1st) Desolation, ruin, waste, destruction. Pl. والي *wālī*.

اوجاړي *ū-jārrī*, s.f. (3rd) Waste, desolation. Pl. ئي *a'ī*. See preceding.

اوجړي *ūjaraey*, s.m. (1st) An entrail, a gut, the stomach. Pl. اوجري *ūjarī*, The entrails, the guts. (HI اوجهه).

اوجه *ū-ja'h*, s.f. (3rd) (E.) Garlic, a leek. Pl. ئي *ey*. See اوږه and اوګه.

اوچت *ū-chat*, adj. High, lofty; raised, lifted; (Fem.) اوچته *ū-chata'h*. اوچت والي *ū-chat-wālaey*, s.m. (1st) Height, altitude, elevation, loftiness. Pl. والي *wālī*. اوچت کيدل *ū-chat kedal*, verb intrans. To become raised or elevated, to become or grow high or lofty. اوچت کول *ū-chat kawul*, verb trans. To raise, to elevate, to render high or lofty. اوچت نيول *ū-chat nī-wal*, verb trans. To hold up, to raise on high. See اچت.

اوچي پوچي *ū-chey pū-chey*, s.f. (3rd) Pl. Twaddle, nonsense, absurdity, foolish talk, ridiculousness.

اودالي *aw-dālī*, s.m. (1st) Pl. The name of an Afghān tribe, the Abdālīs. اودالي *aw-dālaey*, Sing. A male of the tribe. اودالئ *aw-dāla'ī*, s.f. (6th) A female of the tribe. Sing. and Pl. See ابدالي.

اودس *aw-das*, s.m. (2nd) Ablution (performed before prayer). It consists in first washing the hands, then the mouth inside, cleaning the teeth, then throwing water on the forehead, washing the whole face, the arms, and lastly, the feet. Pl. اودسونه *aw-dasūnah*. اودس کول *aw-das kawul*, verb trans. To perform the ablution for prayer (? P آبدست).

اودل *ū-dal*, or (W.) *ao-dal*, verb trans. To weave, to plait, to braid, to mat. Pres. اووي *ū-wī*, or اوي *u-wī*; past وُ اود *wu-ūd*; fut. وُ به اوي *wu bah u-wī*, or اووي *ū-wī*; imp. وُ اووه *wu ū-wah*; act. part. اودونکي *ū-dūnkaey*, or اودوني *ū-dūnaey*; past part. اودلي *ū-dalaey*; verb.n. اودنه *ū-dana'h*. See وودل.

اوده *ū-da'h*, s.f. (3rd) The breath. 2. A charm, an incantation. Pl. ئي *ey*. اوده کول *ū-da'h kawul*, verb trans. To breathe on, to charm, to exorcise. اوده دار *ū-da'h-dār*, adj. An exorcist, one who charms; (Fem.) اوده داره *ū-da'h dāra'h*. See هوده.

اوده *ū-dah*, Asleep, sleeping, fast asleep, sound asleep, napping (Masc. and Fem.) اوده کيدل *ū-dah kedal*, verb intrans. To fall or go to sleep, to slumber, to drop asleep, to take a nap. اوده کول *ū-dah kawul*, verb trans. To make sleep, to put to sleep, to put to bed. See ووده and بيده.

اوډنئ *aoddana'ī*, s.f. (6th) (S اوڑهني) A small veil or mantle worn by women. Sing. and Pl.

اور *aor*, s.m. (2nd) Fire. Pl. اورونه *aor-ūnah*. (H אור light). اور لګيدل *aor lagedal*, or اور بليدل *aor baledal*, verb intrans. To take fire. اور لګول *aor lagawul*, or اور بلول *aor balawul*, verb trans. To set on fire. اور لړوني *aor-larrū-naey*, s.m. (1st) A poker of wood or iron. Pl. ي *ī*. See هور.

A اوراد *aw-rād*, s.m. (6th) (Pl. of ورد) Daily rehearsals, portions of the Ḳur'ān fixed for reading at certain times, devotions, practices.

اوراره *ao-rārah*, s.m. (2nd) A brother's son, a nephew. Pl. اوررونه *ao-rarūnah*. See وراره.

اور اوره کي *aor-aorah-kaey*, sm. (1st) A firefly, a glow-worm. Pl. ي *ī*, or اوره کي, which see.

اوربوشي *aor-būshey*, s.f. (3rd) Pl. Barley; (Sing.) اوربوشه *aor-būshah*, A barleycorn.

اوربشينه *aor-bashīna'h*, s.f. (3rd) Barley-bread. Pl. ئ *ey*.

اوربل *aor-bal*, or *ūr-bal*, s.m. (2nd) The hair plaited on the temples of young women. Pl. اوربلونه *aor-balūnah*, or *ūr-balūnah*. See كوڅي.

اور پښت *aor-pusht* (W.), or *aor-pukht* (E.) s.m. (6th) A moth. Sing. and Pl.

اوره كيَ *ao-rah-kaey*, s.m. (1st) A firefly. Pl. ي *ī*. See اور.

اورلړونيَ *aor-larrūnaey*, s.m. (1st) A poker of iron or wood. Pl. ي *ī*.

اورميږ *aor-mejz* (W.) or اورميګ *aor-meg* (E.), s.m. (2nd) The neck, the throat. Pl. اورميږونه *aor-mejzūnah*, or اور ميګونه *aor-megūnah*. See ورميږ and ورميګ.

اورنړيَ *aor-arrnaey*, s.m. (1st) A swaddling-cloth wrapped round an infant. Pl. ي *ī*. See اونړي.

اورور *ao-ror*, s.m. (2nd) A brother. Pl. اورونړَ *aor-ūrrna*, or اورونړه *aor-ūrrnah*. See ورور.

آورول *āw-rawul*, verb trans. (caus.) To cause to hear. Pres. آوروي *āw-rawī*; past واوراوه *wāw-rāwuh*; fut. وا به وروي *wā bah warawī*; imp. واوروه *wāw-rawah*; act. part. آوروونكيَ *āw-rawūnkaey*, or آوروونيَ *āw-rawūnaey*; past part. آوروليَ *āw-rawulaey*; verb. n. آورونه *āw-rawuna'h*.

اورون *ao-rūn*, s.m. (2nd) The thigh. Pl. اورونونه *ao-rūnūnah*. See ورون.

اوره *o-rah*, s.m. (6th) A cloud, clouds. Sing. and Pl. See ارو, اوريځه and اوريزه.

اورئ *ao-ra'ī*, s.f. (6th) The gums, the quick of the nails. Sing. and Pl.

اوريَ *ao-raey*, s.m. (1st) Mustard, mustard seed. Pl. ي *ī*.

آوريدل *āw-redal*, verb trans. To hear, to hearken, to listen, to attend. Pres. آوري *āw-rī*; past واوريده *wāw-redah*, or واوريدَ *wāw-reda*; fut. وا به وري *wā bah wrī*; imp. واوره *wāw-rah*; act. part. آوريدونكيَ *āw-redūnkaey*, or آوريدونيَ *āw-redūnaey*; past part. آوريدليَ *āw-redalaey*; verb. n. آوريدنه *āw-redana'h*. See آورول.

اوريدل *ao-redal*, verb trans. To rain, to drizzle, to pour with rain. Pres. اوري *ao-rī*; past وُ اوريده *wu-ao-redah*, or وُ اوريدَ *wu-ao-reda*; fut. وُ به اوري *wu bah ao-rī*; imp. وُ اوره *wu-ao-rah*; act. part. اوريدونكيَ *ao-redūnkaey*, or اوريدونيَ *ao-redūnaey*; past part. اوريدليَ *ao-redalaey*; verb. n. اوريدنه *ao-redana'h*. اورول *ao-rawul*, verb trans. To make or cause to rain. Pres. اوروي *ao-rawī*; past وُ اوراوه *wu-ao-rāwuh*, or اوراوو *ao-rāwo*; fut. وُ به اوروي *wu bah ao-rawī*; imp. وُ اوروه *wu-ao-rawah*; act. part. اوروونكيَ *ao-rawūnkaey*, or اوروونيَ *ao-rawūnaey*; past part. اوروليَ *ao-rawulaey*; verb. n. اورونه *ao-rawuna'h*.

آوريده *āw-redah*, s.m. (6th) (verb. n.) Hearing, hearkening, listening, attending. Sing. and Pl.; or آوريدنه *āw-redana'h*, s.f. (3rd). Pl. ئ *ey*.

اوريز *aor-yaz*, s.f. (1st) A cloud. Pl. اوريزِ *aor-yazi*, or اوريزه *aor-yaza'h*, s.f. (3rd). Pl. ئ *ey*. See وريز or وريزه.

اوريځ *aor-yadz*, s.f. (1st) A cloud. Pl. اوريځ *aor-yadzi*, or اوريځه *aor-yadza'h*, s.f. (3rd). Pl. ئ *ey*. See preceding, and وريځ or وريځه.

اوريئ *aor-ya'ī*, s.f. (6th). Sing. and Pl. See اورئ.

اوړ *aorr*, s.m. (2nd) A tool used by weavers. Pl. اوړونه *aorrūnah*.

اوړل *ū-rral*, verb trans. To bear, to carry, to remove, to transport, to carry over, to convey, to waft, etc. Particularly applied to objects inanimate. For inflexions see وړل.

اوړنبيَ *aorr-unbaey*, or *ūrr-unbaey*, adj. Prior, former, previous, preceding, foremost; (Fem.) اوړنبئ *aorr-unba'ī*, or *ūrrunba'ī*. See وړنبي, ړنبي, امړي, and اولني.

اوړنيَ *aorr-naey*, or اوړه نيَ *aorrah-naey*, s.m. (1st) A small size sheet or veil worn by women. Pl. ي *ī*. (HI. اوڑھني.)

اوړوكيَ *ūrrūkaey*, adj. Little, small, less, diminutive. 2. A term of endearment for a child, as "little one" or "wee thing," in English. Pl. ي *ī*; (Fem.) اوړوكئ *ūrrūka'ī*, Sing. and Pl.; or اوړوكِ *ūrrūki*. Pl. ي *ī*. See اوړيكي and وړوكي.

اوړول *ao-rrawul*, verb trans. (E.) To grind, to

triturate, to pulverize, to reduce to powder, to grind into flour (as grain). See اوړه کول.

اوړه *aorr-ah*, s.m. (6th) Flour, meal. Sing. and Pl. Also written at times اوړَ *aorr-a*. اوړه کيدل *aorr-ah kedal*, verb intrans. To become turned into or reduced to flour or meal, to become triturated. اوړه کول *aorr-ah kawul*, verb trans. To grind to flour, to triturate, to make into meal, to pulverize.

اوړه نيَ *aorrah-naey*, s.m. (1st) A small veil or sheet worn by women. Pl. ي *ī*. See اوړنيَ.

اوړيَ *aorraey*, s.m. (1st) The summer season, the spring or summer harvest. Pl. ي *ī*. See ووړي and دوبي.

اوړيدل *aorredal*, verb intrans. To be ground in a mill, to become triturated or pulverized. See اوړه کيدل.

اوړيکيَ *ao-rrekaey*, adj. Small, little, etc.; (Fem.) اوړيکۍ *ao-rreki*. Pl. ي *i*. See اووړوکيَ or ووړوکي.

اوزمکۍ *aoz-mak*. See اوړمکۍ.

اوژړيَ *aojz-raey*, s.m. (1st) The stomach of an animal, the belly. Pl. ي *ī*. See لړي.

اوژغونيَ *aojz-ghūney*, s.f. (3rd) Pl. Goat's hair. Sing. not used.

اوږد *ūjzd* (W.) adj. Long, lengthy, extended, elongated, stretched out, prolonged. Pl. اوږډه *ūjzd-æh*; (Fem.) اوږده *ūjzda'h*. Pl. ې *ey*. See اوګد and اوګده. اوږديدل *ūjzdedal*, verb intrans. To become or grow long, lengthy, extended, or stretched out, to become prolonged or protracted. Pres. اوږديږي *ūjzdejzī*; past اوږد شه *ūjzd shah*, or وُ شه *nu-shah*; fut. اوږد به شي *ūjzd bah shī*, or به وُ شي *bah nu-shī*; imp. اوږد شه *ūjzd shah*, or وُ شه *nu-shah*; act part. اوږديدونکيَ *ūjzdedūnkaey*, or اوږديدونيَ *ūjzdedūnaey*; past part. اوږد *ūjzd*, or اوږد شويَ *ūjzd shawaey*; verb. n. اوږديدنه *ūjzdedana'h*. اوږدول *ūjzdawul*, verb trans. To make long or lengthy, to elongate, to draw or stretch out, to extend, to protract, to prolong. Pres. اوږدوي *ūjzdawī*; past اوږد کړ *ūjzd karr*, or وُ کړ *nu-karr*; fut. اوږد به کړي *ūjzd bah krrī*, or به وُ کړي *bah nu-krrī*; imp. اوږد کړه *ūjzd krrah*, or وُ کړه *wu krrah*; act. part. اوږدوونکيَ *ūjzdawūnkaey*, or اوږدووني *ūjzdawūnaey*; past part. اوږد کړيَ *ūjzd karraey*; verb. n. اوږدونه *ūjzdawuna'h*.

اوږد واليَ *ūjzd-wālaey*, s.m. (1st) Length, elongation, extension, prolongation, protraction. Pl. والي *wālī*. See اوګد واليَ.

اوږده ميږيانه *aojz-da'h mejze-āna'h*, s.f. (3rd) Long pepper (piper longum). Pl. ې *ey*. See پيپلي.

اوږه *ao-jza'h*, s.f. (3rd) (W.) The shoulder. Pl. ې *ey*. See اوګه.

اوږه *ūjza'h*, s.f. (3rd) (W.) Garlic, a leek. Pl. ې *ey*. See هوږه and اوجه or اوګه.

اوږيَ *ao-jzaey*, s.m. (1st) A grain measure of seven seers or fourteen pounds (E.), or (W.) two seers or fourteen pounds. Pl. ي *ī*.

اوږۍ *ao-jza'ī*, s.f. (6th) (W.) A neck ring, a necklace. Sing. and Pl. (E.) اوګۍ *ao-ga'ī*.

اوس *aos*, adv. Now, at present, at this time, yet, still, hitherto, already, even now. تر اوسَ *tar aosa*, or پوري, or تر اوسَ پوري *tar aosa pūri*, or *pūrī*, As yet, so far, hitherto, up to the present time. اوسن *aos-an* or اوسنيَ *aos-anaey*, adj. Actual, existing, present, the present. 2. The people of the present day; (Fem.) اوسنه *aos-ana'h*, or اوسنۍ *aos-ana'ī*.

HI اوسان *au-sān*, s.m. (2nd) Sense, sensation; presence of mind, courage. Pl. اوسانونه *au-sānūnah*. اوسان تلليَ *au-sān t'lalaey*, adj. (past part.) Gone out of one's mind, beside one's self, demented, distracted; (Fem.) اوسان تللي *an-sān t'lali*. Pl. (Masc. and Fem.) ي *ī*.

اوسَپنه *aos-pana'h*, s.f. (3rd) Iron. Also used as an adjective to qualify another noun, signifying, Iron-like, hard. Pl. ې *ey*. اوسپنخړيَ *aos-pankharraey*, s.m. (1st) The dross of iron left after melting. Pl. ي *ī*.

اوسپينه *aos-pīna'h*, s.f. (3rd) Same as preceding. Pl. ې *ey*.

P اوستاد *ūs-tād*, s.m. (5th) A teacher, a tutor, a master (tradesman). Pl. اوستادان *ūs-tādān*. اوستاده *ūs-tāda'h*, s.f. (3rd) A tutoress. Pl. ې *ey*. Also pronounced (corrup.) اوستا *ūs-tā*. Pl. اوستايان *ūs-tāyān*. See استاذ and استاد.

اوستاذ *ūs-tāẕ*, s.m. (5th). Pl. اوستاذان *ūs-tāẕān*. اوستاذه *ūs-tāẕa'h*, s.f. (3rd). Pl. ې *ey*. Same as preceding.

اوستاځَي *aos-tādzaey*, adj. as s.m. (1st) A messenger, a legate, an agent, a peace-maker, an umpire, an apostle. Pl. ي *ī*; (Fem.) اوستاځِ *aos-tādzi*. Pl. ي *ī*. See استاځي.

A اوسط *aow-saṭ*, adj. Middle, middling, intervening. 2. s.m. (2nd) The middle, mean. 3. Medium, mediocrity. Pl. اوسطونه *aow-saṭūnah*; (Fem). اوسطه *aow-saṭa'h*. Pl. ې *ey*.

اوسن *aos-an*, or اوسنَي *aos-anaey*, adj. Actual, existing, present, the people of the present time; recent, late; (Fem.) اوسنه *aos-ana'h*, or اوسنۍ *aos-ana'ī*. 2. Recently, lately, just now. اوسن خلق *aos-an khalḳ*, The people of the present day. See اوس.

اوسَي *ao-saey*, s.m. (1st) An antelope, a gazelle, a small deer. Pl. ي *ī*. اوسۍ *ao-sa'ī*, s.f. (6th) A doe, feminine of the above. Sing. and Pl. See هوسي.

اوسيدل *aose-dal*, verb intrans. To be, to exist, to dwell, to have being, to live. Pres. اوسي *aosī*; past وُ اوسيده *wu-aose-dah*, or وُ اوسيدَ *wu-aoseda*; fut. وُ به اوسي *wu bah aosī*; imp. اوسه *aosah*; act. part. اوسيدونكَي *aose-dūnkaey*, or اوسيدونَي *aose-dūnaey*; past part. اوسيدلَي *aose-dalaey*; verb. n. اوسيدنه *aose-dana'h*, or اوسيده *aose-dah*. اوسول *aosa-wul*, verb trans. To make or cause to dwell, remain, stay, exist, live, etc. Pres. اوسوي *aosawī*; past وُ اوساوه *wu-aosāwuh*, or اوساوو *aosāwo*; fut. وُ به اوسوي *wu bah aosawī*; imp. وُ اوسوه *wu-aosawah*; act. part. اوسوونكَي *aosawūnkaey*, or اوسوونَي *aosawūnaey*; past part. اوسولَي *aosawulaey*; verb. n. اوسونه *aosawuna'h*.

A اوسيده *aosedah*, s.m. (6th) (verb. n.) Being, existing, living, having being; dwelling, staying, tarrying. Sing. and Pl.; or اوسيدنه *aosedana'h*, s.f. (3rd). Pl. ې *ey*.

اوښ *ūsh* (W.), or *ūkh* (E.), s.m. (5th) A camel, a dromedary. Pl. اوښان *ūshān*, or *ūkhān*. اوښه *ūsha'h*, or *ūkha'h*, s.f. (3rd) A female camel or dromedary. Pl. ې *ey*.

اوښبه *ūshbah* (W.), or *ūkhbah* (E.) s.m. (4th) A camel grazier. Pl. اوښبانه *ūshbānah*, or *ūkhbānah*; or اوښپه *ūshpah*, or *ūkhpah*. Pl. اوښپانه *ūshpānah*, or *ūkhpānah*.

آوښتل *ā-wushtal* (W.), or *ā-wukhtal* (E.), verb trans. To turn, to change, to alter, to deviate, to revolve, to change about. Pres. آوړي *ā-wuṛṛī*; past وا وښت *wā-wusht*, or *wā-wukht*; fut. وا به وړي *wā bah wṛṛī*; imp. واوړه *wāwṛṛah*; act. part. آوښتونكَي *ā-wushtūnkaey*, or *ā-wukhtūnkaey*; or آوښتونَي *ā-wushtūnaey*, or *ā-wukhtūnaey*; past part. آوښتلَي *ā-wushtalaey*, or *ā-wukhtalaey*; verb. n. آوښتنه *ā-wushtana'h*, or *ā-wukhtana'h*.

اوښه *ao-sha'h* (W.), or *ao-kha'h* (E.) s.f. (3rd) A tear. Pl. اوښې *ao-shey* or *ao-khey*, Tears. اوښې توييدل *ao-shey*, or *ao-khey toeyedal*, verb intrans. To cry, to weep, to shed tears, to greet, to whimper. اوښې تويول *ao-shey*, or *ao-khey toe-yawul*, verb trans. To cause to weep or cry, to make shed tears. اوښينې سترګې *ao-sheney*, or *ao-kheney stargey*, Tearful eyes, eyes suffused with tears; also written اوښنې سترګې *ao-khaney stargey*, etc.

اوښي *ao-shaey* (W.) or *ao-khaey* (E.) s.m. (1st) A wife's brother, a sister's husband, a brother-in-law. Pl. ي *ī*. See اخښي.

اوښي *ao-khī* (E.) or *ao-shī* (W.) s.m. (1st) Pl. The mane of a horse. See اووي ,يال, and وربر or ورګ.

A اوصاف *au-ṣāf*, s.m. (6th) (Pl. of وصف) Praises, endowments, qualities, qualifications. S. and P.

A اوطاق *aw-ṭāḳ*, s.m. (2nd) A temporary dwelling, a lodging. 2. A tent, a dwelling. اوطاقونه *aw-ṭāḳūnah*.

اوغان *aw-ghān*, s.m. (5th) An Afghān, an inhabitant of Afghānistān. Pl. اوغانان *aw-ghānān*. اوغانه *aw-ghāna'h*, s.f. (3rd) An Afghān female. Pl. ې *ey*. See افغان.

اوغز *ūghz*, s.m. (5th) A walnut with a soft skin. Sing and Pl. See اكوز.

A اوقات *au-ḳāt*, s.m. (6th) (Pl. of وقت) Times, hours, circumstances. Sing. and Pl.

اوګد *ūgd*, adj. (E.) Long, lengthy, extended,

prolonged, protracted, elongated, stretched out; (Fem.) اوګده *ūgda'h*. اوګدیدل *ūgdedal*, verb intrans. To become or grow long, lengthy, elongated, protracted, etc. اوګدول *ūgdawul*, verb trans. To make long or lengthy, to elongate, to extend, to protract, to prolong. For different inflexions see under (W.) اوږد, and substitute ګ for ږ.

اوګدوالی *ūgd-wālaey*, s.m. (1st) (E.) Length, elongation, extension, prolongation, protraction. Pl. والي *wālī*.

اوګره *ao-gra'h*, s.f. (3rd) The name of a dish of grain, generally wheat, boiled to pap. Pl. ئ *ey*.

اوګړائي *ūg-ṟṟā'ī*, s.f. (3rd) An instalment, a fixed portion of the price of goods to be paid at certain fixed periods. Pl. ئي *a'ī*. اوګړائي کول *ūg-ṟṟā'ī kawul*, verb trans. To collect instalments of money.

اوګړه *ūg-ṟṟa'h*, s.f. (3rd) A kind of gruel or pap generally made from wheat. Pl. ئ *ey*. See اوګره (HI اوگرا).

اوګه *ao-ga'h*, s.f. (3rd) (E.) The shoulder. Pl. ئ *ey*. See اوږه.

اوګه *ū-ga'h*, s.f. (3rd) (E.) Garlic, a leek. Pl. ئ *ey*. See اوږه or هوږه, and اوجه.

اوګی *ao-gaey*, s.m. (1st) (E.) A dry measure containing seven seers or fourteen pounds. Pl. ي *ī*. See اوړی.

اوګئ *ao-ga'ī*, s.f. (6th) A collar, a neck ring, a necklace. Sing. and Pl.

A اول *aw-wal*, adj. First, best, principal, proper, fit. 2. Beginning; (Fem.) اوله *aw-wala'h*. اولاً *aw-walan*, adv. At first, in the first place, in the beginning. له اولَ *lah aw-wala*, or له اول نه *lah aw-wal nah*, From the first, from the commencement or beginning. See رنبي, etc. اولنی *aw-walnaey*, or *aw-lanaey*, adj. Prior, former, previous, preceding, foremost, antecedent, foregoing; (Fem.) اولنئ *aw-walna'ī*, or *aw-lana'ī*. See ورنبي, امري, and اورنبي.

A اولاد *au-lād*, or *aw-lād*, s.m. (6th) (Pl. of ولد) Children, descendants, progeny, issue. Sing. and Pl.

اولجه *ūl-ja'h*, s.f. (3rd) Prey, spoil, plunder, booty, pillage. Pl. ئ *ey*. 2. Adj. Entangled, complicated, intricate, perplexed (HI اُلجها). اولجه کول *ūl-ja'h kawul*, verb trans. To plunder, to pillage, to sack, to spoil. 2. To entangle, to perplex, to make or render intricate. اولجه کيدل *ūl-ja'h kedal*, verb intrans. To become plundered or pillaged. 2. To become entangled or intricate. See الجه, اوار, and ګونښي.

اولل *ao-lal*, verb trans. To wash, to cleanse, to purify. Pres. اولي *ao-lī*; past و اوله *wu-ao-lah*; fut. و به اولي *wu bah ao-lī*; imp. و اوله *wu-ao-lah*; act. part. اولونکی *ao-lūnkaey*, or اولونی *ao-lūnaey*; past part. اولی *ao-laey*, or اوللی *ao-lalaey*; verb. n. اولن *ao-lan*, or اولنه *ao-lana'h*. See ولل and وينځل.

اولو *aw-lū*, s.m. (6th) Molasses, treacle. Sing. and Pl. See ککث.

اولوی *aw-lawaey*, adj. Scorched (with grief), much burned, roasted, parched; (Fem.) اولوِ *aw-lawi*. Pl. (Masc. and Fem.) ي *ī*. See الوي and الوويل.

اوله *ao-lah*, s.m. (5th) A flock of lambs kept separate from their mothers. Pl. اولان *ao-lān*. See رمه.

A اولی *au-lā*, adi. (compar. of ولي) Better, best.

A اوليا *au-liyā*, s.m. (6th) (Pl. of ولي) Friends, companions (particularly of the prophets). 2. The saints, the apostles, the holy. Sing. and Pl.

P اوليتر *au-lātar*, adj. (compar. of A اولی and P تر) Best, better, the best; (Fem.) اوليتره *au-lātara'h*.

A اولين *aw-walīn*, adj. (Pl. of اول) The first, the former, the ancients; (Fem.) اولينه *aw-walīna'h*.

اوم *aom*, adj. Unripe, raw, uncooked, crude; (Fem.) اومه *aoma'h*. (HI اومي *ūmī*, An ear of (unripe) corn.)

اومه *ao-mah*, s.m. (5th) The name of a plant which is finely powdered and mixed with snuff to make it pungent; also used in tanning leather. Pl. اومان *ao-mān*.

اوم *u-wam*, adj. Seven. See اووم.

اوميشتيی *ao-mīsh-tiyaey*, s.m. (1st) A seven

months male child. Pl. ي *ī*. اوميشتيي *ao-mīsh-tiya'ī*, s.f. (6th) A female child of seven months. Sing. and Pl.

اوني *ūnaey*, adj. as s.m. (1st) A talker of nonsense, a babbler, a twaddler, a long-tongue; (Fem.) اوني *ūni*. Pl. (Masc. and Fem.) ي *ī*.

اوڼزي *ao-rrnaey*, s.m. (1st) A swaddling cloth wrapped round an infant. Pl. ي *ī*. See اوړنزي.

اووري *ao-wraey*, s.m. (1st) A cloud. Pl. ي *ī*. See اوره.

اووري *ao-ūra'ī*, s.f. (6th) The gums, the quicks of the nails. Sing. and Pl. See اوري.

اووم *ao-wam*, adj. The seventh; (Fem.) اوومه *ao-wama'h*. See اووه.

اووه *ao-wah*, adj. Seven. اووه لس *ao-wah-las*, Seventeen. اووه ويشت *ao-wah-wisht*, Twenty-seven. اووه ديرش *ao-wah-dersh*, Thirty-seven. اووه څلويښت *ao-wah-tsal-wesht*, or *tsal-wekht*, Forty-seven. اووه پنځوس *ao-wah-pindzos*, Fifty-seven. اووه شپيته *ao-wah-shpetah*, Sixty-seven. اووه اويا *ao-wah-ao-yā*, Seventy-seven. اووه اتيا *ao-wah-ati-yā*, Eighty-seven. اووه نو or نوي *ao-wah-nawi*, or *nawī*, Ninety-eight.

اووي *ao-wī*, s.m. (1st) Pl. The mane of a horse, comb of a cock. See اوبي and چارخولك.

اوه *aw-wah*, adj. Seven. See اووه.

اوه *aoh*, or *ūh*, interj. Heigh oh! oh dear!

اوه *ao-wa'h*, s.f. (3rd) A blister, a pustule, a pimple, a freckle, a small-pox mark, a small bladder or bubble on the water. Pl. ي *ey*. See تنراكه.

اوي *ao-ey*, s.m. (2nd) A promise, a pledge, an oath, an agreement, a covenant. Pl اويونه *ao-ey-ūnah*. اوي كول or ترل *ao-ey kawul*, or *tarral*, verb trans. To make a promise, to give a pledge, to enter into an agreement or covenant.

اويا *ao-yā*, adj. Seventy. اويايم *ao-yāyam*, The seventieth; (Fem.) اويايمه *ao-yāyama'h*.

اويزاند *awe-zānd*, adj. (corrup. of P اويز) Suspended, hanging, dangling; (Fem.) اويزانده *awe-zānda'h*. اويزاند كيدل *awe-zānd kedal*, verb intrans. To be suspended, to hang, to dangle. اويزاند كول *awe-zānd kawul*, verb trans. To suspend, to hang up, to make to dangle.

اوينه *aoe-nah*, s.m. (6th) The white ant. Sing. and Pl.

P آه *āh*, s.m. (2nd) A sigh. Pl. آهونه *āh-ūnah*. 2. Interj. Ah! alas! آه كښل *āh kshal* (W.), or آه ښكل *āh khkal* (E.), To sigh. ساړه آهونه *sārrah āh-ūnah*, Cold or deep sighs.

اهاړ *ahārr*, s.m. (9th) The name of the third solar month of the Hindūs, June—July. Sing. and Pl. (s आषाढ). See اهړ.

اهداد *ih-dād*, s.m. (2nd) Punishment, punition, chastisement, correction, infliction, retribution, reward, requital. Pl. اهدادونه *ih-dād-ūnah*. اهداد ور كول *ih-dād war-kawul*, verb trans. To punish, to requite, to chasten, to inflict punishment.

اهړ *aharr*, s.m. (9th) The name of a Hindū month, June—July. Sing. and Pl. See اهاړ.

P آهستگي *āhistagī*, s.f. (3rd) Slowness, tardiness, delay, gentleness, softness. Pl. ئي *a'ī*.

P آهسته *āhistah*, adv. Gently, softly, slowly, tardy, slothful. آهسته كول *āhistah kawul*, verb trans. To do anything slowly, gently, softly, or carefully.

A اهل *ahl*, s.m. (2nd) People, consort, inhabitant, possessor; (in comp.) Possessed of, endowed with. Pl. اهلونه *ahlūnah*. اهل الله *ah-lullah*, The people of God, darweshis, fakirs, etc. اهل ايمان *ahl-i-īmān*, A believer. اهل بيت *ahl-i-bait*, People of the house, family (especially of the Prophet Muhammad). اهل دل *ahl-i-dil*, adj. Liberal, brave, generous. اهل زمان *ahl-i-zamān*, adj. Time-serving. اهل عقل *ahl-i-æakl*, adj. Wise. اهل علم *ahl-i-æilm*, adj. Scientific. اهل كتاب *ahl-i-kitāb*, A learned man, a person of any religion revealed or contained in books.

P آهن *āhan*, s.m. (9th) Iron. Sing. and Pl. آهن گر *āhan gar*, s.m. (5th) A smith, a blacksmith. Pl. آهن گران *āhan-garān*. آهن ربا *āhan-rubā*, s.f. (6th) The magnet or loadstone. (E.) Sing. and Pl.); (W.) Pl. آهن رباوي *āhan-rubāwī*. See اوسپنه.

P آهنګ *āhang*, s.m. (2nd) Intention, design, purpose. 2. Sound, noise. 3. Echo, symphony, melody. Pl. آهنګونه *āhang-ūnah*. آهنګ کول *āhang kawul*, verb trans. To design, to project, to intend, to purport. 2. To sound, to echo. آهنګ په نه آهنګ *āhang pah nah āhang*, Willing or unwilling, nolens volens.

آهنه *āhina'h*, s.f. (3rd) A mirror, a looking-glass. Pl. ې *ey*. See آهينه and آئينه.

P آهو *āhū*, s.m. (5th) A deer. Pl. آهوان *āhūān*. See اوسۍ. آهو چشم *āhū-chashm*, adj. Fawn-eyed, having eyes like a fawn; (Fem.) آهو چشمه *āhū-chashma'h*.

اهورۍ *aho-raey*, s.m. (1st) Mustard seed; also the plant. Pl. ي *ī*. دَ اهوري تيل *da ahorī tel*, The oil extracted from mustard seed. See اوري.

آهينه *āhīna'h*, s.f. (3rd) A mirror, a looking-glass. Pl. ې *ey*. See هنداره and آئينه.

اي *ai*, interj. Used in calling to, or addressing; Oh! Hollo! the sign of the vocative case. See و.

A ايا *ayā*, interj. O! oh! hollo! have a care! look out! mind!

P آيا *āyā*, interj. Wonderful! strange! is it not? whether or not. Used to express doubt or astonishment.

T اياز *ayāz*, s. prop. The name of a favourite of Maḥmūd of Ghaznī; the name of a favourite generally.

A ايام *ai-yām*, s.m. (6th) (Pl. of يوم) Days, times, season, weather. Sing. and Pl.

A آيت *āyat*, s.m. (2nd) A sign, a mark, a verse or paragraph of the Ḳur'ān contained between stops or marks. Pl. آيتونه *āyatūnah*, or A Pl. آيات *āyāt*.

A ايذا *īzā*, s.f. (6th) (inf. IV of اذيت) Hurting, injuring, harm, pain, trouble, vexation, distress, affliction, torment, torture. (E.) Sing. and Pl.; (W.) Pl. ايذاوي *īzāwī*. ايذا رسول *īzā rasawul*, verb trans. To injure, to pain, to distress, to torture, to torment, to afflict.

P ايران *ī-rān*, s. prop. Persia.

ايراني *īrānī*, adj. Persian, a Persian; (Fem.) ايرانۍ *ī-rāna'ī*.

ايرړۍ *aer-rraey*, s.m. (1st) A long-tailed sheep, in contradistinction to the *dumbah*, or fat-tailed species, the common sheep (male). Pl. ي *ī*.

ايرړۍ *aer-rra'ī*, s.f. (6th) An ewe of the above breed. Sing. and Pl. See هر, يري, بيروي, ايري, هيري, هيروي, بري and بيري.

ايرې *īrey*, s.f. (3rd) Pl. Ashes. Sing. ايره *īra'h*. سړې پړې ايرې *sarrey parrey ī-rey*, Cold ashes (fig.), cleared out, gone to the dogs, all gone save cold ashes to sit on; a state of complete ruin and desolation. په سړي پړي ايري کښيناستل *pah sarrey parrey ī-rey k'khenāstal* (E.), or *k'shenāstal* (W.) verb intrans. To sit on cold ashes, to be in a state of utter helplessness and destitution.

ايرړۍ *ae-rraey*, s.m. (1st.) A sheep, a ram. Pl. ي *ī*.

ايرړۍ *ae-rra'ī*, s.f. (6th) An ewe. Sing. and Pl. See ايرړۍ.

P ايزد *ī-zid*, s. prop. God, the Creator. ايزدي *ī-zidī*, adj. Divine.

ايسار *ī-sār*, adj. Surrounded, enclosed, fenced, compassed, invested. 2. s.m. (2nd) Embarrassment, hesitation, demur, intricacy. 3. A fort, a castle, a fortification. Pl. ايسارونه *ī-sārūnah*; (Fem.) ايساره *ī-sāra'h*. ايسار کيدل *ī-sār kedal*, or ايساريدل *ī-sāredal*, verb intrans. To become surrounded, compassed, invested, fenced. 2. To become perplexed or embarrassed. ايسار کول *ī-sār kawul*, or ايسارول *ī-sārawul*, verb trans. To enclose, to surround, to invest. 2. To embarrass, to make to hesitate, to cause to demur, to perplex, to make intricate. See هسار and هساريدل and هسارول.

ايستل *aes-tal*, verb trans. To expel, to reject, to discharge, to cast out, to discard, to exclude, to put off, to put away, to throw out, to give vent to, to let fly, to remove, to free, etc. This infinitive is imperfect, and the greater number of its inflexions are taken from باسل, which see, as also يستل *yas-tal*, the more correct mode of orthography.

ایشنا *aesh-nā*, s.f. (6th) Ebullition, boiling, fusion, agitation, ferment, effervescence (as from heat, etc.) 2. Excitement, passion, agitation, disquietude, vehemence, paroxysm, rage. Pl. وي *wī*. ایشیدل *aeshe-dal*, verb intrans. To boil, to boil over, to become agitated by heat. 2. To become excited, chafed, or disturbed. Pres. ایشیږي *aeshe-jzī* (W.), or ایشیگي *aeshe-gī* (E.); past وُ ایشیده *wu-aeshe-dah*; fut. وُ به ایشیږي *wu bah aeshe-jzī*, or ایشیگي *aeshe-gī*; imp. وُ ایشیږه *wu-aeshe-jzah*, or وُ ایشیگه *wu-aeshe-gah*; act. part. ایشیدونکئ *aeshe-dūnkaey*, or ایشیدونئ *aeshe-dūnaey*; past part. ایشیدلئ *aeshe-dalaey*; verb. n. ایشیدنه *aeshe-danah*. ایشول *aeshawul*, verb trans. To boil, to make hot, to cause ebullition, to excite by means of heat. 2. To chafe, to fret, to disturb, to agitate. Pres. ایشوي *aeshawī*; past وُ ایشاوه *wu-aeshāwuh*, or وُ ایشاوو *wu-aeshāwo*; fut. وُ به ایشوي *wu bah aeshawī*; imp. وُ ایشوه *wu-aeshawah*; act. part. ایشوونکئ *aeshawūnkaey*, or ایشوونئ *aeshawūnaey*; past part. ایشولئ *aeshawulaey*; verb. n. ایشونه *aeshawuna'h*. See یشنا, and یشیدل and یشول.

ایښل *aeshal* (W.), or *aekhal* (E.), verb trans. To place, to put, to set, to lay, to arrange, to dispose, to settle, etc. This infinitive is imperfect, and requires the aid of several other infinitives, imperfect like itself, to complete it. Pres. ږدي *jz'dī* (W.), or گدي *g'dī* (E.), (from ږدل or گدل); past کیښو *ke-sho* (W.), or *ke-kho* (E.) (from کیښول), and کیښود *ke-shod* (W.), or *ke-khod* (E.) (from کیښودل); fut. کښې به ږدي *k'khe* or *k'she bah jz'dī*, or گدي *g'dī* (from کښیږدل); imp. ږده *jz'dah*, or گده *g'dah* (from ږدل or گدل), and کیږده *kejz-dah*, or کیگده *keg-dah* (from کیږدل or کیگدل); act. part. ایښونکئ *aeshūnkaey*, or *aekhūnkaey*, or ایښونئ *aeshūnaey*, or *aekhūnaey*; past part. ایښئ *aeshaey*, or *aekhaey*; verb. n. ایښنه *aeshana'h*, or *aekhana'h*. See ایښول.

ایښودل *aeshodal* (W.), or *aekhodal* (E.), To put, to place, to set, to lay, etc. This infinitive is imperfect. Act. part. ایښودونکئ *aeshodūnkaey* or *aekhodūnkaey*, or ایښودونئ *aeshodūnaey* or *aekhodūnaey*; past part. ایښودلئ *aeshodalaey* or *aekhodalaey*; verb. n. ایښودنه *aeshodana'h* or *aekhodanah*. The other inflexions are taken from the preceding verbs.

ایښوده *aeshodah* or *aekhodah*, s.m. (6th) (verb. n.) Placing, putting, setting; arrangement, settlement, disposition. Sing. and Pl.

ایښول *aeshawul* or *aekhawul*, verb trans. To put, to place, etc. Act. part. ایښوونکئ *aeshawūnkaey* or *aekhawūnkaey*, or ایښوونئ *aeshawūnaey* or *aekhawūnaey*; past part. ایښولئ *aeshawulaey* or *aekhawulaey*; verb. n. ایښونه *aeshawuna'h* or *aekhawuna'h*. This verb is also imperfect, and uses the inflexions of those already mentioned.

ایل *ael* (W.) or *īl* (E.) adj. Tame, domestic, obedient, broken in, mild, gentle, opposite to wild; (Fem.) ایله *aela'h* or *īla'h*. ایلیدل *aeledal* or *īledal*, verb intrans. To become or grow tame, domestic, obedient, to become broken in. Pr. ایلیږي *aelejzī* (W.) or ایلیگي *īl-egī* (E.); past ایل شه *ael* or *īl shah*, or وُ شه *wu-shah*; fut. ایل به شي *ael* or *īl bah shī*, or وُ شي *wu-shī*; imp. ایل شه *ael* or *īl shah*, or وُ شه *wu-shah*; act. part. ایلیدونکئ *aeledūnkaey* or *īledūnkaey*, or ایلیدونئ *aeledūnaey* or *īledūnaey*; past part. ایل *ael* or *īl*, or ایل شوي *ael* or *īl shawaey*; verb. n. ایلیدنه *aeledana'h* or *īledana'h*, or ایلیده *aeledah* or *īledah*. ایلول *aelawul* or *īlawul*, verb trans. To tame, to domesticate, to break in, to make obedient. Pres. ایلوي *aelawī* or *īlawī*; past ایل کړ *ael* or *īl karr*, or وُ کړ *wu-karr*; fut. ایل به کړي *ael* or *īl bah krrī*, or به وُ کړي *bah wu-krrī*; imp. ایل کړه *ael* or *īl krrah*, or وُ کړه *wu-krrah*; act. part. ایلوونکئ *aelawūnkaey* or *īlawūnkaey*, and ایلوونئ *aelawūnaey* or *īlawūnaey*; past part. ایل کړي *ael* or *īl karraey*; verb. n. ایلونه *aelawuna'h* or *īlawuna'h*.

ایل والئ *ael-wālaey*, or *īl-wālaey*, s.m. (1st) Tameness, domestication, obedience. Pl. والي *wālī*, or ایلیدنه *aeledana'h*, or *īledana'h*, s.f.

(3rd) (verb. n.) Pl. ئ *ey*; and ايليده *aeledah*, or *īledah*, s.m. (6th) Sing. and Pl. ايل *ael*, s.m. (2nd) Tribe, sept, clan, family. Pl. ايلونه *aelūnah*.

T ايلاق *ī-lāḳ*, s.m. (2nd) A summer station of the pastoral tribes of the West, in distinction to *ḳish-lāk*, the winter station. Pl. ايلاقونه *ī-lāḳūnah*. See قشلاق.

T ايلچي *īl-chī*, s.m. (5th) An envoy, an ambassador, an agent, or attorney. Pl. ايلچيان *īl-chīān*.

T ايلغار *īl-ghār*, s.m. (2nd) An assault, an attack, an inroad, a foray, an invasion. Pl. ايلغارونه *īl-ghārūnah*. ايلغار كول *īl-ghār kawul*, verb trans. To assault, to invade, to attack, to make an inroad on.

ايلغر *īl-ghar*, s.m. (2nd) Pl. ايلغرونه *īl-gharūnah*. Same as preceding.

ايله *aelah*, adj. Free, liberated, at large, unrestrained, unbridled, irresponsible. 2. Wandering, vagabond, dissolute (Masc. and Fem.). ايله كول *ae-lah kawul*, verb trans. To free, to release, to set at large; to wander about, to make a wanderer or vagabond of. For other combinations of this word, see under يله.

A ايمان *ī-mān*, s.m. (2nd) (inf. IV of امن) Faith, belief, religion, conscience, credit. Pl. ايمانونه *ī-mānūnah*. ايمان دار *ī-mān-dār*, adj. Faithful, conscientious, honest, trusty, a believer; (Fem.) ايمان داره *ī-mān-dāra'h*. ايمان داري *ī-mān-dārī*, s.f. (3rd) Faithfulness, conscientiousness, honesty, fidelity, trustiness. Pl. ئ *a'ī*

A ايمن *ai-min*, adj. More or most happy, fortunate, void of care, free; (Fem.) ايمنه *ai-mina'h*.

ايمن *aey-man*, adj. Quiet, gentle, calm, inexcitable, sober, serene, patient, submissive, inoffensive, peaceful, pacific; (Fem.) ايمنه *aey-mana'h*. ايمن كيدل *aey-man kedal*, verb intrans. To become or grow calm, quiet, gentle; to become appeased, softened, mollified, calmed, pacified, etc. ايمن كول *aey-man kawul*, verb trans. To quiet, to appease, to mollify, to calm, to soothe, to hush, to tranquillize.

ايمن والئ *aey-man-wālacy*, s.m. (1st) Calmness, quietness, tranquillity, peace of mind, composure, placidity, meekness, gentleness, patience, sobriety, sedateness. Pl. والي *wālī*.

A ايمه *ai-mah*, s.f. (3rd) Land given as a reward or favour by a king or chief at a very low rent, a fief. Pl. ئ *ey*. ايمه دار *ai-mah-dār*, A feoffee; (Fem.) ايمه داره *ai-mah-dāra'h*. See سيري and دفتر.

اينده *īn-da'h*, s.f. (3rd) (W.) A gulph, a draught. 2. A mouthful, a sip. Pl. ئ *ey*. See انده.

P آينده *ā-indah*, s.m. (6th) The future, coming. Sing. and Pl. 2. adv. In future, for the future.

اينزر *īn-zar*, s.m. (6th) A fig. Sing. and Pl. دَ اينزر ونه *da īn-zar wanah*, A fig-tree. See انځير.

اينه *īna'h*, s.f. (3rd) The liver, the heart, the vitals. Pl. ئ *ey*. See ځيگر.

ايوازئ *ae-wāzaey*, adj. Alone, etc. See following word.

ايواځئ *ae-wādzaey*, adj. Alone, single, solitary, insular, insulated, isolated, lone; (Fem.) ايواځې *ae-wādzi*. Pl. ي *ī*. ايواځئ كيدل *ae-wādzaey kedal*, verb intrans. To become isolated, lone, solitary. ايواځئ كول *ae-wādzaey kawul*, verb trans. To make or render lonely, single, solitary; to insulate. See يواځئ.

A ايوب *ai-yūb*, s. prop. The prophet Job. 2. The name for a man.

ايوب زي *ai-yūb-zī*, s.m. (1st) Pl. The name of an Afghān tribe. ايوبزئ *ai-yūbzaey*, Sing. A male of the above tribe. ايوبزئ *ai-yūbza'ī*, s.f. (6th) A female of the above. Sing. and Pl.

P آئين *ā'īn*, s.m. (2nd) Regulation, institute, statute, rule, common law. Pl. آئينونه *ā'īnūnah*.

P آئينه *ā'īnah*, s.f. (3rd) A mirror, a looking-glass. Pl. ئ *ey*.

ب

ب *bey* is the second letter of the Pus̲h̲to, as well as of the Arabic, Hebrew, and Persian alphabets. In the Afg̲h̲ān language this letter is sometimes changed for و as in the Persian.

بَ *ba*, a particle, the sign of the future, the doubtful past, and the continuative tenses of verbs. When not prefixed to a word, which is the most general form, it is written به, which see. See also my Grammar.

A بِ *bi*, prep. (always prefixed to another word), By, with, from, near, on, into, in, for, towards, etc.

P بَ *ba*, prep. Generally prefixed to another word, and when standing alone written به, signifying, With, by, for, in, into, to, up to, on, upon.

P با *bā*, prep. With, by. It is only used with a few Persian words such as با ايمان *bā īmān*, Religious, faithful. با مروت *bā murūwat*, With kindness, etc. See په the Pus̲h̲to equivalent for this preposition.

باو *bā-ū*, s.m. (5th) A bracelet, an ornament for the wrist. Pl. باوګان *bā-ū-gān*. See باهو.

A باب *bāb*, s.m. (2nd) A door, a gate. 2. A chapter, section, or division of a book. 3. Subject, head, affair, point, matter, business, reason, manner, mode, species, sort. 4. P Fate, destiny, fortune, lot. Pl. بابونه *bābūnah*. په دا باب *pah dā bāb*, or په دا باب کښې *pah dā bāb kk̲h̲ey*, or *ks̲h̲ey*, On this account, for this reason.

T بابا *bābā*, A term of endearment: Father! dad! sire! sir! child! جان بابا *jān bābā*, The name of a celebrated devotee whose shrine is situated at Jabgarrah in Buner. See بابو ,بابکو, and بچو.

A بابت *bābat*, s.m. (2nd) Account, head, article, item, affair, matter, business. Pl. بابتونه *bābatūnah*.

بابړ *bābarr*, s.m. (6th) The name of an Afg̲h̲ān tribe. Pl. بابړان *bābarr-ān*; (Fem.) (3rd) بابړه *bābarra'h*. Pl. ې *ey*.

بابکو *bābko*, s.m. A term of endearment to a child. See بچو.

A بابل *bābul*, s. prop. Babel, the tower of Babel, Babylon.

بابو *bābū*, A term of endearment from a child to its father, or to a venerable man. بابو جان *bābū jān*, The name of a Pus̲h̲to author, said to have been a converted Sī'āh-pos̲h̲ Kāfir, who again relapsed. For specimen of his works, see Text Book.

بابوزي *bābū zī*, s.m. (1st) Pl. Name of a tribe of Afg̲h̲āns. بابوزی *bābū-zaey*, Sing. A man of the above; (Fem.) (6th) بابوزۍ *bābūza'ī*, A female of the above. Sing. and Pl.

بابي *bābī*, s.f. (3rd) A brother's wife. Pl. ۍ *a'ī*.

بابي *bābī*, s.m. (1st) Pl. The name of an Afg̲h̲ān tribe. بابی *bābaey*, Sing. A man or male of the tribe, or s.m. (5th) Pl. بابيان *bābī-ān*. بابۍ *bā-ba'ī*, s.f. (6th) A female of the above. Sing. and Pl.

باتور *bā-tor*, adj. (corrup. of P بهادر) Bold, brave, courageous, valiant; (Fem.) باتوره *bā-tora'h*. 2. s.m. (5th) A species of falcon remarkable for its sharp sight. Pl. باتوران *bātorān*. باتوري *bā-torī*, s.f. (3rd). Bravery, boldness, gallantry, heroism. Pl. ۍ *a'ī*. باتوري کول *bā-torī kawul*, verb trans. To act with boldness or bravery, to shew courage or gallantry.

باتور *bātor*, s.m. (2nd) The pupil of the eye. Pl. باتورونه *bātorūnah*. See کسي and توره.

باتوره *bātūra'h*, s.f. (3rd) Name of a poisonous plant, the thorn-apple (Datura fastuosa). Pl. ې *ey*. (HI دهاتورا.)

باتۍ *bāta'ī*, s.f. (6th) A wick, a match. Sing. and Pl.

باټیګڼ *bāṭṭey-garrn*, s.m. (5th) The egg-plant. Pl. باټیګڼ *bāṭṭey-gærrn*.

P باج *bāj*, s.m. (2nd) A tribute, a tax, a toll, impost, duty. Pl. باجونه *bāj-ūnah*. باج دار *bāj dār*, s.m. A tax gatherer, a collector of tribute or revenue. باج ګزار *bāj guzār*, A tax payer, one who pays tribute. باج ور کول *bāj war kawul*, verb trans. To pay tribute.

باجوړ *bājawarr*, s. prop. The country of Bājawarr, north west of Peshāwer. باجوړئ bā-jawarrey, s.m. (1st) A native of Bājawarr. Pl. ي ī ; s.f. (6th) ۍ a'ī. Sing. and Pl.

باخملۍ bākhmala'ī, s.f. (6th) A small red caterpillar produced in the rains, generally covered with hair. 2. The name of a bird which cries at night. Sing. and Pl. See بخملۍ

P باد bād, s.m. (2nd) Wind, air, breeze, gale. Pl. بادونه bādūnah. باد آلوتل bād ālwatal, verb trans. To blow as the wind (lit. to fly). د سحر باد da sahar bād, The morning wind. د قبلي باد da kibley bād, The west wind ; or د نور پريواته باد da n'war prewātah bād. د نور خاته باد da n'war khātah bād, The east wind. د قطب باد da kutb bād, The north wind. د سهيل باد da suhail bād, The south wind ; or د نيلاو باد da nīlāo bād, from nīlāo, the name of the Indus ; in Persian, nīl āb, or the blue water. باد فرنگ bād-ī-farang, The pox. باد پيزي bād pezī, s.f. (3rd) Absurdity, nonsense, vanity, unprofitableness, trash, stuff, fiddle-faddle. Pl. ۍ a'ī. باد پيزي کول bād pezī kawul, verb trans. (lit. to sift the wind), To do anything absurd or unprofitable. باد جړۍ bād jarra'ī, s.f. (6th) Driving rain, wind and rain, drift. Sing. and Pl. See جم جکړ or جهم جکړ. بر باد bar-bād, adj. Given to the winds, thrown away, misapplied, lost, wasted, laid waste, ruined. بر باد کيدل bar bād kedal, verb intrans. To become ruined or laid waste. بر باد کول bar bād kawul, verb trans. To ruin, to waste, to give to the winds. باد وهل bād wahal, verb trans. To strike as a hot pestilential wind.

P بادام bādām, s.m. An almond. Pl. بادامونه bādāmūnah. بادامي bādāmī, adj. Almond-shaped.

P بادبان bādbān, s.m. (2nd) A sail, a vessel used to hold a lamp for the purpose of protecting it from the wind, a shade. Pl. بادبانونه bād-bānūnah ; also بادوان, which see.

باد پيزي bād pezī, s.f. (3rd) Absurdity, nonsense, vanity, trash, stuff, fiddle-faddle, unprofitableness. Pl. ۍ a'ī. باد پيزي کول bād pezī kawul, verb trans. To do anything absurd, nonsensical, or unprofitable.

باد خور bād khor, s.m. (6th) The rupture, hernia. (In Persian, a disease in horses, which causes the hair to fall off.) Sing. and Pl.

باد خورک bād khorak, s.m. (6th) The pox. 2. A running at the nose and eyes from cold. Sing. and Pl. 3. s.m. (5th) A kind of hawk or kite. Pl. باد خورکان bād khorakāṇ.

باد خوري bād khūrī, s.f. (3rd) A disease to which horses are subject : they refuse their grain and fall off in condition. Pl. ۍ a'ī.

P باد رنگ bād rang, s.m. (6th) A kind of cucumber. Sing. and Pl.

بادرو bād-rau, s.m. (2nd) A ventilator, a place to admit air, made in the walls of houses. Pl. بادروونه bād-rauūnah.

بادرو bādro, s.m. (9th) The second month of the rainy season—August. (HI بهادون).

P بادشاه bādshāh, s.m. (5th) A king, a sovereign, a ruler, a potentate, a monarch. Pl. بادشاهان bādshāhān.

P بادشاهانه bādshāhānah, adj. Imperial, royal. 2. adv. Royally, princely, kingly.

P بادشاهت bādshāhat, s.m. (2nd) Royalty, empire, kingdom, government, dominion. Pl. بادشاهتونه bādshāhatūnah.

P بادشاهي bādshāhī, adj. Royal, imperial, regal. 2. s.f. (3rd) Empire, reign, sway, sovereignty, dominion, office of a king. Pl. ۍ a'ī.

بادوان bād-wān, s.m. (2nd) A sail, a shade or screen for a lamp. Pl. بادوانونه bād-wānūnah. See بادبان.

P بادوکئ bādūkaey, s.m. (1st) A gentle breeze, a light air, a cat's-paw. Pl. ي ī.

P باده bāda'h, s.f. (3rd) Wine, spirit. Pl. ې ey.

باد هوا bād hawā, s.m. (5th) A paper kite. Pl. باد هواگان bād-hawā-gān. See کاغذ باد.

P بادي bādī, adj. Flatulent, windy ; when applied to a man, it means a useless good-for-nothing fellow, a poltroon.

باډگول bādd-gol, s.m. (2nd) A leading rein, a rope. Pl. باډگولونه bādd-golūnah. See بونړ.

P بار *bār,* s.m. (2nd) A load, a burden, fruit, time, once. Pl. بارونه *bārūnah.* بار بردار *bār-bardār,* Bearing a burthen, a porter, a carrier, a beast of burden. بار برداري *bār-bārdārī,* s.f. (3rd) Means of conveyance, carriage, beasts of burden. Pl. ئي *a'ī.* بارداره خځه *bārdāra'h khadza'h,* s.f. (3rd) A pregnant woman. Pl. ئي *ey.* باري *bārī,* A beast of burden, carriage, fit for a load. هندو بار *hindū bār,* A place where Hindūs assemble, Hindūstān.

S بار *bār,* s.m. (2nd) Time, occasion, a time. Pl. بارونه *bārūnah.* بار بار *bār-bār,* adv. Repeatedly, often. See وار

P باران *bārān,* s.m. (2nd) Rain. Pl. بارانونه *bārānūnah.* د پسرلي باران *da psarlī bārān,* Spring rain or showers. باران سال *bār-ān sāl,* A rainy year; also باران کال *bār-ān-kāl.* د ووري باران *da wo-ṛṛī bārān,* Rain which falls in the summer season injurious to the crops; also called وسه *wasa'h.* رنگئ باران *ran-gaey bārān,* A slight shower, drizzling rain. گڼړ باران *gaṛṛn bārān,* Heavy rain, a heavy shower or fall of rain. باران اوريدل or ووريدل *bārān ao-redal,* or *wo-redal,* verb intrans. To rain, to fall or pour as rain. باران اورول or وورول *bārān ao-rawul,* or *wo-rawul,* verb trans. To make or cause to rain or pour. See اوريدل, etc.

P باراني *bārān-ī,* adj. Relating to or depending on rain, of rain.

بارانئ *bārāna'ī,* s.f. (6th) A coat or cloak for keeping off rain. Sing. and Pl.

بارخو *bārkho,* s.f. (9th) The face, the cheek. Sing. and Pl.

بارخو *bārkhū,* s.m. (5th) (W.) The cheek, the side of the face. Pl. بارخوگان *bār-khūgān.*

بارک *bārak,* s. prop. The name of one of the three sons of Zīrak, the ancestor of the Bārakzīs, of which tribe Dost Muḥammad Khān, the present ruler of Kābul, is the head and chief.

بارکزي *bārak-zī,* s.m. (1st) Pl. The name of an Afghān tribe. بارکزئ *bārak-zaey,* Sing. A male of the tribe; s.f. (6th) ئي *a'ī,* A female of the tribe. Sing. and Pl.

بارکښ *bār-kash* (W.) or *bār-kakh* (E.) adj. (past part.) Burden-bearing or drawing, such as carts, camels, carriers, etc. 2. Meek, humble; (Fem.) بار کښه *bār-kasha'h,* or *bār-kakha'h.* بارکښي *bār-kashī* (W.) or *bār-kakhī* (E.) s.f. (3rd) Carrying loads, porterage, carrying, conveyance. Pl. ئي *a'ī.* بار کښي کول *bār-kashī,* or *bār-kakhī kawul,* verb trans. To carry a burden, to carry, to convey. (P بار کش, etc.)

P بارگاه *bār-gā'h,* s.f. (2nd) A court, a palace, a place of audience. Pl. بارگاهونه *bār-gāhūnah.*

باروزي *bāro-zī,* s.m. (1st) Pl. The name of a tribe of Afghāns. باروزئ *bāro-zaey,* Sing. A male of the tribe; s.f. (6th) باروزئي *bāro-za'ī,* A female of the above. Sing. and Pl.

بارول *bārawul,* verb trans. To load, to pack, to freight, to pack up. Pres. باروي *bārawī;* past بار کړ *bār karr,* or وُ کړ *wu-karr;* fut. بار به کړي *bār bah kṛrī,* or به وُ کړي *bah wu-kṛrī;* imp. بار کړه *bār kṛrah;* act. part. بارونکئ *bārawūnkaey,* or باروونئ *bārawūnaey;* past part. بار کړئ *bār karraey;* verb. n. بارونه *bārawuna'h.*

بارول *bārawul,* verb trans. To set by the ears, to incite, to instigate or animate to action (as a man or animal).

P باره *bāra'h,* s.f. (3rd) A fortification, defence, rampart, a ditch, palisade, an entrenchment, a breastwork. Pl. ئي *ey.* See سنگر

P باري *bārey,* adv. Once, one time; at last, at length. See بهره

A باري *bārī,* act. part. of برأ, (H ברא, Created) The Deity, the Creator, the First Cause. باري تعالي *bārī ta'ææālā,* The Most High God.

P باريک *bārīk,* adj. Fine, slender, subtile, minute; (Fem.) باريکه *bārīka'h.* باريک کول *bārīk kawul,* verb trans. To make or render fine, slender, minute.

P باريکي *bārīkī,* s.f. (3rd) Fineness, niceness, subtilty, minuteness. Pl. ئي *a'ī.* باريکي کول *bārīkī kawul,* verb trans. To manifest or show subtilty, penetration, etc.

S بار *bāṛr,* s.m. (2nd) A volley of musketry. Pl.

بارونه *bā**rr**ūnah*. بار کول *bā**rr** kawul*, verb trans. To fire or give a volley.

P باز *bāz*, s.m. (5th) A hawk, a falcon. Pl. بازان *bāzān*. See باښه and باښين

P بازار *bāzār*, s.m. (2nd) A market. Pl. بازارونه *bāzārūnah*.

P بازارگی *bāzārgaey*, s.m. (1st) A small market. Pl. ي *ī*.

P بازاري *bāzār-ī*, adj. Belonging to the market, a market person.

P بازنده *bāzindah*, s.m. (5th) (act. part. of باختن) A player, the proper name of a pigeon. Pl. بازندهگان *bāzindah-gān*.

P بازو *bāzū*, s.m. (5th) The side of a bedstead, the arm, the fold of a door. Pl. بازوگان *bāzūgān*.

P بازو بند *bāzū band*, s.m. (2nd) An ornament worn on the arm, a bracelet. Pl. بازوبندونه *bāzū-bandūnah*.

P بازي *bāzī*, s.f. (3rd) Play, sport, game, a trick. Pl. ئ *a'ī*. بازي کول *bāzī kawul*, verb trans. To play, to sport, to make merry. بازي وړل *bāzī w'**rr**al*, or بازي گټل *bāzī ga**tt**al*, verb trans. To win at play, to excel.

بازید *bāzīd*, s. prop. (properly بایزید Bāyazīd), the name of the celebrated Derwe**sh**; the name of the founder of the Ro**sh**ānīān sect, Bāyazīd Ansārī; called also Pīr Tarīk, or the Saint of Darkness.

P بازیگر *bāzīgar*, s.m. (5th) A tumbler, one who exhibits feats of activity, a rope-dancer. بازیگر *bāzīgær*; s.f. (3rd) بازیگره *bāzīgara'h*. Pl. ئ *ey*. See نټ

P بازیگري *bāzīgarī*, s.f. (3rd) The art of a tumbler. Pl. ئ *a'ī*.

باس *bās*, s.m. (2nd) A necessary, a privy (s odour, smell). Pl. باسونه *bāsūnah*.

باسل *bāsal*, verb trans. To reject, to expel, to discharge, to cast out, to discard, to exclude, to put off, to put away, to let fly, to remove, to free, to give vent to. This verb is imperfect, and is used to make up the tenses wanting in the verbs ایستل and یستل, which are likewise imperfect. Pres. باسي *bāsī*; fut. وُ به باسي *wu bah bāsī*; imp. وُ باسه *wu bāsah*.

باښه *bā**kh**a'h* (E.) or *bā**sh**a'h* (W.) s.f. (3rd) A sparrow-hawk. Pl. ئ *ey*; and باښين *bā**sh**īn*, or *bā**kh**īn*, s.f. (5th). Pl. باښينان *bā**sh**īnān*, or *bā**kh**īnān*.

A باطل *bā**t**il*, adj. (from بطل) False, vain, absurd, futile, ineffectual, abolished; (Fem). باطله *bā**t**ila'h*.

A باطن *bā**t**in*, s.m. (2nd) (from بطن) The inward part, the inside, the internal, the heart, the mind. Pl. باطنونه *bā**t**inūnah*. 2. adj. Internal, hidden, concealed.

A باطني *bā**t**inī*, adj. Internal, concealed.

A باعث *bā'æi**s***, s.m. (9th) (act. part. of بعث, Productive) Cause, occasion, motive, reason, account, subject. Sing. and Pl.

A باعد *bā'æid*, adj. Far, remote, very distant; (Fem.) باعده *bā'æida'h*.

P باغ *bā**gh***, s.m. (2nd) A garden, an orchard, a grove. Pl. باغونه *bā**gh**ūnah*.

P باغبان *bā**gh**bān*, s.m. (5th) A gardener; also written باغوان *bā**gh**wān*. Pl. باغبانان *bā**gh**bānān*.

P باغباني *bā**gh**bānī*, s.f. (3rd) The science of gardening. Pl. ئ *a'ī*. باغباني کول *bā**gh**-bānī kawul*, verb trans. To carry on the business of a gardener.

A باغي *bā**gh**ī*, act. part. (from بغي or بغاوت) A mutineer, a traitor, a rebel. See ياغي

A باقي *bā**k**ī*, part. act. (of بقا) Remaining, permanent, lasting, extant, eternal; (used substantively), remnant, remainder, balance, arrear. باقي دار *bā**k**ī dār*, Owing a balance; (Fem.) باقي داره *bā**k**ī-dāra'h*. باقيات *bā**k**iyāt*, s.m. (6th) (Pl. of باقي) Remainders, balances, arrears.

P باك *bāk*, s.m. (9th) Fear, dread, care, anxiety, misgiving. Sing. and Pl. بي باك *bey bāk*. Without fear, etc.; (Fem.) بي باکه *bey bāka'h*,

HI باگډور *bāg-**dd**or*, s.m. (2nd) A long rein by which horses are led. Pl. باگډورونه *bāg-**dd**or-ūnah*.

باګو *bā-gū*, s.f. (5th) A bug-bear, a woman dressed up in a frightful manner to frighten children when naughty. Pl. باګوګانِ *bāgū-gāni*, or باګوګاني *bāgū-gānī*.

بگولئي *bāgo-la'ī*, s.f. (6th) Same as preceding. Sing. and Pl.; also بگلولئي *bagalola'ī*.

P بالا خانه *bālā khāna'h*, s.f. (3rd) An upper room, an upper story, a balcony. Pl. ي *ey*.

بالښت *bāliḳht* (E.) or *bālisht* (W.) s.m. (2nd) (P بالشت) A cushion, a pillow, a bolster. Pl. بالښتونه *bāliḳhtūnah* or *bālishtūnah*.

بالښتک *bālishtak* (W.) or *bāliḳhtak* (E.) s.m. (5th) A small pad stuffed with cotton or rags, placed at the back of a buckler to protect the hand. Pl. بالښتکان *bālishtakān* or *bāliḳhtakān*.

A بالغ *bāligh*, adj. (act. part. of بلوغ) Reaching its end, consummate, arrived at the age of maturity; an adult; (Fem.) بالغه *bāligha'h*. See بلوغت

بالړ *bālarrn*, s.m. (5th) A kind of broth or hash. 2. Fuel, firewood. Pl. بالړ *bālærrn*.

P بالين *bālīn*, s.m. (2nd) A pillow, a bolster. Pl. بالينونه *bālīnūnah*.

P بام *bām*, s.m. (2nd) An upper story, the terrace or roof of a house. Pl. بامونه *bāmūnah*. له بام لويدل *lah bāma lwe-dal*, verb trans. To fall from the roof of a house, to plump down.

بامبړ or بامبن *bāmbarrn*, s.m. (5th) A Brāhman. Pl. بامبړان *bāmbarrnān*; s.f. (3rd) بامبړه *bāmbarrna'h*, A female of the above. Pl. ي *ey*; and بامړ or بامن *bāmarrn*. Pl. بامړان or بامنان *bāmarrnān*; and بامړه or بامنه *bāmarrna'h*, s.f. (3rd). Pl. ي *ey*.

بامبړه *bam-barrna'h*, s.f. (3rd) A flame, a blaze with smoke. Pl. ي *ey*. See ډانډئي and لمبه.

HI بانات *bānāt*, s.m. (6th) Broad cloth. Sing. and Pl. See بنات

بانډِ *bāndi*, prep. Above, up, on, upon. Sometimes written باندي *bāndī*. باندِ کول *bāndi kawul*, verb trans. To put or place on or upon, as a pot on the fire, etc.

باندړه *bāndda'h*, s.f. (3rd) A sheep-fold, a cattle pen. 2. A small village or hamlet, a few dwellings collected together. Pl. ي *ey*. See شپول

بانديسي *bānddesaey*, s.m. (1st) A wandering grazier or shepherd. Pl. ي *ī*.

P بانگ *bāng*, s.m. (2nd) Voice, crying out, sound, the voice of the mu'azzin calling the faithful to prayer, the crowing of the cock. Pl. بانگونه *bāngūnah*. بانگ ويل *bāng wa-yal*, or بانگ کول *bāng kawul*, verb trans. To crow as a cock, to cry out with a loud voice, as the mu'azzin when calling to prayer. بانگي چرگ *bāngī chirg*, A crowing cock, a cock kept for the purpose of crowing (generally white), to rouse people to prayer before daybreak.

بانه *bāna'h*, s.f. (3rd) Pretence, evasion, excuse, pretext, feint, contrivance, affectation. Pl. ي *ey* (P بهانه). بانه غوښتل *bā-na'h ghoshtal* (W.) or *ghoḳhtal* (E.) verb trans. To seek or search for a pretext, pretence, or evasion. بانه کول *bā-na'h kawul*, verb trans. To put forward a pretext, or evasion; to evade, to contrive.

بانړو *bārrno*, s.m. (5th) (W.) The eyelash. Pl. بانړوگان *bārrno-gān*. (E.) بانړه, which see.

بانړه or بانه *bārrna'h*, s.f. (3rd) (E.) An eyelash. Pl. ي *ey*. Also written بانړَ or بانَ.

A باوجود *bāwajūd*, adv. Excepting, nevertheless, notwithstanding, particularly, chiefly, especially.

P باور *bāwar*, s.m. (9th) Belief, faith, confidence, trust, credit. Sing. and Pl. باور کول *bā-war kawul*, verb trans. To believe, to trust, to credit. باور لرل *bā-war laral*, verb trans. To have or possess faith, confidence, or trust in. باوري *bā-warī*, adj. Faithful, trustworthy, creditable.

باوسير *bāw-sīr*, s.m. (6th) (corrup. of A بواسير) The piles, hemorrhoids. Sing. and Pl.

S باهر *bāhar*, adv. Without, outside, away. 2. Foreign. See دباندي or دباندِ.

باهو *bāhū*, s.m. (5th) An ornament for the arm or ankles. Pl. باهوگان *bāhū-gān*. See باداو

بايده *bā'īdah*, adv. Perhaps, possibly, may be. (P بايد).

بايده *bāedah*, adj. Necessary, suitable, fit, proper, meet, becoming. 2. adv. Necessarily, it behoveth. دود بايده *dod-bāedah*, Necessaries, or clothes and ornaments furnished to a bride by her father, outfit.

بايلل *bā'e-lal*, verb trans. To lose (at play), to

be overcome, to forfeit by unsuccessful contest; pres. بايلي *bā'e-lī*; past. بايلو *bā'e-lo*, or بايلوي *bā'e-loey*, or بايله *bā'e-lah*; fut. باي به لي *bā-e bah lī* (W.) or با به يلي *bā bah e-lī* (E.); imp. بايله *bā'e-lah*; act. part. بايلونكي *bā'e-lūnkaey*, or بايلوني *bā'e-lūnaey*; past part. بايلوي *bā'e-lawaey*, or بايللي *bā'e-lalaey*; verb. n. بايلنه *bā'e-lana'h*.

بايلول *bā'e-lawul*, verb trans. (caus.) To cause to lose, etc.; pres. بايلوي *bā'e-lawī*; past. بايلو *bā'e-lo*; fut. با به يلوي *bā bah e-lawī*; imp. بايلوه *bā'e-lawah*; act. part. بايلونكي *bā'e-lawūnkaey*, or بايلووني *bā'e-lawūnaey*; past. part. بايلولي *bā'e-lawalaey*, or بايلوي *bā'e-lawaey*; verb. n. بايلونه *bā'e-lawana'h*.

بائيزي *bā-yī zī*, s.m. (1st) Pl. The name of an Afghān tribe; Sing. ي *aey*, s.f. (6th) ئي *a'ī*. Sing. and Pl.

بائيكر *bā-yī-kar*, s.m. (6th) The name of a shrub, producing a fruit about the size of a currant, and from which they make a kind of toothbrush (Salvadora Persica). Sing. and Pl.

ببر *babar*, adj. Hairy, bushy, shaggy, bearded, downy; (Fem.) ببره *babara'h*. ببريدل *babaredal*, verb intrans. To become hairy, bushy, shaggy, ruffled (as a cat when ready to fight). ببرول *babarawul*, verb trans. To render hairy, bushy, shaggy; to bristle up.

ببوزي *babo zaey*, s.m. (1st) A fan, a ventilator. 2. A kind of fishing bird. Pl. ي *ī*. See بهبوزي.

ببئي *baba-a'ī*, s.f. (6th) The name of a worm-eating bird. Sing. and Pl.

P بت *but*, s.m. (5th) An idol, image, statue; a beloved object, a mistress. Pl. بتان *but-ān*. بت پرست *but parast*, adj. An idolator, one who worships images; (Fem.) بت پرسته *but parasta'h*. بت پرستي *but parastī*, s.f. (3rd) Idolatry. Pl. ئي *a'ī*. بت خانه *but khāna'h*, s.f. (3rd) An idol temple. Pl. ي *ey*; also بت كده *but kadah*.

بت *but*, s.m. (2nd) One of the walls of a well with a Persian wheel, two of which support the cross beam. Pl. بتان *butān*.

بتان *batān*, s.m. (5th) The general name by which Afghāns are known in India. Pl. بتانان *batānān*; (Fem.) (3rd) بتانه *batāna'h*. Pl. ي *ey*. See also پتان and the derivation and meaning of the word in the Introduction to my Grammar.

P بتر *batar*, adj. compar. (cont. of بد تر) Very bad, worse; (Fem.) بتره *batara'h*.

بتك *batak*, s.m. (2nd) An earthen or leathern vessel for containing water. Pl. بتكونه *batakūnah*. See also بتكي

A بتول *batūl*, s. prop. A pure virgin, *i.e.* Fātimah, the daughter of Muḥammad and wife of Æalī.

بته *bata'h*, s.f. (3rd) A heron. Pl. بتي *batey*.

بتي *batī*, s.f. (3rd) Glue, starch, paste, a stiffening for cloth, size. Pl. ئي *a'ī*. بتي ډكه *batī ddakah*, adj. Unworn or unwashed cloth (*lit.* full of size). See شډله

بټ *batt*, s.m. (2nd) A large iron pan or cauldron for roasting grain, a furnace, a kiln. 2. Luck, prosperity, felicity. 3. The bark of a tree, bark, rind, peel, husk (S वट or वष, wrap round or entwine). Pl. بټونه *battūnah*. See پټ ,پستكي, and بجه

بټه *batta'h*, s.f. (3rd) Husked or pounded barley. Pl. بټي *battey*.

بڅخه *butskha'h*, s.f. (3rd) A small bundle or parcel, a roll of clothes. (T بقچه). Pl. ي *ey*.

بڅري *batsaraey*, s.m. (1st) A spark of fire. Pl. ي *ī*.

بڅركي *batsar-kaey*, s.m. (1st) A spark of fire. Pl. ي *ī*.

P بجز *bajuz*, prep. With the exception, without, save, besides, except.

بجل *bijal*, s.f. (1st) A knuckle-bone with which a game is played. Pl. بجلِ *bijali*. بجل باز *bijal-bāz*, s.m. (5th) A person who plays at the game of knuckle-bones. Pl. بجل بازان *bijal-bāzān*. بجل بازه *bijal-bāza'h*, s.f. (3rd). Pl. ي *ey*. See تكه and ارغند

بچري *bachraey*, s.m. (1st) A young donkey. Pl. ي *ī*. Fem. (6th) ئي *a'ī*. Sing. and Pl.

بچكري *bachakaraey*, s.m. (1st) The lash of a whip, the end of a sling—the slight part which is let go. Pl. ي *ī*. Also بچوي

بچو *bac͟hū*, A term of endearment to a child. See بابکو.

بچونګړي *bac͟hūngaṟṟaey*, s.m. (1st) A very little child, or the young of an animal. Pl. ي *ī*; s.f. (6th) ئ *a'ī*. Sing. and Pl.

بچوي *bac͟hawaey*, s.m. (1st) The lash of a whip. 2. The slight end of a sling which is let go in throwing. 3. A band or ribbon for fastening the plaited ends of women's hair. Pl. ي *ī*. See پيبوي and بچکري.

P بچي *bac͟haey*, s.m. (1st) An infant, a child, the young of any creature. Pl. ي *ī*; s.f. (6th) بچئ *bac͟ha'ī*. Sing. and Pl. (P بچه).

A بحاث *baḥḥās̤*, adj. (superl. of بحث) A great disputer, controvertist, arguer; (Fem.) بحاثه *baḥḥās̤a'h*.

A بحال *baḥāl*, adj. Unaltered, happy; in office, reinstated, restored; (Fem.) بحاله *baḥāla'h*. بحال کول *baḥāl kawul*, verb trans. To replace, to reinstate, to restore, to re-establish. بحالي *baḥālī*, s.f. (3rd) Restoration, re-instalment. Pl. ئ *a'ī*.

A بحث *baḥs̤*, s.m. (2nd) Inquiry, discussion, dispute, altercation, controversy, debate, argument. Pl. بحثونه *baḥs̤ūna'h*. بحث کول *baḥs̤ kawul*, verb trans. To dispute, to argue, to debate.

A بحر *baḥr*, s.m. (2nd) The ocean, the sea, a bay, a gulf. Pl. بحرونه *baḥrūnah*. بحر و بر *baḥr ow barr*, Ocean and land, water and land.

بحري *baḥ-rī*, adj. Of or relating to the sea, naval.

P بخت *bak͟ht*, s.m. (2nd) Fortune, luck, prosperity, felicity. Pl. بختونه *bak͟htūnah*. بختور *bak͟htawar*, adj. Fortunate, lucky; (Fem.) بختوره *bak͟htawura'h*. بد بخت *bad-bak͟ht* or تور بخت *tor-bak͟ht*, adj. Unfortunate, unlucky; (Fem.) بد بخته *bad-bak͟hta'h* or تور بخته *tor-bak͟hta'h*.

P بختيار *bak͟ht-yār*, s.m. (5th) The name of an Afg͟hān tribe. Pl. بختياران *bak͟ht-yārān*; s.f. (3rd) بختياره *bak͟ht-yāra'h*, A female of the above. Pl. ئ *ey*. 2. adj. Fortunate, lucky; (Fem.) بختياره *bak͟ht-yāra'h*.

بخره *bak͟hra'h*, s.f. (3rd) Share, portion, part, lot. Pl. ئ *ey*. See برخه (P بخرا).

بخښ *bak͟hs͟h*, s.m. (2nd) (from P بخشيدن) Share, portion, lot; forgiveness; imparting, bestowing. Pl. بخښونه *bak͟hs͟hūna'h*.

بخښښ *bak͟hs͟his͟h*, s.m. (2nd) Gift, donation, donative, grant, boon, reward, giving, beneficence, pardon, forgiveness, liberality, generosity, etc. Pl. بخښښونه *bak͟hs͟his͟hūnah*. صاحب د بخښښ *sāḥib da bak͟hs͟his͟h*, adj. Munificent, liberal, or generous person. بخښل *bak͟hs͟hal*, verb trans. To give, to bestow, to grant. See ببښل and ببښنه (P بخشش).

A بخل *buk͟hl*, s.m. (9th) Avarice, stinginess, parsimony. Sing. and Pl. بخل کول *buk͟hl kawul*, verb trans. To act parsimoniously, to manifest avarice.

بخملئ *bak͟hmala'ī*, s.f. (6th) A small insect with a red back and soft like velvet, a scarlet fly or lady-fly. Sing. and Pl. See also باخملئ.

A بخيل *bak͟hīl*, s.m. (5th) A miser, a niggard. Pl. بخيلان *bak͟hīlān*; Fem. (6th) بخيله *bak͟hīla'h*. Pl. ئ *ey*.

A بخيلي *bak͟hīlī*, s.f. (3rd) Stinginess, niggardliness, parsimony, avarice. Pl. ئ *a'ī*.

P بد *bad*, adj. Evil, bad. (Fem.) بده *bada'h*. بد اصل *bad as̤l*, adj. Low born. بد آواز *bad āwāz*, adj. A bad voice, a bad name. بد بخت *bad bak͟ht*, adj. Unlucky, unfortunate, wretched, rascally; (Fem.) بد بخته *bad bak͟hta'h*. بد بختي *bad bak͟htī*, s.f. (3rd) Misfortune, bad luck, adversity. Pl. ئ *a'ī*. بد بوي *bad bū'e*, adj. Fetid, foul, putrid. بد بوئي *bad bū'yī*, s.f. (3rd) Fetor, stench, stink, putrescence. Pl. ئ *a'ī*. بد حال *bad ḥāl*, adj. In bad circumstances, ill-conditioned. بد حالي *bad ḥālī*, s.f. (3rd) Badness of circumstances or condition. Pl. ئ *a'ī*. بدخصلت *bad k͟has̤lat*, adj. Bad in disposition, ill-disposed. بد خوي *bad k͟ho'e*, adj. Of bad habits, ill-disposed, evil-minded. بد خواه *bad k͟h'āh*, adj. Ill-wisher, malignant, malicious, malevolent, wishing evil. بد خوئي *bad k͟ho'ī*, s.f. (3rd) Unmannerliness, ill-nature, badness of disposition. Pl. ئ *a'ī*. بده دعا *bada'h du'ǣā*, s.f. (6th) A curse or imprecation. (E.) Sing.

and Pl.; (W.) Pl. دعاوي *du-'æāwī*. بده دعا پہ بده کول *bada'h du'æā kawul*, verb trans. or پہ بده دعا یادول *pah bada'h du'æā yādawul*, verb trans. To curse, to call down imprecations on. بد ذات *bad ẕāt*, adj. Low born, base, evil-minded, wicked, of bad breed, unprincipled, vicious, a villain. بد ذاتي *bad ẕātī*, s.f. (3rd) Baseness, wickedness, viciousness, villany. Pl. ۍ *a'ī*. بد رنګ *bad rang*, adj. Of a bad colour, of a bad kind. بد سلوک *bad salūk*, adj. Ill-mannered, of bad conduct or mode, ill-behaved. بد سلوکي *bad salūkī*, s.f. (3rd) Misbehaviour, maltreatment, abuse. Pl. ۍ *a'ī*. بد صورت *bad ṣūrat*, adj. Ugly, ill-conditioned. بد صورتي *bad-ṣūratī*, s.f. (3rd) Ugliness, uncomeliness. Pl. ۍ *a'ī*. بد فال *bad fāl*, adj. Ill-omened. بد فالي *bad fālī*, s.f. (3rd) Misfortune, an ill-omened business or affair. Pl. ۍ *a'ī*. بد فالي نیولی *bad fālī nī-walacy*, adj. (past part.) Ill-omened, unlucky; (Fem.) بد فالي نیولې *bad fālī nī-wali*. Pl. (Masc. and Fem.) ي *ī*. بد کار *bad kār*, adj. Sinful, wicked, an evil-doer. بد کاري *bad kārī*, s.f. (3rd) Wickedness, vice, iniquity. Pl. ۍ *a'ī*. بد ګمان *bad gumān*, adj. Suspicious, mistrustful, disaffected. بد ګماني *bad gumānī*, s.f. (3rd) Suspicion, distrust, disaffection. Pl. ۍ *a'ī*. بد ګوي *bad go'e*, adj. Evil speaking, slanderous, an evil speaker, slanderer, calumniator. بد ګوئي *bad go'ī*, s.f. (3rd) Slander, calumny, evil speaking,. Pl. ۍ *a'ī*. بد مذهب *bad maẕhab*, adj. Sectarian, dissenter. بد مزاج *bad mizāj*, adj. Ill-tempered, sour, churlish. بد مزاجي *bad mizājī*, s.f. (3rd) Sourness, churlishness, crossness. Pl. ۍ *a'ī*. بد مزه *bad mazah*, adj. Tasteless, vapid, insipid. بد مزګي *bad mazagī*, s.f. (3rd) Tastelessness, insipidity, vapidness. Pl. ۍ *a'ī*. بد معامله *bad mu'æāmalah*, adj. Unfair in dealing. بد نام *bad nām*, adj. Infamous, ignominious, of bad repute. بد نام کول *bad nām kawul*, verb trans. To asperse, calumniate, traduce, vilify, defame. بد نامي *bad nāmī*, s.f. (3rd) Infamy, scandal, disrepute, traducement, defamation, vilification. Pl. ۍ *a'ī*. بد نصیب *bad naṣīb*, adj. Unfortunate, unlucky, adverse. بد نماي *bad numā'e*, adj. Ill-looking, ungraceful, inelegant, unsightly, unbecoming. بد نمائي *bad numā'ī*, s.f. (3rd) Ungracefulness, inelegance, unsightliness. Pl. ۍ *a'ī*. بد نیتی *bad nī-yataey*, adj. Ill-disposed, malevolent, of bad intention, malicious. (Fem.) بد نیتې *bad nī-yati*. بد نیتي *bad nī-yatī*, s.f. (3rd) Ill-will, maliciousness, malevolence. Pl. ۍ *a'ī*. In forming the feminines of the preceding add ه to the masculine. بد نیول *bad nīwal*, verb trans. To take amiss, to consider as inopportune or unseasonable, unlucky, inauspicious, unpropitious, or unfortunate.

P بد تر *bad tar*, adj. (compar.) Worse, bad. (Fem.) بد تره *bad tara'h*. See بتر

بدخشان *badakhshān*, s. prop. The name of a country north of Hindū Kush, and north-west of Peshāwer, famous for its ruby mines.

A بدر *badr*, s.f. (9th) The full moon. Sing. and Pl.

بدر *badar*, s.m. (6th) The name of a tree, the white poplar. Sing. and Pl.

بدرکاړنۍ *badarkārrna'ī*, s.f. (6th) The name of a fruit which is very bitter. Sing. and Pl.

بدرګه *badraga'h*, s.f. (3rd) An escort, a convoy, a guide, a guard. Pl. ې *ey*. (A بدرقه).

A بدره *bad-ra'h*, s.f. (3rd) A bag of money, a weight equal to ten thousand dirhems. Pl. ې *ey*.

بدرۍ *badra'ī*, s.f. (6th) The name of a small river near Panjtār, in the Yūsufzī country. 2. The name of a female. Sing. and Pl.

بدري *budrī*, s.f. (3rd) A trip, a stumble, a fall. 2. (W.) Injury, damage, detriment, loss, injury; anguish, affliction. Pl. ۍ *a'ī*. بدري خوړل *budrī khwarral*, verb trans. To trip, to stumble. بدري مندل *bud-ra'ī mundal*, verb trans. To sustain loss, injury, detriment.

بدعا *baduæā*, s.f. (6th) An ill wish, imprecation, curse, malediction (corrup. of P بد and A دعا). (E.) Sing. and Pl.; (W.) Pl. بدعاوي *baduæāwī*; also بد دعا *bad-duæā*.

A بدعت *bid-æat*, s.m. (2nd) The introduction

of change or novelty in religion, innovation, heresy, schism; violence, oppression, wrong. Pl. بدعتونه *bid-æatūnah.* بدعتي *bid-æatī*, adj. Tyrant, oppressor, tyrannical, oppressive.

A بدل *badal*, s.m. (2nd) Exchange, substitution, retaliation. Pl. بدلونه *badalūnah.* 2. In exchange for, on account of. ادل بدل *adal-badal*, s.m. (2nd) Exchange, barter, chopping and changing, confusion. Pl. ادل بدلونه *adal badal-ūnah.* بدليدل *badaledal*, verb intrans. To be changed, to change, to alter, to vary, to invert, to reverse. Pres. بدليږي *badalejzī* (W.), or بدليگي *badalegī*; past بدل وُ شه *badal wu-shah*, or بدل شه *badal shah*; fut. بدل به شي *badal bah shī*, or بدل به وُ شي *badal bah wu-shī*; imp. بدل شه *badal shah*, or بدل وُ شه *badal wu shah*; act. part. بدليدونكي *badaledūnkaey*, or بدليدوني *badaledūnaey*; past part. بدل شوي *badal shawaey*; verb. n. بدليدنه *badaledana'h.* بدلول *badalawul*, verb trans. To change, to barter, to alter, to vary, to shift, to diversify. Pres. بدلوي *badalawī*; past بدل كه *badal kah*, or بدل وُ كه *badal wu-kah*; fut. بدل به كړي *badal bah krrī*, or بدل به وُ كړي *badal bah wu-krrī*; imp. بدل كړه *badal krrah*, or بدل وُ كړه *badal wu-krrah*; act. part. بدلوونكي *badalawūnkaey*, or بدلووني *badalawūnaey*; past part. بدل كړي *badal karraey*; verb. n. بدلونه *badalawuna'h.*

بدلمن *bad-laman*, adj. Incontinent, unchaste, wanton, licentious, rakish; (Fem.) بدلمنه *bad-lamana'h.*

بدله *badala'h*, s.f. (3rd) Tunes or words which they sing to musical notes, song, melody. Pl. ې *ey.* بدله ويل *badala'h wa-yal*, verb trans. To sing.

P بدي *badī*, s.f. (3rd) (from بد) Badness, wickedness, evil, ill, mischief, injury, misfortune. Pl. ئ *a'ī.* بدي كول *badī kawul*, verb trans. To sin, to transgress, to err, to do amiss. بديدار *badī-dār*, s.m. (5th) A person who has many enemies. Pl. بديداران *badī-dārān*; (Fem.) بديداره *badī-dāra'h.* Pl. ې *ey.* بديدل *badedal*, verb intrans. To become spoiled or waste, miserable, bad, ruined, injured, etc. Pres. بدېږي *badejzī* (W.) or بديگي *badegī* (E.); past بد شه *bad shah*; fut. بد به شي *bad bah shī*; imp. بد وُ شه *bad wu-shah*, or بد شه *bad shah*; act. part. بديدونكي *badedūnkaey*, or بديدوني *badedūnaey*; past part. بد شوي *bad shawaey*; verb. n. بديدنه *badedana'h.* بدول *badawul*, verb trans. To spoil, to injure, corrupt, vitiate, ruin, mar, desolate. Pres. بدوي *badawī*; past بد كړ *bad karr*, or بد وُ كړ *bad wu-karr*; fut. بد به كړي *bad bah krrī*, or بد به وُ كړي *bad bah wu-krrī*; imp. بد كړه *bad krrah*, or بد وُ كړه *bad wu-krrah*; act. part. بدوونكي *badawūnkaey*, or بدووني *badawūnaey*; past part. بد كړي *bad karraey*; verb. n. بدونه *badawana'h.*

A بديع *badīæ*, adj. Wonderful, surprising, marvellous, strange, astonishing.

بداي *baddā'e*, adj. Great, important, dignified, supreme; (Fem.) بدايه *baddāya'h.* بدائي *baddā-yī*, s.f. (3rd) Greatness, rank, dignity, importance. Pl. ئ *a'ī.* بدائي كول *baddā-yī kawul*, verb trans. To show dignity or greatness (s بدّا). بدگال *badda-gāl*, s.m. (6th) The feathery flower of the لوخه *lūkhah*—a reed or kind of gorse, which see. Sing. and Pl.

بده *badda'h*, s.f. (3rd) A bribe, a douceur. 2. The upper hem of the drawers through which the string passes to fasten them round the loins with. بده آخستل *badda'h ākhistal*, or بده خوړل *badda'h khwarral*, verb trans. To receive or take a bribe.

A بذر *bazr.* s.m. (6th) Seed. Sing. and Pl.

بذ گر *baz gar*, s.m. (5th) A husbandman. Pl. بذ گرٌ *baz-gær.*

بر *bar*, s.m. (9th) A stroke of the moon affecting a wound, a stroke of the moon—moon-blast. Sing. and Pl. بر وهلي *bar-wahalaey*, adj. Affected by a stroke of the moon.

برٌ *bær*, s.m. (6th) The leaf of a carrot, of the tamarisk tree, and such like plants, the leaves of which are small and wiry. Sing. and Pl.

بر *bar*, adj. Victorious, triumphant; (Fem.) بره

bara'h. 2. (P) On, above, upon, up. برپښتون *bar pus͟htūn* (W.) or *bar puk͟htūn* (E.) The name given to the Afghān tribes who inhabit the western portions of Afghānistān—Kābul, Ḳandahār, S͟horā'wak and Pis͟hīn; or Upper Afghāns, in distinction to the Eastern Afghāns, who are termed لرپښتون *lar-pus͟htūn* or *puk͟htūn*, or Lower Afghāns. See under لر. برطرف *bar ṭaraf*, The winning side, the successful side or party. بريَ *baraey*, s.m. (1st) Winning, victory, triumph, success, getting the upper hand. 2. The leaf of the Chīnār or plane-tree. Pl. ي *ī*. بركيدل *bar kedal*, verb intrans. To be mastered, overcome, or conquered. بر كول *bar kawul*, verb trans. To succeed, to accomplish, to triumph, to gain the ascendency, to bring about.

برسير *bar-ser*, adj. Apparent, clear, visible, obvious, palpable, manifest, distinct; (Fem.) برسيره *bar-sera'h*. برسير كيدل *bar-ser kedal*, verb intrans. To become apparent, clear, etc. برسير كول *bar-ser kawul*, verb trans. To make manifest, clear, obvious, to show, to demonstrate.

A بر *barr*, adj. Just, holy, pious, dutiful. See ابرار. 2. Dry land, a desert. بر و بحر *barr-o-bahr*, Land and sea.

P برابر *barābar*, adj. Abreast, even, level, uniform, alike, up to, opposite, equal, on a par, adequate, exact, accurate; (Fem.) برابره *barābara'h*. برابريدل *barābaredal*, verb intrans. To suit, to agree, to equal. برابرول *barābarawul*, verb trans. To adjust, to accord, to assimilate, to match.

P برابري *barābarī*, s.f. (3rd) Equality, exactness, rivalry, competition, emulation. Pl. ئ *a'ī*. برابري كول *barābarī kawul*, verb trans. To oppose, to resist, to withstand, to vie, to equal, to emulate, to rival.

P برات *barāt*, s.m. (2nd) The fourteenth day of the month—S͟hasæ-bān, which is appropriated to the commemoration of deceased ancestors. 2. A commission, an assignment, a warrant. Pl. براتونه *barātūnah*. شب برات *s͟hab-i-barāt*, The night of the day in question. برات آخستل *bar-āt āk͟histal*, verb trans. To receive a warrant or assignment. برات ور كول *bar-āt war kawul*, verb trans. To give an assignment or warrant for money, etc.

برايه *barāyah*, adv. Last or yesternight. برائي شپه *barāyī s͟hpah*, Last or yesternight. See بيكانئ شپه or برنئ شپه

A براق *burāḳ*, s. prop. The ass on which Muḥammad is said to have passed from Jerusalem to heaven. 2. A horse, a steed. Pl. براقونه *burāḳūnah*.

برالبه *brālba'h*, adj. (W.) Pregnant as a woman or animal. برالبه واليَ *brālba'h wālaey*, s.m. (1st) Pregnancy, impregnation. Pl. والي *wālī*. برالبيدل *brālbedal*, verb intrans. To become pregnant. برالبول *brālbawul*, verb trans, To make pregnant, to get with young. See بلاربه.

P برباد *bar-bād*, adj. Given to the winds, misapplied, lost, thrown away, gone to the dogs, destroyed, laid waste, ruined; (Fem.) بربادہ *bar-bāda'h*. برباد كيدل *bar-bād kedal*, verb intrans. To be thrown away, misapplied, lost, etc. برباد كول *bar-bād kawul*, verb trans. To throw away, misapply, lose, waste, destroy.

P بربادي *bar-bādī*, s.f. (3rd) Ruin, waste, destruction, misapplication. Pl. ئ *a'ī*.

بر بست *bar-bast*, s.m. (2nd) Goods, chattels, property, effects. Pl. بربستونه *bar-bastūnah*.

بربري *bar-barī*, s.m. (6th) The leaf of the tamarisk tree, and the like. Sing. and Pl.

P بربط *barbaṭ*, s.m. (2nd) A kind of harp or lute. Pl. بربطونه *bar-baṭūnah*. See غږوونكيَ *g͟hajzawūnkaey*, s.m. (1st) A harper. Pl. ي *ī*.

بربكئ *barbuka'ī*, s.f. (6th) A whirlwind, a devil. See also بربوكئ and بوربوكئ

برېنډ *barbanḍḍ*, adj. Naked, bare, denuded, undressed, stripped, unclothed; (Fem.) برېنډه *barbanḍḍa'h*. See also برمند

برېنډ توب *barbanḍḍ-tob*, s.m. (2nd) or برېنډ تيا *barbanḍḍ-tī'ā*, s.f. (6th), برېنډ واليَ *barbanḍḍ-wālaey*, s.m. (1st) Nakedness, bareness, nudity, undress. Pl. توبونه *tob-ūnah*, تياوي *tī'āwī*, and والي *wālī*. برېنډيدل *barbanḍḍedal*, verb intrans. To become naked, bare, or in a state of nakedness, nude, exposed. Pres. بربنډيږي *barbanddejzī*(W.)or بربنډيګي *barbanddegī*(E.); past بربنډ شه *barbandd shah*; fut. بربنډ به وُ شي *barbandd bah wu-shī*, or بربنډ به شي *barbandd bah shī*; imp. بربنډ وُ شه *barbandd wu-shah*, or بربنډ شه *barbandd shah*; act. part. بربنډيدونکَي *barbanddedūnkaey*, or بربنډيدونيَ *barbanddedūnaey*; past part. بربنډ شويَ *barbandd shawaey*; verb. n. بربنډيدنه *bar-bandde-dana'h*, or بربنډيده *bar-banddedah*. بربنډول *barbanddawul*, verb trans. To divest, uncover, denude, strip, unclothe, undress, unrobe, disrobe, doff. Pres. بربنډوي *barbanddawī*; past بربنډ وُ کړ *barbandd wu-karr*, or بربنډ کړ *barbandd karr*, and بربنډ وُ که *barbandd wu-kah*, or بربنډ که *barbandd kah*; fut. بربنډ به وُ کړي *barbandd bah wu-krrī*, or بربنډ به کړي *barbandd bah krrī*; imp. بربنډ وُ کړه *barbandd wu-krrah*, or بربنډ کړه *barbandd krrah*; act. part. بربنډوونکَي *barbanddawūnkaey*, or بربنډوونيَ *barbanddawūnaey*; past part. بربنډ کړيَ *barbandd karraey*; verb. n. بربنډونه *barbanddawana'h*.

P S بريا *barpā*, adj. Raised, set on foot, established, pitched, produced, commenced; also برپاي *barpā'e*; (Fem.) برپايه *bar-pāya'h*. برپا کيدل *barpā kedal*, verb intrans. To be raised, etc. برپا کول *barpā kawul*, verb trans. To raise, set on foot.

برته *birtah*, adv. After, behind, in the wake of, in the rear of; away, apart, aside, separate. برته کيدل *birtah kedal*, verb intrans. To become separated, parted, detached, disunited. برته کول *birtah kawul*, verb trans. To separate, disjoin, part, disunite, detach, disengage. See also بيرته and بيارته

برڅير *bartser*, adj. Clear, manifest, apparent, distinct, visible, obvious; (Fem.) برڅيره *bartser-a'h*. See برسير. برڅير کيدل *bar-tser kedal*, verb intrans. To become clear, visible, obvious; to appear, present itself, to meet, strike, or catch the eye. برڅير کول *bartser kan.'.* verb trans. To manifest, to show, to indic .e, to

disclose, to set forth, to present. See برسير کيدل and برسير کول

برج *barj*, s.m. (2nd) The bark of a tree, which is very slight and often used as paper. Pl. برجونه *barjūnah*. See بست, پست, and پستکي

A برج *burj*, s.m. (2nd) A tower, a turret, bastion. Pl. برجونه *burj-ūnah*.

برجو *barjū*, s.f. (5th) A whetstone, a hone. Pl. برجوګانِ *barjūgāni*, or برجي *bar-jī*, s.f. (3rd) Pl. ئي *a'ī*.

برخو *barkho*, s.f. (9th) The cheek, the side of the face. Sing, and Pl.; or (W.) s.m. (5th) Pl. برخوګان *barkho-gān*.

برخه *brakha'h*, s.f. (3rd) A share, portion, part. Pl. برخي *brakhey*. See بخره

P برداشت *bardāsht*, s.m. (2nd) Endurance, patience. Pl. برداشتونه *bar-dāshtūnah*. برداشت کول *bardāsht kawul*, verb trans. To endure, to have patience.

P برده *barda'h*, s.f. (3rd) A female slave, a captive, a servant. Pl. ئي *ey*. See وينځه

برسير *barser*, adj. Clear, manifest, apparent, distinct, visible, obvious; (Fem.) برسيره *bar-sera'h*. برسير کيدل *barser kedal*, verb intrans. To become apparent. برسير کول *barser kawul*, verb trans. To make apparent. See برڅير

برسيرن *bar-seran*, adj. Slight (as a flesh wound), trivial, trifling, puerile, light, frivolous, finical; (Fem.) برسيرنه *bar-serana'h*.

P A برطرف *bar-ṭaraf*, adj. Aside, apart, dismissed; (Fem.) برطرفه *bar-ṭarafa'h*. برطرف کيدل *bar-ṭaraf kedal*, verb intrans. To be dismissed, discharged, turned off, cast aside. برطرف کول *bar-ṭaraf kawul*, verb trans. To dismiss, discharge, turn off, cashier.

P برطرفي *barṭarafī*, s.f. (3rd) Dismission, discharge. Pl. ئي *a'ī*.

بر طرف *bar ṭaraf*, s.m. (2nd) The winning side, the upper side. Pl. بر طرفونه *bar-ṭarafūnah*. See بر and لر and لرطرف

برغ *bragh*, s.m. (2nd) Fold, plait, ply, stratum, layer. Pl. برغونه *braghūnah*. برغ په برغ

bragh pah bragh, Fold on fold, plait on plait, layer on layer; also used expressive of multiplication, as دوه برغ *dwah bragh*, Double, دري برغ *drey bragh*, Treble.

برغټ *bar-ghutt*, s.m. (5th) A tom-cat. Pl. برغټان *barghuttān*; برغټه *barghutta'h*, s.f. (3rd) A female cat. Pl. ې *ey*. See پرانګ پيش and برغوټ

برغو *bargho*, s.m. (5th) A rod for boring the barrel of a gun, a cleaning rod. Pl. برغوګان *bargho-gān*.

برغوټ *barghūt*, s.m. (5th) A male cat. Pl. برغوټان *barghūttān*. See also برغټ, etc.

برغوټي *barghottaey*, s.m. (1st) An earring. Pl. ي *ī*, or برغوږي *barghwajzaey*, s.m. (1st) (W.) or برغوګي *barghwagaey*, (E.) Pl. ي *ī*.

برغولي *bar-gholaey*, s.m. (1st) The lid of a pot, a cover. Pl. ي *ī*.

برغوني *braghūnaey*, s.m. (1st) A male twin. Pl. ي *ī*; s.f. (6th) برغوني *braghūna'ī*, A female twin. Sing. and Pl.

برغيدل *braghedal*, verb intrans. To become folded, plaited, stratified, doubled. برغول *braghawul*, verb trans. To fold, to plait, to double, to make or render stratified.

A برق *bark*, s.m. (2nd) Lightning, electric fire. Pl. برقونه *barkūnah*.

برقه *burka'h*, s.f. (3rd) A dress or kind of veil with eye-holes, worn by women, and covering the whole body from head to foot (A برقع). Pl. ې *ey*. See also بولقه

برکه *baraka'h*, s.f. (3rd) A warm kind of cloth made from camel's hair, and the peculiar wool called *pashmīnah*. Pl. ې *ey*.

A برکت *barakat*, s.m. (2nd) Blessing, abundance, prosperity, auspiciousness. Pl. برکتونه *barakatūnah*. برکت ور کول *barakat war-kawul*, or برکت کول *barakat kawul*, verb trans. To bless, to prosper.

برکښ *bar kakh*, s.m. (5th) A puller of the strong bow, drawing to the head. Pl. برکښان *barkakhān*.

برګ *brag*, adj. Spotted, pie-bald, grizzled (as the hair). 2. A leper; (Fem.) برګه *braga'h*. See برګي, چرګ برګ, and کړ

P برګ *barg*, s.m. (2nd) A leaf. 2. Warlike apparatus, provision or necessaries for a journey. 3. Melody. Pl. برګونه *bargūnah*. برګ رژيدل *barg rajzedal*, verb trans. To fall, as the leaves from a tree. برګ رژول *barg rajzawul*, verb trans. To scatter, to cause to fall, to disperse (as the wind in autumn). برګ غوړيدل *barg ghwarredal*, verb intrans. To bud, to unclose, to blow, to bloom. برګ غوړول *barg ghwarrawul*, verb trans. To cause or make to bud or bloom.

P برګزيده *barguzīdah*, adj. Chosen, selected, elect.

برګړندي *bar-grrandī*, s.m. (1st) Pl. Embracing, hugging. برګړندي کول *bar-grrandī kawul*, verb trans. To embrace, to hug, to cuddle. See روغ بر and بره ګره

P برګستوان *bar-gastawān*, s.m. (2nd) Trapping, armour, etc. for a horse. Pl. برګستوانونه *bar-gastawān-ūnah*.

برګستون *bargastawan*, s.m. (2nd) The girth or surcingle of a horse, together with his armour. Pl. برګستونونه *bargastawanūnah*. Also written برګستان (P).

برګويټ *bar-gwett*, s. prop. The name of one of the great ancestors of the Khattak tribe of Afghāns.

برګه *barga'h*, s.f. (3rd) A rafter. Pl. ې *ey*.

برګي *bragey*, s.m. (1st) The leprosy. Pl. ي *ī*. See برګ

برګيدل *bragedal*, verb intrans. To become grizzled (as the hair), to become spotted (particularly from leprosy). برګول *bragawul*, verb trans. To render grey or grizzled (as the hair), to spot (as leprosy).

برم *bram*, s.m. (2nd) Power, strength, vigour, force. Pl. برمونه *bramūnah*. له برمَ پريوتل *lah brama prewatal*, verb intrans. To become or grow powerless, weak, enfeebled, enervated, debilitated.

برمته *bramta'h*, s.f. (3rd) Seizing the persons of one village for the debts of the people of another, as a pledge, or as hostages for the payment. Pl. ي *ey*. See بوته

HI برملا *barmalā*, adj. Public, manifest, obvious, plain, palpable. برملا كيدل *barmalā kedal*, verb intrans. To appear, to present itself, to be public, to manifest itself, to arise, etc. برملا كول *barmalā kawul*, verb trans. To reveal, evince, disclose, discover, manifest. برملا ويل *bar-malā wa-yal*, verb trans. To speak plainly, or publicly.

برمند *barmandd*, adj. Naked, denuded, bare, undressed, stripped, unclothed; (Fem.) برمنده *barmandda'h*. برمنديدل *barmandddedal*, verb intrans. To become naked, bare, nude, exposed. Pres. برمنديږي *barmandddejzī* (W.) or برمنديگي *barmandddegī* (E.); past برمند وُ شه *barmandd wu-shah*, or برمند شه *barmandd shah*; fut. برمند به وُ شي *barmandd bah wu-shī*, or برمند به شي *barmandd bah shī*; imp. برمند وُ شه *barmandd wu-shah*, or برمند شه *barmandd shah*; act. part. برمنديدونكي *barmandddedūnkaey*, or برمنديدوني *barmandddedūnaey*; past part. برمند شوي *barmandd shawaey*; verb. n. برمنديدنه *barmandddedana'h*. See بربند

برمند والي *barmandd wālaey*, s.m. (1st) Nakedness, bareness, nudity, undress; also برمند توب *barmandd tob*, s.m. (2nd); برمند تيا *barmandd tī'ā*, s.f. (6th). Pl. والي *wālī*, توبونه *tobūnah*, and تياوي *tī'āwī*. See بربند, etc.

برمندول *barmanddawul*, verb trans. To divest, uncover, denude, strip, unclothe, undress, unrobe, disrobe, doff. Pres. برمندوي *barmanddawī*; past برمند وُ كړ *barmandd wu-karr*, or برمند كړ *barmandd karr*; fut. برمند به وُ كړي *barmandd bah wu-krrī*, or برمند به كړي *barmandd bah krrī*; imp. برمند وُ كړه *barmandd wu-krrah*, or برمند كړه *barmandd krrah*; act. part. برمندوونكي *barmanddawūnkaey*, or برمندووني *barmanddawūnaey*; past part. برمند كړي *barmandd karraey*; verb. n. برمندونه *barmanddawuna'h*. See بربند etc.

برمه *barmah*, s.f. (3rd) A kind of gimlet or borer worked with a string, an auger or centre-bit. Pl. ي *ey*. (HI برما)

برند *brand*, adj. White-eyed, staring, shameless, amorous. 2. Attentive, intent on; looking towards, regarding stedfastly; (Fem.) برنده *branda'h*. برندي سترگي *brandey stargey*, s.f. (3rd) Pl. Staring or wide-open eyes, gloating eyes.

برندو *brandū*, s. prop. The name of a river in Buner.

برندول *brandawul*, verb trans. To frown, to scowl, to look at angrily. Pres. برندوي *brandawī*; past وُ برنداوه *wu-brandāwuh*, or وُ برنداوو *wu-brandāwo*; fut. وُ به برندوي *wu bah brandawī*; imp. وُ برندوه *wu-brandawah*; act. part. برندوونكي *brandawūnkaey*, or برندووني *brandawūnaey*; past part. برندولي *brandawulaey*; verb. n. برندونه *brandawuna'h*.

برني *baranaey*, adj, Stale, not fresh. 2. adv. Yester-night, last night. برني شپه *barana'ī shpah*, Last night. See also برائي and بيگاني شپه

برووړه *barorra'h*, s.f. (3rd) The name of an insect found in timber something similar to the bug—a sort of wood-louse—whose bite causes irritation for about a month, and from which a yellow matter is discharged. Pl. ي *ey*.

برووړه *brorra'h*, s.f. (3rd) A kind of bread made from various sorts of grain. Pl ي *ey*. See راړه

برونړئ *barwarrna'ī*, s.f. (6th) Part of a Persian wheel: the socket in which the upright beam or axle turns. Sing. and Pl.

بروي *bar-waey*, adj. Adhesive, cohering, sticky, united, inseparable, or indivisible (particularly an importunate person), sticking like a leech, or like wax. 2. Importunate, plaguy, haunting, etc.; (Fem.) برو *bar-wi*. Pl. (Masc. and Fem.) ي *ī*. بروي كول *bar-waey kawul*, verb trans. To stick to, to cleave or adhere to; to importunate, to haunt, to bother. بروي كيدل *bar-waey kedal*, verb intrans. To cleave, to adhere, to hold to, to stick, to cling, etc.

A برهان *burhān*, s.m. (2nd) Demonstration, proof. Pl. برهانونه *burhānūnah*.

بره خان خيل *barah khān khel*, s.m. (6th) The name of an Afghān tribe. 2. A male of the tribe. Sing. and Pl. (Fem.) (3rd) خيله *khela'h.* Pl. ي *ey.*

بره خوا *bara'h khwā*, adj. The upper side. See بر.

بره گره *bara'h garra'h*, s.f. (3rd) Embrace, interview, meeting, shaking hands. بره گره کول *bara'h garra'h kawul*, verb trans. To embrace, to hug. Pl. ي *ey.* See برگرندي and روغ بر

P برهم *barham*, adj. Confused, entangled, spoiled. 2. Angry, vexed, sullen; (Fem.) برهمه *barhama'h.*

برهميدل *barhamedal*, verb intrans. To be entangled, confused, spoiled, etc. برهمول *barhamawul*, verb trans. To confuse, to entangle, to spoil.

S برهمن *brahman*, s.m. (5th) A Brahman. Pl. برهمنان *brahmanān.* See بامبڼ and بامڼ

بري *baraey*, s.m. (1st) Victory, success, triumph. 2. The leaf of the plane-tree. Pl. ي *ī.* بري مندل *baraey mundal*, verb trans. To gain a victory, to triumph. بري کول *baraey kawul*, verb trans. To conquer, to overcome. بري کيدل *baraey kedal*, verb intrans. To be conquered, overcome.

بريت *bret*, s.m. (2nd) A mustache. Pl. بريتونه *bret-ūnah.* بريت آړول *bret ārrawul*, or تاوول *tā-wawul*, verb trans. To twist the moustaches, as a person when excited or enraged.

بريد *b'rīd*, s.m. (2nd) Attack, onset, charge, assault, storm. Pl. بريدونه *b'rīdūnah.* بريد کول *b'rīd kawul*, verb trans. To attack, to assault, to charge.

بريد *burīd*, s.m. (9th) (P بريدن) Separation, absence. Sing. and Pl.

بريږن *bre-jzan*, s.m. (2nd) The bleat of a goat or sheep. Pl. بريږنونه *bre-jzanūnah.* بريږن کول *bre-jzan kawul*, verb trans. To bleat.

بريښ *brekh* (E.) or *bresh* (W.), s.m. (2nd) A twitch of pain, a twinge, a cramp, a spasm, a shoot. Pl. بريښونه *brekh-ūnah*, or *bresh-ūnah.* بريښ کول *brekh*, or *bresh kawul*, verb trans. To affect with a sharp sudden pain, to twinge, to shoot.

بريښنا *breshnā*, (W.) or *brekhnā* (E.) s.f. (6th) Lustre, brightness, brilliancy, sheen, glow. (E.) Sing. and Pl.; (W.) Pl. بريښناوي *breshnāwī.* بريښيدل *breshedal* (W.) or *brekhedal* (E.) verb intrans. To shine, glitter, gleam, glisten, brighten, twinkle. Pres. بريښي *breshī* or *brekhī*; past وُ بريښيده *wu-breshedah* or *wu-brekhedah*; fut. وُ به بريښي *wu bah breshī* or *brekhī*; imp. وُ بريښه *wu-breshah* or *wu-brekhah*; act. part. بريښيدونکي *breshedūnkaey* or *brekhedūnkaey*, or بريښيدوني *breshedūnaey* or *brekhedūnaey*; past part. بريښيدلي *breshedalaey* or *brekhedalaey*; verb. n. بريښيدنه *breshedana'h* or *brekhedana'h.*

بريښول *breshawul* or *brekhawul*, verb trans. To illuminate, to irradiate, cast lustre upon, to cause to glitter. Pres. بريښوي *breshawī* or *brekhawī*; past وُ بريښاوه *wu-breshāwuh* or *brekhāwuh*, or وُ بريښاوو *wu-breshāwo* or *brekhāwo*; fut. وُ به بريښوي *wu bah breshawī* or *brekhawī*; imp. وُ بريښوه *wu-breshawah* or *brekhawah*; act. part. بريښوونکي *breshawūnkaey* or *brekhawūnkaey*; or بريښووني *breshawūnaey* or *brekhawūnaey*; past part. بريښولي *breshawulaey* or *brekhawulaey*; verb. n. بريښونه *breshawuna'h* or *brekhawuna'h.*

بړاس *b'rrās*, s.m. (2nd) Vapour, heat, exhalation, steam. Pl. بړاسونه *b'rrāsūnah.* See بهراس

بړانډه *barrāndda'h*, s.f. (3rd) A blaze of fire with much smoke, a flame. Pl. ي *ey.* See لمبه and داندي.

بړبړ *barr-barr*, adv. Often, frequently, repeatedly, again and again. (S بيربير). بړبړ راشه *barr-barr rāshah*, Come constantly, come often—a compliment to a guest.

بړبوکۍ *barrbūka'ī*, or *burrbūka'ī*, s.f. (6th) A whirlwind, a devil. Sing. and Pl. See also بړبکۍ and بوربوکۍ

بړستن *brrastan*, s.f. (1st) A coverlet, a quilt or counterpane. Pl. بړستنۍ *brrastani.*

بړگړندي *barrgarrandī*, s.m. (1st) Pl. Embrace, salutation, greeting. See برگرندي and روغ بر. بړگړندي کول *barrgarrandī kawul*, verb trans. To embrace, hug, cuddle, salute, greet.

بړنگي *barrangaey*, s.m. (1st) The leathern strap

used for fastening the churning-staff. Pl. ي *ī*. See مندانړو and روګ

برنۍ *barrnaey*, s.m. (1st) The name of a tree. Pl. ي *ī*.

بروا *barrwā*, s.m. (5th) A pimp, a cuckold, a wittol. Pl. برواګان *barrwagān*. (HI بهڑوا).

بروس *b'rros* or *b'rrūs*, adj. Angry, wrath, irritated, nettled, exasperated, wild, furious, savage; (Fem.) بروسه *b'rrosa'h* or *b'rrūsa'h*. بروس والۍ *b'rros-wālaey*, s.m. (1st) Anger, wrath, rage, indignation, fury, resentment. Pl. والي *wālī*. بروسيدل *b'rrosedal* or *b'rrūsedal*, verb intrans. To become or grow angry, enraged, wrathful. بروسول *b'rrosawul* or *b'rrūsawul*, verb trans. To make angry, to chafe, to put out of humour.

برۍ *berraey*, s.m. (1st) A long-tailed sheep. Pl. ي *ī*; s.f. (6th) ۍ *a'ī*. Sing. and Pl. See also بيروي, ايروي, بري, ييري, هيري and هيروي

برېڅي *barretsī*, s.m. (1st) Pl. The name of a tribe of Afghāns. برېڅي *barretsaey*, Sing. A male of the above. برېڅه *barretsa'h*, s.f. (3rd). Pl. ۍ *ey*.

برين چغ *barren chagh*, s.m. (2nd) A kind of whirligig. Pl. برين چغونه *barren-chaghūnah*.

بز *baz*, s.m. (7th) A he-goat. Pl. بزونه *b'zūnah*. See also وز and وزګري

P بزرګ *buzarg*, s.m. (5th) A saint, a religious instructor, an elder, an ancestor. 2. Great, reverend, venerable. Pl. بزرګان *buzargān*. بزرګه *buzarga'h*, s.f. (3rd). Pl. ۍ *ey*. See also زبرګ

P بزرګوار *buzarg-wār*, adj. Great, reverend. 2. An ancestor, an elder, a saint; (Fem.) بزرګواره *buzarg-wāra'h*.

P بزرګي *buzargī*, s.f. (3rd) Grandeur, greatness, eminence, exaltation. Pl. ۍ *a'ī*.

بزغلۍ *buzghalaey*, s.m. (1st) A young shoot, as from an onion, etc., a young plant. Pl. ي *ī*.

بزګر *baz-gar*, s.m. (5th) A husbandman, an agriculturist (A بذر seed). Pl. بزګران *baz-garān*. See دهقان

بزګري *baz-garī*, s.f. (3rd) Husbandry, agriculture. Pl. ۍ *a'ī*.

P بزم *bazm*, s.m. (2nd) An assembly, company, a banquet. Pl. بزمونه *bazmūnah*.

بزو *bizo*, s.m. and s.f. (5th) A monkey. Pl. بزوګان *bizogān*; (Fem.) Pl. بزوګاني *bizogāney*.

بزه *b'za'h*, s.f. (3rd) The name of a bird, the ibis, or royal cerclew. (P بوزه). 2. A she-goat. Pl. بزۍ *b'zey*.

بزه *b'zah*, adj. Torn, severed, separated, cut up, jointed, etc. بزه کول *b'zah kawul*, verb trans. To tear, to sever, to cut up. See بژه

P بزه *baza'h*, s.f. (3rd) A sin, a crime. Pl. ۍ *ey*.

بزه ګار *baza'h-gār*, s.m. (5th) A sinner, a criminal. Pl. بزه ګاران *baza'h-gārān*. بزه ګاره *baza'h-gāra'h*, s.f. (3rd). Pl. ۍ *ey*. بزه کول *baza'h kawul*, verb trans. To sin, to commit a crime or fault.

بژه *b'jza'h*, s.f. (3rd) Slaughter, immolation, sacrifice. Pl. ۍ *ey*. See بزه

P بس *bas*, adj. Enough, sufficient, plenty, abundance, too much, very much. بس کول *bas kawul*, verb trans. To overpower, to bring to submission, to silence.

بس که *bas kah* (imp.) Enough! sufficient! silence! leave off! Also بس کړه *bas krrah*.

A بساط *bisāṭ*, s.m. (2nd) What is spread out; carpeting, bedding, a chess-board, a dice-board, expanse, surface. Pl. بساطونه *bisāṭūnah*.

بسباسه *bisbāsa'h*, s.f. (3rd) The name of a medicinal plant. Pl. ۍ *ey*.

A بسمل *bismil*, adj. Sacrificed; an animal sacrificed; (Fem.) بسمله *bismila'h*. بسمل کول *bismil kawul*, verb trans. To sacrifice. بسمل کيدل *bismil kedal*, verb intrans. To be made a sacrifice of, to become sacrificed.

A بسم الله *bismi-l-lāh*, In the name of God. بسم الله کول *bismi-l-lāh kawul*, verb trans. To begin, to commence.

بسيا *basi-yā*, adj. Cultivated, peopled. بسيا کيدل *basi-yā kedal*, verb intrans. To become peopled, cultivated, inhabited. بسيا کول *basi-yā kawul*, verb trans. To cultivate, to make or render cultivated, to people.

بشپړ *bashparr*, adj. Entire, perfect, complete, whole, thorough; (Fem.) بشپړه *bashparra'h*.

بشپړه بلا *bashparra'h balā,* A great or complete misfortune or calamity. See پوره

A بشر *bashar,* s.m. (2nd) Man, mankind, human being, mortals. Pl. بشرونه *basharūnah.*

A بشري *bashar-ī,* adj. Human, relating to man.

بشکه *bashka'h,* s.f. (3rd) A kind of potherb or greens growing wild. Pl. ې *ey.*

بشنج *bashanj,* s.m. (2nd) Character, reputation, renown, good name. Pl. بشنجونه *bashanjūnah.*

ښتنه *bukhtana'h,* s.f. (3rd) (verb. n. of ښتيدل) A quagmire, a bog, a marsh. 2. Sticking, adhering (as mud). Pl. ې *ey.* See بوښتنه. ښتيدل *bukhtedal* (E.) or *bushtedal* (W.) verb intrans. To stick, adhere (as mud), cohere, hold, cleave to. Pres. ښتيږي *bushtejzī* (W.) or ښتيګي *bukhtegī* (E.); past ښت وُ شه *bukht* or *busht wu-shah,* or ښت شه *bukht* or *busht shah;* fut. ښت به وُ شي *bukht* or *busht bah wu-shī,* or ښت به شي *bukht* or *busht bah shī;* imp. ښت وُ شه *bukht* or *busht wu-shah,* or ښت شه *bukht* or *busht shah;* act. part. ښتيدونکی *bukhtedūnkaey* or *bushtedūnkaey,* or ښتيدونی *bukhtedūnaey* or *bushtedūnaey;* past part. ښت *bukht* or *busht,* or ښت شوی *bukht* or *busht shawaey;* verb. n. ښتنه *bukhtana'h* or *bushtana'h,* or ښتيدنه *bukhtedana'h* or *bushtedana'h.* ښتول *bukhtawul* or *bushtawul,* verb trans. To cause to stick, to embed, to stick in. Pres. ښتوي *bukhtawī* or *bushtawī;* past ښت وُ کړ *bukht* or *busht wu-karr,* or ښت کړ *bukht* or *busht karr;* fut. ښت به کړي *bukht* or *busht bah krrī;* imp. ښت وُ کړه *bukht* or *busht wu-krrah,* or ښت کړه *bukht* or *busht krrah;* act. part. ښتوونکی *bukhtawūnkaey* or *bushtawūnkaey,* or ښتوونی *bukhtawūnaey* or *bushtawūnaey;* past part. ښت کړی *bukht* or *busht karraey;* verb. n. ښتونه *bukhtawuna'h* or *bushtawuna'h.* See بوښتول

ښکال *bashakāl,* s.m. (2nd) The rainy season, a rainy year (s پشکال). Pl. ښکالونه *bashakālūnah.* See پرشکال

ښل *bakhal,* verb trans. (E.) To give, present, bestow, accord, confer, concede, consign. Pres. ښي *bakhī;* past وُ باښه *wu-bākhah;* fut. وُ به ښي *wu bah bakhī;* imp. وُ ښه *wu-bakhah* or ښه *bakhah;* act. part. ښونکی *bakhūnkaey* or ښونی *bakhūnaey;* past part. ښلی *bakhalaey;* verb. n. ښنه *bakhana'h.* See (W.) بخښل

ښنه *bakhana'h,* s.f. (3rd) (E.) verb. n. A gift, donation, grant, boon, reward; giving, bestowing, beneficence, pardon, forgiveness, liberality, generosity. Pl. ې *ey.*

A بصير *baṣīr,* act. part. (from بصر) Seeing, beholding, observing, penetration.

بصير من *baṣīr-man,* adj. A beholder, an observer; (Fem.) بصير منه *baṣīr-mana'h.*

A بط *baṭ,* s.f. (1st) A duck. Pl. بطِ *baṭi.* See هيلۍ

A بطلان *buṭlān,* s.m. (9th) Falseness, vanity, abortion, the becoming of no effect. Sing. and Pl.

A بعث *baæṣ,* s.m. (9th) Excitement, motive, cause. 2. Resurrection. Sing. and Pl. بعث و نشر *baæṣ-o-nashr,* s.m. (9th) The resurrection. Sing. and Pl.

A بعد *ba'æd,* adv. After, afterwards, subsequent. See پس

A بعض *ba'æẓ,* بعضا *ba'æẓā,* or بعضي *ba'æẓe,* adj. Some, certain ones, a few, several. See ځني, ځنِ and دنِ

A بعيد *ba'æīd,* adj. (from بعد) Far, distant, absent, remote; strange, improbable; (Fem.) بعيده *ba'æīda'h.*

بغارګ *b'ghārg,* adj. Double, two-fold, duplex; (Fem.) بغارګه *b'ghārga'h.* See برګ and بغرګ

بغاره *baghāra'h,* s.f. (3rd) A scream, a screech, shriek, squall. Pl. ې *ey.* بغارې وهل *baghārey wahal,* verb trans. To squall, to scream, to shriek.

بغبغو *bagh-bagho,* s.m. (5th) A bird of the sandpiper breed frequenting the banks of rivers. Pl. بغبغوګان *bagh-baghogān.*

بغدر *baghdar,* s.m. (5th) A mallet, a hammer. Pl. بغدر *baghdær.* See دبلۍ.

بغرږ *bagharjz,* s.m. Return, retrogression, reflexion. 2. Returning, coming back, retrograding. بغرږيدل *bagharjz-edal,* verb intrans. To return, rebound, reflex, regrade. Pres. بغرږيږي *bagharjzejzī;* past بغرږ شه *bagharjz shah* ; fut. بغرږ به شي *bagharjz bah shī* ; imp. بغرږ وُ شه *bagharjz wu-shah*, or بغرږ شه *bagharjz shah* ; act. part. بغرږيدونکي *bagharjzedūnkaey*, or بغرږيدوني *bagharjzedūnaey* ; past part. بغرږ *bagharjz*, or بغرږ شوي *bagharjz shawaey* ; verb. n. بغرږيدنه *bagharjzedana'h*.

بغرږول *bagharjzawul*, verb trans. To return, to restore, render ; to cause to return, rebound, regrade. Pres. بغرږوي *bagharjzawī* ; past بغرږ وُ که *bagharjz wu-kah* or وُ کړ *wu-karr*, or بغرږ که *bagharjz kah* or کړ *karr* ; fut. بغرږ به کړي *bagharjz bah krrī*, or بغرږ به وُ کړي *bagharjz bah wu-krrī*, بغرږ به وُ که *bagharjz bah wu-kah*, or بغرږ به که *bagharjz bah kah* ; imp. بغرږ وُ که *bagharjz wu-kah* or وُ کړه *wu-krrah*, or بغرږ که *bagharjz kah* or کړه *krrah* ; act. part. بغرږوونکي *bagharjzawūnkaey* or بغرږووني *bagharjzawūnaey* ; past part. بغرږ کړي *bagharjz karraey* ; verb. n. بغرږونه *bagharjzawuna'h*.

بغرګ *bagharg*, s.m. Return, retrogression, reflexion. 2. Returning, coming back, retrograding. 3. adj. Double, two-fold. بغرګيدل *baghargedal*, verb intrans. To return, to come back ; and بغرګول *baghargawul*, verb trans. To return, to make or cause to return. See preceding infinitive, and substitute ګ for ږ

بغرګه *bgharga'h*, s.f. (3rd) (fem. of بغرګ) A valley between two mountains. 2. A woman who has brought forth twins. Pl. ې *ey*.

بغري *bagharaey*, s.m. (1st) A pimp, cuckold, a term of abuse. Pl. ي *ī* ; s.f. (6th) بغرۍ *baghara'ī*, A mortar, vulva, a term of abuse. Sing. and Pl. See مولي and چندرۍ

A بغض *bughz*, s.m. (9th) Malice, spite, resentment, revenge, hatred, hate. Sing. and Pl.

P بغل *baghal*, s.m. (2nd) The armpit, the embrace. Pl. بغلونه *baghalūnah*. بغل ګيري *baghal-gīrī*, s.f. (3rd) Embracing. Pl. ۍ *a'ī*. بغلګيري کول *baghalgīrī kawul*, verb trans. To embrace. ګنده بغل *gandah baghal*, A person having stinking armpits—a disease ; (Fem.) ګنده بغله *gandah baghala'h*.

A بغي *baghī*, adj. Rebellious, mutinous.

A بغير *baghair*, adv. Without, except, besides, otherwise.

بق بق *bak bak*, s.m. (2nd) Nonsense, prattle, chat, garrulity. Pl. بق بقونه *bak-bakūnah*. بق بق کول *bak bak kawul*, verb trans. To chatter, prattle, prate, twaddle. See بک بک and بربر

A بقا *bakā*, s.f. (6th) Duration, permanence, remaining, eternity, immortality. (E.) Sing. and Pl. ; (W.) Pl. بقاوي *bakāwī*. بقا لرل *bakā laral*, verb trans. To last, endure, to have duration, permanence, or immortality.

T بقچه *buk-cha'h*, s.f. (3rd) A small bundle, a parcel, a roll of clothes. Pl. ې *ey*. See بغچه

S بک *bak*, s.m. (2nd) Prattle, chat, garrulity, foolish talk. Pl. بکونه *bakūna'h*. بک بک کول *bak bak kawul*, verb trans. To prattle, to chatter, to gabble. See بربر and بق بق

بکاينړ *bakā-yarrn*, s.m. (6th) The name of a tree (Melia sempervirens). Sing. and Pl. (HI بکاين).

بکاينړه *bakā-yarrna'h*, s.f. (3rd) The name of a tree or shrub (Melia sempervirens). Pl. ې *ey*. See روي and شندي

بک بک *bak bak*, s.m. Prattle, babble, foolish talk, clack, gabble, twaddle. Pl. بک بکونه *bak-bakūna'h*.

بکرۍ *bakra'ī*, s.f. (6th) Flint, a flint. Sing. and Pl.

بکلولۍ *bagalola'ī*, s.f. (6th) A woman dressed up to frighten naughty children, a bug-bear. Sing. and Pl. See باګو

بګلي *buglaey*, s.m. (1st) An aigrette. 2. A stork, a bittern, a heron. Pl. ي *ī*. (S بګلا).

بګنيدل *bugnedal*, verb intrans. To shy, to start, to fear, to wince. Pres. بګنيږي *bugnejzī* (W.) or بګنيګي *bugnegī* (E.) ; past. وُ بګنيده *wu-bugnedah* ; fut. وُ به بګنيږي *wu bah bugnejzī*, or وُ به بګنيګي *wu bah bugnegī* ; imp. وُ بګنيږه *wu-bugnejzah*, or وُ بګنيګه *wu-bugnegah* ; act. part. بګنيدونکي *bugnedūnkaey*, or بګنيدوني *bugnedūnaey* ; past part. بګنيدلي *bugnedalaey* ; verb. n. بګنيدنه *bugnedana'h*. See also ترهيدل

بګنول *bugnawul*, verb trans. To cause to shy, start, fear, wince, etc. Pres. بګنوي *bugnawī*; past وُ بګناوه *wu-bugnāwuh*, or وُ بګناوو *wu-bugnāwo*; fut. وُ به بګنوي *wu bah bugnawī*; imp. وُ بګنوه *wu-bugnawah*; act. part. بګنوونکَي *bugnawūnkaey*, or بګنوونَي *bugnawūnaey*; past part. بګنولَي *bugnawulaey*; verb. n. بګنونه *bugnawuna'h*. See ترهول

بګوړه *bagorra'h*, s.f. (3rd) Coagulated milk, a kind of cheese, the Persian *ḳurūt*. Pl. ې *ey*. See قرت and کرت. بګوړه زدويل *bagorra'h z'do-yal*, verb trans. To grind, or prepare cheese, etc. by grinding.

ٻل *bæl*, adj. Another, other, different, not the same. Sing. and Pl.; (Fem.) ٻله *bæla'h*. Pl. ٻلې *bæley*. ٻل ٻل *bæl bæl*, Various. ٻله پلا *bæla'h plā*, Another time. ٻل سر *bæl sar*, The other end. ٻل صبا *bæl ṣabā*, The day after to-morrow. ٻله ورځ *bæla'h wradz*, Next day. ٻل هير *bæl heyr*, Another time, etc.

A بل *bal*, adv. Moreover, but, yet, however, upon which, thereupon, likewise, besides. See also بلکه

بل *bal*, adj. Burnt, consumed, lighted, inflamed, set on fire; (Fem.) بله *bala'h*. جل بل *jal bal*, Burnt up or consumed by fire (s).

بليدل *baledal*, verb intrans. To burn, to kindle, to be consumed, to ignite, to take or catch fire. Pres. بليږي *balejzī* (W.) or بليګي *balegī* (E.); past بل وُ شه *bal wu-shah*, or بل شه *bal shah*; fut. بل به وُ شي *bal bah wu-shī*, or بل به شي *bal bah shī*; imp. بل وُ شه *bal wu-shah*, or بل شه *bal shah*; act. part. بليدونکَي *baledūnkaey*, or بلدونَي *baledūnaey*; past part. بل *bal*, or بل شوَي *bal shawaey*; verb. n. بليدنه *baledana'h*.

بلول *balawul*, verb trans. To burn, to set on fire, to light up, enkindle, ignite. Pres. بلوي *balawī*; past بل وُ کړ *bal wu-karr*, or بل وُ که *bal wu-kah*, or بل کړ *bal karr*, or بل که *bal kah*; fut. بل به وُ کړي *bal bah wu-krrī*, or بل به کړي *bal bah krrī*; imp. بل وُ کړه *bal wu-krrah*, or بل وُ که *bal wu-kah*, or بل کړه *bal krrah*, or بل که *bal kah*; act. part. بلوونکَي *balawūnkaey*, or بلوونَي *balawūnaey*; past part. بل کړَي *bal karraey*; verb. n. بلونه *balawuna'h*.

A بلا *balā*, s.f. (6th) Trial, calamity, misfortune, accident, vengeance, evil, ill. (E.) Sing. and Pl.; (W.) Pl. بلاوي *balāwī*. بلا پسيَ *balā pasey* (correctly بلا پس ئي), May calamity follow him or her. بلا زده *balā-zadah*, adj. Overwhelmed with misfortune. بلا کښ *balā-kash* (W.) or *kakh* (E.), adj. Afflicted, sufferer. (Fem.) بلا کښه *balā-kasha'h*, or *kakha'h*.

A بلا *bilā*, prep. Without, unless. بلا توقف *bilā tawakkuf*, Without delay, speedily. بلا طلب *bilā ṭalab*, Without asking, of one's own free-will, uncalled.

بلاربه *blārbah*, adj. Pregnant, as a woman or animal. See also ډکه, شکاره, and برالبه.

بلاربيدل *blārbedal*, verb intrans. To become pregnant, great with young. Pres. بلاربيږي *blārbejzey* (W.) or بلاربيګي *blārbegey* (E.); past بلاربه شوه *blārbah shwah*, or بلاربه وُ شوه *blārbah wu-shwah*; fut. بلاربه به وُ شي *blārbah bah wu-shī*, or بلاربه به شي *blārbah bah shī*; imp. بلاربه وُ شه *blārbah wu-shah*, or بلاربه شه *blārbah shah*; act. part. بلاربيدونکِ *blārbedūnki*, or بلاربيدونِ *blārbedūni*; past part. بلاربه *blārbah*, or بلاربه شو *blārbah shawi*; verb. n. بلاربيدنه *blārbedana'h*.

بلاربول *blārbawul*, verb trans. To render pregnant, impregnate, bring with young, to get with child. Pres. بلاربوي *blārbawī*; past بلاربه وُ کړه or کړله *blārbah wu-krrah*, or *krralah*, or بلاربه کړه or کړله *blārbah krrah* or *krralah*; fut. بلاربه به وُ کړي *blārbah bah wu-krrī*, or بلاربه به کړي *blārbah bah krrī*; imp. بلاربه وُ کړه *blārbah wu-krrah*, or بلاربه کړه *blārbah krrah*; act. part. بلاربوونکَي *blārbawūnkaey*, or بلاربوونَي *blārbawūnaey*; past part. بلاربه کړ *blārbah karri*; verb. n. بلاربونه *blārbawuna'h*. See برالبه, etc.

بلارب والَي *blārb wālaey*, s.m. (1st) Pl. والي *wālī*, or بلارب توب *blārb-tob*, s.m. (2nd) Pregnancy, impregnation. Pl. توبونه *tobūnah*.

A بلاغ *bilāgh*, s.m. (2nd) Whatever is brought; a sufficiency, enough; any vocable implying excellence, as purity, virtue, etc. Pl. بلاغونه *bilāghūnah*.

بلاغند *balā-ghundd*, s.m. (5th) Name of a fruit, and of which snuff-boxes are made (Cratæva or Ægle marmelos). Pl. بلاغندان *balā-ghunddān*. See also بيل تاك and بيپل

بلانړه *bil-ārrnah*, s.m. (9th) A low or faint groan, moan, plaint, etc. Sing. and Pl. بلانړه ختل *bil-ārrnah khatal*, verb intrans. To moan, to utter faint groans, as a person near death.

بُل بُل *bæl bæl*, adj. Various, different, diversified; (Fem.) بُله بُله *bæla'h bæla'h*.

بلبل *bulbul*, s.m. (5th) A nightingale. Pl. بلبلان *bulbulān*; s.f. (3rd) بلبله *bulbula'h*. Pl. بلبلي *bulbuley*.

P بلد *balad*, s.m. (5th) A guide, a conductor. Pl. بلدان *baladān*; s.f. (3rd) بلده *balada'h*. Pl. ې *ey*.

بُل سر *bæl sar*, s.m. (2nd) The other end, as of a plank, stick, etc. Pl. بُل سرونه *bæl-sarūnah*.

بُل صبا *bæl ṣabā*, adj. To-morrow.

بلغاك *bulghāk*, s.m. (2nd) Noise, clamour, uproar, hubbub, din, hullaballoo. 2. The sound of grief or sorrow, wail, lamentation. Pl. بلغاكونه *bul-ghāk-ūnah*. بلغاك كول *bul-ghāk kawul*, verb trans. To grieve, to lament, to bewail, to cry out, to groan audibly.

A بلغم *balgham*, s.m. (6th) Phlegm. 2. A running at the nose from cold. Sing. and Pl.

A بلغمي *balghamī*, adj. Phlegmatic.

بلق *balk*, s.m. (2nd) Lightning. See برق

P بلكه *balkih*, adv. Moreover, but, nay.

بلگه *balga'h*, s.f. (3rd) A clue, a trace, as of stolen property. Pl. ې *ey*. See بيلگه. بلگه مندل *balga'h mun-dal*, verb trans. To obtain a clue or trace.

بلل *balal*, verb trans. To call, to convoke, to summon, cite, call for, invoke, invite, request to meet or come. Pres. بولي *bolī*; past و باله *wu-bālah* or و بالَ *wu bāla*; fut. و به بولي *wu bah bolī*; imp. و بوله *wu bolah* or بوله *bolah*; act. part. بلونكي *balūnkaey* or بلونې *balūnaey*; past part. بللي *balalaey*; verb. n. بلنه *balana'h*.

بلماز *bilmāz*, adj. Profane, unholy, irreligious; (Fem.) بلمازه *bilmāza'h*.

بلمگي *balmagaey*, adj. Saltless, insipid, tasteless, weak, vapid; (Fem.) بلمگې *balmagi* or بلمنكي *balmangey*. Pl. (Masc. and Fem.) ي *ī*.

بلمنگه *bal-mangah*, adj. Saltless, unsavoury, insipid, vapid, tasteless, weak. See بلمنكي

P بلند *buland* or *biland*, adj. High, lofty, elevated, exalted, sublime, tall, loud; (Fem.) بلنده *bulanda'h* or *bilanda'h*.

بلندي *bulandī* or *bilandī*, s.f. (3rd) Height, a height, elevation, loftiness, eminence, loudness. Pl. ئي *a'ī*.

P بلوا *balwā*, s.f. (6th) Tumult, riot, sedition, insurrection; confusion, disturbance, disobedience; a concourse, a crowd. (E.) Sing. and Pl.; (W.) Pl. بلواوي *balwāwī*. بلوا كول *balwā kawul*, verb trans. To create a riot or disturbance, to make or cause a tumult.

بلوڅ *balūts*, s.m. (5th) A Beluch, the tribe of Beluchīs. Pl. بلوڅان *balūtsān*. بلوڅه *balūtsa'h*, s.f. (3rd) A female of the Beluchī tribe. Pl. ې *ey*.

بلوجيان *balūjī-ān*, s.m. (5th) Pl. Ignorant people; Beluchīs.

بلودل *b'lodal*, verb trans. To touch, to graze, to abrade, to come in contact. Pres. بلودي *b'lodī*; past و بلود *wu-b'lod*; fut. و به بلودي *wu bah b'lodī*; imp. و بلوده *wu-b'lodah*; act. part. بلودونكي *b'lodūnkaey* or بلودونې *b'lodūnaey*; past part. بلودلي *b'lodalaey*; verb. n. بلودنه *b'lodana'h*.

بلوس *b'los*, s.m. (2nd) Touch, contact, distress. Pl. بلوسونه *b'losūnah*.

بلوسيدل *b'losedal*, verb trans. To afflict, to distress; to touch, to graze, to abrade, come in contact with. Pres. بلوسي *b'losī*; past و بلوسيدَ *wu-b'loseda*; fut. و به بلوسي *wu bah b'losī*; imp. و بلوسه *wu-b'losah*; act. part. بلوسيدونكي *b'losedūnkaey*, or بلوسيدونې *b'losedūnaey*; past part. بلوسيدلي *b'losedalaey*; verb. n. بلوسيدنه *b'losedana'h*.

بلوسيدنه *b'losedana'h*, s.f. (3rd) (verb. n.) Touch, contact, abrasion, grazing, coming into contact. 2. Affliction; trouble. Pl. ې *ey*.

بلوس والي *b'los-wālaey,* s.m. (1st) Contact, touch, etc. Pl. والي *wāli.*

A بلوط *balūṭ,* s.m. (6th) The oak-tree, an acorn, a chesnut. Sing. and Pl.

A بلوغ *bulūgh,* s.m. (9th) Puberty, adolescence. Sing. and Pl.; also بلوغت *bulūghat,* s.m. (2nd) Pl. بلوغتونه *bulūghatūnah.*

بلول *balawul,* verb trans. To light, burn, set on fire, kindle, ignite. See under بل

بلونګړي *bilūngarraey,* s.m. (1st) A squirrel. See also ګيدړي Pl. ي *ī.*

بلو *balau,* or بلوو *balawū,* s.m. (5th) A barber's hone. Pl. بلوګان *balau-gān,* or بلووګان *bala-wūgān.*

بله پلا *bæla'h plā,* s.f. (6th) Another time. (E.) Sing. and Pl.; (W.) Pl. بله پلاوي *bæla'h plāwī.*

بله روځ *bæla'h rwadz,* or بله ورځ *bæla'h wradz.* Another day.

بل هوس *bul hawas,* adj. The father of desire, avaricious, parsimonious; (Fem.) بل هوسه *bul-hawasa'h.*

بل هير *bæl heyr,* adv. Another time.

بلئي *bala'ī,* s.f. (6th) The eave or eaves of a house; a pole to propel a boat; the bolt or bar of a door (HI بلي). Sing. and Pl.

بليدل *baledal,* verb intrans. To burn, to kindle, to ignite, to be consumed, to take fire. See under بل

بليږدل *blejzdal,* verb trans. To swaddle, to swathe (particularly infants). Pres. بليږدي *blejzdī*; past وُ بليږده *wu-blejzdah*; fem. وُ به بليږدي *wu bah blejzdī*; imp. وُ بليږده *wu-blejzdah*; act. part. بليږدونکي *blejzdūnkaey,* or بليږدوني *blejzdūnaey*; past. part. بليږدلي *blejzdalaey*; verb. n. بليږدنه *blejzdana'h.*

بليږدنه *blejzdana'h,* s.f. (3rd) (verb. n.) Swathing, swaddling (an infant). Pl. ي *ey.*

بمبره *bambara'h,* s.f. (3rd) A large red wasp or hornet. Pl. ي *ey.*

بن *bæn,* s.f. (1st) Rival (wife), cotemporary wife; one of two or more wives are *bæns* to each other. Pl. بنِ *bæni.*

A بنا *binā,* s.f. (6th) Building, foundation, an edifice. (E.) Sing. and Pl.; (W.) Pl. بناوي *bināwī.* بنا كول *binā kawul,* verb trans. To build, to found.

HI بنات *banāt,* s.m. (6th) Woollen cloth, broad cloth. Sing. and Pl. بناتي *banātī,* adj. Woollen.

بنبل *ban-bal,* s.m. (2nd) The beard of grain, the feathery tuft of gorse, etc. Pl. بنبلونه *ban-balūnah.*

A بنت *bint,* s.f. (1st) A daughter. Pl. بنتِ *binti.*

بنج *banj,* s.m. (6th) A chesnut-tree, a chesnut. Sing. and Pl. See بار بنج

S بنج *banj* or *banaj,* s.m. (2nd) Trade, traffic, merchandize, commerce. Pl. بنجونه *banj-ūnah,* or *banajūnah.*

بنجخ *banjakh,* s.m. (6th) The name of a plant, the seed of which contains a sort of cow-itch. Sing. and Pl.

بنجئي *banja'ī,* s.f. (6th) The cassia tree. Sing. and Pl.

P بند *band,* s.m. (2nd) A fastening, imprisonment, confinement, arrest, captivity, a knot, a bond, bandage, belt, roll, joint, knuckle. 2. Twist in wrestling, a dodge, a ruse, an artifice, a wile. Pl. بندونه *bandūnah.* 3. adj. Fastened, bound, shut, stopped; (Fem.) بنده *banda'h.* بند تړل *band tarral,* verb trans. To restrain an inundation with dykes. بند بند *band band,* Joint by joint. بند بند نيول *band band nīwul,* verb trans. To seize (as rheumatism, etc.) all the joints. بند بند كول *band band kawul,* verb trans. To disjoint, to separate joint from joint.

بندخ *bandukh,* s.m. (2nd) A musket, a fire lock. Pl. بندخونه *bandukhūnah.*

P بندر *bandar,* s.m. (2nd) A city, port, harbour, a trading town. Pl. بندرونه *bandarūnah.*

P بندري *bandarī,* adj. Relating to a seaport town. 2. A sort of chintz.

T بندق *banduḳ,* s.m. (2nd) A musket, a fire-lock. Pl. بندقونه *banduḳūnah.* See بندخ and بندوق

بند كړيَ مرغه *band karraey murghah*, s.m. (5th) A decoy bird. Pl. مرغان *murghān*.

P بندگي *bandagī*, s.f. (3rd) Servitude, homage. Pl. ئي *a'ī*. بندگي كول *bandagī kawul*, verb trans. To honour, serve, do homage, reverence, show fealty.

بندوخ *ban-dūkh*, s.m. (2nd) A fire-lock, a musket. Pl. بندوخونه *ban-dūkhūnah*. See بندق

P بنده *bandah*, s.m. (5th) A slave, a servant, a bondsman. Pl. بنده گان *bandahgān*. بندئي *banda'ī*, s.f. (6th) A female slave, a female captive. Sing. and Pl. بنده پرور *bandah parwar*, adj. Cherisher of servants (an expression of respect to a superior); (Fem.) بنده پروره *banda'h parwara'h*. بنده پروري *bandah parwarī*, s.f. (3rd) Cherishing of servants. Pl. ئي *a'ī*. بنده نواز *bandah nawāz*, adj. Cherisher of servants or dependants; (Fem.) بنده نوازه *bandah-nawāza'h*.

P بنده گي *bandah-gī*, s.f. (3rd) Service, etc. Pl. ئي *a'ī*. See بندگي.

P بندوبست *band-o-bast*, s.m. (2nd) Settlement, regulation, disposition, arrangement, economy, management, government. Pl. بندوبستونه *band-o-bastūnah*. بندوبست كول *band-o-bast kawul*, verb trans. To dispose, to arrange, to regulate, etc.

P بندي *bandī*, s.m. (5th) A slave, a captive, a prisoner. Pl. بنديان *bandī-ān*.

S بنديوان *bandī-wān*, s.m. (5th) Same as above. Pl. بنديوانان *bandī-wānān*; (Fem.) (3rd) بنديوانه *bandīwāna'h*. Pl. ئي *ey*.

بندئي *banda'ī*, s.f. (6th) A belt or shoulder ornament worn by women and children. Sing. and Pl.

بن‌زيَ *ban-zaey*, s.m. (1st) The son of a husband by another wife who may be alive, a step-son. Pl. بن‌زي *banzī*; بن‌زئي *ban-za'ī*, s.f. (6th) A daughter as above. Sing. and Pl. See also پركتي, پلندر, and ميره

P بنگ *bang*, s.m. (6th) Hemp (Cannabis sativa). 2. An intoxicating potion made from the leaves of hemp. Sing. and Pl.

بنگول *bangawul*, verb trans. To taint, to corrupt, to make fly blown. Pres. بنگوي *bangawī*; past. وُ بنگاوه *wu-bangāwuh*, or وُ بنگاوو *wu-bangāwo*; fem. وُ به بنگوي *wu bah bangawī*; imp. وُ بنگوه *wu-bangawah*; act. part. بنگوونكيَ *bangawūnkaey*, or بنگوونيَ *bangawūnaey*; past. part. بنگوليَ *bangawulaey*; verb. n. بنگونه *bangawuna'h*. See بونړول.

بنگښ *bangash* (W.) or *bangakh* (E.) s.m. (6th) The name of a tribe claiming Afghān descent, also the name of their district. 2. A male of the tribe. بنگښه *bangasha'h*, or *bangakha'h*, s.f. (3rd) A female of the above. Pl. ئي *ey*.

P بنگي *bangī*, s.m. (5th) One who is in the habit of intoxicating himself with bang. Pl. بنگيان *bangīān*; s.f. (6th) Sing. and Pl. ئي *a'ī*.

بنو *banū*, s. prop. A district in Afghānistān, west of Derah Ismæīl Khān, whose inhabitants are called بنوچيَ *bunūchaey*, s.m. (1st) Pl. ي *ī*; (Fem.) (6th) ئي *a'ī*. Sing. and Pl.

A بنو *bano*, or بني *banī*, s.m. (9th) (Pl. of ابن, H בן), Sons, posterity. بني آدم *banī ādam*, Sons of Adam, men. بني اسرايل *banī isrā-īl*, The children of Israel, Israelites. بني جان *banī jān*, Beings who inhabited the world before Adam, genii, fairies.

بنئي *bana'ī*, s.f. (6th) A bellows made from the skin of a goat or sheep; a wallet, a bag of leather. Sing. and Pl.

A بنياد *bunyād*, s.m. (2nd) Foundation, basis, origin. Pl. بنيادونه *bunyādūnah*. بنياد ختل *bunyād khatal*, verb intrans. To become annihilated, to become erased from foundation. بنياد ښكل or كښل *bunyād khkal* (E.) or *kshal* (W.) verb trans. To root out from the very foundation, to annihilate, to eradicate.

بنير *buner*, s. prop. A district of Afghānistān, north-east from Peshāwer.

بنيروال *buner wāl*, s.m. (6th) An inhabitant of Buner. Sing. and Pl.; (Fem.) (3rd) واله *wāla'h*. Pl. ئي *ey*.

بنړ or بن *barrn*, s.m. (2nd) A forest, a wood (s वन). Pl. بنړونه *barrnūnah*.

بنړكه *barrnaka'h*, s.f. (3rd) A feather (dimin. of following). Pl. ئي *ey*.

بنړه *barrna'h*, s.f. (3rd) The strongest feather in a bird's wing, of which there are two. Pl. بنړي *barrney*.

بنړېچغ *barrne-chagh*, s.m. (2nd) A kind of whirligig. Pl. بنړېچغونه *barrne-chaghūnah*.

بنړئي *barrna'ī*, s.f. (6th) The name of a tree. Sing. and Pl.

بنړيه *barrn-īah*, s.m. (5th) A chandler, a huckster, a shopkeeper. بنړيهګان *barrn-īah-gān* (HI بنيان).

P بو *bū*, s.m. Smell, scent, odour, effluvium. See بوي

بو *bau*, or *bao*, s.m. (2nd) A scare-crow, a bugaboo, a bogie, etc. to frighten children. Pl. بوونه *bau-ūnah*, or *bao-ūnah*; also علي بوبو *æalī-bau-bau*.

بواسير *bawāsīr*, s.m. (6th) The piles or hemorrhoids (Pushto باوسير *bāw-sīr*). Sing. and Pl.

A بوالهوس *bū-l-hawas*, adj. (com. of بو Endowed with, and هوس Desire), Desirous, whimsical, capricious, a wavering or fickle person, a blockhead; (Fem.) بوالهوسه *bū-l-hawasa'h*.

A بوالهوسي *bū-l-hawasī*, s.f. (3rd) Caprice, capriciousness, fickleness. Pl. ئي *a'ī*.

A بوالهوس نـاكي *bū-l-hawas nākī*, s.f. (3rd) Caprice, fickleness, capriciousness. Pl ئي *a'ī*.

بوتكي *būtkī*, s.f. (3rd) A gold coin, a ducat, value about ten shillings English, imported from Russia. Pl. ئي *a'ī*.

بوتلل *botlal*, verb trans. To take along, lead, conduct, convey, remove, transport, peculiar to animate objects. Pres. بوزي *bozī*; past بوت *bot*; fut. بو به زي *bo bah zī*; imp. بوزه *bozah*; act. part. بوتلونكي *botlūnkaey*, or بوتلوني *botlūnaey*; verb. n. بوتلنه *botlana'h*, or بوته *bota'h*. The other inflections are wanting, this infinitive being used to complete the conjugation of بيول, which see.

بوته *bota'h*, s.f. (3rd) Seizing the person of a villager and retaining him as a hostage or pledge for the debts of another, a custom amongst the Afghāns. Pl. ي *ey*. See برمته

بوتي *botaey*, s.m. (1st) A young camel. Pl. بوتي *botī*; s.f. (6th) بوتئي *bota'ī*. Sing. and Pl.

بوټ *būtt*, adj. Ill-tempered, crabbed, morose, surly, stern, sour-tempered; (Fem.) بوټه *būtta'h*. See سوټ بوټ

بوټ سوړي *būtt sūrrī*, s.m. (1st) Pl. Bran, chaff. See also پوټ سوړي

بوټي *būttaey*, s.m. (1st) A bush, a shrub, a flower worked or painted on cloth or paper. Pl. بوټي *būttī*, Drugs, medicine given to children after birth. (HI. بوٹا).

بوښكئي *būtska'ī*, s.f. (6th) The soft part of the ear or nose, the lobe of the ear. Sing. and Pl. Also written بوښئي *būtsa'ī*, and پوښكئي *pūtska'ī*, and پوښئي *pūtsa'ī*.

بوجه *būja'h*, s.f. (3rd) A cork, a stopper. Pl. ي *ey*. (HI.)

P بود *būd*, s.m. (9th) (verb. n. of بودن) Being, existence. Sing. and Pl.

بوده *būda'h*, s.f. (3rd) The woof of the web in weaving. Pl. ي *ey*. Also پوده

بوډاګي *būddā-gaey*, s.m. (1st) (s بڈھا) An old decrepit man, an imbecile (used in a contemptuous sense). Pl. ي *ī*. بوډاګئي *būddā-ga'ī*, s.f. (6th) An old decrepit woman. Sing. and Pl.

بور *bawr*, s.m. (6th) A leopard, a panther. Sing. and Pl. See پړانګ.

بور *bor*, adj. Light grey or brown, a horse of that colour; (Fem.) بوره *bora'h*.

بور *būr*, s.m. (6th) A carrot leaf, the leaf of the tamarisk tree. Sing. and Pl. See بر بري 2. adj. A man who has lost his child by death; (Fem.) بوره *būra'h*.

بورا *bawrā*, s.m. (5th) A large black bee. Pl. بوراګان *bawrā-gān*.

بوربوكئي *bor-būka'ī*, s.f. (6th) A whirlwind, a devil. Sing. and Pl. See بربكي and پربوكي

بورجل *borjal*, s.f. (1st) A house, home, hearth, halting-place, abode, resort. Pl. بورجل *borjali*.

بورنه *bornah*, s.m. (6th) Dredging, dried flour used to sprinkle meat or dough with. Sing. and Pl.

بورڼه *borrrnah*, s.m. (6th) Dredging. See above. Sing. and Pl.

بوره *būra'h*, adj. as s.f. (3rd) A woman who has

lost her child in its infancy. Pl. بوري *būrey.* See بور

بوري *bawra'ī,* s.f. (6th) A gall, a corn or bunion. Sing. and Pl. See رسولي and کلي

بوړه *būrra'h,* s.f. (3rd) Table land, flat mountain land. Pl. ي *ey.* See also ستيزه

بوړی *būrraey,* s.m. (1st) The cog of a Persian wheel. Pl. ي *ī.*

بوړی *būrraey,* adj. One whose nose, lips, ears, or hand has been cut off; a vessel or cup with the lip broken off. 2. Broken, split, reft; (Fem.) بوړ *būrrī.* Pl. (Masc. and Fem.) ي *ī.*

بوړي *būrra'ī,* s.f. (6th) A disorder, in which the intestinum rectum is prolapsed, generally amongst children (Prolapsus ani). Sing. and Pl.

P بوزه *boza'h,* s.f. (3rd) The ibis or royal cerclew. Pl. ي *ey.* See بزه

P بوزه *boza'h,* s.f. (3rd) Anything which has undergone fermentation, such as wine, milk, etc. 2. An intoxicating drink made from the fermented milk of the camel. Pl ي *ey.*

بوزي بنده *būzī bandah,* adj. Simple, foolish. 2. A simple, artless or harmless person, a simpleton.

بوزينه *bozīna'h,* s.f. (3rd) Leather made from the skins of goats, of a red colour; morocco leather. Pl. ي *ey.*

بوږ *bojz,* (W.) adj. Harsh (in sound), bass, hollow, sepulchral; (Fem.) بوږه *bojza'h.* See دد. بوږ غاړی *bojz-ghārraey,* adj. as s.m. (1st) A person having a harsh or hollow voice; (Fem.) بوږ غاړ *bojz-ghārrī.* Pl. (masc. and fem.) ي *ī.* بوږي غاړي *bojzey ghārrey,* Sore-throat. See غاړه

بوس *būs,* s.m. (6th) Bran, chaff. Sing. and Pl. See بهوس.

بوساړه *būsārra'h,* s.f. (3rd) A heap or stack of chopped straw (*būsah*), used as food for cattle and mixed with mud for building purposes, covered over with a mud thatch (s بهسيرا). Pl. ي *ey.*

P بوستان *bos-tān,* s.m. (2nd) A flower-garden. Pl. بوستانونه *bos-tānūnah.*

بوښتنه *bokhtana'h,* s.f. (3rd) (verb. n.) Sticking, cleaving, etc. (as in mud). 2. A quagmire, a bog, a marsh. Pl. ي *ey.* See بښتنه

بوښتيدل *bokh-tedal* (E.), or *bosh-tedal* (W.), verb intrans. To stick, adhere (as mud), cohere, hold, cleave to. Pres. بوښتيږي *bosh-tejzī* (W.), or بوښتيگی *bokh-tegī* (E.); past بوښت وُ شه *bokht* or *bosht wu-shah,* or بوښت شه *bokht* or *bosht shah*; fut. بوښت به وُ شي *bokht* or *bosht bah wu-shī,* or بوښت به شي *bokht* or *bosht bah shī*; imp. بوښت وُ شه *bokht* or *bosht wu-shah,* or بوښت شه *bokht* or *bosht shah*; act. part. بوښتيدونکی *bokhtedūnkaey* or *boshtedūnkaey,* or بوښتيدونی *bokhtedūnaey* or *boshtedūnaey*; past part. بوښت *bokht* or *bosht,* or بوښت شوی *bokht* or *bosht shawaey*; verb. n. بوښتنه *bokhtana'h* or *boshtana'h.* See بښتيدل

بوښتول *bokhtawul* or *boshtawul,* verb trans. To cause to stick, to embed, to stick in, to join, to glue, etc. Pres. بوښتوي *bokhtawī* or *boshtawī*; past بوښت وُ کړ *bokht* or *bosht wu-karr* or وُ که *wu-kah,* or بوښت کړ *bokht* or *bosht karr* or که *kah*; fut. بوښت به کړي *bokht* or *bosht bah krrī* or به وُ کړي *bah wu-krrī*; imp. بوښت وُ کړه *bokht* or *bosht wu-krrah* or وُ که *wu-kah,* or بوښت کړه *bokht* or *bosht krrah* or که *kah*; act. part. بوښتوونکی *bokhtawūnkaey* or *boshtawūnkaey,* or بوښتوونی *bokhtawūnaey* or *boshtawūnaey*; past part. بوښت کړی *bokht* or *bosht karraey*; verb. n. بوښتونه *bokhtawuna'h* or *boshtawuna'h.* See بښتول

بوښت والی *bokht* or *bosht wālaey,* s.m. (1st) Pl. والي *wālī*: or بوښت توب *bokht* or *bosht tob,* s.m. (2nd) Stickiness, tenacity. Pl. توبونه *tobūnah.*

بوغ *būgh,* s.m. (2nd) A wooden bowl, a cup or basin. Pl. بوغونه *būghūnah.* See کنړي

A بوق *būk,* s.m. (9th) A trumpet, a clarion. Sing. and Pl.

A بوقلمون *bū-kalamūn,* s.m. (6th) Changing colour, a chamelion. Also ابوقلمون *abū-kalamūn.* Sing. and Pl.

بوکه *boka'h,* s.f. (3rd) A leather or wooden bucket. Pl. ئ *ey.*

بوکي *bokī,* s.m. (1st) Pl. The name of a tribe of Afghāns. Sing. ي *aey*; s.f. (6th) ئ *a'ī.* Sing. and Pl.

بوګړی *bo-garaey,* s.m. (1st) (W.) Land given to holy men free of rent. Pl. ي *ī.* See سيري

HI بول *bol,* s.m. (2nd) Word, speech, talk. Pl. بولونه *bolūnah.*

A بولِ *bawli,* s.f. (1st) Pl. Urine. بولِ کول *bawli kawul,* verb trans. To urinate.

بولر *bolar,* s.m. (6th) The name of a tribe of Afghāns. Sing. and Pl.; s.f. (3rd) بولره *bolara'h.* Pl. بولرئ *bolarey.*

بولقه *bolka'h,* s.f. (3rd) A dress or kind of veil with eye-holes, worn by women, and covering the whole body from head to foot. Pl. ئ *ey.* See برقه

P بوم *būm,* s.m. (5th) A native, home-bred person, one who has never been abroad. 2. A guide. 3. An owl. 4. A country. Pl. بومان *bū-mān.* 5. s.m. (9th) Earth, ground. Sing. and Pl.; (from s भूमि). Also adj. Acquainted, familiar with (a road, place, etc.), habituated, used to; (Fem.) بومه *būma'h.* نا بوم *nā-būm* and نا بومه *nā-būma'h,* Unacquainted, not accustomed, un-habituated. See ګونګي and چغرو.

بوميا *būmiā,* s.m. and f. (5th) A guide, a conductor, a leader. Pl. بومياګان *būmiā-gān*; Fem. Pl. بومياګانِ *būmiā-gāni.*

S بوند *būnd,* s.m. (2nd) A drop. Pl. بوندونه *būndūnah.*

بونسټ *bon-saṯṯ,* s.m. (2nd) Basis, root, foundation; a term of reproach, as بونسټ دِ وُ خيژه *bon-saṯṯ di wu-khejzah,* 'May thy foundation be destroyed, or rooted out;' 'May destruction overtake thee.' Pl. بونسټونه *bon-saṯṯūnah.* See کونسته

بونګه *būnga'h,* s.f. (3rd) Black-mail, ransom. Pl. ئ *ey.*

بونيدل *bonedal,* verb intrans. To buzz or hum; to swarm as flies. See بونړيدل

بونړ *būrrn,* s.m. (6th) A nose having no smell, a disease of the nose. 2. A person afflicted with this disease. 3. Rope used for bed-lacings. Sing. and Pl.

بونړ *borrn,* s.m. (5th) Buzz, the hum or sound of flies or bees. Pl. بونړهار *borrnahār.*

بونړول *borrnawul,* verb trans. To make a buzzing noise (as flies). 2. To taint, corrupt, putrefy, to make fly-blown. Pres. بونړوي *borrnawī*; past وُ بونړاوه *wu-borrnāwuh,* or وُ بونړاوو *wu-borrnā-wo*; fut. وُ به بونړوي *wu bah borrnawī*; imp. وُ بونړوه *wu-borrnawah*; act. part. بونړوونکی *borrnawūnkaey,* or بونړوونی *borrnawūnaey*; past part. بونړولی *borrnawulaey*; verb. n. بونړونه *borrnawuna'h.* See بنګول

بونړولی *borrnawulaey,* adj. (past part.) Fly-blown, tainted, high, putrid; (Fem.) بونړولِ *borrnawuli.* Pl. (Masc. and Fem.) ي *ī.*

بونړيدل *borrnedal,* verb intrans. To buzz or hum as flies; (fig.) To become fly-blown or tainted, to putrefy, corrupt. Pres. بونړيږي *borrnejzī* (W.), or بونړيګي *borrnegī* (E.); past وُ بونړيدَ *wu-borrneda*; fut. وُ به بونړيږي *wu bah borrnejzī,* or وُ به بونړيګي *wu bah borrnegī*; imp. وُ بونړيږه *wu-borrnejzah*; act. part. بونړيدونکی *borrne-dūnkaey,* or بونړيدونی *borrnedūnaey*; past part. بونړيدلی *borrnedalaey*; verb. n. بونړيدنه *borrnedana'h.*

بونړکی *borrnkaey,* s.m. (1st) A buzzing sound, hum, whispering. Pl. ي *ī.*

بوهار *buhār,* s.m. (9th) (P بهار) Spring, prime, bloom, elegance, delight. Sing. and Pl.

بوهاری *buhāraey,* s.m. (1st) A weanling, an animal newly weaned. Pl. ي *ī*; (Fem.) (6th) ئ *a'ī.* Sing. and Pl.

P بوي *bū-e,* s.m. (2nd) Smell, odour, scent. Pl. بويونه *bū-eūnah.*

بوي تلل *bū-e t'lal,* verb intrans. To smell, to stink. بويول *bū-e-yawul,* verb trans. To smell, scent, snuff. Pres. بويوي *bū-e-yawī*; past بوي وُ کړ *bū-e wu-karr,* or بوي کړ *bū-e karr*; fut. بوي به وُ کړي *bū-e bah wu-krrī,* or بوي به کړي *bū-e bah krrī*; imp. بوي وُ کړه *bū-e wu-krrah,* or بوي کړه *bū-e krrah*; act. part. بويونکی *bū-e-wūnkaey,* or بويوني *bū-e-wūnaey*; past part. بوي کړي *bū-e karraey*; verb. n. بويونه *būe-yawanah*.

بويه *bo-yah*, adj. Necessary, indispensable, needful, meet, obligatory, binding, behoving. 2. adv. As in duty bound, indispensably, necessarily, meetly, fitly, properly. کړلئ بويه *karralaey bo-yah*, It behoveth to be done, *or* Fit or necessary to be done. ويلئ بويه *wayalaey bo-yah*, Fit or necessary to be said, etc.

به *bah*, A particle, the sign of the future, the doubtful past, and the continuative tenses of the Pushto verbs. When prefixed to a word, which it sometimes is, it is written as simple بَ See my Grammar.

A بها *bahā*, s.f. (6th) Price, value. (E.) Sing. and Pl.; (W.) Pl. بهاوي *bahāwī*.

P بهادر *bahādur*, adj. Brave, bold, valiant, courageous. 2. s.m. (5th) A hero, a champion. Pl. بهادران *bahādurān*; (Fem.) (3rd) بهادره *bahādura'h*. Pl. ئ *ey*.

بهادرئ *bahāduraey*, s.m. (1st) A coward (*lit.* a small hero). Pl. ي *ī*; s.f. (6th) ئ *a'ī*. Sing. and Pl.

P بهادري *bahādurī*, s.f. (3rd) Bravery, heroism. Pl. ئ *a'ī*. په بهادري *pah bahādurī*, or په بهادري سره *pah bahādurī sarah*, adv. Bravely, with bravery, valiantly.

P بهار *bahār*, s.m. (9th) Spring, prime, bloom. Sing. and Pl. Also written بوهار *būhār*.

P بهانه *bahāna'h*, s.f. (3rd) Pretence, evasion, contrivance, excuse, pretext, feint. Pl. ئ *ey*. See also بانه. بهانه کول *bahāna'h kawul*, verb trans. To make a pretext, evasion, excuse, etc.

بهاړن *bihārrn*, s.m. (2nd) or (5th) A colt. Pl. بهاړنونه *bihārrnūnah*, or بهاړنان *bihārrnān*; s.f. (3rd) بهاړنه *bihārrna'h*. Pl. بهاړنئ *bihārrney*. Also written بهاڼ

بهانيه *bahā-nīah*, adj. Valuable, high-priced, precious, expensive.

P بهبود *bihbūd*, adj. Healthy, vigorous, perfect, in good order; (Fem.) بهبوده *bihbūda'h*.

بهبودي *bihbūdī*, s.f. (3rd) Health, vigour, goodness, welfare, well-being. 2. A large knife or dagger. Pl. ئ *a'ī*.

بهبوزئ *bahbozaey*, s.m. (1st) A fan, a ventilator. 2. A kind of fishing-bird. Pl. ي *ī*. See also ببوزي. بهبوزي وهل *bahbozaey wahal*, verb trans. To fan, to ventilate, to cool.

A بهتان *buhtān*, s.m. (2nd) Calumny, false imputation, aspersion, defamation. Pl. بهتانونه *buhtānūnah*. بهتان ويل *buhtān wa-yal*, verb trans. To calumniate, to asperse, to defame.

P بهتر *bih-tar*, adj. compar. Better, good, excellent, well, preferable; (Fem.) بهتره *bih-tara'h*.

P بهتري *bih-tarī*, s.f. (3rd) Advantage, welfare, improvement. Pl. ئ *a'ī*.

بهر *bahar*, adv. Without, out, outside, abroad, away. بهر کيدل *bahar kedal*, verb intrans. To come out, outside, or away. بهر کول *bahar kawul*, or بهر يستل *bahar yastal*, verb trans. To put or cast out, or away. بهر ليږل *bahar lejzal* (W.) or بهر ليګل *bahar legal* (E.) verb trans. To send out, or away. بهر لاړل *bahar lārral*, or بهر تلل *bahar t'lal*, verb intrans. To go out, outside. بهر راتلل *bahar rā-t'lal*, or بهر راغلل *bahar rāgh-lal*, verb intrans. To come out, to issue, to come forth.

P بهره *bahra'h*, s.f. (3rd) Profit, gain, advantage. 2. Quota, share, portion. 3. Fortune, property. Pl. ئ *ey*. بهره مند *bahra'h mand*, or بهره ور *bahra'h war*, adj. Fortunate, blessed, prosperous, enjoying one's wish, happy; (Fem.) بهره وره *bahra'h-wara'h*, or منده *mandah*. بهره ياب *bahrah yāb*, adj. Prosperity, profited, gainer; (Fem.) بهره يابه *bahrah-yāba'h*.

P بهره مندي *bahrah-mandī*, s.f. (3rd) Prosperity, happiness, profit. Pl. ئ *a'ī*.

بهره *bahrih*, adv. Once, one time, all at once. 2. At last, at length, at least. See باري.

بهراس *b'harrās*, s.m. (2nd) Vapour, steam, exhalation, heat. بهراسونه *b'harrāsūnah*. See براس

P بهزاد *bihzād*, s. prop. The name of Isfandiyār, son of Kashtāsib. The name also of a Prince of Bulghār, in the tale of Bahrām Gūr.

P بهشت *bihisht*, s.m. (2nd) Paradise, heaven. Pl. بهشتونه *bihishtūnah*. See بهبشت and جنت

بهښت *bihisht* (W.) or *bihikht* (E.), s.m. (2nd) Paradise, heaven. Pl. بهښتونه *bihishtūnah*, or *bihikhtūnah*; بهښتي *bihishtī*, or *bihikhtī*; adj. Celestial, of or relating to Paradise. See بهشت and جنت

بهګنړ or بهګڼ *bhagarrn*, or بهګنړ *bhagærrn*, s.m. (5th) A fly.

بهلول *bhalol*, s. prop. The name of a brother of Maḥmūd of Ghaznī. 2. The name of an Emperor of Hindūstān.

بهم *ba-ham*, adv. (for P باهم), Together, one with another, one against another.

بهنه *bahna'h*, s.f. (3rd) A boy's top. Pl. ئ *ey*. See لاډو

بهوس *bhūs*, s.m. (6th) Bran, husk, chaff. Sing. and Pl. See also بوس (s بهس).

بهول *bahawul*, verb trans. To cause to flow, to glide, float, pass, drive. Pres. بهوي *bahawī*; past وُ بهاوه *wu-bahāwuh*, or وُ بهاوو *wu-bahāwo*; fut. وُ به بهوي *wu bah bahawī*; imp. وُ بهوه *wu-bahawah*; act. part. بهوونکی *bahawūnkaey*, or بهووني *bahawūnaey*; past part. بهولي *bahawulaey*; verb.n. بهونه *bahawuna'h*. See بهيدل

بهئي *baha'ī*, s.f. (6th) A well with steps to go down into. Sing. and Pl.

P بهي *bihī*, s.m. (6th) A quince. Sing and Pl.

بهيانړ *bheārrn*, s.m. (2nd) A colt. Pl. بهيانړونه *bheārrnūnah*; s.f. (3rd) بهيانړه *bheārrna'h*. Pl. بهيانړئ *bheārrney*. See بهانړ

بهيدل *bahedal*, verb intrans. To flow, glide, float, run, pass, drive. Pres. بهيږي *bahejzī* (W.), or بهيګي *bahegī* (E.); past وُ بهيده *wu-bahedah*; fut. وُ به بهيږي *wu bah bahejzī*, or وُ به بهيګي *wu bah bahegī*; imp. وُ بهيږه *wu-bahejzah*, or وُ بهيګه *wu-bahegah*; act. part. بهيدونکی *bahedūnkaey* or بهيدوني *bahedūnaey*; past part. بهيدلي *bahedalaey*; verb. n. بهيدنه *bahedana'h*.

HI بهير *bahīr*, s.m. (2nd) The baggage and materiel of an army. 2. A crowd, a mob, a throng, a multitude. Pl. بهيرونه *bahīrūnah*.

P بي *bey*, prep. Without, out of. When prefixed to words it is equivalent to the English *in*, *un*, *im*, *ir*, *dis*, *less*, etc. بي آب *bey āb*, Without water, lustre, temper, dignity, etc. (See آب). بي آبَ كول *bey āba kawul*, verb trans. To dishonour, disgrace, lower in the estimation of another. بي آبرو *bey āb-rū*, adj. Dishonourable, dishonoured, disgraced. بي آبروي *bey āb-rū-ī*, s.f. (3rd), Disgrace, dishonour. Pl. ئ *a'ī*. بي آبي *bey ābī*, s.f. (3rd) Want of water, lustre, temper, etc. Pl. ئ *a'ī*. بي اتفاق *bey ittifāḳ*, adj. Disagreeing, discordant, at variance, jarring. بي اتفاقي *bey ittifāḳī*, s.f. (3rd) Disagreement, discord, dissonance, discrepancy, discordance. Pl. ئ *a'ī*. بي اثر *bey aṣar*, adj. Without impression, or effect, ineffectual. بي اثري *bey aṣarī*, s.f. (3rd) Inefficiency. Pl. ئ *a'ī*. بي اجل *bey ajal*, Untimely (death). بي احتياط *bey iḥtiyāṭ*, adj. Incautious, improvident, imprudent, rash. بي احتياطي *bey iḥtiyāṭī*, s.f. (3rd) Incautiousness, imprudence, rashness, improvidence. Pl. ئ *a'ī*. بي اختيار *bey ikhtiyār*, adj. Without choice, involuntary. بي اختياري *bey ikhtiyārī*, s.f. (3rd) Without choice or election, helplessness. Pl. ئ *a'ī*. بي ادب *bey adab*, adj. Rude, unmannerly, impudent, presumptuous, disrespectful. بي ادبي *bey adabī*, s.f. (3rd) Rudeness, disrespect, presumptuousness. Pl. ئ *a'ī*. بي آرام *bey ārām*, adj. Restless, uneasy. بي آرامي *bey ārāmī*, s.f. (3rd) Restlessness, uneasiness, disquiet, disease. Pl. ئ *a'ī*. بي اسباب *bey asbāb*, adj. Without necessaries. بي اسبابي *bey asbābī*, s.f. (3rd) Want of goods or necessaries. Pl. ئ *a'ī*. بي اعتبار *bey iætibār*, adj. Of no credit or estimation, not to be relied on. بي اعتباري *bey iætibārī*, s.f. (3rd) Discredit, distrust, dishonesty. Pl. ئ *a'ī*. بي اعتدال *bey iætidāl*, adj. Unequal, unequal. بي اعتدالي *bey iætidālī*, s.f. (3rd) Unevenness, inequality, Pl. ئ *a'ī*. بي اعتقاد *bey iætiḳād*, adj. Incredulous, disbelieving. بي اعتقادي *bey iætiḳādī*, s.f. (3rd) Incredulity, disbelief. Pl. ئ *a'ī*. بي اعتماد *bey iætimād*, adj. Distrustful, diffident, not relying upon. بي اعتمادي *bey* ness. Pl. ئي a'ī. بي توقع bey tawakkuæ, adj. Hopeless. بي ثبات bey ṣabāt, adj. Unstable, inconstant. بي ثباتي bey ṣabātī, s.f. (3rd) Instability, inconstancy. Pl. ئي a'ī. بي ثمر bey ṣamar, adj. Fruitless. بي ثمري bey ṣamarī, s.f. Fruitlessness. Pl. ئي a'ī. بي څاڅ be-tsāfa, or بي څافه be-tsāfah, adv. Suddenly, unawares, all at once, abruptly, unexpectedly. بي جا bey jā, adj. Ill-placed, misplaced, ill-timed, improper, inaccurate; adv. Inopportunely, improperly. بي جان bey jān, adj. Lifeless, dead, inanimate, faint. بي جرأت bey jur'at, adj. Cowardly, pusillanimous. بي جرأتي bey jur'atī, s.f. (3rd) Want of courage, pusillanimity. Pl. ئي a'ī. بي جرم bey jurm, adj. Faultless, innocent. بي جرمي bey jurmī, s.f. (3rd) Innocence. Pl. ئي a'ī. بي جگر bey jigar, adj. Coward, timid, poor-spirited, pusillanimous. بي جگري bey jigarī, s.f. (3rd) Want of courage, poltroonery, spiritlessness. Pl. ئي a'ī. بي جواب bey jawāb. adj. Without answer, unable to answer. بي جوابي bey jawābī, s.f. (3rd) The being without answer. Pl. ئي a'ī. بي چاره bey chārah, adj. Without choice or remedy, helpless, poor. بي چارگي bey chāragī, s.f. (3rd) Helplessness, necessity. Pl. ئي a'ī. بي چون bey chūn, adj. Incomparable, inscrutable. بي چگون bey chigūn, adj. Incomprehensible, unparalleled. بي حال bey ḥāl, adj. Out of condition, ill-circumstanced, indisposed. بي حالي bey ḥālī, s.f. (3rd) Badness of circumstances or condition. Pl. ئي a'ī. بي حجاب bey ḥijāb, adj. Unveiled. بي حجابي bey ḥijābī, s.f. (3rd) Appearing unveiled, immodesty. Pl. ئي a'ī. بي حد bey ḥadd, adj. Boundless. بي حركت bey ḥarakat, adj. Immovable. بي حركتي bey ḥarakatī, s.f. (3rd) Want of motion. Pl. ئي a'ī. بي حرمت bey ḥurmat, adj. Disgrace. بي حرمتي bey ḥurmatī, s.f. (3rd) Disgrace, dishonour. Pl. ئي a'ī. بي حس bey ḥiss, adj. Insensible, senseless. بي حساب bey ḥisāb, adj. Countless, beyond calculation, immoderate, inconsistent. بي حسابي bey ḥisābī, s.f. (3rd) Countlessness, immoderation, inconsistency. Pl. ئي a'ī. بي حكمت bey ḥikmat, adj. Unskilful. بي حواس bey ḥawāss, adj. Out of one's senses, beside one's-self. بي حواسي bey ḥawāssī, s.f. (3rd) Distraction of mind, senselessness, insensibility. Pl. ئي a'ī. بي حيا bey ḥayā, adj. Shameless, immodest, impudent, barefaced. بي حيائي bey ḥayā-ī, s.f. (3rd) Shamelessness, barefacedness, impudence, immodesty. Pl. ئي a'ī. بي خار bey khār, adj. Without anxiety, without thorns, without fear or solicitude. بي خان و مان bey khān ow mān, adj. Houseless, destitute. بي ختي bey khuttey, adj. Castrated, an eunuch. بي ختي كول bey khuttey kawul, verb trans. To castrate, to geld. بي خبر bey khabar, adj. Without intelligence, senseless, incautious, careless, heedless, imprudent, uninformed, ignorant, stupid, unwitting. بي خبري bey khabarī, s.f. (3rd) Imprudence, carelessness, heedlessness, stupidity. Pl. ئي a'ī. بي خرڅه bey khartsah, or بي خرچه bey kharchah, adj. Without money. بي خرڅي bey khartsī, or بي خرچي bey kharchī, s.f. (3rd) Want of pay or wages. Pl. ئي a'ī. بي خطا bey khaṭā, adj. Unerring. بي خطر bey khaṭar, or بي خطره bey khaṭrah, adj. Free from danger, safe, fearless. بي خواب bey khwāb, adj. Sleepless. بي خوابي bey khwābī, s.f. (3rd) Sleeplessness. Pl. ئي a'ī. بي خواهش bey khwāhish, Without inclination or spirit, without pursuit, object, or hobby. بي خود bey khūd, adj. Beside one's-self, out of one's mind, enraptured, senseless, delirious. بي خودي bey khūdī, s.f. (3rd) The being beside one's-self, alienation of mind, ecstacy, rapture, senselessness, delirium. Pl. ئي a'ī. بي خوند bey khwand, adj. Without flavour, insipid, tasteless. بي خوندي bey khwandī, s.f. (3rd) Want of flavour, insipidity, tastelessness. Pl. ئي a'ī. بي خور و خواب bey khūr ow khwāb, adj. Without inclination for sleep or food, restless. بي خويش *bey <u>kh</u>wesh*, adj. Friendless. بي داد *bey dād*, Iniquity, injustice. 2. adj. Unjust, not doing justice, lawless. بي دادگر *bey dād-gar*, adj. An oppressor; (Fem.) بي دادگره *bey dād gara'h*. بي دادگري *bey dād-garī*, s.f. (3rd) Oppression. Pl. ئ *a'ī*. بي دادي *bey dādī*, s.f. (3rd) Injustice, lawlessness. Pl. ئ *a'ī*. بي داغ *bey dāgh*, adj. Spotless. بي دانه *bey dānah*, adj. Grainless, seedless (as fruit). بي درنگ *bey drang*, adj. Without delay. بي دريغ *bey daregh*, adj. Unsparing, ungrudging, liberal. 2. Pitiless, unmerciful. بي دست و پا *bey dast ow pā*, adj. (Having neither hands nor feet), helpless, without power or authority. بي دستور *bey dastūr*, adj. Ill-bred, unusual. بي دعوي *bey daæwā*, adj. Free from claims. بي دل *bey dil*, adj. Heartless, dispirited, dejected, sad. بي دلي *bey dilī*, s.f. (3rd) Heartlessness, dejection. Pl. ئ *a'ī*. بي دم *bey dam*, adj. Breathless. بي دمي *bey damī*, s.f. Breathlessness. Pl. ئ *a'ī*. بي دماغ *bey dimāgh*, adj. Ill-tempered, impatient, irritable, easily provoked. بي دماغي *bey dimāghī*, s.f. (3rd) Ill-temper, irritability, impatience. Pl. ئ *a'ī*. بي دوا *bey dawā*, adj. Incurable. بي دولت *bey dawlat*, adj. Unfortunate. بي دولتي *bey dawlatī*, s.f. (3rd) Bad luck. Pl. ئ *a'ī*. بي دهشت *bey dah<u>sh</u>at*, adj. Fearless. بي ديانت *bey diyānat*, adj. Irreligious, unjust. بي دين *bey dīn*, adj. Irreligious. بي دول *bey <u>dd</u>awl*, adj. Shapeless, ugly, uneducated, ill-bred, unpleasant. بي راه *bey rāh*, adj. Erring, astray, dissolute, unprincipled. بي راهي *bey rāhī*, s.f. (3rd) Error, wandering, dissoluteness. Pl. ئ *a'ī*. بي رتبه *bey rutbah*, adj. Without dignity or rank, worthless. بي رحم *bey raḥm*, adj. Merciless, cruel. بي رحمي *bey raḥmī*, s.f. (3rd) Cruelty. Pl. ئ *a'ī*. بي رضا *bey raẓā*, adj. Without leave. بي روي *bey rū'e*, adj. Without shame, shameless, inhuman. بي روئي *bey rū-ī*, s.f. (3rd) Shamelessness, inhumanity. Pl. ئ *a'ī*. بي ريا *bey ri-yā*, adj. Without guile, guileless, candid, sincere. بي ريائي *bey riyā-ī*, s.f. (3rd) Sincerity, candour. Pl. ئ *a'ī*. بي ريب و ريا *bey raib ow ri-yā*, adj. Without guile or deceit. بي ريشه *bey re<u>sh</u>ah*, adj. Without fibre. بي زبان *bey zabān*, adj. Mute, without language. بي زباني *bey zabānī*, s.f. (3rd) Inability to speak, dumbness. Pl. ئ *a'ī*. بي زر *bey zar*, adj. Poor, helpless. بي زن و فرزند *bey zan ow farzand*, adj. Without wife or children, بي زوال *bey za-wāl*, adj. Imperishable, unchangeable. بي زور *bey zor*, adj. Weak, impotent. بي زهره *bey zahrah*, adj. Without gall or bile, patient, good-tempered, forbearing, indefatigable, shameless. بي زيب و زينت *bey zeb ow zīnat*, adj. Ugly and awkward, inelegant in dress and person. بي زين *bey zīn*, adj. Unsaddled. بي ځان *bey <u>dz</u>ān*, adj. Lifeless, inanimate, faint, dead. بي ځگر *bey <u>dz</u>igar*, adj. Coward, timid, poor-spirited. بي سبب *bey sabab*, adj. Causeless. بي ستر *bey satr*, adj. Unveiled, exposed. بي ستري *bey satrī*, s.f. (3rd) Unveiling, exposure, dishonour. Pl. ئ *a'ī*. بي سترګو *bey stargo*, adj. Blind, without eyes. بي سخن *bey su<u>kh</u>an*, adj. Taciturn. بي سر *bey sar*, adj. Peerless, unequalled. بي سر و پا *bey sar ow pā*, adj. Impotent, destitute, very wretched. بي سلوك *bey sulūk*, adj. Ill-behaved, wicked, sinful. بي شرم *bey <u>sh</u>arm*, adj. Shameless, impudent, immodest. بي شرمي *bey <u>sh</u>armī*, s.f. (3rd) Impudence, shamelessness, immodesty. Pl. ئ *a'ī*. بي شعور *bey <u>sh</u>uæūr*, adj. Ignorant, uninformed; a blockhead. بي شعوري *bey <u>sh</u>uæūrī*, s.f. (3rd) Ignorance, stupidity. Pl. ئ *a'ī*. بي شفقت *bey <u>sh</u>afakat*, adj. Unkind, unmerciful, harsh. بي شكه *bey <u>sh</u>akkah*, adj. Doubtless, indubitable, certain. بي شك و شبه *bey <u>sh</u>akk ow <u>sh</u>ubah*, adj. Doubtless, indubitable, certain. بي شگون *bey <u>sh</u>ugūn*, adj. Ill-omened, unlucky. بي شمار *bey <u>sh</u>umār*, adj. Countless, numberless, much. بي صبر *bey ṣabr*, adj. Impatient, restless. بي صبري *bey* *ṣabr-ī*, s.f. (3rd) Impatience, restlessness. Pl. ئي *a'ī*. بي صرفه *bey ṣarfah*, adj. Unprofitable. بي صلاح *bey ṣalāḥ*, adj. Ill-advised, headstrong. بي ضابطه *bey ẓābiṭah*, adj. Irregular, unlawful. بي طـاقت *bey ṭāḳat*, adj. Powerless, weak. بي طاقتي *bey ṭāḳat-ī*, s.f. (3rd) Weakness. Pl. ئي *a'ī*. بي طالع *bey ṭāliæ*, adj. Unlucky, unfortunate. بي طرح *bey ṭaraḥ*, or بي طور *bey ṭaur*, adj. Ill-mannered, unmannerly, uncivil, rude, awkward. بي طوري *bey ṭaurī*, s.f. Incivility, rudeness. Pl. ئي *a'ī*. بي طمع *bey ṭamaæ*, adj. Free from covetousness, disinterested. بي طمعي *bey ṭamaæī*, s.f. (3rd) Freedom from covetousness, disinterestedness. Pl. ئي *a'ī*. بي عبرت *bey æibrat*, adj. Unawed, not warned by example. بي عدل *bey æadl*, adj. Unjust, lawless. بي عزت *bey æizzat*, adj. Without honour, disgrace. بي عزتي *bey æizzatī*, s.f. (3rd) Dishonour, disgrace. Pl. ئي *a'ī*. بي عقل *bey æaḳl*, adj. Stupid. بي عقلي *bey æaḳlī*, s.f. (3rd) Stupidity. Pl. ئي *a'ī*. بي علم *bey æilm*, adj. Without knowledge, ignorant. بي عمل *bey æamal*, adj. Without practice, or execution. بي عيب *bey æaib*, adj. Faultless, without blemish. بي غايت *bey ghāyat*, adj. Boundless. بي غرض *bey gharaẓ*, adj. Disinterested, impartial, independent, indifferent. بي غرضي *bey gharaẓī*, s.f. (3rd) Disinterestedness, impartiality, indifference. Pl. ئي *a'ī*. بي غـل و غش *bey ghill ow ghishsh*, adj. Without trouble or anxiety, without fraud or hatred. بي غم *bey gham*, adj. Without anxiety or trouble. بي غور *bey ghaur*, adj. Without consideration. بي غيرت *bey ghairat*, adj. Without pride or emulation, spiritless, wanton, impudent, infamous, rude. بي غيرتي *bey ghairatī*, s.f. (3rd) Want of pride, emulation, or spirit; disgrace. Pl. ئي *a'ī*. بي فايده *bey fā-īdah*, adj. Unprofitable, useless, vain. بي فكر *bey fikr*, adj. Thoughtless, contented, tranquil. بي فكري *bey fikr-ī*, s.f. (3rd) Thoughtlessness, contentedness. Pl. ئي *a'ī*. بي فهم *bey fahm*, adj. Stupid, senseless. بي فيض *bey faiẓ*, adj. Unprofitable, possessing but not bestowing. بي قابو *bey ḳābū*, adj. Unable, without, out of one's power, secure against surprise or attack. بي قاعده *bey ḳā-æidah*, adj. Irregular, ungrammatical, unarranged. بي قدر *bey ḳadr*, adj. Worthless, unimportant. بي قدري *bey ḳadrī*, s.f. (3rd) Worthlessness, low estimation. Pl. ئي *a'ī*. بي قرار *bey ḳarār*, adj. Inconstant, variable, unsettled, restless, out of patience, uneasy, anxious, distracted. بي قراري *bey ḳarārī*, s.f. (3rd) Instability, inconstancy, variableness, restlessness, uneasiness, anxiety. Pl. ئي *a'ī*. بي قصور *bey ḳuṣūr*, adj. Faultless, innocent, without fail, entirely, completely. بي قلعي *bey ḳalæ-ī*, adj. Untinned. بي قوت *bey ḳūwat*, adj. Powerless, weak. بي قول *bey ḳaul*, adj. Faithless, perfidious. بي قياس *bey ḳiyās*, adj. Inconceivable, contrary to the common order of things, incomprehensible, immense, exorbitant. بي قيد *bey ḳaid*, adj. Unrestrained, irregular, dissolute, licentious. بي كار *bey kār*, adj. Unemployed. بي كاري *bey kārī*, s.f. (3rd) Want of employment, idleness. Pl. ئي *a'ī*. بي كام *bey kām*, adj. Disappointed. بي كس *bey kas*, adj. Friendless, forlorn. بي كسي *bey kasī*, s.f. (3rd) Forlorn, friendless state, destitution. Pl. ئي *a'ī*. بي كفني *bey kafanī*, s.f. (3rd) The being buried without a shroud. Pl. ئي *a'ī*. بي گاه *bey gāh*, adj. Untimely, unseasonably. بي گمان *bey gumān*, adj. Without doubt or suspicion, doubtless. بي گناه *bey gunāh*, adj. Innocent, guiltless. بي گناهي *bey gunāh-ī*, s.f. (3rd) Innocence, guiltlessness. Pl. ئي *a'ī*. بي لباس *bey libās*, adj. Naked, without clothing. بي لباسي *bey libāsī*, s.f. (3rd) Nakedness. Pl. ئي *a'ī*. بي لحاظ *bey liḥāẓ*, adj. Inattentive, indiscreet, unmannerly. بي لطف *bey lutf*, adj. Unkind, inelegant. بي لطفي *bey luṭ-fī*, s.f. Unkindness. Pl. ئي *a'ī*. بي لگام *bey lagām*, adj. Unbridled, licentious, intemperate. بي مايه *bey māyah*, adj. Without funds or substance, poor. بي مايگي *bey māyagī*, s.f. (3rd) Poverty. Pl. ئي *a'ī*. بي مثال *bey miṡāl*, adj. Incomparable. بي محل *bey maḥall*, adj. Out of place; adv. Improperly. بي مخ *bey makh*, adj. Without face, shameless, inhuman. بي مروت *bey murūwat*, adj. Unkind, inhuman, cruel, unpolite, uncivil. بي مزه *bey mazah*, adj. Insipid, tasteless, displeased. بي مزگي *bey mazagī*, s.f. (3rd) Insipidity, tastelessness; coolness (between friends), disgust. Pl. ئي *a'ī*. بي معني *bey maænī*, adj. Unmeaning, absurd, foolish, idle, vain. بي مقدور *bey maḳdūr*, adj. Without authority, without resource, poor, miserable. بي منت *bey minnat*, adj. Independent, unwilling to incur obligation. بي موجب *bey mūjib*, adj. Causeless, without reason. بي موسم *bey mausim*, adj. Out of season, unseasonably. بي موقع *bey maukiæ*, adj. Out of season, out of place, unapt, inopportune, inconvenient. بي مهر *bey mihr*, adj. Unkind, unfriendly. بي مهري *bey mihr-ī*, s.f. (3rd) Unkindness. Pl. ئي *a'ī*. بي نام *bey nām*, adj. Without character or reputation, inglorious. بي نام و نشان *bey nām ow nishān*, adj. Without name or character. بي ناموسي *bey nāmūsī*, s.f. (3rd) Disgrace, dishonour. Pl. ئي *a'ī*. بي نصيب *bey naṣīb*, adj. Without portion or lot, unfortunate, frustrated. بي نصيبي *bey naṣībī*, s.f. (3rd) Misfortune. Pl. ئي *a'ī*. بي نظير *bey naẓīr*, adj. Incomparable. بي نقصان *bey nuḳṣān*, adj. Without loss or injury. بي نمک *bey namak*, adj. Saltless, insipid, ugly, ordinary. بي ننگ *bey nang*, adj. Shameless. بي ننگ و ناموس *bey nang ow nāmūs*, adj. Without name or character. بي نوا *bey nawā*, adj. Without provisions or furniture, without prosperity, indigent, destitute. بي نوائي *bey nawā'ī*, s.f. (3rd) Indigence, beggary. Pl. ئي *a'ī*. بي نوري *bey nūr-ī*, s.f. Absence or want of light. Pl. ئي *a'ī*. بي نهايت *bey nihāyat*, adj. Without bounds, endless. بي نياز *bey niyāz*, adj. Wanting and asking nothing, not in need, independent. بي نيازي *bey niyāzī*, s.f. (3rd) Independence. Pl. ئي *a'ī*. بي وجه *bey wajah*, adj. Without cause or reason. بي وطن *bey waṭan*, adj. Without a home, an exile. بي وطني *bey waṭanī*, s.f. (3rd) Exile, banishment. Pl. ئي *a'ī*. بي وفا *bey wafā*, adj. Faithless, perfidious, treacherous, traitor, ungrateful, ingrate. بي وفائي *bey wafā-ī*, s.f. (3rd) Infidelity, faithlessness, ingratitude, treachery. Pl. ئي *a'ī* بي وقت *bey waḳt*, adj. Out of season, untimely, ill-timed, at an unusual time. بي وقر *bey waḳr*, adj. Without dignity or character, dishonourable. بي وقري *bey waḳr-ī*, s.f. Want of dignity. Pl. ئي *a'ī*. بي وقوف *bey wuḳūf*, adj. Ignorant, foolish, inexpert, stupid, blockhead. بي وقوفي *bey wuḳūfī*, s.f. (3rd) Ignorance, want of understanding, stupidity, folly, foolishness. Pl. ئي *a'ī*. بي ويري *bey weraey*, adj. Fearless, bold, dauntless. بي همال *bey himāl*, adj. Without compeer, unequalled. بي همت *bey himmat*, adj. Pusillanimous, unambitious, humble, lazy, indolent. بي همتي *bey himmatī*, s.f. (3rd) Pusillanimity. Pl. ئي *a'ī*. بي هنر *bey hunar*, adj, Unskilful, unskilled. بي هنري *bey hunarī*, s.f. (3rd) Unskilfulness. Pl. ئي *a'ī*. بي هنگام *bey hangām*, adj. Untimely. بي هوش *bey hosh*, or بي هوښ *bey hosh*, or *bey hokh*, adj. Senseless, stupefied, intoxicated, delirious. بي هوشي *bey hoshī*, or بي هوښي *bey hoshī*, or *bey hokhī*, s.f. (3rd) Senselessness, stupidity, intoxication, delirium, stupefaction. Pl. ئي *a'ī*. بي هيڅ *bey heṯs*, adj. For nothing, without reason. بي ييري *bey yiraey*, adj. Fearless, bold, dauntless. To form the feminine adjective add ه *a'h*.

بيا *bī-ā*, adv. Again, anew, afresh, repeatedly. په بيا بيا *pah bī-ā bī-ā*, Ever and anon, time after time, oft-times, frequently, repeatedly.

P بيابان *bayā-bān*, s.m. (2nd) A desert, a wilderness. Pl. بيابانونه *bayā-bānūnah*. بياباني *bayā-bānī*, adj. Of the desert, wild.

بياتي *biā-tī*, s.f. (3rd) Scissors, shears. Pl. ئي *a'ī*.

بيارته *bī-ārtah*, adv. Back, again, beyond, apart,

asunder, away, aside. بيارته شه *bī-ārtah shah,* Get away, avaunt! بيارته راغلل *bī-ārtah rāghlal,* verb intrans. To return, to come back. بيارتد كول *bī-ārtah kawul,* verb trans. To put asunder, apart, aside, away. See بيرته.

بياسته *biyāsta'h,* s.f. (3rd) One of the two ropes which cover the water wheel of a Persian wheel, to which the water-pots are fastened. 2. A rope in general, a cable, a line to hang clothes on. Pl. ې *ey.*

A بياض *bayāẓ,* s.m. (9th) Whiteness, brightness; adj. White, bright; (Fem.) بياضه *bayāẓa'h.*

بيامندل *bī-ā-mundal,* verb trans. To recover, acquire, get, gain, win, receive, retrieve, come in for, obtain, derive. Pres. بيامومي *bī-ā-mūmī*; past بياموند *bī-ā-mūnd*; fut. بيا به مومي *bī-ā bah mūmī*; imp. بيامومه *bī-ā-mūmah*; act. part. بياموندونكى *bī-ā-mūndūn-kaey,* or بياموندونى *bī-ā-mūndūnaey*; past part. بياموندلى *bī-ā-mūndalaey*; verb. n. بياموندنه *bī-ā-mūndana'h.*

A بيان *bayān,* s.m. (2nd) Explanation, relation, exposition. Pl. بيانونه *bayānūnah.* په بيان راوړل *pah bayān rā-w'rral,* verb trans. To relate, expose, tell, explain. بيان كول *bayān kawul,* or بيانول *bayānawul,* verb trans. To relate.

بيان *bī-ān,* s.m. (2nd) A colt, a foal, a filly. Pl. بيانونه *bī-ānūnah*; s.f. (3rd) بيانه *bī-āna'h.* Pl. بياني *bī-āney.* See بهانړ or بهاڼ.

P بي بي *bī bī,* or بيبي *bībī,* s.f. (5th) A lady. Pl. بيبيان *bī-bīyāni.*

بيپرتي *be-partey,* adj. Excessive (eating), eating too much; (Fem.) بيپرتِ *be-parti.* Pl. (Masc. and Fem.) ي *ī.* بيپرتي خوړل *be-partey khwarral,* verb trans. To over-eat, to gormandize.

بيپل *bī-pal,* s.m. (6th) Name of a fruit—Cratæva, or Ægle Marmelos. Sing. and Pl. See also تاك بيل and بلغند.

A بيت *bait,* s.m. (2nd) A house, a temple, an edifice. 2. A couplet, a distich, a verse in poetry. Pl. بيتونه *baitūnah.* بيت الله *baitu-l-lah,* The House of God, the temple of Mekka.

بيت الحرم *bait-ul-ḥaram,* The Sacred House, the temple of Mekka. بيت المال *bait-ul-māl,* An escheat, property that falls to the crown in failure of heirs. بيت المقدس *bait-ul-mukaddas,* The Sacred or Holy House, the temple of Jerusalem.

S بيت *bet,* s.m. (2nd) A cane, a rattan. Pl. بيتونه *bet-ūnah.*

بيټ *baitt,* s. prop. According to Khān Jehān, Lūdhī, (Mirāt-ul-Āfaghānah) the name of one of the sons of Æabd-ur-Rashīd, Patān, the great ancestor of the Afghāns, and the progenitor of the division called *baittinī.* Some authors contend that the son of Æabd-ur-Rashīd referred to, was called Tabrī. See Introduction to my Grammar; also بتن and بتني

بيټني *baittanī,* or *baittinī,* s.m. (1st) The name of a division of the Afghāns, of whom Batān, referred to above, is the progenitor. Pl. ى *aey*; s.f. (6th) ئ *a'ī.* Sing. and Pl.

بيچاړه *bey-chārrna'h,* s.f. (3rd) A bed, bedding, bed-clothes. Pl. ې *ey.* (HI. بچهونه).

P بيخ *bekh,* s.m. (2nd) Root, origin, foundation. Pl. بيخونه *bekhūnah.*

بي خرتى *bey khrataey,* s.m. (1st) An unseasonable business or action. Pl. ي *ī.*

P بيد *bed,* s.m. (5th) A willow, a sort of cane. Sing. and Pl.

P بيدار *bedār,* adj. Awake, watching, wakeful, watchful, sleepless; (Fem.) بيداره *bedāra'h.* بيداريدل *bedāredal,* verb intrans. To wake, to wake up, to become awake, to awaken from sleep. بيدارول *bedārawul,* verb trans. To rouse from sleep, to make to get up, to awaken from sleep.

بيداري *bedārī,* s.f. (3rd) Wakefulness, watchfulness, waking. Pl. ئ *a'ī.*

بيدو *be-dū,* adv. The same, the very same, that very individual, etc., exactly, identical.

بيده *bī-dah,* adj. (W.) Asleep, sleeping, fast asleep, sound asleep, napping. بيده كيدل *bī-da'h kedal,* verb intrans. To fall or go to sleep, to drop off to sleep, to slumber, to take a nap. بيده كول *bī-da'h kawul,* verb trans. To put to sleep, to put to bed, to make or cause to sleep. See اوده and وده.

بيده *beda'h,* s.f. (3rd) A bundle of hay twisted at the time of cutting, the better to preserve it in winter. Pl. بيدې *bedey.*

بيد هوه *bed hawah,* s.m. A paper kite. Pl. بيد هوهګان *bed-hawahgān.* See باد هوا.

بيديا *bedīā,* s.f. (6th) A desert, a wilderness. (E.) Sing. and Pl.; (W.) Pl. بيدياوي *bedīāwī.*

بيرته *bi-yartah,* adv. Back again, beyond, apart, asunder, away, aside. بيرته شه *bi-yartah shah,* interj. Get out! get away! avaunt! بيرته راغلل *bi-yartah rāgh-lal,* verb intrans. To return, to come back. بيرته كول *bi-yartah kawul,* verb trans. To put asunder, apart, aside, away. See also بيارته.

بيرغ *bai-ragh,* s.m. (2nd) (corrup. of P بيرق) A banner, an ensign, a standard. Pl. بيرغونه *bai-raghūnah.*

P بيرق *bairak,* s.m. (2nd) A standard, a flag, a banner, an ensign, colours. Pl. بيرقونه *bairakūnah.* See also جنده.

بيرړ or بيرڼ *beyrarrn,* s.m. (6th) A kind of grass. Sing. and Pl.

بيرو *bey-rū,* adj. Uncouth, rude, uncivilized; (Fem.) بيروه *bey-rūa'h.* See بيروي.

بيره *bīra'h,* s.f. (3rd) A fruit—the lote or jujube. Pl. ې *ey.* See بده بيره and كركنره.

بيړه *berra'h,* s.f. (3rd) A raft, a float. (S بيڑا). Pl. ې *ey.*

بيړۍ *berra'ī,* s.f. (6th) A boat, a ship. Sing. and Pl.

بيزل *bezal,* verb trans. To darn, to fine-draw. Pres. بيزي *bezī*; past و بيزه *wu-bezah*; fut. و به بيزي *wu bah bezī*; imp. و بيزه *wu-bezah*; act. part. بيزونكي *bezūnkaey* or بيزوني *bezūnaey*; past part. بيزلي *bezalaey*; verb. n. بيزنه *bezana'h.*

بيزو *bīzo,* s.m. (5th) A monkey. Pl. بيزوګان *bīzogān*; s.f. (5th) بيزو *bīzo.* Pl. بيزوګاني *bīzogānī.* See بزو, بز and شادو.

P بيزار *bezār,* adj. Displeased, angry, out of humour, disgusted, (vulg.) sick; (Fem.) بيزاره *bezāra'h.* بيزار كيدل *bezār kedal,* verb intrans. To become disgusted, displeased. بيزار كول *bezār kawul,* verb trans. To displease, vex, etc. See also ويزار.

P بيزاري *bezārī,* s.f. (3rd) Displeasure, disgust, vexation, anger, ill-humour. Pl. ئ *a'ī.* See ويزاري.

S بيساك *baisākh,* s.m. (9th) The first solar month of the Hindū year: April—May. The people of the Peshāwer valley, in matters referring to agriculture, use the names of the Hindū months. Sing. and Pl.

بيستۍ *beyasta'ī,* s.f. (6th) A kind of coarse cloth. Sing. and Pl.

P بيش *besh,* adj. More, most. 2. Good, proper, well; (Fem.) بيشه *besha'h.* بيشي *beshī,* s.f. (3rd) Excess, surplus. Pl. ئ *a'ī.*

P بيشه *besha'h,* s.f. (3rd) A forest. Pl. ې *ey.*

بيعه *baiæa'h,* s.f. (3rd) Buying and selling, commerce. Pl. ې *ey.* بيعه نامه *baiæa'h nāmah,* s.f. (3rd) A deed of sale. Pl. ې *ey.* بيعه كيدل *baiæa'h kedal,* verb intrans. To be sold. بيعه كول *baiæa'h kawul,* verb trans. To sell, to dispose of. په بيعه آخستل *pah baiæa'h ākhistal,* verb trans. To purchase, to buy. بيعانه *baiæ-āna'h,* s.f. (3rd) Earnest money. Pl. ې *ey.* (Corrup. of A بيع).

A بيعت *baiæat,* s.m. (2nd) Homage, fealty. Pl. بيعتونه *baiæatūnah.* بيعت كول *baiæat kawul,* verb trans. To become the disciple of anyone, to pay homage.

بيك *beyak,* s.m. (5th) A kind of harpoon with five prongs, called by sailors "grains." Pl. بيكونه *beyakūnah.*

بيګا *begā,* s.m. (2nd) The evening. Pl. بيګاونه *begāūnah.* See also بيګاه.

HI بيګار *beygār,* s.m. (2nd) A person forced to work, or impressed, either with or without pay. Pl. بيګارونه *beygārūnah.* په بيګار نيول *pah beygār nī-wal,* verb trans. To seize labourers by force, to press men for work.

P بيګانګي *begānagī,* s.f. (3rd) Strangeness, the being foreign, not domestic. Pl. ئ *a'ī.*

بيگانه *begānah*, adj. Strange, foreign, unknown, not domestic, not an acquaintance.

بيگاني *begānaey*, adj. Yester, last, last past, next before the present. 2. Left, remaining from the day before. Pl. ي *ī*. بيگاني شپه *begāna'ī shpa'h*, adv. Last night, yesternight. See برني شپه

بيگاه *begāh*, s.m. (2nd) The evening. Pl. بيگاهونه *begāhūnah*.

S بيل *bel*, s.m. (6th) The name of a fruit (Cratæva or Ægle Marmelos). 2. A creeper, a climber. Sing. and Pl. See also تاك, بلاغند and بيپل

بيل *beyal*, adj. Separate, different, away, apart, aside, asunder, absent; (Fem.) بيله *beyala'h*. بيليدل *beyaledal*, verb intrans. To become separated. Pres. بيليږي *beyalejzī* (W.), or بيليگي *beyalegī* (E.); past بيل شه *beyal shah*, or بيل وُ شه *beyal wu-shah*; fut. بيل به شي *beyal bah shī*, or به وُ شي *bah wu-shī*; imp. بيل شه *beyal shah*, or بيل وُ شه *beyal wu-shah*; act. part. بيليدونكَيَ *beyaledūnkaey* or بيليدونيَ *beyaledunaey*; past part. بيل *beyal*, or بيل شويَ *beyal shawaey*; verb. n. بيلېدنه *beyaledana'h*.

بيلول *beyalawul*, verb trans. To separate, to put away or asunder. Pres. بيلوي *beyalawī*; past بيل وُ كړ *beyal wu-karr*, or بيل كړ *beyal karr*; fut. بيل به وُ كړي *beyal bah wu-krrī*, or بيل به كړي *beyal bah krrī*; imp. بيل وُ كړه *beyal wu-krrah*, or بيل كړه *beyal krrah*; act. part. بيلوونكَيَ *beyalawūnkaey*, or بيلوونيَ *beyalawūnaey*; past part. بيل كړيَ *beyal karraey*; verb. n. بيلونه *beyalawuna'h*.

بيلاو *belāw*, s.m. (5th) A hone, a sharpening stone. Pl. بيلاوگان *belāwgān*. See بيلهو

بيلتون *beyaltūn*, s.m. (4th) Separation, disjunction, absence. Pl. بيلتانه *beyaltānah*.

بيلك *be-lak*, s.m. (2nd) A gift, a present of clothes, food, etc., sent by a bridegroom to the bride. 2. A rival, a guardian, an enemy, a back-biter. Pl. بيلكونه *be-lak-ūnah*.

بيلگه *belga'h*, s.f. (3rd) Finding a clue to stolen property; a clue, trace, etc. Pl. ي *ey*. See بلگه

بيلماز *belmāz*, adj. Without prayer, profane, irreligious, unholy; (Fem.) بيلمازه *belmāza'h*. See بلماز

بيله *bela'h*, s.f. (3rd) An island, a delta. Pl. ي *ey*.

بي مخ توب *bey-makh-tob*, s.m. (2nd) Immodesty, shamelessness. Pl. توبونه *tobūnah*.

بيلهو *belho*, s.m. (5th) A hone, a sharpening stone. Pl. بيلهوگان *belhogān*. See بيلاو

P بيم *bīm*, s.m. (2nd) Fear, terror, dread, danger. Pl. بيمونه *bīmūnah*.

P بيمار *bīmār*, adj. Sick, indisposed, ill; (Fem.) بيماره *bīmāra'h*.

بيمار خانه *bīmār khānah*, s.f. (3rd) A hospital. Pl. ي *ey*. بيماريدل *bīmāredal*, verb intrans. To fall sick or ill, to become indisposed. بيمارول *bīmārawul*, verb trans. To make ill or sick, to indispose.

بيماري *bīmārī*, s.f. (3rd) Sickness, illness, disorder, disease, distemper. Pl. ئ *a'ī*.

بيماري سترگي *bīmārey stargey*, s.f. (3rd) Pl. Sleepy or amorous eyes.

بي مخه *bey makhah*, adj. Uncouth, rude, uncivilized. See بيرو

A بين *bain*, prep. Between, betwixt. See ما بين

P بينا *bīnā*, adj. (from ديدن) Seeing, clear-sighted, having sight.

بينائي *bīnā'ī*, s.f. (3rd) Sight, eye-sight. Pl. ئ *a'ī*.

A بين الناس *bain-an-nās*, Amongst men or mankind.

بينش *bainsh*, s.m. (2nd) A beam, a large piece of timber. Pl. بينشونه *bainshūnah*.

بيوره *bew-rah*, adj. Plain, clear, distinct, simple, unreserved (as speech), apparent, manifest, distinctly, explicitly.

A P بي وسعت *bey wusæat*, adj. Without opportunity, latitude, amplitude; (Fem.) بي وسعته *bey-wusæata'h*.

بيول *bī-wal*, verb trans. To take along, conduct, lead, convey, remove, transport (peculiar to animate objects). This infinitive is imperfect, and takes many of its inflexions from بوتلل, already noticed. Pres. بيائي *bīā-yī*; past بوت *bot* (from بوتلل); fut. بو به زي *bo bah zī*;

imp. بيايه *bī-āyah*; act. part. بيوونکي *bīwūnkaey*, or بيووني *bīwūnaey*; past part. بيولي *bī-walaey*; verb. n. بيونه *bī-wuna'h*.

P بيوه *bewa'h*, s.f. (3rd) A widow. Pl. ې *ey*. See كنده

بيعه *bai'h*, s.f. (3rd) Price, value. (A بيع) Pl. ې *ey*.

بيهند *behandd*. See بهاڼ

P بيهوده *behūdah*, adj. Absurd, vain, foolish, idle, fruitless, unprofitable.

بيهوده گوي *behūdah go-e*, adj. At alker of nonsense, a babbler; (Fem.) بيهوده گويه *behūdah go-ea'h*. بيهوده گوئي *behūdah go'ī*, s.f. (3rd) Talking nonsense, nonsense, absurdity. Pl. ئ *a'ī*. بيهودگي *behūdagī*, s.f. (3rd) Absurdity, nonsense, vanity, unprofitableness. Pl ئ *a'ī*.

پ

پ *pe* is the third letter of the Pushto and Persian alphabets, and has the same pronunciation as English *p*. It is interchangeable with ف, as پتنه for فتنه, etc. It does not occur in either the Arabic or Hebrew alphabets, but corresponds with Sanskrit प.

پَ *pa*, prep. By, with, for, for the sake of. When used combined with کښي *kshey* or *kkhey*, it signifies in, into, within, etc.; and with باندِ *bāndi* or دپاسه *dapāsah*, in, upon, above, over, etc. See په.

P پا *pā*, s.m. (9th) The leg, the foot. Sing. and Pl. See ښپه or پښه. پا بند *pā band*, s.m. (2nd) A rope by which the hind feet of a horse are tied. Pl. بندونه *bandūnah*. 2. adj. Clogged, fettered, bound; (Fem.) پا بنده *pā-banda'h*.

پاتُ *pāto*, past part. and adj. Remaining, left, left behind, residuary, unconsumed, surviving. Also written پاتِ *pāti*. See پاتو and پاتي.

پاتيدل *pātedal*, verb intrans. To remain, be left behind, to survive, to remain unconsumed. Pres. پاتېږي *pātejzī* (W.) پاتيکي *pātegī* (E.); past پاتي شه *pātey shah*, or پاتو شه *pāto shah*, and پاتي وُ شه *pātey wu-shah* or پاتو وُ شه *pāto wu-shah*; fut. پاتي or پاتو به وُ شي *pātey* or *pāto bah wu-shī*; imp. پاتي or پاتو شه *pātey* or *pāto shah*, or پاتي or پاتو وُ شه *pātey* or *pāto wushah*; act. part. پاتيدونکي *pātedūnkaey*, or پاتيدوني *pātedūnaey*; past part. پاتي *pātey*, or پاتو *pāto*, and پاتي شوي *pātey shawaey*, or پاتو شوي *pāto shawaey*; verb. n. پاتيدنه *pāte-dana'h*.

پاتيکيدل *pātekedal*, verb intrans. To remain, to stay. پاتي کول *pātey kawul*, verb trans. To stop, to stay, to keep back. See preceding.

پاتا *pātā*, s.f. (6th) The funeral service (from A فاتحه) (E.) Sing. and Pl.; (W.) Pl. پاتاوي *pātāwī*. پاتا کول *pātā kawul*, or پاتا ويل *pātā wa-yal*, verb trans. To offer up prayers for the dead, to perform the funeral service, to make an exordium.

پاتو *pāto*, adj. and past part. Remaining, left, surviving, unconsumed, residuary, left behind. See پاتُ and پاتيدل

پاتو *pātū*, s.m. (5th) A small kind of caterpillar with a red back, and soft like velvet; a scarlet fly, or lady-fly. 2. A bird which cries at night. Pl. پاتوگان *pātū-gān*. See بخملي and باخملي

پاتول *pātawul*, verb trans. To cause or make to remain, to leave or cause to be left, to make or cause to stay, to keep back. Pres. پاتوي *pātawī*; past پاتو كه *pāto kah*, or پاتي کړ *pātey karr*; fut. پاتو or پاتي به کړي *pāto* or *pātey bah krrī*; imp. پاتو كه *pāto kah*, or پاتي کړه *pātey krrah*; act. part. پاتوونکي *pātawūnkaey*, or پاتووني *pātawūnaey*; past part. پاتو *pāto*, or پاتي کړي *pātey karraey*; verb. n. پاتونه *pātawuna'h*.

پاتي *pātey*, adj. and past part. Remaining, left, etc. See پاتو

پاتي *pātaey*, s.m. (1st) A dish of cooked peas or other kind of pulse. 2. Pulse, vetches. Pl. ي *ī*. See پيتي

پاټئ *pātta'ī*, s.f. (3rd) The piece of tape or leather fastened to the strings of a pellet bow for holding the ball; the pan or cup of a sling for holding the stone. See جائي and جئي

پاڅول *pātsawul*, verb trans. To raise, awaken, erect, set upright, stir up, stimulate. Pres. پاڅوي *pātsawī*; past وُ پاڅاوه *wu-pātsāwuh*, or وُ پاڅاوو *wu-pātsāwo*; fut. پا به څوي *pā bah tsawī*, or وُ به پاڅوي *wu bah pātsawī*; imp. وُ پاڅوه *wu-pātsawah*; act. part. پاڅوونکي *pātsawūnkaey*, or پاڅووني *pātsawūnaey*; past part. پاڅولي *pātsawulaey*; verb. n. پاڅونه *pātsawuna'h*.

پاڅيدل *pātsedal*, verb intrans. To rise, arise, uprise, get up, to move from a recumbent to a sitting posture, to get up from a sitting posture. Pres. پاڅي *pātsī*; past وُ پاڅيدَ *wu-pātseda*; fut. پا به څي *pā bah tsī*, or وُ به پاڅي *wu bah pātsī*; imp. وُ پاڅه *wu-pātsah*; act. part. پاڅيدونکي *pātsedūnkaey*, or پاڅيدوني *pātsedūnaey*; past part. پاڅيدلي *pātsedalaey*; verb. n. پاڅيدنه *pātsedana'h*.

پاخه *pākhah*, adj. (Pl.) Cooked things. See پوخ and پخه

P پاداش *pādāsh*, s.m. (2nd) Retaliation, recompense, retribution, reward, requital. Pl. پاداشونه *pādāshūnah*.

P پادشاه *pādshāh*, s.m. (5th) A king, sovereign. Pl. پادشاهان *pādshāhān*. See بادشاه

P پادشاهي *pādshāhī*, adj. Royal, regal, imperial. 2. s.f. (3rd) Royalty, empire, reign, sovereignty, kingdom. Pl. ئي *a'ī*.

پارچنګ *pār-chang*, s.m. (2nd) A ladder, steps, a staircase, a flight of steps. Pl. پارچنګونه *pār-changūnah*. See پوړۍ

پارچنګي *pār-changaey*, s.m. (1st) A small ladder or steps (dimin. of پارچنګ). Pl. ي *ī*. See اندر پايه

P پارچه *pārcha'h*, s.f. (3rd) A fragment, a piece, a scrap, a rag, cloth, clothing. 2. The launder or wooden trough that receives the water from the water-wheel of a Persian wheel. Pl. ي *ey*.

S پارس *pāras*, s.m. (9th) The philosopher's stone. Sing. and Pl.

P پارسا *pārsā*, adj. Abstemious, watchful, chaste; پارسائي *pārsā'ī*, s.f. (3rd) Chastity, purity, abstinence, continence. Pl. ئي *a'ī*.

پارو *pārū*, s.m. (5th) A wooden rake or instrument for raking together. Pl. پاروګان *pārū-gān*.

پارول *pārawul*, verb trans. To set on or at (as a dog), to instigate, irritate, vex, excite, to set by the ears. Pres. پاروي *pārawī*; past وُ پاراوه *wu-pārāwuh*, or وُ پاراوو *wu-pārāwo*; fut. وُ به پاروي *wu bah pārawī*; imp. وُ پاروه *wu-pārawah*; act. part. پاروونکي *pārawūnkaey*, or پاروونی *pārawūnaey*; past part. پارولي *pārawulaey*; verb. n. پارونه *pārawuna'h*. See پرول and پاړهول

P پاره *pāra'h*, s.f. (3rd) A strap, a slip, a bit, a piece, a fragment. Pl. ي *ey*. See پاړه

P پاري *pārī*, part. Succeeding well, anything which happens fortunately.

پاريدل *pāre-dal*, verb intrans. To become vexed, excited, irritated, or instigated. Pres. پاريږي *pārejzī* (W.) or پاريګي *páregī* (E.); past وُ پاريدَ *wu-pāreda*; fut. وُ به پاريږي *wu bah pārejzī*, or وُ به پاريګي *wu bah pāregī*; imp. وُ پاريږه *wu-pārejzah*, or وُ پاريګه *wu-pāregah*; act. part. پاريدونکي *pāredūnkaey*, or پاريدوني *pāredūnaey*; past. part. پاريدلي *pāredalaey*; verb. n. پاريدنه *pāredana'h*.

پاړ بنج *pārr banj*, s.m. (6th) The chestnut tree which bears fruit, a chestnut. Sing. and Pl. See بنج

پاړو *pārrū*, s.m. A snake-charmer, a juggler. 2. Charming, juggling. Pl. پاړوګان *pārrū-gān*.

پړول *parrawul*, verb trans. To charm, to juggle.

پاړه *pārra'h*, s f. (3rd), A piece or portion of land left unploughed, or patches left unploughed at the time of ploughing a field. 2. A bad action or affair. 3. A kind of rake. Pl. ي *ey*. See بنج غښي

پاړي *pārraey*, s.m. (3rd) A hog-deer (Cervus porcinus). Pl. ي *ī*.

پازه *pā-zah*, s.m. (6th) Effect, operation (of medicine), impression, result, consequence, force; execution, accomplishment. Sing. and Pl.

پازه لرل *pā-zah laral*, verb trans. To have effect, or impression (to be effective). پازه

کول *pā-zah kawul*, verb trans. To operate, to take effect, to make impression.

پازیکه *pāzīkah*, adj. Clean, pure, chaste. See پاکیزه

پاس *pās*, prep. Above, over, on, aloft, up, at, a-top, upwards. دَ پاسَ *da pāsa*, Upon, over, near, at the top, etc.

پاس *pās*, s.m. (2nd) Anointing a camel with oil and lime as a remedy for mange. 2. The ointment or embrocation used. 3. (P) Guarding, taking care of, respect, observance. Pl. پاسونه *pāsūnah*. See پاسولیَ

پاسته *pāstah*, adj. (Masc. Pl. of پوست *post*) Soft, tender, mild. 2. Gentle, easy; (Fem.) پسته *pasta'h*. Pl. پستيِ *pastey*.

P پاسخ *pā-sukh*, s.m. (2nd) An answer, a reply. Pl. پاسخونه *pā-sukhūnah*.

پاسلول *pās-lawul*, verb trans. To give in charge, to recommend to one's care, to consign, to intrust, to commit, to make over to, to give in trust. Pres. پاسلوي *pāslawī*; past وُ پاسلاوه *wu-pāslāwuh*, or وُ پاسلاوو *wu-pāslāwo*; fut. وُ به پاسلوي *wu bah pāslawī*; imp. وُ پاسلوه *wu-pāslawah*; act. part. پاسلوونکيَ *pāslawūnkaey* or پاسلوونيَ *pāslawūnaey*; past part. پاسلوليَ *pāslawulaey*; verb. n پاسلونه *pāslawuna'h*.

پاسلونه *pāslawuna'h*, s.f. (3rd) (verb. n.) Keeping, charge, care, trust, custody, protection, guarding, preserving. Pl. يِ *ey*.

پاسو *pāsū*, adj. Low-born, mean, ignoble, plebeian, vulgar, obscure.

پاس واليَ *pās wālaey*, s.m. (1st) Partiality, regard, consideration, favoritism, leaning, guardianship. Pl. والي *wālī*.

پاسوان *pāswān*, s.m. (3rd) A sentinel, a watch, a guard, a shepherd. Pl. پاسوانان *pās-wānān*.

پاسواني *pāswānī*, s.f. (3rd) Watch, guard, guarding, the duty of a guard, protection, keeping. Pl. ئِ *a'ī*. پاسواني کول *pāswānī kawul*, verb trans. To keep watch, to guard, to protect.

پاشنه *pāsh-na'h*, s.f. (3rd) The heel of a door which revolves in a socket instead of a hinge. (P. the heel). Pl. يِ *ey*. پاشنه گرد *pāsh-na'h-gard*, s.m. (2nd) The socket in which the heel turns. Pl. پاشنه گردونه *pāsh-na'h-gardūnah*.

پاښ *pāsh* or *pākh*, s. prop. The name of the supposed seat of the Afghān tribes, situate in the district of Rūdah and the highlands of Kāseghar, in the Wuzīrī country, and from which the words Pashto or Pushto, and Pushtūn or Pukhtūn, are supposed to be derived. It is also written پښ *push* and *pukh*.

P پاغنده *pā-ghunda'h*, s.f. (3rd), A roll of carded cotton. Pl. يِ *ey*.

P پاك *pāk*, adj. Pure, clean, holy, innocent, spotless, immaculate, fair; (Fem.) پاکه *pāka'h*.

پاك دامن *pāk dāman*, adj. Pure, chaste, innocent, holy in life, modest; (Fem.) پاك دامنه *pāk dāmana'h*. پاکي *pākī*, s.f. (3rd) Purity, chastity, innocence, spotlessness, fairness. Pl. ئِ *a'ī*.

پاکول *pākawul*, verb trans. To purify, cleanse, clear, wash, make clean. Pres. پاکوي *pākawī*; past پاك وُ کړ *pāk wu-karr*, or پاك کړ *pāk karr*; fut. پاك به کړي *pāk bah krrī*, or پاك به وُ کړي *pāk bah wu-krrī*; imp. پاك وُ کړه *pāk wu-krrah*, or پاك کړه *pāk krrah*; act. part. پاکوونکيَ *pākawūnkaey*, or پاکوونيَ *pāka-wūnaey*; past part. پاك کړيَ *pāk karraey*; verb. n. پاکونه *pākawana'h*.

پاکيدل *pākedal*, verb intrans. To become cleansed, purified, cleared, washed, made clean. Pres. پاکيږي *pākejzī* (W.), or پاکيگي *pākegī* (E.); past پاك وُ شه *pāk wu-shah*, or پاك شه *pāk shah*; fut. پاك به وُ شي *pak bah wu-shī*, or پاك به شي *pāk bah shī*; imp. پاك وُ شه *pāk wu-shah*, or پاك شه *pāk shah*; act. part. پاکيدونکيَ *pākedūnkaey*, or پاکيدونيَ *pākedūn-aey*; past part. پاك *pāk*, or پاك شويَ *pāk shawaey*; verb. n. پاکيدنه *pākedana'h*.

P پاکيزه *pākīzah*, adj. Clean, pure, chaste. پاکيزه خصلت *pākīzah khaṣlat*, Of chaste habits or disposition. See پازيکه

پال *pāl*, s.m. (2nd) Abstinence, continence, forbearance. 2. An omen, augury, presage. 3. Enchantment. Pl. پالونه *pālūnah*. پال

آچول پال *pāl ā͟chawul,* or پال نيول *pāl nī-wul,* verb trans. To take an omen.

پالكانه *pāl-kāna'h,* s.f. (3rd) A high roof. 2. A window. Pl. ي *ey.*

پالل *pālal,* verb trans. To preserve, protect, rear, bring up, cherish, nourish, educate, breed, patronize. Pres. پالي *pālī*; past وُ پاله *wu-pālah,* or وُ پالَ *wu-pāla*; fut. وُ به پالي *wu bah pālī*; imp. وُ پاله *wu-pālah*; act. part. پالونكي *pālūnkaey,* or پالوني *pālūnaey*; past part. پاللي *pālalaey*; verb. n. پالنه *pālana'h.*

پالنگ *pālang,* s.m. (2nd) A bed, a bedstead, a coverlet, a counterpane. (HI پلنگ). Pl. پالنگونه *pālangūnah.* See also پهلنگ

پالنگ پوښ *pālang po͟sh* (W.), or *po͟kh* (E.), s.m. (2nd) A coverlet, a quilt, a counterpane. Pl. پالنگ پوښونه *pālang-po͟khūnah,* or *pālang-po͟shūnah.*

پالنه *pālana'h,* s.f. (3rd) (verb. n. of پالل) Bringing up, preserving, preservation, cherishing, rearing, breeding, nourishing, education. (S पालन). Pl. ي *ey.*

پالوده *pālūda'h,* s.f. (3rd) A kind of sloe. 2. A kind of sweetmeat. Pl. ي *ey.*

پاله *pāla'h,* s.f. (3rd) A kind of plough-share. Pl. ي *ey.* See سسپار

پانښنبه *pān͟shanba'h,* s.f. Friday. (P پنجشنبه). Pl. ي *ey.*

پانه *pāna'h,* s.f. (3rd) A wedge for splitting wood. 2. A mode of torture. Pl. ي *ey.* پانه وركول *pāna'h war-kawul,* verb trans. To split with a wedge. 2. To torture.

پاړ *pā͟rrn,* s.m. (2nd) The steep or scarped bank of a river, etc. Pl. پاړونه *pā͟rrn-ūnah.*

پاړه *pā͟rrna'h,* s.f. (3rd) The leaf of a tree or plant, the leaf of a book. Pl. ي *ey.* د مزري پاړه *da mazarī pā͟rrna'h,* A kind of aloe (Aloe perfoliata).

S پاو *pā-o,* s.m. (2nd) A quarter, a fourth part. Pl. پاوونه *pā-o-ūnah*; Fem. (3rd) پاوه *pāwa'h.* Pl. پاوي *pāwey.* پاو كم دوه *pā-o kam dwah,* One and three-quarters. پنځه پاو *pin͟dzah pā-o,* One and a quarter.

P پائي *pā'e,* s.m. (9th) The foot. 2. Termination, end, extremity, summit. Sing. and Pl. 3. adj. Finished, completed, terminated. پائي بند *pā'e band,* adj. Tied by the leg, encumbered, fettered, captivated. پائي تخت *pā'e ta͟kht,* A royal residence, the seat of government. پائي مال *pā'e māl,* adj. Trampled on, ruined, destroyed. پائي مال كيدل *pā'e māl kedal,* verb intrans. To be ruined, trampled on, destroyed. پائي مال كول *pā'e māl kawul,* verb trans. To ruin, destroy, tread under foot. پائي مالي *pā'e mālī,* s.f. (3rd) Destruction, ravage, ruin. Pl. ئ *a'ī.*

P پاياب *pā-yāb,* adj. Within man's depth, fordable, the depth of water. 2. A ford, the bottom. Pl. پايابونه *pā-yābūnah*; (Fem.) پايابه *pā-yāba'h.*

P پايان *pāyān,* s.m. (2nd) End, extremity, termination, completion. Pl. پايانونه *pāyānūnah.*

پاياو *pā'e-āw,* adj. Fordable, within man's depth, The depth of water; (Fem.) پاياوه *pā'e-āwa'h.* 2. s.m. (2nd) A ford. Pl. پاياوونه *pā'e-āwūnah.*

پايكو *pā'e-ko,* s.f. (5th) A lever for pounding or threshing grain. Pl. پايكوګان *pā'e-ko-gānī,* or پايكوګاني *pā'e-kogānī.*

پايله *pā'e-la'h,* s.f. (3rd) An ornament for the feet with bells. Pl. ي *ey.*

پاينده *pā-yandah,* adj. Durable, permanent, perpetual, constant, firm, remaining.

پاينك *pā'e-nak,* s.m. (2nd) The mounting at the end of the scabbard of a sword, etc. Pl. پاينكونه *pā'e-nakūnah.*

پايه *pā-ya'h,* s.f. (3rd) A step. 2. Rank, dignity. 3. Basis, foundation. Pl. ي *ey.*

پائي *pā'ī,* s.f. (3rd) A halter. Pl. ئ *a'ī.* See كبي, كپي and خپي

پائي خيل *pā'ī ͟khel,* s.m. (6th) The name of a tribe of Afghāns. Sing. and Pl. Fem. (3rd) پائي خيله *pā'ī ͟khela'h,* A female of the above. Pl. ي *ey.*

پائيدل *pā'edal,* verb intrans. To remain, last, endure, stand, survive, dwell, bide, stop, tarry, subsist. Pres. پائي *pā'yī*; past وُ پائيدَ *wu-pā'eda*; fut. وُ به پائي *wu bah pā'yī*; imp. وُ پايه *wu-pā-yah*; act. part. پائيدونكي *pā'e-*

dūnkaey, or پائيدونَي *pā'edūnaey*; past part. پائيدلَي *pā'edalaey*; verb. n. پائيدنه *pā'edana'h*.

پائيدنه *pā'edana'h*, s.f. (3rd) (verb. n.) Permanence, endurance, preservation, stability, dwelling, stopping, tarrying. Pl. ئ *ey*.

پبله باندي *pablah bāndey*, adj. Fold upon fold, piled up, folded (correctly په بله باندي *pah balah bāndey*). See also زبله باندي and پرله باندي

پبي *pabī*, s.m. (1st) Pl. The name of a tribe of Afghāns. پبَي *pabaey*, Sing. A male of the above. 2. The name of a large village 16 miles east of Peshāwer, on the high road to Attak; s.f. (6th) پبئي *pabā'ī*, A female of the above. Sing. and Pl.

s پت *pat*, s.m. (2nd) Good name, honour, character, reputation. Pl. پتونه *patūnah*.

پتاو *pitā-o*, s.m. (2nd) Sunshine, a place exposed to the sun. Pl. پتاوونه *pitā-o-ūnah*. پتاو کول *pitā-o kawul*, or پتاو ته کښيناستل *pitā-o tah kkhenāstal*, or *kshenāstal*, verb trans. To bask in the sunshine.

پترَي *patraey*, s.m. (1st) A clamp or binding of iron or brass, the boss of a shield. (s पत्र). Pl. ي *ī*.

s پتنګ *patang*, s.m. (5th) A moth; a paper kite. Pl. پتنګان *patangān*. See اور پبست and ياد هوه

پتنه *pitna'h*, s.f. (3rd) Sedition, mutiny, mischief, perfidy. (A فتنه). Pl. ئ *ey*. پتنه آچول *pitna'h āchawul*, or پتنه کول *pitna'h kawul*, verb trans. To create a mutiny, to get up a sedition. پتنه انګيز *pitna'h-angez*, A fermenter of disturbances, an incendiary, a mischief-maker; (Fem.) پتنه انګيزه *pitna'h-angeza'h*. پتنه انګيزي *pitna'h-angezī*, s.f. (3rd) Sedition, seditiousness, mischievousness. Pl. ئ *a'ī*.

پتنړ or پتړ *patarrn*, s.m. (2nd) The lower part of a spinning wheel. 2. A ferry, a passage across a river. Pl. پتنړونه *pattarrnūnah*.

پتون *patūn*, s.m. (2nd) The thigh of a man, beast, or bird. Pl. پتنونه *patanūnah*. See رون

پتيره *pate-ra'h*, s.f. (3rd) Unleavened bread. Pl. ئ *ey*.

پټ *patt*, s.m. (9th) Affected by a demon, a kind of delirium, demented. Sing. and Pl. پټ نيول *patt nī-wal*, verb trans. To seize a demon or evil spirit; (Eng. verb intrans.) To become possessed.

پټ *patt*, s.m. (2nd) The bark of a tree. Pl. پټونه *pattūnah*.

پټ *putt*, adj. Concealed, hidden, out of sight, secret, clandestine. 2. Covered, closed, veiled, masked, screened, shrouded, shaded, etc.; (Fem.) پټه *putta'h*. سر پټه *sar-putta'h*, s.f. (3rd) A virgin, a maiden (lit. head concealed). Pl. ئ *ey*. پټ پنهم *putt-pinham*, adj. Totally hidden or concealed; (Fem.) پټ پنهمه *putt-pinhama'h*.

پټ والَي *putt wālaey*, s.m. (1st). Pl. والي *wālī*, or پټ تيا *putt tī'ā*, s.f. (6th) Concealment, secrecy, stealth, stealthiness, hiding. (E.) Sing. and Pl.; (W.) Pl. تياوي *tī'āwī*. See پټيدنه

پټ پټانړي *putt pattārrnaey*, s.m. (1st), or پټ پټونړي *putt pattawrrnaey*, s m. (1st) A kind of game played by boys, something similar to hide and seek. Pl. ي *ī*.

پټ ګنئي *putt-gana'ī*, s.f. (6th) An ambush, an ambuscade, cover, lurking place. Sing. and Pl. پټ ګنئي کول *putt-gana'ī kawul*, verb. trans. To lie in ambush, to lurk, to lie in wait for. See پسوني

پټخ *pattakh*, adj. Tough, hard, horny. 2. Faded, decayed, effete, mellow, declining; (Fem.) پټخه *pattakha'h*. پټخيدل *pattakhedal*, verb intrans. To grow tough, hard, horny; to decay, to become faded, mellow, effete, etc. پټخول *pattakhawul*, verb trans. To make or render hard, tough, or horny; to cause decay, etc. پټخ والَي *pattakh-wālaey*, s.m. (1st) Hardness, stiffness, toughness; de cay, decline, mellowness, etc Pl. والي *wālī*.

پټ سپاهي *putt-spāhī*, s.m. (5th) A heavy-armed soldier (lit. a concealed or hidden soldier). Pl. پټ سپاهيان *putt-spāhīān*.

پټول *puttawul*, verb trans. To conceal, hide, secrete, cover, screen, veil, shroud, shade, ensconce, muffle. پټوي *puttawī*; past پټ ؤ کړ

putt wu-karr, or پټ کړ *putt karr*; fut. پټ به وُ کړي *putt bah wu-krrī*, or پټ به کړي *putt bah krrī*; imp. پټ وُ کړه *putt wu-krrah*, or پټ کړه *putt krrah*; act. part. پټوونکي *puttawūnkaey*, or پټووني *puttawunaey*; past part. پټ کړي *putt karraey*; verb. n. پټونه *puttawana'h*.

پټيدل *puttedal*, verb intrans. To be invisible, hidden, or concealed, to lie hidden or concealed, to be covered, secreted, veiled, ensconced, muffled, shrouded, etc. Pres. پټيږي *puttejzī* (W.), پټيګي *puttegī* (E.); past پټ وُ شه *putt wu-shah*, or پټ شه *putt shah*; fut. پټ به وُ شي *putt bah wu-shī*, or پټ به شي *putt bah shī*; imp. پټ وُ شه *putt wu-shah*, or پټ شه *putt shah*; act. part. پټيدونکي *puttedūnkaey*, or پټيدوني *puttedūnaey*; past part. پټ *putt*, or پټ شوي *putt shawaey*; verb. n. پټيدنه *puttedana'h*.

پټيدنه *puttedana'h*, s.f. (3rd) (verb. n.) Concealment, secrecy, stealth, stealthiness, hiding, concealing, shrouding, veiling, etc. Pl. ې *ey*. See پټ والي and پټ تيا

پټکه *pattka'h*, s.f. (3rd) A cloth worn round the waist, a girdle. (s پټکا). Pl. ې *ey*.

پټکي *pattkaey*, s.m. (1st) A small turban. Pl. ي *ī*.

پټکي *pattikī*, adv. Upon the very spot, in place, properly placed. 2. The same, the very same, self-same, no other, identical, that very, etc.

s پټو *pattū*, s.m. (5th) A kind of woollen cloth, or blanket. Pl. پټوګان *pattūgān*.

پټوسکي *pattūskaey*, adj. A few, some, less, a little, an indefinite quantity, a small portion, scanty, thinly scattered, hardly or scarcely any. Pl. ي *ī*; (Fem.) Sing. and Pl. ې *a'ī*. See لکوټي

پټو مهيرګه *patto mahergah*, interj. A term of imprecation, a malediction. See مهيرګه

پټه *patta'h*, s.f. (3rd) A sword belt, the cross belt of a soldier. Pl. ې *ey*.

پټي *pattaey*, s.m. (1st) A field, a portion of land, an estate, a field sown or prepared for sowing. Pl. ي *ī*.

پټۍ *patta'ī*, s.f. (6th) The alphabet. 2. A bandage for a wound, a fillet. Sing. and Pl.

پټيره *pattera'h*, s.f. (3rd) The upper or roof beam of a building. Pl. ې *ey*. See بينش

پټي لنړ *pattey larrn*, s.m. (2nd) A weaver's beam. Pl. پټي لنړونه *pattey-larrnūnah*. See پلي تنړ

پڅ *pats*, adj. Blunt, obtuse, dull, abrupt; (Fem.) پڅه *patsa'h*. پڅه ژبه *patsa'h jzaba'h*, A blunt or abrupt word, or not plainly spoken.

پڅيدل *patsedal*, verb intrans. To grow or become blunt, dull, obtuse, abrupt, etc. پڅول *patsawul*, verb trans. To make or render blunt, dull, obtuse, abrupt.

پڅ والي *pats wālaey*, s.m. (1st) Bluntness, obtuseness, dullness, stupidity, abruptness. Pl. والي *wālī*.

پڅاړني *patsārrney*, adj. Scarce, not plentiful, few, less, a little, a small portion, an indefinite quantity, thinly scattered, hardly or scarcely any, etc; (Fem.) پڅاړنۍ *patsārrna'ī*. See لږ, پټوسکي and لکوټي

پڅکه *pits-ka'h*, s.f. (3rd) A point, nib, spike, a cone, peak, corner, end, extremity. Pl. ې *ey*.

پڅکي *pits-kaey*, s.m. (1st) (E.) Point, nib, cone, corner, end, extremity. Pl. ي *ī*. See preceding.

پڅړني *patsarrney*, adj. See پڅاړني

پجه *paja'h*, s.f. (3rd) A brick-kiln, a furnace. Pl. ې *ey*.

s پچواړۍ *pachwārra'ī*, s.f. (6th) The heel ropes of a horse. Sing. and Pl. See پيچواړۍ

پچوري *pachoraey*, s.m. (1st) A veil, a sheet, a mantle, generally made of chintz. Pl. ي *ī*. See پروني and چهاپل

پچه *pacha'h*, s.f. (3rd) The orbicular dung of sheep, goats, deer, hares, etc. 2. The fret or agitation on the surface of water from a light air or breeze, ripple, undulation. Pl. ې *ey*. پچه کيدل *pacha'h kedal*, verb intrans. To ripple, to fret on the surface, to become agitated as water. پچه کول *pacha'h kawul*, verb trans. To ripple, or cause to ripple, to agitate the surface of fluids. پچي پچي *pachey pachey*, In ripples.

پخ *pækh*, s.m. (2nd) Scab, mange. Pl. پخونه *pækhūnah*.

پخ pa*kh*, s.m. (5th) The spit or hiss of a cat when making an attack. Pl. پخهار pa*kh*ahār. پخ وهل pa*kh* wahal, verb trans. To spit or make a hissing noise like a cat.

پخپلَ pa*kh*pula, or پخپله pa*kh*pulah, adv. Spontaneously, of one's own accord or free will, voluntarily, of thine, his, or her own accord, of itself, etc. See خپل

پخنگي pu*kh*tagī, s.f. (3rd) Maturity, ripeness, experience, expertness, the being cooked. Pl. ئ a'ī. See پوخ والي

P پخته pu*kh*tah, adj. Dressed (as victuals), baked, ripe; shrewd, knowing, expert, wise, firm, strong, solid. Pl. پختگان pu*kh*tagān.

پخساك pa*kh*sāk, s.m. (2nd) Affliction, distress, sorrow, grief, woe, solicitude, yearning, pining, inclination, care, anxiety. Pl. پخساكونه pa*kh*-sākūnah. See پسخاك and پخشاك

پخسيدل pa*kh*sedal, verb intrans. To grieve, fret, pine, yearn, to be desirous, to have strong inclination. Pres. پخسيږي pa*kh*se*jz*ī (W.), or پخسيگي pa*kh*segī (E.); past وُ پخسيده wu-pa*kh*sedah; fut. وُ به پخسيږي wu bah pa*kh*-se*jz*ī, or وُ به پخسيگي wu bah pa*kh*segī; imp. وُ پخسيږه wu-pa*kh*se*jz*ah, or وُ پخسيگه wu-pa*kh*segah; act. part. پخسيدونكي pa*kh*sedūn-kaey, or پخسيدونيَ pa*kh*sedūnaey; past part. پخسيدليَ pa*kh*sedalaey; verb. n. پخسيدنه pa*kh*sedana'h.

پخسيدنه pa*kh*sedana'h, s.f. (3rd) (verb. n.) Longing, hankering; solicitude, eagerness, anxiety, yearning, pining, grieving. Pl. ئ cy. See پخساك

پخسول pa*kh*sawul, verb trans. To afflict, distress, fret, vex, displease, annoy, irritate, aggrieve, cross. Pres. پخسوي pa*kh*sawī; past وُ پخساوه wu-pa*kh*sāwuh, or وُ پخساوو wu-pa*kh*sāwo; fut. وُ به پخسوي wu bah pa*kh*sawī; imp. وُ پخسوه wu-pa*kh*sawah; act. part. پخسوونكي pa*kh*sawūnkaey, or پخسووني pa*kh*-sawūnaey; past part. پخسوليَ pa*kh*sawulaey; verb. n. پخسونه pa*kh*sawuna'h.

پخسه pa*kh*sa'h, s.f. (3rd) The section or portion of a mud wall, the mud used for building purposes. Pl. ئ cy.

پخسيه pa*kh*sīah, adj. Anything melted, liquid, fluid.

پخشاك pa*kh*s*h*āk, s.m. (2nd) Affliction, distress, sorrow, grief, woe; solicitude, care, anxiety; yearning, pining, inclination. Pl. پخشاكونه pa*kh*s*h*ākūnah. See پخساك and پخسيدنه

پخلا pa*kh*ulā, adj. Reconciled, pacified, made up, settled, arranged, accommodated, tranquilized, composed, hushed up, appeased, propitiated, conciliated. پخلا كيدل pa*kh*ulā kedal, verb intrans. To become reconciled, pacified, appeased, etc. پخلا كول pa*kh*ulā kawul, verb trans. To make peace, to pacify, to reconcile, conciliate, to restore harmony, to heal the breach, etc. پخلا توب pa*kh*ulā tob, s.m. (2nd) or واليَ wālaey, s.m. (1st) Concord, reconciliation. Pl. توبونه tobūnah and والي wālī.

پخليَ pa*kh*alaey, s.m. (1st) Preparation, ripeness, maturity, experience, dressing, cooking. Pl. ي ī. See پختگي

پخليَ pu*kh*alaey, s.m. (1st) The hooping cough. Pl. ي ī; also پخليَ تخليَ pu*kh*alaey *tt*u*kh*alaey. Pl. ي ī. See also توره غاره

پخوا pa-*kh*wā, adj. Prior, previous, preceding, anterior, former. 2. adv. Prior to, before, previously, anteriorly, afore, ere, antecedently, ere now, before now.

پخوانيَ pa*kh*wānaey, adj. Prior, preceding, first, former, ancient, old (as a friend), etc. Pl. ي ī. (Fem.) Sing and Pl. ئ a'ī.

پخول pa*kh*awul, verb trans. To cook, dress, prepare, to ripen, mature, etc. Pres. پخوي pa*kh*awī; past پوخ وُ كړ po*kh* wu-ka*rr*, or پوخ كړ po*kh* ka*rr*; fut. پوخ به وُ كړي po*kh* bah wu-k*rr*ī, or پوخ به كړي po*kh* bah k*rr*ī; imp. پوخ وُ كړه po*kh* wu-k*rr*ah, or پوخ كړه po*kh* k*rr*ah; act. part. پخوونكيَ pa*kh*awūnkaey, or پخووني pa*kh*awūnaey; past part. پوخ كړيَ po*kh* ka*rr*aey; verb. n. پخونه pa*kh*awuna'h.

پخولا pa*kh*olā, adj. Peaceful, reconciled, accommodated, tranquilized. See پخلا

پخونديَ *pakhwandaey*, s.m. (1st) A loop, a noose, a button-hole. Pl. ي ī. See also پلواهه, پل وهه, پل گواهه, and غريبني

پخه *pakha'h*, adj. (Fem.) Cooked, ripe. See پوخ.

پُخيَ *pækhaey*, s.m. (1st) A person or animal affected with the itch, scab, or mange. 2. adj. Mangy, scabby. Pl. ي ī; s.f. (6th) پُخي *pækha'ī*. Sing. and Pl.

پُخي *pækhey*, s.f. (3rd) Pl. Scurf. See پُخ

پخيدل *pakhedal*, verb intrans. To be dressed or cooked, to ripen, suppurate, boil, etc. Pres. پخيږي *pakhejzī* (W.), or پخيگي *pakhegī* (E.); past پوخ وُ شه *pokh wu-shah*, or پوخ شه *pokh shah*; fut. پوخ به وُ شي *pokh bah wu-shī*, or پوخ به شي *pokh bah shī*; imp. پوخ وُ شه *pokh wu-shah*, or پوخ شه *pokh shah*; act. part. پخيدونکيَ *pakhedūnkaey*, or پخيدونيَ *pakhedūnaey*; past part. پوخ *pokh*, or پوخ شويَ *pokh shawaey*; verb. n. پخيدنه *pakhedana'h*, or پخيده *pakhedah*.

پخيل *pakhyal*, s.m. (2nd) Covering a person with bed-clothes to produce perspiration, sweating, sweltering, administering anything hot to produce perspiration. Pl. پخيلونه *pakhyalūnah*. پخيل کول *pakhyal kawul*, verb trans. To sweat, to swelter, to cause perspiration. See also پيخل and پياخله

پخيل واليَ *pakhyal wālaey*, s.m. (1st) Sweatiness, perspiration. Pl. والي *wālī*. See پيخل والي

پدود *padod*, adv. Like, in the same manner, similar, just as, as if, as it were, so to speak. See په دود and دود

P پديد *padīd*, adj. Open, public, clear, evident, manifest, conspicuous, visible; (Fem.) پديده *padīda'h*.

پده *padda'h*, s.f. (3rd) A species of willow. Pl. يْ *ey*.

پر *par*, prep. On, upon, over. پرِ *pri*, or پري *pre*, On him, her, it, etc. See my Grammar, page 48, paragraph 136, for an explanation of this preposition. (s पर).

پر *par*, s.m. (2nd) The wing of a windmill, a paddle, the broad board of a waterwheel, etc. (P A feather, a wing). Pl. پرونه *par-ūnah*.

پراچه *parā-chah*, s.m. (5th) A mercer, a draper, a cloth-merchant. Pl. پراچگان *parā-chagān*. s.f. (6th) پراچي *parācha'ī*. Sing. and Pl. See پرانچه

پراخ *parākh*, adj. (corrup. of P فراخ), Wide, ample, spacious, capacious, large; abundant, plentiful, cheap; (Fem.) پراخه *parākha'h*. پراخي *parākhī*, s.f. (3rd) Amplitude, spaciousness, wideness; cheapness, abundance. Pl. ئ *a'ī*.

پراخ کيدل *parākh kedal*, verb intrans. To become plentiful, cheap, abundant, spacious, wide, large. پراخ کول *parākh kawul*, verb trans. To amplify, to widen, to make or render large or capacious, to cheapen, to make abundant.

P پراگنده *parā-gandah*, adj. Dispersed, scattered, distracted. پراگندگي *parā-gandagī*, s.f. (3rd) Dispersion, distraction. Pl. ئ *a'ī*. پراگنده کول *parā-ganda'h kawul*, verb trans. To disperse, to scatter.

پرانتل *prā-natal*, verb trans. To open, unclose, unbar, unlock, to remove any fastening and set open, to unfold, to separate parts that are close, to cut through, to split, divide, break, to clear or open (a street), to spread, expand, unstop, reveal, unclose, explain. Pres. پرانځي *prā-nadzī*; past پرانت *prā-nat*; fut. پرا به نځي *prā bah nadzī*; imp. پرانځه *prā-nadzah*; act. part. پرانتونکيَ *prānatūnkaey*, or پرانتونيَ *prā-natūnaey*; past part. پرانتيَ *prā-nataey*, or پرانتليَ *prā-natalaey*; verb. n. پرانتنه *prā-natana'h*, or پرانته *prā-natah*.

پرانتنه *prā-natana'h*, s.f. (3rd) (verb. n.) Openness, looseness, expansion. 2. Opening, unclosing, unbarring, etc. Pl. يْ *ey*; or پرانته *prā-natah*, s.m. (6th). Sing. and Pl.

پرانچه *parān-chah*, s.m. (5th) A mercer, a draper, a cloth-merchant. Pl. پرانچهگان *parān-chahgān*; s.f. (6th) پرانچي *parān-cha'ī*, A female of the above class. Sing. and Pl. See پراچه.

پرِ باندِ *pri bāndi*, prep. On him, her, it, etc. See پر and باند.

پرت *prat*, adj. Absurd, vain, foolish, idle, fruitless, unprofitable, delirious, rambling in one's talk, raving. 2. Distant, far, remote; (Fem.) پرته *prata'h*.

P پرتاب *par-tāb*, or تير پرتاب *tīr par-tāb*, s.m. (2nd) Bow-shot, the range of an arrow, musket, etc. Pl. پرتابونه *par-tāb-ūnah*.

P پرتل *par-tal*, s.m. (2nd) A set of household utensils, furniture. 2. The baggage of a horseman carried on a bullock or pony. Pl. پرتلونه *par-talūnah*.

P پرتو *partaw*, s.m. (2nd) Light, rays, sunbeams, moonbeams. Pl. پرتوونه *partawūnah*.

پرتوغاښ *partū-g͟hāsh* (W.), or *partū-g͟hāk͟h* (E.) s.m. (2nd) The string or fastening of a pair of drawers. Pl. پرتوغاښونه *partū-g͟hās͟hūnah* or *partū-g͟hāk͟hūnah*.

پرتوګ *partūg*, s.m. (2nd) Drawers, trowsers. Pl. پرتوګونه *partūgūnah*. See پرتوک

پرته *prata'h*, adj. (Fem.) Absurd, vain, foolish, idle, fruitless, unprofitable. 2. Delirious, rambling in one's talk, raving. 3. Distant, far, remote, far off. پرته پرته *prata'h prata'h*, Very far or remote. پرته ويل *prata'h wa-yal*, verb trans. To ramble in one's talk, to rave.

پرچ *prac͟h*, s.m. (5th) A sneeze. Pl. پرچهار *prac͟hahār*. پرچيدل *prac͟hedal*, verb intrans. To sneeze. پرچول *prac͟hawul*, verb trans. To make or cause to sneeze. See پرنج and پرنجول and پرنجيدل

S پرچتئ *par-c͟hatta'ī*, s.f. (6th) A coping of thatch over a mud wall. 2. A hut with a thatched or wooden roof. Sing. and Pl. See سرماتي

P پرچم *par-c͟ham*, s.m. (2nd) A lock of hair particularly waving over the forehead, the tail of a horse used as a standard. Pl. پرچمونه *par-c͟hamūnah*.

P پرخانه *par-k͟hāna'h*, s.f. (3rd) The place in an arrow where the feathers are inserted. Pl. ې *ey*.

پرخم *par-k͟ham*, s.m. (2nd) The tuft of the tail of a cow or ox. Pl. پرخمونه *par-k͟hamūnah*.

پرخه *park͟ha'h*, s.f. (3rd) Dew. Pl. ې *ey*.

P پرداخت *par-dāk͟ht*, s.m. (2nd) (from پرداختن) Performance, patronizing, relinquishment, proceeding. Pl. پرداختونه *pardāk͟htūnah*.

P پرداز *par-dāz*, s.m. (9th) (from پرداختن) Performance, finishing, completing. 2. Finish, perfection. Sing. and Pl.

P پردازي *par-dāzī*, s.f. (3rd) Performance. Pl. ئ *a'ī*.

P پرده *parda'h*, s.f. (3rd) A curtain, a screen, cover, veil; secrecy, privacy, modesty. Pl. ې *ey*. پرده پوښ *parda'h pos͟h* (W.), or *parda'h pok͟h* (E.), Keeping a secret. پرده پوښي *parda'h pos͟hī* or *parda'h pok͟hī*, s.f. (3rd) Concealment of a blemish. Pl. ئ *a'ī*. پرده دار *parda'h dār*, adj. Confidential; (Fem.) پرده داره *parda'h dāra'h*, and s.f. (3rd) A female kept in strict privacy. Pl. ې *ey*.

P پرده داري *parda'h dārī*, s.f. (3rd) Confidence, trust, dependence. Pl. ئ *a'ī*.

پردئ *pra-daey*, adj. Strange, a stranger. Pl. پردي *pra-dī*; (Fem.) Sing. and Pl. پردئ *pra-da'ī*. پردئ کيدل *pra-daey kedal*, verb intrans. To become strange, shy, undomestic, foreign. پردئ کول *pra-daey kawul*, verb trans. To make or render strange, shy, or undomesticated.

پرزو *pirzo*, adj. Proper, fitting, becoming, suitable, agreeable, just, worthy, reasonable; inclined, partial to, longing, etc.

پرزو والي *pirzo-wālaey*, or پيرزو والي *pīrzo-wālaey*, s.m. (1st) Desire, inclination, leaning, bent, partiality, fancy, hankering, yearning; worth, agreeability, suitableness, fitness, propriety. Pl. والي *wālī*.

پرزول *par-zawul* or *pur-zawul* (W.), verb trans. To throw as in wrestling, to prostrate, to overturn, to overthrow. Pres. پرزوي *par-zawī*; past وُ پرزاوه *wu-par-zāwuh*, or وُ پرزاوو *wu-par-zāwo*; fut. وُ به پرزوي *wu bah par-zawī*; imp. وُ پرزوه *wu-par-zawah*; act. part. پرزوونکي *par-zawūnkaey*, or پرزووني *par-zawūnaey*; past part. پرزولئ *par-zawulaey*; verb. n. پرزونه *par-zawuna'h*.

پرزونه *par-zawuna'h*, s.f. (3rd) (verb. n.) Throwing, overturning, prostrating, overthrow, upset, summerset. Pl. ئ *ey.*

پرزیدل *par-zedal* or *pur-zedal*, (W.) verb intrans. To be thrown as in wrestling, to be prostrated, overturned, overthrown, overset. Pres. پرزیږي *par-zejzī* (W.) or پرزیګي *par-zegī* (E.); past وُ پرزیده *wu-par-zedah*; fut. وُ به پرزیږي *wu bah par-zejzī*, or وُ به پرزیګي *wu bah parzegī*; imp. وُ پرزیږه *wu-par-zejzah*, or وُ پرزیګه *wu-par-zegah*; act. part. پرزیدونکی *par-zedūnkaey*, or پرزیدونی *par-zedūnaey*; past part. پرزیدلی *par-zedalaey*; verb. n. پرزیدنه *par-zedana'h*, or پرزیده *par-zedah*.

پرزوه *pir-zawa'h*, s.f. (3rd) Desire, wish, inclination, etc. Pl. ئ *ey.* پرزوه کول *pir-zawah kawul*, verb trans. To desire, wish for, lean to, to fancy, long for, hanker after, yearn for, etc. See پرزو

P پرست *parast*, part. (in compos.) Adorer, worshipper; devoted to, attentive to. آتش پرست *ātash parast*, A fire-worshipper, a Gabar of the sect of Abraham, Zoroaster, or the Magi. بت پرست *but parast*, An idolater, a worshipper of idols. خدا پرست *khudā parast*, A worshipper of God. خود پرست *khūd parast*, A worshipper or admirer of one's-self, self-conceited, an egotist.

P پرستار *paras-tār*, s.m. (5th) A slave, an adorer. Pl. پرستاران *paras-tārān*; s.f. (3rd) پرستاره *paras-tāra'h*, feminine of the above. Pl. ئ *ey.*

P پرستان *paristān*, s. prop. Fairy land.

P پرستش *paras-tish*, s.m. (2nd) Worship, adoration. Pl. پرستشونه *paras-tishūnah.*

P پرستي *paras-tī*, s.f. (3rd) (in compos.) Worship, adoration. Pl. ئ *a'ī.*

P پرسش *pur-sish*, s.m. (2nd) Inquiry, interrogation, questioning. Pl. پرسشونه *pur-sishūnah.*

پرشکال *par-shakāl*, s.m. (2nd) (E.) The rainy season, a rainy year (s پشکال). Pl. پرشکالونه *par-shakālūnah.*

پرغز *par-ghaz*, s.m. (2nd) A trembling which attacks a person at the commencement of an attack of the small-pox. Pl. پرغزونه *par-ghazūnah.*

P پرکار *pur-kār*, adj. Thick, stout, fat, coarse. 2. Well executed, artful, skilful, well-made; (Fem.) پرکاره *pur kāra'h.*

پرکټی *par-kattaey*, s.m. (1st) A step-son, the son of a wife by a former husband. Pl. ي *ī*; s.f. (6th) پرکټۍ *parkatta'ī*, A step-daughter. See also بن زي and پلندر

پرکښ *pur-kakh*, part. Drawing a bow to the full extent of the arm, raising or stretching out the arm to full length. See also برکښ

P پرګار *par-gār*, s.m. (2nd) A pair of compasses. Pl. پرګارونه *par-gārūnah.*

P پرګنه *par-gana'h*, s.f. (3rd) An inferior division of a country, and less than a ضلع *zilæ* (zillah). Pl. ئ *ey.*

پر له بانډِ *par lah bāndi*, adj. Fold upon fold, folded, piled up. See پبله بانډِ and زبله بانډِ.

پرمخ *par makh*, adj. Fallen (on the face), upset, face downwards; (Fem.) پرمخه *par-makha'h.* See also پرمخ

پرنا *par-nā*, s.f. (6th) Sleepiness, drowsiness, sluggishness, heaviness, listlessness, languidness, nodding, dozing. (E.) Sing. and Pl.; (W.) Pl. پرناوي *par-nāwī.* پرناوړي سترګي *par-nāwarrey stargey*, adj. Sleepy, drowsy, or heavy-eyed. پرنا وړل *par-nā w'rral*, verb trans. (*lit.* to be carried away by sleep), To nod from sleepiness, to doze, to slumber, to fall asleep, to take a nap, etc.

پرناوړي *par-nā w'rrey*, adj. Sleepy, drowsy, heavy, sluggish, heavy-eyed; (Fem.) پرنا وړِ *par-nā w'rri.* Pl. (Masc. and Fem.) ي *ī.*

پرنج *pranj*, s.m. (5th) A sneeze. Pl. پرنجهار *pranjahār.* See پرنچ

پرنجی *pran-jaey*, s.m. (1st) A sneeze. Pl. ي *ī.* See preceding.

پرنجیدل *pran-jedal*, verb intrans. To sneeze. Pres. پرنجیږي *pran-jejzī* (W.) or پرنجیګي *pran-jegī* (E.); past وُ پرنجید *wu-pran-jeda*; fut. وُ به پرنجیږي *wu bah pran-jejzī*, or وُ به پرنجیګي *wu bah pran-jegī*; imp. وُ پرنجیږه *wu-*

pran-jejzah, or وُ پرنجيگه *wu-pran-jegah*; act. part. پرنجيدونكي *pran-jedūnkaey*, or پرنجيدوني *pran-jedūnaey*; past part. پرنجيدلي *pran-jedalaey*; verb. n. پرنجيدنه *pran-jedana'h*.

پرنجيدنه *pran-jedana'h*, s.f. (3rd) (verb. n.) Sneezing. Pl. ي *ey*.

پرنجول *pran-jawul*, verb trans. To make or cause to sneeze. Pres. پرنجوي *pran-ja-wī*; past. وُ پرنجاوه *wu-pran-jāwuh*, or وُ پرنجاوو *wu-pran-jāwo*; fut. وُ به پرنجوي *wu bah pran-jawī*; imp. وُ پرنجوه *wu-pran-jawah*; act. part. پرنجوونكي *pran-jawūnkaey*, or پرنجووني *pran-jawūnaey*; past part. پرنجولي *pran-jawulaey*; verb. n. پرنجونه *pran-jawuna'h*.

پرنړ *prarrn*, s.m. (6th) Milk which has turned sour from heat or by long keeping. Sing. and Pl.

پرو *paro*, s.m. (6th) A hot wind. Sing. and Pl.

P پروا *par-wā*, s.f. (6th) Care, anxiety, concern. 2. Fear, terror. 3. Inclination, affection, desire. 4. Quiet, repose. (E.) Sing. and Pl.; (W.) Pl. پرواوي *par-wāwī*.

P پرواز *par-wāz*, s.m. (2nd) Flight, flying. Pl. پروازونه *par-wāzūnah*. See آلوتل

P پروانگي *par-wānagī*, s.f. (3rd) Command, order, permission.. Pl. ئ *a'ī*.

P پروانه *par-wāna'h*, s.f. (3rd) An order, a pass, a license, leave, command, a precept, a warrant. Pl. ي *ey*.

پروت *prot*, past part. of پريوتل, Fallen, dropped, descended. Pl. پراته *prātah*; (Fem.) پرته *prata'h*. Pl. پرتي *pratey*.

P پرور *par-war*, adj. (act. part. of پروردن) A patron, protector, nourisher; (Fem.) پروره *par-wara'h*.

P پروردگار *par-wardagār* (from پروردن) s. prop. An epithet of the deity, a nourisher of all.

P پرورده *par-wardah*, adj. Bred, reared, brought up, nourished.

P پرورش *par-warish*, s.m. (2nd) Fostering, nourishment, maintenance, support, sustenance. Pl. پرورشونه *par-warishūnah*.

پرورل *par-waral*, verb trans. To nourish, to foster, to feed, to educate, to take care of, to bring up. Pres. پروري *par-warī*; past وُ پروره *wu-par-warah*; fut. وُ به پروري *wu bah par-warī*; imp. وُ پروره *wu-par-warah*; act. part. پرورونكي *par-warūnkaey*, or پروروني *par-warūnaey*; past part. پرورلي *par-waralaey*; verb. n. پرورنه *par-warana'h*.

پروړ *prorr*, s.m. (2nd) (W.) Chaff or *boosa* of wheat and barley straw. Pl. پروړونه *prarr-ūnah*; or پروړه *pro-rra'h*, s.f. (3rd) Pl. ي *ey*.

پروس كال *par-os kāl*, Last year (s كال).

پرول *par-awul*, verb trans. To set on or at (as a dog), to instigate, irritate, vex, excite. Pres. پروي *para-wī*; past وُ پراوه *wu-parā-wuh*, or وُ پراوو *wu-parā-wo*; fut. وُ به پروي *wu bah para-wī*; imp. وُ پروه *wu-parawah*; act. part. پروونكي *para-wūnkaey*, or پرووني *para-wūnaey*; past part. پرولي *parawulaey*; verb. n. پرونه *para-wuna'h*. See پارول and پارهول

پرونه *para-wuna'h*, s.f. (3rd) (verb. n.) Instigating, exciting, instigation, vexation. Pl. ي *ey*.

پرولل *pro-lal*, verb trans. To sell, vend, dispose of, to retail. Pres. پرولي *pro-lī*; past وُ پرولَ *wu-pro-la*, or وُ پروله *wu-pro-lah*; fut. وُ به پرولي *wu bah pro-lī*; imp. وُ پروله *wu-pro-lah*, or پروله *pro-lah*; act. part. پرولونكي *pro-lūnkaey*, or پرولوني *pro-lūnaey*; past part. پروللي *pro-lalaey*, or پرولي *pro-laey*; verb. n. پرولنه *pro-lana'h*. See خرڅول

پرولنه *pro-lana'h*, s.f. (3rd) (verb. n.) Selling, vending, retailing; sale, vent. Pl. ي *ey*.

پروول *pro-wul*, verb trans. To sell, vend, dispose of, retail. Pres. پرووي *pro-wī*; past وُ پرووه *wu-pro-wah*; fut. وُ به پرووي *wu bah pro-wī*; imp. وُ پرووه *wu-pro-wah*, or پرووه *pro-wah*; act. part. پروونكي *pro-wūnkaey*, or پرووني *pro-wūnaey*; past part. پروولي *pro-wulaey*, or پرووي *pro-waey*; verb. n. پروونه *pro-wuna'h*. See پلورل

پروونه *pro-wuna'h*, s.f. (3rd) (verb. n.) Selling, vending, disposing; sale, vent, disposal. Pl. ي *ey*.

پرون *par-ūn*, adv. Yesterday. Also written پارون *pārūn*.

پروني *par-ūnaey*, adj. Yester, last, last past,

next before the present (with reference to time only.) Pl. ي ī; (Fem.) Sing. and Pl. پرونۍ *par-ūna'ī.* پرونۍ شپه *par-ūna'ī shpa'h,* Yester night (*i.e.* the night before the last, the Musalmāns accounting the night before the day). See بيګاني

P پرويز *par-wīz,* s. prop. The name of a prince, the lover of Shīrīn, celebrated in romance.

P پروين *par-wīn,* s.m. (9th) The Pleiades. Sing. and Pl. See also پيروني and جنبق ستوري

پره *para'h,* s.f. (3rd) The broad board of a water wheel. 2. Standing or moving in a line, row, or rank, a line; row, rank, file. 3. Dispersing in search of a thing, or as soldiers at open order. Pl. ې *ey.* په پره تلل *pah para'h t'lal,* verb intrans. To move along in a line or open rank (as soldiers, etc.). په پره دريدل *pah para'h daredal,* verb intrans. To stand in a line, rank, or row. پره كيدل *para'h kedal,* verb intrans. To form in a line or row, to become dispersed as soldiers. پره كول *parah kawul,* or تړل *tarral,* verb trans. To form into a line, to make or cause to stand in a row or file.

پرهار *par-hār,* s.m. (2nd) A wound, a blow, a stroke, the act of striking or beating Pl. پرهارونه *par-hārūnah.* (s प्रहार) پرهار ژن *par-hār jzan,* or پرهار جن *par-hār jan,* adj. Wounded, maimed, mutilated, hurt, injured; (Fem.) پرهار ژنه *par-hār jzana'h,* etc. پرهار جلي *par-hār jaley,* adj. Wounded, hurt, etc. پرهار ژن *par-hār jzan,* پرهار جن *par-hār jan,* or پرهار جلي كيدل *par-hār jalaey, kedal,* verb intrans. To become wounded, hurt, bruised, etc. پرهار ژن كول *par-hār jzan,* etc., *kawul,* verb trans. To wound, hurt, maim.

پرهر *par-har,* s.m. (2nd) A wound, a blow, a stroke. See preceding. Pl. پرهرونه *par-harūnah.*

پرهول *parah-wul,* verb trans. To irritate, to vex, to instigate, to excite. See پرول

P پرهيز *par-hez,* s.m. (2nd) Abstinence, forbearance, continence, abstaining, or keeping aloof, control of the passions, caution, sobriety.

Pl. پرهيزونه *par-hezūnah.* پرهيز كول *par-hez kawul,* verb trans. To control one's passions, to abstain, to keep aloof.

P پرهيزانه *par-hezānah,* adj. Fit for a person under a regimen.

P پرهيزګار *par-hezgār,* adj. Abstinent, continent, abstemious, sober; (Fem.) پرهيزګاره *par-hezgāra'h.*

P پرهيزګاري *par-hezgārī,* s.f. (3rd) Abstinence, control of the passions. Pl. ۍ *a'ī.*

P پري *parī,* s.f. (3rd) A fairy. Pl. پرۍ *para'ī;* or پرۍ *para'ī,* s.f. (6th). Sing. and Pl. پري رخسار *parī rukhsār,* or پري روي *parī rū'e,* or پري مثال *parī-misāl,* adj. Fairy-faced, angelic; (Fem.) رخساره *rukhsāra'h,* etc.

پريدل *pre-dal,* verb intrans. To discontinue, to relinquish, to cease, to leave off, to drop, to desist, etc. Corrup. of پريږدل, which see.

پريږدل *prejz-dal* (W.), or پريګدل *preg-dal* (E.) verb. trans. To discontinue, cease, desist, leave off, drop, lay aside, give over, give up, have done with, relinquish, discard, dismiss, desert, forsake, abandon, renounce, forswear. Pres. پريږدي *prejz-dī,* or پريګدي *preg-dī;* past پريښود *pre-shod* (W.), or *pre-khod* (E.), (from پريښودل); fut. پري به ږدي *pre bah jzdī,* or پري به ګدي *pre bah gdī;* imp. پريږده *prejz-dah,* or پريګده *preg-dah;* act. part. پريښوونكی *pre-showūnkaey,* or *pre-khowūnkaey;* or پريښووني *pre-showūnaey,* or *pre-khowūnaey;* past part. پريښي *pre-yashaey,* or *pre-yakhaey;* verb. n. پريښونه *pre-showuna'h,* or *pre-khowuna'h.* See پريښول and پريښل

P پريشان *pare-shān,* adj. Dispersed, perplexed, confused, troubled, amazed; dishevelled, disordered, deranged; (Fem.) پريشانه *pare-shāna'h.*

P پريشان حال *pare-shān ḥāl,* adj. Distressed in condition. پريشان كيدل *pare-shān kedal,* verb intrans. To be dispersed, or perplexed, etc. پريشان كول *pare-shān kawul,* verb trans. To disperse, confuse, disorder, etc.

پريشاني *pareshānī,* s.f. (3rd) Sleepiness, drowsiness, nodding, dozing. 2. (P) Distraction, perplexity, dispersion, derangement. Pl. ئ *a'ī*.

پريښودل *pre-khodal* (E.), or *pre-shodal* (W.), verb trans. To discontinue, cease, desist, leave off, give over, relinquish, forsake, abandon, renounce, forswear, etc. Pres. (wanting—pres. of پريږدل *prejz-dal*, or پريګدل *preg-dal* used instead); past پريښود *pre-khod*; fut. (wanting—fut. of پريږدل used instead); imp. (wanting—same as preceding); act. part. پريښودونکی *pre-khodūnkaey*, or *pre-shodūnkaey*, or پريښودوني *pre-khodūnaey*, or *pre-shodūnacy*; past part. (wanting — that of پريېښل *pre-yakhal*, or *pre-yashal*, used); verb. n. پريښودنه *pre-khodanah*, or *pre-shodana'h*.

پريښول *pre-shwal* (W.), or *pre-khwal* (E.), verb trans. To discontinue, cease, desist, abandon, renounce, etc. Past پريښو *pre-sho*, or *pre-kho*; act. part. پريښوونکی *pre-shawūnkaey*, or *pre-khawūnkaey*, or پريښووني *pre-shawūnaey*, or *pre-khawūnaey*; verb. n. پريښونه *pre-shwana'h*, or *pre-khwana'h*. The remaining inflexions are wanting, and are taken from the verbs پريېښل *pre-yashal*, or *pre yakhal*, and پريږدل *prejz-dal* (W.), or پريګدل *preg-dal* (E.), which see.

پريکول *pre-kawul*, verb trans. To cut, sever, divide, sub-divide, cut off. Pres. پريکوي *pre-kawī*; past پري که *pre-kah*; fut. پري به کا *pre-bah kā*, or پري به کي *pre-bah kī*; imp. پري که *pre kah*; act. part. پريکوونکی *pre-kawūnkaey*, or پريکووني *pre-kawūnacy*; past part. پريکړي *pre-karraey*; verb. n. پريکونه *pre-kawuna'h*.

پريکړي شول *pre-karrey sh'wal*, verb pass. To be cut, severed, divided, cut off. See شول

پريګدل *preg-dal* (W.), verb trans. To abandon, renounce, etc. See پريږدل and پريدل

پريمشتل *pre-mishtal*, verb trans. To dwell, to reside, to inhabit, to sojourn, to stay, to rest. See ميشته کول

پريو *par-yow*, s.m. (5th) Following, a follower. Pl. پريوان *par-yowān*. See پيرو

پريوار *parī-wār*, adj. Fairy-like; (Fem.) پريواره *parī-wāra'h*. See پيري

پريوان *pre-wān*, s.m. (2nd) The after-birth, or placenta. Pl. پريوانونه *pre-wānūnah* (HI پرين). 2. Adj. (corrup. of P فراوان) Much, great in quantity or amount, many in number, abundant, copious, sufficient, opulent; (Fem.) پريوانه *pre-wāna'h*.

پريواني *pre-wānī*, s.f. (3rd) Abundance, sufficiency, opulence, copiousness. Pl. ئ *a'ī*.

پريوتل *pre-watal*, verb intrans. To fall, come down, drop, drop down, dismount, alight, tumble, to light on, come by chance, to come (as fortune or calamity), to fall in (as an ambuscade), etc. Pres. پريوزي *pre-w'zī*; past پريووت *pre-wot*; fut. پري به وزي *pre bah w'zī*; imp. پريوزه *pre-w'zah*; act. part. پريوتونکی *pre-watūnkaey*, پريوتوني *pre-watūnaey*; past part. پريوتلي *pre-watalaey*, or پريوتي *pre-watey*; verb. n. پريوتنه *pre-watana'h*, or پريواته *pre-wātah*.

پريواته *pre-wātah*, s.m. (6th) Sing. and Pl., or پريوتنه *pre-watana'h*, s.f. (3rd) (verb. n.) Descent, fall, drop, downfall, tumble, descension, slip, falling, dropping, slipping, etc. Pl. ئ *ey*.

پريوستل *pre-wastal*, verb trans. To throw, cast, fling, propel, project, chuck, hurl, dart, discharge, etc. This infinitive is imperfect, and has no present or future tenses or imperative mood, the whole of which are taken from پريباسل *pre-bāsal*, which in the same manner has no past tenses or past participles, so the one makes up the other. Past پريوست *pre-wast*; act. part. پريوستونکی *pre-wastūnkaey*, or پريوستوني *pre-wastūnaey*; past part. پريوستلي *pre-wastalaey*; verb. n. پريوستنه *pre-wastana'h*, or پريواسته *pre-wāstah*.

پريواسته *pre-wāstah*, s.m. (6th) Sing. and Pl.; or پريوستنه *pre-wastana'h*, s.f. (3rd) (verb. n.) Propulsion, push, throw, toss, shy, projection, discharge; throwing, darting, flinging, discharging. Pl. ئ *ey*.

پريوينځل *pre-wīndzal*, verb trans. To wash, lave, purify. See وينځل

پرييستل *pre-yastal*, verb trans. To throw, propel, fling, dart, cast, project, discharge, hurl, chuck, etc. This verb, like پريوستل *pre-wastal*, is imperfect, and takes the present, future, and imperative from پرياسل *pre-bāsal*, which see. Past پرييست *pre-yast*; act. part. پرييستونکي *pre-yastūnkaey*, or پرييستوني *pre-yastūnaey*; past part. پرييستلي *pre-yastalaey*; verb. n. پرييستنه *pre-yastana'h*, or پرياسته *pre-yāstah*.

پرياسته *pre-yāstah*, s.m. (6th) Sing. and Pl.; or پرييستنه *pre-yastana'h*, s.f. (3rd) (verb. n.) Propulsion, push, throw, toss, discharge, projection, etc. Pl. ي *ey*. See پريواسته and پريوستنه

پرييښل *pre-yashal* (W.), or *pre-yakhal* (E.), verb trans. To discontinue, cease, desist, leave off, drop, lay aside, give over, relinquish, abandon, etc. This is another of the imperfect verbs. It has no present, past, future, nor imperative, which are taken from پرېږدل *prejz-dal* and پرېښول *pre-shwal*, which see. Act. part. پرييښونکي *pre-yashūnkaey* or *pre-yakhūnkaey*, or پرييښوني *pre-yashūnaey* or *pre-yakhūnaey*; past part. پرييښلي *pre-yashalaey* or *pre-yakhalaey*, or پرييښي *pre-yashaey* or *pre-yakhaey*; verb. n. پرييښنه *pre-yashana'h* or *pre-yakhana'h*.

پرييښنه *pre-yashana'h* or *pre-yakhana'h*, s.f. (3rd) (verb. n.) Relinquishment, abandonment, desertion, discontinuance, dropping, abandoning, etc. Pl. ي *ey*.

ټړ *pærr*, adj. Conquered, ruined, beaten, overcome. 2. A gambling house. 3. The losing side. (Fem.) ټړه *pærra'h*. See ور

ټړ کيدل *pærr-kedal*, verb intrans. To be overcome, conquered, foiled, worsted, beaten, etc.

ټړ کول *pærr-kawul*, verb trans. To overcome, to conquer, foil, worst, beat, subdue, reduce, discomfit, etc.

پړاق *parr-āk*, s.m. A razor strop. See also پړق

پړان پيش *prrān pīsh*, s.m. (5th) A wild cat. Pl. پړان پيشان *prrān pīshān*; s.f. (3rd) پړان پيشه *prrān pīsha'h*. Pl. پړان پيشي *prrān pīshey*. See غرڅني پيش

پړانګ *prrāng*, s.m. (5th) A tiger, a panther. Pl. پړانګان *prrāngān*; s.f. (3rd) پړانګه *prrāng-a'h*. Pl. پړانګي *prrāngey*.

پړانګ پيش *prrāng pīsh*, s.m. (5th) A wild or tiger cat. Pl. پړانګ پيشان *prrāng pīshān*; s.f. (3rd) پړانګ پيشه *prrāng pīsha'h*. Pl. پړانګ پيشي *prrāng pīshey*.

ټړانه وړانه *pærrāna'h wurrāna'h*, s.f. (3rd) (*lit.* loss and gain), Hazard, venture, gambling, betting, wagering, etc. Pl. ي *ey*. See ټړ

پړپوس *parr-pūs*, s.m. (2nd) The lungs, the heart, liver, and lights of an animal. Pl. پړپوسونه *parr-pūsūnah*. See سګي

پړتوغاښ *parr-tūghākh*, s.m. (2nd) The fastening or string of a pair of drawers. Pl. پړتوغاښونه *parr-tūghākhūnah*.

پړتوګ *parr-tūk*, s.m. (2nd) Trowsers, drawers. Pl. پړتوکونه *parr-tūkūnah*. See also پرتوګ

پړده *parr-da'h*, s.f. (3rd) (corrup. of P پرده) A curtain, a screen, a cover, a veil; secrecy, privacy, modesty. Pl. ي *ey*.

پړسوب *parr-sob*, s.m. (2nd) A swelling; swelling. Pl. پړسوبونه *parr-sobūnah*. Also پاړسوب *pārr-sob*. پړسوب *parr-sob*, or پاړسوب کول *pārr-sob kawul*, verb trans. To swell, to increase in size, to cause to expand, dilate, or increase. Also پړسيدل *parr-sedal*, verb intrans. To swell, expand, enlarge, gather, fill out, dilate. Pres. پړسيږي *parr-sejzī* (W.), or پړسيګي *parr-segī* (E.); past وُ پړسيدَ *wu-parr-seda*; fut. وُ به پړسيږي *wu bah parr-sejzī*, or وُ به پړسيګي *wu bah parr-segī*; imp. وُ پړسيږه *wu-parr-sejzah*, or وُ پړسيګه *wu-parr-segah*; act. part. پړسيدونکي *parr-sedūnkaey*, or پړسيدوني *parr-sedūnaey*; past part. پړسيدلي *parr-sedalaey*; verb. n. پړسيدنه *parr-sedana'h* or پړسيده *parr-sedah*.

پړسول *parr-sawul*, verb trans. To make swell, to increase the size, bulk, dimensions of, to cause to rise, dilate, expand. Pres. پړسوي *parr-sawī*; past وُ پړساوه *wu-parr-sāwuh*, or وُ پړساوو *wu-parr-sāwo*; fut. وُ به پړسوي *wu bah parr-sawī*; imp. وُ پړسوه *wu-parr-sawah*; act. part. پړسوونکي *parr-sawūnkaey*, or

پړسووني *parr-sawūnaey*; past part. پړسولي *parr-sawulaey*; verb. n. پړسونه *parr-sawuna'h*.

پړسونه *parr-sawuna'h*, s.f. (3rd) (verb. n.) Causing to swell, rise, dilate, or expand. Pl. ې *ey*.

پړسيدنه *parr-sedana'h*, s.f. (3rd) (verb. n.) or پړسيده *parr-sedah*, s.m. (6th) Sing. and Pl. Swelling, distension, expansion, enlargement, increase of size, amplification. Pl. ې *ey*.

پړسيدلي *parr-sedalaey*, adj. (past part.) Swelled, expanded, inflated; (Fem.) پړسيدلې *parr-sedali*. Pl. (Masc. and Fem.) ي *ī*.

پړق *parrak*, s.m. (2nd) A razor strop. See براق. Pl. پړقونه *parrakūnah*.

پړک *parrak*, s.m. (2nd) Agitation, palpitation, heaving, flutter, flurry, twitter, tremor, panting, trepidation, wince, going pit-a-pat, etc. Pl. پړکونه *parrak-ūnah*.

پړکيدل *parrakedal*, verb intrans. To flutter, throb, palpitate, wince, writhe from pain, etc. Pres. پړکيږي *parrakejzī* (W.), or پړکيګي *parrakegī* (E.); past وُ پړکيدَ *wu-parrakeda*; fut. وُ به پړکيږي *wu bah parrakejzī*, or وُ به پړکيګي *wu bah parrakegī*; imp. وُ پړکيږه *wu-parrakejzah*, or وُ پړکيګه *wu parrakegah*; act. part. پړکيدونکي *parrakedūnkaey*, or پړکيدوني *parrakedūnaey*; past part. پړکيدلي *parrakedalaey*; verb. n. پړکيدنه *parrakedana'h*. See also پړک خوړل and خړپيدل

پړکول *parrakawul*, verb trans. To agitate, convulse, disturb, perturb, flutter, ruffle, disorder, throw into confusion. Pres. پړکوي *parrakawī*; past وُ پړکاوه *wu-parrakāwuh*, or وُ پړکاوو *wu parrakāwo*; fut. وُ به پړکوي *wu bah parrakawī*; imp. وُ پړکوه *wu-parrakawah*; act. part. پړکوونکي *parrakawūnkaey*, or پړکووني *parrakawūnaey*; past part. پړکولي *parrakawulaey*; verb. n. پړکونه *parrakawuna'h*. See خړپول

پړکونه *parrakawuna'h*, s.f. (3rd) (verb. n.) Agitating, convulsing, fluttering, perturbing, disordering, etc. Pl. ې *ey*.

پړک خوړل *parrak khwarral*, verb trans. To flutter, to tremble, to become agitated (Eng. verb intrans.) See پړکول

پړک *parrk*, s.m. (2nd) A crowd, a throng, a press, a mob, a horde, a posse, a body, a tribe, a gang, a knot, a crew, a swarm, a shoal, a bevy, a flock, a herd, a drove, a corps, a troop, a squad, a company, a squadron, etc. etc. Pl. پړکونه *parrkūnah*. پړک پړک *parrk-parrk*, or پړک په پړک *parrk pah parrk*, In bodies, in knots, in droves, etc.

پړکي *parrkaey*, s.m. (1st) The leg from the ankle to the knee. Pl. ي *ī*.

پړمخ *parr makh*, adj. Fallen (on the face), upset, face downwards; (Fem.) پړمخه *parr makha'h*. See پړمخ and پړمخي. پړمخ پريوتل *parr makh pre-watal*, verb intrans. To fall on the face, to upset, to fall with the face downwards. پړمخي *parr-makhaey*, adj. Upset. پړمخي پريوتل *parr-makhaey pre-watal*, verb intrans. To fall on the face.

پړنګ *prrang*, s.m. (5th) Cry, whine, whimper, Pl. پړنګهار *prrangahār*. پړنګ وهل *prrang wahal*, verb trans. To cry, to whine.

پړنګ *prrang*, s.m. (9th) The leprosy. Sing. and Pl. پړنګي *prrangaey*, s.m. (1st) A leper. Pl. ي *ī*. پړنګۍ *prranga'ī*, s.f. (6th) A female leper. Sing. and Pl. See برګ and پيس

پړوکي *parrū-kaey*, s.m. (1st) A strip, a fillet, a band, a ribbon, a small piece of rope, a shred, bit, a driblet, a tatter. Pl. ي *ī*. پړوکي پړوکي *parrū-kī parrū-kī*, In shreds, in tatters.

پړول *parrawul*, verb trans. To charm by breathing or blowing on, to juggle. Pres. پړوي *parrawī*; past وُ پړاوه *wu-parrāwuh*, or وُ پړاوو *wu-parrāwo*; fut. وُ به پړوي *wu bah parrawī*; imp. وُ پړوه *wu-parrawah*; act. part. پړوونکي *parrawūnkaey*, or پړووني *parrawūnaey*; past part. پړولي *parrawulaey*; verb. n. پړونه *parrawuna'h*.

پړوني *parrū-naey*, s.m. (1st) A veil, a sheet, a mantle worn by women. Pl. ي *ī*. See also چپايل and بچوري

پُړه *pærra'h*, s.f. (3rd) Losing at play, failure, repulse, defeat, fall, discomfiture; a losing game. Pl. ې *ey*. پَړه آړول *pærra'h ārrawul*, verb trans. To discomfit, to make to fail.

پړهه *parr-ha'h*, s.f. (3rd) A shoe, a slipper. Pl. پړهې *parr-hey*. See پنړهه and کوښه

پړئ *parraey*, s.m. (1st) A cord, a small rope, a line, a thread, a string in general. Pl. ي *ī*. See سيلئ , رسئ , and واښکي

پز وهل *paz wahal*, verb trans. To squeeze out, to squash, to mash, to soften, to crush, to beat into a pulp.

پزه *paza'h*, s.f. (3rd) The nose. Pl. پزې *pazey*, چته پزه *chitāh-paza'h*, or پلنه پزه *plana'h paza'h*, or پته پزه *pita'h paza'h*, A flat or broad nose; چت پزئ *chit pazaey*, etc. A person with a broad or flat nose, flat nosed; (Fem.) چته پزې *chita'h pazi*, etc. Pl. (Masc. and Fem.) ي *ī*. See پوزه

پزه وينيدل *paza'h wīnedal*, verb intrans. To fall a bleeding (the nose). پزه وينول *paza'h wīnawul*, verb trans. To cause or make the nose tobleed, to give one a bloody nose.

پس *pas*, adv. After, behind; at length, then, therefore, finally. دغه پس *daghah pas*, After that. په ما پسِ *pah mā pasi*, After me, etc. را پسِ *rā pasi*, After me, or us. در پسِ *dar pasi*, After thee, or you. ور پسِ *war pasi*, After him, etc. or them.

پُس *pæs*, s.m. (5th) A dumb fart. Pl. پُسهار *pæsahār*. پُس آچول *pæs āchawul*, verb trans. To break wind.

پسات *pasāt*, s.m. (2nd) (from A فساد) Depravity, iniquity, wickedness, mischief. 2. Violence, war, sedition, rebellion. Pl. پساتونه *pasātūnah*. پسات کول *pasāt kawul*, verb trans. To make mischief, to rebel, to create sedition.

پس پسي کول *pas pasey kawul*, verb trans. To whisper in the ear, to address in a low voice.

پسان *p'sān*, s.m. (2nd) A sharpening stone, a grinding stone, on which swords are sharpened (s पिष, Grind or reduce to powder). Pl. پسانونه *p'sān-ūnah*.

P پست *past*, adj. Low, abject, lower, below; (Fem.) پسته *pasta'h*.

پستکئ *pustakaey*, s.m. (1st) Rind, bark, etc. Pl. ي *ī*. See پوستکي and پت

پستنه *pastanah*, adv. After, subsequently, since, behind, at the tail of, in the rear of. پستنه جاروتل *pastanah jār-watal*, verb intrans. To retire, to turn back, to recede, to withdraw.

پستو *pas-tū*, s.m. (5th) An inner room with but one entrance. Pl. پستوگان *pas-tūgān*.

پستونئ *pas-tūnaey*, s.m. (1st) The name of a tree. Pl. ي *ī*.

پسته *pasta'h*, adj. (Fem. of پوست) Soft, tender, supple, ductile. 2. After, subsequently. Pl. پستې *pastey*.

P پسته *pista'h*, s.f. (3rd) A pistachio nut. Pl. ې *ey*.

P پستي *pas-tī*, s.f. (3rd) Inferiority, lowness, meanness. Pl. ئ *a'ī*.

پستيدل *pastedal*, verb intrans. To become or grow soft, tender, supple, ductile, yielding, gentle, tractable. پستول *pastawul*, verb trans. To make or render soft, tender, ductile, yielding, etc. Also written پوسيدل *posedal* and پوسول *posawul*. See پوست

پسخاك *pas-khāk*, s.m. (2nd) Sorrow, grief, distress, woe, affliction. Pl. پسخاکونه *pas-khāk-ūnah*. See بخساك

P پس خورده *pas khūrda'h*, s.f. (3rd) Leavings, remnants, relics, refuse, offals. Pl. ې *ey*.

پسخه *paskha'h*, s.f. (3rd) A clod of mud used in building walls, not quite so soft as the usual mud used for mortar. Pl. پسخې *pas-khey*.

پسرلئ *psar-laey*, or *pasar-laey*, s.m. (1st) The spring. Pl. ي *ī*. See also سپرلي

P پس رو *pas rau*, s.m. (5th) A follower. 2. A dependant. 3. Train, equipage. Pl. پس روان *pas rawān*; s.f. (3rd) پس روه *pas-rawa'h*. Pl. ې *ey*. پس روي *pas rawī*, s.f. (3rd) Following. Pl. ئ *a'ī*.

پُسکئ *pæska'ī*, s.f. (6th) A dumb fart. Sing. and Pl. تارغه پُسکئ or دَ كارغه *da kār-ghah*, or *kār-ghah pæska'ī*, s.f. (6th) A small freshwater shell, a snail's shell (*lit.* 'A crow's fart'). Sing. and Pl. See کوجي

P پسند *pasand*, s.m. (9th) Choice, approbation. Sing. and Pl. 2. adj. or part. Approved, grateful, approving, choosing; (Fem.) پسنده pasanda'h. دل پسند dil pasand, adj. Agreeable, grateful to the heart. حق پسند ḥakḳ pasand, adj. Approving what is just and right.

پسنديدل pasand-edal, verb intrans. To be approved or chosen, to please, to like, to prefer. Pres. پسنديږي pasandejzī (W.), or پسنديګي pasandegī (E.); past پسند وُ شه pasand wu-shah, or پسند شه pasand shah; fut. پسند به شي pasand bah shī, or به وُ شي bah wu-shī; imp. پسند وُ شه pasand wu-shah, or پسند شه pasand shah; act. part. پسنديدونکَي pasandedūnkaey or پسنديدونَي pasandedūnaey; past part. پسند شوَي pasand sharaey; verb. n. پسنديدنه pasandedana'h.

پسندول pasand-awul, verb trans. To approve, like, be pleased with, to commend, to choose. Pres. پسندوي pasandawī; past پسند وُ که pasand wu-kah or وُ کړ wu karr, or پسند که pasand kah or کړ karr; fut. پسند به وُ کي pasand bah wu-kī or به وُ کړي bah wu-krrī, or پسند به کي pasand bah kī or به کړي bah krrī; imp. پسند وُ که pasand wu-kah or وُ کړه wu-krrah, or پسند که pasand kah or کړه krrah; act. part. پسندوونکَي pasand-awūnkaey, or پسندوونَي pasandawūnaey; past part. پسند کړَي pasand karracy; verb. n. پسندونه pasandawana'h.

P پسنديده pasandīdah, adj. Chosen, approved of, choice, liked, agreed to.

پسور psor, s.m. (2nd) Breadth, latitude, broadness. Pl. پسورونه psorūnah. پسورور psorawar, adj. Broad, wide; (Fem.) پسورورة psorawara'h.

پسول p'sol, s.m. (2nd) A necklace or belt of gold or silver coins worn by women. Pl. پسلونه p'salūnah, or پسولونه p'solūnah.

پسولول p'solawul, verb trans. To deck (with jewels), to bedeck, to ornament, to adorn, to decorate, to garnish, to bedizen, to embellish, to trick out, etc. Pres. پسولوي p'solawī; past وُ پسولوه wu-p'solāwuh; fut. وُ به پسولوي wu bah p'solawī; imp. وُ پسولوه wu-p'solawah; act. part. پسولوونکَي p'solawūnkaey or پسولوونَي p'solawūnaey; past part. پسولولَي p'solawul-aey; verb. n. پسولونه p'solawuna'h.

پسولولَي p'solawulaey, adj. (past part.) decked out, bedecked, adorned, ornamented, decorated, bedizened, tricked out, embellished; (Fem.) پسولولِ p'solawuli. Pl. (Masc. and Fem.) ي ī.

پسونَي psūnaey, s.m. (1st) An ambush, an ambuscade, a lurking place, a cover. Pl. ي ī. په پسوني کښي کښيناستل pah psūnī kshey, or kkhey kshenāstal, or kkhenāstal, verb trans. To lie in ambush. See پټ ګنيِ

پسه psah, s.m. (2nd) The general name for goats and sheep. Pl. پسونه psūnah. See بزه.

پسينه pasīnah, adj. Late (sown) as a field, last, posterior. (P پسين). See مهينه

پٛش pæsh, s.m. (5th) A blacksmith. 2. Forcing the air out of a bag or bladder. Pl. پٛشان pæshān.

پش پش pash-pash, Words used in calling a cat.

P پشت pusht, s.m. (2nd) The back. 2. Progenitors, ancestry. 3. The reservoir of a kārez. 4. A prop, a second, an assistant. Pl. پشتونه pushtūnah. پشت به پشت pusht bah pusht, From generation to generation. 2. Back to back. See پيږي

پشته pashtah, A word used in driving away a cat.

P پشتي pushtī, s.f. (3rd) Support, a prop. 2. Alliance, aid. Pl. ئِي a'ī. پشتي کول pushtī kawul, verb trans. To assist, to second, to aid, to support. پشت گير pusht-gīr, An aider, a seconder, a support; (Fem.) پشت گيره pusht-gīra'h.

پشرلَي psharlaey, s.m. (1st) A kid or lamb when about a year old. Pl. ي ī; s.f. (6th) پشرلئِي psharla'ī, A female kid or lamb as above. Sing. and Pl.

پشک pishak, s.m. (2nd) A kind of ringworm. 2. A vulture. Pl. پشکونه pishakūnah. See ګنجي, ميرګنج, and بشاك.

پشکالَي pash-kālaey, s.m. (1st) Hay. Pl. ي ī.

P پشم pashm, s.m, (2nd) Fur, hair, wool. Pl. پشمونه pashm-ūnah.

P پشمي pashm-ī, adj. Woollen, hairy.

P پشمينه *pash-mīnah*, adj. Woollen, woollen goods.

پشو *pisho*, s.m. and f. (5th) A cat. Pl. پشوګان *pisho-gān*; Fem. pl. پشوګاني *pisho-gānī*. See پشي

پشو پړانګ *pisho prrāng*, s.m. (5th) A wild cat. Pl. پړانګان *prrāngān*; s.f. (3rd) پشو پړانګه *pisho prrānga'h*, A female wild cat. Pl. ې *ey*. See also غرځني پشو

پشوخټ *pishokhutt*, s.m. (6th) The name of the seed or berry of a tree made into necklaces for cattle. Sing. and Pl.

پشونګړی *pishon-garraey*, s.m. (1st) A male kitten. Pl. ي *ī*; s.f. (6th) ۍ *a'ī*. Sing. and Pl.

پشه *pashah* or *pishah*, and پشي *pashey* or *pishey*, A word used in driving away a cat.

پشی *pishaey*, s.m. (1st) A he cat. Pl. ي *ī*. پشي *pishī*; s.f. (5th) A she cat. Pl. پشيان *pishīāni*, or پشياني *pishīānī*; and پشۍ *pisha'ī*, s.f. (6th). Sing. and Pl.

پښتنخا *pukhtun-khā* (E.) or *pushtun-khā* (W.), or پښتنخوا *pukhtun-khwā* or *pushtun-khwā*, s.f. (6th) The Afghān country, Afghānistān (from پښتن Afghan and خا or خوا side, quarter, locality) (E.), Sing. and Pl.; (W.), Pl. خاوي *khāwī*, or خواوي *khwāwī*.

پښتن والی *pukhtun-wālaey* or *pushtun-wālaey*, s.m. (1st) The manners and customs of the Afghān tribes, the Afghān code. Pl. والي *wālī*. Also پښتن ولي *pukhtun-wulī* or *pushtun-wulī*, s.f. (3rd). Pl. ۍ *a'ī*; and پښتن ګلوي *pukhtun-galwī* or *pushtun-galwī*, s.f. (3rd). Pl. ۍ *a'ī*.

پښتو *pukhto* (E.), or *pushto* (W.), or *pashto*, s.f. (9th) The language of the Afghān tribes, the Afghān language. Sing. and Pl.

پښتورګه *pukhtawarga'h* (E.) or *pushtawarga'h* (W.) and *pakhtawarga'h* or *pashtawarga'h*, s.f. (3rd) A kidney. Pl. ې *ey*.

پښتون *pukhtūn* (E.) or *pushtūn* (W.), s.m. (4th) An Afghān, one whose language is the Pushto or Pukhto. Pl. پښتانه *pukhtānah* or *pushtānah*, پښتنه *pukhtana'h* or *pushtana'h*, s.f. (3rd). An Afghān female. Pl. ې *ey*. بر پښتون *bar-pukhtūn* or *bar-pushtūn*, The Upper or Higher Afghāns, the Western Afghāns, or all those inhabiting the country west of the Khaiber Pass. لر پښتون *lar-pushtūn* or *lar-pukhtūn*. The Lower or Eastern Afghāns, those east of the Khaiber.

پښته *pukhta'h* (E.) or *pushta'h* (W.), s.f. (3rd) A little hill. Pl. ې *ey*. (P پشته).

پښتۍ *pukhta'ī* (E.) or *pushta'ī* (W.), s.f. (6th) A rib, the ribs. Sing. and Pl.

پښتي *pukhtī* (E.) or *pushtī* (W.), s.f. (3rd) Inquiry, search, quest, pursuit, scrutiny, investigation, examination. Pl. ۍ *a'ī*.

پښتيدل *pukh-tedal* (E.) or *push-tedal* (W.), verb trans. To ask, inquire, question, interrogate, require an answer, etc. Pres. پښتي *pukhtī* or *pushtī*; past وُ پښتيدَ *wu-pukhteda* or *wu-pushteda*; fut. وُ به پښتي *wu bah pukhtī* or *pushtī*; imp. وُ پښته *wu-pukhtah* or *wu-pushtah*; act. part. پښتيدونکی *pukhtedūnkaey* or *pushtedūnkaey*, or پښتيدونی *pukhtedūnaey* or *pushtedūnaey*; past part. پښتيدلی *pukhtedalaey* or *pushtedalaey*, or پښتيدی *pukhtedaey* or *pushtedaey*; verb. n. پښتيدنه *pukhtedana'h* or *pushtedana'h*, or پښتنه *pukhtana'h* or *pushtana'h*, or پښتيده *pukhtedah* or *pushtedah*.

پښتيدنه *pukhtedana'h* (E.) or *pushtedana'h* (W.), and پښتنه *pukhtana'h* or *pushtana'h*, s.f. (3rd) (verb. n.) Inquiry, search, quest, pursuit, scrutiny, interrogation, examination, asking, questioning. Pl. ې *ey*; or پښتيده *pukhtedah* or *pushtedah*, s.m. (6th). Sing. and Pl.

پښويه *pakho-ya'h*, s.f. (3rd) The act of naming, orthography, the manner of forming words with letters, spelling. Pl. ې *ey*. See also پيزې

پښه *pkha'h* (E.) or *psha'h* (W.), s.f. (3rd) The foot, a foot-mark, a track. Pl. پښې *pkhey* or *pshey*. پښه ارته *pkha'h arta'h* (E.) or *psha'h arta'h* (W.), s.f. (3rd) (lit. 'foot released') The first visit of the lover to the house of his betrothed. Pl. ې *ey*. پښه په رکاب *psha'h pah rikāb*, adj.

Ready, waiting, foot in stirrup. پښي يبل *pshey yabal,* adj, Bare-footed. See پښه

پښيمان *pakhīmān* (E.) or *pashīmān* (W.), adj. Penitent, sorry, abashed, disgraced, ashamed, repentant; (Fem.) پښيمانه *pakhīmāna'h* or *pashīmāna'h.* پښيمان کيدل *pakhīmān* or *pashīmān kedal,* verb intrans. To repent, to be abashed, to be sorry, etc. پښيمان کول *pakhīmān* or *pashīmān kawul,* verb trans. To abash, to make ashamed, disgrace. (P پشيمان).

پښيماني *pakhīmānī* (E.) or *pashīmānī* (W.), s.f. (3rd) Disgrace, regret, sorrow, penitence, repentance, shame. Pl. ئ *a'ī.*

پغله *pighla'h,* s.f. (3rd) A maiden, a virgin. Pl. ئ *ey.* See پيغله

پقير *pakīr,* s.m. (5th) A beggar, a mendicant. Pl. پقيران *pakīrān,* s.f. (3rd) پقيره *pakīra'h.* Pl. ئ *ey* (A فقير).

پک *puk,* s.m. (9th) Opportunity, suitable or proper time, turn, juncture, crisis, chance, the nick of time. Sing. and Pl. پک خطا شول *puk khaṭā sh'wal,* or کيدل *kedal,* verb intrans. To be lost (as an opportunity, opening, chance), etc.

پکار *pa-kār,* or په کار *pah kār,* adj. Of use, useful, serviceable, helping, conducive, available, effective, effectual. په کار کيدل *pah kār kedal,* verb intrans. To be useful, serviceable, conducive, available, etc. په کار کول *pah kār kawul,* verb trans. To use, to employ, to hold, to turn to account, to make the most of.

پکر *pakr,* s.m. (5th) Poverty, the practice of a fakīr or derwesh. Pl. پکرونه *pakrūnah.* (A فقر).

پکل *pakal,* verb trans. To chuck into the mouth from the palm of the hand, as grain, meal, etc. Pres. پکي *pakī*; past وُ پاکَ *wu-pāka,* or وُ پاکه *wu-pākah*; fut. وُ به پکي *wu bah pakī*; imp. وُ پکه *wu-pakah*; act. part. پکونکي *pakūnkaey,* or پکوني *pakūnaey*; past part. پکلي *pakalaey*; verb. n. پکنه *pakana'h.* See also پکه وهل

پکلئ *pak-la'ī,* s.f. (6th) The name of a small state north of Aṭṭak. پکلئ وال *pak-la'ī wāl,* s.m. (5th) an inhabitant or native of Pak-la'ī. Sing and Pl.; s.f. (3rd) پکلئ واله *pak-la'ī-wāla'h.* Pl. پکلئ والي *pak-la'ī wāley.*

پکو *pako,* adj. Astonished, confounded, amazed, wondering; (Masc. and Fem.) پکو شول *pako sh'wal,* or کيدل *kedal,* verb. intrans. To become astonished, amazed. پکو کول *pako kawul,* verb trans. To confound, to astonish, to make amazed.

پکه *paka'h,* s.f. (3rd) A small quantity sufficient for one throw with the hand into the mouth, as Orientals take physic. Pl. ئ *ey.*

پکه وهل *paka'h wahal,* verb trans. To chuck into the mouth from the palm of the hand, as grain, meal, etc. See پکل and کپه

پګړئ *pag-ṛra'ī,* s.f. (6th) A turband. Sing. and Pl. (HI پگري).

پګڼ *pagaṛṇ,* s.m. (9th) The name of the eleventh month of the Hindū year,—February-March. (HI پهاگن). Sing. and Pl.

پل *pal,* s.m. (4th) A mill-stone, a potter's wheel. 2. The foot of man or beast, a pace, a step, a footstep. 3. A truck, a small wooden wheel. Pl. پلونه *plūnah.*

S پل *pal,* s.m. (9th) A moment, the twinkling of an eye, a short space of time. Sing. and Pl.

P پل *pul,* s.m. (2nd) A bridge, an embankment. Pl. پلونه *pulūnah.*

پل *pæl,* adj. Exempted, absolved, exonerated, acquitted, pardoned, let off, forgiven, passed over. Fem. پله *pæla'h.* See پلول

پلا *plā,* s.f. (6th) A journey, tour, passage from one place to another, trip, excursion, ramble, jaunt. 2. One time, one turn, a moment, time, period. Pl. پلاوي *plāwī* (W.); (E.) Sing. and Pl. پلا کول *plā kawul,* verb trans. To journey, to travel, to go on a journey. يوه پلا *yawa'h plā,* adv. Once, one time.

پلار *plār,* s.m. (2nd) A father. Pl. پلارونه *plār-ūnah,* or (W.) پلرونه *plar-ūnah.* پلارتيا *plār-tī'ā,* s.f. (6th) Paternity, fatherliness. (E.)

Sing. and Pl.; (W.) Pl. تیاوي *tīā-wī*; and پلار گلوي *plār-galwī*, s.f. (3rd) Pl. ئي *a'ī*.

پلار مرئ *plār-marraey*, adj. as s.m. (1st) A child who has lost its father, an orphan; (Fem.) پلار مړ *plār-marri*. Pl. (Masc. and Fem.) ي *ī*. See سیه

پلاله *plāla'h*, s.f. (3rd) Rice-straw. Pl. پلالي *plāley*.

پلاړنه *palārrna'h*, s.f. (3rd) Water brought in skins from a distance, a load of water. Pl. ئ *ey*.

P پلاو *pulāo*, s.m. (2nd) A dish made of flesh, rice, raisins, etc. Pl. پلاوونه *pulāo-ūnah*.

پلټن *palttan*, s.f. (1st) A regiment, a battalion of soldiers. Pl. پلټنې *palttani*.

پلټل *palattal*, verb trans. To twist, to distort, to bend, to involve, to wind, to coil, to screw, to envelope, etc. 2. To look for, seek, search, inquire, to look out for, trace, investigate, pursue. Pres. پلټي *palatti*; past وُ پلاټه *wu palāttah*; fut. وُ به پلټي *wu bah palatti*; imp. وُ پلټه *wu palattah*; act. part. پلټونکي *palattūnkaey*, or پلټونئ *palattūnaey*; past part. پلټلئ *palattalaey*; verb. n. پلټنه *palattana'h*.

پلرگنئ *plar-gana'ī*, s.f. (6th) The relations or family of one's father, paternal relations. Sing. and Pl. See مورگنئ

پلغت *palaghat*, adv. Quickly, sharply, swiftly, speedily, apace. Also written په لغت *pah laghat*.

P پلک *palak* or *pilak*, s.m. (2nd) The eyelid; a moment, an instant. Pl. پلکونه *palakūnah* or *pilakūnah*.

ټلک *pælk*, s.m. (2nd) A sledge-hammer. Pl. ټلکونه *pælkūnah*. See ځټک

پل گواښه *pal gwākha'h* (E.), or *pal-gwāsha'h* (W.), s.f. (3rd) A loop, a noose, the heel ropes to picket a horse by. Pl. ئ *ey*. See also غراشه, پلواښه, غریشي, and بخوندي

پلمه *palma'h*, s.f. (3rd) Falsehood, false pretences, slander, calumny, deception, untruth. Pl. ئ *ey*. پلمه کول *palma'h kawul*, verb. trans. To make false pretences, to practice deception, to tell lies. See تور

پلن *plan*, adj. Broad, wide, extensive, spacious; (Fem.) پلنه *plana'h*. پلن والئ *plan wālaey*, s.m. (1st) Breadth, width, extension, space, latitude. Pl. والي *wālī*.

پلنیدل *plan-edal*, verb intrans. To widen, to extend, to grow wide, to outspread, to dilate, to expand, to become wide. Pres. پلنیږي *plan-ejzī* (W.), or پلنیګي *plan-egī* (E.); past. پلن شه *plan shah*, or پلن وُ شه *plan wu-shah*; fut. پلن به شي *plan bah shī*, or پلن به وُ شي *plan bah wu-shī*; imp. پلن وُ شه *plan wu-shah*; act. part. پلنیدونکئ *planedūnkaey*, or پلنیدونئ *planedūnaey*; past part. پلن *plan*, or پلن شوئ *plan shawaey*; verb. n. پلنیدنه *planedana'h*, or پلنیده *planedah*.

پلنول *plan-awul*, verb trans. To render broad or wide, to widen, to extend, to outspread. Pres. پلنوي *planawī*; past پلن کړ *plan karr* or که *kah*, or پلن وُ که *plan wu-kah* or وُ کړ *wu-karr*; fut. پلن به کړي *plan bah krrī* or به کي *bah kī*, or پلن به وُ کړي *plan bah wu-krrī* or به وُ کي *bah wu-kī*; imp. پلن که *plan kah* or کړه *krrah*, or پلن وُ که *plan wu-kah* or وُ کړه *wu-krrah*; act. part. پلنوونکئ *planawūnkaey*, or پلنوونئ *planawūnaey*; past part. پلن کړئ *plan karraey*; verb. n. پلنونه *planawuna'h*.

پلندر *plan-dar*, s.m. (2nd) A step-father. Pl. پلندرونه *plan-darūnah*. See بنزي

پلنډه *plandda'h*, s.f. (3rd) A load for the head, a bundle carried on the head. Pl. ئ *ey*. See بیټ and بنډه

S پلنګ *palang*, s.m. (5th) A bed, a bedstead. Pl. پلنګان *palangān*, or s.m. (2nd). Pl. پلنګونه *palangūnah*. See پیلنګ

پلو *palau*, s.m. (2nd) The hem or border of a garment; side, margin, border, edge, verge. Pl. پلوونه *palauūnah* (HI پلو *pallū*).

پلواښه *pul-wākhah* (E.), or *pul-wāshah* (W.), s.f. (3rd) A loop, a noose; the heel-ropes for picketing a horse. Pl. ئ *ey*. See پلگواښه, غراشه, پلوښه, غریشي, and بخوندي

پلور *plor*, s.m. (6th) Buying and selling; sale, disposal. Sing. and Pl.

پلورل *ploral*, verb trans. To sell, to dispose of,

to vend, to retail. Pres. پلوري *plorī*; past وُ پلورَ *wu plora*, or وُ پلوره *wu plorah*; fut. وُ به پلوري *wu bah plorī*; imp. وُ پلوره *wu-plorah*, or پلوره *plorah*; act. part. پلورونكيَ *plor-ūnkaey*, or پلوروني *plor-ūnaey*; past part. پلورليَ *ploralaey*; verb. n. پلورنه *plorana'h*. See also پرولل, خرخول, and پيرودل

پلوسه *palū-sa'h*, s.f. (3rd) The name of a thorny tree used for fuel only. Pl. ي *ey*. د غرَ پلوسي *da ghra palū-sey*, The mountain species of the tree, which attains a large size, and from which charcoal is made.

پلوشه *palosha'h*, s.f. (3rd) A ray of light, as of the sun, a lamp, etc. Pl. ي *ey*.

پلوښه *pulwasha'h* (W.), or *pulwakha'h* (E.) s.f. (3rd) A loop, a noose, a button-hole; the heel ropes of a horse. Pl. ي *ey*. See پلواښه, غراشه, etc.

پلول *pulawul*, verb trans. To let off, to let go, to forgive, to remit, to pass over, to absolve, to dispense with, to exempt, to acquit, to set aside, to give dispensation. Pres. پلوي *pulawī*; past پل كړ *pæl karr*, or وُ كړ *wu-karr*; fut. پل به كړي *pæl bah krrī*, or به وُ كړي *bah wu-krrī*; imp. پل كړه *pæl krrah*, or وُ كړه *wu-krrah*; act. part. پلوونكيَ *pulawūnkaey*, or پلووني *pulawūnaey*; past part. پل كړيَ *pæl karraey*; verb. n. پلونه *pulawuna'h*. See پُل

پلوند *pal-wandd*, adj. Foolish, silly, senseless, imbecile, weak-minded, half-witted; (Fem.) پلونده *pal-wanda'h*. پلوند توب *pal-wand-tob*, s.m. (2nd) Stupidity, poverty of intellect, silliness, imbecility. Pl. توبونه *tob-ūnah*, or پلوندي *pal-wandī*, s.f. (3rd). Pl. ئي *a'ī*.

پلونيدل *plonedal*, verb intrans. and پلونول *plon-awul*, verb trans. See پلنيدل

پله *pala'h*, s.f. (3rd) A tendon, sinew, a nerve. 2. (P) The basin of a balance, a scale, the cup of a mill, the sole of the foot, etc. 3. (P) The shutter or fold of a door. 4. One of a pair, one side or part of anything. 5. Margin, side, brink (HI). Pl. ي *ey*.

پله پوري *pala'h porī*, adj. Shut, closed, shut fast as a door, window, etc.; joined, connected, united. پله پوري كيدل *palah porī kedal*, verb intrans. To become shut or closed (as a door), to unite, to become joined or connected. پله پوري كول *palah porī kawul*, verb trans. To shut, shut up, close, put to, join, unite, connect, etc. See پرله پوري

پلئي *pala'ī*, s.f. (6th) A spoke, or the spokes of a wheel. Sing. and Pl.

پليَ *palaey*, s.m. (1st) A pod, the seed vessel of beans, peas, and such like plants, Pl. ي *ī*. See غوره

پلي *palaey*, adj. On foot. له عقلَ پلي *lah æakla palaey*, adj. Foolish, void of understanding, weak in intellect; (Fem.) پلِ *pali*. Pl. (Masc. and Fem.) ي *ī*.

P پليت *palīt*, adj. Unclean, polluted, impure, defiled; (Fem.) پليته *palīta'h*. پليتيدل *palīt-edal*, verb intrans. To become polluted, impure, defiled, etc. Pres. پليتيږي *palīt-ejzī* (W.), or پليتيګي *palīt-egī* (E.); past پليت شه *palīt shah*, or پليت وُ شه *palīt wu-shah*; fut. پليت به شي *palīt bah shī*, or پليت به وُ شي *palīt bah wu-shī*; imp. پليت شه *palīt shah*, or پليت وُ شه *palīt wu-shah*; act. part. پليتيدونكيَ *palīt-edūnkaey*, or پليتيدونيَ *palīt-edūnaey*; past part. پليت شويَ *palīt-shawaey*; verb. n. پليتيدنه *palītedana'h*.

پليتول *palītawul*, verb trans. To defile, to pollute, to render impure. Pres. پليتوي *palītawī*; past پليت كړ *palīt karr* or كه *kah*, or پليت وُ كړ *palīt wu-karr* or وُ كه *wu-kah*; fut. پليت به كړي *palīt bah krrī* or كي *kī*, or پليت به وُ كړي *palīt bah wu-krrī* or به وُ كي *bah wu-kī*; imp. پليت كړه *palīt krrah* or كه *kah*, or پليت وُ كړه *palīt wu-krrah* or وُ كه *wu-kah*; act. part. پليتوونكيَ *palītawūnkaey*, or پليتوونيَ *palītawūnaey*; past part. پليت كړيَ *palīt karraey*; verb. n. پليتونه *palītawuna'h*.

P پليتي *palītī*, s.f. (3rd) Uncleanness, impurity, foulness. Pl. ئي *a'ī*.

پلي تڼر *paley tarrn*, s.m. (2nd) A weaver's beam. Pl. پلي تڼرونه *paley tarrn-ūnah*. See پتي لنړ

P پليد *palīd*, adj. Impure, unclean, defiled,

polluted; (Fem.) پليده *palīda'h*. See پليت, etc.

P پليدي *palīdī*, or پليتي *palītī*, s.f. (3rd) Pollution, impurity, uncleanliness, defilement, etc. Pl. ئ *a'ī*.

پم *pam*, s.m. (2nd) Scab, itch, mange, scurf. Pl. پمونه *pamūnah*.

پمبچه *pam-ba<u>ch</u>a'h*, s.f. (3rd) The stalk of the cotton plant, generally used for fuel. Pl. ئ *ey*. See پمبي چو

پمن *paman*, adj. Scabby, mangy, scurfy, itchy; (Fem.) پمنه *pamana'h*. پمن توب *paman tob*, s.m. (2nd) Pl. توبونه *tobūnah*; or پمن والئ *paman-wālaey*, s.m. (1st) Scabbiness, manginess, scurfiness, the quality of being scabby. Pl. والي *wālī*.

پمنيدل *pamanedal*, verb intrans. To become scabby, mangy, scurfy, to become inoculated with the scab or itch. Pres. پمنيږي *pamanejzī* (W.), or پمنيگي *pamanegī* (E.); past پمن شه *paman <u>sh</u>ah*, or پمن وُ شه *paman wu-<u>sh</u>ah*; fut. پمن به شي *paman bah <u>sh</u>ī*, or پمن به وُ شي *paman bah wu-<u>sh</u>ī*; imp. پمن شه *paman <u>sh</u>ah*, or پمن وُ شه *paman wu-<u>sh</u>ah*; act.part. پمنيدونكئ *pamanedūnkaey*, or پمنيدونئ *pamanedūnaey*; past part. پمن or پمن شوئ *paman <u>sh</u>awaey*; verb. n. پمنيدنه *pamanedana'h*, or پمنيده *pamanedah*.

پمنول *pamanawul*, verb trans. To inoculate with the scab, itch, or mange. Pres. پمنوي *pamanawī*; past پمن كړ *paman ka<u>rr</u>* or كه *kah*, or پمن وُ كړ *paman wu-ka<u>rr</u>* or وُ كه *wu-kah*; fut. پمن به كړي *paman bah k<u>rr</u>ī* or به كي *bah kī*, or پمن به وُ كړي *paman bah wu-k<u>rr</u>ī* or به وُ كي *bah wu-kī*; imp. پمن كړه *paman k<u>rr</u>ah* or كه *kah*, or پمن وُ كړه *paman wu-k<u>rr</u>ah* or وُ كه *wu-kah*; act. part. پمنوونكئ *pamanawūnkaey*, or پمنوونئ *pamanawūnaey*; past part. پمن كړئ *paman ka<u>rr</u>aey*; verb. n. پمنونه *pamanawuna'h*.

P پمبه *pumba'h*, s.f. (3rd) Cotton. Pl. ئ *ey*. See پنبه

پمبي چو *pumbey <u>ch</u>ū*, s.f. (5th) A cotton pod. Pl. پمبي چوگان *pumbey <u>ch</u>ūgāni*. See كالك and پمي جو چو

پمن *paman*, adj. Scabby, itchy, mangy, scurfy, etc.; (Fem.) پمبه *pamana'h*. See پم

پمي چو *pamey <u>ch</u>ū*, s.f. (5th) A cotton pod. Pl. پمي چوگان *pamey <u>ch</u>ūgāni*.

P پناه *panāh*, s.f. (9th) Aid, assistance, shade, shelter, protection, asylum, support. Sing. and Pl.

پنا كول *panā kawul*, verb trans. To aid, to back, to shade, to stand by. پنا نيول *panā nīwal*, verb trans. To take shelter, to seek aid, shelter, protection, or support. پنا وړل *panā w'<u>rr</u>al*, verb trans. To shade, to screen, to shun, to avoid.

P پنبه *pambah*, s.f. (3rd) Cotton. Pl. ئ *ey*. See also پمبه

P پنبئ *pumba'ī*, adj. Made of cotton.

پنج پاو *panj pā'o*, s.m. (5th) One of the two grand divisions of the Abdālī tribe, the descendants of Nūr, <u>Kh</u>okai, and Mākou, sons of Abdāl, and Is'ḥāk and Æalī, the two younger sons of his eldest son Æsau. The other is known as the Zīrak division, from whom the Suddozīs are descended. See Introduction to my Pu<u>sh</u>to Grammar, pp. 12, 13. The word is used both Sing. and Pl.; s.f. (3rd) پنج پاوه *panj pāwa'h*, A female of the above. Pl. پنج پاوئ *panj pāwey*.

پنج پاي *panj pā'e*, s.m. (6th). Sing. and Pl. See preceding word; s.f. (3rd) پنج پايه *panj pā-ya'h*. Pl. پنج پايئ *panj pā-yey*.

پنجره *pinj-ra'h*, s.f. (3rd) A cage. Pl. ئ *ey*. (s پنجرا).

پنج غښئ *panj <u>gh</u>a<u>kh</u>aey*, s.m. (1st) A rake. Pl. ي *ī*. See پاړه

پنجكئ *panjakaey*, s.m. (1st) The cross-bar separating the strings of a pellet-bow. Pl. ي *ī*.

P پنجه *panja'h*, s.f. (3rd) A hand with the five fingers, a claw, the clutch, the grasp, a paw. Pl. ئ *ey*.

پند *pand*, s.m. (2nd) Science, skill, sagacity, art, stratagem, cunning. 2. Distance, remoteness, farness. 3. (P) Advice, counsel, admonition. Pl. پندونه *pandūnah*. پند آخستل *pand ā<u>kh</u>istal*, verb trans. To take advice, to take counsel. پند ورکول *pand war-kawul,* verb trans. To give advice, to admonish.

پند *pand,* s.m. (2nd) Going, departing; marching, decamping. Pl. پندونه *pand-ūnah.* پند کول *pand kawul,* verb trans. To go, to depart, to decamp, to march.

پند تیا *pand-tīā,* s.f. (6th) Artfulness, cunning; skilfulness, sagaciousness. (E.) Sing. and Pl.; (W.) Pl. تیاوي *tīā-wī.*

P پند نامه *pand nāma'h,* s.f. (3rd) A book conveying advice. Pl. ې *ey.*

P پندار *pin-dār,* s.m. (2nd) Thought, imagination, opinion, notion. 2. Self-conceit, pride, arrogance. Pl. پندارونه *pindārūnah.*

پندانه *pun-dāna'h,* s.f. (3rd) Cotton seed. Pl. ې *ey.* (P پنبه دانه).

پندوک *pan-dūk,* s.m. (6th) A bud, a rose-bud. Sing. and Pl.

پندۍ *punda'ī,* s.f. (6th) The heel. 2. The steel or iron haft of a spear or lance. Sing. and Pl.

پنډ *pandd,* s.m. (2nd) A load for the head. Pl. پنډونه *panddūnah.*

پُنډ *pændd,* s.m. (2nd) A body, a band, detachment, party, gang, knot, troop, squad, etc. 2. A swelling, a protuberance, a bump, an excrescence. 3. Vulva. Pl. پُنډان *pænddān.*

پنډ *pundd,* s.m. (2nd) A flint, a flint and steel. Pl. پنډونه *punddūnah.* See خو

پنډ *pundd,* adj. Corpulent, stout, fat, bloated, pot-bellied, puffy, dumpy, pursy, squabby, blowzy. 2. s.m. (5th) A fat person. Pl. پنډان *punddān*; s.f. (3rd) پنډه *pundda'h.* Pl. پنډي *punddey.* پنډيدل *punddedal,* verb intrans. To become larger, to expand, swell, fill out, dilate, to gather flesh, to out-grow. Pres. پنډيږي *punddejzī* (W.), or پنډيګي *punddegī* (E.); past پنډ شه *pundd shah,* or پنډ وُ شه *pundd wu-shah*; fut. پنډ به شي *pundd bah shī,* or پنډ به وُ شي *pundd bah wu-shī*; imp. پنډ شه *pundd shah,* or پنډ وُ شه *pundd wu-shah*; act. part. پنډيدونکې *punddedūnkaey,* or پنډيدونې *punddedūnaey*; past part. پنډ *pundd,* or پنډ شوې *pundd shawaey*; verb. n. پنډيدنه *punddedana'h.* پنډول *punddawul,* verb trans. To render larger, to expand, distend, inflate, puff, etc. Pres. پنډوي *punddawī*; past پنډ کړ *pundd karr* or کړ *kah,* or پنډ وُ کړ *pundd wu-karr* or وُ که *wu-kah*; fut. پنډ به کړي *pundd bah krrī* or به کي *bah kī,* or پنډ به وُ کړي *pundd bah wu-krrī* or به وُ کي *bah wu-kī*; imp. پنډ کړه *pundd krrah* or که *kah,* or پنډ وُ کړه *pundd wu-krrah* or وُ که *wu-kah*; act. part. پنډوونکې *punddawūnkaey,* or پنډوونې *punddawūnaey*; past part. پنډ کړې *pundd karraey*; verb. n. پنډونه *punddawuna'h.*

پنډاو چرګ *panddāw charg,* s.m. (5th) A game fowl, a fowl of a large breed. Pl. پنډاو چرګان *panddāw chargān*; s.f. (3rd) پنډاو چرګه *panddāw charga'h,* or پنډاونه چرګه *panddāw-ana'h chargah,* The hen bird of the above. Pl. پنډاو *panddāw* or پنډاوي چرګي *pandd-āwaney chargey.*

پنډ غالىَ *pandd ghālaey,* s.m. (1st) A plain outside a village, where the whole of the cattle assemble when going out and on returning from the grazing-ground. Pl. پنډ غالي *pandd ghālī.*

پنډ والىَ *pandd-wālaey,* s.m. (1st) Stoutness, corpulence, plumpness, obesity, embonpoint. Pl. والي *wālī.*

پنډوس *panddos,* s.m. (5th) A ball for playing with. Pl. پنډوسان *panddosān.*

پنډوسکىَ *panddoskaey,* s.m, (1st) (dimin. of preceding) A small ball for playing with. Pl. ي *ī.*

پنډوکىَ *panddūkaey,* s.m. (1st) A small bundle for the head. Pl. ي *ī.*

پنډولى *panddolī,* s.f. (3rd) A share or portion of a crop of cotton, the perquisite of females who gather it in. Pl. ۍ *a'ī.*

پنډول ګره *panddol gara'h,* s.f. (3rd) A female who gathers cotton; *lit.,* 'a shareholder of cotton' (from the preceding word). Pl. ې *ey.* See کالک چينه

پنډه *pandda'h,* s.f. (3rd) A small load for the head. Pl. ې *ey.* See پنډ

پنډۍ *pandda'ī,* s.f. (6th) The heel. Sing. and Pl. See پنډۍ and پرکىَ

پنځه *pindzah*, adj. Five. See پينځه

پنځه بنا *pindzah binā*, s.f. (6th) The five foundations of religion—the recital of the belief; prayer; fasting; pilgrimage to Mekka; and giving of alms. (A بنا). (E.) Sing. and Pl.; (W.) Pl. بناوي *binārwī*.

پنځه کلنی *pindzah kalanaey*, adj. Five years old; (Fem.) پنځه کلنۍ *pindzah kalana'ī*.

پنځه لس *pindzah las*, adj. Fifteen. پنځه ويشت *pindzah wisht*, Twenty-five. پنځه ديرش *pindzah dersh*, Thirty-five. پنځه څلويښت *pindzah tsalwekht* or *tsalwesht*, Forty-five.

پنځوس *pindzos*, adj. Fifty. پنځه پنځوس *pindzah pindzos*, Fifty-five. پنځه شپيته *pindzah shpetah*, Sixty-five. پنځه اويا *pindzah ao-yā*, Seventy-five. پنځه اتيا *pindzah at-yā*, Eighty-five. پنځه نوي *pindzah nawī*, Ninety-five.

پنګه *panga'h*, s.f. (3rd) Stock-in-trade, capital, funds, means, reserve, relay, supply, hoard, savings. Pl. ئ *ey*.

پنهم *pinham*, adj. Concealed, hidden, secret; (Fem.) پنهمه *pinhama'h*. پټ پنهم *putt pinham*, Entirely or wholly concealed or hidden. See پټ. (P پنهان).

پنی *panaey*, s.m. (1st) A kind of grass from which brooms are made (Andropogon muricatum). Pl. ي *ī*.

پني *panī*, s.m. Pl. (1st) The name of a tribe of Afghāns (Rī'āz-ul-Muhabbat). پنی *panaey*, Sing. A male of the tribe. پنۍ *pana'ī*, s.f. (6th) A female of the above. Sing. and Pl.

P پنير *panīr*, s.m. (6th) Cheese. Sing. and Pl. پنير مايه *panīr mā-ya'h*, s.f. (3rd) Rennet. Pl. ئ *ey*. See پوڅه

پنړه *parrna'h*, s.f. (3rd) A shoe, a slipper. Pl. ئ *ey*. See پيزار ,کيټۍ ,کوښه ,پنړه ,پڼه, موچنړه, and ګاوله

پنړي *parrnī*, s.m. (1st). Pl. The name given to one of the numerous subdivisions of the Afghāns, in which the Sāfī and Gadūn tribes, as also the Khatānīs, are included. پنړی *parrnaey*, Sing. A male of the above. پنړۍ *parrna'ī*, s.f. (6th) A female of the above. Sing. and Pl. See پني

P پو *pū*, adj. Light, smooth, slight. 2. s.m. (9th) Inquiry, searching, running about. Sing. and Pl. تک و پو کول *tak-o-pū kawul*, verb trans. To enquire diligently, to run about in search of anything.

پو *pū*, s m. (9th) A puff, a blast, act of breathing, inflating, blowing, etc. Sing. and Pl. See پوک

پوپکه *pūpaka'h*, s.f. (3rd) A bump, a swelling, a protuberance. Pl. ئ *ey*. See ماتس

پوپلزي *popal-zī*, s.m. (1st) Pl. The name of an Afghān tribe, the descendants of Popal, son of Zīrak, son of Æsau, son of Malik Abdāl, the progenitor of the Abdālīs. During the Durānī monarchy this tribe furnished the Wuzīrs or Prime Ministers, as a matter of right, being the next in rank to the Suddozīs, the royal tribe. Sing. پوپلزی *popalzaey*, A male of the above. پوپلزۍ *popalza'ī*, s f. (6th) A female of the above. Sing. and Pl.

پوټی *po-taey*, s.m. (1st) A mound, a height, a bluff, a heap of earth. Pl. ي *ī*.

پوټ *pott*, s.m. (2nd) Crust, skin, bark, rind, shell, hide. 2. Disagreement, enmity. Pl. پوټونه *pottūnah*.

پوټسکی *pottuskaey*, adj. A little; small, scarce, few, scanty; seldom, some, less; (Fem.) پوټسک *pottuski*. Pl. (Masc. and Fem.) ي *ī*.

پوټ سوري *pūtt sūrrī*, s.m. (1st) Pl. Bran, chaff. See بوټ سوري

پوټی *pūttaey*, adj. A little, small, scarce, few, scanty, seldom, some, less, etc.; (Fem.) پوټ *pūtti*. Pl. (Masc. and Fem.) ي *ī*. پوټي پوټي *pūttī pūttī*, In pieces, in fragments, in shreds, in crumbs, etc. See پوټسکي

پوڅکۍ *pūtsaka'ī*, s.f. (6th) The lobe of the ear. Sing. and Pl. See پوڅۍ and بوڅۍ

پوڅکۍ *potsaka'ī*, s.f. (6th) A mushroom. Sing. and Pl.

پوڅه *potsa'h*, s.f. (3rd) Cheese, coagulated milk. Pl. ئ *ey*.

بوڅۍ *pūtsa'ī*, s.f. (6th) The lobe of the ear. Sing. and Pl. See بوڅۍ

پوجي *pūjī*, s.f. (3rd) Weeding a field, thinning the lower branches of a tree that it may acquire strength. Pl ئي *a'ī*.. پوجي کول *pūjī kawul*, verb trans. To thin, to weed.

P پوچ *pūch*, adj. Absurd, of no moment or consequence, useless, nonsense, nonsensical, injudicious; (Fem.) پوچه *pūcha'h*. پوچ ويل *pūch wa-yal*, verb trans. To speak foolishly, to make absurd or foolish remarks.

P پوچ گو *pūch go*, Talking nonsense, a speaker of nonsense, or absurdity.

P پوچ گوئي *pūch go'e*, s.f. (3rd) Nonsense, absurdity, folly, rigmarole, inconsistency. Pl. *a'ī*. پوچ گوئي کول *pūch-go'e kawul*, verb trans. To talk absurdly or inconsistently.

پوخ *pokh*, adj. Cooked, dressed (as victuals), ripe. 2. Shrewd, knowing, expert, wise, firm, strong. Pl. پاخه *pākhah*; (Fem.) پخه *pakha'h*. Pl. پخي *pakhey*. See پخيدل and پخول

پوخلي *pūkhuley*, s.f. (3rd) Pl. The hooping cough.

پوده *pūda'h*, s.f. (3rd) The woof of the web in weaving. Pl. ئي *ey*. See تار and بوده

P پوده *pū-dah*, adj. Rotten, decayed, tainted, spoiled, worm-eaten, mildewed, crumbling. پوده کول *pū-dah kawul*, verb trans. To render or make rotten, to destroy, to deteriorate, to corrupt. پوده کيدل *pū-dah kedal*, verb intrans. To turn or grow rotten, to decay, to spoil, to crumble away. پوده والئ *pū-dah wālaey*, s.m. (1st) Decay, rottenness, deterioration, falling to pieces. Pl. والي *wālī*.

پور *por*, s.m. (2nd) A loan, a debt, an advance, etc. Pl. پورونه *porūnah*. پور آخستل *por ākhistal*, verb trans. To borrow, to raise money on loan. پور ورکول *por war-kawul*, verb trans. To lend, to advance money. پور څکل *por kh'kal* (E.), or پور کښل *por k'shal* (W.) verb trans. To collect the amount of a debt, to recover a loan.

پورِ *pori*, adv. To, as far as, near, up to, close to, till, until, during, whilst; over, on that side, beyond, across, opposite. 2. part. Shutting a door, piercing with a spear, stabbing; anointing, putting collyrium into the eyes, colouring the hands with henna; rubbing dirty hands on one. پورِ کول *pori kawul*, verb trans. To apply, to close, to attach, to join, to lay, to put, to place, to plant, to set, to shut, to connect, to fasten, to spread, to plaster, to employ, to engage, to use, to impute, to report anything, such as malice or scandal. پورِ وتل *pori watal*, verb intrans. To pass over, or cross a river, to ferry. پورِ وهل *pori wahal*, verb trans. To push, to impel, to thrust, to drive away, to force. پورِ يستل *pori yastal*, verb trans. To ferry, to carry or transport over a river, brook, etc. 2. To lend, to advance, to accommodate with money. Also written پوري *porī*.

پورِ ژنئ *pori jzanaey*, adj. (past part.) Expelled, driven away, ejected; (Fem.) پورِ ژنِ *pori-jzani*.. Pl. (Masc. and Fem.) ي *ī*. (E.) پورِ جنئ *pori-janaey*; (Fem.) پورِ جنِ *pori-jani*. Pl. (Masc. and Fem.) ي *ī*.

پورِ اورِ *pori aori*, adv. Right through, through and through, from one end or surface to another, here and there, hither and thither. Also پورِ را پورِ *pori rā pori*, پورِ وورِ *pori wori*, and پوري ووري *porī worī*. پورِ اورِ *pori aori*, or پورِ را پورِ وتل *pori rā pori watal*, verb intrans. To pierce, to enter as a pointed instrument, to penetrate, to enter. پورِ اورِ *pori aori*, or پورِ را پورِ يستل *pori rā pori yastal*, verb trans. To pierce, to transfix, to perforate, to transpierce, to impale, to spear, to stick, to spit, to penetrate, to permeate, etc.

پورته *portah*, adv. and prep. Above, on, upon, up, over, a-top, etc. 2. adj. More, greater, greater in quantity. پورته کيدل *portah kedal*, verb intrans. To ascend, to rise, mount, arise, uprise, get up, climb, clamber, scale, escalade. پورته کول *portah kawul*, verb trans, To raise, elevate, lift, upraise, erect, hoist, weigh, exalt, set up, etc.

پورول *porawul*, verb trans. To borrow, to raise money on loan. Pres. پوروي *porawī*; past

پور كه *por kah* or پور وُ كه *por wu-kah*, or پور كړ *por karr* or پور وُ كړ *por wu-karr*; fut. پور به كي *por bah kī*, or به وُ كي *bah wu-kī*; imp. پور كه *por kah* or وُ كه *wu-kah*, or پور كړه *por krrah* or وُ كړه *wu-krrah*; act. part. پورونكيَ *porawūnkaey* or پوروني *porawūnacy*; past part. پور كړيَ *por karraey*; verb. n. پورونه *porawuna'h*.

پوروړيَ *porawurraey*, adj. as s.m. (1st) A creditor, a lender, a dun, a debtor; (Fem.) پوروړِ *porawurri*. Pl. (Masc. and Fem.) ي *ī*.

پوره *pūrah*, adj. Full, complete, entire, exact, perfect, sufficient, just, total, ripe. (s پورا). پوره كيدل *pūrah kedal*, verb intrans. To be completed, ended, fulfilled, perfected, to become full. پوره كول *pūrah kawul*, verb trans. To fill, finish, end, perfect, accomplish, fulfil, perform, execute, terminate, bring to pass, etc.

پوره واليَ *pūrah wālaey*, s.m. (1st) Completion, accomplishment, fulfilment, finish, termination, execution. Pl. والي *wālī*.

پوري *porī*, adv. To, as far as, near, etc. See پورِ.

پوري اوري *porī aorī* or پوري را پوري *porī rā porī*, Right through, etc. See پورِ اور

پوري ژني *porī jzanaey*, adj. (past part.) Expelled, driven away, ejected. See also پورِ ژني and پورِ جني

پوړ *porr*, adj. Half grown, or near puberty (as a boy or girl), nearly ripe (as fruit), half dressed or cooked (as meat); (Fem.) پوړه *porra'h*.

پوړ *pawrr*, s.m. (2nd) A rope for fastening the feet of a cow or other animal. Pl. پوړونه *pawrrūnah*. See also پيكړه

پوړۍ *pawrra'ī*, s.f. (6th) A flight of steps, a staircase, steps, a ladder. Sing. and Pl. See بارجنكي or بارجنګ and اندر پايه

پوزه *poza'h*, s.f. (3rd) The nose of a man or beast. Pl. ې *ey*. چيته پوزه *cheta'h poza'h*, or پته پوزه *pita'h poza'h*, A flat or broad nose. چت پوزيَ *chit-pozaey*, or پت پوزيَ *pit-pozaey*, A person having a flat or broad nose; (Fem.) چته پوز *chita'h-pozi*, or پته پوزِ *pita'h pozi*, A female with a flat or broad nose. Pl. (Masc. and Fem.) ي *ī*. لنډه پوزه *landda'h poza'h*, s.f. (3rd) A short nose. Pl. ې *ey*. لنډ پوزيَ *landd pozaey*, A short-nosed person; (Fem.) لنډ پوزِ *landd pozi*. پوز پري كړي *poz pre karrey*, With the nose cut, cut-nosed, a term of abuse.

پوزيَ *pozaey*, s.m. (1st) A small mat. Pl. ي *ī*. See انديري and بوهر

پوږ *pūjz*, s.m. (2nd) (W.) The act of blowing, a puff, a blast, blowing up a fire, etc. 2. Squirting water on a flower with the mouth to freshen it, or on clothes by washermen or women before folding them, sprinkling. 3. A bellows. Pl. پوږونه *pūjz-ūnah*. See also پوك and پز وهل

پوږ وهل *pūjz wahal*, verb trans. To squirt or sprinkle water, etc.

پوس *pos*, adj. Soft, tender, supple, ductile, easy, gentle, tractable, yielding, bending, silly, etc. Pl. پاسه *pāsa'h*; (Fem.) پوسه *posa'h*. Pl. پوسې *posey*; or پوست *post*, adj. Soft, tender, etc. Pl. پاسته *pāstah*; (Fem.) پوسته *posta'h*. Pl. پوستې *postey*.

P پوست *post*, s.m. (2nd) Crust, shell, skin, hide, bark, etc. 2. Poppy-head or capsule. Pl. پوستونه *postūnah*.

پوست كښل *post k'shal* (W.) or پوست خكل *post kh'kal* (E.), To bark, to shell, to strip of skin, to unskin.

پوستكيَ *postakaey*, s.m. (1st) Skin, hide, untanned leather, crust, bark, peel, rind, etc. Pl. ي *ī*. See پستكي and پت

P پوستي *postī*, s.m. (5th) One who intoxicates himself with infusion of poppy-heads, a sot, a lazy indolent person. Pl. پوستيان *postī-ān*.

پوستيدل *postedal*, verb intrans. To grow or become soft, tender, supple, easy, gentle, tractable. پوستول *postawul*, verb trans. To make or render soft, tender, ductile, tractable, gentle.

P پوستين *postīn*, s.m. (2nd) A fur cloak or coat, a sheepskin coat or vest. Pl. پوستينونه *postīn-ūnah*, or s.m. (5th) Pl. پوستينان *postīnān*.

پوسل *poslal*, verb trans. To clothe, array, enrobe, dress, attire, wrap up, cover, envelope.

Pres. پوسلي *pos-lī*; past وُ پوسلَ *wu-posla*, or وُ پوسله *wu-poslah*; fut. وُ به پوسلي *wu bah poslī*; imp. وُ پوسلَ *wu-posla*, or وُ پوسله *wu-poslah*; act. part. پوسلونکيَ *pos-lūnkaey*, or پوسلونيَ *pos-lūnaey*; past part. پوسليَ *pos-alaey*, or پوسلليَ *poslalaey*; verb. n. پوسلنه *poslana'h*.

پوسل توب *posal tob*, s.m. (2nd) Pl. توبونه *tob-ūnah*; or پوسل تيا *posal tīā*, s.f.(6th). (E.) Sing. and Pl. (W.) Pl. تياوي *tī-ānī*; or پوسل واليَ *posal wālaey*, s.m. (1st) Clothing, dressing, attiring, the act of being clothed. Pl. والي *wālī*.

پوش *posh*, interj. Take care, have a care, look out! (s पश्य).

پوښ *posh* (W.), or *pokh* (E.) s.m. (2nd) (P پوش) Covering, clothed in, wearing, dressed; dress, clothing, apparel. Pl. پوښونه *poshūnah* or *pokhūnah*. پاپوښ *pā-posh* or *pāpokh*, Shoes, slippers, covering for the feet. سبز پوښ *sabz posh* or *sabz pokh*, adj. Clothed in green. پوښ کول *posh* or *pokh kawul*, verb trans. To shape, prepare, or fabricate, as clothes.

پوښاك *poshāk* or *pokhāk*, s.m. (2nd) Vestments, dress, attire, habit, garments, clothes, raiment, accoutrements. Pl. پوښاکونه *posh-ākūnah* or *pokhākūnah*.

پوښښ *poshish* (W.), or *pokhikh* (E.) s.m. (from P پوشيدن) Dress, wear, garments, vestment, covering. Pl. پوښښونه *poshishūnah* or *pokhikh-ūnah*.

پوښتۍ *pūkhta'ī*, s.f. (6th) A rib, the ribs. Sing. and Pl. See پښتۍ

پوښل *pokhal* (E.) or *poshal* (W.) verb trans. To cover in, to roof, to screen, to shelter, to array, to clothe, to attire, to wrap up. 2. To hide, to secrete, etc. 3. To solace, to console, to cheer in grief or calamity. Pres. پوښي *pokhī* or *poshī*; past وُ پوښه *wu-pokhah* or *wu-poshah*; fut. وُ به پوښي *wu bah pokhī* or *poshī*; imp. وُ پوښه *wu-pokhah* or *wu-poshah*; act. part. پوښونکيَ *pokhūnkaey* or *poshūnkaey*, or پوښونيَ *pokhūnaey* or *poshūnaey*; past part. پوښليَ *pokhalaey* or *poshalaey*; verb. n. پوښنه *pokh-ana'h* or *poshana'h*.

پوښيده *poshedah* or *pokhedah*, adj. Concealed, hidden, dressed, clothed, secret. 2. adv. Secretly. پوښيده کول *poshedah* or *pokhedah kawul*, verb trans. To clothe, dress, conceal, hide, secrete.

پوغله *pogh-la'h*, s.f. (3rd) The thin excrement of kids, lambs, etc., before it assumes the orbicular shape. Pl. ې *ey*. See پيخاره

پوك *pūk*, s.m. (2nd) A puff, a blast, the act of blowing. Pl. پوکونه *pūkūnah*. See also پو and پوکي

پوکل *pūkal*, verb trans. To blow, to blow out, to blow up (as a fire), to inflate, to breathe upon, to blow away. Pres. پوکي *pū-kī*; past پوکه *pū-kah*, or وُ پوکه *wu-pū-kah*; fut. وُ به پوکي *wu bah pūkī*; imp. وُ پوکه *wu-pū-kah*, or پوکه *pū-kah*; act. part. پوکونکيَ *pūkūnkaey*, or پوکونيَ *pūkūnaey*; past part. پوکليَ *pūkalaey*; verb. n. پوکنه *pūkana'h*. See پو

پوکنړۍ *pūkarrna'ī*, s.f. (6th) A bladder. Sing. and Pl. See سپوخښه

پوکول *pūkawal*, verb trans. To blow, to blow out, to blow up (as a fire), to inflate, to breathe upon, to blow away. Pres. پوکوي *pūkawī*; past وُ پوکاوه *wu-pūkāwuh*, or وُ پوکاوو *wu-pūkāwo*; fut. وُ به پوکوي *wu bah pūkawī*; imp. پوکوه *pūkawah*, or وُ پوکوه *wu-pūkawah*; act. part. پوکوونکيَ *pūkawūnkaey*, or پوکوونيَ *pūkawūnaey*; past part. پوکوليَ *pūkawulaey*; verb. n. پوکونه *pūkawuna'h*. See پوکل

پوکيَ *pūkaey*, s.m. (1st) A puff, a blast; inflating, blowing. Pl. ي *ī*. See پو

پوګ *pūg*, s.m. (2nd) The act of blowing, a puff, a blast, blowing up a fire, etc. 2. Squirting water on a flower with the mouth to freshen it, or on clothes by washermen or women before folding them, sprinkling. 3. A bellows. Pl. پوګونه *pūgūnah*. پوګ کول or وهل *pūg kawul*, or *wahal*, verb trans. To puff, to blow, to blow up. 2. To squirt water, etc. See پوړ and پړ

P پول *pūl*, s.m. (2nd) or (5th) An aqueduct, a trough, a gutter, a scupper, a launder, etc.

Pl. پولونه *pūlūnah*, or پولان *pūlān*. See بيله and ترناو

پول *pūl*, s.m. (2nd) A film over the eye. Pl. پولونه *pūlūnah*. See گل

پولاد *polād*, s.m. (6th) The finest kind of steel. Sing. and Pl. See فولاد

پولکټ *pū-lak*, s.m. (2nd) A kind of double wedge for fastening the iron ploughshare to the frame of a plough. Pl. پولكونه *pū-lakūnah*.

پوله *pūla'h*, s.f. (3rd) A small embankment of earth in a field for the purpose of regulating the irrigation. Pl. ې *ey*.

پوله *pū-lah*, s.m. (6th) Parched or roasted grain. Sing. and Pl. پوله كول *pūlah kawul*, verb trans. To parch or roast grain.

پون *pūn*, s.m. (9th) The scab or mange. Sing. and Pl. See پم and پمن

پونده *pūnda'h*, s.f. (3rd) The heel. 2. Urging a horse by kicking him with the heels. Pl. ې *ey*. پونده وهل *pūnda'h wahal*, verb trans. To urge a horse by kicking him with the heels. Also written پوندَ *pūnda*.

پونډۍ *pūndda'ī*, s.f. (6th) The heel, the heels. Sing. and Pl. پونډۍ وهل *pūndda'ī wahal*, verb trans. To urge a horse by striking him with the heels. See preceding.

پون سو *pūn sū*, adj. Five hundred. See پنځه سو

پونه *pūna'h*, s.f. (3rd) Small rain, drizzle, mist, sprinkling. 2. Sprinkling water by the mouth. Pl. پونې *pūney*. See پوک

پونړۍ *pūrrna'ī*, s.f. (6th) A roll of cotton for spinning from. Sing. and Pl.

پوول *po-wul*, verb trans. To graze, to browse, to crop. This infinitive is imperfect, and takes some of its tenses from پيايل Pres. پيائي *pīā-yī*; past وُ پوو *wu-po-wū*; fut. وُ به پيائي *wu bah pīā-yī*; imp. وُ پيايه *wu-pīā-yah*, or پيايه *pīā-yah*; act. part. پووونکئ *po-wūnkacy* or پووونئ *po-wūnacy*, or پيايونکئ *pīā-yūnkacy* or پيايونئ *pīā-yūnaey*; past part. پوولئ *po-wulacy* or پيايلئ *pīā-yalaey*; verb. n. پوونه *powana'h* or پوويانه *po-wīāna'h*.

پوه *poh*, adj. Intelligent, knowing, learned, wise; (Fem.) پوهه *poha'h*. پوه نپوه *poh-napoh* or

پوه نه پوه *poh nah poh*, Whether or not, knowingly or unknowingly, etc.

پوهاند *po-hānd*, adj. (W.) Wise, intelligent, learned, clever; (Fem.) پوهانده *po-hānda'h*. See پوه

پوهړ *pūharr*, s.m. (2nd) A large mat. Pl. پوهړونه *pūharrūnah*. See پوزي

پوهړ *poharr*, adj. Foolish, stupid, uncivilized, simple. 2. Slovenly, careless of dress and cleanliness. (H I پهوهڙ). (Fem.) پوهړه *poharra'h*.

پوهړي *poharracy*, adj. as s.m. (1st) (dimin. of پوهړ) A foolish, stupid, uncivilized, or simple person. 2. A sloven, one careless of his person. Pl. ي *ī*; (Fem.) پوهړۍ *poharra'ī*. Sing and Pl.

پوهول *pohawul*, verb trans. To inform, impart, acquaint, apprize, make known, signify, explain, set forth, etc. Pres. پوهوي *pohawī*; past وُ پوهاوه *wu-pohāwuh*, or وُ پوهاوو *wu-pohāwo*; fut. وُ به پوهوي *wu bah pohawī*; imp. وُ پوهوه *wu-pohawah*; act. part. پوهوونکئ *pohawūnkaey*, or پوهوونئ *pohawūnacy*; past part. پوهولئ *pohawulacy*; verb. n. پوهونه *pohawuna'h*.

پوهه *poha'h*, s.f. (3rd) Intellect, understanding, comprehension, reason, sense, capacity, intelligence, conception, judgment, etc. Pl. ې *ey*. پوهيدل *pohedal*, verb intrans. To know, to be informed, to have perception of, to take cognizance of, to examine. Pres. پوهيږي *pohejzī* (W.), or پوهيگي *pohegī* (E.); past وُ پوهيده *wu-pohedah*; fut. وُ به پوهيږي *wu bah pohejzī*, or وُ به پوهيگي *wu bah pohegī*; imp. وُ پوهيږه *wu-pohejzah*, or وُ پوهيگه *wu-pohegah*; act. part. پوهيدونکئ *pohedūnkacy*, or پوهيدونئ *pohedūnaey*; past part. پوهيدلئ *pohedalacy*; verb. n. پوهيدنه *pohedana'h*.

پوهيدنه *pohedana'h*, s.f. (3rd) (verb. n.) Comprehension, intellect; understanding, comprehending, etc. Pl. ې *ey*. See پوهه

P پويه *po-ya'h*, s.f. (3rd) A canter, a hand gallop. Pl. پويې *po-yey*. پويه كول *po-yah kawul*, verb trans. To canter, to gallop.

په *pah*, prep. By, with, upon, on, above, by

means, in company, etc. 2. For, for the sake of, on account of. په بيا بيا *pah bī-ā bī-ā*, adv. Again and again, constantly, frequently, often.

په *pah* or پها *pahā*, interj. Pooh! pooh! a word used to express contempt.

پهار *pahār*, s.m. (2nd) A division of time, a period of three hours. Pl. پهارونه *pahārūnah*. (s پهر).

پهاړئ *pahāṛra'ī*, s.f. (6th) A hog-deer (Cervus porcinus). Sing. and Pl.

s پهر *pahar*, s.m. (2nd) A division of time, a watch or three hours. Pl. پهرونه *paharūnah*. See پهار

پهره *pahra'h*, s.f. (3rd) A watch, a sentinel. 2. Tour of watch. Pl. ې *ey*. پهره كول *pahra'h kawul*, verb trans. To watch. (s پهرا).

پهره دار *pahra'h dār*, s.m. (5th) A watchman, a sentinel. Pl. پهره داران *pahra'h dārān*.

پهړئ *pah-ṛra'ī*, s.f. (6th) A kind of stool or chair made after the fashion of a bedstead. Sing. and Pl. See پيړئ

په لغت *pah laghat*, adv. Quickly, sharply, swiftly, speedily, apace. په سوي لغت *pah sawī laghat*, Very quickly. See also پلغت

پهلواړئ *phul-wāṛraey*, s.m. (1st) A white rose. Pl. ړي *ī*.

P پهلوان *pahlawān*, s.m. (5th) A hero, a champion, a wrestler. Pl. پهلوانان *pahlawānān*. See غښتلئ

P پهلواني *pahlawānī*, s.f. (3rd) Heroism, the business of a champion. Pl. ئ *a'ī*.

پهم *pahm*, s.m. (2nd) Understanding, intellect, mind, sense, capacity, intelligence. Pl. پهمونه *pahmūnah*. See فهم

پهمول *pahmawul*, verb trans. To inform, impart, acquaint, etc. Pres. پهموي *pahmawī*; past وُ پهماوه *wu-pahmāwuh*, or وُ پهماوو *wu-pahmāwo*; fut. وُ به پهموي *wu bah pahmawī*; imp. وُ پهموه *wu-pahmawah*; act. part. پهمونكي *pahmawūnkaey*, or پهموونئ *pahmawūnaey*; past part. پهمولئ *pahmawulaey*; verb. n. پهمونه *pahmawuna'h*.

P پهن دار *pahan dār*, adj. Broad, wide, ample. See سره ور , پلن and پسره ور

پهورته *pahortah*, adj. More, greater, greater in quantity. 2. adv. and prep. Above, on, upon, up, a top, etc, See under پورته

پهه *paha'h*, s.f. (3rd) A plaster, a pledget. Pl. پهي *pahey*.

پهيلول *phelawul*, verb trans. To spread, to open, to unfold, to stretch, to diffuse, to disperse, to scatter, to propagate, to extend, to deploy, etc. Pres. پهيلوي *phelawī*; past وُ پهيلاوه *wu-phelāwuh*; fut. وُ به پهيلوي *wu bah phelawī*; imp. وُ پهيلوه *wu-phelawah*; act. part. پهيلونكئ *phelawūnkaey*, or پهيلوونئ *phelawūnaey*; past part. پهيلولئ *phelawulaey*; verb. n. پهيلونه *phelawuna'h*.

پهيلېدل *pheledal*, verb trans. To spread, to extend itself in length or breadth, to become dispersed, scattered, diffused, to open, to expand, etc. Pres. پهيليږي *phelejzī* (W.), or پهيلېګي *phelegī* (E.); past وُ پهيلېده *wu-pheledah*; fut. وُ به پهيليږي *wu bah phelejzī*, or پهيليګي *phelegī*; imp. وُ پهيليږه *wu-phelejzah*, or پهيليګه *phelegah*; act. part. پهيلېدونكئ *pheledūnkaey*, or پهيلېدونئ *pheledūnaey*; past part. پهيلېدلئ *pheledalaey*; verb. n. پهيلېدنه *pheledana'h*.

s پئ *pa'ī*, s.f. (6th) Milk, the juice of plants. Sing and Pl. See پئ مخي and شوده

P پي *pay*, s.m. (2nd) The foot, the tendon of the foot, a sinew; footing, basis, foundation, track, trace. 2. A ford, a ferry, a place in a river or other water that may be passed by wading. Pl. پيونه *pay-ūnah*.

پي اوبه *pay ao-ba'h*, Water within one's depth, or that is fordable by wading.

پي كول *pay kawul*, verb trans. To ham-string, to cut off a tree close to the ground.

پي وړل *pay w'ṛral*, verb trans. To know, to understand, to catch at a meaning, hint, etc.

P پي *pai*, adv. Behind, after, following in pursuit. پي در پي *pai dar pai*, (P) or پيا پي *paiā pai*, One after the other, successively. پي وهل *pai wahal*, verb trans. To dig, as a piece of a ditch in successive portions, finishing one before commencing the other.

پياڅه *pī-ātsa'h*, s.f. (3rd) Bread made from a kind of millet. Pl. ې *ey.*

پياخله *pī-ākhla'h*, s.f. (3rd) A piece of cloth added to the sleeve or collar of a dress, a collar, a cuff. 2. Exhaling the steam of herbs, etc.; sweating, sweltering, administering anything hot to produce perspiration, covering a person with bed clothes to produce perspiration. Pl. ې *ey.*

پياخله کول *pī-ākhla'h kawul*, verb trans. To sweat, to swelter, to cause perspiration. See پخيل and پېخل

P پياده *pī-ādah*, s.m. (5th) A footman, one on foot, a foot soldier. Pl. پيادگان *pī-āda-gān*. 2. adj. On foot. پياده پا *pī-ādah pā*, adv. A-foot, on foot; also پياده پائي *pī-ādah pā'e*. See also پلي

پيارمه *pī-ārrma'h*, s.f. (3rd) A brace for tightening the tape of a bedstead. 2. The crupper of a saddle for a horse, or the pack-saddle of a bullock. 3. The rope or strap placed on a spinning wheel. Pl. ې *ey.* See لنګه

P پياز *pī-āz*, s.m. (6th) An onion. Sing. and Pl.

پيازکي *pī-āzakaey*, s.m. (1st) (dimin. of پياز) A wild onion, a squill. Pl. ي *ī*.

پيازه *pī-āza'h*, s.f. (3rd) Miscarrying, dropping her young as an animal. 2. Splitting, dividing. Pl. ې *ey.* پيازه کول *pī-āza'h kawul*, verb trans. To miscarry.

P پياله *pī-āla'h*, s.f. (3rd) A cup, a glass; the pan or fire-pan of a musket. Pl. ې *ey.* See کنډولۍ and کنډۍ

پيپنۍ *pepna'ī*, s.f. (6th) A sort of frock or shift worn by young women. Sing. and Pl. See کنډولي and کنډني

پيتي *paitī*, s.f. (3rd) Cooked peas or other kind of pulse. Pl. پيتۍ *paita'ī*. See پاني

پيټ *pett*, s.m. (2nd) A load for the head, a burden. Pl. پيټونه *pettūnah*.

پيټي *pettaey*, s.m. (1st) A load, a burden, a weight. Pl. ي *ī*.

پېځل *petsal*, verb trans. To endure, to suffer, to sustain, to bear (as grief or sorrow). Pres. پېځي *petsī*; past و پېځه *wu-petsah*; fut. و به پېځي *wu bah petsī*; imp. و پېځه *wu-petsah*; act. part. پېځونکی *petsūnkaey*, or پېځونی *petsūnaey*; past part. پېځلي *petsalaey*; verb. n. پېځنه *petsana'h*.

پېځنه *petsana'h*, s.f. (3rd) (verb. n.) Enduring, suffering, sustaining, or bearing grief. Pl. ې *ey.*

پېجمخي *peja-makhaey*, adj. Handsome, beardless, smooth-faced; (Fem.) پېجمخ *peja-makhi*. Pl. (Masc. and Fem.) ي *ī*.

پېجمخ والي *peja-makh-wālaey*, s.m. (1st) Beardlessness, handsomeness, youthfulness, juvenility. Pl. والي *wālī*. See پې مخي

P پيچ *pech*, s.m. (2nd) Twist, revolution; a coil, a plait, a fold, a screw. 2. Perplexity, ambiguity, difficulty, trouble, deceit, complication, etc. Pl. پيچونه *pechūna'h*.

P پيچ پيچ *pech pech*, or پيچ در پيچ *pech dar pech*, adj. Coil within coil, entangled, complex, intricate. پيچ کول *pech kawul*, verb trans. To deceive, to trick, to complicate. 2. To grapple, to seize in wrestling.

پيچ تاب *pech tāb*, or پيچ و تاب *pech-o-tāb*, s.m. (2nd). Perplexity, folds, twisting and twining, contortion, knots, restlessness, alarm, suspense. Pl. پيچ و تابونه *pech-o-tābūnah*.

P پيچک *pechak*, s.m. (2nd) A ball, skein, or clew of thread. 2. The reel or bottom on which thread is wound. Pl. پيچکونه *pechakūnah*.

P پيچ وخم *pech-o-kham*, adj. Twist within twist, curly, curling locks; (Fem.) پيچ وخمه *pech-o-khama'h*. پيچل *pechal*, verb trans. To twist, to involve, to contort, to wind. Pres. پيچي *pechī*; past و پيچه *wu-pechah*; fut. و به پيچي *wu bah pechī*; imp. و پيچه *wu-pechah*; act. part. پيچونکی *pechūnkaey*, or پيچونی *pechūnaey*; past part. پيچلي *pechalaey*; verb. n. پيچنه *pechana'h*.

پيچوارۍ *pechwārra'ī*, s.f. (6th) The heel ropes of a horse. Sing. and Pl. See پچواري

پېچومه *pechūma'h*, s.f. (3rd) Ascent, rise, steepness, elevation. Pl. ې *ey*.

پېچومي *pechūmaey*, s.m. (1st) Ascent, etc. Pl. ي *ī*. See preceding.

پېخاړه *pekhārra'h*, s.f. (3rd) The dung of young goats, sheep, etc., before it assumes the orbicular shape. Pl. ې *ey*.

پېخل *paikhal*, s.m. (2nd). Pl. پېخلونه *paikhalūnah*. See پياخله etc.

P پيدا *paidā*, adj. Born, created, produced, exhibited, discovered, invented. پيدا كول *paidā kawul*, verb trans. To produce, to discover, to breed, to find, to form, to create, to get, earn, gain, invent, procure. پيدا كېدل *paidā kedal*, verb intrans. To be born, to be created, to be found, earned, or produced. پيدا وار *paidā-wār*, s.m. (2nd) Produce of a field, fruit, profit of trade. Pl. پيدا وارونه *paidā-wārūnah*.

پيدايښ *paidā-īsh* (W.), or *paidā-īkh* (E.), s.m. (2nd) Birth, creation, production, earnings, produce, profit. Pl. پيدايښونه *paidā-īshūnah*, or *paidā-īkhūnah*. (P پيدايش)

پيدايښت *paidā-īsht*, or *paidā-īkht*, s.m. (2nd) Creation, production, birth, etc. Pl. پيدايښتونه *paidā-īkhtūnah* or *paidā-īshtūnah*.

پېر *per*, s.m. (2nd) Turning, turn, return, change, meander, curvature. Pl. پېرونه *perūnah* (HI پهير). پېر خوړل *per khwarral*, verb trans. To turn, to wind, to change, meander. پېر ور كول *per war kawul*, verb trans. To change, to alter, avert, convert, divert, drive round, to whirl round. See فير

P پير *pīr*, s.m. (5th) An old man, a saint, a spiritual guide. Pl. پيران *pīrān*.

S پير *pīr*, s.m. (9th) Monday. Sing. and Pl. See گل

P پيراهن *pairāhan*, s.m. (2nd) A long robe, a shirt or shift. Pl. پيراهنونه *pairāhanūnah*.

پېړ *perarr*, adj. Large, stout, fat, gross, corpulent. Sing. and Pl.; (Fem.) پېړه *perarra'h*. Pl. پېړې *perarrey*. See چغانغه, چغاغه, غټ, and پند. پېړ والى *perarr-wālaey*, s.m. (1st). Pl. والي *wālī*; or پېړ توب *perarr-tob*, s.m. (2nd) Corpulence, stoutness, grossness, obesity. Pl. توبونه *tobūnah*.

P پيرزاده *pīr-zādah*, s.m. (5th) The descendant or son of a saint or spiritual guide. Pl. پيرزادگان *pīrzādagān*; s.f. (3rd) پير زادئ *pīrzāda'ī*, The daughter of a saint, etc. Sing. and Pl.

پېرزو *per-zo*, adj. Proper, fitting, becoming, competent, corresponding, suitable, agreeable, just, worthy, reasonable. پېرزو لرل *per-zo laral*, verb trans. To consider as suitable or fitting, to have a desire or wish to bestow anything on another.

پېرزوينه *per-zowyana'h*, s.f. (3rd) Fitness, suitableness, reasonableness, justness, worth, desire, wish, inclination, leaning, bent, fancy, hankering, partiality, longing. Pl. ې *ey*; also پېرزو والى *perzo-wālaey*, s.m. (1st). Pl. والي *wālī*. See پرزو

پيرل *pī-ral*, verb trans. To purchase, to buy. See پيرودل

P پيرو *pai-rau*, s.m. (5th) (act. part.) Following, a follower, a pursuer, Pl. پيروان *pai-rauān*.

پېروان *per-wān*, s.m. (2nd) (W.) The after-birth or placenta. (HI پرين). Pl. پېروانونه *perwānūnah*. See پريوان

P پيروي *pai-rauī*, s.f. (3rd) Following, imitation, prosecution, pursuit, investigation. Pl. ئ *a'ī*. پيروي كول *paī-rawī kawul*, verb trans. To follow, to follow up, to prosecute, to pursue, to investigate.

پيرودل *pīrawdal*, verb trans. To buy, to purchase. Pres. پيري *pīrī*; past وُ پيرود *wu-pīrawda* or وُ پيروده *wu-pīrawdah*, or وُ پير *wu-pīra* or وُ پيره *wu-pīrah* (from پيرل); fut. وُ به پيري *wu bah pīrī*; imp. وُ پيره *wu-pīrah*, or پيره *pīrah*; act. part. پيرودونكى *pīrawdūnkaey*, or پيرودنى *pīrawdūnaey*; past part. پيرودلى *pīrawdalaey*; verb. n. پيرودنه *pīrawdana'h*. See also پيرل

پېروني *perūney*, s.f. (3rd) Pl. The Pleiades. See جمبق ستوري

P پيري *pīrī*, s.f. (3rd) Old age. 2. **The** business of a saint or spiritual guide. Pl. ئ *a'ī*. See زور

پیرَي *peraey*, s.m. (1st) A demon, an evil spirit, one of the genii. Pl. ي *ī*; s.f. (6th) پیرئ *pera'ī*. A female of the above. Sing. and Pl. See ښه پیري or ښاه پیري

پیرياني *pere-ānaey*, s.m. (1st) A person possessed of a devil or evil spirit. Pl. ي *ī*; s.f. (6th) ئ *a'ī*. Sing. and Pl.

پیړ *perr*, adj. Fat, stout, gross, obese; thick, large, etc.; (Fem.) پیړه *perra'h*. See also پیړ

پیړوالی *perr wālaey*, s.m. (1st). Pl. والي *wālī*; or پیړ توب *perr-tob*, s.m. (2nd) Corpulence, stoutness, grossness, obesity, thickness, amplitude, bulk. Pl. توبونه *tob-ūnah*. See also پیړ والي

پیړزه *pīrr-za'h*, s.f. (3rd) A detached hill or mound separated from the higher range. Pl. ئ *ey*. See پیزه and غندي

پیړه *perra'h*, s.f. (3rd) A globular mass of leaven prepared for baking. 2. A kind of sweetmeat made from milk and sugar. Pl. ئ *ey*.

پیړئ *perra'ī*, s.f. (6th) A stool, a chair made after the fashion of a bedstead. 2. A generation of progenitors. Sing. and Pl. پیړئ په پیړئ *perra'ī pah perra'ī*, From generation to generation. See پهړئ (s پیڑهي).

P پیزار *paizār*, s.m. (2nd) A slipper, a shoe. Pl. پیزارونه *paizārūnah*. See پنړه, پنړهه, etc.

پیزل *pezal*, verb trans. To fine-draw, to darn. Pres. پیزي *pezī*; past وُ پیزه *wu-pezah*; fut. وُ به پیزي *wu bah pezī*; imp. وُ پیزه *wu-pezah*; act. part. پیزونکَي *pezūnkaey* or پیزونَي *pezūnaey*; past part. پیزلَي *pezalaey*; verb. n. پیزنه *pezana'h*. See also بیزل

پیزلَي *pezalaey*, adj. (past part.) Darned, fine-drawn, repaired; (Fem.) پیزلِ *pezali*. Pl. (Masc. and Fem.) ي *ī*. See بیزلي

پیزوان *pezwān*, s.m. (2nd) A nose-ring, an ornament for the nose; a rope or ring inserted in a bullock's nose. Pl. پیزوانونه *pezwānūnah*.

پیزوانَي *pezwānaey*, s.m. (1st) A bullock with the nose bored for a ring or bridle, a bullock with a bridle or ring in the nose. Pl. ي *ī*; s.f. (6th) ئ *a'ī*. Sing. and Pl.

پیزه *peza'h*, s.f. (3rd) The peak of a mountain, apex, summit, top, crest, brow, or crown. Pl. ئ *ey*.

پیزَي *pezaey*, adj. Withered, faded, decayed, shrivelled; (Fem.) پیزئ *peza'ī*. پیزَي کیدل *pezaey kedal*, verb intrans. To fade, to wither, decay, etc. See مړاوي and مړام

پیزئ *pai-za'ī*, s.f. (6th) Spelling with the vowel points, syllabling. Sing. and Pl. پیزئ کول *paiza'ī kawul*, verb trans. To syllable.

پیژندل *pejzandal*, verb trans. To distinguish, to recognize by recollection, remembrance, representation or description, to know, to be familiar with, to be no stranger to. Pres. پیژني *pejzanī*; past وُ پیژاند *wu-pejzānd*, or وُ پیژنده *wu-pejzāndah*; fut. وُ به پیژني *wu bah pejzanī*; imp. وُ پیژنه *wu-pejzanah*; act. part. پیژندنکي *pejzandūnkaey*, or پیژندونَي *pejzandūnaey*; past part. پیژندلَي *pejzandalaey*; verb. n. پیژندنه *pejzandana'h*, or پیژانده *pejzāndah*.

پیژانده *pejzāndah*, s.m. (6th) Sing. and Pl.; or پیژندنه *pejzandana'h*, s.f. (3rd) (verb. n.) Recognition, knowledge, cognizance, familiarity, understanding, comprehension; also, knowing, understanding, recognizing. Pl. ئ *ey*.

پیژند گلوي *pejzand galwī*, s.f. (3rd) Acquaintance, knowledge, understanding. Pl. ئ *a'ī*. Also written پیژند گلي *pejzand galī*. Pl. ئ *a'ī*. See preceding.

پیس *pes*, s.m. (5th) Leprosy, also a leper; s.f. (3rd) پیسه *pesa'h*, A female leper. Pl. ئ *ey*. پیسي *pesī*, adj. Leprous. See برګ.

پیسانړي *pīsārrnaey*, s.m. (1st) Somewhat, a little, a small quantity, a barley-corn. Pl ي *ī*.

پیسه *paisa'h*, s.f. (3rd) The name of a copper coin. Pl. ئ *ey*. (HI پیسا).

P پیش *pesh*, adj. Before, in front, advanced. 2. The vowel point (ـُ). پیش بندي *pesh bandī*, s.f. (3rd) Foresight, timely preparation. Pl. ئي *a'ī*. پيش بين *pesh bīn*, adj. Prudent, provident, wise. پيش بيني *peshbīnī*, s.f. (3rd) Prudence, foresight. Pl. ئي *a'ī* پيش خانه *pesh khāna'h*, s.f. (3rd) A tent or other baggage sent on before. Pl. ئي *ey*. پيش دست *pesh dast*, adj. Anticipating, being beforehand, surpassing. پيش دستي *pesh dastī*, s.f. (3rd) The being beforehand, anticipation, excelling, surpassing, aggression. Pl. ئي *a'ī*. پيش رس *pesh ras*, adj. Early (as fruit, grain, etc.) پيش رو *pesh rau*, adj. A precursor, a leader. 2. s.m. (2nd) Fear, doubt, suspense. Pl. پيش رووُنه *pesh-rauūnah*. پيش روي *pesh rawī*, s.f. (3rd) The act of preceding. Pl. ئي *a'ī*. پيش قبضه *pesh ḳabẓa'h*, s.f. (3rd) A kind of dagger. Pl. ئي *ey*. پيشوا *peshwā*, s.m. (5th) A leader, a precursor. Pl پيشوايان *peshwā-yān*.

P پيشان *peshān*, adj. Before, in front, advanced. پيشانه خونه *peshānah khūna'h*, s.f. (3rd) An inner or back room. Pl. ئي *ey*. See پستو

P پيشاني *peshānī*, s.f. (3rd) The forehead, the brow. Pl. ئي *a'ī*. See وچولي

P پيشتر *pesh-tar*, adv. Before, prior, sooner, formerly, heretofore, ago; (Fem.) پيشتره *pesh-tara'h*.

P پيشخور *pesh khor*, adj. A person who lives on credit, or on advance of wages; (Fem.) پيشخوره *pesh khora'h*.

پيشخوري *pesh khorī*, s.f. (3rd) (P) The living on credit. 2. A small quantity of grain taken by the farmer for present use before the threshing of the crop. Pl. ئي *a'ī*.

P پيشكي *peshakī*, s.f. (3rd) An advance of money or wages. Pl. ئي *a'ī*.

پيش لمىَ *pesh lamaey*, s.m. (1st) The meal before the morning during the fast of the Ramazān. Pl. ي *ī*.

پيش منىَ *pesh manaey*, or پيش نمىَ *pesh namaey*, s.m. (1st). See preceding. Pl. ي *ī*.

P پيشور *peshawar*, s.m. (5th) An artificer, a workman, an artizan. Pl. پيشوران *peshawarān*. s.f. (3rd) پيشوره *peshawara'h*. A work-woman, etc. Pl. ئي *ey*. See پيشه ور

P پيشه *peshah*, s.f. (3rd) Trade, profession, custom, habit, practice. Pl. ئي *ey*.

پيشه ور *peshah-war*, s.m. (5th) An artificer, a workman, etc. Pl. پيشه وران *peshah-warān*. s.f. (3rd) پيشه وره *peshah-wara'h*. Pl. ئي *ey*.

پيشئي *pīsha'ī*, s.f. (6th) A small nose ring. 2. A caterpiller in general. Sing. and Pl. ببره پيشئي *babarah pīsha'ī*, A palmer-worm.

پيشيدل *peshedal*, verb intrans. To close itself (as a door or wound), to unite or coalesce. Pres. پيشيږي *peshejzī* (W.), or پيشيگي *peshegī* (E.); past پيش وُ شه *pesh wu-shah*, or پيش شه *pesh shah*; fut. پيش به شي *pesh bah shī*, or به وُ شي *bah wu-shī*; imp. پيش شه *pesh shah*, or وُ شه *wu-shah*; act. part. پيشيدونكىَ *peshedūnkaey*, or پيشيدونىَ *peshedūnaey*; past part. پيش *pesh*, or پيش شوىَ *pesh sharaey*; verb. n. پيشيدنه *peshedana'h*.

پيشول *peshawul*, verb trans. To shut, to close, to fasten, to place. Pres. پيشوي *peshawī*; past پيش كه *pesh kah*, پيش كړ *pesh karr*, or پيش وُ كه *pesh wu-kah*, or پيش وُ كړ *pesh wu-karr*; fut. پيش به كي *pesh bah kī*, or پيش به وُ كي *pesh bah wu-kī*, or پيش به كړي *pesh bah krrī*, or پيش به وُ كړي *pesh bah wu-krrī*; imp. پيش كه *pesh kah*, or وُ كه *wu-kah*, or پيش كړه *pesh krrah*, or وُ كړه *wu-krrah*; act. part. پيشوونكىَ *peshawūnkaey*, or پيشوونىَ or *peshawūnaey*; past part. پيش كړي *pesh karraey*; verb. n. پيشونه *peshawuna'h*.

پيښ *pekh* (E.), or *pesh* (W.), adj. Before, in front, advanced; (Fem.) پيښه *pekha'h*, or *pesha'h*.

پيښاور *pekhāwar* (E.), or *peshāwar* (W.), s. prop. The name of a city and district west of the Indus. پيښاورىَ *pekhāwaraey*, or *peshāwaraey*, s.m. (1st) A native of Peshāwar. Pl. ي *ī*. s.f. (6th) پيښاورئي *pekhāwara'ī* or *peshāwara'ī*, A woman of Peshāwar. Sing. and Pl.

پيښ كښ *pekh-kakh* (E.), or *pesh-kash* (W.), s.m. (2nd) A present, a tribute, a gift. Pl. پيښ كښونه *pekh kakhūnah*, or *pesh kashūnah*. (P پيش كش).

پيښور *pe<u>kh</u>awar* (E.), or *pe<u>sh</u>awar* (W.), s. prop. The city and district of Pe<u>sh</u>āwar. See پيښاور

پيښوري *pe<u>kh</u>awaraey*, or *pe<u>sh</u>awaraey*, s.m. (1st) A native of Pe<u>sh</u>āwar. Pl. ي *ī*. s.f. (6th) ئ *a'ī*. Sing. and Pl.

پيښول *pe<u>kh</u>awul* (E.), or *pe<u>sh</u>awul* (W.), verb trans. To cause or make to meet, or encounter, to introduce, to conduct and make known, to bring to be acquainted, to bring into notice, to import. Pres. پيښوي *pe<u>kh</u>awī*, or *pe<u>sh</u>awī*; past پيښ كړ *pe<u>kh</u>* or *pe<u>sh</u> karr*, or وُ كړ *wu-karr*; fut. پيښ به كړي *pe<u>kh</u>* or *pe<u>sh</u> bah krrī*, or به وُ كړي *bah wu-krrī*; imp. پيښ كړه *pe<u>kh</u>* or *pe<u>sh</u> krrah* or وُ كړه *wu-krrah*; act. part. پيښوونكي *pe<u>kh</u>awūnkaey* or *pe<u>sh</u>awūnkaey*, or پيښووني *pe<u>kh</u>awūnaey* or *pe<u>sh</u>awūnaey*; past part. پيښولي *pe<u>kh</u>awulaey* or *pe<u>sh</u>awulaey*; verb. n. پيښونه *pe<u>kh</u>awuna'h* or *pe<u>sh</u>awuna'h*.

پيښي *pe<u>kh</u>ey* (E.), or *pe<u>sh</u>ey* (W.), s.f. (3rd) Pl. Ridicule, burlesque, caricature, mockery. پيښي كول *pe<u>kh</u>ey* or *pe<u>sh</u>ey kawul*, verb trans. To mock, to mimic, to ape, to personate, to counterfeit, to caricature, to burlesque, to ridicule, to vex, to provoke.

پيښيدل *pe<u>kh</u>edal* (E.), or *pe<u>sh</u>edal* (W.), verb intrans. To meet, to encounter, to have interview with, etc. Pres. پيښيږي *pe<u>sh</u>ejzī* (W.), or پيښيگي *pe<u>kh</u>egī* (E.); past پيښ شه *pe<u>sh</u>* or *pe<u>kh</u> <u>sh</u>ah*, or پيښ وُ شه *pe<u>sh</u>* or *pe<u>kh</u> wu-<u>sh</u>ah*; fut. پيښ به شي *pe<u>sh</u>* or *pe<u>kh</u> bah <u>sh</u>ī*, or پيښ به وُ شي *pe<u>sh</u>* or *pe<u>kh</u> bah wu-<u>sh</u>ī*; imp. پيښ شه *pe<u>sh</u>* or *pe<u>kh</u> <u>sh</u>ah*, or پيښ وُ شه *pe<u>sh</u>* or *pe<u>kh</u> wu-<u>sh</u>ah*; act. part. پيښيدونكي *pe<u>sh</u>e-dūnkaey* or *pe<u>kh</u>edūnkaey*, or پيښيدوني *pe<u>sh</u>e-dūnaey* or *pe<u>kh</u>edūnaey*; past part. پيښ شوي *pe<u>sh</u>* or *pe<u>kh</u> <u>sh</u>awaey*; verb. n. پيښيدنه *pe<u>sh</u>e-dana'h* or *pe<u>kh</u>edana'h*.

P پيغام *pai<u>gh</u>ām*, or پيغم *pai<u>gh</u>am*, s.m. (2nd) A message, an injunction. Pl. پيغامونه *pai<u>gh</u>ām-ūnah*, or پيغمونه *pai<u>gh</u>amūnah*.

P پيغامبر *pai<u>gh</u>ām-bar*, or پيغمبر *pai<u>gh</u>am-bar*, s.m. (5th) A messenger. 2. A prophet. Pl. پيغامبران *pai<u>gh</u>āmbarān*, or پيغمبران *pai<u>gh</u>am-barān*.

P پيغامبري *pai<u>gh</u>āmbarī*, or پيغمبري *pai<u>gh</u>ambarī*, s.f. (3rd) Mission (especially) as a prophet, Pl. ئ *a'ī*.

پيغله *pe<u>gh</u>-la'h*, s.f. (3rd) A virgin, a maid, a maiden, a damsel. Pl. ئ *ey*. See پغله , جنئ , and جل or نجل

پيغور *pe<u>gh</u>or*, s.m. (2nd) Calumny, slander, railing, reproach, opprobrious language, abuse. Pl. پيغورونه *pe<u>gh</u>or-ūnah*. (P پيغار or پيغاره).

پيغور ور كول *pe<u>gh</u>or war-kawul*, verb trans. To reproach, to abuse, to rail at, to calumniate, to slander.

پيكړه *pai-karra'h*, s.f. (3rd) An anklet, a ring, an ornament, a fetter. Pl. پيكړي *pai-karrey*, Fetters, manacles.

پيكل *paykal*, s.m. (2nd) A rope or line used for hanging clothes on. Pl. پيكلونه *paykalūnah*. See سهه and پري and كديكه

پيكوي *pekawaey*, s.m. (1st) A ribbon or band for fastening plaits of women's hair. Pl. ي *ī*. See پيبوي and بچوي

P پيل *pīl*, s.m. (5th) A male elephant. Pl. پيلان *pilān*. s.f. (3rd) پيله *pīla'h*, A female elephant. Pl. ئ *ey*. See هاتي

پيلات *pe-lāt*, s.m. (2nd) (corrup. of A فعلات), Fraud, deceit, artifice, subterfuge, imposture. Pl. پيلاتونه *pe-lāt-ūnah*.

P پيلپا *pīl-pā*, adj. Afflicted with elephantiasis. 2. s.f. (6th) Elephantiasis. (E.) Sing. and Pl.; (W.) Pl. پيلپاوي *pīl-pāwī*.

P پيله *pela'h*, s.f. (3rd) The ball or cocoon which the silkworm forms round itself. Pl. ئ *ey*.

P پيمان *paimān*, s.m. (2nd) A promise, agreement, confirmation, asseveration, an oath. Pl. پيمانونه *paimānūnah*. پيمان كول *paimān kawul*, or پيمان تړل *paimān tarral*, verb trans. To make an agreement, to promise, to give an asseveration, to make or take an oath.

P پيمانه *paimāna'h*, s.f. (3rd) A goblet, a certain dry measure. Pl. پيماني *paimāney*. پيمانه كول *paimānah kawul*, verb trans. To measure.

P پيمايش *paimā-esh*, s.m. (2nd) (verb. n. of P پيمودن), Measure, limit. Pl. پيمايشونه *paimā-eshūnah.*

پئي مخي *pa'ī makhaey*, adj. Handsome, beardless, smoothfaced. Pl. پئي مخي *pa'ī makhī*; (Fem.) پئي مخه *pa'ī makha'h.* Pl. ي *ey.*

پئي مختوب *pa'ī makhtob*, s.m. (2nd) Beardlessness, handsomeness, youthfulness, juvenility. Pl. پئي مختوبونه *pa'ī makhtobūnah*; or (W.) پيجه مخ والئ *peja-makh-wālaey*, s.m. (1st) Pl. والي *wālī.*

پينځه *pīndzah*, adj. Five. See پنځه

پينل *pī-nal*, verb trans. To chuck into the mouth from the palm of the hand, as grain, medicine, etc. Pres. پيني *pīnī*; past وُ پينه *wu-pīnah*, or وُ پين *wu-pīna*; fut. وُ به پيني *wu bah pīnī*; imp. وُ پينه *wu-pīnah*; act. part. پينونکئ *pīnūnkaey*, or پينونئ *pīnūnaey*; past part. پينلئ *pīnalaey*; verb. n. پينته *pīnana'h.* See پکل and خرپت

پينه *pīna'h*, s.f. (3rd) A wooden bowl or trough for making dough in. 2. A piece, a patch. Pl. ي *ey.* See شانک

پيودل *pew-dal*, verb trans. To string, to file, to put on a line, to spit, to pierce, to thrust through. Pres. پيودي *pew-dī*; past وُ پيود *wu-pewd*; fut. وُ به پيودي *wu bah pew-dī*; imp. وُ پيوده *wu-pewdah*; act. part. پيودونکئ *pewd-ūnkaey*, or پيودونئ *pewd-ūnaey*; past part. پيودلئ *pewdalaey*; verb. n. پيودنه *pewdana'h.*

پيودلئ *pewdalaey*, adj. (past part.) Strung, filed, spitted, pierced, thrust through; (Fem.) پيودلِ *pewdali.* Pl. (Masc. and Fem.) ي *ī.*

پيوره *pa'i-wara'h*, adj. as s.f. (3rd) Giving much milk (as a cow, etc.) Pl. ي *ey.* See لنګه

P پيوست *paiwast*, s.m. (2nd) Junction, connexion, friendship. 2. Touching, joining, a join. Pl. پيوستونه *paiwastūna'h.* See کښت

P پيوستګي *paiwastagī*, s.f. (3rd) Junction, proximity, contiguity, closeness, adhesion, attachment. Pl. ئي *a'ī.* پيوستګي کول *paiwastagī kawul*, verb trans. To form attachment, to make or cause closeness or junction.

پيوستون *paiwastūn*, s.m. (6th) Junction, connexion, friendship, attachment, closeness. Sing. and Pl.

P پيوسته *paiwastah*, adj. Joined, contiguous, attached; adv. Always, continually. پيوسته ابرو *paiwastah abrū*, adj. Whose eyebrows join above the nose. پيوسته کيدل *paiwastah kedal*, or پيوستيدل *paiwastedal*, verb intrans. To join, fasten, tie, bind, connect, attach. Pres. پيوستيږي *paiwastejzī* (W.), or پيوستيګي *paiwastegī* (E.); past پيوسته شه *paiwastah shah*, or وُ شه *wu-shah*; fut. پيوسته به شي *paiwastah bah shī*, or به وُ شي *bah wu-shī*; imp. پيوسته شه *paiwastah shah*, or وُ شه *wu-shah*; act. part. پيوستيدونکئ *paiwastedūnkaey*, or پيوستيدونئ *paiwastedūnaey*; past part. پيوسته شوئ *paiwastah shawaey*; verb. n. پيوستيدنه *paiwastedana'h*, or پيوستون *paiwastūn.* پيوسته کول *paiwastah kawul*, verb trans. To join, to fasten, to bind, to connect, to attach.

P پيوند *paiwand*, s.m. (2nd) (part. from پيوستن) Joining, attaching, connecting, linking, junction, conjunction, addition, connexion, relationship. 2. A joint, a patch, a join, a graft, a bud, a scion. Pl. پيوندونه *paiwandūnah.* پيوند کول *paiwand kawul*, verb trans. To graft, to inoculate (as a tree). 2. To join, to patch.

پي هچ *pey huch*, s.m. (6th) A tree of the pine family. Sing. and Pl.

پيوئ *peyawaey*, s.m. (1st) A kind of ribbon or band for fastening the ends of the plaits of hair of young girls and women, generally made of various colours. The plainer bands worn by elderly females are called بچوي. Pl. پيوي *peyawī.* See بچوي and پيکوي

ت

ت *te*, The fourth letter of the Pushto and Persian alphabets, is the third of the Arabic, and pronounced *ta.* It stands for 400 according to the Arabic *abjad*, or appropriation of the letters to represent numbers. In conformity with the rules of the latter language also, when prefixed to a noun, it may be the تاء القسم, denoting an oath; as تا لله, By God.

تَ *ta*, or ته *tah*, The second personal pronoun of the Pushto language. With transitive verbs in the past tenses, and in the oblique cases, it becomes changed to تا *tā*. See my Grammar, page 32.

P تا *tā*, adv. To, until, as far as, whilst, as long as, even to, in order that, to the end that, in such a manner that.

تا *tā*, s.f. (6th) A fold, a plait, a ply, a sheet of paper, etc. 2. A noise, a sound. (E.) Sing. and Pl.; (W.) Pl. تاوي *tāwī*. See also ته. يوه تا *yawah tā*, adj. Simple, single, singular, unique. دوي تا *dwey tā*, Double, two-fold. دري تا *drey tā*, Triple, three-fold, etc.

P تاب *tāb*, s.m. (2nd) Heat, light, splendour. 2. Power, strength, endurance. 3. Rage, fury. 4. Burning, inflaming, illuminating. Pl. تابونه *tābūnah*. تاب دار *tāb dār*, adj. Bright, luminous. 2. Twisted; (Fem.) تاب داره *tāb-dāra'h*. See تاو

P تابان *tābān*, adj. (from تافتن) Resplendent, splendid, glittering, burning, refulgent; (Fem.) تابانه *tābāna'h*.

P تاب دان *tāb dān*, s.m. (2nd) A lattice, a sky-light. Pl. تاب دانونه *tāb-dānūnah*.

P تابستان *tābistān*, s.m (2nd) The hot season, summer. Pl. تابستانونه *tābistānūnah*. See اوري and دوبي

A تابع *tābiæ*, s.m. (5th) (act. part. from تبع) A dependant, a follower, a subject. Pl. تابعان *tābiæ-ān*. تابعه *tā-biæ'h*, s.f. (3rd). Pl. ې *ey*.

P تابنده *tābindah*, s m. (5th) Shining, a giver of light. Pl. تابندگان *tābindagān*.

A تابوت *tābūt*, s.m. (2nd) A coffin, a bier. 2. The ark of the covenant, presented by God to Adam. Pl. تابوتونه *tābūtūnah*.

تابين *tābīn*, s.m. (5th) A dependant, a follower, a subject. (A تابع). Pl. تابينان *tābīnān*. تابينه *tābīna'h*, s.f. (3rd) A female follower or dependant. Pl. ې *ey*.

P تاتار *tātār*, s.m. (9th) The name of a country, Tartary. 2. A Tartar, a native of Tartary. Sing. and Pl.

تاتنگ *tā-tang*, s.m. (2nd) The girth of a saddle. 2. The name of a Durrah or valley in the Kohistān of Kābul. Pl. تاتنگونه *tā-tangūnah*.

A تاثير *tā-ṣīr*, s.m. (2nd) (inf. II of اثر) The making an impression, operation, penetration. Pl. تاثيرونه *tāṣīrūnah*. (A Pl. تاثيرات).

P تاج *tāj*, s.m. (2nd) A crown, a diadem, a tiara, a crest, the comb of a bird. Pl. تاجونه *tājūnah*.

P تاج بخش *tāj-bakhsh*, adj. (used as a substantive) An emperor, a giver of kingdoms. تاج دار *tāj dār*, s.m. (5th) One who wears a crown, a king, a prince. Pl. تاج داران *tāj dārān*; s.f. (3rd) تاج داره *tāj dāra'h*. Pl. ې *ey*.

P تاج خروس *tāj-i-kharūs*, s.m. (6th) The comb of a cock. 2. The cockscomb flower (Amaranthus, or Celosia). Sing. and Pl.

A تاجر *tājir*, s.m. (5th) (part. act. of تجارت) A trader, a merchant. Pl. تاجران *tājirān*.

تاجک *tājik*, s.m. (5th) A name applied to descendants of Arabs, numbers of whom reside about the chief towns of W. Afghānistān. Pl. تاجکان *tājikān*. تاجکه *tājika'h*, s.f. (3rd). A female of the above. Pl. ې *ey*. See تاژک

P تاخت *tākht*, s.m. (2nd) Plunder, ravage, assault, attack, inroad, invasion. 2. A run, a gallop, a foray. Pl. تاختونه *tākhtūna'h*. تاخت کول *tākht kawul*, verb trans. To attack, to assault, to invade, to ravage; to run, to gallop.

P تاخت تاراج *tākht tārāj*, s.m. (9th) Assault and plunder, depredation, devastation. Sing. and Pl. تاخت تاراج کول *tākht tārāj kawul*, verb trans. To ruin, to depopulate.

A تاخير *tākhīr*, s.m. (2nd) (inf. II of آخرت) Delay, procrastination, impediment. Pl. تاخيرونه *tākhīrūnah*. تاخير کول *tākhīr kawul*, verb trans. To delay, procrastinate, postpone, retard.

A تاديب *tādīb*, s.m. (2nd) (inf. II of ادب) Correction, chastisement, amendment, discipline, erudition. Pl. تاديبونه *tādībūnah*. تاديب کول *tādib kawul*, verb trans. To instruct, to correct, to chastise.

P تار *tār*, s.m. (2nd) A thread, a lace, a yarn, the string of a musical instrument, the warp or threads placed lengthwise in weaving a piece of cloth. Pl. تارونه *tārūnah*.

تار تار *tār tār*, or تار په تار *tār pah tār*, adj. Dispersed, scattered, dishevelled, streaming, loose (as the hair).

P تاراج *tārāj*, s.m. (2nd) Plunder, devastation. Pl. تاراجونه *tārājūnah*. تاراج کول *tārāj kawul*, verb trans. To plunder, to spoil.

تار په تارول *tār pah tārawul*, verb trans. To disperse, to scatter, to spread, to distribute; to perplex, to confuse, to derange, to disorder, to distract, to perturb. See تار په تار

A تارک *tārik*, s.m. (5th) (act. part. of ترک) Leaving, deserting. 2. A deserter. Pl. تارکان *tārikān*; s.f. (3rd) تارکه *tārika'h*. Pl. ې *ey*.

تارک الدنيا *tārik-ud-dunyā*, adj. Abandoning the world, sober, chaste. 2. An anchoret, a hermit.

تارو *tā-rū*, s.m. (5th) A black partridge. Pl. تاروگان *tārūgān*.

تارول *tārawul*, verb trans. To disperse, to spread, to scatter, etc.

A تاريخ *tārīkh*, s.m. (2nd) Date, epoch, era, day of a month. 2. Annals, history. Pl. تاريخونه *tārīkhūnah*.

P تاريخ وار *tārīkh wār*, adv. Daily, at stated periods.

P تاريک *tārīk*, adj. Dark, obscure; (Fem.) تاريکه *tārīka'h*.

P تاريکي *tārīkī*, s.f. (3rd) Darkness, obscurity, gloom. Pl. ئې *a'ī*. See تياره and تاريکه

تاړ *tāṟr*, s.m. (2nd) A gang of robbers, a band, a company. 2. Plunder, spoil, robbery. Pl. تاړونه *tāṟrūnah*; or تاړاک *tāṟrāk*, s.m. (2nd). Pl. تاړاکونه *tāṟrākūnah*. تاړ پريوتل *tāṟr prewatal*, verb intrans. To fall on in a gang, to fall on as brigands, to attack. تاړ *tāṟr* or تاړاک کول *tāṟrāk kawul*, verb trans. To plunder, to spoil. See داړ

تاړه *tāṟrah*, adj. Ruined, spoiled, poor, wretched, distressed, abject.

تاړي *tāṟrī*, s.m. (1st) Pl. Clapping the hands to express approbation, and to keep time in music. (s ताली).

تاز *tāz*, s.m. (5th) A species of edible locust produced in the autumn. They alight on trees in swarms, and are captured by smoking them from beneath. Pl. تازان *tāzān*.

تازک *tāzik*, s.m. (5th) A Tājik. Pl. تازکان *tāzikān*; s.f. (3rd) تازکه *tāzika'h*. Pl. ې *ey*. See تاجک

P تازه *tāzah*, adj. Fresh, new, young, green, tender. 2. Fat. 3. Happy, pleased. تازه کيدل *tāzah kedal*, verb intrans. To increase, to flourish, to be in good case. تازه کول *tāzah kawul*, verb trans. To renew, to refresh, to recreate. تازگي *tāzagī*, s.f. (3rd) Freshness, newness, greenness. 2. Fatness, plumpness. 3. Pleasure, happiness. Pl. ئې *a'ī*.

P تازه په تازه *tāzah pah tāzah*, adj. Fresh and blooming.

P تازيانه *tāzi-yāna'h*, s.f. (3rd) A whip, a scourge. Pl. تازيانې *tāzi-yāney*. تازيانه وهل *tāzi-yāna'h wahal*, verb trans. To whip, to scourge. See کروړې

P تازي *tāzī*, s.m. (5th) A greyhound. Pl. تازيان *tāzī-ān*. تازئ *tāza'ī*, s.f. (6th) A greyhound bitch. Sing. and Pl.

P تاس *tās*, s.m. (2nd) A brass cup or vessel. Pl. تاسونه *tāsūnah*. See کټورې

A تاسف *tāssuf*, s m. (2nd) (inf. v of اسف) Pining, lamenting, grief, regret, remorse, sighing, bemoaning, brooding over affliction. Pl. تاسفونه *tāssufūnah*. تاسف خوړل *tāssuf khwaṟral*, verb trans. To grieve, to lament, to pine, to regret.

تاسو *tāso*, The plural form of the second personal pronoun, ye or you. It may also be written تاسُ *tāsu*, تاسي *tāsī*, and تاسِ *tāsi*. See my Grammar, page 32.

تاغه *tāghah*, s.m. (6th) The name of a tree, the elm or poplar, pieces of which are strung together and hung round horses' necks to avert the evil eye. Sing. and Pl.

P تافته *tāftah*, s.f. (3rd) A kind of silk, taffeta. Pl. ي *ey*. See تاوته

P تاك *tāk*, s.m. (2nd) A vine, the branch of any tree growing or trained like a vine. Pl. تاكونه *tākūnah*; or s.m. (5th) Pl. تاكان *tākān*.

تاك *tāk*, s.m. (2nd) A precipice, the steep side of a mountain pass. Pl. تاكونه *tākūnah*. See كرنك

تاك *tāk*, adj. (corrup. of A طاق) Odd, single, unique; (Fem.) تاكه *tāka'h*.

A تاكيد *tākīd*, s.m. (2nd) (inf. II of اكد) Confirmation, emphasis. 2. Injunction, ascertaining, superintendence. Pl. تاكيدونه *tākīdūnah*. تاكيد كول *tākīd kawul*, verb trans. To urge, insist, enjoin, to press.

A تاكيدي *tākīdī*, adj. Emphatic, decided, dogmatic.

S تال *tāl*, s.m. (2nd) Beating time in music by striking or slapping the fingers or hands together. Pl. تالونه *tālūnah*. تال كول *tāl kawul*, verb trans. To chime, to beat or clap the hands, to keep time.

تالا *tālā*, s.f. (6th) Plunder, spoil, sack, booty, prey, devastation, destruction, ravage, waste, pillage. (E.) Sing. and Pl.; (W.) Pl. تالاوي *tālāwī*. تالا كول *tālā kawul*, verb trans. To ravage, to plunder, to sack, to pillage, to lay waste, to devastate. See تاله and تالان

P تالاب *tālāb*, or تالاو *tālāo*, s.m. (2nd) A pond, a tank, a reservoir. Pl. تالابونه *tālābūnah*, or تالاوونه *tālāoūnah*. See ناور

تالاش *tālāsh*, s. prop. The name of a district north-west of Peshāwar.

P تالان *tālān*, s.m. (2nd) Plunder, spoil, pillage, sack, booty, prey, devastation, ravage, waste, destruction. Pl. تالانونه *tālānūnah*. See تالا and تاله

تالنده *tālanda'h*, s.f. (3rd) Thunder, thundering. Pl. ي *ey*. See تنا

S تالو *tālū*, s.m. (5th) The palate, the ridge or slit in the roof of the mouth. Pl. تالوكان *tālūgān*. See كومي

تاله *tāla'h*, s.f. (3rd) Plunder, spoil, booty, sack, prey, devastation, ravage, waste, pillage, destruction. Pl. ي *ey*. تاله كول *tālah kawul*, verb trans. To ravage, to plunder, to sack, to pillage, to lay waste. See also تالا and تالان

تاله *tāla'h*, s.f. (3rd) A kind of delicate short grass which grows only in the spring months. Pl. ي *ey*.

تالى *tālaey*, s.m. An iron or brass plate. Pl. تالي *tālī*. (S تهالي).

A تام *tāmm*, adj. (act. part. of تمام) Perfect, entire, complete, full.

S تامبه *tāmba'h*, s.f. (3rd) Copper. Pl. تامبي *tāmbey*.

A تامل *tā'ammul*, s.m. (2nd) (inf. V of امل) Meditation, reflection, consideration, hesitation, purpose. Pl. تاملونه *tā'ammulūnah*. تامل كول *tā'ammul kawul*, verb trans. To consider, to reflect, to meditate.

S تان *tān*, s.m. (2nd) A tune, a key note in music. تانونه *tānūnah*.

S تانبه *tānba'h*, s.f. (3rd) Copper. Pl. ي *ey*. See تامبه

تاندوله *tāndola'h*, s.f. (3rd) A kind of vegetable, greens. Pl. ي *ey*. See سوركلي

تانده *tānda'h*, adj. Green, fresh, verdant, flourishing, recently grown.

P تانسته *tānista'h*, s.f. (3rd) The warp in weaving. Pl. تانستي *tānistey*. See كنري

تانك *tāng*, s.m. (2nd) The girth of a saddle, a band, a brace. Pl. تانكونه *tāngūnah*.

تانړه *tārrna'h*, s.f. (3rd) A police station, a picquet, a guard. Pl. ي *ey*.

P تاو *tā'o*, s.m. (2nd) Heat, warmth. 2. (S) Passion, rage, anger. 3. Twist, contortion. 4. Strength, power. Pl. تاوونه *tā'o-ūnah*. په تاو *pah tā'o*, or په تاو سره *pah tā'o sarah*, adv. Quickly, swiftly, speedily, apace. تاويدل *tāwedal*, verb trans. To twist, to writhe, to become distorted or contorted. Pres. تاويږي *tāwejzī* (W.), or تاويګی *tāwegī* (E.); past تاو شه *tā'o shah*, or تاو ؤ شه *tā'o wu-shah*; fut. تاو به شي *tā'o bah shī*, or به ؤ شي *bah wu-shī*; imp. تاو شه *tā'o shah*, or ؤ شه *wu-shah*; act. part. تاويدونكى *tā'o-edūnakaey*, or تاويدونى *tā'o-edūnaey*; past part. تاو شوى

tā'o shawaey; verb. n. تاويدنه *tā'o-edana'h.* Also تاو خورل *tā'o khwarral,* verb trans. تاوول *tā'o-awul,* verb trans. To twist, to writhe, to wind, to encircle, to weave, to unite, to screw as the keys of a musical instrument. Pres. تاووي *tāwawī*; past تاو که *tā'o kah,* or وُ که *wu-kah,* or تاو کړ *tā'o karr,* or وُ کړ *wu-karr*; fut. تاو به کي *tā'o bah kī,* or به وُ کي *bah wu-kī,* or تاو به کړي *ta'o bah krrī,* or به وُ کړي *bah wu-krrī*; imp. تاو که *tā'o kah,* or وُ که *wu-kah,* or تاو کړه *tā'o krrah,* or وُ کړه *wu-krrah*; act. part. تاووونکَي *tāwawūnkaey,* or تاووونَي *tāwawūnaey*; past part. تاو کړي *tā'o karraey*; verb. n. تاوونه *tā'o-wawana'h.* Also تاو ور کول *tā'o war kawul,* verb trans.

P تاوان *tāwān,* s.m. (2nd) Retaliation, recompense, amends. 2. Debt. 3. Fine, mulct. 4. Injury, loss. Pl. تاوانونه *tāwānūnah.* تاوان کيدل *tāwān kedal,* verb trans. To sustain injury or loss, to lose. تاوان آخستل *tāwān ākhistal,* verb trans. To amerce, to mulct, to fine. تاوان ور کول *tāwān war-kawul,* verb trans. To give compensation, to make amends, to pay a fine.

تاوته *tāwta'h,* s.f. (3rd) Taffeta, a kind of cloth. Pl. يْ *ey.* See تافته

A تاوس *tā'ūs,* s.m. (5th) A peacock. Pl. تاوسان *tā-ūsān.*

تاوون *tā-wūn,* s.m. (5th) The plague (A طاعون). Pl. تاوونونه *tā-wūnūnah.*

تاوونَي *tā-wūnaey,* s.m. (1st) The plague. See preceding. Pl. ي *ī.*

تاويتک *tāwī-tak,* s.m. (2nd) A kind of ornament of silver in the shape of an almond, etc., containing a talisman or charm, worn by females. Pl. تاويتکونه *tāwī-takūnah.*

تاويل *tā-wīl,* s.m. (2nd) Change, transfer, return, trusts (corrup. of A تحويل). Pl. تاويلونه *tāwīlūnah.*

A تاويل *tā-wīl,* s.m. (2nd) (inf. II of اول) Explanation, elucidation, interpretation, paraphrase. Pl. تاويلونه *tā-wīlūnah.* تاويل کول *tā-wīl kawul,* verb trans. To elucidate, to explain.

P تاه *tāh,* s.f. (1st) A plait, a fold, a ply; multiplicity, perplexity, confusion. Pl. تاهِ *tāhi.* See تا and ته

تاهر *tāhar,* s.m. (5th) The name of a clan of the Ghalzīs. Pl. تاهران *tāharān.* تاهره *tāhara'h,* s.f. (3rd). Pl. يْ *ey.*

A تايب *tā-īb,* adj. (act. part. of توبه) Repentant, penitent; (Fem.) تايبه *tā-ība'h.*

تب *tab,* s.m. (2nd), An antidote, a sedative, a fomentation, a poultice, an embrocation. Pl. تبونه *tabūnah.* تبل *tabal,* verb trans. To foment, to poultice, to apply an embrocation or antidote. Pres. تبي *tabī*; past وُ تابه *wu-tābah*; fut. وُ به تبي *wu bah tabī*; imp. وُ تبه *wu-tabah*; act. part. تبونکَي *tabūnkaey,* or تبونَي *tabūnaey*; past part. تبلَي *tabalaey*; verb. n. تبنه *tabana'h.* See ټکور

P تبار *tabār,* s.m. (2nd) Race, tribe, family, people, nation. Pl. تبارونه *tabārūnah.* See also تبر

P تباه *tabāh,* adj. Abject, ruined, spoiled, wretched; bad, wicked, depraved. تباه حال *tabāh ḥāl,* adj. Ruined, wretched, spoiled. تباه کيدل *tabāh kedal,* verb intrans. To become ruined, abject, wretched, etc. تباه کول *tabāh kawul,* verb trans. To ruin, to spoil, to make wretched.

P تباهي *tabāhī,* s.f. (3rd) Ruin, wreck, perdition, depravity, wickedness. Pl. ئي *a'ī.*

تبجن *tab-jan,* adj. Feverish, a person labouring under fever; (Fem.) تبجنه *tab-janah.* See تبه

تبخَي *tabakhaey,* s.m. (1st) The pelvis, the abdomen, the pubes. 2. An iron dish for baking cakes on. Pl. ي *ī.*

A تبدل *tabaddul,* s.m. (2nd) (inf. V of بدل), Alteration, change, difference, transposition. Pl. تبدلونه *tabaddalūnah.*

A تبديل *tabdīl,* s.m. (2nd) (inf. II of بدل), Alteration, change, difference, transposition. Pl. تبديلونه *tabdīlūnah.* تبديل کيدل *tabdīl kedal,* verb intrans. To change, to alter, to differ. تبديل کول *tabdīl kawul,* verb trans. To alter, to change, to transpose. See بدليدل and بدلول

P تبر *tabar,* s.m. (2nd) An axe, a hatchet. Pl.

تبرونه *tabarūnah*. تبر زين *tabar zīn*, s.m. (5th) A horseman's battle axe. Pl. تبر زينان *tabar-zīnān*; or s.m. (2nd). Pl. تبر زينونه *tabar-zīnūnah*.

A تبرا *tabarrā*, s.f. (6th) Being absent, remote, or at a distance. 2. Being acquitted, cleared, or absolved. (E.) Sing. and Pl.; (W.) Pl. تبراوي *tabarrāwī*.

A تبرك *tabarruk*, s.m. (2nd) (inf. v of برکت), Benediction, congratulation. Pl. تبركونه *tabarrukūnah*.

تبرى *tubraey*, s.m. (1st) The head of an arrow. Pl. ي *ī*. See توبري

A تبسم *tabassum*, s.m. (2nd) (inf. v of بسم), A smile. Pl. تبسمونه *tabassum-ūnah*. تبسم كول *tabassum kawul*, verb trans. To smile. See مسكي.

A تبع تابعين *tabæ-i-tābiæ'īn*, s.m. (Pl.) The friends of the friends of Muhammad. See تابعين

تبق *tabaḳ*, or تبخ *tabakh*, s.m. (2nd) A disease in cattle, a running at the nose, the glanders. Pl. تبقونه *tabaḳūnah*, or تبخونه *tabakhūnah*.

تبه *taba'h*, s.f. (3rd) Fever, heat. Pl. تبې *tabey*. See تبجن تبه نيول *taba'h nīwul*, verb trans. To take a fever. زيړي تبه *z'yarra'ī taba'h*, or واره گري تبه *wāra'h garey taba'h*, A tertian fever. Also دريمه تبه *dre-yama'h taba'h*, and سه يكه تبه *sih yaka'h taba'h*. سړه تبه *sarra'h taba'h*, An ague. شبره تبه *shabara'h taba'h*, لو تبه *lo taba'h*, or اوچكي تبه *ūchaku'ī taba'h*, A burning fever. سكاروي تبه *skārwa'ī taba'h*, A burning fever with a pain in the liver. همه روزه تبه *hamah roza'h taba'h*, or دائره تبه *dā'era'h taba'h*, A quotidian fever.

تبي *taba'ī*, s.f. (6th) An earthen plate or dish for baking cakes on. Sing. and Pl. See also تبخي

تپ تپ *tap tap*, A word or words used to make a dog go into a hole. (T تب تب).

ټپ *tæp*, s.m. (2nd) (W.) A mole, a wart. Pl. ټپونه *tæp-ūnah*. تور ټپ *tor-tæp*, A black mole. تور ټپي *tor-tæpaey*, adj. Marked with a black mole; (Fem.) تور ټپ *tor-tæpi*. Pl. (Masc. and Fem.) ي *ī*.

S تپاس *tapās*, s.m. (2nd) Toil, labour, search, enquiry. Pl. تپاسونه *tapāsūnah*. تپاس كول *tapās kawul*, verb trans. To search for, to make enquiry, to toil.

P تپاك *tapāk*, s.m. (2nd) Affection, esteem, regard, love, ardour, zeal. Pl. تپاكونه *tapāk-ūnah*. تپاك لرل *tapāk laral*, verb trans. To regard, to esteem, to love, to have affection for.

تپاند *tapānd*, pres. part. Palpitating, growing hot or warm (corrup. of P تپان from تپيدن).

تپړا *taprrā*, s.f. (6th) A wooden instrument used by potters for tapping. (E.) Sing and Pl.; (W.) Pl. تپړاوي *taprrāwī*. See تپڼرا

تپك *tapak*, s.m. (2nd) The sound of a drum. تپكونه *tapakūnah*.

تپل *tapal*, verb trans. To heap, to pile, to pack, to amass, to accumulate. Pres. تپي *tapī*; past و تاپه *wu-tāpah*; fut. و به تپي *wu bah tapī*; imp. و تپه *wu-tapah*; act. part. تپونكي *tap-ūnkaey*, or تپوني *tapūnaey*; past part. تپلي *tapalaey*; verb. n. تپنه *tapana'h*.

تپلي *tapalaey*, adj. (past part.) Heaped up, piled, amassed, accumulated; (Fem.) تپل *tapali*. Pl. (Masc. and Fem.) ي *ī*.

تپڼرا *taprrnā*, s.f. (6th) A wooden instrument used by potters for tapping. (E.) Sing. and Pl.; (W.) Pl. تپڼراوي *taprrnāwī*. See تپړا

تپور *tapor*, s.m. (2nd) A kind of ornamental stomacher worn by young women. Pl. تپورونه *taporūnah*.

تپوس *tapa'ūs*, s.m. (2nd) Search, investigation, examination, labour (corrup. of A تفحص). Pl. تپوسونه *tapa'ūsūnah*. See تپاس

تپه *tapa'h*, s.f. (3rd) A division, a district, a parish, a ward, a tribe, a clan. Pl. تپې *tapey*. (HI تپا).

تپي *tapaey*, s.m. (1st) A wart, a mole or spot on the face. Pl. ي *ī*. تور تپي *tor tapaey*, A black mole. See زخه

تت *tat*, adj. Thick, dense, close, compact, thick-set; lisping. Pl. تتونه *tatūnah*. See گنر

تتيدل *tatedal*, verb intrans. To grow dense, thick, close, or compact, as leaves, corn, hay, etc. Pres. تتيږي *tatejzī* (W.), or تتيگي *tategī*

(E.); past تت شه *tat shah*, or ۇ شه *wu-shah*; fut. تت به شي *tat bah shī*, or به ۇ شي *bah wu-shī*; imp. تت شه *tat shah*, or ۇ شه *wu-shah*; act. past تتيدونكي *tatedūnkaey*, or تتيدونې *tatedūnaey*; past part. تت *tat*, or تت شوې *tat shawaey*; verb. n. تتيدنه *tatedana'h*, or تتيده *tatedah*.

تت والې *tat wālaey*, s.m. (1st) Thickness, denseness, closeness, compactness. Pl. ي *ī*.

تتول *tatawul*, verb trans. To make dense or close, to bring together, to thicken. Pres. تتوي *tatawī*; past تت كړ *tat karr*, or ۇ كړ *wu-karr*; fut. تت به كي *tat bah kī*, or به ۇ كي *bah wu-kī*, and تت به كړي *tat bah krrī*, or به ۇ كړي *bah wu-krrī*; imp. تت كه *tat kah*, or كړه *krrah*, and تت ۇ كه *tat wu-kah*, or ۇ كړه *wu-krrah*; act. part. تتونكي *tatawūnkaey*, or تتونې *tatawūnaey*; past part. تت كړې *tat karraey*; verb. n. تتونه *tatawuna'h*.

تترې *tataraey*, s.m. (1st) Porphyry. Pl. ي *ī*.

تتړې *tatarraey*, adj. Lisping, speaking imperfectly. 2. One who lisps. Fem. ۍ *a'ī*. See also ترې , ترترې , ګانګوري, and تته

A تتمه *tatimma'h*, s.f. (3rd) An appendix, supplement, continuation. Pl. ې *ey*.

تتوه *tatawa'h*, s.f. (3rd) A turtle dove, a ring dove. Pl. ې *ey*.

تته *tata'h*, adj. (Fem. of تت), Thick, dense, compact. تتې خبرې *tatey khabarey*, Lisping words. تته اوريځ *tata'h aoredz*, A thick or dense cloud.

A تجارت *tijārat*, s.m. (2nd) Commerce, trade. تجارتونه *tijāratūnah*.

A تجاوز *tajāwuz*, s.m. (2nd) (inf. VI of جوز), Departing, passing, transgressing, surpassing, excess, deviating, offending. Pl. تجاوزونه *tajāwuzūnah*. تجاوز كول *tajāwuz kawul*, verb trans. To offend, to transgress, to depart.

A تجاهل *tajā-hul*, s.m. (2nd) (inf. VI of جهل), Pretended ignorance, connivance, apathy, indifference. Pl. تجاهلونه *tajā-hulūnah*. تجاهل كول *tajā-hul kawul*, verb. trans. To pretend, or affect ignorance.

A تجربه *tajriba'h*, s.f. (3rd) (inf. II of جرب), Experiment, trial, proof, experience, assay, probation. Pl. ې *ey*. تجربه كار *tajriba'h kār*, adj. Expert, experienced, conversant in; (Fem.) تجربه كاره *tajriba'h kāra'h*. تجربه كاري *tajriba'h kārī*, s.f. (3rd) Experience, expertness, etc. Pl. ۍ *a'ī*. تجربه كول *tajriba'h kawul*, verb trans. To experience, to try, to make trial of.

A تجسس *tajassus*, s.m. (2nd) (inf. V of جس), Spying, exploring, search, enquiry, investigation, inquisitiveness. Pl. تجسسونه *tajassusūnah*. A تجسس كول *tajassus kawul*, verb trans. To explore, to investigate, to pry into.

A تجله *tajalla'h*, s.f. (3rd) Pl. ې *ey*; or تجلي *tajallī*, s.f. (3rd) (inf. V of جلا), Splendour, brilliancy, lustre, clearness. Pl. ۍ *a'ī*.

A تجويز *tajwīz*, s.m. (2nd) (inf. II of جوز), Approbation, permission. 2. Inquiring into, examining, investigation, considering. 3. Contrivance, scheme, plan; sentence, judgment, determination, trial. Pl. تجويزونه *tajwīzūnah*. تجويز كول *tajwīz kawul*, verb trans. To investigate, to examine, to enquire into, to sentence, to plan, to contrive.

S تچ *tach*, adj. Void, empty. 2. Contemptible, worthless, despicable; (Fem.) تچه *tacha'h*.

تچ *tich*, s.m. (2nd) The sheath or scabbard of a sword, dagger, etc. Pl. تچونه *tich-ūnah*.

A تحت *taht*, s.m. (2nd) The inferior part, below, under. 2. Subjection, possession. Pl. تحتونه *tahtūnah*.

A تحرير *tahrīr*, s.m. (2nd) (inf. II of حر), Writing correctly, writing, description. 2. Written, dated. Pl. تحريرونه *tahrīrūnah*. تحرير كيدل *tahrīr kedal*, verb intrans. To be written. تحرير كول *tahrīr kawul*, verb trans. To write, to describe.

A تحسين *tahsīn*, s.m. (2nd) (inf. II of حسن), Approbation, applause, acclamation. Pl. تحسينونه *tahsīnūnah*. تحسين كول *tahsīn kawul*, verb trans. To praise, to applaud, to approve.

A تحصيل *tahsīl*, s.m. (2nd) (inf. II of حصول),

Gain, profit, attainment, learning, acquisition. Pl. تحصيلونه *taḥṣīlūnah*. تحصيل كول *taḥṣīl kawul*, verb trans. To acquire, to gain, to learn, to collect.

P تحصيلدار *taḥṣīldār*, s.m. (5th) A collector, a tax-gatherer. Pl. تحصيلداران *taḥṣīldārān*.

P تحصيلداري *taḥṣīldārī*, s.f. (3rd) Collectorship, tax-gathering. Pl. ئي *a'ī*.

A تحفه *tuḥfah*, s.f. (3rd) A curiosity, a rarity, a present. Pl. تحفي *tuḥfey*. 2. adj. Rare, excellent, uncommon, admirable; nice, choice, beautiful, odd, singular.

A تحقيق *taḥḳīḳ*, adj. Authentic, ascertained, apparent, indubitable. adv. Truly, indeed. 3. s.m. (2nd) Exactness, precision, verification, trial. Pl. تحقيقونه *taḥḳīḳūnah*. تحقيق كول *taḥḳīḳ kawul*, verb trans. To ascertain, to investigate, to inspect.

A تحقيقات *taḥḳīḳāt*, s.m. (Pl. of تحقيق), Investigations, inquiries. Pl. تحقيقاتونه *taḥḳīḳātūnah*. تحقيقات كول *taḥḳīḳāt kawul*, verb trans. To investigate, to inquire into.

A تحمل *taḥammul*, s.m. (2nd) (inf. v of حمل), Patience, endurance, long-suffering, resignation, forbearance, peace, meekness, humility. Pl. تحملونه *taḥammulūnah*. تحمل كول *taḥammul kawul*, verb trans. To endure, forbear, bear, be patient.

A تحويل *taḥwīl*, s.m. (2nd) (inf. II of حول), Change, transfer. 2. Trust, charges, cash in charge. Pl. تحويلونه *taḥwīlūnah*.

A تحويلدار *taḥwīldār*, s.m. (5th) A treasurer, a cash-keeper. Pl. تحويلداران *taḥwīldārān*.

P تحويلداري *taḥwīldārī*, s.f. (3rd) The business of a cash-keeper. Pl. ئي *a'ī*.

P تخت *taḵẖt*, s.m. (2nd) A throne. Pl تختونه *taḵẖtūnah*. تخت نشين *taḵẖt nishīn*, A king, a ruler. تخت يا تخته *taḵẖt yā taḵẖtah*, Either a throne or a bier (spoken on entering on a desperate enterprise), "Death or victory," "a Peerage or Westminster Abbey," etc. تخت گاه *taḵẖt-gāh*, s.m. (2nd) A metropolis, the capital of a country, the seat of government. Pl. تخت گاهونه *taḵẖt-gāhūnah*.

P تخته *taḵẖta'h*, s.f. (3rd) A plank, a board, a stool, a bench, a bier, a sheet of paper. Pl. تختي *taḵẖtey*. تخته بندي *taḵẖta'h bandī*, s.f. (3rd) Wainscot, boarding. Pl. ئي *a'ī*. تخته پوښ *taḵẖta'h posh* or *poḵẖ*, s.m. (2nd) A stage, a platform, a wooden floor. Pl. پوښونه *poshūnah* or *poḵẖūnah*.

P تخته نرد *taḵẖtah-nard*, s.m. (2nd) Backgammon. Pl. تخته نردونه *taḵẖtah-nardūnah*.

تخرگ *t'ḵẖarg*, s.m. (2nd) The armpit. Pl. تخرگونه *t'ḵẖargūnah*.

تخرگي *t'ḵẖargaey*, s.m. (1st) A gusset in the armpit of a dress. Pl. ي *ī*.

تخځ *taḵẖadz*, s.f. (1st) An adze, a carpenter's tool. Pl. تخځ *taḵẖadzi*. See ترښز

A تخفيف *taḵẖfīf*, s.m. (2nd) (inf. II of خف) Making light, alleviating. 2. Alleviation, abatement, relief, remission, mitigation. Pl. تخفيفونه *taḵẖfīfūnah*. تخفيف كول *taḵẖfīf kawul*, verb trans. To alleviate, to remit, to assuage, to abate. Also تخفيف ور كول *taḵẖfīf war kawul*, or تخفيف غوښتل *taḵẖfīf ghoḵẖtal* or *ghoshtal*, verb trans. To request abatement, relief, or remission.

A تخليق *taḵẖlīḳ*, s.m. (2nd) (inf. II of خلق) Forming well, completing, creating. Pl. تخليقونه *taḵẖlīḳūnah*.

P تخم *tuḵẖm*, s.m. (2nd) Seed, sperm. Pl. تخمونه *tuḵẖmūnah*. تخم بد *tuḵẖm-i bad*, adj. Low-bred. تخم ريحان *tuḵẖm-i rīhān*, s.m. (6th) The seed of the sweet basil, etc. Sing. and Pl. تخم ريزي *tuḵẖm rezī*, s.f. (3rd) Sowing, casting seed. Pl. ئي *a'ī*. تخم ريزي كول *tuḵẖm rezī kawul*, verb trans. To sow. تخم كاهو *tuḵẖm-i kāhū*, s.m. (9th) The seed of lettuce. Sing. and Pl. تخم كتان *tuḵẖm-i katān*, s.m. (6th) Linseed. Sing. and Pl.

تخ مخ *taḵẖ maḵẖ*, interj. O fie! for shame!

A تخمينا *taḵẖmīnan*, adv. (from خمن) By guess, by conjecture. 2. Nearly, about.

P تخمه *tuḵẖma'h*, s.f. (3rd) Origin, principle. 2. (A) Indigestion. Pl. ئي *ey*.

تخنول *taḵẖnawul*, verb trans. To tickle, to

titillate. Pres. تخنوي *ta<u>kh</u>nawī*; past وُ تخناوه *wu-ta<u>kh</u>nāwuh*, or وُ تخناوو *wu-ta<u>kh</u>nāwo*; fut. وُ به تخنوي *wu bah ta<u>kh</u>nawī*; imp. وُ تخنوه *wu-ta<u>kh</u>nawah*; act. part. تخنوونكَي *ta<u>kh</u>nawūnkaey*, or تخنووني *ta<u>kh</u>nawūnaey*; past part. تخنولَي *ta<u>kh</u>nawulaey*; verb. n. تخنونه *ta<u>kh</u>nawuna'h*. See تخول

تخنونه *ta<u>kh</u>nawuna'h*, s.f. (3rd) (verb. n.) Tickling, titillating. Pl. يْ *ey*.

تخنيدل *ta<u>kh</u>nedal*, verb intrans. To feel tickling or titillation. Pres. تخنيږي *ta<u>kh</u>nejzī* (W.) or تخنيگي *ta<u>kh</u>negī* (E.); past وُ تخنيده *wu-ta<u>kh</u>nedah*; fut. وُ به تخنيږي *wu bah ta<u>kh</u>nejzī*, or وُ به تخنيگي *wu bah ta<u>kh</u>negī*; imp. وُ تخنيږه *wu-ta<u>kh</u>nejzah*, or وُ تخنيگه *wu-ta<u>kh</u>negah*; act. part. تخنيدونكَي *ta<u>kh</u>nedūnkaey*, or تخنيدونَي *ta<u>kh</u>nedūnaey*; past part. تخنيدلَي *ta<u>kh</u>nedalaey*; verb. n. تخنيدنه *ta<u>kh</u>nedana'h*. See تخيدل

تخول *ta<u>kh</u>awul*, verb trans. To tickle, to titillate. Pres. تخوي *ta<u>kh</u>awī*; past وُ تخاوه *wu-ta<u>kh</u>ā-wuh*, or وُ تخاوو *wu-ta<u>kh</u>ā-wo*; fut. وُ به تخوي *wu bah ta<u>kh</u>awī*; imp. وُ تخوه *wu-ta<u>kh</u>awah*; act. part. تخوونكَي *ta<u>kh</u>awūnkaey*, or تخوونَي *ta<u>kh</u>awūnaey*; past part. تخولَي *ta<u>kh</u>awulaey*; verb. n. تخونه *ta<u>kh</u>awuna'h*.

تخه *ta<u>kh</u>a'h*, s.f. (3rd) Tickling, titillation. Pl. تخيْ *ta<u>kh</u>ey*. تخيدل *ta<u>kh</u>edal*, verb intrans. To tickle, to titillate, to feel titillation. Pres. تخيږي *ta<u>kh</u>ejzī* (W.) or تخيگي *ta<u>kh</u>egī* (E.); past وُ تخيده *wu-ta<u>kh</u>edah*; fut. وُ به تخيږي *wu bah ta<u>kh</u>ejzī*, or وُ به تخيگي *wu bah ta<u>kh</u>egī*; imp. وُ تخيږه *wu-ta<u>kh</u>ejzah*, or وُ تخيگه *wu-ta<u>kh</u>egah*; act. part. تخيدونكَي *ta<u>kh</u>edūnkaey*, or تخيدونَي *ta<u>kh</u>edūnaey*; past part. تخيدلَي *ta<u>kh</u>edalaey*; verb. n. تخيدنه *ta<u>kh</u>edana'h*.

تخَي *ta<u>kh</u>aey*, s.m. (1st) Tickling, titillation. Pl. ي *ī*. See تخه

A تدارك *tadāruk*, s.m. (2nd) (inf. VI of درك) Reparation, remedy, an expedient, precaution, provision, preparation. 2. Chastisement, retaliation. Pl. تداركونه *tadārukūnah*. تدارك كول *tadāruk kawul*, verb trans. To provide against, to make preparation, to take precaution, to chastise, to redress.

A تدبير *tadbīr*, s.m. (2nd) (inf. II of دبر) Deliberation, counsel, contrivance, expedient, opinion, advice. 2. Arrangement, order, management, policy, prudence. Pl. تدبيرونه *tadbīrūnah*. تدبير كول *tadbīr kawul*, verb trans. To contrive, to deliberate, to counsel.

A تدريج *tadrīj*, s.m. (2nd) (inf. II of درج) Gradation, scale. Pl. تدريجونه *tadrījūnah*.

تر *tar*, adv. and prep. To, until, as far as, as long as, even to, in order that, to the end that. This word is generally followed by پورِ or پوري; thus تر ابدَ پورِ *tar abada pori*, To all eternity. تر اوسَ *tar aosa*, or تر اوسَ پوري *tar aosa porī*, Yet, hitherto, till, as yet, so far. تر دغه پورِ *tar daghah pori*, or تر دي پورِ *tar dey pori*, So far, as far as this. تر كله پورِ *tar kalah pori*, Till when? how long? تر كمه *tar kamah*, or تر كمَ پورِ *tar kama pori*, How far? to where? تر هغه پورِ *tar haghah pori*, As far as that.

تر *tar*, prep. From, of, than, by, with, etc. In the oblique cases it becomes ترِ *tri*. See Grammar, page 48.

تراپ *tarāp*, s.m. (2nd) A leap, a jump, a bound, a spring. Pl. تراپونه *tarāpūnah*. See ترپ *trap*.

تراټ *trāṯ*, s.m. (2nd) A kind of whip, a goad. Pl. تراټونه *trāṯūnah*.

تراټه *trāṯa'h*, s.f. (3rd) An edging or piping added to a dress. Pl. يْ *ey*.

تراړه *tarāṟa'h*, s.f. (3rd) Stony or gravelly ground; a pebble, a piece of stone. Pl. يْ *ey*.

P ترازو *tarāzū*, s.m. (5th) A scale, a balance. Pl. ترازوگان *tarāzūgān*. تول ترازو *tol tarāzū*, The sign Libra.

ترازه *tarāza'h*, s.f. (3rd) A slice, a bit, a piece, a shred, a ribbon. Pl. يْ *ey*. ترازه كيدل *tarāza'h kedal*, verb intrans. To become split, splintered, torn to shreds or ribbons. ترازه كول *tarāza'h kawul*, verb trans. To tear in shreds, to cut to pieces, to slice, to splinter.

P تراش *tarā<u>sh</u>*, s.m. (2nd) (part. of تراشيدن)

Cutting, forming, shaping. 2. A cutter, carver. 3. Shape, cut, form, fashion. Pl. تراشونه *tarā<u>sh</u>ūnah*. تراشل *tarā<u>sh</u>al*, verb trans. To pare, to clip, to prune, etc. Pres. تراشي *tarā<u>sh</u>ī*; past وُ تراشه *wu-tarā<u>sh</u>ah*; fut. وُ به تراشي *wu bah tarā<u>sh</u>ī*; imp. وُ تراشه *wu-tarā<u>sh</u>ah*; act. part. تراشونكي *tarā<u>sh</u>ūnkaey*, or تراشوني *tarā<u>sh</u>ūnaey*; past part. تراشلي *tarā<u>sh</u>alaey*; verb. n. تراشنه *tarā<u>sh</u>ana'h*.

P تراشه *tarā<u>sh</u>a'h*, s.f. (3rd) A shaving, a paring, a splinter, a chip, a shred, a scrap. Pl. ي *ey*. See ترازه

تراغ *tarā<u>gh</u>*, s.m. (2nd) A twist, a coil, a plait, a fold. Pl. تراغونه *tarā<u>gh</u>ūnah*.

تراك *trāk*, s.m. (2nd) A crack, a split, a fissure, a breach, a rent, a slit. 2. The noise of a thing cracking or splitting. (A تراك). Pl. تراكونه *trākūnah*.

P ترانه *tarāna'h*, s.f. (3rd) Modulation, harmony, voice, song, melody, symphony, quaver, trill, etc. Pl. ي *ey*. ترانه ويل *tarāna'h wayal*, verb trans. To sing, to modulate.

تراوي *tarāwey*, s.f. (3rd) Pl. A prayer for the month of Ramazān, consisting of twenty genuflexions repeated at bed-time.

A تربت *turbat*, s.m. (2nd) A tomb, a monument, a sepulchre. Pl. تربتونه *turbatūnah*.

A تربد *turbid* or *tarbud*, s.m. (2nd) A purgative root brought from India—turbith (Convolvulus turpethum). Pl. تربدونه *turbidūnah* or *tarbudūnah*.

تربور *turbūr*, s.m. (2nd) A father's brother's son, a cousin. Pl. تربورونه *turbūrūnah*. See تربله

تربور گلوي *turbūr galwī*, s.f. (3rd) Pl. ئي *a'ī*, or تربور والي *turbūr wālaey*, s.m. (1st) Nepotism, fondness for nephews, favoritism, or undue fondness for nephews, or other relatives. 2. Enmity to relations also, very common amongst the Af<u>gh</u>āns. Pl. والي *wālī*.

A تربيت *tarbiyat*, s.m. (2nd) (inf. II of ربي) Education, instruction, tuition, breeding, bringing up, correction. Pl. تربيتونه *tarbiyatūnah*. تربيت كول *tarbiyat kawul*, verb trans. To instruct, to educate, to bring up.

ترپ *trap*, s.m. (6th) A leap, a jump, a spring, a bound, a caper, a vault. Sing. and Pl.; and s.m. (5th) The sound produced on a person jumping, etc., thump, bump, jolt, smack, dowse, etc. Pl. ترپهار *trapahār*. ترپ وهل *trap wahal*, verb trans. To jump, to leap, to bound, to spring.

ترپيدل *trapedal*, verb intrans. To jump, to leap, to bound, to spring, etc. Pres. ترپيږي *trapejzī* (W.), or ترپيگي *trapegī* (E.); past وُ ترپيده *wu-trapedah*, or وُ ترپيد *wu-trapeda*; fut. وُ به ترپيږي *wu bah trapejzī*, or وُ به ترپيگي *wu bah trapegī*; imp. وُ ترپيږه *wu-trapejzah*, or وُ ترپيگه *wu-trapegah*; act. part. ترپيدونكي *trapedūnkaey*, or ترپيدوني *trapedūnaey*; past part. ترپيدلي *trapedalaey*; verb. n. ترپيدنه *trapedana'h*.

ترپيدنه *trapedana'h*, s.f. (3rd) (verb. n.) Jumping, leaping, bounding, springing, capering, vaulting, etc. Pl. ي *ey*.

ترپول *trapawul*, verb trans. To make or cause to jump, bound, spring, etc. Pres. ترپوي *trapawī*; past وُ ترپاوه *wu-trapāwuh*, or وُ ترپاوو *wu-trapāwo*; fut. وُ به ترپوي *wu bah trapawī*; imp. وُ ترپوه *wu-trapawah*; act. part. ترپوونكي *trapawūnkaey*, or ترپووني *trapawūnaey*; past part. ترپولي *trapawulaey*; verb. n. ترپونه *trapawuna'h*.

ترپ *turp* or *tarp*, s.m. (5th) A radish. Pl. ترپان *turpān* or *tarpān*.

ترپچه *tarpu<u>ch</u>ah* or *turpu<u>ch</u>a'h*, s.f. (3rd) A radish leaf. Pl. ي *ey*; or (W.) s.m. (6th). Sing. and Pl. See also مولي

ترپلل *traplal*, verb trans. To leap, to jump, to run with swiftness, to vault. Pres. ترپلي *traplī*; past ترپلو *traplo*, or وُ ترپله *wu-traplah*; fut. وُ به ترپلي *wu bah traplī*; imp. ترپله *traplah*; act. part. ترپلونكي *traplūnkaey*, or ترپلوني *traplūnaey*; past part. ترپللي *traplalaey*; verb. n. ترپلنه *traplana'h*.

ترپه *trapa'h*, s.f. (3rd) A jump, a leap, a bound, a spring, a vault. Pl. ي *ey*. See also ترپ, دنگل, تيندك, غرزنگ, and

ترپي *trapaey*, s.m. (1st) A foot-fall, the sound

of the feet of either man or animal in walking or running. Pl. ي *ī*.

ترتاب *tar-tāb*, s.m. (2nd) Sorrow, regret, repining, lamenting, deploring. Pl. ترتابونه *tar-tābūnah*. ترتاب کول *tar-tāb kawul*, verb trans. To regret, to deplore, to rue, to bewail.

ترترئ *tartarraey*, s.m. (1st) A stammerer, a lisper, one who speaks imperfectly. 2. Stammering, lisping. 3. The name of a bird. Pl. ترتري *tartarrī*.

ترتلو *tar talo*, adv. Always, ever, continually, perpetually, constantly. See تل تر تله

A ترتيب *tartīb*, s.m. (2nd) (inf. II of رتب) Arrangement, disposition, method, order. Pl. ترتيبونه *tartībūnah*. ترتيب کول *tartīb kawul*, verb trans. To order, to arrange, to compose, etc.

ترتيزک *tar-tezak*, s.m. (6th) A cress, water cresses. Sing. and Pl. See تيزک

ترټل *trattal*, verb trans. To scold, to reprimand, to treat harshly or disrespectfully, to taunt. 2. To drive away, to turn adrift, to bundle out, to drive from one's door. Pres. ترټي *trattī*; past وُ ترټه *wu-trāttah*, or تراټ *trātta*; fut. وُ به ترټي *wu bah trattī*; imp. وُ ترټه *wu-trattah*; act. part. ترټونکئ *trattūnkaey*, or ترټونئ *trattūnaey*; past part. ترټلئ *trattalaey*; verb. n. ترټنه *trattana'h*. See رټل

A ترجمان *tarjumān*, s.m. (5th) An interpreter. ترجمانان *tarjumānān*.

A ترجمه *tarjuma'h*, s.f. (3rd) Translation, interpretation. Pl. ئ *ey*. ترجمه کول *tarjuma'h kawul*, verb trans. To translate, to interpret.

A ترجيح *tarjīḥ*, s.m. (2nd) (inf. II of رجوح) Gaining a superiority, pre-eminence, excellence, preference. Pl. ترجيحونه *tarjīḥūnah*. ترجيح کول *tarjīḥ kawul*, verb trans. To prefer, to show preference for. ترجيح لرل *tarjīḥ laral*, verb trans. To surpass, to excel, to have or hold superiority.

ترخ *trakh*, s.m. (2nd) The armpit, the embrace. Pl. ترخونه *trakhūnah*. See تخرگ

P ترخان *tarkhān*, s.m. (5th) Free, exempted from tribute or taxes. 2. The herb dragon's-wort. 3. A tribe of Turks. Pl. ترخانان *tarkhānān*.

ترخه *tarkha'h*, s.f. (3rd) The herb dragon's-wort, or wormwood. Pl. ئ *ey*. ترخه ککوره *tarkha'h kakora'h*, s.f. (3rd) The bitter apple, the colocynth. Pl. ئ *ey*. See also مرغوني and ترخه هندوانه

ترخئ *tar-kha'ī*, s.f. (6th) A wild shrub that bears a flower like chamomile (Chrysanthemum). Sing. and Pl. See شستي

ترخيدل *trikhedal*, verb intrans. To grow or become bitter, nauseous, or unpalatable. ترخول *trikhawul*, verb trans. To make or render bitter, nauseous, or unpalatable. See تريخ

A تردد *taraddud*, s.m. (2nd) (inf. II of رد) Application, labour, investigation. 2. Irresolution, indecision, hesitation, wavering, debating, etc. Pl. ترددونه *taraddudūnah*. تردد کول *taraddud kawul*, verb trans. To labour, to show application, etc.

ترز *tarz*, s.m. (2nd) Form, manner. (A طرز). Pl. ترزونه *tarzūnah*.

P ترس *tars*, s.m. (2nd) Fear, terror, dread. (H) Compassion Pl. ترسونه *tarsūnah*. See ويره

P ترسا *tarsā*, s.m. (5th) A pagan, an infidel, a fire-worshipper, a Christian. Pl. ترسايان *tarsāyān*.

P ترسان *tarsān*, adj. (act. part. of ترسيدن) Fearful, timid; (Fem.) ترسانه *tarsāna'h*.

P ترس ناک *tars nāk*, adj. Timid, cowardly, terrified; (Fem.) ترس ناکه *tars-nāka'h*.

ترسرئ *tar-saraey*, s.m. (1st) A head-stall for a horse. Pl. ي *ī*.

ترسري *tar-sarī*, s.m. (1st) Pl. Freckles, small yellowish spots on the skin of the face, etc. Sing. not used. ترسري مخئ *tar-sarī makhaey*; adj. Freckled, having a face full of freckles; (Fem.) ترسري مخې *tar-sarī makhi*. ترسري کيدل *tar-sarī kedal*, verb intrans. To become freckled. ترسري کول *tar-sarī kawul*, verb trans. To freckle.

P ترش *tursh*, adj. Sour acid, harsh. 2. Gruff, ill-tempered, crabbed; (Fem.) ترشه *tursha'h*. ترش روي *tursh rū'e*, adj. Cynical, morose, surly, stern, hard-favoured, gruff, ugly; (Fem.) ترش رویه *tursh rū'ea'h.* ترش روئي *tursh rū-yī,* s.f. (3rd) Moroseness, sternness, gruffness, ugliness. Pl. ئي *a'ī.*

P ترشي *turshī,* s.f. (3rd) Sourness, acidity, harshness. Pl. ئي *a'ī.*

ترهز *tarkhaz,* s.f. (1st) An adze. 2. A gore or piece of cloth for enlarging a vest, the pieces in a vest cut transversely or diagonally. Pl. ترهزِ *tarkhazi.* See ترهځ

ترهزه *tarkhaza'h,* s.f. (3rd) The same as the preceding. Pl. ي *ey.* See ترشه

ترهځ *tarshadz* or *tarkhadz,* s.f. (1st) An adze. 2. A gore, a gusset. Pl. ترهځ *tar-shadzi* or *tar-khadzi.* See تيشه and تخځ Also written ترهز *tarkhaz* or *tarshaz,* which see.

A ترغيب *targhīb,* s.m. (2nd) (inf. II of رغبت) Incitement, instigation, temptation, stimulation. Pl. ترغيبونه *targhībūnah.* ترغيب کول *targhīb kawul,* verb trans. To incite, to excite, to set agog, to tempt, to entice, to induce.

A ترقي *taraḳḳī,* s.f. (3rd) (inf. V of رقي) Promotion, preferment, advancement, elevation. 2. Increase, improvement; making progress in learning, proficiency. Pl. ئي *a'ī.* ترقي ور کول *taraḳḳī war kawul,* verb trans. To promote, to advance, to elevate, to increase.

P ترک *turk,* s.m. (5th) A Turk, a soldier. A word used by poets to express beautiful youth. Pl. ترکان *turkān.* ترکه *turka'h,* s.f. (3rd) A mistress. Pl. ي *ey.*

A ترک *tark,* s.m. (2nd) Abandoning, abdication, deserting, leaving, omission, abandonment. Pl. ترکونه *tarkūnah.* ترک کول *tark kawul,* verb trans. To leave, to forsake, to give up, to desert, to resign, to omit, to cease, etc.

ترک *tark,* s.m. (2nd) A split, a crack, a cleft. 2. The noise made in splitting. 3. A disease in the hoofs of horses, mules, asses, etc.; sand-crack. Pl. ترکونه *tarkūnah.*

ترک *trak,* s.m. (2nd) The opening of a bud or sprout; a shoot, a sprout. 2. A blow with a hammer or any hard substance, a stroke, a tap, a knock, a rap, a pat, a hit, etc. 3. The sound of footsteps on hard ground. Pl. ترکونه *trakūnah.* ترک وهل *trak wahal,* verb trans. To shoot out, to sprout, to open as a bud.

ترکيدل *trakedal,* verb intrans. To be struck, hit, knocked, tapped, etc. Pres. ترکيږي *trakejzī* (W.), or ترکيګي *trakegī* (E.); past وُ ترکيده *wu-trakedah,* or وُ ترکيدَ *wu-trakeda*; fut. وُ به ترکيږي *wu bah trakejzī,* or ترکيګي *trakegī*; imp. وُ ترکيږه *wu-trakejzah,* or وُ ترکيګه *wu-trakegah*; act. part. ترکيدونکی *trakedūnkaey,* or ترکيدونی *trakedūnaey*; past part. ترکيدلی *trakedalaey*; verb. n. ترکيدنه *trakedana'h.*

ترکيدنه *trakedana'h,* s.f. (3rd) (verb. n.) Striking, thumping, tapping, hitting, rapping, etc. Pl. ي *ey.*

ترکول *trakawul,* verb trans. To strike, to knock, to tap, to hit, to smite, etc. Pres. ترکوي *trakawī*; past وُ ترکاوه *wu-trakāwuh,* or وُ ترکاوو *wu-trakāwo*; fut. وُ به ترکوي *wu bah trakawī*; imp. وُ ترکوه *wu-trakawah*; act. part. ترکوونکی *trakawūnkaey,* or ترکووني *trakawūnaey*; past part. ترکولی *trakawulaey*; verb. n. ترکونه *trakawuna'h.* See تک

ترکاړ *tarkārrn,* s.m. (5th) A carpenter. Pl. ترکاړان *tarkārrnān.* (Panjābī).

ترکښ *tar kash* (W.), or *tar kakh* (E.), s.m. (2nd) A quiver for arrows. Pl. ترکښونه *tar kashūnah,* or *tarkakhūnah.* (P ترکش)

ترکلاړي *tarkalārrnī,* s.m. (1st) Pl. The name of an Afghān tribe. ترکلاړی *tarkalārrnaey,* Sing. A man of the Tarkalarrnī tribe. ترکلاړئي *tarkalārrna'ī,* s.f. (6th) A female of the above. Sing. and Pl.

A ترکه *tarka'h,* s.f. (3rd) What is left, the effects of a deceased person, a legacy. Pl. ي *ey.*

P ترکي *turkī,* adj. The Turkish language.

A ترکيب *tarkīb* (2nd) (inf. II of رکب), Form, fashion, mechanism, make, cement, composition. Pl. ترکيبونه *tarkībūnah.* ترکيب کول *tarkīb kawul,* verb trans. To form, to fashion, to organize.

ترګمئي *targ-ma'ī,* s.f. (6th) A dark night, a night

without moonlight. 2. Darkness. Sing. and Pl. See تورگمي

ترله *tarla'h*, s.f. (3rd) A father's brother's daughter, a cousin. Pl. ې *ey*. See also تربور

ترم *turum*, s.m. (2nd) A stallion kept particularly for breeding purposes. Pl. ترمونه *turumūnah*. Also s.m. (5th) Pl. ترمان *turumān*.

ترمنه *taramna'h*, s.f. (3rd) A bog, a quagmire, wet or damp ground. Pl. ې *ey*. See also ترمه , بوښتنه , and لهه

ترمي ترمي *tar-mey tar-mey*, adj. Dispersed, scattered, dishevelled, streaming. ترمي ترمي كيدل *tar-mey tar-mey kedal*, verb intrans. To become dispersed, scattered, dispelled, scattered to the winds. ترمي ترمي كول *tar-mey tar-mey kawul*, verb trans. To disperse, to dispel, to dishevel, to scatter to the winds.

ترناو *tarnāo*, s.m. (2nd) A trough, a gutter, a scupper, a launder, an aqueduct. Pl. ترناوونه *tar-nāo-ūnah*. See پول and بيله

A ترنج *turunj*, s.m. (5th) The citron. Pl. ترنجان *turunjān*; or s.m. (6th). Sing and Pl.

ترنج *taranj*, s.m. (6th) The name of several plants of the species Euphorbia, Asclepias, and the like, containing a milky juice. Sing. and Pl.

P ترنجبين *taranjubīn*, s.m. (6th) Manna, produced from the Hedysarum Alhagi. Sing. and Pl. See د خوزكوړئ

ترنجوكئ *tranjūkaey*, s.m. (1st) A twisted skein of silk or thread. Pl. ي *ī*.

ترنجئ *tranjaey*, s.m. (1st) Same as preceding. Pl. ي *ī*.

ترنځ *trandz*, adj. Slight, thin, spare, delicate, emaciated; (Fem.) ترنځه *trandza'h*. ترنځيدل *trandzedal*, verb trans. To become emaciated, thin, slight, or spare. Pres. ترنځيږي *trandzejzī* (W.), or ترنځيګي *trandzegī* (E.); past وُ ترنځيده *wu-trandzedah*, or ترنځ شه *trandz shah*; fut. وُ به ترنځيږي *wu bah trandzejzī*, or وُ به ترنځيګي *wu bah trandzegī*; imp. وُ ترنځيږه *wu-trandzejzah*, or وُ ترنځيګه *wu-trandzegah*; act. part. ترنځيدونكئ *trandzedūnkaey*, or ترنځيدونئ *trandzedūnaey*; past part. ترنځيدلئ *trandzedalaey*; verb. n. ترنځيدنه *trandzedana'h*.

ترنك *tarnak*, s. prop. The name of a river to the south of Kandahār.

ترنكوڅه *trankūtsa'h*, s.f. (3rd) A sling. Pl. ې *ey*. See مچوغنه and مچلوغزه

ترنګ *trang*, s.m. (5th) Twang, intonation, the sound of the strings of a musical instrument, etc. Pl. ترنګهار *trangahār*. ترنګيدل *trangedal*, verb intrans. To twang, to intonate, to sound as the strings of a musical instrument. Pres. ترنګيږي *trangejzī* (W.), or ترنګيګي *trangegī* (E.); past وُ ترنګيده *wu-trangedah*; fut. وُ به ترنګيږي *wu bah trangejzī*, or وُ به ترنګيګي *wu-bah trangegī*; imp. وُ ترنګيږه *wu-trangejzah*, or وُ ترنګيګه *wu-trangegah*; act. part. ترنګيدونكئ *trangedūnkaey*, or ترنګيدونئ *trangedūnaey*; past part. ترنګيدلئ *trangedalaey*; verb. n. ترنګيدنه *trangedana'h*.

ترنګول *trangawul*, verb trans. To make sound, or twang. Pres. ترنګوي *trangawī*; past وُ ترنګاوه *wu-trangāwuh*, or وُ ترنګاوو *wu-trangāwo*; fut. وُ به ترنګوي *wu bah trangawī*; imp. وُ ترنګوه *wu-trangawah*; act. part. ترنګوونكئ *trangawūnkaey*, or ترنګوونئ *trangawūnaey*; past part. ترنګولئ *trangawulaey*; verb. n. ترنګونه *trangawuna'h*. See شرنګ

ترنګړ *trangarr*, s.m. (2nd) A net used for carrying grass, straw, etc. Pl. ترنګړونه *trangarrūnah*.

ترو *tro*, adv. Then, at that time, afterwards, continually, at the same time, at length, therefore, for as much, for that, consequently.

P تروتازه *tar-o-tāzah*, adj. Green, fresh, cheerful.

P تر و تازګي *tar-o-tāzagī*, s.f. (3rd) Greenness, newness, freshness. Pl. ې *a'ī*.

تروټ *trott*, s.m. (2nd) Loss, defect, deficiency, detriment, injury, damage, blemish, prejudice, etc. Pl. تروټونه *trottūnah*. تروټ خوړل *trott khwarral*, or رسيدل *rasedal*, verb trans. verb intrans. To sustain loss, etc.

تروټه *trotta'h*, s.f. (3rd) Loss, deficiency, detriment. Pl. ې *ey*. See تروټ

ترور *tror*, s.f. (5th) A father's or mother's sister, an aunt. Pl. تروراني *trorāney*. Also trorey *trorey*. Pl. تروريگاني *trorey-gānī*.

تروړۍ *tarorra'ī*, s.f. (6th) A fox. Sing. and Pl.

ترورمۍ *tarojzma'ī*, s.f. (6th) A moonless or dark night, the opposite of moonlight. Sing. and Pl.

تروکه *tarūka'h*, s.f. (3rd) A kind of sorrel. Pl. ې *ey*.

تروکې *tarūkaey* or ترووکې *tarwūkaey*, s.m. (1st) A kind of sorrel. Pl. ي *ī*.

جوگا تروکې *jawgā tarūkaey*, s.m. (1st) A species of sorrel, with a root similar to a potato, and of mountain growth. Pl. ي *ī*. See preceding words.

تروۍ *tarwaey* or *turwaey*, s.m. (1st) Turpeth, an Indian plant which has a cathartic power, the Ipomœa turpethum. Pl. ي *ī*.

تره *trah*, s.m. (2nd) A paternal or maternal uncle. Pl. ترونه *trūnah*. See اکا

P تره *tara'h*, s.f. (3rd) A cucumber. 2. Pottage, greens, garden herbs. Pl. ې *ey*.

تره *tara'h*, s.f. (3rd) Fear, dismay, awe, alarm, timidity. Pl. ې *ey*. See ترهره and ويره

ترهيدل *tarhedal*, verb intrans. To take alarm, to start, to wince, to cower, to be afraid, to be terrified, to become frightened, to be disturbed or agitated, to fly in terror. This is almost peculiar to animals. Pres. ترهيږي *tarhejzī* (W.), or ترهيگي *tarhegī* (E.); past وُ ترهيده *wu-tarhedah*, or وُ ترهيدَ *wu-tarheda*; fut. وُ به ترهيږي *wu bah tarhejzī*, or وُ به ترهگيي *wu bah tarhegī*; imp. وُ ترهيږه *wu-tarhejzah*, or وُ ترهيگه *wu-tarhegah*; act. part. ترهيدونکې *tarhedūnkaey*, or ترهيدونې *tarhedūnaey*; past part. ترهيدلې *tarhedalaey*; verb. n. ترهيدنه *tarhedana'h*.

ترهول *tarhawul*, verb trans. To alarm, to terrify, to frighten, to disturb, to agitate, to cause to start, etc. (peculiar to animals.) Pres. ترهوي *tarhawī*; past وُ ترهاوه *wu-tarhāwuh*, or وُ ترهاوو *wu-tarhāwo*; fut. وُ به ترهوي *wu bah tarhawī*; imp. وُ ترهوه *wu-tarhawah*; act. part. ترهوونکې *tarhawūnkaey*, or ترهوونې *tarhawūnaey*; past part. ترهولې *tarhawulaey*; verb. n. ترهونه *tarhawuna'h*.

ترهاو *tirhāo*, s.m. (2nd) The third part of an *ūgaey* containing eight *sīrs*. Pl. ترهاوونه *tirhāoūnah*. See اوگي

ترهره *tarhara'h*, s.f. (3rd) Fear, dismay, timidity, awe, alarm, etc. Pl. ې *ey*.

ترهور *tar-hūr*, adj. Timid, fearful, nervous, diffident, overawed, dismayed; (Fem.) ترهوره *tarhūra'h*.

P تري *tarī*, s.f. (3rd) Moisture, freshness, water (in opposition to dry land). Pl. ۍ *a'ī*. 2. adv. By water. شکر تري *shakar tarī*, Soft sugar. See نمي

ترۍ *traey*, s.m. (1st) A kind of cucumber (Cucumis utilissimus). 2. A mountain stream or rivulet, brought from one mountain to another for the purposes of irrigation. Pl. ي *ī*.

ترۍ *tara'ī*, adv. Clandestinely, in secret, under the rose, confidentially, comprehensively, tacitly. (s تري and تلي). په ترۍ ويل *pah tara'ī wa-yal*, verb trans. To speak clandestinely, etc. ترۍ والې *tara'ī walaey*, s.m. (1st) Secrecy, etc. Pl. ي *ī*.

تري *trī* or ترِ *tri* (from the prep. تر), From him, her, it, that, etc. See my Grammar, page 48, para. 136, and تر

ترياك *taryāk*, s.m. (6th) Opium, an antidote for poisonous snake bites. (A ترياق *tiryāq*). Sing. and Pl.

A تريج *tarīj*, adj. Violent (as wind), strong or powerful (as a man); (Fem.) تريجه *tarīja'h*.

تريخ *trīkh*, adj. Bitter, nauseous. Pl. ترخه *tarkhæh*; (Fem.) ترخه *tarkha'h*. Pl. ترخې *tarkhey*. تريخ توب *trīkh-tob*, s.m. (2nd). Pl. *tobūnah*; or تريخ تيا *trīkh tīā*, s.f. (6th) (E.) Sing. and Pl.; (W.) Pl. تياوي *tīāwī*; and تريخ والې *trīkh-walaey*, s.m. (1st) Bitterness, nauseousness. Pl. والي *wālī*. تريخيدل *trīkhedal*, verb intrans. To become bitter or nauseous. تريخول *trīkhawul*, verb trans. To make or render bitter or nauseous.

تريخې *trīkhaey*, s.m. (1st) The gall bladder;

gall, bitterness. 2. Anger, bitterness of mind, rancour, malignity. Pl. ي *ī*. تريخي لرل *trīkhaey laral*, verb trans. To bear malice against one, to regard with malignity, to regard with bitterness, to be rancorous, or spiteful towards.

تريو *trīw*, adj. Sour, acid, tart, crabbed, rough. Pl. تروه *tarwæh*; (Fem.) تروه *tarwa'h*. Pl. تروې *tarwey*. تريو مخي *trīw-makhaey*, adj. Morose, surly, stern, hard-favoured, gruff, ugly, cynical; (Fem.) تريو مخ *trīw-makhi*. Pl. (Masc. and Fem.) ي *ī*. تريويدل *trīwedal*, verb intrans. To grow or become sour, tart, crabbed, etc. تريوول *trīwawul*, verb trans. to make or render sour, tart, crabbed.

تريو توب *trīw-tob*, s.m. (2nd). Pl. توبونه *tobūnah*; or تريو والي *trīw-wālaey*, s.m. (1st). Pl. والي *wālī*; and تريو تيا *trīw-tī'ā*, s.f. (6th) Sourness, acidity, tartness, crabbedness, sternness, moroseness, gruffness, ugliness, roughness. (E.) Sing. and Pl.; (W.) Pl. تياوي *tī'āwī*.

تريه *tær-yah*, A word used to drive sheep.

ترازه *tarrāza'h*, s.f. (3rd) A slice, a piece, a bit, a thin piece. Pl. ې *ey*. See تارزه

تراق *trrāk*, s.m. (5th) A tap, rap, pat, a knock, etc., a stroke with anything hard, as on a door, etc. Pl. تراقهار *trrāka-hār*. تراق تراق *trrāk-trrāk*, A tapping, knocking, or rapping. تراق تراق كول *trrāk-trrāk kawul*, or تراق وهل *trrāk wahal*, verb trans. To tap, to knock, etc. See ترق

تراقئ *tarrāka'ī*, s.f. (6th) A cloth worn between the legs, a langotie. Sing. and Pl. See چوتي

ترانكه *tarrānka'h*, s.f. (3rd) A blister, a pustule, a bubble. Pl. ې *ey*. See تنراكه

ترپ *trrap*, s.m. (5th) Bump, thump, haste, hurry. 2. Bustle, noise. Pl. ترپهار *trrapahār*. (HI ترپ). ترپيدل *trrapedal*, verb intrans. To bump, to thump. 2. To flutter, to flounce, to palpitate, to writhe, to be agitated, to wriggle, to toss, to spring, to bound, to jump, to leap. Pres. ترپيږي *trrapejzī* (W.), or ترپيکي *trrapegī* (E.); past و ترپيده *wu-trrapedah*, or و ترپيدَ *wu-trrapeda*; fut. و به ترپيږي *wu bah trrapejzī*, or ترپيکي *trrapegī*; imp. و ترپيږه *wu-trrapejzah*, or و ترپيکه *wu-trrapegah*; act. part. ترپيدونکي *trrapedūnkaey*, or ترپيدوني *trrapedūnaey*; past. part. ترپيدلي *trrapedalaey*; verb. n. ترپيدنه *trrapedanah*. See ترپيدل

ترپول *trrapawul*, verb trans. To flutter, to agitate, to cause to flounce, to cause to writhe or wriggle, to cause to spring, jump, or bound. Pres. ترپوي *trrapawī*; past و ترپاوه *wu-trrapāwuh*, or و ترپاوو *wu-trrapāwo*; fut. و به ترپوي *wu bah trrapawī*; imp. و ترپوه *wu-trrapawah*; act. part. ترپوونکي *trrapawūnkaey*, or ترپووني *trrapawūnaey*; past part. ترپولي *trrapawulaey*; verb. n. ترپونه *trrapawuna'h*.

ترق *trrak*, s.m. (5th) A tap, rap, pat, knock, a slight sound. Pl. ترقهار *trrakahār*. ترق وهل *trrak wahal*, verb trans. To tap, to pat, to rap.

ترل *tarral*, verb trans. To bind, to fasten, to attach, to make fast, to secure, to tie, to pinion, to strap, to lash, to gird, to affix, etc. Pres. تري *tarrī*; past و تاره *wu-tārrah*; fut. و به تري *wu bah tarrī*; imp. و تره *wu-tarrah*; act. part. ترونكي *tarrūnkaey*, or تروني *tarrūnaey*; past part. ترلي *tarralaey*; verb. n. ترنه *tarrana'h*, or ترون *tarrūn*.

ترم *tarram*, adj. Lukewarm, warm as milk from the cow, tepid; (Fem.) ترمه *tarrama'h*.

ترون *tarrūn*, s.m. (9th) (verb. n. of ترل) Binding, fastening, attaching, securing, lashing, girding, affixing. 2. A compact, contract, agreement, bargain, covenant, treaty. Sing. and Pl. ترون كول *tarrūn kawul*, verb trans. To covenant, to contract, to bargain, to agree for, to treat, to negociate, to come to terms. See تره and ترنه

تره *tarra'h*, s.f. (3rd) A compact, covenant, contract, agreement, bargain, treaty. Pl. ترې *tarrey*. See preceding.

تري *tarraey*, s.m. (1st) Lisping, speaking imperfectly. 2. One who lisps. Pl. ڀ *ī*; s.f. (6th) ترڀ *tarra'ī*. Sing. and Pl. See تترڀ, ترترڀ, تته and ګانکوڀ

A تزلزل *tazalzul*, s.m. (2nd) (inf. II of زلزله) Commotion, agitation, trepidation. 2. An earthquake. Pl. تزلزلونه *tazalzulūnah*.

تزن *tu-zan*, adj. Poor-spirited, cowardly, faint-hearted, base, craven, dastard; (Fem.) تزنه *tu-zana'h*. تزن والئ *tu-zan wālaey*, s.m. (1st) Cowardliness, supineness, baseness, dastardliness, spiritlessness. Pl. والي *wālī*.

A تزوير *tazwīr*, s.m. (2nd) (inf. II of زور) Imposture, fraud, deceit, deception, stratagem, lie. Pl. تزويرونه *tazwīrūnah*.

A تزئين *taz'īn*, s.m. (2nd) (inf. II of زينت) Decoration, ornament; honour, jewel; dressing one's-self. Pl. تزئينونه *taz'īnūnah*.

تږئ *tajzaey*, adj. Thirsty; (Fem.) تږې *tajzi*. Pl. (Masc. and Fem.) ي *ī*. تږئ کيدل *tajzaey kedal*, verb intrans. To become thirsty. تږئ کول *tajzaey kawul*, verb trans. To make thirsty. See تنده

A تسبيح *tasbīḥ*, s.m. (2nd) (inf. II of سبح, He praised) The act of praising God. 2. A rosary, a chaplet of beads. Pl. تسبيحونه *tasbīḥūnah*. See تسپه and تسبه

تسبه *tasba'h*, s.f. (3rd) The bead of a rosary. Pl. تسبئ *tasbey*, A rosary, a chaplet of beads. (corrup. of A تسبيح).

تسبي آړول *tasbey ārrawul*, verb trans. To tell one's beads; also تسبيح ويل *tasbīḥ wayal*, verb trans. See above.

تسپه *taspa'h*, s.f. (3rd). Pl. ئ *ey*. See above.

تسخير *taskhīr*, s.m. (2nd) (inf. II of سخر) Imprisoning, taking a stronghold or fortress, subduing, capturing; capture, subjection, subjugation.. Pl. تسخيرونه *taskhīrūnah*. تسخير کيدل *taskhīr kedal*, verb intrans. To become captured, subdued, or subjugated. تسخير کول *taskhīr kawul*, verb trans. To captivate, to capture, to subdue, to subjugate, to conquer.

A تسکين *taskīn*, s.m. (2nd) (inf. II of سکن) Consolation, comfort, pacifying, assuaging, soothing, appeasing. Pl. تسکينونه *taskīnūnah*. تسکين ور کول *taskīn war kawul*, verb trans. To sooth, to comfort, to solace, to cheer, to sustain, to encourage, to support.

A تسلي *tasallī*, s.f. (3rd) Pl. ئ *a'ī*; or تسلي *tasallā*, s.f. (6th) (inf. v of سلي or سلا, He was quiet), Consolation, comfort, solace. Pl. تسلاوي *tasallāwī*. تسلي کيدل *tasallā kedal*, verb intrans. To be consoled or comforted. تسلي کول *tasallā kawul*, verb trans. To comfort, to console, to assure, to animate; also تسلي ور کول *tasallā war kawul*, verb trans.

A تسليم *taslīm*, s.m. (2nd) (inf. II of سلم) Surrender, resignation, cession. 2. Salutation, homage, obeisance, health, security. Pl. تسليمونه *taslīmūnah*. (Pl. A تسليمات *taslīmāt*). تسليم کيدل *taslīm kedal*, verb intrans. To be resigned or committed. تسليم کول *taslīm kawul*, verb trans. To resign, to surrender, to cede, to commit, to salute, to make obeisance, to do homage.

P تسمه *tasma'h*, s.f. (3rd) A thong, a strap of leather. Pl. ئ *ey*.

تش *tash*, adj. Empty, void, devoid, having no sense or ideas, foolish, useless. 2. Mere, only, unmixed. 3. adv. Merely, only, solely, simply; (Fem.) تشه *tasha'h*. تش په تشَ *tash pah tasha*, or تش په تورَ *tash pah tora* or تش تور *tash tor*, Completely or entirely empty, void, or useless. تش لاس *tash lās*, Empty handed. تش توب *tash-tob*, s.m. (2nd) Pl. توبونه *tobūnah*; or تش والئ *tash wālaey*, s.m. (1st) Pl. والي *wālī*; or تش تيا *tash tī-ā*, s.f. (6th) Emptiness, voidness, uselessness, foolishness, ignorance, etc. (E.) Sing. and Pl.; (W.) Pl. تياوي *tī'āwī*.

تشيدل *tashedal*, verb intrans. To become empty, void, useless. Pres. تشيږي *tashejzī* (W.) or تشيګي *tashegī* (E.); past تش شه *tash shah*, or تش وُ شه *tash wu-shah*; fut. تش به شي *tash bah shī*, or به وُ شي *bah wu-shī*; imp. تش شه *tash shah*, or تش وُ شه *tash wu-shah*; act. part. تشيدونکئ *tashedūnkaey*, or تشيدونئ

tashedūnaey ; past part. تش شوي *tash*, or *tash sharvaey* ; verb. n. تشيدنه *tashedana'h*.

تشول *tasharvul*, verb trans. To empty, to make void or destitute, to pour out contents, to waste. Pres. تشوي *tasharvī* ; past تش كه *tash kah* or كړ *karr*, or تش وُ كه *tash rvu-kah* or وُ كړ *rvu-karr* ; fut. تش به كي *tash bah kī*, or به كړي *bah krrī*, or تش به وُ كي *tash bah rvu-kī*, or به وُ كړي *bah rvu-krrī* ; imp. تش كه *tash kah*, or كړه *krrah*, or تش وُ كه *tash rvu-kah*, or وُ كړه *rvu-krrah* ; act. part. تشوونكي *tasharvūnkaey*, or تشووني *tasharvūnaey* ; past part. تش كړي *tash karraey* ; verb. n. تشونه *tasharvuna'h*.

A تشبيه *tashbīh*, s.m. (2nd) (inf. II of شبه) A simile, comparison, allegory, metaphor. Pl. تشبيهونه *tashbīhūnah*. حرف تشبيه *ḥarf-i-tashbīh*, Adverb of similitude. تشبيه لرل *tashbīh laral*, verb trans. To hold or have comparison, to be like, equal, or similar. تشبيه كول *tashbīh karvul*, verb trans. To compare, to contrast, to place side by side, to draw a parallel.

P تشت *tasht*, s.m. (2nd) A large flat vessel or ewer, a wash-hand basin. Pl. تشتونه *tashtūnah*.

تشخانه *tashkhāna'h*, s.f. (3rd) The pan of a gun or matchlock. Pl. ي *ey*. See آتشخانه and ماشه

A تشخيص *tashkhīṣ*, s.m. (2nd) (inf. II of شخص) Distinguishing perfectly, ascertainment, valuation, assessment. Pl. تشخيصونه *tashkhīṣūnah*. تشخيص كول *tashkhīṣ karvul*, verb trans. To ascertain, assess, value, appraise.

A تشديد *tashdīd*, s.m. (2nd) (inf. II of شد) Consolidating, corroboration. 2. Putting the orthographical mark *tashdīd* (ّ) over letters, denoting that the letter should be doubled. 3. The name of the character itself. Pl. تشديدونه *tashdīdūnah*.

A تشريح *tashrīḥ*, s.m. (2nd) (inf. II of شرح) Explanation, declaration. 2. Anatomy. Pl. تشريحونه *tashrīḥūnah*.

A تشريف *tashrīf*, s.m. (2nd) (inf. II of شرف) Honouring, exalting. 2. Investing with a robe of honour. Pl. تشريفونه *tashrīfūnah*.

A تشكيك *tashkīk*, s.m. (2nd) (inf. II of شك) Creating doubt. Pl. تشكيكونه *tashkīkūnah*. ماضي تشكيك *māẓī-i-tashkīk*, The Doubtful Past Tense in Grammar.

A تشويش *tashrvīsh*, s.m. (2nd) (inf. II of شوش) Anxiety, grief, disquietude, alarm, apprehension, distraction. 2. Confusion. Pl. تشويشونه *tashrvīshūnah*.

A تشهد *tashahhud*, s.m. (2nd) (inf. V of شهادت) Making a profession of religious sentiments, avowing belief in the unity of the Deity, and the mission of Muḥammad. Pl. تشهدونه *tashahhudūnah*.

A تشهير *tashhīr*, s.m. (2nd) (inf. II of شهرت) Proclaiming, publishing, reciting in public. 2. Marking a criminal, public exposure on an ass. Pl. تشهيرونه *tashhīrūnah*. تشهير موندل *tashhīr mūndal*, verb trans. To be publicly exposed on an ass. تشهير كول *tashhīr karvul*, verb trans. To proclaim, to publish, to expose on an ass as a punishment.

تشي *tashaey*, s.m. (1st) The side, the space between the lower ribs and the hips ; the hypochondria. Pl. ي *ī*.

تښتن *tashtan* (W.) or *takhtan* (E.), s.m. (5th) A lord, master, possessor, owner, proprietor. Pl. تښتنان *tashtanān* or *takhtanān*. تښتنه *tashtana'h* or *takhtana'h*, s.f. (3rd) A mistress, a lady, a proprietress. Pl. ي *ey*. See خښتن

تښتيدل *tashtedal* (W.) or *takhtedal* (E.) verb intrans. To flee, to fly, to escape, to decamp, to bolt, to run away. Pres. تښتي *tashtī* or *takhtī* ; past وُ تښتيده *rvu-tashtedah* or *rvu-takhtedah*, or وُ تښتيدَ *rvu-tashteda* or *rvu-takhteda* ; fut. وُ به تښتي *rvu bah tashtī* or *takhtī* ; imp. وُ تښته *rvu-tashtah* or *rvu-takhtah* ; act. part. تښتيدونكي *tashtedūnkaey* or *takhtedūnkaey*, or تښتيدوني *tashtedūnaey* or *takhtedūnaey* ; past part. تښتيدلي *tashtedalaey* or *takhtedalaey* ; verb. n. تښتيدنه *tashtedana'h* or *takhtedana'h*.

تښتول *ta<u>sh</u>tawul* or *ta<u>kh</u>tawul*, verb trans. To put to flight, to cause to flee or fly, to cause to bolt, to run away with, to elope with. Pres. تښتوي *ta<u>sh</u>tawī* or *ta<u>kh</u>tawī*; past وُ تښتاوه *wu-ta<u>sh</u>tāwuh* or *wu-ta<u>kh</u>tāwuh*, or وُ تښتاوو *wu-ta<u>sh</u>tāwo* or *wu-ta<u>kh</u>tāwo*; fut. وُ به تښتوي *wu bah ta<u>sh</u>tawī* or *ta<u>kh</u>tawī*; imp. وُ تښتوه *wu-ta<u>sh</u>tawah* or *ta<u>kh</u>tawah*; act. part. تښتوونکي *ta<u>sh</u>tawūnkaey* or *ta<u>kh</u>tawūnkaey*, or تښتووني *ta<u>sh</u>tawūnaey* or *ta<u>kh</u>tawūnaey*; past part. تښتولي *ta<u>sh</u>tawulaey* or *ta<u>kh</u>tawulaey*; verb. n. تښتونه *ta<u>sh</u>tawuna'h* or *ta<u>kh</u>tawuna'h*.

تښتل *t'<u>sh</u>al* (W.) or *t'<u>kh</u>al* (E.) verb intrans. To fly from, to decamp, to retreat, to retire, to move off. Pres. تښي *t'<u>sh</u>ī* or *t'<u>kh</u>ī*; past وُ تښ *wu-ti<u>sh</u>* or *wu-ti<u>kh</u>*; fut. وُ به تښي *wu bah t'<u>sh</u>ī* or *t'<u>kh</u>ī*; imp. وُ تښه *wu-t'<u>sh</u>ah* or *wu-t'<u>kh</u>ah*; act. part. تښونکي *t'<u>sh</u>ūnkaey* or *t'<u>kh</u>ūnkaey*, or تښوني *t'<u>sh</u>ūnaey* or *t'<u>kh</u>ūnaey*; past part. تښلي *t'<u>sh</u>alaey* or *t'<u>kh</u>alaey*; verb. n. تښنه *t'<u>sh</u>ana'h* or *t'<u>kh</u>ana'h*. See تښتيدل and تيښتيدل, etc.

تښول *t'<u>sh</u>awul* or *t'<u>kh</u>awul*, verb trans. To put to flight, to make or cause to retire, to send to the right about. See also تښتول and تيښتول

A تصدق *taṣadduḳ*, s.m. (2nd) (inf. v of صدق) Giving alms. 2. Sacrificing, sacrifice, devoting. Pl. تصدقونه *taṣadduḳūnah*. تصدق كيدل *taṣadduḳ kedal*, verb intrans. To become devoted, sacrificed. تصدق كول *taṣadduḳ kawul*, verb trans. To devote, to sacrifice.

A تصديع *taṣdīæ*, s.m. (2nd) (inf. II of صدع) The headache. 2. Affliction, trouble, annoyance, vexation, toil, perplexity. Pl. تصديعونه *taṣdīæūnah*. تصديع ور كول *taṣdīæ war kawul*, verb trans. To trouble, vex, tease, harass, plague, annoy. تصديع كول *taṣdīæ kawul*, verb trans. To take trouble.

A تصديق *taṣdīḳ*, s.m. (2nd) (inf. II of صدق) Verifying, attesting, verification, appeal, acknowledging as true. Pl. تصديقونه *taṣdīḳūnah*. تصديق كيدل *taṣdīḳ kedal*, verb intrans. To become attested or verified. تصديق كول *taṣdīḳ kawul*, verb trans. To attest, to verify, to acknowledge as true. تصديق ور كول *taṣdīḳ war kawul*, verb trans. To give attestation or verification.

A تصرف *taṣarruf*, s.m. (2nd) (inf. v of صرف) Possession, use, sway. 2. Expenditure, disposal, embezzlement, extravagance. Pl. تصرفونه *taṣarrufūnah*. تصرف كول *taṣarruf kawul*, verb trans. To expend, to appropriate to one's own use, to embezzle, to occupy.

A تصنيف *taṣnīf*, s.m. (2nd) (inf. II of صنف) Invention, composition, writing of a book. Pl. تصنيفونه *taṣnīfūnah*. تصنيف كول *taṣnīf kawul*, verb trans. To compose, to write a book.

A تصور *taṣawwur*, s.m. (2nd) (inf. v of صورت) Imagination, contemplation, meditation, reflection, fancy, idea, conception, preconception. Pl. تصورونه *taṣawwurūnah*. تصور كول *taṣawwur kawul*, verb trans. To imagine, to fancy, to conceive.

A تصوف *taṣawwuf*, s.m. (2nd) (inf. v of صوف) The theology of the Ṣūfīs, mystics, mystery, contemplation. Pl. تصوفونه *taṣawwufūnah*.

A تصوير *taṣwīr*, s.m. (2nd) (inf. II of صورت) A picture, a portrait, an image. Pl. تصويرونه *taṣwīrūnah*. تصوير ښكل *taṣwīr <u>kh</u>kal*, or كښل *k<u>sh</u>al*, verb trans. To draw, to paint. See خيره

A تعالي *taæālā*, adj. (from علو) Most high. تعالي الله *taæālā-llah*, The Most High.

A تعبير *taæbīr*, s.m. (2nd) (inf. II of عبر) Explanation, interpretation (particularly of dreams), attribute, quality. Pl. تعبيرونه *taæbīrūnah*. تعبير ويل *taæbīr wayal*, or كول *kawul*, verb trans. To interpret, to explain. تعبير ويونكي *taæbīr wayūnkaey*, or كوونكي *kawūnkaey*, s.m. (1st) An interpreter of dreams; (Fem.) ويونكِ *wayūnki*, or كوونكِ *kawūnki*; Pl. (Masc. and Fem.) ي *ī*.

A تعجب *taæjjub*, s.m. (2nd) (inf. v of عجب) Admiration, astonishment, wonder, amazement, surprise, wondering. Pl. تعجبونه *taæj-*

jubūnah. تعجب كول *taæjjub kawul* or لرل *laral,* verb trans. To wonder, to admire, to be filled with admiration or astonishment.

A تعجيل *taæjīl,* s.m. (2nd) (inf. II of عجل) Agility, haste, despatch, expedition. Pl. تعجيلونه *taæjīlūnah.* تعجيل كول *taæjīl kawul,* verb trans. To make haste, to hasten, to expedite.

A تعدي *taæddā,* s.f. (6th) (inf. V of عدو) Extortion, oppression, wrong, injury, tyranny, violence, cruelty. Pl. تعديوي *taæddāwī.* تعدي كول *taæddā kawul,* verb trans. To oppress, to extort, to injure, to tyrannize over.

A تعريف *taærīf,* s.m. (2nd) (inf. II of عرف) Explanation, description. 2. Praise, praising. Pl. تعريفونه *taærīfūnah.* تعريف كول *taærīf kawul,* verb trans. To praise, to laud, to extol.

P تعريفي *taærīfī,* adj. Commendable, notable, worthy of praise.

A تعزير *taæzīr,* s.m. (2nd) (inf. II of عزر) Punishment, correction, reproof, censure, reprimand. Pl. تعزيرونه *taæzīrūnah.* تعزير كول *taæzīr kawul,* verb trans. To punish, to correct, to reprimand.

A تعطيل *taæṭīl,* s.m. (2nd) (inf. II of عطل) Abandoning, neglecting. 2. Vacation. Pl. تعطيلونه *taæṭīlūnah.* تعطيل كول *taæṭīl kawul,* verb trans. To neglect, to abandon.

A تعظيم *taæẓīm,* s.m. (2nd) (inf. II of عظم) Reverence, respect, honour, treating with ceremony and respect, honoring, gentility, politeness, Pl. تعظيمونه *taæẓīmūnah.* تعظيم كول *taæẓīm kawul,* verb trans. To honor, to reverence, to show respect. تعظيم ويل *taæẓīm wayal,* verb trans. To present one's respects.

A تعلق *taælluḳ,* s.m. (2nd) (inf. V of علق) Relationship, connection, concern, dependence, appertaining, possession, property. 2. Commerce, correspondence. 3. A lordship, a manor. Pl. تعلقونه *taælluḳūnah.* تعلق كول *taælluḳ kawul,* verb trans. To make connection or dependence, to hold commerce or correspondence. تعلق لرل *taælluḳ laral,* verb trans. To appertain, to depend, to belong.

A تعلقه *taælluḳa'h,* s.f. (3rd) Connection, relationship. 2. Possession of land, fee, manor, lordship. Pl. ې *ey.*

A تعلم *taællum,* s.m. (2nd) (inf. V of علم) Learning, knowledge, being taught. 2. Study. Pl. تعلمونه *taællumūnah.*

A تعليم *taælīm,* s.m. (2nd) (inf. II of علم) Teaching, instruction, tuition. Pl. تعليمونه *taælīmūnah.* تعليم كول *taælīm kawul,* verb trans. To teach, to instruct.

A تعمير *taæmīr,* s.m. (2nd) (inf. II of عمر) Building, structure, repairing. Making a place habitable and populous. Pl. تعميرونه *taæmīrūnah.* تعمير كول *taæmīr kawul,* verb trans. To build, to repair, to construct.

A تعويذ *taæwīẕ,* s.m. (2nd) (inf. II of عوذ) Having recourse to the Deity, asking protection. 2. A charm, an amulet. Pl. تعويذونه *taæwīẕūnah.*

تغ *tag͟h,* s.m. (2nd) A helmet. Pl. تغونه *tag͟hūnah.* See خول

تغ *tug͟h,* s.m. (2nd) A flag, an ensign, a standard, a banner. 2. A mark, a welt, a scar, etc. Pl. تغونه *tug͟hūnah.* See توغ and تغمه

P تغار *tag͟hār,* s.m. (2nd) A tub, a bucket, a trough, a pail, a platter. Pl. تغارونه *tag͟hārūnah.* See بهانك

P تغارك *tag͟hārak,* s.m. (2nd) The dropsy. Pl. تغاركونه *tag͟hārakūnah.*

P تغاري *tag͟hāraey,* s.m. (1st) A large flat earthen dish. 2. A small tub or bucket, a small pail or platter. Pl. ي *ī.*

تغاري *tag͟hāraey,* adj. A glutton, a gormandizer; (Fem.) تغاري *tag͟hāra'ī.*

A تغافل *tag͟hāful,* s.m. (2nd) (inf. VI of غفلت) Negligence, neglect, indifference, inattention, inadvertency. Pl. تغافلونه *tag͟hāfulūnah.* تغافل كول *tag͟hāful kawul,* verb trans. To neglect, to manifest negligence.

P تغافلي *tag͟hāfulī,* s.f. (3rd). See تغافل Pl. ئي *a'ī.*

A تغلب *tag͟hallub,* s.m. (2nd) Cheating, imposition, forgery, falsification, embezzlement. Pl. تغلبونه *tag͟hallubūnah.* تغلب كول *tag͟hallub kawul*, verb trans. To embezzle, to cheat, to falsify accounts, to impose on.

A تغمه *taghma'h*, s.f. (3rd) A mark, a welt, a scar, a blemish. Pl. ئ *ey*. See موره and توغ or تخ

A تغير *taghīr*, s.m. (2nd) (inf. II of غير) Alternation, change. Pl. تغيرونه *taghīrūnah*. 2. adj. Changed, altered, discharged, dismissed; (Fem.) تغيره *taghīra'h*. تغير كول *taghīr kawul*, verb trans. To remove, to dismiss, to change, to alter. تغير و تبديل *taghīr-o-tabdīl*, Change for better for worse.

P تف *tuf*, s.m. (9th) Spittle, the sound of spitting. Sing. and Pl. See تو

A تفاوت *tafāwut*, s.m. (2nd) (inf. VI of فوت) Distance, difference, distinction, disparity. Pl. تفاوتونه *tafāwutūnah*.

A تفحص *tafaḥḥuṣ*, s.m. (2nd) Investigation, inquiry, search, disquisition. Pl. تفحصونه *tafaḥḥuṣūnah*. See تپوس

A تفرقه *tafriḳa'h*, s.f. (3rd) (inf. II of فرق) Separation, dispersion, distinction. Pl. ئ *ey*.

A تفريق *tafrīḳ*, s.m. (2nd) (inf. II of فرق). See preceding. Pl. تفريقونه *tafrīḳūnah*.

A تفسير *tafsīr*, s.m. (2nd) (inf. II of فسر) Explanation, commentary, paraphrase, an interpretation. Pl. تفسيرونه *tafsīrūnah*. تفسير كول *tafsīr kawul*, verb trans. To interpret, to explain.

A تفصيل *tafṣīl*, s.m. (2nd) (inf. II of فصل) Explanation, analysis, separation, division, detail. Pl. تفصيلونه *tafṣīlūnah*. تفصيل كول *tafṣīl kawul*, verb trans. To explain, to detail, to separate. تفصيل وار *tafṣīl wār*, adv. Distinctly, in detail.

A تفضيل *tafẓīl*, s.m. (2nd) (inf. II of فضل) Excellence, pre-eminence. Pl. تفضيلونه *tafẓīlūnah*.

A تفويض *tafwīẓ*, s.m. (2nd) (inf. II of فوض) Resigning, committing to another, cession, confiding. Pl. تفويضونه *tafwīẓūnah*. تفويض كول *tafwīẓ kawul*, verb trans. To commit, to confide, to resign.

A تقاضا *taḳāẓā*, s.f. (6th) (inf. VI of تقضي) Dunning, exacting, exigence, urgency, importunity. Pl. تقاضاوي *taḳāẓāwī*. تقاضا كول *taḳāẓā kawul*, verb trans. To dun, to exact. تقاضا لرل *taḳāẓā laral*, verb trans. To be in distress or necessity (*lit.* to hold or possess distress).

A تقدير *taḳdīr*, s.m. (2nd) (inf. II of قدر) Fate, destiny, divine decree, lot, predestination. Pl. تقديرونه *taḳdīrūnah*.

A تقرير *taḳrīr*, s.m. (2nd) (inf. II of قر) Relation, detail, recital, narration, confirmation, exposition, confession. Pl. تقريرونه *taḳrīrūnah*. تقرير كول *taḳrīr kawul*, verb trans, To relate, to recite, to avow.

A تقسيم *taḳsīm*, s.m. (2nd) (inf. II of قسم) Dividing, division, distributing, distribution. Pl. تقسيمونه *taḳsīmūnah*. تقسيم كول *taḳsīm kawul*, verb trans. To divide, to distribute, to share, to part, to portion, to assort.

A تقصير *taḳṣīr*, s.m. (2nd) (inf. II of قصر or قصور) Fault, crime, offence, error. Pl. تقصيرونه *taḳṣīrūnah*. تقصير كول *taḳṣīr kawul*, verb trans. To commit a crime, fault, or offence. تقصير دار *taḳṣīr-dār*, adj. Blamable, faulty, criminal, guilty, culpable; (Fem.) تقصيرداره *taḳṣīr-dāra'h*.

A تقليد *taḳlīd*, s.m. (2nd) (inf. II of قلد) Imitation, forgery, counterfeiting. Pl. تقليدونه *taḳlīdūna'h*. تقليد كول *taḳlīd kawul*, verb trans. To imitate, to counterfeit, to mimic, to ape.

A P تقليدي *taḳlīdī*, adj. Imitated, forged, false, counterfeit.

A تقوي *taḳwā*, s.f. (6th) Piety, the fear of God, abstinence. Pl. تقويوي *taḳwāwī*. آهل تقوي *āhl-i-taḳwā*, Pious, God-fearing.

A تقه *tuḳḳa'h*, s.f. (3rd) A blunt-headed arrow, an arrow with a round head. Pl. ئ *ey*. See توقه (P تكا or تكه).

P تک *tak* (part. of تكيدن) Running about. تک و پو *tak-o-pū*, Searching or examining, bustle. تک و پو كول *tak-o-pū kawul*, verb trans. To search or examine carefully.

تک *tak*, adv. Altogether, quite, entirely, wholly,

totally, utterly, thoroughly, out and out, outright. This word is only applicable with respect to colour; thus, تک تور *tak tor*, Entirely or wholly black. تک سپین *tak spīn*, Quite or altogether white, etc.

A تکبیر *takbīr*, s.m. (2nd) (inf. II of کبر) Repeating the Musalmān belief, and saying by way of exclamation on particular occasions, "God is great." Pl. تکبیرونه *takbīrūnah*.

A تکرار *takrār*, s.m. (2nd) (inf. II of کر) Altercation, contention, dispute, wrangle, cavil, repetition, tautology. Pl. تکرارونه *takrārūnah*. تکرار کول *takrār kawul*, verb trans. To debate, to dispute, to argue, to wrangle, to cavil, to repeat.

A P تکراري *takrārī*, adj. Importuning, seizing, fond of argument, wrangling. 2. A wrangler, a carper, a caviller; (Fem.) ئي *a'ī*.

A تکریم *takrīm*, s.m. (2nd) (inf. II of کرم) Honour, reverence, respect. Pl. تکریمونه *takrīmūnah*. تعظیم و تکریم *taǽzīm-o-takrīm*, Treating with reverence and respect.

تکړه *takaṟṟa'h*, s.f. (3rd) A flat smooth stone or pebble found in rivers, from the size of a walnut upwards. Pl. ئي *ey*. See تیږه and تیکه

تکړه *takṟṟah*, adj, Strong, active, healthy. تکړه کیدل *takṟṟah kedal*, verb intrans. To become or grow strong, active, healthy. تکړه کول *takṟṟah kawul*, verb trans. To make or render strong, active, or healthy.

تکل *takal*, s.m. (2nd) Endeavour, attempt, effort, essay, application, study. Pl. تکلونه *takalūnah*. تکل کول *takal kawul*, verb trans. To endeavour, to attempt, to essay, to make effort, to study.

تک لاستي *tak-lāstaey*, adj. Active, quick, nimble, alert, agile, smart, spirited; (Fem.) تک لاستِ *tak-lāsti*. Pl. (Masc. and Fem.) ي *ī*.

A تکلیف *taklīf*, s.m. (2nd) (inf. II of کلف) Ceremony. 2. Trouble, difficulty, distress, inconvenience, ailment, affliction, annoyance. Pl. تکلیفونه *taklīfūnah*. تکلیف کول *taklīf kawul*, verb trans. To take the trouble. تکلیف ور کول *taklīf war kawul*, verb trans. To annoy, to molest, incommode, trouble.

A تکیه *takīa'h*, s.f. (3rd) A pillow, a bolster. Pl. ئي *ey*. تکیه کول *takīa'h kawul*, verb trans. To support, to encourage, تکیه ور کول *takīa'h war kawul*, verb trans. To receive respectfully. تکیه کلام *takīa'h kalām*, s.m. A cant word, an expletive. تکیه وهل *takīa'h wahal*, verb trans. To lean on, to bolster, to support.

P تګ *tag*, s.m. (9th) Running, gait, pace, walk, motion. Sing. and Pl. تګ کول *tag kawul*, verb trans. To run.

P تګاپو *tagā-pū*, s.m. (9th) Bustle, search, toil, labour. Sing. and Pl. تګاپو کول *tagā-pū kawul*, verb trans. To bustle, to search, to toil, to labour. تګ و دو *tag-o-daw*, s.m. (9th) Bustle, etc. Sing. and Pl. See تګ

تګيَ *tagaey*, adj. (W.) Thirsty; (Fem.) تګِ *tagi*. Pl. (Masc. and Fem.) ي *ī*. See تږي

تل *tal*, adv. Always, ever, perpetually, eternally, every day, etc., invariably, without exception. تل تتله *tal tatalah*, تل ته تله *tal tah talah*, تل تر تله *tal tar talah*, تل تا تله *tal tā talah*, or تل دَ تله *tal da talah*, Always, at all times, ever, for ever and a day, for ever and ever, time without end, till doomsday, to the end of time, for evermore.

A تل *tall*, s.m. (2nd) A hill, a hillock, a mound, a heap. Pl. تلونه *tallūnah*.

S تل *tal*, s.m. (2nd) Bottom, the bottom of anything, the base, the foot, the sole. Pl. تلونه *talūnah*.

A تلاش *talāsh*, s.m. (2nd) Search, pursuit, quest, investigation. Pl. تلاشونه *talāshūnah*. تلاش کول *talāsh kawul*, verb trans. To search, to seek for, to pursue.

P تلاو *talāo*, s.m. (2nd) (corrup. of تالاب) A pond, a reservoir of water. Pl. تلاوونه *talāo-ūnah*. See ناور and ونګره

A تلاوت *talāwat*, s.m. (2nd) Meditating, reading (particularly the Kur'ān, as a devotional act). Pl. تلاوتونه *talāwatūnah*.

تلب *talab*, s.m. (2nd) Wages, salary, hire. Pl. تلبونه *talabūnah*. (corrup. of A طلب).

تلتک *taltak*, s.m. (2nd) A coverlet, a counterpane. Pl. تلتکونه *taltakūnah*.

P تلخ *talkh*, adj. Bitter, acrid, rancid; (Fem.) تلخه *talkha'h*. See تریخ

P تلخان *talkhān*, s.m. (6th) Parched wheat reduced to meal and made into paste, which is generally taken on a journey. Sing. and Pl.

A تلف *talaf*, s.m. (2nd) Ruin, destruction, loss. 2. Prodigality, consumption, expense. Pl. تلفونه *talafūnah*. تلف کول *talaf kawul*, verb trans. To ruin, to waste, to consume, to destroy. تلف کیدل *talaf kedal*, verb intrans. To be unfortunate, to meet with a loss, to be destroyed, wasted.

A تلفظ *talaffuẓ*, s.m. (2nd) (inf. v of لفظ) Utterance, expression, pronunciation. Pl. تلفظونه *talaffuẓūnah*. تلفظ کول *talaffuẓ kawul*, verb trans. To utter, to pronounce.

تلکه *talaka'h*, s.f. (3rd) A kind of snare or trap made from the horns or ribs of a cow, also of wood and iron, for catching birds, rats, etc., a gin. Pl. ې *ey*. (P تلکث).

تلل *t'lal*, verb intrans. To go, to depart, to set out, to quit, to retire, to leave a place, etc. This infinitive is irregular and imperfect. Pres. ځي *dzī*; past لاړ *lārr*; fut. به ځي *bah dzī*, or لاړ به شي *lārr bah shī*, or به وُ شي *bah wu shī*; imp. ځه *dzah*, لاړ شه *lārr shah*, or وُ لاړ شه *wu lārr shah*; act. part. تلونکي *t'lūnkaey* or تلونې *t'lūnaey*; past part. تللي *t'lalaey* or تلې *talaey*; verb. n. تله *t'lah* or تلنه *t'lana'h*.

تله *t'lah*, s.m. (6th) (verb. n.) Departure, exit, exodus, removal. 2. Going, departing, setting out. Sing. and Pl.

تلل *talal*, verb trans. To weigh, to measure, to value, to rate, to estimate, to balance, to take into account. Pres. تلي *talī*; past وُ تاله *wu-tālah*; fut. وُ به تلي *wu bah talī*; imp. تله *talah* or وُ تله *wu-talah*; act. part. تلونکي *talūnkaey* or تلونې *talūnaey*; past part. تللي *talalaey*; verb. n. تلنه *talana'h*. See تول

تلوار *talwār*, s.m. (2nd) Speed, swiftness, rapidity, fleetness, quickness, velocity, haste, precipitation. Pl. تلوارونه *talwārūnah*. تلوار کول *talwār kawul*, verb trans. To haste, to hurry, to hasten, to make haste, to precipitate, to urge, to accelerate, to expedite, to quicken pace. په تلوار *pah talwār* or په تلوار سره *pah talwār sarah*, adv. Swiftly, speedily, full speed, slap-dash, apace, head-long, post-haste. تلوار گرندي *talwār grandaey*, adj. Hasty, rash, inconsiderate, precipitate, reckless, desperate; (Fem.) تلوار گرندِ *talwār-grandi*. Pl. (Masc. and Fem.) ي *ī*.

تلواري *talwārī*, adj. Fast, speedy, swift, rapid, quick, nimble, agile, expeditious, prompt.

تلوسه *talwasa'h*, s.f. (3rd) Commotion, astonishment, trouble, distraction, superstition, melancholy. Pl. ې *ey*. تلوسه لرل *talwasa'h laral*, verb trans. To become distracted (*lit.* to have distraction), troubled, astonished, etc. تلوسه کول *talwasa'h kawul*, verb trans. To astonish, to trouble, to distract, to fill with commotion. (P تلواسه).

تلول *tal-wal*, s.m. (6th) Quickness, swiftness, speed, dispatch, promptitude, haste, precipitation; hastiness, irascibility, rashness. 2. Perturbation, restlessness. Sing. and Pl. تلول کول *tal-wal kawul*, verb trans. To act with promptitude, quickness, speed, rashness, precipitation, etc.

تلول *talawul*, verb trans. To fry. Pres. تلوي *talawī*; past وُ تلاوه *wu-talāwuh* or وُ تلاوو *wu-talāwo*; fut. وُ به تلوي *wu bah talawī*; imp. وُ تلوه *wu-talawah*; act. part. تلوونکي *talawūnkaey* or تلوونې *talawūnaey*; past part. تلولي *talawulaey*; verb. n. تلونه *talawuna'h*.

تلولې *tal-walaey*, s.m. (1st) A small active person, one who acts with rashness or precipitation, a person of a quick or irascible temper. Pl. ي *ī*. تلولِي *tal-wala'ī*, s.f. (6th) A quick irascible female. Sing. and Pl.

تلې *talaey*, s.m. (1st) The sole of a shoe, the

bottom of anything, the hollow of the hand, as much as may be contained in the hollow of the hand, the bottom of the sea. Pl. ي *ī*.

تله *tala'h*, s.f. (3rd) A scale, a balance. Pl. ې *ey*. See تلل

تله *tala'h*, s.f. (3rd) The sole of the foot. Pl. ې *ey*. (s तल).

تلئ *tila'ī*, s.f. (6th) The shaft of an arrow, the stalks of corn after separating the heads. Sing. and Pl.

تم *tam*, adv. A word added by way of emphasis to the adjective تور *tor*, 'black *or* dark,' to express total or complete darkness. (s तम: The third of the qualities incident to humanity, the *tama gun*, or property of darkness, from whence proceed folly, ignorance, mental darkness, and the like. 2. Gloom, darkness). تورتم *tor tam*, adj. Total or complete darkness. See تورکمي or تربمي

تم *tam*, s.m. (2nd) Continuance, permanence, settledness, rest. Pl. تمونه *tamūnah*. 2. As adj. Staying, stopping, tarrying, holding, abiding, keeping. Fem. Sing. تمه *tama'h*; Pl. تمې *tamey*. تم کيدل *tam kedal*, verb intrans. To keep one's footing, to stand fast, to take root, to remain, to tarry, to stay. تم کول *tam kawul*, verb trans. To aid, to support, to prop; to make or cause to stay.

A تماشا *tamāshā*, s.f. (6th) Pl. تماشاوي *tamāshāwī*, or تماشه *tamāsha'h*, s.f. (3rd) An entertainment, show, a spectacle. 2. Sight, amusement, show. Pl. ې *ey*. تماشه کول *tamāsha'h kawul*, verb trans. To behold, to look at for amusement, to see, to take a walk. تماشه بين *tamāsha'h bīn*, A spectator, a traveller, a pilgrim; (Fem.) تماشه بينه *tamāsha'h-bīna'h*.

تماکو *tamākū* or تمباکو *tambākū*, s.m. (6th) Tobacco. Sing. and Pl.

A تمام *tamām*, adj. (from تم) Entire, perfect, complete; (Fem.) تمامه *tamāma'h*.

تمامي *tamāmī*, s.f. (3rd) Completion, end, accomplishment, perfection. Pl. ئ *a'ī*. تمام توب *tamām-tob*, s.m. (2nd) Pl. توبونه *tobūnah*, or تمام تيا *tāmām-tī'ā*, s.f. (6th) (E.) Sing. and Pl.; (W.) Pl تياوي *tī'āwī*, or تمام والئ *tamām wālaey*, s.m. (1st) Completeness, completion, accomplishment, the state of being complete, perfect state. Pl. والي *wālī*. تماميدل *tamāmedal*, verb intrans. To be finished, to be ended, to be perfected, to be completed, to become concluded. Pres. تماميږي *tamāmejzī* (W.) or تماميګي *tamāmegī* (E.); past تمام شه *tamām shah*, or تمام وُ شه *tamām wu-shah*; fut. تمام به شي *tamām bah shī*, or به وُ شي *bah wu-shī*; imp. تمام شه *tamām shah*, or تمام وُ شه *tamām wu-shah*; act. part. تماميدونکئ *tamāmedūnkaey*, or تماميدونئ *tamāmedūnaey*; past part. تمام شوئ *tamām shawaey*; verb. n. تماميدنه *tamāmedana'h*.

تمامول *tamāmawul*, verb trans. To perfect, to complete, to finish, to end, to conclude. Pres. تماموي *tamāmawī*; past تمام کړ *tamām karr* or که *kah*, or تمام وُ کړ *tamām wu-karr* or وُ که *wu-kah*; fut. تمام به کړي *tamām bah krrī* or به کي *bah kī*, or تمام به وُ کړي *tamām bah wu-krrī* or به وُ کي *bah wu-kī*; imp. تمام کړه *tamām krrah* or وُ کړه *wu-krrah*; act part. تمامونکئ *tamāmawūnkaey* or تامونئ *tamāmawūnaey*; past part. تمام کړئ *tamām karraey*; verb. n. تمامونه *tamāmawuna'h*.

تمانچه *tamāncha'h*, s.f. (3rd) A pistol. Pl. ې *ey*. (corrup. of طمانچه).

تمبګئ *tambaga'ī*, s.f. (6th) The leaf of a door or a window. Sing. and Pl. See also تمبه

تمبل *tambal*, s.m. (2nd) A tambourine, a small drum. Pl. تمبلونه *tambalūnah*. تمبل باز *tambal bāz*, s.m. (5th) A kettle-drum player. Pl. تمبل بازان *tambal-bāzān*; Fem. (3rd) تمبل بازه *tambal bāza'h*. Pl. ې *ey*. See دومبکي ,دومکي ,تنبل and تمل (corrup. of A طبل).

تمبوزک *tambūzak*, s.m. (2nd) (W.), or s.m. (5th) The muzzle of anything, the mouth and nose of an animal. 2. A fastening for the mouth. 3. The bridge of the nose. Pl. تمبوزکونه *tambūzakūnah* and تمبوزکان *tambū-*

zakān; also تنبوزک tanbūzak. Pl. تنبوزکان tanbūzakān, etc.

تمبوزي tambūzaey, s.m. (1st) The bridge of the nose. Pl. ي ī.

تمبه tamba'h, s.f. (3rd) The leaf of a door or window. Pl. ې ey. See تمبکي

تمبه tamba'h, s.f. (3rd) The prop of a door, etc. 2. A party, a group, knot, or small body of people. Pl. ې ey. تمبې تمبې tambey tambey, In parties, in bodies, in knots, party by party, etc. See تمن تمن

تمبيزه tambezah, s.f. (3rd) The bridge of the nose, the muzzle. 2. A muzzle for an animal. Pl. ې ey. See تنبيزه

تمبيزي tambezey, s.m. (1st) The bridge of the nose, the muzzle. Pl. ي ī. See preceding word, and also تمبوزک and تنبيزي

تمتراق tamtarāḳ, s.m. (2nd) (corrup. of طمطراق) Grandeur, magnificence, pomp. Pl. تمتراقونه tamtarāḳūnah.

A تمثيل tams̤īl, s.m. (2nd) (inf. II of مثل) Comparison, similitude, allegory, parable, example, counterpart, fac-simile. Pl. تمثيلونه tams̤īlūnah. تمثيل ويل tams̤īl wayal, verb trans. To allegorise, to speak by parable.

A تمر هندي tamr-i-hindī, s.m. (9th) The tamarind. Sing. and Pl.

A تمسک tamassuk, s.m. (2nd) (inf. V of مسک) A note of hand, a bond, obligation, receipt. Pl. تمسکونه tamassukūnah.

A تملک tamalluk, s.m. (2nd) (inf. V of ملک) Cajoling, flattery, caressing, dalliance, adulation. Pl. تملکونه tamallukūnah. تملک کول tamalluk kawul, verb trans. To cajole, flatter, caress.

P تمن tuman, s.m. (2nd) Brotherhood, connexion. 2. Bevy, crowd, troop, squadron, company, party, etc. Pl. تمنونه tumanūnah. تمن تمن tuman tuman, In parties, in bodies, in knots, party by party, troop by troop, etc. See تمبه

A تمنا tamannā, s.f. (6th) (inf. V of مني) Request, wish, prayer, supplication, inclination, petition. Pl. تمناوي tamannāwī. تمنا لرل tamannā laral, verb trans. To be inclined, to have a request or supplication. تمنا کول tamannā kawul, verb trans. To request, to pray, to wish, to supplicate, to petition.

SYR تموز tamoz, s.m. (2nd) The name of a month. A Syrian month—July. 2. Heat, warmth. Pl. تموزونه tamozūnah.

تمه tama'h, s.f. (3rd) (corrup. of A طمع) Avidity, greediness, ambition, avarice, covetousness. Pl. ې ey. تمه لرل tama'h laral, verb trans. To be greedy, to have greediness, to be ambitious, covetous. تمه کول tama'h kawul, verb trans. To covet, to desire, to hanker after, to lust after, etc.

A تمهيد tamhīd, s.m. (2nd) (inf. II of مهد) Arrangement, settlement, introduction, disposition. Pl. تمهيدونه tamhīdūnah.

A تميز tamīz, s.m. (2nd) (for تمييز, inf. II of ميز) Discernment, judgment, discretion, distinction, sense. Pl. تميزونه tamīzūnah. تميز لرل tamīz laral, verb trans. To have discretion, judgment, etc. تميز کول tamīz kawul, verb trans. To distinguish, to discern.

P تن tan, s.m. (2nd) The body, the person. Pl. تنونه tanūnah. تن پرور tan parwar, Careful of the body, self-indulgent; (Fem.) تن پروره tan-parwara'h. تن پروري tan-parwarī, s.f. (3rd) Self-indulgence. Pl. ۍ a'ī. تن درست tan durust, adj. Healthy, vigorous; (Fem.) تن درسته tan-durusta'h. تن درستي tan durustī, s.f. (3rd) Health, vigour. Pl. ۍ a'ī. تن ور کول tan war kawul, verb trans. To pay attention.

تن په تنا tan pah tanā, s.f. (6th) Self-preservation, self-defence. Pl. تن په تناوي tan pah tanāwī.

تنا tanā, s.f. (6th) Thunder. (E.) Sing. and Pl.; (W.) Pl. تناوي tanāwī. See تالندء

تناو tanāw, s.m. (2nd) The cord or strap of a spinning-wheel, a line for hanging clothes on, a line for measuring land. Pl. تناوونه tanāwūnah. See بياسته

تنبل tanbal, s.m. (2nd) A small kettle drum. Pl. تنبلونه tanbalūnah. See تمبل

تنبه tanba'h, s.f. (3rd) A party, a knot, a group, a small body of people. 2. The prop of a door. 3. The panel or leaf of a door or window. Pl. ي *ey*. تنبي تنبي *tanbey-tanbey*, In knots, in groups, in small parties. See تمبه

تنبيزه *tanbeza'h*, s.f. (3rd) The bridge of the nose, the muzzle. Pl. ي *ey*. See تمبيزه

تنبيزي *tanbezaey*, s.m. (1st) Pl. ي *ī*; or تنبوزک *tanbūzak*, s.m. (2nd) The bridge of the nose. Pl. تنبوزکونه *tanbūzakūnah*. See تمبيزي

A تنبيه *tanbīh*, s.m. (2nd) (inf. II of نبه) Admonition, advice, animadversion, correction, punishment. Pl. تنبيهونه *tanbīhūnah*. تنبيه ور کول *tanbīh war kawul*, verb trans., or تنبيه کول *tanbīh kawul*, verb trans. To admonish, to punish, to correct.

تنتنا *tantanā*, s.f. (6th) Noise, vociferation, clamour. 2. Fame, rumour, pomp. 3. News, report. 4. Sound, resounding, echo. (corrup. of A طنطنه). (E.) Sing. and Pl.; (W.) Pl. تنتناوي *tantanāwī*.

P تند *tund*, adj. Active, quick, sharp, fast, swift, hot, spirited, furious, severe, acrid, pungent; (Fem.) تنده *tunda'h*. تند خوي *tund-kho'e*, adj. Irascible, of a fiery disposition, furious, passionate, fretful; (Fem.) تند خويه *tund-kho'ea'h*. تند خوئي *tund kho'ī*, s.f. (3rd) Irascibility, passion, furiousness, peevishness. Pl. ئي *a'ī*. تند زبان *tund zabān*, adj. Eloquent, speaking rapidly, long-tongued. تند مزاج *tund mizāj*, adj. Hot-headed, passionate. تند کيدل *tund kedal*, verb intrans. To be angry, to be displeased. تند کول *tund kawul*, verb trans. To quicken, to make angry.

تندر *tandar*, s.m. (2nd) Thunder, a thunderbolt, Pl. تندرونه *tandarūnah*. Also تندره *tandara'h*, s.f. (3rd). Pl. ي *ey*.

تندک *tindak*, s.m. (2nd) A jump, a leap, a bound, a spring, a vault. Pl. تندکونه *tindakūnah*. See تيندک

تندور *tandor*, s.f. (1st) A father's brother's wife. Pl. تندور *tandori*. See تنديارہ

P تندور *tandūr*, s.m. (2nd) An oven. Pl. تندورونه *tandūrūnah*. See تنور

تندوره *tandūra'h*, s.f. (3rd) A cascade, a waterfall. Pl. ي *ey*.

تنده *tanda'h*, s.f. (3rd) Thirst, thirstiness. Pl. ي *ey*.

تندوري *tindoraey*, s.m. (1st) The bone or bridge of the nose, the cartilage of the nose. Pl. ي *ī*. See تنبيزه and تندوري or تمبيزي

تندوي *tandwaey*, s.m. (1st) Gristle, cartilage; the cartilage of the nose. Pl. ي *ī*. See also کرچوني

P تندي *tundī*, s.f. (3rd) Activity, acrimony, impetuosity, fierceness, sharpness. Pl. ئي *a'ī*.

تندي *tandaey*, s.m. (1st) A suckling of an animal, a babe, a young tree, a shoot, a sprout. 2. The forehead. Pl. ي *ī*. s.f. (6th) Sing. and Pl. ئي *a'ī*.

تنديارہ *tund-yāra'h*, s.f. (3rd) A father's brother's wife, a paternal aunt. Pl. ي *ey*. See تندور

تندل *tan-ddal*, verb trans. To make, to form, to fashion, to prepare, to adapt, to arrange, to rectify, to put in order, to repair, to mend, to restore, etc. Pres. تندي *tan-ddī*; past وُ تانده *wu-tān-ddah*; fut. وُ به تندي *wu bah tan-ddī*; imp. وُ تنده *wu-tan-ddah*; act. part. تندونکي *tan-ddūnkaey*, or تندوني *tan-ddūnaey*; past part. تندلي *tan-ddalaey*; verb. n. تندنه *tan-ddana'h*.

تنذري *tanzaraey*, s.m. (1st) A grey partridge. Pl. ي *ī*. See تنکذري

تنسته *tanista'h*, s.f. (3rd) The web of a loom, a spider's web. Pl. ي *ey*. See also تانسته

تنکي *tankaey*, s.m. (1st) A babe, a suckling of any animal, a young ox unfit for the plough, a young horse too young for the saddle, a colt. 2. adj. Unripe, tender, immature, green. Pl. ي *ī*. See تندي

P تنگ *tung*, s.m. (5th) A vessel with a long narrow neck. Pl. تنگان *tungān*.

P تنگ *tang*, adj. Straight, narrow, tight, confined. 2. Scarce, wanting, scanty, barren. 3. Distressed, pressed by want, dejected, sad; (Fem.) تنگه *tanga'h*. تنگ چشم *tang chashm*, adj. Miserly, niggardly. تنگ چشم والي *tang-chashm wālaey*, s.m. (1st) Niggardliness, parsimony, miserliness, stinginess, avarice. Pl. ي *ī*. تنگ چشمي *tang chashmī*, s.f. (3rd) Same as preceding. Pl. ئ *a'ī*. تنګ حال *tang ḥāl*, adj. Poor, distressed, straitened in circumstances. تنګ حالي *tang ḥālī*, s.f. (3rd) Poverty, distress, narrow circumstances. Pl. ئ *a'ī*. تنګ حوصله *tang ḥauṣilah*, adj. Unable to keep anything secret, a blab. تنګ دست *tang dast*, adj. Poor, distressed; miserly, parsimonious, stingy, avaricious. تنګ دستي *tang dastī*, s.f. (3rd) Poverty, distress, want. 2. Parsimony, avarice, niggardliness. Pl. ئ *a'ī*. تنګ دل *tang dil*, adj. Narrow-hearted, miserly, niggard, illiberal. تنګ دلي *tang dilī*, s.f. (3rd) Narrow-minded, or narrow-heartedness, stinginess, parsimony. Pl. ئ *a'ī*. په تنګ راغلل *pah tang rāghlal*, verb intrans. To be distressed, incommoded, distracted, dejected, or exhausted. تنګ کول *tang kawul*, verb trans. To straiten, to narrow, to tighten, to confine, to contract. See تنګول . تنګ کيدل *tang kedal*, verb intrans. To be tightened, straitened, contracted, distressed, etc. See تنګيدل . تنګ نيول *tang nīwul*, verb trans, To importune, to dun, to beset, to reduce to extremity, to straiten, to distress, to press for payment (as a creditor).

تنګ توب *tang tob*, s.m. (2nd) Pl. توبونه *tobūnah*; تنګ والئ *tang wālaey*, s.m. (1st) Pl. والي *wālī*; or تنګ تيا *tang tī'ā*, s.f. (6th) Narrowness, closeness, tightness, distress, poverty, want. (E.) Sing. and Pl; (W.) Pl. تياوي *tī'āwī*.

تنګسه *tangsa'h*, s.f. (3rd) Distress, helplessness, poverty, distress, scarcity, famine. 2. Narrowness, tightness. Pl. ئ *ey*. See تنګسيا and کاخت

تنګسيا *tangsī'ā*, s.f. (6th) Distress, helplessness, poverty, scarcity, famine. 2. Narrowness, tightness. See preceding. (E.) Sing. and Pl.; (W.) Pl. تنګسياوي *tangsī'āwī*.

تنګول *tangawul*, verb trans. To tighten, to confine, to narrow, to contract. Pres. تنګوي *tangawī*; past تنګ کړ *tang karr* or که *kah*, or تنګ و کړ *tang wu-karr* or و که *wu-kah*; fut. تنګ به کړي *tang bah krrī* or به کي *bah kī*, or تنګ به و کي *tang bah wu-kī* or به و کړي *bah wu-krrī*; imp. تنګوه *tangawah*, or تنګ کړه *tang krrah* or که *kah*, or تنګ و کړه *tang wu-krrah* or و که *wu-kah*; act. part. تنګوونکي *tangawūnkaey*, or تنګووني *tangawūnaey*; past part. تنګ کړي *tang karraey*; verb. n. تنګونه *tangawuna'h*. See تنګ کول

تنګيدل *tangedal*, verb intrans. To be tightened, distressed, contracted, confined, incommoded, etc. Pres. تنګيږي *tangejzī* (W.), or تنګيګي *tangegī* (E.); past تنګ شه *tang shah*, or تنګ و شه *tang wu-shah*; fut. تنګ به شي *tang bah shī* or به و شي *bah wu-shī*; imp. تنګ شه *tang shah*, or تنګ و شه *tang wu-shah*; act. part. تنګيدونکي *tangedūnkaey*, or تنګيدونئ *tangedūnaey*; past part. تنګ *tang*, or تنګ شوئ *tang shawaey*; verb. n. تنګيدنه *tangedana'h*. See تنګ کيدل

P تنګه *tanga'h*, s.f. (3rd) The trunk, stem, stalk, or stock of a tree. 2. The body or centre width of a garment. 3. The name of a coin, about one-third of a rupee. Pl, ئ *ey*.

تنګئ *tangaey*, s.m. (1st) A pass, a gorge, a road between two mountains. Pl. ي *ī*. See کوتل

P تنګي *tangī*, s.f. (3rd) Tightness, narrowness, straitness. 2. Poverty, distress, want. 3. Parsimony, stinginess, avarice. Pl. ئ *a'ī*. See تنګ توب etc.

P تنور *tanūr*, s.m. (4th) An oven, a stove, a furnace. Pl. تناره *tanāra'h* or تنارَ *tanāra*. (W.) s.m. (2nd) Pl. تنرونه *tanarūnah*. See تندور

P تنها *tanhā*, adj. Alone, singular, solitary, unique, single. 2. adv. Only, merely. See بيل and يواخي

P تنهائي *tanhā-ī*, s.f. (3rd) Loneliness, solitude, privacy. Pl. ئ *a'ī*.

تنړاکه *tarrnā-ka'h*, s.f. (3rd) A blister, a pustule, a bubble. Pl. ئ *ey*. تنړاکه کيدل *tarrnā-ka'h kedal*, verb intrans. To blister, to rise in pustules or blisters. تنړاکه کول *tarrnā-ka'h kawul*, verb trans. To blister, to raise blisters by hurt, burn, or any violent action upon the skin.

تنړکار *tarrnakār*, s.m. (9th) Borax. Sing. and Pl.

تڼر *ta<u>rr</u>n*, s.m. (5th) The roar of a lion, tiger, etc. Pl. تڼرهار *ta<u>rr</u>na-hār*. تڼرهار کول *ta<u>rr</u>na-hār kawul*, or تڼرهار لرل *ta<u>rr</u>na-hār laral*, verb trans. To roar (as a lion, etc.). See غرنب

تڼرۍ *ta<u>rr</u>na'ī*, s.f. (6th) A string or tape with which garments are fastened. Sing. and Pl.

تو *tū*, s.m. (9th) Spittle. Sing. and Pl. تو کول *tū kawul*, verb trans. To spit. تو *tū* is also used to express contempt.

تو تو *to to*, The sound of calling a dog. (s تُو تُو).

A تواريخ *tawārī<u>kh</u>*, s.m. (2nd) (Pl. of تاريخ) History, histories, dates, annals. Pl. تواريخونه *tawārī<u>kh</u>ūnah*.

A تواضع *tawāẓuæ*, s.m. (2nd) (inf. VI of وضع) Humility, attention, civility, pretended kindness, empty compliments. Pl. تواضعونه *tawāẓuæūnah*.

P توان *tuwān*, s.m. (2nd) Power, strength, vigour, force, stamina, nerve, brute force. Pl. توانونه *towānūnah*. توانيدل *tuwānedal*, verb intrans. To be able, powerful, equal to, to be vigorous, robust, hardy, muscular, etc. Pres. توانيږي *tuwāne<u>jz</u>ī* (W.) or توانيګي *tuwānegī* (E.); past وُ توانيده *wu-tuwānedah*, or وُ توانيدَ *wu-tuwāneda*; fut. وُ به توانيږي *wu bah tuwāne<u>jz</u>ī*, or وُ به توانيګي *wu bah tuwānegī*; imp. وُ توانيږه *wu-tuwāne<u>jz</u>ah*, or وُ توانيګه *wu-tuwānegah*; act. part. توانيدونکَي *tuwānedūnkaey*, or توانيدونَي *tuwānedūnaey*; past part. توانيدلَي *tuwānedalaey*; verb. n. توانيدنه *tuwānedana'h*, or توانيده *tuwāneda'h*.

توانول *tuwānawul*, verb trans. To strengthen, to make strong, to invigorate, to confirm, to establish, to animate, to encourage. Pres. توانوي *tuwānawī*; past وُ تواناوه *wu-tuwānāwuh*; fut. وُ به توانوي *wu bah tuwānawī*; imp. وُ توانوه *wu-tuwānawah*; act. part. توانوونکَي *tuwānawūnkaey*, or توانوونَي *tuwānawūnaey*; past part. توانولَي *tuwānawulaey*; verb. n. توانونه *tuwānawuna'h*.

توان لرل *tuwān laral*, verb trans. To have or possess power, strength, force, vigour, etc.

P توانا *tuwānā*, adj. Powerful, strong, able, vigorous, sturdy, energetic.

P تواني *tuwān'ī*, s.f. (3rd) Power, ability, strength, force, nerve, stamina. Pl. ئي *a'ī*.

توب *tob*, A particle affixed to nouns and adjectives, together with تيا, والي etc., to denote state or quality, in the same manner as English *ness*.

توبره *tobra'h*, or *tūbra'h*, s.f. (3rd) A nose-bag for horses' grain, a beggar's wallet, a saddle bag. Pl. توبرې *tobrey* or *tūbrey* (HI توبڑا).

توبرَي *tobraey*, s.m. (1st) The head of an arrow or dart. Pl. ي *ī*.

A توبه *toba'h*, s.f. (3rd) Penitence, conversion, contrition, repentance, remorse. Pl. ې *ey*. توبه توبه *toba'h toba'h*, interj. Tush! fy! foh! for shame! توبګار *tobagār*, adj. Penitent, contrite, repentant, restrained by a vow; (Fem.) بوبګاره *tobagāra'h*. توبه کول *toba'h kawul*, verb trans. To repent, to regret, to rue, to repine, to deplore. توبه ښکل *toba'h <u>kh</u>'kal* (E.) or کښل *k'<u>sh</u>al* (W.) To repent, to deplore. See preceding.

T توپ *top*, s.m. (2nd) A cannon, a gun. Pl. توپونه *topūnah*. توپچي *top-<u>ch</u>ī*, s.m. (5th) A cannonier, an artilleryman. Pl. توپچيان *top-<u>ch</u>īān*. توپ خلاصول *top <u>kh</u>alāṣawul*, ويشتل *wī<u>sh</u>tal*, ييله *yelah*, or ايله کول *aelah kawul*, verb trans. To cannonade, to bombard, to fire upon, to discharge a cannon.

توپان *tū-pān*, s.m. (2nd) (corrup. of A طوفان) A hurricane, a storm of wind and rain, an inundation. Pl. توپانونه *tū-pān-ūnah*.

توپک *topak* or *tūpak*, s.m. (5th) A musket. Pl. توپکان *topakān* or *tūpakān*. See توپک

توپنګچه *topang-<u>ch</u>a'h*, s.f. (3rd) A pistol. Pl. ې *ey*. See توفنګچه and تمانچه

A توت *tūt*, s.m. (5th) A mulberry. Pl. توتان *tūtān*. ابراهيم خاني توت *ibrāhīm <u>kh</u>ānī tūt*, A kind of mulberry, half white and half purple. بي دانه توت *bey dāna'h tūt*, The seedless mulberry. تور توت *tor tūt*, The purple mulberry. دانه دار توت *dāna'h dār tūt*, The seedy mulberry. سيميا توت *sīmī-ā tūt*, The vermicelli mulberry. شه توت *<u>sh</u>ah tūt*, The royal mulberry. کشمشي *ki<u>sh</u>mi<u>sh</u>ī*, or مرواري

تُوت *marwārī tūt*, The raisin, or pearl mulberry.

HI توتا *totā*, s.m. (5th) A parrot. Pl. توتايان *totā-yān*. See توتي

توتكي *totakaey*, or توتكري *totakaraey*, s.m. (1st) A swallow. Pl. ي *ī*; (W.) توتكۍ *totaka'ī*, s.f. (6th) Sing. and Pl.

توتنكي *tūtankaey*, s.m. (1st) A shaving, a chip, a clip, a filing, a fragment. Pl. ي *ī*. See also تراشه and دړه

توتي *tūtī*, s.f. (5th) A parrot. Pl. توتيان *tūtīān*. See توتا

PS توتيا *totī-yā*, s.f. (6th) Tutty, protoxyd of zinc. (E.) Sing. and Pl.); (W.) Pl. توتياوي *totī'āwī*. نيل توتيا *nīl totī-yā*, s.f. (6th) Blue vitriol, sulphate of copper. سبز توتيا *sabz totī-yā*, s.f. (6th) Green vitriol, or sulphate of iron.

A توجه *tawajjuh*, s.m. (2nd) (inf. V of وجه) Countenancing, regarding, turning towards, undertaking a journey, attending to, attention, regard, tendency. 2. Kindness, favour, obligation. Pl. توجهونه *tawajjuh-ūnah*. توجه كول *tawajjuh kawul*, verb trans. To countenance, to regard, to attend to, to show kindness to, to turn towards.

A توجيه *taujīh*, s.m. (2nd) (inf. II of وجه) Calling one's attention, explaining, accounting for. 2. Adjustment of accounts, assessment, a description roll, a statement. Pl. توجيهونه *taujīhūnah*. توجيه كول *taujīh kawul*, verb trans. To explain, to account for, to adjust, to assess.

A توحيد *tauḥīd*, s.m. (2nd) (inf. II of وحد) Unity; believing in the unity of the Deity. Pl. توحيدونه *tauḥīdūnah*.

توخي *to-khī*, s.m. (1st) The name of an Afghān tribe. Sing. توخي *tokhaey*, a male of the tribe. توخۍ *tokha'ī*, s.f. (6th) A female, or females, of the tribe. Sing. and Pl.

تود *tod*, adj. Hot, warm, sultry, close; (Fem.) توده *toda'h*.

تود والي *tod-wālaey*, s.m. (1st) Heat, warmth, fervour, glow, temperature. Pl. ي *ī*. توديدل *todedal*, verb intrans. To grow warm or heated, to become close or sultry. Pres. توديږي *todejzī* (W.) or توديگي *todegī* (E.); past تود شه *tod shah*, or تود وُ شه *tod wu-shah*; fut. تود به شي *tod bah shī* or به وُ شي *bah wu-shī*; imp. تود شه *tod shah* or وُ شه *wu-shah*; act. part. توديدونكي *todedūnkaey*, or توديدوني *todedūnaey*; past part. تود *tod*, or تود شوي *tod shawaey*; verb. n. توديدنه *todedana'h*, or توديده *todedah*.

تودوخه *tawdūkha'h*, or *todūkha'h*, s.f. (3rd) Heat, warmth, fervour, glow, temperature, closeness, sultriness. Pl. ې *ey*. See under تود

تودوكي *todūkaey*, adj. (dimin. of تود) Somewhat warm, hot, heated, close, sultry, etc.; (Fem.) تودوكۍ *todūki*; Pl. (Masc. and Fem.) ي *ī*.

تودول *todawul*, verb trans. To make hot, to heat, to warm. Pres. تودوي *todawī*; past تود كړ *tod karr* or كه *kah*, or تود وُ كړ *tod wu-karr* or وُ كه *wu-kah*; fut. تود به كي *tod bah kī* or به كړي *bah krrī*, or تود به وُ كي *tod bah wu-kī* or به وُ كړي *bah wu-krrī*; imp. تود كړه *tod krrah* or كه *kah*, or تود وُ كړه *tod wu-krrah* or وُ كه *wu-kah*; act. part. تودوونكي *todawūnkaey*, or تودووني *todawūnaey*; past part. تود كړي *tod karraey*; verb. n. تودونه *todawuna'h*.

تور *tor*, s.m. (2nd) A net, a snare. 2. False accusation, aspersion, slander, imputation. Pl. تورونه *torūnah*, or (W.) (5th) توران *torān*.

تور *tor*, adj. Black, sable, swarthy, sombre, dark, murky, (Fem.) توره *tora'h*. تك تور *tak tor*, Coal black, entirely or wholly black, dark, etc. تور بخت *tor bakht*, adj. Unfortunate, unlucky; (Fem.) تور بخته *tor bakhta'h*. تور بختي *tor bakhtey*, s.m. (1st) An unlucky or unfortunate person; (Fem.) تور بختِ *tor bakhti*. Pl. (M. and F.) ي *ī*. تور بخت والي *tor bakht wālaey*, s.m. (1st) Pl. والي *wālī*; or تور بختي *tor bakhtī*, s.f. (3rd) Ill-luck, bad fortune, adversity, disaster, calamity. Pl. ۍ *a'ī*. See بد بختي. تور تم *tor tam*, s.m. (2nd) Total or complete darkness. ټپ تور *ṭap tor*, adj. Completely or totally black. تور ديو *tor dīw*, s.m. (5th) A demon, a black demon. تور شان *tor shān*, adj. Blackish, darkish, dusky. تور مخ *tor makh*, adj. Black-faced, disgraced. تور مخي

tor makhaey, s.m. (1st) A baboon, a criminal, a culprit. Pl. ي *ī*; (Fem.) Sing. and Pl. ۍ *a'ī*. مخ توري *makh toraey*, s.m. (1st) A culprit, a disgraced person, a criminal; (Fem.) مخ تور *makh-tori*. Pl. (Masc. and Fem.) ي *ī*. تور ويښته *tor wekhtah*, s.m. (6th) The hair on the pubes. Sing. and Pl. See زنبه. تور والي *tor wālaey*, s.m. (1st) Blackness, darkness, dinginess, swarthiness, inkiness, etc. Pl ي *ī*. تور پوري کول *tor pūrey kawul*, verb trans. To slander, to calumniate, to accuse falsely. توريدل *toredal*, verb intrans. To blacken, to grow black, dark, murky, dingy, etc. Pres. توريږي *torejzī* (W.), or توريګي *toregī* (E.); past تور شه *tor shah* or تور وُ شه *tor wu-shah*; fut. تور به شي *tor bah shī* or به وُ شي *bah wu-shī*; imp. تور شه *tor shah* or وُ شه *wu-shah*; act. part. توريدونکي *toredūnkaey* or توريدوني *toredūnaey*; past part. تور *tor* or تور شوي *tor shawaey*; verb. n. توريدنه *toredana'h*. تورول *torawul*, verb trans. To blacken, to darken, to sully reputation, to make infamous, to cloud, to soil. Pres. توروي *torawī*; past تور کړ *tor karr* or که *kah*, or تور وُ کړ *tor wu-karr* or وُ که *wu-kah*; fut. تور به کړي *tor bah krrī* or به کي *bah kī*, or تور به وُ کړي *tor bah wu-krrī* or به وُ کي *bah wu-kī*; imp. تور کړه *tor krrah* or که *kah*, or تور وُ کړه *tor wu-krrah* or وُ که *wu-kah*; act. part. توروونکي *torawūnkaey* or تورووني *torawūnaey*; past part. تور کړي *tor karraey*; verb. n. تورونه *torawuna'h*. تور تپ *tor tap* or تور ټپ *tor ttap*, s.m. (2nd) A black spot or mole. Pl. تپونه *tapūnah* or ټپونه *ttapūnah*. See تپ. تور تپي *tor tapaey* or تور ټپي *tor ttapaey*, adj. Spotted, marked, scarred. تور غوږي *tor ghwajzaey* (W.), or تور غوګي *tor ghwagaey* (E.), s.m. (1st) A person who will not take advice, a dolt, a ninny, a fool, a blockhead, etc. Pl. ي *ī*; Fem. (3rd) تور غوږه *tor ghwajza'h* or غوګه *ghwaga'h*. Pl. ې *ey*. تورکي *torkaey*, s.m. (1st) Lamp-black, soot, smut; smut or blight in corn. Pl. ي *ī*. تورګمي

tor-gamaey, s.m. (1st) Darkness, murkiness. Pl. ي *ī*. توره تياره *tora'h tī-āra'h*, s.f. (3rd) Total or complete darkness, etc. Pl. ې *ey*. See تور تم

تور *tor*, s.m. (2nd) Fright, affright, terror, horror, panic, fear, stampede. Pl. تورونه *torūnah*. See ترهره and تره. تور خوړل *tor khwarral*, verb trans. To take fright, to be seized with panic, to be affected with stampede. توريدل *tor-edal*, verb intrans. To be seized with panic, to be seized with terror, etc. Pres. توريږي *tor-ejzī* (W.) or توريګي *tor-egī* (E.); past وُ توريده *wu-toredah* or وُ توريد *wu-toreda*; fut. وُ به توريږي *wu bah torejzī* or توريګي *toregī*; imp. وُ توريږه *wu-torejzah* or توريګه *toregah*; act. part. توريدونکي *toredūnkaey* or توريدوني *toredūnaey*; past part. توريدلي *toredalaey*; verb. n. توريدنه *toredana'h*. See ترهيدل. تورول *torawul*, verb trans. To frighten, to terrify, to strike with panic (particularly horses, and the like). Pres. توروي *torawī*; past وُ توراوه *wu-torāwuh* or وُ توراوو *wu-torāwo*; fut. وُ به توروي *wu bah torawī*; imp. وُ توروه *wu-torawah*; act. part. توروونکي *torawūnkaey* or تورووني *torawūnaey*; past part. تورولي *torawulaey*; verb. n. تورونه *torawuna'h*. See ترهول

تورغړي *tor-gharraey*, s.m. (1st) The arm from the elbow to the shoulder. Pl. ي *ī*. See ګردي ليچي

تورلمي *tor-lamaey*, s.m. (1st) The name of an animal that feeds on dead bodies. Pl. ي *ī*.

توره *tora'h*, s.f. A copper coin, in value about two pice, or one penny. Pl. ې *ey*.

توره *tūrah*, s.f. A sword, a scimetar. Pl. ې *ey*. تورزن *tūrzan* or توريالي *tūr-yālaey*, adj. A swordsman, warlike, a gallant soldier.

توره آنا *tora'h-ānā*, s.f. (6th) The name of a blackbird with a club-tail. Also called دانګ لکي. Sing. and Pl.

توره غاړه *tora'h ghārra'h*, s.f. (3rd) The hooping cough. Pl. ې *ey*. See توخلي

توري *toraey*, s.m. (1st) The spleen. 2. The pupil of the eye. Pl. ي *ī*.

توري *to-raey*, adj. Simple, plain, unmixed, pure; (Fem.) تور *to-ri*. Pl. (Masc. and Fem.) ي *ī*. تور اوبه *to-ri ao-ba'h*, Plain, pure, or unadulterated water.

توري *tora'ī*, s.f. (6th) The name of a vegetable. Sing. and Pl. (HI توري).

A توريت *torīt* or *tauret* (A توراة, H תורה), s.m. (2nd) The Pentateuch, the Old Testament. Pl. توريتونه *torītūnah*.

توږل *tojzal* (W.) verb trans. To shave, to plane, to smooth, to furbish, to scour, to polish. See توګل

P توسن *tosan*, s.m. (2nd) A horse, a high blooded or noble steed, a war-horse. Pl. توسنونه *tosanūnah*.

توسند *to-sand*, adj. Dry, droughty, requiring much water (as land); (Fem.) توسنده *to-sanda'h*.

P توشدان *tosh-dān*, s.m. (2nd) A pouch, a cartouch-box. Pl. توشدانونه *tosh-dān-ūnah*. See كمر كيسه

P توشک *toshak*, s.m. (2nd) A mattress, a coarse carpet for sitting on. Pl. توشكونه *toshakūnah*.

P توشه *tosha'h*, s.f. (3rd) Provision for a journey, necessaries, viaticum. Pl. ئ *ey*. See توښه and خوري

P توشه خانه *tosha'h khāna'h*, s.f. (3rd) A wardrobe, a place where furniture is kept. Pl. ئ *ey*. See فراش خانه

توښه *tosha'h* (W.) or *tokha'h* (E.), s.f. (3rd) Necessaries, provisions for a journey. Pl. ئ *ey*. See توشه

توغ *togh*, s.m. (2nd) A flag, a standard. Pl. توغونه *toghūnah*. See بيرغ and جنده

توغم *togham*, s.m. (2nd) A saddle cloth, a namad. Pl. توغمونه *toghamūnah*. Also written توغل *toghal* and توغلونه *toghalūnah*.

A توفيق *tofīḳ* or *taufīḳ*, s.m. (2nd) (inf. II of وفق) Completion of one's wishes, the divine grace, the favour of God, prosperity. Pl. توفيقونه *taufīḳūnah*.

A توقع *tawaḳḳuæ*, s.m. (2nd) (inf. V of وقوع) Expectation, hope, desire, wish, trust, reliance. 2. Request. توقع لرل *tawaḳḳuæ laral*, verb trans., or توقع كول *tawaḳḳuæ kawul*, verb trans. To expect, to hope, to place trust or reliance on.

A توقف *tawaḳḳuf*, s.m. (2nd) (inf. V of وقف) Delay, pause, hesitation, cessation, tediousness, patience. توقف كول *tawaḳḳuf kawul*, verb trans. To pause, to hesitate, to wait, to dally, to delay.

توقه *toḳa'h*, s.f. (3rd) A blunt arrow with which boys learn to shoot. Pl. ئ *ey*. See also تقه

توک *tūk*, s.m. (2nd) Spittle. Pl. توكونه *tūkūnah*. توک كول *tūk kawul*, verb trans. To spit; also توكول *tūkawul* or توكل *tūkal*, which see.

توكل *tūkal*, verb trans. To spit. Pres. توكي *tūkī*; past وُ توكل *wu-tūkal*; fut. وُ به توكي *wu bah tūkī*; imp. وُ توكه *wu-tūkah*; act. part. توكونكې *tūkūnkaey* or توكونې *tūkūnaey*; past part. توكلې *tūkalaey*; verb. n. توكنه *tūkana'h*. See also تو

A توكل *tawakkul*, s.m. (2nd) (inf. V of وكل) Reliance, trust in God, faith, resignation to God's will. Pl. توكلونه *tawakkulūnah*. توكل كول *tawakkul kawul* or لرل *laral*, verb trans. To have faith or reliance, to put trust in God.

توكې *tūkaey*, s.m. (1st) Spittle. Pl. ي *ī*. See تو and توک

توګل *to-gal* (E.) or توږل *tojzal* (W.) verb trans. To shave, to plane, to smoothe, to polish, to scour, to furbish. Pres. توګي *togī* or توږي *tojzī*; past وُ توګه *wu-togah* or وُ توګ *wu-toga*, or وُ توږه *wu-tojzah* or وُ توږ *wu-tojza*; fut. وُ به توګي *wu bah togī* or وُ به توږي *wu bah tojzī*; imp. وُ توګه *wu-togah* or وُ توږه *wu-tojzah*; act. part. توګونكې *togūnkaey* or توږونكې *tojzūnkaey*, or توګونې *togūnaey* or توږونې *tojzūnaey*; past part. توګلې *togalaey* or توږلې *tojzalaey*; verb. n. توګنه *togana'h* or توږنه *tojzana'h*.

توګه *to-ga'h*, s.f. (3rd) Method, way, manner, wise, course. Pl. ئ *ey*. په څه توګه *pah tsah to-ga'h*, adv. How? in what manner? after what fashion?

توګې *to-gaey*, s.m. (1st) Manner, way, method, course, fashion, practice. Pl. ي *ī*.

تول *tol*, s.m. (2nd) Weight, weighing, ponderousness, heaviness, etc. Pl. تولونه *tolūnah*. تول لرل *tol laral*, verb intrans. To weigh, to have weight, to sink by its own weight. تول كول *tol kawul*, verb trans. To weigh, to ascertain the weight of a thing; also تولول *tolawul*, verb trans. To weigh, to examine by weight, to ascertain the weight of. Pres. تولوي *tolawī*; past وُ تولاوه *wu-tolāwuh* or وُ تولاوو *wu-tolāwo*; fut. وُ به تولوي *wu bah tolawī*; imp. وُ تولوه *wu-tolawah*; act. part. تولوونكےَ *tolawūnkaey* or تولوونےَ *tolawūnaey*; past part. تولولےَ *tolawulaey*; verb. n. تولونه *tolawuna'h*. See تلل

تول *tūl*, s.m. (9th) A field of corn, etc., almost ready for reaping or gathering. Sing. and Pl.

تول *twal*, adj. Equal in weight, equal, even, coequal, on a par with, six of one and half-a-dozen of the other; (Fem.) توله *twala'h*. تول كيدل *twal kedal*, verb intrans. To be equal, to match, to cope with, to amount to. تول كول *twal kawul*, verb trans. To make or render equal, to balance, to adjust.

تولاند *tūlānd*, s.m. (2nd) The gait of a partridge, slipping along over any smooth surface, gliding or sliding along. Pl. تولاندونه *tūlāndūnah*. په تولاند تلل *pah tūlānd t'lal*, verb intrans. To slip, to glide, to slide along (as on ice), etc. See تول

تولائي *tolā-ī*, s.f. (5th) A mattress, a quilted bed. Pl. تولايانِ *tolā-yāni*. See نهالي

A تولد *tawallud*, s.m. (9th) (inf. v of ولد) Birth, nativity; adj. Born, generated. Sing. and Pl.

توله *tola'h*, s.f. (3rd) A denomination of weight about 12½ mashas. Pl. ي *ey*. (s تولا).

P تومان *to-mān*, s.m. (2nd) A myriad, ten thousand. 2. A sum equal to 20 rupees, or about £2 English. Pl. تومانونه *tomān-ūnah*.

تومنه *tom-na'h*, s.f. (3rd) Rennet, leaven, ferment. The root, origin, principle, essence, seed, foundation, etc. Pl. ي *ey*. Also تُومنه *twamnah*. Pl. ي *ey*. See سيلي and مايه

تومه *to-ma'h*, s.f. (3rd) Same as preceding. Pl. ي *ey*.

تونبيا *ton-bīyā*, s.m. (9th) Thread made from carded cotton; cleaning or picking cotton or flax previous to giving it to the weaver. Sing. and Pl. تونبيا كول *ton-bīyā kawul*, verb trans. To card wool, cotton, or flax. (HI توميا and تومنا).

تونگ *tawang*, s.m. (2nd) A kind of basket with a cover for keeping clothes in, a kind of portmanteau. Pl. تونگونه *tawang-ūnah*.

P تونگ *tūng* or *tuwang*, s.m. (5th) A treasury, a store, a magazine. Pl. تونگان *tūngān* or *tuwangān*.

تونگ *tūng*, s.f. (1st) A young girl. Pl. تونگِ *tūngi*. See لور

P تونگر *tawangar*, adj. Rich, wealthy, powerful. Pl. تونگران *tawangarān*; s.f. (3rd) تونگره *tawangara'h*. Pl. تونگرې *tawangarey*.

P تونگري *tawan-garī*, s.f. (3rd) Wealth, riches. Pl. ئي *a'ī*.

تونگےَ *tawan-gaey*, s.m. (1st) A small basket or portmanteau. Pl. ي *ī*. See تونگ

تونړئي *torrna'ī*, s.f. (6th) A kind of box for keeping clothes in, which opens with a sliding cover like a paint box, a kind of casket. Sing. and Pl.

توهړ *to-harr*, s.m. (2nd) The prickly pear tree, or cactus. Pl. توهړونه *toharrūnah*.

توي *to'e*, past part. Spilt, scattered, dispersed, shed, overflowed, etc.; (Fem.) تويه *to'e-a'h*.

توئيدل *to-yedal*, verb intrans. To spill, to shed, to scatter, to disperse, to overflow, to sweat, to percolate, to roll, to well, etc. Pres. توئيږي *to-yejzī* (W.) or توئيگي *to-yegī* (E.); past توي شه *to'e shah* or وُ شه *wu-shah*; fut. توي به شي *to'e bah shī* or به وُ شي *bah wu-shī*; imp. توي شه *to'e shah* or وُ شه *wu-shah*; act. part. توئيدونكےَ *to-yedūnkaey* or توئيدونےَ *to-yedūnaey*; past part. توي *to'e* or توي شوےَ *to'e shawaey*; verb. n. توئيدنه *to-yedana'h*.

توئيدنه *to-yedana'h*, s.f. (3rd) Spilling, shedding, scattering, dispersing, overflowing, percolating, welling. Pl. ي *ey*. تويول *to-yawul*, verb trans. To spill, to shed, to scatter, to let fall, to disperse, to strew, to sprinkle, to diffuse, to dispel. Pres. تويوي *to-yawī*; past

توي کړ *to'e karr* or که *kah*, or توي وُ کړ *to'e wu-karr* or وُ که *wu-kah*; fut. توي به کړي *to'e bah krrī* or به وُ کړي *bah wu-krrī*, or توي به که *to'e bah kah* or به وُ که *bah wu-kah*; imp. توي کړه *to'e krrah* or که *kah*, or توي وُ کړه *to'e wu-krrah* or وُ که *wu-kah*; act. part. تويوونکی *to-yawūnkaey* or تويووني *to-yawūnaey*; past part. توي کړي *toey karraey*; verb. n. تويونه *to-yawana'h*.

تويونه *to-yawana'h*, s.f. (2nd) (verb. n.) Causing or making to diffuse, sprinkle, scatter, shed, etc. Pl. ې *ey*.

ته *tah*, The singular form of the 2nd personal pronoun, 'thou.' Inflected تا *tā*. Pl. تاسو *tāso* or تاسُ *tāsu*, and تاسي *tāsey* or تاسِ *tāsi*. ته چرته زه چرته *tah chartah zah chartah*, "Where thou, and where I?" meaning that there is no similarity between us. See تَ, and Grammar, page 32.

P ته *tah*, s.f. (1st) A fold, a plait, a layer, a stratum. 2. The bottom, under, beneath. Pl. تهِ *tahi*; and تهه *taha'h*, s.f. (3rd). Pl. تهې *tahey*. See تا

ته *tah*; (Fem.) تله *t'la'h*, (part. pres., and imp. tense of تلل *t'lal*, To go) Walking, going along; or ته ته *tah tah*.

P ته و بالا *tah-o-bālā*, adj. Topsy-turvy, upside down. ته و بالا کول *tah-o-bālā kawul*, verb trans. To subvert, to overthrow, to turn upside down.

H تهاپېړه *thāperra'h*, s.f. (3rd) A slap, a box, a clout, a buffet. Pl. ې *ey*. See ځاپېړه

A تهجد *tahajjud*, s.m. (2nd) (inf. v of هجد) A form of prayer said during the night. 2. Wakefulness. 3. Sleeping sound. Pl. تهجدونه *tahajjudūnah*.

A تهجي *tahajjī*, part. (inf. v of هجو) Spelling, naming the letters of a word. تهجي کول *tahajjī kawul*, verb trans. To spell. حروف تهجي *huruf-i-tahajjī*, The letters of the alphabet. See پيزي, هجکي and هيڅکي

P ته خانه *tah khāna'h*, s.f. (3rd) A room under ground used in the hot season, a cellar, a vault. Pl. ې *ey*.

A تهديد *tahdīd*, s.m. (2nd) (inf. II of هد) Terrifying, threatening, menace, threat. Pl. تهديدونه *tahdīdūnah*.

A تهلکه *tah-luka'h*, s.f. (3rd) (inf. v of تهلک) Ruin, perdition. 2. Consternation, alarm. 3. Pang, agony. Pl. ې *ey*.

A تهليل *tahlīl*, s.m. (9th) (inf. II of هل) Praising God). Sing. and Pl. تهليل ويل *tahlīl wayal*, verb trans. To praise God.

A تهمت *thumat*, s.m. (2nd) Suspicion of guilt, calumny, slander, false accusation, aspersion, imputation. Pl. تهمتونه *thumatūnah* (vulgarly تومت *tomat*). تهمت تړل *thumat tarral* or ويل *wayal*, verb trans. To slander, to accuse, to belie, to asperse, to traduce, to calumniate, to slander.

تهمتي *thumatī*, adj. Suspicious. 2. Ignominious, calumniated. (Masc. and Fem.)

تهنال *tahnāl*, s.m. (2nd) The mounting at the end of the scabbard of a sword. Pl. تهنالونه *tahnālūnah*. See پاينک and مونال

تهنه *tahana'h*, s.f. (3rd) Low or marshy ground. Pl. ې *ey*.

P تهي *tihī*, adj. Empty, void, vain. پهلو تهي کول *pahlū tihī kawul*, verb trans. To abstain, to avoid, to refrain, to shun. تهي دماغ *tihī dimāgh*, adj. Ignorant, vain, foolish; (Fem.) دماغه *dimāgha'h*.

A تهيه *tahī-ya'h*, s.f. (3rd) (inf. II of هياة or هي) Preparation, provision, putting in order. تهيه کول *tahī-ya'h kawul*, verb trans. To prepare, to make preparation, to put in order.

تي *taey*, s.m. (1st) A teat, a dug, the nipple of a woman's breast. Pl. ي *ī*. د تي ورور *da tī w'ror*, A foster-brother. د تي خور *da tī khor*, A foster-sister.

P تيار *tai-yār*, adj. Ready, prepared, finished, complete; (Fem.) تياره *tai-yāra'h*. تياريدل *tai-yāredal*, verb intrans. To prepare, to become ready, to mature, to make one's-self ready. Pres. تيارېږي *tai-yārejzī* (W.), or تياريګي *tai-yāregī* (E.); past تيار شه *tai-yār shah* or وُ شه *wu-shah*; fut. تيار به شي *tai-yār bah shī* or به وُ شي *bah wu-shī*; imp. تيار شه *tai-yār shah* or وُ شه *wu-shah*; act.

part. تیاریدونکي tai-yāredūnkaey or تیاریدوني tai-yāredūnaey; past part. تیار tai-yār or تیار شوي tai-yār shawaey; verb. n. تیاریدنه tai-yār-edana'h; s.f. (3rd) Preparation, maturity, becoming ready or prepared. Pl. ي ey.

تیارول tai-yārawul, verb trans. To prepare, to make ready, to get up, to arrange, to put in order, to provide, to equip, to fit up. Pres. تیاروي tai-yārawī; past تیار کړ tai-yār karr or وُ کړ wu-karr; fut. تیار به کړي tai-yār bah krrī or به وُ کړي bah wu-krrī; imp. تیار کړه tai-yār krrah or که kah, or تیار وُ کړه tai-yār wu-krrah or وُ که wu-kah; act. part. تیاروونکي tai-yārawūnkaey or تیاروونې tai-yārawūnaey; past part. تیار کړي tai-yār karraey; verb. n. تیارونه tai-yārawuna'h.

تیارونه tai-yārawuna'h, s.f. (3rd) Making preparation, getting ready, arranging. Pl. ي ey.

تیاره t'yāra'h, s.f. (3rd) Darkness, obscurity, dusk, gloom, gloominess, want or absence of light. Pl. ي ey. توره تیاره tora'h t'yāra'h, Total darkness, the palpable obscure, dark as Erebus. See تور تم

تیاري tai-yārī, s.f. (3rd) Readiness, preparation, provision, arrangement, disposal, training, maturation. Pl. ئي a'ī.

تیبون tey-būn or tai-būn, s.m. (2nd) Purifying with clean dust, before prayer, when no water is procurable. Pl. تیبونونه tey-būnūnah. تیبون وهل tey-būn or tai-būn wahal, verb trans. To purify one's-self before prayer. See A تیمم

تیڅل te-tsal, verb trans. To pierce, to perforate, to transfix, to spear, to gore, to stab. 2. To stuff, to cram, to ram in. 3. To eat voraciously. Pres. تیڅي te-tsī; past وُ تیڅه wu te-tsah; fut. وُ به تیڅي wu bah te-tsī; imp. وُ تیڅه wu-te-tsah; act. part. تیڅونکي te-tsūnkaey or تیڅوني te-tsūnaey; past part. تیڅلي te-tsalaey; verb. n. تیڅنه te-tsana'h.

تیڅنه te-tsana'h, s.f. (3rd) Perforating, transfixing, spearing, stabbing. Pl. ي ey. See مندل and څیخل

تیر ter, adj. Passed, gone by, done, accomplished, spent (as time), over, lapsed, that has been; (Fem.) تیره tera'h. تیر و بیر ter-o-ber, More or less. تیر تر تیره ter tar terah, adj. Excessive, much, extravagant, outrageous, prodigious, tremendous.

تیر هیر ter-her, adj. Gone and passed, forgotten, out of date; (Fem.) تیره هیره tera'h-hera'h.

تیري teraey, s.m. (1st) Excess, superiority, majority, maximum, acme, transcendence. 2. Passing, going on, passing away, proceeding, advancing, going forward; progress, course, progression. 3. Excelling, surpassing, beating. Pl. ي ī. تیري کول teraey kawul, verb trans. To surpass, to exceed, to excel, to beat.

تیریدل teredal, verb intrans. To pass, to pass away, to pass by, to precede, to proceed, to go on, to advance, to ascend, to surpass, to die. Pres. تیریږي terejzī (W.) or تیریګي teregī (E.); past تیر شه ter shah or تیر وُ شه ter wu-shah; fut. تیر به شي ter bah shī or به وُ شي bah wu-shī; imp. تیر شه ter shah or وُ شه wu-shah; act. part. تیریدونکي teredūnkaey or تیریدوني teredūnaey; past part. تیر ter or تیر شوي ter shawaey; verb. n. تیریدنه teredana'h.

تیرول terawul, verb trans. To pass over, to cross, to cause to advance, to cause to proceed, etc. Pres. تیروي terawī; past تیر کړ ter karr or وُ کړ wu-karr; fut. تیر به کړي ter bah krrī or به وُ کړي bah wu-krrī; imp. تیر کړه ter krrah or وُ کړه wu-krrah; act. part. تیروونکي terawūnkaey or تیروونې terawūnaey; past part. تیر کړي ter karraey; verb. n. تیرونه terawuna'h.

P تیر tīr, s.m. (2nd) An arrow. Pl. تیرونه tīrūnah. See غشي. تیر انداز tīr-andāz, s.m. (5th) An archer, a bowman. Pl. تیر اندازان tīr-andāzān. See غشي لاستي. تیر اندازي tīr-andāzī, s.f. (3rd) Archery. Pl. ئي a'ī. تیر رس tīr ras, A bow-shot, the range of an arrow; or تیر پرتاب tīr-par-tāb, s.m. (2nd). Pl. تیر پرتابونه par-tābūnah. تیر کش tīr kash or تیر کښ tīr-kakh (E.), or kash (W.), s.m. (2nd) A loop-hole for arrows. Pl. تیرکښونه tīr-kakhūnah, or kashūnah.

P تیر tīr, s.m. (2nd) A beam, a ridge pole, a mast, the ridge pole of a plough. Pl. تیرونه

tīrūnah; or (5th) تیران *tīrān*. دَ پوزي تیر *da pozey tīr*, The bridge of the nose. دَ شا تیر *da shā tīr* or دَ ملا تیر *da m'lā tīr*, The back or waist-bone, the spine.

تیر سرَي *ter saraey*, s.m. (1st) A freckle, a mole on the face. 2. A head-stall for a horse. Pl. ي *ī*.

تیر سو *ter-sū*, adj. Three hundred.

تیرک *tīrak*, s.m. (2nd) The iron axle on which the stones of a mill turn or revolve. Pl. تیرکونه *tīrakūnah*.

تیره *te-ra'h*, adj. Sharp, keen, acute, fiery, sharpened. تیره والَي *tera'h-wālaey*, s.m. (1st) Sharpness, keenness, acuteness. Pl. ي *ī*. تیره کیدل *tera'h kedal*, verb intrans. To become sharp or keen, to become sharpened. تیره کول *tera'h kawul*, verb trans. To sharpen, to give an edge to, to make keen, to whet.

تیره *terah*, adj. Ready for the male (as a cow, donkey, etc.) See سیمه

P تیره *tīrah*, adj. Dark, obscure, turbid, sad. تیره بخت *tīrah bakht*, adj. Unfortunate, unlucky. تیره بختي *tīrah bakhtī*, s.f. (3rd) Misfortune, mishap, reverse. Pl. ئي *a'ī*. تیره کیدل *tīra'h kedal*, verb intrans. To turn black, turbid, or obscure. تیره کول *tīra'h kawul*, verb trans. To make black, turbid, obscure. تیره والَي *tīra'h wālaey*, s.m. (1st) Darkness, obscurity, turbidness. 2. Sadness. Pl. والي *wālī*.

تیرَي *teraey*, adj. Nine, or تیر تر اته *ter tar a-tah*. See نه

تیریدل and تیرول See under تیر

تیریستل *ter-yastal*, verb trans. to evade, to elude, to dodge, to quibble, to equivocate, to prevaricate, to put off.

P تیز *tez*, adj. Sharp, acute, hot, fiery, caustic, acrid, violent, swift, etc.; (Fem.) تیزه *teza'h*. تیز آب *tez āb*, s.m. (2nd) Nitric acid or aqua fortis. Pl. آبونه *ābunah*. تیز فهم *tez fahm*, adj. Acute, intelligent, apt, quick of apprehension; (Fem.) تیز فهمه *tez fahama'h*. تیز فهمي *tez fahmī*, s.f. (3rd) Acumen, intelligence, acuteness, aptness. Pl. ئي *a'ī*. تیزي *tezī*, s.m. (1st) Sharpness, keenness, acrimony, pungency, swiftness, impetuosity. Pl. ئي *a'ī*.

تیز *tīz*, s.m. (2nd) a fart. Pl. تیزونه *tīzūnah*. تیز آچول *tīz āchawul*, verb trans. To break wind. تیزارتَي *tīz-ārataey*, adj. A farter, a coward, a poltroon; (Fem.) تیزارتِ *tīz-ārati*. Pl. (Masc. and Fem.) ي *ī*; or تیزاونړ *tīz-āwarrn*, s.m. (6th) Same as preceding. Pl. تیزاوُنړ *tīz-āwærrn*. تیزاونړه *tīz-āwarrna'h*, s.f. (3rd). Pl. ي *ey*.

تیزل *tezal*, verb trans. To run or gallop (as a horse), to urge. Pres. تیزي *tezī*; past. وُ تیزه *wu-tezah*; fut. وُ به تیزي *wu bah tezī*; imp. وُ تیزه *wu-tezah*; act. part. تیزونکَي *tezūnkaey*, or تیزونَي *tezūnaey*; past. part. تیزلَي *tezalaey*; verb. n. تیزنه *tezana'h*.

تیزندئي *tezanda'ī*, s.f. (6th) A piece of rope with a running noose, a halter, a hangman's rope. Sing. and Pl.

تیږه *tīẕa'h* (W.), s.f. (3rd) A flat round stone, a flat stone on which condiments are ground. Pl. ي *ey*. See تیکه

P تیشه *tesha'h*, s.f. (3rd) An adze, a kind of axe used by carpenters. Pl. ي *ey*. See ترښز

تیښته *teshta'h* (W.) or *tekhta'h* (E.), s.f. (3rd) Overthrow, defeat, flight, decampment, retreat. Pl. ي *ey*. تیښتیدل *teshtedal* or *tekhtedal*, verb intrans. To flee, to decamp, to bolt, to run away, to elope. تیښتول *teshtawul* or *tekhtawul*, verb trans. To put to flight, to cause to run away, to run away or elope with. See تښتیدل etc.

P تیغ *tegh*, s.m. (2nd) A sword or scimitar. 2. A young plant, a sprout, a shoot. Pl. تیغونه *teghūnah*. تیغ وهل *tegh wahal*, verb trans. To smite with a sword. 2. To sprout out, to shoot (as a plant).

تیغنه *teghna'h*, s.f. (3rd) A sword. 2. An iron plate for baking cakes of bread on. Pl. ي *ey*. See تبخي

تیک *t'yak*, adj. Distended, developed, inflated, expanded, stretched, drawn tight, etc.; (Fem.) تیکه *t'yaka'h*. تیکیدل *t'yakedal*, verb intrans. To expand, to swell, to become distended or stretched. تیکول *t'yakawul*, verb trans. To distend, to expand, to stretch, to draw tight, to develope, to inflate, to magnify. تیک والَي *t'yak wālaey*, s.m. (1st)

Expansion, distension, spread, extension, enlargement, dispansion, etc. Pl. والي *wālī.*

تيکه *teka'h,* s.f. (3rd) The sheath or scabbard of a sword, etc. Pl. ئ *ey.*

تيکئ *tekaey,* s.m. (1st) A scabbard, a sheath. Pl. ي *ī.*

تيګه *tīga'h* (E.), s.f. (3rd) A round flat stone, a flat stone on which condiments are ground. Pl. ئ *ey.* See تيږه

HI تيل *tel,* s.m. (6th) Oil. Sing. and Pl. تيلئ *telaey,* s.m. (1st) An oilman. Pl. ي *ī.* تيلئ *tela'ī,* s.f. (6th) The wife of an oilman. Sing. and Pl.

P تيمار *tīmār,* s.m. (2nd) Care, attention. 2. Regimen of the sick. 3. Infirmity, sickness, indisposition. Pl. تيمارونه *tīmārūnah.* تيمار کول *tīmār kawul,* verb trans. To take care of, to tend, to foster, to attend to.

A تيمم *tayammum,* s.m. (2nd) Purifying one's-self before prayer with dust or sand, when water is not procurable. Pl. تيممونه *tayammumūnah.* تيمم وهل *tayammum wahal,* verb trans. To purify one's-self, as above.

تينبوزک *ten-būzak,* s.m. (2nd) (W.) The bridge of the nose, the muzzle. Pl. تينبوزکونه *tenbūzakūnah.* See تنبوزک and تنبيزي

تينبوزي *ten-būzaey,* s.m. (1st) Same as preceding. Pl. ي *ī.*

تيندوړي *tīn-doṛraey,* s.m. (1st) The cartilage of the nose. Pl. ي *ī.*

تينکي *ten-kaey,* s.m. (1st) (W.) Same as preceding. Pl. ي *ī.*

تيندک *tīndak,* s.m. (2nd) A jump, a leap, a bound, a spring, a vault. Pl. تيندکونه *tīndakūnah.* تيندک وهل *tīndak wahal,* verb trans. To jump, to leap, to bound, to vault, to spring. تيندک په تيندک زغاستل *tīndak pah tīndak z'ghāstal,* verb intrans. To bound or jump along, to run along, now rising now falling, as when pursued, to rush along, etc. See تندک

تبيل *te-yal,* verb trans. To roast, to fry, to grill, to parch, to char, etc. Pres. تيبي *te-yī*; past وُ تيبه *wu-te-yah*; fut. وُ به تيبي *wu bah te-yī*; imp. وُ تيبه *wu-te-yah*; act. part. تيبونکي *te-yūnkaey,* or تيبونی *te-yūnaey*; past part. تيبلي *te-yalaey*; verb. n. تيبنه *te-yana'h.*

تيبني *te-yanaey,* s.m. (1st) A fry, a broil, a grill, etc. Pl. ي *ī.*

ټ

ټ *ṭṭe,* The fifth letter of the Pushto alphabet, and similar in sound to the Sanskrit ट. It is pronounced by reverting the tip of the tongue to the palate. There is no letter of this sound in any of the Semitic dialects.

HI ټاپو *ṭṭāpo,* s.m. (5th) An island. Pl. ټاپوګان *ṭṭāpo-gān.*

ټاپوړه *ṭṭā-poṛra'h,* s.f. (3rd) A crutch, a stilt, a kind of wooden rake. 2. A washerman's board. Pl. ئ *ey.* See پاړه

ټاټ *ṭṭāṭṭ,* s.m. (2nd) Coxcombry, vanity, conceit, swagger, gasconade, puppyism, pertness, assumption. Pl. ټاټونه *ṭṭāṭṭūnah.* 2. Canvas, sackcloth (HI). ټاټ کول *ṭṭāṭṭ kawul,* verb trans. To show off, to flaunt, to strut, to swagger, to flourish, to look big, to assume, to act the puppy. ټاټي *ṭṭāṭṭ-ī,* s.m. (5th) A coxcomb, a puppy, a fop, a dandy, a spark, a swell, a beau, an exquisite, a jackanapes; Fem. (3rd) ټاټئ *ṭṭāṭṭa'ī,* Sing. and Pl. See پيس and دول

ټاټوب *ṭṭā-ṭṭob,* s.m. (2nd), Calmness, composure, tranquillity, rest, peace of mind, repose. Pl. ټاټوبونه *ṭṭā-ṭṭobūnah.* ټاټوب کيدل *ṭṭā-ṭṭob kedal,* verb intrans. To be composed, to be tranquil in mind, etc. ټاټوب کول *ṭṭā-ṭṭob kawul,* verb trans. To rest, to compose, to lull, to quiet, to tranquillize, to soothe. ټاټوب نيول *ṭṭā-ṭṭob nī-wul,* verb trans. To rest, to take repose.

ټاټوبه *ṭṭā-ṭṭoba'h,* s.f. (3rd) Calmness, etc. Same as preceding, which see. Pl. ئ *ey.*

ټاټوکه *ṭṭā-ṭṭuka'h,* s.f. (3rd) A kind of white edible ground nut. Pl. ئ *ey.*

ټاټئ *ṭṭā-ṭṭa'ī,* s.f. (6th) Lullaby. 2. The act of swinging, rocking, moving to and fro, vibrating, oscillating. Sing. and Pl. ټاټئ وهل *ṭṭaṭṭa'ī wahal,* verb trans. To swing, to rock, to move to and fro, to vibrate, to oscillate. ټاټي خورل *ttatta'ī khwarral*, verb trans. To move to and fro, to wave, to vibrate, to swing, to oscillate (verb intrans. in English).

ټاس *ttās*, s.m. (2nd) A slight report or explosion from a gun or musket containing a small charge only, a pop, a snap. Pl. ټاسونه *ttāsūnah*.

ټاق *ttāḳ*, s.m. (2nd) A discharge, a report, a crack, a slam, a bang, a clap, an explosion, a crash, a burst, a salvo. Pl. ټاقونه *ttāḳūnah*. ټاق وهل *ttāḳ wahal*, verb intrans. To explode, to crack, to burst, to go off, to slam, to utter a report with sudden violence. ټاق کول *ttāḳ kawul*, verb trans. To explode, to discharge, to let off, to crack, to slam, to burst. See تق and دز

ټاقر *ttā-ḳarr*, s.m. (5th) An old or decrepid man. Pl. ټاقران *ttāḳarrān*; (Fem.) ټاقره *ttā-ḳarra'h*. Pl. ې *ey*. Also written ټاقر *ttā-ḳar*. See توقر (s ټهاکر ?).

ټاک *ttāk*, s.m. (2nd) The fruit or kernel of a tree (Cratæva, or Ægle marmelos), which is made into snuff-boxes, etc. 2. A discharge, explosion, burst, report. Pl. ټاکونه *ttāk-ūnah*. See also بيل , بيپل , and بلاغند

ټاکو *ttā-kū*, s.m. (5th) One who takes whatever he can lay his hands on, and to whom nothing is amiss. Pl. ټاکوګان *ttākū-gān*. ټاکو *ttā-kū*, s.m. (9th) The name of a disease among buffaloes. Sing. and Pl. 2. adj. Assiduous, plodding, persevering, meddling, pushing, intriguing; (Fem.) ټاکوه *ttā-kawa'h*.

ټال *ttāl*, s.m. (2nd) A swing, ropes fastened to the branch of a tree as a swing. 2. The branch or bough of a tree. Pl. ټالونه *ttāl-ūnah*. ټال خورل *ttāl khwarral*, verb trans. To swing, to dangle, to hang, to be pendent, to wave, to vibrate. ټال وهل *ttāl wahal*, verb trans. To swing, to hang, to suspend, to move to and fro, to wave. دَ بوډۍ ټال *da būdda'ī ttāl*, s.m. (2nd) A rainbow. Pl. ټالونه *ttālūnah*. See شنه کاسه سره کاسه

ټانټه *ttān-tta'h*, s.f. (3rd) Straw of the Jowar (Holcus sorgum). Pl. ې *ey*.

ټانګ *ttāng*, s.m. (2nd) A fixed period, a term, space, spell, season. Pl. ټانګونه *ttāng-ūnah*.

ټانګو *ttāngū*, s.m. (5th) The name of a tree bearing a fruit like the apple in appearance. 2. The name of the fruit. Pl. ټانګوان *ttān-gū-ān*.

ټانګه *ttānga'h*, s.f. (3rd) The name of the fruit of the above. Pl. ې *ey*.

ټانګۍ *ttān-ga'ī*, s.f. (6th) The name of the wild tree and fruit of the preceding, and from the branches of which sticks and clubs are made. Sing. and Pl. See دانګي

ټبر *ttabar*, s.m. (2nd) Family, household, including parents, children, and servants. Pl. ټبرونه *ttabar-ūnah*.

ټبر *ttabar*, s.f. (1st) A wife. Pl. ټبرِ *ttabari*.

ټبر *ttabarr*, s.m. (2nd) Family, etc. Pl. ټبرونه *ttabarrūnah*. See also کدر

ټبکَی *ttub-kaey*, s.m. (1st) A hole, a pit, a deep trench or ditch. Pl. ي *ī*. ټبکي ټبکي *ttubkī-ttubkī*, adj. Up and down, irregular, uneven, full of hollows and irregularities.

ټبلَی *ttublaey*, s.m. (1st) A hole, a pit. See preceding. Pl. ي *ī*. ټبلي ټبلي *ttub-lī ttub-lī*, adj. See preceding.

ټپ *ttap*, s.m. (5th) A sound, the sound of anything coming into contact with any soft body, as the sound of a horse's feet on a muddy road, the closing of a book, etc. 2. A thump, a whack, a hit. Pl. ټپهار *ttapa-hār*. ټپ کول *ttap kawul*, verb trans. To beat, to thump, to baste, to whack, to smack, to belabour. ټپ ټپ کول *ttap ttap kawul*, verb trans. To clap the hands. 2. To chastise a child.

ټپ *ttap*, s.m. (2nd) A wound, cut, injury, sore, hurt. Pl. ټپونه *ttapūnah*. ټپي *ttap-ī*, adj. Wounded, hurt, scarred, injured. ټپي کول *ttap-ī kawul*, verb trans. To wound, to injure, to hurt.

ټپ *ttap*, adv. of emphasis, used with adjectives to denote intensity or emphasis; as, Wholly, entirely, totally, throughout, altogether, perfectly, really, verily, truly, etc.; (Fem.) Sing. ټپه *ttapa'h*. Pl. ې *ey*: as, ټپه تغره *tta-*

pa'h ttaghara'h, s.f. (3rd) Perfect poverty, helplessness, beggary, etc. Pl. ئ *ey*. تپ تيټ *ttap ttītt*, adj. Entirely or perfectly crooked, bent, curved, etc.; (Fem.) تپه تيټه *ttapa'h ttītta'h*. تپ دريدلئ *ttap dare-dalaey*, adj. Wholly tired out, completely knocked up, thoroughly jaded or wearied. تپ روند *ttap rrūnd*, adj. Totally blind, blind as a bat. تپ زوړ *ttap zorr*, adj. Quite old or aged, as old as the hills. تپ کوڼ *ttap korrn*, adj. Deaf as a post. تپ گونګ *ttap gūng*, adj. Dumb, mute as a fish. تپ گران *ttap girān*, adj. Very, or exceedingly dear. تپ گمراه *ttap gum-rāh*, adj. Totally lost, gone to the dogs. تپ ليوني *ttap le-wanaey*, adj. Mad as a March hare. تپ لوغړن *ttap lū-gharran*, adj. Smoked black. تپ لويدلئ *ttap l'wedalaey*, adj. Entirely useless, fit for nothing. تپ لوند *ttap lūnd*, adj. Wet through, perfectly soaked. تپ مړ *ttap-marr*, adj. Quite dead, dead as a door nail. تپ موړ *ttap morr*, adj. Perfectly satiated. تپ نږدې *ttap nijz-dey*, adj. Quite close, very near. تپ وچ *ttap wuch*, adj. Quite dry, entirely dried up, dry as a bone. تپ وږي *ttap wajzey* or وگي *wagey*, adj. Hungry as a hunter. تپ وران *ttap wa-rān*, adj. Totally deserted, ruined, desolate. تپ ويريدلئ *ttap were-dalaey*, adj. Frightened out of one's wits. تپ هير *ttap her*, adj. Wholly forgotten.

تپتپاړني *ttap-ttapārrnaey*, s.m. (1st) The name of a game played by children. Pl. ي *ī*.

تپريدل *ttapar-edal*, verb intrans. To totter along (as an aged person), to creep, to plod, to move slowly, to mince, to falter, to stagger, to lounge, to saunter. Pres. تپريږي *ttapar-ejzī* (W.) or تپريگي *ttapar-egī* (E.); past و تپريده *wu-ttapar-edah* or و تپريدَ *wu-ttapar-eda*; fut. و به تپريږي *wu bah ttapar-ejzī* or و به تپريگي *wu bah ttapar-egī*; imp. و تپريږه *wu-ttapar-ejzah* or و تپريگه *wu-ttapar-egah*; act. part. تپريدونکئ *ttapar-edūnkaey* or تپريدونئ *ttapar-edūnaey*; past part. تپريدلئ *ttapar-edalaey*; verb. n. تپريدنه *ttapar-edana'h*.

تپړ *ttaprr*, s.m. (2nd) Sackcloth, canvas. Pl. تپړونه *ttaprr-ūnah*.

تپس *ttapus*, s.m. (5th) A kite, a bird of prey. Pl. تپسان *ttapus-ān*. Fem. (3rd) تپسه *ttapus-a'h*. Pl. ئ *ey*. See تپوڅ

تپل *ttapal*, verb intrans. To loiter, to plod, to dally, to tarry, to procrastinate, to move along lazily. Pres. تپيږي *ttape-jzī* (W.) or تپيگي *ttape-gī* (E.); Fut. و به تپيږي *wu bah ttape-jzī* or تپيگي *ttape-gī*; imp. و تپيږه *wu-ttap-ejzah* or تپيگه *ttap-egah*; act. part. تپونکئ *ttapūnkaey* or تپونئ *ttapūnaey*; past part. تپلئ *ttapalaey*; verb. n. تپنه *ttapana'h*. The other tenses are wanting.

تپوڅ *ttapūts*, s.m. (5th) A kite, a bird of prey. Pl. تپوڅان *ttapūts-ān*. Fem. (3rd) تپوڅه *ttapūtsa'h*. Pl. ئ *ey*. See تپس

تپي *ttapaey*, s.m. (1st) A black mole, a black spot on a sheep, goat, or other animal. Pl. ي *ī*. See تپ and تپي

تټ *ttat*, s.m. (2nd) Boasting, conceit, vanity. Pl. تټونه *ttatūnah*; Fem. (3rd) تټه *ttata'h*. Pl. ئ *ey*. تټي *ttatacy*, s.m. (1st) A boaster (*lit.* a farter), a coxcomb, a puppy, a beau, a fop, a swaggerer, a jackanapes, a poltroon. Pl. ي *ī*. Fem. (6th). Sing. and Pl. تټئ *ttata'ī*. تټاوړن *ttatāwarrn*, s.m. (5th) Same as preceding. Pl. تټاوُړن *ttatāwærrn*; (Fem.) تټاوړنه *ttatāwarrna'h*. Pl. ئ *ey*.

تټ *ttitt*, adj. Bent, bowed, crooked. 2. Helpless, distressed; (Fem.) تټه *ttitta'h*. See تيټ

تټاريَ *ttattā-raey*, s.m. (1st) A sandpiper, the pewit. Pl. ي *ī*. See تټوغي and تيټاري

تټر *ttattar*, s.m. (2nd) The breast. 2. The crown of the head. Pl. تټرونه *ttattarūnah*.

تټو *ttattū*, s.m. (5th) A pony, a small horse (HI). 2. The bridge of a fiddle. Pl. تټوان *ttattū-ān*; (Fem.) (3rd) تټوه *ttattawa'h*. Pl. ئ *ey*. See خرکي

تټوغيَ *ttatto-ghaey*, s.m. (1st) A sandpiper. Pl. ي *ī*. See تټاري (s ٹٹهارا).

تټئ *ttatt-a'ī*, s.f. (6th) A screen, a matted shutter. Sing. and Pl. (HI. ٹٹی).

تچ *ttach*, s.m. (5th), A pop, a snap, a slight

report as from a gun lightly charged. Pl. ټچهار *ttachahār*. See ټاس

ټخ *ttukh*, s.m. (5th) A cough, expectoration. Pl. ټخهار *ttukhahar*. ټخ وهل *ttukh wahal*, verb trans. To cough, to expectorate. Also written ټخه *ttukha'h*, s.f. (3rd). Pl. ئ *ey*; and ټخي *ttukhaey*, s.m. (1st). Pl. ي *ī*. ټخيدل *ttukhedal*, verb intrans. To cough. Pres. ټخيږي *ttukhe-jzī* (W.), or ټخيګي *ttukhe-gī* (E.); past وُ ټخيده *wu-ttukhedah*, or وُ ټخيدَ *wu-ttukheda*; fut. وُ به ټخيږي *wu bah ttukhe-jzī*, or وُ به ټخيګي *wu bah ttukhe-gī*; imp. وُ ټخيږه *wu-ttukhejzah*, or وُ ټخيګه *wu-ttukhe-gah*; act. part. ټخيدونکيَ *ttukhe-dūnkaey*, or ټخيدونيَ *ttukhe-dūnaey*; past part. ټخيدليَ *ttukhe-dalaey*; verb. n. ټخيدنه *ttukhedana'h*. See توخي and توخيدل

ټخول *ttukhawul*, verb trans. To cause to cough or expectorate, to make cough. Pres. ټخوي *ttukha-wī*; past وُ ټخاوه *wu-ttukhā-wuh* or وُ ټخاوو *wu-ttukhā-wo*; fut. وُ به ټخوي *wu bah ttukha-wī*; imp. وُ ټخوه *wu-ttukhawah*; act. part. ټخوونکيَ *ttukha-wūnkaey*, or ټخوونيَ *ttukha-wūnaey*; past part. ټخوليَ *ttukha-wulaey*; verb. n. ټخونه *ttukha-wuna'h*. (HI تهوک). See توخول

ټخلئ *ttukhala'ī*, s.f. (6th) A cap, a hat. Sing. and Pl.

ټخليَ *ttukhalaey*, s.f. Pl. (3rd) The hooping cough. Pl. ي *ī*. Also written پخليَ ټخليَ *pukhalaey ttukhalaey*. See also پخلي and توره غاره

ټخه *ttukha'h*, s.f. (3rd) A cough. Pl. ئ *ey*. See ټخ and ټخي

ټخيَ *ttukhaey*, s.m. (1st) A cough. Pl. ي *ī*. See preceding.

ټر *ttar*, s.m. (5th) A fart. 2. A word applied to denote contempt, as in English, bosh, fudge, stuff, palaver, fiddlestick, fiddle faddle, humbug. Pl. ټرهار *ttara-hār*. ټرو *ttarū*, s.m. (5th) A farter, a humbug, a donkey, an ass, a twaddler. Pl. ټروګان *ttarū-gān*. ټريدل *ttare-dal*, verb intrans. To fart. ټرهار لرل *ttarahār laral*, verb trans. To twaddle, to humbug, to talk nonsensically.

ټرټر *ttar-ttar*, s.m. (2nd) Chattering, garrulity, prattle, talkativeness. Pl. ټرټرونه *ttar-ttarūnah*, ټرټر کول *ttar-ttar kawul*, verb trans. To chatter, to gabble, to jabber. See ټر

ټريَ *ttaraey*, s.m. (1st) A farter, a humbug, an ass, a twaddler, a fool. Pl. ي *ī*. See ټرو

ټرق *ttrak*, s.m. (2nd) A blow, a bang, a slap, a discharge, an explosion, etc. Pl. ټرقونه *ttrak-ūnah*. See تاق and تق

ټريدل *ttare-dal*, verb intrans. To chatter, to jabber, to gabble. Pres. ټريږي *ttare-jzī* (W.), or ټريګي *ttare-gī* (E.); past وُ ټريده *wu-ttare-dah*, or وُ ټريدَ *wu-ttareda*; fut. وُ به ټريږي *wu bah ttare-jzī*, or وُ به ټريګي *wu bah ttare-gī*; imp. وُ ټريږه *wu-ttare-jzah*, or وُ ټريګه *wu-ttare-gah*; act. part. ټريدونکيَ *ttare-dūnkaey*, or ټريدونيَ *ttare-dūnaey*; past part. ټريدليَ *ttare-dalaey*; verb. n. ټريدنه *ttare-dana'h*.

ټز *ttaz*, s.m. (2nd) A pop, a sound, a fart. Pl. ټزونه *ttazūnah*. See ټر and تيز

ټس *ttas*, s.m. (2nd or 5th) A dumb fart, a puff, a slight sound. Pl. ټسونه *ttas-ūnah*, or ټسهار *ttasa-hār*. See ټپ

ټس ټوس *ttas ttūs*, s.m. (9th) The pop, or crack of fire-arms. 2. A brush, a shindy, a skirmish, a fracas, a rumpus. 3. The exchange of a few shots between two parties, without coming to a pitched battle. Sing. and Pl. ټس ټوس کول *ttas-ttūs kawul*, verb trans. To skirmish, to get up or kick up a row, to quarrel, to wrangle, to fight.

ټسکي *ttaskī*, or *ttiskī*, s.f. (3rd) Laziness, sluggishness, dullness, apathy, callousness. Pl. ئ *a'ī*. ټسکيَ *ttaskaey*, s.m. (1st) A poltroon, a dastard, a milksop, a coward. Pl. ي *ī*. s.f. (6th) ئ *a'ī*. Sing. and Pl.

ټس مس *ttas-mas*, adj. Apathetic, phlegmatic, sluggish, dull; (Fem.) ټسه *ttasa'h*.

ټغ *ttagh*, s.m. (2nd) The pupil of the eye. 2. The jay (coracias bengalensis). Pl. ټغونه *ttaghūnah*. شين ټغ *shīn-ttagh*, s.m. (2nd) A blue jay. ټغي سترګي *ttaghey star-gey*, s.f. Pl. (3rd) Staring eyes, a stare, fixed look. په ټغو سترګو ليدل *pah ttagho stargo lī-dal*, verb trans. To stare at, to gaze, to look at with a fixed look.

تغ _tt_ag_h_, s.m. (5th) A creak, a croak, a sharp sound. Pl. تغهار _ttagha-hār_.

تغر _ttaghar_, s.m. (2nd) A carpet or kind of cloth made from wool. 2. A piece of felt placed beneath the saddle. 3. An old rag, a clout. Pl. تغرونه _ttagharūnah_.

تغن _ttaghan_, s.m. (5th) A coward, a poltroon, a mean apathetic fellow, a milk-sop. Pl. تغن _ttaghæn_.

تغول _ttaghawul_, verb trans. To set the teeth on edge, to jar, to grate, to displease. Pres. تغوي _ttaghawī_; past وُ تغاوه _wu-ttaghāwuh_, or وُ تغاوو _wu-ttaghāwo_; fut. وُ به تغوي _wu bah ttaghawī_; imp. وُ تغوه _wu-ttaghawah_; act. part. تغوونكي _ttaghawūnkaey_, or تغووني _ttaghawūnaey_; past part. تغولي _ttaghawulaey_; verb. n. تغونه _ttaghawuna'h_.

تق _ttaḳ_, s.m. (5th) A blow, a slap, a smack, a bang, a whack, a squash, a thump, a punch, a yerk, etc. Pl. تقهار _ttaḳahār_. تق وهل _ttaḳ wahal_, verb trans. To bump, to clash, to beat against, to crack. تق كول _ttaḳ kawul_, verb trans. To thump, to baste, to dab, to hit, to slam, to whack, to butt, to rap, to pelt, to yerk, etc. See تاق and ترق.

تقول _ttaḳawul_, verb trans. To blame, to censure, to rate, to reprove, to lecture, to scold, to upbraid, to accuse, to castigate, to reprobate, to calumniate. Pres. تقوي _ttaḳawī_; past وُ تقاوه _wu-ttaḳāwuh_, or وُ تقاوو _wu-ttaḳāwo_; fut. وُ به تقوي _wu bah ttaḳawī_; imp. وُ تقوه _wu-ttaḳawah_; act. part. تقوونكي _ttaḳa-wūnkaey_, or تقووني _ttaḳawūnaey_; past part. تقولي _ttaḳa-wulaey_; verb. n. تقونه _ttaḳawuna'h_.

تكت _ttuk_, s.m. (2nd) A piece, a bit, a shred, an atom, a particle, etc. Pl. تكونه _ttukūnah_. See توكت and تكي

تكت _ttak_, s.m. (2nd) A murrain amongst cattle. Pl. تكونه _ttakūnah_.

تكت _ttak_, s.m. (5th) The sound of the footsteps of man or animal, a thump, a slam, a rap, a bang, a report, etc. Pl. تكهار _ttaka-hār_. See تكا _ttakā_. تكت وهل _ttak wahal_, verb trans. To strike, to beat, to thump, to drive in, to crack, to split, to hit, to pound, to shake, to shake as fruit from a tree, to sting. تكول _ttakawul_, verb trans. To beat, to thump, to bruise, to knock, to cudgel, to drive a peg. Pres. تكوي _ttakawī_; past وُ تكاوه _wu-ttakā-wuh_, وُ تكاوو _wu-ttakā-wo_; fut. وُ به تكوي _wu bah ttakawī_; imp. وُ تكوه _wu-ttakawah_; act. part. تكوونكي _ttaka-wūnkaey_, or تكووني _ttaka-wūnaey_; past part. تكولي _ttaka-wulaey_; verb. n. تكونه _ttaka-wuna'h_. تكت كول _ttak kawul_, verb trans. To discharge (as a gun), to fire off.

تكا _ttakā_, s.f. (6th) The sound of the footsteps of man or beast, report of fire-arms, a slam, a bang, a thump, a rap, crack, etc. (E.) Sing. and Pl.; (W.) Pl. تكاوي _ttakā-wī_. See تكت and تهكالو

تكاركي _ttikārkaey_, s.m. (1st) A small spot of ground hard and free from grass and weeds. Pl. ي _ī_. See also داكت and داكه

تكانه _ttikā-na'h_, s.f. (3rd) A place, abode, residence, dwelling. 2. Boundary, limit, fixing. Pl. ي _ey_. (s تهكانا). تكانه كيدل _ttikā-na'h kedal_, verb intrans. To rest, to repose, to settle, to desist. تكانه كول _ttikā-na'h kawul_, verb trans. To stop, to remain, to stay. تكانه لگيدل _ttikā-na'h lage-dal_, verb intrans. To settle down, to reach one's level, to become stationary. تكانه لگول _ttikā-na'h lagawul_, verb trans. To decide, to fix, to bring to adjustment.

تكتو _ttaka-tū_, s.m. prop. The name of a mountain east of Ḳandahār.

تكتكت _ttak-ttak_, The sound of feet, etc. See تكت

تكتكاڑي _ttak-ttakārrnaey_, s.m. (1st) The name of a game played by children. 2. The clapper of a mill, the piece of wood that strikes the mill hopper. 3. The wood-pecker (Picus). Pl. ي _ī_.

تكر _ttakar_, s.m. (2nd) Shoving, pushing, push, knocking against, collision, a butt, butting, the knocking of head against head. Pl. تكرونه

ttakar-ūnah. (HI ٹکر). ٹکر خوړل *ttakar khwarral*, verb trans. To receive a butt, to be dashed against anything. ٹکر وهل *ttakar wahal*, verb trans. To butt, to knock against, to shove.

ٹکړ *ttukrr*, s.m. (5th) A piece, a morsel, a bit, a portion, a slice or morsel of bread. Pl. ٹکړان *ttukrr-ān*; Fem. (3rd) ٹکړه *ttukarra'h*. Pl. ئ *ey*. (S ٹکړا).

ټکسرَی *ttak-saraey*, adj. (Masc.) Murrain, a term of abuse, tabid, mangy; (Fem.) ټکسرِ *ttak-sari*. Pl. (Masc. and Fem.) ي *ī*. ټکسرَی شي *ttak-sarey shey*, A murrain seize thee! See ټک

ټککه *ttakaka'h*, s.f. (3rd) A piece of wood placed across the handle of a shovel or spade above the iron part, to place the foot on for shoving it into the ground. Pl. ئ *ey*.

ټککړنه غرمه *ttakkarrna'h gharma'h*, s.f. (3rd) Noon, mid-day. Pl. ئ *ey*. 2. adj. Noon, exactly noon, meridional. See ټکنده غرمه

ټک لاستَی *ttak lās-taey*, adj. Nimble-handed, nimble, handy, fine-fingered (as a thief), quick, smart, ingenious, light-footed. 2. Striking or firing rapidly or with vehemence. ټک لاستَی والَی *ttak-lāstaey wālaey*, s.m. (1st) Nimbleness, handiness, quickness, smartness, ingeniousness, adroitness. Pl. ي *ī*. Also ټک لاستَی توب *ttak-lāstaey tob*, s.m, (2nd) Pl. توبونه *tobūnah*.

ټکنده غرمه *ttakanda'h gharma'h*, s.f. (3rd) Noon, noon-day, mid-day. Pl. ئ *ey*. 2. adj. Exactly noon, noon, meridional. Also ټکنئ غرمه *ttakana'ī gharma'h*, s.f. (6th), and adj. See ټککړنه غرمه

ټکړنَی *ttakarrnaey*, adj. Stubborn, contumacious, obstinate, restive. 2. s.m. (1st) A restive or obstinate horse. Pl. ي *ī*; (Fem.) ئ *a'ī*. Sing. and Pl.

ټکور *ttakor*, s.m. (2nd) An antidote, a sedative, a panacea, embrocation, a poultice, a cataplasm, a fomentation. Pl. ټکورونه *ttakorūnah*. ټکور کول *ttakor kawul*, verb trans. To apply an antidote or embrocation, to poultice, to foment, etc. (HI ٹکور). See also تبل and ضماد.

ټکه *ttaka'h*, s.f. (3rd) Enmity, hatred, jealousy, animosity, pique. 2. A thunderbolt. Pl. ئ *ey*. ټکه لرل *ttaka'h laral*, verb trans. To hate, to be jealous of, to be at enmity with.

ټکه *ttakah*, s.m. (5th) A mountain goat, or species of the ibex. Pl. ټکهګان *ttakah-gān*. ټکه ارغند *ttakah arghund*, s.m. (5th) The knuckle-bone of the mountain-sheep, with which a kind of game is played. Pl. ارغندان *arghundān*. See ارغند. ټکه پوست *ttakah post*, The leather prepared from the skin of the ibex or mountain goat.

ټکَی *ttakaey*, s.m. (1st) A spot, a dot, a mark, a streak, a stripe. 2. A drop, a sprinkling, a molecule. 3. A bullock with a spot on the forehead. 4. An appointed time or place. Pl. ټکي *ttakī*. ټکي ټکي *ttakī-ttakī* or *ttikī-ttikī*, adj. Spotted, dotted, speckled, studded. Also ټکيالَی *ttakī-ālaey*, adj. Pl. ي *ī*; (Fem.) ئ *a'ī*. Sing. and Pl.

ټکئ *ttika'ī*, s.f. (6th) A small cake or biscuit. 2. An orb, the disk of the sun or moon. 3. A small mark or butt for arrows. 4. A loud laugh. Sing. and Pl.

ټکي ټکي *ttukī-ttukī*, adj. Ragged, in tatters, in pieces, in shreds, in drops (as rain). See ټک

ټګ *ttag*, s.m. (5th) A cheat, an impostor. 2. A robber, an assassin, cut-throat. Pl. ټګان *ttagān*; s.f. (3rd) ټګه *ttaga'h*. Pl. ئ *ey*.

ټګي *ttagī*, s.f. (3rd) Robbery, theft, cheating. Pl. ئ *a'ī*. ټګل *ttagal*, verb trans. To rob, to cheat, to deceive. Pres. ټګي *ttagī*; past وُ ټاګه *wu-ttā-gah* or وُ ټاګ *wu-ttā-ga*; fut. وُ به ټګي *wu bah ttagī*; imp. وُ ټګه *wu-ttagah*; act. part. ټګونکَی *ttagūnkaey* or ټګونَی *ttagūnaey*; past part. ټګلَی *ttagalaey*; verb. n. ټګنه *ttagana'h*. (HI ٹهگ).

ټګي کول *ttagī kawul*, verb trans. To cheat, to rob, to plunder, to deceive. See preceding.

ټل *ttal*, s.m. (2nd) Thickness or closeness of

grain in a field, or of trees in a grove or forest, or hair of the head. 2. The ward or division of a town or village. 3. A large field, the fourth part of the lands of a village, a bed of flowers, etc., a plot or plat of land. Pl. تلونه *ttalūnah.* تلگي *ttal-gaey*, s.m. (1st) The diminutive of the preceding—a small field, a few houses close to each other. Pl. ي *ī.*

تل *ttal*, adj. Full, replete, having as much as it can contain. 2. Abundant, plenteous, replete; (Fem.) تله *ttala'h.* تل كيدل *ttal kedal*, verb intrans. To fill, to grow or become full, replete, etc. تل كول *ttal kawul*, verb trans. To fill, to pour into the thing until it will hold no more, to render replete, abundant, etc. تل والي *ttal wālaey*, s.m. (1st) Fullness, abundance, repletion, plenitude. Pl. والي *wālī.*

تم *ttam*, s.m. (5th) The bark or growl of a dog or other beast. Pl. تمهار *ttama-hār.* تم وهل *ttam wahal*, verb trans. To bark, to growl.

تم تيل *ttam-ttīl*, s.m. (5th) The name of a water bird with long beak and legs. Pl. تم تيلان *ttam-ttīlān.* تم تيلا *ttam-ttīlā* (5th), Same as preceding. Pl. تم تيلاگان *ttam-ttīlāgān.*

تمک *ttimak*, s.m. (5th) One of the cross poles of a tent, which support the sides and cross each other. Pl. تمكان *ttimak-ān.* See كړدۍ

تنبل *ttunbal*, verb trans. To pick, to cleanse (as the teeth, ears, nails, etc.), to pull off or pluck out with the fingers anything which sticks (as a thorn, etc.) Pres. تنبي *ttunbī*; past وُ تنبه *wu-ttunbah*; fut. وُ به تنبي *wu bah ttunbī*; imp. وُ تنبه *wu-ttunbah*; act. part. تنبونكي *ttunbūnkaey*, or تنبوني *ttunbūnaey*; past part. تنبلي *ttunbalaey*; verb. n. تنبنه *ttunbana'h.* غاښ تنبونكي *ghash* (W.) or *ghakh* (E.) *ttunbūnkaey*, s.m. (1st) A toothpick. Pl. ي *ey.*

تند *ttandd*, adj. Fat, stout, corpulent, pot-bellied; (Fem.) تنده *ttandda'h*, A fat or stout woman, also a woman big with child. تند والي *ttandd wālaey*, s.m. (1st) Corpulence, obesity, stoutness. Pl. ي *ī.* See پړس

تنگ *ttang*, s.m. (5th) A sound, twang, jar, creak, clank, jingle (as of dishes), ring. Pl. تنگهار *ttanga-hār.* Also s.m. (2nd) Pl. تنگونه *ttang-ūnah.* تنگيدل *ttange-dal*, verb intrans. To sound, to grate, to jar, to creak, to ring. Pres. تنگيږي *ttangejzī* (W.) or تنگيگي *ttangegī* (E.); past وُ تنگيده *wu-ttangedah* or وُ تنگيدَ *wu-ttangeda*; fut. وُ به تنگيږي *wu bah ttangejzī* or وُ به تنگيگي *wu bah ttangegī*; imp. وُ تنگيږه *wu-ttangejzah* or وُ تنگيگه *wu-ttangegah*; act. part. تنگيدونكي *ttange-dūnkaey* or تنگيدوني *ttange-dūnaey*; past part. تنگيدلي *ttange-dalaey*; verb. n. تنگيدنه *ttange-dana'h.* تنگول *ttangawul*, verb trans. To sound, to make to ring, to make a grating sound, to jingle. Pres. تنگوي *ttangawī*; past وُ تنگاوه *wu-ttangāwuh* or وُ تنگاوو *wu-ttangāwo*; fut. وُ به تنگوي *wu bah ttangawī*; imp. وُ تنگوه *wu-ttangawah*; act. part. تنگوونكي *ttanga-wūnkaey* or تنگووني *ttanga-wūnaey*; past part. تنگولي *ttanga-wulaey*; verb. n. تنگونه *ttanga-wuna'h.* See غرول

تنگ تونگ *ttang-ttūng*, s.m. (2nd) The sound of a musical instrument (as of a violin, etc.) Pl. تنگ تونگهار *ttang-ttūngahār.*

تنگه *ttanga'h*, s.f. (3rd) A copper coin. 2. Money, wealth. Pl. ي *ey.* See يكي

توپ *ttop*, s.m. (2nd) A leap, a jump, a spring, a hop, a bound, a caper, a curvet, a caracole. 2. A stack of dried cakes of cow-dung for fuel, a stack in general. 3. Overplus or measure, a small quantity over and above the measure given to purchasers of cloth, grain, etc. Pl. توپونه *ttopūnah.* توپ كول *ttop kawul* or توپ وهل *ttop wahal*, verb trans. To leap, to spring, to bound, to caper, to curvet.

توپک *ttopak*, s.m. (2nd) A matchlock, a musket. Pl. توپكونه *ttopak-ūnah.* See also توپک and بندوخ

توپل *ttopal*, s.m. (2nd) The crown of the head. 2. A cap, a covering for the head. Pl. توپلونه *ttopalūnah.*

توپۍ *ttopa'ī*, s.f. (6th) A cap, a hat, a helmet,

a bowl, the cup of a pipe, etc. Sing. and Pl. (HI ٹوپي). See خولۍ

ټوټي *ttottaey*, s.m. (1st) A piece, a bit, a scrap, a rag, a shred, a tatter, a splinter, a cutting, a slice, a chip, a driblet, a paring, a shaving. Pl. ي *ī*; s.f. (3rd) ټوټه *ttotta'h*, Pl. ې *ey*. ټوټي ټوټي *ttottī ttottī*, adj. In pieces, in shreds, in tatters, in rags. See ټکي ټکي

ټوخ *ttūkh*, s.m. (5th) A cough, expectoration. Pl. ټوخهار *ttūkhahār*. See also ټخ. ټوخ وهل *ttūkh wahal*, verb trans. To cough, to expectorate. ټوخيدل *ttūkhedal*, verb intrans. To cough. ټوخول *ttūkhawul*, verb trans. To cause to cough. See also ټخيدل and ټخول

ټوخه *ttūkha'h*, s.f. (3rd) A cough. Pl. ې *ey*. Also written ټوخی *ttūkhaey*, s.m. (1st) Pl. ي *ī*. See preceding.

ټوخلۍ *ttūkhala'ī*, s.f. (6th) A cap, a covering for the head, generally padded with cotton. Sing. and Pl. See ټخلۍ

ټوخلی *ttūkhalaey*, s.m. (1st) The hooping-cough. Pl. ي *ī*. See ټخلي and توره غاره

ټوکړ *ttūkarr*, s.m. (5th) An old or decrepid man. Pl. ټوکړان *ttūkarrān*. See ټاکړ

ټوکړه *ttūkarra'h*, s.f. (3rd) An old woman. Pl. ې *ey*.

ټوکه *ttoka'h*, s.f. (3rd) Ridicule, derision, mockery, quiz, banter, scoffing, satire, pleasantry, joking, Pl. ې *ey*. ټوکه کول *ttoka'h kawul*, verb trans. To ridicule, to deride, to quiz, to roast, to scoff, to mock. ټوکي *ttokī*, s.m. (5th) A wag, a wit, a quiz, a satirist. Pl. ټوکيان *ttokī-ān*, and s.f. (5th) Pl. ټوکيانِ *ttokī-āni*. See ملنډه and مسخره

ټوک *ttok*, adj. Closely or thickly woven (as cloth); (Fem.) ټوکه *ttoka'h*.

s ټوک *ttūk*, s.m. (2nd) A piece, a little, a particle, an atom, a bit. Pl. ټوکونه *ttūkūnah*. ټوک ټوک *ttūk ttūk*, adj. In pieces, in bits, in atoms. See ټک.

ټوکيدل *ttūkedal*, verb intrans. To grow, to germinate, to bud, to shoot, to sprout, to vegetate, to become large. Pres. ټوکيږي *ttūkejzī* (W.) or ټوکيګي *ttūkegī* (E.); past وُ ټوکيده *wu-ttūkedah* or وُ ټوکيدَ *wu-ttūkeda*; fut. وُ به ټوکيږي *wu bah ttūkejzī* or وُ به ټوکيګي *wu bah ttūkegī*; imp. وُ ټوکيږه *wu-ttūkejzah* or وُ ټوکيګه *wu-ttūkegah*; act. part. ټوکيدونکی *ttūkedūnkaey* or ټوکيدونی *ttūkedūnaey*; past part. ټوکيدلی *ttūkedalaey*; verb. n. ټوکيدنه *ttūkedana'h* or ټوکيده *ttūkedah*.

ټوکيدنه *ttūke-dana'h*, s.f. (3rd) (verb. n.) Pl. ې *ey*; or ټوکيده *ttūkedah*, s.m. (6th) Growing, germinating, sprouting, budding, increasing. Sing. and Pl.

ټوکول *ttūkawul*, verb trans. To cause or make grow or germinate, to sprout or bud, to expand, to inflate. Pres. ټوکوي *ttūkawī*; past وُ ټوکاوه *wu-ttūkāwuh* or وُ ټوکاوو *wu-ttūkā-wo*; fut. وُ به ټوکوي *wu bah ttūkawī*; imp. وُ ټوکوه *wu-ttūkawah*; act. part. ټوکوونکی *ttūkawūnkaey* or ټوکوونی *ttūkawūnaey*; past part. ټوکولی *ttūkawulaey*; verb. n. ټوکونه *ttūkawuna'h*.

ټوکه *ttoka'h*, s.f. (3rd) Ridicule, derision, mockery, quiz, banter, pleasantry, joking, fun, etc. Pl. ې *ey*. See ټوقه

ټوکرۍ *ttokra'ī*, s.f. (6th) A small basket. Sing. and Pl. See کواره. (HI ٹوکري).

ټوکی *tto-kaey*, s.m. (1st) A patch, a vamp, a repair. 2. A piece of cloth. Pl. ي *ī*.

ټول *ttol*, adj. All, the whole, the gross, the sum total, every one, the whole quantity, extent, duration, amount, quality, or degree; (Fem.) ټوله *ttola'h*. Sing. and Pl. ټوليدل *ttoledal*, verb intrans. To assemble, to congregate, to gather together, to crowd, to flock, to herd, to collect, to accumulate, to convene, to convoke, to truss, to stack, etc. Pres. ټوليږي *ttolejzī* (W.) or ټوليګي *ttolegī* (E.); past ټول شه *ttol shah* or وُ شه *wu-shah*; fut. ټول به شي *ttol bah shī* or وُ به شي *bah wu shī*; imp. ټول شه *ttol shah* or وُ شه *wu-shah*; act. part. ټوليدونکی *ttole-dūnkaey* or ټوليدونی *ttole-dūnaey*; past part. ټول شوی *ttol shawaey* or ټول *ttol*; verb. n. ټوليدنه *ttole-dana'h*. ټولول *ttolawul*, verb trans. To assemble, to muster, to collect, to bring together, to convoke, to crowd or get together. Pres. تولوي *ttolawī*; past تول کړ *ttol karr* or وُ کړ *wu-karr*; fut. تول به کړي *ttol bah krrī* or به وُ کړي *bah wu-krrī*; imp. تول کړه *ttol krrah* or وُ کړه *wu-krrah*; act. part. تولوونکَي *ttolawūnkaey* or تولووني *ttolawūnaey*; past part. تول کړي *ttol karraey*; verb. n. تولونه *ttolawuna'h*.

تولټال *ttol-ttāl*, adj. All, the whole, the sum total, the gross, etc.; (Fem.) توله ټاله *ttola'h-ttāla'h*. See تول and درست

تول *ttol*, s.m. (2nd) A crowd, a body or company of men or beasts, a throng, a mob, a multitude, a horde, a tribe, a gang, a crew, a knot, a band, a bevy, a flock, a drove, a troop, a corps, etc. Pl. تولونه *ttol-ūnah*. See جرګه

تولګَي *ttol-gaey*, s.m. (1st) The diminutive of the preceding—A small party, band, knot, etc. Pl. ي *ī*.

تولَي *ttolaey*, s.m. (1st) A company, a society, an assembly, a congress, a levy, a gathering, a concourse, a party. Pl. ي *ī*; s.f. (6th) تولۍ *ttola'ī*. Sing. and Pl. (HI ٹولي).

تونګ *ttong*, s.m. (2nd) Irritation, excitement, provocation, setting against, exciting, provoking. Pl. تونګونه *ttongūnah*.

تونګاره *ttongāra'h*, s.f. (3rd) Irritating or provoking language, abuse previous to a quarrel. Pl. ې *ey*. تونګاره آچول *ttongāra'h āchawul*, verb trans. To excite, to insult, to nettle, to provoke, to stir one's bile.

تيپر *ttepær*, s.m. (2nd) A turnip. Pl. تيپرونه *ttepærūnah*.

تيت *ttitt*, adj. Crooked, bent, curved, bowed, awry, wry, deformed, hump-backed; (Fem.) تيته *ttitta'h*. تپ تيت *ttap-ttitt*, adj. Entirely crooked or bent, quite crooked, much curved. سر تيت کول *sar ttitt kawul*, verb trans. To bend the head, to stoop. تيتيدل *ttittedal*, verb intrans. To bend, to be crooked, to incline, to lean, to bow. Pres. تيتيږي *ttittejzī* (W.) or تيتيګي *ttittegī* (E.); past تيت شه *ttitt shah* or وُ شه *wu-shah*; fut. تيت به شي *ttitt bah shī* or به وُ شي *bah wu-shī*; imp. تيت شه *ttitt shah* or وُ شه *wu-shah*; act. part. تيتيدونکَي *ttittedūnkaey* or تيتيدونَي *ttittedūnaey*; past part. تيت شوَي *ttitt* or تيت شوَي *ttitt shawaey*; verb. n. تيتيدنه *ttittedana'h*. تيتول *ttittawul*, verb trans. To bend, to curve, to incurvate, to arch, to bow. Pres. تيتوي *ttittawī*; past تيت کړ *ttitt karr* or وُ کړ *wu-karr*; fut. تيت به کړي *ttitt bah krrī* or به وُ کړي *bah wu-krrī*; imp. تيت کړه *ttitt krrah* or وُ کړه *wu-krrah*; act. part. تيتوونکَي *ttittawūnkaey* or تيتوونَي *ttittawūnaey*; past part. تيت کړَي *ttitt karraey*; verb. n. تيتونه *ttittawuna'h*.

تيت والَي *ttitt wālaey*, s.m. (1st) Crookedness, wryness, curvature, bend, deformity. Pl. ي *ī*.

تيتَي *ttittaey*, adj. (The diminutive of تيت *ttitt*) Slightly or a little curved or bent. Pl. ي *ī*; (Fem.) Sing. and Pl. تيتۍ *ttitta'ī*.

تيتارَي *ttittāraey*, s.m. (1st) A sand-piper, the pewit. Pl. ي *ī*. See تتاري. (S ٹٹري).

تيټال *ttī-ttāl*, s.m. (2nd) Duplicity, guile, deception, deceit, stratagem, trick, fraud, cheat, etc. Pl. تيټالونه *ttī-ttāl-ūnah*. تيټال کول *ttī-ttāl kawul*, verb trans. To deceive, to impose upon, to beguile, to mislead, to throw dust in the eyes. تيټال خوړل *ttī-ttāl khwarral*, verb trans. (*lit.* 'to eat deception'), To become deceived or misled, to be imposed upon. The word is also written طيطال

تيغ *ttegh*, s.m. (2nd) A belch, eructation. Pl. تيغونه *tteghūnah*. تيغ کښل *ttegh k'shal* (W.) or *k'khal* (E.), verb trans. To belch. See اروي

تيکاو *ttikā-o*, s.m. (9th) Rest, stay, staying, resting, remaining, tarrying. Sing. and Pl.

تيک *ttek*, s.m. (2nd) The temple, the side of the head. Pl. تيکونه *ttekūnah*.

تيک *ttik*, s.m. (2nd) An ornament for the forehead. Pl. تيکونه *ttikūnah*. (S ٹیکا).

تيکه *ttika'h*, s.f. (3rd) Same as preceding. 2. A round piece of cloth sown in front of a cap as an ornament. Pl. ې *ey*.

تيک تاکه *ttik ttā-ka'h*, s.f. (3rd) A kind of carpet made of wool, and very stiff and hard, brought from Herāt and Hazārah. Pl. ې *ey*.

تيل *tteyl*, s.m. (2nd) A shove, a push, a jog, a thrust; shoving, pushing, thrusting. Pl. تيلونه *tteyl-ūnah*. تيل وهل *tteyl wahal*, verb trans. To push, to shove, to remove by pushing. (HI ٹهيل). See also ټه پير

تيل ټال *tteyl ttāl*, s.m. (9th) Romping, fun, frolic, prank, antic, etc. 2. Dalliance. Sing. and Pl. تيل ټال كول *tteyl ttāl kawul*, verb trans. To romp, to gambol, to dally, to fondle.

تينگ *tting*, adj. Coherent, cohesive, compact, close, thickset, coagulated, thick, curdled, clotted, inspissated, stiff. 2. Tight, firm, strong; (Fem.) تينگه *ttinga'h*. تپ تينگ *ttap tting*, adj. Very thick, tight, firm, strong, etc. تينگ ترل *tting tarral*, verb trans. To tighten, to fasten tightly or firmly; also تينگ كول *tting kawul*, verb trans. تينگ والي *tting wālaey*, s.m. (1st) Coagulation, inspissation, thickening, compactness, consistence, thickness, solidity, cohesivess, stiffness, firmness. Pl. ي *ī*. تينگيدل *ttingedal*, verb intrans. To become solid, to congeal, to coagulate, to curdle, to clot, to cohere, to concrete, to thicken, to constipate. 2. To stand, to rise, to stand up. Pres. تينگيږي *ttingejzī* (W.) or تينگيگي *ttingegī* (E.); past تينگ شه *tting shah* or وُ شه *wu-shah*; fut. تينگ به شي *tting bah shī* or به وُ شي *bah wu-shī*; imp. تينگ شه *tting shah* or وُ شه *wu-shah*; act. part. تينگيدونكي *ttingedūnkaey* or تينگيدوني *ttingedūnaey*; past part. تينگ *tting* or تينگ شوي *tting shawaey*; verb. n. تينگيدنه *ttingedana'h*. تينگول *ttingawul*, verb trans. To harden, to stiffen, to render or make solid, to squeeze, to ram down, to compress, to condense, etc. 2. To erect, to raise, to cause to stand. Pres. تينگوي *ttingawī*; past تينگ كړ *tting karr* or وُ كړ *wu-karr*; fut. تينگ به كړي *tting bah krrī* or به وُ كړي *bah wu-krrī*; imp. تينگ كړه *tting krrah* or وُ كړه *wu-krrah*; act. part. تينگوونكي *ttingawūnkaey* or تينگووني *ttingawūnaey*; past part. تينگ كړي *tting karraey*; verb. n. تيگونه *ttingawuna'h*.

ث

ث *s* or lisped *s*, is the fourth letter of the Arabic alphabet. It does not occur in words of either Pushto or Persian origin. In the Arabic it denotes the number 500.

A ثابت *sābit*, adj. (from ثبوت) Ascertained, constant, firm, durable, stable, proved, sure, valid, confirmed, established; (Fem.) ثابته *sābita'h*. ثابت قدم *sābit kadam*, adj. Resolute, constant, immovable, permanent, true to one's word. ثابت كيدل *sābit kedal*, verb intrans. To be proved or confirmed, to be verified or established. ثابت كول *sābit kawul*, verb trans. To prove, to show, to verify, to substantiate, to bring home to, to evince. See زباد

A ثالث *sālis*, s.m. (5th) (from ثلث) An umpire, an arbitrator, a mediator. 2. The third. Pl. ثالثان, *sā-lisān*. ثالث بالخير *sālis bi-l-khair*, An unprejudiced arbitrator.

A ثاني *sānī*, adj. Second. 2. s.m. (9th) The second. Sing. and Pl. s.f. (3rd) ثانيه *sānīa'h*. Pl. ې *ey*.

A ثبات *sabāt*, s.m. (9th) Stability, permanency, firmness. Sing. and Pl.

A ثبت *sabt*, s.m. (2nd) Firmness, stability, constancy. Pl. ثبتونه *sabt-ūnah*. 2. adj. Firm, constant, inscribed; (Fem.) ثبته *sabta'h*. ثبت كيدل *sabt kedal*, verb intrans. To be inscribed or written. ثبت كول *sabt kawul*, verb trans. To inscribe, to subscribe, to write.

A ثبوت *subūt*, s.m. (9th) Firmness, stability, constancy, conviction, proof, confirmation by evidence. Sing. and Pl. 2. adj. Firm, proved; (Fem.) ثبوته *subūta'h*.

A ثريا *surai-yā*, s.f. (6th) The Pleiades. Sing. and Pl.

ثعلب مصري *saælab misrī*, s.m. (9th) Salep, the root of a species of orchis (Orchis mascula) considered a restorative. Sing. and Pl.

A ثقيل *sakīl*, adj. (ثقل) Heavy. 2. Lazy, phlegmatic. 3. Indigestible; (Fem.) ثقيله *sakīla'h*.

A ثلث s̤ulṡ, s.m. (5th) The third part, one-third. Pl. ثلثان s̤ulṡān.

A ثمر s̤amar, s.m. (9th) Fruit. 2. Produce, advantage, profit. 3. Offspring. Sing. and Pl. ثمر دار s̤amar dār, adj. Fruit bearing; (Fem.) ثمر داره s̤amar-dārah. ثمره s̤amara'h, s.f. (3rd) Fruit. 2. Profit, result, reward, 3. Offspring. Pl. ې ey.

A ثنا s̤anā, s.f. (6th) Praise, applause. (E.) Sing. and Pl. (W.) Pl. ثناوي s̤anāwī. ثنا خوان s̤anā khwān, Repeating praise, one who praises. ثنا خواني s̤anā khwānī, s.f. (3rd) Praise, applause, plaudit, praising, extolling. Pl. ئي a'ī. ثنا ويل s̤anā wayal, or ثنا خواني كول s̤anā khwānī kawul, verb trans. To commend, to applaud, to laud, to magnify.

A ثواب s̤awāb, s.m. (2nd) The future reward of virtue. 2. A good or virtuous action or reward. Pl. ثوابونه s̤awābūnah.

A ثواب گټل s̤awāb gattal, verb trans. To obtain a reward or recompense for good actions. ثواب لرل s̤awāb laral, verb trans. To reward, to give recompense, to have a reward.

A ثوابت s̤awābit, s.m. (Pl. of ثابت) The fixed stars.

A ثور s̤aur, s.m. (9th) A bull; Taurus, the sign of the Zodiac. Sing. and Pl.

A ثيبه s̤a-yeba'h, s.f. (3rd) A young woman who has consummated her marriage. Pl. ې ey.

ځ

ځ tse or tze, the seventh letter of the Pushto alphabet, similar in sound to the letter צ tsode of the Hebrew and other Semitic dialects. There is no equivalent for it in the Sanskrit.

ځاپېړه tsā-perra'h, s.f. (3rd) A slap, a box, a wipe, a buffet, a clout, a tap, a cuff. Pl. ې ey. (HI تهپېړا). See څپېړه

ځاڅكي tsātskaey, s.m. (1st) A drop, a sprinkling, a minim. Pl. ي ī. See څڅوكي

ځادر tsā-dar, s.m. (2nd) A sheet, a veil. Pl. ځادرونه tsādarūnah. (P چادر).

ځار tsār, s.m. (2nd) The business of a scout, watching, looking out. Pl. ځارونه tsār-ūnah. ځار كول tsār kawul, verb trans. To keep a look out, to discover, to act as a scout, to keep watch and ward.

ځاري tsārī, s.m. (5th) A scout, a look out. Pl. ځاريان tsārī-ān. Also ځاركوونكي tsār-kawūnkaey, s.m. (1st) (act. part.) A scout. Pl. ي ī.

ځارښكه tsār-shaka'h (W.) or tsār-khaka'h (E.) s.f. (3rd) The name of a bird known as the tā-ler in the Panjāb. Pl. ې ey. See ځاښكه

ځاروي tsār-waey, s.m. (1st) An animal, a quadruped, a horse, a camel, a beast of burthen, cattle. Pl. ي ī.

ځاره tsāra'h, s.f. (3rd) Remedy, cure, expedient, help, aid. Pl. ې ey. ځاره كول tsāra'h kawul, verb trans. To remedy, to cure, to rectify, to remove (as an evil). ځاره گر tsāra'h-gar, adj. Remedial, healing, curing. ځاره گري tsārah-garī, s.f. (3rd) Remedying, curing, cure, removing. Pl. ئي a'ī. (P چاره).

ځاړي tsārraey, s.m. (1st) A bustard, a florican (Otis bengalensis). Pl. ي ī.

ځاشي tsā shaey, s.m. (1st) A spindle, the rod or pin on which anything turns. 2. A kind of reel or spindle for winding or twisting cotton or thread. Pl. ي ī. See جلك

ځاښت tsāsht (W.) or tsākht (E.) s.m. (2nd) The intermediate hour between sunrise and the meridian. Pl. ځاښتونه tsāshtūnah or tsākhtūnah. (P چاشت).

ځاښتي tsāshtī (W.) or tsākhtī (E.) s.f. (3rd) Luncheon, collation, early dinner. Pl. ئي a'ī.

ځاښكه tsā-shaka'h (W.) or tsā-khaka'h (E.) s.f. (3rd) The name of a bird in India and the Panjāb, the tā-ler. Pl. ې ey. See ځارښكه

ځاښي tsā-shaey (W.) or tsā-khaey (E.) s.m. (1st) A spindle, the rod or pin on which anything turns. Pl. ي ī.

ځاك tsāk, s.m. (2nd) A slit, a rent, a fissure, a narrow opening left in the clothes. 2. The corner of a sheet or skirt of a dress. Pl. ځاكونه tsākūnah. See بڅكه

ځانګ tsāng, s.m. (2nd) The wing of a bird, the

branch or bough of a tree. Pl. څانګونه *t̲sāng-ūnah*. څانګ غوڅ *t̲sāng g̲h̲wat̲s*, adj. Broken winged, distressed, afflicted. See ددړه

څانګه *t̲sānga'h*, s.f. (3rd) The wing of a bird, the branch or bough of a tree. 2. Acute pain. Pl. ې *ey*. څانګه غوڅه *t̲sānga'h g̲h̲wat̲sa'h*, Broken winged, afflicted, distressed. See preceding.

څاه *t̲sāh*, s.m. (2nd) A well, a pit. Pl. څاهونه *t̲sāhūnah*. Also څه *t̲sah*, s.m. (5th). Pl. څهان *t̲sahān*. See چاه

څپ *t̲sap*, s.m. (2nd) A kind of basket for winnowing corn with. Pl. څپونه *t̲sapūnah*. See چج or چچ (s सूपं). څپ وهل *t̲sap wahal*, and څپول *t̲sapawul*, verb trans. To winnow or clean grain, to rinse. Pres. څپوي *t̲sapawī*; past وُ څپاوه *wu-t̲sapāwuh*, or وُ څپاوو *wu-t̲sāpawo*; fut. وُ به څپوي *wu bah t̲sapawī*; imp. وُ څپوه *wuh-t̲sapawah*; act. part. څپوونکی *t̲sapawūnkaey*, or څپووني *t̲sapawunaey*; past part. څپولی *t̲sapawulaey*; verb. n. څپونه *t̲sapawuna'h*.

څپتي *t̲sapat̲t̲aey*, s.m. (1st) A flat cake of unleavened bread. Pl. ي *ī*. (HI چپاتي).

څپر *t̲sapar*, s.m. (2nd) A thatched roof, the thatch of a house, a hut of reeds or grass (HI چهپر). 2. A frame work of wood rendered heavy, which is drawn about by bullocks as a sort of threshing machine to separate the grain from the straw. Pl. څپرونه *t̲saparūnah*.

څپرکی *t̲sapar-kaey*, s.m. (1st) A flake, a pellicle, a scale, a shaving, a film, a layer, a stratum, any scaly matter in layers. Pl. ي *ī*.

څپړ *t̲saparr*, s.f. (1st) A blow or tap with the soft foot of a camel or similar animal. 2. The flat soft foot of the camel, elephant, etc. Pl. څپړ *t̲saparri*.

څپق *t̲sapaḳ*, s.m. (2nd) A hand's, or four fingers' breadth, a palm, a lineal measure of three inches. Pl. څپقونه *t̲sapaḳūnah*. Also څپک *t̲sapak*. Pl. څپکونه *t̲sapakūnah*. See څپرکي and ورغوي

څپک *t̲sapak*, s.m. (2nd) A flake of snow, a pellicle, etc. Pl. څپکونه *t̲sapakūnah*. See څپرکي

څپلاک *t̲sap-lāk*, adj. Crushed, squashed, pressed with the foot; (Fem.) څپلاکه *t̲sap-lāka'h*. څپلاک والی *t̲saplāk wālaey*, s.m. (1st) Squashiness, softness, etc. Pl. ي *ī*. څپلاک کيدل *t̲saplāk kedal*, verb intrans. To become squashed or crushed, pressed with the foot. څپلاک کول *t̲saplāk kawul*, verb trans. To squash, to press with the foot, to crush.

څپلۍ *t̲sapla'ī*, s.f. (6th) A sandal, made generally of leather, but sometimes of a coarse grass called مزري *mazarey* by the Afg̲h̲āns about Pes̲h̲āwer. Sing. and Pl. See کنړاوه

څپوټکی *t̲sapūt̲t̲kaey*, s.m. (1st) A small turban, a sort of handkerchief or short veil worn by women when occupied in household affairs. Pl. ي *ī*. See سربسته

څپولی *t̲sapolaey*, adj. Entangled, matted (as the hair); a person with matted hair; (Fem.) څپولِ *t̲sapoli*. Pl. (Masc. and Fem.) ي *ī*. څپولی کيدل *t̲sapolaey kedal*, verb intrans. To become entangled or matted. څپولی کول *t̲sapolaey kawul*, verb trans. To make entangled.

څپه *t̲sapa'h*, adj. Inverted, upside down, topsy turvy, inversed, turned in a contrary direction. 2. s.f. (3rd) A wave, a billow, a surge, 3. A gust of wind, a blast. Pl. ې *ey*. څپه وهل *t̲sapa'h wahal*, verb trans. To roll, to strike (as a wave), to blow in gusts or puffs.

څپياکه *t̲sap-yāka'h*, s.f. (3rd) A cake of dried cow dung, a cake in general, anything flattened. Pl. ې *ey*. See څپلاک

څپيره *t̲saperæh*, adj. A greyish brown colour, earth-coloured. 2. int. May you be miserable, wretched, or may ill luck attend you; a word or term of abuse.

څپيړه *t̲saperra'h*, s.f. (3rd) A slap, a box, a buffet, a wipe, a clout, a tap, a cuff, striking with the flat of the hand. Pl. ې *ey*. څپيړه وهل *t̲saperra'h wahal*, verb trans. To slap, to box (as the ears), to buffet, to strike with the open hand. See چاپيړه

څپېدل *tsapedal*, verb intrans. To flutter, to move or flap the wings without flying, to hover. Pres. څپېږي *tsapejzī* (W.), or څپېګي *tsapegī* (E.); past وُ څپېده *wu-tsapedah*, or وُ څپېدَ *wu-tsapeda*; fut. وُ به څپېږي *wu bah tsapejzī*, or وُ به څپېګي *wu bah tsapegī*; imp. وُ څپېږه *wu-tsapejzah*, or وُ څپېګه *wu-tsapegah*; act. part. څپېدونکَي *tsapedūnkaey*, or څپېدونَي *tsapedūnaey*; past part. څپېدلَي *tsapedalaey*; verb. n. څپېدنه *tsapedana'h*. څپول *tsapawul*, verb trans. To cause to flutter, to drive in disorder. Pres. څپوي *tsapawī*; past وُ څپاوه *wu-tsapāwuh*, or وُ څپاوو *wu-tsapāwo*; fut. وُ به څپوي *wu bah tsapawī*; imp. وُ څپوه *wu-tsapawah*; act. part. څپوونکَي *tsapawūnkaey*, or څپوونَي *tsapawūnaey*; past part. څپولَي *tsapawulaey*; verb n. څپونه *tsapawuna'h*. See رپيدل

څټ *tsatt*, s.m. (2nd) The back of the neck. Pl. څټونه *tsattūnah*.

څټک *tsuttak* or *tsattak*, s m. (5th) A sledge hammer. Pl. څټکان *tsattakān*. See پلک

څټکَي *tsattakaey*, s.m. (1st) (the diminutive of the above) A small hammer. Pl. ي *ī*.

څټل *tsattal*, verb trans. To lick, to lap. Pres. څټي *tsattī*; past وُ څاټه *wu-tsāttah*, or وُ څاټَ *wu-tsātta*; fut. وُ به څټي *wu bah tsattī*; imp. وُ څټه *wu-tsattah*; act. part. څټونکَي *tsattūnkaey*, or څټونَي *tsattūnaey*; past part. څټلَي *tsattalaey*; verb. n. څټنه *tsattana'h*.

څټول *tsattawul*, verb trans. (caus.) To cause to lick or lap.

څټوټ *tsatt-watt*, s.m. (2nd) Apoplexy, sudden death. Pl. څټوټونه *tsatt-wattūnah*.

څټ وټ *tsatt watt*, adv. Suddenly, all at once, abruptly, at short notice, instanter.

څټه *tsatta'h*, s.f. (3rd) A bag of coarse cloth either of hair or hemp, a sack in general. 2. A sack-full. Pl. ې *ey*.

څڅوبَي *tsatsobaey*, s.m. (1st) The eave of a roof or wall which throws off the water. 2. A leak, dropping of water from the eaves of the roof. Pl. ي *ī*.

څڅوئِکَي *tsatsūe-kaey*, s m. (1st) A drop of water as of (rain or a tear), a sprinkling, a droplet, a minim. Pl. ي *ī*. See also څاڅکَي

څڅېدل *tsatsedal*, verb intrans. To leak, to drop, to distil, to fall, to let fall by drops. Pres. څاڅي *tsātsī*; past وُ څڅېده *wu-tsatsedah*, or وُ څڅېدَ *wu-tsatseda*; fut. وُ به څاڅي *wu bah tsātsī*; imp. وُ څاڅه *wu-tsātsah*; act. part. څڅېدونکَي *tsatsedūnkaey*, or څڅېدونَي *tsatsedūnaey*; past part. څڅېدلَي *tsatsedalaey*; verb. n. څڅېدنه *tsatsedana'h*. څڅول *tsatsawul*, verb trans. To pour, to drop, to distil, to discharge by drops. Pres. څڅوي *tsatsawī*; past وُ څڅاوه *wu-tsatsāwuh*, or وُ څڅاوو *wu-tsatsāwo*; fut. وُ به څڅوي *wu bah tsatsawī*; imp. وُ څڅوه *wu-tsatsawah*; act. part. څڅوونکَي *tsatsawūnkaey*, or څڅوونَي *tsatsawūnaey*; past part. څڅولَي *tsatsawulaey*; verb. n. څڅونه *tsatsawuna'h*. See also زهيدل and زوهيدل

څخو *tsakho*, adj. Somewhat, a few, some, something, more or less, a certain quantity or degree indeterminate, a part greater or less. 2. adv. In some degree or quantity, slightly, not much. څخو څخو *tsakho-tsakho*, A little, little by little, by degrees. See لږ and لکٔ

څخه *tsakhah*, postpos. At the side, near, at, beside, about; a word affixed to the ablative case, thus, را څخه *rā tsakhah*, near me or us; در څخه *dar tsakhah*, near thee or you; ور څخه *war tsakhah*, near him, her, it, or them; also from, etc., as له ما څخه *lah mā tsakhah*, from me; له تا څخه *lah tā tsakhah*, from thee, etc. See څنګه

څخېدل *ts'khedal*, verb intrans. To creep, to crawl, to move slowly, to advance slowly and slily, to move on all fours. Pres. څخېږي *ts'khejzī* (W.), or څخېګي *ts'khegī* (E.); past وُ څخېده *wu-ts'khedah*, or وُ څخېدَ *wu-ts'kheda*; fut. وُ به څخېږي *wu bah ts'khejzī*, or وُ به څخېګي *wa bah ts'khegī*; imp. وُ څخېږه *wu-ts'khejzah*, or وُ څخېګه *wu-ts'khegah*; act. part. څخېدونکَي *ts'khedūnkaey*, or څخېدونَي *ts'khedūnaey*; past part. څخېدلَي *ts'khedalaey*; verb. n. څخېدنه *ts'khedana'h*. څخول *ts'khawul*, verb trans. To attract, to draw along or towards one's-self, to drag, to extract, to take to one's arms. Pres. څخوي *ts'khawī*; past وُ څخاوه *wu-ts'khāwuh*, or وُ څخاوو *wu-ts'khāwo*; fut. وُ به څخوي *wu bah ts'khawī*; imp. وُ څخوه *wu-ts'khawah*; act. part. څخوونکَي *ts'khawūnkaey*, or څخووني *ts'khawūnaey*; past part. څخولَي *ts'khawulaey*; verb n. څخونه *ts'khawuna'h*. Also څکول, which see.

څر *tsar*, s.m. (9th) Forage, pasture, food. Sing. and Pl. (s चर).

څر *tsar*, s.m. (2nd) Pasture, forage, pasturing, grazing. Pl. څرونه *tsarūnah*. څريدل *tsaredal*, verb intrans. To graze, browse, crop. Pres. څري *tsarī*; past وُ څريده *wu-tsaredah*, or وُ څريدَ *wu-tsareda*; fut. وُ به څري *wu bah tsarī*; imp. وُ څره *wu-tsarah*; act. part. څريدونکَي *tsare-dūnkaey*, or څريدونَي *tsare-dūnaey*; past part. څريدلَي *tsaredalaey*; verb. n. څريدنه *tsaredana'h*. Also څر کول *tsar kawul*, or څرول *tsarawal*, verb trans. To graze, to feed or supply cattle with grass, etc., to take out for the purpose of feeding, to feed on, to tend grazing cattle. Pres. څروي *tsarawī*; past وُ څراوه *wu-tsarāwuh*, or وُ څراوو *wu-tsarāwo*; fut. وُ به څروي *wu bah tsarawī*; imp. وُ څروه *wu-tsarawah*; act. part. څروونکَي *tsarawūnkaey*, or څرووني *tsarawūnaey*; past part. څرولَي *tsarawulaey*; verb. n. څرونه *tsarawuna'h*. See پوول

څر *tsir*, s.m. (5th) The sound produced by ejection of anything liquid and in small quantities, (as in flux or diarrhœa), squirt, spurt, sputter, the sound produced from a lamp when there may be water mixed with the oil. Pl. څرهار *tsira-hār*. څر وهل *tsir wahal*, verb trans. and څريدل *tsiredal*, verb intrans. To sputter, to squirt, to eject, to emit with a sharp sound, to let fly. Pres. څريږي *tsirejzī* (W.) or څريګي *tsiregī* (E.); past وُ څريده *wu-tsiredah*, or وُ څريدَ *wu-tsireda*; fut. وُ به څريږي *wu bah tsirejzī*, or وُ به څريګي *wu bah tsiregī*; imp. وُ څريږه *wu-tsirejzah*, or وُ څريګه *wu-tsiregah*; act. part. څريدونکَي *tsiredūnkaey*, or څريدونَي *tsiredūnaey*; past part. څريدلَي *tsiredalaey*; verb. n. څريدنه *tsiredana'h*. See ريځ

څربښت *tsar-basht* (W.) or *tsar bakht* (E.) s.m. (2nd) Fatness, stoutness, corpulency, plumpness, obesity. Pl. څربښتونه *tsar-bashtūnah*, or *tsar-bakhtūnah*. See څورب

څرپ *tsrap*, s.m. (5th) A flap, or flapping (as the wings of a bird), flutter, whir, etc. Pl. څرپهار *tsrapahār*. څرپ وهل *tsrap wahal*, verb trans. or څرپيدل *tsrapedal*, verb intrans. To flap the wings, to flutter or flop, to whir (as a bird in flying). Pres. څرپيږي *tsrapejzī* (W.) or څرپيګي *tsrapegī* (E.); past وُ څرپيده *wu-tsrapedah*, or وُ څرپيدَ *wu-tsrapeda*; fut. وُ به څرپيږي *wu bah tsrapejzī*, or وُ به څرپيګي *wu bah tsrapegī*; imp. وُ څرپيږه *wu-tsrapejzah*, or وُ څرپيګه *wu-tsrapegah*; act. part. څرپيدونکَي *tsrapedūnkaey*, or څرپيدونَي *tsrapedūnaey*; past part. څرپيدلَي *tsrapedalaey*; verb. n. څرپيدنه *tsrapedana'h*. څرپول *tsrapawul*, verb trans. To flutter, to agitate, to make to flutter (as a bird). Pres. څرپوي *tsrapawī*; past وُ څرپاوه *wu-tsrapā-wuh*, or وُ څرپاوو *wu-tsrapā-wo*; fut. وُ به څرپوي *wu bah tsrapawī*; imp. وُ څرپوه *wu-tsrapawah*; act. part. څرپوونکَي *tsrapwūnkaey*, or څرپووني *tsarpawūnaey*; past part. څرپولَي *tsrapawulaey*; verb. n. څرپونه *tsrapawuna'h*.

څرخ *tsarkh*, s.m. (2nd) A wheel (particularly a potter's, or of a water-mill or well). 2. A grindstone. 3. Circular motion, turn, revolution, the act of turning. 4. Fortune, chance. 5. The heavens, the sphere, the celestial globe. 6. A kind of hawk or falcon, an eagle. 7. A stab, a puncture, a prick, a wound produced by a spear, an arrow, or the like. Pl. څرخونه *tsarkh-ūnah*; 8. adj. Punctured, pricked, pierced, stabbed; (Fem.) څرکه *tsarka'h*. څرخيدل *tsarkhedal*, verb intrans. To revolve, to turn round, to wheel. 2. To dance. Pres. څرخيږي *tsarkhejzī* (W.) or څرخيګي *tsarkhegī* (E.); past وُ څرخيده *wu-tsarkhedah* or وُ څرخيدَ *wu-tsarkheda*; fut. وُ به څرخيږي *wu bah tsarkhejzī* or وُ به څرخيګي

wu bah tsarkhegī; imp. وُ څرخيږه *wu-tsarkhejzah* or وُ څرخيګه *wu-tsarkhegah*; act. part. څرخيدونکي *tsarkhedūnkaey* or څرخيدوني *tsarkhedūnaey*; past part. څرخيدلي *tsarkhedalaey*; verb. n. څرخيدنه *tsarkhedana'h*.

څرخول *tsarkhawul*, verb trans. To turn, to make revolve, to wheel round. 2. To sharpen. Pres. څرخوي *tsarkhawī*; past وُ څرخاوه *wu-tsarkhāwuh* or وُ څرخاوو *wu-tsarkhāwo*; fut. وُ به څرخوي *wu bah tsarkhawī*; imp. وُ څرخوه *wu-tsarkhawah*; act. part. څرخوونکي *tsarkhawūnkaey* or څرخووني *tsarkhawūnaey*; past part. څرخولي *tsarkhawulaey*; verb. n. څرخونه *tsarkhawuna'h*. (P چرخ).

څرخ کول *tsarkh kawul*, verb trans. To pierce, to stab, to puncture. څرخ کيدل *tsarkh kedal*, verb intrans. To enter (as a pointed instrument), to penetrate, to stab, to pierce.

څرخه *tsarkha'h*, s.f. (3rd) A spinning-wheel, a large reel. Pl. ئ *ey*. (P چرخه).

څرخي *tsarkhaey*, s.m. (1st) A kind of reel for winding cotton on, a ball of cotton, silk, etc. 2. A species of falcon. Pl. ي *ī*. See خاشي

څرخلګي *tsarkhal-gaey*, s.m. (1st) A piece of wood, stone, etc., on which thread is wound, a reel. Pl. ي *ī*. Also څرخلرګي *tsarkhlargaey*. Pl. ي *ī*.

څرخندوکي *tsarkhandūkaey*, s.m. A tee-totum, a child's top. Pl. ي *ī*. See لادو, چرلندي and چلنغي

څرګند *tsargand*, adj. Apparent, manifest, plain, evident, obvious, clear, distinct, visible, discernible, conspicuous, exposed to view; (Fem.) څرګنده *tsarganda'h*. څرګند توب *tsargandtob*, s.m. (2nd) Pl. توبونه *tobūnah*; and څرګند والي *tsargand wālaey*, s.m. (1st) Distinctness, appearance, conspicuity, conspicuousness, visibility. Pl. ي *ī*. څرګنديدل *tsargandedal*, verb intrans. To appear, to come to sight, to be visible, to present itself, etc. to meet the view, to come out, to come to light. Pres. څرګنديږي *tsargandejzī* (W.) or څرګنديګي *tsargandegī* (E.); past څرګند شه *tsargand shah* or وُ شه *wu-shah*; fut. څرګند به شي *tsargand bah shī* or به وُ شي *bah wu-shī*; imp. څرګند شه *tsargand shah* or وُ شه *wu-shah*; act. part. څرګنديدونکي *tsargandedūnkaey* or څرګنديدوني *tsargandedūnaey*; past part. څرګند *tsargand* or څرګند شوي *tsargand shawaey*; verb. n. څرګنديدنه *tsargandedana'h*.

څرګندول *tsargandawul*, verb trans. To make visible, to show, to reveal, to disclose, to bring to view, to make to appear. Pres. څرګندوي *tsargandawī*; past څرګند کړ *tsargand karr* or وُ کړ *wu-karr*; fut. څرګند به کړي *tsargand bah krrī* or به وُ کړي *bah wu-krrī*; imp. څرګند کړه *tsargand krrah* or وُ کړه *wu-krrah*; act. part. څرګندوونکي *tsargandawūnkaey* or څرګندووني *tsargandawūnaey*; past part. څرګند کړي *tsargand karraey*; verb. n. څرګندونه *tsargandawuna'h*.

څرمښکي *tsar-masha'ī* (W.) or *tsar-makha'ī* (E.) s.f. (6th) A kind of lizard. Sing. and Pl. See چرمښکي and شرمښکي

څرمن *tsarman*, s.f. (1st) Skin, leather, the hide of an animal. Pl. څرمنِ *tsarmani*.

څرمه *tsarma'h*, s.f. (3rd) Side, margin, extremity, towards. Pl. ئ *ey*. This word is also used in some instances adverbially: as له څرمي *lah tsarmey* or له څرمي نه *lah tsarmey nah*, From beginning to end, from first to last, wholly, altogether, all in all. See my Grammar, p. 8, example 3rd; also څيلمه

څروټکه *tsarwattkah*, s.f. (3rd) A live coal, an ember, burning charcoal. Pl. ئ *ey*. See سکروټه

څريکه *tsirī-ka'h*, s.f. (3rd) A throb, a beat or strong pulsation, palpitation (as from a wound or boil), throbbing, beating. 2. A spot, a splash, a sprinkle (as of mud), a gush, flow, etc. Pl. ئ *ey*. See څريکه

څړني *tsarrna'ī*, s.f. (6th) A top knot of hair, the tuft of hair on the crown of the head of Hindūs, etc. Sing. and Pl. See څړني

څړه *tsarrah*, adj. Single, unmarried. 2. Alone, solitary. 3. Unique. 4. Light, simple, unincumbered, light as to baggage (as a force in light marching order).

څړه لار *tsarra'h lār*, s.f. (1st) A foot-path, a by-path, a narrow road impracticable for horses, etc. Pl. څره لاړِ *tsarra'h lāri*. څره وري *tsarra'h-warraey*, adj. A traveller unincumbered with baggage, or unattended; one who can travel by a foot or by-path; (Fem.) څره وړ *tsarra'h-warri*. Pl. (Masc. and Fem.) څره وړي *tsarra'h-warrī*.

څرهوات *tsarra'h-watt*, s.f. (1st). A foot-path, a narrow road for foot-passengers only. Pl. څرهواتِ *tsarrah-wātti*. See وات

څرۍ *tsarra'ī*, s.f. (6th) A top-knot, a tuft of hair on the crown of the head. Sing. and Pl. See څرني

څريكه *tsirrīka'h*, s.f. (3rd) A throb, a beat or strong pulsation or palpitation (as from a wound or boil), throbbing, beating. A spot, a splash, a sprinkle (as of mud, etc.), a gush, a flow. Pl. ې *ey*. څريكه *tsirrīkah* or څريك *tsirrīk* وهل *wahal*, verb trans. To throb, to beat, to palpitate (as a wound). 2. To gush out, to splash, to spot, to sprinkle.

څزی *tsajzaey*, s.m. (1st) The lungs, or light. Pl. ي *ī*. See څكي and سكي or سږي.

څشكلَ *tsashkala* or څشكله *tsashkalah*, adv. How? in what manner? by what means? by what mode?

څښاك *ts'shāk* (W.) or *ts'khāk* (E.) s.m. (2nd) Drink, beverage, liquor, potion. Pl. څښاكونه *ts'shākūnah* or *ts'khākūnah*. خوراك و څښاك *khwarāk ow ts'shāk* or *ts'khāk*, Food, aliment, sustenance, meat and drink.

څښتن *tsashtan* (W.) or *tsakhtan* (E.) s.m. (5th) A master, a lord, a possessor, a proprietor, an owner. Pl. څښتنان *tsáshtanān* (W.) or *tsakhtanān* (E.) څښتنه *tsashtana'h* or *tsakhtana'h*, s.f. (3rd) A lady, a mistress, a proprietress. Pl. ې *ey*. څښتن كول *tsashtan* or *tsakhtan kawul*, verb trans. To marry (as a woman), to take a husband. See تښتن

څښتيدل *tsashtedal* (W.) or *tsakhtedal* (E.), verb intrans. To fly, to flee, to escape, to take to flight, to retreat, to elope, to run away, to decamp. Pres. څښتي *tsashtī* or *tsakhtī*; past وُ څښتيده *wu-tsashtedah* or *wu-tsakhtedah*, or وُ څښتيدَ *wu-tsashteda* or *wu-tsakhteda*; fut. وُ به څښتي *wu bah tsashtī* or *wu bah tsakhtī*; imp. وُ څښته *wu-tsashtah* or *wu-tsakhtah*; act. part. څښتيدونكي *tsashtedūnkaey* or *tsakhtedūnkaey* or څښتيدوني *tsashtedūnaey* or *tsakhtedūnaey*; past part. څښتيدلي *tsashtedalaey* or *tsakhtedalaey*; verb. n. څښتيدنه *tsashtedana'h* or *tsakhtedana'h*. See تښتيدل.

څښتول *tsashtawul* (W.) or *tsakhtawul* (E.) verb trans. To cause to flee, to put to flight, to cause to decamp, etc. Pres. څښتوي *tsashtawī* or *tsakhtawī*; past وُ څښتاوه *wu-tsashtāwuh* or *wu-tsakhtāwuh* or وُ څښتاوو *wu-tsashtāwo* or *wu-tsakhtāwo*; fut. وُ به څښتوي *wu bah tsashtawī* or *wu bah tsakhtawī*; imp. وُ څښتوه *wu-tsashtawah* or *wu-tsakhtawah*; act. part. څښتوونكي *tsashtawūnkaey* or *tsakhtawūnkaey* or څښتووني *tsashtawūnaey* or *tsakhtawūnaey*; past part. څښتولي *tsashtawulaey* or *tsakhtawulaey*; verb. n. څښتونه *tsashtawuna'h* or *tsakhtawuna'h*. See تښتول

څښكله *tsash-kalah*, adv. (W.) How? in what manner? by what mode or means? See څشكله and سشكله

څښكو *tsash-kū* (W.) or *tsakh-kū* (E.), s.m. (9th) A black seed used in medicine, a remedy for sore eyes. Sing. and Pl. See also څكشو (چاكسو P).

څښكوړي *tsashkorraey* (W.) or *tsakhkorraey* (E.) s.m. (1st) The skin or hide of an animal in general. Pl. ي *ī*. See څرمي

څښل *ts'shal* (W.), verb trans. To drink, to quaff, to imbibe, to drink up. Pres. څښي *ts'shī*; past وُ څښل *wu-ts'shal*; fut. وُ به څښي *wu bah ts'shī*; imp. وُ څښه *wu-ts'shah*; act. part. څښونكي *ts'shūnkaey* or څښوني *ts'shūnaey*; past part. څښلي *ts'shalaey*; verb. n. څښنه *ts'shana'h*. See سكل and څكل

څك *tsak*, adj. Straight, unbent, regular, undistorted; (Fem.) څكه *tsakah*.

څكشو *tsakshū*, s.m. (9th) A black seed used in medicine. Sing. and Pl. See څښكو

څكل *tskal*, verb trans. To drink. See څښل and سكل

څكندن *tsakindan*, s.m. (2nd) Taste, tasting, flavour, savour, relish. Pl. ځکندنونه *tsakindan-ūnah*. See preceding. ځکندن وهل *tsakindan wahal*, verb trans. To taste, to flavour, to try by eating a little, to eat a little of.

ځکول *tskawul*, verb trans. To cause to drink, suck, inhale, to water (as cattle). 2. To lengthen, to stretch, to unsheathe. Pres. ځکوي *tskawī*; past وُ ځکاوه *wu-tskāwuh*, or وُ ځکاوو *wu-tskāwo*; fut. وُ به ځکوي *wu bah tskawī*; imp. وُ ځکوه *wu-tskawah*; act. part. ځکوونکَي *tskawūnkaey*, or ځکوونَي *tskawūnaey*; past part. ځکولَي *tskawulaey*; verb. n. ځکونه *tskawuna'h*.

ځکولي *tsakolaey*, s.m. (1st) The hide or skin of any animal. Pl. ي *ī*. See څهکوري

ځکوندل *tskonddal*, verb trans. To pinch, to squeeze. Pres. ځکوندي *tskonddī*; past وُ ځکونده *wu-tskonddah*, or وُ ځکوندَ *wu-tskondda*; fut. وُ به ځکوندي *wu bah tskonddī*; imp. وُ ځکونده *wu-tskonddah*; act. part. ځکوندونکَي *tskonddūnkaey*, or ځکوندونَي *tskonddūnaey*; past part. ځکوندلَي *tskondd-alaey*; verb. n. ځکوندنه *tskonddana'h*.

ځکه *tsakah*, s.f. (3rd) Taste, flavour, relish, savour, tasting. Pl. ئ *ey*. 2. A cliff, a precipice. ځکل *tsakal*, verb trans. To taste, to savour, to flavour. Pres. ځکي *tsakī*; past وُ ځاکه *wu-tsākah*, or وُ ځاکَ *wu-tsāka*; fut. وُ به ځکي *wu bah tsakī*; imp. وُ ځکه *wu-tsakah*; act. part. ځکونکَي *tsak-ūnkaey*, or ځکونَي *tsakūnaey*; past part. ځکلَي *tsakalaey*; verb. n. ځکنه *tsakana'h*.

ځکه *tskah*, adv. So, then, therefore, in like manner, thus, on these terms, well, the fact being such, etc. See سکه

ځکي *tsakaey*, s.m. (1st) A rope or line suspended from the roof of a house for hanging clothes on. Pl. ي *ī*.

ځکيدل *tskedal*, verb intrans. To crawl, to creep, to move along slowly. Pres. ځکيږي *tskejzī* (W.) or ځکيګي *tskegī* (E.); past وُ ځکيده *wu-tskedah*, or وُ ځکيدَ *wu-tskeda*; fut. وُ به ځکيږي *wu bah tskejzī*, or وُ به ځکيګي *wu bah tskegī*; imp. وُ ځکيږه *wu-tskejzah*, or وُ ځکيګه *wu-tskegah*; act. part. ځکيدونکَي *tskedūnkaey*, or ځکيدونَي *tskedūnaey*; past part. ځکيدلَي *tskedalaey*; verb. n. ځکيدنه *tskedana'h*.

ځګَي *tsagaey*, s.m. (1st) The lungs or lights. 2. A word used in calling or driving cattle. Pl. ي *ī*. See also ځري and سکي

ځلور *tsalor*, adj. Four; ځلورم *tsaloram*, The fourth; (Fem.) ځلورمه *tsalorama'h*. ځوار لس or ځور *tswar* or *tswār las*, Fourteen. ځلير ويشت *tsaler wīsht*, or ځلر ويشت *tsalir wīsht*, Twenty-four. ځلور ديرش *tsalor dersh*, Thirty-four. ځلور ځلويښت *tsalor tsalwesht*, or *tsal-wekht*, Forty-four. ځلور پنځوس *tsalor pindzos*, Fifty-four. ځلور شپيته *tsalor shpetah*, Sixty-four. ځلور اويا *tsalor ow-yā*, Seventy-four; ځلور اتيا *tsalor atīyā*, Eighty-four. ځلور نوِ or نيوي *tsalor-nawi* or *nīwī*, Ninety-four. ځوار لسم or ځور *tswar* or *tswār-lasam*, The fourteenth; (Fem.) ځوار لسمه *tswār-lasama'h*, etc.

ځلويښت *tsalwesht* (W.) or *tsalwekht* (E.) adj. Forty. يو ځلويښت *yow tsalwesht*, or *tsalwekht*, Forty-one. دو ځلويښت *do tsal-wesht* or *tsal-wekht*, Forty-two, etc.

ځلويښتي *tsalweshtī* (W.) or *tsalwekhtī* (E.) s.f. (3rd) The forty days after child-birth. Pl. ئِي *a'ī*. 2. s.m. (5th) A magistrate elected by the Maliks and heads of families amongst the tribes of Dāmān. They were at first designed to make up the number of forty, hence the name. The president, when they are in any number, is called the Mīr. See Elphinstone's "Kābul," vol. ii., p. 74. Pl. ځلويښتيان *tsalweshtīān* or *tsalwekhtīān*.

ځله *tsila'h*, s f. (3rd) Forty days of extreme heat, cold, or rain, in their respective seasons. 2. A period of forty days, during which the religious fraternities of the East pass their time in fasting and prayer. Pl. ئ *ey*. (P چله)

ځلَي *tsalaey*, s.m. (1st) A ring for the finger. 2. A pillar of mud or stones as a mark for land. 3. A butt or mark for arrows. 4. A mound or platform for watching a field. 5. A temporary building or shed. Pl. ي *ī*. See منا

ځليبښ tsalesh (W.) or tsalekh (E.) s.m. (2nd) Glue, starch, etc. 2. Stickiness, gumminess, adhesiveness, cohesion. Pl. ځليبښونه tsaleshūnah or tsalekhūnah. ځليبښ ناك tsalesh-nāk or tsalekh-nāk, adj. Sticky, adhesive, viscous, clammy, glutinous, etc.; (Fem.) ځليبښ ناكه tsalesh-nāka'h or tsalekh-nāka'h; also ځليښت tsalesht (W.) or tsalekht (E.); and ځليخت tsalekht, s.m. (2nd). Pl. ځليختونه tsalekhtūnah. See سليبښ , سليخ and سليښت

ځمڅي tsamtsa'ī, s.f. (6th) A ladle made of wood, brass, or iron. Sing. and Pl. (P چمچه). See كړيڅي , كاچوغه and خونځي

ځملاستل tsam-lāstal, verb intrans. To lie down, to recline, to repose, to be recumbent. Pres. ځملي tsamlī; past ځملاست tsamlāst; fut. وُ به ځملي wu bah tsamlī; imp. ځمله tsamlah; act. part. ځملاستونكي tsamlāstūnkaey, or ځملاستوني tsamlāstūnaey; past part. ځملاستلي tsamlāstalaey; verb. n. ځملاستنه tsamlāstana'h. ځملول tsamlawul, verb trans. To make recline, to put to rest, to make lie down. Pres. ځملوي tsamlawī; past وُ ځملاوه wu-tsamlāwuh, or وُ ځملاوو wu-tsamlāwo; fut. وُ به ځملوي wu bah tsamlawī; imp. وُ ځملوه wu-tsamlawah; act. part. ځملوونكي tsamlawūnkaey, or ځملووني tsamlawūnaey; past part. ځملولي tsamlawulaey; verb. n. ځملونه tsamlawuna'h.

ځميار tsam-yār, s.m. (5th) A tanner, a currier. Pl. ځمياران tsam-yārān. See چميار

ځند tsandd, s.m. (9th) Shake, agitation, waving motion. Sing. and Pl. په ځند وهل pah tsandd wahal, verb trans. To shake, to agitate; or ځندل tsanddal, To shake, to clean by shaking, to agitate. Pres. ځندي tsanddī; past وُ ځانده wu-tsānddah, or وُ ځاندَ wu-tsāndda; fut. وُ به ځندي wu bah tsanddī; imp. وُ ځنده wu-tsanddah; act. part. ځندونكي tsanddūnkaey, or ځندوني tsanddūnaey; past part. ځندلي tsanddalaey; verb. n. ځندنه tsanddana'h.

ځنده tsandda'h, s.f. (3rd) Side, brim, edge, brink, margin, rim, verge, fringe, edging, hem. Pl. ي ey.

ځنده وهل tsandda'h wahal, verb trans. To shake, to toss, to agitate. 2. To jerk, to twitch, to pull or snatch away (as a garment). See ځندل

ځنگ tsang, s.m. (2nd) The side, the flank. Pl. ځنگونه tsangūnah. ځنگ په ځنگ tsang pah tsang, adv. Side by side, abreast. See اړخ

ځنگل tsangal, s.m. (1st) The arm from the elbow to the wrist, or to the end of the fingers. Pl. ځنگل tsangali. Also ځنگله tsangala'h, s.f. (3rd). Pl. ي ey.

ځنگه tsangah, adv. How? in what manner? by what means? in what state? It is also used in exclamation, as "How are the mighty fallen!"

ځنړكه tsarrnaka'h, s.f. (3rd) A ringlet, a side lock, a curl, a lock of hair. Pl. ي ey. Also ځنړه tsurrna'h, s.f. (3rd). Pl. ي ey, and څونړه, which see.

څو tso, adj. Any, some, something, somewhat, a little. 2. adv. and prep. Till, until, to the event mentioned, or the time of it. څو څو tso-tso, Various, several, different, manifold, diverse. څو چند tso chand, A great number, several, manifold. څو شان tso shān, or څو طور tso taur, etc. Various modes, different ways or conditions. څومره tsomrah, How much? what quantity? څوني tsoney, How much? په څو څو رنگَ pah tso tso ranga, In various ways, of different colours, in divers ways, etc. په څو شانَ pah tso shāna, In different conditions or states, in various modes, manners, or fashions. په څو قسمَ pah tso ḳisma, Of, or in divers sorts, species, etc. تر څو or تر څو پوري tar tso or tar tso porī, How long? till when? ته څو or ته څو پوري tah tso or tah tso porī, How long? till when? to what time? هر څو har tso, How much soever, to whatever degree, etc.

څوارلس or څور tswar or tswār-las, adj. Fourteen. څوارلسم or څور tswar or tswār lasam, The fourteenth; (Fem.) څور لسمه tswar-lasama'h, etc.

څوب tswab, s.m. (2nd) Longing, hankering, eagerness, anxiety, yearning, mania, passion, craving. Pl. څوبونه tswabūnah. څوب لرل tswab laral, verb trans. To have a longing or hankering after anything, to yearn after, to crave.

څوباړی tsobārraey, s.m. (1st) A wooden instrument used by washermen for beating clothes. Pl. ي ī.

څوټ tsott, s.m. (2nd) Attack, onset, charge, onslaught, sally, raid, foray, sortie, etc. Pl. څوټونه tsott-ūnah. څوټ کول tsott kawul, verb trans. To attack, to charge, to assault, to make a sortie, onslaught, etc.

څوڅه tsūtsa'h, s.f. (3rd) A porpoise. Pl. ې ey. (سوس s).

څورب tsorb; adj. Fat, stout, corpulent, plump, in good condition. Pl. څاربه tsārba'h; (Fem.) څربه tsarba'h. Pl. څربې tsarbey. څورب تیا tsorb tī'ā, s.f. (6th) (E.) Sing. and Pl.; or (W.) Pl. تیاوي tī-ā-wī; or څورب والی tsorb wālaey, s.m. (1st) Plumpness, fatness, corpulence. Pl. ي ī. څربیدل tsarbedal, verb intrans. To become fat, stout, or plump, to fatten. Pres. څربیږي tsarbejzī (W.) or څربیګي tsarbegī (E.); past څورب شه tsorb shah or ؤ شه wu-shah; fut. څورب به شي tsorb bah shī or به ؤ شي bah wu-shī; imp. څورب شه tsorb shah or ؤ شه wu-shah; act. part. څربیدونکی tsarbedūnkaey or څربیدونی tsarb-edūnaey; past part. څورب شوی tsorb or څورب tsorb shawaey; verb. n. څربیدنه tsarbedana'h. څربول tsarbawul, verb trans. To fatten, to make fat, to make plump. Pres. څربوي tsarbawī; past څورب کړ tsorb karr or ؤ کړ wu-karr; fut. څورب به کړي tsorb bah krrī or به ؤ کړي bah wu-krrī; imp. څورب کړه tsorb krrah or ؤ کړه wu-krrah; act. part. څربوونکی tsarbawūnkaey or څربوونی tsarb-awūnaey; past part. څورب کړی tsorb karraey; verb. n. څربونه tsarbawuna'h.

څورلی tswurlaey, s.m. (1st) A gimlet, an auger. Pl. ي ī.

څورنګ tsowrang, adj. Thrashed, bruised, beaten, drubbed, cudgeled. څورنګ کول tsowrang kawul, verb trans., or څورنګول tsowrangawul, verb trans. To thrash, to beat, to drub, to bruise, to cudgel. Pres. څورنګوي tsowrangawī; past څورنګ کړ tsowrang karr or ؤ کړ wu-karr; fut. څورنګ به کړي tsowrang bah krrī or به ؤ کړي bah wu-krrī; imp. څورنګ کړه tsowrang krrah or ؤ کړه wu-krrah; act. part. څورنګوونکی tsowrangawūnkaey or څورنګوونی tsowrangawūnaey; past څورنګ کړی tsowrang karraey; verb. n. څورنګونه tsowrangawuna'h.

څورنګونه tsowrangawunah, s.f. (3rd) (verb. n.) Pl. ې ey; or څورنګ تیا tsowrang tī'ā, s.f. (6th) A thrashing, a beating, a drubbing, a cudgeling. (E.) Sing. and Pl., (W.) Pl. تیاوي tī'āwī; or څورنګ توب tsowrang-tob, s.m. (2nd), Pl. توبونه tobūnah; and څورنګ والی tsowrang wālaey, s.m. (1st), Pl. والي wālī.

څوری tsowraey, s.m. (1st) Provisions for a journey. Pl. ي ī. See توشه and توښه

څور tsorr, adj. Crooked, crump, wry. 2. A bullock with crumpled horns; (Fem.) څوړه tsorra'h.

څوړی tsorraey, adj. as s.m. (1st) A bullock with his horns curling downwards over his ears. Pl. ي ī. څوړئ tsorra'ī, s.f. (6th) A cow as above. Sing. and Pl.

څوښئ tso-sha'ī (W.) or tso-kha'ī (E.) s.f. (6th) The spout of a vessel, a pipe, a tube, the pipe or spout of an ewer. 2. The penis of a boy. Sing. and Pl. Also څوښه tso-sha'h or tso-kha'h, s.f. (3rd), Pl. ې ey.

څوښکه tsūshka'h (W.) or tsūkhka'h (E.) s.f. (3rd) The spout or pipe of an ewer, a tube, a pipe. Pl. ې ey.

څوښکی tsūshkaey (W.) or tsūkhkaey (E.) s.m. (1st) A spout, etc. See preceding. Pl. ي ī.

څوښه tso-sha'h (W.) or tso-kha'h (E.) s.f. (3rd) The penis of a boy. Pl. ې ey. See چولک

څوک tsok, An interrogative pronoun applied chiefly to persons, and rarely to inanimate things—Who? which? what? It is both Masc. and Fem., Sing. and Pl., and becomes چا chā in the oblique cases. هر څوک har tsok, Whoever, whichever, or whatever.

څوکه tsūka'h, s.f. (3rd) The point of anything, the peak of a mountain, a beak, a snout, a proboscis, the nozzle. Pl. ې ey. څوکه دار tsūka'h dār, adj. Pointed, acute, peaked, spiked; (Fem.) څوکه داره tsū-ka'h dāra'h.

څوکۍ tsoka'ī, s.f. (6th) A post where a guard is stationed, a station-house. 2. Guard or watch, watching. 3. Binding one's-self by a vow to visit or perform some duty at a shrine. Sing. and Pl. څوکۍ آخستل tsoka'ī ākhistal, verb trans. To make a vow to visit some shrine until one's wishes are fulfilled. (HI چوکي). څوکۍ کول tsoka'ī kawul, verb trans. To keep watch, to keep guard. څوکيدار tsokī-dār, s.m. (5th) A watchman, a guard, a policeman. Pl. څوکيداران tsokī-dārān.

څول tswal, adj. Torn, rent; (Fem.) څوله tswala'h; 2. s.m. (2nd) A piece, a portion, a bit, a fragment, a morsel. Pl. څولونه tswalūnah. څول څول tswal-tswal, adj. In tatters, in bits, in pieces, in rags.

څومره tsomrah, adv. How much? what quantity? etc. Also څوني tsonī or tsoney.

څونځۍ tson-tsa'ī, s.f. (6th) A spoon or ladle made of wood, iron, or brass. Sing. and Pl. See ځمڅۍ, کاچوغه, and کربڅۍ

څوني tsonī or tsoney, adv. How much? what quantity? See څومره

څوړنه tsūrrna'h, s.f. (3rd) A curl, a ringlet, a side lock, a lock of hair. Pl. ې ey. See also څنرکه

څوی tsawaey, s.m. (1st) An ambush, ambuscade, retreat, cover, lurking-hole. Pl. ي ī. څوی کول tsawaey kawul, verb trans. To lay an ambuscade, to lie in ambush, to lurk or lie in wait for.

څه tsah, A pronoun used both in an interrogative as well as in an indefinite sense, What? or a, an, any, some, etc. Sing. and Pl. هرڅه har tsah, pron. Whatever, whatsoever. څه چه tsah chih or څچه tsachih, Whatsoever that, whatever that. څه دی tsah daey, Who is it? what is it? څه دپاره tsah da-pārah, adv. Why? wherefore? for what reason? on what account? څه رنګه tsah rangah or څنګه tsangah, adv. How? in what manner? by what means? in what state or condition? څه شو tsah shū, adv. What matter? of what consequence is it? no matter, never mind. څه ښه tsah shah (W.) or tsah khah (E.) interj. How good! how fine! how excellent! څه قدر tsah kadar, adv. How much? how many? څه لره tsah larah or څلره tsalarah, or څه له tsah lah, adv. Why? on what account? wherefore? په څه pah tsah, adv. For what reason? wherefore? څه شکل tsah sh'kal, or په څه رنګه pah tsah rangah, or څنګه tsangah, adv. How? in what manner? after what mode, method, wise, fashion? etc.

څه tsah, s.m. (5th) A well. Pl. څهان tsahān. See څاه

څهره tsihra'h, s.f. (3rd) Face, visage, image, countenance. Pl. ې ey. (P چهره).

څيخل tse-khal, verb trans. To thrust, to probe, to stab, to pink, to stuff into, to cram, to force or ram in, to press or squeeze into, etc. Pres. څيخي tsekhī; past و څيخه wu-tsekhah or و څيخ wu-tsekha; fut. و به څيخي wu bah tsekhī; imp. و څيخه wu-tsekhah; act. part. څيخونکی tsekhūnkaey or څيخونی tsekhūnaey; past. part. څيخلی tsekhalaey; verb. n. څيخنه tsekhana'h. See سيخل

څير tser, adj. Similar, like, resembling, analogous, alike, near, something like, such like, etc. It is for the most part used with the preposition په pah before it. See غند, شان, and دود

څيره tse-ra'h, s.f. (3rd) A scarecrow. Pl. ې ey.

څيره tsīra'h, s.f. (3rd) An incision, a cut, a slit, a strip, a ribbon, a slip, a shred. Pl. څيرې tsīrey. څيره جورول tsīra'h jorrawul, verb trans. To divide into slips or shreds, to tear into strips or ribbons. څيرې tsīrey, adj. Torn into strips, split, torn in shreds. څيريدل tsīredal, verb intrans. To be torn, rent, or lacerated, to be torn in shreds or ribbons.

Pres. ځیریږي *tsīrejzī* (W.) or ځیریګي *tsīregī* (E.); past ځیري شه *tsīrey shah* or وُ شه *wu shah*; fut. ځیري به شي *tsīrey bah shī* or به وُ شي *bah wu shī*; imp. ځیري شه *tsīrey shah* or وُ شه *wu-shah*; act. part. ځیریدونکَي *tsīredūnkaey* or ځیریدونَي *tsīredūnaey*; past part. ځیري شوَي *tsīrey shawaey*; verb. n. ځیریدنه *tsīredana'h.*

ځیرول *tsīrawul,* or ځیري کول *tsīrey kawul,* verb trans. To rend, to tear, to lacerate, to divide. ځیرل *tsīral,* verb trans. To rend, to tear, to lacerate, to tear asunder. Pres. ځیري *tsīrī*; past وُ ځیره *wu-tsīrah,* or وُ ځیرَ *wu-tsīra*; fut. وُ به ځیري *wu bah tsīrī*; imp. وُ ځیره *wu-tsīrah*; act. part. ځیرونکَي *tsīrūnkaey,* or ځیرونَي *tsīrūnaey*; past part. ځیرلَي *tsīralaey*; verb. n. ځیرنه *tsīrana'h.*

ځیړه *tsīṛra'h,* s.f. (3rd) A line of men arranged in small knots or parties for battle or for hunting, either halted or walking. Pl. ئ *ey.* په ځیړه تلل *pah tsīṛra'h t'lal,* verb intrans. To move in a line as above.

ځیز *tsīz,* s.m. (2nd) A thing, an object, an article, matter, commodity. Pl. ځیزونه *tsīzūnah.* (P چیز). په لږ څه ځیز *pah lajz tsah tsīz,* For, or with a trifle, a rush, a small matter, a bulrush, etc.

ځیښته *tsekhta'h,* s.f. (3rd) Flight, fleeing, decampment, retreat, running away. Pl. ئ *ey.* ځیښتیدل *tsekhtedal,* verb intrans. To fly, to flee, to decamp, to run away. ځیښتول *tsekhtawul,* verb trans. To put to flight, to cause to fly, to cause to retreat. See ښتیدل for inflections.

ځیښل *tseshal* (W.) verb trans. To drink, to imbibe, to quaff. Pres. ځیښي *tseshī*; past وُ ځیښه *wu-tseshah,* or وُ ځیښَ *wu-tsesha*; fut. وُ به ځیښي *wu bah tseshī*; imp. وُ ځیښه *wu-tseshah*; act. part. ځیښونکَي *tseshūnkaey,* or ځیښونَي *tseshūnaey*; past part. ځیښلَي *tseshalaey;* verb.n. ځیښنه *tseshana'h.* See ښل

ځیلمه *tselma'h,* s.f. (3rd) Side, margin, extremity, towards. Pl. ئ *ey.* This word is at times used adverbially, as له ځیلمي *lah tselmey,* or له ځیلمي نه *lah tselmey nah,* From beginning to end, from first to last, wholly, altogether, entirely, all in all. See also خرمه

ځینځښ *tsīndzakh,* s.m. (2nd) or (5th) (E.) A bull frog. Pl. ځینځښونه *tsīndzakhūnah,* or ځینځښان *tsīndzakhān.* s.f. (3rd) ځینځښه *tsīndzakha'h.* Pl. ئ *ey.*

ځینګښ *tsīngakh* (E.) or *tsīngash* (W.), s.m. (2nd) A frog. Pl. ځینګښونه *tsīngakhūnah,* or *tsīngashūnah.* s.f. (3rd) ځینګښه *tsīngakha'h.* Pl. ئ *ey.* See چنګښه

ج

ج *jīm,* the fifth letter of the Arabic, and the sixth of the Persian, is the eighth of the Pushto alphabet. It stands for three in arithmetic, and is equivalent to English *j* in the word 'judge.' In Persian and Arabic it is sometimes interchangeable with ژ, ز, ش, and sometimes چ. In Pushto it is interchangeable with ځ *dze* and ږ *jze.*

A جابر *jā-bir,* s.m. (5th) (from جبر) A despot, a tyrant. Pl. جابران *jābirān*; s.f. (3rd) جابره *jābira'h.* Pl. ئ *ey.*

S جاپ *jāp,* s.m. (2nd) Muttering one's prayers, reciting to one's-self, a recitation. Pl. جاپونه *jāpūnah.*

جات *jāt,* A termination or affix added to Persian and Arabic words ending in ه to denote the plural; thus, میوه جات *mewah-jāt,* Fruits.

P جادو *jādū,* s.m. (9th) Enchantment, incantation, juggling, conjuring. Sing. and Pl. جادو کول *jādū kawul,* verb trans. To conjure, to juggle, to charm, to enchant, to practice incantations. جادوګر *jādū-gar,* s.m. (5th) A conjurer, a juggler, an enchanter, a wizard, a magician, a sorcerer. Pl. جادوګران *jādū-garān*; s.f. (3rd) جادوګره *jādūgara'h,* A witch, a sorceress, an enchantress. Pl. ئ *ey.* جادوګري *jādū-garī,* s.f. (3rd) Magic, sorcery, necromancy, enchantment. Pl. ئ *a'ī.*

جادئي *jā<u>dd</u>a'ī*, s.f. (6th) An old female camel very thin and ugly. Applied to old women also. Sing. and Pl.

جار *jār*, s.m. (2nd) A proclamation, notification, announcement, hue and cry. Pl. جارونه *jārūnah*. جار وهل *jār wahal*, verb trans. To make proclamation, to notify, to proclaim, to publish, to advertise. جارچي *jār<u>ch</u>ī*, s.m. (5th) A herald, a crier, a pursuivant. Pl. جارچيان *jār<u>ch</u>ī-ān*. جارچي باشي *jār<u>ch</u>ī bā<u>sh</u>ī*, A head pursuivant, a herald. Pl. جارچي باشيان *jār<u>ch</u>ī bā<u>sh</u>īān*.

جار *jār*, s.m. (9th) Sacrifice, consecration, redemption, offering, oblation, victim, devoting one's-self to save or preserve another, ransom, cartel, exchange. Sing. and Pl. See خار. جاريدل *jāredal*, verb intrans. To be sacrificed or devoted, to sacrifice one's-self. Pres. جاريږي *jārejzī* (W.) or جاريگي *jāregī* (E.); past جار شه *jār <u>sh</u>ah*, or وُ شه *wu-<u>sh</u>ah*; fut. جار به شي *jār bah <u>sh</u>ī*, or به وُ شي *bah wu-<u>sh</u>ī*; imp. جار شه *jār <u>sh</u>ah*, or وُ شه *wu-<u>sh</u>ah*; act. part. جاريدونکَي *jāre-dūnkaey*, or جاريدونَي *jāre-dūnaey*; past part. جار شوَي *jār <u>sh</u>awaey*; verb. n. جاريدنه *jāre-dana'h*. جارول *jārawul*, To sacrifice, to devote, to offer as an oblation, to make a victim of, to victimize. Pres. جاروي *jārawī*; past جار کړ *jār ka<u>rr</u>*, or وُ کړ *wu-ka<u>rr</u>*; fut. جار به کړي *jār bah k<u>rr</u>ī*, or به وُ کړي *bah wu-k<u>rr</u>ī*; imp. جار کړه *jār k<u>rr</u>ah*, or وُ کړه *wu-k<u>rr</u>ah*; act. part. جاروونکَي *jārawūnkaey*, or جاروونَي *jārawūnaey*; past part. جار کړَي *jār ka<u>rr</u>aey*; verb. n. جارونه *jārawuna'h*.

جارو *jārū*, s.m. (5th) A broom, a besom. Pl. جاروگان *jārūgān*. (P جاروب). جارو کول *jārū kawul*, verb trans. To sweep, to brush out.

جارواته *jār-wātah*, s.m. (6th) (verb .n.) Return, returning, retrogression, the act of coming or going back. Sing. and Pl. See جاروتنه

جاروتل *jār-watal*, verb intrans. To return, to come or go back, to retrograde, to revert, to come again, to turn back. Pres. جاروزي *jārwuzī*; past وُ جارووت *wu-jārwot*, or وُ جاروت *wu-jārwut*, or وُ جاروت *wu-jārwat*; fut. وُ به جاروزي *wu bah jārwuzī*; imp. وُ جاروزه *wu-jārwuzah*; act. part. جاروتونکَي *jārwatūnkaey*, or جاروتونَي *jārwatūnaey*; past part. جاروتلَي *jārwatalaey*, or جاروتَي *jārwataey*; verb. n. جاروتنه *jārwatana'h*, or جارواته *jārwātah*.

جاروتنه *jārwatana'h*, s.f. (3rd) (verb. n.) Returning, return, retrogression, the act of coming or going back. Pl. ئ *ey*. See also جارواته

جارول *jārawul*, verb trans. To collect the threads together previously to preparing the web in weaving. Pres. جاروي *jārawī*; past جار کړ *jār ka<u>rr</u>* or وُ کړ *wu-ka<u>rr</u>*; fut. جار به کړي *jār bah k<u>rr</u>ī* or به وُ کړي *bah wu-k<u>rr</u>ī*; imp. جار کړه *jār k<u>rr</u>ah* or وُ کړه *wu-k<u>rr</u>ah*; act. part. جاروونکَي *jārawūnkaey* or جاروونَي *jārawūnaey*; past part. جار کړَي *jār ka<u>rr</u>aey*; verb. n. جارونه *jārawuna'h*.

جار ياسته *jār-yāstah*, s.m. (6th) (verb. n.) Diversion, diverting, turning aside, bringing or turning back, causing to retrograde, etc. Sing. and Pl. See جاريستنه

جاريستل *jār-yastal*, verb trans. To divert, to turn aside, to bring or turn back, to turn aside from a thing or matter, to cause to retrograde or recede. Pres. جارباسي *jār-bāsī*; past وُ جاريوست *wu-jār-yost* or جاريست *jār-yast*; fut. وُ به جارباسي *wu bah jār-bāsī*; imp. جارباسه *jār-bāsah* or وُ جارباسه *wu-jār-bāsah*; act. part. جاريستونکَي *jār-yastūnkaey* or جاريستونَي *jār-yastūnaey*; past part. جاريستلَي *jār-yastalaey*; verb.n. جاريستنه *jār-yastana'h*.

جاريستنه *jār-yastana'h*, s.f. (3rd)(verb.n.) Diversion, diverting, turning aside, bringing or turning back, causing to retrograde, etc. Pl. ئ *ey*. Also جارياسته, which see.

A جاري *jārī*, adj. Running, flowing, proceeding, current, usual. جاري کول *jārī kawul*, verb trans. To begin, to set on foot, to introduce (custom), to issue or put in force (an order). جاري كيدل *jārī kedal*, verb intrans. To flow, to issue. 2. To pass current, to prevail, to be in force, to proceed (as business or work).

جاړ *jāṟṟ*, s.m. (2nd) A wood, a patch of bushes, a brake, underwood. Pl. جاړونه *jāṟṟūnah*. (HI جهاړ).

جاړه *jāṟṟa'h*, s.f. (3rd) A bush, a bramble, any thorny shrub (such as the wild Ber or Jujube), etc. Pl. ي *ey*. (HI جهاړي).

A جاسوس *jāsūs*, s.m. (5th) A spy, an emissary. Pl. جاسوسان *jāsūsān*.

جاسوسي *jāsūsī*, s.f. (3rd) The action or business of a spy, spying. Pl. ئي *a'ī*. جاسوسي كول *jāsūsī kawul*, verb trans. To act the spy.

P جاگير *jāgīr*, s.m. (2nd) Land granted by the ruling power as a reward for services or as a fee, a fief, a pension, a grant. Pl. جاگيرونه *jāgīr-ūnah*. جاگيردار *jāgīr-dār*, s.m. (5th) A feoffee, the holder of a *jāgīr* or grant. Pl. جاگيرداران *jāgīr-dār-ān*; s.f. (3rd) جاگيرداره *jāgīr-dāra'h*. Pl. ي *ey*.

S جال *jāl*, s.m. (2nd) A net, a sash. Pl. جالونه *jālūnah*. 2. adj. Forged, counterfeit. (A جعل). See تور

A جالوت *jālūt*, s. prop. The Muḥammadan name for Goliath.

جاله *jāla'h*, s.f. (3rd) The nest of a bird. 2. A raft of wood or inflated hides. 3. A large coarse sheet used for catching mulberries in. 4. (S جالي) Lace used for veils. Pl. جالي *jāley*. See ځاله

جالئ *jāla'ī*, s.f. (6th) Cobweb. Sing. and Pl.

P جام *jām*, s.m. (2nd) A cup, a goblet, a glass, a bowl, a drinking vessel. Pl. جامونه *jām-ūnah*. جام جم *jām-i-jam*, s.m. (2nd) The mirror of Jamshīd, which showed him all he wished to see. ډك جام *ḍḍak jām*, s.m. (2nd) A bumper. Pl. ډك جامونه *ḍḍak-jāmūnah*.

جامباز *jāmbāz*, s.m. (5th) A rough draught camel, unused to the riding saddle. Pl. جامبازان *jāmbāzān*; s.f. (3rd) جامبازه *jām-bāza'h*. Pl. ي *ey*. See جمبازه and جنبازه

P جامداني *jāmadānī*, s.f. (3rd) A kind of muslin in which the flowers are wove and not worked in. Pl. ئي *a'ī*.

A جامع *jāmiʿ*, act. part. (from جمع) Completing, comprehending, collecting; a collector, a compiler, compriser. 2. adj. All, universal, whole, collective. 3. A synagogue, a mosque or cathedral, where the prayer called the خطبه *khuṭba'h* is read on Fridays.

P جامه *jāma'h*, s.f. (3rd) A garment, robe, dress. 2. The jaw-bone. Pl. ي *ey*. جامه وار *jāma'h-wār*, adj. Enough for a suit or *jāma'h*, fit to make clothes of.

جامه ټولول *jāma'h ṭṭolawul*, verb trans. To gather up the clothes or garments about one (as a woman her petticoats). جامه ماتول *jāma'h mātawul*, verb trans. To crumple, to pucker, to crease the clothes or garments.

P جامي *jāmī*, s. prop. The name of a celebrated Persian poet.

P جان *jān*, s.m. (2nd) Life, soul, spirit, a sweetheart. 2. The private parts. Pl. جانونه *jānūnah*. 3. adj. Dear, beloved. جانان *jānān*, s.m. (5th) Pl. Lives, sweethearts. Used singularly, as a sweetheart, one beloved. جان فشان *jān-fishān*, adj. Ready to lay down one's life, zealous, fervent; (Fem.) جان فشانه *jān-fishāna'h*. جان فشاني *jān fishānī*, s.f. (3rd) Devotion, zeal, extreme diligence or labour. Pl. ئي *a'ī*. جان فشاني كول *jān fishānī kawul*, verb trans. To strain every nerve, to show great devotion or zeal. See ځان

A جانب *jānib*, s.m. (9th) Part, side. Sing. and Pl. 2. adv. Towards, near at hand. جانبين *jānibain*. (A dual of جانب) Mutual, on both sides.

جانجي *jānjī*, s.m. (5th) The marriage guest of a man, who accompanies him to bring home the bride. Pl. جانجيان *jānjīān*. See ورا, وراباندي, مانجي, ويبزه and جنج

P جانور *jān-war*, s.m. (5th) An animal, a bird. Pl. جانوران *jānwarān*. See ځان

جانوله *jān-wala'h*, s.f. (3rd) Gum, gum-arabic. Pl. ي *ey*. See جاوله, ژاوله, and كندري

جانهٔ *jānah* or جانَ *jāna*, interj. Beloved! sweetheart! my dear! a term of endearment (From P).

جاوجي *jāw-ja'ī*, s.f. (6th) The skirt or hem of a garment. Sing. and Pl.

P جاودان *jāwidān*, adj. Eternal, endless, perpetual. جاوداني *jāwidānī*, s.f. (3rd) Eternity, perpetuity, immortality. Pl. ئي *a'ī*. See جاويد

جاوله *jāwla'h*, s.f. (3rd) Gum, gum-arabic. Pl. ئي *ey*. See ژاوله

P جاويد *jāwīd*, adj. } Eternal, endless, perpetual. جاويدان *jāwīdān*, } See جاودان

جاويداني *jāwīdānī*, s.f. (3rd) Eternity, perpetuity, immortality. Pl. ئي *a'ī*.

P جاه *jāh*, s.m. (2nd) Dignity, rank, grandeur, pomp. Pl. جاهونه *jāhūnah*. جاه و جلال *jāh-ow-jalāl*, Dignity, pomp, grandeur, magnificence.

A جاهل *jā-hil*, adj. (from جهل) Ignorant, illiterate, barbarous, brutal. 2. s.m. (5th) A fool, an illiterate person. Pl. جاهلان *jāhilān*; s.f. (3rd) جاهله *jāhila'h*. Pl. ئي *ey*. جاهلي *jāhilī*, s.f. (3rd) Ignorance, emptiness, want of sense or knowledge. Pl. ئي *a'ī*.

P جاي *jā'e*, s.m. (2nd) A place, a room, a dwelling, etc. Pl. جايونه *jā'eūnah*. See ځاي. جاي ضرور *jā'e ẓarūr*, A privy, a necessary. جاي غم *jā'e-g͟ham*, The place or time of grief. جاي نشين *jā'e nis͟hīn*, A successor, a locum tenens.

جائي *jā'a'ī*, s.f. (6th) A bowstring. See جي

P جائيداد *jā'edād*, s.m. (2nd) An assignment in land as a maintenance. 2. Property. Pl. جائيدادونه *jā'edādūnah*.

A جايز *jā'iz*, adj. (from جواز) Lawful, right, permitted, proper, warrantable, allowable, authorized; (Fem.) جايزه *jā'iza'h*. جايز کول *jā'iz kawul*, verb trans. To warrant, to justify, to tolerate.

A جبار *jabbār*, adj. superl. (from H גבור) Omnipotent, mighty. 2. Conqueror.

A جبر *jabr*, s.m. (2nd) (from H גבר 'was strong') Oppression, violence, strength, force, power. Pl. جبرونه *jabr-ūnah*. په جبر سره *pah jabr sarah*, adv. By violence, forcibly. له جبرَ *lah jabra*, or له جبر نه *lah jabr nah*, adv. Compulsively, forcibly. جبراً *jabran*, adv. By main force, forcibly, by compulsion, or from compulsion.

A جبرئيل *jabra-yīl*, s. prop. The archangel Gabriel. (from H.)

A جبلت *jibillat*, s.m. (2nd) Essence, quality, disposition, temperament, constitution, creation, form. Pl. جبلتونه *jibillat-ūnah*.

A جبلي *jibillī*, adj. Natural, innate, essential, in general.

جبه *jaba'h*, s.f. (3rd) A mere, a marsh, a bog. Pl. ئي *ey*.

A جبه *juba'h*, s.f. A kind of long vest or shirt, a coat of mail. Pl. ئي *ey*.

A جبين *jabīn*, s.m. (5th) The forehead. Pl. جبينان *jabīnān*. See تندي

S جت *jat*, s.m. (2nd) Manner, fashion, kind. Pl. جتونه *jatūnah*, s.m. (5th). 2. The name of a tribe inhabiting Persia and western parts of Afg͟hānistān and Seistān, supposed to be gipseys. Pl. جتان *jatān*; s.f. (3rd) جته *jata'h*. Pl. ئي *ey*.

HI جټ *jat̤t̤*, s.m. (5th) The name of a tribe of Rājputs, numbers of whom dwell in the southern and eastern parts of the Panjāb. Pl. جټان *jat̤t̤ān*; s.f. (3rd) جټه *jat̤t̤a'h*. Pl. ئي *ey*.

ججوره *jajūra'h*, s.f. (3rd) The crop of a bird, the maw or first stomach, the dew-lap of an animal. 2. A double chin. Pl. ئي *ey*. See غبغب

ججوري *jajūraey*, s.m. (1st) Same as the preceding. Pl. ي *ī*. Also جج *jaj*, s.m, (2nd). Pl. ججونه *jajūnah*.

ججوي *jajū'ī*, s.m. (5th) The anemone. Pl. ججويان *jajū-ī-ān*.

ججي *juja'ī*, s.f. (6th) A kind of pheasant. Sing. and Pl. See جوجي

جخ *jak͟h*, s.m. (5th) A froth bubble on the water. Pl. جخان *jak͟hān*; or 2. s.m. (2nd) A small fly which moves along on the surface of the water. Pl. جخونه *jak͟hūnah*.

جخت *juk͟ht*, adj. Right, exact, even, accurate,

fair, equable, fit; (Fem.) جخته *jukhta'h*. See جوښت

A جد *jadd*, s.m. (2nd) A grandfather, an ancestor, Pl. جدان *jaddān*. See نيکه

P جدا *judā*, adj. Separate, apart, distinct, aside, asunder, absent, different, peculiar, extraordinary. جدا جدا *judā judā*, adj. Various, one by one, several, separate. 2. adv. Separately, severally. جدا جدا کول *judā judā kawul*, verb trans. To particularize, to individualize, to enumerate. جدا کول *judā kawul*, verb trans. To divide, to separate, to part, to disengage, to disjoin, to distinguish. جدا کيدل *judā kedal*, verb intrans. To part, to separate, to become disjoined or divided. جدائي *judā'ī*, s.f. (3rd) Separation, absence, parting, disjoining. Pl. ئ *a'ī*.

A جدال *jidāl*, s.m. (2nd) (inf. III of جدل), Contention, strife, altercation, squabble, contest. Pl. جدالونه *jidālūnah*. جنګ و جدال *jang-ow-jidāl*, s.m. (2nd) Fighting, contention, strife. جنګ و جدال کول *jang-ow-jidāl kawul*, verb trans. To quarrel, to contend, to fight.

جدال *jadāl*, s.m. (5th) Antichrist. See also دجال and خرجدال

A جدل *jadal*, s.m. (2nd) Altercation, strife, battle, encounter. Pl. جدلونه *jadalūnah*. See جدال

A جدوار *jadwār*, s.m. (2nd) Zedoary (Kœmpferia zedoar). Pl. جدوارونه *jadwār-ūnah*.

A جدول *jadwal*, s.m. (2nd) Lines drawn in a book or on the margin. Pl. جدولونه *jadwalūnah*. جدولي *jadwalī*, adj. A book marked with lines.

A جدي *jadd-ī*, adj. Ancestral, belonging to ancestors.

A جديد *jadīd*, adj. New, modern, fresh.

A جذام *juzām*, s.m. (2nd) Leprosy. Pl. جذامونه *juzāmūnah*. See پيس and پون

A جذب *jazb*, s.m. (2nd) Absorption, drawing (as a blister), attraction, allurement. Pl. جذبونه *jazbūnah*. جذب کول *jazb kawul*, verb trans. To imbibe, to draw (as a blister), to attract, to absorb. جذب کيدل *jazb kedal*, verb intrans. To be absorbed.

جذبه *jazba'h*, s.f. (3rd) Fury, passion, rage, desire. Pl. ي *ey*. See جذب

P جر *jar*, s.m. (2nd) A drain, a small ditch for carrying off water and for draining lands. 2. A crack, a cleft, a fissure in the ground. Pl. جرونه *jarūnah*.

A جرأت *jur'at*, s.m. (2nd) Courage, boldness, audacity, bravery, temerity, valour. Pl. جرأتونه *jur'ātūnah*. جرأت کول *jur'āt kawul*, verb trans. To dare, to have the courage, or temerity.

A جراح *jarrāḥ*, s.m. (5th) A surgeon, a healer of wounds. Pl. جراحان *jarrāḥān*.

جراحي *jarrāḥ-ī*, s.f. (3rd) Surgery. Pl. ئ *a'ī*.

A جرار *jarrār*, adj. Warlike, bold, brave.

جرده *jardah*. See چرده

جړه *jir-ṛra'h*, s.f. (3rd) A rag, a tatter. Pl. ي *ey*. See چړه

A جرس *jaras*, s.m. (2nd) A bell. Pl. جرسونه *jarasūnah*.

A جرعه *jur'æa'h*, s.f. (3rd) One draught, a drop. Pl. ي *ey*.

جرکاڼي *jur-kāṛṛney*, s.m. (1st) To boot, into the bargain, over and above. Pl. ي *ī*. See سر

جرګتو *jirgatū*, s.m. (5th) The member of a *jirga'h* or assembly amongst the Yūsufzī's. Pl. جرګتوګان *jirgatūgān*.

جرګه *jirga'h*, or جيرګه *jeyrga'h*, s.f. (3rd) An assembly, a party met for consultation, a sort of democratic council amongst the Yūsufzī's. Pl. ي *ey*. See معرکه (P جرګه ?).

A جرم *jirm*, s.m. (2nd) The body, substance, mass; residue, or refuse of anything. Pl. جرمونه *jirmūnah*. See وسپينخري

A جرم *jurm*, s.m. (2nd) A crime, sin, fault. Pl. جرمونه *jurmūnah*.

جرموړه *jar-moṛra'h*, s.f. (3rd) A kind of rash or eruption caused by the sting of any venomous insect, or from excess of blood. Pl. ي *ey*. جرموړه کيدل *jar-moṛra'h kedal*, verb intrans. To become afflicted or affected with the preceding. جرموره کول *jar-morra'h kawul*, verb trans. To affect with, or cause *jar-morra'h*.

جرندگري *jarandgaraey*, adj. as s.m. (1st) A miller. Pl. ي *ī*; (Fem.) جرنده گرِ *jaranda'h-gari*. Pl. ي *ī*.

جرنده *jaranda'h*, s.f. (3rd) A water-mill or a wind-mill, also a mill turned by camels or bullocks. Pl. ې *ey*. See also ژرنده and زرنده

جره *jurrah*, s.m. (5th) A species of hawk or falcon, a tercel goshawk. Pl. جره‌گان *jurrah-gān*. Also جره باز *jurrah bāz*.

A جريان *jir-yān*, s.m. (2nd) Running, flowing, flux (as of blood, matter, etc.) Pl. جريانونه *jir-yānūnah*. جريان آب *jir-yān-i-āb*, Fluor albus. جريان شکم *jir-yān-i-shikam*, Dysentery, flux. جريان مذي *jir-yān-i-mazī*, Fluor albus. جريان مني *jir-yān-i-manī*, Gonorrhœa simplex, gleet.

A جريب *jarīb*, s.m. (2nd) A land measure, a corn measure of 384 *mudds*, or as much land as will produce so much. Pl. جريبونه *jarīb-ūnah*.

A جريده *jarīdah*, adj. Alone, separate, solitary, unattended, unincumbered.

A جريمانه *jarī-māna'h*, s.f. (3rd) A fine, a penalty, a forfeit. Pl. ې *ey*. جريمانه کول *jarī-māna'h kawul*, verb trans. To fine, to mulct.

جړ *jurr*, s.m. (5th) Bubbling, murmuring, gurgling or purling, as a brook or running water, the sound of falling water, as from a cascade or waterfall. Pl. جړهار *jurrahār*. جړ کول *jurr kawul*, verb trans. To bubble, to gurgle, to purl, to murmur as a brook, to foam or boil as a cascade. جړ جړ *jurr jurr*, A rumbling in the belly or intestines, purling or murmuring as a brook. جړ جړ کول *jurr-jurr kawul*, verb trans. To rumble.

جړانگو *jarrāngū*, s.m. (5th) The cassia fistula. Pl. جړانگان *jarrāngān*. Also لانديس and پلوس

جړا *jarrā*, s.f. (6th) Weeping, lamentation, crying, bewailing. (E.) Sing. and Pl.; or (W.) Pl. جړاوي *jarrānī*. See ژړا. جړل *jarral*, verb trans. To cry, to weep, to bewail, to whimper. See ژړل

S جړاو *jarrāo* or *jarrāw*, adj. Set, studded with jewels, fixed, placed, composed; (Fem.) جړاوه *jarrāo-a'h* or *jarrāwa'h*. جړاو کول *jarrāo kawul*, verb trans. To set, to ornament, to stud with jewels, to fix in metal (as a jewel).

جړنگ *jurrang*, s.m. (5th) A creeping-plant, a creeper (as of cucumbers, melons, etc.) Pl. جړنگان *jurrangān*.

جړۍ *jarra'ī*, s.f. (6th) The root of a medicinal plant used as a remedy for snake bites. Sing. and Pl. (s जटा). 2. Continual or down-pouring rain, or cloudy weather. Sing. and Pl. See داره and ليندي

P جز *juz*, s.m. (5th or 2nd) A part, a portion, a division of a book, containing eight leaves. Pl. جزان *juzān* or جزونه *juzūnah*. جزبندي *juz-bandī*, s.f. (3rd) Binding a book. Pl. ۍ *a'ī*. جزدان *juz-dān*, s.m. (2nd) A portfolio, a cloth in which books are wrapped up, a wrapper. Pl. جزدانونه *juz-dānūnah*. جز و کل *juz-o-kul*, adv. Totally, entirely, one and all, great and small.

A جزا *jazā*, s.f. (6th) Retaliation, requital, return, compensation, reward, recompense. (E.) Sing. and Pl.; (W.) جزاوي *jazāwī*. جزا ور کول *jazā war-kawul*, verb trans. To give compensation, to requite, to return.

A جزايل *jazā'yil* or جرزايل *jar-zā'yil*, s.m. (5th) A large musket, a wall piece, a swivel. Pl. جزايلان *jazā'yilān* or جرزايلان *jar-zā'yilān*.

جزبز *jiz-biz*, s.f. (1st) A game played with knuckle-bones. Pl. جزبز *jiz-bizi*. See بجل

A جزم *jazm*, s.m. (2nd) Decision, determining, resolving. 2. Amputating. 3. The orthographical character *jazm* (ـْـ), which is placed over a letter to show that it is quiescent, or has no vowel following it. Pl. جزمونه *jazm-ūnah*.

A جزيره *jazīra'h*, s.f. (3rd) An island, a peninsula. Pl. ې *ey*. See تاپو

A جزيه *jizya'h*, s.f. (3rd) A tribute, capitation-tax levied on individuals, a poll tax. Pl. ې *ey*.

جس *jas*, s.m. (6th) Pewter. Sing. and Pl. See also HI جست *jast*, s.m. (6th) Pewter. Sing. and Pl.

P جست *jast*, s.m. (2nd) A leap, a jump, a bound, a spring. Pl. جستونه *jastūnah*. جست وهل *jast wahal*, verb trans. To jump, to leap, to spring, to bound. See ترپ

P جست و جوي *just-o-jū'e*, s.m. (2nd) Search, inquiry, quest, scrutiny, investigation, examination, searching, seeking. Pl. جست و جويونه *just-o-jū'e-ūnah*. جست و جوي کول *just-o-jū'e kawul*, verb trans. To search, to inquire, to scrutinize, to investigate.

جسته *jis-ta'h*, s.f. (3rd) A shoe or slipper with high heels worn by the females of Kābul and Pes͟hāwer out of doors. 2. (P) *jasta'h*, Pewter, Pl. ې *ey*.

A جسد *jasad*, s.m. (2nd) The body. Pl. جسدونه *jasadūnah*.

A جسر *jisr*, s.m. (2nd) A bridge of boats. Pl. جسرونه *jisrūnah*.

A جسم *jism*, s.m. (2nd) The body of any being. Pl. جسمونه *jismūnah*. جسماني *jism-ānī*, adj. Belonging to the body, corporeal, material, carnal.

جسه *jussa'h*, s.f. (3rd) The body, the shape or figure of the human form. Pl. ې *ey*. (corrup. of جثه A).

A جسيم *jasīm*, adj. (from جسم) Corpulent, stout.

جشي *jis͟haey*, s.m. (1st) The name of a prickly thorn or shrub which adheres to one's clothes. Pl. ي *ī*.

A جعفري *jaæ-farī*, s.m. (6th) The name of a yellow flower, the Linum trigynum. Sing. and Pl.

A جعل *jaæl*, adj. Forged, counterfeit, a forgery; also جعلي *jaælī*. See جال

جغ *jug͟h*, s.m. (2nd) The yoke of a plough, a yoke for oxen in general. Pl. جغونه *jug͟hūnah*. جغ ترل *jug͟h tar͟ral*, verb trans. To yoke. (S युग).

جغانغه *jug͟hān-g͟ha'h*, s.f. (3rd) The name of a species of shrub. Pl. ې *ey*.

جغندر *jug͟handar*, s.m. (5th) Beet-root. Pl. جغندران *jug͟handarān*. (P چقندر).

جغه *jag͟ha'h* or جوغه *jog͟ha'h*, s.f. (3rd) A plume, an ornament worn by kings and princes in the East Pl. ې *ey*.

A جفا *jafā*, s.f. (6th) Oppression, injustice, injury. (E.) Sing. and Pl.; (W.) Pl. جفاوي *jafāwī*. جفا ورل *jafā w'r͟ral*, verb trans. To suffer or endure oppression or injustice. جفا کول *jafā kawul*, verb trans. To oppress, to tyrannize over. جفا کار *jafā-kār*, adj. Oppressive, unjust, cruel. 2. s.m. (5th) An oppressor, a tyrant; s.f. (3rd) جفاکاره *jafā-kāra'h*. جفاکاري *jafā-kārī*, s.f. (3rd) Tyranny, oppression, injustice, cruelty. Pl. ئې *a'ī*.

P جفت *juft*, adj. Right, exact, even, fair, equitable, fit, accurate; (Fem.) جفته *jufta'h*. See جخت

P جفت *juft*, s.m. (2nd) A pair, a couple, a match. 2. Evenness, a party. Pl. جفتونه *juftūnah*.

جفتک *juftak*, s.f. (1st) A kick with both the hind legs of a horse, ass, etc, Pl. جفتکې *juftaki*. جفتک وهل *juftak wahal*, verb trans. To kick with both hind legs.

جق جق *jaḳ jaḳ*, s.m. (2nd) The noise made by fowls. 2. Prattle, chatter, gabble. Pl. جق جقونه *jaḳ jaḳūnah*. جق جق کول *jaḳ jaḳ kawul*, verb trans. To chatter, to prattle, to clack. See بق بق and چغ چغ

جک *jak*, s.m. (2nd) The name of a kind of fly or beetle which skims along the surface of the water and difficult to strike, hence foolish talk, nonsense, a useless matter. Pl. جکونه *jakūnah*. جک وهل *jak wahal*, verb trans. To talk nonsense, to chatter, to prattle, to do any useless thing. (? HI جهک, absurdity, etc.)

جک جک *jig-jig*, A word used to incite or instigate a bull to fight. جک جک کول *jig-jig kawul*, verb trans. To incite a bull to fight.

جکړه *jagr͟ra'h* or *jagar͟ra'h*, s.f. (3rd) Strife, contention, altercation, quarrel, squabble. Pl.

ئي *ey*. جګړه کول *jagaṟṟa'h kawul*, verb trans. To quarrel, to contend, to dispute, to wrangle. (HI جهګړا).

جګناتئي *jagnāta'ī*, s.f. (6th) A kind of fine cloth or muslin. Sing. and Pl.

جګي جګي *jigī-jigī*, s.f. (3rd) Coaxing, entreating, wheedling. 2. (HI) An expression indicative of pleasure or surprise. Pl. ئي *a'ī*. جګي جګي کول *jigī-jigī kawul*, verb trans. To crave, to entreat, to coax, to beseech.

جل *jal*, s.m. (7th) A hedge of thorns around a dwelling or a village. 2. A kind of screen made of thorns to close the entrance to a thorny hedge, a stop-gap. Pl. جلونه *j'lūnah*.

جل *jal*, s.m. (5th) A skylark. Pl. جلان *jalān*.

جَل *jæl*, s.f. (1st) A damsel, a virgin, a young girl from the age of puberty. Pl. جلِ *jæli*. See جن and نجل

A جلا *jilā*, s.f. (6th) Leaving one's country, exile, departure, desertion. 2. Separation, separating. 3. (*jalā*) Anything clear and distinct. 4. Scouring, polishing. (E.) Sing. and Pl.; (W.) Pl. جلاوي *jilāwī* and *jalāwī*. 5. adj. Separate, distinct, away, apart, aside, asunder, absent. جلا کيدل *jilā kedal*, verb intrans. To part, to be disunited, to separate. جلا کول *jilā kawul*, verb trans. To disunite, to disconnect, to separate, to divide, to detach. جلا وطن *jilā waṭan*, s.m. (2nd) Emigration, leaving one's country. Pl. جلا وطنونه *jilā waṭanūnah*. جلاوطني *jilā waṭanī*, s.f. (3rd) Banishment, leaving one's country. Pl. ئي *a'ī*. جلا وطن کول *jilā waṭan kawul*, verb trans. To banish, to exile. جلا وطن کيدل *jilā waṭan kedal*, verb intrans. To emigrate, to leave one's native land, to be exiled.

A جلاب *julāb*, s.m. (2nd) A purge, a cathartic. Pl. جلابونه *julābūnah*. جلاب کول *julāb kawul*, verb trans. To take a purging dose or aperient. جلاب ور کول *julāb war-kawul*, verb trans. To purge, to give aperient medicine.

جلات *jal-āt*, s. prop. The name of a celebrated lover, whose mistress's name was Shahā.

جلات *jallāt*, s.m. (5th) An executioner. Pl. جلاتان *jallāt-ān*. 2. adj. Cruel, hard-hearted. جلاتي *jallāt-ī*, s.f. (3rd) The office of executioner. 2. Cruelty. Pl. ئي *a'ī*. (A جلاد).

جلاجل *julā-jil*, s.m. (5th) A small globular bell, strings of which are hung about the heads or necks of cattle, or worn about the feet by women. Pl. جلاجلان *julājil-ān*.

A جلال *jalāl*, s.m. (2nd) Dignity, grandeur, state, power, splendour, glory, majesty. Pl. جلالونه *jalālūnah*. جلاله *jalālah*, adj. Grand, great, high.

جلالي و کمالي *jalāley ow kamāley*, s. The name of two hills on the Indus a little below Aṭṭak.

جلب *jalab*, s.m. (2nd) The rope or rein by which horses are picketed, head ropes of a horse. Pl. جلبونه *jalabūnah*. See جلو

A جلباب *jalbāb*, s.m. (2nd) A long veil, a pavilion or awning of net-work to keep off flies. Pl. جلبابونه *jalbābūnah*.

جل بنګ *jal-bang*, s.m. (9th) A kind of plant which stings on touching it, a kind of stinging nettle, the tops and leaves of which are cooked and eaten. Sing. and Pl. Also جلبنګئ *jalbanga'ī*, s.f. (6th) The small species of the above. Sing. and Pl. See سوربلي

جلت *jalt*, adj. Quick, precipitate, rash, abrupt, impetuous, hasty; (Fem.) جلته *jalta'h*. 2. adv. Quickly, briskly. (corrup. of P جلد).

جلته *jalata'h*, s.f. (3rd) A kind of hamper or large basket with a cover for keeping grain in. Pl. ئي *ey*. See خمبه

P جلد *jald*, adj. Quick, nimble, brisk, fast, hasty, impetuous, rash, fierce, quickly; (Fem.) جلده *jalda'h*.

P جلدي *jaldī*, s.f. (3rd) Haste, hurry, abruptness, quickness, celerity, precipitation, impetuosity. Pl. ئي *a'ī*. 2. adv. Quickly, briskly. جلدي کول *jaldī kawul*, verb trans. To hasten, to hurry, to be rash or impetuous. See زر and ژر

جلک *jalak*, s.m. (2nd) A kind of reel used in spinning cotton, thread, etc. Pl. جلکونه *jalakūnah*. See شاهی and څرخي

جلنانۍ *jal-nāna'ī*, s.f. (6th) A cookhouse, a kitchen. Sing. and Pl.

جلندرۍ *jalandara'ī*, s.f. (6th) A whirligig. Sing. and Pl. See also چرلي and برين چغ

A جلو *jalaw*, s.m. (2nd) The head ropes of a horse, the rein for picketing a horse with. 2. Retinue, train. Pl. جلوونه *jalawūnah*. See جلب

جلو دار *jalaw-dār*, s.m. (5th) An attendant. Pl. جلو داران *jalaw-dārān*.

A جلوه *jalwa'h*, s.f. (3rd) Splendour, lustre, adornment. 2. The bridal bed or ornaments. Pl. ي *ey*. جلوه گاه *jalwa'h gāh*, s.m. (2nd) The nuptial throne, place of display. Pl. جلوه گاهونه *jalwa'h gāhūnah*. جلوه گر *jalwa'h-gar*, adj. Splendid, lustrous; (Fem.) جلوه گره *jalwa'h-gara'h*. جلوه گري *jalwa'h-garī*, s.f. (3rd) Blandishment, affectation. 2. Splendour, conspicuity. Pl. ۍ *a'ī*.

جلۍ *jala'ī*, s.f. (6th) A scream, a shriek, a roar, a bellow. 2. Calling with a loud voice. جلۍ وهل *jala'ī wahal* or کول *kawul*, verb trans. To scream, to shriek, to bellow.

جليا *jaliyā*, adj. Burnt, consumed. (From HI جلنا.)

A جليل *jalīl*, adj. (from جلال) Great, glorious, illustrious; (Fem.) جليله *jalīla'h*.

جم *jam* or *jamm*, s.m. (9th) Falling on in a body. 2. The small shot of a fowling piece striking the object in a mass, or compact. Sing. and Pl. (? A جَمّ a multitude.)

جم *jum*, s.m. (5th) A turf, turf used in strengthening the banks of a canal or pond, a clod of earth. Pl. جمان *jumān*.

A جماد *jamād*, s.m. (2nd) Whatever is incapable of growth, a stone, a fossil, etc. Pl. جمادونه *jamādūnah*. (A جمادات)

A جماظ *jamāẓ*, s.m. (5th) A runner, a person who decamps. Pl. جماظان *jamāẓān*.

A جماع *jimāæ*, s.f. (1st) Coitus, copulation. Pl. جماعِ *jimāæi*. See غو

A جماعت *jamā-æt*, s.m. (2nd) A crowd, an assembly, a troop, a meeting, a congregation, a masjid. Pl. جماعتونه *jamā-æatūnah*.

د جماعت نمونځ *da jamā-æt namūndz*, Public prayers along with the congregation.

A جمال *jamāl*, s.m. (2nd) Beauty, elegance. Pl. جمالونه *jamālūnah*.

HI جمال گوټه *jamāl goṯṯa'h*, s.f. (3rd) The name of a purgative root (Croton tiglium). Pl. ي *ey*. Also جمال کوټه *jamāl koṯṯah*.

جمدر *jamdar*, s.m. (2nd) A tare, the darnel (Vicia sativa). Pl. جمدرونه *jamdarūnah*. See جودر

جمرود *jamrūd*, s.prop. The name of a river or stream flowing from the Khaiber Pass, and giving name to a village and fort west of Peshāwar, near the Pass.

P جمشيد *jamshīd*, s. prop. The name of a famous king of Persia.

جمعه *jamæa'h*, s.f. (3rd) A congregation, collection, assembly, amount, sum total, whole, the plural number. Pl. ي *ey*. (Corrupt. of A جمع). جمعه کيدل *jamæa'h kedal*, verb intrans. To be collected, to assemble, to flock. جمعه کول *jamæa'h kawul*, verb trans. To collect, to amass, to gather together, add together, to assemble, to heap. جمعدار *jamædār*, s.m. (5th) A native officer, a rank in the army. Pl. جمعداران *jamædārān*. جمعداري *jamædārī*, s.f. (3rd) The business of a *jamædār*. Pl. ۍ *a'ī*. جمع خرچ *jamæ-kharch*, s.m. (2nd) Account of receipt and disbursement, account current.

P جمعگي *jumaægī*, s.f. (3rd) The weekly allowance to schoolboys paid on a Friday, the present given on a Friday by schoolboys to their master. Pl. ۍ *a'ī*.

A جمعه *jumæa'h*, s.f. (3rd) Friday. Pl. ي *ey*. See جمه

A جمعيت *jamæī-yat*, s.m. (2nd) Collection, assemblage, accumulation of persons. 2. Wealth. 3. Recollection, reflection. 4. Peace of mind. Pl. جمعيتونه *jamæī-yatūnah*.

A جمله *jumla'h*, s.f. (3rd) The whole, the sum, the aggregate, total amount. Pl. ي *ey*. في الجمله *fi-l-jumla'h*, adv. Upon the whole, in short. من جمله *min-jumla'h*, adv. Out of the whole;

جملي څخه لـه *lah jumley dzakhah*, or لـه جملي نه *lah jumley nah*, Upon the whole, in short.

جمعه *juma'h*, s.f. (3rd) Friday, the Muhammadan sabbath. Pl. ې *ey*. See جمعه

جمي *jamaey*, s.m. (1st) The winter, the cold season. Pl. ي *ī*. See ژمي

جن *jæn*, s.f. (1st) A virgin, a maiden, spinster. Pl. جني *jæni*. See جل

A جن *jinn*, s.m. (5th) A demon, a spirit, a genius, one of the genii. Pl. جنان *jinnān*. جن نيولي *jinn nīwalaey*, adj. Possessed of an evil spirit; also جني *jinnī*, adj. Stubborn, possessed of a devil.

A جناب *janāb*, s.m. (2nd) Majesty, highness, excellency. 2. Power, dignity. 3. Brink, side, margin. 4. A threshold, a vestibule. Pl. جنابونه *janābūnah*. جناب عالي *janāb-i-æālī*, Your majesty, your excellency, the most high.

A جنازه *jināza'h* or *janāza'h*, s.f. (3rd) A bier, a funeral. Pl. ې *ey*.

P جناور *janāwar*, s.m. (5th) An animal in general, a bird. Pl. جناوړ *janāwær*, or (P) Pl. جناوران *janāwarān*.

A جنب *janb*, s.m. (2nd) A side, part, a tract of country, etc. Pl. جنوبه *janbūnah*.

A جنب *junub*, adj. Polluted, defiled, spotted; (Fem.) جنبه *junuba'h*. جنب كيدل *junub kedal*, verb intrans. To become defiled or polluted. جنب كول *junub kawul*, verb trans. To defile, to pollute.

جنبازه *junbāza'h*, s.f. (3rd) The going rough, as a camel unaccustomed to the saddle. Pl. ې *ey*. جنبازه وهل *junbāza'h wahal*, verb trans. To go roughly, as an unbroken camel; also written جمبازه *jumbāzah*.

P جنبان *junbān*, adj. Moving, tremulous, vibrating. 2. act. part. Moving, shaking.

جنبق *jambak*, adj. Close, dense, clustered, grouped, assembled, collected, amassed; also written جمبق *jambak*. جنبق ستوري *janbak storī*, The Pleiades. See پيروني

جنبه *janba'h*, s.f. (3rd) A party, a horde, an assemblage, a collection, a clan, a brotherhood, a group, a pack. Pl. ې *ey*. 2. s.m. (6th) A partizan, an auxiliary, a help, an adherent. Sing. and Pl. See تولي

A جنت *jannat*, s.m. (2nd) Paradise, the garden. Pl. جنتونه *jannatūnah*. جنتي *jannatī*, s.m. (5th) An inhabitant of Paradise. Pl. جنتيان *jannatī-ān*. 2. adj. Of Paradise, heavenly, celestial. جنت الفردوس *jannat-ul-firdous*, The garden of Paradise.

جنج *janj*, s.m. (2nd) A marriage procession, a party of men, friends of the bridegroom, who go with him to fetch the bride home. Pl. جنجونه *janjūnah*. جنجي *janjī*, s.m. (5th) One of a marriage procession, a wedding guest. Pl. جنجيان *janjīān*. See جانجي

S جنجال *janjāl*, s.m. (2nd) Trouble, difficulty, perplexity, embarrassment, plague. 2. Strife, etc. Pl. جنجالونه *janjālūnah*. جنجال كول *janjāl kawul*, verb trans. To trouble, to plague, to distress, to embarrass. جنجالي *janjālī*, s.m. (5th) A molester, a plaguer, a perplexer, a disturber. Pl. جنجاليان *janjālī-ān*.

جنجل *janjal*, s.m. (2nd) A kind of tree. Pl. جنجلونه *janjalūnah*.

جنجړ *janjarrn*, s.m. (6th) A plant producing a kind of pulse (Cytisus cajan). Sing. and Pl. See جيانجړ

جندره *jandra'h*, s.f. (3rd) A padlock. 2. An instrument for drawing wire. Pl. ې *ey*. See راښكو

جنډه *jandda'h*, s.f. (3rd) A flag, a standard, a banner. Pl. ې *ey*. (S جهنڈا). See بيرق

A جنس *jins*, s.m. (2nd) Family, race. 2. Genus, kind, gender, species, sort. 3. Drapery. Pl. جنسونه *jinsūnah*. (A Pl. اجناس *ajnās*). جنس په جنس *jins pah jins*, adv. Separately, kind by kind. جنسي *jinsī*, adj. In kind.

جنغوزي *janghozaey*, s.m. (1st) A kind of nut like the pistachio, the kernel of the pine. Pl. ي *ī*. See چلغوزي

جنكۍ *jinaka'ī*, s.f. (6th) A little, or very young girl; the diminutive of جني. Sing. and Pl. See جونكۍ

P جنگ *jang*, s.m. (2nd) Battle, war, combat, fight. Pl. جنگونه *jangūnah*. جنگ آزموده

jang āzmūdah, adj. Tried in war, a veteran, warlike, brave. جنګ آور *jang āwur*, or جنګ يالي *jang yālaey*, adj. A hero, a champion, a fighter. جنګ آوري *jang-āwarī*, s.f. (3rd) Battle, warfare. Pl. ئي *a'ī*. جنګ جوي *jang jūey*, adj. Contentious, litigious. جنګ ديده *jang dīdah*, adj. Veteran, tried in war, warlike. جنګ و جدل *jang-o-jadal*, s.m. (2nd) Altercation, strife, squabble, conflict, battle. جنګوړي *jangūrraey*, s.m. (1st) A skirmish, a squabble (dimin. of جنګ). Pl. ي *ī*. جنګ ځاي *jang dzā'ey*, s.m. (2nd) A battle-field. Pl. ځايونه *dzā-eyūnah*. جنګ ريز *jang-rez*, s.m. (9th) Retreating with the face to the enemy, facing about and fighting. Sing. and Pl. جنګ کول *jang kawul*, verb trans. To fight, to combat, to make war. جنګ نښتل *jang n'khatal* (E.) or *n'shatal* (W.), verb trans. To commence to fight, to fall-to, to fight, to assail, to assault, to join in battle. جنګ نښلول *jang n'khalawul* (E.) or *n'shalawul* (W.), verb trans. To fight, to contend, to war against, to set to. جنګيدل *jangedal*, verb intrans. To fight, to contend, to war. Pres. جنګيږي *jangejzī* (W.) جنګيګي *jangegī* (E.); past وُ جنګيده *wu-jangedah* or وُ جنګيدَ *wu-jangeda*; fut. وُ به جنګيږي *wu bah jangejzī* or وُ به جنګيګي *wu bah jangegī*; imp. وُ جنګيږه *wu-jangejzah* or وُ جنګيګه *wu-jangegah*, ; act. part. جنګيدونکَي *jangedūnkaey* or جنګيدونَي *jangedūnaey*; past part. جنګيدلَي *jangedalaey*; verb. n. جنګيدنه *jangedana'h*. جنګول *jangawul*, verb trans. To fight, to contend with, to bait, etc. Pres. جنګوي *jangawī*; past وُ جنګاوه *wu-jangāwuh* or وُ جنګاوو *wu-jangāwo*; fut. وُ به جنګوي *wu bah jangawī*; imp. وُ جنګوه *wu-jangawah*; act. part. جنګوونکَي *jangawūnkaey* or جنګوونَي *jangawūnaey*; past جنګولَي *jangawulaey*; verb. n. جنګونه *jangawuna'h*.

جنګ *jung*, s.m. (2nd) or (5th) A young camel ready for carrying a burden. Pl. جنګونه *jungūnah* or جنګان *jungān*; s.f. (3rd) جنګه *junga'h*. Pl. جنګي *jungey*.

جنګ *jung*, s.m. (2nd) A miscellany, a chrestomathy, a book of extracts. Pl. جنګونه *jungūnah*.

جنګړه *jungarra'h*, s.f. (3rd) A hut, a hovel. Pl. ئي *ey*. See جونګړه *jongarra'h*.

جنګي *jungaey*, s.m. (1st) A young camel, from his birth until able to bear a load. Pl. ي *ī*; Fem. (6th) جنګئ *junga'ī*. Sing. and Pl. See جنګ

P جنګي *jangī*, s.m. (5th) A combatant, a warrior, a fighter. Pl. جنګيان *jangīān*; adj. Warlike, of war, martial.

A جنوب *janūb*, s.m. (9th) The south. Sing. and Pl.

A جنوبي *junūbī*, adj. Southern.

A جنون *junūn*, s.m. (9th) Madness, insanity, phrenzy. 2. A demoniac, a madman. Sing. and Pl. جنوني *junūnī*, adj. Mad, insane, passionate. See ليونتوب

جنئ *jina'ī*, s.f. (6th) A girl not yet arrived at puberty, a daughter, a damsel. Sing. and Pl. See also جنګئ and جونګئ

جنړه جنړه *jarrna'h jarrna'h* or جنړَ جنړَ *jarrna jarrna*, s.f. (3rd) Shift, subterfuge, evasion, shuffling, equivocation. Pl. ئي *ey*. جنړه جنړه کول *jarrna'h jarrna'h kawul*, verb trans. To evade, to shuffle, to equivocate, to make shift. په جنړه جنړه *pah jarrna'h jarrna'h*, adv. Evasively.

P جو *jau*, s.m. (6th) Barley. Sing. and Pl. See اوربشه

A جواب *jawāb*, s.m. (2nd) An answer, a reply. Pl. جوابونه *jawābūnah*. جواب ده *jawāb dih*, An answerer, a replier. جواب دهي *jawāb dihī*, s.f. (3rd) Amenable, accountable, responsible, answerable. Pl. ئي *a'ī*. جواب سوال *jawāb suwāl*, Altercation, conversation. جواب کول *jawāb kawul*, verb trans. To answer, to reply to. جواب مندل *jawāb mundal*, verb trans. To get an answer, to be dismissed or discharged. جواب نامه *jawāb nāma'h*, s.f. (3rd) A written reply, an answer. Pl. ئي *ey*. جواب ور کول *jawāb war kawul*, verb trans. To discharge, to dismiss, to disband, to answer to, to reply to. حاضر جواب *ḥāẓir jawāb*, Echo. 2. A ready reply or answer. 3. adj. Pert. قطعي جواب *kaṭæī jawāb*, A definite reply or answer.

HI جوار *j'wār*, s.m. (6th) The name of a grain (Holcus sorgum). Sing. and Pl.

جوارگر *jū'-ār-gar*, s.m. (5th) A gambler. Pl. جوارګر *jū-'ār-gær*. جوارګره *jū'-ār-gara'h*, s.f. (3rd). Pl. ي *ey*.

جواري *j'wārī*, s.m. (1st) Pl. A species of grain (Holcus sorgum). See جوار

S جواري *jū'-ārī*, s.m. (5th) A gamester, a gambler. Pl. جواريان *jū'ārī-ān*.

جواري *jū'-ārī*, s.f. (3rd) Gambling. Pl. ي *a'ī*. جواري كول *jū'-ārī kawul*, verb trans. To gamble, to game.

P جوال *juwāl*, s.m. (2nd) A sack or bag woven of wool or hair for holding things. Pl. جوالونه *juwālūnah*.

P S جوان *jawān*, adj. Young, juvenile; (Fem.) جوانه *jawāna'h*. See ځوان

جوانوان *jawānwān*, s.m. (6th) A kind of grain like mustard seed from which a kind of bitter oil is expressed. Sing. and Pl.

A جواهر *jawāhir*, s.m. (2nd) A jewel, a gem, etc. Pl. جواهرونه *jawāhirūnah*, or (A جواهرات *jawāhirāt*).

A جواهري *jawāhirī*, s.m. (5th) A jeweller. Pl. جواهريان *jawāhirīān*.

جوبل *jobal*, adj. Wounded, maimed, mutilated, hamstrung; (Fem.) جوبله *jobla'h*. جوبليدل *jobaledal*, verb intrans. To become wounded, maimed, mutilated, etc. جوبلول *jobalawul*, verb trans. To hamstring, to maim, to mutilate. See ژوبل

جوبله *jobala'h*, s.f. (3rd) Injury, hurt, detriment, scath. 2. Retaliation, revenge. Pl. ي *ey*. See ژوبله

P جوبه *joba'h*, s.f. (3rd) A mart, a market, an emporium. Pl. ي *ey*.

جوتۍ *jūta'ī*, s.f. (6th) A shoe, a slipper. Sing. and Pl. See پنړۍ (HI جوتي).

S جوټه *jūṯṯa'h*, s.f. (3rd) Refuse, leavings, remains, scourings. 2. Base, false, as coin or gems, etc. Pl. ي *ey*.

جوټۍ *jūṯṯa'ī*, s.f. (6th) The act of swinging, rocking, moving to and fro, vibrating, oscillating, nodding, as from sleep. Sing. and Pl. جوټۍ خوړل *jūṯṯa'ī khwaṟṟal*, verb trans. To take (*lit.* consume) a swing, to rock, to move, to vibrate, to oscillate, to nod from drowsiness (verb intrans. in English). جوټۍ وركول *jūṯṯa'ī war-kawul*, verb trans. To rock, to swing, to give a swing to, to set a swinging. See ټال and ټالۍ

جوجه ماجوجه *jūja'h mājūja'h*, s.f. (3rd) Gog and Magog. Pl. ي *ey*. (A ياجوج و ماجوج). See ئوځه ماځوځه

P جو دانه *jo-dāna'h*, s.f. (3rd) The mark in the teeth of horses by which the age may be ascertained. 2. The quantity of grain consumed in a stable. Pl. ي *ey*.

جودر *jawdar*, s.m. (2nd) A tare, the darnel (Vicia sativa), particularly those growing amongst barley. Pl. جودرونه *jawdarūnah*. See جمدر and ماردندان

A جور *jawr*, s.m. (2nd) Violence, oppression. Pl. جورونه *jawrūnah*. جور كول *jawr kawul*, verb trans. To act with oppression or violence.

جور *jawar*, adj. Deep, profound, not shallow; (Fem.) جوره *jawara'h*.

جور تيا *jawar tī-ā*, s.f. (6th) Depth, deepness, profundity, depression. (E.) Sing. and Pl.; (W.) Pl. جور تياوي *jawar-tī-ā-wī*, or جور والي *jawar wālaey*, s.m. (1st) Pl. والي *wālī*. See ژور

جوره *jawara'h*, s.f. (3rd) A leech. Pl. ي *ey*.

جوړ *joṟṟ*, adj. Healthy, well, in good health, vigorous, strong. 2. Arranged, prepared, framed, devised, effected. 3. adv. Exactly, precisely. روغ جوړ *rogh joṟṟ*, adj. Well, healthy and strong, etc.; (Fem.) روغه جوړه *rogha'h-joṟṟa'h*. جوړ والي *joṟṟ wālaey*, s.m. (1st) Pl. والي *wālī*, or جوړ تيا *joṟṟ-tī-ā*, s.f. (6th) Health, sanity, healthfulness, haleness, heartiness, vigour, soundness. 2. Preparation, arrangement. (E.) Sing. and Pl.; (W.) Pl. تياوي *tī-ā-wī*.

جوريدل *jorredal*, verb intrans. To recover, to grow healthy or strong, to become vigorous. 2. To become arranged or effected (as peace, or a dispute). Pres. جوريږي *jorrejzī* (W.), or جوريګي *jorregī* (E.); past جوړ شه *jorr shah*, or جوړ وُ شه *jorr wu-shah*; fut. جوړ به شي *jorr bah shī*, or به وُ شي *bah wu-shī*; imp. جوړ شه *jorr shah*, or وُ شه *wu-shah*; act. part. جوړيدونكَي *jorre-dūnkaey*, or جوړيدونيَ *jorre-dūnaey*; past part. جوړ شوىَ *jorr shawaey*; verb. n. جوړيدنه *jorredana'h*.

جوړول *jorrawul*, verb trans. To arrange (as a dispute), to set in order, to devise, frame, contrive, to mature, to organize, to adjust, to accommodate. 3. To cure, to heal, to restore, Pres. جوړوي *jorrawī*; past جوړ كړ *jorr karr*, or وُ كړ *wu-karr*; fut. جوړ به كړي *jorr bah krrī*, or به وُ كړي *bah wu-krrī*; imp. جوړ كړه *jorr krrah*, or وُ كړه *wu-krrah*; act. part. جوړوونكَي *jorrawūnkaey*, or جوړوونيَ *jorrawūnaey*; past part. جوړ كړيَ *jorr karraey*; verb. n. جوړونه *jorrawuna'h*.

جوړاب *jorrāb*, s.m. (2nd) Beauty, gracefulness, good looks, grace, neatness, spruceness, comeliness. Pl. جوړابونه *jorrābūnah*. See كړه وړه

جوړښت *jorrikht* (E.) or *jorrisht* (W.), s.m. (2nd) Combination, union, junction, connection, alliance, concord, coalition, confederacy, conspiracy. Pl. جوړښتونه *jorrikhtūnah* or *jorrishtūnah*. (s جوړِن).

جوړه *jorra'h*, s.f. (3rd) A pair, a set, a couple. 2. A suit of clothes sent to the house of the bride by the bridegroom. Pl. ىْ *ey*. (s. جوړا)

A جوز *jawz*, s.m. (2nd) A nut, the middle or marrow of anything. Pl. جوزونه *jawzūnah*. جوز رومي *jawz-i-rūmī*, A walnut. جوز بويه *jawz būya'h*, A nutmeg. جوز مائل *jawz-i-mā-sil*, or نائل *nā-sil*, A deleterious herb. جوز هندي *jawz-i-hindī*, Betel nut.

جوزه *jawza'h*. s.f. (3rd) A nutmeg. Pl. ىْ *ey*.

جوس *jawas*, s.m. (2nd) A courtyard, an area. Pl. جوسونه *jawas-ūnah*.

P جوش *josh*, s.m. (2nd) Ebullition, effervescence; heat, emotion, lust, passion. Pl. جوشونه *joshūnah*. جوش خروش *josh kharosh*, s.m. (2nd) Anger, rage, passion. جوش خون *josh-i-khūn*, Ebullition of the blood, the name of a disease. په جوش راتلل *pah josh rātlal*, verb intrans., or جوش خوړل *josh khwarral*, or جوش وهل *josh wahal*, verb trans. To boil or bubble up, to be agitated by the action of heat. جوش ور كول *josh war-kawul*, verb trans. To boil, to heat, to stew, to cook, to seethe, to scald. جوشانده *joshānda'h*, s.f. (3rd) A decoction. Pl. ىْ *ey*.

جوكل *jokal*, verb trans. To weigh, to measure. Pres, جوكي *jokī*; past وُ جوكه *wu-jokah* or وُ جوكَ *wu-joka*; fut. وُ به جوكي *wu bah jokī*; imp. وُ جوكه *wu-jokah*; act. part. جوكونكَي *jokūnkaey* or جوكونيَ *jokūnaey*; past part. جوكليَ *jokalaey*; verb. n. جوكنه *jokana'h*.

P جوكوب *jau-kob*, adj. (from جو and act. part. of كوفتن) Half-pounded, coarsely ground. جوكوب كول *jau-kob kawul*, verb trans. To pound or grind coarsely.

S جوګي *jogī*, s.m. (5th) A Hindū fakīr, a devotee. 2. A kind of pigeon. Pl. جوګيان *jogīān*. s.f. (3rd) جوګړنه *jogarrna'h*. Pl. ىْ *ey*.

جولا *jolā*, s.m. (5th) A weaver, a spider. Pl. جولاګان *jolāgān*.

P جولان *jau-lān*, s.m. (9th) Moving about (as horses in a place of exercise), coursing, springing, wandering. Sing. and Pl. جولان كول *jau-lān kawul*, verb trans. To make to spring or jump about, to exercise (as horses). جولان ګاه *jau-lān-gāh*, s.m. (2nd) A place of exercise (of an army, or for horses). Pl. ګاهونه *gāh-ūnah*.

جولانګري *jau-lān-garī*, s.f. (3rd) Galloping fast, fleetness. Pl. ئي *a'ī*.

P جولاه *jolāh*, s.m. (5th) A weaver. Pl. جولاګان *jolā-gān*. See جولا

جوله *jola'h*, s.f. (3rd) (HI جهولا) A stroke of the sun. Pl. ىْ *ey*. جوله وهلي *jola'h wahalaey*, adj. (past part.) Sun-struck; (Fem.) جوله وهلي *jola'h wahali*. Pl. (Masc. and Fem.) يَ *ī*.

جولئي *jola'ī*, s.f. (6th) A wallet, a sack, a bag, a

scrip, a haversack, the skirt of a dress when anything is carried in it. Sing. and Pl. See خولۍ

جونکۍ *jūnaka'ī*, s.f. (6th) A little girl, the diminutive of جنۍ *jina'ī*, which see. Sing. and Pl.

جونګ *jong*, s.m. (2nd) or (5th) A young camel ready for carrying a burden. Pl. جونګونه *jong-ūnah*, or جونګان *jong-ān*. جونګه *jonga'h*, s.f. (3rd) The feminine of the above. Pl. ې *ey*, See جنګ and جنګي

جونګړه *jūngarra'h*, s.f. (3rd) A hut, a hovel. Pl. ې *ey*. See جنګړه

جونګي *jūngaey*, s.m. (1st) A young camel not yet able to carry a load, the diminutive of جونګ Pl. ي *ī*; (Fem.) (6th) Sing. and Pl. جونګۍ *jūnga'ī*. See جنګ and جنګي

جونۍ *jūna'ī*, s.f. (6th) A young girl, a girl, a young unmarried woman. Sing. and Pl.

جوول *jowul*, verb trans. To masticate, to chew, to champ. Pres. جووي *jowī* (rare, the pres. of جويل viz. جويي being generally used instead); past وُ جووه *wu-jo-wuh*, or وُ جووو *wu-jo-wo*; fut. وُ به جووي *wu bah jo-wī* or جويي *jo-yī*; imp. وُ جووه *wu-jo-wah*, or وُ جويه *wu-jo-yah*; act.part. جووونکي *jowūnkaey* or جووونی *jo-wūnaey*; past part. جوولی *jowulaey*; verb. n. جوونه *jowuna'h* or جوينه *jo-yana'h*. See جويل and ژوول

جووه *jowa'h*, s.f. (3rd) A narrow pit or trough for admitting water to melon-plants and grapes. Pl. جووې *jowey*.

AP جوهر *jawhar*, s.m. (9th) A gem, a jewel, a pearl. 2. Matter, substance, essence. 3. Virtue, worth, merit. 4. The blackish marks or water on scimitars. Sing. and Pl. جوهر دار *jawhardār*, adj. A scimitar marked with *jawhar*. جوهري *jawharī*, s.m. (5th) A jeweller. Pl. جوهريان *jawharī-ān*.

جوهړه *jūharra'h*, s.f. (3rd) A wrinkle, a furrow in the face or body. 2. A crease, a crumple, a pucker, a rumple, a plait. Pl. ې *ey*. See ګنځه ,ګنجه ,کرتۍ and چيچر

جويل *jo-yil*, verb trans. To chew, to masticate, to champ. Pres. جويي *jo-yī*; past وُ جويه *wu-jo-yah*; fut. وُ به جويي *wu bah jo-yī*; imp. وُ جويه *wu-jo-yah*; act. part. جويونکی *jo-yūnkaey*, or جويونی *jo-yūnaey*; past part. جويلی *jo-yalaey*; verb. n. جوينه *jo-yana'h*. See جوول and ژويل

جه *jah*, adj. Stubborn, resistive, refractory (as an animal). 2. At bay, standing with the face to one's foes, determining to resist to the death. جه جه *jah jah*, Words used to drive cattle. جه کيدل *jah kedal*, verb intrans. To stand at bay, to take one's stand before an enemy, with the intention of fighting to the last.

A جهاد *jihād*, s.m. (2nd) (inf. III of جهد) War, battle, particularly with infidels. Pl. جهادونه *jihādūnah*. See غزا

جهاړ بوټي *jhārr-būttaey*, s.m. (1st) A kind of wild rue. Pl. ي *ī*. See زار بوټي

P جهاز *jahāz*, s.m. (2nd) A ship, also a boat. Pl. جهازونه *jahāzūnah*.

A جهالت *jahālat*, s.m. (2nd) Ignorance, barbarism, brutality. Pl. جهالتونه *jahālatūnah*.

P جهان *jahān*, s.m. (9th) The world, the universe. 2. People. جهان ديده *jahān-dīdah*, adj. One who has seen the world, a great traveller, experienced. جهان سوز *jahān-soz*, adj. World-inflaming. جهان ګير *jahān-gīr*, adj. World-conquering, world-subduing. جهان ګرد *jahān-gard*, adj. Going round the world, a traveller.

A جهت *jihat*, s.m. (2nd) Cause, reason, account. 2. Side, surface, form, mode, manner. Pl. جهتونه *jihatūnah*.

A جهد *jahd*, s.m. (2nd) Effort, exertion, endeavour, struggle, diligence, care, application, assiduity, earnestness. Pl. جهدونه *jahdūnah*.

جهر *jihr*, s.m. (2nd) A kind of dance performed by men. Pl. جهرونه *jihrūnah*.

A جهل *jahl*, s.m. (2nd) Ignorance, want of sense. Pl. جهلونه *jahlūnah*. جهل کول *jahl kawul*, verb trans. To show ignorance or want of sense.

جهم جکړ *jahm jakarr*, s.m. (2nd) Wind and rain, drift. Pl. جهم جکړونه *jahm jakarrūnah*. (HI جهم جهم).

A جهميه *jhami-yah*, s.m. (6th) The name of a sect of Muḥammadans. Sing. and Pl.

A جهنم *jahannam*, s. prop. Hell.

A جهنمي *jahannamī*, adj. Hellish, infernal, belonging to hell.

P جهود *jahūd*, s.m. (5th) A Jew. Pl. جهودان *jahūdān*. (A يهود)

جهوله *jahūla'h*, s.f. (3rd) The name of a disease. Pl. ې *ey*.

جي *jaey*, s.m. (1st) A leathern bag for carrying water in, a water bag. Pl. ي *ī*.

جئي *ja'ī*, s.f. (6th) Sheep-gut, or goats' entrails, used for bow strings and the strings of musical instruments, catgut. 2. Border, edge, margin, brink, brow, skirt, rim, side, verge. Sing. and Pl. See پيزه ,ژنري ,پاتئي ,جائي ,ژئي and څنډه

T جيب *jeb*, s.m. (2nd) A pocket. Pl. جيبونه *jebūnah*.

جيټ *jeṯṯ*, s.m. (6th) The name of a tree from which tooth brushes or tooth cleaners are made. Sing. and Pl.

S جيټ *jeṯṯ*, s.m. (2nd) The name of the second month of the Hindū year, the month of May—June. Pl. جيټونه *jeṯṯ-ūnah*.

جبرمه *jejzma'h*, s.f. (3rd) The eyelid. Pl. ې *ey*. See څيزمه

P جيغه *jīgha'h*, s.f. (3rd) An ornament of gold worn in the turban, a plume. Pl. ې *ey*. See قرقره

جيل *jel*, s.m. (2nd) (corrup. of A جهل), Ignorance, want of sense, nescience. 2. (HI) A string or line of captives. 3. A string of buckets turned by a Persian wheel. Pl. جيلونه *jelūnah*. جيل کول *jel kawul*, verb trans. To show or manifest ignorance or stupidity. See جهل and څيل

جين جنړ *jīn jarrn*, s.m. (6th) A plant producing a kind of pulse (Cytisus cajan). Sing. and Pl. See جنجنړ

چ

چ *che*, also called *chīm* or *jīm-i-fārsī*, and *jīm-aejamī*, is the seventh letter of the Persian, and the ninth of the Pushto alphabet, and is never found in Arabic words. Its sound is as *ch* in the English word 'cheek.' As a numeral it stands for 3, like the letter ج

P چابک *chābuk*, adj. Alert, quick, agile. چابک دست *chābuk dast*, adj. Active, alert, quick, adroit. چابک دستي *chābuk-dastī*, s.f. (3rd) Activity, alertness, quickness, adroitness. Pl. ئي *a'ī*. See گرندي

P چابکي *chābuk-ī*, s.f. (3rd) Activity, alertness, agility, dispatch, celerity. Pl. ئي *a'ī*. چابکي کول *chābuk-ī kawul*, verb trans. To dispatch, to make haste, to act with celerity.

چاپ *chāp*, s.m. (2nd) Print, copy, impression, stamp. 2. An edition. Pl. چاپونه *chāpūnah*. 3. adj. Printed, stamped, impressed; (Fem.) چاپه *chāpa'h*. 2. s.f. (3rd) A stamp, the stone or letters set up from which an impression is taken. Pl. ې *ey*. چاپ کول *chāp kawul*, verb trans. To print, to stamp. (HI چهاپ)

P چاپلوس *chāp-lūs*, s.m. (5th) A flatterer, a wheedler, a fawner. Pl. چاپلوسان *chāp-lūsān*; s.f. (3rd) چاپلوسه *chāp-lūsa'h*. Pl. ې *ey*.

P چاپلوسي *chāp-lūsī*, s.f. (3rd) Flattery, sycophancy, adulation, wheedling. Pl. ئي *a'ī*. چاپلوسي کول *chāp-lūsī kawul*, verb trans. To flatter, to wheedle, to coax.

چاپه *chāpa'h*, s.f. (3rd) A stamp, the stone or letters from which the impression is taken. Pl. ې *ey*. چاپه وهل *chāpa'h wahal*, verb trans. To print, to stamp, to take an impression. See چاپ

چاپي *chāpī*, s.f. (5th) Kneading the limbs, shampooing. Pl. چاپيگان *chāpī-gānī*. چاپي کول *chāpī kawul*, verb trans. To knead the limbs, to shampoo.

چاپير *chāper*, or چاپيره *chā-perah*, adv. On all sides, round about, on every side, all round, around, about. چار چاپيره *chār-chāperah*, On all sides, right and left. See چوپير and چوپيره

چاپير ځان ځان کيدل *chā-per dzān dzān kedal*, verb intrans. To disperse, or take up a position round about or on all sides of a building or other place, but separate one from each other (as soldiers skirmishing, etc.) چاپير ځان ځان

کول *chāper dzān dzān kawul*, verb trans. To station or post persons round about a place, as above.

P چادر *chādar*, s.m. (2nd) A sheet, a veil worn by women. Pl. چادرونه *chādar-ūnah*. See شادر

چار *chār*, s.f. (1st) Action, business, affair, work, profession, labour, occupation, operation. 2. Remedy, cure, expedient, help, aid. Pl. چار *chāri*. See چاره 3. (P.) adj. Four. Used in composition; as چار آبرو *chār ābrū*, s.m. (5th) A young man whose beard is just appearing. Pl. چار آبروان *chār ābrūān*. چار آينه *chār ā'īna'h*, s.f. (3rd) Steel armour. Pl. ې *ey*. چار پا *chār-pā*, s.m. (5th) A quadruped. Pl. چار پايان *chār-pāyān*. چار پاره *chār pāra'h*, s.f. (3rd) Broken rice, the bullet of a gun, divided into four. Pl. ې *ey*. چار چشم *chār chashm*, s.m. (5th) Expectation, meeting, interview. 2. The eyes of two persons meeting. 3. A dog with white spots above the eyes. Pl. چار چشمان *chār chashmān*. چار پايي *chār pā-yī*, s.f. (5th) A cot, a bed. Pl. چار پايیگان *chār pā-yī-gāni*. چار چوب *chār chob*, s.m. (2nd) The frame of a door, window, etc. Pl. چار چوبونه *chār chobūnah*. چار چوبۍ *chār choba'ī*, s.f. (6th) A privy, a bath, a doorpost. Sing. and Pl. See باس . چار خانه *chār khāna'h*, s.f. (3rd) Chequered cloth. Pl. ې *ey*. چار خول *chār khwal*, s.m. (2nd) Pl. چار خولونه *chār khwalūnah*, or خولي *khwalaey*, s.m. (1st) The comb of the cock, the hood of the hoopoe or the lark, etc. Pl. ي *ī*. چار خولک *chār khwalak*, The diminutive of the preceding. چار زانو *chār zānū*, A mode of sitting like a tailor, squatting. چار زانو كيناستل *chār zānū kenāstal*, verb intrans. To squat. چار سال *chār sāl*, A horse of four years old. چار سو *chār sū*, A cross road, two roads crossing each other, a court, or square, a market-place. چار شانه *chār shāna'h*, adj. Tough, hardy, brawny. چار شمبه *chār shamba'h*, Wednesday. چار صده *chār ṣada'h*, s.prop. The name of a small village in the Do'ābah of Peshāwar. چار گل *chār gul*, s.m. (5th) An ornament for the nose. Pl. چار گلان *chār gulān*. چار مغز *chār maghz*, s.m. (2nd) A walnut. Pl. چار مغزونه *chār maghzūnah*. چار يار *chār yār*, s. prop. The four Khalīfs, the four successors of Muḥammad. چار ياري *chār yārī*, s.m. (5th) A sect of Muḥammadans who venerate the above. Pl. چار ياريان *chār yārīān*. چاريک *chār yek*, s.m. (2nd) A quarter, a fourth part. Pl. چاريكونه *chār yekūnah*. چار نا چار *chār nā chār*, adv. Certainly, inevitably, by force, right or wrong, nolens volens. See خواه ما خواه

P چاره *chāra'h*, s.f. (3rd) Remedy, expedient, cure, aid, help. Pl. ې *ey*. چاره ساز *chāra'h sāz*, or چاره گر *chāra'h gar*, s.m. (5th) Applying remedies, a restorer, a helper, an aider. Pl. چاره سازان *chāra'h sāzān* or گران *garān*, چاره سازي *chāra'h sāzī* or گري *garī*, s.f. (3rd) Remedying, aiding, helping, applying remedies. Pl. ئي *a'ī*.

چاړا *chārrā*, adj. Dumb, stammering. See گنگي

چاړه *chā-rra'h*, s.f. (3rd) A knife, a long knife or dagger, a cleaver. Pl. چاړې *chā-rrey* or چړې *charrey*. Also چړوكۍ *churrūka'ī*, s.f. (6th) A small knife. Sing. and Pl.

چاغ *chāgh*, adj. Alert, active, in spirits, healthy, vigorous, fat, stout, obese; (Fem.) چاغه *chāgha'h*. (T چاق)

چاغيدل *chāghedal*, verb intrans. To become fat, stout, or in good condition, to become active and vigorous. Pres. چاغيږي *chāghejzī* (W.), or چاغيكي *chāghegī* (E.); past چاغ شه *chāgh shah*, or وُ شه *wu-shah*; fut. چاغ به شي *chāgh bah shī*, or به وُ شي *bah wu-shī*; imp. چاغ شه *chāgh shah*, or وُ شه *wu-shah*; act. part. چاغيدونكي *chāghedūnkaey*, or چاغيدونی *chāghedūnaey*; past part. چاغ *chāgh*, or چاغ شوي *chāgh shawaey*; verb. n. چاغيدنه *chāghedana'h*. چاغول *chāghawul*, verb trans. To fatten, to make fat, to make fleshy or plump. Pres. چاغوي *chāghawī*; past چاغ كړ *chāgh karr*, or وُ كړ *wu-karr*; fut. چاغ به كړي *chāgh bah krrī*, or به وُ کړي *bah wu-krrī*; imp. چاغ کړه *chāgh krrah*, or وُ کړه *wu-krrah*; act. part. چاغوونکَي *chāghawūnkaey*, or چاغووني *chāghawūnaey*; past part. چاغ کړي *chāgh karraey*; verb. n. چاغونه *chāghawuna'h*.

T چاقو *chākū*, s.m. (5th) A penknife, a clasp-knife. Pl. چاقوګان *chākūgān*. See چاکو

P چاك *chāk*, s.m. (2nd) A rent, a slit, a fissure, a crack, a chap, an opening left in the clothes, a chink, a gash. Pl. چاکونه *chāk-ūnah*. 2. adj. Rent, torn, slit, gashed, cracked; (Fem.) چاکه *chāka'h*. چاك کيدل *chāk kedal*, verb intrans. To be rent, torn, cracked, slit, etc. چاك کول *chāk kawul*, verb trans. To rend, to split, to crack, to gash. چاك چاك *chāk-chāk*, adj. Rent and torn, broken, etc. چاك ګريبان *chāk girībān*, adj. Sad, afflicted (*lit.*, having the collar rent).

P چاکر *chākar*, s.m. (5th) A servant, a retainer, a help. Pl. چاکران *chākarān*; s.f. (3rd) چاکره *chākara'h*, A female servant. Pl. ئ *ey*. چاکري *chākarī*, s.f. (3rd) Service, servitude, dependence. Pl. ئ *a'ī*.

چاکو *chākū*, s.m. (5th) A penknife, a clasp-knife. Pl. چاکوګان *chākūgān*. See چاقو

S چال *chāl*, s.m. (2nd) Gait, motion, movement, procedure, habit, custom, way, method. 2. Contrivance, trick. Pl. چالونه *chālūnah*. چال کول *chāl kawul*, verb trans. To contrive, to trick. چالباز *chāl-bāz*, s.m. (5th) A contriver, a cheat, a deceiver. Pl. چالبازان *chāl-bāzān*; s.f. (3rd) چالبازه *chālbāza'h*. Pl. ئ *ey*. See چل

P چالاك *chālāk*, adj. Active, alert, clever, ingenious, dexterous, expert, fleet; (Fem.) چالاکه *chālāka'h*. چالاکي *chālākī*, s.f. (3rd) Activity, alertness, nimbleness, celerity, dexterity, fleetness, agility. Pl. ئ *a'ī*. چالاکي کول *chālākī kawul*, verb trans. To act with alertness or activity, etc.

S چاندني *chāndanī*, s.f. (3rd) A cloth spread over a carpet to preserve it, generally white; a counterpane or cloth spread over a bed. Pl. ئ *a'ī*.

چانړ *chārrn*, adj. Sifted, strained, filtered, percolated; (Fem.) چانړه *chārrna'h*. 2. s.m. (2nd) Siftings, precipitate. Pl. چانړونه *chārrnūnah*. چانړيدل *chārrnedal*, verb intrans. To percolate, to become sifted or strained. Pres. چانړيږي *chārrnejzī* (W.), or چانړيګي *chārrnegī* (E.); past چانړ شه *chārrn shah*, or وُ شه *wu-shah*; fut. چانړ به شي *chārrn bah shī*, or به وُ شي *bah wu-shī*; imp. چانړ شه *chārrn shah*, or وُ شه *wu-shah*; act. part. چانړيدونکَي *chārrnedūnkaey*, or چانړيدوني *chārrnedūnaey*; past part. چانړ شوي *chārrn shawaey*; verb. n. چانړيدنه *chārrnedana'h*. چانړول *chārrnawul*, verb trans. To filter, to sift, to percolate, to strain. Pres. چانړوي *chārrnawī*; past چانړ کړ *chārrn karr*, or وُ کړ *wu-karr*; fut. چانړ به کړي *chārrn bah krrī*, or به وُ کړي *bah wu-krrī*; imp. چانړ کړه *chārrn krrah*, or وُ کړه *wu-krrah*; act. part. چانړوونکي *chārrnawūnkaey*, or چانړووني *chārrnawūnaey*; past part. چانړ کړي *chārrn karraey*; verb. n. چانړونه *chārrnawuna'h*. See چنړل

S چانړه *chārrna'h*, s.f. (3rd) A small rafter laid across the beams of a roof. Pl. ئ *ey*. See دستکي

چاود *chāwd*, s.m. (2nd) A split, a crack, a fissure, a rent. Pl. چاودونه *chāwdūnah*. Also چاوده *chāwda'h*, s.f. (3rd). Pl. ئ *ey*.

چاودل *chāwdal*, verb intrans. To split, to crack, to slit, to splinter. Pres. چوي *ch'wī*; past وُ چاود *wu-chāwd*; fut. وُ به چوي *wu bah ch'wī*; imp. وُ چوه *wu-ch'wah*; act. part. چاودونکَي *chāwdūnkaey*, or چاودوني *chāwdūnaey*; past part. چاودلَي *chāwdalaey*, or چاودَي *chāwdaey*; verb. n. چاودنه *chāwdana'h*. See چول

چاودينك *chāwdīnak*, adj. Bold, saucy, or mischievous (as a child); (Fem.) چاودينکه *chāwdīnaka'h*. See ويته and ويتکي

چاول *chāwul*, s.m. (2nd) A plumb-line, a plummet. Pl. چاولونه *chāwul-ūnah*.

P چاه *chāh*, s.m. (5th) A pit, a well. Pl. چاهان

chahān. چاه زنخ chāh-i-zanakh, The dimple of the chin.

چایل chā-yal, s.m. (2nd) A sheet or veil of chintz, worn by women. Pl. چایلونه chā-yalūnah. See چهایل and پروني

P چپ chap, adj. The left, the opposite to the right of the body, the left hand, etc. چپ وراس chap-o-rās, or چپ و راست chap-o-rāst, Right and left, on all sides. See کینړ

چپ chip, adj. Silent. 2. interj. Silence! hush!

T چپاول chapāwul, s.m. (5th) An advanced guard of cavalry. Pl. چپاولان chapāwulān.

چپاو chapā'o, s.m. (2nd) A raid, a foray, a coup de main, an inroad. Pl. چپاوونه chapā'o-ūnah. چپاو پریوتل chapā'o prewatal, verb trans. To fall on suddenly and attack, to fall upon. چپاو کول chapā'o kawul, verb trans. To plunder, to make a raid or foray.

چپر chapar, s.m. (2nd) A royal messenger, a courier. Pl. چپرونه chaparūnah.

چپړدخ chaparr-dakh, s.m. (2nd) The name of a game played with round flat stones or pebbles, a kind of pitch and toss. 2. The name of the stones with which the game is played. Pl. چپړدخونه chaparr-dakhūnah.

چپړوسي chap-rrūsī, s.f. (3rd) Flattery, sycophancy, adulation, wheedling. Pl. ئ a'ī. چپړوسي کول chap-rrūsī kawul, verb trans. To flatter, to wheedle, to coax.

چپک chapak, adj. Squint-eyed, a person with a squint or cast in the eye; (Fem.) چپکه chapaka'h. سترگي چپکي کول stargey chapakey kawul, verb trans. To squint, to look in an oblique direction.

چپلئ chapla'ī, s.f. (6th) Sandals made of leather or grass. Sing. and Pl. See څپلئ

چپه chapah, adj. Inverted, upside down. چپه کیدل chapah kedal, verb intrans. To become inverted. چپه کول chapah kawul, verb trans. To invert, to turn upside down.

چپه chapa'h, s.f. (3rd) A wave, a billow, a surge, a ripple. 2. A gust of wind, a puff, a blast. 3. The swoop of a falcon or other bird of prey. 4. The height of a disease. 5. An oar, a paddle. Pl. ي ey. چپه وهل chapa'h wahal, verb trans. To flow, to cover with water, to well. 2. To blow, to whiff, to waft as the wind. 3. To swoop as a falcon. 4. To row. See څپه, وکم and ورمه or وکمه

چت chit, adj. Squeezed, pressed, quashed, crushed; (Fem.) چته chita'h. 2. s.m. (2nd) Mind, life, soul, heart, memory. Pl. چتونه chit-ūnah. چت پت chit pit, adj. Quashed, crushed, smashed, trodden under foot. چت پت کول chit pit kawul, verb trans. To crush, to smash, to squash, etc.

چت chat, s.m. (2nd) The roof of a house or room, a ceiling, a platform. Pl. چتونه chat-ūnah. (s چهت).

چتر chatr, s.m. (2nd) A bare place left by a wound or pimple on which the hair does not grow, a bald place on the head. Pl. چترونه chatrūnah. چتري chatraey, adj. A person having a bare or bald place on the head or body; (Fem.) چترئ chatra'ī. Sing. and Pl.

P چتر chatr, s.m. (2nd) An umbrella, a canopy, a shade. Pl. چترونه chatrūnah.

چترک chatrak, s.m. (6th) The name of a tribe of Afghāns. Sing. and Pl. s.f. (3rd) چترکه chatraka'h. Pl. ي ey.

چتي chitey, s.m. (1st) A titmouse. Pl. ي ī.

چتي chitī or چت کول chit kawul, verb trans. To bruise, to crush, to squeeze, to quash.

چټ chatt, s.m. (5th) A libertine, a rake, a debauchee, a vagabond, a profligate, a rollicking blade, a puppy. Pl. چټان chattān; s.f. (3rd) چټه chatta'h, A harlot, a piece, a quean. Pl. ي ey. چټي chattī, s.f. (3rd) Libertinism, licentiousness, debauchery, lewdness. Pl. ئ a'ī. چټي کول chattī kawul, verb trans. To practise libertinism, etc. See also لوند

چټ chatt or چټ پټ chatt-patt, adv. Entirely, wholly, totally, utterly, outright, completely, out and out, clean.

چټک chuttak, s.m. (2nd) A hammer. Pl. چټکونه chuttakūnah. See څټک

چټکه chittka'h, s.f. (3rd) A kind of coarse cotton cloth dyed red. Pl. ي ey.

HI چټکي *chuṭṭkī*, s.f. (3rd) Snapping of the fingers. Pl. ئ *a'ī*. چټکي کول *chuṭṭkī kawul*, verb trans. To snap the fingers.

چټي *chaṭṭī*, s.f. (3rd) Libertinism, profligacy, vagabondism, puppyism, etc. Pl. ئ *a'ī*.

چج *chaj*, s.m. (2nd) A kind of basket for winnowing corn. Pl. چجونه *chajūnah*. Also written چچ *chach*. چج *chaj* or چچ کول *chach kawul*, verb trans. To winnow grain, to clean, to rinse. See څب

چجه *chaja'h*, s.f. (3rd) A stake driven into the ground for catching fish. 2. The ribs on one side, the side ribs. 3. The leaf of the carrot. Pl. ئ *ey*.

چچل *chichal*, verb trans. To bite, to gnaw, to chew, to masticate, to gnash the teeth. Pres. چچي *chichī*; past و چچه *wu-chichah*; fut. و به چچي *wu bah chichī*; imp. چچه *chichah* or و چچه *wu-chichah*; act. part. چچونکے *chichūnkaey* or چچونے *chichūnaey*; past part. چچلے *chichalaey*; verb. n. چچنه *chichana'h*. See also چیچل

چچونکے *chichūnkaey*, act. part. as s.m. (1st) A biter (a horse or other animal); (Fem.) چچونکې *chichūnki*. Pl. (Masc. and Fem.) ي *ī*. See خروري

چچه *chachah*, A word used to drive away goats. See چکر

P چخ *chikh* or چخي *chikhey*, interj. Avaunt! begone! get out! generally used to drive away a dog.

چخربه *chakhrraba'h*, s.f. (3rd) Prodigality, dissipation, extravagance, waste. Pl. ئ *ey*. چخربه کول *chakhrraba'h kawul*, verb trans. To lavish, to waste, to mis-spend, to throw away money.

چخړه *chikhrra'h*, s.f. (3rd) Rheum, watery matter or humour in the eyes. Pl. ئ *ey*. See چخي

چخن *chikhan*, adj. Rheumy, full of rheum or watery matter, running. 2. Dull, dim, or clouded, as a mirror. 3. A person with rheumy eyes, dirty, unclean; (Fem.) چخنه *chikhana'h*.

چخه *chikhah*, interj. Begone! a word used to drive away a dog, and sometimes used contemptuously. 2. *chakhah*, post-p. At the side, near, at, beside. See څنګه

چخے *chikhaey*, s.m. (1st) Rheum, matter from the eyes. Pl. ي *ī*. 2. adj. A few, some.

چدام *chadām*, s.m. (2nd) The eighth part of a *tola*, a weight. Pl. چدامونه *chadāmūnah*.

چرِ *chari* or چري *charey*, adv. One time, once, at any time, some time or other, ever. 2. Never, at no time, on no occasion. 3. Where? in what place? چرِ چرِ *chari-chari* or چري چري *charey-charey*, Now and then, at times, occasionally, sometimes, from time to time.

چر *char*, s.m. (5th) The chirp or chirrup of a sparrow, etc. 2. Chatter, twitter, nonsense. Pl. چرهار *charahār*. چر چر کول *char-char kawul*, verb trans. To chirp, to chirrup, to twitter, to talk nonsense. چر چرے *chir-chiraey*, s.m. (1st) A twitterer, a talker of nonsense, a tattler. Pl. ي *ī*. چرچرئ *chir-chira'ī*, s.f. (6th) A tattling, chatter-box woman. 2. A squib, a kind of firework. Sing. and Pl.

چر *chur*, s.m. (5th) A furrow or ravine made by running water, a channel, a gutter, a gulley. Pl. چران *churān*. چر کيدل *chur kedal*, verb intrans. To become furrowed or channeled by water. چر کول *chur kawul*, verb trans. To channel, to furrow.

P چراغ *chirāgh*, s.m. (2nd) A lamp, a light. Pl. چراغونه *chirāghūnah*. چراغان کول *chirāghān kawul*, verb trans. To illuminate with lamps. چراغ بلول *chirāgh balawul*, verb trans. To light a lamp. چراغ مړ کول *chirāgh marr kawul*, verb trans. To extinguish a lamp.

P چرب *charb*, adj. Fat, thick, gross, viscous, oily. چرب دست *charb dast*, adj. Active, ingenious. چرب زبان *charb zabān*, adj. Smooth-tongued, plausible, fair-spoken, flattering. چرب زباني *charb zabānī*, s.f. (3rd) Plausibility, fairness of speech, speciousness. Pl. ئ *a'ī*. See خورب

چر بانګ *char bāng*, s.m. (2nd) Cock-crow,

early dawn. Pl. چر بانګونه char bāngūnah. See چرګ بانګ

P چربي charbī, s.f. (3rd) Fat, grease, suet. Pl. ۍ a'ī.

HI چرت churt or chart, s.m. (2nd) A nap, drowsiness, nodding. Pl. چرتونه churtūnah. چرت وهل churt wahal, verb trans. To nod, to be drowsy. See پرنا

چرته chartah, adv. Where? in what place?

چرته charta'h, s.f. (3rd) Colour, complexion. Pl. ې ey. See جرده and چرده

چرچڼر char-charrn, s.m. (6th) A cock-sparrow. Pl. چرچڼر char-charrn. s.f. (3rd) چر چڼړه char-charrna'h, A hen-sparrow. Pl. ې ey. See چڼرچڼر and چغکه

P چرخ charkh, s.m. (2nd) A wheel. 2. Turn, motion, turning, circular motion. Pl. چرخونه charkhūnah. See څرخ

چرخولي char-khwalaey, s.m. (1st) The comb of a cock, the crest on the head of birds. Pl. ي ī. See چارخول and چارخولک

چرده charda'h, s.f. (3rd) Colour, complexion. Pl. ې ey. See جرده and چرته

چرړه chir-rra'h, s.f. (3rd) A rag, a tatter, a shred, a fraction. Pl. ې ey. See جرړه

HI چرس chars, s.m. (6th) A preparation made from the flowers of hemp, and used as an intoxicating drug. Sing. and Pl.

چرسي charsī, s.m. (5th) A consumer of chars, intoxicated with chars. Pl. چرسيان charsī'ān.

P چرک chirk, s.m. (2nd) Dirt, filth, ordure. 2. Pus, matter. Pl. چرکونه chirkūnah.

P چرکين chirkīn, adj. Filthy, dirty, foul, unclean; (Fem.) چرکينه chirkīna'h. چرکين کول chirkīn kawul, verb trans. To soil, to make dirty, etc.

چرکلي charkulaey, s.m. (1st) A kind of greens. Pl. ي ī.

چرګ chirg, s.m. (5th) A cock. Pl. چرګان chirgān; s.f. (3rd) چرګه chirgah, A hen. Pl. ې ey. چرګ بانګ chirg bāng, s.m. (2nd) Cock-crow or cock-crowing, early morning. Pl. چرګ بانګونه chirg-bāngūnah.

چرګ chirg, adj. Acute, astute, apt, sharp, clever, keen, long-headed, shrewd. 2. Spotted, or having a spot on the forehead (as a cow, horse, etc.) (Fem.) چرګه chirga'h.

چرګ برګ chrag brag, adj. Spotted, piebald; (Fem.) چرګه برګه chraga'h braga'h.

چرګک chirgak, s.m. (5th) The hoopoe. Pl. چرګکان chirgakān. Also ملا چرګک mullā-chirgak.

چرګوړي chirgūrraey, s.m. (1st) A chicken. Pl. ي ī; s.f. (6th) ۍ a'ī, A pullet. Sing. and Pl.; or چرګوړ chirgurri. Pl. ي ī.

چرګه برګه chragah bragah, adj. Staring or rolling (as the eye, when a person is enraged).

چرګي برګي chragaey bragaey, s.m. (1st) Any thing or animal piebald, striped, or spotted. Pl. ي ī; s.f (6th) ۍ a'ī. Sing. and Pl. چرګي برګي سترګي chragey bragey stargey, Rolling or staring eyes.

چرګي chirgaey or chargaey, s.m. (1st) An animal with a white face (as a horse, etc.). Pl. ي ī; s.f. (6th) Sing. and Pl. ۍ a'ī. See چرګ

چرلندي churlandaey, s.m. (1st) A child's plaything, consisting of a piece of wood with a hole and string, which is wound round the head, producing a buzzing or humming sound, a humming top. Pl. ي ī.

چرلندۍ churlanda'ī, s.f. (6th) A whip-top, a teetotum. Sing. and Pl. See څرخندوکي and جلنغۍ

چرلنډ charlandd, s.m. (5th) A rascal, a knave, a blackguard, a miscreant, a ruffian. Pl. چرلنډان charlanddān. چرلنډه charlandda'h, s.f. (3rd) A jade, a Jezebel. Pl. ې ey.

چرلول churlawul, verb trans. To make revolve, to cause to turn (as the earth) on its own axis. See چرليدل

چرلۍ churla'ī, s.f. (6th) A kind of game played with walnuts, a child's game. 2. A toy which children spin or whirl round, a whirligig. Sing. and Pl. See جلندرۍ

چرليدل churledal, verb intrans. To revolve, to turn, to spin, to circumvolve, to whirl, to gyrate, to twirl. Pres. چرلي churlī, or چرليږي churlejzī (W.) or چرليګي churlegī (E.); past

وُ چرليدَ *wu-churleda* or وُ چرليدهٔ *wu-churledah*; fut. وُ به چرلي *wu bah churlī*, etc.; imp. وُ چرله *wu-churlah*, etc.; act. part. چرليدونكيَ *churledūnkaey* or چرليدونيَ *churledūnaey*; past part. چرليدليَ *churledalaey*; verb. n. چرليدنه *churledana'h*. چرلول *churlawul*, verb trans. To whirl, to make to spin, to make revolve, to turn round, to gyrate. Pres. چرلوي *churlawī*; past وُ چرلاوهٔ *wu-churlāwuh* or وُ چرلاوو *wu-churlāwo*; fut. وُ به چرلوي *wu bah churlawī*; imp. وُ چرلوهٔ *wu-churlawah*; act. part. چرلوونكيَ *churlawūnkaey* or چرلوونيَ *churlawūnaey*; past part. چرلوليَ *churlawulaey*; verb. n. چرلونه *churlawuna'h*.

چرمباز *charambāz*, s.m. (5th) The outer or outside bullock of a pair when treading out corn. The inner one is called مندي . Pl. چرمبازان *charambāzān*.

چرمښكۍ *charmushka'ī* (W.) or *charmukha'ī* (E.) s.f. (6th) A species of lizard. Sing. and Pl. See شرمښكۍ and خرمښكۍ

چرمينه *charmena'h*, s.f. (3rd) Strips of raw hide twisted together and made into rope. Pl. يْ *ey*. See سرباندي

چرنک *charanak*, s.m. (5th) Name of a species of plant with milky juice, of the Asclepias or Euphorbia family. Pl. چرنګ *charanæk*.

چره *chara'h*, s.f. (3rd) Small shot, langrage, grape shot. Pl. يْ *ey*. (HI چهرا)

چري *charey*, adv. At any time, some time or other, ever, once, one time. 2. Never, at no time, on no occasion. 3. Where? in, or at what place? چري چري *charey charey*, Now and then, at times, occasionally, sometimes, from time to time. See چرِ

چريكار *charey-kār*, s.m. (5th) A cultivator who merely supplies his own labour in the cultivation, the farmer furnishing seed, etc.; a ploughman, a man-servant. Pl. چريكاران *charey-kārān*. 2. s.m. (2nd) The hair under the lower lip. Pl. چريكارونه *charey-kārūnah*. Also written چريكار *charikār*. See بزگر

چړ *charr*, s.m. (2nd) A cascade, a waterfall. 2. The bread of charity, collecting the bread for the poor. 3. The staff of a pike or short spear used by infantry. Pl. چړان *charrān*. چړ كول *charr kawul*, verb trans. To collect the bread or other contributions for the travellers or mullās of the masjid, from the different houses.

چړي *charrī*, s.m. (5th) A person who goes from house to house collecting the bread, etc., as above. Pl. چړيان *charrīān*.

چړ *churr*, s.m. (2nd) The part of a door which revolves in a socket in the lintel or threshold, and serves the purpose of a hinge. Pl. چړونه *churrūnah*. See چنځ

چړچه *charrcha'h*, s.f. (3rd) Excess, luxury, dissipation, debauchery, sensuality. Pl. يْ *ey*. چړچيي *charr-cha-yī*, s.m. (5th) A free-liver, a voluptuary, a Sybarite. Pl. چړچيان *charrcha-yīān*. چړچه كول *charrcha'h kawul*, verb trans. To indulge, to revel, to plunge into dissipation.

چړق *charrak*, s.m. (2nd) A waterspout. Pl. چړقونه *charrakūnah*.

چړق *charrak*, s.m. (5th) The noise of water splashing on the ground. Pl. چړقهار *charrakahār*.

چړقاو *charrkā'o*, s.m. (2nd) Sprinkling water. Pl. چړقاوونه *charrkā'o-ūnah*. چړقاو كول *charrkā'o kawul*, verb trans. To sprinkle water on the ground, etc. See چنكاو and چنړكاو

چړوكۍ *churrūka'ī*, s.f. (6th) A small knife. Sing. and Pl.

P چسپ *chasp*, s.m. (2nd) Stickiness, tenacity, cohesion, adhesiveness, gumminess. Pl. چسپونه *chaspūnah*. چسپان *chaspān*, adj. Adhesive, sticky, viscous, sticking together; (Fem.) چسپه *chaspa'h*. چسپيدل *chaspedal*, verb intrans. To cohere, to stick, to adhere, to cling, to cleave, to hold, to hang together. Pres. چسپيږي *chaspejzī* (W.) or چسپيګي *chaspegī* (E.); past وُ چسپيدَ *wu-chaspeda* or وُ چسپيدهٔ *wu-chaspedah*; fut. وُ به چسپيږي *wu bah chaspejzī* or وُ به چسپيګي *wu bah chaspegī*; imp. وُ چسپېږه *wu-chaspejzah* or وُ چسپېګه *wu-chaspegah*; act.part. چسپېدونکئ *chaspedūnkaey* or چسپېدونئ *chaspedūnaey*; past part. چسپېدلئ *chaspedalaey*; verb. n. چسپېدنه *chaspedana'h*. چسپول *chaspawul*, verb trans. To fasten by causing to adhere, to make stick, to glue, to cement. Pres. چسپوي *chaspawī*; past وُ چسپاوه *wu-chaspāwuh* or وُ چسپاوو *wu-chaspāwo*; fut. وُ به چسپوي *wu bah chaspawī*; imp. وُ چسپوه *wu-chaspawah*; act. part. چسپوونکئ *chaspawūnkaey* or چسپوونئ *chaspawūnaey*; past part. چسپولئ *chaspawulaey*; verb. n. چسپونه *chaspawuna'h*. See سليښت.

P چست *chust*, adj. Active, quick, ingenious, alert. 2. Tight fitting as a garment, straight; (Fem.) چسته *chusta'h*. چست او چالاک *chust aw chālāk*, adj. Fleet, alert, sharp. چستي *chustī*, s.f. (3rd) Activity, fleetness, nimbleness, alertness. Pl. ئ *a'ī*.

چستي *chustaey*, s.m. (1st) The tripe or rectum. Pl. ي *ī*. (P چستا).

چشكله *chashkalah*. See څشكله and څښكله

چشل *ch'shal*, verb trans. See څښل

P چشم *chashm*, s.m. (5th) The eye. Pl. چشمان *chashmān*. Used in composition, as آهو چشم *āhū chashm*, adj. Fawn-eyed, soft-eyed. چشم براه *chashm ba-rāh*, Expecting, waiting for. چشم پوشي *chashm poshī*, s.f. (3rd) Turning away the eyes, connivance, pretending not to see or notice. Pl. ئ *a'ī*. See سترګه

P چشمک *chashmak*, s.m. (2nd) A wink, winking. Pl. چشمکونه *chashmakūnah*. چشمک وهل *chashmak wahal*, verb trans. To wink the eye, to make a sign unto.

چشمکه *chashmaka'h*, s.f. (3rd) An eye-glass. Pl. چشمکي *chashmakey*, A pair of spectacles.

P چشمه *chashma'h*, s.f. (3rd) A fountain. 2. An eye-glass, a spectacle. Pl. چشمي *chashmey*, A pair of spectacles. See چينه

چشي *chashaey*, s.m. (1st) A kind of thistle which sticks to the clothes, the caltrop. Pl. ي *ī*.

چښتن *chakhtan* (E.) or *chashtan* (W.) s.m. (5th) A master, a lord, a possessor, a proprietor, an owner. Pl. چښتنان *chakhtanān* or *chashtanān*; s.f. (3rd) چښتنه *chakhtana'h* or *chashtana'h*, A mistress, a lady, a proprietress. Pl. ې *ey*. See څښتن

چغ *chagh* or *chigh*, s.m. (5th) Noise, din, tumult, disturbance, altercation, dispute. Pl. چغهار *chaghahār* or *chighahār*. چغ چغ *chigh chigh*, s.m. (2nd) The noise made by fowls, cackling, prattle, chatter, gabble. Pl. چغ چغونه *chigh chighūnah*. See جق جق.

چغ چوغ *chigh chūgh*, s.m. (2nd) Noise, tumult, clamour, din, hullaballoo. Pl. چغ چوغونه *chigh chūghūnah*. چغېدل *chighedal*, verb intrans. To become noisy or tumultuous, to dispute, etc. Pres. چغېږي *chighejzī* (W.) or چغېګي *chighegī* (E.); past وُ چغېدَ *wu-chigheda* or وُ چغېده *wu-chighedah*; fut. وُ به چغېږي *wu bah chighejzī* or وُ به چغېګي *wu bah chighegī*; imp. وُ چغېږه *wu-chighejzah* or وُ چغېګه *wu-chighegah*; act. part. چغېدونکئ *chighedūnkaey* or چغېدونئ *chighedūnaey*; past part. چغېدلئ *chighedalaey*; verb. n. چغېدنه *chighedana'h*. چغول *chighawul*, verb trans. To create a din, tumult, or disturbance, to make a noise, to cause an altercation, etc. Pres. چغوي *chighawī*; past وُ چغاوه *wu-chighāwuh* or وُ چغاوو *wu-chighāwo*; fut. وُ به چغوي *wu bah chighawī*; imp. وُ چغوه *wu-chighawah*; act. part. چغوونکئ *chighawūnkaey* or چغوونئ *chighawūnaey*; past part. چغولئ *chighawulaey*; verb. n. چغونه *chighawuna'h*.

چغار *chughār*, s.m. (2nd) The song of a bird, particularly of the nightingale; the sound of an instrument. Pl. چغارونه *chughārūnah*.

چغاره *chighāra'h*, s.f. (3rd) Noise, disturbance, din, tumult, hullaballoo, cry, scream, outcry, uproar. Pl. ې *ey*. چغاره کول *chighāra'h kawul*, verb trans. To raise an outcry, uproar, disturbance, etc.

چغاغه *chaghā-gha'h*, s.f. (3rd) The name of a plant growing near water, of which pickles are made, and also used in medicine. There are two sorts پيروه چغاغه *per-ṟṟa'h chaghā-gha'h* (bitter and sweet), and نرئي چغاغه *nara'ī chaghā-gha'h* (thin and bitter). Pl. ې *ey*. See چغانغه

چغال *chaghāl*, s.m. (5th) A jackal. Pl. چغالان *chaghālān*. (P شغال).

چغانغه *chaghāngha'h*, s.f. (3rd) The name of a plant. Pl. ې *ey*. See چغاغه

P چغانه *chaghāna'h*, s.f. A violin. Pl. ې *ey*.

T چغتا *chaghattā*, s.m. (6th) The name of a Mughal family to which Tīmūr belonged.

چغتي *chaghattaey*, s.m. (1st) A man of the above tribe. Pl. ي *ī*; s.f. (3rd) ئي *a'ī*, A female of the tribe. Sing. and Pl.

P چغر *chaghar*, adj. Wall-eyed (as a horse); (Fem.) چغره *chaghara'h*.

چغرزي *chaghar-zī*, s.m. (1st) Pl. The name of a tribe of Afghāns dwelling in Buner.

چغرزئ *chaghar-zaey*, A man of the above tribe; s.f. (6th) ئي *a'ī*, A female of the above. Sing. and Pl.

چغرو *chagharū*, s.m. (5th) An owl. Pl. چغروگان *chagharū-gān*. See گونگي

چغرئي *chigh-ra'ī*, s.f. (6th) The name of a river near Kandahār. Sing. and Pl.

چغزئي *chaghza'ī*, s.f. (6th) A kind of soft walnut, of which there are two sorts. Sing. and Pl. See متاك and اوغز

چغزي *chaghzī*, s.m. (5th) The sound of an arrow passing through the air, the crackling of wood when splitting. 2. Any wood of a brittle or stiff kind which cannot be bent. Pl. چغزيان *chaghzī-ān*. See کروسند, سړ and شر

P چغک *chughuk*, s.m. (5th) A sparrow. Pl. چغکان *chughukān*; s.f. (3rd) چغکه *chughuka'h*. Pl. ې *ey*. See چرچڼر

P چغل *chughul*, s.m. (5th) A tell-tale, a tale-bearer, a backbiter, a spy, an informer. Pl. چغلان *chughulān*; s.f. (3rd) چغله *chughula'h*. Pl. ې *ey*.

چغلي *chughulī*, s.f. (3rd) Tale-bearing, back-biting, informing. Pl. ئي *a'ī*. چغلي کول *chughulī kawul*, verb trans. To back-bite, to carry tales, to inform.

چغي *chughaey*, adj. as s.m. (1st) Blinkard, seeing with the eyes half shut. 2. A blinkard. Pl. ي *ī*. چغي *chugha'ī*, s.f. (6th) Sing. and Pl. چغي سترګي *chaghey stargey*, Blinking eyes.

چف *chuf*, s.m. (2nd) A breath, a puff, charming by breathing on a thing, or as a juggler when exorcising. Pl. چفونه *chufūnah*. See چپ and دم. چف کول *chuf kawul*, verb trans. To breathe, to breathe on by way of a charm.

چقړ *chikaṟṟ*, s.m. (2nd) Mud, mire, slime. Pl. چقړونه *chikaṟṟūnah*. See چکړ and خټه (HI چيکړ).

T چقماق *chakmāk* or چقمق *chak-mak*, s.m. (2nd) A flint lock for a gun. Pl. چقماقونه *chakmāk-ūnah* or چقمقونه *chakmakūnah*. چقماقي توپک *chakmākī topak*, s.m. (2nd) A firelock. Pl. توپکونه *topakūnah*.

P چقندر *chukundur*, s.m. (5th) Beet-root (Beta vulgaris). Pl. چقندرونه *chukundurūnah*. See چغندر

چقه *chu-ka'h*, s.f. (3rd) The clucking of a cock or hen when angry, cackle. Pl. ې *ey*. چقه وهل *chu-ka'h wahal*, verb trans. To cackle, to make a noise, as fowls when angry.

چکچکه *chak-chaka'h*, s.f. (3rd) A clap of the hand. Pl. چکچکي *chakchakey*, Clapping the hands by way of applause. چکچکي کول *chak-chakey kawul*, verb trans. To clap the hands by way of applause.

چکر *chikar*, A word used to call goats. See چچه

چکړ *chikaṟṟ*, s.m. (2nd) Mud, mire, slime. Pl. چکړونه *chikaṟṟ-ūnah*. See چقړ and خټه

چکس *chakas*, s.m. (2nd) A perch for birds, a roost for a falcon. Pl. چکسونه *chakasūnah* (HI چکس).

چکښو *chakshū* (W.) or *chakkhū* (E.), s.m. (9th) A black seed used in medicine as a remedy for sore eyes. Sing. and Pl. See څکښو (P چاکسو).

چکله *chikla'h*, s.f. (3rd) A small quantity, particularly liquids, as a thimbleful, a sprinkling, a droplet, a dash, etc. Pl. ې *ey*.

چکلۍ *chakla'ī*, s.f. (6th) The large cog wheel of a Persian wheel which turns perpendicularly. 2. The name of a plaything, a whirligig. Sing. and Pl.

T چکمک *chakmak*, s.m. (2nd) Pl. چکمکونه *chakmakūnah*. See چقمق

HI چکمه *chakma'h*, s.f. (3rd) A boot, a stocking. Pl. ې *ey*.

P چکن *chikan*, s.m. (2nd) A mode of working flowers on muslin or other cloth, embroidery. Pl. چکنونه *chikanūnah*. چکن دوز *chikan-doz*, s.m. (5th) An embroiderer. Pl. چکن دوزان *chikan-dozān*. چکن دوزي *chikan-dozī*, s.f. (3rd) The making of embroidery on muslin, etc. Pl. ۍ *a'ī*.

چکه *chaka'h*, s.f. (3rd) The hand. Pl. ې *ey*. چک چکي *chak-chakī*, Clapping the hands. چک چکي کول *chak-chakī kawul*, verb trans. To clap the hands. چک په چک *chak pah chak*, Hand in hand.

چکه *chaka'h*, s.f. (3rd) Coagulated milk, curd. Pl. ې *ey*. (S چکا).

چکه *chakah*, adj. Perfect, expert, experienced, applied to a robber; as چکه غل *chakah ghal*, A perfect or experienced thief, the son of a thief, etc. چکه آغزن *chakah āghzan*, Very thorny, full of or covered with thorns. See اچکه غل

چکوری *chikoraey*, s.m. (1st) A new-born calf until weaned. Pl. ي *ī*; s.f. (6th) چکورۍ *chikora'ī*, The feminine of the above. Sing. and Pl. See څکوري

چکۍ *chaka'ī*, s.f. (6th) A cake, a lump, a clot, a stick, a mass of matter concreted. 2. The tail of the *dūmba'h* or flat-tailed sheep. Sing. and Pl.

P چکیده *chakīdah*, adj. Coagulated, clotted as curds, etc. (P چکیدن To drop, to distil).

S چل *chal*, s.m. (2nd) Deception, fraud, imposition, artifice, trickery, juggle, humbug, gammon, imposture. Pl. چلونه *chalūnah*. چل باز *chal bāz* or چلي *chalī*, s.m. (5th) A deceiver, a cheat, a quack, an imposter, etc. Pl. چل بازان *chal-bāzān*, or چلیان *chalī-ān*; s.f. (3rd) چلبازه *chal-bāza'h*. Pl. ې *ey*. چل کول *chal kawul*, verb trans. To cheat, to deceive, to impose on, to bamboozle, to defraud, to swindle, etc.

S چلان *chalān*, s.m. (2nd) Remittance, utterance, advancing, impelling. Pl. چلانونه *chalānūnah*. 2. adj. Current, prevailing, usual, existing.

چلاؤ *chalā'ū*, s.m. (2nd) Boiled rice. Pl. چلاؤونه *chalā'ū-ūnah*.

S چل‌چل *chal-chal*, s.m. (9th) Bustle, hurry, stir, tumult. Sing. and Pl.

چل‌چلا *chal-chalā*, s.f. (6th) The bustle of setting out on a journey, preparation for a journey. (E.) Sing. and Pl., or (W.) Pl. چل‌چلاوي *chal-chalāwī*.

چلخۍ *chalkha'ī*, s.f. (6th) A teetotum, a child's top, a whirligig. Sing. and Pl. See also چرلۍ and څرخندوکي

چلر *chulur*, s.m. (5th) A mean ignoble person, a blackguard. Pl. چلران *chulurān*; s.f. (3rd) چلره *chulura'h*. Pl. ې *ey*.

P چلغوزی *chalghozaey*, s.m. (1st) A kind of nut like the pistachio, or the kernels of the pine. Pl. ي *ī*. See جنغوزي

چلقت *chalkat*, s.m. (2nd) A thick padded coat for soldiers, a coat of mail. Pl. چلقتونه *chalkat-ūnah*.

HI چلم *chilam*, s.m. (2nd) or (5th) A tobacco-pipe, a smoking apparatus, the part of a *hukka*, which contains the tobacco and fire. Pl. چلمونه *chilamūnah* or چلمان *chilamān*.

S چلن *chalan*, s.m. (2nd) Habit, custom, conduct, behaviour. 2. Currency. Pl. چلنونه *chalanūnah*. 3. adj. Current.

چله *chala'h*, s.f. (3rd) An ear-ring. Pl. ې *ey*.

چلۍ *chala'ī*, s.f. (6th) A head or ear of corn. Sing. and Pl. See وږي

چلیدل *chaledal*, verb intrans. To move, to go, to proceed, to walk, to go off, to pass (as coin), to pass (as time away), to be discharged (as a gun), to flow, to drive, to blow, to answer, to succeed, to avail, to stand. Pres.

چليږي chalejzī (W.) or چليگي chalegī (E.); past وُ چليدَ wu-chaleda or وُ چليده wu-chaledah; fut. وُ به چليږي wu bah chalejzī or وُ به چليگي wu bah chalegī; imp. وُ چليږه wu-chalejzah or وُ چليگه wu-chalegah; act. part. چليدونكَي chaledūnkaey or چليدونَي chaledūnaey; past part. چليدلَي chaledalaey; verb. n. چليدنه chaledana'h. چلول chalawul, verb trans. To impel, to hasten, to set a-going, to actuate, to direct, to make to go or pass, to fire or shoot at, to utter (as coin), to advance. Pres. چلوي chalawī; past وُ چلاوه wu-chalāwuh or وُ چلاوو wu-chalāwo; fut. وُ به چلوي wu bah chalawī; imp. وُ چلوه wu-chalawah; act. part. چلوونكَي chalawūnkaey or چلوونَي chalawūnaey; past part. چلولَي chalawulaey; verb. n. چلونه chalawana'h.

چم cham, s.m. (2nd) A division, a district, a parish, a ward or quarter of a town or city. 2. A tribe, a clan, a family. 3. A clod of earth used in building purposes. 4. Deception, fraud, artifice, imposition, trickery, imposture. See جم and چوم

P چم cham, s.m. (9th) Gait, mode of walking. Sing. and Pl.

چم و خم cham-o-kham, s.m. (9th) A graceful gait, leaning from side to side in walking. Sing. and Pl.

P چمبر chambar, s.m. (2nd) A sphere, an orb, a circle, a disc, a wheel, a globe. Pl. چمبرونه chambarūnah.

چمته chamta'h, s.f. (3rd) A beggar's wallet, a haversack, a bag. Pl. ئ ey.

P چمچه chamcha'h, s.f. (3rd) A spoon. Pl. ئ ey. Also چمچئ chamcha'ī, s.f. (6th). Sing. and Pl. See خونچئ

چمكني chamkanī, s. prop. The name of a large village or small town, about five miles east from Peshāwar.

چمله chamla'h, s.f. (3rd) The name of a small district about twenty miles north of Attak, near the right bank of the Indus, and south of Buner.

P چمن chaman, s.m. (2nd) A parterre, a flower bed, a garden, a meadow. Pl. چمنونه chamanūnah.

P چمني chamanī, adj. Of or relating to a meadow. 2. Green, verdant.

چميار chamyār, s.m. (5th) A currier, a skinner, a worker in leather. Pl. چمياران chamyārān. See خميار

چميارڙئ chamyārra'ī, s.f. (6th) The name of a mountain tree bearing a fruit of which birds are fond. Sing. and Pl.

P چنار chinār or chunār, s.m. (5th) The poplar or plane tree. Pl. چناران chinārān.

HI چنبلي chanbelī, s.m. (9th) The name of a flower (Jasminum grandiflorum). Sing. and Pl.

چنجري chanjaraey, s.m. (1st) A partridge. Pl. ي ī. See تنزري

چنجي chinjaey, s.m. (1st) A worm, an insect. Pl. ي ī. د پشكال چنجي da pashakāl chinjaey, s.m. (1st) An earth worm of a red colour, the common worm. د ريښمو چنجي da reshamo (W.) or rekhamo (E.) chinjaey, s.m. (1st) A silk-worm. Pl. ي ī.

چنجيدل chinjedal, verb intrans. To be disgusted, to feel disgust, to conceive an antipathy against or dislike to, to nauseate. Pres. چنجيږي chinjejzī (W.) or چنجيگي chinjegī (E.); past وُ چنجيدَ wu-chinjeda or وُ چنجيده wu-chinjedah; fut. وُ به چنجيږي wu bah chinjejzī or وُ به چنجيگي wu bah chinjegī; imp. وُ چنجيږه wu-chinjejzah or وُ چنجيگه wu-chinjegah; act. part. چنجيدونكَي chinjedūnkaey or چنجيدونَي chinjedūnaey; past part. چنجيدلَي chinjedalaey; verb. n. چنجيدنه chinjedana'h. چنجول chinjawul, verb trans. To disgust, to detest, to abhor, to surfeit, to abominate, to loathe, to nauseate, to disrelish. Pres. چنجوي chinjawī; past وُ چنجاوه wu-chinjāwuh or وُ چنجاوو wu-chinjāwo; fut. وُ به چنجوي wu bah chinjawī; imp. وُ چنجوه wu-chinjawah; act. part. چنجوونكَي chinjawūnkaey or چنجوونَي chinjawūnaey; past part. چنجولَي chinjawulaey; verb. n. چنجونه chinjawuna'h.

چن چڼري chan-charrnaey, s.m. (1st) A child's

rattle, a rattle fixed on the head of a spear. Pl. ي ī. See ګرنجاوو

P چند chand, adj. Several, various, some, a few. 2. adv. How much? how many? چندان chandān, adj. So much, much, many, so much as, as much as, how many soever. څو چند tso chand, Several times, often. 2. How much? to what degree? هر چند har chand or هر چند چه har chand chih, adv. Although, nevertheless, notwithstanding, however, with all that.

چندخه chandakha'h, s.f. (3rd) A frog. Pl. ئ ey. See چنګښه

چندنړ chandarrn, s.m. (2nd) Sandal wood or sandars. Pl. چندنړونه chandarrnūnah. د چندنړ رباب da chandarrn rabāb, A rebeck made of sandal wood.

چندنړ هار chandarrn hār, s.m. (2nd) A necklace of circular pieces of gold each in the shape of a moon (corrup. of s چندر هار). Pl. چندنړ هارونه chandarrn hārūnah.

چنده chindah, adj. Picked, selected, chosen, assorted. چنده کول chindah kawul, verb trans. To pick, to select.

چنډال chanddāl, s.m. (5th) A low, mean, or base person, an outcast, a wretch, a miser (HI A man of the lowest Hindū caste). Pl. چنډالان chanddālān.

T چنډاول chanddāwal, s.m. (5th) The rear-guard of an army, a name by which the Ḳazalbāshes of Kābul are known. Pl. چنډاولان chanddāwalān.

چنډاولي chanddāwalaey, s.m. (1st) A man of the Ḳazalbāsh clan. Pl. ي ī; (Fem.) Sing. and Pl. ئ a'ī. Also written چندولي chandawalaey, etc.

چنغاله changhāla'h, s.f. (3rd) A betrothed girl, a girl arrived at puberty. Pl. ئ ey.

چنغله changhala'h, s.f. (3rd) Same as preceding. Pl. ئ ey.

چنغول changhol, s.m. (4th) A betrothed youth, a young man. Pl. چنغاله changhālah.

چنکاو chan-kā'o, s.m. (2nd) Sprinkling water. Pl. چنکاوونه chan-kā'o-ūnah. See چړکاو and چنړکاو

P چنګ chang, s.m. (2nd) A musical instrument, a guitar. 2. The hand expanded, a claw, a talon, the fingers. Pl. چنګونه changūnah.

چنګاښ changāsh (W.) or changākh (E.), s.m. (5th) A crab. Pl. چنګاښان changāshān or changākhān. See کبر and کوني

P چنګال changāl, s.m. (2nd) A claw, a talon, the fingers, the hand expanded. Pl. چنګالونه changālūnah. See چنګ

چنګښه chungasha'h or chungakha'h, s.f. (3rd) A frog, a toad. Pl. ئ ey. See چندخه

P چنګل changul, s.f. (1st) The talon of a bird, the claw of a wild beast, the fingers. Pl. چنګلِ changuli.

چنګل changul, s.m. (2nd) A measure of land equal to fifteen jarībs, or quarter of a plough. Pl. چنګلونه changulūnah.

چنه chana'h, s.f. (3rd) The back part or back wall of a house, the mud wall of a house. 2. Haggling, chaffering, bartering. Pl. ئ ey. چنه وهل chana'h wahal, verb trans. To haggle, to bargain, to chaffer, to beat down, to cheapen, etc.

چنړاسه charrnāsa'h, s.f. (3rd) Mildew, mould, decay. Pl. ئ ey. چنړاسي کول charrnāsey kawul, verb trans. To mildew, to put forth mildew. Also written چنړاشه

چنړچنړ charrn-charrn, s.m. (5th) A cock-sparrow. Pl. چنړچنړ charrn-charrn. چنړچنړه charrn-charrna'h, s.f. (3rd) A hen-sparrow. Pl. ئ ey. See also چنړچنړک, etc.

چنړکاو charrn-kā'o, s.m. (2nd) Sprinkling water. Pl. چنړکاوونه charrn-kā'o-ūnah. See چنکاو. چنړکاو کول charrn-kā'o kawul, verb trans. To sprinkle.

چنړچنړک charrn-charrnak, s.m. (5th) A sparrow, a cock-sparrow, the diminutive of the preceding. Pl. چنړچنړک charrn-charrnæk. s.f. (3rd) چنړچنړکه charrn-charrnaka'h, A hen-sparrow. Pl. ئ ey.

چنړل churrnal, verb trans. To sift, to separate, to part, to choose, to select. 2. To crease, to fold, to plait. Pres. چنړي churrnī; past وُ چنړه wu-churrnah; fut. وُ به چنړي wu bah churrnī;

imp. وُ چنړه *wu-churrnah*; act. part. چنړونکَي *churrnūnkaey*, or چنړونَي *churrnūnaey*; past part. چنړلَي *churrnalaey*; verb. n. چنړنه *churrnana'h*. چنړيدل *churrnedal*, verb intrans. To separate, to become sifted, to become selected, etc. Pres. چنړيږي *churrnejzī* (W.) or چنړيگي *churrnegī* (E.); past وُ چنړيدَ *wu-churrneda*, or وُ چنړيده *wu-churrnedah*; fut. وُ به چنړيږي *wu bah churrnejzī*, or وُ به چنړيگي *wu bah churrnegī*; imp. وُ چنړيږه *wu-churrnejzah*, or وُ چنړيگه *wu-churrnegah*; act. part. چنړيدونکَي *churrnedūnkaey*, or چنړيدونَي *churrnedūnaey*; past part. چنړيدلَي *churrnedalaey*; verb. n. چنړيدنه *churrnedana'h*. (HI چهاننا).

چنړه *charrna'h*, s.f. (3rd) A kind of pulse, chick-pea, vetches (Cicer arietinum). Pl. ئ *ey*. (HI چنا).

چو *cho*, adv. How many? See څو

چو *chau*, s.m. (2nd) A canal for carrying off and distributing over fields the water of a *kārez*, which see. Pl. چوونه *chau-ūnah*.

P چوب دار *chob-dār*, s.m. (5th) A mace-bearer, a servant who announces visitors. Pl. چوب داران *chob-dārān*.

چوب چيني *chob chīnī*, s.m. (9th) The name of a medicine. Sing. and Pl.

S چوپاړ *cho-pārr*, s.m. (2nd) A summer-house, a temporary dwelling, a pavilion, generally made of the branches of trees. Pl. چوپاړونه *chopārrūnah*. Also (S) چوپال *chopāl*, s.m. (2nd). Pl. چوپالونه *chopālūnah*. See څپر

چوپړ وهل *choparr wahal*, verb trans. To drudge, to strive, to take pains, to toil.

چوپل *chūpal*, verb trans. To suck, to imbibe, to inhale. Pres. چوپي *chūpī*; past وُ چوپه *wu-chūpah*, or وُ چوپَ *wu-chūpa*; fut. وُ به چوپي *wu bah chūpī*; imp. وُ چوپه *wu-chūpah*; act. part. چوپونکَي *chūpūnkaey*, or چوپونَي *chūpūnaey*; past part. چوپلَي *chūpalaey*; verb. n. چوپنه *chūpana'h*. See زبيښل

چوپير *chawper*, adv. On all sides, all around, round about. (HI چوپهير). See چاپير

چوتَي *chotaey*, s.m. (1st) A cloth wound round the loins, a cloth worn between the legs to conceal the privities. 2. Two ropes used in fastening a camel's load. Pl. ي *ī*.

چوټي *choṭṭī*, adj. Unplaited, unraveled, disheveled, let loose (as the hair). 2. A head of hair unplaited or disheveled, or چوټي سر *choṭṭī-sar*.

چوچۍ *chūcha'ī*, s.f. (6th) A kind of pheasant. Sing. and Pl. Also written چچۍ *chuja'ī*. See چچۍ

چور *chūr*, s.m. (2nd) Powder, filings. 2. An atom, a bit, a scrap. (S) 3. Plunder, pillage, sack, devastation, ravage, desolation, ruin, destruction. Pl. چورونه *chūrūnah*. 4. adj. Bruised, broken, shattered. چر چور *char chūr*, Broken to atoms, shattered to pieces, in bits. چور کول *chūr kawul*, verb trans. To plunder, to sack, to ravage, to pillage, to ruin. چر چور کول *char chūr kawul*, verb trans. To shatter to atoms, to break to bits, to bruise, etc.

چور *chūr*, s.m. (5th) A ravine, a chasm, a fissure, a gully. Pl. چوران *chūrān*. See چر

چورلول *chūrlawul*, verb trans. To whirl, to make to spin, to make revolve, to turn round. چورليدل *chūrledal*, verb intrans. To turn, to spin, to revolve, to gyrate, to twirl round, to circumvolve. See چرلول and چرليدل

چور مچور *chor-machor*, adj. Broken to atoms, in fragments, in bits. 2. A disconsolate lover; (Fem.) چور مچوره *chor-machora'h*.

S چورنگ *chawrang*, s.m. (2nd) A practice of the sword exercise. 2. Cutting off the four legs of an animal at one blow. Pl. چورنگونه *chawrangūnah*. چورنگ پريکول *chawrang pre-kawul*, verb trans. To cut clean off the legs of an animal at a blow, to cut clean off, to sever completely at a blow. See څورنگ

چوړَي *chū-raey*, s.m. (1st) A servant, a servitor, a dependant, an attendant. Pl. ي *ī*. چوړۍ *chū-ra'ī*, s.f. (6th) A hand-maid, a female servant, an abigail, a waiting maid. Sing. and Pl.

چوړۍ *chawra'ī*, s.f. (6th) An instrument for driving away flies, made from horse hair, or the tail of the Thibet ox. Sing. and Pl. (HI چونري).

HI چوړ chawrr, adj. Ruined, destroyed, desolated, pillaged, deserted. كور د چوړ شه kor di chawrr shah, "May thy house be desolated!" an ill wish. چوړيدل chawrredal, verb intrans. To become desolate, ruined, destroyed, uninhabited, etc. Pres. چوړيږي chawrrejzī (W.) or چوړيگي chawrregī (E.); past چوړ شه chawrr shah, or چوړ وُ شه chawrr wu-shah; fut. چوړ به شي chawrr bah shī, or به وُ شي bah wu-shī; imp. چوړ شه chawrr shah, or وُ شه wu-shah; act. part. چوړيدونکَي chawrredūnkaey or چوړيدونَي chawrredūnaey; past part. چوړ chawrr, or چوړيدلَي chawrr-edalaey; verb. n. چوړيدنه chawrredana'h. چوړول chawrrawul, verb trans. To destroy, to ruin, to desolate, to depopulate. Pres. چوړوي chawrrawī; past چوړ کړ chawrr karr, or چوړ وُ کړ chawrr wu-karr; fut. چوړ به کړي chawrr bah krrī, or به وُ کړي bah wu-krrī; imp. چوړ کړه chawrr krrah, or وُ کړه wu-krrah; act. part. چوړوونکَي chawrrawūnkaey, or چوړوونَي chawrrawūnaey; past part. چوړ کړَي chawrr karraey; verb. n. چوړونه chawrrawunah.

چوړ chūrr, s.m. (2nd) The part of a door which revolves in a socket in the lintel and serves the purpose of a hinge. Pl. چوړونه chūrrūnah. See چړ

S چوړا chūrrā, s.m. (9th) An ornament for the wrist, a bangle. Sing. and Pl.

P چوز chūz, s.m. (5th) A young hawk under a year old that has not yet been flown. Pl. چوزان chūz-ān. چوزه chūza'h, s.f. (3rd) The hen of the preceding. Pl. ئ ey.

چوسار chawsār, s.m. (2nd) A file, a rasp, a grater. Pl. چوسارونه chawsārūnah.

چوشکه chūshka'h, s.f. (3rd) The spout of an ewer, a tube, a pipe. Pl. ئ ey. See څوښکه and څوښکي

چوغي chughaey, adj. Hump-backed, bent from age or weakness; (Fem.) چوغ chūghi. Pl. (Masc. and Fem.) ي ī.

چوک chūk, s.m. (2nd) Diminution, abbreviation, subsidence, abatement, mitigation, etc., as of passion, anger, etc. 2. Loss, waste, damage. 3. (HI) Error, fault, mistake, blunder. چوک ختل chūk khatal, verb intrans. To become alleviated, sobered down, tempered, blunted, curbed, checked, softened. چوک يستل chūk yastal, verb trans. To allay, to lull, to curb, to tame, to repress.

چوک chok, adj. Seated on all fours, particularly a camel, etc., squatting on all fours. چوکيدل chokedal, verb intrans. To squat down as a camel, to sit or recline as a camel or other animal. Pres. چوکيږي chokejzī (W.) or چوکيگي chokegī (E.); past چوک شه chok shah or وُ شه wu-shah; fut. چوک به شي chok bah shī or به وُ شي bah wu-shī; imp. چوک شه chok shah or وُ شه wu-shah; act. part. چوکيدونکَي chokedūnkaey or چوکيدونَي chok-edūnaey; past part. چوک chok or چوک شوَي chok shawaey; verb. n. چوکيدنه chokedana'h. چوکول chokawul, verb trans. To make to sit or squat. Pres. چوکوي chokawī; past چوک کړ chok karr or وُ کړ wu-karr; fut. چوک به کړي chok bah krrī or به وُ کړي bah wu-krrī; imp. چوک کړه chok krrah or وُ کړه wu-krrah; act. part. چوکوونکَي chokawūnkaey or چوکوونَي chokawūnaey; past part. چوک کړَي chok karraey; verb. n. چوکونه chokawuna'h.

HI چوک chawk, s.m. (2nd) A market, a square, a court-yard, a square place before the door of a house or shop. Pl. چوکونه chawkūnah.

چوکل chokal, verb trans. See جوکل

چوکه chūka'h, s.f. (3rd) A goad, a prick, a spur. 2. Sharp, stinging pain. 3. Moistening, dipping, or seasoning with anything. Pl. ئ ey. چوکه کول chūkah kawul, verb trans. To goad, to stimulate, to excite, to irritate. 2. To moisten or dip bread in soup, etc., to season with.

HI چوکي chawka'ī, s.f. (6th) A stool, a chair, a bench. 2. Guard, watch, watching. Sing. and Pl.

چوکي دار chawkī-dār, s.m. (5th) A watchman, a guard. Pl. چوکي داران chawkī-dārān.

چوکي داري *chawkī dārī*, s.f. (3rd) The business of a watchman, the pay or hire of one. Pl. ئ *a'ī*. چوکئي کول *chawka'ī kawul*, verb trans. To watch, to guard, to mount guard.

P چوګان *chawgān*, s.m. (2nd) A bat or club with which a game resembling cricket is played, but on horseback. Pl. چوګانونه *chawgānūna'h*. چوګان بازي *chawgān bāzī*, s.f. (3rd) A game like cricket played on horseback, playing at the game. Pl. ئ *a'ī*.

چول *chol*, s.m. (2nd) A tract of country where no water is procurable, a waste. Pl. چولونه *cholūnah*.

چول *cha-wul*, verb trans. To split, to disjoin, to divide, to sunder, to cleave, to rend, to splinter, to split. Pres. چوي *chawī*; past وُ چاوه *wu-chāwuh* or وُ چاوو *wu-chāwo*; fut. وُ به چوی *wu bah chawī*; imp. وُ چوه *wu-chawah*, act. part. چوونکی *chawūnkaey* or چووني *chawūnaey*; past part. چولی *chawulaey*; verb. n. چونه *chawuna'h*.

چولک *cholak*, s.m. (2nd) The penis of a child until circumcised. Pl. چولکونه *cholakūnah*. See څوبني and څوبنوتي

چوم *chom*, s.m. (2nd) A clod of earth used for building purposes. Pl. چومونه *chomūnah*. See جم and چم

چونکي *chūnkaey*, adj. Shameless, impudent, bold, assuming, pert, saucy, forward. 2. Sensitive, easily affected to tears; (Fem.) چونکۍ *chūnki*. Pl. (Masc. and Fem.) ي *ī*.

HI چونګي *chūn-gaey*, s.m. (1st) A toll, a fee, a tax, duty, tythe, a share of grain to village servants, such as the barber, washerman, etc. Pl. ي *ī*.

چونګي ټولول *chūngaey ttolawul*, verb trans. To collect a toll or tythe. چونګي آخستل *chūngaey ákhistal*, verb trans. To take or receive a toll, fee, or perquisite.

چونه *chūnah*, s.f. (3rd) Lime, mortar. Pl. ئ *ey*. See کوني (S چونا).

چوني *chūnaey*, s.m. (1st) A dwarf, an elf, a mannikin. Pl. ي *ī*; (Fem.) Sing. and Pl. ئ *a'ī*.

چونئي *chūna'ī*, s.f. (6th) A spark or small ruby or other gem inserted in a دري—an ornament for the forehead. Sing. and Pl. (HI چوني).

چونړ *chūrrn*, s.m. (2nd) A fold, a plait, a wrinkle, a crease. 2. Selecting, picking, choosing, sifting. 3. The bottom part of a door which revolves in a socket in the lintel and serves in the place of a hinge. Pl. چونړونه *chūrrnūnah*. چونړل *chūrrnal*, verb trans. To choose, to pick, to sift, etc. See چنړ

چوهړی *chūh-rraey*, s.m. (1st) A person of the lowest caste, a sweeper, one employed in the meanest and dirtiest occupations. Pl. ي *ī*. چوهړئ *chūh-rra'ī*, s.f. (6th) The female of the preceding. Sing. and Pl. (HI چوهڑا).

چه *chah*, s.m. (6th) Shade, shadow, shelter, Sing. and Pl.

چه *chih*, conj. Because, whether, or that, as, whereas, etc.

چهايل *chahā-yal*, s.m. (2nd) A veil, a sheet, a mantle, a sheet made of chintz for women. Pl. چهايلونه *chahā-yalūnah*. See چايل and پروني

چهلئ *chah-la'ī*, s.f. (6th) A head or ear of corn or millet. Sing. and Pl. See جلئ and جلئ

S چيت *chait*, s.m. (9th) The Hindū name of the twelfth month, April—May.

چيت *chīt*, adj. Flat, pressed, crushed, quashed, low, squat. چيت پيت *chīt-pīt*, adj. Crushed, smashed, quashed, flattened, trodden under foot. چيت پيت کول *chīt-pīt kawul*, verb trans. To crush, to flatten, to level, etc. چيته پوزه *chītah pozah*, adj. A flat nose. چيت پوزی *chīt-pozaey*, Flat-nosed; (Fem.) چيت پوزۍ *chīt-pozi*. Pl. (Masc. and Fem.) ي *ī*.

چيتر *chaitr*, s.m. (9th) The twelfth month of the Hindū year, commencing in the month of March. See چيت

چيټئ *chītta'ī*, s.f. (6th) A letter, a note, a writing. Sing. and Pl. (HI چيٹهي)

چيچړ *chīcharr*, s.m. (5th) A wrinkle or furrow on the face or body, a crease, a crumple, a pucker. Pl. چيچړ *chīchærr*. چيچړ کيدل *chīcharr kedal*, verb intrans. To become wrinkled or furrowed. چيچړ کول *chīcharr kawul*, verb trans. To wrinkle. See جوهړه

چیچل che-chal, verb trans. To bite, to gnaw, to chew, to masticate, to gnash the teeth. See چچل

چیخل chīkhal, verb trans. To poke, to push, to goad, to jog, to thrust, to urge, to punch, to impel, etc. Pres. چیخي chīkhī ; past وُ چیخه wu-chīkhah or وُ چیخَ wu-chīkha ; fut, وُ به چیخي wu bah chīkhī ; imp. وُ چیخه wu-chīkhah ; act. part. چیخونکي chīkhūnkaey or چیخونيَ chīkhūnaey ; past part. چیخليَ chīkhalaey ; verb. n. چیخنه chīkhana'h. See چوکه

چیخن chīkhan, adj. Rheumy, foul, nasty, dirty, unclean, untidy, soiled, unwashed ; (Fem.) چیخنه chīkhana'h. چیخن توب chīkhan-tob, s.m. (2nd) or چیخن واليَ chīkhan-wālaey, s.m. (1st) Dirtiness, uncleanness, untidiness, mustiness, purulence, etc. Pl. چیخن توبونه chīkhan tobūnah, or والي wālī. چیخي chīkhaey, s.m. (1st) Dirt, filth, nastiness, offal, ordure, Pl. ي ī.

S چیره chīra'h, s.f. (3rd) A kind of turban, the folds of which are very small. Pl. ې ey.

P چیز chīz, s.m. (2nd) A thing, a commodity, an object, an article. Pl. چیزونه chīzūnah. See خیز

چیغه chīgha'h, s.f. (3rd) Noise, clamour, outcry, disturbance, tumult, din, uproar, hullaballoo. Pl. چیغې chīghey. چیغې کول chīghey kawul, verb trans. To make an uproar, to raise a din, tumult, clamour, etc. See چغ and چغاره

HI چیکړ chīkarr, s.m. (2nd) Mud, slime, mire. Pl. چیکړونه chīkarrūnah. See چقړ

چیلو chīlū, s.m. (5th) A kind of herb or vegetable. Pl. چیلوګان chīlūgān.

چیلی chīlaey, s.m. (1st) A young male kid. Pl. ي ī ; (Fem.) Sing. and Pl. ۍ a'ī. See ارغومي

چین chīn, s. prop. (9th) The name of a country, China. چیني chīnī, s.m. (5th) A Chinese. 2. The article called china. Pl. چینیان chīnī-ān ; (Fem.) Sing. and Pl. (6th) چینۍ chīna'ī.

چینچلۍ chīnchala'ī, s.f. (6th) The name of a village in the Yūsufzī district. چینجي

chīnjaey, s.m. (1st) A worm. Pl. ي ī. See چنجي

چیندخ chīndakh, s.m. (5th) A bull frog. Pl. چیندخان chīndakhān. چیندخه chīndakha'h, s.f. (3rd) The female frog. Pl. ې ey. See چندخه and خیښس

چینګ chīng, adj. Wide open, unclosed, open, grinning, opening the mouth ; (Fem.) چینګه chīnga'h. چینګ خلي chīng khulaey, Open-mouthed, grinning. چینګي داړي chīngey dārrey, adj. Grinning, open-mouthed, snarling. چینګ داړي chīng dārraey, s.m (1st) A grinner, a snarler. Pl. ي ī ; (Fem.) Sing. and Pl. (6th) ۍ a'ī. چینګیدل chīngedal, verb intrans. To grin, to open, to unclose, to grind the teeth, to open the mouth, to snarl. Pres. چینګیږي chīngejzī (W.) or چینګیګي chīngegī (E.) ; past چینګ شه chīng shah, or وُ شه wu-shah ; fut. چینګ به شي chīng bah shī, or به وُ شي bah wu-shī ; imp. چینګ شه chīng shah, or وُ شه wu-shah ; act. part. چینګیدونکي chīngedūnkaey, or چینګیدونيَ chīngedūnaey ; past part. چینګ chīng, or چینګ شويَ chīng shawaey ; verb. n. چینګیدنه chīngedana'h. چینګول chīngawul, verb trans. To open wide, to unclose, to grin, to make snarl, or show the teeth. Pres. چینګوي chīngawī ; past چینګ کړ chīng karr, or وُ کړ wu-karr ; fut. چینګ به کړي chīng bah krrī, or به وُ کړي bah wu-krrī ; imp. چینګ کړه chīng krrah, or وُ کړه wu-krrah ; act. part. چینګوونکي chīngawūnkaey, or چینګوونيَ chīngawūnaey ; past part. چینګ کړيَ chīng karraey ; verb. n. چینګوونه chīngawuna'h.

چینه chīna'h, s.f. (3rd) A spring, a fountain. Pl. ې ey.

ح

ح he or hā, commonly called hā-i-muhmalah or hā-i-huttī, the sixth letter of the Arabic, is the tenth of the Pushto alphabet, but will not be found in any other than pure Arabic words introduced into the language. It is one of the six guttural letters of the Arabic, and its sound is formed deeper in the throat than ه , and with an aspiration much stronger. It stands for eight in the *abjad*.

A حاتم *ḥātim*, s. prop. The name of a most liberal Arabian, and surnamed طائي *ṭā'yī*, hence adj. Liberal, generous, bountiful.

A حاجت *ḥājat* (from حاج, H חוג, Stood in need of), s.m. (2nd) Need, want, necessity, poverty. 2. Hope, wish. Pl. حاجتونه *ḥājat-ūnah*. حاجت مند *ḥājat mand*, adj. Necessitous, indigent. 2. Hoping, depending. حاجت مندي *ḥājat mandī*, s.f. (3rd) Indigence, poverty, adversity. Pl. ئي *a'ī*. حاجت كول *ḥājat kawul*, verb trans. To relieve one's necessities, to go to the necessary. حاجت لرل *ḥājat laral*, verb trans. To wish, to desire, to be in need of anything.

A حاجي *ḥā-jī*, s.m. (5th) (part. act. of حج, He turned round, danced, celebrated a festival), A pilgrim to Mekka. Pl. حاجيان *ḥājī-ān*.

A حادث *ḥādis*, adj. (from حدث, Was new, existed for the first time), New, just appearing.

A حادثه *ḥādisa'h*, s.f. (3rd) A novelty, incident, adventure, calamity, misfortune, occurrence. Pl. ئي *ey*. حادثه پيښيدل *ḥādisa'h peshedal* (W.) or *pekhedal* (E.), verb intrans. To sustain misfortune or calamity, to befal, to happen.

حازي *ḥāzī*, or حازي خيل *ḥā-zī khel*, s. prop. The name of a clan of the Yūsufzīs.

A حاسد *ḥāsid*, s.m. (5th) An enemy, an envier, a rival. Pl. حاسدان *ḥāsidān*. 2. adj. Envious, invidious; (Fem.) حاسده *ḥāsida'h*.

A حاشيه *ḥāshiya'h*, s.f. (3rd) A margin, border, hem. 2. A marginal note. Pl. ئي *ey*.

A حاصل *ḥāṣil*, s.m. (2nd) Produce, profit, result. 2. Corn, crops. 3. Acquiring, producing. 4. Revenue, tax, duty. Pl. حاصلونه *ḥāṣil-ūnah*. حاصل د خبري *ḥāṣil da khabarey*, or حاصل د كلام *ḥāṣil da kalām*, adv. In short, in a word, briefly. حاصل لرل *ḥāṣil laral*, verb trans. To produce, to give, to yield, to afford, to impart. حاصليدل *ḥāṣiledal*, verb intrans. To be acquired or obtained, to result, to accrue. Pres. حاصليږي *ḥāṣilejzī* (W.) or حاصليگي *ḥāṣilegī* (E.); past حاصل شه *ḥāṣil shah*, or و شه *wu-shah*; fut. حاصل به شي *ḥāṣil bah shī*, or به و شي *bah wu-shī*; imp. حاصل شه *ḥāṣil shah*, or و شه *wu-shah*; act. part. حاصليدونكي *ḥāṣiledūnkaey*, or حاصليدونى *ḥāṣiledūnaey*; past part. حاصليدلى *ḥāṣiledal-aey*; verb. n. حاصليدنه *ḥāṣiledana'h*. حاصلول *ḥāṣilawul*, verb trans. To gain, collect, acquire, derive, obtain. Pres. حاصلوي *ḥāṣilawī*; past حاصل كړ *ḥāṣil karr*, or و كړ *wu-karr*; fut. حاصل به كړي *ḥāṣil bah krrī*, or به و كړي *bah wu-krrī*; imp. حاصل كړه *ḥāṣil krrah*, or و كړه *wu-krrah*; act. part. حاصلوونكي *ḥāṣilawūn-kaey*, or حاصلوونى *ḥāṣilawūnaey*; past part. حاصل كړى *ḥāṣil karraey*; verb. n. حاصلونه *ḥāṣilawuna'h*.

A حاضر *ḥāẓir*, adj. (act. part. of حضور) Present, ready, at hand, content, willing; (Fem.) حاضره *ḥāẓira'h*. حاضران *ḥāẓirān*, Pl. The people present. حاضر جواب *hāẓir jawāb*, adj. Pert, smart, answering wittily. حاضر جوابي *ḥāẓir jawābī*, s.f. (3rd) Repartee, witticism. Pl ئي *a'ī*.

حاضر اوسيدل *ḥāẓir aosedal*, verb intrans. To attend, to be in attendance, present, ready. حاضرو ناظر *ḥāẓir-o-nāẓir*, adj. Present and seeing. حاضريدل *ḥāẓiredal*, verb intrans. To be at hand, to be ready, to consent. Pres. حاضريږي *ḥāẓirejzī* (W.) or حاضريگي *ḥāẓiregī* (E.); past حاضر شه *ḥāẓir shah*, or و شه *wu-shah*; fut. حاضر به شي *ḥāẓir bah shī*, or به و شي *bah wu-shī*; imp. حاضر شه *ḥāẓir shah*, or و شه *wu-shah*; act. part. حاضريدونكي *ḥāẓiredūnkaey*, or حاضريدونى *ḥāẓiredūnaey*; past part. حاضر شوى *ḥāẓir shawaey*; verb. n. حاضريدنه *ḥāẓiredana'h*. حاضرول *ḥāẓirawul*, verb trans. To bring, to produce, to make present. Pres. حاضروي *ḥāẓirawī*; past حاضر كړ *ḥāẓir karr*, or و كړ *wu-karr*; fut. حاضر به كړي *ḥāẓir bah krrī*, or به و كړي *bah wu-krrī*; imp. حاضر كړه *ḥāẓir krrah*, or و كړه *wu-krrah*;

act. part. حاضروونكيَ *ḥāẓiravūnkaey*, or حاضرووني *ḥāẓiravūnaey*; past part. حاضر كړيَ *ḥāẓir karraey*; verb. n. حاضرونه *ḥāẓira-wuna'h*. Also written حضريدل *ḥaẓiredal*, and حضرول *ḥaẓirawul*.

A حافظ *ḥāfiẓ*, s.m. (5th) A governor, preserver, a guardian. 2. A blind man. 3. Having a good memory, remembering the whole Ḳur'ān. Pl. حافظان *ḥāfiẓān*; s.f. (3rd) حافظه *ḥāfiẓa'h*. Pl. ې *ey*. Also memory, recollection, etc.

A حاكم *ḥākim*, s.m. (5th) A ruler, a commander, a judge, a master. Pl. حاكمان *ḥākimān*. حاكمانه *ḥākimānah*, adv. Judicially, in a legal manner.

A حال *ḥāl* (from حال, Passed, H הול, Turned, passed), s.m. (2nd) State, condition, case. 2. Affair, business, matter. 3. The present, present time. Pl. حالونه *ḥālūnah*. حال احوال *ḥāl aḥwāl*, State, condition, affairs, matters, etc.

A حالت *ḥālat*, s.m. (2nd) State, circumstance, posture of affairs, case. Pl. حالتونه *ḥālatūnah*.

A حالي *ḥālī*, adj. Aware of, acquainted with, apprized of, informed. 2. Careful. 3. Modern, new, current.

A حب *ḥubb*, s.m. (2nd) Love, friendship, affection. Pl. حبونه *ḥubbūnah*. حب الوطن *ḥubbu-l-waṭan*, Patriotism, love of one's country.

A حباب *ḥubāb*, s.m. (2nd) A bubble. Pl. حبابونه *ḥubābūnah*. See كوبئ

A حبشي *ḥabshaey*, s.m. (1st) A negro, an Abyssinian, an Ethiop. Pl. ي *ī*; s.f. (6th) ئ *a'ī*, A negress, etc. Sing. and Pl.

حبطه *ḥabaṭah*, adj. Useless, of no use, fruitless, vain, futile. حبطه كيدل *ḥabaṭah kedal*, verb intrans. To be useless, futile, vain. حبطه كول *ḥabaṭah kawul*, verb trans. To render useless, void, fruitless, nugatory.

A حبيب *ḥabīb* (from حب) adj. Beloved, dear. Also used substantively, A beloved one, a sweetheart, a friend, a mistress.

A حتي *ḥatta*, conj. Up to, until, so that, in such a manner, etc. حتي المقدور *ḥatta-l-maḳdūr* or الامكان *l-imḳān*, adv. To one's utmost, to the best of one's ability.

حتياط *ḥatī-āṭ* (corrup. of A احتياط) s.m. (2nd) Caution, care, circumspection, foresight. Pl. حتياطونه *ḥatī-āṭūnah*.

A حج *ḥaj*, s.m. (2nd) Act of walking or going round a place. 2. Pilgrimage to Mekka. Pl. حجونه *ḥajūnah*.

A حجاب *ḥijāb*, s.m. (2nd) (from حجب) Modesty, bashfulness, shame, concealment. 2. A veil, a curtain. Pl. حجابونه *ḥijābūnah*. حجاب آخستل *ḥijāb ākhistal*, verb trans. To remove (as a screen or a veil). حجاب كول *ḥijāb kawul*, verb trans. To cover, conceal, hide. 2. To shame.

A حجام *ḥajjām*, s.m. (5th) A cupper, a phlebotomist, a shaver. Pl. حجامان *ḥajjāmān*.

A حجامت *ḥajjāmat*, s.m. (2nd) Cupping, shaving. Pl. حجامتونه *ḥajjāmatūnah*.

A حجت *ḥujjat*, s.m. (2nd) An argument, reason, proof. 2. Altercation, disputation. Pl. حجتونه *ḥujjatūnah*. حجت كول *ḥujjat kawul*, verb trans. To argue, to dispute.

A حجتي *ḥujjatī*, s.m. (5th) A sound reasoner, a wrangler, a caviller. Pl. حجتيان *ḥujjatī-ān*. 2. adj. Quarrelsome, litigious, wrangling. (Masc. and Fem.)

A حجره *ḥujra'h*, s.f. (3rd) A cell, a closet, a chamber; at Peshāwar and vicinity—a public apartment or hall, a resting-place for travellers, one of which is generally attached to a *kandey* or quarter. Pl. ې *ey*.

A حجم *ḥajm* or *ḥujm*, s.m. (2nd) Bigness, size, thickness (particularly of a book). Pl. حجمونه *ḥajamūnah* or *ḥujmūnah*.

A حد *ḥadd*, s.m. (2nd) Boundary, extent, limit, extremity. 2. An impediment. 3. A definition. 4. A starting post. 5. Lashes inflicted for certain crimes, prescribed by the laws of Islām. Pl. حدونه *ḥaddūnah*. حد بلوغ *ḥadd-i-bulūgh*, The time of puberty, youth. حد ترل *ḥadd tarral*, verb trans. To bound, to terminate, to fix bounds. په حد كول *pah ḥadd kawul*, verb trans. To punish with stripes. تر حدَ تير *tar ḥadda ter*, تر حدَ پهورته *tar ḥadda pahortah.* له حدَ زيات *lah ḥadda zī-āt* or تر حد تيري *tar ḥadd terey,* Beyond bounds, out and out. تر داسي حدَ پوري *tar dāsī ḥadda pūrī,* adv. So far, to this degree. تر حد تيريدل *tar ḥadd teredal,* verb intrans. To exceed bounds, to exceed, to infringe, to overshoot the mark, etc. تر حد تيري كول *tar ḥadd terey kawul,* verb trans. To exceed, to encroach, to trespass, to infringe.

A حديث *ḥadīṣ,* s.m. (2nd) (from حدث) A history, a tradition, the traditional sayings of the Prophet. Pl. حديثونه *ḥadīṣūnah.*

A حذر *ḥaẕar,* s.m. (2nd) Fear, caution, prudence. Pl. حذرونه *ḥaẕarūnah.* حذر كيدل *ḥaẕar kedal,* verb intrans. To be aware, to be cautious. حذر كول *ḥaẕar kawul,* verb trans. To take care, to avoid, to be cautious of.

A حذف *ḥaẕf,* s.m. (2nd) Taking away, cutting off a letter or syllable, elision, emission. Pl. حذفونه *ḥaẕfūnah.* حذف كول *ḥaẕf kawul,* verb trans. To omit, to contract, to cut off, to drop (a letter), etc.

A حرارت *ḥarārat* (from حر), s.m. (2nd) Heat, warmth, fervour, fieriness, zeal. Pl. حرارتونه *ḥarāratūnah.*

A حراست *ḥirāsat* (from حرس), s.m. (2nd) Care, watching, guarding. حراست كول *ḥirāsat kawul,* verb trans. To govern, to guard, to take care of.

A حرام *ḥarām,* adj. (from حرم) Forbidden, unlawful, prohibited, excluded, sacred, wrong; (Fem.) حرامه *ḥarāma'h.* حرام خور *ḥarām khor,* s.m. (5th) One who lives on the wages of iniquity. Pl. خوران *khorān*; s.f. (3rd) حرام خوره *ḥarām khora'h.* Pl. ي *ey.* حرام خوري *ḥarām khorī,* s.f. (3rd) Iniquity, baseness, unlawfulness. Pl. ئي *a'ī.* حرام خوړل *ḥarām khwaṛṛal,* verb trans. To receive the wages of iniquity. حرام زاده *ḥarām zādah,* adj. Illegitimate, base-born, bastard. 2. (Masc. and Fem.) A rascal, a blackguard Pl. زادگان *zādagān.* حرام زادگي *ḥarām zādagī,* s.f. (3rd) Wickedness, rascality, blackguardism. Pl. ئي *a'ī.* حرام زادگي كول *ḥarām zadagī kawul,* verb trans. To act in a rascally or blackguardly manner, to abuse. حرام مغز *ḥarām maghz,* s.m. (2nd) Spinal marrow. Pl. مغزونه *maghzūnah.* حرام نفقه *ḥarāma'h nafaka'h,* s.f. (3rd) Unlawful food. Pl. ي *ey.*

A حرامي *ḥarāmī,* s.m. (5th) A robber, an assassin, a rascal, a cheat, etc. Pl. حراميان *ḥarāmī-ān.* حراميدل *ḥarāmedal,* verb intrans. To become unlawful or prohibited. Pres. حراميږي *ḥarāmejzī* (W.) or حراميگي *ḥarāmegī* (E.); past حرام شه *ḥarām shah* or وُ شه *wu-shah*; fut. حرام به شي *ḥarām bah shī* or به وُ شي *bah wu-shī*; imp. حرام شه *ḥarām shah* or وُ شه *wu-shah*; act. part. حراميدونكَي *ḥarāmedūnkaey* or حراميدونَي *ḥarāmedūnaey*; past part. حرام *ḥarām* or حرام شوَي *ḥarām shawaey*; verb. n. حراميدنه *ḥarāmedana'h.* حراموَل *ḥarāmawul,* verb trans. To make unlawful, to prohibit, to interdict. Pres. حراموي *ḥarāmawī*; past حرام كړ *ḥarām kaṛṛ* or وُ كړ *wu-kaṛṛ*; fut. حرام به كړي *ḥarām bah kṛṛī* or به وُ كړي *bah wu-kṛṛī*; imp. حرام كړه *ḥarām kṛṛah* or وُ كړه *wu-kṛṛah*; act. part. حراموونكَي *ḥarāmawūnkaey* or حراموونَي *ḥarāmawūnaey*; past part. حرام كړَي *ḥarām kaṛṛaey*; verb. n. حرامونه *ḥarāmawuna'h.*

حراموني *ḥarāmūnaey,* adj. (past part.) Baseborn, bastard, illegitimate. Pl. ي *ī*; (Fem.) حرامونِ *ḥarāmūni.* Pl. ي *ī.* See حراه زاده

A حرص *ḥirṣ,* s.m. (2nd) Desiring eagerly, greediness, avidity, avarice, ambition. Pl. حرصونه *ḥirṣūnah.* حرص كول *ḥirṣ kawul,* verb trans. To covet, to desire, to be ambitious.

A حرف *ḥarf,* s.m. (2nd) A letter, a word, a particle. Pl. حرفونه *ḥarfūnah.*

A حركت *ḥarakat,* s.m. (2nd) Motion, procedure, gesture, action. 2. Hinderance, interruption, prevention. 3. A short vowel. Pl. حركتونه *ḥarakatūnah.* حركت كول *ḥarakat kawul,* verb trans. To move, to stir, to agitate, to commit (an improper) action.

A حرم *ḥaram,* adj. Sacred, forbidden. 2. s.m. (2nd) A wife, a concubine. 3. A seraglio, a harem, women's apartments. 4. The temple of Mekka, a sanctuary. Pl. حرمونه *ḥaramūnah.* حرمين *ḥaramain,* The sacred cities, Mekka and Madīnah. حرم سراي *ḥaram sarā'e,* A seraglio, a harem.

A حرمت *ḥurmat,* s.m. (2nd) Dignity, character, chastity, honour, reverence, esteem. Pl. حرمتونه *ḥurmatūnah.*

حريان *ḥar-yān,* حريانيدل *ḥar-yānedal,* and حريانول *ḥar-yānawul* (corrup. of حيران), which see.

A حريص *harīṣ,* adj. (from حرص) Covetous, voracious, greedy, gluttonous; (Fem.) حريصه *ḥarīṣa'h.*

A حريف *ḥarīf,* adj. (from حرف) Rival, adverse, opposed. 2. s.m. (5th) A rival, an enemy, an adversary, an antagonist. Pl. حريفان *ḥarīfān*; (Fem.) حريفه *ḥarīfa'h,* s.f. (3rd) Pl. ې *ey.* حريفي *ḥarīfī,* s.f. (3rd) Enmity, rivalry, opposition. Pl. ئ *a'ī.*

A حساب *ḥisāb,* s.m. (2nd) Account, reckoning, accounts, calculation, computation. Pl. حسابونه *ḥisābūnah.* حساب پاك كول *ḥisāb pāk kawul,* verb trans. To clear off, or settle (as accounts). حساب كتاب *ḥisāb kitāb,* Accounts. حساب آخستل *ḥisāb ākhistal,* verb trans. To take an account. حساب كول *ḥisāb kawul,* verb trans. To calculate, to add up. حساب لرل *ḥisāb laral,* verb trans. To have transactions together, to keep an account with. حساب وركول *ḥisāb war-kawul,* verb trans. To furnish an account, to render an account. حسابي *ḥisābī,* adj. Proper, accountable, correct, accurate, just.

A حسد *ḥasad,* s.m. (2nd) Envy, malice; emulation, ambition. Pl. حسدونه *ḥasadūnah.* حسد كول *ḥasad kawul,* or حسد لرل *ḥasad laral,* verb trans. To covet, to envy.

A حسرت *ḥasrat,* s.m. (2nd) (from حسر), Regret, grief, sorrow; desire. Pl. حسرتونه *ḥasratūnah.* حسرت خورل *ḥasrat khwarral,* verb trans. To regret, to grieve.

A حسن *ḥasan,* adj. (from حسن) Beautiful, good. 2. A proper name. حسن حسين *ḥasan ḥusain,* The names of the two sons of Æalī. 2. The name of a book. 3. The name of an Afghān month—Muharram.

A حسن *ḥusn,* s.m. (9th) Beauty, elegance, goodness. Sing. and Pl. حسن خلق *ḥusn-i-khulḳ,* A good disposition. حسن ظن *ḥusn-i-ẓann,* A good opinion, a favorable judgment.

A حسين *ḥasīn,* adj. (from حسن) Beautiful; (Fem.) حسينه *ḥasīna'h.*

A حسين *ḥusain,* adj. Good, beautiful. 2. A proper name, the younger brother of Ḥasan son of Æalī.

A حشر *ḥashr,* s.m. (9th) A meeting, a concourse. 2. The resurrection. Sing. and Pl. روځ د حشر *rwadz da ḥashr,* The day of resurrection.

A حشري *ḥashr-ī,* adj. Violent and impetuous (as a horse for a mare). Also written هشري *hashrī.*

A حشمت *ḥashmat,* s.m. (2nd) State, dignity; train, retinue, equipage. Pl. حشمتونه *ḥashmatūnah.*

A حصار *ḥiṣār,* s.m. (2nd) A fort, a fortress. بالا هسار *bālā hisār,* or بالا سار *bālā-sār* (corrup. of بالا حصار) A fort, a fortification. Pl. حصارونه *ḥiṣārūnah.*

A حصه *ḥiṣṣa'h,* s.f. (3rd) (from حص to cut) Share, portion, lot, part, division. Pl. ې *ey.* حصه دار *ḥiṣṣa'h dār,* s.m. (5th) A sharer. Pl. داران *dārān.* s.f. (3rd) حصه داره *ḥiṣṣa'h dāra'h.* Pl. ې *ey.* حصه كول *ḥiṣṣa'h kawul,* verb trans. To share, to distribute, to apportion, to divide, to part. See بخره.

A حضرت *ḥaẓrat,* s.m. (9th) Presence, dignity. 2. Majesty, highness, etc., a title of respect. Sing. and Pl. حضرت عيسي *ḥaẓrat æīsā,* Jesus Christ.

A حضور *ḥuẓūr,* s.m. (9th) (from حضر) Presence, appearance, attendance. Sing. and Pl. په حضور *pah ḥuẓūr,* adv. In the presence of, before. 2. (respectfully) Your worship.

A حظ *ḥaẓẓ,* s.m. (2nd) Pleasure, delight. 2. Flavour, taste. 3. Good fortune, felicity. Pl. حظونه *ḥaẓẓūnah.* حظ نفساني *ḥaẓẓ-i-nafsānī,* Sensual pleasure. حظ آخستل *ḥaẓẓ ākhistal,* To derive pleasure, delight, etc.

A حفاظت *hifāzat*, s.m. (2nd) (from حفظ) Custody, guarding, keeping, care, protection, preservation. Pl. حفاظتونه *hifāzatūnah*. حفاظت كول *hifāzat kawul*, verb trans. To guard, to defend, to preserve.

A حفظ *hifz*, s.m. (2nd) Memory. 2. Custody, keeping, guarding, protection. Pl. حفظونه *hifzūnah*.

A حق *hakk*, s.m. (2nd) The truth, justice, rectitude, right, equity, just claim, portion, etc. Pl. حقونه *hakkūnah*. 2. adj. Just, right, true. حق آدا كول *hakk ādā kawul*, verb trans. To render every one his due. حق تعالي *hakk tæālā*, The Almighty God who is the Most High. حق جلّ جلالُهُ *hakk jalla-jalāluhu*, The Deity in all his splendour. حق حيران *hakk hairān*, Exceedingly astonished. حق دار *hakk dār*, adj. Rightful, having right. 2. s.m. (5th) Proprietor, owner. Pl. داران *dārān*; (Fem.) حق داره *hakk-dāra'h*, and s.f. (3rd). Pl. ئي *ey*. حق شناس *hakk shinās*, adj. Grateful, rendering every one his due, knowing and performing one's duty. حق شناسي *hakk shināsī*, s.f. (3rd) Gratitude, knowledge of right and wrong. Pl. ئي *a'ī*. حق گوي *hakk go'e*, A speaker of the truth. حق نا حق *hakk nā hakk*, adv. Right or wrong, nolens volens. حق نمك *hakk-i-namak*, Fidelity. په حق د *pah hakk da*, With regard to, concerning, for. د خداي حق *da khudā'e hakk*, The rights of God, punishment for offences against religion. د خلقو حق *da khalko hakk*, The rights of man, punishment for offences against society. نا حق *nā-hakk*, adj. Unjust, improper. نا حقي *nā-hakkī*, s.f. (3rd) Injustice. Pl. ئي *a'ī*. نا حقي كول *nā hakkī kawul*, verb trans. To act unjustly, or with injustice.

حق *huk*, s.m. (5th) The sound produced when vomiting. Pl. حقهار *hukahār*. حق وهل *huk wahal*, verb trans. To retch, to vomit.

A حقا *hakkā*, adv. Really, truly, by God.

A حقاني *hakkānī*, adj. Divine, of the Deity. حقاني معني *hakkānī mæa'nā*, The real or accepted meaning (of anything). حقاني مينه *hakkānī mīna'h*, Love of the Deity.

A حقير *hakīr*, adj. (from حقارت) Contemptible, vile. 2. Thin, lean; (Fem.) حقيره *hakīra'h*. حقيرګنړل *hakīr garrnal*, verb trans. To contemn, to despise. حقيري *hakīrī*, s.f. (3rd) Contemptibleness, vileness. Pl. ئي *a'ī*.

A حقيقت *hakīkat*, s.m. (2nd) (from حق) Truth, rightness, sincerity, fact, reality. 2. Relation, story, state, condition, narration, explanation. Pl. حقيقتونه *hakīkatūnah*. حقيقتاً *hakīkataṇ*, adv. Really, in truth, truly, in reality.

A حقيقي *hakīkī*, adj. Real, true, certain, just, actual, accurate.

A حكاك *hakkāk*, s.m. (5th) A polisher of precious stones, a lapidary. Pl. حكاكان *hakkākān*.

A حكايت *hikāyat*, s.m. (2nd) (from حكو or حكي to narrate) A history, a tale, a story, a romance. Pl. حكايتونه *hikāyatūnah*.

A حك پك *hak-pak*, adj. Perplexed, astonished, confused, etc. See هك پك

A حكم *hukm*, s.m. (2nd) Command, order, decree, sentence, award, authority, doom, jurisdiction, article of faith, etc. Pl. حكمونه *hukmūnah*. حكم د شرعي *hukm da sharæey*, A judicial decree, a decision according to law. حكم راني *hukm rānī*, s.f. (3rd) Sway, sovereignty, rule. Pl. ئي *a'ī*. حكم كول *hukm kawul*, verb trans. To judge, decide, sentence, decree, regulate, determine, to adjudge, to award. حكم وركول *hukm war-kawul*, verb trans. To command, to order, to request, to direct. الحكم لله *al-hukmo-lillah*, God is the judge, heaven must decide.

A حكمت *hikmat*, s.m. (2nd) Wisdom, knowledge. 2. Skill, contrivance, device, cleverness, address. 3. Philosophy, mystery. Pl. حكمتونه *hikmatūnah*. علم حكمت *æilm-i-hikmat*, Philosophy, physics, medicine. حكمت د خداي *hikmat da khudā'e*, Divine mystery. حكمتي *hīkmatī*, adj. Skilful, clever, artful, wise, philosophical.

A حكومت *hukūmat*, s.m. (2nd) Authority, sway, dominion, sovereignty, government, jurisdiction. Pl. حکومتونه *ḥukūmatūnah.* حکومت کول *ḥukūmat kawul,* verb trans. To govern, to rule, to sway.

A حکیم *ḥakīm,* s.m. (5th) A sage, a physician, a philosopher. Pl. حکیمان *ḥakīmān.* (A Pl. حکما *ḥukamā*). حکیمانه *ḥakīmānah,* adj. Physician-like, sage-like, philosophical. حکیمي *ḥakīmī,* s.f. (3rd) The practice of medicine, physic. Pl. ئي *a'ī.*

A حلاج *ḥalāj,* s.m. (5th) A comber or carder of cotton. Pl. حلاجان *ḥalājān.* See also الې کړ

A حلال *ḥalāl,* adj. (from حل) Legal, lawful, allowable, right. 2. Pure, clean; (Fem.) حلاله *ḥalāla'h.* حلال کول *ḥalāl kawul,* verb trans. To make lawful; to slay according to the forms prescribed by the Muḥammadan religion. حلالیدل *ḥalāledal,* verb intrans. To become lawful, legal, allowable. Pres. حلالیږي *ḥalālejzī* (W.) or حلالیګي *ḥalālegī* (E.); past حلال شه *ḥalāl shah* or وُ شه *wu-shah*; fut. حلال به شي *ḥalāl bah shī* or به وُ شي *bah wu-shī*; imp. حلال شه *ḥalāl shah* or وُ شه *wu-shah*; act. part. حلالیدونکئ *ḥalāledūnkaey* or حلالیدونئ *ḥalāledūnaey*; past part. حلال *ḥalāl* or حلال شوئ *ḥalāl shawaey*; verb. n. حلالیدنه *ḥalāledana'h.* حلالول *ḥalālawul,* verb trans. To make lawful, to slay, to make pure, to permit. Pres. حلالوي *ḥalālawī*; past حلال کړ *ḥalāl karr* or وُ کړ *wu-karr*; fut. حلال به کړي *ḥalāl bah krrī* or به وُ کړي *bah wu-krrī*; imp. حلال کړه *ḥalāl krrah* or وُ کړه *wu-krrah*; act. part. حلالونکئ *ḥalālawūnkaey* or حلالونئ *ḥalālawūnaey*; past part. حلال کړئ *ḥalāl karraey*; verb. n. حلالونه *ḥalālawuna'h.*

A حلف *ḥalf,* s.m. (2nd) An oath. Pl. حلفونه *ḥalfūnah.* See قسم and سوګند

A حلق *ḥalḳ,* s.m. (2nd) The throat, the wind-pipe. Pl. حلقونه *ḥalḳūnah.* See ستوني

A حلقه *ḥalḳa'h,* s.f. (3rd) A circle, a ring, an assembly, a fraternity. 2. A knocker for a door. Pl. حلقي *ḥalḳey.* حلقه به ګوش *ḥalḳa'h bah gosh,* A servant, a slave, one who wears a ring in his ear as a badge of servitude.

A حلم *ḥilm,* s.m. (9th) (from حلم, was mild and long-suffering) Gentleness, mildness, clemency, affability, wisdom. Sing. and Pl. بي حلم *bey ḥilm,* adj. Harsh, severe, merciless. حلم کول *ḥilm kawul,* verb trans. To show clemency, mildness, or gentleness.

A حلوا *ḥalwā,* s.f. (6th) A kind of sweetmeat made of flour, *ghī,* and sugar. (E.) Sing. and Pl.; (W.) Pl. حلواوي *ḥalwāwī.*

A حلوائي *ḥalwā-ī,* s.m. (5th) A confectioner. Pl. حلوایان *ḥalwā-ī-ān.*

حله *ḥala'h,* s.f. (3rd) Pl. ئي *ey.* See هله

A حلیم *ḥalīm,* adj, (from حلم) Mild, clement, affable, gentle, tractable. (Fem.) حلیمه *ḥalīma'h.* حلیمي *ḥalīmī,* s.f. (3rd) Mildness, clemency, gentleness, affability. Pl. ئي *a'ī.*

A حلیه *ḥulia'h,* s.f. (3rd) A set of jewels or ornaments for women. Pl. ئي *ey.*

A حماقت *ḥimāḳat,* s.m. (2nd) Stupidity, folly, ignorance. Pl. حماقتونه *ḥimāḳatūnah.*

A حمام *ḥamām,* s.m. (2nd) A bath, a hot bath, a bathing house. Pl. حمامونه *ḥamāmūnah.* حمامي *ḥamāmī,* s.m. (5th) The keeper of a bath. Pl. حمامیان *ḥamāmīān.* حمام کول *ḥamām kawul,* verb trans. To bathe.

A حمایت *ḥimā-yat,* s.m. (2nd) (from حما) Defence, protection, countenance, guardianship. Pl. حمایتونه *ḥimāyat-ūnah.* حمایت کول *ḥimā-yat kawul,* verb trans. To defend, to guard, to protect, to patronise.

A حمد *ḥamd,* s.m. (2nd) Praise, blessing, praising (God). Pl. حمدونه *ḥamdūnah.* حمد کول or ویل *ḥamd kawul* or *wayal,* verb trans. To praise, to bless (God).

A حمل *ḥaml,* s.m. (9th) Pregnancy, a child in the womb. 2. A burden, a load. Sing. and Pl. حمل آخستل *ḥaml ākhistāl,* verb trans. To carry a load, to bear (a child), to generate.

A حمله *ḥamla'h,* s.f. (3rd) Attack, assault, storm, onset. Pl. ئي *ey.* حمله کول *ḥamla'h kawul,* verb trans. To attack, to assail, to attempt, to storm, to assault.

A حنا *ḥinnā,* s.f. (9th) The juice of a tree with which the hands and feet are stained (Lawsonia inermis). Sing. and Pl. حنا بند *ḥinnā band*, s.m. (2nd) A cloth with which the stain is applied. Pl. بندونه *bandūnah*. حنائي *ḥinnā'ī*, adj. The colour of *ḥinnā*.

A حنظل *ḥanẓal*, s.m. (9th) The colocynth, the bitter apple. Sing. and Pl. See مرغوني

A P حوالدار *ḥawāl-dār* or *ḥawāla-dār*, s.m. (5th) A military officer of inferior rank, a sergeant. Pl. حوالداران *ḥawāl-dārān*.

A حواله *ḥawāla'h*, s.f. (3rd) Care, custody, charge, possession, delivery, consignment, trust. Pl. ې *ey*.

A حواله كول *ḥawāla'h kawul*, verb trans. To give in charge, to commit, to consign, to intrust, to deliver. 2. To instigate, to incite (as a dog).

حوره *ḥūra'h*, s.f. (3rd) (from A حور) A virgin of paradise, a black-eyed nymph. Pl. ې *ey*.

A حوصله *ḥauṣila'h*, s.f. (3rd) (from حصل) The stomach, crop, maw. 2. (met.) Capacity, resolution, ambition, desire, spirit, courage. Pl. ې *ey*. حوصله دار *ḥauṣila'h-dār*, s.m. (5th) A person of capacity, resolution. Pl. داران *dārān*. داره *dāra'h*, s.f. (3rd). Pl. ې *ey*.

A حوض *ḥauẓ*, s.m. (2nd) A reservoir, a cistern, the basin of a fountain, a pond, a vat, a tank. Pl. حوضونه *ḥauẓūnah*. حوض كوثر *ḥauẓ-i-kawṣar*, A river of nectar in Paradise.

A حويلي *ḥawelī*, s.f. (3rd) A house, a mansion, a habitation. Pl. ئ *a'ī*.

A حيا *ḥayā*, s.f. (6th) Modesty, shame, bashfulness. (E.) Sing. and Pl.; (W.) Pl. حياوي *ḥayāwī*. حيا كول *ḥayā kawul*, verb trans. To show modesty or shame, to act modestly. حيا دار *ḥayā-dār* or حيا ناك *ḥaya-nāk*, adj. Modest, bashful; (Fem.) حيا داره *ḥayā dāra'h* or ناكه *nāka'h*.

A حيات *ḥayāt*, s.m. (9th) (from حي) Life, vitality, animation. Sing. and Pl. See ژوندون

A حيران *ḥairān*, adj. Confounded, amazed, perplexed, astonished, disturbed; (Fem.) حيرانه *ḥairāna'h*. حق حيران *ḥakk ḥairān*, adj. Extremely perplexed or astonished. حيران كول *ḥairān kawul*, verb trans. To perplex, to astonish, to amaze. حيرانيدل *ḥairānedal*, verb intrans. To become perplexed, astonished, amazed, discomposed, etc. Pres. حيرانيږي *ḥairānejzī* (W.) or حيرانيگي *ḥairānegī* (E.); past حيران شه *ḥairān shah* or و شه *wu-shah*; fut. حيران به شي *ḥairān bah shī* or به و شي *bah wu-shī*; imp. حيران شه *ḥairān shah* or و شه *wu-shah*; act. part. حيرانيدونكي *ḥairānedūnkaey* or حيرانيدوني *ḥairānedūnaey*; past part. حيران *ḥairān* or حيران شوي *ḥairān shawaey*; verb. n. حيرانيدنه *ḥairānedana'h*. حيرانول *ḥairānawul*, verb trans. To perplex, to astonish, to amaze, to discompose. Pres. حيرانوي *ḥairānawī*; past حيران كړ *ḥairān karr* or و كړ *wu-karr*; fut. حيران به كړي *ḥairān bah krrī* or به و كړي *bah wu-krrī*; imp. حيران كړه *ḥairān krrah* or و كړه *wu-krrah*; act. part. حيرانوونكي *ḥairānawūnkaey* or حيرانووني *ḥairānawūnaey*; past part. حيران كړي *ḥairān karraey*; verb. n. حيرانونه *ḥairānawuna'h*. See حريان

A حيراني *ḥairānī*, s.f. (3rd) Confusion, astonishment, amazement, perturbation, stupor. Pl. ئ *a'ī*.

A حيرت *ḥairat*, s.m. (2nd) Amazement, confusion, astonishment, perturbation. Pl. حيرتونه *ḥairatūnah*.

A حيض *ḥaiẓ*, s.m. (2nd) The menses. Pl. حيضونه *ḥaiẓūnah*. حيضه *ḥaiẓah*, adj. (used substantively) s.f. (3rd) A menstruous woman. Pl. ې *ey*.

A حيف *ḥaif*, interj. Alas! ah! sorrow! 2. adj. Useless, futile, good for nothing, inutile.

A حيله *ḥīla'h*, s.f. (3rd) Artifice, deceit, pretence, trick, wile, chicane, stratagem. Pl. ې *ey*. حيله باز *ḥīla'h bāz*, حيله ساز *ḥīla'h sāz*, or حيله گر *ḥīla'h-gar*, adj. Artful, cunning, deceitful, wily, preparing deceit, etc.; (Fem.) حيله بازه *ḥīla'h bāza'h*, etc. Pl. ې *ey*. حيله بازي or سازي or گري *ḥīla'h bāzī, sāzī,* or *garī*, s.f. (3rd) Artfulness, deceit, wile, trickery, chicanery. Pl. ئ *a'ī*. حيله كول *ḥīla'h kawul*, verb trans. To act deceitfully, artfully, cunningly, etc.

A حين *ḥīn*, s.m. (9th) Time, interval of time.

Sing. and Pl. حين حيات *ḥīn-i-ḥaiyāt*, Time or period of life. 2. During, or for life.

A حيوان *ḥaiwān*, s.m. (5th) (from حي) An animal, a brute, a beast. Pl. حيوانان *ḥaiwānān* or (A حيوانات *ḥaiwānāt*). حيوان توب *ḥaiwān-tob*, s.m. (2nd) Brutality, beastliness, savageness, brutishness. Pl. توبونه *tobūnah*. Also حيوانيت *ḥaiwān-iyat*.

خ

خ *khe*, called خاي منقوطه and معجمه, is the seventh letter of the Arabic, and the eleventh letter of the Pushto alphabet. It is a guttural letter, and is uttered by compressing the upper part of the throat near the mouth. It has no corresponding sound in English, but the Scottish pronunciation of *ch* in 'loch' is equivalent to it, as is also the German *ch*. It stands for 600 in the *abjad* system of numerals.

خاپش *khā-pash*, s.prop. The name of a mountain of Gandāb, in the country of the Upper Mohmands.

A خاتم *khātim*, s.m. (2nd) (from ختم to seal) A seal, a ring worn on the fingers. Pl. خاتمونه *khātimūnah*. See گوته and مهر

A خاتمه *khātima'h*, s.f. (3rd) Conclusion, end, finish, finis. Pl. ې *ey*.

خاته *khātah*, s.m. (6th) (verb. n. of ختل) Ascending, ascent, steepness, rise, ascension, mounting. Sing. and Pl.

A خادم *khā-dim*, s.m. (5th) A servant, a help. Pl. خادمان *khādimān*; s.f. (3rd) خادمه *khādima'h*. Pl. ې *ey*.

خادمه *khādama'h*, s.f. (3rd) A kind of lizard with spikes or bristles on the back and a large head. Pl. خادمې *khādamey*. See سمسره

خادمي *khādama'ī*, s.f. (6th) A kind of lizard smaller than the preceding. Sing. and Pl.

خاده *khāda'h*, s.f. (3rd) A pole, the piece of wood placed as a mark at the head of a grave. Pl. ې *ey*.

A خار *khār*, s.m. (2nd) A thorn, a thistle, a bramble. 2. A spike, a splinter. Pl. خارونه *khārūnah*. خاردار *khār-dār*, adj. Thorny, barbed, troublesome. خارگيري *khār-gīrī*, s.f. (3rd) A fence, a temporary defence made of thorns. Pl. ئ *a'ī*. See اغزن

خارپوځه *khārpotsa'h*, s.f. (3rd) Going on all fours (as a child). Pl. ې *ey*. See خروځه and خارپوسه

A خارج *khā-rij*, adj. (from خرج being out, etc.) Excluded, expelled, outcast, without, out, struck off. خارج کول *khārij kawul*, verb trans. To expel, to exclude, dispense, strike off, turn off.

A خارجي *khārijī*, s.m. (5th) A sect of Muḥammadans who do not reckon Æalī among the lawful successors of the Prophet. Pl. خارجيان *khārijīān*. Also خارجي مارجي *khārijī mārijī* (from A مارج *mā-rij*, a flame without smoke) A Khārijī schismatic, only fit for the flames.

A خارش *khārish*, or خارشت *khārisht* (W.), s.m. (2nd) The itch, the scab. Pl. خارشونه *khārishūnah*, or خارشتونه *khārishtūnah*. خارش کول *khārish kawul*, verb trans. To scratch, to rub gently with the nails.

خارښت *khārisht* (W.) or *khārikht* (E.) s.m. (2nd) The itch, the scab. Pl. خارښتونه *khārishtūnah* or *khārikhtūnah*. خارښتيدل *khārishtedal* (W.) or *khārikhtedal* (E.) verb intrans. To itch, to tickle, to scratch. Pres. خارښتيږي *khārishtejzī* or خارښتيګي *khārikhtegī*; past وُ خارښتيدَ *wu-khārishteda* or *wu-khārikhteda* or وُ خارښتيده *wu-khārishtedah* or *wu-khārikhtedah*; fut. وُ به خارښتيږي *wu bah khārishtejzī* or وُ به خارښتيګي *wu bah khārikhtegī*; imp. وُ خارښتيږه *wu-khārishtejzah* or وُ خارښتيګه *wu-khārikhtegah*; act. part. خارښتيدونکَي *khārishtedūnkaey* or *khārikhtedūnkaey* or خارښتيدونَي *khārishtedūnaey* or *khārikhtedūnaey*; past part. خارښتيدلَي *khārishtedalaey* or *khārikhtedalaey*; verb. n. خارښتيدنه *khārishtedana'h* or *khārikhtedana'h*. خارښتول *khārishtawul* or *khārikhtawul*, verb trans. To scratch, to rub with the nails. Pres.

خارښتوي *khārishtawī* or *khārikhtawī*; past وُ خارښتاوه *wu-khārishtāwuh* or *wu-khārikht-āwuh* or وُ خارښتاوو *wu-khārishtāwo* or *wu-khārikhtāwo*; fut. وُ به خارښتوي *wu bah khārishtawī* or *wu bah khārikhtawī*; imp. وُ خارښتوه *wu-khārishtawah* or *wu-khārikhta-wah*; act. part. خارښتونکَي *khārishtawūnkaey* or *khārikhtawūnkaey* or خارښتونَي *khārisht-awūnaey* or *khārikhtawūnaey*; past part. خارښتولَي *khārishtawulaey* or *khārikhtawulaey*; verb. n. خارښتونه *khārishtawuna'h* or *khār-ikhtawuna'h*.

خارښتي *khārikhtī* (E.) or *khārishtī* (W.) adj. Mangy, itchy, scabby. Used substantively, s.m. (5th). Pl. خارښتيان *khārikhtīan* or *khārishtīān*. s.f. (5th) خارښتي *khārikhtī* or *khārishtī*. Pl. خارښتيانِ *khārikhtīāni* or *khārishtīāni*. خارښتي بزه or وز *khārikhtī* or *khārishtī b'zah* or *wuz*, A scabby sheep.

P خاشاك *khāshāk*, s.m. (6th) Sweepings, leaves, chips, rubbish. Sing. and Pl. See خزله and ور خمه

خاش خاش *khāsh-khāsh* or خش خاش *khash-khāsh*, s.m. (6th) Poppy seeds. Sing. and Pl. د خش خاش غوټۍ *da khash-khāsh ghūṭṭa'ī*, s.f. (6th) A poppy. Sing. and Pl. See كوكنار

خارك *khārak*, s.m. (2nd) A stretcher used in stretching the skin or leather bag in which the coagulated milk is placed in making butter. Pl. خاركونه *khārakūnah*.

خاشه *khāsha'h*, s.f. (3rd) A little, somewhat, a small quantity. 2. Any useless stick or chip, straw, etc. 3. The name of a disease amongst children, during which the face turns yellow and the belly increases in size. Pl. ۍ *ey*.

خاشه خښ *khāshah-khash* (W.) or *khakh* (E.) s.m. (5th) One who cures the *Khāsha'h* disease (generally practised by old women). خاشه خښه *khāsha'h-khasha'h* or *khakha'h*, s.f. (3rd) An old woman who cures the *Khāsha'h*. Pl. ۍ *ey*.

A خاص *khāṣṣ*, adj. (from خص) Excellent, pure, unmixed, noble. 2. Particular, private, own, proper, peculiar, single, sole; adv. Particularly, solely, peculiarly. خاص و عام *khāṣṣ-o-ææm*, Noble and plebeian, high and low, rich and poor.

A خاصه *khāṣṣa'h*, adj. Excellent, pure, noble, good, delightful, charming, nice, pretty, fine, virtuous. 2. s.f. (3rd) A kind of bread. 3. A kind of muslin. Pl. ۍ *ey*. خاصه وردار *khāṣṣa'h wardār*, s.m. (5th) A servant who carries a firelock, a servant in a great man's retinue. Pl. ورداران *wardārān*.

A خاصيت *khāṣṣiyat*, s.m. (2nd) Attribute, natural disposition, peculiarity, innate property, quality. Pl. خاصيتونه *khāṣṣiyatūnah*.

A خاطر *khāṭir*, s.m. (9th) The heart, soul, inclination, mind, memory, sake, behalf, will, choice, propensity, etc. Sing. and Pl. خاطر آزرده *khāṭir āzurdah*, adj. Dejected, distressed, melancholy. خاطر پريشان *khāṭir pareshān*, adj. Troubled or distressed in mind. خاطر جمع *khāṭir jamæ*, adj. Comforted, collected, confidant, contented, at ease, tranquil. خاطر جمعي *khāṭir jamæī*, s.f. (3rd) Comfort, tranquility, ease of mind. Pl. ئ *a'ī*. خاطر خواه *khaṭir khwāh*, adj. Satisfactory, agreeable to one's wishes. خاطر خواهي *khāṭir khwāhī*, s.f. (3rd) Satisfaction, contentment, peace of mind, serenity. Pl. ئ *a'ī*. خاطر دار *khāṭir-dār*, adj. Encouraging, comforting; comforter, encourager; (Fem.) خاطر داره *khāṭir-dāra'h*. خاطر داري *khāṭir-dārī*, s.f. (3rd) Comfort, encouragement, satisfaction, gratification. Pl. ئ *a'ī*. خاطر داري كول *khāṭir-dārī kawul*, verb trans. To comfort, to encourage, to please, to gratify. خاطر مانده *khāṭir māndah*, adj. Distressed, dejected, melancholy. خاطر نشان or نشين *khāṭir nishān* or *nishīn*, adj. Impressed in the memory, by heart, fixed in the memory. 2. Beloved, chosen, selected.

P خاك *khāk*, s.m. (9th) Ashes, earth, dust. Sing. and Pl. See خاوري . خاك پا *khāk-i-pā*, Dust of the feet, the lowest or humblest thing. خاك سار *khāk-sār*, adj. Humble, low-born, mean, base; (Fem.) خاك ساره *khāk-sāra'h*. خاك ساري *khāk-sārī*, s.f. (3rd)

Humbleness, lowness, meanness. Pl. ئ *a'ī.*

P خاك شور *khak shor,* s.m. (5th) A washer of gold, or sand from which gold dust is extracted. Pl. خاك شوران *khāk shorān.*

خاكه *khāka'h,* s.f. (3rd) Particle of gems, stones, or the like; broken rice unfit for use. Pl. ئ *ey.*

P خاكي *khākī,* adj. Dusty, earthy, of ashes. 2. The colour of earth or dust. 3. Humble, worthy. (Masc. and Fem.)

خاګلي *khāgaley,* adj. Praised, commended, popular, approved, deserving. See ښاګلي and ستايلي

P خاګينه *khāgīna'h,* s.f. (3rd) (from خاګ, an egg) Fried eggs, a kind of dish made from eggs, an omelet. Pl. ئ *ey.*

A خال *khāl,* s.m. (2nd) A mole on the face, an artificial spot made on the face for ornament. Pl. خالونه *khālūnah.* خال خال *khāl khāl,* adj. Little, scarce; adv. Here and there, rarely. خال دار *khāl-dār,* adj. Spotted, marked with or having moles; (Fem.) خال داره *khāl-dāra'h.*

A خالص *khāliṣ,* adj. (from خلص) Pure, genuine, a friend; (Fem.) خالصه *khāliṣa'h.*

A خالصه *khāliṣa'h,* s.f. (3rd) Fallow or uncultivated land. Pl. ئ *ey.*

A خالق *khāliḳ,* part. act. (from خلق) used substantively, The Creator.

P خالي *khālī,* adj. Desert, void, empty, vacant, exempt. 2. Pure, unmixed, without effect. 3. Unoccupied, unemployed, idle. 4. The first day of the week, Saturday. 5. The eleventh month of the Afghān year, also called ميانه, which see. خالي توب *khālī-tob,* s.m. (2nd) or خالي والیَ *khālī-wālaey,* s.m. (1st) Emptiness, vacuity, voidness, vacancy. Pl. (2nd) توبونه *tobūnah*; (1st) والي *wālī.* خالي كيدل *khālī kedal,* verb intrans. To become empty or void. خالي كول *khālī kawul,* verb trans. To empty, to make void, to evacuate. خالي لاس *khālī lās,* Empty handed, penniless, unarmed.

P خام *khām,* adj. Raw, unripe, green; inexpert, vain; of unbaked earth or mud. خام كار *khām kār,* adj. Awkward, unskilful, inexpert, bungler. خام كاري *khām kārī,* s.f. (3rd) Awkwardness, unskilfulness, inexpertness. Pl. ئ *a'ī.*

خامتا *khām-tā,* s.f. (6th) A kind of coarse cotton cloth. (E.) Sing. and Pl.; (W.) Pl. خامتاوي *khāmtāwī.* See كرباس

خام سوز *khām-soz,* adj. Half-cooked, raw inside and burnt out; (Fem.) خام سوزه *khām-soza'h.*

P خاموش *khāmosh,* adj. Silent, mute, still. خاموشي *khāmoshī,* s.f. (3rd) Silence, stillness, taciturnity. Pl. ئ *a'ī.*

P خامي *khāmī,* s.f. (3rd) Rawness, unripeness, immaturity, inexperience. 2. Loss. Pl. ئ *a'ī.*

T خان *khān,* s.m. (5th) A lord, a prince, a title principally used by Afghāns or Paṭṭāns. Pl. خانان *khānān*; خان ملا *khān mullā,* s.m. (5th) The head *mullā* or priest who distributes the allowance to the clergy. Pl. ملايان *mullāyān.*

خانتما *khān-tamā,* adj. Proud, arrogant, vain.

P خاندان *khānadān,* s.m. (2nd) Family, house, race, household. Pl. خاندانونه *khānadānūnah.*

A خانقه *khānaḳā'h* or *khānḳā'h,* s.f. (3rd) A monastery, the shrine of a saint. Pl. ئ *ey.*

P خانمان *khānomān* or خان و مان *khān-o mān,* s.m. (9th) Household furniture, everything belonging to the house, family, household, house, etc. Sing. and Pl.

P خانواده *khānawāda'h,* s.f. (3rd) A family, a house, a race, a tribe of people. Pl. ئ *ey.*

P خانه *khāna'h,* s.f. (3rd) A house, place, room, etc. Pl. ئ *ey.* خانه آباد *khāna'h-ābād,* adj. Prosperous. 2. May you flourish! may your house prosper! خانه آبادي *khāna'h ābādī,* s.f. (3rd) Prosperity. Pl. ئ *a'ī.* خانه خانه *khāna'h khāna'h,* adj. Cellular, formed with cells. خانه خراب *khāna'h kharāb,* adj. Ruined, destroyed. 2. Base, mean. 3. A vain or empty person. 4. Be thy house desolate! خانه خرابي *khāna'h kharābī,* s.f. (3rd) Ruin, destruction. Pl. ئ *a'ī.* خانه دار *khāna'h dār,* s.m. (5th) A householder, the master of a family. Pl. خانه داران *khāna'h dārān.* خانه داري *khāna'h dārī,* s.f. (3rd) Housekeeping, care of domestic concerns. Pl. ئ *a'ī*. خانه زاد *khāna'h zād*, adj. The child of a slave; (Fem.) خانه زاده *khāna'h-zāda'h*. خانه نشين *khāna'h nishīn*, adj. Sitting in the house, retired, unemployed. باد خانه *bād khana'h*, s.f. (3rd) A ventilator. Pl. ئ *ey*. بالا خانه *bālā khāna'h*, s.f. (3rd) A balcony, an upper room. Pl. ئ *ey*. جبه خانه *jabbah khāna'h*, s.f. (3rd) A magazine, store, arsenal. Pl. ئ *ey*. رود خانه *rūd khana'h*, s.f. (3rd) The bed or channel of a river, a stream. Pl. ئ *ey*. فيل خانه *fīl khāna'h*, s.f. (3rd) A place where elephants are kept. Pl. ئ *ey*. كتاب خانه *kitāb khāna'h*. s.f. (3rd) A library. Pl. ئ *ey*. گرم خانه *garam khāna'h*, s.f. (3rd) A room in which they sit and sleep in winter, and under which a fire is lighted. Pl. ئ *ey*.

خاوره *khāwra'h*, s.f. (3rd) Earth, dust, clay, etc. Pl. ئ *ey*. The plural form is most generally used. خاور گاړي *khāwr gāṛraey*, s.m. (1st) A hole made in the ground by digging clay for making pots, a clay-pit, etc. Pl. ي *ī*. متټه خاوره *matta'h khāwra'h*, s.f. (3rd) Clay. Pl. ئ *ey*. See خوري and خورين

خاورين *khāwrīn*, adj. Clay, made of clay. 2. Grain containing particles of dirt or earth; (Fem.) خاورينه *khāwrīna'h*.

P خاوند *khāwand*, s.m. (5th) A lord, master, husband. Pl. خاوندان *khāwandān*.

A خاين *khā-īn*, adj. (from خيانت) A traitor, a deceiver, fraudulent, treacherous.

P خايه مال *khā-ya'h māl*, s.m. (5th) A fawner, a flatterer (from خايه, a testicle, and مال, a rubber). Pl. خايه مالان *khā-ya'h mālān*. خايه مالي *khā-ya'h mālī*, s.f. (3rd) Flattery, cringing, fawning. Pl. ئ *a'ī*. خايه مالي كول *khā-ya'h mālī kawul*, verb trans. To curry favour, to fawn, to flatter.

A خبث *khubs*, s.m. (2nd) Malice, malignity, perfidy. Pl. خبثونه *khubsūnah*.

A خبر *khabar*, s.m. (2nd) Advice, news, information, intelligence, rumour, report, account. Pl. خبرونه *khabarūnah*. خبر كول *khabar kawul*, verb trans. To apprise, to inform, to acquaint, to report, to advise. خبردار *khabar dār*, adj. Careful, cautious; informed, acquainted; (Fem.) خبر داره *khabar-dāra'h*. خبر دار كول *khabar dār kawul*, verb trans. To put on one's guard, to warn, to caution, to alarm. خبردار اوسيدل *khabar dār aosedal*, verb intrans. To take care, to be on one's guard, to be on the look out. خبرداري *khabar dārī*, s.f. (3rd) Caution, care, carefulness. 2. Informing, obtaining information. Pl. ئ *a'ī*. خبرداري كول *khabar dārī kawul*, verb trans. To take care, to act with caution. خبرلرل *khabar laral*, verb trans. To have or possess information, to be informed or acquainted. خبر رسول *khabar rasawul*, verb trans. To apprize, to inform, to report, to advise, to acquaint. خبرگير *khabar gīr*, s.m. (5th) A spy, an informer. 2. A protector, a patron. Pl. خبرگيران *khabar gīrān*. خبرگيري *khabar gīrī*, s.f. (3rd) Informing, spying. 2. Aid, protection, care. Pl. ئ *a'ī*. خبر آخستل *khabar ākhistal*, verb trans. To inquire into, to look after, to take care or notice of. خبر لوڅ *khabar lots* or خبر لوڅي *khabar lotsacy* (W.), adj. Eloquent, long-tongued, talkative, entertaining; (Fem.) خبر لوڅه *khabar lotsa'h*. خبريدل *khabaredal*, verb intrans. To be informed, acquainted, aware, advised. Pres. خبريږي *khabarejzī* (W.) or خبريگي *khabaregī* (E.); past خبر شه *khabar shah* or و شه *wu-shah*; fut. خبر به شي *khabar bah shī* or به و شي *bah wu-shī*; imp. خبر شه *khabar shah* or و شه *wu-shah*; act. part. خبريدونكَي *khabaredūnkaey* or خبريدونَي *khabaredūnaey*; past part. خبر شوَي *khabar shawaey*; verb. n. خبريدنه *khabaredana'h*. خبرول *khabarawul*, verb trans. To inform, to apprize, to report, to rumour. Pres. خبروي *khabarawī*; past خبر كړ *khabar kaṛ* or و كړ *wu-kaṛ*; fut. خبر به كړي *khabar bah kṛī* or به و كړي *bah wu-kṛī*; imp. خبر كړه *khabar kṛah* or و كړه *wu-kṛah*; act. part. خبروونكَي *khabarawūn-*

kaey or خبرووني *khabarawūnaey*; past part. خبر کړي *khabar karraey*; verb. n. خبرونه *khabarawuna'h.*

خبره *khabara'h*, s.f. (3rd) Speech, language. 2. Affair, matter, thing. Pl. ي *ey*. خبره کول *khabara'h kawul*, verb trans. To speak, to say.

A خبيث *khabīs*, adj. (from خبپ) Wicked, impure, malignant, without prayer. 2. s.m. (5th) An evil spirit. Pl. خبيثان *khabīsān*; (Fem.) خبيثه *khabīsa'h*, and s.f. (3rd). Pl. ي *ey*.

خپړ *khaparr*, s.f. (1st) The palm of the hand, the sole of the foot. Pl. خپړ *khaparri*.

خپسه *khapasa'h*, s.f. (3rd) The nightmare. Pl. ي *ey*. Also خپسکي *khapaskaey*, s.m. (1st) (W.) Pl. ي *ī*.

خپل *khpul*, the reflective or reciprocal pronoun, Self, myself, thyself, himself, herself, own, etc. Sing. and Pl. خپل سر *khpul sar*, adj. Self-opinionated, obstinate, headstrong, uncontrolled, having one's own way, unfettered. خپل سري *khpul saraey*, An obstinate or uncontrolled person; (Fem.) خپل سر *khpul sari*. Pl. (Masc. and Fem.) ي *ī*. په خپل سر *pah khpul sar*, Of one's own accord, authority, or free will. له خپلَ اندَ *lah khpula anda*, adv. Unwittingly, spontaneously, of one's own accord, freely, voluntarily, ignorantly. خپل ولي *khpul-walī*, s.f. (3rd), or والي *wāley*, s.m. (1st), or گلوي *galwī*, s.f. (3rd) Connection, relationship, affiliation, kindred, family connexion. Pl. ولئ *wala'ī*, والي *wālī*, or گلوئ *galwa'ī*. خپليدل *khpuledal*, verb intrans. To become one's own, to become connected, to become bound by ties of friendship, to become biased, swayed, influenced, engaged, drawn over, inclined, etc. Pres. خپليږي *khpulejzī* (W.) or خپليگي *khpulegī* (E.); past خپل شه *khpul shah* or و شه *wu-shah*; fut. خپل به شي *khpul bah shī* or به و شي *bah wu-shī*; imp. خپل شه *khpul shah* or و شه *wu-shah*; act. part. خپليدونکي *khpuledūnkaey* or خپليدوني *khpuledūnaey*; past part. خپل شوي *khpul shawaey*; verb. n. خپليدنه *khpuledana'h*. خپلول *khpulawul*, verb trans. To make one's own, to win over, to influence, to bias, to sway, to incline, to predispose, to prevail upon. Pres. خپلوي *khpulawī*; past خپل کړ *khpul karr* or و کړ *wu-karr*; fut. خپل به کړي *khpul bah krrī* or به و کړي *bah wu-krrī*; imp. خپل کړه *khpul krrah* or و کړه *wu-krrah*; act. part. خپلوونکي *khpulawūnkaey* or خپلووني *khpulawūnaey*; past part. خپل کړي *khpul karraey*; verb. n. خپلونه *khpulawuna'h*.

خپلوي *khpulawī*, s.f. (3rd) Connection, friendship, relationship, family connexion. Pl. ئ *a'ī*. خپلوي کول *khpulawī kawul*, verb trans. To form connexion by marriage, to make or contract friendship.

خپه *khpah*, s.m. (6th) Tinder, touchwood. Sing. and Pl. See خو

خپور *khpor*, adj. Opened, or blown as a flower, spread out, unclosed, blooming, expanded, florid. 2. Dispersed, scattered, dishevelled, loose, streaming. Pl. خپاره *khpārah*; (Fem.) خپره *khpara'h*. Pl. خپري *khparey*. خپور والي *khpor wālaey*, s.m. (1st) Openness, expansion, looseness, etc. Pl. والي *wālī*. خپريدل *khparedal*, verb intrans. To open, to bloom, to spread, to expand, to dishevel, to become dispersed. Pres. خپريږي *khparejzī* (W.) or خپريگي *khparegī* (E.); past خپور شه *khpor shah* or و شه *wu-shah*; fut. خپور به شي *khpor bah shī* or به و شي *bah wu-shī*; imp. خپور شه *khpor shah* or و شه *wu-shah*; act. part. خپريدونکي *khparedūnkaey* or خپريدوني *khparedūnaey*; past part. خپور *khpor* or خپور شوي *khpor shawaey*; verb.n. خپريدنه *khparedana'h* or خپريده *khparedah*. خپرول *khparawul*, verb trans. To cause to open, unclose, or expand. 2. To dishevel, to scatter, to loosen. Pres. خپروي *khparawī*; past خپور کړ *khpor karr* or و کړ *wu-karr*; fut. خپور به کړي *khpor bah krrī* or به و کړي *bah wu-krrī*; imp. خپور کړه *khpor krrah* or و کړه *wu-krrah*; act. part. خپروونکي *khparawūnkaey* or خپرووني *khparawūnaey*; past part. خپور کړي *khpor karraey*; verb. n. خپرونه *khparawuna'h*. See خور etc.

خپه *khapah*, adj. Angry, vexed, offended, displeased. 2. s.f. (3rd) Suffocation, strangulation. Pl. ې *ey*. خپه کول *khapah kawul*, verb trans. To vex, offend, displease, to enrage. 2. To suffocate, to strangle, to choke. خپه کيدل *khapah kedal*, verb intrans. To be offended, to be vexed, to be displeased. 2. To choke, to become suffocated. See خفه

خپگي *khapagī*, s.f. (3rd) Anger, vexation, displeasure, pet, rage. Pl. ئ *a'ī*. See خفگي

خپي *khapī*, s.f. (3rd) A rope of cotton, hair, or hemp. 2. A halter for a horse. Pl. ئ *a'ī*. See پائي and کپي or گپي

ختائي *khatā'ī*, s.f. (3rd) (corrup. of A and H خطي) Fault, error, neglect, sin, mistake. Pl. ئ *a'ī*. ختائي کول *khatā'ī kawul*, verb trans. To err, to miss, to mistake, to sin, to blunder.

ختر *khatar*, s.m. (2nd) (corrup. of A خطر) Danger, risk, venture. 2. Thought, remembrance. Pl. خترونه *khatar-ūnah*. خترناك *khatar-nāk*, adj. Dangerous, hazardous, frightful; (Fem.) خترناکه *khatar nāka'h*. خترناکي *khatar nākī*, s.f. (3rd) Dangerousness. Pl. ئ *a'ī*; also خطره *khatara'h*, s.f. (3rd). Pl. ې *ey*. په خترکښي آچول *pah khatar k'shey* or *k'khey āchawul*, verb trans. To endanger, to throw into, or expose to danger, to risk.

ختل *khatal*, verb intrans. To ascend, rise, mount, arise, uprise, get up, climb, scale, surmount, aspire, shoot up. خيژي *khejzī* (W.) or خيجي *khejī* (E.); past ؤ خوت *wu-khot*; fut. ؤ به خيژي *wu bah khejzī* or خيجي *khejī*; imp. ؤ خيژه *wu-khejzah* or ؤ خيجه *wu-khejah*; act. part. ختونکي *khatūnkaey* or ختوني *khatūnaey*; past part. ختلي *khatalaey*; verb. n. ختنه *khatana'h* or خاته *khātah*. See خيژول

A ختم *khatm*, s.m. (2nd) Conclusion, end, seal. Pl. ختمونه *khatmūnah*. 2. adj. Done, finished. completed. ختم کول *khatm kawul*, verb trans. To finish, end, complete, conclude.

P ختن *khutan*, s. prop. Name of a country in Tūrkestān, famous for its musk, and the beauty of its women.

ختنه *khatana'h*, s.f. (3rd) (verb. n.) Ascending, rising, mounting, arising, surmounting, shooting up. Pl. ې *ey*; and خاته *khātah*, s.m. (6th). Sing. and Pl.

A ختنه *khatna'h*, s.f. (3rd) Circumcision. Pl. ې *ey*. ختنه کول *khatna'h kawul*, verb trans. To circumcise.

خته *khata'h*, s.f. (3rd) Plain apparel, a shirt or shift of coarse cloth. Pl. ې *ey*.

خٹ *khætt*, s.m. (2nd) A hill, a hillock, a mound, a knoll, a mount. 2. A bank of clouds. Pl. خٹونه *khættūnah*.

خٹ *khutt*, s.m. (5th) Ebullition, effervescence, agitation, bubbling, boiling. 2. Paroxysm, convulsion, vehemence, rage, wildness, etc. Pl. خٹهار *khuttahār*. خٹ کيدل *khutt kedal*, verb intrans. To boil, to effervesce, to become agitated, to bubble, to purl, to boil with rage, passion, grief, etc. خٹ کول *khutt kawul*, verb trans. To make boil, bubble, or effervesce, to agitate, to enrage, to put into a passion. See خوٹ etc.

خٹبيل *khattbel*, s.m. (6th) Dregs, sediment, lees. Sing. and Pl. Also خٹبيله *khattbela'h*, s.f. (3rd). Pl. ې *ey*.

خٹک *khattak*, s.m. (6th) The name of a tribe of Afghāns who occupy the district to the south and west of Attak, and whose chief town is Akorra'h. 2. A male of the tribe. Sing. and Pl. خٹکه *khattaka'h*, s.f. (3rd) A female of the above. Pl. ې *ey*.

خٹک *khattak*, s.m. (5th) A kind of beetle which infests houses. 2. A green unripe water melon of which pickles are made. Pl. خٹکان *khattakān*.

خٹکي *khattakaey*, s.m. (1st) A species of water melon, peculiar to Afghānistan. Pl. ي *ī*.

خٹکي *khuttkaey*, s.m. (1st) Ebullition, etc., the diminutive of خٹ Pl. ي *ī*.

خٹولی *khattoley*, s.f. (3rd) Pl. Muddy, or turbid water. See خړي اوبه

خٹه *khatta'h*, s.f. (3rd) Mud, slush, mire. Pl. ې *ey*. خٹه کيدل *khatta'h kedal*, verb intrans. To become muddy, miry. خٹه کول *khatta'h karwul*, verb trans. To make or render muddy or miry.

خته *khutta'h*, s.f. (3rd) Clay, marl. Pl. ې *ey*.

خڅوزه *khatsoza'h*, s.f. (3rd) A bit, a fragment. Pl. ې *ey*.

خڅه *khatsah*, post-pos. At the side, near, at, beside, about, etc. See څخه

A خجل *khijil*, adj. (from خجالت) Modest, bashful, ashamed, abashed; (Fem.) خجله *khijila'h*.

خجونکو *khajūnko*, adj. Frisky, prancing, capering (as a horse), rolling from side to side in walking. 2. Rebounding (as a ball).

خجه *khwajah*, s.m. (5th) An eunuch. Pl. خجگان *khwaja-yān*. See خوجه

خچخچوني *khach-khachūnacy*, s.m. (1st) Turning over and over, or head over heels, rebounding. Pl. ي *ī*. په خچخچوني تلل *pah khach-khachūnacy t'lal*, verb intrans. To turn head over heels, to turn over and over, to rebound. په خچخچوني ويشتل *pah khach-khachūnī wishtal*, verb trans. To throw so as to rebound, to make turn over and over. See تيندك

خچر *khachar*, s.m. (5th) A mule. Pl. خچران *khach-arān*. s.f. (3rd) خچره *khachara'h*. Pl. ې *ey*.

خچن *khachan*, adj. Rheumy, full of rheum or watery matter, dirty, unclean, filthy. 2. Dull, dim, clouded (as a mirror); (Fem.) خچنه *khach-ana'h*. See ججن

خچه *khacha'h*, s.f. (3rd) The little finger. 2. A bound, a rebound, a skip, a dip, a duck, a plunge, a glide; rebounding along the ground as a ball, or over the surface of the water as a flat stone, or duck and drake. Pl. ې *ey*. خچل *khachal*, verb trans. To hurl, to shy, to propel with a skimming motion, to bowl along, to trundle, to roll along, to throw as a stone in the game of duck and drake. Pres. خچي *khachī*; past و خاچه *wu-khāchah*; fut. و به خچي *wu bah khachī*; imp. و خچه *wu-khachah*; act. part. خچونکی *khachūnkaey*, or خچونی *khach-ūnaey*; past part. خچلی *khachalaey*; verb. n. خچنه *khachana'h*.

P خدا *khudā*, s.m. (5th) God. Pl. خدايان *khu-dāyān*.

خداي *khudā-e*, s.m. (5th) God. Pl. خدايان *khudāiyān*. This word is used almost exclusively by the Afghāns. خداي پرست *khudā-e parast*, adj. Godly, pious, worshipper of God. خداي پرستي *khūdā-e parastī*, s.f. (3rd) Piety, godliness, the worship of God. Pl. ې *a'ī*. خداي ترس *khudā-e tars*, adj. Virtuous, fearing God. خداي شناس *khudā-e shinās*, adj. Knowing God. خداي شناسي *khudā-e shināsī*, s.f. (3rd) Knowledge of God. Pl. ې *a'ī*. خداي د و كي *khudā-e di wu-kī*, Please God! God grant! خداي د نه كي *khudā-e di nah kī*, God forbid! God forfend! خداي څه و كي *khudā-e tsah wu-kī*, What will destiny produce? what may God decree?

P خدائي *khudā-ī*, s.f. (3rd) Providence, divinity, godhead. Pl. ې *a'ī*.

P خدايا *khudāyā*, interj. Oh God!

A خدايتعلي *khudā-e-tæalā*, The Most High God.

خدرزي *khadar-zī*, s.m. (1st) Pl. The name of a tribe of Afghāns. خدرزی *khadarzaey*, sing. A man of the tribe. s.f. (6th) ې *a'ī*, A female of the tribe. Sing. and Pl.

A خدمت *khidmat*, s.m. (2nd) Employment, duty, attendance, office, service. Pl. خدمتونه *khidmatūnah*. خدمت كول *khidmat karwul*, verb trans. To attend, to serve, to do duty. 2. To beat (met.). خدمتگار *khidmat-gār*, s.m. (5th) A servant, an attendant. Pl. خدمتگاران *khidmatgārān*. خدمتگاري *khidmatgārī*, s.f. (3rd) Service, duty, attendance. Pl. ې *a'ī*. خدمتي *khidmatī*, adj. Attentive, diligent, heedful, mindful (Masc. and Fem.).

P خدنگ *khadang*, s.m. (9th) An arrow or lance of poplar wood; the poplar tree. Sing. and Pl.

خدو خيل *khado-khel*, s.m. (6th) The name of an Afghān clan. Sing. and Pl. خدو خيله *khado-khela'h*, s.f. (3rd) A female of the above. Pl. ې *ey*.

خديجه *khadīja'h*, s. prop. The name of Muhammad's first wife.

خدل *khaddal*, adj. as s.m. (5th) A large dog in good condition. Pl. خدلان *khaddalān.* خدله *khaddala'h*, s.f. (3rd) A bitch as above. Pl. ې *ey.*

خرٌ *khær*, s.m. (5th) A snore, a purr, a snort; snoring, purring, etc. Pl. خرهار *khærahār.* خر وهل *khær wahal*, verb trans. To snore, to purr, to snort. See خركي

خر *khar*, s.m. (4th) (Push. and Pers.) An ass, a donkey. Pl. خره *kh'rah.* خره *khara'h*, s.f. (3rd) A female donkey. Pl. ې *ey.* گوره خر *gorah-khar*, s.m. (4th) The onager or wild ass. Pl. گوره خره *gorah-kh'rah.* خر توب *khar-tob*, s.m. (2nd) Stupidity, dullness, stolidity. Pl. خر توبونه *khar-tobūnah.*

A خراب *kharāb*, adj. Bad, depraved. 2. Ruined, abandoned, spoiled, lost, deserted, depopulated, waste. خرابيدل *kharābedal*, verb intrans. To become spoiled, ruined, desolated, laid waste, vitiated, corrupted. Pres. خرابيږي *kharābejzī* (W.) or خرابيګي *kharābegī* (E); past خراب شه *kharāb shah* or وُ شه *wu-shah*; fut. خراب به شي *kharāb bah shī* or به وُ شي *bah wu-shī*; imp. خراب شه *kharāb shah* or وُ شه *wu-shah*; act. part. خرابيدونكَي *kharābedūnkaey* or خرابيدونَي *kharābedūnaey*; past part. خراب *kharāb* or خراب شوَي *kharāb shawaey*; verb. n. خرابيدنه *kharābedana'h.* خرابول *kharābawul*, verb trans. To spoil, to mar, to ruin, to destroy, to vitiate, to waste, to desolate. Pres. خرابوي *kharābawī*; past خراب كړ *kharāb karr* or وُ كړ *wu-karr*; fut. خراب به كړي *kharāb bah krrī* or به وُ كړي *bah wu-krrī*; imp. خراب كړه *kharāb krrah* or وُ كړه *wu-krrah*; act. part. خرابونكَي *kharābawūnkaey* or خرابونَي *kharābawūnaey*; past part. خراب كړَي *kharāb karraey*; verb. n. خرابونه *kharābawuna'h.*

P A خراباتي *kharābātī*, s.m. (5th) A debauchee, a rake, a libertine. Pl. خراباتيان *kharābātīān.*

A خرابه *kharāba'h*, s.f. (3rd) Ruin, destruction, desolation. Pl. ې *ey.* 2. adj. Ruined, waste, bad, spoiled.

A P خرابي *kharābī*, s.f. (3rd) Ruin, desolation, ill, mischief, evil, destruction. Pl. ئ *a'ī.*

A خراج *khirāj*, s.m. (2nd) (from خرج) Rent, tax, duty, revenue, tribute. Pl. خراجونه *khirājūnah.* خراجي *khirājī*, s.f. (3rd) Land paying tribute to government, paying revenue. Pl. ئ *a'ī.*

خراړه *kharārra'h*, s.f. (3rd) The name of a bird, the skylark. Pl. ې *ey.*

خراسان *khurāsān*, s. prop. The name of a country, Afghānistān.

خراشكَي *kharāshkaey*, s.m. (1st) Phlegm, mucus from the throat. Pl. ي *ī.* See also كرولبي

خربشوي *kharbushoey*, s.m. (5th) A hog, a swine, a boar. Pl. خربشويان *kharbushoeyān.* (Fem.) خربشويه *kharbushoea'h*, A sow, etc. Pl. ې *ey.*

خرپوڅه *kharpotsa'h*, s.f. (3rd) Crawling on all fours (as a child). Pl. ې *ey.* خرپوڅه كول *kharpotsa'h kawul*, verb trans. To move on all fours. See خارپوڅه and خرپوسه

خرپټ *khar-patt*, s.m. (2nd) A powder; medicine taken simply, not mixed but dry, in opposition to an electuary; sufficient to lie in the palm of the hand and fill the mouth. Pl. خرپټونه *khar-pattūnah.* خرپټ كول *khar-patt kawul*, verb trans. To take medicine or anything dry, as above, by throwing or jerking it into the mouth. See كپه

خرپوسه *kharposa'h*, s.f. (3rd) Going on all fours (as a child). Pl. ې *ey.* See خرپوشه and خرپوڅه

خر تيزه *khar tīza'h*, s.f. (3rd) The capering of a horse or an ass, cutting capers. Pl. ې *ey.*

خرټ *kharatt*, adj. Fat, stout; (Fem.) خرټه *kharatta'h*, A fat or stout woman. 2. s.f. (3rd) A large turban worn by mullās. Pl. ې *ey.* 3. *kharattah*, s.m. (5th) A knave, a cheat, a hypocrite, an impostor, a wolf in sheep's clothing. Pl. خرټان *kharattān.*

خرڅ *kharts*, s.m. (2nd) Expense, price, outlay, expenditure, spending, outgoing. 2. Fee, duty. Pl. خرڅونه *khartsūnah* (A خرج). خرڅيدل *khartsedal*, verb intrans. To be expended.

Pres. خرڅيږي *khartsejzī* (W.) or خرڅيګي *khartsegī* (E.); past خرڅ شه *kharts shah* or وُ شه *wu-shah*; fut. خرڅ به شي *kharts bah shī* or به وُ شي *bah wu-shī*; imp. خرڅ شه *kharts shah* or وُ شه *wu-shah*; act. part. خرڅيدونکي *khartsedūnkaey* or خرڅيدوني *khartsedūnaey*; past part. خرڅ شوي *kharts shawaey*; verb. n. خرڅيدنه *khartsedana'h*.

خرڅول *khartsawul*, verb trans. To expend, to disburse, to spend. Pres. خرڅوي *khartsawī*; past خرڅ کړ *kharts karr* or وُ کړ *wu-karr*; fut. خرڅ به کړي *kharts bah krrī* or به وُ کړي *bah wu-krrī*; imp. خرڅ کړه *kharts krrah* or وُ کړه *wu-krrah*; act. part. خرڅوونکي *khartsawūnkaey* or خرڅووني *khartsawūnaey*; past part. خرڅ کړي *kharts karraey*; verb. n. خرڅونه *khartsawuna'h*.

خرڅي *khartsī*, adj. Prodigal, lavish, extravagant. (Masc. and Fem.)

خرڅوړي *khartsorraey*, s.m. (1st) A rag, a clout, a piece of tattered cloth, etc. Pl. ي *ī*.

خرجدال *khar-jadāl*, s.m. (5th) Antichrist. 2. An evil disposed or wicked person. Pl. خرجدالان *khar-jadālān*. See خردجال

خرجګجګلي *khar-jagjagalaey*, s.m. (1st) The name of a game played by children. Pl. ي *ī*.

خرچ *khrach*, s.m. (5th) The sound produced by the splitting of wood, crack. Pl. خرچهار *khrachahār*.

خرخاري *khar-khāraey*, s.m. (1st) Asses' play, nonsense, foolishness. Pl. ي *ī*.

P خرخښه *kharkhasha'h* (W.) or *kharkhakha'h* (E.) s.f. (3rd) Tumult, noise, encounter, riot, quarrelling. 2. A crowd. Pl. ې *ey*. خرخښه کول *kharkhasha'h* or *kharkhakha'h kawul*, verb trans. To create a disturbance or riot, to quarrel.

خردجال *khar-dajāl*, s.m. (5th) Antichrist. 2. A wicked or depraved person. Pl. خردجالان *khar-dajālān*. See خرجدال

P خرس *khirs*, s.m. (5th) A bear. Pl. خرسان *khirsān*. See ميلو and يږ or يګ

خر سور *khar-sor*, s.m. (5th) A fool, a blockhead, an idiot, (*lit.*) a rider on an ass. Pl. خر سوران *khar-sorān*; (Fem.) خرسوره *khar-sora'h*.

خرشن *kharshin*, s.m. (4th) The dung of a horse. Pl. خرشنَ *kharshna* or خرشنه *kharshnah*. The plural form is mostly used.

خرشبون *kharshabūn*, s. prop. The second and youngest son of Sarī, eldest son of Æabd-ur-Rashīd, Pattān, from whom are descended the Yusūfzīs, Mhomands, Khalīls, and other tribes at present dwelling in the plain of Peshāwer. See the Introduction to my Grammar, p. 9.

خرغيړني *khargherrnaey*, s.m. (1st) A toadstool, a poisonous mushroom. Pl. ي *ī*.

P خرفه *khurfa'h*, s.f. (3rd) Purslain. Pl. ې *ey*. See خلفه

A خرقه *khirka'h*, s.f. (3rd) A patched garment, a religious habit, a darwesh's dress. Pl. ې *ey*.

خرکي *kharkaey*, s.m. (1st) A snore, a purr, a snort. 2. Snoring, purring, snorting. Pl. خرکي *kharkī*. خرکي کول *kharkey kawul*, verb trans. To snore, to purr (as a cat), to snort. See خو

خرګټ *khargatt*, s.m. (5th) A species of grouse, or ortolan. Pl. خرګټان *khargattān*; (Fem.) خرګټه *khargattah*. Pl. ې *ey*. See خراره

خرګي *khargaey*, s.m. (1st) A young ass. 2. A piece of ivory let into the stock of a matchlock behind the breech. 3. The bridge of a violin, etc. Pl. ي *ī*. See تتو

P خرم *khurram*, adj. Pleasant, agreeable, delightful, cheerful, pleased, gay, glad, merry, joyful. خش و خرم *khush-o-khurram*, Pleased and delighted, merry and gay; (Fem.) خرمه *khurrama'h*.

P خرما *khurmā*, s.f. (6th) A date. (E.) Sing. and Pl. (W.) Pl. خرماوي *khurmāwī*.

خرمستي *khar-mastī*, s.f. (3rd) Foolish play, pranks, capers. Pl. ئ *a'ī*. خرمستي کول *khar-mastī kawul*, verb trans. To play pranks, to cut capers, etc.

خرمندي *kharmandey*, adj. Wee, miniature, tiny, little, small, small in size but in proportion; (Fem.) ئ *a'ī*. Sing. and Pl.

P خرمهره *khar-muhra'h*, s.f. (3rd) A small shell called *kawdie* in India, used as a coin. Pl. ې *ey*. See کنجکه

P خروار *khar-wār*, s.m. (2nd) An ass load. Pl. خروارونه *kharwārūnah*.

خرورګ *khar-warg*, adj. A four-year old sheep or goat, from that age upwards. Sing. and Pl. (Fem.) خرورګه *kharwarga'h*. Pl. ې *ey*. See پشرلي and ورګ

خروړی *kharorraey*, adj. A biter (as a dog, horse, snake, etc.); (Fem.) خروړ *kharorri*. Pl. (Masc. and Fem.) ي *ī*.

خروسک *kharosak*, s.m. (9th) A disease of the throat, which swells inside, and finally becomes closed altogether, and death ensues. Sing. and Pl.

P خروش *kharosh*, s.m. (9th) Noise, clamour, tumult, cry, crash. Sing. and Pl. جوش و خروش *josh-o-kharosh*, Tumult, disturbance.

خری *kharaey*, s.m. (1st) A small whitlow, a blister, an excoriation, a pustule. Pl. ي *ī*.

خريان *khar-yān*, s.f. (6th) An ass, a donkey. Sing. and Pl.

P خريت *kharī-yat*, s.m. (2nd) Stupidity, asinine quality. Sing. and Pl. See خرتوب

P خريد *kharīd*, part. (from خريدن) Bought, purchased. s.m. (2nd) Purchase, goods bought. Pl. خريدونه *kharīdūnah*. خريد کول *kharīd kawul*, verb trans. To purchase, to buy. خريدار *kharīd-ār*, s.m. (2nd) A buyer, purchaser. Pl. خريداران *kharīd-ārān*. خريد و فروخت *kharīd-o-farokht*, Buying and selling, barter, exchange, trade and traffic.

خرېړی *kharerraey*, s.m. (1st) Thick sour milk, or coagulated milk mixed with fresh milk; a kind of junket; buttermilk. 2. A mushroom, a toad-stool. Pl. ي *ī*.

خريز *khirīz*, s.m. (2nd) Stubble of the cotton plant or grain left in the ground after reaping. Pl. خريزونه *khirīzūnah*. Also خرند and نار which see.

خريل *kh'riyal*, verb trans. To shave, to shear. Pres. خريي *kh'riyī*; past و خريه *wu-kh'riyah*; fut. و به خريي *wu bah kh'riyī*; imp. و خريه *wu-kh'rīyah*; act. part. خريونکی *kh'riyūnkaey*, or خريونی *kh'riyūnaey*; past part. خريلی *kh'riyalaey*; verb. n. خرينه *kh'riyana'h*.

خريلی *kh'riyalaey*, adj. (past part.) Shaved, shorn.

خړ *khærr*, adj. Muddy, miry, turbid, puddly, dirty, dusty, smoky, soiled, etc. 2. Mud-coloured, brown. 3. Plain, humble in dress; (Fem.) خړه *khærra'h*. خړې اوبه *khærrey aoba'h*, Muddy or turbid water. خړه اوريځ *khærra'h aor-yadz*, A dark or murky cloud. خړوالی *khærr wālaey*, s.m. (1st) Muddiness, turbidness, foulness. Pl. والي *wālī*, or تيا *tī a*, s.f. (6th) (E.) Sing. and Pl. (W.) Pl. تياوي *tī-āwī*. خړجن *khær-jan*, adj. Dirty, foul, turbid, dusty; (Fem.) خړجنه *khærr-jana'h*. خړېدل *khærredal*, verb intrans. To become muddy, dirty, dusty, foul, puddly. 2. To become angry, troubled, disturbed, excited, irritated, etc. Pres. خړيږي *khærrejzī* (W.) or خړيګي *khærregī* (E.); past خړ شه *khærr shah* or و شه *wu-shah*; fut. خړ به شي *khærr bah shī* or به و شي *bah wu-shī*; imp. خړ شه *khærr shah* or و شه *wu-shah*; act. part. خړېدونکی *khærredūnkaey* or خړېدونی *khærr-edūnaey*; past part. خړ *khærr*, or خړ شوی *khærr shawaey*; verb. n. خړېدنه *khærr-edana'h*. خړول *khærrawul*, verb trans. To puddle, to dirty, to make foul or dusty. 2. To seek a pretext, to use as a plea, etc. Pres. خړوي *khærrawī*; past خړ کړ *khærr karr* or و کړ *wu-karr*; fut. خړ به کړي *khærr bah krrī* or به و کړي *bah wu-krrī*; imp. خړ کړه *khærr krrah* or و کړه *wu-krrah*; act. part. خړوونکی *khærrawūnkaey* or خړوونی *khærr-awūnaey*; past part. خړ کړی *khærr karraey*; verb. n. خړونه *khærrawuna'h*.

خړ *khurr*, s.m. (5th) The sound produced when vomiting or retching, the sound produced by hawking or expectorating. Pl. خړهار *khurra-hār*. Pl. خړ وهل *khurr wahal*, verb trans. To puke, spew, retch, hawk, etc.

خړ *khurr*, s.m. (2nd) A watercourse; a ravine dry in summer; the sandy bed of a river or rivulet; the dry bed of a river. Pl. خړونه *khurrūnah*. Also خړه *khwarra'h*, s.f. (3rd) Pl. ې *ey*. See خور and مانده

خړپ *khrrap*, s.m. (5th) The sound produced

by chewing carrots and the like, a crunch or craunch, a smash, quash, crash, the sound of a sudden blow, or of a sword on the flesh, etc. Pl. خرپهار *khrrapahār*. خرپ وهل *khrrap wahal*, verb trans. To crunch, to smash, to quash, to strike suddenly.

خرپوڅه *kharrpotsa'h*, s.f. (3rd) Crawling on all-fours (as a child). Pl. ې *ey*. خرپوڅه کول *kharrpotsa'h kawul*, verb trans. or په خرپوڅه تلل *pah kharrpotsa'h t'lal*, verb intrans. To move along on all-fours, to crawl along. See خرپوسه or خرپوڅه and خارپوڅه

خرتم *kharrtam*, s.m. (2nd) (from A خرطوم) The trunk of an elephant. Pl. خرتمونه *kharrtamūnah*. خرتم آچول *kharrtam āchawul*, verb trans. To blow the nose on, to crow over, To talk big.

خرس *khrras*, s.m. (5th) Clash, crash, shock, blow, thump, click, clap, slam, etc. Pl. خرسهار *khrrasahār*. خرس وهل *khrras wahal*, verb trans. To clash, to crash, to click, to thump, etc. or خرسهار لرل *khrrasahār laral*, verb trans.

خرکَی *khurrkaey*, s.m. (1st) The sound produced by vomiting or retching, or by hawking or spitting (dimin. of خر). Pl. خرکي *khurrkī*. خرکَی کول *khurrkaey kawul*, verb trans. To puke, to spew, to retch, to hawk.

خرل *kharral*, verb trans. To ease one's-self, to go to stool, to dung. Pres. خري *kharrī*; past و خرل *wu-kharral*; fut. و به کري *wu bah kharrī*; imp. و خره *wu-kharrah*; act. part. خرونکَی *kharrūnkaey*, or خرونَی *kharrūnaey*; past part. خرلَی *kharralaey*; verb. n. خرنه *kharrana'h*. See غل کول

خرند *kharrandd*, s.m. (2nd) The stump of a tree or shrub, a branch, stubble left in the ground after reaping, etc. Pl. خرندونه *kharranddūnah*. See خريز and نار

خروب *kharrob*, adj. Saturated, watered, irrigated, wetted with water, watered (as a horse or cow); (Fem.) خروبه *kharroba'h*. خروب کول *kharrob kawul*, verb trans. To water, to saturate, to irrigate, to water (as cattle).

خريس *khrrīs*, s.m. (5th) A large and bulky person, tall and stout, a stalwart or strapping fellow. Pl. خريسان *khrrīsān*. s.f. (3rd) خريسه *khrrīsa'h*. Pl. ې *ey*. 2. adj. Large, big, great, stalwart, spanking, burly, brawny. خريس والَی *khrrīs wālaey*, s.m. (1st) Bigness, stoutness, stalwartness, brawniness, strength. Pl. والي *wālī*.

خرين *khurrīn*, adj. Softened, sodden, ripe, risen (as bread with yeast), festered (as a boil), unsound (as fruit), well boiled (as meat). 2. Angry, enraged, wroth. 3. Mortified, hurt; (Fem.) خرينه *khurrīna'h*. خرين والَی *khurrīn-wālaey*, s.m. (1st) or خرين توب *khurrīn-tob*, s.m. (2nd) Softness, ripeness, unsoundness, mellowness. Pl. والي *wālī* or توبونه *tobūnah*. خرينيدل *khurrīnedal*, verb intrans. To soften, to sodden, to ripen, to become soft by boiling. Pres. خرينيږي *khurrīnejzī* (W.), or خرينيگي *khurrīnegī* (E.); past خرين شه *khurrīn shah* or و شه *wu-shah*; fut. خرين به شي *khurrīn bah shī* or به و شي *bah wu-shī*; imp. خرين شه *khurrīn shah* or و شه *wu-shah*; act. part. خرينيدونکَی *khurrīnedūnkaey* or خرينيدونَی *khurrīnedūnaey*; past part. خرين *khurrīn* or خرين شوَی *khurrīn shawaey*; verb. n. خرينيدنه *khurrīnedana'h*. خرينول *khurrīnawul*, verb trans. To sodden, to make soft, ripe, or festered. Pres. خرينوي *khurrīnawī*; past خرين کړ *khurrīn karr* or و کړ *wu-karr*; fut. خرين به کړي *khurrīn bah krrī* or به و کړي *bah wu-krrī*; imp. خرين کړه *khurrīn krrah* or و کړه *wu-krrah*; act. part. خرينوونکَی *khurrīnawūnkaey* or خرينوونَی *khurrīnawūnaey*; past part. خرين کړَی *khurrīn karraey*; verb. n. خرينونه *khurrīnawunah*.

P خزان *khazān*, s.m. (2nd) Autumn. Pl. خزانونه *khazānūnah*. See مني

A خزانه *khizāna'h*, s.f. (3rd) A treasury, a magazine, a repository, a granary; the chamber of a rifle or gun. Pl. ې *ey*. خزانه دار *khizāna'h-dār*, or خزانهي *khizāna'h'ī*, A rifle or musket, a matchlock with a chamber.

خزانه چي khizāna'h-chī, s.m. (5th) A treasurer. Pl. خزانه چيان khizāna'h-chīān.

خزله khazala'h, s.f. (3rd) Rubbish, sweepings, litter of anything. Pl. ي ey. See ورخره and خاشاك

P خزنده khazanda'h, s.f. (3rd) A creeping thing, an insect, a reptile. Pl. ي ey.

خږ khujz, adj. (W.) Lame, crippled, wounded, bruised, injured, mauled, etc.; (Fem.) خږه khujza'h. 2. s.m. (6th) A hurt, an injury, a wound, a bruise, scath, mutilation; disease, ailment, malady, ill. Sing. and Pl. خږ مند khujz mand, adj. Diseased, ill, lame, out of sorts, crippled, bruised, etc.; (Fem.) خږ منده khujz-manda'h. خږ والي khujz-wālaey, s.m. (1st) Painfulness, uneasiness. Pl. والي wālī.

خږيدل khujzedal (W.) or خګيدل khugedal (E.) verb intrans. To pain, to twinge, to ache, to smart, to tingle, to shoot. Pres. خږيږي khujzejzī (W.) or خګيګي khugegī (E.); past خږ شه khujz shah or خګ شه khug shah or ؤ شه wu-shah; fut. خږ به شي khujz bah shī or خګ به شي khug bah shī or به ؤ شي bah wu-shī; imp. خږ شه khujz shah or خګ شه khug shah or ؤ شه wu-shah; act. part. خږيدونکی khujzedūnkaey or خګيدونکی khugedūnkaey or خږيدونی khujzedūnaey or خګيدونی khugedūnaey; past part. خږ khujz or خګ khug or خږ شوی khujz shawaey or خګ شوی khug shawaey; verb. n. خږيدنه khujzedana'h or خګيدنه khugedana'h. خږول khujzawul (W.) or خګول khugawul (E.) verb trans. To pain, to inflict pain, to pinch, to wring, to torture, to agonize, etc. Pres. خږوي khujzawī or خګوي khugawī; past خږ کړ khujz karr or خګ کړ khug karr or ؤ کړ wu-karr; fut. خږ به کړي khujz bah krrī or خګ به کړي khug bah krrī or به ؤ کړي bah wu-krrī; imp. خږ کړه khujz krrah or خګ کړه khug krrah or ؤ کړه wu-krrah; act. part. خږوونکی khujzawūnkaey or خګوونکی khugawūnkaey or خږووني khujzawūnaey or خګووني khugawūnaey; past part. خږ کړی khujz karraey or خګ کړی khug karraey; verb. n. خږونه khujzawuna'h or خګونه khugawuna'h. See خګ and خوږ

خږ khajz, s.m. (5th) A rattling or gurgling sound produced in the throat of a dying animal, etc.; the death rattle. Pl. خږهار khajzahār. خږ کول khajz kawul, verb trans. To rattle or gurgle, as a goat or sheep with its throat cut.

P خس khass, s.m. (2nd) Any useless stick or herb, dry grass, etc. Pl. خسونه khasūnah. خس و خاشاك khas-o-khāshāk, Litter of anything, rubbish, sweepings.

خسا khsā, adj. Fetid, strong-smelling, putrid, stinking, foul, rank, musty, noisome, etc. (Masc. and Fem.) خسا والی khsā-wālaey, s.m. (1st) Fetor, strong smell, stench, stink, foulness, rancidity. Pl. والي wālī. See سخا خسا کيدل khsā kedal, verb intrans. To stink, to smell, to become noisome. خسا کول khsā kawul, verb trans. To make to stink, to make rancid.

P خسر khusar, s.m. (5th) A father-in-law. Pl. خسران khusarān. See سخر

خسرړی khasarraey, s.m. (1st) A straw, or anything of no value or little consequence, rubbish, etc. Pl. ي ī. خسرړي آچول khasarrey āchawul, verb trans. To cast lots (with straws).

خسمانه khasamāna'h, s.f. (3rd) Protection, care, custody, support, assistance, aid. Pl. ي ey. خسمانه کول khasamāna'h kawul, verb trans. To assist, to protect, to give aid or succour, to render assistance.

خسرړنی khasarrnaey, s.m. (1st) A straw, or anything of no value. Pl. ي ī. خسرړني آچول khasarrnaey āchawul, verb trans. To cast lots with straws. See preceding.

خسی khsaey, s.m. (1st) A young sucking calf. Pl. خسي khsī; s.f. (6th) خسۍ khsa'ī. Sing. and Pl. See سخی

خسي khasī, s.m. (5th) A castrated animal, as a horse, sheep, etc. Pl. خسيان khasīān. 2. adj. Castrated, gelt. خسي کول khasī kawul, verb trans. To castrate, to geld. See آخته, (A خصي).

A خسيس khasīs, adj. (from خست) Sordid, penurious, avaricious. 2. Mean, ignoble.

P خسيل khasīl, s.m. (2nd) Green corn given to cattle. Pl. خسيلونه khasīlūnah. See also خويد

خشاوزه khushāw-za'h, s.f. (3rd) Orris root, the sweet cane, the galingale. Pl. ئ ey. See سخاوزه

خشت khusht or khisht, adj. Damp, wet, soaked, drenched, dripping, reeking, dank, humid; (Fem.) خشته khushta'h or khishta'h. خشت پشت khusht-pusht or khisht-pisht, adj. Dripping wet, soaked through, reeking, very damp or humid. خشتيدل khushtedal, verb intrans. To become wet, damp, soaked, humid, etc. Pres. خشتيږي khushtejzī (W.) or خشتيگي khushtegī (E.); past خشت کړ khusht karr or وُ کړ wu-karr; fut. خشت به شي khusht bah shī or به وُ شي bah wu-shī; imp. خشت شه khusht shah or وُ شه wu-shah; act. part. خشتيدونکَي khushtedūnkaey or خشتيدونَي khushtedūnaey; past part. خشت khusht or خشت شوَي khusht shawaey; verb.n. خشتيدنه khushtedana'h. خشتول khushtawul, verb trans. To make wet, to damp, to soak, to make humid, etc. Pres. خشتوي khushtawī; past خشت کړ khusht karr or وُ کړ wu-karr; fut. خشت به کړي khusht bah krrī or به وُ کړي bah wu-krrī; imp. خشت کړه khusht krrah or وُ کړه wu-krrah; act. part. خشتونکَي khushtawūnkaey or خشتونَي khushtawūnaey; past part. خشت کړَي khusht karraey; verb. n. خشتونه khushtawuna'h.

P خشک khushk, adj. Dry, withered; (Fem.) خشکه khushka'h. خشکاوه khushkāwa'h, s.f. (3rd) A dry year, a drought. 2. Dry, sterile land. Pl. ئ ey. خشک دماغ khushk damāgh or خشک مغز khushk maghz, adj. Hot-brained, hot-headed, crazy, crack-brained. خشک دماغی khushk damāghī or مغزي maghzī, s.f. (3rd) Craziness, hot-headedness. Pl. ئ a'ī. خشک سالي khushk sālī, s.f. (3rd) Drought, a drought, sterility. Pl. ئ a'ī. خشکه khushka'k, s.f. (3rd) Boiled rice. Pl. ئ ey.

P خشکه khushkah or خشکي adv. By land, in opposition to تري tarī, by water.

P خشنود khushnūd, adj. Pleased, gratified, contented, satisfied. خشنودي khushnūdī, s.f. (3rd) Contentment, pleasure, gratification, satisfaction. Pl. ئ a'ī.

خشَي khushaey, adj. Crazy, weak-minded, lunatic, demented, daft, giddy, flighty, beside one's-self. 2. A mad-cap, a lunatic, a dreamer. 3. Undefended, open to assault, exposed, vulnerable. 4. Defenceless, unaided, unassisted, unfriended; (Fem.) خشِ khushi. See خوشي

خښ khakh (E.) adj. Buried, interred, inhumed, entombed, under ground. 2. Embedded, implanted, inserted, stuck in; (Fem.) خښه khakha'h. خښيدل khakhedal (E.) verb intrans. To enter, to penetrate, to sink into, to insinuate itself, to be absorbed or swallowed. Pres. خښيگي khakhegī; past خښ شه khakh shah or وُ شه wu-shah; fut. خښ به شي khakh bah shī or به وُ شي bah wu-shī; imp. خښ شه khakh shah or وُ شه wu-shah; act. part. خښيدونکَي khakhedūnkaey or خښيدونَي khakhedūnaey; past part. خښ khakh or خښ شوَي khakh shawaey; verb. n. خښيدنه khakhedana'h or خښيده khakhedah. خښول khakhawul, verb trans. To bury, inter, inhume, entomb, to introduce, to insert, to implant, to embed, to stick into, to plant. Pres. خښوي khakhawī; past خښ کړ khakh karr or وُ کړ wu-karr; fut. خښ به کړي khakh bah krrī or به وُ کړي bah wu-krrī; imp. خښ کړه khakh krrah or وُ کړه wu-krrah; act. part. خښوونکَي khakhawūnkaey or خښوونَي khakhawūnaey; past part. خښ کړَي khakh karraey; verb. n. خښونه khakhawuna'h. See also مَښ

خښتګ khashtag (W.) or khakhtag (E.) s.m. (2nd) A square piece of cloth inserted in a pair of drawers, a gore, a gusset. Pl. خښتګونه khashtagūnah or khakhtagūnah.

خښتګي *khashtagaey* (W.) or *khakhtagaey* (E.) s.m. (1st) A gore, a gusset (the dimin. of above.) Pl. ي *ī*.

خښته *khashta'h* (W.) or *khakhta'h* (E.) s.f. (3rd) A brick, burnt or otherwise. Pl. ې *ey*.

خښي *khakhī* (E.) or *khashī* (W.) s.m. (1st) (Pl.) The name given to the whole Yūsufzī tribe of Afghāns. خښي *khakhaey* or *khashaey* (Sing.) A male of the above. خښۍ *khakha'ī* or *khasha'ī*, s.f. (6th) A female or females of the above. Sing. and Pl.

A خصلت *khaṣlat*, s.m. (2nd) Habit, custom, disposition, nature, virtue, quality, mode. Pl. خصلتونه *khaṣlatūnah*.

A خصوصاً *khuṣūṣan*, adv. Particularly, especially.

A خصوصيت *khuṣūṣiyat*, s.m. (2nd) Attachment, friendship, peculiarity, singularity. Pl. خصوصيتونه *khuṣūṣiyatūnah*.

A خضر *khizr*, s. prop. A companion of Moses, Phineas, or the prophet Elias.

A خط *khaṭṭ*, s.m. (2nd) A letter, epistle, note. 2. A line, lineament. 3. Writing, handwriting. 4. Down on the face, youthful beard. Pl. خطونه *khaṭṭūnah*. خط کښل *khaṭṭ k'shal* or *k'khal*, verb trans. To draw, to write, to draw a line; or خط وهل *khaṭṭ wahal*.

A خطا *khaṭā*, s.f. (6th) Mistake, error, fault, crime. (E.) Sing. and Pl.; (W.) Pl. خطاوي *khaṭāwī*. خطا کيدل *khaṭā kedal*, verb intrans. To miss, err, fail, miscarry, to wander, to ramble, to fail to hit. خطا کول *khaṭā kawul*, verb trans. To err, to blunder, to miss, to fail in aim, to mislead, to cause to deviate.

A خطاب *khiṭāb*, s.m. (2nd) (from خطب) Title, address. Pl. خطابونه *khiṭābūnah*. خطاب ورکول *khiṭāb war-kawul*, verb trans. To bestow a title.

A خطبه *khuṭba'h*, s.f. (3rd) An oration or sermon delivered after every Friday's service, in which the preacher blesses God, Muḥammad, and his successors, and prays for the reigning sovereign. Pl. ي *ī*.

A خطر *khaṭar*, s.m. (2nd) Danger, risk, thought, recollection, remembrance. خطرونه *khaṭarūnah*. خطر ناک *khaṭar-nāk*, adj. Frightful, hazardous, dangerous; (Fem.) خطر ناکه *khaṭar-nāka'h*. د ځان خطر *da dzān khaṭar*, Danger of life, hazard of life. د مال خطر *da māl khaṭar*, Danger, or hazard of property, etc.

A خطره *khaṭra'h*, s.f. (3rd) Danger, fear, risk, venture. Pl. ې *ey*.

A خطيب *khaṭīb*, s.m. (5th) A preacher, a public speaker. Pl. خطيبان *khaṭībān*.

A خفت *khiffat*, s.m. (2nd) Lightness of weight, levity in conduct, want of dignity, disgrace, indignity, slight, affront. Pl. خفتونه *khiffatūnah*.

A خفقان *khafaḳān*, s.m. (2nd) (from خفق) Palpitation of the heart, palpitation, vibration. 2. Displeased, vexed. Pl. خفقانونه *khafaḳānūnah*.

A خفه *khafah*, adj. Angry, enraged, displeased. 2. Strangled, choked. خفه کيدل *khafah kedal*, verb intrans. To become angry, displeased. 2. To choke, or become choked. خفه کول *khafah kawul*, verb trans. To make angry, to enrage. 2. To strangle, to choke. خفگي *khafagī*, s.f. (3rd) Displeasure, anger, pet. Pl ۍ *a'ī*.

خګ *khug*, adj. Lame, crippled, wounded, bruised, injured, mauled, etc. s.m. (6th) A hurt, injury, wound, bruise, disease, ailment, malady. Sing. and Pl. (Fem.) خګه *khuga'h*. خګ مند *khug-mand*, adj. Diseased, ill, lame, out of sorts, crippled, etc. خګ والی *khug-wālaey*, s.m. (1st) Painfulness, uneasiness. Pl. ي *ī*. خګيدل *khugedal*, verb intrans. To pain, ache, smart, etc. خګول *khugawul*, verb trans. To pain or inflict pain, to agonize, to pinch, to wring, to torture. See conjugations of خږيدل and خږول which are exactly the same meaning, the Western tribes using ږ and the Eastern substituting ګ

خګ لن *khug-lan*, s.m. (2nd) Hot ashes, live coals, cinder, etc. Pl. خګ لنونه *khug-lanūnah*. See خوګ and سخوبښتن

خل *khal*, s.m. (2nd) Faith, confidence, trust, hope. Pl. خلونه *khalūnah*.

خلات khalāt, s.m. (2nd) A dress, or robe of honor presented to a person by a prince (corrup. of A خلعت). Pl. خلاتونه khalātūnah.

A خلاص khalāṣ, adj. (from خلص) Free, liberated, redeemed, done, finished out. خلاصي khalāṣ-ī, s.f. (3rd) Discharge, deliverance, liberation, release, freedom, redemption. Pl. ئي a'ī.

خلاصيدل khalāṣedal, verb trans. To be freed or set free, emancipated, etc.; to be released or discharged, to emit. 2. To be brought to bed, to calve, etc. 3. Emissio seminis. Pres. خلاصيږي khalāṣejzī (W.) or خلاصيګي khalāṣegī (E.); past خلاص شه khalāṣ shah or وُ شه wu-shah; fut. خلاص به شي khalāṣ bah shī or به وُ شي bah wu-shī; imp. خلاص شه khalāṣ shah or وُ شه wu-shah; act. part. خلاصيدونکَي khalāṣedūnkaey or خلاصيدونَي khalāṣedūnaey; past part. خلاص khalāṣ or خلاص شوَي khalāṣ shawaey; verb. n. خلاصيدنه khalāṣedana'h or خلاصيده khalāṣedah.

خلاصول khalāṣawul, verb trans. To release, to set free, to liberate, to discharge, to redeem, to ransom, to emit, to let loose, to discharge (as a gun). Pres. خلاصوي khalāṣawī; past خلاص کړ khalāṣ karr or وُ کړ wu-karr; fut. خلاص به کړي khalāṣ bah krrī or به وُ کړي bah wu-krrī; imp. خلاص کړه khalāṣ krrah or وُ کړه wu-krrah; act. part. خلاصونکَي khalāṣawūnkaey or خلاصونَي khalāṣawūnaey; past part. خلاص کړَي khalāṣ karraey; verb. n. خلاصونه khalāṣawuna'h.

A خلاصه khulāṣa'h, s.f. (3rd) Conclusion, inference, moral, sum, thes hort and the long of, essence, abstract, etc, Pl. ئي ey.

خلاصيدنه khalāṣedana'h, s.f. (3rd) or خلاصيده khalāṣedah, s.m. (6th) (verb. n.) Release, liberation, freedom, emancipation, exemption, independence, escape, discharge, dismissal. Pl. (3rd) ئي ey; (6th) Sing. and Pl.

A خلاف khalāf, s.m. (9th) (from خلف) Contrariety, opposition, antagonism, in opposition, contrary to, against. 2. Falsehood. Sing. and Pl. خلاف له رائَ khalāf lah rā'ya, Against one's will or opinion. خلاف له شرعي khalāf lah sharæey, Illegal, unlawful, contrary to orthodox law. خلاف له عقلَ khalāf lah æakla, Contrary to reason. خلاف له قياسَ khalāf lah ḳiyāsa, Absurd, improbable, irregular, anomalous. خلاف له وعدي khalāf lah waædey, Breaking one's promise.

A خلافت khilāfat, s.m. (2nd) (from خلف) Deputyship, lieutenancy, the office of a Khalīfah. 2. Dignity, monarchy. Pl. خلافتونه khilāfatūnah.

خلا ملا khalā-malā, adj. Unfeigned (friendship), unreserved, frank, candid, sincere, free spoken. په خلا ملا ويل pah khalā-malā wa-yal, verb trans. To speak one's mind, to speak frankly, to speak without mincing matters.

خلبوري khulboraey, s.m. (1st) A stopper, a plug, a cork, a bung, a spigot, a lid. Pl. ي ī.

خلپه khulpa'h, s.f. (3rd) Purslain (Portulaca oleracea). Pl. ئي ey. See خرفه

خلته khalta'h, s.f. (3rd) A bag, a wallet, a scrip, a satchel, a haversack. Pl. ئي ey. See خليته

P خلش khalish, s.m. (2nd) Suspicion, doubt, solicitude, interruption, putting a stop to. Pl. خلشونه khalishūnah.

A خلط khilṭ, s.m. (2nd) One of the four humours of the human body. Pl. خلطونه khilṭūnah.

A خلط khalṭ, s.m. (2nd) Confusion, mixture, medley, mixing. Pl. خلطونه khalṭūnah.

A خلعت khalæat or khilæat, s.m. (2nd) A dress or robe of honour, which princes confer on their subjects. Pl. خلعتونه khalæatūnah. See خلات

خلعه khalæa'h, s.f. (3rd) (corrup. of A خلع) Deposing, removing from office, stripping. 2. Repudiating a wife, when desired by herself from dislike to her husband, at which time she is entitled to residue of dowry. 3. Disinheriting a son. Pl. خلعي khalæey.

A خلق khulḳ, s.m. (2nd) Nature, disposition, quality, civility, politeness. Pl. خلقونه khulḳūnah. (A Pl. اخلاق akhlāḳ).

A خلق khalḳ, s.m. (6th) Creation, people, mankind, the world. Sing. and Pl. (A Pl. خلايق khalāyiḳ).

A خلقت *khalkat*, s.m. (2nd) The creation, people, the world, the populace. Pl. خلقتونه *khalkatūnah*.

خلقه *khalka'h*, s.f. (3rd) People, mankind, creation. Pl. خلقي *khalkey*, A multitude, a crowd, a throng.

A خلقي *khilkī*, adj. Natural, innate.

A خلل *khalal*, s.m. (2nd) (from خل) Interruption, confusion, disturbance, damage, injury, defect, breach, prejudice, hiatus. Pl. خللونه *khalalūnah*. خلل کول *khalal kawul*, verb trans. To interrupt, confuse, prejudice, disturb, injure.

A P خللي *khalal-ī*, adj. a disturber, an interrupter, a mischief-maker.

خلنج *khalanj*, s.m. (5th) A kind of mulberry, red and white, with seeds. Pl. خلنجان *khalanjān*.

A خلوت *khalwat*, s.m. (2nd) Retirement, privacy, solitude, a closet, a private apartment, private conference. Pl. خلوتونه *khalwatūnah*. خلوت خانه *khalwat khāna'h*, s.f. (3rd) A closet, a cabinet, a private apartment. Pl. خانې *khāney*. حلوت کول *khalwat kawul*, verb trans. To closet, or be closeted. خلوت نشين *khalwat nishīn*, adj. Retired. 2. s.m. (5th) A hermit, a recluse. Pl. خلوت نشينان *khalwat nishīnān*. خلوتي *khalwatī*, s.m.(5th) A confidant, an intimate friend, a hermit. Pl. خلوتيان *khalwatīān*.

خله *khula'h*, s.f. (3rd) The mouth, orifice, entrance. Pl. خلې *khuley*. پټه خله *putta'h khula'h*, adj. Silent, mute, mum, taciturn, still, 2. interj. Silence! hush! keep silent! پټه خله اوسيدل *putta'h khula'h aosedal*, verb intrans. To become silent, to remain mute, etc. پټه خله کول *putta'h khula'h kawul*, verb trans. To silence, to hush. پټ خلي *putt khulaey*, s.m. (1st) A silent or taciturn person. (Fem.) پټ خل *putt khuli*. Pl. (Masc. and Fem.) ي *ī*.

خلگۍ *khulga'ī*, s.f. (6th) A small mouth (dimin. of خله). Sing. and Pl.

خلی *khalaey*, s.m. (1st) A sprout, a shoot, a blade of grass, etc., a straw, anything proverbially worthless, rubbish, refuse, sweepings. Pl. ي *ī*.

خليته *khalīta'h*, s.f. (3rd) A bag, a haversack, a wallet. Pl. ې *ey*. See خلته

A خليفه *khalīfah*, s.m. (5th) (from خلف, H חלף, To succeed) A successor, a sovereign, particularly applied to Muḥammad's successors. 2. A monitor. Pl. خليفگان *khalīfagān*.

A خليق *khalīk*, adj. (from خلق) Kind, benign, of good disposition, civil, polite.

خليل *khalīl*, s.m. (6th) The name of a tribe of Afghāns inhabiting the plains of Peshāwer between Tahkāl and Jumrūd. 2. (A) A friend, a sincere friend (Abraham). Sing. and Pl.; s.f. (3rd) خليله *khalīla'h*, A female of the Khalīl tribe. Pl. ې *ey*.

P خم *khum*, s.m. (5th) A large jar, a boiler, a still or alembic. Pl. خمان *khumān*.

P خمار *khumār*, s.m. (9th) (from خمر) Sickness, headache after a debauch. 2. Intoxicating, languishing appearance of the eyes from love, drinking, or drowsiness. Sing. and Pl.

خماري *khumārī*, adj. Drunken, languishing, intoxicating. خماري سترگي *khumārī stargey*, Sleepy eyes.

خمار *khumār*, s.m. (9th) (corrup. of قمار) Dice, a game, any game of hazard. Sing. and Pl. خمار باز *khumār-bāz*, s.m. (5th) A gambler. Pl. خمار بازان *khumār-bāzān*. خمار بازي *khumār-bāzī*, s.f. (3rd) Gaming, gambling. Pl. ئ *a'ī*. خمار کول *khumār kawul*, verb trans. To game, to gamble.

خمبه *khamba'h*, s.f. (3rd) A kind of hamper or large basket with a cover for keeping grain in. Pl. ې *ey*. See خلته

خمټ *khamatt*, adj. Fair and chubby (as a baby); (Fem.) خمټه *khamatta'h*.

خمچه *khamachah*, adj. Puny, petty, little, short (particularly for the little finger and short ribs); thus خمچه گته *khamacha'h guta'h*, The little finger. خمچه پښتۍ *khamacha'h pushta'ī* or *pukhta'ī*, s.f. (6th) The short ribs. Sing. and Pl.

خمچي *khamachey*, s.f. (3rd) Pl. Broken rice or millet, ground and made into bread.

خمرۍ *khumra'ī*, s.f. (6th) A small earthen or brass narrow-mouthed vessel for drinking out of, a drinking cup. Sing. and Pl. See کنجۍ

خمسور *khamsor*, adj. Free, easy, unceremonious, unconstrained, familiar, not formal; (Fem.) خمسوره *khamsora'h*. خمسور تيا *khamsor-tī'ā*, s.f. (6th) Familiarity, freedom from ceremony, affability. (E.) Sing. and Pl.; (W.) Pl. خمسور تياوي *khamsor-tī'āwī*. See خمخور

خمن *khaman*, adj. Twisted, bent, curled, crooked, curved; (Fem.) خمنه *khamana'h*.

خميدل *khamedal* (from خم) verb intrans. To grow or become crooked, curved, wry, deformed, bowed, bent, etc, خمول *khamawul*, verb trans. To make or render crooked, curved, wry, or deformed; to pervert.

A خمير *khamīr*, adj. Leavened, raised by fermentation; (Fem.) خميره *khamīra'h*. خميره دوډۍ *khamīra'h ḍoḍa'ī*, Leavened bread. See پتير

خميره *khamīra'h*, s.f. (3rd) Dough, leaven, a mass of sour dough. Pl. ې *ey*.

خميز *khamez*, adj. Slightly curved, crooked, somewhat wry or deformed, etc.; (Fem.) خميزه *khameza'h*. خميزيدل *khamezedal*, verb intrans. To grow or become twisted, curled, bent, crooked, curved. خميزول *khamezawul*, verb trans. To make or render twisted, curled, bent, crooked, curved.

خنجاړه *khan-jāṛra'h*, s.f. (3rd) A species of grain, small in size, from which bread is made: the straw is given to cattle. Pl. ې *ey*.

A خنجر *khanjar*, s.m. (2nd) A dagger. Pl. خنجرونه *khanjarūnah*.

خنجک *khanjak*, s.m. (2nd) The mastic tree, and the fruit thereof. Pl. خنجکونه *khanjakūnah*. See د شنو ونه

خند *khand*, s.m. (2nd) A ring drawn on the ground for playing the game called خند خند *khand-khand*, or game of knuckle-bones. Pl. خندونه *khandūnah*. See تکه آرغند

خندا *khandā*, s.f. (6th) Laughter, a laugh. (E.) Sing. and Pl.; (W.) Pl. خنداوي *khandāwī*. خندا کول *khandā kawul*, verb trans. To laugh, to giggle. (P خنده).

A خندق *khandaḳ*, s.m. (2nd) A ditch, a moat, a fosse. Pl. خندقونه *khandaḳūnah*.

خندل *khandal*, verb trans. To laugh, to ridicule. Pres. خاندي *khāndī*; past وُ خندل *wu-khandal*; fut. وُ به خاندي *wu bah khāndī*; imp. وُ خانده *wu-khāndah*; act. part. خندونکۍ *khandūnkaey* or خندونۍ *khandūnaey*; past part. خندلي *khandalī*; verb. n. خندنه *khandana'h*.

خندول *khandawul*, verb trans. (causal) To cause to laugh, to make to laugh. Pres. خندوي *khandawī*; past وُ خنداوه *wu-khandāwuh* or وُ خنداوو *wu-khandāwo*; fut. وُ به خندوي *wu bah khandawī*; imp. وُ خندوه *wu-khandawah*; act. part. خندوونکۍ *khandawūnkaey* or خندوونۍ *khandawūnaey*; past part. خندولۍ *khandawulaey*; verb. n. خندونه *khandawuna'h*.

خندي *khundī*, adj. Preserved, protected, secure, taken care of. 2. Adjusted settled, arranged, put to rights. خندي کول *khundī kawul*, verb trans. To keep, preserve, protect, secure; to adjust, to settle. خندي والۍ *khundī-wālaey*, s.m. (1st), or خندي توب *khundī-tob*, s.m. (2nd) Preservation, protection, security, care. 2. Putting to rights, adjustment. Pl. والي *wālī* and توبونه *tobūnah*.

خنديدل *khandedal*, verb intrans. To laugh, giggle, titter, etc. Pres. خنديږي *khandejzī* (W.) or خنديگي *khandegī* (E.); past وُ خنديده *wu-khandedah* or وُ خنديدَ *wu-khandeda*; fut. وُ به خنديږي *wu bah khandejzī* or وُ به خنديگي *wu bah khandegī*; imp. وُ خنديږه *wu-khandejzah* or وُ خنديگه *wu-khandegah*; act. part. خنديدونکۍ *khandedūnkaey* or خنديدونۍ *khandedūnaey*; past part. خنديدلۍ *khandedalaey*; verb. n. خنديدنه *khandedana'h*.

خنديل *khundi-yal*, verb trans. To keep, preserve, protect, secure, adjust, settle, arrange. 2. To intrust to, to make over to, to confide to. Pres. خنديي *khundi-yī*; past وُ خنديه *wu-*

khundi-yah; fut. وُ به خندیي wu bah khundi-yī; imp. وُ خندیه wu-khundi-yah; act. part. خندیونکَي khundi-yūnkaey or خندیونَي khundi-yūnaey; past part. خندیلَي khundi-yalaey; verb. n. خندینه khundi-yana'h. See خندي

خند khandd, s.m. (2nd) The trunk or root of a tree or shrub which has been left standing in the ground. Pl. خندونه khanddūnah.

خندن khanddan, s.m. (9th) The name of a plant, zedoary (curcuma zerumbet), Sing. and Pl.

P خنک khunuk, adj. Cold, cool, temperate; (Fem.) خنکه khunuka'h. خنکي khunukī, s.f. (3rd) Coldness, coolness, temperateness. Pl. ئ a'ī. See سور

خو khū, s.m. (9th) Tinder. Sing. and Pl. 2. kho, adv. Certainly, undoubtedly, surely. See خپه

خوا khwā, s.f. (6th) Side, margin, extremity, quarter, corner; towards. 2. Constitution, temperament, nature, health. (E.) Sing. and Pl.; (W.) Pl. خواوي khwāwī. دا خوا dā khwā, adv. This side, hither. هغه خوا haghah khwā, adv. That side, thither. خوابخوا khwā pa-khwā, adv. Abreast, side by side, opposite, breast to breast. خوا بدي khwā-badī, s.f. (3rd) Indigestion, dyspepsia. 2. Offence, affront, pique, umbrage, dudgeon, huff. Pl. ئ a'ī. خوا بدیدل khwā badedal, verb intrans. To become offended, to take umbrage, to take huff, to be piqued. خوا بدول khwā badawul, verb trans. To give umbrage, to incense, to provoke, to irritate, to fret, to discompose. خوا بدي کول khwā badī kawul, verb trans. To give umbrage, to put out of humour, to stir up one's bile. خوا خوږي khwā-khojzaey, adj. (as s.m. 1st) (W.) A comforter, a friend, a condoler, a sympathizer, a consoler. Pl. ي ī; also خوا خوگي khwā khogaey (E.); (Fem.) خوا خوږ khwā-khojzi or خوگ khogi. Pl. (Masc. and Fem.) ي ī. خوا خوږي khwā-khojzī or خواخوگي khwā-khogī, s.f. (3rd) Comfort, condolence, sympathy, friendship, etc. Pl. ئ a'ī. خوا و شا khwā-o-shah, adv. Round about, on all sides, all round. خوا گرزنَي khwā garzanaey, s.m. (1st) An emetic. Pl. ي ī. 2. adj. Emetic, producing vomiting. خوا گرزیدل khwā garzedal, verb intrans. To vomit, to puke. خوا گرزول khwā garzawul, verb trans. To cause to vomit.

خواجوزي khwā-jūzī, s.m. (1st) Pl. The name of a tribe of Afghāns. خواجوزَي khwā-jūzaey, Sing. A man of the above tribe; s.f. (6th) خواجوزئ khwā-jūza'ī, A female or females of the above. Sing. and Pl.

P خواجه khwājah, s.m. (5th) A man of distinction, a rich merchant, a gentleman. Pl. خواجگان khwājagān. خواجه خضر khwājah khiẓr, s. prop. A prophet skilled in divination, who is said to have discovered the water of life, Phineas or Elias.

P خوار khwār, adj. Poor, distressed, wretched, friendless, deserted, abandoned, ruined, abject. 2. Thin, lean, poor in condition. (Fem.) خواره khwāra'h. خوار و زار khwār-o-zār or خوار خسته khwār-khastah, adj. Abject, ruined, distressed, hard pinched, destitute, etc. خواري khwārī, s.f. (3rd) Meanness, contemptibleness, abjectness, distress, ruin. Pl. ئ a'ī. خواري کول khwārī kawul, verb trans. To strive, to take pains. خواریدل khwāredal, verb intrans. To become poor, destitute, wretched, distressed, ruined. 2. To grow lean or thin. Pres. خواریږي khwārejzī (W.) or خواریگي khwāregī (E.); past خوار شه khwār shah or وُ شه wu-shah; fut. خوار به شي khwār bah shī or به وُ شي bah wu-shī; imp. خوار شه khwār shah or وُ شه wu-shah; act. part. خواریدونکَي khwār-edūnkaey or خواریدونَي khwāredūnaey; past part. خوار شوَي khwār shawaey; verb. n. خواریدنه khwāredana'h or خواریده khwāredah. خوارول khwārawul, verb trans. To distress, to make wretched, to reduce to poverty, to ruin, etc. 2. To reduce in flesh, to make lean or thin. Pres. خواروي khwārawī; past خوار کړ khwār karr or وُ کړ wu-karr; fut. خوار به کړي khwār bah krrī or به وُ کړي bah wu-krrī; imp. خوار کړه khwār krrah or وُ کړه wu-krrah; act. part. خواروونکَي khwārawūnkaey or خواروونَي

khwārawūnaey; past part. خوار کړي khwār karraey; verb. n. خوارونه khwārawuna'h.

خوارهکَي khwārah-kaey, adj. (dimin. of خوار) Very contemptible, most vile or mean. 2. Poor, destitute (person). 3. Thin, lean. Pl. ي ī; (Fem.) خوارهکَي khwārahka'ī. Sing. and Pl. خوارهکَي شان khwārakaey shān, Poorish, thinnish, leanish, etc.

خوارړه khwārrah, s.m. (6th) Food, victuals, provision, eating. Sing. and Pl. څښنه خوارړه ts'shah (W.) or ts'khah (E.) khwārrah, Meat and drink, food, victuals. See خوړل

خوارږه ولني khwājzah-walanī (W.) s.m. (1st) Pl. Anise seed. See ګاګه ويلني and خواګه ولني

P خواست khwāst, s.m. (2nd) Desire, wish, inclination, want, request. Pl. خواستونه khwāstūnah. خواست ګر khwāst-gar, s.m. (5th) A candidate, aspirant, bidder, votary. Pl. خواست ګرٌ khwāst-gær; خواست ګره khwāst-gara'h, s.f. (3rd). Pl. ې ey. خواست کول khwāst kawul, verb trans. To desire, wish, ask for, to solicit, to want, to set one's heart on. See غوښت and غوښتل

خواښه khwāsha'h (W.) or khwākha'h (E.) s.f. (3rd) A mother-in-law, the mother of a husband or wife. Pl. ې ey.

خواله khwāla'h, s.m. (6th) Outpouring or revealing one's troubles to another, disclosing, letting the cat out of the bag, disburdening one's mind or conscience, unbosoming one's-self. Sing. and Pl. خواله کيدل khwāla'h kedal, verb intrans. To transpire, to become known, to ooze out, to become laid open, to be let out. خواله کول khwāla'h kawul or خواله ويل khwāla'h wa-yal, verb trans. To open one's mind, to unbosom one's-self, to disburden one's mind, heart, or conscience, to let the cat out of the bag.

P خوان khwān, s.m. (2nd) A tray. Pl. خوانونه khwānūnah. خوانچه khwāncha'h, s.f. (3rd) A small tray. Pl. ې ey; also خونچه khūncha'h. Pl. خونچې khūnchey. خوانچه khwāncha'h or خونچه پوښ khūncha'h posh or pokh, s.m. (2nd) A napkin for covering a tray. Pl. پوښونه poshūnah or pokhūnah. دستر خوان dastar khwān, s.m. (2nd) A table-cloth or cover of cloth or leather. Pl. دستر خوانونه dastar khwānūnah.

P خواه khwāh (part. act. of خواستن) Wishing, requiring, desiring. Used in composition, as دولت خواه dau-lat khwāh, Wishing prosperity. خاطر خواه khāṭir khwāh, The desire of one's heart, a beloved object. خير خواه khair khwāh, A friend, a well-wisher. خواه نخواه khwāh na-khwāh or خواه مخواه khwāh ma-khwāh, adv. Willing or not willing, nolens volens, absolutely, at all events.

P خواهش khwāhish, s.m. (2nd) (from خواستن) Desire, wish, inclination, demand. Pl. خواهشونه khwāhishūnah. خواهش لرل or کول khwāhish laral or kawul, verb trans. To wish for, to desire. خواهش مند khwāhish mand, s.m. (5th) A wisher, a desirer, a seeker. 2. adj. Desirous. Pl. مندان mandān; منده manda'h, s.f. (3rd). Pl. ې ey.

خوب khūb, s.m. (2nd) Sleep, slumber, a nap, a dream. 2. Sleepiness, drowsiness, somnolence. Pl. خوبونه khūbūnah. خوب زنګول khūb zangawul, verb trans. To make to nod, to cause to sleep. خوب زنګيدل khūb zangedal, verb intrans. To nod, to doze, to fall asleep. خوب کول khūb kawul, verb trans. To sleep, to slumber, to fall asleep. خوب راغلل khūb rāghlal, verb intrans. To become sleepy or drowsy. خوب ليدل khūb līdal, verb trans. To dream. خوب وړل khūb w'rral, verb trans. To make drowsy or sleepy, to carry off to sleep, to overpower with sleep.

P خوب khūb, adj. Good, excellent, beautiful, pleasant, amiable. Pl. (used substantively) (5th) خوبان khūbān, The fair. خوب روي khūb-rū'e, adj. Beautiful; as s.m. (5th) a beauty. Pl. خوب رويان khūb-rū'e-ān; (Fem.) خوب رويه khūb-rūea'h. Pl. ې ey. خوب صورت khūb ṣūrat, adj. Pretty, beautiful. Pl. خوب صورتان khūb ṣūratān. خوب سيرت khūb-sīrat, adj. Good morals or manners.

P خوبي khūbī, s.f. (3rd) Beauty, goodness, excellence, merit, pleasantness. Pl. ئي a'ī. په خوبي pah khūbī or په خوبي سره pah khūbī sarah, adv. Excellently, well.

خوټ khūṯṯ, s.m. (5th) Ebullition, bubbling, effervescence, agitation. 2. Paroxysm, convulsion, vehemence, wildness, rage. Pl. خوټهار khūṯṯahār; also خوټکي khūṯṯkaey, s.m. (1st) Pl. ي ī. خوټ کيدل khūṯṯ kedal, verb intrans. To boil, to become agitated, to throb, etc. خوټ کول khūṯṯ kawul, verb trans. To agitate, to make to bubble, to make to throb, to make angry. See خټ

خوټه khoṯṯa'h, s.f. (3rd) A testicle. Pl. ې ey.

خوټي khoṯṯaey, adj. Small, diminutive, puny, dwarfish, undersized. Pl. ي ī; (Fem.) Sing. and Pl. ئي a'ī.

خوټ خوټئي khoṯṯ khūṯṯa'ī, s.f. (6th) A game of bowls. Sing. and Pl.

خود khūd, adv. Certainly, without doubt, verily, surely, assuredly. See خو

P خود khūd, pron. Self (used in compos.); as خود آرا khūd ārā, adj. Setting one's-self off, dressing finely. 2. Proud, arrogant. خود بخود khūd bakhūd, Of thine, his, or her, etc., own accord, of itself, voluntarily. خود بين khūd bīn, adj. Self-conceited, proud, arrogant, presumptuous. خود بيني khūd bīnī, s.f. (3rd) or خودي khūdī, s.f. (3rd) Self-pride, arrogance, vanity, self-conceit. Pl. ئي a'ī. خود پرست khūd parast, adj. Self-conceited. خود پرستي khūd parastī, s.f. (3rd) Self-sufficiency, self-conceit. Pl. ئي a'ī. خود پسند khūd pasand, adj. Self-complacent, self-conceited. خود پسندي khūd pasandī, s.f. (3rd) Self-conceit, self-complacency. Pl. ئي a'ī. خود راي khūd-rā'e, Self-conceited. خود رائي khūd-rā'ī, s.f. (3rd) Self-conceit. Pl. ئي a'ī. خود روي khūd-ro'e, adj. Wild, spontaneous, growing of itself without being sown. خود روئي khūd-ro'ī, s.f. (3rd) The growing of one's-self, or of itself. Pl. ئي a'ī. خود رنګ khūd rang, adj. Preserving the natural colour, unchanged. خود ستاي khūd satā'e, adj. An egotist. خود ستائي khūd satā'ī, s.f. (3rd) Self-praise, egotism. Pl. ئي a'ī. خود سر khūd sar, adj. Obstinate, self-conceited, self-willed, wilful, absolute. خود سري khūd-sarī, s.f. (3rd) Obstinacy, self-conceit, independence. Pl. ئي a'ī. خود غرض khūd gharaz, adj. Selfish, self-interested, designing. خود غرضي khūd gharazī, s.f. (3rd) Selfishness, self-love. Pl. ئي a'ī. خود کام khūd kām, adj. Following one's own desires, libertine, self-willed. خود کامي khūd kāmī, s.f. (3rd) Self-will, doing what is pleasing to one's-self. Pl. ئي a'ī. خود کرده khūd-kardah, adj. Done or made of one's-self, brought on one's-self. خودي khudī, s.f. (3rd) Pride, vanity, selfishness. Pl. ئي a'ī.

خور khor, s.f. (5th) A sister. Pl. خويندي khwendī. خور ځه khor-dza'h, s.f. (3rd) A sister's daughter, a niece. Pl. ې ey. خور لنړه khor-larrna'h, s.f. (3rd) A sister's daughter, or niece, the name given by a whole clan to any daughter of the members after marriage. Pl. ې ey. خور والي khor-wālaey, s.m. (1st) Sisterliness. Pl. ي ī. خورينګه khorīnga'h, s.f. (3rd) An adopted sister, or a female companion. Pl. ې ey. خورينګئي khorīnga'ī, s.f. (6th) Friendship between adopted sisters or female friends, sisterliness. Sing. and Pl. د تي خور da tī khor, A foster sister.

خور khor, adj. Opened or blown (as a flower), spread out, unclosed, blooming, opened, expanded, florid. 2. Dispersed, scattered, dishevelled, loose, streaming. Pl. خواره khwārah; (Fem.) خوره khwara'h. Pl. خورې khwarey. خورې زلفې khwarey zulfey, Dishevelled or streaming locks. خور وور khor-wor or خور ور khor-wur Completely dishevelled, scattered, or dispersed. Pl. خواره واره khwārah-wārah; (Fem.) خوره وره khwara'h-wara'h. Pl. خورې ورې khwarey-warey. خوريدل khwaredal, verb intrans. To open, to bloom; to become dispersed, to spread, to expand, to dishevel. Pres. خوريږي khwarejzī (W.) or خوريګي khwaregī (E.); past خور شه khor shah or و شه wu-shah; fut. خور به شي khor bah shī or به وُ شي bah wu-shī; imp. خور شه khor shah or وُ شه wu-shah; act. part. خوريدونکيَ khoredūnkaey or خوريدونيَ khoredūnaey; past part. خور khor or خور شويَ khor shawaey; verb. n. خوريدنه khwaredana'h. خورول khwar-awul, verb trans. To open, to unclose, to expand, to spread, to dishevel, to loosen, to scatter, to disperse. Pres. خوروي khwarawī; past خور کړ khor karr or وُ کړ wu-karr; fut. خور به کړي khor bah krrī or به وُ کړي bah wu-krrī; imp. خور کړه khor krrah or وُ کړه wu-krrah; act. part. خوروونکيَ khorawūnkaey or خوروونيَ khorawūnaey; past part. خور کړيَ khor karraey; verb. n. خورونه khwarawuna'h. See خپور

خور khwar, s.m. (2nd) Skin, bark, tegument, cuticle, scurf-skin, crust, peel, rind, scale, shell, husk, cortex, etc. Pl. خورونه khwar-ūnah; also خوروکيَ khwarūkaey, s.m. (1st) Pl. ي ī. خور خور khwar-khwar, adj. Scaly, skinny, cuticular, husky. خور آوښتل khwar āwokhtal (E.) or āwoshtal (W.), verb intrans. To peel off, to lose the skin. خور آړول khwar ārrowal, verb trans. To bark, to flay, to strip off skin, to excoriate. خور آچول khwar āchawul, verb trans. To throw off the skin, to moult, to peel off. خور نيول khwar nīwal, verb trans. To take skin (to become covered with). خور خور کيدل khwar-khwar kedal, verb intrans. To become scaly, scabby, husky, etc.

خوراك khwarāk, s.m. (2nd) Food, victuals, eating, daily food, aliment, diet, eatables. Pl. خوراکونه khwarākūnah. (P khūrāk.) See خواړه

خوراکي khwarākī, adj. Edible, esculent, eatable.

P خورجين khūrjīn, s.m. (5th) A portmanteau, a wallet. Pl. خورجينان khūrjīnān.

خورجينه khūrjīna'h, s.f. (3rd) A large wadded cap with flaps for the ears. Pl. ې ey. Also توپ ttop, s.m. (2nd) Pl. توپونه ttopūnah. (HI).

خور خل khor-khal, s.m. (2nd) (E.) A shears for shearing sheep, etc. Pl. خور خلونه khor-khalūnah; also خور خول khwar-khwal (W.), s.m. (2nd) Pl. خور خولونه khwar-khwalūnah;

and خورخور khor-khor, s.m. (2nd) (Sing.) Pl. خورخورونه khor-khorūnah. See سکستل

P خورده فروش khūrdah farosh, s.m. (5th) A huckster, a retailer. Pl. خورده فروشان khūrdah faroshān. خورده فروشي khūrdah faroshī, s.f. (3rd) Retailing, selling, by retail. Pl. ئ a'ī. خورده فروشي کول khūrdah faroshī kawul, verb trans. To sell by retail, to retail.

خورمه khorma'h, s.f. (3rd) Down on the chin and face, preceding the beard. Pl. ې ey. See زوانکه

P خورنده khūrandah, adj. (act. part. of خوردن), used substantively, An eater, a gormandizer, a glutton. Sing. and Pl. and Masc. and Fem.

خورول khūrawul or خوړول khūrrawul, verb trans. (caus. of خوړل) To feed, to supply or furnish with provisions, to fill up, to provision. Pres. خوروي khūrawī; past وُ خوراوه wu-khūrāwuh or وُ خوراوو wu-khūrāwo; fut. وُ به خوروي wu bah khūrawī; imp. وُ خوروه wu-khūrawah; act. part. خوروونکيَ khūrawūnkaey or خوروونيَ khūrawūnaey; past part. خوروليَ khūrawulaey; verb. n. خورونه khūrawuna'h.

خوره khūra'h, s.f. (3rd) Anything that eats or corrodes, as rust, gangrene, leprosy, acids, etc. Pl. ې ey. See خواړه

خوريَ khaw-raey, s.m. (1st) Clay. 2. Origin, family, lineage. Pl. ي ī. خورين khaw-rīn, adj. Clay, made of clay (as a pot or vessel). 2. Grain with which small particles of earth are mixed. (Fem.) خورينه khaw-rīna'h. See متـه خاوره and ليتي

خورئ khawra'ī, s.f. (6th) Alum. Sing. and Pl.

خوره ييَ khorah-yaey, s.m. (1st) A sister's son, a nephew. Pl. ي ī; also s.m. (5th) Pl. خورديان khorah-yān.

خوړ khwarr, s.m. (2nd) A watercourse, a ravine, the dry bed of a river. Pl. خوړونه khwarrūnah. See شيله and مانده

خوړل khwarral, verb trans. To eat, to devour, to feed, to bite, to gnaw, to nibble, to crop, etc. Pres. خوري khūrī; past وُ خوړ wu-khorr; fut. وُ به خوري wu bah khūrī; imp. خوره khūrah or وُ خوره wu-khūrah; act. part. خوړونکيَ

khwarrūnkaey or خوړونيَ *khwarrūnaey* ; past part. خوړلیَ *khwarralaey* ; verb. n. خوړنه *khwarrana'h*. See خوړول

خوړه *khwarra'h*, s.f. (3rd) A donation, contribution, subscription, a gratuity, a benefaction, meed, etc. 2. A gift given to a spiritual guide or mullā. 3. The sandy bottom of a ravine or watercourse, the dry bed of a river. Pl. يْ *ey*. See خړ and خوړ

خوځېدل *khwadzedal*, verb intrans. To shift, to move or remove, to recede, to move out of the way, to move to one side, to draw back. Pres. خوځېږي *khwadzejzī* (W.) or خوځيګي *khwadzegī* (E.) ; past وُ خوځېدَ *wu-khwadzeda* or وُ خوځېده *wu-khwadzedah* ; fut. وُ به خوځېږي *wu bah khwadzejzī* or وُ به خوځيګي *wu bah khwadzegī* ; imp. وُ خوځېږه *wu-khwadzejzah* or وُ خوځيګه *wu-khwadzegah* ; act. part. خوځېدونکيَ *khwadzedūnkaey* or خوځېدونيَ *khwadzedūnaey* ; past part. خوځېدليَ *khwadzedalaey* ; verb.n. خوځېدنه *khwadzedana'h*. خوځول *khwadzawul*, verb trans. To shift, to remove, to put on one side, to transplant, to transpose. Pres. خوځوي *khwadzawī* ; past وُ خوځاوه *wu-khwadzāwuh* or وُ خوځاوو *wu-khwadzāwo* ; fut. وُ به خوځوي *wu bah khwadzawī* ; imp. وُ خوځوه *wu-khwadzawah* ; act. part. خوځوونکيَ *khwadzawūnkaey* or خوځوونيَ *khwadzawūnaey* ; past part. خوځوليَ *khwadzawulaey* ; verb. n. خوځونه *khwadzawuna'h*.

خوږ *khojz*, adj. Sweet, saccharine ; (Fem). خوږه *khwajzah*. خوږ واليَ *khojz wālaey*, s.m. (1st) Sweetness. Pl. ي *ī* ; also خوږ توب *khojz tob*, s.m. (2nd) Pl. خوږ توبونه *khojz-tobūnah* ; or خوږ تيا *khojz-tīā*, s.f. (6th) (E.) Sing. and Pl. ; (W.) Pl. خوږ تياوي *khojz-tī-āwī*. See خوږ. خوږه غاړه *khwajza'h ghārra'h*, A sweet or melodious voice, a sweet sound (*lit.* 'sweet-throat'). See غاړه

خوږېدل *khojzedal* (W.) or خوګيدل *khogedal* (E.) verb intrans. To become sweet. Pres. خوږېږي *khwajzejzī* (W.) or خوګيګي *khwagegī* (E.) ; past خوږ شه *khojz shah* or خوګ شه *khog shah* or وُ شه *wu-shah* ; fut. خوږ به شي *khojz bah shī* or خوګ به شي *khog bah shī*, or به وُ شي *bah wu-shī* ; imp. خوږ شه *khojz shah* or خوګ شه *khog shah*, or وُ شه *wu-shah* ; act. part. خوږېدونکيَ *khojzedūnkaey* or خوګيدونکيَ *khogedūnkaey*, or خوږېدونيَ *khojzedūnaey* or خوګيدونيَ *khogedūnaey* ; past part. خوږ *khojz* or خوګ *khog*, or خوږ شويَ *khojz shawaey* or خوګ شويَ *khog shawaey* ; verb. n. خوږېدنه *khwajzedana'h* or خوګيدنه *khwagedana'h*, or خوږېده *khwajzedah* or خوګيده *khwagedah*.

خوږېده *khwajzedah* or خوګيده *khwagedah*, s.m. (6th) Sweetness. Sing. and Pl. ; also خوږېدنه *khwajzedana'h* or خوګيدنه *khwagedana'h*, s.f. (3rd) Pl. يْ *ey*. See خوګ والي or خوږ

خوږول *khwajzawul* (W.) or خوګول *khwagawul* (E.), verb trans. To sweeten, to make sweet. Pres. خوږوي *khwajzawī* or خوګوي *khwagawī* ; past خوږ کړ *khojz karr* or خوګ کړ *khog karr* or وُ کړ *wu-karr* ; fut. خوږ به کړي *khojz bah krrī* or خوګ به کړي *khog bah krrī*, or به وُ کړي *bah wu-krrī* ; imp. خوږ کړه *khojz krrah* or خوګ کړه *khog krrah*, or وُ کړه *wu-krrah* ; act. part. خوږېدونکيَ *khwajzedūnkaey* or خوګيدونکيَ *khwagedūnkaey* or خوږېدونيَ *khwajzedūnaey* or خوګيدونيَ *khwagedūnaey* ; past part. خوږ کړيَ *khojz karraey* or خوګ کړيَ *khog karraey* ; verb. n. خوږونه *khwajzawuna'h* or خوګونه *khwagawūna'h*. See خوګ

خوږ لوړيَ or خوږه *khojzah* or *khojza-lorraey*, adj. Sour and sweet, agreeable, sourish, acidulous. Also خوګَ لوړيَ *khoga-lorraey*, etc.

خوږه وله *khwajza'h wala'h*, s.f. (3rd) Liquorice root. Pl. خوږه ولې *khwajza'h waley* ; also خوګه وله *khwaga'h wala'h* and خوګه ولې *khwaga'h waley*.

خوږ *khūjz*, adj. Lamed, crippled, wounded, hurt, etc. See خږ and خږېدل, etc. خوږ or خوګ مند *khūjz* or *khūg-mand*, adj. Diseased, lame, ill, crippled, bruised ; (Fem.) خوږ or خوګ منده *khūjz* or *khūg-manda'h*. خوږ or خوګ واليَ *khūjz* or *khūg-wālaey*, s.m. (1st) Lameness, painfulness. Pl. والي *wālī*.

خوست khost, s. prop. The name of a province in Afghānistān. خوستي khostaey, s.m. (1st) A man of Khost. Pl. ي ī; (Fem.) Sing. and Pl. ۍ a'ī, A female or females of Khost.

P خوش khūsh, adj. Pleased, pleasing, acceptable, cheerful, etc.; used in compos., as خوش اطوار khūsh-atwār, adj. Mannerly, well-bred. خوش آمد khūsh-āmad, s.m. (2nd) Flattery, compliments. Pl. خوش آمدونه khūsh-āmadūnah. خوش آمد كول khūsh-āmad kawul, verb trans. To flatter, to compliment. خوش آمد گر khūsh-āmad gar, s.m. (5th) A flatterer. Pl. گرٌ gær; گره gara'h, s.f. (3rd). Pl. ې ey. خوش اندام khūsh-andām, adj. Well-formed, well-made. خوش آواز khūsh-āwāz, With a sweet voice. خوش آوازي khūsh-āwāzī, s.f. (3rd) Sweetness of voice. Pl. ۍ a'ī. خوش بو khūsh-bū, adj. Fragrant, pleasant smelling, sweet. خوش بوئي khūsh-bū'ī, s.f. (3rd) Perfume, fragrance. Pl. ۍ a'ī. خوش بيان khūsh-bayān, adj. Eloquent, perspicuous. خوش بياني khūsh-bayānī, s.f. (3rd) Eloquence. Pl. ۍ a'ī. خوش پوشاك khūsh poshāk, adj. Well dressed. خوش تركيب khūsh tarkīb, adj. Elegant in form. خوش تقرير khūsh taḳrīr, adj. Eloquent. خوش حال khūsh ḥāl, adj. Happy, fortunate, blissful, in pleasant circumstances. خوش حالي khūsh ḥālī, s.f. (3rd) Happiness, bliss, felicity. Pl. ۍ a'ī. خوشحاليدل khūsh-ḥāledal, verb intrans. To be pleased, happy, blissful, overjoyed, enraptured, etc. Pres. خوشحاليږي khūshḥālejzī (W.) or خوشحاليگي khūshḥālegī (E.); past خوشحال شه khūshḥāl shah or وُ شه wu-shah; fut. خوشحال به شي khūshḥāl bah shī or به وُ شي bah wu-shī; imp. خوشحال شه khūshḥāl shah or وُ شه wu-shah; act. part. خوشحاليدونكي khūshḥāledūnkaey or خوشحاليدوني khūshḥāledūnaey; past part. خوشحال khūshḥāl or خوشحال شوي khūshḥāl shawaey; verb.n. خوشحاليدنه khūshḥāledana'h or خوشحاليده khūshḥāledah. خوشحالول khūshḥālawul, verb trans. To delight, to charm, to rejoice, to transport, to enchant. Pres. خوشحالوي khūshḥālawī; past خوشحال كړ khūshḥāl karr or وُ كړ wu-karr; fut. خوشحال به كړي khūshḥāl bah krrī or به وُ كړي bah wu-krrī; imp. خوشحال كړه khūshḥāl krrah or وُ كړه wu-krrah; act. part. خوشحالونكي khūshḥālawūnkaey or خوشحالووني khūshḥālawūnaey; past part. خوشحال كړي khūshḥāl karraey; verb. n. خوشحالونه khūshḥālawuna'h. خوش خبري khūsh khabarī, s.f. (3rd) Glad tidings, good news. Pl. ۍ a'ī. خوش خط khūsh khatt, Fine writing. خوش خطي khūsh khattaey, A good writer. خوش خلق khūsh khulḳ or خوش خوي khūsh kho-e, adj. Affable, well-bred, of good disposition. (Fem.) خوش خويه khūsh-kho-ea'h. خوش خور khūsh-khor, adj. A good liver. 2. Pleasant to the taste. خوش رنگ khūsh rang, adj. Pleasant in colour. خوش طبع khūsh tabæ, adj. Jocular, merry. خوش گذران khūsh-guzrān, adj. A good liver, an extravagant fellow. خوش گذراني khūsh guzrānī, s.f. (3rd) Good living. Pl. ۍ a'ī. خوش مزه khūsh mazah, adj. Delicious. خوش نويس khūsh-nawīs, adj. Writing an elegant hand, a fine writer. خوش نويسي khūsh-nawīsī, s.f. (3rd) Caligraphy, fine writing. Pl. ۍ a'ī. خوش و خرم khūsh-o-khurram, adj. Cheerful, gay.

خوشوي khūsho-e, s.m. (4th) Horse dung, cow dung, etc. Pl. خوشايه khoshā-yah, or (W.) (5th) خوشايي khoshā-yī. See غشوي

P خوشه khosha'h, s.f. (3rd) An ear of corn, a bunch (as of grapes, etc.) Pl. ې ey. خوشه چين khosha'h-chīn, s.m. (5th) A gleaner. Pl. چينان chīnān; (Fem.) خوشه چينه khosha'h-chīna'h.

خوشي khūshaey, adj. Crazy, weak-minded, daft, giddy, flighty, beside one's-self. 2. A mad-cap, a lunatic, a dreamer. 3. Undefended, open to assault, exposed, vulnerable. 4. Defenceless, unaided, unassisted. 6. Idle, free, without employment or occupation; (Fem.) خوشې khūshi. Pl. (Masc. and Fem.) ي ī. See خشي

خوښ khwash (W.) or khwakh (E.), adj. Pleased, delighted, delightful, charming, captivating, attractive, pleasant, causing or giving pleasure; (Fem.) خوښه khwasha'h or khwakha'h.

خوښي khwashī or khwakhī, s.f. (3rd) Delight, pleasure, cheerfulness, gaiety, happiness, gladness, mirth, joy, will, choice. Pl. ئ a'ī. خوښي كول khwashī kawul or khwakhī kawul, verb trans. To rejoice, to make merry. خوښيدل khwashedal or khwakhedal, verb intrans. To charm, to rejoice, to delight, to gladden, to captivate, to bewitch, to enrapture, to take one's fancy. Pres. خوښيږي khwashejzī (W.) خوښيگي khwakhegī (E.); past خوښ شه khwash or khwakh shah, or وُ شه wu-shah; fut. خوښ به شي khwash or khwakh bah shī, or به وُ شي bah wu-shī; imp. خوښ شه khwash or khwakh shah, or وُ شه wu-shah; act. part. خوښيدونكي khwashedūnkaey or khwakhedūnkaey, or خوښيدونيَ khwashedūnaey or khwakhedūnaey; past part. خوښ khwash or khwakh, or خوښ شويَ khwash or khwakh shawaey; verb. n. خوښيدنه khwashedana'h or khwakhedana'h. خوښول khwashawul or khwakhawul, verb trans. To charm, to gladden, to transport, to delight, to captivate. Pres. خوښوى khwashawī or khwakhawī; past خوښ كړ khwash or khwakh karr, or وُ كړ wu-karr; fut. خوښ به كړي khwash or khwakh bah krrī, or به وُ كړي bah wu-krrī; imp. خوښ كړه khwash or khwakh krrah, or وُ كړه wu-krrah; act. part. خوښوونكيَ khwashawūnkaey or khwakhawūnkaey, or خوښوونيَ khwashawūnaey or khwakhawūnaey; past part. خوښ كړيَ khwash or khwakh karraey; verb. n. خوښونه khwashawuna'h or khwakhawuna'h.

خوښينه khoshīna'h or khokhīna'h, s.f. (3rd) A wife's sister. Pl. ئ ey. See ښينه

A خوف khof, s.m. (2nd) Fear, distrust, hesitation, apprehension. Pl. خوفونه khofūnah. خوف رجا khof rajā, Suspense, fear and hope. خوف كول khof kawul, verb trans. To alarm, to affright, to frighten, to terrify, to dismay. خوف كيدل khof kedal, verb intrans. To become apprehensive, frightened, alarmed, dismayed, terrified.

خوګ khūg, adj. (E.) Lame, crippled, wounded, hurt; (Fem.) خوګه khūgah. خوګ مند khūg-mand, adj. Lame, ill, diseased, bruised, crippled; (Fem.) خوګ منده khūg-manda'h. خوګ والیَ khūg-wālaey, s.m. (1st) Lameness, painfulness, disease, etc. Pl. والي wālī. خوګول khūgawul, verb trans. To hurt, to lame, to cripple, etc. See under خږ and خوږ

خوګ khog, adj. (E.) Sweet, etc. See خوږ

خوګ khūg, s.m. (5th) A hog, a swine. Pl. خوګان khūgān (P خوګ). خوګه khūga'h. s.f. (3rd). Pl. ئ ey.

S خول khol, s.m. (2nd) A helmet, a steel-cap; a case, a sheath. Pl. خولونه kholūnah.

خوله khwala'h, s.f. (3rd) Sweat, perspiration. Pl. ئ ey. خوله كيدل khwala'h kedal, verb intrans. To sweat, to perspire, to swelter. خوله كول khwala'h kawul, verb trans. To sweat, to cause to perspire.

خوله پريكول khūla'h pre-kawul, verb trans. To open the mouth, (to speak), to open one's lips, to declaim, etc.

خولئ khola'ī, s.f. (6th) A cap, a covering for the head. Sing. and Pl.

P خون khūn, s.m. (2nd) Murder, killing. 2. Blood. Pl. خونونه khūnūnah. خوني khūnī, s.m. (5th) A murderer, a shedder of blood. Pl. خونيان khūnī-ān. خون آلوده khūn-ālūdah. adj. Stained with blood, bloody. خون بها khūn-bahā, s.f. (6th) The price of blood, forfeit or retaliation for murder, (E.) Sing. and Pl. (W.) Pl. خون بهاوي khūn bahāwī. خون جگر خوړل khūn-i-jigar khwarral, verb trans. To work one's-self to death. خون خوار khūn-khwār, adj. An animal that devours blood, a murderer. 2. Bloodthirsty, murderous, sanguinary, cruel; (Fem.) خون خواره khūn-khwāra'h. خون خواري khūn-khwārī, s.f. (3rd) Bloodshed, slaughter, murder. Pl. ئ a'ī. خون دار khūn-dār, adj. Bloody, sanguine. 2. One who has killed another in a feud, and also one who has to take revenge for the death of a clansman. خون ريز khūn-rez, adj. Cut-throat, assassin, murderous, bloodshedding. خون ريزي *khūn-rezī*, s.f. (3rd) Bloodshed, carnage, slaughter. Pl. ۍ *a'ī*. خون ريزي كول *khūn-rezī kawul*, verb trans. To slaughter, to shed blood. خون كار *khūn-kār*, s.m. (5th) A murderer, an assassin. Pl. خون كاران *khūn-kārān*. خون كاره *khūn-kārah*, s.f. (3rd) A murderess. Pl. ې *ey*. خون كول *khūn kawul*, verb trans. To kill, to assassinate, to commit murder.

خوناق *khonāk*, s.m. (6th) The quinsey or inflammation of the throat (corrup. of A خناق). Sing. and Pl.; and (E.) at times, s.m. (2nd). See اسپه

خوند *khwand*, s.m. (2nd) Taste, flavour, twang. Pl. خوندونه *khwandūnah*. خوند كول *khwand kawul*, verb trans. To taste, savour, flavour. خوند وركول *khwand war-kawul*, verb trans. To flavour, to give savour.

خوندي *khūndī*, adj. Kept, protected, preserved, secured, taken care of, stored, husbanded. 2. Adjusted, settled, set to rights, arranged. خوندي كول *khūndī kawul*, verb trans. To keep, protect, preserve, store, husband; to adjust, settle, put to rights, etc. خوندي والئ *khūndī wālaey*, s.m. (1st) Preservation, protection, security, keep, care. Pl. والي *wālī*. Also خوندي توب *khūndī tob*, s.m. (2nd). Pl. توبونه *tobūnah*.

خوندي *khūndī*, s.m. (1st) Pl. The name of a tribe of Afghāns who are dispersed in small numbers throughout the country. خوندئ *khūndaey*, Sing. A man of the above tribe; خوندۍ *khūnda'ī*, s.f. (6th) A female or females of the tribe. Sing. and Pl.

خونه *khūna'h*, s.f. (3rd) A room, a chamber, an apartment, a hall, a court, or saloon, a receptacle, a dormitory. Pl. خونې *khūney*. خونه مري *khūnah marrey*, An ill wish—May death take place in thy house or dwelling! خونه ودانه *khūna'h wadāna'h*, A benediction—May your house flourish!

خوي *kho-e*, s.m. (2nd) Disposition, temper, manner, habit, custom. Pl. خويونه *kho-e-ūnah*. بد خوي *bad kho-e*, Of bad disposition. نيك خوي *nek kho-e*, Of good disposition; (Fem.) خويه *kho-e-a'h*. (P خو).

P خويد *khwīd* or خيد *khīd*, s.m. (2nd) Unripe or green grain cut for cattle, green corn, a green field. Pl. خويدونه *khwīdūnah* or *khīdūnah*.

خوئيدل *khū-yedal*, verb intrans. To fester, to rankle, to suppurate. Pres. خوئيږي *khū-yejzī* (W.) or خوئيگي *khū-yegī* (E.); past وُ خوئيده *wu-khū-yedah*; fut. وُ به خوئيږي *wu bah khū-yejzī* or خوئيگي *khū-yegī*; imp. وُ خوئيږه *wu-khū-yejzah* or وُ خوئيگه *wu-khū-yegah*; act. part. خوئيدونكئ *khū-yedūnkaey* or خوئيدونئ *khū-yedūnaey*; past part. خوئيدلئ *khū-yedal-aey*; verb. n. خوئيدنه *khū-yedana'h* or خوئيده *khū-yedah*. خويول *khū-yawul*, verb trans. To fester or cause to fester, to rankle or cause to rankle, to make to suppurate. Pres. خويوي *khū-yawī*; past وُ خوياوه *wu-khū-yāwuh* or وُ خوياوو *wu-khū-yāwo*; fut. وُ به خويوي *wu bah khū-yawī*; imp. وُ خويوه *wu-khū-yawah*; act. part. خويوونكئ *khū-yawūnkaey* or خويوونئ *khū-yawūnaey*; past part. خويولئ *khū-yawulaey*; verb. n. خويونه *khū-yawuna'h*.

P خيابان *khiyābān*, s.m. (2nd) A flower-bed, a parterre, the path in a garden. Pl. خيابانونه *khiyābānūnah*.

A خيار *khiyār*, s.m. (2nd) Choice, election, selection. Pl. خيارونه *khiyārūnah*.

A خياط *khiyāṭ*, s.m. (5th) A tailor. Pl. خياطان *khiyāṭān*; s.f. (3rd) خياطه *khiyāṭa'h*. Pl. ې *ey*. خياطي *khiyāṭī*, s.f. (3rd) Tailoring, the business of a tailor. Pl. ۍ *a'ī*. خياطي كول *khiyāṭī kawul*, verb trans. To tailor, to practice making clothes.

A خيال *khayāl* or *khiyāl*, s.m. (2nd) Fancy, thought, imagination, idea, consideration, apprehension, conceit, suspicion, notion, opinion. 2. Delusion, vision. Pl. خيالونه *khayālūnah*. خيال پلاو وهل *khayāl pulā'o wahal*, verb trans. To build castles in the air, to indulge in vain speculations or absurd ideas. خيال وهل *khayāl wahal,* verb trans. To think, to imagine, to fancy. خيالي *khayālī,* adj. Fanciful, visionary, ideal, capricious, fantastical; or خيالَ من *khayāla man.* خيالو *khayālo,* interj. Oh beloved!

A خيانت *khayānat,* s.m. (2nd) Treachery, perfidy, treason, knavery, embezzlement. Pl. خيانتونه *khayānatūnah.* خيانت کول *khayānat kawul,* verb trans. To play false, to act treacherously or perfidiously, to embezzle.

خيبر *khaibar,* s. prop. The name of a famous pass and range of mountains about twelve miles W. of Peshāwer.

خيټه *khetta'h,* s.f. (3rd) The belly. Pl. ئ *ey.* خيټور *khettawar,* adj. Pot-bellied, a glutton; (Fem.) خيټوره *khettawara'h.* See کيډور

خيڃول *khejawul,* verb trans. (E.) (trans. of ختل) To elevate, to raise, to lift, to upraise, to set up, to erect, to lift, to exalt, to make climb, to make ascend. Pres. خيڃوي *khejawī*; past وُ خيڃاوه *wu-khejāwuh* or وُ خيڃاوو *wu-khejāwo*; fut. وُ به خيڃوي *wu bah khejawī*; imp. وُ خيڃوه *wu-khejawah*; act. part. خيڃوونکيَ *khejawūnkaey* or خيڃووني *khejawūnaey*; past part. خيڃوليَ *khejawulaey*; verb. n. خيڃونه *khejawuna'h.* See خيژول

خيدک *khaidak,* s.m. (2nd) Sour milk. Pl. خيدکونه *khaidakūnah.*

خير *khīr,* adj. Sick at heart, sorrowful. 2. Passionate, rageful; (Fem.) خيره *khīra'h.*

A خير *khair,* adj. Good, well, best. 2. adv. Well. 3. s.m. (2nd) Health, happiness, goodness. 4. Alms, charity, poverty, beggary, begging. Pl. خيرونه *khairūnah.* د خير خبر *da khair khabar,* Good news, glad tidings. خير خواه *khair khwāh,* Well-wishing, a well-wisher, a friend. خير خواهي *khair khwāhī,* s.f. (3rd) Friendship, good-will, wishing well. Pl. ئ *a'ī.*

A خيرات *khairāt,* s.m. (2nd) Alms, charity. Pl. خيراتونه *khairātūnah.* خيرات کول *khairāt kawul,* verb trans. To give alms, to bestow charity. خيراتي *khairātī,* adj. Intended for charitable purposes, a charitable person.

خيريت *khairiyat,* s.m. (2nd) Welfare, success, prosperity. Pl. خيريتونه *khairiyat-ūnah.*

خيره *khīra'h,* s.f. (3rd) Filth, dirt, etc., of the body. Pl. ئ *ey.* خيرن *khīran,* adj. Dirty, filthy, unclean, soiled; (Fem.) خيرنه *khīrana'h.* خيرن کول *khīran kawul,* verb trans. To soil, to make filthy.

خيريَ *khīraey,* s.m. (1st) Dirt, filth, uncleanliness (particularly of the body). Pl. ي *ī.* See خيره. خيرنيدل *khīranedal,* verb intrans. To be unclean, dirty, soiled. Pres. خيرنيږي *khīranejzī* (W.) or خيرنيگي *khīranegī* (E.); past خيرن شه *khīran shah* or وُ شه *wu-shah*; fut. خيرن به شي *khīran bah shī* or به وُ شي *bah wu-shī*; imp. خيرن شه *khīran shah* or وُ شه *wu-shah*; act. part. خيرنيدونکيَ *khīranedūnkaey* or خيرنيدونيَ *khīranedūnaey*; past part. خيرن *khīran* or خيرن شويَ *khīran shawaey*; verb. n. خيرنيدنه *khīranedana'h* or خيرنيده *khīranedah.* خيرنول *khīranawul,* verb trans. To soil, to dirt, to render unclean, to foul, to pollute. Pres. خيرنوي *khīranawī*; past خيرن کړ *khīran karr* or وُ کړ *wu-karr*; fut. خيرن به کړي *khīran bah krrī* or به وُ کړي *bah wu-krrī*; imp. خيرن کړه *khīran krrah* or وُ کړه *wu-krrah*; act. part. خيرنوونکيَ *khīranawūnkaey* or خيرنووني *khīranawūnaey*; past part. خيرن کړيَ *khīran karraey*; verb. n. خيرنونه *khīranawuna'h.*

P خيري *khairī,* s.m. (9th) A kind of violet. Sing. and Pl.; or خيرو *khairo* (9th), Sing and Pl.

P خيز *khez,* s.m. (2nd) Rising, leaping, bounding, etc. Pl. خيزونه *khezūnah.* خيز وهل *khez wahal,* verb trans. To leap, to bound, to jump, to rise, to caper, to frisk about.

خيژول *khejzawul,* verb trans. (W.) (trans. of ختل) To raise, to elevate, to lift, to upraise, to erect, to set up, to exalt, to make climb, etc. See the conj. of خيڃول, and substitute the ږ *jz* for the ڃ *j.*

خيږ *khejz,* s.m. (2nd) The scab of a wound. Pl. خيږونه *khejzūnah.* See ور and خيک

خيشکي *kheshkī,* s.m. (Pl.) A tribe of Afghāns. خيشکيَ *kheshkaey* (Sing.) A man of the above tribe; s.f. (6th) ئِي a'ī, A female or females of the above. Sing. and Pl.

خيښ *kheṣh* (W.) or *khekh* (E.), s.m. (5th) A kinsman, the relation or kinsman of one's wife. Pl. خيښان *kheṣhān* or *khekhān*. خيښه *kheṣhah* or *khekhah*, s.f. (3rd) A female relation, a kinswoman by marriage. Pl. ئي *ey*.

خيښي *kheṣhī* or *khekhī*, s.f. (3rd) Relationship by marriage. Pl. ئِي *a'ī*.

خيښي كول *kheṣhī* or *khekhī kawul*, verb trans. To contract relationship by marriage.

خيك *khīk*, s.m. (2nd) A bag of leather or inflated hide, on which rivers are crossed. Pl. خيكونه *khīkūnah*. Also خيك *khīg* and خيگونه *khīgūnah*. See شناز and زي

خيگ *khīg*, s.m. (2nd) (E.) The fresh scab on a wound. Pl. خيگونه *khīgūnah*. See خير and ور.

خيل *khel*, s.m. (2nd) A tribe, a clan, a sept, the division or part of a clan. Pl. خيلونه *khelūnah*. (H חַיִל).

خيل خانه *khel khāna'h*, s.f. (3rd) Kindred, clansmen. Pl. ئي *ey*.

A خيمه *khaima'h*, s.f. (3rd) A tent, a pavilion. Pl. ئي *ey*. خيمه درول *khaimah darawul*, verb trans. To encamp, to pitch a tent.

د

د *dāl*, called دال مهمله or غير معجمه, is the eighth letter of the Arabic, the tenth of the Persian, and the twelfth of the Puṣhto alphabet. According to the numerical application of the former alphabet it stands for four.

دَ *da*, or occasionally ده *dah*, the particle governing the genitive case, which always precedes the noun. It is not affected by gender. 2. Another particle written in the same manner, but quite distinct, is sometimes used to govern the ablative case, instead of له *lah* or له نه *lah nah*. It is, however, rare. See my Grammar, page 10, paragraph 38.

دِ *di*, A remote demonstrative pronoun applicable to persons and things, used in the singular number. See دغه, دا and دي. 2. A form of personal pronoun for the 2nd person Sing., used in all past tenses of the active voice, as the actor or instrumental case, and to point out the object or possessive case with intransitive verbs, signifying—'thou,' 'thine,' or 'to thee,' and is not subject to any change for gender. 3. A particle the peculiar sign of the third person Sing. and Pl.; of the Precative or 1st Future Tense; and the third persons of the Imperative.

دا *dā*, one of the five different forms of the proximate demonstrative pronouns, signifying 'this,' and applicable to both persons and things. Used in composition, as دا خواه *dā khwāh*, adv. This side, hither. دا رنگ *dā rang*, adv. In this way or manner, so, thus, therefore. دا وخت *dā wakht*, adv. Now, at this time. دا هسي *dā hasey* or داسي *dā'sī*, adv. Thus, so, in this way or manner, therefore. دا هومره *dā homrah* or دومره *domrah*, adv. This much.

داب *dāb*, s.m. (2nd) The large wooden axle of a Persian wheel, which has a cog, and sets the other wheels in motion. Pl. دابونه *dābūnah*.

A دابه *dāba'h*, s.f. (3rd) The genus quadruped, cattle, beast, reptile, etc., applied to the whole species. Pl. ئي *ey*.

A داج *dāj*, s.m. (2nd) Darkness, obscurity. 2. A dark night. Pl. داجونه *dājūnah*.

A داخل *dākhil*, act. part. (of دخل). 1. Entering, arriving, penetrating. 2. adj. Entered, penetrated. 3. Inside, within, interior. داخليدل *dākhiledal*, verb intrans. To enter, to penetrate, to arrive, to appertain to, to belong. Pres. داخليږي *dākhilejzī* (W.) or داخليگي *dākhilegī* (E.); past داخل شه *dākhil shah* or وُ شه *wu-shah*; fut. داخل به شي *dākhil bah shī* or به وُ شي *bah wu-shī*; imp. داخل شه *dākhil shah* or وُ شه *wu-shah*; act. part. داخليدونكَي *dākhiledūnkaey* or داخليدونَي *dākhiledūnaey*; past part. داخل *dākhil* or داخل شوَي *dākhil shawaey*; verb. n. داخليدنه

dā*kh*iledana'h or داخليده dā*kh*iledah. داخلول dā*kh*ilawul, verb trans. To cause to enter or arrive, to place or fix in, to insert, to introduce, to put in. Pres. داخلوي dā*kh*ilawī; past داخل كړ dā*kh*il karr or وُ كړ wu-karr; fut. داخل به كړي dā*kh*il bah krrī or به وُ كړي bah wu-krrī; imp. داخل كړه dā*kh*il krrah or وُ كړه wu-krrah; act. part. داخلوونكَي dā*kh*ilawūnkaey or داخلووني dā*kh*ilawūnaey; past part. داخل كړي dā*kh*il karraey; verb. n. داخلونه dā*kh*ilawuna'h.

P داد *dād*, s.m. (2nd) Justice, law, equity. 2. Crying out for justice, complaint. Pl. دادونه dādūnah. داد خواه dād *kh*wāh, s.m. (5th) A demander of justice, a plaintiff, a suitor. Pl. داد خواهان dād *kh*wāhān. داد خواهي dād *kh*wāhī, s.f. (3rd) Demanding of justice. Pl. ئي a'ī. داد خواهي كول dād *kh*wāhī kawul, verb trans. To demand or ask for justice. داد رس dād-ras, adj. A redresser of grievances, administering justice. داد رسي dād rasī, s.f. (3rd) Redress of grievances, the administering of justice. Pl. ئي a'ī. داد رسي كول dād rasī kawul, verb trans. To administer justice. داد كول dād kawul, verb trans. To make complaint of injustice. دادگر dād gar, s.m. (5th) An administrator of justice, a just prince, etc. Pl. داد گران dād garān. داد و بيداد dād-o-bedād, Crying out for help or justice.

دادا *dādā*, A term of endearment to a father or elder brother (E.), and also for an elder sister (W.)

P دار *dār*, s.m. (2nd) A gibbet, a gallows, a stake. Pl. دارونه dārūnah. په دار كول pah dār kawul, verb trans. To hang, to gibbet, to impale.

P دار *dār*, verb. n. (of داشتن), Possessing, a possessor, a lord, a master. Used in compos. آب دار āb dār, s.m. (5th) A person who has charge of the water for drinking. Pl. آب داران āb dārān. adj. Resplendent. حصه دار ḥiṣṣa'h dār, s.m. (5th) A sharer, a partaker. Pl. حصه داران ḥiṣṣa'h dārān. چوب دار *ch*ob dār, s.m. (5th) A mace-bearer, a servant who announces company. Pl. چوب داران *ch*ob dārān. دار و مدار dār-o-madār, s.m. (9th) Dissimulation, circumvention. 2. Agreement, stipulation. Sing. and Pl.

P دارچيني *dār-chīnī*, s.m. (6th) Cinnamon. Sing. and Pl. Also دال چيني dāl-chīnī (corrup.)

P دارو *dārū*, s.m. (9th) Medicine, physic. 2. Gunpowder (HI). Sing. and Pl.

P داروغه *dārog͟hah*, s.m. (5th) An overseer, a manager, the intendant of the camels. Pl. داروغگان dārog͟hagān.

داره *dāra'h*, s.f. (3rd) A spirt, a jet, a spout, a rush, a gush, a cascade, a cataract. Pl. ې ey. داره وهل dāra'h wahal, verb trans. To spirt, jet, or gush out. See شترکه

درياال *dāriyāl*, s.m. (2nd) A tambourine. Pl. داريالونه dāriyālūnah or دريا, which see.

داړ *dārr*, s.m. (2nd) A company, a band, a gang of thieves. Pl. داړونه dārrūnah. (s دَارِه)

S داړه *dārra'h*, s.f. (3rd) A jaw tooth, a grinder. 2. An attack made on a village by day or night, with open violence. 3. A gang, company, or band (E.) Pl. ې ey. See هپه.

داړل *dārral*, verb trans. To bite as a dog, etc. Pres. داړي dārrī; past وُ داړه wu-dārrah or وُ داړَ wu-dārra; fut. وُ به داړي wu bah dārrī; imp. وُ داړه wu-dārrah; act. part. داړونكَي dārrūnkaey or داړوني dārrūnaey; past part. داړلي dārralaey; verb. n. داړنه dārrana'h. Also written دهړل dharral by the Western Afg͟hāns.

P داستان *dāstān*, s.m. (2nd) A tale, a story, a fable. Pl. داستانونه dāstānūnah.

داښت *das͟ht* (W.) or *dakht* (E.) s.m. (2nd) A potter's furnace, an oven. 2. Strength, durability. Pl. داښتونه dās͟htūnah or dā*kh*tūnah. داښت لرل dās͟ht or dā*kh*t laral, verb trans. To last, to endure, to remain permanent (*lit.* 'To retain durability').

A داعي *dā'æī*, s.m. (5th) (act. part. of دعا) An instigator, author, cause; a plaintiff, a claimant. Pl. داعيگان dā'æī-gān.

P داغ *dāgh*, s.m. (2nd) A blemish, scar, spot, stain, mark, brand, stigma. Pl. داغونه *dāgh-ūnah*. داغ دار *dāgh dār*, adj. Spotted, marked, branded, blemished, etc.; (Fem.) داغ داره *dāgh-dāra'h*. داغ يښول *dāgh yishawul* (W.) or *yikhawul* (E.), verb trans. To brand, to scar, to stain, to mark, to vilify, to defame. داغ وركول *dāgh war-kawul*, verb trans. To mark by a hot iron, to cauterize, to brand, to scar. داغل *dāghal*, verb trans. To burn, to brand, to scar, to cauterize, to mark, to stain, to blemish, to vilify. Pres. داغي *dāghī*; past وُ داغه *wu-dāghah* or وُ داغَ *wu-dāgha*; fut. وُ به داغي *wu bah dāghī*; imp. وُ داغه *wu-dāghah*; act. part. داغونكي *dāghūnkaey* or داغوني *dāghūnaey*; past part. داغلي *dāghalaey*; verb. n. داغنه *dāghana'h*. داغيدل *dāghedal*, verb intrans. To be or become spotted, scarred, stained, cauterized, vilified, branded, etc. Pres. داغيږي *dāghejzī* (W.) or داغيگي *dāghegī* (E.); past داغ شه *dāgh shah* or وُ شه *wu-shah*; fut. داغ به شي *dāgh bah shī* or به وُ شي *bah wu-shī*; imp. داغ شه *dāgh shah* or وُ شه *wu-shah*; act. part. داغيدونكي *dāghedūnkaey* or داغيدوني *dāghedūnaey*; past part. داغ شوي *dāgh shawaey*; verb. n. داغيدنه *dāghedana'h* or داغيده *dāghedah*. داغول *dāghawul*, verb trans. To burn, to brand, to scar, to cauterize, to stain, to vilify, to defame. Pres. داغوي *dāghawī*; past داغ كړ *dāgh karr* or وُ كړ *wu-karr*; fut. داغ به كړي *dāgh bah krrī* or به وُ كړي *bah wu-krrī*; imp. داغ كړه *dāgh krrah* or وُ كړه *wu-krrah*; act. part. داغوونكي *dāghawūnkaey* or داغووني *dāghawūnaey*; past part. داغ كړي *dāgh karraey*; verb. n. داغونه *dāghawuna'h*.

P دالان *dālān*, s.m. (2nd) A hall, a vestibule. Pl. دالانونه *dālānūnah*.

P دام *dām*, s.m. (2nd) A net, a snare, a trap. Pl. دامونه *dāmūnah*. دام آچول *dām āchawul*, verb trans. To lay a snare, to set a trap.

P دامان *dāmān*, s.m. (2nd) The skirt, foot, or declivity of a mountain. 2. A plain. 3. The Afghān country between the eastern branches of the Sūlimān range and the hills south of the Salt range. Pl. دامانونه *dāmānūnah*. Also دامانه *dāmāna'h*, s.f. (3rd). Pl. ې *ey*. داماني *dāmānaey*, s.m. (1st) An inhabitant of Dāmān. Pl. ي *ī*; s.f. (6th) ۍ *a'ī*, A female or females of Dāmān. Sing. and Pl.

P دانا *dānā*, adj. Wise, learned, sage. (Pl. as a subs. دانايان *dānāyān*). دانائي *dānā'ī*, s.f. (3rd) Wisdom, sagacity, learning, intelligence. Pl. ۍ *a'ī*. دانست *dānist*, s.m. (9th) (from دانستن), Knowledge, opinion. Sing. and Pl. دانسته *dānistah*, adj. (past part.) Known, knowing.

P دانش *dānish*, s.m. (2nd) Knowledge, intelligence, learning, science. Pl. دانشونه *dānish-ūnah*. دانش مند *dānish-mand*, adj. Learned, intelligent, wise. دانشمندي *dānishmandī*, s.f. (3rd) Learning, wisdom. Pl. ۍ *a'ī*.

P دانه *dāna'h*, s.f. (3rd) A grain, seed, berry, corn; speck, pimple, boil. Pl. ې *ey*. دانه دار *dāna'h-dār*, adj. Granulated, containing grain. توره دانه *tora'h dāna'h*, s.f. (3rd) A black-head, a boil, a bubo. Pl. ې *ey*. Also د كال دانه *da kāl dānah* (*lit.* 'a boil which remains a year').

A داود *dā'ūd*, s. prop. The name of a Prophet, David. (H דוד Beloved).

داودزي *dā'ūdzī*, s.m. (1st) Pl. The name of an Afghān tribe inhabiting the northern part of the plain of Pesh'āwer. داودزي *dā-ūdzaey*, A man of the above tribe. s.f. (6th) ۍ *a'ī*, A female of the above. Sing. and Pl.

داوي *dāwī*, s.m. (1st) Pl. A tribe of Afghāns. داوي *dāwaey*, s.m. (Sing.) A man of the above tribe. ۍ *a'ī*, s.f. (6th) A female or females of the tribe. Sing. and Pl.

A دائره *dā'ira'h*, s.f. (3rd) A ring, a circle, an orbit, circumference. 2. A monastery. Pl. ې *ey*.

A دايم *dā'īm*, adj. (act. part. of دوم), Perpetual, permanent, ceaseless, eternal, always, continual. دائم الخمر *dā'īm-ul-khamar*, adj. Sot, drunkard, constantly drunk. دائمي *dā'īmī*,

Perpetual, continual, enduring, lasting, unchanging.

داٸي *dā'ī*, s.f. (5th) A nurse, a midwife, Pl. داٸيکانِ *dā'īgāni*. (P دايه).

P دبارا *dubārā* or دباره *dubārah*, adv. Twice, again, another time.

P دباغ *dabāgh*, s.m. (5th) A tanner, a currier. Pl. دباغان *dabāghān*. دباغ خانه *dabāgh khāna'h*, s.f. (3rd) A tan-pit. Pl. ې *ey*. دباغي *dabāghī*, s.f. (3rd) The business of a tanner or currier. Pl. ٸ *a'ī*. دباغي کول *dabāghī kawul*, verb trans. To curry, to tan.

دباندِ *dabāndi* or دباندي *dabāndī*, adv. Outside, without, out, externally.

A دبدبه *dabdaba'h*, s.f. (3rd) Pomp, parade, state, dignity. Pl. ې *ey*.

دبلي *dabley*, s.m. (1st) A small round box for keeping anything in, a casket. Pl. ي *ī*.

A دبه *daba'h*, s.f. (3rd) A leathern bottle for holding oil, etc. Pl. ې *ey*.

دبي *dabī*, adj. Fruit made ripe by laying it in straw, or layers of leaves.

دپاره *dapārah* or دپارَ *dapāra*, prep. For, for the sake of, on account of, by reason of.

A دجاج *dujāj*, s.m. (6th) A fowl, the domestic fowl. Sing. and Pl. See چرګ

A دجال *dajjāl*, s. prop. (from دجل, He lied), Antichrist, an imposter, a liar.

A دخل *dakhl*, s.m. (2nd) Entrance, access. 2. Intrusion, interference, molestation. 3. Profit, income, advantage. Pl. دخلونه *dakhlūnah*. دخل لرل *dakhl laral*, verb trans. To have access (*lit.* 'to hold or retain entrance'). دخل کول *dakhl kawul*, verb trans. To intrude, to enter, to interrupt, to intermeddle, to interfere, to meddle, to concern one's-self, to encroach, to take possession.

دخمه *dakhma'h*, s.f. (3rd) A corner, a secluded place, a place of concealment, a lurking place, ambush. 2. A tomb. Pl. ې *ey*. دخمه نيول *dakhma'h nīwal*, verb trans., or په دخمه کښيناستل *pah dakhma'h k'shenāstal*, or *k'khenāstal*, verb intrans. To lie in ambush, to lurk.

A دخيل *dakhīl*, adj. (from دخل) Admitted, allowed entrance. 2. Intimate, familiar, a friend, confidant, adopted.

P دد *dad*, s.m. (5th) A fierce or rapacious animal, a beast of prey, a reptile. Pl. ددان *dad-ān*. دده *dada'h*, s.f. (3rd) The female of the above. Pl. ې *ey*.

P در *dar*, s.m. (2nd) A door. Pl. درونه *darūnah*. در بدر *dar badar*, From door to door. در بدري *dar badarī*, s.f. (3rd) Begging, vagrancy, begging from door to door. Pl. ٸ *a'ī*. در بدر کول *dar badar kawul*, verb trans. To ruin, to reduce to poverty and distress.

در *dar*, pron. or pronominal dative prefix of the second person, used to point out the object in a sentence. It is both singular and plural, has no independent meaning, and is used like را and ور with all verbs: it signifies, 'to thee or you.' See Grammar, page 46, paragraph 132. Also در ته *dar tah*, در لره *dar larah*, or در له *dar lah*, To thee or you.

درَ *dara* or دره *darah*, imp. of درلل, which see.

A در *durr*, s.m. (2nd) A pearl. Pl. درونه *durr-ūnah*. See مرغلره

درِ *dri* or دري *drey*, adj. Three. دريم *dreyam*, The third; (Fem.) دريمه *dreyama'h*. در ويشت *dar-wīsht* (W.) or *dri-wīsht* (E.) Twenty-three. درِ ديرش *dri-dersh*, Thirty-three. درِ څلويښت *dri-tsalwesht* (W.) or *dri-tsalwekht* (E.) Forty-three. درِ پنځوس *dri-pindzos*, Fifty-three. درِ شپيته *dri-shpetah*, Sixty-three. درِ اويا *dri-awyā*, Seventy-three. درِ اتيا *dri-atī'ā*, Eighty-three. درِ نوِ *dri nawi*, Ninety-three. درِ کنجي *dri-kunjey*, adj. Three-cornered; (Fem.) درِ کنجه *dri kunja'h*.

دراني *durānī*, s.m. (1st) Pl. One of the great divisions of the Afghāns, of which there are two branches—Zīrak and Panj-pā'o, and amongst which is included the royal tribe. They are also called Abdālīs. See the Introduction to my Grammar. درانی *durānaey*, Sing. A man of the above tribe. ٸ *a'ī*, s.f. (6th) A female or females of the tribe. Sing. and Pl.

دراٸي *darā'ī*, s.f. (3rd) A kind of red silk. Pl. ٸ *a'ī*.

درب *drab*, s.m. (2nd) A kind of sacrificial grass (Poa cynosuroides). Pl. دربونه *drabūnah*.

درب *drab*, s.m. (5th) A crash, smash, roll, rumble, thump, bang, dab, beat, etc. Pl. دربهار *drabahār*. درب وهل *drab wahal*, verb trans. To make a rumbling, rolling, crashing noise.

P دربار *darbār*, s.m. (2nd) The holding of a court, a hall of audience, a court. Pl. دربارونه *darbārūnah*. دربار کول *darbār kawul*, verb trans. To hold a court, to give audience, to consult on affairs of state.

P درباري *darbārī*, s.m. (5th) A courtier. Pl. درباريان *darbārī'ān*.

P دربان *dar-bān*, s.m. (5th) A porter, a door-keeper. Pl. دربانان *darbānān*.

دربچه *dar-bacha'h*, s.f. (3rd) A window, a pantry, a cupboard. Pl. ئ *ey*. See دريچه

دربل *drabal*, verb trans. To shake or press down, as flour, etc.) Pres. دربي *drabī*; past و درابه *wu-drābah* or و درابَ *wu-drāba*; fut. و به دربي *wu bah drabī*; imp. دربه *drabah* or و دربه *wu-drabah*; act. part. دربونکيَ *drabūnkaey* or دربونيَ *drabūnaey*; past part. دربليَ *drabalaey*; verb. n. دربنه *drabana'h*.

دربل *drabal*, verb intrans. To fall in (as the roof of a house), to come down, to break down, to give way. Pres. دربي *drabī*; past و دربل *wu-drabal*; fut. و به دربي *wu bah drabī*; imp. و دربه *wu-drabah*; act. part. دربونکيَ *drabūnkaey* or دربونيَ *drabūnaey*; past part. دربليَ *drabalaey*; verb. n. دربنه *drabana'h*. دربول *drabawul*, verb trans. To bring down, to break down, to cause or make fall in, to cause to give way, to cast down. 2. To thrash, to take down a peg. Pres. دربوي *drabawī*; past و درباوه *wu-drabāwuh*; fut. و به دربوي *wu bah drabawī*; imp. و دربوه *wu-drabawah*; act. part. دربوونکيَ *drabawūnkaey* or دربوونيَ *drabawūnaey*; past part. دربوليَ *drabawulaey*; verb. n. دربونه *drabawuna'h*.

دربليَ *drabalaey*, adj. (past part.) Fallen in, come down by the run, given way, broken down; (Fem.) دربلې *drabali*. Pl. (Masc. and Fem.) دربلي *drábalī*.

دربلئ *dar-bala'ī*, s.f. (6th) A tripod or trivet of wood. Sing. and Pl.

دربيَ *drabaey*, s.m. (1st) A crash, a smash, rumble, thump, etc. Pl. ي *ī*. See درب

A درج *darj*, s.m. (9th) A place for writing, a closet, anything written on, a volume. Sing. and Pl. درج کول *darj kawul*, verb trans. To enter, to insert, to copy, to write, to record.

A درجه *dar-ja'h* or *daraja'h*, s.f. (3rd) Degree, rank, dignity, station, step, gradation. 2. Division, act of a play, etc. 3. A degree of a circle. Pl. ئ *ey*; or (A) Pl. درجات *darajāt*. درجه په درجه *darja'h pah darja'h*, adv. Gradually, by degrees, step by step.

درخته *drakhtah*, s.f. (3rd) (corrup. of P درخت) A tree. Pl ئ *ey*. See ونه

P درخواست *darkhwāst*, s.m. (2nd) Request, application, demand, petition, appeal, wish, desire, proposal. Pl. درخواستونه *darkhwāstūnah*. درخواست کول *darkhwāst kawul*, verb trans. To request, require, seek, beg, demand, propose.

P درد *dard*, s.m. (2nd) Pain, affliction, ache. 2. Pity, affection, sympathy, compassion. 3. Anger, passion, vexation. Pl. دردونه *dardūnah*. د لنګالوه درد *da langālwa'h dard*, The pains of child-birth. د سر درد *da sar dard*, The head-ache; vexation, trouble. د زړه درد *da z'rrah dard*, The belly-ache, colic. دردمن *dard-man*, adj. Afflicted, pained. 2. Compassionate, sympathizing; (Fem.) دردمنه *dard-mana'h*. دردمندي *dard-mandī*, s.f. (3rd) Affliction, sorrow, compassion. Pl. ئ *a'ī*. درد کول *dard kawul*, verb trans. To ache, to smart, to pain. درديدل *dardedal*, verb intrans. To become, angry, vexed, or displeased. Pres. درديږي *dardejzī* (W.) or درديګي *dardegī* (E.); past و درديده *wu-dardedah* or و درديدَ *wu-dardeda*; fut. و به درديږي *wu bah dardejzī* or و به درديګي *wu bah dardegī*; imp. و درديږه *wu-dardejzah* or و درديګه *wu-dardegah*; act. part. درديدونکيَ *dardedūnkaey* or درديدونيَ

dardedūnaey; past part. درديدلي *dardedalaey*; verb. n. درديدنه *dardedana'h* or درديده *dardedah.* دردول *dardawul*, verb trans. To make angry, to vex, to displease. Pres. دردوي *dardawī*; past وُ درداوه *wu-dardāwuh* or وُ درداوو *wu-dardāwo*; fut. وُ به دردوي *wu bah dardawī*; imp. وُ دردوه *wu-dardawah*; act. part. دردوونكي *dardawūnkaey* or دردووني *dardawūnaey*; past part. دردولي *dardawulaey*; verb. n. دردونه *dardawuna'h.*

دردر *dar-dar* or در *dar*, s.m. (5th) The sound of falling rain, patter. Pl. درهار *darahār.* دردر كول *dar-dar kawul*, verb trans. To patter, as rain, hail, etc.

P A درز *darz*, s.m. (2nd) A seam or suture, a crack, a cleft, a flaw, a narrow strip of cloth. Pl. درزونه *darz-ūnah.*

P درزي *darzī*, s.m. (5th) A tailor. Pl. درزيان *darzīān.*

A درس *dars*, s.m. (2nd) A lesson, a lecture, reading, learning to read. Pl. درسونه *dars-ūnah.* درس لولول *dars l'walawul* or درس وركول *dars war-kawul*, verb trans. To instruct, to teach to read.

درست *drast*, adj. All, the whole, entire. 2. adv. Wholly, entirely; (Fem.) درسته *drasta'h.*

درسته *darasta'h*, s.f. (3rd) Arms, implements of war, armour, a set or stand of arms. Pl. ي *ey.* See وسله

درستيدل *drastedal*, verb intrans. To become complete, perfect, finished, accomplished, fulfilled, etc. درستول *drastawul*, verb trans. To render or make complete, to perfect, to finish, to accomplish, to fulfil.

P درشت *durusht*, adj. Hard, harsh, rough, fierce, oppressive, surly, morose, stern, stiff, rigid; (Fem.) درشته *durushta'h.* See زبر and زګ

P درشتي *durushtī*, s.f. (3rd) Harshness, severity, sternness, asperity, roughness, moroseness. Pl. ئي *a'ī.* درشتي كول *durushtī kawul*, verb trans. To treat with asperity, harshness, severity, etc.

درشل *darshal*, s.f. (1st) The frame of a door. Pl. درشل *darshali.* Also درشاهي *darshāhī*, s.f. (3rd). Pl. ئي *a'ī.*

درغل *darghal*, s.m. (5th). A liar, a false speaker, a hypocrite, a deceiver. 2. Astray, erring, wandering, misled, bewildered, lost, seduced. Pl. درغلان *darghalān.* درغله *darghala'h*, s.f. (3rd). Pl. ي *ey.*

درغوګ *dar-ghwag*, s.m. (2nd) (E.) (from غوګ 'the ear'), A mark to distinguish cattle, generally made by cutting the ears in a peculiar manner. Pl. درغوګونه *dar-ghwagūnah.* See درور

درغول *dar-ghol*, s.m. (2nd) A gap or cleft in the bank of a *nāla'h* or water-course through which the water breaks out during floods or heavy rains. Pl. درغولونه *darghol-ūnah.*

درغيدل *dar-ghedal*, verb intrans. To slip, to tumble, to trip, to stumble, to slide, to plump down. درغول *dar-ghawul*, verb trans. To cause or make to slip, trip, stumble, slide, etc.

درک *darak*, s.m. (2nd) A place, abode. 2. Trace, sign, mark, indication. Pl. درکونه *darakūnah.* درک كول *darak kawul*, verb trans. To trace, to discover, to find out.

درکړ *drakarr*, s.f. (1st) The outside rim or felly of a wheel. Pl. درکړ *drakarri.*

درګه *darga'h*, s.m. (3rd) A copse, a place where the trees and brushwood grow close together. Pl. ي *ey.*

در ګور كول *dar gor kawul*, verb trans. To abandon, to give up entirely, to forget, to think no more about (*lit.* 'To bury in the grave').

درګه *dargah*, s.m. (2nd) (corrup. of P درګاه), A threshold, a door. 2. A mosque, a shrine. 3. A court, a palace. Pl. درګهونه *dargah-ūnah.*

درلول *darlawul*, verb trans. To have, to retain, to possess, to maintain. Past وُ درلو *wu-darlo*; act. part. درلوونكي *darla-wūnkaey* or درلووني *darla-wūnaey*; past part. درلولي *darlawulaey*; verb. n. درلونه *darlawuna'h.* This verb is imperfect, and all the other tenses are taken from لرل, which see.

P درمان *darmān*, s.m. (2nd) Medicine, drug, remedy. Pl. درمانونه *darmānūnah.*

P درماندگي *darmāndagī*, s.f. (3rd) Misery, distress, misfortune, adversity, penury. Pl. ئ *a'ī*.

P درمانده *darmānda'h*, adj. Helpless, destitute, without remedy, distressed.

درمتوړ *daramtawaṟr*, s. prop. The name of a small district north-east of Hazārah in the Panjāb.

درمند *darmand*, s.m. (2nd) Harvest, a heap or stack of unthreshed corn. 2. A threshing floor, a place for treading out corn. 3. Smooth, even, level (ground). Pl. درمندونه *darmandūnah*, or (5th) Pl. درمندان *darmandān*.

درمنده *darmunda'h*, s.f. (3rd) A skein of twisted wool, a hank. Pl. ئ *ey*.

درمه *durma'h* or *darma'h*, s.f. (3rd) A reed from which mats are made. 2. A shepherd's pipe. Pl. ئ *ey*. See دورمه , دروي and نل

درناوي *daranāwey*, s.m. (1st) Solidity, heaviness, weight, load, burden. 2. Steadiness, constancy. Pl. ي *ī*. See دره ناوي and دروند والي

P درنده *darindah*, adj. (from دريدن), Rapacious, fierce, ravenous, tearing. 2. s.m. (5th) A beast of prey, a ravenous beast. Pl. درندگان *darindagān*.

P درنګ *dirang*, s.m. (9th) Delay, hesitation, procrastination. درنګ کول *dirang kawul*, verb trans. To defer, to delay, to put off, to postpone, to protract, to suspend. See ځنډ. بي درنګَ *be dranga*, adv. Without delay, immediately.

P دروازه *darwāza'h*, s.f. (3rd) A door, an entrance, a gate. Pl. ئ *ey*. دروازه ټکول *darwāza'h ṯṯakawul*, verb trans. To knock at the door. دروازه پيشول *darwāza'h peshawul*, verb trans. To close a door. دروازه تړل *darwāza'h taṟral*, verb trans. To fasten or shut a door.

دروازوان *darwāzawān*, s.m. (5th) A door-keeper, a gate-keeper, a warden. Pl. دروازوانان *darwāzawānān*. دروازوانه *darwāzawāna'h*, s.f. (3rd) A porteress. Pl. ئ *ey*.

P درود *darūd*, s.m. (2nd) Congratulation, blessing, salutation, benediction. Pl. درودونه *darūdūnah*. درود ويل *darūd wa-yal*, verb trans. To congratulate, to bless.

درور *dror*, s.f. (5th) A husband's sister. Pl. درندِ *drandi*. See ندرور

دروزګر *darūz-gar*, s.m. (5th) A carpenter, a joiner. Pl. دروزګران *darūzgarān* (corrup. of P درود گر).

دروزه *drūza'h*, s.f. (3rd) Stubble, stumps of wheat, etc., left by the sickle; the hard part of the head of corn left after threshing. Pl. ئ *ey*. See ګشاره and خريز

درووږ *darwajz*, s.m. (2nd) A mark made in the ears of cattle to distinguish them. Pl. درووږونه *darwajzūnah*. See درغوګ

درووږی *darwajzaey*, s.m. (1st) The term applied to a male child of a woman supposed to have become pregnant through the prayers of some priest or holy man (*lit.* 'marked one'). Pl. ي *ī*. s.f. (6th) ئ *a'ī*. Sing. and Pl.

P دروغ *darogh*, s.m. (6th) A falsehood, a lie, an untruth. Sing. and Pl. 2. adj. False, untrue; (Fem.) دروغه *darogha'h*. دروغ جن *darogh-jan* (E.) or دروغ ژن *darogh jzan* (W.), s.m. (5th) A liar. Pl. دروغ جَن or ژَن *darogh jæn* or *jzæn*, and دروغ ګوي *darogh-go-e*, s.m. (5th). Pl. دروغ ګويان *darogh go-e-ān*. دروغ ګوئي *darogh go'ī*, s.f. (3rd) Lying, false speaking. Pl. ئ *a'ī*.

درومل *drūmal*, verb intrans. To go, to depart, to set out, to quit. Pres. درومي *drūmī*; fut. وُ به درومي *wu bah drūmī*; imp. وُ درومه *wu-drūmah*. The past tenses are wanting, and are taken from دروميدل, which is deficient in the present tenses.

درميدل *drūmedal*, verb intrans. To go, to depart, etc. This infinitive is also imperfect with regard to the present tenses, which, added to the preceding, completes it. Past وُ درومیده *wu-drūmedah* or وُ درومیدَ *wu-drūmeda*; act. part. درومیدونکی *drumedūnkaey* or درومیدونی *drumedūnaey*; past part. درومیدلی

drūmedalaey ; verb. n. درومیدنه *drūmedana'h*. See preceding infinitive.

P درون *darūn*, adv. In, within.

P درونه *darūna'h*, s.f. (3rd) The heart, core. Pl. ئي *ey*.

دروند *drūnd*, adj. Heavy, weighty, ponderous, massive, unwieldy. Pl. درانه *drānah*; (Fem.) درنه *drana'h*. Pl. درني *draney*. دروند والي *drūnd wālaey*, s.m. (1st) or دروند تیا *drūnd tī'ā*, s.f. (6th) Weight, heaviness, ponderousness, load, burden, ballast. Pl. دروند والي *drūnd wālī*; (W.) Pl. دروند تیاوي *drūnd-tī'āwī*. See درناوي

دروه *droh*, s.m. (2nd) Fraud, deceit, imposture, artifice, evasion. 2. (s) Spite, malice, hatred. Pl. دروهونه *drohūnah*. دروه خوړل *droh khwarral*, verb trans. To be deceived, cheated, defrauded. دروه ورکول *droh war-kawul*, verb trans. To cheat, to defraud, to deceive. دروهیدل *drohedal*, verb intrans. To be deceived, cheated, defrauded. Pres. دروهیږي *drohejzī* (W.) or دروهیګي *drohegī* (E.); past ؤ دروهیده *wu-drohedah*; fut. ؤ به دروهیږي *wu bah drohejzī* or ؤ به دروهیګي *wu bah drohegī*; imp. ؤ دروهیږه *wu-drohejzah* or ؤ دروهیګه *wu-drohegah*; act. part. دروهیدونکي *drohedūnkaey* or دروهیدوني *drohedūnaey*; past part. دروهیدلي *drohedalaey*; verb. n. دروهیدنه *drohedana'h* or دروهیده *drohedah*. دروهول *drohawul*, verb trans. To cheat, to deceive, to defraud. Pres. دروهوي *drohawī*; past ؤ دروهاوه *wu-drohāwuh* or ؤ دروهاوو *wu-drohāwo*; fut. ؤ به دروهوي *wu bah drohawī*; imp. ؤ دروهوه *wu-drohawah*; act. part. دروهوونکي *drohawūnkaey* or دروهووني *drohawūnaey*; past part. درهولي *drohawulaey*; verb. n. دروهونه *drohawuna'h*. دروهل *drohal*, verb trans. To cheat, to deceive, to defraud. Pres. دروهي *drohī*; past ؤ دروهه *wu-drohah* or ؤ دروهَ *wu-droha*; fut. ؤ به دروهي *wu bah drohī*; imp. ؤ دروهه *wu-drohah*; act. part. دروهونکي *drohūnkaey* or دروهوني *drohūnaey*; past part. دروهلي *drohalaey*; verb. n. دروهنه *drohana'h*.

دروهلي *drohalaey*, adj. (past part.) Cheated, deceived, defrauded. Sometimes used to signify a cheat, a deceiver, but it is incorrect, and the act. part. should be used instead.

دروي *darwaey*, s.m. (1st) A reed from which mats are made. 2. A shepherd's pipe. Pl. Pl. ي *ī*. See درمه , دورمه and شپیلي

درویزه *darweza'h*, s.f. (3rd) Beggary, mendicancy. Pl. ئي *ey*. درویزګر *darwez-gar*, s.m. (5th) A beggar, a mendicant. Pl. درویزګران *darwez-garān*.

درویزه *darwezah*, s. prop. The name of a celebrated Afghān Akhūnd, or teacher, who, with his son Karīm Dād, wrote the work known as Makhzan Pushto, in refutation of the doctrines of Bāyizīd Anṣārī, the founder of the Roshāniān sect. The work in question is one of the earliest compositions in the Pushto language. See my Pushto Text Book.

P درویش *darwesh*, s.m. (5th) A darwesh, a beggar. Pl. درویشان *darweshān*.

P درویشي *darweshī*, s.f. (3rd) The way of life, doctrine, or office of a darwesh or religious mendicant. Pl. ئي *a'ī*.

درویشت *dar-wīsht*, n. adj. Twenty-three. See under در

A دره *dura'h* or *dirra'h*, s.f. (3rd) A scourge. Pl. ئي *ey*.

دره *dara'h*, s.f. (3rd) A valley between two hills or ranges of mountains, through which a stream flows; a pass or way between two mountains. Pl. ئي *ey*.

دره *darah* or درَ *dara*, imp. of verb trans. درلل, which see.

دره ناوي *darah-nāwaey*, s.m. (1st) Weight, etc. Pl. ي *ī*. See درناوي and دروند

درهیسته *dar-hīstah*, adv. Towards or near thee or you. See راهسته, etc.

دري *drey*, adj. Three. دریم *dreyam*, Third; (Fem.) دریمه *dreyama'h*. See در, etc.

دریاب *dar-yāb*, s.m. (2nd) A sea, a river, the waters in general. Pl. دریابونه *dar-yābūnah*. دریابي *daryābī*, adj. Aquatic, of the sea or river. قهري دریاب *kaharey dar-yāb*, The ocean, the sea. Also قالي درياب *ḳāley dar-yāb.*

P درياقت *dary-āft*, s.m. (2nd) (from دريافتن) Discovery, investigation, finding out, comprehension, understanding. Pl. دريافتونه *dary-āftūnah.* دريافت کول *dary-āft kawul*, verb trans. To discover, to find out, to detect, to perceive, to understand.

P دريچه *darīcha'h*, s.f. (3rd) A window. Pl. ې *ey.* See دربچه

دريدل *daredal*, verb intrans. To stand, to be upon the feet, to abide, to stay, to halt, to remain. Pres. دريږي *darejzī* (W.) or دريګي *daregī* (E.); past ودريده *wud-redah* or ودريد *wud-reda*; fut. وُ به دريږي *wu bah darejzī* or وُ به دريګي *wu bah daregī*; imp. ودريږه *wud-arejzah* or ودريګه *wudaregah*; act. part. دريدونکَي *dare-dūnkaey* or دريدونيَ *dare-dūnaey*; past part. دريدليَ *daredalaey*; verb. n. دريدنه *daredana'h* or دريده *daredah.* درول *darawul*, verb trans. To cause to stand, to make abide, to cause to stay, halt, or remain, to pitch (as a tent), to support, to fix. Pres. دروي *darawī*; past ودراوه *wudar-āwuh* or ودراوو *wudar-āwo*; fut. وُ به دروي *wu bah darawī*; imp. ودروه *wudar-awah*; act. part. درونکَي *darawūnkaey* or دروونيَ *darawūnaey*; past part. درولیَ *darawulaey*; verb. n. درونه *darawuna'h.* See also ودريدل

دري ښاخي *draey-shākhaey* (W.) or *draey-khākhaey* (E.), s.m. (1st) A kind of pitchfork, an instrument used in winnowing corn. Pl. ي *ī.* See ښانکي , ښاخه , چار, etc.

P دريغ *daregh* or *dregh*, s.m. (9th) Sorrow, a sigh, disinclination. Sing. and Pl. دريغ خوړل *daregh* or *dregh khwarral*, verb trans. To grieve, to lament, to mourn. دريغَ *daregha* or *dregha*, and دريغه *dareghah* or *dreghah*, interj. Alas! sorrow! would to God! alack-a day!

دريه *dar-ya'h*, s.f. (3rd) A tambourine. Pl. ې *ey.* See داريال

دړ دړ *darr-darr*, adj. Broken to bits, shattered, torn, piecemeal, in fragments, in shreds, splintered, shivered to atoms, etc.; (Fem.) دړه دړه *darra'h-darra'h.* دړ دړ کيدل *darr-darr kedal*, verb intrans. To become broken, shattered, splintered, shivered. دړ دړ کول *darr-darr kawul*, verb trans. To break to bits, to tear, to splinter, to shiver to atoms.

دړديدل *darrdedal*, verb intrans. To ache, to suffer pain, to be in pain. دړدول *darrdawul*, verb trans. To pain, to make or render uneasy, to agonize, to torture, to afflict, to trouble. See under درد

دړه *darra'h*, s.f. (3rd) A split, a crack, a fissure. 2. Wood split for firewood. 3. A long split piece of wood or stone, a chip, a shaving. 4. An allowance in weight, tare. Pl. ې *ey.* See توتنکي

دړئ *darra'ī*, s.f. (6th) Gilt or ornamented paper used by females in place of ornaments and jewellery, and stuck on the forehead, etc. Sing. and Pl.

P دست *dast*, s.m. (2nd) Stool, purge, evacuation. 2. Hand, cubit, a measure. Pl. دستونه *dast-ūnah.* See لاس. Used in compos., as دست انداز *dast andāz*, s.m. (5th) An oppressor, a plunderer, one who interferes, free with one's hands. Pl. دست اندازان *dast andāzān.* دست اندازي *dast andāzī*, s.f. (3rd) Interference, insertion. Pl. ئ *a'ī.* دست اندازي کول *dast andāzī kawul*, verb trans. To interfere, to intrude, to insert. دست آويز *dast āwez*, s.m. (2nd) A note of hand, a bond, a certificate. Pl. دست آويزونه *dast āwezūnah.* دست بردار کيدل *dast bardār kedal*, verb intrans. To resign, desert, abstain, desist, cease, relinquish, retire, decline. دست بردار کول *dast bardār kawul*, verb trans. To withdraw, to take away, to make abstain or relinquish. دست بسته *dast bastah*, adj. Respectful (*lit.* 'with closed hands'). دست پناه *dast panāh*, s.m. (2nd) The guard of a sword. Pl. پناهونه *panāh-ūnah.* دست تنګ *dast-tang*, adj. Poor, indigent. دست تنګي *dast-tangī*, s.f. (3rd) Poverty, indigence, adversity. Pl. ئ

a'ī. دست خط *dast khatt*, s.m. (2nd) Signature, a manuscript. Pl. دست خطونه *dast khattūnah*. دست خط کول *dast khatt kawul*, verb trans. To sign, to attach one's signature. دست رس *dast ras*, s.m. (9th) Ability, power, means, skill, attainment. Sing. and Pl. دست رس لرل *dast ras laral*, verb trans. To have or hold ability, means, or power. دست شوئي *dast sho'e*, s.m. (2nd) A wash-hand basin. Pl. دست شويونه *dast sho'e-ūnah*. دست فروش *dast farosh*, s.m. (5th) A pedlar. Pl. دست فروشان *dast faroshān*. دست فروشي *dast faroshī*, s.f. (3rd) The business of a pedlar. Pl. ئي *a'ī*. دست کښ *dast kash* or *kakh*, s.m. (2nd) A glove, a gauntlet. Pl. کښونه *kashūnah* or *kakhūnah*; or دست کله *dast kala'h*, s.f. (3rd). Pl. کلئ *kaley*. دست گير *dast gīr*, s.m. (2nd) Taking by the hand, an aider, a patron saint, a protector. Pl. دست گيران *dastgīrān*, 2. adj. Laying hands on. دست گيري *dast gīrī*, s.f. (3rd) Aid, help, support, patronage, etc. Pl. ئي *a'ī*. دست لاف *dast lāf*, s.m. (9th) The first money received from sale of goods in the morning. Sing. and Pl. دست مال *dast māl*, s.m. (2nd) A towel, a handkerchief. Pl. دست مالونه *dast-mālūnah*.

P دستار *dastār*, s.m. (2nd) A turband. Pl. دستارونه *dastārūnah*.

P دستر خوان *dastar khwān*, s.m. (2nd) A covering for the table, a table-cloth. Pl. دستر خوانونه *dastar-khwānūnah*.

P دستک *dastak*, s.m. (2nd) An account-book, a day-book, a summons, a citation. Pl. دستکونه *dastakūnah*.

دستکئ *dastakaey*, s.m. (1st) A small rafter placed over the beams. Pl. ي *ī*.

P دستگاه *dast-gāh*, s.m. (2nd) Power, ability, means. Pl. دستگاهونه *dast-gāhūnah*.

دستمايه *dast-māya'h*, s.f. (3rd) A strap or handle for a shield. Pl. ئ *ey*. See د کډئ لړ

دستمبول *dastambol*, s.m. (5th) A musk melon. Pl. دستمبولان *dastambolān*.

P دستور *dastūr*, s.m. (2nd) Custom, usage, mode, manner, model, regulation. 2. A syringe, injection pipe. Pl. دستورونه *dastūrūnah*. دستور العمل *dastūr-l-aæmal*, s.m. (9th) A rule, law, regulation. Sing. and Pl. دستور کول *dastūr kawul*, verb trans. To syringe, to inject.

P دستوري *dastūrī*, s.f. (3rd) Perquisites paid to servants. Pl. ئي *a'ī*.

P دسته *dasta'h*, s.f. (3rd) A handle, a pestle, a muller. 2. A quire of paper. 3. A nosegay of flowers. 4. A bundle of twenty-four arrows. 5. A handful. 6. A skein of thread or silk. 7. A division, brigade, squadron, or company of an army. Pl. ئ *ey*.

P دسته دار *dasta'h-dār*, s.m. (5th) The commander of a division, etc. Pl. دسته داران *dasta'h-dārān*.

P دستي *dastī*, adj. Manual, of the hand. 2. adv. Quickly, immediately, instantly. پيش دستي *pesh dastī*, s.f. (3rd) Anticipating, being before hand, aggressive, surpassing. Pl. ئي *a'ī*. پيش دستي کول *pesh dastī kawul*, verb trans. To anticipate, to be before hand with, etc.

دښت *dasht* (W.) or *dakht* (E.), s.m. (2nd) A desert, a barren plain. Pl. دښتونه *dashtūnah* or *dakhtūnah*. (P دشت)

دښمن *dushman* (W.) or *dukhman* (E.), s.m. (5th) An adversary, an enemy, a foe. Pl. دښمنان *dushmanān* or *dukhmanān*. دښمني *dushmanī* (W.) or *dukhmanī* (E.), s.f. (3rd) Enmity, hostility, hatred, detestation. Pl. ئي *a'ī*. دښمني کول *dushmanī* or *dukhmanī kawul*, verb. trans. To act hostile to, to show hatred or enmity towards.

دښني *dushnī* or *dukhnī*, s.f. (3rd) Enmity, hostility (corrup. of دښمني). Pl. ئي *a'ī*. دښني کول *dukhnī* or *dushnī kawul*, verb trans. To manifest hostility towards.

A دعا *du'æā*, s.f. (6th) Blessing, benediction, congratulation, invocation, prayer, wish, imprecation. (W.) Pl. دعاوي *du'æā-wī*. (E.) Sing. and Pl. دعا کول *du'æā kawul*, verb trans. To bless or pray for, to invoke blessings. دعا گوي *du'æā go'e*, s.m. (5th) A blesser, invoker, one who blesses or prays. Pl. دعا

گويان *du'æā go'e-ān.* دعا گوئي *du'æā go'ī,* s.f. (3rd) Blessing, benediction, invocation. Pl. ئي *a'ī.*

A دعوت *daæ-wat,* s.m. (2nd) Invitation, convocation. 2. A feast, entertainment. Pl. دعوتونه *daæ-watūnah.* دعوت كول *daæ-wat kawul,* verb trans. To invite, to convoke. See ميلمستيا

دعوه *daæ-wa'h,* s.f. (3rd) A claim, action at law, plaint, accusation, law-suit (corrup. of A دعوي). Pl. ئي *ey.* دعوه دار *daæ-wa'h dār,* s.m. (5th) A claimant, plaintiff, accuser, pretender. Pl. دعوه داران *daæ-wa'h dārān.* دعوه كول *daæ-wa'h kawul,* verb trans. To claim, to accuse, to make claim.

A دغدغه *dagh-dagha'h,* s.f. (3rd) Alarm, disturbance, care, fear, dread, awe, tumult, suspicion. Pl. دغدغي *dagh-daghey.* دَغه *daghah,* prox. dem. pron. This, or these (applied to persons and things). Sing. and Pl. In the oblique it becomes دِغِه *dighih* for the Fem. Sing., and دغو or دغوي *dagho* or *daghoey* for the Masc. and Fem. Pl. The other prox. dem. pronouns are دا, دِ, دي, and دَه. See Grammar, p. 34. دغه سي *daghah-sey* or دا سي *dā-sey,* adv. Thus, so, in this way, in this manner. See هسي

P دف *daf,* s.m. (2nd) A small tambourine. Pl. دفونه *dafūnah.*

P دفتر *daftar,* s.m. (2nd) A book, record, register, account book, archive, roll. Pl. دفترونه *daftarūnah.* دفتر دار *daftar dār,* s.m. (5th) A record keeper. Pl. دفتر داران *daftar dārān.*

A دفتي *dafta'ī,* s.f. (6th) A copy slip, pasteboard, the binding of a book. Sing. and Pl.

A دفعتاً *dafæa-taṇ,* adv. Often, all at once, suddenly, at one time.

دفعه *dafæa'h,* s.f. (3rd) (from A دفع) Averting, preventing, repelling, repulsion. Pl. دفعي *dafæey.* دفعه كول *dafæa'h kawul,* verb trans. To avert, to repel, to ward off, to remove. دفعه كيدل *dafæa'h kedal,* verb intrans. To return, to be averted, to be repelled.

A دفعه *dafæa'h,* s.f. (3rd) A time, turn, one time, one turn, a moment. Pl. دفعي *dafæey.*

A دفعه دار *dafæa'h-dār,* s.m. (5th) An officer of cavalry. Pl. دفعه داران *dafæa'h-dārān.*

A دق *dikḳ,* s.m. (9th) Teasing, trouble, vexation. 2. A hectic fever. Sing. and Pl. 3. adj. Vexed, irritated. دق كيدل *dikḳ kedal,* verb intrans. To be irritated, vexed, troubled. دق كول *dikḳ kawul,* verb trans. To irritate, annoy, plague, tease, exasperate.

A دقت *dikḳat,* s.m. (9th) Difficulty, trouble, abstrusity, close application, diligence. 2. Accuracy, exactitude, industry. 3. A subtle or minute matter or thing. Sing. and Pl.

A دقيقه *dakīḳa'h,* s.f. (3rd) A moment, a minute, a portion of time. 2. A particle, any thing or matter subtle or trifling. Pl. ئي *ey.*

P دكان *dukān,* s.m. (2nd) A shop. Pl. دكانونه *dukānūnah.* دكان دار *dukān dār,* s.m. (5th) A shop keeper. Pl. دكان داران *dukān dārān.*

دكث *duk,* s.m. (2nd) (corrup. of S دكهه) Pain, ache, grief, affliction. 2. Labour, fatigue, distress, annoyance. 3. The iron pin of a spinning wheel by which the thread is twisted. Pl. دكونه *dukūnah.* دكث زغمل *duk z'ghamal,* verb trans. To sustain labour or toil, to endure grief, to suffer distress, etc. See دوكث

P دكانچه *dukāncha'h,* s.f. (3rd) A bench before a door for exposing goods, or for sleeping on. 2. A mound or terrace for sitting and conversing on. Pl. ئي *ey.* (E.) دنكاچه *dunkācha'h.* Pl. ئي *ey.*

دكهن *dakhan,* s.prop. The southern part of India, the Dakhan. Also دكن *dakan.*

دل *dal,* s.m. (9th) A dish made of split or bruised grain, split grain in general. Sing. and Pl. See اوګره

P دل *dil,* s.m. (5th) Heart, soul, mind. Sing. and Pl. (Used in comp.) دلارام *dil-ārām,* s.m. (6th) A sweetheart, a heart-easer. Sing. and Pl. دلارامه *dil-ārāma'h,* s.f. (3rd). Pl. ئي *ey.* دلازار *dil-āzār,* s.m. (6th) A sweetheart. Sing. and Pl. دلازاره *dil-āzāra'h,* s.f. (3rd). Pl. ئي *ey.* دلازاري *dil-āzārī,* s.f. (3rd) Torment, anxiety, trouble. Pl. ئي *a'ī.* دل آزرده

dil āzurdah, adj. Vexed, troubled in mind, dejected. دلاسا ***dilāsā***, s.f. (6th) Comfort, consolation, soothing. (W.) Pl. دلاساوي ***dil-āsā-wī***. (E.) Sing. and Pl. دلاسا كول ***dilāsā kawul***, verb trans. To soothe, to comfort, to console. دلبر ***dil-bar***, s.m. (5th) Heart-ravisher, beloved, a sweetheart. Pl. دلبران ***dilbarān***. دلبره ***dilbara'h***, s.f. (3rd). Pl. ئي ***ey***. دل بستگي ***dil bastagī***, s.f. (3rd) Affliction or anguish of mind, attachment. Pl. ئي ***a'ī***. دل بسته ***dil bastah***, adj. Afflicted, attached, enamoured. دل بند ***dil band***, s.m. (2nd) The lights, the lungs. Pl. دل بندونه ***dil band-ūnah***. دل پذير ***dil pazīr*** or دل پسند ***dil pasand***, adj. Agreeable, plausible, pleasant, amiable, satisfactory. دل تنگ ***dil tang***, adj. Distressed, mournful, sad. دل تنگي ***dil tangī***, s.f. (3rd) Distress, grief, sadness. Pl. ئي ***a'ī***. دل جوي ***dil jo'e***, adj. Grateful, studious of pleasing. دل جوئي ***dil jo'ī***, s.f. (3rd) Attention, gratitude, study to please. Pl. ئي ***a'ī***. دل خسته ***dil khastah***, adj. Heart-broken. دل خواه ***dil khwāh***, s.m. (5th) Affection, desire. Pl. دل خواهان ***dil khwāhān***. دل دار ***dil-dār***, adj. Charming, delighting; a lover; (Fem.) دل داره ***dil-dāra'h***, A mistress, a sweetheart. دلداري ***dil-dārī***, s.f. (3rd) Kindness, consolation, encouragement, blandishment. Pl. ئي ***a'ī***. دلربا ***dil-rubā***, adj. Alluring, bewitching; a sweetheart, a charmer. دلربائي ***dil-rubā'ī***, s.f. (3rd) Heart-stealing, ravishing. Pl. ئي ***a'ī***. دل سوز ***dil-soz***, adj. Inflaming the heart, ardent, fervent, pathetical; (Fem.) دل سوزه ***dil-soza'h***, A mistress, a friend. دل سوزي ***dil-sozī***, s.f. (3rd) Ardour, fervour, sympathy, affection. Pl. ئي ***a'ī***. دلكش ***dil-kash***, adj. Alluring, heart-attracting, winning, lovely, pleasant. دلكشه ***dil-kusha'h***, adj. Blissful, charming, delightful, heart-expanding. دلگير ***dil-gīr***, adj. Afflicted, grieved, sad, low-spirited. دلگيري ***dil-gīrī***, s.f. (3rd) Melancholy, affliction, concern, sadness, sorrow. Pl. ئي ***a'ī***. دلنشين ***dil-nishīn***, adj. Grateful to the mind, impressed on the mind. See زړه

دلازاك ***dalāzāk***, s.m. (6th) The name of a tribe of Afghāns residing in the plain of Peshāwer to the south, once very powerful. 2. A male of the tribe. Sing. and Pl. دلازاكه ***dalāzā-ka'h***, s.f. (3rd) A female of the above tribe. Pl. ئي ***ey***.

A دلال ***dallāl***, s.m. (5th) A broker, a salesman. Pl. دلالان ***dallālan***. دلالي ***dallālī***, s.f. (3rd) Brokerage, the business of a salesman. Pl. ئي ***a'ī***. دلالي كول ***dallālī kawul***, verb trans. To carry on the business of a broker.

A دلاله ***dallāla'h***, s.f. (3rd) A female broker, a go-between, a procuress. Pl. ئي ***ey***.

دلانډِ ***dalāndi***, or دلاندي ***dalāndey***, prep. Under, beneath, below. Also لاندي ***lāndey***.

P دلاور ***dilāwar***, adj. Brave, gallant, intrepid.

P دلاوري ***dilāwarī***, s.f. (3rd) Bravery, intrepidity, gallantry, boldness. Pl. ئي ***a'ī***. دلاوري كول ***dilāwarī kawul***, verb trans. To act intrepidly, bravely, etc.

دلته ***daltah***, adv. Here, hither. Also دلِ ***dali***, which see.

دلدل ***dal-dal***, adj. Broken in pieces, in fragments; (Fem.) دلدله ***dal-dala'h***. See دل

دلوه ***dalwa'h***, s.f. (3rd) (corrup. of A دلو) A bucket of leather, wood, etc., an urn. Pl. ئي ***ey***.

دلۍ ***dala'ī***, s.f. (6th) A stack of corn, a store, a granary, a magazine. Sing. and Pl. See امبار

دلي ***daley*** or دلِ ***dali***, adv. Here, hither. Also دلِ ***dali*** or دلي وته ***daley watah***. See دلته

P دلير ***diler***, adj. Brave, bold, intrepid, daring, courageous, valiant; insolent, impudent; (Fem.) دليره ***dilera'h***.

P دليري ***dilerī***, s.f. (3rd) Intrepidity, boldness, courage, valour, bravery, hardihood; insolence, etc. Pl. ئي ***a'ī***. دليري كول ***dilerī kawul***, verb trans. To act with bravery, valour, etc.

A دليل ***dalīl***, s.m. (2nd) Demonstration, argument, proof. 2. A director or guide. Pl. دليلونه ***dalīlūnah***. دليلي ***dalīlī***, s.f. (3rd) Argumentative, demonstrative. Pl. ئي ***a'ī***.

P دم ***dam***, s.m. (2nd) Breath, life. 2. Boasting, pride, ambition. 3. A moment of time. 4. The edge of a sword, knife, etc. 5. The steam from a pot, kettle, etc. 6. Deceit, coaxing. 7. A bellows. 8. Breathing on by way of charm. Pl. دمونه *damūnah.* دمل *damal,* verb trans. To blow with the breath (as in breathing, or charming, or as the wind). 2. To appear (as the dawn). Pres. دمي *damī*; past وُ دمل *wu-damal*; fut. وُ به دمي *wu bah damī*; imp. وُ دمه *wu-damah*; act. part. دمونکَي *damūnkaey* or دمونَي *damūnaey*; past part. دملَي *damalaey*; verb. n. دمنه *damana'h.* See چف. دم بخود *dam bakhūd,* adj. Silent. دم پدم *dam padam,* adv. Constantly, every moment, at every breath. دم پخت *dam pukht,* s.m. (9th) A kind of *pulā'o,* or stew. Sing. and Pl. دم تر دمَ *dam tar dama,* adv. Frequently, constantly. دم درحال *dam dar ḥāl,* adv. Immediately, instantly, in an instant, quick as thought, in less than no time. Also written دم در حل *dam dar ḥal.* دم دلاسا *dam dilāsā,* s.m. (6th) Encouragement, comfort, soothing, coaxing. Pl. دلاساوي *dilāsāwī.* دم دلاسا ورکول *dam dilāsā war-kawul,* verb trans. To encourage, to coax, to soothe. دم ورکول *dam war-kawul,* verb trans. To deceive, to wheedle, to coax, to inveigle. دم زدن *dam zadan,* Speaking, breathing, boasting. دم ساز *dam sāz,* adj. Harmonious, concordant, assenting, intimate. 2. A confidant, a friend, an intimate. دم سازي *dam sāzī,* s.f. (3rd) Concord, harmony, intimacy. Pl. ۍ *a'ī.* دم کول *dam kawul,* verb trans. To blow (as a fire); to blow (as an old woman when charming). دمگري *dam-garaey,* s.m. (1st) A charmer, one who charms away pain, etc., a juggler. Pl. ي *ī.* دمگرۍ *dam-gara'ī,* s.f. (6th) Sing. and Pl., or دم گرِ *dam-gari.* Pl. ي *ī.*

A دماغ *dimāgh,* s.m. (2nd) The brain. Pl. دماغونه *dimāghūnah.* تازه دماغ *tāzah dimāgh,* adj. Pleased, delighted. دماغي *dimāghī,* adj. Vain, conceited, proud, frivolous.

P دمبال *dumbāl,* adv. After, behind, in the rear. Also دنبال *dunbāl.*

دمباله *dumbāla'h,* s.f. (3rd) A rear-guard. Pl. ې *ey.* Also written دنباله *dunbāla'h.*

دمچي *dumchī,* s.f. (3rd) A crupper. Pl. ۍ *a'ī.*

دمدمه *dam-dama'h,* s.f. (3rd) A mound, a raised battery, a cavalier. Pl. ې *ey.*

دمړۍ *damṟra'ī,* s.f. (6th) The eighth part of a pice. Sing. and Pl. (s دمړي).

دمول *damawul,* verb trans. To breathe on, to inspire or blow into, to charm by breathing on. Pres. دموي *damawī*; past دم کړ *dam-karr* or وُ کړ *wu-karr*; fut. دم به کړي *dam bah krrī* or به وُ کړي *bah wu-krrī*; imp. دم کړه *dam krrah* or وُ کړه *wu-krrah*; act. part. دمونکَي *damawūnkaey* or دمونَي *damawūnaey*; past part. دم کړي *dam karraey*; verb. n. دمونه *damawana'h.*

دمه *dama'h,* s.f. (3rd) Breath, respiration. 2. Resting, rest, ease, repose. Pl. ې *ey.* دمه نيول *dama'h nīwal,* verb trans. To take breath, to recover breath, to repose, to breathe. دمه ورکول *dama'h war-kawul,* verb trans. To breathe (as a horse, etc.), to give breath to, to ease, to repose.

دند *dund* or *dand,* s.m. (2nd) Injustice, oppression (*lit.* darkness, obscurity, gloom). 2. Noise (as of thunder or fire), the report of a cannon, noise, tumult. 3. Haze, mist, smoke, vapour, clouds of dust. Pl. دندونه *dundūnah* or *dandūnah.*

دندوکار *dandūkār,* s.m. (2nd) The noise of fire or thunder, the report of cannon, tumult, noise, roar, disorder, turbulence, tornado. 2. Mist, smoke, haze. Pl. دندوکارونه *dandūkārūnah.*

دندانه *dandāna'h,* s.f. (3rd) The tooth of a saw or comb 2. (P) A small waterfall or linn, the place in the bed of the river causing the fall of the water. Pl. ې *ey.*

دنکاچه *dankācha'h,* s.f. (3rd) A terrace, a bench. Pl. ې *ey.* See دکانچه

دنګ *dang,* adj. (as s.m.) Tall, long, tall in stature. 2. s.m. (6th) A tall man. Sing. and Pl. دنګه *danga'h,* s.f. (3rd) A tall woman. Pl. دنګې *dangey.*

دنګ *dang,* s.m. (5th) A leap, a jump, a spring, a bound, a hop, a vault, etc. Pl. دنګان

dangān. دنګل *dangal,* verb trans. To take a jump, to make a jump, to make a spring or bound. Pres. دنګي *dangī*; past وُ دنګل *wu-dangal*; fut. وُ به دنګي *wu bah dangī*; imp. وُ دنګه *wu-dangah*; act. part. دنګونکي *dangūnkaey* or دنګوني *dangūnaey*; past part. دنګلي *dangalaey*; verb. n. دنګنه *dangana'h.* دنګول *dangawul,* verb trans. (caus.) To cause to leap, jump, bound, etc. Pres. دنګوي *dangawī*; past وُ دنګاوه *wu-dangāwuh* or وُ دنګاوو *wu-dangāwo*; fut. وُ به دنګوي *wu bah dangawī*; imp. وُ دنګوه *wu-dangawah*; act. part. دنګوونکي *dangawūnkaey* or دنګووني *dangawūnaey*; past part. دنګولي *dangawulaey*; verb. n. دنګونه *dangawuna'h.*

دننه *dananah,* prep. Within, in the inner part. 2. Adv., Inwardly, internally.

A دنيا *dunyā,* s.f. (6th) The world, people, goods of the world. (E.) Sing. and Pl. (W.) Pl. دنياوي *dunyā-wī.* دنيا پرست *dunyā parast,* adj. Worldly, earthly, mundane. دنيا دار *dunyā dār,* adj. Rich, opulent, possessing worldly goods. دنيا داري *dunyā dārī,* s.f. (3rd) Economy, worldliness, opulence, wealth. Pl. ئي *a'ī.* دنياوي *dunyāwī,* or دنيوي *dunyawī,* adj. Worldly, pertaining to the world.

P دو *do,* noun adj. Two. Used in Pus͟hto composition, as دو باره *do bārah,* adj. Twice, again, double. دو بدو *do bado,* or *dū badū,* Face to face, tête-à-tête. دو پاي *do pā-e,* adj. Twolegged (as a man). دو پټه *do paṯṯa'h* s.f. (3rd) A veil or scarf in which there are two breadths. Pl. ئ *ey.* دو چار *do c͟hār,* s.m. (9th) Interview, meeting. Sing. and Pl. دو چندان *do chandān,* or دو چند *do chand,* adj. Double, as much again, twofold. دو راهي *do rāh'ī,* s.f. (3rd) A road leading two different ways. Pl. ئي *a'ī.* دو راسته *do rāsta'h,* adj. Right and left, on both sides (as a street, row of trees, etc.) دو رګه *do ragah,* adj. Mongrel, of double breed, of two natures; also دو رګ *do rag.* دو زانو کښيناستل *do zānū k's͟henāstal,* (W.) or *k'k͟henāstal* (E.) To kneel. دو زبان *do zabān,* adj. Double-tongued, cunning. دو زباني *do zabānī,* s.f. (3rd) Duplicity, equivocation, hypocrisy. Pl. ئي *a'ī.* دو زباني کول *do zabānī kawul,* verb trans. To equivocate, to act with duplicity. دو ساله *do sālah,* adj. Two years old (a horse, etc.), biennial. دو شنبه *do s͟hanba'h,* Monday. دو طرفه *do ṯarf-ah,* adj. On both sides. دو لړه *do laṟṟah,* Two stringed, double.

دو *daw,* s.m. (2nd) A stroke at play, a game, a venture, a hit, a single match at play. Pl. دوونه *daw-ūnah.* (P. داو). دو کول *daw kawul,* verb trans. To stake, to hazard, to play a match or game. دو ګټل *daw gaṯṯal,* verb trans. To win a game or stake.

A دوا *dawā,* s.f. (6th) A medicine, a remedy. 2. An amulet, a charm, a square piece of silver worn round the neck by women. (E.) Sing. and Pl. (W.) Pl. دواوي *dawāwī.* دوا خوړل *dawā k͟hwaṟṟal,* verb trans. To take physic. دوا کول *dawā kawul,* verb trans. To cure, to remedy, to heal, to physic.

دوابه *do'āba'h,* s.f. (3rd) A country between two rivers, twice irrigated land. 2. The name of a pargana'h of Pes͟hāwer, called also دواوه *do-āwa'h.* Pl. ئ *ey.*

A دوات *dawāt,* s.m. (2nd) An inkstand. Pl. دواتونه *dawātūnah.*

دواړه *dwāṟṟah,* adj. Both, both one and the other. دواړه جهانَ *dwāṟṟah jahāna,* Both worlds, this world and the next.

دوبي *dobey,* s.m. (1st) Summer, the summer season. Pl. ي *ī.* See اوړي.

دوبي *dobī,* s.m. (5th) A washerman, a dyer. Pl. دوبيان *dobī-ān.* دوبئ *doba'ī,* s.f. (6th) A washerwoman. (W.) Sing. and Pl., or دوبنړه *dobaṟṟna'h,* s.f. (1st) Pl. دوبنړي *dobaṟṟney.* (s. دهوبي)

دوتر *dawtar,* s.m. (2nd) (corrup. of P دفتر). A fief, estate, hereditary provision in land (in opposition to سيرئ *sera'ī*) granted to soldiers and relations in lieu of service by the ruling power. Pl. دوترونه *dawtarūnah.*

دود *dod,* s.m. (2nd) Custom, manner, way,

fashion. 2. Vestments and furniture given with a bride, dowry. 3. Entertainment of a guest. Pl. دودونه *dodūnah*. 4. adj. Like, similar, resembling. 5. adv. Like, in the same manner; also دوديه *dodeyah*.

P. دود *dūd*, s.m. (2nd) Smoke. Pl. دودونه *dūdūnah*, دود آلوده *dūd ālūdah*, adj. Smoky. د زړه دود *da z'rrah dūd*, A deep sigh. دود كښ *dūd kash* or *kakh*, s.m. (2nd) A chimney. Pl. دود كښونه *dūd kashūnah* or *kakhūnah*. دوده *dūda'h* or دوهه *doha'h*, s.f. (3rd) A fire-place for cooking, etc. 2. Lamp-black. Pl. ې *ey*. See لو and لوګي

P دور *dūr*, adj. Far, distant, remote, at a distance. دور انديش *dūr andesh*, adj. Circumspect, foreseeing, provident, wise, sagacious, prudent. دور انديشي *dūr andeshī*, s.f. (3rd) Prudence, foresight, sagacity, wisdom, etc. Pl. ئ *a'ī*. دور انديشي كول *dūr andeshī kawul*, verb trans. To act with prudence or sagacity. دور بين *dūr bīn*, s.m. (2nd) A spy-glass, a telescope. Pl. دور بينونه *dūr bīnūnah*. 2. adj. Far-seeing, prudent. دور بيني *dūr bīnī*, s.f. (3rd) Foresight, prudence, sagacity. Pl. ئ *a'ī*. دور و دراز *dūr-o-darāz*, adj. Far, distant, long. 2. Useless, unprofitable. دور كيدل *dūr kedal*, verb intrans. To be removed, or remote. دور كول *dūr kawul*, verb trans. To remove, to dispel, to divert, to keep at a distance.

A دور *daur*, s.m. (2nd) Revolution, circular motion. 2. Age, period, cycle, turn, time, circuit. Pl. دورونه *daurūnah*.

A دوران *daurān*, s.m. (2nd) Time, age, revolution, period, cycle. 2. Fortune, vicissitude. Pl. دورانونه *daurānūnah*.

P دوري *dūrī*, s.f. (3rd) Distance, separation, absence. Pl. ئ *a'ī*.

دورستو *da-wrusto*, adv. Behind, in the rear, out of sight. 2. prep. At the back, in the rear, opposite the front. See ورستو

دوړاندِ *d'wrrāndi*, prep. Before, in front, opposite. 2. adv. Before, in time preceding. See وړاندِ and following words.

دوړه *dūrra'h*, s.f. (3rd) Fine dust, dust in general. 2. A devil, a whirlwind. Pl. ې *ey*. دوړيدل *dūrredal*, verb intrans. To become dusty, to be covered with dust, to become diffused, sprinkled, scattered (as dust or powder on a wound), etc. Pres. دوړيږي *dūrrejzī* (W.) or دوړيګي *dūrregī* (E.); past وُ دوړيده *wu-dūrredah* or وُ دوړيدَ *wu-dūrreda*; fut. وُ به دوړيږي *wu bah dūrrejzī* or وُ به دوړيګي *wu bah dūrregī*; imp. وُ دوړيږه *wu-dūrrejzah* or وُ دوړيګه *wu-dūrregah*; act. part. دوړيدونكَي *dūrredūnkaey* or دوړيدونَي *dūrredūnaey*; past part. دوړيدلَي *dūrredalaey*; verb n. دوړيدنه *dūrredana'h*. دوړول *dūrrawul*, verb trans. To raise the dust, to make dusty, to cover with dust, to sprinkle, scatter, diffuse (as dust or powder on a wound, etc.) Pres. دوړوي *dūrrawī*; past وُ دوړاوه *wu-dūrrāwuh* or وُ دوړاوو *wu-dūrrāwo*; fut. وُ به دوړوي *wu bah dūrrawī*; imp. وُ دوړوه *wu-dūrrawah*; act. part. دوړوونكَي *dūrrawūnkaey* or دوړوونَي *dūrrawūnaey*; past part. دوړولَي *dūrrawulaey*; verb n. دوړونه *dūrrawuna'h*.

P دوزخ *dozakh*, s.m. (2nd) Hell. Pl. دوزخونه *dozakhūnah*. دوزخي *dozakhī*, adj. Hellish, infernal, damnable. See دوغبس

دوزه *dūza'h*, s.f. (3rd) Nonsense, foolish talk, folly, absurdity. Pl. ې *ey*. دوزي *dūzaey*, s.m. (1st) A talker of nonsense, a fool, a blockhead, a simpleton, a booby. Pl. ي *ī*. s.f. (6th) دوزۍ *dūza'ī*, Sing and Pl. دوزي بلل *dūzey bal-al*, verb trans. To boast, to brag, to vaunt, to swagger, to exult, to talk big. See also دوزه, دوزي and دوږخ

دوږخ *do-jzakh*, s.m. (2nd) (W.) Hell, the infernal regions. Pl. دوږخونه *do-jzakhūnah*. See دوغبس

P دوست *dost*, s.m. (5th) A friend, a lover. Pl. دوستان *dostān*. دوسته *dosta'h*, s.f. (3rd). Pl. ې *ey*. دوستدار *dostdār*, s.m. (6th) A friend, a sweetheart. Pl دوستداران *dostdārān*. دوستداره *dostdāra'h*, s.f. (3rd) A sweetheart, a mistress. Pl. ې *ey*. دوستداري *dostdārī*, s.f. (3rd) Friendship, love. Pl. ئ *a'ī*. دوستي

كول *dostī kawul*, verb trans. To make friends with.

P دوشخانه *dosh-khāna'h*, s.f. (3rd) A vessel in which skins are placed before tanning. Pl. ئ *ey*.

دوشرل *do-sharl*, or *do-sharal*, adj. A two-year-old ram or he-goat. Sing. and Pl. دوشرله *do-sharla'h* or *do-sharala'h*, s.f. (3rd) An ewe or she-goat of two years old. Pl. ئ *ey*.

P دوشنبه *doshamba'h*, s.f. (3rd) Monday. Pl. ئ *ey*.

دوغښ *doghakh*, s.m. (2nd) Hell, the infernal regions. Pl. دوغښونه *doghakhūnah*. See دوزخ. دوغښي *doghakhī*, adj. Hellish, infernal, damnable. See دوزخي

دوک *dwak*, s.m. (5th) A foal of two years old. Pl دوکان *dwakān* (A دوک).

P دوک *dūk*, s.m. (2nd) A spindle. Pl. دوکونه *dūkūnah*.

P دوکان *dūkān*, s.m. (2nd) A shop, a workshop. Pl. دوکانونه *dūkānūnah*. دوکان دار *dūkān dar*, s.m. (5th) A shopkeeper. Pl. دوکان داران *dūkān-dārān*. دوکان داري *dūkān dārī*, s.f. (3rd) Shopkeeping. Pl. ئ *a'ī*.

دوکړه *dūkrra'h*, s.f. (3rd) A kind of kettle drum. Pl. ئ *ey*.

P دوګانه *dogānah*, adj. Double, two together. 2. A prayer in which two inclinations or genuflexions are made.

A دولت *daulat*, s.m. (2nd) Wealth, riches, fortune, prosperity. 2. Empire, state, government. Pl. دولتونه *daulatūnah*. دولت خواه *daulat khwāh*, A well wisher, loyal. دولت خواهي *daulat khwāhī*, s.f. (3rd) Loyalty, good will, good wishes. Pl. ئ *a'ī*. دولت مند *daulat mand*, adj. Wealthy, opulent, rich, fortunate. دولتمندي *daulat-mandī*, s.f. (3rd) Opulence, wealth, happiness, prosperity. Pl. ئ *a'ī*. دولت خيل *daulat khel*, s.m. (5th) The name of an Afghān clan. 2. A man of the above clan. Sing. and Pl. دولت خيله *daulat khela'h*, s.f. (3rd) A female of the above. Pl. ئ *ey*.

دولتزي *do-lat-zī*, s.m. (1st) Pl. The name of a tribe of Afghāns. دولتزئ *dolat-zaey*, (Sing.) A man or male of the above tribe. دولتزئ *do-lat-za'ī*, s.f. (6th) A female or females of the above. Sing. and Pl.

دولتئ *do-lata'ī*, s.f. (6th) A kick from the two hind legs of any animal. Sing. and Pl. دولتئ وهل *do-lata'ī wahal*, verb trans. To kick with the hind legs.

دومئ *dū-maey*, s.m. (1st) A cold, indisposition from cold. Pl ي *ī*.

A دون *dūn*, adj. Base, mean, inferior, ignoble, vile. دون همت *dūn himmat*, adj. mean-spirited, low-minded, vile.

دونه *dūna'h*, s.f. (3rd) A bonfire, a fire lighted in the cold weather to give warmth. Pl. ئ *ey*.

دوني *dūnī* or *donī*, adv. This much, to this degree. See همبره

دونړئ *dūrrna'ī*, s.f. (6th) A milk pail (of earthenware), a vessel for holding milk. Sing. and Pl. (s دوهني). See لوغوني

دوه *dwah*, n. adj. Two; (Fem.) دوي *dwey*. دوه برغه *dwah braghah* or دوه بغرګه *dwah bghargah* or دوه غبرګه *dwah ghbargah*, adj. Double. 2. *dwah bgharga'h* or *dwah ghbarga'h*, A woman who has given birth to twins. See برغه and بغرګه. دوه تا *dwah tā*, adj. Double. دوه غښئ *dwah ghashaey* (W.) or *ghakhaey*, (E.) s.m. (1st) A young camel, bull, or buffalo of two teeth. Pl. ي *ī*. s.f. (6th) ئ *a'ī*. Sing. and Pl. دوه کونه *dwah kawnah*, Both worlds, this and the next. دوه لاړ *dwah lārra*, adj. Two stringed, double. دوه لس *dwah-las*, adj. Twelve. دوه لسم *dwah-lasam*, adj. Twelfth. دوه نيم *dwah-nīm*, adj. Two-and-a-half, in two halves. دوه ويشت *dwah-wīsht*, adj. Twenty-two. دوه ديرش *dwah-dersh*, adj. Thirty-two, etc.

دوهئ *do-ha'ī*, s.f. (6th) A fireplace, a temporary chimney. Sing. and Pl.; or دوهه *dūha'h*, s.f. (3rd). Pl. ئ *ey*.

دوي *dū'ī*, Pl. of the prox. dem. pron. دي *dey*, 'These' (persons and things). See Grammar, page 35, paragraph 113.

دوي *do'e*, s.m (2nd) Custom, usage, fashion,

mode, manner, model, regulation. Pl. دويونه *do'e-ūnah.* د مهر دوي *da mihr do'e,* The manner or custom of friendship, kindness, or affection. See دود

دويي *dū-yī,* s.f. (3rd) Disunion, separation. 2. Serving two masters (as God and Mammon). Pl. ئي *a'ī.* دوبين *dū-bīn,* s.m. (5th) A server of two masters. Pl. دوبينان *dūbīnān.* (P دوي).

ده *dah,* prox. dem. pron. 'This' (person or thing.) The other pronouns of this class, of which there are five, are دي, دِ, دا, دغه. دَ *da,* the sign of the genitive case, is sometimes thus written. For declension, see Grammar, page 35.

ده *dah,* A word used in driving or urging a horse. 2. 'Is,' fem. of present tense of 'to be.' See دي

P ده *dih,* s m. (2nd) A village. Pl. دهونه *dih-ūnah.* See كلي

ده مرده *dah-marda'h,* s.f. (3rd) A lever. Pl. ئي *ey.* 2. adj. Strong, bold, brave.

دهتوره *dahtūra'h,* s.f. (3rd) Name of a poisonous plant (Datura fastuosa, or thorn-apple). Pl. ئي *ey.* (s دهتورا)

دهج *dhaj,* s.m. (9th) Vestments and furniture given to a bride, dowry. Sing. and Pl. See دهځ and دود

A دهر *dahr,* s.m. (9th) Time, the world, an age. 2. Custom, habit, mode, care, solicitude. 3. Fortune, chance, danger, adversity. 4. Atheism. Sing. and Pl. دهري *dah-rī,* s.m. (5th) An atheist. Pl. دهريان *dahrī-ān.*

دهړه *dahṟṟa'h,* s.f. (3rd) A jaw tooth, a grinder, a tusk. Pl. ئي *ey.* چينكي دهاړي *chīngey dahāṟṟey,* adj. Showing the teeth, grinning. دهاړي چينكول *dahāṟṟey chīngawul,* verb trans. To grind the teeth, to snarl. دهړل *dahṟṟal,* verb trans. To bite as a dog, etc. Pres. دهړي *dahṟṟī* ; past و داهړه *wu-dāharrah* or و داهړَ *wu-dāhaṟṟa* ; fut. و به دهړي *wu bah dhaṟṟī* ; imp, و دهړه *wu-dahṟṟah* ; act. part. دهړونكَي *dahṟṟūnkaey* or دهړونَي *dahṟṟūnaey* ; past part. دهړلَي *dahṟṟalaey* ; verb. n. دهړنه *dahṟṟana'h,* See داړه

دهځ *dhadz,* s.m. (9th) Vestments or garments given to a bride, dowry. Sing and Pl. See دهج and دود

A دهشت *dahshat,* s.m. (3nd) Awe, alarm, fear, fright, dread, terror, dismay. Pl. دهشتونه *dahshatūnah.* دهشت زده *dahshat zadah,* adj. Alarmed, frightened, panic-struck, terrified. دهشت ناك *dahshat nāk,* adj. Alarming, afraid, terrified, fearful, frightened. دهشت خوړل *dahshat khwaṟṟal,* verb trans. To take fright, to become terrified or dismayed.

A P دهقان *dih-ḳān,* s.m. (5th) A husbandman, a villager. Pl. دهقانان *dih-ḳānān.* دهقاني *dih-ḳānī,* s.f. (3rd) Husbandry, agriculture, Pl. ئي *a'ī.*

دهلا *dahlā,* s. prop. Name of a village or town near Ḳandahār.

دهليج *dah-līj,* s.m. (2nd) or (P) دهليز *dah-līz,* A portico, a threshold. Pl. دهليجونه *dahlījūnah* or دهليزونه *dahlīzūnah.*

دهليدل *dhaledal,* verb intrans. To fear, to quake, to be afraid, to tremble, to apprehend. دهلول *dhalawul,* verb trans. To frighten, to terrify, to alarm, to awe, to dismay.

دهنه *dahana'h,* s.f. (3rd) (corrup. of P دهانه) The bit of a bridle. 2. The mouth of a river or water-course, the mouth of a water bag, the covering of a mouth. Pl. ئي *ey.*

دهور *da-hor,* s.m. (5th) A weaver. Pl. دهوران *dahorān.* دهوره *da-hora'h,* s.f. (3rd) The female of the above. Pl. ئي *ey.*

دهه *daha'h,* s.f. (3rd) The first ten days of the Muḥarram. 2. The models of the tombs of Ḥasan and Ḥusain carried about in procession. Pl. ئي *ey.* (P دها).

دي *dey,* prox. dem. pron. 'This' (applied to persons and things). See دغه *daghah,* and Grammar, page 35.

دَي *daey,* The 3rd person Sing. (Masc.) of the present tense of the verb, To be—'Is'; Fem. ده *dah.* Pl. (Masc. and Fem.) دي *dī.*

ديار لس *di-yār-las,* adj. Thirteen. ديار لسم *di-yār-lasam,* The thirteenth.

A ديانت *diyānat,* s.m. (2nd) Honesty, probity,

integrity, piety, virtue. Pl. ديانتونه *diyānat-ūnah.* ديانت دار *diyānat-dār,* adj. Just, honest, conscientious; (Fem.) ديانت داره *diyānat-dāra'h.* ديانت داري *diyānat dārī,* s.f. (3rd) Honesty, integrity, probity, conscientiousness. Pl. ئي *a'ī.*

P ديبا *debā,* s.f. (6th) Brocade, gold tissue. (E.) Sing. and Pl. (W.) Pl. ديباوي *debāwī.*

A ديباچه *dībā<u>ch</u>a'h* or ديباجه *dībāja'h,* s.f. (3rd) A preface or introduction to a book, the commencement. Pl. ئي *ey.*

A ديت *di-yat,* s.m. (2nd) The law of retaliation, the price of blood, a fine paid for murder, maiming, etc. Pl. ديتونه *di-yatūnah.*

ديچكه *de<u>ch</u>ka'h,* s f. (3rd) A pot or vessel for cooking purposes. Pl. ئي *ey.* (corruption of P ديگچه, which see).

P ديد *dīd,* s.m. (2nd) (from P ديدن) Sight, show, seeing, spectacle. Pl. ديدونه *dīdūnah.* ديد وان *dīd-wān,* s.m. (2nd) The sight of a gun, etc. Pl. ديد وانونه *dīd-wānūnah.*

P ديدار *dīdār,* Sight, interview. Pl. ديدارونه *dīdār-ūnah.*

P ديدن *dīdan,* s.m. (2nd) (P inf. and verb. n.) Seeing, sight, interview. Pl. ديدنونه *dīdan-ūnah.*

P ديدنامي *dīd-nāmī,* s.f. (3rd) Respect for one's character, etc. Pl. ئي *a'ī.*

P ديده *dīdah,* adj. Seen, observed. 2. s.f. (3rd) The eye. Pl. ئي *ey.* ديده و دانسته *dīdah-aw-dānistah,* Wilfully, purposely, wittingly.

ديرش *der<u>sh</u>,* n. adj. Thirty. ديرشم *der<u>sh</u>am,* The thirtieth.

ديره *dera'h,* s.f. (3rd) A tent, a dwelling. Pl. ئي *ey.* ديره كول *dera'h kawul,* verb trans. To pitch one's tent, to take up one's dwelling. (HI ديرا)

P ديگ *deg,* s.m. (2nd) A caldron, a large pot. Pl. ديگونه *degūnah.* ديگ دان *deg-dān,* s.f. (2nd) A fire-place, a trivet. Pl. ديگ دانونه *deg-dānūnah.*

P ديگچه *deg-<u>ch</u>a'h,* s.f. (3rd) A small pot or caldron. Pl. ئي *ey.* See ديچكه

A دين *dīn,* s.m. (2nd) Faith, religion. Pl. دينونه *dīnūnah.* دين پناه *dīn panāh,* A defender or protector of the faith, or دين پرور *dīn parwar*; (Fem.) دين پروره *dīn-parwara'h.* دين دار *dīn-dār,* adj. Religious, virtuous; (Fem.) دين داره *dīn-dāra'h.* دين داري *dīn-dārī,* s.f. (3rd) Religiousness, piety, virtue. Pl. ئي *a'ī.* بي دين *be-dīn,* adj. Impious, irreligious.

A دينار *dīnār,* s.m. (2nd) The name of a gold coin, a ducat. 2. The tenth part of a *pice.* Pl. دينارونه *dīnārūnah.*

A ديني *dīnī,* adj. Spiritual, religious. 2. Well acquainted, very friendly.

P ديو *dew,* s.m. (5th) A demon, a devil. Pl. ديوان *dew-ān.*

P ديوال *dīwāl,* s.m. (2nd) A wall. Pl. ديوالونه *dīwālūnah.*

P ديوان *dīwān,* s.m. (2nd) A book of poetry ending with each letter of the alphabet from A to Y. 2. A tribunal, a divan. Pl. ديوانونه *dīwānūnah.* ديوان خانه *dīwān <u>kh</u>āna'h,* s.f. (3rd) A court, hall, hall of audience. Pl. ئي *ey.* ديواني *dīwānī,* adj. Relating to the court or darbār.

P ديوانه *dīwāna'h,* adj. Mad, insane, out of one's wits. 2. Inspired. ديوانگي *dīwānagī,* s.f. (3rd) Madness, insanity. Pl. ئي *a'ī.* See ليوني

ډ

ډ *<u>dd</u>āl,* called also دال ثقيله *dāl-i-ṣaḳelah,* or heavy *d,* is the thirteenth letter of the Pu<u>sh</u>to alphabet, and is similar in sound to ड which is the twenty-ninth letter of the Sanskrit. It is pronounced by applying the tip of the tongue inverted to the palate.

ډاډ *<u>dd</u>ā<u>dd</u>,* s.m. (2nd) Comfort, solace, consolation. Pl. ډاډونه *<u>dd</u>ā<u>dd</u>ūnah.* ډاډ وركول *<u>dd</u>ā<u>dd</u> war-kawul,* verb trans. To comfort, to solace, to console, to cheer, to soothe.

ډاډه *<u>dd</u>ā<u>dd</u>a'h,* s.f. (3rd) An unripe head of corn roasted on the fire and eaten. Pl. ئي *ey.* See الووي

دار *ddār*, s.m. (2nd) Fear, dread, awe, fright, alarm, disquietude, anxiety. Pl. دارونه *ddārūnah*. داريدل *ddāredal*, verb intrans. To fear, to be afraid, to apprehend, to take alarm. Pres. داريږي *ddārejzī* (W.) or داريګي *ddāregī* (E.); past ؤ داريده *wu-ddāredah* or ؤ داريدَ *wu-ddāreda*; fut. ؤ به داريږي *wu bah ddārejzī* or ؤ به داريګي *wu bah ddāregī*; imp. ؤ داريږه *wu-ddārejzah* or ؤ داريګه *wu-ddāregah*; act. part. داريدونکيَ *ddāredūnkaey* or داريدونيَ *ddāredūnaey*; past part. داريدليَ *ddāredalaey*; verb. n. داريدنه *ddāredana'h* or داريده *ddāredah*. داروُل *ddārawul*, verb trans. To frighten, to terrify, to alarm, to disquiet, etc. Pres. داروي *ddārawī*; past ؤ داراوه *wu-ddārāwuh* or ؤ داراوو *wu-ddārāwo*; fut. ؤ به داروي *wu bah ddārawī*; imp. ؤ داروه *wu-ddārawah*; act. part. داروونکيَ *ddārawūnkaey* or داروونيَ *ddārawūnaey*; past part. داروليَ *ddārawulaey*; verb. n. داروُنه *ddārawuna'h*. See ويره

داګ *ddāg*, s.m. (2nd) A dry hard piece of ground, an open piece of ground, a level or arid plain. Pl. داګونه *ddāgūnah*; or داګه *ddāga'h*, s.f. (3rd). Pl. ې *ey*. See تکارکي

دادر *ddāddar*, s. prop. The name of a town in Kachī, at the mouth of the Bolān Pass.

دال *ddāl*, s.m. (2nd) A shield, a target, a buckler. Pl. دالونه *ddālūnah*. (HI ڈھال).

داندت *ddānddat*, s.m. (2nd) A cotton cleaner's bow. Pl. داندتونه *ddānddatūnah*.

داندۍ *ddāndda'ī*, s.f. (6th) The beam of a balance. Sing. and Pl. Also دندۍ

داندۍ *ddāndda'ī*, s.f. (6th) A flame, a blaze with smoke. Sing. and Pl. See لمبه , لوخړه , بامبڼه , برانده , غرانده , and غرغره

HI دانګ *ddāng*, s.m. (2nd) A club, a stick, a bludgeon. Pl. دانګونه *ddāngūnah*. دانګ لکۍ *ddāng laka'ī*, s.f. (6th) The name of a bird with a club-tail. Sing. and Pl. See توره آنا

دانګوړۍ *ddāngora'ī*, s.f. (6th) A small walking-stick, a small club. Sing. and Pl. (The dimin. of the above).

دانګۍ *ddānga'ī*, s.f. (6th) The name of a tree from which clubs or sticks are made, and which bears a fruit like an apple. Sing. and Pl. See ټانګو and ټانګۍ

دب *ddab*, s.m. (2nd) A blow, thump, or slap with the fist. Pl. دبونه *ddabūnah*. 2. s.m. (5th) The sound of a blow, etc. Pl. دبهار *ddabahār*.

دب *ddab*, s.m. (2nd) A whirlpool, a vortex or eddy. 2. A pool of water, a stoppage of water, a place where water collects. 3. (HI) Power, strength, authority. 4. Shape, form; behaviour, breeding; mode, method, manner, knack, fashion, style, way. Pl. دبونه *ddabūnah*. دبې اوبه *ddabey aoba'h*, Standing water. (HI ڈھب).

دبوُل *ddabawul*, verb trans. To thump, to beat, to chastise, to punish. Pres. دبوي *ddabawī*; past ؤ دباوه *wu-ddabāwuh* or ؤ دباوو *wu-ddabāwo*; fut. ؤ به دبوي *wu bah ddabawī*; imp. ؤ دبوه *wu-ddabawah*; act. part. دبوونکيَ *ddabawūnkaey* or دبوونيَ *ddabawūnaey*; past part. دبوليَ *ddabawulaey*; verb. n. دبونه *ddabawuna'h*.

دبدبنيَ *ddabddabanaey*, adj. Irresolute, vacillating, wavering, disturbed, distracted, chagrined, anxious; (Fem.) ۍ *a'ī*.

دبدوب *ddab-ddūb*, adj. Senseless, apathetic, paralyzed, fainting; (Fem.) دبه دوبه *ddaba'h-ddūba'h*.

دبره *ddabara'h*, s.f. (3rd) A stone, a rock, a pebble. Pl. ې *ey*. دبرينه *ddabarīnah*, adj. Stony, rocky, abounding with stones (ground), hard.

دبليَ *ddabalaey*, s.m. (1st) (W.) A beetle or hammer used by washermen, a wooden mallet. Pl. ي *ī*. Also دبلۍ *ddabala'ī*, s.f. (6th) (E.) Sing. and Pl. See بغدر

دټيَ *ddattaey*, s.m. (1st) A boaster, a coward, a puppy, a swaggerer, a jackanapes, a poltroon (*lit.* a farter). Pl. ي *ī*. 2. adj. Cowardly, boasting (farting). دټۍ *ddatta'ī*, s.f. (6th) Sing. and Pl. See تتي

دچکو *ddachko*, s.m. (5th) The rough pace of a horse, a trot, jog, or amble. 2. A man or horse who trots. 3. Trotting. Pl. ډچکوګان *ddachko-gān* (W.) (E.) Sing. and Pl.

ډچکه *ddachka'h,* s.f. (3rd) A trot, a jolt, the trotting of a horse. Pl. ې *ey.* Also ډچکي *ddichkī,* s.f. (3rd). Pl. ئ *a'ī.* په ډچکي تلل *pah ddach-key t'lal,* verb trans. To trot, to amble. په ډچکي وهل *pah ddachkey wahal,* verb trans. To make trot or amble, to trot. See ډګلند

ډډ *ddadd,* adj. Empty, vacant, void. 2. Harsh (in sound), bass, deep sounding, sepulchral, hollow; (Fem.) ډډه *ddadda'h.* See بوږ

ډډوزه *ddaddūza'h,* s.f. (3rd) Thick smoke and fire, smoke from a cannon, mist, haze, smoke, gloom. Pl. ې *ey.*

ډډه *ddadda'h,* s.f. (3rd) The side, edge, verge, margin, border, the part of an animal between the back, face, and belly. Pl. ې *ey.* ډډه لګول *ddadda'h lagawul,* verb trans. To lean or lie on one side, or with one side to the ground. په ډډه کول *pah ddadda'h kawul,* verb trans. To put anything on its side. په ډډه پريوتل *pah ddadda'h prewatal,* verb intrans. To fall on the side.

ډران *ddarān,* s.m. (9th) A bellow, or unpleasant sound like that of a bull, a harsh or braying noise. Sing. and Pl.

ډرپل *ddirpal,* s.m. (5th) A flatterer, a toady, a sycophant, a parasite. Pl. ډرپلان *ddirpalān.* ډرپله *ddirpala'h,* s.f. (3rd). Pl. ې *ey.* ډرپلي *ddirpalī,* s.f. (3rd) Flattery, toadyism, sycophancy. Pl. ئ *a'ī.* ډرپلي کول *ddirpalī kawul,* verb trans. To flatter, to fawn upon, to pay court to.

ډرپلي *ddarpaley,* s.m. (1st) A kind of greens. Pl. ي *ī.*

ډز *ddaz,* s.m. (5th) A strong or ferocious looking fellow without courage. Pl. ډزان *ddazān.*

ډز *ddaz,* s.m. (5th) The report of a cannon, pop, bang, burst, explosion, discharge, salvo. Pl. ډزهار *ddazahār.* ډز ډوز *ddaz ddūz,* The discharge of firearms or artillery, the clash of arms, a report, crash, discharge, etc. ډز وهل *ddaz wahal,* To go off, to discharge (*lit.* to

strike a bang, etc.) ډز کول *ddaz kawul,* verb trans. To discharge or fire off, to fire a salvo. ډزول *ddazawul,* verb trans. To drub, to thrash, to beat or chastise with a stick or club. Pres. ډزوي *ddazawī*; past وډزاوه *wu-ddazāwuh* or و ډزاوو *wu-ddazāwo*; fut. به و ډزوي *wu bah ddazawī*; imp. و ډزوه *wu-ddazawah*; act. part. ډزوونکی *ddazawūnkaey* or ډزووني *ddazawūn-aey*; past part. ډزولی *ddazawulaey*; verb. n. ډزونه *ddazawuna'h.*

ډغره *ddaghara'h,* s.f. (3rd) Shoving, pushing, knocking of head to head, butting; a butt, a blow with the head, a push. Pl. ې *ey.* ډغره خوړل *ddaghara'h khwarral,* verb trans. To receive a butt or push. ډغره وهل *ddaghara'h wahal,* verb trans. To butt, to push with the head. See ټکر and ډقره

ډقره *ddaḳara'h,* s.f. (3rd). See preceding word. Pl. ې *ey.*

ډک *ddak,* adj. Full, replete, saturated, etc; (Fem.) ډکه *ddaka'h.* ډک والی *ddak-wālaey,* s.m. (1st) Fullness, repletion. Pl. والي *wālī.* ډکيدل *ddakedal,* verb intrans. To fill, to grow or become full, to become replete. Pres. ډکيږي *ddakejzī* (W.) or ډکيګي *ddakegī* (E.) past ډک شه *ddak shah* or و شه *wu-shah*; fut. ډک به شي *ddak bah shī* or به و شي *bah wu-shī*; imp. ډک شه *ddak shah* or و شه *wu-shah*; act. part. ډکيدونکی *ddakedūnkaey* or ډکيدونی *ddakedunaey*; past part. ډک *ddak* or ډک شوی *ddak shawaey*; verb. n. ډکيدنه *ddakedana'h* or ډکيده *ddakedah.* ډک کول *ddak kawul* or ډکول *ddakawul,* verb trans. To fill, to fill up, to make replete; Pres. ډکوي *ddakawī*; past ډک کړ *ddak karr* or و کړ *wu-karr*; fut. ډک به کړي *ddak bah krrī* or به و کړي *bah wu-krrī*; imp. ډک کړه *ddak krrah* or و کړه *wu-krrah*; act. part. ډکوونکی *ddakawūnkaey* or ډکووني *ddaka-wūnaey*; past part. ډک کړی *ddak karraey*; verb n. ډکونه *ddakawuna'h.*

ډکال *ddukāl,* s.m. (2nd) Famine, dearth. Pl. ډکالونه *ddukālūnah.*

ډکه *ddaka'h,* s.f. (3rd) A shove, a jolt, a push.

a jog (HI دهکا). 2. The shadow of a fairy or genii which falls on any one, supposed to cause sickness. 3. Shutting up a person in a house, imprisonment, confinement (HI ڈھکنا). Pl. ې *ey*. دکه خوړل *ddaka'h khwarral*, verb trans. To receive a shove, push, or jolt. 2. To become overshadowed by a fairy or genii. دکه وهل *ddaka'h wahal*, verb trans. To push, to shove, to precipitate. 2. To overshadow.

دکه *ddaka'h*, adj. (Fem. of دک full) Pregnant, being with young. دکه ښځه *ddaka'h khadza'h*, A pregnant woman (vulgar).

دکی *ddakaey*, s.m. (1st) Any useless herb or stick, a piece of straw, a small shoot, or branch of a tree cut off. Pl. ي *ī*.

دګلند *ddugland*, s.m. (6th) A trot, jog, amble, the rough pace of a horse. Sing. and Pl. 2. adj. A trotter or ambler. په دګلند تلل *pah ddugland t'lal*, verb intrans. To trot, to amble. په دګلند وهل *pah ddugland wahal*, verb trans. To make trot or amble.

دګه *ddaga'h*, s.f. (3rd) The penis. Pl. ې *ey*.

دګۍ *ddaga'ī*, s.f. (6th) (dimin. of preceding). Sing. and Pl. See غیټر

دګی *ddagaey*, s.m. (1st) A thin worthless bullock. Pl. ي *ī*. دګۍ *ddaga'ī*, s.f. (6th) A thin worthless cow. Sing. and Pl.

دل *ddal*, s.m. (2nd) A kind of rake of wood or iron. Pl. دلونه *ddalūnah*.

دله *ddala'h*, s.f. (3rd) An assembly, concourse, a crowd, a mob, a party, a gang. Pl. ې *ey*.

دلی *ddilaey*, s. prop. (1st) The name of a city in Hindūstān, the city of Dihlī.

دم *ddum*, s.m. (5th) A caste of singers and musicians, the females of which dance and sing in public. Pl. دمان *ddumān*. دمه *dduma'h*, s.f. (3rd) A female of the above class. Pl. ې *ey*.

دم دوم *ddam ddūm*, s.m. (5th) The sound of a drum. Pl. دم دومهار *ddam ddūmahār*. دمامه *ddamāma'h*, s.f. (3rd) A kettle drum. Pl. ې *ey*. (P دمامه).

دنبره *ddanbara'h*, s.f. (3rd) A large red wasp or hornet. 2. The name of a tree producing a small black berry somewhat like pepper in size and flavour; a species of the *nigella*, probably the black cumin of Scripture. In the mountain districts north of Peshāwer, where pepper is not obtainable, it is used as such. Pl. ې *ey*. See دنداره and غالبوزه

دنبری *ddanbaraey*, s.m. (1st) Cubebs. Pl. ي *ī*.

دند *ddand*, s.m. (2nd) A pond, a cistern, a pool of water, a mere. Pl. دندونه *ddanddūnah*. See ناور, وسته and دنده

دنداره *ddanddāra'h*, s.f. (3rd) A large red wasp or hornet. Pl. ې *ey*. See دنبره and غالبوزه

دندوکی *ddanddūkaey*, s.m. (1st) A small pool or cistern, a small mere (dimin. of دند). Pl. ي *ī*.

دنده *ddandda'h*, s.f. (3rd) A small pond, a cistern, a pool of water, a hole dug for water, a small well. 2. A staff, a pole, a rod, a bar. Pl. ې *ey*. See دند. (S ڈنڈا).

S دندۍ *ddandda'ī*, s.f. (6th) The beam of a balance. Sing. and Pl. See داندۍ

دنګ *ddang*, s.m. (5th) The sound of a musical instrument, strain, intonation. Pl. دنګهار *ddangahār*. دنګ دنګ *ddang-ddang*, Musical sounds. دنګ دنګ کول *ddang-ddang kawul*, verb trans. To sound, to produce sound, to intonate; or دنګهار لرل *ddangahār laral*, verb trans.

دنګر *ddangar*, s.m. (5th) A bullock or buffalo. Pl. دنګر *ddangær*. دنګره *ddangara'h*, s.f. (3rd). Pl. ې *ey*. 2. adj. Thin, weak, lean, meagre, emaciated, scraggy, attenuated.

دنګرۍ *ddingara'ī*, s.f. (6th) A machine for drawing water, a lever supported on a post with a bucket suspended at one end and a weight of earth or a stone at the other. Sing. and Pl. See also یک لنګه

دنګلۍ *ddingala'ī*, s.f. (6th) Same as preceding (HI ڈھینکلی). Sing. and Pl.

دو *ddaw*, s.m. (2nd) A fart. Pl. دوونه *ddawūnah*. دوا *ddawā*, adj. A farter, a dastard, a mean cowardly fellow (E.). دوی *ddawey* (W.); (Fem.) دوۍ *ddawa'ī* (E.). دوا *ddawā*

(W.). دو آچول *ddaw āchawul*, verb trans. To break wind. See تیز and تر

دوب *ddūb*, adj. Sunk, immersed, submerged, deluged, drowned, plunged in the water, sunk (in grief), etc. (HI ڈوب, a dip, a plunge, etc.); (Fem.) دوبه *ddūba'h*. دوبيدل *ddūbedal*, verb intrans. To sink, to be immersed, to be submerged; Pres. دوبيږي *ddūbejzī* (W.) or دوبيگي *ddūbegī* (E.); past دوب شه *ddūb shah* or وُ شه *wu-shah*; fut. دوب به شي *ddūb bah shī* or به وُ شي *bah wu-shī*; imp. دوب شه *ddūb shah* or وُ شه *wu-shah*; act. part. دوبيدونکي *ddūbedūnkaey* or دوبيدوني *ddūbedūnaey*; past part. دوب *ddūb* or دوب شوي *ddūb shawaey*; verb. n. دوبيدنه *ddūbedana'h* or دوبيده *ddūbedah*.

دوبيده *ddūbedah*, s.m. (6th) verb. n. Sing. and Pl. or دوبيدنه *ddūbedana'h*, s.f. (3rd) verb. n. Immersion, submersion, plunging, sinking, drowning. Pl. ې *ey*.

دوبول *ddūbawul*, verb trans. To sink, to submerge, to immerse, to plunge or dip into water, etc.; to drown; Pres. دوبوي *ddūbawī*; past دوب کړ *ddūb karr* or وُ کړ *wu-karr*; fut. دوب به کړي *ddūb bah krrī* or به وُ کړي *bah wu krrī*; imp. دوب کړه *ddūb krrah* or وُ کړه *wu-krrah*; act. part. دوبوونکي *ddūbawūnkaey* or دوبووني *ddūbawūnaey*; past part. دوب کړي *ddūb karraey*; verb. n. دوبونه *ddūbawuna'h*.

دود *ddūdd*, s.m. (2nd) The lotus flower. Pl. دودونه *ddūddūnah* (P نيلوفر).

دوده *ddūdda'h*, s.f. (3rd) The hip, the loin, the haunch. Pl. ې *ey*. Also دودي *ddūddaey*, s.m. (1st). Pl. ي *ī* (W.)

دوډۍ *ddodda'ī*, s.f. (6th) Bread, a cake of bread. Sing. and Pl. See مړۍ and روټۍ

دوزک *ddūzak*, adj. as s.m. (5th) A tattler, a chatterer, a talker of nonsense, a boaster. Pl. دوزکان *ddūzakān*; (Fem.) دوزکه *ddūzaka'h*, s.f. (3rd). Pl. ې *ey*. Also دوزي *ddūzaey* (Masc.) and دوزۍ *ddūza'ī* (Fem.) (dimin. of the preceding).

دوزه *ddūza'h*, s.f. (3rd) Nonsense, tattle, chatter, foolish talk. 2. Boasting. Pl. ې *ey*. See دوزه

دوغ *ddūgh*, s.m. (5th) The sound produced by discharging phlegm, hawking. Pl. دوغهار *ddūghahār*. دوغن *ddūghan*, s.m. (5th) A person constantly hawking, or who is troubled with phlegm. Pl. دوغن *ddūghæn*. دوغنه *ddūghana'h*, s.f. (3rd). Pl. ې *ey*.

دوغل *ddoghal*, s.m. (2nd) A cavity, a hole, a pit, a cavern, an abyss. Pl. دوغلونه *ddoghalūnah*.

HI دول *ddaul*, s.m. (2nd) Mode, manner, fashion, shape, form, dress. Pl. دولونه *ddaulūnah*. دولي *ddaulī*, adj. A puppy, a coxcomb. (Masc. and Fem.)

دول *ddol*, s.m. (2nd) The hopper of a mill of either wood or iron. 2. A large drum. 3. A bucket for drawing water. 4. The large cogwheel of a Persian wheel which is nearest the bullocks. Pl. دولونه *ddolūnah* (HI ڈهول).

دهولکي *ddolkaey*, s.m. (1st) A small drum. Pl. ي *ī* (dimin. of the above). دول وهل *ddol wahal*, verb trans. To beat a drum.

دومبکي *ddombakaey*, s.m. (1st) or دومکي *ddomkaey*, A tambourine, kettle drum, or gong. Pl. ي *ī*. See تمبل and تمل

ديده *ddīda'h*, s.f. (3rd) A bottle stopper, a piece of wood in the centre of the lower millstone on which the upper one revolves. Pl. ې *ey*. See خلبوري and تيرک

دير *dder*, adj. Much in quantity or degree, long in duration, abundant, enough, many in number (Fem.) ديره *ddera'h* (HI ڈهير). دير والي *dder wālaey*, s.m. (1st) Abundance, amplitude, plenitude, enough. 2. Length of time, number, prevalence. Pl. ي *ī*. Also دير توب *dder tob*, s.m. (2nd). Pl. توبونه *tob-ūnah*, and دير تيا *dder tīā*, s.f. (6th) (E.) Sing. and Pl. (W.) Pl. تياوي *tī-awī*. ديريدل *dderedal*, verb intrans. To be great or much in quantity or degree, to increase, to augment, to become prevalent. Pres. ديريږي *dderejzī* (W.) or ديريگي *dderegī* (E.); past دير شه *dder shah* or وُ شه *wu-shah*; fut. دير به شي *dder bah shī* or به وُ شي *bah wu-*

shī ; imp. دير شه dder shah or وُ شه wu-shah ; act. part. ديريدونكي dderedūnkaey or ديريدوني dderedūnaey ; past part. دير dder or دير شوي dder shawaey ; verb. n. ديريدنه dderedana'h, or ديريده dderedah. ديرول dderawul, verb trans. To increase, to augment, to add to, to enhance, to multiply. Pres. ديروي dderawī ; past دير كړ dder karr or وُ كړ wu-karr ; fut. دير به كړي dder bah krrī or به وُ كړي bah wu-krrī ; imp. دير كړه dder krrah or وُ كړه wu-krrah ; act. part. ديروونكي dderawūnkaey or ديرووني dderawūnaey ; past part. دير كړي dder karraey ; verb. n. ديرونه dderawuna'h.

ديران dderān, s.m. (2nd) A dunghill. 2. A cloth worn by women during the period of the menses. Pl. ديرانونه dderānūnah.

ديره ddera'h, s.f. (3rd) A tent, a temporary dwelling. Pl. ي ey (HI ڈيرا).

ديرئ ddera'ī, s.f. (6th) A sand hill, a height, a mound, a heap, a pile. Sing. and Pl.

ديري dderaey, s.m. (1st) A crowd, a throng, a multitude. Pl. ي ī.

ديل ddīl, s.m. (2nd) Mode, manner, fashion, shape, form, dress. 2. Body, bulk, size. Pl. ديلونه ddīlūnah. See دول ddaul.

ديل دول ddīl-ddaul, Dress and fashion, preparation and appearance. ديل دول جوړول ddīl-ddaul jorrawul, verb trans. To make great show in dress, living, etc. ديل دول كول ddīl-ddaul kawul, verb trans. To adorn one's-self and show off, to cut a swell.

دينك ddīng, s.m. (5th) A kind of stork, a paddy bird. Pl. دينكان ddīngān.

دينك دينكي ddīng ddīngaey, s.m. (1st) Lullaby, modulation, a song. Pl. ي ī. په دينك دينكي ويل pah ddīng ddīngī wayal, verb trans. To sing, to modulate, to sing lullaby, to sing to a child whilst rocking it in the arms. See لاني and للو

ديوالي ddīwālī, adj. Bankrupt, one who has dissipated his fortune (s ديواليا)

ديوټ ddīwatt, s.m. (2nd) A candlestick, a lamp stand. Pl. ديوټونه ddīwattūnah (s. ديوٹ).

ديود ddīwadd, s.m. (2nd) A kind of perfumed candle, lighted at weddings. 2. A lamp stand of wood or earth. Pl. ديودونه ddīwaddūnah.

P ديوه ddewa'h, s.f. (3rd) A lamp. Pl. ي ey. (s دِوا). ديوه بلول ddewa'h balawul or لكول lagawul, verb trans. To light a lamp.

ذ

ذ zāl, called ذال معجمه is the ninth letter of the Arabic alphabet, and the eleventh of the Persian. Its existence is very doubtful, unless it be considered a substitute for د. It is the fourteenth letter of the Pushto alphabet, but merely with regard to those Arabic words used in Pushto beginning with that letter. It stands for 700 in denoting numbers by letters in the former language, and is also written as an abbreviation for the month, ذوالحجه

A ذات zāt, s.m. (2nd) The essence, nature, soul, self, substance, body, person, caste, breed, race. Pl. ذاتونه zātūnah. ذاتي zātī, adj. Essential, innate, natural, intrinsic, inherent, bred in the bone.

A ذاكر zā-kir, s.m. (5th) (act. part. of ذكر) Remembering, grateful, a praiser of God, a pious person. Pl. ذاكران zā-kirān. ذاكره zā-kira'h, s.f. (3rd) A pious female, etc. 2. The name of a village near Kandahār. Pl. ي ey.

A ذبحه zab'ha'h, s.f. (3rd) A sacrifice, slaughter, Pl. ي ey. ذبحه كول zab'ha'h kawul, verb trans. To sacrifice, to immolate, to kill, to slaughter (according to the Muhammadan law).

A ذخيره zakhīra'h, s.f. (3rd) Treasure, store, magazine, victuals, provisions, munitions. Pl. ي ey.

A ذره zarra'h, s.f. (3rd) An atom, a jot, a particle, a little, a mote. Pl. ي ey.

A ذريه zuria'h, s.f. (3rd) Family, race, progeny, descendants. Pl. ي ey.

A ذكاوت zakāwat, s.m. (2nd) Acuteness, ingenuity, acumen, sagacity. Pl. ذكاوتونه *zakā-watūnah.* ذكي *zakī*, adj. Acute, etc.

A ذكر *zikr*, s,m. (2nd) Remembrance, memory, mention, commemoration, fame, praise, recital. 2. Reading the Ḳur'ān, and reciting the names and praises of God. Pl. ذكرونه *zikr-ūnah.* ذكر كول *zikr kawul*, verb trans. To mention, to relate, to recite, to express, to commemorate.

A ذلت *zillat*, s.m. (2nd) (from ذل) Abjectness, abasement, affront, dishonour, baseness, vileness, contemptibleness, meanness. Pl. ذلتونه *zillat-ūnah.*

A ذليل *zalīl*, adj. (from ذل) Abject, mean, base, contemptible, wretched; (Fem.) ذليله *zalīla'h.* ذليل كيدل *zalīl kedal*, verb intrans. To become debased, abject, contemptible, etc. ذليل كول *zalīl kawul*, verb trans. To abase, to debase, to make wretched or contemptible, ذليل والیَ *zalīl wālaey*, s.m. (1st) Abjectness, baseness, meanness, contemptibleness, wretchedness. Pl. ي *ī*; also ذليل توب *zalīl tob*, s.m. (2nd). Pl. توبونه *tobūnah*, or ذليل تيا *zalīl tī'ā*, s.f. (6th). (E.) Sing. and Pl. (W.) Pl. تياوي *tī'ā-wī.*

A ذم *zamm*, s.m. (9th) Blame, detraction, reproach, accusation. Sing. and Pl. ذم كول *zamm kawul*, verb trans. To blame, to reproach, to accuse.

A ذمه *zimma'h*, s.f. (3rd) Trust, charge, obligation, subjection, duty, service. Pl. ې *ey.* ذمه آخستل *zimma'h ākhistal*, verb trans. To take in charge, to take on one's-self, to be answerable for, to take care of. په ذمه كول *pah zimma'h kawul*, verb trans. To make over to, to make one answerable for.

A ذوق *zauḳ*, s.m. (2nd) Pleasure, joy, delight, taste, voluptuousness. Pl. ذوقونه *zauḳūnah.* په ذوق سره *pah zauḳ sarah*, adv. With pleasure, willingly, joyfully.

A ذهن *zihn*, s.m. (2nd) Ability, acuteness, acumen, sagacity, wit, mind, understanding, genius. Pl. ذهنونه *zihnūnah.* ذهن نشين *zihn nishīn*, adj. Fixed in the mind, impressed on the memory. ذهن نشين كول *zihn nishīn kawul*, verb trans. To impress on the mind, or memory.

A ذهين *zahīn*, adj. Acute, sagacious, ingenious; (Fem.) ذهينه *zahīna'h.*

A ذي هوش *zī-hosh*, adj. Sensible, of sharp parts, acute, witty.

A ذي حجه *zī ḥijja'h*, or ذوالحجه *zū-l-ḥijja'h*, s.f. (3rd) The name of the last month of the Muḥammadan year. Pl. ې *ey.* See د لوي اختر مياشت

ر

ر *rey*, called راي مهمله, is the tenth letter of the Arabic, the twelfth of the Persian, and the fifteenth of the Pushto alphabet, and corresponds with र of the Sanskrit. Its pronunciation is the same as English *r* when sounded fully. It stands for 200 according to the Arabic system of using letters for numerals.

را *rā*, A pronominal dative prefix for the first person singular and plural, used generally with the verbs, and is not subject to change for gender or number, and signifies 'me' or 'to me,' 'us' or 'to us.' The particles governing the dative case are also used with it, as را ته, را لره, را له. 2. Also the imperative of را كول *rā-kawul*, 'to give,' used chiefly in poetry. See my Grammar, page 46.

A رابطه *rābiṭa'h*, s.f. (3rd) Connection, bond, link. Pl. ې *ey.* رابطه لرل *rābiṭa'h laral*, verb trans. To have or hold connection with, to be acquainted or connected. رابطه كول *rābiṭa'h kawul*, verb trans. To form connection, link, or bond, to make acquaintance.

رابيا *rābiyā*, s.f. (6th) A large double bag of leather for carrying water on bullocks, camels, etc. (E.) Sing. and Pl. (W.) Pl. رابياوي *rā-bīyā-wī.*

راپوري *rā-pūrī*, adv. (from را and پوري) On this side, here, hither, near me, or us, etc.

راتلل *rā-t'lal*, verb intrans. To come, to reach,

to attain, to go to, to get to, to arrive. This infinitive is imperfect. Pres. راځي *rā-dzī*; past راغي *rāghaey* (from راغلل); fut. را به شي *rā bah shī*; imp. را شه *rā shah*; act. part. راتلونکي *rā-t'lūnkaey* or راتلوني *rā-t'lūnaey*; past part. راغلي *rāghalaey*; verb. n. راتلنه *rā-t'lana'h*.

S راجا *rājā*, s.m. (5th) A prince, a lord, a noble. Pl. راجاګان *rājā-gān*.

S راجپوت *rāj-pūt*, s.m. (5th) The name of a Hindū tribe. Pl. راجپوتان *rāj-pūtān*. راجپوته *rāj-pūta'h*, s.f. (3rd) A female of the above. Pl. ې *ey*.

S راجپوتانه *rājpūtāna'h*, s. prop. The name of the province of Ajmīr.

HI راجواړه *rājwāṛra'h*, s. prop. The name of a country of Hindūstān—Rājwārah.

A راحت *rā-ḥat*, s.m. (2nd) (from روح) Repose, quiet, ease, tranquillity, pleasure. Pl. راحتونه *rāḥatūnah*. راحت کول *rāḥat kawul*, verb trans. To take ease or repose.

راخ *rākh*, s.m. (2nd) The cheek. 2. Face, side, quarter. Pl. راخونه *rākh-ūnah*.

راړه *rāṛra'h*, s.f. (3rd) Bread made from different kinds of grain or pulse. 2. The name of a venomous insect. Pl. ې *ey*. See بروره

P راز *rāz*, s.m. (2nd) A secret, a mystery. Pl. رازونه *rāz-ūnah*. رازدار *rāz-dār*, adj. Trusty, faithful. 2. A keeper of a secret, an abettor; (Fem.) رازداره *rāz-dāra'h*. رازداري *rāz-dārī*, s.f. (3rd) Secrecy, keeping a secret. Pl. ئې *a'ī*. راز ساتل *rāz sātal*, verb trans. To keep a secret. راز ويل *rāz wayal*, verb trans. To tell a secret. پټ راز *puṭṭ rāz*, A great secret.

A رازق *rā-ziḳ*, s.m. (9th) (from رزق) A sustainer, giver of daily bread, the Deity. Sing. and Pl.

P راست *rāst*, adj. Right, true, good, just, upright. 2. Straight, even, level. 3. Right (not left). 4. adv. Certainly, truly; (Fem.) راسته *rāsta'h*. راست ګوي *rāst go-e*, adj. A speaker of the truth; (Fem). راست ګويه *rāst-go-e-a'h*. راست ګوئي *rāst go'ī*, s.f. (3rd) Probity, honesty, veracity, truth, sincerity, candour, rectitude, straightness. Pl. ئې *a'ī*. راستي کول *rāstī kawul*, verb trans. To act with sincerity, candour, honesty, etc. See رښتيا

P راشبيل *rāsh-bel*, s.m. (2nd) An instrument for cleaning grain, a wooden rake, a wooden shovel. Pl. راشبيلونه *rāshbelūnah*.

راشتلي *rāshtalaey*, s.m. (1st) The grain remaining on the ground or threshing floor, after carrying the corn, and which is the right of the tiller of the soil. Pl. ي *ī*. Also رشتلي *rishtalaey*, s.m. (1st). Pl. ي *ī*. See ګهاري

راشه *rāsha'h*, s.f. (3rd) A heap of grain, provision, supplies. Pl. ې *ey*. See رشه

راشه درشه *rā-shah dar-shah*, s.f. (9th) Intercourse, ingress and egress, acquaintance. Sing. and Pl.

راښکو *rāshko* (W.) or *rākhko* (E.) s.m. (5th) An instrument for drawing anything out with, a wire-drawer. Pl. راښکوګان *rāshkogān* or *rākhkogān*. See جندره

A راضي *rāẓī*, adj. (act. part. of رضو) Agreed, pleased, approving, contented, satisfied, willing. راضى نامه *rāẓī nāma'h*, s.f. (3rd) A deed of acknowledgement given by a plaintiff when he gives up a cause, or when it is settled. Pl. ې *ey*. راضي کيدل *rāẓī kedal*, verb intrans. To assent, acquiesce, agree, accede, consent, to be content. راضي کول *rāẓī kawul*, verb trans. To satisfy, please, gratify, to make consent or accede.

P راغ *rāgh*, s.m. (2nd) A meadow, a garden, a desert. Pl. راغونه *rāghūnah*.

A راغب *rāghib*, adj. Desirous, willing; (Fem.) راغبه *rāghiba'h*.

راغلل *rāghlal*, verb intrans. To come, to arrive, to reach, to attain. Pres. راځي *rādzī*; past راغي *rāghaey*; fut. را به شي *rā bah shī*; imp. راشه *rāshah* or راځه *rādzah*; act. part. راتلونکي *rā-t'lūnkaey* or راتلوني *rā-t'lūnaey*; past part. راغلي *rāghalaey*; verb. n. راتلنه *rā-t'lana'h* or راتله *rā-t'lah*.

راغه *rāghah*, s.m. (2nd) The skirt of a mountain near a desert. Pl. راغونه *rāghūnah* or رغونه *raghūnah*.

A رافضي *rāfiẓī*, s.m. (5th) A heretic. Pl.

رافضيان *rāfizī-ān*. رافضئ *rāfiza'ī*, s.f. (6th) Sing. and Pl.

S راکس *rā-kas*, s.m. (5th) A demon, an evil spirit, a fiend. 2. (A) *rā-kis*, An ox in the middle of a barn round which the others turn in treading out corn. Pl. راکسان *rā-kasān* or *rā-kisān*.

را کول *rā-kawul*, verb trans. To give (*lit.* To do or make to me). Pres. را کوي *rā-kawī*; past را که *rā-kah*; fut. را به کي *rā bah kī*; imp. را که *rā-kah*; act. part. را کونکئ *rā-kawūnkaey* or را کونئ *rā-kawūnaey*; past part. را کړئ *rā-karraey* (from کړل); verb. n. را کونه *rā-kawuna'h*. See my Grammar, p. 92.

S راګ *rāg*, s.m. (2nd) A musical mode, song, tune, music. Pl. راګونه *ragūnah*. راګ ويل *rāg wa-yal*, verb trans. To sing, to modulate.

رامزده‌ګي *rāmzadah-gī*, s.f. (3rd) A wooden roller by which a millstone is removed. Pl. ئ *a'ī*.

راموسئ *rā-mūsaey*, s.m. (1st) The musk-deer. Pl. ي *ī*. راموسئ *rā-mūsa'ī*, s.f. (6th) The female of the above. Sing. and Pl. See سرژه and سژه

رانجه *rānjah*, s.m. (6th) Collyrium, a lotion for the eyes. Sing. and Pl. رانجونونئ *rānjūnūnaey*, s.m. (1st) A box for containing the collyrium. Pl. ي *ī*. See رنجرومي and رنجرومه

P رانده *rāndah*, adj. Rejected, driven out, expelled. رانده کول *rāndah kawul*, verb trans. To expel, to reject, to repel.

را نيول *rā-nīwal*, verb trans. To seize, to take by force, to take, to appropriate, to lay hands on. 2. To purchase. Pres. را نسي *rā-nisī*; past را نيوه *rā-nīwah*; fut. را به نسي *rā bah nasī* or را وُ به نسي *rā wu bah nisī*; imp. را نسه *rā-nisah*; act. part. را نيونکئ *rā-nīwūnkaey* or را نيونئ *rā-nīwūnaey*; past part. را نيولئ *rā-nīwulaey*; verb. n. را نيونه *rā-nīwuna'h* or را نيوه *rā-nīwah*. Also written را نول *rā-niwal*.

رانړيزئ *rāṟṟnīzaey*, s.m. (1st) A man of the Rāṟṟnīzī tribe. Pl. ي *ī*, The whole tribe; s.f. (6th) ئ *a'ī*, A female of the tribe. Sing. and Pl.

راوړل *rā-w'ṟṟal*, verb trans. To bring, to fetch, to bear, to convey, to carry, etc. (applied only to things inanimate); Pres. راوړي *rā-w'ṟṟī*; past راوړ *rā-wuṟṟ*; fut. را به وړي *rā bah w'ṟṟī*; imp. راوړه *rā-w'ṟṟah*; act. part. راوړونکئ *rā-wuṟṟūnkaey* or راوړونئ *rā-wuṟṟūnaey*; past part. راوړلئ *rā-wuṟṟalaey* or راوړئ *rā-wuṟṟaey*; verb. n. راوړنه *rā-wuṟṟana'h* or راوړه *rā-wuṟṟah*.

راوستل *rā-wustal* or *rā-wastal*, verb trans. To bring, to lead along, to convey, etc. (applied to objects animate). Pres. راولي *rā-walī*; past راوست *rā-wast* or *rā-wust*; fut. را به ولي *ra bah walī*; imp. راوله *rā-walah*; act. part. راوستونکئ *rā-wastūnkaey* or راوستونئ *rā-wastūnaey*; past part. راوستلئ *rā-wastalaey* or راوستئ *rā-wastaey*; verb. n. راوستنه *rāwastana'h* or راوسته *rā-wastah*.

P راه *rāh*, s.m. (9th) Road, way, manner. Sing. and Pl. (Used in composition.) راه بر *rāh-bar*, s.m. (5th) A guide, a conductor. Pl. راه بران *rāh-barān*. راه بره *rāh-bara'h*, s.f. (3rd) A conductress. Pl. ئ *ey*. راه بري *rāh barī*, s.f. (3rd) Guiding, conducting, guidance. Pl. ئ *a'ī*. راه بري کول *rāh barī kawul*, verb trans. To guide, to conduct, to lead. راه دار *rāh-dār*, s.m. (5th) A collector of transit duties. Pl. راه داران *rāh-dārān*. راه داري *rāh-dārī*, s.f. (3rd) Collection of transit duties on roads. Pl. ئ *a'ī*. راه داري کول *rāh-dārī kawul*, verb trans. To collect duties. راه روئ *rāh-rawaey*, s.m. (1st) A traveller. Pl. ي *ī*. s.f. (6th) ئ *a'ī*. Sing. and Pl. راه رو *rāh-rau*, s.m. (2nd) A vestibule, a gallery, a passage. 2. A launder. Pl. راه روونه *rāh-rauūnah*. راه زن *rāh-zan*, s.m. (5th) A highway robber, a footpad. Pl. راه زنان *rāh-zanān*. راه زني *rāh-zanī*, s.f. (3rd) Highway robbery. Pl. ئ *a'ī*. راه ګذر *rāh-guzar*, s.m. (2nd) A road, a way. 2. A traveller. Pl. راه ګذرونه *rāh-guzarūnah*. راه نماي *rāh-numā-e*, s.m. (5th) A guide, a conductor, a leader. Pl. راه نمایان *rāh-numā-e-ān*. راه نمائي *rāh-numā'ī*, s.f. (3rd) Guidance, leading. Pl. ئي *a'ī*. راه وار *rāh-wār*, adj. Ambling. 2. s.m. (5th) An ambling horse. Pl. راه واران *rāh-wārān*. راهي *rā-hī*, adj. Departed, embarked, set out. راهي کيدل *rāhī kedal*, verb intrans. To depart, to set out, to embark. راهي کول *rā-hī kawul*, verb trans. To despatch, to send away.

A راهب *rā-hib*, s.m. (5th) A monk. Pl. راهبان *rāhibān*.

راهسته *rā-histah*, adv. Near me, towards me, here. Also used with هسته, and در, and ور

راهيټ *rāhīṯṯ*, s.m. (5th) The head-man of a village. Pl. راهيټان *rāhīṯṯān*.

A رب *rabb*, s.m. (5th) A lord, protector, preserver, the name of the Deity. Pl. ربان *rabbān*.

P رب *rub*, s.m. (9th) Juice, syrup. Sing. and Pl.

A ربا *ribā*, s.f. (6th) Usury. (E.) Sing. and Pl. (W.) Pl. رباوي *ribāwī*. ربا خور *ribā khor*, s.m. (5th) An usurer. Pl. ربا خوران *ribā khorān*. See سود

P رباب *rabāb*, s.m. (2nd) A kind of violin, a rebeck. Pl. ربابونه *rabābūnah*. ربابي *rabābī*, s.m. (5th) A player on the *rabāb*, a fiddler. Pl. ربابيان *rabābī-ān*. رباب وهل *rabāb wahal*, verb trans. To play on the *rabāb*.

A رباط *ribāṯ*, s.m. (2nd) An inn, a caravansary. Pl. رباطونه *ribāṯūnah*.

ربړيدل *rab-ṟredal*, verb intrans. To become astonished, amazed, perplexed, discomposed. 2. To become deceived, imposed on, to be amused, etc. Pres. ربړيږي *rab-ṟrejzī* (W.) or ربړيګي *rab-ṟregī* (E.); past وُ ربړيده *wu-rab-ṟredah* or ربړيدَ *rab-ṟreda*; fut. وُ به ربړيږي *wu bah rab-ṟrejzī* or ربړيګي *rab-ṟregī*; imp. وُ ربړيږه *wu-rab-ṟrejzah* or وُ ربړيګه *wu-rab-ṟregah*; act. part. ربړيدونکي *rab-ṟredūnkaey* or ربړيدوني *rab-ṟredūnaey*; past part. ربړيدلي *rab-ṟredalaey*; verb. n. ربړيدنه *rab-ṟredanā'h* or ربړيده *rab-ṟredah*. ربړول *rab-ṟrahwul* or ربړول *rab-ṟrawul*, verb trans. To

astonish, to amaze, to perplex, to discompose. 2. To deceive, to impose on, to amuse, to put off with fair words, etc. Pres. ربړوي *rab-ṟrawī*; past وُ ربړاوه *wu-rab-ṟrāwuh* or ربړاوو *rab-ṟrāwo*; fut. وُ به ربړوي *wu bah rab-ṟrawī*; imp. وُ ربړوه *wu-rab-ṟrawah*; act. part. ربړوونکي *rab-ṟrawūnkaey* or ربړووني *rab-ṟrawūnaey*; past part. ربړولي *rab-ṟrawulaey*; verb. n. ربړونه *rab-ṟrawuna'h*.

A ربط *rabṯ*, s.m. (2nd) Connection, habit, use, friendship, familiarity, construction (in grammar). Pl. ربطونه *rabṯūnah*.

ربړنه *rabarrna'h*, s.f. (3rd) Moonshine, the light of the moon, moonlight. Pl. ئي *ey*. See سپوږمي

رپ *rap*, s.m. (2nd) An arched ornament in a wall, a sort of shelf round a room for placing things on. Pl. رپونه *rapūnah* (A رف)

رپيدل *rapedal*, verb intrans. To shake, to shiver, to tremble, to flutter, to agitate, to shudder, to quake, to twitter, to writhe. Pres. رپيږي *rapejzī* (W.) or رپيګي *rapegī* (E.); past وُ رپيده *wu-rapedah* or وُ رپيدَ *wu-rapeda*; fut. وُ به رپيږي *wu bah rapejzī* or رپيګي *rapegī*; imp. وُ رپيږه *wu-rapejzah* or رپيګه *rapegah*, act. part. رپيدونکي *rapedūnkaey* or رپيدوني *rapedūnaey*; past part. رپيدلي *rapedalaey*; verb. n. رپيدنه *rapedana'h* or رپيده *rapedah*. رپول *rapawul*, verb trans. To agitate, to ruffle, to startle, to cause to shudder or shiver, to wriggle, to shake, to cause to quake. Pres. رپوي *rapawī*; past وُ رپاوه *wu-rapāwuh* or وُ رپاوو *wu-rapāwo*; fut. وُ به رپوي *wu bah rapawī*; imp. وُ رپوه *wu-rapawah*; act. part. رپوونکي *rapawūnkaey* or رپووني *rapawūnaey*; past part. رپولي *rapawulaey*; verb. n. رپونه *rapawuna'h*. See لړزيدل and پرکيدل

S رپئي *rupa'ī*, s.f. (6th) or رپي *rupī*, s.f. (3rd) A coin so called. (E.) Sing. and Pl. (W.) Pl. ئي *a'ī*.

رت *rat*, A particle applied to adjectives to denote intensity (particularly of colour), together with تپ and تک, as رت تور *rat-tor*, Quite black, coal-black.

A رتبه *rutba'h*, s.f. (3rd) Rank, dignity, degree, step. Pl. ې *ey*.

رتي *rata'ī*, s.f. (6th) A weight equal to eight barley-corns. 2. A red grain used as a weight. Sing. and Pl. (s رتي)

رټ *raṯṯ*, s.m. (9th) A flood of tears, a gush of tears, an outburst of crying. Sing and Pl. په رټ رټ ژړل *pah raṯṯ raṯṯ jzaṟṟal*, verb trans. To cry violently, to burst into tears, to cry one's-self blind.

رټل *raṯṯal*, verb trans. To expel, to drive away, to cast out, to turn adrift, to bundle out. 2. To scold, to abuse, to treat harshly or disrespectfully, to reprimand, to taunt. Pres. رټي *raṯṯī*; past وُ راټه *wu-rāṯṯah* or راټَ *rāṯṯa*; fut. وُ به رټي *wu bah raṯṯī*; imp. وُ رټه *wu-raṯṯah*; act. part. رټونکي *raṯṯūnkaey* or رټوني *raṯṯūnaey*; past part. رټلي *raṯṯalaey*; verb. n. رټنه *raṯṯana'h*. See ترټل.

رټلي *raṯṯalaey*, adj. (past part.) Expelled, cast out, scolded, abused, reprimanded, taunted. (Fem.) رټلې *raṯṯali*. Pl. (Masc. and Fem.) ي *ī*.

A رجوع *rujūæ*, s.f. (1st) Return, recourse, turning, bent, bias, appearing. Pl. رجوع *rujuæi*. رجوع کول *rujūæ kawul*, verb trans. To have recourse to, to repair to, to appeal, to refer, to return.

S رچ *ruch*, s.m. (2nd) Desire, avidity, pleasure, or desire for eating. Pl. رچونه *ruchūnah*; also رچَ *rucha*, s.f. (3rd). Pl. رچِ *ruchi*.

رچَ *richa* or رچه *richa'h*, s.f. (3rd) A tick or louse, a nit, the egg of a louse. Pl. رچِ *richi* or رچې *richey*. See ريچه and سپګه

رچې رچې *richey richey*, s.f. (3rd) Pl. In atoms, in fragments, in pieces, in shreds. Sing. رچه *richa'h*. رچې رچې کيدل *richey richey kedal*, verb intrans. To be smashed, broken to atoms, shivered to pieces, crushed, etc. رچې رچې کول *richey richey kawul*, verb trans. To break to atoms, to smash to fragments, to crush, to shiver to pieces, etc.

A رحلت *riḥlat*, s.m. (2nd) Departure, marching, death, decease. Pl. رحلتونه *riḥlatūnah*. رحلت کول *riḥlat kawul*, verb trans. To depart, to die.

A رحم *raḥm*, s.m. (9th) Compassion, mercy, pity, kindness. Sing. and Pl. رحم دل *raḥm dil*, adj. Merciful, compassionate. رحم لرل *raḥm laral*, verb trans. To have compassion for, to entertain pity towards, etc. رحم کول *raḥm kawul*, verb trans. To pity, to commiserate, to sympathize with.

A رحم *riḥim*, s.m. (2nd) The womb. Pl. رحمونه *riḥimūnah*.

A رحمان *raḥmān*, adj. Merciful, forgiving, pitying, an epithet of God. عبدالرحمان *æabd-ur-raḥmān*, s. prop. The name of a celebrated Afghān poet. رحماني *raḥmānī*, adj. Divine, heavenly, merciful.

A رحمت *raḥmat*, s.m. (2nd) Kindness, pity, compassion, mercy. Pl. رحمتونه *raḥmatūnah*. رحمت کول *raḥmat kawul*, verb trans. To pity, to show mercy or compassion.

A رحيم *raḥīm*, adj. Merciful, compassionate, an epithet of the Almighty; (Fem.) رحيمه *raḥīma'h*.

P رخ *rukh*, s.m. (5th) Point, face, side, quarter. 2. The castle at chess. Pl. رخان *rukhān*. 3. adj. Fit, proper, suitable, expedient, necessary. See روغ

P رخت *rakht*, s.m. (2nd) Apparel, furniture, goods. 2. A plough. 3. Tanned leather. Pl. رختونه *rakhtūnah*.

P رخسار *rukhsār*, s.m. (2nd) The cheek, the face. Pl. رخسارونه *rukhsārūnah*.

A رخصت *rukhṣat*, s.m. (2nd) (from رخص) Discharge, dismission, leave, indulgence. Pl. رخصتونه *rukhṣatūnah*. رخصت ورکول *rukhṣat war-kawul*, verb trans. To permit, to give leave, to dismiss. رخصت کول *rukhṣat kawul*, verb trans. To dismiss, to permit. رخصت کيدل *rukhṣat kedal*, verb intrans. To be dismissed, to have leave. رخصت آخستل *rukhṣat ākhistal*, verb trans. To take leave.

P رخنه *rakhna'h*, s.f. (3rd) A hole, a fracture, cleft, notch, flaw, crevice. Pl. ې *ey*.

رخه *rakha'h*, s.f. (3rd) Malice, spite, rancour,

hatred, grudge, resentment. Pl. ي *ey*. رخه کول *ra<u>kh</u>a'h kawul*, verb trans. To show spite, malice, or resentment, to act rancorously. رخه کړونکي *ra<u>kh</u>a'h k<u>rr</u>ūnkaey* or کړوني *k'<u>rr</u>ūnaey*, adj. (past part.) Malicious, spiteful, rancorous, revengeful (person); (Fem.) رخه کړونکې *ra<u>kh</u>a'h k'<u>rr</u>ūnki* or کړونې *k'<u>rr</u>ūni*. Pl. (Masc. and Fem.) ي *ī*.

A رد *rad*, s.m. (2nd) Rejection, repulsion, refutation, resistance. Pl. ردونه *radūnah*. 2. adj. Rejected, repulsed, turned back; (Fem.) رده *rada'h*. رد و بدل *rad-o-badal*, Argument, altercation, controversy, discussion. رد جواب *rad-i-jawāb*, A rejoinder, a reply, a retort. رد خلق *rad-i-<u>kh</u>alḳ*, The dregs of the people. رد کيدل *rad kedal*, verb intrans. To be rejected or turned back, to be repulsed. رد کول *rad kawul*, verb trans. To reject, to turn back, to refute, to dispel, to disprove.

P رده *rada'h*, s.f. (3rd) A layer of mud on a mud wall, a layer of bricks, the work of a day, a line, a series, a row. Pl. ي *ey*.

A رديف *radīf*, s.m. (2nd) Following each other in succession, the rhyming word of a poem, a man riding behind another. Pl. رديفونه *radīfūnah*.

رړۍ *ra<u>rr</u>a'ī*, s.f. (6th) The flower of a tree (Melia sempervirens). Sing. and Pl. See also شندۍ and بکاينړه

رزا *razā* (corrup. of A رضا) s.f. (6th) Consent, assent, etc. which see. Pl. (W.) رزاوي *razāwī*.

A رزاق *razzāḳ*, adj. (from رزق) The provider of daily bread, the Deity.

A رزاله *rizālah*, adj. Low, mean, vile, worthless.

رزړ *raza<u>rr</u>*, s.m. (6th) The name of a clan of Af<u>gh</u>āns, a man of the clan. Sing. and Pl. رزړه *raza<u>rr</u>a'h*, s.f. (3rd) A woman of the above. Pl. ي *ey*.

A رزق *rizḳ*, s.m. (2nd) Support, subsistence, daily bread, food, allowance. Pl. رزقونه *rizḳūnah*, رزق رسول *rizḳ rasawul*, verb trans. To support, to feed, to give daily bread. See روزي

رژيدل *ra<u>jz</u>edal*, verb intrans. To moult, to cast off, to shed or cast hair, feathers, etc. (as an animal), to fall as the leaves of a tree in autumn, or as fruit; to let fall, to be dispersed, scattered. Pres. رژيږي *ra<u>jz</u>e<u>jz</u>ī* (W.) or رژيگي *ra<u>jz</u>egī* (E.); past و رژيده *wu-ra<u>jz</u>edah*; fut. و به رژيږي *wu bah ra<u>jz</u>e<u>jz</u>ī* or رژيگي *ra<u>jz</u>egī*; imp. و رژيږه *wu-ra<u>jz</u>e<u>jz</u>ah* or رژيگه *ra<u>jz</u>egah*; act. part. رژيدونکي *ra<u>jz</u>edūnkaey* or رژيدوني *ra<u>jz</u>edūnaey*; past part. رژيدلي *ra<u>jz</u>edalaey*; verb. n. رژيدنه *ra<u>jz</u>edana'h* or رژون *ra<u>jz</u>ūn*. رژول *ra<u>jz</u>awul*, verb trans. To shed, to cast, to strew, to sprinkle, to disperse. Pres. رژوي *ra<u>jz</u>awī*; past و رژاوه *wu-ra<u>jz</u>āwuh* or *wu-ra<u>jz</u>āwo*; fut. و به رژوي *wu bah ra<u>jz</u>awī*; imp. و رژوه *wu-ra<u>jz</u>awah*; act. part. رژوونکي *ra<u>jz</u>awūnkaey* or رژووني *ra<u>jz</u>awūnaey*; past part. رژولي *ra<u>jz</u>awulaey*; verb. n. رژونه *ra<u>jz</u>awuna'h*.

رس *ras*, s.m. (9th) A kind of collyrium made from the root of the Amomum anthorhizum. Sing. and Pl. (HI رسوت)

P رسا *rasā*, past part. (from رسيدن) Attaining, arriving, reaching. 2. adj. Penetrating, skilful, capable. 3. A long sword.

A رساله *risāla'h*, s.f. (3rd) Mission. 2. A book, a treatise, an essay. 3. A troop of horse. Pl. ي *ey*. رساله دار *risāla'h dār*, s.m. (5th) The commander of a troop of horse. Pl. رساله داران *risāla'h dārān*.

رستم خيل *rustam <u>kh</u>el*, s.m. (6th) The name of a clan of Af<u>gh</u>āns. Sing. and Pl. رستم خيله *rustam <u>kh</u>ela'h*, s.f. (3rd) A woman of the above clan. Pl. ي *ey*.

P رسد *rasad*, s.m. (2nd) Store of grain or other provisions, share, provision, 2. The time of harvest. Pl. رسدونه *rasadūnah*.

A رسم *rasm*, s.m. (2nd) Custom, law, model, plan. Pl. رسمونه *rasmūnah*. رسم کول *rasm kawul*, verb trans. To act according to custom or law.

رسوا *ruswā*, adj. Infamous, disgraced, dishonoured. رسوا کيدل *ruswā kedal*, verb intrans. To become infamous or dishonoured. رسوا کول *ruswā kawul*, verb trans. To disgrace, to dishonour. رسوائي *ruswā'ī*, s.f. (3rd) Infamy, ignominy, disgrace, dishonour. Pl ئي *a'ī*.

A رسول *rasūl*, s.m. (5th) A messenger, the prophet Muḥammad. Pl. رسولان *rasūlān*.

رسولئي *raswala'ī*, or *rasola'ī* s.f. (6th) A corn, a bunion, a gall, an excrescence, a wen, a swollen gland. Sing. and Pl. See بورئي and كلئي

A رسوم *rusūm*, s.m. (6th) (Pl. of رسم) Customs, laws, etc.: duties, fees, taxes, etc. Sing. and Pl.

رسئي *rasa'ī*, s.f. (6th) String, cord, rope. Sing. and Pl. (s رسي)

P رسيد *rasīd*, s.m. (2nd) A receipt, acknowledgment. Pl. رسيدونه *rasīdūnah*.

رسيدل *rasedal*, verb intrans. To arrive, to reach, to attain, to come to, to get to, to come up with, to light upon, to bounce upon. Pres. رسيږي *rasejzī* (W.) or رسيكي *rasegī* (E.); past وُ رسيده *wu-rasedah* or وُ رسيدَ *wu-raseda*; fut. وُ به رسيږي *wu bah rasejzī* or رسيكي *rasegī*; imp. وُ رسيده *wu-rasedah*; act. part. رسيدونكَي *rasedūnkaey* or رسيدونَي *rasedūnaey*; past part. رسيدلَي *rasedalaey*; verb. n. رسيدنه *rasedana'h* or رسيده *rasedah*. رسول *rasawul*, verb trans. To cause to attain, arrive, reach, come to, etc. Pres. رسوي *rasawī*; past وُ رساوه *wu-rasāwuh* or رساوو *rasāwo*; fut. وُ به رسوي *wu bah rasawī*; imp. وُ رسوه *wu-rasawah*; act. part. رسوونكَي *rasawūnkaey* or رسوونَي *rasawūnaey*; past part. رسولَي *rasawulaey*; verb. n. رسونه *rasawuna'h*.

رش *rash*, s.m. (2nd) Dirt, filth, ordure. 2. Matter or pus from a wound. Pl. رشونه *rash-ūnah*. رش لري كول *rash lirī kawul*, verb trans. To cleanse or free from dirt, etc., to purify.

رشتلي *rishtalaey*. See راشتلي

P رشك *rashk*, s.m. (2nd) Malice, envy, emulation, jealousy, grudge. Pl. رشكونه *rashk-ūnah*.

A رشوت *rishwat*, s.m. (2nd) A bribe. Pl. رشوتونه *rishwatūnah*. رشوت خور *rishwat khor*, s.m. (5th) One who takes bribes. Pl. رشوت خوران *rishwat khorān*. رشوت خوري *rishwat khorī*, s.f. (3rd) The taking of bribes. Pl. ئي *a'ī*. رشوت وركول *rishwat war-kawul*, verb trans. To give a bribe. رشوت آخستل *rishwat ākhistal*, verb trans. To take a bribe.

رشه *rasha'h*, s.f. (3rd) A heap of grain, provision, supply. Pl. ئي *ey*. See راشه

A رشيد *rashīd*, adj. Eloquent. 2. Guiding, or guided in the right way (from رشد ?).

رښتونَي *rishtūnaey* (W.) or *rikhtūnaey* (E.) adj. True, veracious, honest, upright, free from falsehood. (Fem.) رښتونِ *rishtūni* or *rikhtūni*. Pl. (Masc. and Fem.) ي *ī*. See رښتيني

رښتيا *rishtī'ā* (W.) or *rikhtī'ā* (E.) adj. True, veracious, free from falsehood. See preceding. 2. s.f. (6th) Truth, veracity, fact, reality, gospel, accuracy, exactness. (E.) Sing. and Pl. (W.) Pl. رښتياوي *rishtī'āwī* or *rikhtī'āwī*. رښتيا گوي *rishtī'ā* or *rikhtī'ā go-e*, s.m. (5th) A true speaker, a veracious person. Pl. رښتيا گويان *rishtī'ā* or *rikhtī'ā go-e-ān*. رښتيا ويل *rishtī'ā* or *rikhtī'ā wayal*, verb trans. To speak the truth, to speak truly.

رښتينَي *rishtī-naey* (W.) or *rikhtī-naey* (E.) adj. True, veracious, honest, free from falsehood; (Fem.) رښتينِ *rishtī-ni* or *rikhtī-ni*. Pl. (Masc. and Fem.) ي *ī*.

رښكئي *rishka'ī* (W.) or *rikhka'ī* (E.) s.f. (6th) A strip, a band, a shred, a ribbon, a fillet, a strap. Sing. and Pl.

A رضا *raẓā*, s.f. (6th) Acquiescence, consent, assent, will, leave, permission. (E.) Sing. and Pl. (W.) Pl. رضاوي *raẓā-wī*. رضا مند *raẓā mand*, adj. Consenting, permitting, wishing, willing, acquiescing. (Fem.) رضا منده *raẓā-manda'h*. رضا مندي *raẓā-mandī*, s.f. (3rd) Consent, willingness, good pleasure, permission. Pl. ئي *a'ī*.

رضاعي ورور *raẓā'æī w'ror*, s.m. (5th) A foster-brother. Pl. رضاعي وروڼه *raẓā'æī w'rūṛṛnah*.

A رطب *raṭb* or *ruṭb*, adj. Fresh, green, moist, verdant. 2. Green herbage of a tree. 3. Ripe dates. رطوبت *ruṭūbat*, s.m. (2nd)

Humidity, freshness, greenness. Pl. رطوبتونه *ruṭubat-ūnah.*

A رعايت *ri-æāyat,* s.m. (2nd) (from رعي) Attention, regard, respect, honour, kindness, favour, indulgence. Pl. رعايتونه *ri-æāyatūnah.* رعايت كول *ri-æāyat kawul,* verb trans. To take care of, to show kindness towards.

رعنا زيبا *ra-æanā zebā,* s.f. (6th) The name of a red and yellow flower. (E.) Sing. and Pl. (W.) Pl. زيباوي *zebāwī.*

A رعيت *ra-æiyat,* s.m. (2nd) A subject, a tenant, subjects in general. Pl. رعيتونه *raæiyatūnah.*

A رغبت *ra**gh**bat,* s.m. (2nd) Desire, avidity, curiosity, wish. 2. Esteem, affection, pleasure. Pl. رغبتونه *ra**gh**batūnah.* رغبت كيدل *ra**gh**bat kedal,* verb intrans. To be desirous, to be curious. رغبت كول *ra**gh**bat kawul,* verb trans. To desire, wish for, covet.

رغړيدل *r'**gh**arredal,* verb intrans. To roll, to wallow (as a child), to trundle, to turn over and over. Pres. رغړي *r'**gh**arrī*; past ؤ رغړيده *wu-r'**gh**arredah*; fut. ؤ به رغړي *wu bah r'**gh**arrī*; imp. ؤ رغړه *wu-r'**gh**arrah*; act. part. رغړيدونكي *r'**gh**arredūnkaey* or رغړيدوني *r'**gh**arredūnaey*; past part. رغړيدلي *r'**gh**arredalaey*; verb. n. رغړيدنه *r'**gh**rredana'h* or رغړيده *r'**gh**rredah.* رغړول *r'**gh**arrawul,* verb trans. To roll, to turn over and over, to trundle or bowl along the ground. Pres. رغړوي *r'**gh**arrawī*; past ؤ رغړاوه *wu-r'**gh**arrāwuh* or رغړاوو *r'**gh**arrāwo*; fut. ؤ به رغړوي *wu bah r'**gh**arrawī*; imp. ؤ رغړوه *wu-r'**gh**arrawah*; act. part. رغړوونكي *r'**gh**arrawūnkaey* or رغړووني *r'**gh**arrawūnaey*; past part. رغړولي *r'**gh**arrawulaey*; verb. n. رغړونه *r'**gh**arrawuna'h.*

رغښتل *r'**gh**a**sh**tal* (W.) or *r'**gh**a**kh**tal* (E.) verb intrans. To roll, to wallow, to trundle, to turn over and over. This infinitive is imperfect, and is the same in meaning as رغړيدل from which it supplies its own deficiencies. Past ؤ رغښت *wu-r'**gh**a**sh**t* or *wu-r'**gh**a**kh**t*; act. part. رغښتونكي *r'**gh**a**sh**tūnkaey* or *r'**gh**a**kh**tūnkaey* or رغښتوني *r'**gh**a**sh**tūnaey,* or *r'**gh**a**kh**tūnaey*; past part. رغښتي *r'**gh**a**sh**taey* or *r'**gh**a**kh**taey,* and رغښتلي *r'**gh**a**sh**talaey* or *r'**gh**a**kh**talaey.*

رغي *ra**gh**aey,* s.m. (1st) A small plate or saucer, a salver. Pl. ي ī. See بشقاب

رغيدل *ra**gh**edal,* verb intrans. To amend, to recover, to improve, to mend, to get better, to be independent. Pres. رغيږي *ra**gh**ejzī* (W.) or رغيگي *ra**gh**egī* (E.); past روغ شه *ro**gh** **sh**ah* or ؤ شه *wu-**sh**ah*; fut. روغ به شي *ro**gh** bah **sh**ī* or ؤ به شي *bah wu-**sh**ī*; imp. روغ شه *ro**gh** **sh**ah* or ؤ شه *wu-**sh**ah*; act. part. رغيدونكي *ra**gh**edūnkaey* or رغيدوني *ra**gh**edūnaey*; past part. روغ *ro**gh*** or روغ شوي *ro**gh** **sh**awaey*; verb. n. رغيدنه *ra**gh**edana'h* or رغيده *ra**gh**edah.* رغول *ra**gh**awul,* verb trans. To recover, to cure, to heal, to mend, to improve, to restore to health and strength. 2. To render independent. Pres. رغوي *ra**gh**awī*; past روغ كړ *ro**gh** karr* or ؤ كړ *wu-karr*; fut. روغ به كړي *ro**gh** bah krrī* or ؤ به كړي *bah wu krrī*; imp. روغ كړه *ro**gh** krrah* or ؤ كړه *wu-krrah*; act. part. رغوونكي *ra**gh**awūnkaey* or رغووني *ra**gh**awūnaey*; past part. روغ كړي *ro**gh** karraey*; verb. n. رغونه *ra**gh**awuna'h.* See روغ

P رفتار *raftār,* s.m. (1st) (from رفتن) Pace, gait, walk, going, motion, procedure. Pl. رفتارونه *raftārūnah.* رفتاني *raftānī,* adj. Departing, transient, fit or ready to go.

رفعه *rafæ'h,* s.f. (3rd) (corrup. of A رفع) Repelling, removing, settling, completing, finishing. Pl. ي *ey.* رفعه دفعه *rafæ'h dafæ'h,* Settling, deciding, finishing. رفعه كيدل *rafæ'h kedal,* verb intrans. To be decided, removed, or repelled. رفعه كول *rafæ'h kawul,* verb trans. To settle, to repel, to finish.

A رفعت *rafæ-at,* s.m. (2nd) Eminence, dignity, nobility, elevation, altitude. Pl. رفعتونه *rafæ-atūnah.*

A رفو *rafū,* s.m. (9th) A darn, darning. Sing. and Pl. رفوگر *rafū-gar,* s.m. (5th) A darner, one who darns. Pl. رفوگران *rafū-garān.*

رفو کول *rafū kawul*, verb trans. To darn, to mend.

A رفيق *rafīḳ*, s.m. (5th) A companion, comrade, accomplice, associate, friend, ally. Pl. رفيقان *rafīḳān*. رفيقه *rafīḳa'h*, s.f. (3rd). Pl. ې *ey*.

A رقص *raḳṣ*, s.m. (2nd) A dance, a ball, dancing. Pl. رقصونه *raḳṣūnah*. رقصيدل *raḳṣedal*, verb intrans. To dance. رقصول *raḳṣawul*, verb trans. To make or cause to dance. See گډيدل *gaḏḏedal* and گډول *gaḏḏawul*.

A رقعه *ruḳæa'h*, s.f. (3rd) A note, a letter, a billet. 3. A piece, a bit, a patch. Pl. ې *ey*.

A رقم *raḳam*, s.m. (2nd) A royal edict. 2. A character, entry, mark, sign. Pl. رقمونه *raḳamūnah*. رقوم *ruḳūm*, Arithmetic.

A رقيب *raḳīb*, s.m. (5th) A guardian, a rival, an enemy. Pl. رقيبان *raḳībān*. See ركيب

A رکاب *rikāb*, s.m. (2nd) A stirrup. 2. Train. Pl. رکابونه *rikāb-ūnah*.

رکات *rakāt*, s.m. (2nd) (corrup. of A رکعت) A genuflexion in prayer, a prostration Pl. رکاتونه *rakātūnah*.

رکښ *rakṉ͟h* (W.) or *rakḵh* (E.) Rut, track, path, mark of anything drawn along, course of a stream or current, a mark left by anything that has passed along, a line, a mark. Pl. رکښونه *rakṉ͟hūnah* and *rakḵhūnah*.

A رکن *rukn*, s.m. (2nd) A prop, a pillar, aid, support. Pl. رکنونه *ruknūnah*.

A رکوع *rukūæ*, s.f. (1st) Bowing the body in prayer. Pl. رکوع *rukūæi*.

رکيب *rikeb*, s.m. (2nd) A stirrup iron. Pl. رکيبونه *rikebūnah*. رکيب تسمه *rikeb tasma'h*, s.f. (3rd) A stirrup leather. Pl. ې *ey*.

P. رگ *rag*, s.m. (2nd) A vein, a fibre, a tendon. Pl. رگونه *ragūnah*. رگ وهل *rag wahal*, verb trans. To bleed, to open a vein.

رگړي *rigaṟṟaey*, adj. as s.m. (1st) A child stinted in milk. Pl. ي *ī*. (Fem.) رگړۍ *rigaṟṟa'ī*, s.f. (6th). Sing. and Pl.

رگي *ragaey*, s.m. (1st) Relationship, connexion, kindred, consanguinity, family tie, filiation. Pl. ي *ī*. رگي کول *ragaey kawul*, verb trans. To link, to affiliate, to connect, to make connexion, to form relationship.

رمباړه *rambāṟṟa'h*, s.f. (3rd) The bellow of a bull or cow, low, bleating as a calf. Pl. ې *ey*. رمباړه وهل *rambāṟṟa'h wahal*, verb trans. To bellow, low, bleat, etc.

رمبکي *rambakaey*, s.m. (1st) The bellow of a bull (only). Pl. ي *ī*.

رمبه *ramba'h*, s.f. (3rd) A centre-bit, a borer. Pl. ې *ey*.

رمبي *rambaey*, s.m. (1st) A hoe, a grass cutter's hoe, an instrument for cutting leather. Pl. ي *ī*. رمبي کول *rambaey kawul* or رمبي وهل *rambaey wahal*, verb trans. To hoe, to weed, to clean with a hoe.

P رمز *ramz*, s.m. (2nd) A wink, sign, nod, hint, sarcasm. Pl. رمزونه *ramzūnah*.

A رموز *ra-mūz*, s.m. (9th) (Pl. of رمز) A wink, nod, sign, hint, riddle, enigma, an ambiguous expression, or allusion. Sing. and Pl.

P رمه *rama'h*, s.f. (3rd) A herd, a flock. Pl. ې *ey*. See کندک

رمي *ramey*, s.f. (3rd) Pl. Mucus, bile, the whitish matter voided in tenesmus, the discharge before labour. 2. A bowel complaint, dysentery. See کانګه and رپ

رميدل *ramedal*, verb intrans. To behave, to comport. To proceed as cattle when going to graze, going in a flock or herd. 2. To become terrified or disturbed (from P رميدن). Pres. رميږي *ramejẕī* (W.) or رميګي *ramegī* (E.); past و رميده *wu ramedah* or رميدَ *ramedu*; fut. و به رميږي *wu bah ramejẕī* or رميګي *ramegī*; imp. و رميږه *wu-ramejẕah* or رميګه *ramegah*; act. part. رميدونکيَ *ramedūnkaey* or رميدونيَ *ramedūnaey*; past part. رميدليَ *ramedalaey*; verb. n. رميدنه *ramedana'h* or رميده *ramedah*. رمول *ramawul*, verb trans. To conduct, to manage, to conduct as cattle to graze. 2. To terrify, to disturb. Pres. رموي *ramawī*; past و رماوه *wu ramāwuh* or رماوو *ramāwo*; fut. و به رموي *wu bah ramawī*; imp. و رموه *wu-ramawah*; act. part. رموونکيَ *ramawūnkaey* or رمووني *ramawūnaey*; past part. رمولي *ramawulaey*; verb. n. رمونه *ramawuna'h*.

رنجرومه *ranjarrūma'h*, s.f. (3rd) A box for containing collyrium or antimony. Pl. ي *ey*.

P رنجک *ranjak*, s.m. (2nd) Priming powder. Pl. رنجکونه *ranjakūnah*. رنجک آلوزول *ranjak ālwūzawul*, verb trans. To burn priming, to flash in the pan. رنجک آلوتل *ranjak ālwatal*, verb intrans. To flash in the pan, to miss fire. رنجک آچول *ranjak āchawul*, verb trans. To prime. رنجک دان *ranjak dān*, s.m. (2nd) The priming pan of a firelock or matchlock. Pl. رنجک دانونه *ranjak dānūnah*.

رنجونونه *runjūnūna'h*, s.f. (3rd) A box for collyrium or antimony. Pl. ي *ey*. See رنجرومه

P رند *rind*, s.m. (5th) A reprobate, a drunkard, a debauchee, a libertine, a rake, a profligate, a blackguard. Pl. رندان *rindān*. رنده *rinda'h*, s.f. (3rd) Pl. ي *ey*. رندي *rindī*, s.f. (3rd) Licentiousness, debauchery, lewdness, lust. Pl. ئ *a'ī*.

رندار *rundār*, s.f. (1st) (E.) A brother's wife. Pl. رندارِ *rundari*, or رنداره *rundāra'h* (W.), s.f. (3rd). Pl. ي *ey*. See وررندار and وريندار

P رنده *ran-da'h*, s.f. (3rd) A plane used by carpenters for smoothing wood. Pl. ي *ey*.

رنځ *randz*, s.m. (2nd) Grief, affliction, pain, anguish, toil, disgust. Pl. رنځونه *randzūna'h*. رنځور *randzūr*, adj. Afflicted, pained, grieved, disgusted, troubled in mind, sick; (Fem.) رنځوره *randzūra'h*. رنځنړي *randzarrnaey*, adj. (past part.) Sickly, unhealthy, constantly ailing, invalided; (Fem.) رنځنړ *randzarrni*. Pl. (Masc. and Fem.) ي *ī*. رنځيدل *randzedal*, verb intrans. To be grieved, afflicted, pained, troubled in mind. Pres. رنځيږي *randzejzī* (W.) or رنځيګي *randzegī* (E.); past و رنځيده *wu-randzedah*; fut. و به رنځيږي *wu bah randzejzī* or رنځيګي *randzegī*; imp. و رنځيږه *wu-randzejzah* or رنځيګه *randzegah*; act. part. رنځيدونکي *randzedūnkaey* or رنځيدوني *randzedūnaey*; past part. رنځيدلي *randzedalaey*; verb. n. رنځيدنه *randzedana'h* or رنځيده *randzedah*. رنځول *randzawul*, verb trans. To grieve, to afflict, to pain, etc. Pres. رنځوي *randzawī*; past و رنځاوه *wu-randzāwuh* or رنځاوو *randzāwo*; fut. و به رنځوي *wu bah randzawī*; imp. و رنځوه *wu-randzawah*; act. part. رنځوونکي *randzawūnkaey* or رنځووني *randzawūnaey*; past part. رنځولي *randzawulaey*; verb. n. رنځونه *randzawuna'h*. رنځوريدل *randzūredal*, verb intrans. To hurt, injure, pain, distress, irritate, nauseate, displease, grieve, disgust. Pres. رنځوريږي *randzūrejzī* (W.) or رنځوريګي *randzūregī* (E.); past رنځور شه *randzūr shah* or و شه *wu-shah*; fut. رنځور به شي *randzūr bah shī* or به و شي *bah wu-shī*; imp رنځور شه *randzūr shah* or و شه *wu-shah*; act. part. رنځوريدونکي *randzūredūnkaey* or رنځوريدوني *randzūredūnaey*; past part. رنځور *randzūr* or رنځور شوي *randzūr shawaey*; verb. n. رنځوريدنه *randzūredana'h* or رنځوريده *randzūredah*. رنځورول *randzūrawul*, verb trans. To hurt, injure, distress, pain, irritate, displease, grieve; to disgust, to nauseate. Pres. رنځوروي *randzūrawī*; past رنځور کړ *randzūr karr* or و کړ *wu-karr*; fut. رنځور به کړي *randzūr bah krrī* or به و کړي *bah wu-krrī*; imp. رنځور کړه *randzūr krrah* or و کړه *wu-krrah*; act. part. رنځوروونکي *randzūrawūnkaey* or رنځورووني *randzūrawūnaey*; past part. رنځور کړي *randzūr karraey*; verb. n. رنځورونه *randzūrawuna'h*.

P رنګ *rang*, s.m. (2nd) Colour, hue, tint, sort; method, manner, kind, way, etc. Pl. رنګونه *rangūnah*. رنګا رنګ *rangā-rang* or رنګ په رنګ *rang pah rang*, adj. Various, various colours, hues, or sorts. رنګ ريز *rang-rez*, s.m. (5th) A dyer, one whose business is to dye. Pl. رنګ ريزان *rang-rezān*. رنګ ريزه *rang-reza'h*, s.f. (3rd). Pl. ي *ey*. رنګ ريزي *rang-rezī*, s.f. (3rd) Dying, tinging. Pl. ئ *a'ī*. رنګول *rangawul*, verb trans. To dye, to colour, to stain, to tinge. Pres. رنګوي *rangawī*; past رنګ کړ *rang karr* or و کړ *wu-karr*; fut. رنګ به کړي *rang bah krrī* or

بہ وُ کړي *bah wu-krrī*; imp. رنگ کړه *rang krrah* or وُ کړه *wu-krrah*; act. part. رنگوونکی *rangawūnkaey* or رنگوونی *rangawūnaey*; past part. رنگ کړی *rang karraey*; verb. n. رنگونه *rangawūna'h*.

رنگت *rangatt*, s.m. (2nd) Weeping, blubbering, whimpering. Pl. رنگتونه *rangattūnah*. رنگت وهل *rangatt wahal*, verb trans. To whimper, to greet, to blubber, to weep.

رنگړی *ringarraey*, adj. Beaten down by the rain (as corn), laid low (as a field of grain). رنگړی کیدل *ringarraey kedal*, verb intrans. To be beaten down or laid low by rain or wind. رنگړی کول *ringarraey kawul*, verb trans. To beat down, to lay low.

رنگی *rangaey*, adj. Thin, scanty (as hair, etc.), scarce, scattered, thinly scattered, not dense (as grain sown, or corn in a field), slight (as rain); (Fem.) رنگۍ *ranga'ī*. رنگی باران *rangaey bārān*, Scattered rain, a slight shower. رنگی فصل *rangaey fașl*, A scanty crop, a slight harvest. رنگۍ ویښته *ranga'ī weshta'h* (W.) or *wekhta'h* (E.) Thin or scattered hair. See ورنگی

P رنگین *rangīn*, adj. Coloured, gaudy, painted, variegated, fine, showy, various; (Fem.) رنگینه *rangīna'h*. رنگین کول *rangīn kawul*, verb trans. To colour, to tint, to stain, to variegate.

رنړا *rarrnā* or *rurrnā*, s.f. (6th) Brightness, lustre, shine, brilliancy, splendour, refulgence, luminousness, glare, flare, glow, glitter, glisten, spark, blaze, flash, coruscation, halo, glory, the light of day, daylight. (W.) Pl. رنړاوي *rarrnāwī*. (E.) Sing. and Pl. Also رونړا *rūrrnā*, and رونړاوي *rūrrnāwī*, and رنړائي *rarrnā'ī*, s.f. (3rd). Pl. ئي *a'ī*.

رو *ro*, adj. Easy, slow, soft, not quick, quiet, placid, demure, serene. رو رو *ro-ro*, adv. Softly, gently, gradually, slowly, easily, leisurely, deliberately. See ورو , قرار قرار , and قلار قلار

P رو *rū*, s.m. (9th) Face, surface. Sing. and Pl. See روي

P روا *rawā*, adj. (pres. part. of رفتن), Lawful, allowable, right, proper, worthy, current, going, passing. روا دار *rawā-dār*, s.m. (5th) An approver, chooser, consenter; approving, consenting, holding right. Pl. روا داران *rawā-dārān*. روا داره *rawā-dāra'h*, s.f. (3rd). Pl. ې *ey*. روا داري *rawā-dārī*, s.f. (3rd) Approbation, consent. Pl. ئي *a'ī*. روا کیدل *rawā kedal*, verb intrans. To become lawful or right. روا کول *rawā kawul*, verb trans. To make lawful, to make worthy or approved, to render proper, right, etc.

روا *r'wā*, s.f. (6th) The marriage procession of women who accompany the bridegroom to the house of the bride. Sing. and Pl. See ورا

رویزي *ruwezey*, s.f. (3rd) The female guests invited to accompany the bridegroom in a marriage procession. Sing. رویزه *ruweza'h*. See ورابانړي and جنجي

A رواج *rawāj*, s.m. (2nd) Custom, usage, fashion, currency, vent, sale, etc. Pl. رواجونه *rawājūnah*. 2. adj. Current, customary, fashionable, vendible; (Fem.) رواجه *rawāja'h*. رواج لرل *rawāj laral*, verb trans. To have or hold currency, to be current or fashionable, to be in use, to have sale. رواج ورکول *rawāj warkawul*, verb trans. To make current or customary, to render saleable.

روان *ruw-ān*, adj. Desolate, ruined, destroyed, ravaged, laid waste, devastated; (Fem.) روانه *ruw-āna'h*. See وران

P روان *rawān*, adj. (pres. part. of رفتن), Moving, going, flowing, running, current, fluent, on the move. روانیدل *rawānedal*, verb intrans. To go, run, flow, move, set out, depart, to be set a-going, to become current, to glide along, to slide, to find its way, etc. Pres. روانیږي *rawānejzī* (W.) or روانیګي *rawānegī* (E.); past روان شه *rawān shah* or وُ شه *wu-shah*; fut. روان به شي *rawān bah shī* or به وُ شي *bah wu-shī*; imp. روان شه *rawān shah* or وُ شه *wu-shah*; act. part. روانیدونکی *rawānedūnkaey* or روانیدونی *rawānedūnaey*; past part. روان شوی *rawān shawaey*; verb. n. روانیدنه *rawānedana'h* or روانیده *rawānedah*.

روانول *rawānawul*, verb trans. To despatch, to cause to flow, to make move, to cause to depart, to make current, to make slide, etc. Pres. روانوي *rawānawī*; past روان كړ *rawān karr* or وُ كړ *wu-karr*; fut. روان به كړي *rawān bah krrī* or به وُ كړي *bah wu-krrī*; imp. روان كړه *rawān krrah* or وُ كړه *wu-krrah*; act. part. روانونكَي *rawānawūnkaey* or روانونَي *rawānawūnaey*; past part. روان كړي *rawān karraey*; verb. n. روانونه *rawānawuna'h*.

P روانه *rawānah*, adj. Despatched, departed, proceeding. 2. s.f. (3rd) A passport. Pl. ي *ey*. روانه كيدل *rawānah kedal*, verb intrans. To flow, to be despatched. روانه كول *rawānah kawul*, verb trans. To despatch, to send away, to set a-going.

P رواني *rawānī*, s.m. (3rd) Reading, commencing to read, as a child or pupil. Pl. ي *a'ī*.

A روايت *riwāyat*, s.m. (2nd) A narrative, tale, history, fable, fiction. Pl. روايتونه *riwāyat-ūnah*. روايت كول *riwāyat kawul*, verb trans. To relate, to recite, to narrate.

P روبرو *rūbarū*, adv. Face to face, before, over against. See مخامخ

S روپئي *rūpa'ī*, s.f. (6th) A silver coin so called. Sing. and Pl. (E.) See رپئي

S روټئي *roṯṯaī*, s.f. (6th) Bread, leavened or unleavened. Sing. and Pl. See ډوډئي

A روح *rūḥ*, s.m. (5th) The soul, the spirit. Pl. روحان *rūḥān*. روحاني *rūḥānī*, adj. Spiritual, of the soul. روح الله *rūḥu-l-lah*, The Spirit of God, Jesus Christ, the Holy Ghost.

روخ *rokh*, s.m. (2nd) Side, part, quarter, extremity, towards. Pl. روخونه *rokhūnah*. 2. adj. Fit, proper, worthy (E.); (Fem.) روخه *rokha'h*.

روخَي *rokhaey*, s.m. (1st) (W.) Side, part, etc. Pl. ي *ī*. See preceding.

رود *rod*, s.m. (2nd) (from P رود) A river, a stream, Pl. رودونه *rodūnah*. See سيند

رود بار *rod-bār*, s.m. (2nd) A place from whence many streams run, a river in a valley. Pl. رود بارونه *rod-bārūnah*. رود خانه *rod-khāna'h*, s.f. (3rd) A river, the bed of a river. Pl. ي *ey*.

رودل *raw-dal*, verb trans. To suck, to draw out (as milk from the breast), to inhale, to imbibe. 2. To reap, to cut corn, to cut, to sever, to divide. Pres. روي *rawī*; past وُ رود *wu-rawd*; fut. وُ به روي *wu bah rawī*; imp. وُ روه *wu-rawah*; act. part. رودونكَي *rawdūnkaey* or رودونَي *rawdūnaey*; past part. رودلَي *rawdalaey*; verb. n. رودنه *rawdana'h* or روده *rawdah*. See ريبل

رور *ror*, s.m. (5th) (E.) A brother. Pl. رونړه *rūrrnah*. رور والَي *ror wālaey*, s.m. (1st) Brotherhood, fraternity, brotherliness. Pl. والي *wālī*. See ورور

P روز *roz*, s.m. (9th) A day; used only in composition, as روزانه *rozāna'h*, s.f. (3rd) A daily allowance, daily wages. Pl. ي *ey*. 2. adj. or adv. Daily, day by day, by day. روز گار *roz-gār*, s.m. (2nd) Service, earning. 2. Time, fortune, age. Pl. روزگارونه *roz-gārūnah*. روز گار كول *roz-gār kawul*, verb trans. To earn, to serve. روز مره *roz marrah*, adv. Always, daily, continually.

P روژه *roza'h*, s.f. (3rd) Fast, Lent. Pl. ي *ey*. روژه نيول *roza'h nīwal*, verb trans. To fast, to keep a fast. روژه ماتول *roza'h mātawul*, verb trans. To break a fast. روژه دار *roza'h dār*, s.m. (5th) One who fasts or keeps a fast, a faster. Pl. روژه داران *roza'h dārān*. روژه داره *roza'h dāra'h*, s.f. (3rd) A woman who keeps Lent. Pl. ي *ey*.

P روزي *rozī*, s.f. (3rd) Employment, daily food. Pl. ي *a'ī*. روزي خور *rozī khor*, s.m. (5th) A living creature. Pl. روزي خوران *rozī khorān*; or روزي خوره *rozī khora'h*, s.f. (3rd). Pl. ي *ey*.

روځ *rwadz*, s.f. (1st) A day. Pl. روځِ *rwadzi*; or ورځ *wradz* and ورځِ *wradzi*. روځ په روځ *rwadz pah rwadz*, adv. Constantly, daily, every day. روځ و شپه *rwadz-o-shpa'h*, adv. Day and night, always, constantly. د قيامت روځ *da ḳī-ā-mat rwadz*, s.f. (1st) The day of judgment. Pl. روځِ *rwadzi*. هره روځ *hara'h rwadz*, adv. Daily, every day. پرون روځ *parūn rwadz*, Yesterday. ورمه روځ *warrma'h rwadz*, adv. The day before yesterday. لا ورمه

روغ *lā warrma'h rwadz*, adv. Three days since. See ورغ

روژه *rojza'h*, s.f. (3rd) A fast, Lent. Pl. ئ *ey*. روژه تئ *rojza'h-taey*, s.m. (1st) A faster, one who keeps Lent. Pl. ي *ī*. s.f. (6th) ئ *a'ī*. Sing. and Pl. روژه نيول *rojza'h nīwal*, verb trans. To keep a fast, to keep Lent. روژه ماتول *rojza'h mātawul*, verb trans. To break a fast. د روژي مياشت *da rojzey mī-āsht*, The fast month, Lent, or month of Ramazān. Also روجه *roja'h* and روجي *rojey* amongst some tribes. See روزه

روږد *rūjzd*, adj. Habituated, accustomed, used to, addicted to, given to, in the habit of, hardened, inured, seasoned, acclimatized; (Fem.) روږده *rūjzda'h*. روږدئ *rūjzdaey*, s.m. (1st) A person given to any habit, addicted to or hardened in anything. Pl. ي *ī*. s.f. (6th) ئ *a'ī*. Sing. and Pl. روږد والئ *rūjzd wālaey*, s.m. (1st) Habitualness, addictedness, acclimation. Pl. ي *ī*. Also روږد توب *rūjzd-tob*, s.m. (2nd). Pl. توبونه *tob-ūnah*; and روږد تيا *rūjzd tī'ā*, s.f. (6th) (E.) Sing. and Pl. (W.) Pl. تياوي *tī'ā-wī*. روږديدل *rūjzdedal*, verb intrans. To become habituated, addicted to, given to, inured, hardened, used to, etc. Pres. روږديږي *rūjzdejzī* (W.) or روږديگي *rūjzdegī* (E.); past روږد شه *rūjzd shah* or وُ شه *wu-shah*; fut. روږد به شي *rūjzd bah shī* or به وُ شي *bah wu-shī*; imp. روږد شه *rūjzd shah* or وُ شه *wu-shah*; act. part. روږديدونكئ *rujzdedūnkaey* or روږديدونئ *rūjzdedūnaey*; past part. روږد *rūjzd* or روږد شوئ *rūjzd shawaey*; verb. n. روږديدنه *rūjzdedana'h* or روږديده *rūjzdedah*. روږدول *rūjzdawul*, verb trans. To teach, to habituate, to addict, to inure, to harden, to train, to form, to accustom, to render used to, to acclimate. Pres. روږدوي *rūjzdawī*; past روږد كړ *rūjzd karr* or وُ كړ *wu-karr*; fut. روږد به كړي *rūjzd bah krrī* or به وُ كړي *bah wu-krrī*; imp. روږد كړه *rūjzd krrah* or وُ كړه *wu-krrah*; act. part. روږدوونكئ *rujzdawūnkaey* or روږدوونئ *rūjzdawūnaey*; past part. روږد كړئ *rūjzd karraey*; verb. n. روږدونه *rūjzdawuna'h*.

روږه *rojza'h*, s.f. (3rd) A fast, Lent. Pl. ئ *ey*. روږه نيول *rojza'h nī-wal*, verb trans. To fast, to keep Lent. روږه تي *rojza'h-taey*, s.m. (1st) A faster, one who keeps Lent. Pl. ي *ī*. s.f. (6th) ئ *a'ī*. Sing. and Pl. See under روزه and روژه

روست *rost*, adj. (4th) Rotten, decayed, corrupt, putrid, noisome, fetid, stinking, carious, etc. Pl. روسته *r'wastah*; (Fem.) روسته *rosta'h*. Pl. روستئ *rostey*. See وروست

روست والئ *rost-wālaey*, s.m. (1st) Rottenness, putrescence, decay, taint, cariousness, etc. Pl. والي *wālī*.

روستو *rwasto*, adv. In the rear, after, behind. روستي كال *rwastey kāl*, Last year. See also ورستو and دورستو

روستيدل *rostedal*, verb intrans. To become or turn rotten, fetid, putrid, noisome or carious, to stink, to rot, to decay, to putrefy. Pres. روستيږي *rostejzī* (W.) or روستيگي *rostegī* (E.); past روست شه *rost shah* or وُ شه *wu-shah*; fut. روست به شي *rost bah shī* or به وُ شي *bah wu-shī*; imp. روست شه *rost shah* or وُ شه *wu-shah*; act part. روستيدونكئ *rostedūnkaey* or روستيدونئ *rostedūnaey*; part part. روست *rost* or روست شوئ *rost shawaey*; verb. n. روستيدنه *rostedanah*. روستول *rostawul*, verb trans. To make or turn rotten, putrid, noisome, fetid, stinking, etc. Pres. روستوي *rostawī*; past روست كړ *rost karr* or وُ كړ *wu-karr*; fut. روست به كړي *rost bah krrī* or به وُ كړي *bah wu-krrī*; imp. روست كړه *rost krrah* or وُ كړه *wu-krrah*; act. part. روستوونكئ *rostawūnkaey* or روستوونئ *rostawūnaey*; past part. روست كړئ *rost karraey*; verb. n. روستونه *rosta-wuna'h*.

روښان *roshān* (W.) or *rokhān* (E.) adj. Bright, light, luminous, shining, vivid, lustrous, radiant, sunny, clear, resplendent, refulgent, splendid; (Fem.) روښانه *roshāna'h* or *rokhāna'h*. Pl. ئ *ey*. روښان كيدل *roshān* or *rokhān kedal*, verb intrans. To shine, to glitter, to cast a lustre, to become luminous. روښان کول *roshān* or *rokhān kawul*, verb trans. To light, to render luminous or lustrous, to illuminate, to brighten. روښنائي *roshnā'ī* or *rokhnā'ī*, s.f. (3rd) Light, brightness, lustre, brilliancy, effulgence, glow, glare, flare, etc. Pl. ئي *a'ī*.

روښن *ro-shan* (W.) or *ro-khan* (E.) (from P روشن) adj. Light, luminous, bright, shining, splendid; manifest, conspicuous; (Fem.) روښنه *ro-shana'h* or *ro-khana'h*. See روښان

A روضه *rauza'h*, s.f. (3rd) A garden, mausoleum. Pl. ئي *ey*.

روغ *rogh*, adj. Healthy, in health, well, sound, hearty, hale, fresh, whole, robust, vigorous. Sing. and Pl.; (Fem.) روغه *rogha'h*. Pl. ئي *ey*. روغ والي *rogh wālaey*, s.m. (1st) Health, soundness, heartiness, haleness, vigour. Pl. والي *wālī*. Also روغ توب *rogh tob*, s.m. (2nd). Pl. توبونه *tobūnah*. روغ بړ *rogh barr*, s.m. (2nd) Asking after health, inquiring after circumstances, etc. Pl. روغ بړونه *rogh barrūnah*. روغ بړ کول *rogh barr kawul*, To inquire after another's health, to salute. See رغيدل and رغول

روغه *rogha'h*, s.f. (3rd) Amity, peace, unanimity, friendship, affection, harmony, intercourse, fellowship, etc. Pl. ئي *ey*. روغه کيدل *rogha'h kedal*, verb intrans. To fraternize, to sympathize. روغه کول *rogha'h kawul*, verb trans. To make peace, to act in harmony, to show unanimity.

S روك *rok*, s.m. (2nd) Ready money, cash. Pl. روکونه *rokūna'h*. 2. adj. One who pays ready cash; (Fem.) روکه *roka'h*.

روګ *rog*, s.m. (2nd) A strap for a sandal, a belt, a thong, a strap, the strap of a churning stick. Pl. روګونه *rogūnah*.

روګه *rwaga'h*, s.f. (3rd) A flea, (E.), or روږه *rwajza'h* (W.) Pl. ئي *ey*. See ورګه

A روم *rūm*, s. prop. Rome, Roum, the Turkish empire, Roumelia.

P رومال *rūmāl*, s.m. (2nd) A handkerchief, a towel, a napkin. Pl. رومالونه *rūmālūnah*.

رون *rūn*, s.m. (2nd) The thigh. Pl. رونونه *rūnūnah*. See ورون

A رونق *ronaḳ* or *raunaḳ*, s.m. (2nd) Splendour, elegance, ornament, beauty. Pl. رونقونه *ronaḳūnah* or *raunaḳūnah*.

رونړا *rūrrnā* or *rorrnā*, s.f. (6th) Brightness, brilliancy, lustre, etc. Pl. رونړاوي *rūrrnāwī* or *rorrnāwī* (W.) (E.) Sing. and Pl. See رڼا

رونړ *rūrrn*, adj. Bright, luminous, shining, vivid, lustrous, radiant, lambent, sunny, clear, blazing; (Fem.) رونړه *rūrrna'h*. رونړه شپه *rūrrna'h shpa'h*, s.f. (3rd) Watching by night. Pl. شپې *shpey*. رونړيدل *rūrrnedal*, verb intrans. To shine, glitter, glisten, glow, gleam, flare, sparkle, coruscate, brighten. Pres. رونړيږي *rūrrnejzī* (W.) or رونړيګي *rūrrnegī* (E.); past رونړ شه *rūrrn shah*, or ؤ شه *wu-shah*; fut. رونړ به شي *rūrrn bah shī* or به ؤ شي *bah wu-shī*; imp. رونړ شه *rūrrn shah* or ؤ شه *wu-shah*; act. part. رونړيدونکي *rūrrnedūnkaey* or رونړيدونې *rūrrnedūnaey*; past part. رونړ *rūrrn* or رونړ شوې *rūrrn shawaey*; verb. n. رونړيدنه *rūrrnedana'h* or رونړيده *rūrrnedah*. رونړول *rūrrnawul*, verb trans. To illuminate, lighten, make bright, to make clear, to cause to gleam, glitter, or sparkle, to throw light on, to make coruscate. 2. To watch by night. Pres. رونړوي *rūrrnawī*; past رونړ کړ *rūrrn karr* or ؤ کړ *wu-karr*; fut. رونړ به کړي *rūrrn bah krrī* or به ؤ کړي *bah wu-krrī*; imp. رونړ کړه *rūrrn krrah* or ؤ کړه *wu-krrah*; act. part. رونړوونکي *rūrrnawūnkaey* or رونړوونې *rūrrnawūnaey*; past part. رونړ کړې *rūrrn karraey*; verb. n. رونړونه *rūrrnawuna'h*.

روه *roh*, s. prop. The mountainous district of Afghānistān and part of Balūchistān. روهيله *rohelah*, s.m. (6th) The name of the people of Roh, and, at times, erroneously applied to all Afghāns. Sing. and Pl.

روهلې *rohilaey*, s.m. (1st) An Afghān, so called from Roh, a name given to the country between Ḳandahār and Ghaznī, and the Indus. Pl. ي *ī*. s.f. (6th) Sing. and Pl. ئي *a'ī*. See under روه

روهيلي rohelaey, s.m. (1st) A Rohelah. Pl. ي ī; (Fem.) Sing. and Pl. ئ a'ī. See روهلي

P روي rū'e, s.m. (2nd) The face, countenance, surface. 2. Sake, cause, reason. Pl. رويونه rū'eūnah. روي بند rū'e band, s.m. (2nd) A veil worn by females. Pl. روي بندونه rū'e-bandūnah. روي دار rū'e dār, s.m. (5th) A person of rank or dignity. Pl. روي داران rū'e dārān. روي داره rū'e dāra'h, s.f. (3rd) A woman of rank. Pl. ئ ey. روي داري rū'e-dārī, s.f. (3rd) Rank, dignity, reputation. Pl. ئ a'ī. روي گردان rū'e gardān, adj. Abandoning, deserting, adverse, backward. روي گردان كول rū'e gardān kawul, verb trans. To abandon, to turn away the face.

A رويت rū-yat, s.m. (2nd) Shape, appearance, aspect. 2. Seeing, regarding, consideration. Pl. رويتونه rū-yat-ūnah.

رويدل rū'e-dal, verb intrans. To dispute, to wrangle, to altercate, to brawl, to cavil. Pres. رويږي rū'e-jzī (W.) or رويگي rū'e-gī (E.); past وُ رويده wu-rū'e-dah or رويدَ rū'e-da; fut. وُ به رويږي wu bah ru'e-jzī or رويگي rū'e-gī; imp. وُ رويږه wu-rū'e-jzah or رويگه rū'e-gah; act. part. رويدونكي rū'e-dūnkaey or رويدوني ru'e-dūnaey; past part. رويدلي rū'e-dalaey; verb. n. رويدنه rū'e-dana'h or رويده rū'e-dah.

رويره rawera'h, s.f. (3rd) A brother's daughter. Pl. ئ ey. See وريره

رويزي r'wezey, s.f. (3rd) Pl. The female guests at a marriage invited by the bridegroom (E.); Sing. رويزه r'weza'h, A marriage guest. See وريزه

روي rawaey, s.m. (1st) A demon, a goblin, a fabulous being supposed to sit on one's breast in sleep—nightmare. Pl. ي ī. s.f. (3rd) رويه rawea'h. Pl. ئ ey.

رهته rahata'h, s.f. (3rd) Ease, tranquillity, content, happiness, easy circumstances. Pl. ئ ey. رهته كول rahata'h kawul, verb trans. To take repose, to take rest.

HI رهټ rahaṯṯ, s.m. (2nd) A wheel for drawing water. Pl. رهټونه rahaṯṯūnah.

رهيل rahel, s.m. (2nd) A sort of reading desk, a support for a book. Pl. رهيلونه rahelūnah.

ري raey, s.m. (1st) Price current, rate, price, tariff. Pl. ي ī. See نرخ

A ريا riyā, s.f. (6th) Hypocrisy, dissimulation, subterfuge, affectation. (E.) Sing. and Pl.; (W.) Pl. رياوي riyā-wī. ريا كار riyā-kār, s.m. (5th) A hypocrite, a dissembler. Pl. ريا كاران riyā-kārān; s.f. (3rd) ريا كاره riyā-kāra'h. Pl. ئ ey. روي ريا rū'e riyā, s.f. (6th) Hypocrisy, dissimulation. Pl. رياوي rī'āwī.

ريا rayā, s.f. (6th) The braying of an ass. (W.) Pl. رياوي rayā-wī; (E.) Sing. and Pl. ريل ra-yal, verb trans. To bray (as an ass). Pres. رايي rā-yī; past وُ ريل wu ra-yal; fut. وُ به رايي wu bah rā-yī; imp. وُ رايه wu-rāyah; act. part. ريونكي ra-yūnkaey or ريوني ra-yūnaey; past part. ريلي ra-yalaey; verb. n. رينه ra-yana'h. See نرا

A رياست ri-yāsat, s.m. (2nd) Command, sway, dominion, government. Pl. رياستونه ri-yāsat-ūnah. رياست كول ri-yāsat kawul, verb trans. To rule, to command.

رياشه ri-yāsha'h, s.f. (3rd) (W.) A heap of grain, provision, supplies. Pl. ئ ey. See راشه (E.)

A رياضت ri-yāẕat, s.m. (2nd) Austerity, abstemiousness, abstinence, continence. Pl. رياضتونه ri-yāẕatūnah. رياضتي ri-yāẕatī, s.m. (5th) A devotee, a practiser of austerities. Pl. رياضتيان ri-yāẕatī-ān. رياضت كول ri-yāẕat kawul, verb trans. To practise austerities.

ريبار re-bār, s.m. (5th) A person who acts as go-between or match-maker in cases of marriage or betrothal. Pl. ريباران re-bārān. ريباره re-bāra'h, s.f. (3rd) A female go-between. Pl. ئ ey.

ريباري re-bārī, s.f. (3rd) Match-making, the business of a match-maker, or of a marriage compact. Pl. ئ a'ī. ريباري كول re-bārī kawul, verb trans. To act the go-between or match-maker in cases of betrothal (the business of an old woman, generally).

ريبل re-bal, verb trans. To reap, to cut grain or grass, and the like, with a sickle. Pres. ريبي re-bī; past وُ ريبه wu-rebah or ريبَ reba;

fut. وُ به ريبي *wu bah re-bī*; imp. وُ ريبه *wu-rebah*; act. part. ريبونكيَ *rebūnkaey* or ريبونيَ *rebūnaey*; past part. ريبليَ *rebalaey*; verb. n. ريبنه *rebana'h*. See رودل

A ريحان *rī-ḥān*, s.m. (2nd) An odoriferous plant, sweet basil (Acymum pilosum). Pl. ريحانونه *rī-ḥānūnah*. تخم ريحان *tukhm-i-rī-ḥān*, The seed of the above.

P ريخ *rīkh*, s.m. (2nd) Thin excrement voided in diarrhœa or dysentery, looseness of the bowels, the dung of birds. Pl. ريخونه *rīkhūnah*. ريخن *rīkhan*, adj. Loose in the bowels, troubled with alvine discharges; (Fem.) ريخنه *rīkhana'h*; also ريخيَ *rīkhaey*; (Fem.) ريخۍ *rīkha'ī*. ريخ وهل *rīkh wahal*, verb trans. To void thin excrement, to dung (as birds).

ريخيَ *rīkhaey*, s.m. (1st) A hole in a reservoir, or a place where water is collected for purposes of irrigation. Pl. ي *ī*.

ريديَ *redaey*, s.m. (1st) The poppy tulip, the wild tulip, of a red colour. Pl ي *ī*.

P ريز *rez*, act. part. (of ريختن) in compos. Scattering, pouring, shedding, dropping. خون ريز *khūn-rez*, s.m. (5th) A murderer, a shedder of blood. Pl. خون ريزان *khūn-rezān*; s.f. (3rd) خون ريزه *khūn-reza'h*. Pl. ې *ey*. خون ريزي *khūn-rezī*, s.f. (3rd) Murder, slaughter, bloodshed. Pl. ۍ *a'ī*. خون ريزي كول *khūn-rezī kawul*, verb trans. To slaughter, to shed blood. ريز مريز *rez-ma-rez*, adj. Bruised, in pieces, in fragments, piecemeal. ريز مريز كول *rez-ma-rez kawul*, verb trans. To bruise, to break in pieces, to tear piecemeal.

P ريزه *reza'h*, s.f. (3rd) A piece, a bit, a scrap, a fragment, a filing. Pl. ې *ey*; also ريزگۍ *rezga'ī*, s.f. (6th) A small piece or fragment. Sing. and Pl. ريزه ريزه *reza'h-reza'h*, adj. In pieces, small, broken in pieces. 2. adv. Piecemeal. ريزه ريزه كول *reza'h-reza'h kawul*, verb trans. To reduce to fragments, to break in pieces.

ريږون *rejzūn* or رږون *rajzūn*, s.m. (9th) (verb. n. of رږيدل *rejzedal*), Scattering, dispersing, shedding, casting, etc. Sing. and Pl.

ريږديدل *rejzdedal*, verb intrans. (W.) To tremble, to shake, to quiver, to palpitate, to flutter, to beat, to shake from cold, fear, or emotion. Pres. ريږدي *rejzdī*; past وُ ريږديده *wu-rejzdedah* or ريږديدِ *rejzdeda*; fut. وُ به ريږدي *wu bah rejzdī*; imp. وُ ريږده *wu-rejzdah*; act. part. ريږديدونكيَ *rejzdedūnkaey* or ريږديدونيَ *rejzdedūnaey*; past part. ريږديدليَ *rejzdedalaey*; verb. n. ريږديدنه *rejzdedana'h* or ريږدون *rejzdūn*. ريږدول *rejzdawul*, verb trans. To agitate, to shake, to convulse, to cause to tremble. Pres. ريږدوي *rejzdawī*; past وُ ريږداوه *wu-rejzdāwuh* or ريږداوو *rejzdāwo*; fut. وُ به ريږدوي *wu bah rejzdawī*; imp. وُ ريږدوه *wu-rejzdawah*; act. part. ريږدوونكيَ *rejzdawūnkaey* or ريږدوونيَ *rejzdawūnaey*; past part. ريږدوليَ *rejzdawulaey*; verb. n. ريږدونه *rejzdawunah*. See ريگديدل

A رئيس *ra'īs*, s.m. (5th) A prince, a chief, a lord. Pl. رئيسان *ra'īsān*.

P ريش *rīsh*, s.m. (2nd) A beard. Pl. ريشونه *rīshūnah*. Used only in compos., as ريش خند *rīsh khand*, adj. Laughing, risible, ridiculous. ريش خندي *rīsh khandī*, s.f. (3rd) A laughing-stock, anything done unworthy of one's beard. Pl. ۍ *a'ī*. See ريږه

ريشل *reshal*, verb trans. To spin, to twist into threads. Pres. ريشي *reshī*; past وُ ريشه *wu-reshah* or ريشَ *resha*; fut. وُ به ريشي *wu bah reshī*; imp. وُ ريشه *wu-reshah*; act. part. ريشونكيَ *reshūnkaey* or ريشونيَ *reshūnaey*; past part. ريشليَ *reshalaey*; verb. n. ريشنه *reshana'h*. See وريشل

ريښم *resham* (W.) or *rekham* (E.), s.m. (6th) Silk. Sing. and Pl. ريښمين *reshmīn* or *rekhmīn*, adj. Silken, of silk; also ريښمي *reshamī* or *rekhamī*. (P ريشم). See وريښم

ريښه *resha'h* (W.) or *rekha'h* (E.), s.f. (3rd) A fibre, a fibril, a thread, a yarn, a strip, a shred, a slip, a fillet, a ribbon. 2. Stringiness (as of meat, a turnip, etc.) Pl. ې *ey*. ريښي ريښي *reshey reshey* or *rekhey rekhey*, adj. Fibrous, stringy, in shreds, in tatters. ريښي ريښي كول *reshey reshey kawul*, verb trans. To reduce to tatters or fibres.

P ريګ *reg*, s.m. (2nd) Sand. Pl. ريګونه *regūnah*. ريګ مال *reg māl*, s.m. (2nd) The weeping nycanthus. Pl. ريګ مالونه *reg mālūnah*. ريګستان *registān*, s.m. (2nd) A sandy place or region. Pl. ريګستانونه *registānūnah*. ريګ ماهي *reg-māhaey*, s.m. (1st) A skink (Lacerta scincus). Pl. ي *ī*.

ريګديدل *regdedal*, verb intrans. (E.) To shake, etc.; and ريګدول *regdawul*, verb trans. (E.) To agitate. See ريږديدل and ريږدول for inflections, and substitute ګ for ږ

P ريم *rīm*, s.m. (2nd) Pus, matter, humour, rheum, dregs, dross, lees. Pl. ريمونه *rīmūnah*. ريمن *rīman*, adj. Mattery, rheumy, impure, dirty, filthy, unclean. See خيرن

رينه *rīna'h*, s.f. (3rd) or نيره *nīra'h*, An awl, a shoemaker's instrument. Pl. ې *ey*.

ريودل *ri-yawdal*, verb trans. To raise, to elevate, to lift, to uplift, to upraise. Pres. ريوي *ri-yawī*; past وريود *war-yawd*; fut. وُ به ريوي *wu bah ri-yawī*; imp. وريوه *war-yawah*; act. part. ريودونکي *ri-yawdūnkaey* or ريودوني *ri-yawdūnaey*; past part. ريودلي *ri-yawdalaey*; verb. n. ريودنه *ri-yawdana'h*.

ړ

ړ *rrey*, is the sixteenth letter of the Pushto alphabet, and has no equivalent in either Arabic, Persian, or Sanskrit. Some parties unacquainted with the language have considered it similar in sound to the Sanskrit lingual ड, which is the same in sound as Pushto ډ *dd*; but it is merely necessary to hear it pronounced by an Afghān mountaineer to be convinced to the contrary. It is hardly possible to give the exact pronunciation in writing, and the broad Northumbrian *r* is the nearest approach to it. With, perhaps, the harsh Ռ ռ *rh* or *rr* of the Armenian, there is no equivalent to be found for it in any alphabet of the Old World.

ړانځړ *rrāndzarra* or ړانځړه *rrāndzarrah*, s.m. (6th) Tar, the resinous substance obtained from the pine tree. Sing. and Pl. See زرنړه

ړپ *rrap*, s.m. (2nd) Mucus, bile, whitish matter voided in dysentery or tenesmus, discharge before childbirth. Pl. ړپونه *rrapūnah*. See رمي

ړپيدل *rrapedal*, verb intrans. To shake, to move, to tremble, to be agitated, to writhe, to toss about, to bob, to wag, to palpitate, etc. Pres. ړپيږي *rrapejzī* (W.) or ړپيګي *rrapegī* (E.); past وُ ړپيده *wu-rrapedah* or ړپيدَ *rrapeda*; fut. وُ به ړپيږي *wu bah rrapejzī* or ړپيګي *rrapegī*; imp. وُ ړپيږه *wu-rrapejzah* or ړپيګه *rrapegah*; act. part. ړپيدونکي *rrapedūnkaey* or ړپيدوني *rrapedūnaey*; past part. ړپيدلي *rrapedalaey*; verb. n. ړپيدنه *rrapedana'h* or ړپيده *rrapedah*.

ړپول *rrapawul*, verb trans. To agitate, to toss, to tumble, to buffet, to wallop. 2. To wag the tongue, to prate, to chatter, to cackle, to jabber, to talk nonsense. 3. To wag or move the tongue as a horse, etc. when afflicted with a disease to which that animal is liable. 4. To rinse or cleanse (as clothes). Pres. ړپوي *rrapawī*; past وُ ړپاوه *wu-rrapāwuh* or ړپاوو *rrapāwo*; fut. وُ به ړپوي *wu bah rrapawī*; imp. وُ ړپوه *wu-rrapawah*; act. part. ړپوونکي *rrapawūnkaey* or ړپووني *rrapawūnaey*; past part. ړپولي *rrapawulaey*; verb. n. ړپونه *rrapawuna'h*. See ړپيدل and ربول

ړته ږيره *rrata'h jzīra'h* (W.) or ړته ګيره *rrata'h gīra'h* (E.) s.f. (3rd) A beard of an absurd or inordinate length. Pl. ې *ey*. 2. adj. Foolish, cowardly, nonsensical, dastardly; a poltroon, a milksop, a coward.

ړقول *rrakawul*, verb trans. To mix, to stir, to mingle, to amalgamate. Pres. ړقوي *rrakawī*; past وُ ړقاوه *wu-rrakāwuh* or ړقاوو *rrakāwo*; fut. وُ به ړقوي *wu bah rrakawī*; imp. وُ ړقوه *wu-rrakawah*; act. part. ړقوونکي *rrakawūnkaey* or ړقووني *rrakawūnaey*; past part. ړقولي *rrakawulaey*; verb. n. ړقونه *rrakawuna'h*. See لړل and ګډول

ړمبي *rrumbaey* or ړنبي *rrunbaey*, adj. First, primary; (Fem.) ړمبۍ *rrumba'ī*. 2. adv. In the first place, firstly. See لمري, امري, and ورنبي or ورمبي

ړنديدل rrandedal, verb intrans. To grow or become blind, to lose the sight. ړندول rrandawul, verb trans. To render blind, to blind, to deprive of sight. For inflections, etc., see under ړوند

ړنګ rrang, adj. Ruined, deserted, depopulated, abandoned, spoiled, laid waste; (Fem.) ړنګه rranga'h. ړنګ والي rrang wālaey, s.m. (1st) Ruination, destruction, desolation, depopulation, laying waste. Pl. والي wālī. ړنګيدل rrangedal, verb intrans. To become ruined, depopulated, desolated, etc. ړنګول rrangawul, verb trans. To ruin, to desolate, to destroy, to depopulate, to lay waste. خرنګ و ړنګ khrrang-o-rrang, adj. Entirely ruined, gone to the dogs.

ړواندي rruwāndey, prep. Before, in front, in sight or presence of. See وړاندي

ړوند rrūnd, adj. Blind, sightless, dark, obscure, not easily found. Pl. ړانده rrūndah; (Fem.) ړنده rranda'h. Pl. ئ ey. ړوند والَي rrūnd wālaey, s.m. (1st) Blindness, darkness. Pl. والي wālī; also ړوند توب rrūnd tob, s.m. (2nd). Pl. توبونه tobūnah; or ړوند تيا rrūnd-tī'ā, s.f. (6th). (E.) Sing. and Pl. (W). Pl. تياوي tī'ā-wī. تپ ړوند ttap-rrūnd, adj. Totally or quite blind, blind as a bat, etc; (Fem.) تپه ړنده ttapa'h rranda'h. See تپ. ړنديدل rrandedal, verb intrans. To become blind, to lose the sight. Pres. ړنديږي rrandejzī (W.), or ړنديږي rrandegī (E.); past ړوند شه rrūnd shah or و شه wu-shah; fut. ړوند به شي rrūnd bah shī or به و شي bah wu-shī; imp. ړوند شه rrūnd shah or و شه wu-shah; act. part. ړنديدونکي rrandedūnkaey or ړنديدوني rrandedūnaey; past part. ړوند rrūnd or ړوند شوي rrūnd shawaey; verb. n. ړنديدنه rrandedana'h or ړنديده rrandedah. ړندول rrandawul, verb trans. To blind, to render blind, to deprive of sight. Pres. ړندوي rrandawī; past ړوند کړ rrūnd karr or و کړ wu-karr; fut. ړوند به کړي rrūnd bah krrī or به و کړي bah wu-krrī; imp. ړوند کړه rrūnd krrah or و کړه wu-krrah; act. part. ړندوونکی rrandawūnkaey or ړندووني rrandawūnaey; past part. ړوند کړي rrūnd karraey; verb. n. ړندونه rrandawuna'h.

ړي rrī, A word used in calling or driving cattle, as ړي ړي rrī rrī.

ړَي rraey, A particle of diminution affixed to nouns to denote smallness in size, or by way of endearment, thus, کوزه ړئ kūza'h rra'ī, (Fem.) A small goglet. Sing. and Pl. (Masc.) ي aey. Pl. ي ī. See Grammar, page 29, paragraph 97.

ز

ز zey, called زاي معجمه and زاي منقوطه, is the eleventh letter of the Arabic, the thirteenth of the Persian, and the seventeenth of the Pushto alphabet. It has no corresponding sound in the Sanskrit, but it is equivalent to English z. According to the Arabic system of letters for numbers, it represents 7.

P زاد zād, s.m. (2nd) Food, provisions. Pl. زادونه zādūnah. زاد راه zād-i-rāh, Provisions for travelling, way charges.

P زاد zād, past part. (from زادن) used in composition. Born. 2. (as a substantive) a child, a son. ادمي زاد adamī-zād, Born of man, a man. پري زاد parī-zād, Born of a fairy or angel, a beautiful woman. شهزاده shah-zādah, s.m. (5th) A prince. Pl. شهزادګان shah-zādagān. شهزادئ shah-zāda'ī, s.f. (6th) A princess. Sing. and Pl. اصيل زاده aṣīl zādah, adj. Well born, of good family or descent. حرام زاده ḥarām zādah, adj. Base-born, a bastard. حلال زاده halāl-zādah, adj. Born in wedlock, legitimate. زاد په زاد zād-pah-zād, From generation to generation. ز زاد za-zād, or زهو زاد żaho-zād, Race, lineage, descent, family, offspring.

P زار zār, s.m. (9th) Groan, lamentation, supplication, complaint. Sing. and Pl. 2. adj. Afflicted, groaning, lamenting. 3. One who groans or laments ; (Fem.) زاره *zāra'h*. زار زار *zār zār*, Great lamentation. زاري *zārī*, s.f. (3rd) Crying, groaning, lamenting, supplication, crying out for help. Pl. ئ *a'ī*. زاري كول *zārī kawul*, verb trans. To cry for help, to supplicate for aid.

زار *zār*, s.m. (9th) Sacrifice, oblation, consecration, offering, a victim, ransom, etc. Sing. and Pl. See جار and ځار

زار بوټي *zār būṯṯaey*, s.m. (1st) A kind of wild rue. Pl. ي *ī*. See جهار بوټي

زاړي *zāṟṟaey*, adj. (Masc.) The young of any animal from the age of two or three months, up to which time it is called تندي *tandaey*, until it leaves off sucking its mother. 2. Late crops ; (Fem.) زاړِ *zāṟṟi*. Pl. (Masc. and Fem.) ي *ī*.

زاړِ *zāṟṟi*, adj. as s.f. (8th) An animal or woman whose milk has run short and become impure; late, run out, former. Pl. ي *ī*. From زوړ old, etc., which see.

زازي *zāzī*, s.m. (1st). Pl. The name of a tribe of Afghāns. زازي *zāzaey*, Sing. A male of the above tribe. زازئ *zāza'ī*, s.f. (6th) A female or females of the above. Sing. and Pl.

زامه *zāma'h*, s.f. (3rd) The jaw-bone. Pl. ې *ey*.

زانگو *zāngo*, s.f. (9th) A cradle for a child, a swing. Sing. and Pl. See زنگيدل *zangedal*.

P زانو *zānū*, s.m. (5th) The knee, the lap. Pl. زانوگان *zānūgān*. زانو وهل *zānū wahal*, verb trans. To kneel on one knee. په زانو کښيناستل *pah zānū k'khenāstal* (E.) or *k'shenāstal* (W.) verb intrans. To sit or squat on one knee. دو زانو کښيناستل *do zānū k'khenāstal* or *k'shenāstal*, verb intrans. To sit with both knees on the ground. چار زانو کښيناستل *chār zānū k'khenāstal* or *k'shenāstal*, verb intrans. To sit on both knees, with the feet under one. See زنگون

A زاني *zānī*, s.m. (5th) (act. part of زنا) An adulterer, a whoremonger. Pl. زانيان *zānīān*, زانيه *zānīa'h*, s.f. (3rd) An adultress, a strumpet, a whore. Pl. ې *ey*. See کاسير

زانړه *zāṟṟna'h*, s.f. (3rd) A heron, a crane, a bird of a large breed, a *kulang*. Pl. ې *ey*.

زاوو *zā'wū*, s. prop. The name of a pass leading into Roh.

A زاهد *zāhid*, s.m. (5th) A monk, a hermit, a recluse, a zealot. Pl. زاهدان *zāhidān*. زاهده *zāhida'h*, s.f. (3rd) A female recluse, etc. Pl. ې *ey*. 2. adj. Religious, devout. زاهدي *zāhidī*, s.f. (3rd) Devotion, the life of a recluse. Pl. ئ *a'ī*.

P زاي *zāi*, pres. part. (from زادن to be born). 'Son of,' a word applied to Afghān surnames, to denote the tribe or clan, as Mac, Ap, and O', thus يوسفزاي *yūsuf-zāi*, The tribe or clan of Yūsuf. Also written زي *zaey*, s.m. (1st) Pl. زي *zī* ; (Fem.) Sing. and Pl. زئ *za'ī*. (corrup. also of ځوي, which see.)

A زائد *zā'īd*, adj. (act. part. of زيد) Redundant, superfluous, exceeding.

A زائل *zā'il*, adj. (act. part. of زوال) Deficient, failing, perishing, declining.

زباد *z'bād*, adj. Proved, verified, assayed, tried, tested, etc. ; (Fem.) زباده *z'bāda'h*. زباديدل *z'bādedal*, verb intrans. To be proved, verified, tested, tried, assayed. Pres. زباديږي *z'bādejzī* (W.) or زباديگي *z'bādegī* (E.) ; past زباد شه *z'bād shah* or وُ شه *wu-shah* ; fut. زباد به شي *z'bād bah shī* or به وُ شي *bah wu-shī* ; imp. زباد شه *z'bād shah* or وُ شه *wu-shah* ; act. part. زباديدونکي *z'bādedūnkaey* or زباديدوني *z'bādedūnaey* ; past part. زباد *z'bād* or زباد شوي *z'bad shawaey* ; verb. n. زباديدنه *z'bādedana'h* or زباديده *z'bādedah*. زبادول *z'bādawul*, verb trans. To prove, to verify, to test, to try. Pres. زبادوي *z'bādawī* ; past زباد کړ *z'bād karr* or وُ کړ *wu-karr* ; fut. زباد به کړي *z'bād bah krrī* or به وُ کړي *bah wu-krrī* ; imp. زباد کړه *z'bād krrah* or وُ کړه *wu-krrah* ; act. part. زبادوونکي *z'bādawūnkaey* or زبادووني *z'bādawūnaey* ; past part. زباد کړي *z'bād karraey* ; verb. n. زبادونه *z'bādawuna'h*.

P زبان *zabān*, s.m. (2nd) The tongue ; language, dialect, speech. Pl. زبانونه *zabānūnah*. Used only in composition, as زبان آور *zabān āwar*, adj. Eloquent, voluble, fluent. زبان آوري *zabān āwarī*, s.f. (3rd) Fluency, eloquence. Pl. ئي *a'ī*. زبان دان *zabān dān*, adj. A linguist, a poet, skilled in language. زبان دراز *zabān darāz*, adj. Long-tongued, abusive. زبان درازي *zabān darāzī*, s.f. (3rd) Abuse. Pl. ئي *a'ī*. زبان درازي كول *zabān darāzī kawul*, verb trans. To abuse, to give abuse, زباني *zabānī*, adj. By word, of or from the tongue, traditional, oral, verbal. زباني ويل *zabānī wayal*, verb trans. To give a verbal message. See ژبه or زبه

A زبده *zubda'h*, s.f. (3rd) (from زبد) The cream of milk, the best of anything. Pl. ئي *ey*.

A زبر *zabar*, adj. Above, superior. 2. The vowel point (ـَـ) pronounced *a*. زبر دست *zabar dast*, adj. Powerful, vigorous, violent, oppressive, victorious; (Fem). زبردسته *zabar dasta'h*. زبر دستي *zabar dastī*, s.f. (3rd) Violence, oppression, powerfulness. Pl. ئي *a'ī*. 2. adv. Violently, forcibly. زبر دستي كول *zabar dastī kawul*, verb trans. To force, to oppress.

A P زبرجد *zabar-jad*, s.m. (6th) A kind of emerald, a topaz, a jasper. Sing. and Pl.

زبرگ *z'barg*, adj. Great, large, reverend, venerable, grand. 2. s.m. (5th) A great man, a noble, a saint, an elder, an ancestor. Pl. زبرگان *z'bargān*. زبرگه *z'barga'h*, s.f. (3rd). An ancestress, etc. Pl. ئي *ey*. زبرگي *z'bargī*, s.f. (3rd) Grandeur, greatness, eminence, seniority, nobleness. Pl. ئي *a'ī*. See بزرگ

زبله *zablah*, adv. Together, in company. زبله بانڊِ *zablah bāndi*, Fold on fold, etc. See څبله

P زبون *zabūn*, adj. Bad, evil, wicked, faulty, ill, unlucky. زبوني *zabūnī*, s.f. (3rd) Badness, vileness, vice, evil, ill, unluckiness. Pl. ئي *a'ī*. زبوني كول *zabūnī kawul*, verb trans. To act with vileness, to cause evil.

زبه *zaba'h*, s.f. (3rd) (corrup. of ژبه) The tongue, language, dialect, speech. Pl. ئي *ey*. See جبه

زبيښل *z'beshal* (W.) or *z'bekhal* (E.) verb trans. To suck, to draw into the mouth, to draw out, to imbibe, to inhale. Pres. زبيښي *z'beshī*; or *z'bekhī*; past وُ زبيښه *wu-z'beshah* or *z'bekhah*; fut. وُ به زبيښي *wu bah z'beshī* or *z'bekhī*; imp. وُ زبيښه *wu-z'beshah* or *z'bekhah*; act. part. زبيښونكَي *z'beshūnkaey* or *z'bekhūnkaey*, or زبيښونَي *z'beshūnaey* or *z'bekhūnaey*; past part. زبيښلَي *z'beshalaey* or *z'bekhalaey*; verb. n. زبيښنه *z'beshana'h* or *z'bekhana'h*.

A زحمت *zahmat*, s.m. (2nd) Affliction, sickness, pain, disquietude. Pl. زحمتونه *zahmatūnah*. زحمت كښل *zahmat k'shal* (W.) or *k'khal* (E.), verb trans. To suffer affliction or sickness, to bear or sustain pain or disquietude. زحمتي *zahmatī*, adj. Sick, afflicted.

P زخم *zakhm*, s.m. (2nd) A wound, a sore, a scar, a cut. Pl. زخمونه *zakhmūnah*. See پرهر and پرهار. زخم كول *zakhm kawul*, verb trans. To make or cause a wound. زخمي *zakhmī*, adj. Wounded, scarred, cut. زخمي كيدل *zakhmī kedal*, verb intrans. To be wounded. زخمي كول *zakhmī kawul*, verb trans. To wound.

زخه *zakha'h*, s.f. (3rd) A wart; an excrescence on the trunk of a tree. Pl. ئي *ey*.

A زخيره *zakhera'h*, s.f. (3rd) A heap, a store, a granary, provision. Pl. ئي *ey*.

P زد *zad*, s.m. (2nd) (from زدن) Striking, conflict, combat. 2. Effect, consequence, impression. Pl. زدونه *zadūnah*. زد كول *zad kawul*, verb trans. To strike, to effect, to cause or make impression.

زدايت *zadāyat*, s.m. (2nd) Family, race, genealogy, descent. Pl. زدايتونه *zadāyatūnah*.

زدويل *z'do-yal*, verb trans. To rub, to grind, to grate, to rasp, to rub down, to pare, to scour, to wear away, to smooth, to polish. 2. To draw. Pres زدوئي *z'do-yī*; past وُ زدويه *wu-z'do-yah*; fut. وُ به زدوئي *wu-bah z'do-yī*; imp. وُ زدويه *wu-z'do-yah*; act. part. زدويونكَي *z'do-yūnkaey* or زدويونَي *z'do-yūnaey*; past part. زدويلَي *z'do-yalaey*; verb. n. زدوينه *z'do-yana'h*.

P زده *zadah*, adj. (from زدن) Stricken, smitten, injured by heat, cold, etc., withered.

زده *z'dah*, adj. Remembered, recollected, unforgotten, imprinted in the memory, etc., 2. Acquired, learned, mastered (as a book or language), known.

زده کېدل *z'dah kedal*, verb intrans. To be learned, acquired, retained in the memory, to be recollected. زده کول *z'dah kawul*, verb trans. To commit to memory, to get or learn by heart, to acquire, to learn, to retain, to remember, to recollect, to know by heart.

P زر *zar*, s.m. (6th) Gold, riches, wealth, money. Sing. and Pl. سپين زر *spīn zar*, Silver (*lit.* white gold). سره زر *sarah zar*, Gold. زرافشان *zar afshān*, adj. Strewing gold. زرخريد *zar kharīd*, adj. Purchased (as a slave).

زر *zær*, adj. A thousand. 2. s.m. (2nd). Pl. زرونه *zærūnah*. 3. adj. Swift, speedy, quick, nimble, rapid. زر زر *zær-zær*, Speedily, swiftly, fleetly, suddenly. زرګوني *zærgūnī* or زرګونه *zærgūna'h*, Thousands. See زر and زغرد

A زراعت *zirā-æat*, s.m. (2nd) (from زرع) Agriculture, husbandry, sowing, a crop, a sown field. Pl. زراعتونه *zirā-æatūnah*. زراعت کول *zirā-æat kawul*, verb trans. To sow, to prepare land, to bring under cultivation.

زربرخ *zar-barakh*, s.m. (6th) Talc. Sing. and Pl. See also د شکي ګل

زر بيانګ *zar-bī'āng*, s.m. (2nd) An instrument for scraping and cleaning leather. Pl. زر بيانګونه *zar-bī'āngūnah*.

P زرد آلو *zard-ālū*, s.m. (5th) An apricot. Pl. زرد آلوګان *zard-ālūgān*.

زردکه *zardaka'h*, s.f. (3rd) A carrot. Pl. ې *ey*. (P زردک).

زرغاله *zar-ghāla'h*, adj. (used as subs.) A lying-in woman during forty days after child-birth. 2. The forty days of child-birth during which a woman is impure. Pl. ې *ey*. See لنګه and ځلوينښتي

زرغون *zarghūn*, adj. Green, verdant, fresh. 2. Grown up, come up (as vegetation, etc.). 3. Anything enshrined or imprinted in the heart or recollection. (Fem.) زرغونه *zarghūna'h*. Pl. ې *ey*. زرغون والي *zarghūn wālaey*, s.m. (1st) Greenness, verdancy, freshness. 2. Recollection. Pl. والي *wālī*; also زرغون توب *zarghūn tob*, s.m. (2nd). Pl. توبونه *tobūnah*, and زرغون تيا *zarghūn tī'ā*, s.f. (6th) (E.) Sing. and Pl. (W.) Pl. تياوي *tī'ā-wī*.

زرغونېدل *zarghūnedal*, verb intrans. To grow, to enlarge, to vegetate, to sprout, to spread, to shoot out, to become green, fresh, verdant (as a field) Pres. زرغونېږي *zarghūnejzī* (W.) or زرغونېګي *zarghūnegī* (E.); past زرغون شه *zarghūn shah* or وُ شه *wu-shah*; fut. زرغون به شي *zarghūn bah shī* or به وُ شي *bah wu-shī*; imp. زرغون شه *zarghūn shah* or وُ شه *wu-shah*; act. part. زرغونېدونکئ *zarghūnedūnkaey* or زرغونېدونئ *zarghūnedūnaey*; past part. زرغون *zarghūn* or زرغون شوئ *zarghūn shawaey*; verb. n. زرغونېده *zarghūneda'h* or زرغونېدنه *zarghūnedanah*. زرغونول *zarghūnawul*, verb trans. To make green, fresh, or verdant, to cause or make shoot up, sprout, vegetate, or shoot out. Pres. زرغونوي *zarghūnawī*; past زرغون کړ *zarghūn karr* or وُ کړ *wu-karr*; fut. زرغون به کړي *zarghūn bah krrī* or به وُ کړي *bah wu-krrī*; imp. زرغون کړه *zarghūn krrah* or وُ کړه *wu-krrah*; act. part. زرغونوونکئ *zarghūnawūnkaey* or زرغونوونئ *zarghūnawūnaey*; past part. زرغون کړئ *zarghūn karraey*; verb. n. زرغونونه *zarghūnawuna'h*.

زرکه *zarka'h*, s.f. (3rd) The *chikor*, the bartavelle or Greek partridge. Pl. ې *ey*.

P زرګر *zar-gar*, s.m. (5th) A goldsmith, a worker in gold. Pl. زرګران *zargarān*.

زرګير *zar-gīr*, s.m. (2nd) A thumbstall made of leather, worn by archers to defend the thumb in pulling the string of a bow. Pl. زرګيرونه *zar-gīrūnah*.

P زرمست *zar-mast*, adj. Independent, purse-proud; (Fem.) زرمسته *zar-masta'h*. Pl. ې *ey*.

P زرنباد *zarunbād*, s.m. (6th) The name of a plant, zedoary (Circumba zerumbet). Sing. and Pl.

زرنده *zaranda'h*, s.f. (3rd) (W.) A water-mill, or windmill, or a mill turned by camels or bullocks. Pl. ې *ey*. See ژرنده and جرنده

زرنۍ *zarana'ī*, s.f. (6th) Peeping, ogling, eyeing, leer, glimpse, espionage. Sing. and Pl. (E.); or زرني *zaranī*, s.f. (3rd) (W.). Pl. ۍ *a'ī*. په زرني *pah zaranī* or زرنۍ *zarana'ī* كتل *katal* or ليدل *līdal*, verb trans. To look intently, to strain one's eyes, to gaze, to pore over, to ogle, to leer, to take a peep or glimpse at. See زير كول and په خير كتل

P زرنيخ *zar-nīkh*, s.m. (6th) Orpiment, arsenic. Sing. and Pl.

زرنړه *zararrnah*, s.m. (6th) Tar, the resinous substance obtained from the pine. Sing. and Pl. See رانخره

زرنړه *zararrna'h*, s.f. (3rd) Black mud at the bottom of a pond, slime. Pl. ۍ *ey*.

P زره *zira'h*, s.f. (3rd) Iron armour made with rings, chain armour. Pl. ۍ *ey*. زره پوښ *zira'h posh* or *pokh*, s.m. (5th) A man in chain armour. Pl. زره پوښان *zira'h poshān* or *pokhān*. See زغره

زرئ *zaraey*, s.m. (1st) A scout, a spy, a vedette, one who peeps or ogles. Pl. ي *ī*. زرۍ *zara'ī*, s.f. (6th). Sing. and Pl. See زرنۍ

P زري *zarī*, adj. (from زر) Anything woven from gold or with gold thread.

زرئ *zaraey*, s.m. (1st) The sight of a gun. Pl. ي *ī*. See ديدوان

زري زري *zarey zarey*, adj. In pieces, in atoms, in shreds or fragments (corrup. of ذره).

P زرين *zarīn*, adj. Golden; (Fem.) زرينه *zarīna'h*.

زړګوټئ *zarrgūttaey*, s.m. (1st) Clothes, dress, garments. Pl. ي *ī*. See زړوكي

زړګئ *zarrgaey*, s.m. (1st) The heart (*lit.* a little heart), the dimin. of زړه, which see. Pl. ي *ī*.

زړند *zurrand*, adj. Hanging, dangling, suspended. زړنديدل *zurrandedal*, verb intrans. and زړندول *zurrandawul*, verb trans. To hang, etc. See خوړند

زړوالئ *zarr-wālaey*, s.m. (1st) Oldness, age, antiquity, decline, decay, maturity. Pl. والي *wālī*, also زړ توب *zarr-tob*, s.m. (2nd). Pl. توبونه *tobūnah* or زړ تيا *zarr-tī-ā*, s.f. (6th). (E.) Sing. and Pl. (W.) Pl. تياوي *tī'āwī*. See زوړ

زړوكئ *zarrūkaey*, s.m. (1st) Clothes, dress, garments. 2. An old rag or piece of cloth of no value. Pl. ي *ī*. See زړګوټي

زړه *z'rrah*, s.m. (2nd) The heart, mind, soul. Pl. زړونه *z'rrūnah*. زړګئ *zarrgaey* or زړګوټئ *zarrgottaey*, s.m. (1st) A little heart (dimin. of زړه). Pl. ي *ī*. بې زړه *bey z'rrah*, adj. Dispirited, heartless, dejected, sad. زړه سوئ *z'rrah s'waey*, s.m. (1st) Sympathy, compassion, pity. Pl. ي *ī*. زړه سوئ *z'rrah sawaey*, adj. Afflicted, troubled in mind. د زړه ايشنا *da z'rrah aeshnā*, s.f. (6th) The heart-burn. (E.) Sing. and Pl. (W.) Pl. ايشناوي *aeshnāwī*. زړه ور *z'rrah-war*, adj. Bold, brave, intrepid; (Fem.) زړه وره *z'rrah-wara'h*. زړه ور توب *z'rrah-war tob*, s.m. (2nd) Boldness, bravery, gallantry, courage, valour, daring, intrepidity; nerve, pluck, mettle, bottom, firmness, fortitude, resolution, heroism. Pl. توبونه *tob-ūnah*; or زړه ور تيا *z'rrah-war-tī'ā*, s.f. (6th). (E.) Sing. and Pl. (W.) Pl. تياوي *tī'āwī*. د زړه بداوي *da z'rrah badāwī*, Annoyance, irritation, disquietude of mind, dejection; chagrin, mortification. زړه شين *z'rrah shīn*, adj. (*lit.* green-hearted) (fig.) Enraged, angry, furious. زړه و بدو ته شين *z'rrah wa bado tah shīn*, Ready for any mischief or desperate action, from rage, fury, or chagrin, desperate.

زړئ *zarraey*, s.m. (1st.) A seed, a kernel in general. Pl. ي *ī*. (E.) زنړي

زړئ *zirraey*, s.m. (1st) The jaundice. Pl. ي *ī*. See زيړي

زړيدل *zarredal*, verb intrans. To grow or become old, aged, antique, antiquated, ancient, elderly, grey-headed, venerable, time-worn, decrepid, superannuated, worn out, stricken in years, advanced in life. Pres. زړيږي *zarrejzī* (W.) or زړيګي *zarregī* (E.); past زوړ شه *zorr shah* or وُ شه *wu-shah*; fut. زوړ به شي *zorr bah shī* or به وُ شي *bah wu-shī*; imp. زوړ شه *zorr shah* or وُ شه *wu-shah*; act.

part. زړيدونکي *zarredūnkaey* or زړيدوني *zarredūnaey*; past part. زوړ *zorr* or زوړ شوي *zorr shawaey*; verb. n. زړيدنه *zarredana'h* or زړيده *zarredah*. زړول *zarrawul*, verb trans. To make or render old, aged, venerable, to render decrepid, to wear out (as clothes), to weaken by age. Pres. زړوي *zarrawī*; past زوړ کړ *zorr karr* or وُ کړ *wu-karr*; fut. زوړ به کړي *zorr bah krrī*; or به وُ کړي *bah wu-krrī*; imp. زوړ کړه *zorr krrah* or وُ کړه *wu-krrah*; act. part. زړوونکي *zarrawūnkaey* or زړووني *zarrawūnaey*; past part. زوړ کړي *zorr karraey*; verb. n. زړونه *zarrawuna'h*. See زوړ

زږ *zijz*, adj. Rough, hard, stiff, rigid, stern, harsh; (Fem.) زږه *zijza'h*. زږيدل *zijzedal*, verb intrans. To become or grow rough, hard, stiff, rigid, harsh, severe, etc. زږول *zijzawul*, verb trans. To make or render rough, hard, harsh, rigid, etc. See زيګ

زږګي *zijzgaey*, s.m. (1st) A porcupine, a hedgehog. Pl. ي *ī*. زږګۍ *zijzga'ī*, s.f. (6th) The female hedgehog or porcupine. Sing. and Pl.

زست *zist*, s.m. (9th) (corrup. of P زيست) Life, living, existence. 2. Employment. Sing. and Pl. زست کول *zist kawul*, verb trans. To live, to exist. See ژوندون

زشکله *zash-kalah*, adv. Whenever, at whatever time.

زښا *zakhā*, s.f. (6th) The sound produced by roasting meat, etc. Sing. and Pl. (E.), See سښا and جز

زښت *zikht* (E) or *zisht* (W.), adj. Ugly, deformed, hideous. 2. Stern, severe; (Fem.) زښته *zikhta'h* or *zishta'h* (P زشت). Also written زيښت *zekht* or *zesht*.

A زعفران *zaæfarān*, s.m. (6th) Saffron. Sing. and Pl.

P زعفراني *zaæfarānī*, adj. Saffron-coloured, a yellow colour.

زغ *zagh*, s.m. (2nd) A yoke for oxen. Pl. زغونه *zaghūnah*. زغونډي *zghūnddaey*, s.m. (1st) A peg of the yoke, of which there are four. Pl. ي *ī*.

زغاست *z'ghāst*, s.m. (6th) (verb. n.) Assault and plunder, incursion, inroad, invasion, foray. Sing. and Pl. See زغاستل

زغاستل *z'ghās-tal*, verb intrans. (W.) To run, to move quickly, to take flight. This infinitive is imperfect, and is completed from زغليدل Past وُ زغاست *wu-z'ghāst*; act. part. زغاستونکي *z'ghāstūnkaey* or زغاستوني *z'ghāstūnaey*; past part. زغاستلي *z'ghāstalaey*; verb. n. زغاستنه *z'ghāstana'h* or زغاسته *z'ghāstah*. The other tenses are wanting.

زغاښتل *z'ghākhtal*, verb intrans. (E.) To run. This is also imperfect like the preceding, from which it only differs in substituting ښ for س. See زغليدل

زغرد *zghard*, adj. Quick, fleet, alert, nimble; (Fem.) زغرده *zgharda'h*. 2. adv. Quickly, fleetly, nimbly, alertly, actively.

زغره *z'ghara'h*, s.f. (3rd) Chain armour. Pl. ي *ey*. زغر يالي *z'ghar yālaey*, s.m. (1st) A man in armour. Pl. ي *ī*.

زغليدل *zghaledal*, verb intrans. To run, to move along quickly, to take flight. Pres. زغلي *zghalī*; past وُ زغليده *wu-zghaledah* or زغليدَ *zghaleda*; fut. و به زغلي *wu-bah zghalī*; imp. وُ زغله *wu-zghalah*; act. part. زغليدونکي *zghaledūnkaey* or زغليدوني *zghaledūnaey*; past part. زغليدلي *zghaledalaey*; verb. n. زغليدنه *zghaledana'h* or زغليده *zghaledah*. زغلول *zghalawul*, verb trans. To cause to run, to put to flight, to put to the rout. Pres. زغلوي *zghalawī*; past وُ زغلاوه *wu-zghalāwuh* or وُ زغلاوو *zghalāwo*; fut. وُ به زغلوي *wu bah zghalawī*; imp. وُ زغلوه *wu-zghalawah*; act. part. زغلوونکي *zghalawūnkaey* or زغلووني *zghalawūnaey*; past part. زغلولي *zghalawulaey*; verb. n. زغلونه *zghalawuna'h*.

زغمل *z'ghamal*, verb trans. To bear, to suffer, to endure, to sustain, to undergo, to put up with, to go through. Pres. زغمي *z'ghamī*; past وُ زغامه *wu-z'ghāmah* or زغامَ *z'ghāma*; fut. وُ به زغمي *wu bah z'ghamī*; imp. وُ زغمه *wu-z'ghamah*; act. part. زغمونکي *z'ghamūnkaey* or زغموني *z'ghamūnaey*; past part. زغملي

z'ghamalaey; verb. n. زغمنه z'ghamana'h.

P زغن zaghan, s.m. (5th) A kite. Pl. زغنان zaghanān.

زغورل z'ghoral, verb trans. To keep to preserve, to sustain, to support, to defend, to protect, to guard, to shield. Pres. زغوري z'ghorī; past وُ زغوره wu-z'ghorah; fut. وُ به زغوري wu bah z'ghorī; imp. وُ زغوره wu-z'ghorah; act. part. زغورونکَي z'ghorūnkaey or زغوروني z'ghorūnaey; past part. زغورلَي z'ghoralaey; verb. n. زغورنه z'ghorana'h. See ژغورل

زغوندَي z'ghūndaey, s.m. (1st) The peg of the yoke for oxen, of which there are four. Pl. ي ī.

A زقوم zakūm, s.m. (2nd) A thorny tree, the Indian prickly pear. Pl. زقومونه zakūmūnah.

زگ zik, s.m. (5th) An inflated leather bag used to cross rivers, called also *mask*, and made of the hide of a buffalo, cow, sheep, etc. 2. A bag or bottle made of leather for holding water and other articles. Pl. زکان zikān. See شناز and ژي

A زکاة, or زکات, or زکوت zakāt, s.m. (2nd) The portion of a man's property given in charity according to the rules laid down in the Ḳur'ān, alms. Pl. زکاتونه zakātūnah.

A زکام zukām, s.m. (2nd) Defluxion, rheum, catarrh, a cold. Pl. زکامونه zukāmūnah.

زکوزي zako-zī, s.m. (1st) Pl. The name of a tribe of Afghāns. زکوزَي zako-zaey, Sing. A man or male of the above. زکوزۍ zako-za'ī, s.f. (6th) A woman or female of the above tribe. Sing. and Pl.

زکه zakah, conj. For, because, therefore, on this account that. See ځکه and سکه

A زکي zakī, adj. (from زکا) One who regularly gives the زکاة zakāt, or alms, pious. 2. Pure, continent.

زگ zig (E.), adj. Rough, hard, harsh, rigid, severe; (Fem.) زگه ziga'h. زگیدل zigedal, verb intrans. To become or grow rough, stiff, harsh, severe. زگول zigawul, verb trans. To make or render rough, stiff, etc. See زږ and زیگ

زگ zag, s.m. (2nd) Froth, foam, head, spume. Pl. زگونه zagūnah. زگ لوستل zag lawastal, verb trans. To foam at the mouth, as a camel when angry.

زگر zigar, s.m. (2nd) The liver. 2. Boldness, bravery, courage. Pl. زگرونه zigarūnah. See ځگر

زگیروَي zgerwaey, s.m. (1st) A moan, a whine, a groan, complaint, lamentation. Pl. ي ī. زگیروَي کول zgerwaey kawul, verb trans. To moan, to groan, to whine, to wail, to bemoan, to complain, to lament.

زل zal, s.m. (5th) A horse-cloth, a covering for any animal. Pl. زلان zalān.

زل zal, s.m. (6th) (from زنل) Piercing, stabbing, impaling, pricking, sticking, puncturing, goring. Sing. and Pl. See زننه

A زلزله zalzala'h, s.f. (3rd) An earthquake. Pl. ې ey.

زلفه zulfa'h, s.f. (3rd) A curl, a lock of hair, a ringlet. Pl. ې ey. پریشاني زلفي pareshāney zulfey, Dishevelled locks, the hair unconfined or hanging about the neck or shoulders.

زلفۍ zulfa'ī, s.f. (6th) A staple, a hook of iron. Sing. and Pl. (from P).

A زلل zalal, s.m. (2nd) Blundering, erring. 2. Falling, stumbling. 3. Deficiency, loss. Pl. زللونه zalalūnah.

زلمَي zalmaey, s.m. (1st) A youth, a young man, a bridegroom. Pl. ي ī. زلمۍ zalma'ī, s.f. (6th) A young girl, a damsel, a bride. Sing. and Pl.

زلیچه zalīcha'h, s.f. (3rd) A carpet, a rug of cotton, silk, or wool. Pl. ې ey. See قالیچه

P زلیخا zulīkhā, s. prop. The name of Potiphar's wife.

زم zam, s.m. (2nd) A wound, a hurt, an injury. Pl. زمونه zamūnah. زم زمولَي zam z'molaey, adj. Helpless through wounds or injuries. 2. Carrying away the wounded from a field of battle, taking up a person and carrying him by seizing both hands and feet; (Fem.) زم زمولِ zam-z'moli. Pl. (Masc. and Fem.) ي ī.

A زمانه zamāna'h, s.f. (3rd) Time, an age. 2. The heavens. 3. The world. 4. Fortune, destiny. Pl. ې ey.

P زمرد *zumurrud*, s.m. (2nd) An emerald. Pl. زمردونه *zumurrudūnah*.

زمرئ *z'maraey*, s.m. (1st) A panther. Pl. ي *ī*; s.f. (6th) Sing. and Pl. ئ *a'ī*. See مزري

A زمزم *zamzam*, s. prop. A well at Makka, Hagar's well.

A زمزمه *zamzama'h*, s.f. (3rd) Singing, modulation, a concert. Pl. ې *ey*. زمزمه كول *zamzama'hkawul*, verb trans. To sing, to modulate.

زمكه *z'maka'h*, s.f. (3rd) Ground, land, soil, the earth. Pl. ې *ey*. زمكه ختته لاي *z'maka'h khatta'h lā'e*, Quagmire, soft muddy ground, bog.

زمند *zamand*, s.m. (6th) The name of an Afghān tribe, a male of the above. Sing. and Pl. زمنده *zamanda'h*, s.f. (3rd) A female of the tribe. Pl. ې *ey*.

زموخ *z'mokh*, adj. Astringent, binding, dry to the taste; also written زموخت *z'mokht*; (Fem.) زموخه *z'mokha'h* or زموخته *z'mokhta'h*.

زمول *z'mol*, adj. Helpless, unfortunate, afflicted, ruined, troubled, annoyed; (Fem.) زموله *z'mola'h*. زمولئ *z'molaey*, adj. as s.m. (1st) A person helpless or unfortunate; (Fem.) زمولِ *z'moli*. Pl. (Masc. and Fem.) ي *ī*. زم زمولئ *zam-z'molaey*, adj. Helpless through wounds or other injuries. See زم. زموليدل *z'moledal*, verb intrans. To become afflicted, annoyed, distressed, troubled, ruined, etc. Pres. زموليږي *z'molejzī* (W.) or زموليگي *z'molegī* (E.); past زمول شه *z'mol shah* or وُ شه *wu-shah*; fut. زمول به شي *z'mol bah shī* or به وُ شي *bah wu-shī*; imp. زمول شه *z'mol shah* or وُ شه *wu-shah*; act. part. زموليدونكئ *z'moledūnkaey* or زموليدونئ *z'moledūnaey*; past part. زمول *z'mol* or زمول شوئ *z'mol shawaey*; verb. n. زموليدنه *z'moledana'h* or زموليده *z'moledah*. زمولول *z'molawul*, verb trans. To afflict, to distress, to annoy, to trouble, to aggrieve, to ruin, etc. Pres. زمولوي *z'molawī*; past زمول كړ *z'mol karr* or وُ كړ *wu-karr*; fut. زمول به كړي *z'mol bah krrī* or به وُ كړي *bah wu-krrī*; imp. زمول كړه *z'mol krrah* or وُ كړه *wu-krrah*; act. part. زمولونكئ *z'molawūnkaey* or زمولونئ *z'molawūnaey*; past part. زمول كړئ *z'mol karraey*; verb. n. زمولونه *z'molawuna'h*.

زمئ *zamaey*, s.m. (1st) The winter, the cold season. Pl. ي *ī*. See ژمي

زمئ *z'ma'ī*, s.f. (6th) An alkaline tree, the seed or berry and leaves of which are used in washing. Sing. and Pl.

P زميندار *zamīndār*, s.m. (5th) (from زمين) A landlord, a holder of land, a farmer. Pl. زمينداران *zamīndārān*. زمينداره *zamīndāra'h*, s.f. (3rd) The wife of a farmer. Pl. ې *ey*. زميداري *zamīndārī*, s.f. (3rd) A fief, a landed estate. Pl. ئ *a'ī*. زميداري كول *zamīndārī kawul*, verb trans. To practice farming.

A زنا *zinā*, s.m. (9th) Adultery, fornication. Sing. and Pl. زنا كار *zinā-kār*, s.m. (5th) A fornicator, an adulterer. Pl. زنا كاران *zinā-kārān*. زنا كاره *zinā-kāra'h*, s.f. (3rd) An adultress, a fornicatress. Pl. ې *ey*. زنا كاري *zinā-kārī*, s.f. (3rd) Adultery, fornication. Pl. ئ *a'ī*. زنا كاري كول *zinā-kārī kawul*, verb trans. To fornicate, to commit adultery.

G A زنار *zunnār*, s.m. (2nd) A belt worn by Eastern Christians, Jews, and Magi; the sacred or brāhmanical cord worn by Hindūs, a Hindū rosary. Pl. زنارونه *zunnārūnah*.

زنازه *zanāza'h*, s.f. (3rd) A bier, a funeral. Pl. ې *ey*. See جنازه

P زنانه *zanāna'h*, adj. Female, feminine, effeminate, womanly. 2. s.f. (3rd) Women in general. 3. Female apartments, the ḥaram. Pl. ې *ey*.

P زنبق *zanbaķ*, s.m. (6th) The name of the white jasmine, a lily, or iris. 2. A flower worked on the border of a dress. Sing. and Pl.

زنبك *zunbuk*, s.m. (5th) A tassel, a knot, a rosette, a flower. Pl. زنبكان *zunbukān*. See زندي

زنبل *zanbal*, verb trans. To wink, to blink, to close the eyelids (as a cat in the sunlight), etc. See خمل for conjugation.

زنبه *zunba'h*, s.f. (3rd) Hair on the body. Pl. ئ *ey*. See تور ويښته

P زنجير *zanjīr*, s.m. (2nd) A chain. Pl. زنجيرونه *zanjīrūnah*.

P زنخ *zanakh* or زنخدان *zanakhdān*, s.m. (2nd) The chin, the pit in the chin. Pl. زنخونه *zanakhūnah* or زنخدانونه *zanakhdānūnah*. See زنه

P زندان *zindān*, s.m. (2nd) A jail, a prison. Pl. زندانونه *zindānūnah*. زنداني *zindānī*, adj. Imprisoned, confined, a prisoner.

P زندگاني *zindagānī* or زندگي *zindagī*, s.f. (3rd) Life, living, existence, livelihood. Pl. ئ *a'ī*. زندگاني کول *zindagānī kawul*, verb trans. To exist, to live, to gain a livelihood.

زندئ *zinda'ī*, s.f. (6th) A halter, a noose for hanging criminals. Sing. and Pl. See تيزندئ

زنډي *zanddaey*, s.m. (1st) A tassel, a pendant, an ornament. Pl. ي *ī*. See زنبک

زنزه *zanzā'h*, s.f. (3rd) A centipede. Pl. ئ *ey*.

زنځير *zandzīr*, s.m. (2nd) A chain. Pl. زنځيرونه *zandzīrūnah*. See زنجير

زنکئ *zanka'ī*, s.f. (6th) Cummin seed. Sing. and Pl.

زنګ *zang*, s.m. (2nd) A bell, a bell which dancing women fasten to their feet, a cymbal. Pl. زنګونه *zangūnah*. See زنګوله

P زنګ *zang*, s.m. (9th) Rust, mould, scum, dirt. Sing. and Pl. زنګ کيدل *zang kedal*, verb intrans. To rust, to become rusty. زنګ کول *zang kawul*, verb trans. To make rusty. زنګ شوی *zang shawaey* or زنګ خوړلی *zang khwarralaey*, adj. Rusty, covered with rust.

زنګل *zangal*, s.m. (2nd) A forest, a wood, a wild. Pl. زنګلونه *zangalūnah*. See ځنګل

زنګل *zangal*, verb intrans. To swing, to move to and fro, to vibrate, to wave, to hang. Pres. زانګي *zāngī*; fut. وُ به زانګي *wu bah zāngī*; imp. وُ زانګه *wu-zāngah*. The other tenses are wanting, and are taken from the infinitive زنګيدل, which see.

P زنګوله *zangūla'h*, s.f. (3rd) A small bell, the bell of a tambourine, a cymbal. Pl. ئ *ey*. See زنګ

زنګون *zangūn*, s.m. (2nd) The knee. Pl. زنګنونه *zanganūnah*. د زنګانه سترګه *da zangāna'h starga'h*, s.f. (3rd) The knee-cap. Pl. ئ *ey*. زنګون لګول *zangūn lagawul*, verb trans. To support, to aid, to assist. زنګنونه وهل *zanganūna'h wahal*, verb trans. To beat or slap the knees, *i.e.*, to show extreme grief or sorrow, as at the decease of any relation or friend.

P زنګي *zangī*, s.m. (5th) An Ethiop, a negro. Pl. زنګيان *zangīān*.

زنګيدل *zangedal*, verb intrans. To swing, to wave, to move to and fro, to vibrate, to hang, etc. Pres. زنګيږي *zangejzī* (W.) or زنګيګي *zangegī* (E.); past وُ زنګيده *wu-zangedah* or زنګيدَ *zangeda*; fut. وُ به زنګيږي *wu bah zangejzī* or زنګيګي *zangegī*; imp. وُ زنګيږه *wu-zangejzah* or زنګيګه *zangegah*; act. part. زنګيدونکی *zangedūnkaey* or زنګيدونی *zangedūnaey*; past part. زنګيدلی *zangedalaey*; verb. n. زنګيدنه *zangedana'h* or زنګيده *zangedah*.

زنګول *zangawul*, verb trans. To swing, to wave, to rock, to brandish, to move to and fro, to vibrate, etc. Pres. زنګوي *zangawī*; past وُ زنګاوه *wu-zangāwuh* or زنګاوو *zangāwo*; fut. وُ به زنګوي *wu bah zangawī*; imp. وُ زنګوه *wu-zangawah*; act. part. زنګوونکی *zangawūnkaey* or زنګووني *zangawūnaey*; past part. زنګولی *zangawulaey*; verb. n. زنګونه *zangawuna'h*.

زنل *zanal*, verb trans. To insert, to implant, to embed, to stick into, to plant, to stab, to pierce, to prick, to impale. Pres. زني *zanī*; past وُ زانه *wu-zānah* or زانَ *zāna*; fut. وُ به زني *wu bah zanī*; imp. وُ زنه *wu-zanah*; act. part. زنونکی *zanūnkaey* or زنونی *zanūnaey*; past part. زنلی *zanalaey*; verb. n. زننه *zanana'h*. See منډل and خرخول

زننه *zanana'h*, s.f. (3rd) (verb. n.) Piercing, stabbing, impaling, pricking, sticking, goring, puncturing, etc. Pl. ئ *ey*. See زل and خرخول

زنه *zana'h*, s.f. (3rd) The chin, the pit of the chin. Pl. ئ *ey*. See زنخ

P زنهار *zinhār* or زينهار *zīnhār*, adv. By no means, never. 2. interj. Beware! take care!

زنړغوزه *zarrnghoza'h*, s.f. (3rd) The cone of the pine tree, the tree itself. (E.) Pl. ې *ey*; also زنړغوزي *zarrnghozaey*, s.m. (1st). (W.) Pl. ي *ī*. See جلغوزه

زنړی *zarrnaey*, s.m. (1st) A seed or kernel in general. 2. A lad, a boy not arrived at puberty. Pl. ي *ī*. زنړکی *zarrnkaey*, s.m. (1st) A little boy or young lad (dimin. of the preceding). Pl. ي *ī*. See زوي

A زوال *zawāl*, s.m. (2nd) (from زول) Decline, declination, wane, cessation, wretchedness, the setting (as of the sun.) Pl. زوالونه *zawālūnah*.

P زود *zūd*, adv. Quick, quickly, nimbly, suddenly. See ژر. زودي *zūdī*, s.f. (3rd) Quickness, nimbleness, activity. Pl. ئي *a'ī*. زودي کول *zūdī kawul*, verb trans. To act with quickness, to make haste, to act rashly.

P زور *zor*, s.m. (2nd) Power, force, strength, vigour, violence, weight. Pl. زورونه *zorūnah*. 2. adv. Violently, forcibly, extremely. زور آور *zor-āwar* or زوروور *zorawar*, adj. Powerful, strong, violent; (Fem.) زور آوره *zor-āwara'h* or زوروره *zorawara'h*. Pl. ې *ey*. زور آوري *zor-āwarī* or زورووري *zorawarī*, s.f. (3rd) Force, power, violence. Pl. ئي *a'ī*. زور آوري کول *zor-āwarī kawul*, verb trans. To force, to compel, to act violently towards. زور کول *zor kawul*, verb trans. To use effort, to exert one's-self. زور زور *zor zor*, adj. Strong, mighty.

زورل *zoral*, verb trans. To vex, to provoke, to fret, to irritate. 2. To compel, to force, to coerce, to constrain, to use compulsion, main force, etc. 3. To digest, to cause digestion. Pres. زوري *zorī*; past و زوره *wu-zorah*; fut. و به زوري *wu bah zorī*; imp. و زوره *wu-zorah*; act. part. زورونکی *zorūnkaey* or زوروني *zorūnaey*; past part. زورلی *zoralaey*; verb. n. زورنه *zorana'h*.

زور *zawr*, s.m. (2nd) Grief, pain, anxiety, sorrow, affliction, trouble. Pl. زورونه *zawrūnah*. زوريدل *zawredal*, verb intrans. To become afflicted, pained, or grieved, to be sorrowful. Pres. زوريږي *zawrejzī* (W.) or زوريگي *zawregī* (E.); past و زوريده *wu-zawredah* or زوريدَ *zawreda*; fut. و به زوريږي *wu bah zawrejzī* or زوريگي *zawregī*; imp. و زوريږه *wu-zawrejzah* or زوريگه *zawregah*; act. part زوريدونکی *zawredūnkaey* or زوريدونی *zawredūnaey*; past part. زوريدلی *zawredalaey*; verb. n. زوريدنه *zawredana'h* or زوريده *zawredah*. زوروِل *zawrawul*, verb trans. To aggrieve, to trouble, to afflict, to make anxious or sorrowful. Pres. زوروي *zawrawī*; past و زوراوه *wu-zawrāwuh* or زوراوو *zawrāwo*; fut. و به زوروي *wu bah zawrawī*; imp. و زوروه *wu-zawrawah*; act. part. زوروونکی *zawrawūnkaey* or زوروونی *zawrawūnaey*; past part. زورولی *zawrawulaey*; verb. n. زوروونه *zawrawuna'h*. See خور

زور *zwar*, s.m. (2nd) The vowel point (ـَـ). Pl. زورونه *zwarūnah*.

زوړ *zawarr*, s.m. (9th) Declivity, dip, slope, fall, devexity, downhill. Sing. and Pl. 2. adj. Oblique, slanting, sloping, shelving; (Fem.) زوړه *zawarra'h*. لوړ زوړ *lawarr zawarr* or لوړه زوړه *lawarra'h zawarra'h*, Ascent and descent, rough or uneven ground.

زوړ *zorr*, adj. Old, aged, ancient, antiquated, of long standing, venerable, primitive, worn out (as clothes). Pl. زاړه *zārrah*; (Fem.) زړه *zarra'h*. Pl. زړې *zarrey*. زوړ or زړ والي *zorr* or *zarr-wāley*, s.m. (1st) Age, old age, senility, oldness, seniority, dotage, venerableness. Pl. والي *wālī*; also زوړ or زړ توب *zorr* or *zarr tob*, s.m. (2nd). Pl. توبونه *tobūnah*. زوړ or زړ تيا *zorr* or *zarr tī'ā*, s.f. (6th) (E.) Sing. and Pl. (W.) Pl. تياوي *tī'āwī*. See زړيدل and زړول

زوز *zoz*, s.m. (5th) A prickly bush, the camel thorn (Hedysarum altragi). Pl. زوزان *zozān*. See خوز

زوزات *zū-zāt*, s.m. (2nd) Progeny, issue, species, posterity. Pl. زوزاتونه *zū-zātūnah*. See زوزاد

P زوزاد *za-o-zād* or زهوزاد *zah-o-zād*, s.m. (2nd) Progeny, posterity, issue, descendants, species. Pl. زوزادونه *za-o-zādūnah* or زهوزادونه *zah-o-zādūnah*.

زوږ *zwajz*, s.m. (2nd) Noise, sound, din, uproar, cry, clamour, exclamation; the murmuring of a brook, rippling, rustling of leaves, noise of a high wind, the noise of cattle feeding or walking along. 2. Concern, grief, sorrow, distress, affliction, woe, bitterness; agony, anguish. Pl. زوږونه *zwajzūnah*. See زوګ.

زوږ کول *zwajz kawul*, verb trans. To make a noise, din, uproar, etc.; to rustle, to murmur.

زوښه *zokha'h*, s.f. (3rd) A kind of syrup, or beverage made from the juice of the *ber* or jujube and sweetened. Pl. ې *ey*.

زوګ *zwag*, s.m. (2nd) Noise, sound, clamour, murmur, rustling, etc. Pl. زوګونه *zwagūnah*. زوګ کول *zwag kawul*, verb trans. To make a noise, din, uproar, outcry, etc.; to murmur, to rustle, to moan or whistle as the wind, etc. See زوږ *zwajz*.

زولانه *zolāna'h* or زولنه *zolana'h*, s.f. (3rd) A fetter, a chain for criminals. Pl. ې *ey*. See ځولنه

زوم *zūm*, s.m. (5th) A son-in-law. Pl. زومان *zūmān*. زومګی *zūmgaey*, s.m. (1st) A son-in-law (dimin. of the above). Pl. ي *ī*.

زوم *z'wam*, adj. Deficient, less, little, scanty, rarely, seldom. 2. Lessened, reduced, curtailed, abated, removed, subtracted, withdrawn. 3. Lost, deducted, taken away; (Fem.) زومه *z'wama'h*. زوم کیدل *z'wam kedal*, verb intrans. To become less, reduced, deducted, removed, to lessen, to decrease, to abate, etc. زوم کول *z'wam kawul*, verb trans. To remove, to reduce, to lessen, to withdraw, to subtract, to deduct, to diminish, to make or render less, to depreciate.

زومنه *z'wamna'h*, s.f. (3rd) Soup, broth. Pl. ې *ey*. See ښوروا

زوول *zowul*, verb intrans. To be born, to be brought forth (as young). Past وُ زوو *wu-zonū*; past part. زوولی *zowulaey*. The remaining tenses are wanting. See زیږیدل

زوه *zawa'h*, s.f. (3rd) Pus, matter, rheum. Pl. ې *ey*. زولن *zaw-lan*, adj. Rheumy, covered with pus or matter; (Fem.) زولنه *zaw-lana'h*. زوي بهیدل *zawey bahedal* or زوي وتل *zawey watal*, verb intrans. To ooze, as matter from a wound.

زوی *zo-e*, s.m. (5th) A son. Pl. زامن *zāman* or زهمن *zahman*. زوي مړی *zo-e marraey* or زومړی *zo-marraey*, A person who has lost his son; (Fem.) زوي مړ *zoey marri*. Pl. (Masc. and Fem.) ي *ī*.

زه *zah*, pers. pron. 1st person 'I.' It becomes changed by inflection into ما *mā*. Pl. موږ *mūjz*, and منګا *mungā* or منګ *munga*. See Grammar, p. 30.

A زهد *zuhd*, s.m. (2nd) Continence, devotion, abstinence. Pl. زهدونه *zuhdūnah*. زهد کول *zuhd kawul*, verb trans. To act devoutly, to practice abstinence. See زاهد

P زهر *zahr*, s.m. (6th) Poison. Sing. and Pl. زهر آلود *zahr ālūd*, adj. Poisoned, mixed with poison. زهر قاتل *zahr-i-ḳātil*, Deadly poison. زهر مهره *zahr muhrah*, s.f. (3rd) The bezoar, an antidote for poison. Pl. ې *ey*.

P زهره *zahra'h*, s.f. (3rd) The gall-bladder, bile. 2. Courage, boldness. Pl. ې *ey*. زهره چودل *zahra'h chawdal*, verb intrans. To be much distressed or terrified.

زهګیر *zih-gīr*, s.m. (2nd) The notch at each extremity of a bow for fastening the bow-string. Pl. زهګیرونه *zih-gīrūnah*.

زهوب *zahūb*, s.m. (2nd) Matter, pus, discharge, rheum. Pl. زهوبونه *zahūbūnah*. See زوه

زهیدل *zahedal*, verb intrans. To lessen, or grow less, to decrease, to waste away through sickness or grief, to become thin, etc. Pres. زهيږي *zahejzī* (W.) or زهیګي *zahegī* (E.); past وُ زهیده *wu-zahedah* or زهیدَ *zahedā*; fut. وُ به زهيږي *wu bah zahejzī* or زهیګي *zahegī*; imp. وُ زهیده *wu-zahedah*; act. part. زهیدونکی *zahedūnkaey* or زهیدونی *zahedūnaey*; past part. زهیدلی *zahedalaey*; verb. n. زهیدنه *zahedana'h* or زهیده *zahedah*.

زهول *zahawul*, verb trans. To lessen, to reduce by sickness, grief, or affliction. Pres. زهوي *zahawī*; past وُ زهاوه *wu-zahāwuh* or زهاوو *zahāwo*; fut. وُ به زهوي *wu bah zahawī*; imp. وُ زهوه *wu-zahawah*; act. part. زهوونکی

zahawūnkaey or زهووني *zahawūnaey*; past part. زهولي *zahawulaey*; verb. n. زهونه *zahawuna'h.*

A زهير *zahīr*, adj. (from زهر) Reduced by sickness or distress, thin. 2. Sad, melancholy, troubled in mind, low-spirited, dejected; (Fem.) زهيره *zahīrā'h.* زهير والي *zahīr wālaey*, s.m. (1st) Distress, sadness, trouble, dejection. Pl. والي *wālī*, also زهيرتوب *zahīr tob*, s.m. (2nd). Pl. توبونه *tobūnah.* زهير تيا *zahīr tīā*, s.f. (6th). (E.) Sing. and Pl. (W.) Pl. تياوي *tīāwī.* زهيريدل *zahīredal*, verb intrans. To become thin or emaciated through sickness, to become sad, down-hearted, or melancholy. Pres. زهيريږي *zahīrejzī* (W.) or زهيريگي *zahīregī* (E.); past زهير شه *zahīr shah* or وُ شه *wu-shah*; fut. زهير به شي *zahīr bah shī* or به وُ شي *bah wu-shī*; imp. زهير شه *zahīr shah* or وُ شه *wu-shah*; act. part. زهيريدونكي *zahīredūnkaey* or زهيريدوني *zahīredūnaey*; past part. زهير *zahīr* or زهير شوي *zahīr shawaey*; verb. n. زهيريدنه *zahīredana'h* or زهيريده *zahīredah.* زهيرول *zahīrawul*, verb trans. To distress, to aggrieve, to reduce, to make thin or emaciated (as disease). Pres. زهيروي *zahīrawī*; past زهير كړ *zahīr karr* or وُ كړ *wu karr*; fut. زهير به كړي *zahīr bah krrī* or به وُ كړي *bah wu-krrī*; imp. زهير كړه *zahīr krrah* or وُ كړه *wu-krrah*; act. part. زهيروونكي *zahīrawūnkaey* or زهيرووني *zahīrawūnaey*; past part. زهيركړي *zahīr karraey*; verb. n. زهيرونه *zahīrawuna'h.*

زي *zaey*, s.m. (1st) (In composition) A son, a descendant, as Mc, Fitz, O', etc. It is generally affixed to the names of Afghān tribes, as باركزي *bārakzaey*, A man of the Bārakzī tribe. Pl. ي *ī.* ئي *a'ī*, s.f. (6th). Sing. and Pl. See زوي

زيات *zī'āt*, adj. More, additional, excessive, too much, too many, etc.; (Fem.) زياته *zī'āta'h.* له حدَ زيات *lah hada zī'āt*, Beyond bounds, excessive; or زيات والي *zī-āt-wālaey*, s.m. (1st). Pl. والي *wālī*; or زيات توب *zī'āt-tob*, s.m. (2nd) Augmentation, increase, addition, excess, surplus. Pl. توبونه *tobūnah.* زياته بخره *zī'āta'h bakhra'h*, s.f. (3rd) The largest or lion's share. Pl. ئي *ey.* زياتيدل *zī'ātedal*, verb intrans. To increase, to grow, to become greater in bulk or quantity, to swell (as water of rivers), to become larger, to enlarge. Pres. زياتيږي *zī'ātejzī* (W.) or زياتيگي *zī'ātegī* (E.); past زيات شه *zī'āt shah* or وُ شه *wu-shah*; fut. زيات به شي *zī'āt bah shī* or به وُ شي *bah wu-shī*; imp. زيات شه *zī'āt shah* or وُ شه *wu-shah*; act. part. زياتيدونكي *zī'ātedūnkaey* or زياتيدوني *zī'ātedūnaey*; past part. زيات *zī'āt* or زيات شوي *zī'āt shawaey*; verb. n. زياتيدنه *zī'ātedana'h* or زياتيده *zī'ātedah.* زياتول *zī'ātawul*, verb trans. To increase, to augment, to extend, to spread, to aggravate, to add to. Pres. زياتوي *zī'ātawī*; past زيات كړ *zī'āt karr* or وُ كړ *wu-karr*; fut. زيات به كړي *zī'āt bah krrī* or به وُ كړي *bah wu-krrī*; imp. زيات كړه *zī'āt krrah* or وُ كړه *wu-krrah*; act. part. زياتوونكي *zī'ātawūnkaey* or زياتووني *zī'ātawūnaey*; past part. زيات كړي *zī'āt karraey*; verb. n. زياتونه *zī'ātawuna'h.*

زياتي *zī'ātī*, adj. More, excessive. See زيات

A زياد *ziyād* or زياده *ziyādah*, adj. More, additional, etc. See زيات

A زيارت *zi-yārat*, s.m. (2nd) A pilgrimage, visiting a shrine. 2. A shrine, the tomb of a saint. Pl. زيارتونه *zi-yāratūnah.* زيارت كول *zi-yārat kawul*, verb trans. To make or perform a pilgrimage, to go on a pilgrimage. د زيارت روځ *da zi-yārat rwadz*, The Day of Pilgrimage, Thursday.

P زيان *zi-yān*, s.m. (2nd) Injury, hurt, harm, mischief, detriment, loss, damage, deficiency. Pl. زيانونه *zi-yānūnah.* زيان كار *zi-yān kār*, adj. Doing mischief, hurtful, injurious; (Fem.) زيان كاره *zi-yān kāra'h.* زيان كاري *zi-yān kārī*, s.f. (3rd) The doing mischief, damage or injury, hurtfulness. Pl. ئي *a'ī.* زيان كاري كول *zi-yān kārī kawul*, verb trans. To commit injury, to do or make mischief, damage, etc. زيان کول *zi-yān kawul*, verb trans. To cause harm, hurt, injury, etc.; to injure. زيان من *zi-yān man*, adj. Injured, harmed, hurt; (Fem.) زيان منه *zi-yān mana'h*. Pl. ې *ey*; also زياني *zi-yānī*. (Masc. and Fem.)

P زيب *zeb*, s.m. (2nd) Beauty, elegance, ornament, adornment. Pl. زيبونه *zebūnah*. زيب و زينت *zeb-o-zī-nat*, Adornment, ornament. زيبا *zebā*, adj. Beautiful, adorned, decorated, ornamented. زيبائي *ze-bā'ī*, s.f. (3rd) Gracefulness, beauty, elegance. Pl. ئې *a'ī*.

زيتونه *zaitūna'h*, s.f. (3rd) The olive tree. Pl. ې *ey*. (A زيتون).

P زير *zer*, adv. Under, below. 2. The vowel point (ِ), called also کسره *kasra'h*, sounded as Italian or short *i*. زير و زبر *zer-o-zabar*, adv. Topsy turvy, upside down. زير و زبر کول *zer-o-zabar kawul*, verb trans. To invert, to overturn, to ruin, to destroy. زير دست *zer-dast*, adj. Powerless, under command, vanquished; a subject, a vassal. زير کول *zer kawul*, verb trans. To subdue, to vanquish, to overpower. زير تنګ *zer tang*, s.m. (2nd) The under girth of a saddle. Pl. زير تنګونه *zer tangūnah*.

P زير *zīr*, s.m. (5th) The fine or highest note of a lute; the treble in music. Pl. زيران *zīrān*.

زير *zīr*, s.m. (9th) Contemplation, view, survey, etc. Sing. and Pl. زير کول *zīr kawul*, verb trans. To view, to contemplate. See خير

زير استر *zer-āstar*, s.m. (2nd) A lining in general, Pl. زير استرونه *zer-āstarūnah*.

P زيرک *zī-rak*, adj. Acute, shrewd, penetrating, sagacious, intelligent, ingenious; (Fem.) زيرکه *zī-raka'h*. 2. s.m. (6th) The name of one of the great divisions of the Durānī Afghāns. Sing. and Pl. See Introduction to my Grammar, page 12. زيرکي *zī-rakī*, s.f. (3rd) Acumen, sagacity, ingenuity, acuteness, discernment. Pl. ئې *a'ī*.

زيرمه *zerma'h*, s f. (3rd) Preparation, making ready, providing, provision, putting in order, arrangement, disposal; make, formation. Pl. ې *ey*. زيرمه کول *zerma'h kawul*, verb trans. To arrange, to set or put in order, to organize, to dispose, to provide, etc.

زيره ګري *zerah-garey*, s.m. (1st) A person who brings glad tidings or good news. Pl. ي *ī*. s.f. (8th) زيره ګرِ *zerah-gari*. Pl. ي *ī*.

زيرئ *zeraey*, s.m. (1st) Good news, glad tidings, Pl. ي *ī*. زيرئ کول *zeraey kawul* or ورل *w'rral*, verb trans. To give good news, to carry glad tidings.

زيړ *zi-yarr*, s.m. (6th) Brass. Sing. and Pl. 2. adj. Yellow; (Fem.) زيړه *zi-yarra'h*. زيړئ *zi-yarraey*, s.m. (1st) Yellowness. 2. The jaundice. Pl. ي *ī*. زيړيدل *zi-yarredal*, verb intrans. To become of a yellow colour through sickness, to be dyed yellow. Pres. زيړيږي *zi-yarrejzī* (W.) or زيړيګي *zi-yarregī* (E.); past زيړ شه *zi-yarr shah* or و شه *wu-shah*; fut. زيړ به شي *zi-yarr bah shī* or به و شي *bah wu-shī*; imp. زيړ شه *zi-yarr shah* or و شه *wu-shah*; act. part. زيړيدونکئ *zi-yarredūnkaey* or زيړيدونئ *zi-yarredūnaey*; past part. زيړ *zi-yarr* or زيړ شوئ *zi-yarr shawaey*; verb. n. زيړيدنه *zi-yarredana'h* or زيړيده *zi-yarredah*. زيړول *zi-yarrawul*, verb trans. To make yellow, to dye of a yellow colour, to yellow or make yellow (as sickness). Pres. زيړوي *zi-yarrawī*; past زيړ کړ *zi-yarr karr* or و کړ *wu-karr*; fut. زيړ به کړي *zi-yarr bah krrī* or به و کړي *bah wu krrī*; imp. زيړ کړه *zi-yarr krrah* or و کړه *wu-krrah*; act. part. زيړوونکئ *zi-yarrawūnkaey* or زيړوونئ *zī-yarrawūnaey*; past part. زيړ کړئ *zi-yarr karraey*; verb. n. زيړونه *zi-yarrawunah*.

زيړانکه *zi-yarrānaka'h*, s.f. (3rd) The yellow-wagtail. Pl. ې *ey*. The common grey bird is called شين توپئ *shīn-topa'ī*, s.f. (6th). Sing. and Pl.

زيزمه *zezma'h*, s.f. (3rd) The eyelid. Pl. ې *ey*. See جيرمه

زيږيدل *zejzedal* (W.) or زيګيدل *zegedal* (E.) verb intrans. To be born, to be brought forth. Pres. زيږي *zejzī* or زيګي *zegī*; past و زيږيده *wu-zejzedah* or و زيګيده *wu-zegedah*; fut.

وُ به زيږي *wu bah zejzī* or وُ به زيګي *wu bah zegī*; imp. وُ زيږه *wu-zejzah* or وُ زيګه *wu-zegah*; act. part. زيږيدونكَي *zejzedūnkaey* or زيږيدونيَ *zejzedūnaey* or زيګيدونكَي *zegedūnkaey* or زيګيدونيَ *zegedūnaey*; past part. زيږيدليَ *zejzedalaey* or زيګيدليَ *zegedalaey*; verb. n. زيږيدنه *zejzedana'h* or زيګيدنه *zegedana'h* or زيږيده *zejzedah* or زيګيده *zegedah*.

زيږول *zejzawul* (W.) or زيګول *zegawul* (E.) To procreate, to beget, to propagate. Pres. زيږوي *zejzawī* or زيګوي *zegawī*; past وُ زيږاوه *wu-zejzāwuh* or وُ زيږاوو *zejzāwo* or وُ زيګاوه *wu-zegāwuh* or زيګاوو *zegāwo*; fut. وُ به زيږوي *wu bah zejzawī* or وُ به زيګوي *wu bah zegawī*; imp. وُ زيږوه *wu-zejzawah* or وُ زيګوه *wu-zegawah*, act. part. زيږوونكَي *zejzawūnkaey* or زيږوونيَ *zejzawūnaey* or زيګوونكَي *zegawūnkaey* or زيګوونيَ *zegawūnaey*; past part. زيږوليَ *zejzawulaey* or زيګوليَ *zegawulaey*; verb. n. زيږونه *zejzawuna'h* or زيګونه *zegawuna'h*.

P زيست *zīst* and زيست كول *zīst kawul*, verb trans. See زست

زيګ *zīg*, adj. (E.) Rough, hard, stiff, rigid; stern, harsh; (Fem.) زيګه *zīga'h*. زيګيدل *zīgedal*, verb intrans. To become or grow rough, hard, harsh, etc. زيګول *zīgawul*, verb trans. To make or render hard, harsh, rough, stiff, etc. See زږ

زيګګي *zīggaey*, s.m. (1st) (E) A porcupine, a hedge-hog. Pl. ي *ī*. See زږګي

زيله *zela'h*, s.f, (3rd) The branch, or tendril of a creeper, a creeping plant in general. Pl. ې *ey*. See جرنګ

زيلۍ *zela'ī*, s.f. (6th) A creeper. Sing. and Pl. Also written زيل *zeyl*, s.m. (2nd). Pl. زيلونه *zeylūnah*. See preceding.

زيم *z'yam*, s.m. (2nd) Dampness of the ground, moisture, humidity, dankness, wetness. Pl. زيمونه *z'yamūnah*. زيم ناك *z'yam-nāk*, adj. Moist, damp, humid, dank, swampy, wet; (Fem.) زيم ناكه *z'yam-nāka'h*. زيم والىَ *z'yam-wālaey*, s.m. (1st) Dampness, moisture, humidity, wetness. Pl. والي *wālī*. زيم كول *z'yam kawul*, verb trans. To show dampness or humidity (as a wall, etc.)

P زين *zīn*, s.m. (5th) A saddle. Pl. زينان *zīnān*. زين ييښول *zīn yeshawul* (W.) or *yekhawul* (E.) or زينول *zīnawul*, verb trans. To saddle. زين پوښ *zīn-posh* (W.) or *pokh* (E.) s.m. (2nd) A cloth fastened over the saddle, a housing. Pl. زين پوښونه *zīn poshūnah* or *pokhūnah*. زين ساز *zīn-sāz*, s.m. (5th) A saddler. Pl. سازان *sāzān*.

A زينت *zīnat*, s.m. (2nd) Ornament, decoration, dress, elegance, adornment, beauty. Pl. زينتونه *zīnatūnah*. زينت كول *zīnat kawul*, verb trans. To adorn, to ornament, to decorate.

P زينه *zīna'h*, s.f. (3rd) A ladder, stairs, a pair or set of steps. Pl. ې *ey*. See اندرپايه

P زيور *zewar*, s.m. (2nd) An ornament of gold, or silver, jewelry. Pl. زيورونه *zewarūnah*.

څ

څ *dze* or *dse* is the eighteenth letter of the Pushto alphabet, and is pronounced as *dz* or *ds* in English. There is no equivalent for it in either Arabic, Persian, or Sanskrit, but most of the Semitic languages have a letter of the same sound, and so have several of the Tartārian dialects. It is used with some foreign words for ج and چ

څار *dzār* or *dsār*, s.m. (9th) Sacrifice, oblation, consecration, an offering, a victim, redemption, offering or devoting one's-self to save or preserve another, ransom, cartel. Sing. and Pl. څاريدل *dzārredal* or *dsāredal*, verb intrans. To be sacrificed or devoted, to be offered as an oblation, to be consecrated. څارول *dzārawul* or *dsārawul*, verb trans. To sacrifice, to devote, to offer as a sacrifice or oblation. For conjugation, see جار and زار

څاله *dzāla'h*, s.f. (3rd) The nest of a bird, the web of a spider. Pl. ې *ey*.

څان *dzān*, s.m. (2nd) Life, soul, spirit, mind,

self. 2. A sweetheart. 3. The private parts. Pl. ځانونه dzānūnah. 4. adj. Dear, beloved. ځان خورګي dzān khūragī, s.f. (3rd) Exhaustion, dejection, vexation. Pl. ئ a'ī. ځان خورګي كول dzān khūragī kawul, verb trans. To exhaust, to deject, to vex, to oppress.

ځان دار dzān dār, adj. Having life, an animal; (Fem.) ځان داره dzān dāra'h. ځان داري dzān dārī, s.f. (3rd) Animation, spirit, spiritedness. Pl. ئ a'ī. ځان ځاني dzān dzānī, s.f. (3rd) Selfishness, egotism, taking care of number one, self interest. Pl. ئ a'ī. ځان سپارل dzān spāral, verb trans. To resign one's life, or risk the life on any matter or thing. ځان كندن dzān kandan, s.m. (2nd) Gasping in the agonies of death, agony, torture. Pl. ځان كندنونه dzān kandanūnah, or ځن كندن dzan kandan, etc. خپل ځان khpul dzān, He, himself, etc. خپل ځان وجلل khpul dzān wajlal, verb trans. To commit suicide, to take anything much to heart, to grieve excessively. See P جان

ځاي dzā'e, s.m. (2nd) A place, situation, site, station, direction, whereabouts. Pl. ځايونه dzā'e-ūna'h. ځاي په ځاي dzā'e pah dzā'e, adv. Every place, from place to place, everywhere. ځاي لري dzā'e larī, adj. Fit, proper, suitable, advisable, becoming. ځاي لرل dzāe laral, verb trans. To fit, to suit, to adapt, to be fitted to. ځاي مانده dzā'e māndah, adj. Impotent, incapable, remaining in a place through sickness, etc. ځاي نيول dzā'e nīwal, verb trans. To take up a situation, to take up a residence, to locate one's-self, to inhabit. 2. To take effect (as advice). په ځاي راوړل pah dzā'e rā-w'rral, verb trans. To finish, to accomplish, to fulfil, to obey, to carry out. ځايدل dzā'edal, verb intrans. To retain, to contain, to hold, to take in, to admit, to embrace, to include, etc. Pres. ځايږي dzā'ejzī (W.) or ځايګي dzā'egī (E.); past ځاي شه dzā'e shah or وُ شه wu-shah; fut. ځاي به شي dzā'e bah shī or به وُ شي bah wu-shī; imp. ځاي شه dzā'e shah or وُ شه wu-shah; act. part. ځايدونكي dzā'edūnkaey or ځايدوني dzā'edūnaey; past part. ځاي شوي dzā'e shawaey; verb. n. ځايدنه dzā'edana'h or ځايده dzā'edah. ځايول dzā'eawul, verb trans. To make or cause to contain, embrace, take in, hold, admit, include, etc.. Pres. ځايوي dzā'eawī; past ځاي كړ dzā'e karr or وُ كړ wu-karr; fut. ځاي به كړي dzā'e bah krrī or به وُ كړي bah wu-krrī; imp. ځاي كړه dzā'e krrah or وُ كړه wu-krrah; act. part. ځايونكي dzā'e-awūnkaey or ځايوني dzā'e-awūnaey; past part. ځاي كړي dzā'e karraey; verb. n. ځايونه dzā'eawuna'h.

ځبل dzabal, verb trans. To pound, to bruise, to reduce to powder. Pres. ځبي dzabī; past وُ ځابه wu-dzābah; fut. وُ به ځبي wu bah dzabī; imp. وُ ځبه wu-dzabah; act. part. ځبونكي dzabūnkaey or ځبوني dzabūnaey; past part. ځبلي dzabalaey; verb. n. ځبنه dzabana'h.

ځبله dzab-lah, adv. Together, along with, in company, one with another. ځبله باندِ dzab-lah bāndi, adj. Fold on fold, plait on plait, etc. See زبله

ځبن dzaban, adj. Ill-bred, brutish, barbarous; (Fem.) ځبنه dzabana'h. 2. s.m. (5th) A dolt, a lout, a clown, a fool. Pl. ځبُن dzabæn. ځبنه dzabana'h, s.f. (3rd) A fat, brutish woman. Pl. ئ ey.

ځبيښل dzbe-shal (W.) or dzbe-khal (E.) verb trans. To suck, to draw into the mouth, to draw out, to imbibe, to inhale. For conjugation, see زبيښل

ځنځه dzakhah, post-pos. added to the ablative case, Near, hard by, with, close to, neighbouring, contiguous. را ځنځه rā dzakhah, Near or close to me or us. در ځنځه dar dzakhah, With or near thee or you. ور ځنځه war dzakhah, With or near him or them.

ځري dzaraey, s.m. (1st) A spy, a scout, a vidette, one who ogles or peeps. Pl. ي ī. ځرئ dzaru'ī, s.f. (6th) Sing. and Pl. See زرئ and زري

ځريدل dzarredal, verb intrans. To hang, to

dangle, to swing, to be pendulous or pendant. Pres. ځړيږي dza̱rrejzī (W.) or ځړيږي dza̱rregī (E.); past وُ ځړيده wu-dza̱rredah or ځړيدَ dza̱rreda; fut. وُ به ځړيږي wu bah dza̱rrejzī or ځړيږي dza̱rregī; imp. وُ ځړيږه wu-dza̱rrejzah or ځړيږه dza̱rregah; act. part. ځړيدونکي dza̱rredūnkaey or ځړيدوني dza̱rredūnaey; past part. ځړيدلي dza̱rredalaey; verb. n. ځړيدنه dza̱rredana'h. ځړول dza̱rrawul, verb trans. To hang, to sling, to suspend, to hook up, to fasten to. Pres. ځړوي dza̱rrawī; past وُ ځړاوه wu-dza̱rrāwuh or وُ ځړاوو wu-dza̱rrāwo; fut. وُ به ځړوي wu bah dza̱rrawī; imp. وُ ځړوه wu-dza̱rrawah; act. part. ځړوونکي dza̱rrawūnkaey or ځړووني dza̱rrawūnaey; past part. ځړولي dza̱rrawulaey; verb. n. ځړونه dza̱rrawunah. See ځوړنديدل and ځوړندول

ځز dza̱z, s.m. (5th) A hissing sound produced by sprinkling water on fire, etc., fizz, fizzle, spitting (as meat ejecting gravy when roasting). Pl, ځزهار dza̱zahār. ځزکي dza̱z-kaey, s.m. (1st) (the dimin. of the preceding), *lit.* a little or slight fizz. Pl. ي ī. ځزلرل or وهل dza̱z laral or wahal, verb trans. To hiss, to fizz, to spit, to fizzle.

ځکه dza̱kah, adv. For this reason, on this account, consequently.

ځگر dzi̱gar, s.m. (2nd) The liver, the vitals, the heart, mind, courage, etc. Pl. ځگرونه dzi̱gar-ūnah. (P جگر) ځگر سوخته dzi̱gar sokhtah, adj. Heart inflamed, in love. ځگر سوز dzi̱gar soz, adj. Moving, afflicting, heart inflaming, tormenting; (Fem.) ځگر سوزه dzi̱gar soza'h. ځگري dzi̱garī, adj. Belonging to the liver, hepatic. 2. The colour of the liver.

ځل dza̱l, s.m. (5th) The clothing for a horse, a horse-cloth. Pl. ځلان dza̱lān.

ځل dza̱l, adv. Once, at one time; or يو ځل yow-dza̱l. دوه ځله dwah dza̱lah, Twice, etc.

ځله dza̱la'h, s.f. (3rd) Distraction of mind, perplexity, hesitation, apprehension. Pl. ې ey.

ځليدل dza̱ledal, verb intrans. To shine, to glitter, to glow, to glisten, to gleam, to glare, to sparkle, to coruscate. Pres. ځليږي dza̱lejzī (W.) or ځليکي dza̱legī (E.); past وُ ځليده wu-dza̱ledah or ځليدَ dza̱leda; fut. وُ به ځليږي wu bah dza̱lejzī or ځليکي dza̱legī; imp. وُ ځليږه wu-dza̱lejzah or ځليکه dza̱legah; act. part. ځليدونکي dza̱ledūnkaey or ځليدوني dza̱ledūnaey; past part. ځليدلي dza̱ledalaey; verb. n. ځليدنه dza̱ledana'h or ځليده dza̱ledah. ځلول dza̱lawul, verb trans. To cause to shine or glitter, to make to gleam, glisten, flare, sparkle, etc. Pres ځلوي dza̱lawī; past وُ ځلاوه wu-dza̱lāwuh or ځلاوو dza̱lāwo; fut. وُ به ځلوي wu bah dza̱lawī; imp. وُ ځلوه wu-dza̱lawah; act. part. ځلوونکي dza̱lawūnkaey or ځلووني dza̱lawūnaey; past part. ځلولي dza̱lawulaey; verb. n. ځلونه dza̱lawuna'h.

ځما dza̱mā, The genitive case of the first personal pronoun زه, 'Mine, of me.' See Grammar, page 30. Pl. ځموږ dza̱mūjz or ځمونګ dza̱mūnga, Ours, of us.

ځمل dza̱mal, verb trans. To wink, to blink, to close the eyelids (as a cat in the sunlight). Pres. ځمي dza̱mī; past وُ ځامه wu-dzā̱mah or ځامَ dzā̱ma; fut. وُ به ځمي wu bah dza̱mī; imp. وُ ځمه wu-dza̱mah; act. part. ځمونکي dza̱mūnkaey or ځموني dza̱mūnaey; past part. ځملي dza̱malaey; verb. n. ځمنه dza̱mana'h. See زنبل and ځنبل

ځنِ dzi̱ni or ذنِ zi̱ni, indef. pron. Some, any, a few, etc. Sing. and Pl. See ځني

ځناور dza̱nāwar, s.m. (5th) An animal, a beast. Pl. ځناوران dza̱nāwarān. (P جانور).

ځنبل dza̱mbal, verb trans. To wink, to blink, to close the eyes (as a cat in the sunlight). See ځمل for conjugation, and substitute نب for م.

ځنډ dza̱ndd, s.m. (2nd) Delay, slowness, tardiness, lateness, procrastination. Pl. ځنډونه dza̱nddūnah. ځنډ کيدل dza̱ndd kedal, verb intrans. To be late or tardy. ځنډ کول dza̱ndd kawul, verb trans. To tarry, to delay, to procrastinate, to dawdle, to linger, to loiter, etc. ځنډيدل dza̱nddedal, verb intrans. To delay, to linger, to loiter, to move slowly, to stop for a time, to be tardy or late. Pres. ځنډيږي dza̱nddejzī (W.) or ځنډيکي dza̱nddegī (E):

past وُ څنډيده *wu-dzanddedah*; fut. وُ به څنډيږي *wu bah dzanddejzī* or څنډيګي *dzanddegī*; imp. وُ څنډيږه *wu-dzanddejzah* or څنډيګه *dzanddegah*; act. part. څنډيدونکَي *dzanddedūnkaey* or څنډيدونَي *dzanddedūnaey*; past part. څنډيدلَي *dzanddedalaey*; verb. n. څنډيدنه *dzanddedana'h*. څنډول *dzanddawul*, verb trans. To delay, to detain, to hinder, to cause detention or delay. Pres. څنډوي *dzanddawī*; past وُ څنډاوه *wu-dzanddāwuh* or څنډاوو *dzanddāwo*; fut. وُ به څنډوي *wu bah dzanddawī*; imp. وُ څنډوه *wu-dzanddawah*; act. part. څنډوونکَي *dzanddawūnkaey* or څنډوونَي *dzanddawūnaey*; past part. څنډولَي *dzanddawulaey*; verb. n. څنډونه *dzanddawuna'h*.

څنځير *dzandzīr*, s.m. (2nd) A chair. Pl. څنځيرونه *dzandzīrūnah*. See (P زنجير).

څنګل *dzangal*, s.m. (2nd) A forest, a wood, a wild tract of country. Pl. څنګلونه *dzangalūnah*. څنګلي *dzangalī*, adj. Wild, savage, barbarian, clown, boor; (Fem.) څنګلۍ *dzangala'ī*.

څني *dzinī* or ذني *zinī*, indef. pron. Some, any, a few, etc. Sing. and Pl. Masc. and Fem. See ذنِ and څنِ

څنړَي *dzarrnaey*, s.m. (1st) A lad, a boy not arrived at puberty. Pl. ي *ī*. څنړکَي *dzarrnakaey*, s.m. (1st) A small lad or boy (the dim. of the above). Pl. ي *ī*.

څوان *dzwān*, adj. Young, youthful. 2. s.m. (5th) A youth, a lad, a young man. Pl. څوانان *dzwānān*. څوانه *dzwāna'h*, s.f. (3rd) A young woman. Pl. ئ *ey*. څوان مرد *dzwān mard*, s.m. (5th) A bold, brave, or generous man. Pl. څوان مردان *dzwān mardān*. څوان مرګ *dzwān-i-marg*, Untimely death, dying in the bloom of youth. څوان مرګ شي *dzawān-i-marg shaey*, Mayest thou die in thy youth! (an ill wish). څواني *dzawānī*, s.f. (3rd) Youth, the season of youth, juvenility, childhood, minority, tender age. Pl. ئ *a'ī*.

څور *dzawr*, s.m. (2nd) Grief, pain, anxiety, sorrow, affliction, trouble. Pl. څورونه *dzawrūnah*. څوريدل *dzawredal*, verb intrans. To become afflicted, pained, or grieved, to be sorrowful. څورول *dzawrawul*, verb trans. To aggrieve, to trouble, to afflict, to make anxious or sorrowful. For conjugation see زور

څوړند *dzwarrand*, adj. Hanging, pendent, pendulous, swinging, loose, flowing, etc.; (Fem.) څوړنده *dzwarranda'h*. څوړنديدل *dzwarrandedal*, verb intrans. To hang, to dangle, to swing, to be pendulous or pendent. Pres. څوړنديږي *dzwarrandejzī* (W.) or څوړنديګي *dzwarrandegī* (E.); past څوړند شه *dzwarrand shah* or وُ شه *wu-shah*; fut. څوړند به شي *dzwarrand bah shī* or به وُ شي *bah wu-shī*; imp. څوړند شه *dzwarrand shah* or وُ شه *wu-shah*; act. part. څوړنديدونکَي *dzwarrandedūnkaey* or څوړنديدونَي *dzwarrandedūnaey*; past part. څوړند *dzwarrand* or څوړند شوَي *dzwarrand shawaey*; verb. n. څوړنديدنه *dzwarrandedana'h* or څوړنديده *dzwarrandedah*. څوړندول *dzwarrandawul*, verb trans. To suspend, to hang, to sling, to hook up, to fasten to. Pres. څوړندوي *dzwarrandawī*; past څوړند کړ *dzwarrand karr* or وُ کړ *wu-karr*; fut. څوړند به کړي *dzwarrand bah krrī* or به وُ کړي *bah wu-krrī*; imp. څوړند کړه *dzwarrand krrah* or وُ کړه *wu-krrah*; act. part. څوړندوونکَي *dzwarrandawūnkaey* or څوړندوونَي *dzwarrandawūnaey*; past part. څوړند کړَي *dzwarrand karraey*; verb. n. څوړندونه *dzwarrandawuna'h*.

څوز *dzoz*, s.m. (5th) A prickly bush, the camel-thorn (Hedysarum altragi). Pl. څوزان *dzozān*. See زوز. د څوز ګوړۍ *da dzoz gūrra'ī*, s.f. (6th) Manna. Sing. and Pl. څوځي ماڅوځي *dzūdzaey mā-dzūdzaey*, s. prop. Gog and Magog. See جوجي ماجوجي

څولۍ *dzola'ī*, s.f. (6th) A wallet, a sack, a bag, a scrip, a haversack, the skirt of a dress or anything carried in it. Sing. and Pl. See جولۍ

څير dzīr, s.m. (5th) The fine or highest note of a lute; the treble in music. Pl. څيران dzīrān.

څير dzīr, s.m. (2nd) A kind of soft leather brought from Persia. Pl. څيرونه dzīrūnah.

څير dzīr, s.m. (9th) Contemplation, regard, survey, sight, view, glance. څير كول dzīr kawul, verb trans. or په څير څير كتل pah dzīr dzīr katal, verb trans. To view, to contemplate, to eye, to cast the eyes on, to look intently, to strain one's eyes, to stare at, to gloat on. See زير and سهي

څيرمه dzerma'h, s.f. (3rd) Condolence, sympathy, consolation, pity, commiseration, comforting. 2. Recommendation. Pl. ې ey. څيرمه كول dzerma'h kawul, verb trans. To offer condolence, to sympathize, to pity, to commiserate.

څيزمه dzezma'h, s.f. (3rd) The eyelid. Pl. ې ey. See زيزمه

څيل dzīl, s.m. (2nd) The string of pots or buckets over a Persian wheel. 2. A line or string of captives chained together. Pl. څيلونه dzīlūnah. See جيل

څيل dzel, s.m. (2nd) Ignorance, nescience, inexperience, emptiness. 2. Contradiction, perversity, contrariety, opposition. Pl. څيلونه dzelūnah. څيل كول dzel kawul, verb trans. To show or manifest ignorance, to oppose, to show perversity or opposition. څيلي dzelī, s.m. (6th) An ignorant, foolish, stubborn, or perverse person. Pl. څيليان dzelī'ān. څيلۍ dzela'ī, s.f. (6th). Sing. and Pl.

ژ

ژ jzey, called the زاي عجمي or زاي فارسي, is the fourteenth letter of the Persian, and being also used in Pushto, is the nineteenth of that alphabet. It has no corresponding letter in either Arabic or Sanskrit. Its sound is the same as soft French j, or s in pleasure. The Eastern Afghāns change it to ج, and the Ghalzīs to ز.

P ژاله jzāla'h, s.f. (3rd) Hail, hoar frost. Pl. ې ey. See ږلۍ

ژامه jzāma'h, s.f. (3rd) The jaw, or jaw bone. Pl. ې ey. د ژامي غاښ da jzāmey ghāsh (W.) or ghakh (E.) s.m. (2nd) A back or double tooth, a jaw tooth, or grinder. Pl. غاښونه ghāshūnah or ghākhūnah. See زامه

ژانه jzāna'h, s.f. (3rd) Coaxing, supplication, fawning, adulation, flattery, cajolery, wheedling, etc. Pl. ې ey. ژاني كول jzāney kawul, verb trans. To wheedle, to cajole, to flatter, to pander, to curry favour with, to lick the dust.

ژاوله jzāwla'h, s.f. (3rd) Resin, pitch, wax, etc. Pl. ې ey.

ژاولن jzāwlan, adj. A fool, a milksop, a loon, a dolt, an ass (lit. one who chews resin or wax, and unable to give a clear or plain answer); (Fem.) ژاولنه jzāwlana'h.

ژبه jzaba'h, s.f. (3rd) The tongue, language, dialect. Pl. ې ey. See جبه and زبه. ژبه ور jzaba'h-war, adj. Long-tongued, abusive; (Fem.) ژبه وره jzaba'h wara'h. ژبه د لباس jzaba'h da libās, Flattery, deceit, adulation. د ژبي په سر da jzabey pah sar, On the tip of the tongue.

ژبونكی jzabūnkaey, s.m. (1st) A piece of cloth let in under the collar of a dress, the false seam of the breast of a garment. Pl. ي ī.

ژر jzir, adv. Quickly, speedily, quick, soon. See زر

ژرنده jzaranda'h, s.f. (3rd) A water-mill or wind-mill. Pl. ې ey, See جرنده and زرنده

ژړا jzarrā, s.f. (6th) Crying, weeping, mourning, whimpering. (E.) Sing. and Pl. (W.) Pl. ژړاوي jzarrāwī. ژړل jzarral, verb trans. To cry, to weep, to whimper, to mourn. Pres. ژاړي jzārrī; past وژړل wu-jzarral; fut. و به ژاړي wu bah jzārrī; imp. وژاړه wu-jzārrah; act. part. ژړونكی jzarrūnkaey or ژړونی jzarrūnaey; past part. ژړلی jzarralaey; verb. n. ژړنه jzarrana'h. ژړول jzarrawul, verb trans. To cause to cry or weep, to make cry, sob, or lament. Pres. ژړوي jzarrawī; past وژړاوه wu-jzarrāwuh or ژړاوو jzarrāwo; fut. و به ژړوي wu bah jzarrawī; imp. وژړوه

wu-jzarrawah; act. part. ژړوونکيَ *jzarrawūnkaey* or ژړوونيَ *jzarrawūnaey*; past part. ژړوليَ *jzarrawulaey*; verb. n. ژړونه *jzarrawuna'h*.

ژړاند *jzarrānd*, adj. A blubbering or ill-tempered child always crying; (Fem.) ژړانده *jzarrānda'h*. Also (Masc.) ژړندو *jzarrandū*; (Fem.) ژړندۍ *jzarranda'ī*.

ژغرل *jz'gharal*, verb trans. To keep, to preserve, to protect, to shield, to nourish. It is sometimes written زغرل See ژغورل

ژغند *jzghandd*, s.m. (2nd) A dent, a notch, a socket, a notch made in a piece of wood to split it. Pl. ژغندونه *jzghanddūnah*. ژغند ور کول *jzghandd war-kawul*, verb trans. To make a notch or dent, to notch. ژغند جوړول *jzghandd jorrawul*, verb trans. To scoop out or make a socket in anything, to dent, to mortice.

ژغنډيَ *jzaghunddaey*, s.m. (1st) A peg in a yoke, which prevents it slipping from the neck of the animal. 2. A term of abuse. Pl. ي *ī*. See ژغونډي

ژغورل *jzghoral*, verb trans. To keep, to preserve, to sustain, to support; to defend, to protect, to guard, to shield, to house. Pres. ژغوري *jzghorī*; past وُ ژغوره *wu-jzghorah* or ژغورَ *jzghora*; fut. وُ به ژغوري *wu bah jzghorī*; imp. وُ ژغوره *wu-jzghorah*; act. part. ژغورونکيَ *jzghorūnkaey* or ژغوروني *jzghorūnaey*; past part. ژغورليَ *jzghoralaey*; verb. n. ژغورنه *jzghorana'h*.

ژغورنه *jzghorana'h* (verb. n.) s.f. (3rd) Preservation, support, rescue, conservation, safeguard, security. Pl. ۍ *ey*. See ژغورل and زغورل

ژغوريَ *jz'ghoraey*, s.m. (1st) A keeper, a protector, a preserver, a defender, a guardian. Pl. ي *ī*. ژغورۍ *jz'ghora'ī*, s.f. (6th) A female keeper, a guardian, a protectress. Sing. and Pl.

ژلۍ *jzala'ī*, s.f. (6th) Hail, hoar frost. Sing. and Pl. See ژاله , ږلۍ , and ګلۍ

ژميَ *jzamaey*, s.m. (1st) The winter, the cold season. Pl. ي *ī*. See زمي , جمي , and ژومي

ژنړيَ *jzarrnaey*, s.m. (1st) A lad, a boy not arrived at puberty. Pl. ي *ī*. ژنړ *jzarrni* s.f. (8th) A young girl not arrived at puberty. Pl. ي *ī*. ژنړکيَ *jzarrnkaey*, s.m. (1st) A little boy (dimin. of the above). Pl. ي *ī*. ژنړکۍ *jzarrnka'ī*, s.f. (6th) A little girl. Sing. and Pl. See زنړي and زنړکي

ژنړيَ *jzarrnaey*, s.m. (1st) Catgut, the entrails of sheep or goats used for bow-strings and musical instruments. See جي

ژواك *jzwāk*, s.m. (2nd) Life, existence, being, entity, subsistence, animation. Pl. ژواکونه *jzwākūnah*. مرګ و ژواك *marg o jzwāk*, Life and death, living and dying. See ژوند

ژوبل *jzobal*, adj. Hurt, bruised, scratched, mutilated, injured, ham-strung; (Fem.) ژوبله *jzobala'h*. ژوبليدل *jzobledal*, verb intrans. To be hurt, bruised, wounded, mutilated, injured. Pres. ژوبليږي *jzoblejzī* (W.) or ژوبليګي *jzoblegī* (E.); past ژوبل شه *jzobal shah* or وُ شه *wu-shah*; fut. ژوبل به شي *jzobal bah shī* or به وُ شي *bah wu-shī*; imp. ژوبل شه *jzobal shah* or وُ شه *wu-shah*; act. part. ژوبليدونکيَ *jzobaledūnkaey* or ژوبليدونيَ *jzobaledūnaey*; past part. ژوبل *jzobal* or ژوبل شويَ *jzobal shawaey*; verb. n. ژوبليدنه *jzobledana'h* or ژوبليده *jzobledah*. ژوبلول *jzoblawul*, verb trans. To wound, to hurt, to mutilate, to injure. Pres. ژوبلوي *jzobalawī*; past ژوبل کړ *jzobal karr* or وُ کړ *wu-karr*; fut. ژوبل به کړي *jzobal bah krrī* or به وُ کړي *bah wu-krrī*; imp. ژوبل کړه *jzobal krrah* or وُ کړه *wu-krrah*; act. part. ژوبلوونکيَ *jzobalawūnkaey* or ژوبلوونيَ *jzobalawūnaey*; past part. ژوبل کړيَ *jzobal karraey*; verb. n. ژوبلونه *jzobalawuna'h*.

ژور *jzawar*, adj. Deep, sunk, buried, profound, underground, subterranean; (Fem.) ژوره *jzawara'h*. ژور واليَ *jzawar wālaey*, s.m. (1st) Depth, deepness, profundity, depression. Pl. والي *wālī*. Also ژور توب *jzawar-tob*, s.m. (2nd). Pl. توبونه *tobūnah*; and ژور تيا *jzawar tī'ā*, s.f. (6th). (E.) Sing. and Pl. (W.) Pl. تياوي *tī'āwī*. ژوريدل *jzawaredal*, verb intrans.

To deepen, to sink, to become submerged. Pres. ژوريږي *jzawarejzī* (W.) or ژوريگي *jzaw-aregī* (E); past ژور شه *jzawar shah* or وُ شه *wu-shah*; fut. ژور به شي *jzawar bah shī* or به وُ شي *bah wu-shī*; imp. ژور شه *jzawar shah* or وُ شه *wu-shah*; act. part. ژوريدونكَي *jzawar-edūnkaey* or ژوريدونَي *jzawaredūnaey*; past part. ژور *jzawar* or ژور شوَي *jzawar shawaey*; verb. n. ژوريدنه *jzawaredana'h* or ژوريده *jzawaredah*. ژورول *jzawarawul*, verb trans. To deepen, to make deep, to sink, to hollow, to scoop out. Pres. ژوروي *jzawarawī*; past ژور كړ *jzawar karr* or وُ كړ *wu-karr*; fut. ژور به كړي *jzawar bah krrī* or به وُ كړي *bah wu-krrī*; imp. ژور كړه *jzawar krrah* or وُ كړه *wu-krrah*; act. part. ژورونكَي *jzawarawūnkaey* or ژوروونَي *jzawarawūnaey*; past part. ژور كړَي *jzawar karraey*; verb. n. ژورونه *jzawarawuna'h*. See جور

ژور غالَي *jzawar ghālaey*, s.m. (1st) A little pit or furrow, a hole cut round the root of a tree, a small pit or hole made for planting. Pl. ي *ī*.

ژوره *jzawara'h*, s.f. (3rd) A leech. Pl. ې *ey*. See جوره

ژوژ *jzwajz*, s.m. (2nd) Noise, tumult, din, uproar, sound, cry, clamour, exclamation. 2. The rippling or murmuring of a brook, the rustling of leaves, the moaning of the wind, etc. Pl. ژوژونه *jzwajzūnah*. See زوژ

ژوند *jzwand*, s.m. (9th) Life, living, existence, being, vitality, animation, the vital spark, a flame, the science of life. Sing. and Pl. Also ژوندون *jzwandūn*, s.m. (9th). Sing. and Pl. ژوند كول *jzwand kawul* or ژوندون كول *jzwandūn kawul*, verb trans. To live, to obtain a livelihood. ژوندَي *jzwandaey*, adj. Alive, living, in life, breathing. Pl. ي *ī*; (Fem.) ژوندۍ *jzwanda'ī*. Sing. and Pl. ژوندي كيدل *jzwandaey kedal*, verb intrans. To be alive, to exist, to live, to breathe. ژوندي كول *jzwandaey kawul*, verb trans. To revive, to bring or restore to life, to reanimate.

ژوول *jzo-wul* (W.) verb trans. To masticate, to chew, to champ. For tenses see جوول (E.)

ژويل *jzo-yal*, verb trans. To chew, to masticate, to gnaw. Pres. ژويي *jzo-yī*; past وُ ژويه *wu-jzo-yah*; fut. وُ به ژويي *wu bah jzo-yī*; imp. وُ ژويه *wu-jzo-yah*; act. part. ژويونكَي *jzo-yūnkaey* or ژويونَي *jzo-yūnaey*; past part. ژويلَي *jzo-yalaey*; verb. n. ژوينه *jzo-yana'h*. See جويل and جوول

ژۍ *jza'ī*, s.f. (6th) Catgut, the string of a musical instrument, the string of a bow. Sing. and Pl.

ژي *jzaey*, s.m. (1st) A bag made of leather for holding water. Pl. ي *ī*.

ژبه *jze-ba'h*, s.f. (3rd) The tongue. 2. Language, speech, dialect. Pl. ې *ey*. See ژبه

ژير *jzi-yarr*, adj. Yellow; (Fem.) ژيړه *jzi-yarra'h*. ژيړيدل *jzi-yarredal*, verb intrans. To become or grow yellow. ژيړول *jzi-yarrawul*, verb trans. To make yellow. For conjugation see زير

ږ

ږ *jzey*, the twentieth letter of the Pushto alphabet, is pronounced by reverting the point of the tongue on the palate as French *j* in *jour*. It is commonly substituted for Persian ژ and vice versâ, but is slightly harsher in sound.

ږدل *jz'dal* (W.), verb trans. To place, to put, to lodge, to post, to fix, to establish, to plant, to lay, to set. Pres. ږدي *jz'dī*; past كيښو *kesho* or كښيښو *k'shesho* (W.); fut. كښي *k'she* or كي به ږدي *ke bah jz'dī*; imp. ږده *jz'dah* or كيږده *ke-jz'dah* or كښيږده *k'shejz'dah*; act. part. ږدونكَي *jz'dūnkaey* or ږدونَي *jz'dūnaey*; past part. ييښَي *yeshaey* or ييښلَي *yeshalaey*; verb. n. ييښنه *yeshana'h*. See كدل

ږدن *jz'dan*, s.m. (6th) The name of a grain (arzan), millet. Sing. and Pl.

ږغ *jzagh*, s.m. (2nd) A sound, sound, noise, voice, accent, strain, intonation. Pl. ږغونه *jzaghūnah*. ږغيدل *jzaghedal*, verb intrans. To sound, to make a noise, to give out or emit sound, to resound. Pres. ږغيږي *jzaghejzī* (W.) or ږغيګي *jzaghegī* (E.); past وُ ږغيده *wu-jzaghedah*; fut. وُ به ږغيږي *wu bah jzaghejzī* or ږغيګي *jzaghegī*; imp. وُ ږغيږه *wu-jzaghejzah* or ږغيګه *jzaghegah*; act. part. ږغيدونکي *jzaghedūnkaey* or ږغيدوني *jzaghedūnaey*; past part. ږغيدلي *jzaghedalaey*; verb. n. ږغيدنه *jzaghedana'h*.

ږغل *jzghal*, s.m. (2nd) Gravel, a gravel bed. Pl. ږغلونه *jzghalūnah*.

ږغول *jzaghawul*, verb trans. To make a noise, to play or sound a musical instrument, to cause to speak or raise the voice. Pres. ږغوي *jzaghawī*; past وُ ږغاوه *wu-jzaghāwuh* or ږغاوو *jzaghāwo*; fut. وُ به ږغوي *wu bah jzaghawī*; imp. وُ ږغوه *wu-jzaghawah*; act. part. ږغوونکي *jzaghawūnkaey* or ږغووني *jzaghawūnaey*; past part. ږغولي *jzaghawalaey*; verb. n. ږغونه *jzaghawuna'h*. See غږ and غګ

ږغورل *jz'ghoral*, verb trans. To keep, to preserve, to sustain, to support, to defend, to protect, to guard, to shield, to house. For conjugation see ژغورل and زغورل

ږلئي *jzala'ī*, s.f. (6th) Hail, hoar frost. Sing. and Pl. See ژلئي and ګلي

ږمنز *jz'manz*, s.f. (1st) A comb. Pl. ږمنزِ *jz'manzi*. See ګمنز, etc.

ږو *jzo*, adv. A word or exclamation used by way of affirmation or oath; as خداي ږو *khudā'e jzo*, By God! so help me God! ستا په سر ږو *stā pah sar jzo*, I swear or vow by thy head!

ږوند *jz'wand* or ږوندون *jzwandūn*, s.m. (9th) Life, living, existence, being, vitality animation, the vital spark; the science of life. Sing. and Pl. ږوند *jz'wand* or ږوندون کول *jz'wandūn kawul*, verb trans. To live, to exist, to obtain a livelihood. ږوندي *jzwandaey*, adj. Alive, living, in life, breathing. Pl. ي *ī*; (Fem.) ږوندي *jz'wanda'ī*. Sing. and Pl. ږوندي کيدل *jz'wandaey kedal*, verb intrans. To exist, to live, to breathe, to be alive. ږوندي کول *jz'wandaey kawul*, verb trans. To revive, to bring or restore to life, to reanimate. See ژوند and ژوندون

ږواك *jz'wāk*, s.m. (2nd) Life, existence, being, entity, subsistence, animation. Pl. ږواکونه *jz'wākūnah*. مرګ ږواك *marg jz'wāk*, Life and death, living and dying. See ژواك

ږوږ *jz'wajz*, s.m. (2nd) Noise, tumult, din, uproar, clamour, outcry, exclamation. Pl. ږوږونه *jz'wajzūnah*. See ژوږ and زوږ or زوګ

ږوي *jzawaey*, s.m. (1st) A person, an individual, a body, a creature, a mortal, a party. Pl. ي *ī*. See وګړي

ږيره *jzīra'h*, s.f. (3rd) The beard. Pl. ئ *ey*. سپين ږيري *spīn jzīraey*, s.m. (1st) An elder (*lit.* a white beard). Pl. ي *ī*. پست ږيري *past jzīraey*, s.m. (1st) A low or mean person, a coward, a poltroon (*lit.* a soft beard). Pl. ي *ī*. ړته ږيره *rrata'h jzīra'h*, adj. Long-bearded, having a beard of an absurd or inordinate length; foolish, cowardly, dastardly. ړتي ږيري *rrataey jzīraey*, s.m. (1st) A poltroon, a milksop, a coward. Pl. ي *ī*. See ګيره

س

س *sīn*, called سين غير منقوطه or سين مهمله, the twelfth letter of the Arabic and fifteenth in the Persian alphabet, is the twenty-first letter of the Pushto, and corresponds to स of the Sanskrit. It is sounded as English *s*, and stands for 60 according to the *abjad* system of the Arabs. It is changed for Pushto څ *ts* in many instances.

سا *sā*, s.f. (6th) The breath, life, the vital spark. (E.) Sing. and Pl. (W.) Pl. ساوي *sāwī*. See ساه and سمه

ساو *sā'ū*, adj. Noble, excellent, well-born. See ساوو and ساهو

A سابق *sābiķ*, adj. Former, preceding, foregoing, anterior; (Fem.) سابقه *sābiķa'h*. سابقاً *sābiķan*, adv. Formerly, of yore, heretofore, ago, beforetime.

P سابون *sābūn*, s.m. (2nd) Soap. Pl. سابونونه *sābūnūnah*. See صابون

سابو *sābū*, s.m. (5th) A species of grass growing in the hills of which mats are made. Pl. سابوگان *sābūgān*.

سابه *sā-bah*, s.m. (6th) A kind of grass, very nourishing, growing wild on the hills of Afghānistān and adjacent countries, produced in the spring. Sing. and Pl.

سابه *sābuh*, s.m. (6th) A vegetable in general, greens, dressed greens. Sing. and Pl.

ساپټ *sā-paṭṭ*, adv. Entirely, wholly, completely; also written ثاپټ *ṣā-paṭṭ*.

ساپي *sāpī*, s.m. (1st). Pl. The name of an Afghān tribe; *sāpaey*, Sing. A male of the above. ساپۍ *sapa'ī*, s.f. (6th) A female of the Sāpī tribe. Sing. and Pl.

ساتل *sātal*, verb trans. To keep, to preserve, to protect, to defend, to guard, to shelter, to shield. Pres. ساتي *sātī*; past وُ ساته *wu-sātah*; fut. وُ به ساتي *wu bah sātī*; imp. وُ ساته *wu-sātah*; act part. ساتونکَي *sātūnkaey* or ساتونَي *sātūnaey*; past part. ساتلَي *sātalaey*; verb. n. ساتنه *sātana'h*. See خندي کول

ساتندوي *sātandoaey*, s.m. (5th) or ساتونکَي *sātūnkaey* or ساتونَي *sātūnaey*, s.m. (1st); (act. part.) A preserver, a protector, a guardian, a defender. Pl. ي *ī*. ساتندويه *sātandoeya'h*, s.f. (3rd). Pl. ې *ey*, and ساتونکې *sātūnki* or ساتونې *sātūni*, A protectress, defendress. Pl. ي *ī*.

ساتَنه *sātana'h*, s.f. (3rd) (verb. n.) Preservation. safety, defence, protection, shelter, safeguard, escape. Pl. ې *ey*.

ساتول *sātūl*, s.m. (2nd) A large crooked knife, a cleaver, a chopper. Pl. ساتولونه *sātūlūnah*.

A ساحر *sāḥir*, s.m. (5th) An enchanter, a magician, a conjurer, a necromancer. Pl. ساحران *sāḥirān*. ساحره *sāḥira'h*, s.f. (3rd) An enchantress, a sorceress. Pl. ې *ey*. ساحري *sāḥirī*, s.f. (3rd) Enchantment, magic, sorcery, conjuration. Pl. ۍ *a'ī*. See سحر

P ساخت *sākht*, s.m. (9th) (from ساختن), Make, making, formation, fashion, construction, fabrication, pretence. Sing. and Pl. See جوړښت. ساختگي *sākhtagī*, s.f. (3rd) Machination, fabrication, pretence, romance, fiction. Pl. ۍ *a'ī*. ساختگي کول *sākhtagī kawul*, verb trans. To fabricate, to machinate, to plan, to contrive. See جوړښت والي

ساخت *sākht*, s.m. (2nd) Morocco leather, coloured sheep or goat's skin. Pl. ساختونه *sākhtūnah*.

ساخه *sākha'h*, s.f. (3rd) (corrup. of A صاخة) A sound which grates or stuns the ear, discord. 2. A calamity. 3. The judgment day. Pl. ې *ey*.

ساد *sād*, adj. Respectable (man), trustworthy; (Fem.) ساده *sāda'h*. (S साधु Good, virtuous).

سادو *sādū*, adj. An impostor, a cheat, a knave, a swindler, a sharper.

P ساده *sādah*, adj. Plain, unadorned, simple; white; beardless. 2. Open, sincere, artless. ساده دل *sādah-dil*, adj. Simple, artless, stupid, slow; (Fem.) ساده دله *sādah-dila'h*. ساده دلي *sādah dilī*, s.f. (3rd) Simplicity, stupidity, artlessness. Pl. ۍ *a'ī*. ساده روي *sādah-rū'e*, adj. Beardless. ساده کار *sādah-kār*, s.m. (2nd) Plain work (as that of a tailor or goldsmith). Pl. کارونه *kārūnah*. ساده کاري *sādah kāraey*, adj. (used as subs.) (1st) A plain worker, one who does plain work only (as a tailor, etc.). Pl. ي *ī*. ساده لوح *sādah lauḥ*, adj. Artless, simple, a simpleton, a ninny; (Fem.) ساده لوحه *sādah lauḥa'h*. ساده لوحي *sādah lauḥī*, s.f. (3rd) Simplicity, artlessness, stupidity. Pl. ۍ *a'ī*. سادگي *sādagī*, s.f. (3rd) Plainness, artlessness, simplicity, openness, frankness, sincerity. Pl. ۍ *a'ī*. سادگي کول *sādagī kawul*, verb trans. To act with simplicity, frankness, or sincerity.

سادين *sādīn*, s.m. (2nd) Ground prepared or ready for sowing wheat, etc. Pl. سادينونه *sādīnūnah*. See شدياره

سار *sār*, s.m. (2nd) Good news, happy tidings. Pl. سارونه *sārūnah*.

سار *sār*, s.m. (2nd) (E). The business of a scout, looking out, watching. Pl. سارونه *sārūnah*. سار کول *sār kawul*, verb trans. To keep a look out, to act the scout, to discover, to keep watch and ward. ساري *sārī*, s.m. (5th) A scout, a look-out. Pl. ساريان *sārī-ān*; or سار

كړونكَي *sār-ka*r*r*ūnkaey*, s.m. (1st). Pl. ي *ī*. See خار

P ساربان *sār-bān*, s.m. (5th) A camel keeper. Pl. ساربانان *sārbānān*. See ساروان

ساركه *sāraka'h*, s.f. (3rd) The name of a bird (Turdus salica), also a maina (Gracula religiosa). Pl. ې *ey*.

سارمه *sārma'h*, s.f. (3rd) A kind of pot-herb. Pl. ې *ey*; or سارمَي *sārmaey* (E.), s.m. (1st). Pl. ي *ī*.

سارنده *sārinda'h*, s.f. (3rd) A violin. Pl. ې *ey*. See سرنده

P ساروان *sārwān*, s.m. (5th) The keeper or owner of a camel. Pl. ساروانان *sārwānān*.

ساري *sāraey*, adj. (from P سار) Equal, on a par with. 2. s.m. (1st) An equal, a match, a compeer, a mate; (Fem.) سارِ *sāri*. Pl. (Masc. and Fem.) ي *ī*. سار توب *sār-tob*, s.m. (2nd) Equality, parity, equalization. Pl. توبونه *tobūnah*; or سار تيا *sār-tīā*, s.f. (6th) (E.). Sing. and Pl. (W.) Pl. تياوي *tīāwī*.

ساړه *sā*r*ra'h*, s.f. (6th) The cold season, cold, coldness, frigidity, chillness, inclemency. Sing. and Pl. See سوړ

P ساز *sāz*, s.m. (2nd) Ornament, apparatus, accoutrement, furniture. 2. A musical instrument. Pl. سازونه *sāzūnah*. ساز كول *sāz kawul* or ساز وهل *sāz wahal*, verb trans. To play on a musical instrument. سازيدل *sāzedal*, verb intrans. To become adorned, or ornamented, to become furnished, accoutred, etc. Pres. سازيږي *sāzejzī* (W.) or سازيكي *sāzegī* (E.); past ساز شه *sāz* *sh*ah or وُ شه *wu-*sh*ah*; fut. ساز به شي *sāz bah* *sh*ī or به وُ شي *bah wu-*sh*ī*; imp. ساز شه *sāz* *sh*ah or وُ شه *wu-*sh*ah*; act. part. سازيدونكَي *sāzedūnkaey* or سازيدونَي *sāzedūnaey*; past part. ساز شوَي *sāz* *sh*awaey; verb. n. سازيدنه *sāzedana'h* or سازيده *sāzedah*. سازول *sāzawul*, verb trans. To adorn, to ornament, to make ready, to dress up, to accoutre. Pres. سازوي *sāzawī*; past ساز كړ *sāz ka*r*r* or وُ كړ *wu-ka*r*r*; fut. ساز به كړي *sāz bah k*r*rī* or به وُ كړي *bah wu-k*r*rī*; imp. ساز كړه *sāz k*r*rah* or وُ كړه *wu-k*r*rah*; act. part. سازوونكَي *sāzawūnkaey* or سازوونَي *sāzawūnaey*; past part. ساز كړَي *sāz ka*r*raey*; verb. n. سازونه *sāzawunah*.

P سازش *sāzi*sh**, s.m. (2nd) (from ساختن) Collusion, combination, confederacy, conspiracy, plot, cabal. Pl. سازشونه *sāzi*sh*ūnah*. سازش كول *sāzi*sh* kawul*, verb trans. To plot, to combine, to get up a conspiracy.

P سازنده *sāzindah*, s.m. (5th) (act. part. of ساختن) A maker, a furnisher, an adorner. 2. A musical performer. Pl. سازندگان *sāzindagān*.

A ساعت *sā'œat*, s.m. (2nd) An hour, a moment, a minute. Pl. ساعتونه *sā'œatūnah*. ساعت په ساعت *sā'œat pah sā'œat*, Hour by hour, every moment, continually.

A ساعي *sā'œī*, adj. (act. part. of سعي) Earnest, eager, endeavouring, assiduous, zealous. 2. s.m. (5th) An attempter, an endeavourer, a zealous person. Pl. ساعيان *sā-œīān*; (Fem.) Pl. ساعيانِ *sā'œīāni*.

P ساغَر *sā*gh*ar*, s.m. (2nd) A cup, a bowl, a goblet. Pl. ساغرونه *sā*gh*arūnah*.

P ساغري *sā*gh*arī*, s.f. (3rd) The space between the anus and the tail of a horse, the leather of the hind-quarters of an ass, from which shoes are made. Pl. ۍ *a'ī*.

A ساقي *sāḳī*, s.m. (5th) A cup-bearer, a page. Pl. ساقيان *sāḳī-ān*. ساقيا *sāḳī-yā*, O cup-bearer!

A ساكت *sākit*, adj. (from سكت) Silent, quiet.

ساكن *sākin*, adj. (from سكن) Quiet, peaceable, quiescent (letter). 2. s.m. (5th) An inhabitant, a dweller. Pl. ساكنان *sākinān*.

S ساگ *sāg*, s.m. (6th) Greens, edible vegetables, culinary herbs, potherb. Sing. and Pl.

ساگيڼړَي *sāgī*r*rnaey*, s.m. (1st) A dish of rice and greens. Pl. ي *ī*.

A سالك *sālik*, s.m. (5th) (act. part. of سلك) Going. 2. A traveller, a devotee. Pl. سالكان *sālikān*.

A سالم *sālim*, adj. (act. part. of سلم) Safe, sound, perfect, unimpaired, uninjured; (Fem.) سالمه *sālima'h*.

HI سالن *sālan*, s.m. (2nd) Fish, meat, etc. eaten with bread or rice. Pl. سالنونه *sālanūnah*.

S سالو *sālū*, s.m. (5th) A kind of red cloth dyed with morinda, a muslin sheet or veil. Pl. سالوگان *sālūgān*.

P ساله *sālah* (in composition) A termination affixed to numeral adjectives to denote the number of years old, as يو ساله *yow-sālah*, Of one year, etc.

P سالیانه *sāliyāna'h* (corrup. of سال *sāl*, and the particle آنه *ānah*), s.f. (3rd) An annual stipend, a salary, an annuity. Pl. ي *ey*. 2. adj. Annual, yearly. سالیانه دار *sāliyāna'h-dār*, An annuitant, a pensioner.

P سامان *sāmān*, s.m. (2nd) Apparatus, instruments, tools, necessaries, furniture, accoutrements. Pl. سامانونه *sāmānūnah*. سامان جنگي *sāmān-i-jangī*, Warlike apparatus, ammunition. بي سر و سامان *be sar-o-sāmān*, adj. Destitute, indigent, helpless. 2. Brainless, stupid.

سامانه *sāmāna'h*, s.f. (3rd) Parade, pomp, state. Pl. ي *ey*. See سهمانه

A سامع *sāmiæ*, s.m. (5th) (act. part. of سمع, to hear) A hearer. Pl. سامعان *sāmiæān*. سامعه *sāmiæa'h*, s.f. (3rd) The sense of hearing, or power to hear. Pl. ي *ey*,

P سان *sān*, s.m. (2nd) Muster, review of an army. 2. Calico. Pl. سانونه *sānūnah*. سان نیول *sān nīwal*, verb trans. To make or take muster (as of an army). سان ورکول *sān war-kawul*, verb trans. To give muster (as troops).

ساندہ *sānda'h*, s.f. (3rd) Lamenting, complaining, bewailing, wail, lamentation. Pl. ي *ey*. ساندي ویل *sāndey wa-yal*, verb trans. To lament, to bewail.

HI سانڈا *sānḏḏā*, s.m. (6th) A kind of lizard from which oil is extracted. (E.) Sing. and Pl. (W.) Pl. سانڈاوي *sānḏḏāwī*. See خادمي

سانڈہ *sānḏḏah*, s.m. (5th) A male buffalo. Pl. سانڈگان *sānḏḏagān*. سانڈہ *sānḏḏa'h*, s.f. (3rd) A female buffalo when ready for the male. Pl. ي *ey*. سانڈہ کیدل *sānḏḏa'h kedal*, verb intrans. To become ready for the male buffalo. سانڈہ ختل *sānḏḏah khatal* or سانڈہ ور کول *sānḏḏah-war-kawul*, verb trans. To give the male buffalo. See سنڈہ

سانگه *sānga'h*, s.f. (3rd) A *ḳāfila'h* or caravan in which all travel on horseback, and carry their goods on ponies or horses. 2. A spear, a javelin (s). 3. The branch of a tree, a bough. Pl. ي *ey*.

سانگي *sānga'ī*, s.f. (6th) A kind of pitchfork made of wood, used in winnowing and threshing corn. Sing. and Pl. See دوي ښاخي

ساو *sāw*, s.m. (9th) A tax, a tribute. Sing. and Pl. See باج

ساونړ *sāwarrn*, s.m. (2nd) The name of the fourth Hindū month, July—August. (s ساون) Pl. ساونړونه *sāwarrnūnah*.

ساوو *sāwū*, adj. Noble, well-born, or ساهو *sa-hū*. See ساو

ساه *sāh*, s.m. (2nd) The breath, life. Pl. ساهونه *sāhūnah*. (W.) s.f. (9th) Sing. and Pl. ساه ښکل *sah sh'kal* (W.) or *kh'kal* (E.), or ساه شړل *sāh sharral*, verb trans. To breathe, to draw breath, to puff, to blow, to pant. ساه ختل *sāh khatal*, verb intrans. To die, to cease to breathe, to gasp for breath, to swoon. ساه ختلي *sāh khatalaey*, adj. Gasping for breath, breathless through grief or desire, at the last gasp; (Fem.) ساه ختل *sāh khatali*. Pl. (Masc. and Fem.) ي *ī*. See سهه

ساه لنډي *sāh-lanḏḏī*, s.f. (3rd) The asthma. Pl. ئ *a'ī*. ساه لنډي *sāhlanḏḏaey*, adj. Asthmatic; (Fem.) ساه لنډ *sāh-lanḏḏi*. Pl. (Masc. and Fem.) ساه لنډي *sāh-lanḏḏī*.

ساه ویساه *sāh-wisāh*, s.f. (9th) Faith, confidence, trust, reliance, credit, belief. Sing. and Pl. Also ساه ویسا *sāh-wisā*.

A سایر *sā'ir*, adj. (act. part. of سیر), A rambler, a rascal, a man of bad character; (Fem). سایره *sā'īra'h*.

A سایل *sā'il*, s.m. (5th) (from سال, to ask), An interrogator, an asker, a beggar. Pl. سایلان *sā'īlān*. سایله *sā'īla'h*, s.f. (3rd) Pl. ي *ey*.

P سایه *sāya'h*, s.f. (3rd) Shade, shadow, shelter, protection. 2. A spectre, an apparition. Pl. ي *ey*. سایه دار *sāya'h-dār*, adj. Shady. 2.

A protector. سايه وان *sāya'h wān*, s.m. (2nd) An umbrella, a canopy. Pl. سايه وانونه *sāya'h wānūnah*.

A سب *sibb* or *sabb*, s.m. (2nd) Reviling, reproaching, reproach. Pl. سبونه *sibbūnah* or *sabbūnah*. سب کول *sibb kawul* or ورکول *war-kawul*, verb trans. To revile, to reproach.

سبا *sabā*, s.m. (9th) (corrup. of A صباح), The morning, the dawn of day, to-morrow. Sing. and Pl. سباي محال *sabā'e maḥāl*, adj. Early, soon, not late. See صباح and صبح

A سبب *sabab*, s.m. (2nd) Cause, reason, motive. 2. Affinity, connexion, relationship. 3. Instrument, means. Pl. سببونه *sababūnah*.

A سبحان *sub-ḥān*, s.m. (9th) Praising, glorifying (God). Sing. and Pl. سبحان الله *sub-ḥān-llah*, interj. O God! Good God! Ha! سبحانه *sub-ḥāna-hu*, Praise to Him!

سبزوار *sabz-wār* or *sabzawār*, s. prop. The name of a district between Ḳandahār and Herāt.

P سبزه *sabza'h*, s.f. (3rd) (from سبز), Verdure, herbage. 2. Incipient beard, bloom. Pl. ې *ey*. 3. adj. Sallow, dark complexioned.

P سبزي *sabzī*, s.m. (1st) Pl. Greens, vegetables. culinary vegetables. (Sing. not used). سبزي کار *sabzī-kār*, s.m. (5th) A kitchen-gardener. Pl. کاران *kārān*. سبزي کاري *sabzī-kārī*, s.f. (3rd) Kitchen-gardening, the business of a kitchen-gardener. Pl. ئي *a'ī*.

سبق *sabaḳ*, s.m. (2nd) (from سبق) A lesson, a lecture, reading. Pl. سبقونه *sabaḳūnah*. سبق آخستل *sabaḳ ākhistal*, verb trans. To take a lesson. سبق ورکول *sabaḳ war-kawul*, verb trans. To give a lesson, to teach. سبق ويل *sabaḳ wayal*, verb trans. To repeat a lesson. سبق هيرول *sabaḳ herawul*, verb trans. To forget one's lesson. سبق يادول *sabaḳ yādawul*, verb trans. To learn one's lesson.

P سبوس *sabūs*, s.m. (9th) Bran. Sing. and Pl.

A سبيل *sabīl*, s.m. (9th) Road, way, path, mode, manner. Sing. and Pl. See لار

P سپارش *sipārish* or *supārīsh*, s.m. (2nd) (from سپردن), Recommendation, intercession, inducement, etc. Pl. سپارشونه *sipārishūnah*. د سپارش کاغذ *da sipārish kāghiz*, s.m. (2nd) A letter of recommendation. Pl. کاغذونه *kāghizūnah*. سپارش کول *sipārish kawul*, verb trans. To intercede for, to recommend. See سفارش

سپارل *spāral*, verb. trans. To give in charge, to consign, to intrust, to commit, to recommend to, or make over to one's care. Pres. سپاري *spārī*; past وُ سپاره *wu-spārah* or سپارَ *spāra*; fut. وُ به سپاري *wu bah spārī*; imp. وُ سپاره *wu spārah*; act. part. سپارونکي *spārūnkaey* or سپارونَي *spārūnacy*; past. part. سپارلَي *spāralaey*; verb. n. سپارنه *spārana'h*.

سپارلي *spāralaey*, adj. (past part.) made over, given in charge, delivered in trust, committed to the care or hands of another; (Fem.) سپارلِ *spārali*. Pl. (Masc. and Fem.) ي *ī*.

سپاره *spāra'h*, s.f. (3rd) A ploughshare, the part of a plough shod with iron. Pl. ې *ey*.

سپانده *spānda'h*, s.f. (3rd) The wild rue, the seed of which is burnt as a charm. Pl. ې *ey*. See سپلني

HI سپاري *supārī*, s.m. (6th) Betel-nut (Areca catechu). Sing. and Pl.

P سپاه *sipāh*, s.m. (9th) An army, a soldier. Sing. and Pl. سپاه سالار *sipāh-sālār*, A general, the commander of an army. سپاه گري *sipāh-garī*, s.f. (3rd) Soldiership, tactics, the profession of a soldier. Pl. ئي *a'ī*.

P سپاهي *sipāh-ī*, s.m. (5th) A soldier. Pl. سپاهيان *sipāh-īān*.

سپخزه *spukhza'h*, s.f. (3rd) The belly below the navel, the pubes. 2. The bladder. Pl. ې *ey*. See سپوخته and پوکنړي

سپر *spar*, s.m. (2nd) A shield, a target. Pl. سپرونه *sparūnah* (from P سپر).

سپرخي *sparkhaey*, s.m. (1st) A skewer, a packing needle, the peg of a plough of iron or wood. Pl. ي *ī*.

سپرغه *spargha'h*, s.f. (3rd) A well. Pl. ې *ey*.

سپرلنَي *sparlanaey*, (W.) s.m. (1st) A rider, a horseman. Pl. ي *ī*. See سپور

سپره *sapara'h*, s.f. (3rd) The month Ṣafar (corrup. of صفر). Pl. ې *ey*.

سپره *supra'h*, s.f. (3rd) The anus. Pl. ې *ey*. See سفره

سپريدل *sparedal*, verb intrans. To get on horseback, to leap on any animal, to mount. Pres. سپريږي *sparejzī* (W.) or سپريګي *sparegī* (E.); past سپور شه *spor shah* or وُ شه *wu-shah*; fut. سپور به شي *spor bah shī* or به وُ شي *bah wu-shī*; imp. سپور شه *spor shah* or وُ شه *wu-shah*; act. part. سپريدونکی *sparedūnkaey* or سپريدونی *sparedūnaey*; past part. سپور *spor* or سپور شوی *spor shawaey*; verb. n. سپريدنه *sparedana'h* or سپريده *sparedah*. سپرول *sparawul*, verb trans. To place one's-self on horseback, to mount, to ascend. Pres. سپروي *sparawī*; past سپور کړ *spor karr* or وُ کړ *wu-karr*; fut. سپور به کړي *spor bah krrī* or به وُ کړي *bah wu-krrī*; imp. سپور کړه *spor krrah* or وُ کړه *wu-krrah*; act. part. سپروونکی *sparawūnkaey* or سپروونی *sparawūnaey*; past part. سپرولی *sparawulaey*; verb. n. سپرونه *sparawuna'h*. See سپور

سپړدل *sparrdal* or سپړل *sparral*, verb trans. To undo, to unravel, to unfold, to unclose, to unloose, to open the eyes (as the young of a cat or dog). Pres. سپړي *sparrī*; past وُ سپړد *wu-sparrd*; fut. وُ به سپړي *wu bah sparrī*; imp. وُ سپړه *wu-sparrah*; act. part. سپړدونکی *sparrdūnkaey* or سپړدونی *sparrdūnaey*; past part. سپړدلی *sparrdalaey* or سپړدی *sparrdaey* and سپړلی *sparralaey* or سپړی *sparraey*; verb. n. سپړدنه *sparrdana'h* or سپړنه *sparrana'h*.

سپړلی *sparralaey* or سپړی *sparraey*, adj. (past part. of the above), Opened, unloosed, unravelled, unfolded; (Fem.) سپړل *sparrali* or سپړِ *sparri*. Pl. (Masc. and Fem.) ي *ī*.

سپږمه *spajzma'h* (W.) s.f. (3rd) The nostril, or سپګمه *spagma'h* (E.) Pl. ې *ey*. See سپيرمه

سپږن *spajzan* (W.) adj. Lousy, swarming with lice. 2. Mean, low; (Fem.) سپږنه *spajzana'h*. See سپږه

سپږه *spajza'h*, s.f. (3rd) A louse. Pl. ې *ey*. See سپګه

سپق *sapak*, s.m. (2nd) A hand's breadth, four fingers' breadth, a palm, a lineal measure of three inches. Pl. سپقونه *sapakūnah*. See څپق

سپک *spuk*, adj. Light, flimsy, meagre, little, small, soft, easy, mean, cheap. 2. A trifle, a small matter, a straw, a pin. 3. Trash, stuff; (Fem.) سپکه *spuka'h*. سپکاوي *spukāwaey*, s.m. (1st) Lightness, flimsiness, littleness, slenderness, meagreness, meanness, mediocrity. Pl. ي *ī*; also سپک والی *spukwālaey*, s.m. (1st). Pl. والي *wālī*; or سپک توب *spuk-tob*, s.m. (2nd). Pl. توبونه *tobūnah*; and سپک تيا *spuk-tīā*, s.f. (6th). (E.) Sing. and Pl. (W.) Pl. تياوي *tīāwī*.

سپکيدل *spukedal*, verb intrans. To become light, flimsy, meagre, little, small, mean, to become demeaned, to become trifling, etc. Pres. سپکيږي *spukejzī* (W.) or سپکيګي *spukegī* (E.); past سپک شه *spuk shah* or وُ شه *wu-shah*; fut. سپک به شي *spuk bah shī* or به وُ شي *bah wu-shī*; imp. سپک شه *spuk shah* or وُ شه *wu-shah*; act. part. سپکيدونکی *spukedūnkaey* or سپکيدونی *spukedūnaey*; past part. سپک *spuk* or سپک شوی *spuk shawaey*; verb. n. سپکيدنه *spukedana'h* or سپکيده *spukedah*. سپکول *spukawul*, verb trans. To make light, to diminish (in quantity or in consideration), to demean or render mean, to render despicable. Pres. سپکوي *spukawī*; past سپک کړ *spuk karr* or وُ کړ *wu-karr*; fut. سپک به کړي *spuk bah krrī* or به وُ کړي *bah wu-krrī*; imp. سپک کړه *spuk krrah* or وُ کړه *wu-krrah*; act. part. سپکوونکی *spukawūnkaey* or سپکوونی *spukawūnaey*; past part. سپک کړي *spuk karraey*; verb. n. سپکونه *spukawuna'h*.

سپګه *spaga'h*, s.f. (3rd) A louse. Pl. ې *ey*.

سپګن *spagan*, adj. Lousy, infested with lice. 2. Mean, low, contemptible; (Fem.) سپګنه *spagana'h*. See سپږه and رچه

سپلم *spalam*, s.m. (5th) A fox. Pl. سپلمان *spalamān*. سپلمه *spalama'h*, s.f. (3rd) A female or bitch fox. Pl. ې *ey*. See سپيرلم

سپلمه *spalama'h*, s.f. (3rd) A ring-dove, the turtle-dove. Pl. ې *ey*.

سپلمۍ *spalma'ī*, s.f. (6th) The milk-bush, gigantic swallow-wort (Asclepias gigantea). Sing. and Pl.

سپلنۍ *spalanaey*, s.m. (1st) A seed of the wild rue burnt to drive away evil spirits, or as a charm. Pl. ي *ī*. See سپانده

سپم *spam*, s.m. (2nd) The eye of a needle, a small hole or perforation made in the flesh (as in the ears and nose), the perforation of the penis. Pl. سپمونه *spamūnah*.

سپندخ *spandakh*, s.m. (2nd) A large ball of worsted or cotton. Pl. سپندخونه *spandakh-ūnah*. 2. s.m. (5th) A stuffed calf placed by a cow who may have lost her calf, to make her give milk. Pl. سپندخان *spandakhān*.

سپړنسۍ *sparrnsaey*, s.m. (1st) String, thread, twine, a lace, a yarn, untwisted thread. Pl. ي *ī*.

سپوخز *spokhz*, s.m. (2nd) The belly below the navel, the pubes. 2. The bladder. Pl. سپوخزونه *spokhzūnah*. See سپوخځه and سپخزه

سپوخزه *spokhza'h*, s.f. (3rd) The belly below the navel, the bladder, the pubes. Pl. ې *ey*. Also written سپخز *spakhz*, s.m. (2nd). Pl. سپخزونه *spakhzūnah*. See سپخزه and سپخځه

سپوخځه *spokhdza'h*, s.f. (3rd) The pubes, etc. See preceding. Pl. ې *ey*. See سپخزه and پوکنړۍ

سپور *spor*, adj. Dry, stale, withered, flat. 2. Plain, simple, rough, pure, unmixed (particularly food), unsalted; (Fem.) سپوره *spora'h*. سپوره ډوډۍ *spora'h ddodda'ī*, s.f. (6th) Dry bread. Sing. and Pl.

سپور *spor*, adj. Mounted, seated on horseback, raised. 2. s.m. (4th) A horseman, a cavalier. Pl. سپاره *spārah*; (Fem.) سپره *spara'h*. Pl. سپرې *sparey*. سپارلي *spārlī*, s.f. (3rd) Riding on horseback. Pl. ۍ *a'ī*. سپارلي کول *spārlī kawul*, verb trans. To ride, to take exercise on horseback. See سور and سپریدل

سپوږمۍ *spojzma'ī*, s.f. (6th) (W.) The moon, moonlight. Sing. and Pl. سپوږمۍ تندره نیول *spojzma'ī tandara'h nīwul*, verb trans. To have an eclipse (as the moon); or سپوګمۍ *spogma'ī*, s.f. (6th) (E.) Sing. and Pl.

سپوړنۍ *sporrnaey*, s.m. (1st) The ring-worm, a dry scab. Pl. ي *ī*.

P سپه *sipah*, s.m. (9th) An army, soldiers. Sing. and Pl سپه ګري *sipah-garī*, s.f. (3rd) The profession of a soldier, military tactics. Pl. ۍ *a'ī*. See سپاه

P سپهر *sipahr*, s.m. (9th) The sphere, the celestial globe, the sky, fortune, time, the world. Sing. and Pl.

سپۍ *spaey*, s.m. (1st) A dog. Pl. ي *ī*. سپۍ *spa'ī*, s.f. (6th) A bitch. Sing. and Pl. سپیتانه *spī-tāna'h*, s.f. (3rd) The nature of a dog, currishness. Pl. ې *ey*; or سپي توب *spaey-tob*, s.m. (2nd). Pl. توبونه *tobūnah*. سپیمه *speyama'h*, s.f. (3rd) A bitch in heat. Pl. ې *ey*. سپیمه کیدل *speyama'h kedal*, verb intrans. To get in heat (as a bitch). سپیم توب *speyam-tob*, s.m. (2nd) The heat of a bitch, animal heat. Pl. توبونه *tobūnah*.

سپیازه *speyāza'h*, s.f. (3rd) Miscarrying, dropping the young (peculiar to animals). 2. adj. Raw, unripe, useless, ill-advised, foolish, wild.

سپیټه *sapetta'h*, adv. Never, at no time, on no occasion, positively.

P سپید *saped*, adj. White; (Fem.) سپیده *sapeda'h*. سپید پوستي *saped postaey*, adj. Fair, white; (Fem.) سپید پوستې *saped posti*. Pl. (Masc. and Fem.) ي *ī*. سپید دار *saped-dār*, s.m. (5th) A willow, the wood. Pl. سپیداران *saped-dārān*.

سپیده *sapeda'h*, s.f. (3rd) White-lead, ceruse. Pl. ې *ey*.

سپیدي *sapedī*, s.f. (3rd) Whiteness, fairness. Pl. ۍ *a'ī*.

سپیدي *sapedey*, s.f. (3rd) Pl. The dawn of day, the first light of day. سپیدي داغ *sapedey dāgh*, s.m. (2nd) The dawn, the time of dawn. Pl. داغونه *dāghūnah*.

سپیرکۍ *sper-ka'ī* or سپیره کۍ *sperah-ka'ī*, s.f. (6th) Dill seed (Ligusticum ajowan). Sing. and Pl.

سپیره *speræh*, adj. Gray coloured, hoary, the colour of ashes; (Fem.) *spera'h*. سپیره مخ *speræh makh*, adj. Abject, mean, submissive, wretched, base. سپیره کیدل *speræh kedal*, verb intrans. To be anointed, to become daubed, to be smeared. 2. To become hoary. سپېره کول speræh kawul, verb trans. To anoint, to daub, to smear. 2. To make hoary.

سپېرکئ sper-kaey, adj. Grayish, of a hoary or ash colour (dimin. of سپېره speræh), also سپېره شان speræh-shān; (Fem.) سپېره شانه spera'h shāna'h.

سپېرکئ spera-kaey, s.m. (1st) (dimin. of سپېره) A poltroon, a low, mean, or miserable fellow, a term of abuse. Pl. ي ī. سپېرکئ spera-ka'ī, s.f. (6th) A mean, wretched, miserable, or worthless female. Sing. and Pl.

سپڅل spetsal or spedzal, verb trans. To clear, to clean, to purify, to render spotless. Pres. سپڅي spedzī; past و سپڅه wu-spedzah or سپڅ spedza; fut. و به سپڅي wu bah spedzī; imp. و سپڅه wu-spedzah; act. part. سپڅونکئ spedzūnkaey or سپڅونئ spedzūnaey; past part. سپڅلئ spedzalaey; verb. n. سپڅنه spedzana'h.

سپڅلئ spedzalaey or spetsalaey, adj. (act. part.) Cleaned, purified, cleared, rendered spotless. سپين سپڅلئ spīn spedzalaey, Spotless white.

سپږمه spejzma'h, s.f. (3rd) The nostril. Pl. ې ey. See سږمه and سپېگمه, or سږکمه

سپېښته speshta'h (W.) or spekhta'h (E.), s.f. (3rd) The membraneous covering of the stomach. Pl. ې ey. سپېښته آړول speshta'h or spekhta'h ārrawul, verb trans. To betray the secrets or reveal the faults of another.

سپېگمه spegma'h or سپږمه spejzma'h, s.f. (3rd) The aperture or passage through the nose, the nostril. Pl. ې ey. See سږمه or سږکمه

سپېلنئ spelanaey, s.m. (1st) A seed of the wild rue, burnt to drive away evil spirits. Pl. ي ī. See سپلني

سپېمه speyama'h, s.f. (3rd) A bitch seeking the male, being in heat, animal heat. Pl. ې ey. سپېمه کېدل speyama'h kedal, verb intrans. To get in heat (as a bitch). سپېمه توب speyama'h tob, s.m. (2nd) Animal heat of a bitch. Pl. توبونه tobūnah.

سپين spīn, adj. White, fair, pure, spotless; (Fem.) سپينه spīna'h. سپين والئ spīn-wālaey, s.m. (1st) Whiteness, fairness, purity. 2. Innocence. Pl. والي wālī; or سپين توب spīn-tob, s.m. (2nd). Pl. توبونه tobūnah; or سپين تيا spīn-tī'ā, (E.) Sing. and Pl. (W.) Pl. تياوي tī'āwī. سپين ږيرئ spīn-jzīraey (W.) or سپين گيرئ spīn-gīraey (E.), s.m. (1st) A white-beard, an elder, a patriarch. Pl. ي ī. سپين زړه spīn z'rrah, adj. True, just, sincere, (lit.) white-hearted. سپين شان spīn shān (Masc.) or سپينه شان spīna'h shān (Fem.), Whitish, of a whitish colour. سپين مخ spīn makh, adj. Fair, of good complexion; sincere, true; (Fem.) سپين مخه spīn makha'h. سپين مخئ spīn makhaey, adj. A person of fair complexion, sincere, true, etc.; (Fem.) سپين مخ spīn makhi. Pl. (Masc. and Fem.) سپين مخي spīn makhī. سپين وشئ spīn washaey, s.m. (1st) A silver bracelet. Pl. ي ī. تک سپين tak spīn, adj. Very or quite white, as white as a sheet, white as the driven snow. سپين سپڅلئ spīn spedzalaey or spetsalaey, adj. Clear, pure, or spotless white. سپين زر spīn zar, s.m. (6th) Silver. Sing. and Pl.

سپينېدل spīnedal, verb intrans. To become or grow white, to become bleached or blanched. 2. To peel off, to be skinned or decorticated. Pres. سپينېږي spīnejzī (W.) or سپينېگی spīnegī (E.); past سپين شه spīn shah or و شه wu-shah; fut. سپين به شي spīn bah shī or به و شي bah wu-shī; imp, سپين شه spīn shah or و شه wu-shah; act. part. سپينېدونکئ spīnedūnkaey or سپينېدونئ spīnedūnaey; past part. سپين spīn or سپين شوئ spīn shawaey; verb. n. سپينېدنه spīnedana'h or سپينېده spīnedah.

سپينول spīnawul, verb trans. To make white, to whiten, to whitewash, to bleach, to blanch. 2. To peel, to pare, to flay, to skin, to decorticate. Pres. سپينوي spīnawī; past سپين کړ spīn karr or و کړ wu-karr; fut. سپين به کړي spīn bah krrī or به و کړي bah wu-krrī; imp. سپين کړه spīn krrah or و کړه wu-krrah; act. part. سپينوونکئ spīnawūnkaey or سپينوونئ spīnawūnaey; past part. سپين کړئ spīn karraey; verb. n. سپينونه spīnawuna'h.

سپينګه *spenga'h* (E.) s.f. (3rd) The aperture or passage through the nose, the nostril. Pl. ئ *ey.* See سپيرمه and سپيګمه

سپينه *spīna'h*, s.f. (3rd) (from سپين) Fat, suet, tallow. 2. The tendon Achilles. Pl. ئ *ey.*

سَت *sat*, s.m. (2nd) Reverence, respect, kindness, politeness, favour. 2. Invitation, asking a person who drops in unexpectedly to join at dinner, asking one to take pot-luck. Pl. ستونه *satūnah.* ست کول *sat kawul*, verb trans. To treat with respect or kindness, to invite.

ست *sat*, adj. Straight, flat, level, on the broad of the back, flat as a flounder; (Fem.) سته *sata'h.* See ستون ستغ

ستا *stā*, The genitive case Sing. of the 2nd pers. pron. ته *tah*, Thine, of thee. Also written occasionally دِ تا *di tā.* Pl. ستاسو *stāso* or ستاسي *stāsey*, Yours, of you. See Grammar, page 32.

A ستار *sattār*, adj. (supr. of ستر) One who covers, an attribute of God.

P ستار *sitār*, s.m. (2nd) A guitar with three strings. Pl. ستارونه *sitārūnah.* ستاري *sitārī*, s.m. (5th) A player on the guitar. Pl. ستاريان *sitārī-ān.* ستارئ *sitāra'ī*, s.f. (6th) A female who plays the guitar. Sing. and Pl.

ستاره *stāra'h*, s.f. (3rd) Diffidence, timidity, hesitation, qualm, misgiving, awe, reserve, coyness, shyness. Pl. ئ *ey.* ستاره لويدل *stāra'h l'wedal* or ستاره پريوتل *stāra'h prewatal*, verb intrans. To become diffident, to be overcome with qualms or misgivings, to become shy or coy, to be filled with awe.

ستاسو *stāsū* or ستاسي *stāsey.* Pl. of ستا *stā*, which see.

ستانه *stāna'h*, s.f. (3rd) A threshold, the inside of a house. 2. Family, progeny (particularly of saints or holy persons). Pl. ئ *ey.* See آستانه

ستايل *stā-yal*, verb trans. To praise, to laud, to commend, to applaud, to extol, to eulogize, to glorify, to magnify, to bless. Pres. ستايي *stā-yī*; past وُ ستايه *wu-stā-yah*; fut. وُ به ستايي *wu-bah stā-yī*; imp. وُ ستايه *wu-stā-yah*; act. part. ستايونکي *stā-yūnkaey* or ستايوني *stā-yūnaey*; past part. ستايلي *stā-yalaey*; verb. n. ستاينه *stā-yana'h.*

ستاينه *stā-yana'h*, s.f. (3rd) (verb. n.) Praise, commendation, meed, eulogium, encomium, approbation, laud, applause, blessing, benison. Pl. ئ *ey.*

ستايلي *stā-yalaey*, adj. (past part.) Praised, commended, admired, popular, praiseworthy, plausible, etc.; (Fem.) ستايلِ *stā-yali.* Pl. (Masc. and Fem.) ستايلي *stā-yalī.* See خاګله and ښاګلي

ستخ *stukh* or ستوخ *stūkh*, adj. Bad, ill, prejudicial, sinister, obnoxious, untoward, hurtful, injurious, noxious, baneful, abominable, hateful; (Fem.) ستخه *stukha'h* or ستوخه *stūkha'h.* ستخ *stukh* or ستوخ لګيدل *stūkh lagedal*, verb intrans. To take in bad part, to be distasteful, obnoxious, hurtful, untoward, baneful, etc.

A ستر *satr* or *sitr*, s.m. (2nd) Concealing, covering, veiling, suppressing. 2. Privities. Pl. سترونه *satrūnah* or *sitrūnah.* ستر پوښ *satr-posh* (W.) or *pokh* (E.) adj. One who conceals the faults or failings of others; (Fem.) ستر پوښه *satr posha'h* or *pokha'h.* ستر پوښي *satr-poshī* or *pokhī*, s.f. (3rd) Concealing or veiling the faults of others. Pl. ئ *a'ī.* ستر کول *satr kawul*, verb trans. To conceal, to veil, to suppress. بي ستري کول *be-satrī kawul*, verb trans. To uncover or reveal the faults of another.

ستر *star*, adj. Great, large, big, bulky, wide, capacious. 2. Deep (as a well); (Fem.) ستره *stara'h.* ستر والي *star wālaey*, s.m. (1st) Size, bulk, bigness, magnitude, wideness, extent. 2. Depth, profundity. Pl. والي *wālī.*

ستراو *satrāo*, s.m. (2nd) Fruit fallen from the trees, or strewed on the ground by the wind, the leaves of a tree scattered by the wind, etc. Pl. ستراوونه *satrāo-ūnah.*

سترغلي *starghalaey*, s.m. (1st) The eye-ball including the white and black portions. Pl. ي *ī.* See ليمه

سترګخوږي *starg-khojzaey*, s.m. (1st) A disorder of the eye, ophthalmia. Pl. ي *ī*.

سترګه *starga'h*, s.f. (3rd) The eye, the organ of sight. 2. A planet. Pl ې *ey*. په سترګو *pah stargo* or په سترګو باندِ *pah stargo bāndi*, With heart and soul, with pleasure. برندي سترګي *brandey stargey*, بيماري سترګي *bīmārey stargey*, مړاوي سترګي *m'rrāwey stargey*, or خماري سترګي *khumārey stargey*, adj. Sleepy, or wanton-eyes, eyes marked by debauch or intoxication. سترګ خوږي *starg-khūjzaey* (W.) or سترګ خوګي *starg-khūgaey* (E.) adj. Disease-eyed (person); (Fem.) سترګ خوږِ *starg-khūjzi* or سترګ خوګِ *starg-khūgi*. ردي سترګي *raddey stargey*, سپوري سترګي *sporey stargey*, غټي سترګي *ghattey stargey*, or شوخي سترګي *shokhey stargey*, adj. Lascivious, wanton, large, or immodest eyes. رد سترګي *radd stargaey*, سپور سترګي *spor stargaey*, غټ سترګي *ghatt stargaey*, وا سترګي *wā stargaey*, or شوخ سترګي *shokh stargaey*, adj. Large-eyed, an immodest person; (Fem.) رد سترګِ *radd stargi*, سپور سترګِ *spor stargi*, غټ سترګِ *ghatt stargi*, وا سترګِ *wā stargi*, or شوخ سترګِ *shokh stargi*. پټي سترګي *puttey stargey*, adj. With the eyes closed. پټ سترګي *putt stargaey*, adj. A hardened, impious, or irreverent person, fearless, callous; (Fem.) پټ سترګِ *putt stargi*. چغر سترګي *chaghar stargaey*, adj. Wall-eyed (as a man or animal); (Fem.) چغر سترګِ *chaghar stargi*. Pl. (Masc. and Fem.) ي *ī*. چغره سترګه *chaghara'h starga'h*, s.f. (3rd) An eye with a spot in it, a wall eye. Pl. ې *ey*. سري سترګي *sarey stargey*, adj. Fiery-eyed, red-eyed (through anger); سور سترګي *sor stargaey*, adj. A person with angry or red eyes, an irritable, choleric, or ill-tempered person; (Fem.) سور سترګِ *sor stargi*. لېچني سترګي *lechaney stargey*, Sore or rheumy eyes. لېچن سترګي *lechan stargaey*, adj. Having a disease of the eyes, disordered eyes. چيخني سترګي *chīkhaney stargey*, adj. Rheumy eyes, blear eyes. چوغي *chūghaey* or چوغ سترګي *chūgh stargey*, adj. Short sighted, seeing at small distance. چپکي سترګي *chapakey stargey*, adj. Squinting eyes. سترګي کښل *stargey k'shal*, (W.) or *k'khal* (E.) verb trans. To blind. 2. To look at angrily, to roll the eyes at one. سترګي رپول *stargey rapawul*, verb trans. To wink, to blink. سترګه غورزيدل *starga'h ghorzedal*, verb intrans. To feel a pulsation in the eye (considered a good or bad omen). سترګه وهل *starga'h wahal*, verb trans. To wink as a hint, to communicate a secret by signs. سترګي خوږي کول *stargey khojzey kawul* (W.) or سترګي خوګي کول *stargey khogey kawul* (E.) verb trans. To contemplate the beauty of any one (*lit.* to sweeten the eyes). 2. To take a nap. سترګي آړول *stargey ārrawul*, verb trans. To turn away the eyes (as from grief, displeasure, etc.). سترګي سري کول *stargey sarey kawul*, verb trans. To show rage or anger (to become enraged), (*lit.* to redden the eyes). سترګي تورول *stargey torawul*, verb trans. To blacken the eyelids, to apply antimony to the eyes. په سترګو ختل *pah stargo khatal*, verb intrans. To become an eyesore. د سترګو نور *da stargo nūr*, The light of the eyes; a term of love to a child. د سترګي کاسه *da stargey kāsa'h*, s.f. (3rd) The socket of the eye. Pl. ې *ey*. د سترګو تور *da stargo tor*, The black part of the eye. له سترګو لويدل *lah stargo l'wedal*, verb intrans. (to fall from the eyes) To become mean, or contemptible, to be disgraced or out of favour. له بدو سترګو لري شي *lah bado stargo larey shey*, Be thou far from malicious eyes! په غټو سترګو ويده *pah ghatto stargo wīdah*, adj. Negligent, asleep with the eyes open. په غټو سترګو اوديدل *pah ghatto stargo aodedal* or ويديدل *wīdedal*, verb intrans. To be negligent (*lit.* to sleep with the eyes open).

A ستره *satra'h*, s.f. (3rd) A curtain, a veil, a covering. Pl. ې *ey*. ستره کول *satra'h kawul*, verb trans. To conceal, to veil, to cover.

ستري *satraey*, s.m. (1st) A cut field of grain, a heap of grain, a stock of grain strewed or heaped on the ground. Pl. ي *ī*. ستري وتري

satrī watrī, adj. In heaps, as grain or corn in a field, as bodies on a field of battle, or as fruit fallen from a tree.

ستړی *starraey*, adj. Tired, wearied, fatigued, bored, disgusted, jaded, knocked up, fagged, used up; (Fem.) ستړ *starri*. Pl. (Masc. and Fem.) ي *ī*. ستړيه *starrī-a'h*, s.f. (3rd) Weariness, fatigue, tedium, exhaustion, prostration. Pl. ئ *ey*; or ستړي تيا *starrey tī'ā*, s.f. (6th) (E.) Sing. and Pl. (W.) Pl. تياوي *tī'āwī*. ستړي کيدل *starrey kedal*, verb intrans. To be fatigued, to become tired, jaded, wearied, knocked up, etc. ستړي کول *starrey kawul*, verb trans. To tire, to fag, to fatigue, to jade, to harass, to overwork.

ستغ *stagh*, adj. Sordid, mean, avaricious; astringent, binding, opposed to laxative, rough to the taste, producing dryness in the mouth; (Fem.) ستغه *stagha'h*. 2. s.m. (2nd) A gland, a swelling, a tumour, a bubo, etc. 3. Any astringent remedy applied to a wound. Pl. ستغونه *staghūnah*. See زموخت and مرغړي

ستل *satal*, s.m. (2nd) A bucket or large vessel formed like a bucket, made of copper. Pl. ستلونه *satalūnah*.

P ستم *sitam*, s.m. (2nd) Tyranny, oppression, injury, outrage, violence, vexation. Pl. ستمونه *sitamūnah*. ستم رسيده *sitam rasīdah* or ديده *dīdah*, adj. Oppressed, injured, outraged. ستم گار *sitam-gār*, s.m. (5th) A tyrant, an oppressor. Pl. گاران *gārān*; or ستم گر *sitam-gar*, s.m. (5th). Pl. گر *gær*. ستم گره *sitam gara'h* or گاره *gāra'h*, s.f. (3rd). Pl. ئ *ey*. ستم گري *sitam-garī*, s.f. (3rd) Tyranny, oppression, violence, injustice. Pl. ئ *a'ī*. ستم کول *sitam kawul*, verb trans. To tyrannize over, to oppress, to act with violence or injustice.

ستم *stam*, s.m. (2nd) Exertion of one's powers (as a woman in childbirth), labour, travail, parturition. Pl. ستمونه *stamūnah*. ستم وهل *stam wahal*, verb trans. To labour with pain, as a woman in childbirth.

ستن *stan*, s.f. (1st) A needle, a post, a pillar, a prop, a column. Pl. ستنې *stani*.

ستن پيبودل *stan pe-yodal* or پيبل *pe-yal*, verb trans. To thread a needle.

ستنه *stana'h*, s.f. (3rd) Recession, retirement, withdrawal, retreat, retrocession, etc. Pl. ئ *ey*. په ستنه تلل *pah stana'h t'lal*, verb intrans. To step back (as soldiers at drill), to retire without turning round. په ستنه پوري وتل *pah stana'h pūrī watal* or کيدل *kedal*, verb intrans. To retreat, to retire before.

ستوان *satwān*, s.m. (5th) Pl. Parched grain made into meal. The singular form ستو *sato*, is merely used to express a small quantity. (ستو).

ستوخ *stokh*, adj. Bad, ill, obnoxious, sinister, prejudicial, injurious, baneful, hateful, abominable; (Fem.) ستوخه *stokha'h* or *stūkhah*. ستوخ لگيدل *stokh* or *stūkh lagedal*, verb intrans. To take in bad part, to be distasteful to, obnoxious, etc. See سخ

P ستور *sutūr*, s.m. (5th) An animal, a quadruped, a beast of burden, cattle, etc. Pl. ستوران *sutūrān*.

ستوری *storaey*, s.m. (1st) A star, constellation, Pl. ي *ī*. جمبق ستوري *jambak storī*, s.m. (1st) Pl. The Pleiades. د قطب ستوري *da kutb storaey*, The north-star. د سهيل ستوري *da suhail storaey*, The star Canopus.

ستوگه *stogah*, s.f. (3rd) Ease, rest, repose, quiet, tranquillity, peace; a dwelling. Pl. ئ *ey*. See استوگه

ستومان *stomān*, adj. Tired, wearied, fagged, worn out, fatigued, bored, disgusted, jaded, knocked up; (Fem.) ستومانه *stomāna'h*. ستوماني *stomānī*, s.f. (3rd) Weariness, fatigue, prostration, exhaustion, tedium. Pl. ئ *a'ī*. ستوماني آچول *stomānī āchawul*, verb trans. To stretch out, to gape, to yawn. See ستړي

ستون *stūn*, adj. (past part.) Turned, changed, called back, turned back, returned, come back; (Fem.) ستونه *stūna'h*. ستونيدل *stūnedal*, verb intrans. To return, to come back, to be called back. Pres. ستونيږي *stūnejzī* (W.) or ستونيگي *stūnegī* (E.); past ستون شه *stūn shah* or وُ شه *wu-shah*; fut. ستون به شي *stūn bah shī* or به وُ شي *bah wu-shī*; imp. ستون شه *stūn* shah or وُ شه wu-shah; act part. ستونيدونكيَ stūnedūnkaey or ستونيدونيَ stūnedūnaey; past part. ستون stūn or ستون شويَ stūn shawaey; verb. n. ستونيدنه stūnedana'h or ستونيده stūnedah. ستونول stūnawul, verb trans. To turn back, to call back, to make return, turn, or turn back. Pres. ستونوي stūnawī; past ستون كړ stūn karr or وُ كړ wu-karr; fut. ستون به كړي stūn bah krrī or به وُ كړي bah wu-krrī; imp. ستون كړه stūn krrah or وُ كړه wu-krrah; act. part. ستونوونكيَ stūnawūnkaey or ستونوونيَ stūnawūnaey; past part. ستون كړيَ stūn karraey; verb. n. ستونونه stūnawuna'h.

ستونيَ stūnaey, s.m. (1st) The larynx, Adam's apple. Pl. ي ī.

ستون stūn or ستوني ستغ stūnī stagh, adj. Lying flat on the back, on the broad of the back, turned over, supine. ستوني ستغ پريوتل stūnī-stagh prewatal, verb intrans. To fall on the flat or broad of the back. ستوني ستغ آچول stūnī-stagh āchawul, verb trans. To throw on the broad or flat of the back.

S ستي sata'ī, s.f. (6th) A woman who burns on her husband's funeral pyre. Sing. and Pl.

ستيزه steza'h, s.f. (3rd) Controversy, conflict, altercation, quarrel, battle, dispute. 2. A table-land, flat land. Pl. يْ ey. ستيزه كول steza'h kawul, verb trans. To quarrel, to dispute, to raise a controversy. See بوره

ستټ satt, s.m. (2nd) A cutler's block, a block of wood on which an anvil is placed, the root or trunk of a tree remaining in the ground, a log of wood, a crooked, knotty piece of wood only fit for the fire. 2. A sudden attack. Pl. ستټونه sattūnah. Also ستټه satta'h, s.f. (3rd). Pl. يْ ey. See سوټ , ستټكي and كونسټ

ستټ satt, s.m. (5th) The back or nape of the neck. Pl. ستټان sattān. See څټ

ستټك sattak, s.m. (5th) A hammer. Pl. ستټكان sattakān. See څټك

ستټكوريَ sattkūracy, adj. scorched, burnt (as bread in an oven), shrunk up, wrinkled, scarified, frost-bitten, contracted, shrivelled; (Fem.) ستټكورِ sattkūri. Pl. (Masc. and Fem.) ي ī.

ستټكوريَ كيدل sattkūraey kedal, verb intrans. To become scorched or burnt (as bread, etc.), to become shrivelled, scarified, wrinkled, frost-bitten, etc. ستټكوريَ كول sattkūraey kawul, verb trans. To scorch, to scarify, to wrinkle, to contract, etc. See كونسټ and سونكټ

A سجاده sajjāda'h, s.f. (3rd) (from سجد) A carpet or mat on which Muhammadans kneel at prayers, an altar, a masjid. Pl. يْ ey.

A سجاده نشين sajjāda'h nishīn, s.m. (5th) The prior or superior of an order of monks, the chief priest at a shrine. Pl. نشينان nishīnān.

A سجده sijda'h, s.f. (3rd) Bowing the head so that the forehead may touch the ground, adoration, especially to God. Pl. يْ ey.

سجده گاه sijda'h gāh, s.m. (2nd) The place for performing the sijda'h or adoration. Pl. گاهونه gāhūnah. سجده كول sijda'h kawul, verb trans. To prostrate one's-self in prayer by placing the forehead to the ground, to bow in adoration.

A سجل sijill, s.m. (2nd) A register, a decree of a judge, seal of a judge or court, attestation of a notary. 2. The recording angel. Sing. and Pl. Pl. سجلونه sijillūnah.

A سجود sujūd, Pl. of سجده which see.

S سچ such, adj. Pure, undefiled, unpolluted, clean, unadulterated, without flaw; or سچه suchæh; (Fem.) سچه sucha'h.

A سحاب sahāb, s.m. (6th) A cloud. Sing. and Pl. See اوريځ

A سحار sahār or سحر sahr, s.m. (9th) The dawn of the morning, dawn of day. Sing. and Pl.

A سحر sihr, s.m. (2nd) Enchantment, sorcery, necromancy, magic. Pl. سحرونه sihrūnah. ساحر sāhir, s.m. (5th) A sorcerer, an enchanter, a magician, a conjuror. Pl. ساحران sāhirān. ساحره sāhira'h, s.f. (3rd) A sorceress, an enchantress. Pl. يْ ey. Also سحرگر sihr-gar, s.m. (5th). Pl. سحرگران sihr-garān سحر گره sihr-gara'h, s.f. (3rd). Pl. يْ ey. سحر كول sihr kawul, verb trans. To enchant, to fascinate, to charm.

P سحر خیز *saḥr-khez*, s.m. (5th) One who rises with the dawn, an early riser. Pl. خیزان *khezān*. سحر خیزه *saḥr kheza'h*, s.f. (3rd). Pl. ې *ey*. سحر خیزي *saḥr khezī*, s.f. (3rd) Rising with the dawn, early rising. Pl. ئ *a'ī*. سحر خیزي لرل *saḥr khezī laral* or سحر خیزي کول *saḥr khezī kawul*, verb trans. To rise with the dawn.

A P سحر گاه *saḥr-gāh*, s.m. (2nd) The dawn of day, day-break. Pl. گاهونه *gāhūnah*.

سخ *sakh*, interj. Good! well done! excellent! See آخ.

سخ *sakh*, or سخ *sakh* or سخني کال *sakhanaey kāl*, adv. The present year. See سږ or سګ

A سخا *sakhā*, s.f. (6th) Liberality, generosity, munificence. (E.) Sing. and Pl. (W.) Pl. سخاوي *sakhāwī*; or سخاوت *sakhāwat*, s.m. (2nd). Pl. سخاوتونه *sakhāwatūnah*. سخاوت کول *sakhāwat kawul*, verb trans. To act with liberality or generosity. سخي *sakhī*, adj. Liberal, generous, munificent; (Masc. and Fem.)

سخا *skhā*, adj. Rotten, decayed, putrid, rank, stinking, offensive. سخا والی *skhā wālaey*, s.m. (1st) Rottenness, mustiness, putrescence, foulness, rancidity, stink. Pl. والي *wālī*; or سخا توب *skhā-tob*, s.m. (2nd). Pl. توبونه *tobūnah*; and سخا تیا *skhā tī'ā*, s.f. (6th) (E.) Sing. and Pl. (W.) Pl. تیاوي *tī'āwī*. سخا کیدل *skhā kedal*, verb intrans. To smell, to stink, to become rotten, putrid, offensive, etc. سخا کول *skhā kawul*, verb trans. To make rotten or putrid, to make or cause to stink or smell. See وروست and ورستیدل

سخاوږه *skhāw-jza'h*, s.f. (3rd) Orris root, the sweet cane, the galingale. Pl. ې *ey*. See خشاوږه

P سخت *sakht*, adj. Hard, strong. 2. Difficult. 3. Obdurate. 4. Stingy. 5. Rigid, severe, harsh, violent, vehement, cruel, austere, painful, troublesome; (Fem.) سخته *sakhta'h*. سختیدل *sakhtedal*, verb intrans. To become or get hard, to become or grow stingy, to become harsh, severe, cruel, austere, etc. Pres. سختیږي *sakhtejzī* (W.) or سختیګي *sakhtegī* (E.); past سخت شه *sakht shah* or وُ شه *wu-shah*; fut. سخت به شي *sakht bah shī* or به وُ شي *bah wu-shī*; imp. سخت شه *sakht shah* or وُ شه *wu-shah*; act. part. سختیدونکی *sakhtedūnkaey* or سختیدونی *sakhtedūnaey*; past part. سخت *sakht* or سخت شوی *sakht shawaey*; verb. n. سختیدنه *sakhtedana'h* or سختیده *sakhtedah*. سختول *sakhtawul*, verb trans. To make hard, to harden, to make rigid, to render austere, cruel, severe, etc. Pres. سختوي *sakhtawī*; past سخت کړ *sakht karr* or وُ کړ *wu-karr*; fut. سخت به کړي *sakht bah krrī* or به وُ کړي *bah wu-krrī*; imp. سخت کړه *sakht krrah* or وُ کړه *wu-krrah*; act. part. سختوونکی *sakhtawūnkaey* or سختووني *sakht-awūnaey*; past part. سخت کړی *sakht karraey*; verb. n. سختونه *sakhtawuna'h*.

P سختي *sakhtī*, s.f. (3rd) Hardness, firmness, obduracy, intenseness, vehemence, severity, asperity, cruelty, hardness of heart, harshness. 2. Stinginess, indigence, distress, difficulty. Pl. ئ *a'ī*. سختي کول *sakhtī kawul*, verb trans. To act with severity or harshness, to treat with asperity, etc.

سخر *skhar*, s.m. (5th) A father-in-law. Pl. سخران *skharān*. See خسر

سخر *skhar*, s.m. (6th) A stone, a rock, a pebble. Pl. سخر *skhær*. See دبره

A سخره *sakhra'h*, s.f. (3rd) A rock, a large hewn stone. Pl. ې *ey*.

P سخن *sukhun*, s.m. (5th) Speech, language, thing, business, matter, affair. Pl. سخنان *sukhunān*. Used in compos. سخن آراي *sukhun-ārā'e*, adj. Eloquent, adorning language; (Fem.) سخن آرایه *sukhun ārāya'h*. سخن آرائي *sukhun ārā'ī*, s.f. (3rd) Eloquence, display of language. Pl. ئ *a'ī*; or سخن آور *sukhun āwar*; (Fem.) سخن آوره *sukhun āwara'h*. سخن دان *sukhun dān*, adj. Intelligent, skilled in language, a poet; (Fem.) سخن دانه *sukhun dāna'h*. سخن چین *sukhun chīn*, s.m. (5th) A spy, a tale-bearer, an informer. Pl. چینان *chīnān*. سخن چینه *sukhun chīna'h*, s.f.

(3rd). Pl. ي *ey*. سخن ساز *sukhun sāz*, s.m. (5th) An orator, a speaker, a poet. Pl. سازان *sāzān*. سخن سازه *sukhun sāza'h*, s.f. (3rd). Pl. ي *ey*. سخن سازي *sukhun sāzī*, s.f. (3rd) Eloquence, elocution, oratory, composition. Pl. ئي *a'ī*. سخن سازي كول *sukhun sāzī kawul*, verb trans. To compose. سخن شناس *sukhun shinās*, adj. Knowing or conversant in language; (Fem.) سخن شناسه *sukhun shināsa'h*. سخن فهم *sukhn fahm*, adj. Intelligent, quick of apprehension; (Fem.) سخن فهمه *sukhn fahma'h*. سخن فهمي *sukhn fahmī*, s.f. (3rd) Intelligence, understanding. Pl. ئي *a'ī*.

سخوښتن *skhwashtan* (W.) *skhwakhtan* (E.) s.m. (2nd) Hot ashes, live coals, a cinder, etc. Pl. سخوښتنونه *skhwashtanūnah* or *skhwakhtanūnah*. See خكلن

سخوندر *skhwandar*, s.m. (6th) A steer, a young bullock. Pl. سخوندر *skhwandær*. Also s.m. (5th) Pl. سخوندران *skhwandarān*. سخوندره *skhwandara'h*, s.f. (3rd) A heifer. Pl. ي *ey*. See سوندر and سخي

سخه *sakha'h*, s.f. (3rd) Joy, delight, gladness, glee, pleasure, gratification, bliss, transport, rapture, joy at the misfortune of an enemy. Pl. ي *ey*.

A سخي *sakhī*, adj. Liberal, generous, munificent. سخي توب *sakhī-tob*, s.m. (2nd) Liberality, generosity, munificence. Pl. توبونه *tobūnah*. See سخا

سخي *skhaey*, s.m. (1st) A calf. Pl. ي *ī*. سخئ *skha'ī*, s.f. (6th) A female calf, a young cow. Sing. and Pl.

سد *sud*, s.m. (2nd) Memory, remembrance, understanding, sense, consciousness, notice, care, intelligence, judgment. Pl. سدونه *sudūnah*. (W.) سُد *sæd*. Pl. سُدونه *sædūnah* (s سدھ). بي سد *be-sud*, adj. Beside one's-self. سد بد *sud bud*, Correct knowledge, sense, perception (s سدھ بدھ). سد كول *sud kawul*, verb trans. To inquire into, to exercise one's judgment or intellect, etc.

A سد *sadd*, s.m. (2nd) A wall, a barrier, impediment, an obstacle, etc. Pl. سدونه *saddūnah*.

سدم *sudam*, s. prop. The name of a hill and village in the Yūsufzī country towards Buner.

سدوزي *sado-zī* or سدوزاي *sadū-zā'ī*, s.m. (1st) (Pl.) The name of a tribe of Afghāns, the royal tribe. سدوزی *sado-zaey* or سدوزاي *sado-zāaey*. (Sing.) A male of the above tribe. سدوزئ *sadū-za'ī*, s.f. (6th) A female of the above. Sing. and Pl. See Introduction to Grammar, page 4.

S سده *sudah*, adj. Pure, unsullied, real, entire.

A سده *sudda'h*, s.f. (3rd) (from سد) (in medicine) A stoppage, an obstruction in the bowels, nose, etc. Pl. ي *ey*. See سوده

سدړ *suddar*, adj. Bald, bare-headed or scald-headed, from the disease Tinea capatis; (Fem.) سدړه *suddara'h*. 2. s.m. (5th) A pig, a hog, a wild boar. Pl. سدُړ *suddær* or سدړان *suddarān*. سدړه *suddara'h*, s.f. (3rd) A sow, a wild sow. Pl. ي *ey*. See سودر and كنجي

P سر *sar*, s.m. (2nd) The head, the top, the point of anything. Pl. سرونه *sarūnah*. سر آخستل *sar ākhistal*, verb trans. To rebel, to rise up against one. په سر آخستل *pah sar ākhistal*, verb trans. To turn the brains, to overcome (as with lust or desire). سر په سر *sar pah sar*, adj. Head to head, equal with, all the while. 2. adv. Entirely, from one end to the other. سر بسته *sar bastah*, adj. Closed, shut, hidden, 2. Inextricable. سر پرست *sar parast*, adj. Protector, aider; (Fem.) سر پرسته *sar parasta'h*. سر پرستي *sar parastī*, s.f. (3rd) Aid, protection. Pl. ئي *a'ī*. سر پرستي كول *sar parastī kawul*, verb trans. To aid, to protect. سرماتوك *sar-mātūk*, adj. A head-breaker, a quarrelsome fellow; (Fem.) سر ماتوكه *sar-mātūka'h*. سر مغزن *sar maghzan*, s.m. (5th) A chatter-box. 2. Vexation, perplexity, fatigue. Pl. سر مغزُن *sar maghzæn*. سر مغزنه *sar maghzana'h*, s.f. (3rd) A chattering, long-tongued woman. Pl. ي *ey*. سر ماتي *sar mātaey*, adj. A head-breaker, a quarrelsome fellow, quarrelsome. 2. A person with his head broken, broken-headed; (Fem.) سرماتې

sar-māti. Pl. (Masc. and Fem.) يِ *ī*. سرخيل *sar khel*, s.m. (5th) The chief or head man of a tribe. Pl. خيلان *khelān*; or سر كرده *sar kardah*, s.m. (5th) Pl. كردهگان *kardahgān*. سر تور *sar tor*, adj. Debased, degraded, naked headed, roofless (as a house), uncovered; (Fem.) سر توره *sar tora'h*. سر توري *sar torī*, s.f. (3rd) Debasement, degradation, nakedness of the head, unroofing, uncovering. Pl. ئِ *a'ī*. سر توري كول *sar torī kawul*, verb trans. To debase, to degrade, to uncover or unroof (as a house). سر تور والیَ *sar-tor wālaey*, s.m. (1st) Nakedness of the head. Pl. والي *wālī*. سر هوا *sar hawā*, adj. Vain, foolish, proud, ambitious. سر و پا *sar-o pā*, s.m. (9th) A dress of honour. Sing. and Pl. 2. adv. From head to foot. سر تر پايه *sar tar pāyah*, adv. From head to foot, cap-à-pie. سر و تن *sar-o-tan*, adj. Equal, on a par, straight (as accounts), exact. سر درد *sar dard* or *sar-i-dard*, s.m. (2nd) Headache, trouble, anxiety. Pl. دردونه *dardūnah*; or سر دردي *sar dardī*, s.f. (3rd) Vexation, trouble, toil. Pl. ئِ *a'ī*. سر پري كړیَ *sar pre-karraey*, adj. Beheaded, decapitated. سر پريكول *sar pre-kawul*, verb trans. To behead, to decapitate. سر زوري *sar zoraey*, adj. Headstrong, rebellious, stubborn, mutinous; (Fem.) سر زورِ *sar zori*. Pl. (Masc. and Fem.) يِ *ī*. سر زوري *sar-zorī*, s.f. (3rd) Disobedience, rebellion, stubbornness. Pl. ئِ *a'ī*. سر زوري كول *sar zorī kawul*, verb trans. To rebel, to disobey. سرفراز *sar-farāz* or سر افراز *sar-afrāz* or سر لوړي *sar l'warraey* or سر بلند *sar buland*, adj. Exalted, promoted, eminent, glorious. سر افرازي *sar-afrāzī* or سر بلندي *sar bulandī*, s.f. (3rd) Eminence, exaltation. Pl. ئِ *a'ī*; or سر لوړ تيا *sar l'warr-tī'ā*, s.f. (6th). (E.) Sing. and Pl. (W.) Pl. تياوي *tī'āwī*. سر باز *sar-bāz*, adj. Bold, intrepid, risking one's head. سر بازي *sar-bāzī*, s.f. (3rd) Intrepidity, risking life. Pl. ئِ *a'ī*. سر بازي كول *sar bāzī kawul*, verb trans. To act intrepidly. سر براه *sar ba-rāh*, adj. Set a-going, being in the way of performing or completing any matter. سر براه كول *sar ba-rāh kawul*, verb trans. To set a-going, to commence. سر بمهر *sar ba-muhr*, adj. Sealed. سر تيره *sar terah*, adj. Sharp-pointed. سر خود *sur-i-khūd*, adj. Independent, being one's own master; (Fem.) سر خوده *sar-i-khūda'h*. سر خوش *sar khūsh*, adj. Cheerful, gay, merry; (Fem.) سر خوشه *sar khūsha'h*. سر خوشي *sar khūshī*, s.f. (3rd) Gaiety, cheerfulness, mirth. Pl. ئِ *a'ī*. سر درختي *sar darakhtī*, s.f. (3rd) Produce of trees, part of a garden containing fruit-trees. Pl. ئِ *a'ī*. سر زمين *sar zamīn*, s.m. (2nd) The earth, country, territory. Pl. زمينونه *zamīnūnah*. سر كښ *sar kash* (W.) or *kakh* (E.) adj. Stubborn, mutinous. 2. s.m. (2nd) A covering for a horse reaching from head to foot. Pl. سر كښونه *sar kashūnah* or *kakhūnah*; (Fem.) سر كښه *sar kasha'h* or *kakha'h*. سر كښي *sar kashī* (W.) or *kakhī* (E.), Stubbornness, mutiny, rebellion. Pl. ئِ *a'ī*. سر كښي كول *sar kashī* or *kakhī kawul*, verb trans. To act stubbornly or mutinously. سر كول *sar kol*, s.m. (2nd) The part of a trough of a mill where the water enters. 2. The name of a lake in Pāmir, the source of the Oxus. Pl. كولونه *kolūnah*. سر گذشت *sar-guzasht*, s.m. (2nd) An event, an adventure, an accident, a narrative, a transaction. Pl. سر گذشتونه *sur-guzashtūnah*. سر كار *sar-i-kār*, s.m. (2nd) Affair, matter, concern. Pl. كارونه *kārūnah*. سر گردان *sar-gardān*, adj. Distressed, humbled, confounded, stupified, straying, wandering; (Fem.) سر گردانه *sar gardāna'h*. سر گرداني *sar gardānī*, s.f. (3rd) Distress, confusion, amazement. Pl. ئِ *a'ī*. سر گردان كول *sar-gardān kawul*, verb trans. To distress, to confuse, to confound. سر گرم *sar-garm*, adj. Intent on, eager, earnest, attentive, zealous, inflamed with love, etc.; (Fem.) سر گرمه *sar-garma'h*. سر گرمي *sar-garmī*, s.f. (3rd) Attention, application, diligence, eagerness, zeal, love. Pl. ئِ *a'ī*. سر گرمي كول *sar garmī kawul*, verb trans. To attend to, to act with diligence, to show zeal or application. سر گروه *sar-guroh*, s.m. (5th) A leader, a ringleader. Pl. گروهان *gurohān*. سرمو *sar-i-mū*, The breadth of a hair, a hair's breadth. سر نگون *sar-nigūn*, adj. Abashed, hanging the head, downcast, ashamed. 2. Upside down, topsy-turvy; (Fem.) سر نگونه *sar-nigūna'h*. See نسکور. سر له سرَ *sar lah sara*, Renewal, recommencement. سر نوشت *sar nawisht*, s.m. (2nd) Fortune, destiny, fate. Pl. نوشتونه *nawishtūnah*. سرچشمه *sar-chashma'h*, s.f. (3rd) A fountain. Pl. ې *ey*. سر غوړ *sar-ghwarr*, s.m. (6th) Pomatum, grease for the hair. Sing. and Pl. تر سر تیر *tar sar tera*, In danger of one's life, desperate. د سر په زور *da sar pah zor*, With all one's might. سر کول *sar kawul*, verb trans. To begin, to commence. 2. To finish, to complete. 3. To appoint a chief or head man, to elect. سر کیدل *sar kedal*, verb intrans. To become completed or finished. په سر خاوري دوړول *pah sar khāwrey dūrrawul*, verb trans. To throw dust on the head, to lament. سر ماتول *sar mātawul*, verb trans. To break one's head. سر وهل *sar wahal*, verb trans. To take great pains (as in teaching, etc.), to search diligently. سرځړول *sar dzarrawul*, verb trans. to hang the head through modesty, shame, etc. سر کوټل *sar kūttal*, verb trans. To bruise the head (as of a snake), to strike on the head. سر تړل *sar tarral*, verb trans. To bandage the head. سر تړوني *sar tarrūnaey*, s.m. (1st) (act. part.) A bandage for the head. Pl. ي *ī*. سر بر کول *sar bur kawul*, verb trans. To strip a tree of its branches. سر خریل *sar khareyal*, verb trans. To shave the head. سرگرول *sar garawul*, verb trans. To scratch one's head (as at a loss what to do).

A سر *sirr*, s.m. (2nd) A secret, a mystery. Pl. سرونه *sirrūnah*. سر ساتل *sirr sātal*, verb trans. To keep a secret. سر ویل *sirr wa-yal* or سرفاش کول *sirr fāsh kawul*, verb trans. To reveal or betray a secret. See راز

سرا *sarā*, s.f. (6th) (E). Manure, dung. Sing. and Pl. See سره and جوره

A سراب *sarāb*, s.m. (2nd) Vapour resembling water at a distance, seen on sandy plains, mirage. Pl. سرابونه *sarābūnah*.

A سراج *sarrāj*, s.m. (5th) A saddler, a groom. Pl. سراجونه *sarrājūnah*. سراجي *sarrājī*, s.f. (3rd) The business of a saddler. Pl. ئ *a'ī*.

P سراچه *sarā-cha'h*, s.f. (3rd) A small enclosure, a small caravansary. Pl. ې *ey*.

P سراسر *sarā-sar*, adj. All, the whole. 2. adv. Wholly, entirely, from beginning to end. سراسري *sarāsarī*, adj. Summary, short, brief.

سراسر *sarāsar*, s.m. (6th) The juniper tree. Sing. and Pl. See ناجو

P سراسیمه *sarā-sīmah*, adj. Amazed, confounded, distracted, disturbed, beside one's-self. سراسیمه کیدل *sarā-sīmah kedal*, verb intrans. To become amazed, to grow distracted, confounded, etc. سراسیمه کول *sarā-sīmah kawul*, verb trans. To disturb, to amaze, to distract, to confound.

P سراسیمگي *sarā-sīmagī*, s.f. (3rd) Amazement, distress, confusion or distraction of mind. Pl. ئ *a'ī*.

P سراغ *surāgh*, s.m. (2nd) Sign, mark, trace, intelligence. 2. Search, inquiry, spying, etc. Pl. سراغونه *surāghūnah*. سراغ پیدا کول *surāgh paidā kawul*, verb trans. To discover trace, intelligence, etc. سراغ یستل *surāgh yastal*, verb trans. To discover, to gain trace of (as property). سراغي *surāghī*, A tracker of thieves. Pl. سراغیان *surāghī-ān*.

سرانه *sarāna'h*, s.f. (3rd) The wood at the upper part of a door in which are two holes or sockets for the door to revolve in instead of hinges. Pl. ې *ey*.

P سرانجام *sarānjām*, s.m. (2nd) Apparatus, utensils, furniture, goods and chattels, stores, materials, requisites. 2. Conclusion, end. Pl. سرانجامونه *sarānjāmūnah*. سرانجام کول *sarānjām kawul*, verb trans. To accomplish, to finish, to prepare.

P سرانداز *sarāndāz*, s.m. (2nd) The foot and head pieces of a bed. 2. The carpet spread at the head of a room. سراندازونه *sarāndāzūnah*.

P سراۍ *srā'e* or *sarā'e*, s.m. (2nd) A house, an inn, a caravansary. Pl. سرايونه *sarā'e-ūnah*. كاروان سراۍ *kārwān sarā'e*, A caravansary. د دنيا سراۍ *da dunyā sarā'e*, The inn of the world, the world, the earth. سراۍ دار *sarā'e-dār*, s.m. (5th) The keeper, or attendant at a caravansary. Pl. داران *dārān*.

سربانديؤ *sar-bāndey*, s.f. (3rd) Pl. A piece of land or portion of a field left unploughed or uncut. 2. The fastening of the yoke of a plough. (Sing. not used.) See سرواندي

سربانډي *sar-bānḍḍey*, s.f. (3rd) Pl. Rope made of strips of leather. 2. The rope for fastening the yoke to the plough. See چرمينه

سر بسته *sar basta'h*, s.f. (3rd) A small turban, a kind of handkerchief or veil worn by women during household duties. Pl. ۍ *ey*. See څپوټکي

سرپ *surup*, s.m. (6th) Lead. Sing. and Pl. (P سرب).

سرپ *sirp*, adv. (corrup. of صرف) Solely, merely, purely, only, alone.

سر پاړي *sar-pājzaey*, s.m. (1st) The name of a disease in which the face swells. Pl. ي *ī*. (Pl.) The name of a tribe of Afghāns. سرپاړی *sarpājzaey*, (Sing.) A man of the above tribe. سرپاړۍ *sarpājza'ī*, s.f. (3rd) A woman of the above. Sing. and Pl.

سرپوټه *sar pūṯṯa'h*, s.f. (3rd) A virgin, a young unmarried woman (*lit.* head-concealed). Pl. ۍ *ey*.

سرپوښ *sar-posh* (W.) or *sar-pokh* (E.), s.m. (2nd) The cover or lid of a pot or other vessel. Pl. سرپوښونه *sar-poshūnah* or *sar-pokhūnah*. (P سرپوش).

سر تير *sar-i-tīr*, adv. Quickly, speedily.

P A سرحد *sar-ḥadd*, s.m. (2nd) Boundary, limits, confines, frontier, extremity. Pl. سرحدونه *sar-ḥaddūnah*.

P سرخ *surkh*, adj. Red. (In composition). سرخ باد *surkh bād*, s.m. (2nd) Erysipelas, St. Anthony's dance, or fire. Pl. بادونه *bādūnah*. سرخ روي *surkh rū'e*, adj. Honorable, unabashed (person); (Fem.) سرخ رويه *surkh rū'ea'h*. سرخ روي *surkh rū'ī*, s.f. (3rd) Honour, character, fame. Pl. ۍ *a'ī*. سرخه *surkhah*, adj. Fair, cream coloured (as a horse).

سرخاب *surkhāb* or سرخاو *surkh-āo*, s. prop. The name of a river between Kābul and Jelālābād, a river in the Afrīdī country, which joins the Bārah river.

سرخچه *surkhcha'h*, s.m. (6th) A kind of apricot. Pl. ۍ *ey*.

سرخكه *sarkhaka'h*, s.f. (3rd) The name of a small bird, the *tā-ler*. Pl. ۍ *ey*.

سرخي *surkhī*, s.f. (3rd) Blight in corn, mildew. 2. The yellow jaundice. 3. (P) Redness, red paint, or red ink. Pl. ۍ *a'ī*.

سرخۍ *surkha'ī*, s.f. (6th) An embroidered fur-below, a piece of cloth sewed on to the legs of women's trousers, a frill. Sing. and Pl. See also سروزنه

P سرد *sard*, adj. Cool, cold, damp, (only in composition). سرد و گرم *sard-o-garm*, A cold in the head. سرد سير *sard-ser*, adj. Very cold. سردي *sardī*, s.f. (3rd) Coldness, coolness, dampness. Pl. ۍ *a'ī*. See سور

P سردار *sardār*, s.m. (5th) A chief, a commander, a head man. Pl. سرداران *sardārān*.

P سرداري *sardārī*, s.f. (3rd) Chiefship, rule, domination, lordship, supremacy. Pl. ۍ *a'ī*. سرداري كول *sardārī kawul*, verb trans. To command, to rule over, to sway.

P سررشته *sar-rishta'h*, s.f. (3rd) Connection, affinity. 2. Office, employment. 3. The end of a cord, a rope, a thread, a series. Pl. ۍ *ey*.

P سر رو *sar-i-rū* or سرارو *sarā-rū*, s.m. (5th) The cephalic vein in the arm. Pl. سر روگان *sar-i-rūgān* or سراروگان *sarā-rūgān*.

P سرزنش *sar-zanish*, s.m. (2nd) Reproof, rebuke. Pl. سرزنشونه *sar-zanishūnah*.

سر زوړه *sar-z'warra'h*, s.f. (3rd) A declivity, a slope, descent. Pl. ۍ *ey*. See سر ځوړه and سر لوړه

سر ځوړه *sar-dz'warra'h*, s.f. (3rd) A declivity, a slope; dip, descent, slope. Pl. ۍ *ey*. See سر زوړه

سرژه *sar-jza'h*, s.f. (3rd) (W.) A species of

mountain deer similar to the musk-deer. Pl. ي *ey*. See راموسي

سرسام *sar-sām*, s.m. (2nd) Delirium, phrensy. 2. A tumour or inflammation of the brain. Pl. سرسامونه *sar-sāmūnah*.

سرسايه *sar-sāya'h*, s.f. (3rd) Alms given to the poor on the breaking up of the Muḥammadan Lent. 2. A veil given to a daughter by the father on the last day of her marriage festivities. Pl. ي *ey*.

سرسر *sar-sar*, s.m. (9th) A cold boisterous wind (corrup. of A صرصر). Sing. and Pl. Also باد سرسر *bād-i-sarsar*.

P سرسري *sarsarī*, adj. Easy, trivial, trifling, facile, careless.

سرشاهي *sar-shā-hī*, s.f. (3rd) A weight of about half-an-ounce. Pl. ئي *a'ī*.

P سرشت *sarisht* or *sirisht*, s.m. (2nd) Nature, temperament, constitution, disposition, complexion. Pl. سرشتونه *sarisht-ūnah*, etc.

سرغ *sargh*, s.m. (2nd) A saddle (prob. from A سرج). Pl. سرغونه *sarghūnah*.

P سرغنه *sarghanah*, s.m. (6th) A head man, a chief, a great person. Sing and Pl.

سرغوند *sar-ghūndd*, s.m. (9th) A glandular swelling of the neck. Sing. and Pl.

سرفه *sarfa'h*, s.f. (3rd) Gain, profit, advantage. 2. Sparing or frugal in expense. 3. Deficiency, shortcoming, default, remissness, forbearance. 4. (P) A cough. Pl. ي *ey*.

P سركار *sarkār*, s.m. (5th) Government, estate, property, a district of several *parganahs*. 2. A superintendent. Pl. سركاران *sarkārān*.

P سركاري *sarkārī*, s.f. (3rd) Superintendence, government. Pl, ئي *a'ī*. 2. adj. Belonging to the state or to government.

سركاڼي *sarkārrnī*, s.m. (1st) Pl. The name of a tribe of Durānīs. سركاڼۍ *sarkārrnaey* (Sing.) A male of the above tribe. سركاڼئ *sarkārrna'ī*, s.f. (3rd) A female of the above. Sing. and Pl.

سركنډئ *sar-kundda'ī*, s.f. (6th) A girl with hair cropped, cropped hair, allowing the hair to grow altogether. Sing. and Pl. سركنډي *sar-kunddaey*, s.m. (1st) A cropped head of hair on a male, the hair cut short; a boy or man with short hair. Pl. ي *ī*. 2. adj. Hanging with the heels in the air and head undermost. سركنډي كول *sar-kunddaey kawul*, verb trans. To hang up by the heels.

P سركوب *sar-kob*, adj. Overlooking, commanding, overtopping (as a fort). 2. An overlooker, a superintendent, a foreman.

سركوزۍ *sar-kūzaey*, s.m. (1st) A hog. سر كوز *sar kūzi*, s.f. (8th) A sow. Pl. (Masc. and Fem.) ي *ī*. See خربوشو

سركوزي *sar-kūzī*, s.f. (3rd) Meekness, humility, lowliness, modesty, submission. Pl. ئي *a'ī*. سر كوزي كول *sar-kūzī kawul*, verb trans. To act with or display meekness, humility, or submission.

P سركه *sir-ka'h*, s.f. (3rd) Vinegar. Pl. ي *ey*.

سركئ *sirka'ī*, s.f. (6th) A scarlet fly or lady fly. Sing. and Pl. See خملئ

P سرگردان *sar-gardān*, adj. Distressed, humbled, confounded, stupified, straying, wandering; (Fem.) سرگردانه *sar-gardāna'h*.

سرگرداني *sar-gardānī*, s.f. (3rd) Distress, confusion, amazement. Pl. ئي *a'ī*. سرگردان كول *sar-gardān kawul*, verb trans. To distress, to confound, to perplex, to annoy.

سرگړۍ *sar-garraey*, s.m. (1st) A kind of sweet-scented grass used for fodder. Pl. ي *ī*.

P سرگشته *sar-gashtah*, adj. Head-turned, giddy, affected in the head, wandering, at a loss. سرگشته كول *sar-gashtah kawul*, verb trans. To turn one's head, to make giddy, to cause to wander in mind. سرگشتگي *sar-gashtagī*, s.f. (3rd) Affliction, wandering, giddiness. Pl. ئي *a'ī*.

سرگله *sar-gala'h*, s.f. (3rd) A grazing tax levied on all cattle. Pl. ي *ey*.

سرمال *sar-māl*, s.m. (2nd) A rope for fastening a load on a camel, that one part may not separate from the other. Pl. سرمالونه *sar-mālūnah*.

P سرمايه *sar-māya'h*, s.f. (3rd) Capital, stock-in-trade, fund, means, etc. Pl. ي *ey*.

P سرمه *surma'h*, s.f. (3rd) Black antimony, or an ore of lead applied to the eyelids. Pl. ي *ey*. سرمائي *surmā'ī*, adj. Greyish, of the colour of *surma'h*. See رانجه

P سرنا *surnā*, s.f. (6th) A clarion, a hautboy. (E.) Sing. and Pl., (W.) Pl. سرناوي *surnāwī*. سرناچي *sur-nāchī*, s.m. (5th) A clarion or hautboy player. Pl. سرناچيان *sur-nāchī-ān*; or سرنائي *surnā'ī*. Pl. سرنائيان *surnā'īān*.

P سر نامه *sar-nāma'h*, s.f. (3rd) A title-page, address, superscription of a letter, direction. Pl. ي *ey*.

سرنده *sarinda'h*, s.f. (3rd) A kind of violin. Pl. ي *ey*. See غچكه

سرنگي *sarangaey*, s.m. (1st) A mine, a gallery, a subterranean passage, an adit. Pl. ي *ī*. (s سرنگ).

سرواښ *sar-wāsh* (W.) or *sar-wākh* (E.) s.m. (2nd) A fastening for a cow or ox. Pl. سرواښونه *sar-wāshūnah* or *sar-wākhūnah*. Also سرواښي *sar-wāshaey* or *sar-wākhaey*, s.m. (1st). Pl. ي *ī*. See واښ

سرواندِ *sar-wāndi* or سرواندي *sarwāndey*, s.f. (3rd) Pl. A piece of land or portion of a field left uncut or unploughed. 2. The fastening of the yoke to a plough. (Sing. not used.) See سربانڊِ

سروتكه *sarwat-ka'h* or سړوتكه *sarrwat-ka'h*, s.f. (3rd) A spark of fire, a particle of live coal, etc. Pl. ي *ey*. See سكروټه

P سرود *sarod*, s.m. (2nd) A song, modulation, melody. Pl. سرودونه *sarodūnah*. سرودي *sarodī*, s.m. (5th) A singer. Pl. سروديان *sarodī-ān*.

P سرور *sarwar*, s.m. (5th) A leader, a chief, a principal. Pl. سروران *sarwarān*. سخي سرور *sakhī-sarwar*, s. prop. The name of a saint, and shrine in the Derajāt, west of Derah Ghāzī Khān. سروري *sarwarī*, s.f. (3rd) Leadership, rule, sway. Pl. ئي *a'ī*.

سروزنه *sar-wazana'h*, s.f. (3rd) The part of the drawers through which the waist string runs. 2. An embroidered furbelow, a frill, a piece of cloth sewn to the legs of women's drawers, or trousers. Pl. ي *ey*. See سرخڼي

P سروسامان *sar-o-sāmān*, s.m. (2nd) Goods and chattels, property, etc. Pl. سامانونه *sāmān-ūnah*.

سروه *sarwa'h*, s.f. (3rd) The cypress tree. Pl. ي *ey* (from P سرو). سروشان *sarw-shān*, adj. Like a cypress. سرو قد *sarw-i-kadd* or *sarw-kadd* or سرو قامت *sarw-kāmat*, adj. Tall and graceful, like the cypress in stature. سرو روان *sarw-i-rawān*, A moving cypress, a sweetheart moving gracefully.

سره *sara'h*, s.f. (3rd) Manure, dung. Pl. ي *ey*. سره كول *sara'h kawul* or سره وركول *sara'h war-kawul*, or سره آچول *sara'h āchawul*, verb trans. To manure (as land). See سرا. 2. adj. Pure, prime, best sort, genuine, honest, sincere, candid, strict. (s كهرا). See كره

سره *sarah*, adv. With, along with, together, in company, society, etc. It is often prefixed by له, the particle governing the ablative case; thus, له ما سره *lah mā sarah*, Along with me. را or در or ور سره *rā, dar,* or *war sarah*, Along with me or us, together with thee or you, and with him or them.

سره شنه *sara'h shna'h* or سره و شنه *sara'h-o-shna'h*, s.f. (3rd) A rainbow. Pl. ي *ey*. See د بودي تال

سره مخه *sara'h makha'h*, s.f. (3rd) An eruption of the body. Pl. ي *ey*.

سره ور *sarah-war*, adj. Broad, wide, ample, extended; (Fem.) سره وره *sara'h-wara'h*. See سور

سره ور توب *sarah-war-tob*, s.m. (2nd) Breadth, width, amplitude, latitude, broadness, extent. Pl. توبونه *tob-ūnah*.

سرياني *suri-yānī*, s.m. (1st) Pl. The name of an Afghān tribe. سرياني *suri-yānaey*, Sing. A male of the above tribe. سريانۍ *suri-yāna'ī*, s.f. (6th) A female of the above. Sing. and Pl.

سريخ *srīkh*, s.m. (2nd) The name of a tree (Seris mimosa). Pl. سريخونه *srīkhūnah*.

سريښ *saresh* (W.) or *sarekh* (E.) s.m. (2nd) Glue, birdlime. 2. Stickness, adhesiveness, cohesion. Pl. سريښونه *sareshūnah* or *sarekh-ūnah*. See سليخ

سري صاف *sirī ṣāf*, s.m. (6th) A kind of muslin. Sing. and Pl.

A سريع *sariæ*, adj. (from سرع) Quick, nimble, ready.

سري ورخ *sarī-warakh*, s.m. (2nd) The head of a stream, the part from whence the water flows. 2. The commencement of any work or business. Pl. سري ورخونه *sarī-warakhūnah*. See ورخ and ورخه

سربنی *sarr-banī*, s.m. (1st) Pl. The name of a tribe of Afghāns. سربنَي *sarr-banaey* (Sing.) A male of the above tribe. سربنۍ *sarr-bana'ī*, s.f. (6th) A female of the above. Sing. and Pl.

سرپ *srrap*, s.m. (5th) The sound of walking in mire, the sound of a smack or thump, the sound from striking with a sword or spear. 2. Slapping, clapping sound. 3. Vox congressus in coitu. Pl. سرپهار *srrapa-hār*. سرپهار لرل *srrapa-hār laral*, verb trans. To emit a squashy sound as from walking in mud, etc.; or سرپ سرپ کول *srrap-srrap kawul*, verb trans.

سرزي *sarr-zī* (W.) or سرزي *sar-zī* (E.) s.f. (3rd) Cold, coldness, frigidity, chillness. Pl. ۍ *a'ī*. See سوړ

سروتکه *sarr-watka'h* or سروتکه *sar-watka'h*, s.f. (3rd) A spark, an ember, a live coal, a piece of lighted charcoal, etc. Pl. ۍ *ey*. See also سکروټه

سره *sarrah*, adj. Free, liberated, relieved, done, finished, out. 2. Pure, genuine. Also written سر *sarra*.

سره بنړ *sarrah-barrn*, s.m. (6th) The name of one of the two grand divisions of the Afghāns, a number of the tribes of which dwell in the plain of Peshāwer, and to the north. See Introduction to Grammar, page 9. Sing. and Pl. سره بنړَي *sarrah-barrnaey*, s.m. (1st) A man of one of the tribes of the above division of the Afghāns, an Eastern Afghān. Pl. ي *ī*. سره بنړۍ *sarrah-barrna'ī*, s.f. (6th) A female of the above. Sing. and Pl.

سره ککره *sarra'h-kakarra'h*, adj. Stone dead, dead as a door-nail (*lit.* cold and dry).

سره لري *sarra'h-lirey*, s.f. (3rd) Pl. Fever and ague. Also written سره لوي *sarra'h-lawey*.

سړَي *sarraey*, s.m. (1st) A man, a human being, an individual. Pl. ي *ī*. سړي توب *sarraey tob*, s.m. (2nd) Humanity, the nature of man as distinguished from the brute, human nature. Pl. توبونه *tobūnah*. Also سړي هوښ *sarraey hosh* or *hokh*, s.m. (9th). Sing. and Pl.

P سزا *sazā*, s.f. (6th) Punishment, correction, penalty, chastisement, retribution. (E.) Sing. and Pl. (W.) Pl. سزاوي *sazāwī*. سزا ورکول *sazā war-kawul*, verb trans. To punish, to chastise, to correct, to avenge.

P سزاوار *sazā-wār*, adj. Worthy, deserving, fit, suitable, excellent, proper, applicable; (Fem.) سزاواره *sazā-wāra'h*.

سزاواري *sazāwārī*, s.f. (3rd) Worthiness, suitableness, excellence, justness, merit. Pl. ۍ *a'ī*.

T سزاول *sazāwul*, s.m. (5th) A tax-gatherer, a bailiff, a land steward. Pl. سزاولان *sazāwulān*.

سږه *sajza'h*, s.f. (3rd) (W.). See سرږه Pl. ۍ *ey*.

سږ *sajz*, s.m. (5th) The whiz, whistle, hiss, ring, crack, etc. of a bullet, cannon ball, or the like. Pl. سږهار *sajzahār*. See شغ and سغ

سږ *sajz*, adv. The present year; or سږني کال *sajzanaey kāl*. See سږ and سکڅ

سږَي *sajzaey*, s.m. (1st) (W.) The lungs, the lights. Pl. ي *ī*. Also سګي *sagaey* (E.) Pl. ي *ī*.

سږمه *sajz-ma'h*, s.f. (3rd) The nostril, the aperture through the nose. Pl. ۍ *ey*. See سپږمه and سپينګه

سسپار *saspār* or *sispār*, s.m. (2nd) A ploughshare. Pl. سسپارونه *saspārūnah* or *sispārūnah*. See پاله

سسپور *saspor*, s.m. (2nd) A mattock, a hoe. Pl. سسپورونه *sasporūnah*. See سپنسوره and کودالي

P سست *sust* or *sast*, adj. Loose, relaxed, weak, lazy, slothful, idle, neglectful, slow, tardy, inactive, indolent, feeble, languid, soft, frail, remiss, impotent; (Fem.) سسته *susta'h* or *sasta'h*. سست دام *sust-dām*, s.m. (2nd) A net for catching birds, left loose and not drawn tight. Pl. سست داmونه *sust-dāmūnah*. سست کول *sust kawul*, verb trans. To relax, to loosen, to make weak or languid, to effeminate. سستي *sustī* or *sastī*, s.f. (3rd) Laziness, slothfulness, idleness, slowness, negligence, dilatoriness, remissness, relaxation, languor, slothfulness. Pl. ئي *a'ī*. سستي کول *sustī* or *sastī kāwul*, verb trans. To idle away, to do nothing, to fiddle-faddle, to dawdle, to act with remissness, negligence, sluggishness, etc.

سشکله *sash-kalah*, adv. Always, at all times, ever. See زشکله , هرکله , تل and تل تله

سښا *sashā* (W.) or *sakhā* (E.) s.f. (6th) The sound produced by meat roasting, fizz, etc. (E.) Sing. and Pl. (W.) Pl. سښاوي *sashāwī*.

سښسوره *sashsora'h* (W.) or *sakhsora'h* (E.) s.f. (3rd) A mattock, a hoe. Pl. ئي *ey*. See سسپوره and کوداڵي

A سطر *saṭar*, s.m. (2nd) A line, a rank, a row, a series, a lineament. Pl. سطرونه *saṭarūnah*. سطر کښل *saṭar k'shal* (W.) or *k'khal* (E.) To draw a line or mark for writing on, etc.

A سعادت *sa'æā-dat*, s.m. (2nd) (from سعد) Felicity, happiness, good fortune, prosperity, etc. Pl. سعادتونه *sa'æā-datūnah*. سعادت من *sa'æā-dat-man* or مند *mand*, adj. Happy, fortunate, prosperous; (Fem.) سعادت منه *sa'æā-dat-mana'h* or منده *manda'h*. سعادت مندي *sa'æā-dat-mandī*, s.f. (3rd) Prosperity, happiness, felicity. Pl. ئي *a'ī*.

A سعد *suæd*, s.m. (2nd) The name of a leaf used in medicine. Pl. سعدونه *suædūnah*.

سعيه *sa'æya'h*, s.f. (3rd) (corrup. of A سعي), Attempt, effort, endeavour, essay, purpose, enterprise, etc. Pl. ئي *ey*. سعيه کول *sa'æya'h kawul*, verb trans. To endeavour, to strive, to attempt, to essay.

سغ *sagh*, s.m. (5th) The hiss, whiz or whistle of a bullet, rustle, whir, etc.; the whizzing sound produced by the flying of a partridge, pigeon, or wild duck. Pl. سغهار *sagha-hār*. سغهار لرل *sagha-hār laral* or سغ سغ کول *sagh-sagh kawul*, verb trans. To whiz, to hiss, to whistle, to whir, to make a rustling, whirring sound.

سغيدل *sughedal*, verb trans. To become perforated, stabbed, probed, stuck, punctured, impaled, drilled, etc. Pres. سغيږي *sughejzī* (W.) or سغيګي *sughegī* (E.); past وُ سغيده *wu-sughedah* or وُ سغيدَ *wu-sugheda*; fut. وُ به سغيږي *wu bah sughejzī* or وُ به سغيګي *wu bah sughegī*; imp. وُ سغيږه *wu-sughejzah* or سغيګه *sughegah*; act. part. سغيدونکي *sughedūnkaey* or سغيدوني *sughedūnaey*; past part. سغيدلي *sughedalaey*; verb. n. سغيدنه *sughedana'h* or سغيده *sughedah*. سغول *sughawul*, verb trans. To stick, to pierce, to stab, to pink, to prick, to probe, to puncture, to impale, to spear. Pres. سغوي *sughawī*; past وُ سغاوه *wu-sughāwuh* or وُ سغاوو *sughāwo*; fut. وُ به سغوي *wu bah sughawī*; imp. وُ سغوه *wu-sughawah*; act. part. سغوونکي *sughawūnkaey* or سغووني *sughawūnaey*; past part. سغولي *sughawulaey*; verb. n. سغونه *sughawuna'h*.

سغولي *sughawulaey*, adj. (past part.) Stuck, stabbed, punctured, probed, speared, etc.; (Fem.) سغولې *sughawali*. Pl. (Masc. and Fem.) ئي *ī*.

A سفر *safar*, s.m. (2nd) Journey, travel, voyage, campaign, travelling, journeying, etc. Pl. سفرونه *safarūnah*. سفر کول *safar kawul*, verb trans. To travel, to journey, to make a voyage, to retire, to depart. په سفر تلل *pah safar t'lal*, verb intrans. To go a journey, to set out to travel, to go a voyage, etc. سفري *safarī*, s.f. (3rd) Travelling, provisions. Pl. ئي *a'ī*.

P سفره *sufra'h*, s.f. (3rd) The anus. Pl. ئي *ey*. See سپره

A سفوف *sufūf*, s.m. (6th) A medicine taken dry and unmixed, a powder (in opposition to an electuary). Sing. and Pl. See کپه and خريت

P سفيدار *safedār*, s.m. (5th) The white poplar tree, the wood of the poplar. Pl. سفيداران *safedār-ān*. See سپيدار

سقاو *sakkāo* or سقو *sakkow*, s.m. (5th) A water

carrier. Pl. سقاوان sakḳāo-ān or سقوان sakḳow-ān (corrup. of A سقا).

A سقاوه sakḳāwa'h, s.f. (3rd) A reservoir, a cold bath. Pl. ي ey.

A سقر sakar, s.m. (9th) (from سقر) Hell, the infernal regions. Sing. and Pl.

A سقف sakf, s.m. (2nd) Roof, ceiling, canopy a platform. سقفونه sakfūnah.

P سقلات saklāt, s.m. (2nd) A kind of red or scarlet cloth. Pl. سقلاتونه saklātūnah.

سكاروي skārwaey, s.m. (1st) The pleurisy. Pl. ي ī.

سكالوه skāl-wah, s.m. (6th) Discourse, mention, talk, discussion. 2. The sound of conversation, muttering, buzz, hum, murmur. 3. The sound of footsteps, etc. Sing. and Pl. سكالوه كول skāl-wah kawul, verb trans. To discuss, to mention. 2. To murmur, to hum, to make a muttering, buzzing sound. 3. To sound as footsteps. See هكالوه and كنكوسي

سكاړ skāṟṟn, adj. Dark complexioned, agreeable, fresh, healthy looking. 2. A bay coloured horse; (Fem.) سكاړه skāṟṟna'h.

A سكته sakta'h, s.f. (3rd) (from سكت), Apoplexy, a pause, a trance, vacancy, hiatus. Pl. ي ey.

A سكر sukr, s.m. (9th) (from سكر) Intoxicating drink, wine, intoxication. Sing. and Pl.

A سكرات sakarāt, s.f. (1st) Agency, fainting, senselessness. Pl. سكراتِ sakarāti. سكرات موت sakarāt-i-maut, The pangs or agony of death, the point of death.

سكروټه skarwaṯṯa'h, s.f. (3rd) Burning charcoal, a live coal, an ember. Pl. ي ey. See also سروټكه

سكړك sukṟṟuk, adj. Lame of a hand or hands, having lost the use of hands and feet, lame, powerless in the limbs; (Fem.) سكړكه sukṟṟuka'h. سكړك كيدل sukṟṟuk kedal, verb trans. To become powerless in the limbs, to lose the use of hands and feet, etc. سكړك كول sukṟṟuk kawul, verb trans. To render powerless, etc.

سكستل skustal, verb trans. To shear, to prune, to clip, to thin (as the hair of a horse, camel, etc.) Pres. سكلي skulī; past وُ سكست wu-skust; fut. وُ به سكلي wu bah skulī; imp. وُ سكله wu-skulah; act. part. سكستونكي skustūnkaey or سكستونَي skustūnaey; past part. سكستلي skustalaey; verb. n. سكستنه skustana'h.

سكښتل skashtal (W.) or skakhtal (E.) verb trans. To cut out, to shape (as clothes), to plan, to design, etc. Pres. سكڼري skarrnī; past وُ سكښت wu-skasht or wu-skakht; fut. وُ به سكڼري wu bah skarrnī; imp. وُ سكڼره wu-skarrna'h; act. part. سكښتونكي skashtūnkaey or skakhtūnkaey or سكښتونَي skashtūnaey or skakhtūnaey; past part. سكښتلي skashtalaey or skakhtalaey; verb. n. سكښتنه skashtana'h or skakhtana'h.

سكل s'kal, verb trans. To drink, to quaff, to imbibe, to drink up. For conjugation see څښل

سكنډل skunḏḏal, verb trans. To pinch, to tweak, to pain, to hurt, to gall. Pres. سكنډي skunḏḏī; past وُ سكنډه wu-skunḏḏah or وُ سكنډَ wu-skunḏḏa; fut. وُ به سكنډي wu bah skunḏḏī; imp. وُ سكنډه wu-skunḏḏah; act. part. سكنډونكي skunḏḏūnkaey or سكنډونَي skunḏḏūnaey; past part. سكنډلي skunḏḏalaey; verb. n. سكنډنه skunḏḏana'h.

P سكنجبين sikanjabīn, s.m. (6th) Lime-juice or other acid mixed with sugar or honey, oxymel. Sing. and Pl.

P سكندر sikandar, s. prop. Alexander the Great. Also written اسكندر iskandar.

سكو sko, s.m. (2nd) Sewing, a stitch, a seam. Pl. سكوونه sko-ūnah. See سكوي

سكور skor, s.m. (4th) Charcoal, fuel. Pl. سكاره skārah.

سكول skwal, s.m. (2nd) Shearing, clipping, cutting off wool, hair, nap, etc. by shears. Pl. سكولونه skwalūnah. سكول كول skwal kawul, verb trans. To shear, to clip. See سكستل

سكول s'kawul, verb trans. (caus.) To cause to drink, imbibe, drink up, to water as a horse, cattle, etc. 2. To draw out, to unsheath. See څكول

A سكون sukūn, s.m. (9th) Quietude, rest, peace, tranquillity. Sing. and Pl.

A سکونت *sukūnat*, s.m. (2nd) (from سکن) Residence, habitation, dwelling. 2. Tranquility, rest. Pl. سکونتونه *sukūnatūnah*. سکونت کيدل *sukūnat kedal*, verb trans. To dwell, to reside, to sojourn, to abide, to continue, to rest. See آستيدل. سکونت کول *sukūnat kawul*, To take up one's residence, to inhabit, to occupy, to dwell in.

سکوي *sko-e*, s.m. (2nd) Sewing a seam, a stitch. 2. Solicitude, anxiety. Pl. سکويونه *sko-eūnah*. See سکو

سکويل *sko-yal*, verb trans. To scrape, to rub, to clean by scraping, to remove or take off by rubbing, to scratch (as the flesh when itching). Pres. سکويي *sko-yī*; past وُ سکويه *wu-sko-yah*; fut. وُ به سکويي *wu bah sko-yī*; imp. وُ سکويه *wu-sko-yah*; act. part. سکويونکيَ *sko-yūnkaey* or سکويونيَ *sko-yūnaey*; past part. سکويليَ *sko-yalaey*; verb. n. سکوينه *sko-yana'h*.

سکوينه *sko-yana'h*, s.f. (3rd) (verb. n.) Scraping, rubbing, scratching, cleaning, etc. Pl. ئ *ey*.

P A سکه *sika'h*, s.f. (3rd) A stamped coin, a coining die, an impression on money. 2. Lead. Pl. ئ *ey*. 3. adj. Current, sterling,. 4. Heavy, weighty, respectable. 5. Dull, stupid, heavy (corrup. of A.)

سکه *sakah*, adj. A full brother of the same parent, related, akin (s سگا).

سکه *shah*, adv. Then, therefore, moreover, finally. 2. As if, as it were. See وسکه

S سکه *sikh* or سيکه *sīkh*, s.m. (5th) A Sikh, a disciple, a follower of Nānak. Pl. سکهان *sikhān* or سيکهان *sīkhān*. Also written سيک *sīk*. Pl. سيکان *sīkān*.

سکښ *sag* or سکني کال *sagnaey kāl*, adv. The present year. See سږ and سږ

سکل *sugul*, s.f. (1st) A kind of buskin made of the fresh skin of any animal, worn during the winter season when snow is on the ground. Pl. سکل *suguli*.

P سگال *sigāl*, s.m. (2nd) Thought, suspicion, imagination. 2. Enmity, hatred. 3. Word, speech. P. سگالونه *sigālūnah*. بد سگال *bad-sigāl*, adj. Evil-minded, malevolent, malignant; (Fem.) بد سگاله *bad-sigāla'h*.

سگلاوو *saglā-wo*, s.m. (5th) An otter, the water-dog. Pl. سگلاووگان *saglā-wo-gān*.

سگلئ *sugala'ī*, s.f. (6th) A hiccough, the hiccough, a sob. 2. The death-rattle in the throat. سگلئ وهل *sugala'ī wahal*, verb trans. To hiccough, to sob, to give a convulsive sigh.

سگه *saga'h*, s.f. (3rd) Stock, capital, means, profit. 2. A share or portion of land. Pl. ئ *ey*. 3. adj. Acquired, gained, collected.

سگيَ *sagaey*, s.m. (1st) The lungs, the lights. Pl. ي *ī*. See سږي

سل *sal* or *sil*, adj. A hundred; or سو *sau*. سل کلنيَ *sal* or *sil kalanaey*, adj. A hundred years old; (Fem.) ئ *a'ī*. سل خبري سر ئي يو دي *sal khabarey sir yey yow daey*, A hundred words and one meaning, "A long story about nothing."

A سل *sill*, s.m. (2nd) A consumption, hectic fever. Pl. سلونه *sillūnah*.

سلارزي *salārzī*, s.m. (1st) Pl. The name of a tribe of Afghāns. سلارزيَ *salār-zaey*, Sing. A male of the above tribe. سلارزئ *salārza'ī*, s.f. (6th) A female of the above. Sing. and Pl.

سلاره *salāra'h*, s.f (3rd) A kind of striped cloth. Pl. ئ *ey*.

A سلام *salām*, s.m. (2nd) Peace, safety. 2. Salutation. Pl. سلامونه *salāmūnah*. سلام کول *salām kawul*, verb trans. To salute, to hail, to accost, to bid good bye, to say adieu. سلام عليکم *salāmun ælaikum*, "Peace be unto you," a form of salutation the reply to which is عليکم السلام *ælaikum-us-salām*, "Unto you be peace." سلام آخستل *salām ākhistal*, verb trans. To return a salutation. سلام آچول *salām āchawul*, verb trans. To salute.

A سلامت *salāmat*, s.m. (2nd) (from سلم) Safety, salvation, health, recovery, tranquility. Pl. سلامتونه *salāmatūnah*. 2. adj. In safety, well, safe. سلامتي *salāmatī*, s.f. (3rd) Safety, health, in health or in safety. Pl. ئ *a'ī*. سلامت واليَ *salāmat wālaey*, s.m. (1st)

Health, safety, recovery, tranquility. Pl. والي *wālī*.

S سلائي *salā'ī*, s.f. (3rd) A needle, a bodkin, a piece of wire used in depriving a person of sight. Pl. ئي *a'ī*.

سلائي *salā'ī*, s.m. (5th) The upright pillar of a Persian wheel which sets the wheels in motion. Pl. سلائيګان *salā-īgān*.

سلټ *salaṯṯ*, s.m. (2nd) A shield, a target, made deep and round. Pl. سلټونه *salaṯṯ-ūnah*.

A سلسل بول *silsil-i-baul*, s.m. (9th) A diabetes, morbid copiousness of urine. Sing. and Pl.

A سلسله *silsila'h*, s.f. (3rd) A series, a set, a chain, a concatenation; succession, descent of a family, pedigree, genealogy. Pl. ئي *ey*.

A سلطان *sulṯān*, s.m. (5th) (from سلط) A sovereign, a prince, an emperor, a king. Pl. سلطانان *sulṯānān*. سلطاني *sulṯānī*, adj. Royal, regal, princely, belonging to a sultan.

A سلطنت *salṯanat*, s.m. (2nd) Empire, dominion, sway, sovereignty, kingdom, reign. Pl. سلطنتونه *salṯanatūnah*. سلطنت کول *salṯanat kawul*, verb trans. To rule, to reign, to exercise sovereignty or dominion.

A سلف *salaf*, s.m. (6th) (from سلف) An ancestor, a predecessor. Sing. and Pl.

سلګئي *salga'ī*, s.f. (6th) A hiccough, a sigh, a sob. Sing. and Pl. 2. The death rattle in the throat. سلګئي کول *salga'ī kawul*, verb trans. To hiccough, to sigh, to sob. See also سکلئي

سلمچي *silamchī*, s.m. (5th) A wash-hand basin of metal with a cover to it, a basin. Pl. سلمچيان *silamchīān*.

A سلوک *sulūk*, s.m. (2nd) Mode, manner, conduct, way, road. 2. Intercourse, usage, treatment, civility, kindness, attention. Pl. سلوکونه *sulūkunah*. سلوک کول *sulūk kawul*, verb trans. To treat, to proceed with, to hold intercourse, etc.

A سلوم *sulūm*, adj. Celebrated, famous, noted, well known, notorious; (Fem.) سلومه *sulūmu'h*.

سله *sala'h*, s.f. (3rd) A pig or mass of iron or other metal. Pl. ئي *ey*.

سلي *salaey*, s.m. (1st) A ring for the finger. Pl. ي *ī*.

سليخ *salekh*, s.m. (2nd) Glue, bird-lime. 2. Cohesion, stickiness, adhesiveness, gumminess. Pl. سليخونه *salekhūnah*. Also سليښ *salesh* (W.) or *salekh* (E.) Pl. سليښونه *saleshūnah* or *salekhūnah*. Also سليخت *salekht* (E.) or سليښت *salesht* (W.) Pl. *salekhtūnah* or *saleshtūnah*.

سليخت ناك *salekht-nāk* or سليښت ناك *salesht-nāk* (W.) or *salekht-nāk* (E.), adj. Sticky, adhesive, viscous, clammy, glutinous; (Fem.) سليخت *salekht* or سليښت ناکه *salekht* or *salesht-nāka'h*.

A سليقه *salīka'h*, s.f. (3rd) Nature, taste, good disposition, genius, method, knack, address, dexterity, knowledge. Pl. ئي *ey*.

A سليم *salīm*, adj. Mild, meek, humble, pacific, affable. 2. Healthy, perfect; (Fem.) سليمه *salīma'h*. سليم الطبع *salīm-uṯ-ṯabæ*, adj. Mild or gentle in disposition, pacific, mild.

A سليمان *suleymān* or *sulīmān*, s. prop. Solomon the son of David. تخت سليمان *takht-i-sulīmān*, The name of a mountain in Afghānistān, part of the range so called, near the Indus, on which Solomon's throne is said to have rested, and in the vicinity of which the Afghāns first dwelt on their immigration from the west. See Introduction to Grammar, p. 7. سليمان خيل *sulīmān khel*, s.m. (6th) The name of a tribe of Afghāns, a male of the tribe. Sing. and Pl. سليمان خيله *sulīmān khela'h*, s.f. (3rd) A female of the above. Pl. ئي *ey*. سليماني *sulīmānī*, s.f. (5th) A name sometimes given to Afghāns in general. Pl. سليمانيان *sulīmānī-ān*. s.f. (6th) سليمانئي *sulīmāna'ī*. Sing. and Pl.

P سم *sum*, s.m. (2nd) The hoof of a horse, ass, mule, etc. Pl. سمونه *sumūnah*. See سوه

S سم *sam*, adj. Level, straight, flat, even, plane, flush, etc.; (Fem.) سمه *sama'h*. سره سم *sarah-sam*, adv. Equally, in the same manner or degree. سميدل *samedal*, verb intrans. To become level, flat, even, plane, etc. Pres.

سميږي *samejẕī* (W.) or سميګي *samegī* (E.); past سم شه *sam shah* or وُ شه *wu-shah*; fut. سم به شي *sam bah shī* or به وُ شي *bah wu-shī*; imp. سم شه *sam shah* or وُ شه *wu-shah*; act. part. سميدونکي *samedūnkaey* or سميدوني *samedūnaey*; past part. سم *sam* or سم شوي *sam shawaey*; verb. n. سميدنه *samedana'h* or سميده *samedah*. سمول *samawul*, verb trans. To level, to flatten, to make even, to smooth. Pres. سموي *samawī*; past سم کړ *sam karr* or وُ کړ *wu-karr*; fut. سم به کړي *sam bah krrī* or به وُ کړي *bah wu-krrī*; imp. سم کړه *sam krrah* or وُ کړه *wu-krrah*; act. part. سموونکي *samawūnkaey* or سمووني *samawūnaey*; past part. سم کړي *sum karraey*; verb. n. سمونه *samawuna'h*.

سم والي *sam-wālaey*, s.m. (1st) Flatness, evenness, level, smoothness. Pl. والي *wālī*.

A سم *samm*, s.m. (2nd) Venom, poison, virus. 2. *sam*, A description of arrow. Pl. سمونه *samm-ūnah* or *samūnah*.

A سماع *samāæ*, s.f. (1st) or سماعه *samāæa'h*, s.f. (3rd) Hearing, listening, the sense of hearing or listening. 2. A song, singing. Pl. سماع *samāæi* or سماعي *samāæey*. سماعت *samāæat*, s.m. (2nd) Hearing. Pl. سماعتونه *samāæat-ūnah*. سماعت کول *samāæat kawul*, verb trans. To hear.

A سماق *sumāḳ*, s.m. (2nd) Sumac (Rhus coriaria). 2. The hardest marble, porphyry. Pl. سماقونه *sumāḳ-ūnah*; or سماغ *sumāgh*, etc.

سمت *simt* or *samt*, s.m. (6th) A way, path, side, quarter, part, towards. Sing. and Pl.

سمڅ *smats*, s.f. (1st) A cavern, a cave, a grotto, a cavity. 2. A mine, an excavation, a subterranean passage. Pl. سمڅ *smatsi*. Also سمڅه *smatsa'h*, s.f. (3rd). Pl. ې *ey*. See سمست. (P سمچ)

A سمر *samar*, s.m. (9th) Narration, relation, evening conversations. Sing. and Pl.

سمساره *samsāra'h*, s.f. (3rd) A large lizard or iguana, a land crocodile, or alligator. Pl. ې *ey*. See سيمسار and خادمي

سمست *samist*, s.f. (1st) A cave, a cavern, a mine. Pl. سمست *samisti*. سمسته *simista'h*, s.f. (3rd). Pl. ې *ey*. See سمڅ. Also سمسره *samsara'h*, s.f. (3rd) A large lizard or iguana, a chamelion. Pl. ې *ey*.

سمسوري *sam-soraey*, s.m. (1st) An equal, one having the same rank, power, etc. Pl. ي *ī*. سمسوره *samsora'h*, s.f. (3rd). Pl. ې *ey*.

A سمک *samak*, s.m. (6th) The fish on which the earth is supposed to rest, the sign Pisces. Sing. and Pl.

سم له لاسه *sam lah lāsah*, adv. Speedily, with haste or celerity, soon, without delay.

P سمن *saman*, s.m. (6th) The jasmine. 2. The lily of the valley. Sing. and Pl. سمن بوي *saman-bo-e*, adj., as s.m. (5th) A lover. Pl. سمن بويان *saman-bo-e-ān*. سمن بويه *saman-bo-e-a'h*, s.f. (3rd) A mistress, a sweetheart. Pl. ې *ey*.

P سمند *samand*, adj. A horse of a yellow colour; (Fem.) سمنده *samanda'h*.

P سمندر *samandar*, s.m. (5th) A salamander. Pl. سمندران *samandarān*.

سمندروز *samand-roz*, s.m. (6th) A kind of silk taffeta. Sing. and Pl.

A سمور *samūr*, s.m. (5th) A sable, a martin, a weasel. Pl. سموران *samūrān*. د سمور پوست *da samūr post*, s.m. (2nd) Sable-skin. Pl. پوستونه *postūnah*.

سمه *sama'h*, s.f. (3rd) A plain, a level tract of country. 2. The name of the country of the Yūsufzīs between the Kābul river and the mountains of Suwāt and Buner. Pl. ې *cy*. See سم

سن *san*, s.m. (9th) A year, age, year. Sing. and Pl. And سنه *sana'h*, s.f. (3rd). Pl. ې *ey* (A سنة).

S سنار *sunār*, s.m. (5th) A goldsmith, a worker in precious metals. Pl. سناران *sunārān* (E.)

S سناري *sunārī*, adj. Golden, gilded, gilt.

P سنبل *sunbul*, s.m. (6th) The hyacinth, the spikenard. 2. A flower (of an odoriferous plant). Sing. and Pl.; or د سنبل گل *da sunbul gul*.

A سنت *sunnat*, s.m. (2nd) Circumcision. 2. The

traditions of Muhammad, ordinance, institute, rite. Pl. سنتونه *sunnatūnah.* سنت کول *sunnat kawul,* verb trans. To circumcise. 2. To act up to the rites and ordinances of the Prophet. سنت جماعت *sunnat jamāeat,* The name of a class of Muhammadans. اهل سنت *ahl-i-sunnat,* One who obeys the tenets of the Sunnah, one circumcised. سنتي *sunnatī,* s.f. (3rd) Circumcision. Pl. ئي *a'ī.*

P سنج *sanj,* adj. (act. part. of P سنجیدن) A weigher, examiner, one who considers, who looks before he leaps; (Fem.) سنجه *sanja'h.* سنجول *sanjawul,* verb trans. To weigh, to examine, to consider, to ponder on.

سنج *sunj,* adj. Void, dreary, deserted, desolate; (Fem.) سنجه *sunja'h.* سنج کیدل *sunj kedal,* verb intrans. To become void, empty, desolate, deserted, etc. سنج کول *sunj kawul,* verb trans. To desolate, to ruin, to make void or empty. سنج والئ *sunj-wālaey,* s.m. (1st) Desolation, dreariness, voidness, emptiness, destitution. Pl. والي *wālī.* Also سنج توب *sunj-tob,* s.m. (2nd). Pl. توبونه *tobūnah.* And سنج تیا *sunj tī'ā,* s.f. (6th) (E.) Sing. and Pl. (W.) Pl. تیاوي *tī'āwī.*

P سنجاب *sanjāb* or سنجاپ *sanjāp,* s.m. (2nd) Ermine, the grey squirrel. Pl. سنجابونه *sanjābūnah* or سنجاپونه *sanjāpūnah.*

سند *sind,* s.m. (2nd) A river. 2. The country of Sindh, extending from the Salt Range to Karāchī (S سندھ). See سیند

A سند *sannad,* s.m. (2nd) A deed, a grant, a diploma, a signature, a document, proof, or certificate. Pl. سندونه *sannadūnah.*

P سندان *sandān,* s.m. (2nd) An anvil. Pl. سندانونه *sandānūnah.* See بلک

سندره *sandara'h,* s.f. (3rd) A song, a melody, modulation. Pl. ې *ey.*

S سندوري *sandūrī,* adj. A scarlet colour obtained from Thuia articulata.

سنډ *sundd,* s.m. (6th) Green ginger. Sing. and Pl. Also s.m. (5th) The lip. Pl. سنډان *sunddān.* See سونډ

S سنډاسي *sanddāsī,* s.m. (5th) A mendicant, a devotee, a caste of Hindū fakīrs. Pl. سنډاسیان *sunddāsīān.* See also سناسي

سنډه *sanddah,* s.m. (5th) A male buffalo. Pl. سنډگان *sanddagān.* See سانډه

سنځل *sandzal,* verb trans. To bale out, to empty, to pour out, to eject water, etc. Pres. سنځي *sandzī*; past و سانځه *wu-sāndzah* or و سانځ *wu-sāndza*; fut. و به سنځي *wu bah sandzī*; imp. و سنځه *wu-sandzah*; act. part. سنځونکئ *sandzūnkaey* or سنځونئ *sandzūnaey*; past part. سنځلئ *sandzalaey*; verb. n. سنځنه *sandzana'h.*

سنکیا *sankeā,* s.f. (6th) (corrup. of S سنکھیا) Arsenic. (E.) Sing. and Pl. (W.) Pl. سنکیاوي *sankeā-wī.*

P سنګ *sang,* s.m. (9th) A stone, weight. Sing. and Pl. (used in composition). سنګ اسود *sang-i-aswad,* The name of a black stone at Makka. سنګ دل *sang dil,* adj. Hard-hearted, stony-hearted, cruel, obdurate, severe; (Fem.) سنګ دله *sang dila'h.* سنګ دلي *sang-dilī,* s.f. (3rd) Hard-heartedness, cruelty. Pl. ئي *a'ī.* سنګ ریزه *sang-reza'h,* s.f. (3rd) Gravel, pebble. Pl. ې *ey.* سنګ ریزي *sang-rezī,* s.f. (3rd) Flinging or throwing stones. Pl. ئي *a'ī.* سنګ سماق *sang-i-samāķ,* Porphyry. سنګ سار *sang-sār,* s.m. (6th) Stoning to death. Sing. and Pl. سنګسار کول *sangsār kawul,* verb trans. To stone to death. سنګ مثانه *sang-i-maṣāna'h,* The stone, the gravel. سنګ مرمر *sang-i-marmar,* s.m. (6th) Marble. Sing. and Pl. See کانړي

S سنګار *singār,* s.m. (2nd) Ornament, dress, embellishment, decoration. Pl. سنګارونه *singārūnah.* سنګار کول *singār kawul,* verb trans. To ornament, to decorate, to embellish.

سنګاوړن *singāwarrn,* s.m. (5th) A pole for steering, turning, or propelling a boat. Pl. سنګاوړنان *singāwarrnān.*

سنګ بر *sang-bar* or سنګ تراش *sang-tarāsh,* s.m. (5th) A stone cutter. Pl. سنګ بران *sang barān* or تراشان *tarāshān.* سنګ شوئي *sang-sho'ī,* s.f. (3rd) Washing rice, etc.

before dressing. Pl. ئي *a'ī.* سنګ شوئ کول *sang-sho'ī kawul,* verb trans. To wash or clean rice, etc. سنګ ملتانه *sang-multānah,* s.f, (3rd) (corrup. of P سنګ مثانه *sang-i-maṣāna'h*) The gravel, the stone. Pl. ئي *ey.*

سنګ پاژه *sang-pājza'h,* s. prop. The name of a mountain in the Khaiberī country, to the south, towards Tīrāh, and separating the latter from the country of the Ismā-æīl-zīs, a branch of the tribe of Orūkzī, one of the three divisions of the Khaiberīs. It is at present called سنګ پګه *sang-paga'h.*

S سنګر *sangar,* s.m. (2nd) A breastwork of stones, etc., erected to close a pass or road; lines, entrenchments. Pl. سنګرونه *sangarūnah.* See باره

سنګزن *sang-zan,* adj. Top-heavy, lop-sided, overbalanced; (Fem.) سنګزنه *sang-zana'h.*

سنګل *sangal,* s.f. (1st) The arm from the elbow to the wrist, or to the end of the fingers. Pl. سنګلِ *sangali.* Also سنګله *sangala'h,* s.f. (3rd). Pl. ئي *ey.* See څنګل

سنګ لاخ *sang-lākh,* adj. Stony, rocky. 2. Arduous, difficult; (Fem.) سنګ لاخه *sang-lākha'h.*

P سنګين *sangīn,* adj. Weighty, heavy, of stone, stony, solid, thick; (Fem.) سنګينه *sangīna'h.* سنګين دل *sangīn dil,* adj. Hard-hearted; (Fem.) سنګين دله *sangīn dila'h.*

سنه مکي *sanah makī,* s.m. (9th) Senna leaves (*lit.* Makka senna). Sing. and Pl. See سنا

A سني *sunnī,* adj. as s.m. (5th) An orthodox Muḥammadan who reveres the four successors of the Prophet, in opposition to the Shī'æahs, who revere Æalī. Pl. سنيان *sunnīān*; (Fem.) سني *sunnī.* Pl. سنيانِ *sunnīāni.* سنت سنيه *sunnat-i-sunīah,* Holy or orthodox law.

سني توب *sunnī-tob,* s.m. (2nd) Orthodoxy, true faith, exactness in religion according to the tenets of the Sunnīs, in oppostion to Shī-æahs. Pl. توبونه *tobūnah.* Also سني ګلوي *sunnī-galwī,* s.f. (3rd). Pl. ګلوئ *galwa'ī*; and سني والَي *sunnī-wālaey,* s.m. (1st). Pl. والي *wālī.*

سرړ *sarrn,* s.m. (6th) The name of a plant from which tow is made (Crotolaria juncea). Sing. and Pl. (S سن).

S سو *sau,* adj. (E.) One hundred. This word is only used with reference to more than one hundred, the Pushto for one hundred only being سل *sal,* which see.

A سوا *siwā,* prep. or post-p. Besides, except, but, without.

سوات *suwāt* or سواد *sewād,* s. prop. The name of a valley north of the Kābul river, to the north-east of Peshāwer, inhabited by Yūsufzīs, once a flourishing Bhuddist kingdom, called Udjānā, mentioned by the Chinese historians.

A سواد *sa-wād,* s.m. (2nd) Environs of a city, villages or territory belonging to a city or town. 2. (S) *sawād* or *s'wād,* Relish, sweetness, flavour, taste, pleasure. Pl. سوادونه *sa-wād-ūnah.*

A سوال *suwāl,* s.m. (2nd) (from سأل) Question, interrogation, query, request, proposition, begging, questioning, interrogating. Pl. سوالونه *suwālūnah.* سوال کول *suwāl kawul,* verb trans. To question, to interrogate, to beg.

سوالي *suwālī,* s.m. (5th) A questioner, a beggar, an interrogator. Pl. سواليان *suwālīān.*

S سوانګ *sawāng* or *swāng,* s.m. (2nd) Acting, disguise, imitation, mimicry, sham. Pl. سوانګونه *swāngūnah.* سوانګي *swāngey,* s.m. (1st) A mimic. Pl. ي *ī.* سوانګئ *swānga'ī,* s.f. (6th). Sing. and Pl. سوانګ کول *swāng kawul,* verb trans. To mimic, to imitate, to sham.

S سوائ *sawā'ī,* s.f. (3rd) A quarter more. 2. Profit, interest. Pl. ئي *a'ī.*

سوباړي *so-bārraey,* s.m. (1st) A plank on which washermen beat clothes. Pl. ي *ī.* See څوباړي

H سوپاري *sūpārī,* s.m. (6th) Betel nut. Sing. and Pl.

سوټ بوټ *sūtt-būtt,* adj. Ill-natured, ugly, disagreeable, ill-favoured, grim, repulsive. 2. Tying firmly, tightening, pinioning. 3. All of a heap; (Fem.) سوټه بوټه *sūtta'h-būtta'h.* سوټ بوټ ترړل *sūtt-būtt tarral,* verb trans. To pinion, to tie firmly.

سوټه *sūṯṯa'h*, s.f. (3rd) Fresh or hard dung of any animal in a heap. Pl. ي *ey*.

سوچه *sūchah*, adj. Unadulterated, pure, without flaw, simple, sheer, unsophisticated, exclusive. 2. Unlucky, sinister, bad, evil, hurtful (s سوچهه).

P سوخته *sokhtah*, adj. Burnt, consumed, scorched. Used in composition, as دل سوخته *dil sokhtah* or ځان سوخته *dzān-sokhtah*, adj. Inflamed in mind, distressed, grieved, vexed, heart-burnt.

P سود *sūd*, s.m. (2nd) Profit, interest, usury. Pl. سودونه *sūdūnah*. سود من *sūd-man* or مند *mand*, adj. Profitable, beneficial, useful, lucrative, benefited, profited. سود مندي *sūd-mandī*, s.f. (3rd) Benefit, profitableness, advantage. Pl. ئي *a'ī*.

P سودا *saudā*, s.f. (6th) Trade, commerce, traffic, marketing. (E.) Sing. and Pl. (W.) Pl. سوداوي *saudāwī*. سود سودا *sūd saudā*, Buying and selling, barter, trade, traffic, etc. سودا كول *saudā kawul*, verb trans. To trade, to traffic, to barter, to buy, to sell. سوداګر *saudā-gar*, s.m. (5th) A trader, a merchant. Pl. سوداګران *saudā-garān*. سوداګري *saudāgarī*, s.f. (3rd) Trade, commerce, merchandise. Pl. ئي *a'ī*.

P سودا *saudā*, s.f. (6th) Melancholy, madness. 2. Love, desire, ambition. (E.) Sing. and Pl. (W.) Pl. سوداوي *saudāwī*.

A P سودائي *saudā'ī*, adj. Insane, mad, melancholic.

P سوده *sūdah*, adj. (past part. of سودن) Rubbed, abraded, scraped, frayed. 2. Dissolved. سوده كيدل *sūdah kedal*, verb intrans. To become rubbed, abraded, excoriated, frayed, etc. سوده كول *sūdah kawul*, verb trans. To rub, to abrade, to fray. سوده وريجي *sūda'h w'rījī*, Boiled rice (s سودها).

سوده *sūda'h*, s.f. (3rd) A stoppage, an obstruction in the bowels, nose, etc. Pl. ي *ey*. See سده

سوده *sawada'h*, s.f. (3rd) A basket, a hamper, a kind of cover for covering food, a sort of dish cover. Pl. ي *ey*.

سوډر *soḏḏar*, s.m. (5th) A pig, a wild pig, a hog, a boar. Pl. سوډران *soḏḏarān*. 2. adj. Bald, scald-headed; (Fem.) and s.f. (3rd) سوډره *soḏḏara'h*. Pl. ي *ey*. See سډر and ګنجي

سور *sor*, s.m. (2nd) Breadth, width, latitude, extent, expanse. Pl. سورونه *sorūnah*. سرَ ور *sarawar* or سره ور *sarah-war*, adj. Broad, wide, ample, extended; (Fem.) سرَ وره *sarah wara'h* or سره وره *sarah-wara'h*. سره ور كول *sarah-war kawul*, verb trans. To widen, to make broad, to extend. See پسور and بر

سور *sor*, adj. Mounted, seated on horseback, raised. 2. as s.m. (4th) A horseman, a cavalier. Pl. سواره *swārah*. سوره *swara'h*, adj; (Fem.), and s.f. (3rd) A horse-woman, a female mounted on horseback. Pl. ي *ey*. سوريدل *swaredal*, verb intrans. To ascend, to mount on horseback, to mount, to bestride, to cover. Pres. سوريږي *swarejzī* (W.) or سوريګي *swaregī* (E.); past سور شه *sor shah* or و شه *wu-shah*; fut. سور به شي *sor bah shī* or و به شي *bah wu-shī*; imp. سور شه *sor shah* or و شه *wu-shah*; act. part. سوريدونكي *swaredūnkaey* or سوريدوني *swaredūnaey*; past part. سور or سور شوي *sor shawaey*; verb. n. سوريدنه *swaredana'h* or سوريده *swaredah*. سورول *swarawul*, verb trans. To mount, to place on horseback, to place one's-self on horseback, to climb. Pres. سوروي *swarawī*; past سور كړ *sor karr* or و كړ *wu-karr*; fut. سور به كړي *sor bah krrī* or و به كړي *bah wu-krrī*; imp. سور كړه *sor krrah* or و كړه *wu-krrah*; act. part. سوروونكي *swarawūnkaey* or سوروونى *swarawūnaey*; past part. سور كړي *sor karraey*; verb. n. سورونه *swarawuna'h*. See سپور and سپريدل

سورلي *swarlī*, s.f. (3rd) Riding, passing or travelling on horseback; cavalcade, suite. Pl. ئي *a'ī*. سورلي كول *swarlī kawul*, verb trans. To take exercise on horseback, to go for a ride. 2. To accompany on horseback.

سور *sūr*, adj. Red, of a red colour; (Fem.) سره *sara'h*. سور كيدل *sūr kedal*, verb intrans. To become red, to redden, to blush, to become red-hot. سور كول *sūr kawul*, verb trans. To redden, to make red, to make blush, to make red-hot. سور والي *sūr-wālaey*, s.m. (1st) Redness, rosiness, ruddiness, blush. Pl. والي *wālī*. تک سور *tak sūr*, adj. Very red, red as fire, red as a turkey-cock, red-hot; (Fem.) تکه سره *taka'h-sara'h*. سور بنړي *sūr barrnaey*, adj. Red-haired. 2. s.m. (1st) A person with red or auburn hair and florid complexion. Pl. ي *ī*. سور بنړ *sūr barrni* s.f. (8th) A female with red hair. Pl. ي *ī*. Also written سور بونړي *sūr burrney*, etc. سور په وينو *sūr pah wīno*, adj. Covered or smeared with blood, blood-stained. سور پوستي *sur postaey*, adj. Red-skinned, scarlet-skinned; (Fem.) سور پوستِ *sur posti*. Pl. (Masc. and Fem.) ي *ī*. سور گلي *sūr-gulaey*, s.m. (1st) A kind of vegetable or greens. Pl. ي *ī*. سور غوږي *sūr-ghwajzaey* (W.) or غوگي *ghwagaey* (E.) s.m. (1st) Red sorrel, a kind of vegetable (Amaranthus polygamus). Pl. ي *ī*.

سور *sūr* or *sor*, s.m. (6th) The name of a tribe of Afghāns from whom Shīr Shāh, Salīm Shāh, and Muḥammad Shāh, Adilī, emperors of Hindūstān, were descended. Sing. and Pl.

سورپلي *sūr-palaey*, s.m. (1st) A kind of stinging nettle. Pl. ي *ī*. See جلبنگ

سورت *sūrat*, s.m. (2nd) The body (corrup. of A صورت) only so pronounced in conversation. Pl. سورتونه *sūratūnah*. See صورت

A سورت *sūrat* (2nd) A chapter or division of the Kur'ān. Pl. سورتونه *sūratūnah*.

P سورسات *sūr-sāt*, s.m. (2nd) Collecting stores or provisions for an army, stores, etc. Pl. سورساتونه *sūr-sātūnah*.

سورسانده *sūr sānda'h*, s.f. (3rd) Heath, heather. Pl. ي *ey*.

سورلگي *sūr-lakaey*, s.m. (1st) A small bird of the size of a robin, red under the tail, a kind of warbler. Pl. ي *ī*.

سورلنډ *sūr-landd*, s.m. (5th) A jackal. 2. The name of a tribe of Afghāns. Pl. سورلنډان *sūr-landdān*. سورلنډه *sūr-landda'h*, s.f. (3rd) A female jackal. 2. A female of the above tribe. Pl. ي *ey*. Also سور لنډي *sūr-landdaey*, adj. as s.m. (1st) (*lit.* red-back); (Fem.) لنډِ *landdi*. Pl. (Masc. and Fem.) ي *ī*.

سورمل *sūr-mal*, s.m. (2nd) A kind of prickly grass. Pl. سورملونه *sūrmalūnah*.

سور میږي *sūr-mejzī*, s.m. (5th) (W.) A red ant. Pl. سره میږیان *sara'h mejzīān*. Also سور میگي *sūr-megī* (E.) Pl. سره میگیان *sara'h megīān*.

A سورنجان *sūrinjān*, s.m. (6th) The name of a medicine (Hermodactylus). Sing. and Pl.

سوري *sūraey*, s.m. (1st) A hole, passage, orifice, etc. Pl. ي *ī*. سوري کیدل *sūraey kedal*, verb intrans. To become perforated, mined, or drilled out. سوري کول *sūraey kawul*, verb trans. To bore, to mine, to perforate, to make a hole or passage in anything.

سوري *sūrey*, s.f. (3rd) Pl. A shout, a call, a bawl, a noise, a loud sound, tumult, disturbance. The Sing. is سوره *sūra'h*, but it is seldom or never used. See زوږ. ناري سوري *nārey sūrey*, A great tumult or disturbance, hullaballoo.

سوري *sewraey* or *soraey*, s.m. (1st) Shade, shadow, cloud. Pl. ي *ī*. Also سیوري *sewraey* or *sīoraey*. Pl. ي *ī*.

سوریته *sūr-yata'h*, s.f. (3rd) A female slave who has borne a child to her master. Pl. ي *ey*.

سوړ *sorr*, adj. Cold, cool, frigid, chill, frosty. Pl. ساړه *sārrah*; (Fem.) سړه *sarra'h*. Pl. سړې *sarrey*. سوړ والي *sorr-wālaey* or سړ والي *sarr wālaey*, s.m. (1st) Coldness, coolness, frigidity, chillness, inclemency. Pl. والي *wālī*. See ساړه. سړیدل *sarredal*, verb intrans. To freeze, to congeal, to become cool, cold, frigid, etc. Pres. سړیږي *sarrejzī* (W.) or سړیگي *sarregī* (E.); past سوړ شه *sorr shah* or ؤ شه *wu-shah*; fut. سوړ به شي *sorr bah shī* or به ؤ شي *bah wu-shī*; imp. سوړ شه *sorr shah* or ؤ شه *wu-shah*; act. part. سړیدونکي *sarredūnkaey* or سړیدوني *sarredūnaey*; past part. سوړ *sorr* or سوړ شوي *sorr shawaey*; verb. n. سړیدنه *sarredana'h* or سړیده *sarredah*. سړول *sarrawul*, verb trans. To cool, to chill, to congeal, to freeze, to make cold, to benumb. Pres. سړوي *sarrawī*; past سوړ کړ *sorr karr* or ؤ کړ *wu-karr*; fut. سوړ به شي *sorr bah shī* or به ؤ شي *bah wu-shī*; imp. سوړ شه *sorr shah* or ؤ شه *wu-shah*; act. part. سړوونکيَ *sarrawūnkaey* or سړوونيَ *sarrawūnaey*; past part. سوړ کړيَ *sorr karraey*; verb. n. سړونه *sarrawuna'h*.

سوړ بوئي *sorr bū-ī*, s.m. (2nd) Stink, smell, effluvium, stench, fetor, foulness, etc. Pl. سوړ بويونه *sorr bu-īūnah*.

سوړه *sūrra'h*, s.f. (3rd) A hole, a burrow, an opening, a chasm, a fissure. Pl. ې *ey*. See سهوړه

سوړيَ *sūrraey*, s.m. (1st) A fissure, a chasm, an opening, a hole. Pl. ي *ī*. See preceding.

سوړيَ کول *sūrraey kawul*, verb trans. To bore, to mine, to perforate, to cause or make a chasm or fissure.

P سوز *soz*, s.m. (2nd) Burning. 2. Ardour, passion. 3. Vexation, heart-burning. Pl. سوزونه *sozūnah*. Used in composition. سوزگداز *soz gudāz*, Burning and melting, impassioned. په سوز راغلل *pah soz rāgh-lal*, verb intrans. To become excited. سوزان *sozān*, Burning. سوزش *sozish*, s.m. (2nd) (verb. n. of سوختن) Burning, inflammation, ardour, vexation, solicitude, pain. Pl. سوزشونه *sozishūnah*.

P سوزاك *sozāk*, s.m. (2nd) A clap, the gonorrhœa. Pl. سوزاكونه *sozākūnah*.

P سوزني *sozanī* or *soznī*, s.f. (3rd) A kind of small embroidered carpet, quilted linen. Pl. ئي *a'ī*.

سوزه *sūza'h*, s.f. (3rd) A gusset or gore of a shirt or coat. 2. An adze. Pl. ې *ey*. See ترهزه and تيشه

سوسر *sūsar*, s.m. (5th) A fish, a porpoise. Pl. سوسرونه *sūsarūnah*. (s سوس).

A سوسن *sosan* or *sausan*, s.m. (5th) A lily. Pl. سوسنان *sosanān*.

سوغ *sogh* or *sūgh*, s.m. (5th) A sniff, a snort, a snuff, the sound produced in blowing the nose, or smelling. Pl. سوغهار *soghahār*. سوغيدل *soghedal*, verb intrans. To smell, to scent, to snuff, to sniff. Pres. سوغيږي *soghejzī* (W.) or سوغيگي *soghegī* (E.); past ؤ سوغيده *wu-soghedah* or سوغيده *sogheda*; fut. ؤ به سوغيږي *wu bah soghejzī* or سوغيگي *soghegī*; imp. ؤ سوغيږه *wu-soghejzah* or سوغيگه *soghegah*; act. part. سوغيدونکيَ *soghedūnkaey* or سوغيدونيَ *soghedūnaey*; past part. سوغيدليَ *soghedalaey*; verb. n. سوغيدنه *soghedana'h* or سوغيده *soghedah*. سوغول *soghawul*, verb trans. To cause to smell, to give to smell, or sniff. Pres. سوغوي *soghawī*; past ؤ سوغاوه *wu-soghāwuh* or سوغاوو *soghāwo*; fut. ؤ به سوغوي *wu bah soghawī*; imp. ؤ سوغوه *wu-soghawah*; act. part. سوغوونکيَ *soghawūnkaey* or سوغوونيَ *soghawūnaey*; past part. سوغوليَ *soghawulaey*; verb. n. سوغونه *soghawuna'h*.

سوغ *sogh*, s.m. (2nd) A pinch (as of snuff) anything taken between the finger and thumb. Pl. سوغونه *soghūnah*. سوغ کول *sogh kawul*, verb trans. To take snuff, etc.

P سوغات *saughāt*, s.m. (2nd) A rarity, a present, a curiosity. Pl. سوغاتونه *saughātūnah*.

سوغاتي *saughātī*, adj. Fit for a present, rare, given as a present.

سوغاليَ *so-ghālaey*, s.m. (1st) A hare's form or burrow. Pl. ي *ī*. See سوي

سوغن *sūghan*, adj. as s.m. (5th) A sniveller, one who is constantly sniffing, through a cold, etc. Pl. سوغنُ *su-ghæn*; (Fem.) سوغنه *sūghana'h*. Pl. ې *ey*.

سوغيدل *sūghedal*, verb intrans. To become probed, pierced, stabbed, pinked, perforated, etc. سوغول *sūghawul*, verb trans. To perforate, to stab, to pierce, to probe. For tenses see سغيدل and سغول

سوك *sūk*, s.m. (2nd) The fist, a blow with the fist, a box, a buffet. 2. The root of a tree remaining in the ground. Pl. سوكونه *sūkūnah*; or s.m. (5th) Pl. سوكان *sūkān* (W.). په سوك وهل *pah sūk wahal*, verb trans. To strike with the fist, to box, to buffet. سوك وركول *sūk warkawul*, verb trans. To knead, to mash, to soften, to pommel, to beat to a mummy.

سوكړ *sūkarr*, s.m. (5th) A man with a thin beard and whiskers. Pl. سوكړان *sūkarrān*.

سوكړك *sūkarrak*, s.m. (2nd) Bread made from

jū'ar or maize (Holcus sorgum). Pl. سوکړکونه *sūkarrakūnah.*

P سوګند *saugand,* s.m. (2nd) An oath, an affirmation. Pl. سوګندونه *saugandūnah.* سوګند خوړل *saugand khwarral,* verb trans. To take an oath, to swear. سوګند ورکول *saugand warkawul,* verb trans. To administer an oath, to put on one's oath.

سول *swal,* verb intrans. To burn, to be on fire, to flame, to be heated, consumed, to take fire, to ignite, to kindle. This infinitive is also used as a transitive verb—To burn, to consume, to set on fire, to kindle, to ignite. Pres. سوځي *swadzī*; past وُ سه *wu-sah*; fut. وُ به سوځي *wu bah swadzī*; imp. وُ سوځه *wu-swadzah*; act. part. سوونکےَ *swūnkaey* or سوونےَ *swūnaey*; past part. سوےَ *sawaey*; verb. n. سونه *swana'h* or سوي *swaey.* See سیځل

سولاغه *solāgha'h,* s.f. (3rd) A bucket for drawing water, generally made of leather. Pl. ئ *ey.* See بوکه and دلوه

سولئ *sūla'ī,* s.f. (6th) An empaling stake, a pale, a stake, a gibbet. 2. A cold wind. Sing. and Pl. په سولئ کول *pah sūla'ī kawul,* verb trans. To empale. (s سولي). See سیلئ

سولیدل *sūledal,* verb intrans. To become ground, grated, rasped, to become abraded, rubbed down, to be filed, to be worn or smoothed. Pres. سولیږي *sūlejzī* (W.) or سولیګي *sūlegī* (E.); past وُ سولیده *wu-sūledah* or وُ سولیدَ *wu-sūleda*; fut. وُ به سولیږي *wu bah sūlejzī* or سولیګي *sūlegī*; imp. وُ سولیږه *wu-sūlejzah* or وُ سولیګه *wu-sūlegah*; act. part. سولیدونکےَ *sūledūnkaey* or سولیدونےَ *sūledūnaey*; past. part. سولیدلےَ *sūledalaey*; verb. n. سولیدنه *sūledana'h* or سولیده *sūledah.* سولول *sūlawul,* verb trans. To rub, to rub down, to grate, to file, to abrade, to smoothe, to wear away, to rasp, etc. Pres. سولوي *sūlawī*; past وُ سولاوه *wu-sūlāwuh* or وُ سولاوو *wu-sūlāwo*; fut. وُ به سولوي *wu bah sūlawī*; imp. وُ سولوه *wu-sūlawah*; act. part. سولوونکےَ *sūlawūnkaey* or سولوونےَ *sūluwūnaey*; past part. سولولےَ *sūlawulaey*; verb. n. سولونه *sūlawuna'h.*

سوم *swam,* s.m. (2nd) The eye of a needle, a small hole or perforation made in the ears or nose, the perforation of the penis; (Fem.) سومونه *swamūnah.* See سپم

سونبه *sūnba'h,* s.f. (3rd) A socket, the haft of a spear or lance, the head of an axe, or the like, in which the handle is placed. Pl. ئ *ey.* See پوندئ

سوندر *swandar,* s.m. (6th) A steer, a young bullock. Pl. سونډر *swandær* (E.); or s.m. (5th) (W.) Pl. سوندران *swandarān.* سوندره *swandara'h,* s.f. (3rd) A heifer, a young cow. Pl. ئ *ey.* See سخوندر

سونده *sūndah,* adj. Jealous, suspicious, emulous, apprehensive of rivalship.

s سونډ *sūndd,* s.m. (5th) The lip. Pl. سونډان *sūnddān.* See شونډ

سونډ *sūndd,* s.m. (6th) Dry ginger. Sing. and Pl.

سونډک *sūnddak,* s.m. (5th) The proboscis of an elephant. Pl. سونډکان *sūnddakān* (from s سونډ).

سونګټ *sūngatt,* adj. burnt or scorched (as bread in an oven), shrunk up, shrivelled, scarified, wrinkled, contracted, frost-bitten. سونګټ کیدل *sūngatt kedal,* verb intrans. To become scorched, shrunk up, shrivelled, etc. سونګټ کول *sūngatt kawul,* verb trans. To scorch, to shrivel, to contract, to scarify. See کونسټ and سټکوري

سونګےَ *songaey,* s.m. (1st) A dwarf, a pigmy. Pl. ي *ī.* سونګئ *songa'ī,* s.f. (6th) A female dwarf. Sing. and Pl.

سونړ *sūrrn,* s.m. (5th) A sniff, a snort, a snuff, the act of smelling or blowing the nose. Pl. سونړهار *sūrrnahār.* 2. s.m. (2nd) A pinch of snuff, etc. Pl. سونړونه *sūrrn-ūnah.* سونړ کول *sūrrn kawul,* verb trans. To take a pinch (as of snuff, etc.) سونړیدل *sūrrnedal,* verb intrans. To smell, to scent, to snuff, to sniff. Pres. سونړیږي *sūrrnejzī* (W.) or سونړیګي *sūrrnegī* (E.); past وُ سونړیده *wu-sūrrnedah* or وُ سونړیدَ *wu-sūrrneda*; fut. وُ به سونړیږي *wu bah sūrrnejzī* or سونړیګي *sūrrnegī*; imp.

وُ سونړيږه *wu-sūrrnejzah* or سونړيگه *sūrrnegah*; act. part. سونړيدونکي *sūrrnedūnkaey* or سونړيدوني *sūrrnedūnaey*; past. part. سونړيدلي *sūrrnedalaey*; verb. n. سونړيدنه *sūrrnedana'h* or سونړيده *sūrrnedah*. سونړول *sūrrnawul*, verb trans. To cause to smell, to give to smell or sniff. Pres. سونړوي *sūrrnawī*; past وُ سونړاوه *wu-sūrrnāwuh* or وُ سونړاوو *wu-sūrrnāwo*; fut. وُ به سونړوي *wu bah sūrrnawī*; imp. وُ سونړوه *wu-sūrrnawah*; act. part. سونړوونکي *sūrrnawūnkaey* or سونړووني *sūrrnawūnaey*; past part. سونړولي *sūrrnawulaey*; verb. n. سونړونه *sūrrnawuna'h*.

سوور *swor*, adj. Mounted, seated on horseback, raised. 2. s.m. (4th) A horseman, a cavalier, Pl. سواره *swāra'h*; (Fem.) سوره *swara'h*, and s.f. (3rd). Pl. ۍ *ey*. سووريدل *sworedal*, verb intrans. To ascend or mount on horseback, to mount, to bestride, to cover. سوورول *sworawul*, verb trans. To mount, to place on horseback, to place one's-self on horseback, to climb. See under سور and سپور

سوود *sowa'h*, s.f. (3rd) The name of a plant, small anise. Pl. ۍ *ey*. See خواږه ولني

سوه *soa'h*, s.f. (3rd) Ornament, dress, decoration, Pl. ۍ *ey*. (s शोभा)

سوه *swa'h*, s.f. (3rd) The hoof of a horse, ass, mule, etc. Pl. ۍ *ey*. See بهونگري and سم

سوهاگن *sohāgan*, s.f. (1st) A woman beloved by her husband, a favourite wife, a newly married woman, a bride. Pl. سوهاگنِ *sohāgani*. (s سهاگن)

P سوهان *sohān*, s.m. (2nd) A file, a rasp. Pl. سوهانونه *sohānūnah*. سوهان کول *sohān kawul*, verb trans. To file, to rasp, to reduce by filing.

سوَي *sawaey*, adj. Burnt, consumed, on fire, heated, set on fire, ignited. (past part. of سول). سوَي لوغړن *sāwaey lūgharran*, adj. Smoked black, burnt black, half burnt. 2. Vexed, afflicted, heart-burnt, heart broken, etc.; (Fem.) سوي لوغړنه *sawey lūgharrana'h*.

سوَي *swaey*, s.m. (1st) (verb. n. of سول) Burning, heat, warmth, ardour, inflammation, pain, vexation, solicitude, fervour, flush, etc. Pl. ي *ī*. زړه سوَي *z'rrah swaey* or زړ سوَي *z'rr-swaey*, s.m. (1st) Sympathy, compassion, pity, commiseration, tenderness. Pl. ي *ī*. سوَي کول *swaey kawul*, verb trans. To inflame, to ache, to burn, to pain, to cause vexation, to flush, to make blush, etc.

سوي لړمون *sawaey larr-mūn* or سوخته لړمون *sokhtah larr-mūn*, adj. Heart consumed, half dead; (Fem.) سو لړمونه *sawi larrmūna'h* or سوخته لړمونه *sokhtah larrmūna'h*.

سوي *soe*, s.m. (5th) A hare, the general term for the species. Pl. سويان *soe-ān*. سويه *soeya'h*, s.f. (3rd) A female hare. Pl. ۍ *ey*. This is the Western form: the tribes of Peshāwer use the feminine سويه *soeya'h*, for the species, and when mentioning the male or female make the difference as above. سوي غالي *soe-ghālaey*, s.m. (1st) A hare's form or burrow. Pl. ي *ī*. See سوغالي

سويشل *sweshal*, verb trans. To milk. See لوشل

سويه *soeya'h*, s.f. (3rd) A hare in general. 2. A female hare (E.). 2. Young crops for the first month or six weeks until watered. Pl. ۍ *ey*. See سوي

P سه *sih* or *si*, adj. Three. In composition as سه شنبه *sih shamba'h*, Tuesday. سه فصله *sih-fasalah*, adj. Having three harvests. سه تار *sih-tār*, s.m. (2nd) A guitar. Pl. سه تارونه *sih-tārūnah*. See ستار

سهره *suhrra'h*, s.f. (3rd) A hole, a cleft, a fissure, a chasm, an opening. Pl. ۍ *ey*. سهره کول *suhrra'h kawul*, verb trans. To bore, to mine, to make a cleft, fissure, chasm, etc. See سوره

A سهل *sahl*, adj. Easy, not difficult, trifling, simple. adv. Easily.

سهل *sahal*, verb intrans. To bear, to endure, to suffer, to support, to put up with, to undergo. Pres. سهي *sahī*; past وُ ساهه *wu-sāhah* or وُ ساهَ *wu-sāha*; fut. وُ به سهي *wu bah sahī*; imp. وُ سهه *wu-sahah*; act. part. سهونکي *sahūnkaey* or سهوني *sahūnaey*; past part. سهلي *sahalaey*; verb. n. سهنه *sa-hana'h*. See سهيدل

P سهم *sahm*, s.m. (2nd) Fear, dread, terror,

awe, horror. Pl. سهمونه *sahm-ūnah*. سهم ناك *sahm-nāk*, adj. Horrible, terrible, dreadful; (Fem.) سهم ناكه *sahm-nāka'h*. سم گر *sahm-gar*, adj. Causing terror, terrific, horrible; (Fem.) سهم گره *sahm-gara'h*. سهم كول *sahm kawul*, verb trans To terrify, to horrify, to frighten, to fill with awe or dread.

سهمانه *sahmāna'h*, s.f. (3rd) Pomp, parade, state. Pl. ي *ey*. See سامانه

سهوه *sahwa'h*, s.f. (3rd) (corrup. of A سهو) An error, mistake, fault, blunder, omission, inadvertency. Pl. ي *ey*. سهوه كول *sahwa'h kawul*, verb trans. To commit a fault, to make a mistake or blunder, to make an omission. په سهوه *pah sahwa'h*, adv. Erroneously, inadvertently, by mistake.

سهه *saha'h*, s.f. (3rd) The breath, life, the vital spark. 2. A line or pole for hanging clothes on, a clothes' horse. Pl. ي *ey*. See پيكل and ګډيكه. سهه كښل *saha'h k'shal* (W.) or سهه ښكل *saha'h kh'kal* (E.) verb trans. To breathe, to draw breath. سهه شړل *saha'h sharral* or وهل *wahal*, verb trans. To pant, to puff, to breathe with difficulty, to breathe. سهه ختل *saha'h khatal*, verb intrans. To die, to cease to breathe, to give up the ghost. See ساه

سهي *sahī*, adj. Straight, true. 2. adv. True! well! good! (corrup. of A صحيح). سهي كول *sahī kawul*, verb trans. To look at attentively, to mark, to observe, to notice. See زير كول

سهيدل *sahedal*, verb intrans. To endure, to bear, to support, to undergo, to put up with. Pres. سهيږي *sahejzī* (W.) or سهيګي *sahegī* (E.); past وُ سهيده *wu-sahedah* or وُ سهيدَ *wu-saheda*; fut. وُ به سهيږي *wu bah sahejzī* or سهيګي *sahegī*; imp. وُ سهيږه *wu-sahejzah* or وُ سهيګه *wu-sahegah*; act. part. سهيدونكَى *sahedūnkaey* or سهيدونَى *sahedūnaey*; past part. سهيدلَى *sahedalaey*; verb. n. سهيدنه *sahedana'h* or سهيده *sahedah*.

A P سهيل *suhail*, s.m. (9th) The star Canopus. See ستوري

S سهيلي *suhelī*, s.f. (3rd) A woman's female companion, a handmaid, a damsel, a concubine. Pl. ي *a'ī*.

سيا *siyā*, s.f. (6th) Shade, shadow, obscurity, gloom, shadiness, duskiness, umbrage. (E.) Sing. and Pl. (W.) Pl. سياوي *siyāwī*. See سياه

A سياح *saiyāḥ*, s.m. (5th) A pilgrim, a traveller, travelling much. Pl. سياحان *saiyāḥān*. سياحه *saiyāḥa'h*, s.f. (3rd) A female pilgrim or traveller. Pl. ي *ey*. سياحت *saiyāḥat*, s.m. (2nd) Travelling, a voyage, a journey, a tour, a pilgrimage. Pl. سياحتونه *saiyāḥatūnah*; or سياحي *saiyāḥī*, s.f. (3rd). Pl. ي *a'ī*. سياحت *saiyāḥat* or سياحي كول *saiyāḥī kawul*, verb trans. To travel, to make a journey or go on a pilgrimage.

سياځه *sīā-dza'h*, s.f. (3rd) A large flat stone or pebble used for grinding condiments on, a cobbler's lapstone, etc. Pl. ي *ey*. See دسته

A سياست *siyāsat*, s.m. (2nd) (from سوس) Punishment, chastisement, pang, agony. 2. Administration of justice, government. Pl. سياستونه *siyāsatūnah*. په سياست كول *pah siyāsat kawul*, verb trans. To punish, to chastise.

سيال *sī-āl*, adj. Of the same tribe or clan. Pl. سيالان *sī-ālān*. 2. s.m. (5th) An equal, equal, alike, resembling; s.f. (3rd) سياله *sī-āla'h*. Pl. ي *ey*.

سيالي *sī-ālī*, s.f. (3rd) Equality, resemblance, parity, sameness of degree or quantity. Pl. ي *a'ī*. سيالي كول *sī-ālī kawul*, verb trans. To equal, to match, to come up to, to cope with. سيالي كيدل *sī-ālī kedal*, verb intrans. To match, to be of equal size, degree, or equality; or سيالي لرل *sī-ālī laral*, verb trans. To have or hold equality.

P سياه *sī-āh*, adj. Black, unfortunate, bad. Used only in composition. سياه بخت *sī-āh bakht*, adj. Unfortunate; (Fem.) سياه بخته *sī-āh bakhta'h*. سياه بختي *sī-āh bakhtī*, s.f. (3rd) Misfortune, ill-luck. Pl. ي *a'ī*. سياه پوښ *sī-āh posh* (W.) or pokh (E.) s.m. (5th) The name of the inhabitants of Kāfiristān, a country to the north of Jelālābād (*lit.* black-clad). 2. A male of the above. Pl. سیاه پوښان *sī-āh poshān* or *pokhān*. سیاه پوښه *sī-āh posha'h* or *pokha'h*, s.f. (3rd) A female of the above tribe. Pl. ې *ey*.

P سیاه گوش *sī-āh gosh*, s.m. (5th) A lynx. Pl. سیاه گوشان *sī-āh goshān*.

P سیاهي *sī-āhī*, s.f. (3rd) Blackness, ink. Pl. ئ *a'ī*. Also vulg. سیهي *sī-hī*. Pl. ئ *a'ī*. سیاهي د لښکر *sī'āhī da lashkar* (W.) or *lakhkar* (E.) The blackness or shade of an army, with reference to a force in which the non-combatants are in greater numbers than the fighting men, as in Indian armies.

P سیب *seb*, s.m. (2nd) An apple. Pl. سیبونه *sebūnah*. See منړه

P سیپاره *sī-pāra'h* or *se-pāra'h*, s.f. (3rd) Each one of the thirty sections into which the Ḳur'ān is divided. Pl. ې *ey*.

سیپئ *sīpa'ī*, s.f. (6th) A shell. 2. The edge or side of a hill, or any high or lofty thing. Sing. and Pl.

S سیټه *setth* or سیټ *sett*, s.m. (5th) A banker, a merchant. Pl. سیټهان *setthān* or سیټان *settān*.

P سیخ *sīkh*, s.m. (2nd) A spit, a skewer, a ram-rod. Pl. سیخونه *sīkhūnah*. Also s.m. (5th). Pl. سیخان *sīkhān*. See سپرکي. په سیخ پییل *pah sīkh peyal*, verb trans. To spit, to pierce. سیخ وهل *sīkh wahal*, verb trans. To probe, to search, to sound, to explore, to search for.

P سیخچه *sekh-cha'h*, s.f. (3rd) A skewer, a small spit. 2. A long bayonet which is sometimes fixed on to a matchlock. Pl. ې *ey*.

سیخل *sīkhal*, verb trans. To probe, to pink, to stab, to perforate, to spit, to thrust, to stuff into (as clothes into a bag), to cram or force into, to press or squeeze into. For tenses, see ځخل

A سید *saiyid* or *suyed*, s.m. (5th) A lord, a prince. 2. A descendant of Ḥusain, the grandson of Muḥammad. Pl. سیدان *saiyidān* or *suyedān*. سیده *siayida'h*, s.f. (3rd) A female descendant of Ḥusain. Pl. ې *ey*.

A سیر *sair*, s.m. (2nd) Perambulation, excursion, an airing, taking the air, a walk, recreation, amusement, going about. Pl. سیرونه *sairūnah*. سیر کول *sair kawul*, verb trans. To take the air, travel, rove, walk.

S سیر *ser*, s.m. (2nd) The name of a weight of about the fifth of an English pound; in India two pounds. Pl. سیرونه *serūnah*.

P سیراب *ser-āb*, adj. Full of water, saturated, moist, succulent, satisfied with drink. 2. Fresh, blooming; (Fem.) سیرابه *ser-āba'h*. سیراب کول *ser-āb kawul*, verb trans. To saturate, to moisten, to fill with water. سیرابي *ser-ābī*, s.f. (3rd) Moistness, freshness, juiciness. Pl. ئ *a'ī*.

A سیرت *sī-rat*, s.m. (2nd) Way of life, morals, manners, conduct. Pl. سیرتونه *sī-ratūnah*.

سیرلی *ser-laey*, s.m. (1st) A kid during the first year. Pl. ي *ī*. سیرلئ *ser-la'ī*, s.f. (6th) A female kid as above. Sing. and Pl.

سیرئ *sīra'ī*, s.f. (6th) Rent-free land given to holy men, a fief, an estate, a temporary pension. Sing. and Pl. See دوتر and بوکري

سیزل *se-zal*, verb trans. To burn, to consume, to set on fire, to ignite. For tenses, see سیځل

سیزني *sez-nī*, s.f. (8th) A swaddling band. Pl. ئ *a'ī*. See اونړي or اورنړي

سیځل *sedzal*, verb trans. To burn, to consume, to set on fire, to ignite, to fire, to kindle. Pres. سیځي *sedzī*; past وسیځه *wu-sedzah* or وسیځَ *wu-sedza*; fut. و به سیځي *wu bah sedzī*; imp. وسیځه *wu-sedzah*; act. part. سیځونکی *sedzūnkaey* or سیځونی *sedzūnaey*; past part. سیځلی *sedzalaey*; verb. n. سیځنه *sedzana'h*. See سیزل

سیستان *sīstān*, s. prop. The name of a country, —the ancient Drāngīānah—eastward of Persia Proper.

سیسه *sī-sa'h*, s.f. (3rd) (s सीसक) Lead. Pl. ې *ey*. Also written سیسَ *sī-sa*. Pl. سیسِ *sī-si*.

سیکړه *saikarra'h*, s.f. (3rd) A hundred, per cent. 2. A piece of coarse cloth to the extent of one hundred yards. Pl. ې *ey* (s سیکړا).

سیکل *sekal*, verb trans. To toast, to warm, to

foment, to cherish with heat, to bathe with or apply warm lotions, etc. Pres. سيكي *sekī*; past وُ سيکه *wu-sekah*; fut. وُ به سيكي *wu bah sekī*; imp. وُ سيکه *wu-sekah*; act. part. سيكونكَي *sekūnkaey* or سيكونَي *sekūnaey*; past part. سيكلَي *sekalaey*; verb. n. سيكنه *sekana'h* (H سينكنا). See also تكور

سيكن *sai-kan* (E.) or *se-kan* (W.) s.m. (5th) Disgust, aversion, loathing, antipathy, dislike, abhorrence, nausea, repulsiveness. Pl. سيكُن *sai-kæn* or *se-kæn*.

سيكه *sīka'h*, s.f. (3rd) Lead. Pl. ي *ey*. See سكه

A سيل *sail*, s.m. (2nd) Flowing, walking, creeping, walking or going about for amusement. 2. A current, a torrent, a flood. 3. A flock of birds, a shoal of fishes. Pl. سيلونه *sailūnah*. Also pronounced *sel* by the Afghāns of the west. سيل كول *sail kawul*, verb trans. To walk about, to view, to take amusement or recreation. سيلاب *sailāb*, s.m. (2nd) A flood, a torrent, a stream, a deluge. Pl. سيلابونه *sailābūnah*. 2. adj. Abounding with water.

سيلمه *selma'h*, s.f. (3rd) End, point, extremity, summit. Pl. ي *ey*. See څيلمه

سيلوه *sel-wa'h*, s.f. (3rd) Friendship, affection. 2. Partiality, assistance, aid. Pl. ي *ey*. سيلوي لرل *sel-wey laral*, verb trans. To like, to hold dear, to have friendship for, to be partial unto. See سيله

سيله *se-la'h*, s.f. (3rd) Friendship, affection. 2. Partiality, assistance, aid. Pl. ي *ey*. سيله لرل *se-la'h laral* or سيلي لرل *se-ley laral*, verb trans. To hold dear, to like, to have partiality for, etc. سيله كول *sela'h kawul*, verb trans. To favour, to lean towards, to show partiality. See سيلوه

سيلَي *siyalaey*, s.m. (1st) Rennet, the prepared stomach of a kid, lamb, etc. containing the concreted milk from which cheese is made. Pl. ئي *ī*.

سيلئي *sīla'ī*, s.f. (6th) A slap, a blow with the flat of the hand. 2. High wind with dust, a storm, a tempest. 3. Rope made from the hair of goats, camels, etc. Sing. and Pl.

P سيم *sīm*, s.m. (2nd) Silver. 2. Wire of any kind. Pl. سيمونه *sīmūnah*. سيم بر *sīm bar*, adj. Silver-bosomed, with a bosom like silver; (Fem.) سيم بره *sīm bara'h*. سيم بدن *sīm badan* or سيم تن *sīm tan*, adj. Silver-bodied, with a body fair as silver; (Fem.) سيم بدنه *sīm badana'h* or سيم تنه *sīm tana'h*.

P سيماب *sīm-āb*, s.m. (6th) Mercury, quicksilver. Sing. and Pl. سيمابي *sīmābī*, adj. Of mercury, made of mercury, mercurial.

P سيمرغ *sī-murgh*, s.m. (5th) A fabulous bird, a griffin. Pl. سيمرغان *sī-murghān*.

سيمسار *sīm-sār*, s.m. (2nd) A species of lizard or iguana, a land crocodile or aligator. Pl. سيمسارونه *sīm-sārūnah*. سيمساره *sīm-sāra'h*, s.f. (3rd) A female of the above. Pl. ي *ey*. See سمسره

P سيمک *sīmak*, s.m. (5th) A long iron needle used by weavers, a knitting needle. Pl. سيمكان *sīmakān*.

سيمه *sīma'h*, s.f. (3rd) A way, a path; a part, side, quarter, towards. Pl. ي *ey*. Also written سيمَ *sīma*.

سيمه *sema'h*, s.f. (3rd) A mare or ass seeking the male. Pl. ي *ey*.

سيميا *sīmī-ā*, s.f. (6th) Vermicelli. Sing. and Pl. See ماچي. سيميا توت *sīmī-ā-tūt*, The vermicelli mulberry. See توت

سيند *sīnd*, s.m. (2nd) A river, the sea, the ocean. Pl. سيندونه *sīndūnah*. Also written and pronounced سين *sīn* (S سندھ). آبا سيند *ābā sīnd* or سين *sīn*, The father of rivers—the Indus. لندي سيند *landdaey sīnd*, The little river, the river of Kābul, which joins the Indus a little north of Attak.

سيندلاوُ *sīnd-lā-o*, s.m. (5th) An otter, the water dog. Pl. سيندلاوُگان *sīnd-lā-o-gān*. The feminine form merely takes (ے) in the plural. See سگلاوو

سينگار *sīngār*, s.m. (2nd) Ornament, adornment, decoration, dress, etc. Pl. سينگارونه *sīngārūnah*. سينگار كول *sīngār kawul*, verb trans. To ornament, to decorate, to embellish, to deck one's-self out. See سنگار

سينه *sīna'h*, s.f. (3rd) The breast, the bosom. Pl. ې *ey*. سينه بند *sīna'h band*, s.m. (2nd) Stays, a bodice. Pl. بندان *bandān*. سينه سوخته *sīna'h sokhtah* or سينه سوز *sīna'h soz*, adj. Tormented, distressed. سينه وهل *sīna'h wahal*, verb trans. To beat the breast. سينه دار *sīna'h dār*, adj. Calm, patient, cool in temper; (Fem.) سينه داره *sīna'h dāra'h*. سينه داغي *sīna'h dāghaey*, adj. Distressed, troubled in mind; (Fem.) سينه داغ *sīna'h dāghi*. Pl. (Masc. and Fem.) ي *ī*. See تتر

P سيني *sīnī*, s.f. (3rd) A salver, a tray, a trough. Pl. ئي *a'ī*.

P سيو *sew*, s.m. (6th) An apple. Sing. and Pl.

سيوري *sew-raey* or *seo-raey*, s.m. (1st) Shadow, shade, cloud. Pl. ي *ī*. See سوري. سيوري لرل *sew-raey* or *seo-raey laral*, verb trans. To have shade or shadow, to cast or throw shadow. سيوري كول *sew-raey* or *seo-raey kawal*, verb trans. To shade, to overshadow, to screen.

ش

ش *shīn*, called the شين منقوطه or شين معجمه is the thirteenth letter of the Arabic, the sixteenth of the Persian, and the twenty-second of the Pushto alphabet. The sound is the same as English *sh*, French *ch*, or Italian *sc*. In denoting numbers by the letters of the Arabic alphabet it stands for 300. Sometimes this letter is changed for the Pushto ښ *khīn* or *shey* in words taken from the Persian, as خوښ for خوش, پيښ for پيش, etc.

شا *shā*, s.f. (6th) The back. (E.) Sing. and Pl. (W.) Pl. شاوي *shā-wī*. پسي شا *pasey shā*, Behind the back, in one's absence. شا په شا *shā pah shā*, Back to back, at enmity with each other. شا كول *shā kawul*, verb trans. To turn the back on, to reject, to abandon, to treat with contempt; also تر شا كول *tar shā kawul*. شا وركول *shā war kawul*, verb trans. To flee, to run away, to turn tail.

P شاباز *shā-bāz*, s.m. (2nd) The bass string of a violin or other stringed instrument. 2. A royal falcon. Pl. شابازونه *shā-bāzūnah*; or s.m. (5th). Pl. شابازان *shā-bāzān*.

P شاباش *shā-bāsh*, interj. Bravo! well done! excellent! contracted and corrupted, at times, into شاباس *shā-bās*. See شاه

شاپيټي *shā-peṭṭaey*, s.m. (1st) A snail. Pl. ي *ī*. and د كارغه پسكي كوجي

شاتر *shā-tar*, s.m. (5th) A man who runs before one's horse and holds him when the rider alights, a running footman or groom. Pl. شاتران *shā-tarān*.

شاټينګه *shā-ṭṭenga'h*, s.f. (3rd) The gizzard of a fowl, or bird in general. Pl. ې *ey*. See شاټيغي

شادو *shādo*, s.m. (5th) A monkey, an ape. Pl. شادوګان *shādo-gān*. This noun is also used as s.f. (5th). Pl. شادوګاني *shādo-gāni*. See بيزو

شاربل *shār-bal*, verb trans. To churn. Pres. شاربي *shārbī*; past و شاربه *wu-shārbah*; fut. و به شاربي *wu-bah shārbī*; imp. و شاربه *wu shārbah*; act. part. شاربونكي *shār-būnkaey* or شاربوني *shār-būnaey*; past part. شاربلي *shār-balaey*; verb. n. شاربنه *shār-bana'h*. See مندانړو

شاړ *shāṛṛ*, adj. Rude, clownish (person), unmannered, a clodhopper, a clown. 2. Out of work, unemployed, fallow; (Fem.) شاړه *shāṛṛa'h*. Also as s.f. (3rd) Waste or fallow land. Pl. ې *ey*.

A شاعر *shā'ær*, s.m. (5th) A poet. Pl. شاعران *shā'ærān*. شاعره *shā'æra'h*, s.f. (3rd) A poetess. Pl. ې *ey*. شاعري *shā'ærī*, s.f. (3rd) Poetry, the art or practice of poetry. Pl. ئي *a'ī*. شاعري كول *shā'ærī kawul*, verb trans. To make or compose poetry.

A شاغل *shā-ghil*, adj. (past part. of شغل), Occupied, employed, attentive; (Fem.) شاغله *shā-ghila'h*.

A شافع *shāfiæ*, s.m. (5th) (act. part. of A شفع) Deprecating, interceding; an advocate, an intercessor, a patron. Pl. شافعان *shāfiæ-ān*.

A شافعي *shāfi-æī*, s.m. (5th) One of the chiefs of the four principal sects of the Muḥammadan faith. 2. Following the sect of Shāfi'æī. Pl. شافعيان *shāfi-æī-ān*.

A شاكر *shā-kir*, adj. (act. part. of شكر) Grateful, praising, thankful; (Fem.) شاكره *shā-kira'h*.

P شاگرد *shā-gird*, s.m. (5th) A scholar, a pupil, a disciple, an apprentice, a servant. Pl. شاگردان *shā-girdān*; also شاگړد *shā-girrd* and شاگړدان *shā-girrdān*. شاگرده *shā-girda'h* or شاگړده *shāgirrda'h*, s.f. (3rd) A female pupil or scholar. Pl. ې *ey*.

شاگردي *shā-girdī* or شاگړدي *shā-girrdī*, s.f. (3rd) Pupilage, studying, learning, apprenticeship. Pl. ئ *a'ī*. شاگردي کول *shā-girdī kawul* or شاگړدي کول *shā-girrdī kawul*, verb trans. To study, to learn, to act as a pupil, to serve apprenticeship.

S شال *shāl*, s.m. (2nd) A shawl. Pl. شالونه *shālūnah*. شال باف *shāl-bāf*, s.m. (5th) A shawl weaver. Pl. شال بافان *shāl-bafān*.

S شالئ *shāla'ī*, s.f. (6th) Rice before it is reaped or threshed. Sing. and Pl. شالئ زاره *shāla'ī zāra'h*, s.f. (3rd) Rice-ground, ground in which rice has been sown. Pl. ې *ey*. See also شول and شول کره

P شام *shām*, s. prop. Syria, شامي *shāmī*, s.m. (5th) A Syrian. Pl. شاميان *shāmī-ān*. شامئ *shāma'ī*, s.f. (6th) A Syrian female. Sing. and Pl.

A شامت *shā-mat*, s.m. (2nd) (from شوم) Mischance, adversity, bad luck. Pl. شامتونه *shā-matūnah*.

A شامل *shā-mil*, adj. (act. part. of شمل) Comprising, containing, including, extending, communicating; included, blended, united, comprised, common. 2. adv. Together, in company with. 3. prep. With, along with. شامل کيدل *shā-mil kedal*, verb intrans. To be blended, comprised, included, to partake. شامل کول *shā-mil kawul*, verb trans. To blend, to include, to unite, etc.

شاموزي *shāmo-zī*, s.m. (1st) Pl. The name of a tribe of Afghāns. Sing. شاموزی *shāmo-zaey*, A male of the above tribe. شاموزئ *shāmoza'ī*, s.f. (6th) A female of the above tribe. Sing. and Pl.

شامئ *shāma'ī*, s.f. (6th) A tomb, a sepulchre, a charnel house, a small tomb or house made of stones in which dead bodies are deposited instead of being interred. This is generally adopted in mountainous districts where there is no available ground, or where it may not be soft enough, and in places where it is soft and sandy. Sing. and Pl.

A شان *shān*, s.m. (from شأن) Business, affair. 2. Dignity, state, pomp, degree, condition. 3. Nature, disposition, constitution. Pl. شانونه *shān-ūnah*.

شان *shān*, adv. of similitude, Like, as, similar, etc. 2. adj. Resembling, like, or (adjunct of similitude), for English *ish*, as تور شان *tor shān*, Blackish. سپين شان *spīn-shān*, Whitish. 3. s.m. (2nd) Way, manner, method, etc. Pl. شانونه *shānūnah*. (Fem.) شانه *shāna'h*. په بل شان *pah bal shān*, In a different mode or manner. په څه شان *pah tsah shān* In what manner? after what fashion? how? په څو شان *pah tso shān*, In different ways. په څو څو شان *pah tso tso shān*, In manifold ways, in various manners. په دغه *pah daghah*, په دا *pah dā*, or په دي شان *pah dey shān*, In this way, after this fashion. په هغه شان *pah haghah shān*, In that way? after that fashion? هر شان *har shān*, By every means, in some way or other. The postposition سره *sarah*, is also often used with it, as well as the preposition په *pah*; thus, په هر شان سره *pah har shān sarah*, By hook or by crook, by every means. بي شانَ *bey-shāna*, adj. Unequalled, incomparable. See لکه, غندِ, and دود

شانگئ *shānga'ī*, s.f. (6th) A kind of pitchfork, an instrument used for winnowing corn. Sing. and Pl. See چار ښاخه, دري ښاخي, and ښانگئ

شانه *shāna'h*, s.f. (3rd) A comb. Pl. ې *ey*. See ږمنځ and كمنځه, etc.

شاول *shāwul*, s.m. (6th) A plumb-line, a plummet. Pl. شاولونه *shā-wulūnah.* See خاول شاولي واولي *shāw-laey-wāw-laey,* adj. Careless, foolish, indiscreet, without sense or discernment. 2. A careless foolish person; (Fem.) شاولِ واولِ *shāw-li-wāw-li.* Pl. (Masc. and Fem.) ي *ī.*

P شاه *shāh,* s.m. (5th) A king, a prince, an emperor. Pl. شاهان *shāh-ān.* شاه باز *shāh-bāz,* s.m. (2nd) The bass string of a musical instrument. 2. A royal falcon. Pl. شاه بازونه *shāh-bāzūnah.* See شاباز. شاه باش *shāh bāsh,* interj. Bravo! well done! شاه باشي *shāh-bāshī,* s.f. (3rd) Praise, applause, approbation, commendation. Pl. ئ *a'ī.* شاه باشي or (corrup.) شاباسي كول *shāh-bāshī* or (corrup.) *shā-bāsī kawul,* verb trans. To praise, to applaud, to commend, to hail. د شاه باشي غرهار *da shāh-bāshī ghara-hār,* Shouts of praise, cheers, plaudits, huzzas. شاه توت *shāh-tūt,* s.m. (5th) A royal mulberry. Pl. شاه توتان *shāh tūtān.* شاه تير *shāh-tīr,* s.m. (5th) A beam. Pl. شاه تيران *shāh-tīrān.* See بينش. شاه زاده *shāh-zādah,* s.m. (5th) A prince, a prince royal. Pl. شاه زادهگان *shāh-zādah-gān.* شاه زادئ *shāh-zāda'ī,* s.f. (6th) A princess. Sing. and Pl.

شاه تره *shāh-tara'h,* s.f. (3rd) Fumitory (Oldenlandia biflora). Pl. ئ *ey.*

A شاهد *shā-hid,* s.m. (5th) (from H, CH, and A شهد) A witness. Pl. شاهدان *shā-hidān.* 2. (P) شاهده *shā-hida'h,* s.f. (3rd) A sweetheart, a female friend, a beloved object, a female witness. Pl. ئ *ey.*

A شاهدي *shā-hidī,* s.f. (3rd) Evidence, testimony, witness, deposition, attestation. Pl. ئ *a'ī.* شاهدي وركول *shā-hidī war-kawul,* شاهدي لل or شاهدي لودل *shā-hidī lal* or *shā-hidī lau-dal,* verb trans. To give evidence or testimony, to testify, to depose.

P شاهنشاه *shāhan-shāh,* s.m. (5th) The King of kings, a title of the old kings of Persia. Pl. شاهنشهان *shāhan-shahān.*

P شاهي *shāh-ī,* s.f. (3rd) Reign, sovereignty, royalty. Pl. ئ *a'ī.* 2. adj. Royal, regal, kingly.

P شاهين *shā-hīn,* s.m. (5th) A royal white falcon. Pl. شاهينان *shā-hīnān.* See شهين

P شايان *shā-yān,* adj. Legal, worthy, suitable, agreeable; (Fem.) شايانه *shā-yāna'h.*

P شايد *shā-yad,* adv. Perhaps, perchance, possibly, may be, probably. See بهائي

P شب *shab,* Night. Used only in Pushto composition, as شب خون *shab-khūn* or شب گير *shab-gīr,* s.m. (2nd) A night attack. Pl. شب خونونه *shab-khūnūnah* or شب گيرونه *shab-gīrūnah.* شب خون *shab-khūn* or شب گير كول *shab-gīr kawul,* verb trans. To attack by night, to make a night attack on. شب خيز *shab-khez,* s.m. (5th) A person who rises at night to pray. Pl. شب خيزان *shab-khezān.* شب خيزه *shab kheza'h,* s.f. (3rd) A female who rises at night to pray. Pl. ئ *ey.* شب خيزي *shab-khezī,* s.f. (3rd) Rising at night for prayer. Pl. ئ *a'ī.* شبخيزي كول *shab-khezī kawul,* verb trans. To rise at night to pray. See شپه

A شباهت *shabā-hat,* s.m. (2nd) Similarity, resemblance, likeness. Pl. شباهتونه *shabā-hatūnah.*

شب بو *shab-bo* or (corrup.) شبو *shabo,* s.m. (9th) The Polianthes tuberosa. Sing. and Pl. Also د شبو گل *da shabo gul,* s.m. (5th). Pl. گلان *gulān.*

P شبكه *shabaka'h,* s.f. (3rd) A lattice, a window of lattice work. 2. A net, a reticulated veil. Pl. ئ *ey.*

P شبنم *shab-nam,* s.m. (9th) Dew. Sing. and Pl.

P شبه *shaba'h,* s.f. (3rd) A species of jet or black coral used as beads, black shells or glass beads. Pl. ئ *ey.*

A شبهه *shub-ha'h,* s.f. (3rd) (from شبه) Doubt, uncertainty, suspicion, ambiguity, hesitation. Pl. ئ *ey.* شبهه كول *shub-ha'h kawul,* verb trans. To doubt, to suspect, to have scruple, etc.

شپاړس *shpā-rras,* adj. Sixteen. شپاړسم *shpā-rrasam,* Sixteenth; (Fem.) شپاړسمه *shpā-rrasama'h.*

شپږ *shpajz*, adj. (W.) Six. شپږم *shpajzam*, Sixth. شپږويشت *shpajz-wisht*, Twenty-six. شپږ ديرش *shpajz-dersh*, Thirty-six. شپږ څلويښت *shpajz-tsalwesht* (W.) or *tsalwekht* (E.) Forty-six. شپږ پنځوس *shpajz-pin-dzos*. Fifty-six. شپږ شپيته *shpajz-shpetah*, Sixty-six. شپږ اويا *shpajz-ao-yā*, Seventy-six. شپږ اتيا *shpajz-ati-yā*, Eighty-six. شپږ نوِ *shpajz-niwi*, Ninety-six. See شپګ

شپشتي *shpishtaey*, s.m. (1st) The spoke of a wheel. Pl. ي *ī*.

شپګ *shpag*, adj. (E.) Six. شپګم *shpagam*, The sixth. For the other numbers see شپږ, which are all the same with the difference of ګ for ږ in pronunciation.

شپنغوده *shpan-ghoda'h*, s.f. (3rd) The name of a bird, called the shepherd's deceiver. Pl. ې *ey* (P شبان فريب).

شپنکي *shpankaey*, s.m. (1st) A little shepherd, a shepherd boy (dimin. of شپون, which see). Pl. ي *ī*. شپنکۍ *shpanka'ī*, s.f. (6th) A shepherd girl, a little shepherdess. Sing. and Pl.

شپني *shpanī*, s.f. (3rd) Tending sheep, shepherdism, pastoral life. Pl. ۍ *a'ī*. شپني کول *shpanī kawul*, verb trans. To tend sheep, to graze flocks.

شپول *shpol*, s.m. (2nd) A hedge of thorns, a sheep-fold. 2. A halo round the moon. Pl. شپلونه *shpalūnah*. See شپال

شپون *shpūn*, s.m. (4th) A shepherd. Pl. شپانه *shpānah*. شپنکي *shpankaey*, s.m. (1st) A little shepherd, a shepherd boy. Pl. ي *ī*. شپنه *shpana'h*, s.f. (3rd) A shepherdess. Pl. ې *ey*. شپنکۍ *shpanka'ī*, s.f. (6th) A shepherd girl, a little shepherdess (dimin. of شپنه). Sing. and Pl.

شپه *shpah*, s.m. (4th) A shepherd (W.) Pl. شپانه *shpānah*.

شپه *shpa'h*, s.f. (3rd) Night. Pl. ې *ey*. شپه په شپه *shpa'h pah shpa'h*, adv. Night by night, nightly, every night. شپې ته, لره or له *shpey tah, larah* or *lah*, At night, at night time, in the night. شپه و روځ *shpa'h-ow-rwadz* or شپه و ورځ *shpa'h-ow-wradz*, Day and night, always, constantly. توره شپه *tora'h shpa'h*, Dark night, midnight. 2. s.f. (3rd) A dark night. Pl. ې *ey*. د برات شپه *da barāt shpa'h*, The 14th of the month of Shaebān, on which offerings and oblations are made in the names of deceased relations. هره شپه *hara'h shpa'h*, adv. Nightly, every night. په شپه *pah shpa'h*, In the night, at night time.

شپيته *shpetah*, adj. Sixty. شپيتم *shpetam*, The sixtieth; (Fem.) شپيتمه *shpetama'h*.

شپيتي *shpetaey*, s.m. (1st) A wedge to cleave wood with. Pl. ي *ī*. (E.)

شپيشته *shpeshta'h*, s.f. (3rd) (W.) A wedge. 2. A kind of vetch, lucerne. Pl. ې *ey*. See preceding.

شپيشتري *shpeshtaraey* or شپيشتي *shpeshtaey*, s.m. (1st) (E.) A wedge of wood. 2. A kind of vetch, lucern. Pl. ي *ī*. See preceding.

شپيلۍ *shpela'ī*, s.f. (6th) A flute, a fife, a pipe, a blow-pipe, the barrel of a gun, a whistle. Sing. and Pl. شپيلۍ مار *shpela'ī mār*, s.m. (5th) A fifer. Pl. شپيلۍ ماران *shpela'ī mārān*. شپيلۍ ماره *shpela'ī māra'h*, s.f. (3rd) A female who whistles or plays on a pipe. Pl. ې *ey*. شپيلۍ وهل *shpela'ī wahal*, verb trans. To play on a flute, pipe, etc.

شپيلي *shpelaey*, s.m. (1st) A whistle, a hiss, whistling. 2. A mean, ignoble, or stingy person. Pl. ي *ī*. شپيلۍ *shpela'ī*, s.f. (6th) A low, mean, contemptible woman, a term of abuse. Sing. and Pl. شپيلي کول *shpelaey kawul*, verb trans. To whistle, to hiss. شپيلکي *shpelkaey*, s.m. (1st) (dimin. of شپيلي), A whistle, a hiss, whistling, hissing. Pl. ي *ī*. شپيلکي کول *shpelkaey kawul*, verb trans. To whistle, to hiss.

P شتاب *shitāb*, s.m. (2nd) Haste, quickness, speed. Pl. شتابونه *shitāb-ūnah*. 2. adj. Quick, speedy. شتابي *shitābī*, s.f. (3rd) Quickness, haste, despatch, expedition. Pl. ۍ *a'ī*. شتابي کول *shitābī kawul*, verb trans. To make haste, to use despatch. په شتابي سره *pah shitābī sarah*, adv. Quickly, hastily, speedily, with despatch.

شتاه *shat-āh*, adj. A deceitful, insidious, or artful person, a chatter-box, one without shame; (Fem.) شتاهه *shat-āha'h*.

شترلړ *shutar-larr*, s.m. (2nd) The pieces of wood placed to keep the ropes, on which the pots of a Persian wheel are fastened, from coming in contact with each other. Pl. شترلړونه *shutar-larrūnah*.

شترکه *shuturaka'h*, s.f. (3rd) A spirt, a jet, a spout, a gush, a rush, or cascade of water, a cataract. Pl. ئ *ey*. شترکه وهل *shuturaka'h wahal*, verb trans. To spirt, to jet or gush out. See داره

P شتر مرغ *shutur-murgh*, s.m. (5th) An ostrich. Pl شتر مرغان *shutur-murghān*. شتر مرغه *shutur-murgha'h*, s.f. (3rd) A female ostrich. Pl. ئ *ey*.

P شتري *shutur-ī*, adj. Of a camel—a name given to a kind of cloth, called *barak*, made from camel's hair.

شته *shtah*, The third person singular and plural of the present tense of the substantive verb "to be," together with دي *dey* and دي *dī*, signifying, being, existing. The infinitive is unknown. شته که نشته *shtah kih nashtah* or شته نشته *shtah nashtah*, At all events, whether or no, happen what may, etc.

شتئ *shat-a'ī*, s.f. (6th) A barbed arrow. 2. The green scum on stagnant pools, green mould sticking to walls, fur, etc. 3. The ear of maize without the grain. Sing. and Pl.

شتل *shattal*, adj. Slow, indolent, lazy, languid, tardy, relaxed, heavy, dull; (Fem.) شتله *shattala'h*. شتل والَي *shattal wālaey*, s.m. (1st) Indolence, languor, sloth, apathy, tardiness, dullness, heaviness. Pl. والي *wālī*. See شلت and شدل

شڅرلَي *shats-arlaey*, s.m. (1st) A carpenter's chisel. Pl. ي *ī*. See سکنه

شجاع *shujā'æ*, adj. (from شجع) Brave, bold, courageous. شجاعت *shujā-æt*, s.m. (2nd) Bravery, boldness, courage. Pl. شجاعتونه *shujā-æt-ūnah*. شجاعت لرل *shujā-æt laral*, verb trans. To be possessed of or have bravery or courage (to be brave). شجاعت کول *shujā-æt kawul*, verb trans. To manifest or show courage or bravery, to act intrepidly or courageously.

A P شجره *shajara'h*, s.f. (3rd) A list of saints, a genealogical tree. Pl. ئ *ey*; or شجر نامه *shujar-nāma'h*. Pl. ئ *ey*.

P شخ *shakh*, adj. Anything hard, stiff, tough, not to be bent, hard (as ground), etc; (Fem.) شخه *shakha'h*. See ټخ

شخره *shkharra'h*, s.f. (3rd) Nonsense, useless talk, gibberish, twaddle, stuff. Pl. ئ *ey*. شخره ويل *shkharra'h wa-yal*, verb trans. To talk nonsense, absurdity, etc.

شخلَي *shkhulaey*, s.m. (1st) A quiver for arrows. Pl. ي *ī*. See جعبه and شخولي

شخند *shkhand*, s.m. (2nd) Chewing the cud, ruminating, musing. 2. A ruminating animal. Pl. شخندونه *shkhandūnah*. شخند کول or وهل *shkhand kawul* or *wahal*, verb trans. To ruminate, to chew the cud. See شخوند

P شخوده *shukhūdah*, adj. Scratched with the nails, scored, grooved. شخوده کول *shukhūdah kawul*, verb trans. To scratch with the nails, to score, to groove.

شخول *shkhwal*, s.m. (2nd) Noise, uproar, din, clamour, tumult, outcry, rustling of leaves from the wind, the murmuring or rippling of a brook, the noise of cattle grazing in a forest. Pl. شخولونه *shkhwalūnah*. شخول کول *shkhwal kawul*, verb trans. To make a noise, to raise a tumult, or uproar, etc.

شخولي *shkhwalaey*, s.m. (1st) A quiver for arrows. Pl. ي *ī*. See شخلي

شخوند *shkhwand*, s.m. (2nd) Ruminating, chewing the cud, musing. 2. A ruminating animal. Pl. شخوندونه *shkhwandūnah*. شخوند کول or وهل *shkhwand kawul* or *wahal*, verb trans. To ruminate, to chew the cud.

A شد *shadd*, s.m. (2nd) The mark (ـّـ) which signifies that the letter must be doubled; also A تشديد. Pl. شدونه *shaddūnah*.

A شدت *shiddat* or *shidat*, s.m. (2nd) Violence,

force, vehemence. 2. Fighting with missiles. Pl. شدتونه shiddatūnah or shidatūnah.

P شدني shudan-ī, adj. Practicable, possible.

شديارہ shud-yāra'h, s.f. (3rd) Land ploughed and ready for sowing. Pl. ي ey. (P شديار)

A شديد shad-īd, adj. (from شد), Difficult. 2. Violent, acute, strong, intense, vehement; afflicting, atrocious; (Fem.) شديده shad-īda'h.

شدل shaddal, adj. Slow, indolent, lazy, languid, tardy. 2. Fat, stout, heavy. 3. Unbleached, unwashed (cloth); (Fem.) شدله shaddala'h. See شتل and بتي دكه

A شر sharr, s.m. (2nd) Depravity, wickedness, villany, malignancy, evil. Pl. شرونه sharr-ūnah. شر و شور sharr-o-shor, Tumult, riot, disturbance. شر كول sharr kawul, verb trans. To offend, to trespass, to transgress, to act depravedly or viciously.

شر shir, s.m. (5th) Pattering of rain, rushing, splash, rush, gush, gurge. 3. The sound made by an arrow passing through the air. Pl. شرهار shirahār. شرهار كول shirahār kawul, verb trans. To patter (as rain), to splash, to rush, to gush, to gurge; or شرهار لرل shirahār laral, verb trans. See سړ and سغ

A شراب sharāb, s.m. (6th) Wine, any spirituous liquor. Sing. and Pl. شراب خانه sharāb khāna'h, s.f. (3rd) A tavern, a wine-shop. Pl. ي ey. شراب خور sharāb khor, s.m. (5th) A wine-drinker, drinking wine. Pl. شراب خوران sharāb khorān. شراب خوره sharāb-khora'h, s.f. (3rd) A woman who drinks wine. Pl. ي ey. شراب خوري sharāb-khorī, s.f. (3rd) Drunkenness, wine-drinking. Pl. ي a'ī. شرابي sharābī, s.m. (5th) A drunkard. Pl. شرابيان sharābī-ān. 2. adj. Intoxicated, drunk.

A شرارت sharārat, s.m. (2nd) Wickedness, vice, mischief, depravity, villany. Pl. شرارتونه sharārat-ūnah.

A شرافت sharāfat, s.m. (2nd) Nobility. Pl. شرافتونه sharāfat-ūnah.

A شراكت sharā-kat, s.m. (2nd) (from شرك), Partnership, participation, fellowship. Pl. شراكتونه sharā-katūnah. شراكت كول sharākat kawul, verb trans. To enter into partnership, or connection. شراكت لرل sharākat laral, verb trans. To hold partnership or participation in any thing or matter.

P شربت shar-bat, s.m. (2nd) Beverage, drink, sherbet. Pl. شربتونه sharbat-ūnah.

شرحه sharḥa'h, s.f. (3rd) (corrup. of A شرح) Explanation, commentary, annotation, description. 2. Rate, pay, allowance. Pl. شرحي sharḥ-ey. شرحه كول sharḥa'h kawul, verb trans. To explain, to describe, to comment on.

شرخبون sharkhabūn, s.m. (6th) The name of a division of the Afghān tribes, so called from one of the two sons of Sarī, son of Æabd-ur-Rashīd, Pattān, the great progenitor of the Afghāns. Sing. and Pl. See Introduction to Grammar, page 10; (Fem.) شرخبونه shar-khabūna'h. Pl. ي ey.

A شرخشت shar-khásht or shir-khisht, s.m. (6th) A kind of manna which falls on trees. Sing. and Pl. See د خوزكوري

شرشائي shar-shā'ī, s.f. (3rd) The weight of 12 māssas, about the weight of an Indian tola. Pl. ي a'ī.

A شرط sharṭ, s.m. (2nd) Condition, stipulation, bargain, agreement. 2. Wager, bet. 3. Mark, sign, signal. Pl. شرطونه sharṭ-ūnah. شرط كول sharṭ kawul, verb trans. To stipulate, to agree, to bargain, to wager, to bet. شرطي sharṭī, adj. Conditional. 2. A whore, a bad woman. Sing. and Pl.

شرعه sharæa'h, s.f. (3rd) (corrup. of A شرع) The precepts of the prophet Muḥammad; law, equity. Pl. ي ey. شرعي sharæī, adj. Lawful, religious, conformable to the Sharæ.

شرغشي shar-ghashaey, s.m. (1st) A kind of reed, from which baskets and stools are made, and the shafts of arrows. 2. The leaves of the above, reed grass (Saccharum sara). Pl. ي ī.

T شرغه *sharghah*, adj. A horse with white eyes or white forehead.

A شرف *sharaf*, s.m. (9th) Nobility, eminence, rank, honor. Sing. and Pl.

A شرق *shark*, s.m. (9th) The east. Sing. and Pl.

A شرقي *shark-ī*, adj. Eastern, oriental.

A شرك *shirk*, s.m. (2nd) Paganism, partnership, polytheism. Pl. شركونه *shirk-ūnah*.

A شركت *shir-kat*, s.m. (2nd) Society, partnership, connection. Pl. شركتونه *shir-katūnah*. شركت كول *shir-kat kawul*, verb trans. To enter into partnership, to make a connection. شركت لرل *shir-kat laral*, verb trans. To have connection or partnership in any matter. See شراكت

P شرم *sharm*, s.m. (9th) Bashfulness, modesty, shame. Sing. and Pl. شرم ناك *sharm-nāk*, adj. Bashful, modest, coy; (Fem.) شرم ناكه *sharm nāka'h*. بي شرم *bey sharm*, adj. Shameless, immodest; (Fem.) بي شرمه *be-sharma'h*. شرم لرل *sharm laral*, verb trans. To have modesty or bashfulness (Eng., verb intrans. To be bashful or coy). شرم كول *sharm kawul*, verb trans. To shew bashfulness, shame, or modesty. شرميدل *sharmedal*, verb intrans. To become abashed, bashful, or modest. Pres. شرمېږي *sharmejzī* (W.) or شرميګي *sharmegī* (E.); past وُ شرميده *wu-sharmedah* or شرميدَ *sharmeda*; fut. وُ به شرمېږي *wu bah sharmejzī* or شرميګي *sharmegī*; imp. وُ شرمېږه *wu-sharmejzah* or شرميګه *sharmegah*; act. part. شرميدونكَي *sharmedūnkaey* or شرميدونَي *sharmedūnaey*; past part. شرميدلَي *sharmedalaey*; verb. n. شرميدنه *sharmedana'h* or شرميده *sharmedah*. شرمول *sharmawul*, verb trans. To abash, to shame, to make bashful, to put to the blush, to disconcert. 2. To ravish, to rape. Pres. شرموي *sharmawī*; past وُ شرماوه *wu-sharmāwuh* or وُ شرماوو *wu-sharmāwo*; fut. وُ به شرموي *wu bah sharmawī*; imp. وُ شرموه *wu-sharmawah*; act. part. شرموونكَي *sharmawūnkaey* or شرموونَي *sharmawūnaey*; past part. شرمولَي *sharmawulaey*; verb. n. شرمونه *sharmawuna'h*.

P شرمسار *sharm-sār*, adj. Abashed, ashamed, coy; (Fem.) شرمساره *sharm-sāra'h*.

شرمښ *shar-mash* (W.), or *shar-makh* (E.), s.m. (5th) A wolf. Pl. شرمښان *shar-mashān* or *shar-makhān*. See ليوه

شرمښكَي *shar-mashka'ī* (W.) or *shar-makhka'ī* (E.), s.f. (6th) A lizard. Sing. and Pl. See خرمښكَي

P شرمنده *sharmindah*, adj. Blushing, abashed, ashamed, bashful, modest, coy (Masc. and Fem). شرمنده كيدل *sharmindah kedal*, verb intrans. To become ashamed, abashed, bashful, coy, etc. شرمنده كول *sharmindah kawul*, verb trans. To abash, to make ashamed, to put to the blush, etc.

P شرمندګي *sharmindagī*, s.f. (3rd) Bashfulness, modesty, coyness. 2. Shame, repentance, disgrace. Pl. ئي *a'ī*.

شرنګ *shrang*, s.m. (5th) Ring, jingle, chink, tinkle, chime, clink, reverberation. Pl. شرنګهار *shrang-hār* or *shranga-hār*. شرنګيدل *shrang-edal*, verb intrans. To ring, to jingle, to clink, to tinkle. Pres. شرنګيږي *shrangejzī* (W.) or شرنګيګي *shrangegī* (E.); past وُ شرنګيده *wu-shrangedah* or شرنګيدَ *shrangeda*; fut. وُ به شرنګيږي *wu bah shrangejzī* or شرنګيګي *shrang-egī*; imp. وُ شرنګيږه *wu-shrangejzah* or شرنګيګه *shrangegah*; act. part. شرنګيدونكَي *shrang-edūnkaey* or شرنګيدونَي *shrangedūnaey*; past part. شرنګيدلَي *shrangedalaey*; verb. n. شرنګيدنه *shrangedana'h* or شرنګيده *shrang-edah*. شرنګول *shranganwul*, verb trans. To cause or make to ring, jingle, tinkle, clink, etc. Pres. شرنګوي *shrangawī*; past وُ شرنګاوه *wu-shrangāwuh* or شرنګاوو *shrangāwo*; fut. وُ به شرنګوي *wu bah shrangawī*; imp. وُ شرنګوه *wu-shrangawah*; act. part. شرنګوونكَي *shrang-awūnkaey* or شرنګوونَي *shrangawūnaey*; past part. شرنګولَي *shrangawulaey*; verb. n. شرنګونه *shrangawuna'h*.

A شروع *shurūæ*, s.f. (1st) (from شرع) Commencement, beginning. Pl. شروعِ *shurūæi*.

شروع کيدل *shurūæ kedal*, verb intrans. to be begun or commenced. شروع کول *shurūæ kawul*, verb trans. To begin, to commence, to set a going.

شرئ *sharaey*, s.m. (1st) The measles, a slight cutaneous eruption. Pl. ي *ī*. (A شرا). شري نيول *sharī nīwal*, verb trans. To take or fall sick of the measles, to get the measles.

A شرير *sharīr*, adj. Wicked, depraved, vicious; (Fem.) شريره *sharīra'h*.

A شريعت *sharī-æat*, s.m. (2nd) (from شرع) The laws of Muḥammad. 2. Law, equity, justice. Pl. شريعتونه *sharī-æatūnah*. شريعت کول *sharī-æat kawul*, verb trans. To administer justice. 2. To prefer a claim before a judge.

A شريف *shar-īf*, adj. (from شرف) Noble, eminent, honourable, exalted, etc.; (Fem.) شريفه *sharīfa'h*.

شريفه *sharīfa'h*, s.f. (3rd) A ledge extending out from a wall to keep off rain, the eave of a roof. Pl. ې *ey*. See بلئ

A شريک *sharīk*, s.m. (5th) (from شرک) A partner, an associate, ally, comrade, accomplice. Pl. شريکان *sharīkān*. شريکه *sharīka'h*, s.f. (3rd) A female partner, associate, etc. Pl. ې *ey*. شريک کيدل *sharīk kedal*, verb intrans. To partake, to participate, to become a partner. شريک کول *sharīk kawul*, verb trans. To make a partner, ally, or accomplice of.

شړته *sharrata'h*, s.f. (3rd) Barley, a barley-corn, a small quantity. Pl. شړتې *sharratey*, Barley. See شړهته

شړشم *sharr-sham*, s.m. (6th) The mustard plant, mustard. Sing. and Pl.

شړل *sharral*, verb trans. To drive away, to repel, to repulse, to eject, to turn out of doors, to drive, etc. Pres. شړي *sharrī*; past وُ شاړه *wu-shārrah*; fut. وُ به شړي *wu bah sharrī*; imp. وُ شړه *wu-sharrah*; act. part. شړونکئ *sharrūnkaey* or شړونئ *sharrūnaey*; past part. شړلئ *sharralaey*; verb. n. شړنه *sharr-ana'h*.

شړلئ *sharralaey*, adj. Expelled, driven out, turned adrift, bundled out, banished, exiled; (Fem.) شړلې *sharrali*. Pl. (Masc. and Fem.) شړلي *sharralī*.

شړهته *sharr-hata'h*, s.f. (3rd) Barley, a grain of barley. Pl. ې *ey*. See اوربشي and شړته

شړهيدل *sharr-hedal*, verb intrans. To rot or grow rotten, to decay, to crumble to bits (as cloth), to decompose. 2. To be overcooked (as meat, etc). Pres. شړهيږي *sharr-hejzī* (W.) or شړهيګي *sharr-hegī* (E.); past وُ شړهيده *wu-sharr-hedah* or شړهيدَ *sharr-heda*; fut. وُ به شړهيږي *wu bah sharr-hejzī* or شړهيګي *sharr-hegī*; imp. وُ شړهيده *wu-sharr-hedah*; act. part. شړهيدونکئ *sharr-hedūnkaey* or شړهيدونئ *sharr-hedūnaey*; past part. شړهيدلئ *sharr-hedalaey*; verb. n. شړهيدنه *sharr-hedana'h* or شړهيده *sharr-hedah*. شړهول *sharr-hawul*, verb trans. To decompose, to bring to corruption, to cause to decay or rot. 2. To spoil meat by overcooking. Pres. شړهوي *sharr-hawī*; past وُ شړهاوه *wu-sharr-hāwuh* or شړهاوو *sharr-hāwo*; fut. وُ به شړهوي *wu bah sharr-hawī*; imp. وُ شړهوه *wu-sharr-hawah*; act. part. شړهوونکئ *sharr-hawūnkaey* or شړهوونئ *sharr-huwūnaey*; past part. شړهولئ *sharr-hawulaey*; verb. n. شړهونه *sharr-hawunah*.

شړهيدلئ *sharr-hedalaey*, adj. (past part. of شړهيدل) Rotten, decayed, decomposed, overdone (as meat); (Fem.) شړهيدلې *sharr-hedali*. Pl. (Masc. and Fem.) ي *ī*.

شړۍ *sharra'ī*, s.f. (6th) A blanket. Sing. and Pl.

شستۍ *shasta'ī*, s.f. (6th) The name of a flower (Chrysanthemum Indiena). Sing. and Pl.

ششنئ *shishnaey*, s.m. (1st) The neigh of a horse (W.) Pl. ي *ī*. ششنئ کول *shishnaey kawul*, verb trans. To neigh. See ششړئ

ششړئ *shashrrnaey*, s.m. (1st) The neigh of a horse (E.) Pl. ي *ī*. ششړيدل *shash-rrnedal*, verb trans. To neigh as a horse when he sees another. Pres. ششړيږي *shash-rrnejzī* (W.) or ششړيګي *shash-rrnegī* (E.); past وُ ششړيده *wu shash-rrnedah* or ششړيدَ *shash-rrneda*; fut. وُ به ششړيږي *wu bah shash-rrnejzī* or

ششنړيگي shash-rrnegī ; imp. وُ ششنړيږه wu-shash-rrnejzah or ششنړيگه shash-rrnegah ; act. part. ششنړيدونکي shash-rrnedūnkaey or ششنړيدوني shash-rrnedūnaey ; past part. ششنړيدلي shash-rrnedalaey ; verb. n. ششنړيدنه shash-rrnedana'h or ششنړيده shash-rrnedah.

A شطرنج shaṭ-ranj, s.m. (6th) The game of chess. Sing. and Pl. شطرنج باز shaṭ-ranj-bāz, s.m. (5th) A chess player. Pl. شطرنج بازان shaṭ-ranj-bāzān. شطرنج کول shaṭ-ranj kawul, verb trans. To play at chess.

شعاعه shuæā-æa'h, s.f. (3rd) (from شع) Light, splendor, lustre, rays of the sun, radiance, sunshine, etc. Pl. ې ey.

A شعر shiær, s.m. (2nd) Poetry, verse. Pl. شعرونه shiær-ūnah. شعر کول shiær kawul, verb trans. To compose or write poetry or verses.

A شعله shuæla'h, s.f. (3rd) (from شعل) Flame, blaze, light, flash, lustre. Pl. ې ey. شعله کول shuæla'h kawul, verb trans. To shine, to flash, to blaze, etc. See شغله

A شعور shu-æūr, s.m. (9th) (from شعر) Wisdom, intelligence, knowledge, discernment. Sing. and Pl.

شغ shagh, s.m. (5th) Whiz, whistle of a bullet or arrow, ring, the noise of birds flying. Pl. شغهار shaghahār. See سر and سغ

P شغال shaghāl, s.m. (5th) A jackal. Pl. شغالان shaghālān. See چغال

شغرب مغرب shagharib-magharib, From east to west, the east and west (A مشرق مرغب).

A شغل shughl, s.m. (2nd) Employment, occupation. Pl. شغلونه shughlūnah. شغل کول shughl kawul, verb trans. To practice some employment or occupation.

شغله shughla'h, s.f. (3rd) Blaze, light, lustre, flash. Pl. ې ey. (corrup. of شعله) which see.

A شفا shifā, s.f. (6th) (from CH שפה) Remedy, cure, recovery, healing, convalescence. (W.) Pl. شفاوي shifā-wī. (E.) Sing. and Pl.

A شفاعت shafā-æat, s.m. (2nd) (from شفع) Deprecation, intercession, recommendation, entreaty. Pl. شفاعتونه shafā-æatūnah. شفاعت کول shafā-æat kawul, verb trans. To intercede for, to deprecate.

A شفاف shaffāf, adj. (from شف) Transparent, clear, pellucid, very thin ; (Fem.) شفافه shaffāfa'h.

P شفتالو shuftālū, s.m. (5th) A peach, the colour of peach blossom. Pl. شفتالوگان shuftālūgān.

A شفق shafaḳ, s.m. (9th) (from H and CH ספק) Evening, twilight. Sing. and Pl.

A شفقت shafaḳat, s.m. (2nd) Clemency, compassion, mercy, kindness, affection. Pl. شفقتونه shafaḳatūnah. شفقت کول shafaḳat kawul, verb trans. To show kindness or clemency.

A شفيع shafī-æ, adj. (from شفع) Advocate, mediator, patron ; (Fem.) شفيعه shafīæa'h.

A شقاوت shaḳāwat, s.m. (2nd) Misery, poverty, distress. 2. Vice, villany. Pl. شقاوتونه shaḳāwat-ūnah.

A شقي shaḳī, adj. Wretched, miserable. 2. Vicious, villanous. (Masc. and Fem.)

A شک shakk, s.m. (2nd) Doubt, suspense, hesitation, uncertainty. Pl. شکونه shakkūnah. شک و شبهه shakk-aw-shubaha'h, Doubt, suspense, uncertainty. شک من shakk-man, adj. Doubtful, uncertain, suspicious. 2. A suspicious person, a person of a suspicious temperament ; (Fem.) شک منه shakk mana'h. بي شکه bey shakkah or بي شکَ bey shakka, adv. Without doubt, doubtless, certainly. شک راوړل shakk rā-w'rral or شک کول shakk kawul, verb trans. To doubt, to mistrust, to hesitate, to suspect.

P شکال sh'kāl, s.m. (2nd) A string for fastening the fore feet of a restive horse. Pl. شکالونه sh'kālūnah. See شکيل

A شکايت shikā-yat, s.m. (2nd) (from شکو) Accusation, complaint, lamentation, etc. Pl. شکايتونه shikā-yatūnah. شکايت کول shikā-yat kawul, verb trans. To accuse, to lament, to complain. See گله

A شکر shukr, s.m. (2nd) Thanks, gratitude. Pl. شکرونه shukrūnah. شکر کول shukr kawul, verb trans. To thank, to acknowledge a favour, to return thanks; or شكرپه ځاي راورل shukr pah dzā-e rā-w'rral, verb trans. شکرگذار shukr guzār, adj. Grateful, thankful; (Fem.) شکرگذاره shukr guzāra'h. شکرگذاري shukr guzārī, s.f. (3rd) Thanksgiving, gratitude, thanks, thankfulness. Pl. ئي a'ī. شكرانه shukr-āna'h, s.f. (3rd) Thanksgiving, gratitude, acknowledgment of thanks. Pl. ې ey. شكريت shuk-riyat, s.m. (2nd) Thanks, gratitude. Pl. شكريتونه shuk-riyatūnah.

شكره shakara'h or shakkara'h, s.f. (3rd) Sugar (from P شكر). Pl. ې ey. شكر خند shakar-khand, adj. Smiling sweetly, smiling, amiable; (Fem.) شكرخنده shakar-khanda'h. شکرلب shakar-lab, adj. Sugar-lipped; (Fem.) شكر لبه shakar-laba'h.

شكرى shikraey, s.m. (1st) (from P شكره) A hawk, a falcon. Pl. ي ī. شكره shikra'h, s.f. (3rd) The female of the above. Pl. ې ey.

شكرى sh'karaey, s.m. (1st) A kind of flat basket like a tray. Pl. ي ī. شكرئي sh'kara'ī, s.f. (6th) A basket smaller than the preceding for holding nicknacks, or trifles. Sing. and Pl. See شكوري and ټكري

P شكست shikast, s.m. (2nd) Breaking, fracture, defeat. Pl. شكستونه shikastūnah. 2. adj. Broken, odd, uneven, defeated. شكست خوړل shikast khwarral, verb trans. To become broken or defeated, to sustain a defeat.

P شكسته shikastah, adj. Broken, sick, bankrupt, defeated. See مات

A شكل shakl, s.m. (2nd) Shape, figure, effigy, appearance, semblance, mode. Pl. شكلونه shaklūnah.

شكلي shak-laey, s.m. (1st) The end or tail of a turban. Pl. ي ī.

P شكنجه shikanja'h, s.f. (3rd) Stocks for the legs. 2. A bookbinder's press. 3. A press in general. 4. Torture, rack, torment, etc. Pl. ې ey. شكنجه كول shikanja'h kawul, verb trans. To press. 2. To torment, to put in the stocks, to put to the rack.

شكنځه shikandza'h, s.f. (3rd) Pl. See preceding.

شكنړ shkurrn, s.m. (4th) A porcupine. Pl. شكانړه shkārrnah or شكنړ shkarrn, s.m. (5th). Pl. شكنړيان shkarrnīān. (W.) See شكونړ

شكوری shkoraey, s.m. (1st) A flat basket without a cover like a tray, made of cane, grass, or wood. Pl. ي ī. شكورئي shkora'ī, s.f. (6th) A basket like the above but smaller. Sing. and Pl. See شكري

P شكوفه shikūfa'h or shigūfa'h, s.f. (3rd) A flower, a blossom, a bud. Pl. ې ey.

شكونړ shkorrn, s.m. (4th) A porcupine. Pl. شكانړه shkārrnah. See شكنړ

شكول sh'kawul, (W.) verb trans. To extract, to pluck or tear out, to wrench or wring from, to pull out (as hair by the roots), to gather, to pluck fruit from a tree. Pres. شكوي sh'kawī; past وُ شكاوه wu-sh'kāwuh or وُ شكاوو wu-sh'kāwo; fut. وُ به شكوي wu bah sh'kawī; imp. وُ شكوه wu sh'kawah; act part. شكوونكى sh'kawūnkaey or شكوونى sh'kawūnaey; past part. شكولى sh'kawulaey; verb. n. شكونه sh'kawuna'h. See شوكول

A شكوه shakwa'h, s.f. (3rd) Complaint, upbraiding. Pl. ې ey. شكوه كول shakwa'h kawul, verb trans. To complain, to upbraid, to blame.

شګاره shigāra'h, s.f. (3rd) A pregnant animal, a pregnant woman. Pl. ې ey. See بلاربه

شګرى shigraey, s.m. (1st) A priming horn. Pl. ي ī; or شكرى shikraey. Pl. ي ī. See ټكري

شګلن shig-lan, adj. Sandy, gravelly, full of sand; (Fem.) شګلنه shig-lana'h.

شګه shiga'h, s.f. (3rd) Sand, gravel, small pebbles. Pl. ې ey. د شګې ګل da shigey gul, Talc. (lit. the sand flower). شګلنه shiglana'h, adj. as s.f. (3rd) Sandy or gravelly soil. Pl. ې ey; or شګئي shig-a'ī, s.f. (6th). (E.) Sing. and Pl. See رغل

A شل shall, adj. One who is unable to take anything in his hands (from sickness), paralytic, palsied; (Fem.) شله shalla'h. شل و شول shall-o-shūl, Palsied, paralytic.

P شل shil or shal, s.m. (2nd) A small spear, a javelin. Pl. شلونه shilūnah or shalūnah.

شل shil, adj. Twenty, a score. شلم shilam, The twentieth; (Fem.) شلمه shilama'h. شل شلي

shil shiley, Twenty-score; or شل شلکه *shil-shilakah*.

شلانده *shlānda'h*, s.f. (3rd) A frog, a toad. Pl. ئ *ey*.

شلت *shalat*, adj. Lazy, indolent, heavy, dull; (Fem.) شلته *shalata'h*. See شڅل

شلخي *shalkhaey*, s.m. (1st) The name of a species of potherb. Pl. ي *ī*.

شل دانه *shal-dāna'h*, s.f. (3rd) A species of white grain made into necklaces for females (*lit.* forty-grain). Pl. ئ *ey*. See مرغچجي

P شلغم *shalgham*, s.m. (6th) A turnip. Sing. and Pl. See تيپر

شلک *shilak*, s.m. (2nd) (corrup. of A شلخ or شلق) A round, a discharge, a volley, a salute. Pl. شلکونه *shilakūnah*. شلک کول *shilak kawal*, To discharge, to salute. شلک ورکول *shilak war-kawul*, verb trans. To give or pour in a volley, or a round (as of musketry, etc.)

شلگي *shal-gaey*, s.m. (1st) A small spear, a javelin. 2. A flag, a standard (dimin. of شل which see). Pl. ي *ī*.

P شلوار *shalwār*, s.m. (2nd) Trousers. Pl. شلوارونه *shalwār-ūnah*.

شلوم *shlom* or شلونب *shlonb*, s.m. (2nd) The dregs or refuse of melted butter. 2. Butter-milk. Pl. شلومونه *shlomūnah* or شلونبونه *shlonbūnah*. شلومبَي *shlombaey*, s.m. (1st) (W.) Buttermilk, sour milk. Pl. ي *ī*; or شلومبي *shlombey*, (E.) s.f. (Pl.) Sing. not used. Also written شلونبي *shlonbaey*, etc. See شوملي

شليدل *shle-dal*, verb intrans. To break or be torn asunder (as a rope), to part, to tear, to burst, to separate (as rope, string, or the like). Pres. شليږي *shle-jzī* (W.) or شليگي *shle-gī* (E.); past وُ شليدَ *wu-shledah* or شليدَ *shleda*; fut. وُ به شليږي *wu bah shle-jzī* or شليگي *shle-gī*; imp. وُ شليږه *wu-shle-jzah* or شليگه *shle-gah*; act. part. شليدونکَي *shle-dūnkaey* or شليدونَي *shle-dūnaey*; past part. شليدلَي *shle-dalaey*; verb. n. شليدنه *shle-dana'h* or شليده *shle-dah*. شلول *shlawul*, verb trans. To part (as rope), to break, to tear asunder, to burst, to separate (as rope, string, etc.) Pres. شلوي *shla-wī*; past وُ شلاوه *wu-shlāwuh* or شلاوو *shlāwo*; fut. وُ به شلوي *wu bah shlawī*; imp. وُ شلوه *wu-shlawah*; act. part. شلوونکَي *shlawūnkaey* or شلوونَي *shlawūnaey*; past part. شلولَي *shlawulaey*; verb. n. شلونه *shlawuna'h*.

P شمار *shumār*, s.m. (9th) Counting, computing, numbering; number, account, estimation. Sing. and Pl. Also pronounced *sh'mār*. شمار کول *shumār* or *sh'mār kawul*, verb trans. To reckon, to number, to count, to compute, to regard; also شمارل *shmāral*, verb trans. (for tenses of which see شميرل *shmeral*, and substitute ا for ي).

A شمال *shamāl* or *shimāl*, s.m. (9th) The north, the north wind. Sing. and Pl. شمالي *shamālī*, adj. Northern, of the north. (Masc. and Fem.)

A شمايل *shamā-īl*, s.m. (6th) Disposition, virtues, customs, good qualities. Sing. and Pl.

شمځي *sham-dza'ī*, s.f. (6th) The back bone, the spine. Sing. and Pl. See د ملا تير

P شمشاد *sham-shād*, s.m. (6th) The box tree. Sing. and Pl.

شمشتي *sham-shata'ī*, s.f. (6th) A tortoise, a turtle. Sing. and Pl. See کشپ

شمعه *shamæa'h*, s.f. (3rd) (from A شمع) A candle, a lamp. Pl. ئ *ey*. شمعه دان *shamæa'h-dān*, s.m. (2nd) A candlestick, a lamp-stand. Pl. شمعه دانونه *shamæa'h-dānūnah*. شمعه ساز *shamæa'h-sāz*, s.m. (5th) A candle maker, a chandler. Pl. شمعه سازان *shamæa'h-sāzān*.

شمکلَي *sham-kalaey*, s.m. (1st) A cloth for cleaning a millstone, made of the unwoven end of a web. Pl. ي *ī*.

شمکوري *sham-korī*, s.f. (3rd) Night-blindness. Pl. ئ *a'ī*. شمکور *sham-kor*, adj. Night-blind, one troubled with night-blindness; (Fem.) شمکوره *sham-kora'h*. See شو کور

شمکَي *shamkaey*, s.m. (1st) The name of a medicinal plant. Pl. ي *ī*.

A شمله *shamla'h*, s.f. (3rd) The end of a turban, A shawl for the waist. Pl. ئ *ey*.

شمند روز *shamand-roz*, s.m. (6th) A kind of taffeta. 2. The name of a bird. Sing. and Pl.

A شمه *shama'h*, s.f. (3rd) An atom, a particle, the smallest quantity (of perfume, etc.); a smack, a smatter. Pl. ې *ey*.

شموخه *shamūkha'h* or شماخه *shamākha'h*, s.f. (3rd) The name of a small grain bitter to the taste. (Panicum frumentaceum, Rox.) (s श्यामाक). Pl. ې *ey*.

شميرل *shmeral*, verb trans. To count, to reckon, to number, to compute, to regard. Pres. شميري *shmerī*; past وُ شميره *wu-shmerah*; fut. وُ به شميري *wu bah shmerī*; imp. وُ شميره *wu-shmerah*; act. part. شميرونکَي *shmerūnkaey* or شميرونَي *shmerūnaey*; past part. شميرلَي *shmeralaey*; verb. n. شميرنه *shmerana'h*. See شمارل

شناخت *sh'nākht*, s.m. (2nd) (from P شناختن), Knowledge, acquaintance, understanding. Pl. شناختونه *sh'nākhtūnah*. شناخت لرل *sh'nākht laral*, verb trans. To have or hold acquaintance with, to know. شناخته *sh'nākhtah*, adj. Known, acquainted, understood.

شناز *shināz*, s.m. (2nd) A water-bag made of goat-skin. 2. The inflated skin of a goat, sheep, or other animal, used in crossing rivers. Pl. شنازونه *shināz-ūnah*. See ژي and زك

P شنبه *shambah* or شنبي *shambey*, s.m. (9th) Saturday. Sing. and Pl. See د خالي روځ

شنده *shanda'h*, s.f. (3rd) Impossible, desperate, unheard of, incredible, inconceivable (action or affair). Pl. ې *ey*. شنده کول *shanda'h kawul*, verb trans. To commit any incredible or unheard of action.

شنډ *shandd*, adj. Barren, impotent, sterile, unproductive, unprolific, infecund; (Fem.) شنډه *shandda'h*. شنډ والَي *shandd wālaey*, s.m. (1st) Barrenness, sterility, futility, unfruitfulness, impotence, infecundity. Pl. والي *wālī*.

شنډ پاره *shundd-pārah*, adj. Having the upper lip formed like a hare, hare-lipped. (Masc. and Fem.)

شنډۍ *shandda'ī*, s.f. (6th) The name of a tree (Melia sempervirens). Sing. and Pl. See بکاينرنه and روي

شنګرپ *shin-girip*, s.m. (6th) (P شنگرف) Vermilion, cinnabar. Sing. and Pl.

P شنگرف *shan-garf*, s.m. (6th) Cinnabar, vermilion. Sing. and Pl.

شنګرۍ *shingra'ī*, s.f. (6th) A tower, the outwork to the gate of a fort. 2. A mould for casting or forming earthen vessels. Sing. and Pl.

شنل *shanal*, verb trans. To rummage, to ransack, to look or go over, to explore, to sound, to grope for, to feel for, to search, seek, or look for, to reconnoitre, to look, to peer, to pry into every hole and corner, to beat the bushes, to leave no stone unturned; to mouse, to hunt, to dodge, to track; to overhaul, to fathom, to dip into; to canvass, to agitate, to sound, to analyze; to seek a clue, to pass in review; to pump, to cross-question, to catechise, to pop, start or put forth (a question), etc. Pres. شني *shanī*; past وُ شانه *wu-shānah*; fut. وُ به شني *wu bah shanī*; imp. وُ شنه *wu-shanah*; act. part. شنونکَي *shanūnkaey* or شنونَي *shanūnaey*; past part. شنلَي *shanalaey*; verb. n. شننه *shanana'h*.

شننه *shanana'h*, s.f. (3rd) (verb. n.) Inquiry, search, research, quest, scrutiny, investigation, inquest, study, sifting; examination, cross-examination, catechism; reconnoitring, reconnaissance, espionage, spying, prying. Pl. ې *ey*.

P شنوا *shanawā*, adj. A hearer, hearing.

شنواري *shinwārī*, s.m. (1st) Pl. The name of an Afghān tribe. شنوارَي *shinwāraey*, Sing. A male of the above tribe. شنوارۍ *shinwāra'ī*, s.f. (6th) A female of the above. Sing. and Pl.

شنونکَي *shanūnkaey* or شنونَي *shanūnaey*, adj. (act. part.) An inquirer, a querist, an examiner, a quidnunc; (Fem.) شنونکِ *shanūnki* or شنونِ *shanūni*. Pl. (Masc. and Fem.) ي *ī*.

شنه زرغونه *shna'h zarghūna'h*, s.f. (3rd) A rainbow. Pl. ې *ey*. Also شنه کاسه سره کاسه *shna'h-kāsa'h sara'h-kāsa'h*, s.f. (3rd) (*lit.* a green and red cup). Pl. ې *ey*. See د بوډۍ تال

شنيَ *shinaey*, s.m. (1st) A whitlow, a blister, a pustule. 2. A tick full of blood. Pl. ي *ī*. See كنړ

شني *shney*, s.f. (3rd) Pl. The fruit of the mastic tree. د شنو ونه *da shno wana'h*, s.f. (3rd) The mastic tree. Pl. ۍ *ey*.

شنيدل *shanedal*, verb intrans. To shake, to tremble, to become agitated, to quaver, to flutter, to beat, to throb, to palpitate, to go pit-a-pat, to toss about, to writhe, to wag, to flop, to totter, to flicker, to shake like an aspen leaf. Pres. شنيږي *shanejzī* (W.) or شنيګي *shanegī* (E.); past وُ شنيده *wu-shanedah*; fut. وُ به شنيږي *wu bah shanejzī* or شنيګي *shanegī*; imp. وُ شنيږه *wu-shanejzah* or شنيګه *shanegah*; act. part. شنيدونکيَ *shanedūnkaey* or شنيدونيَ *shanedūnaey*; past.part. شنيدليَ *shanedalaey*; verb. n. شنيدنه *shanedana'h*. شنول *shanawul*, verb trans. To agitate, to shake, to convulse, to flap, to disturb, to shake up, to jolt, to jog, to jostle, to tumble, to wield, to make or cause to throb, flutter, etc. Pres. شنوي *shanawī*; past وُ شناوه *wu-shanāwuh*; fut. وُ به شنوي *wu bah shanawī*; imp. وُ شنوه *wu-shanawah*; act. part. شنوونکيَ *shanawūnkaey* or شنوونيَ *shanawūnaey*; past part. شنوليَ *shanawulaey*; verb. n. شنونه *shanawuna'h*.

شوپا *sho-pā*, adj. Uncircumcised, a term of abuse. See نا سولت

شوپرک *shau-parak*, s.m. (5th) A bat (from P شب پره). Pl. شوپرکان *shau-parakān*.

P شوخ *shokh*, adj. Mischievous, pert, saucy, playful, brisk, cheerful, humorous, insolent, wanton, presumptuous, sly, etc.; (Fem.) شوخه *shoka'h*. شوخ چشم *shokh chashm* or شوخيَ ستړګيَ *shokhaey stargaey*, adj. Wanton-eyed, having a humorous or saucy eye. شوخ و شخ *shokh-ow-shakh*, adj. Impudent, immodest. شوخ و شنګه *shokh-ow-shanga'h*, adj. Playful and wanton, elegant and sweet in manners (as a mistress).

P شوخي *shokhī*, s.f. (3rd) Mischief, playfulness, pertness, fun, forwardness, sauciness, wantonness, coquetry. Pl. ۍ *a'ī*. شوخي کول *shokhī kawul*, verb trans. To display mischief, playfulness, fun; to act with wantonness, forwardness, pertness, etc.

شوخون *sho-khūn*, s.m. (2nd) A night attack, a nocturnal invasion. Pl. شوخونونه *sho-khūn-ūnah*. See شب خون and شب ګير

شوده *shaudæh*, s.m. (6th) Milk. Sing. and Pl. ټينګ شوده *ttīng-shaudæh*, Thick or rich milk. سپور شوده *spor-shaudæh*, Thin or bad milk.

P شور *shor*, s.m. (2nd) Noise, uproar, din, disturbance, tumult, clamor, clangor, riot, outcry, etc. Pl. شورونه *shor-ūnah*. شور کول *shor kawul*, verb trans. To raise a tumult, or disturbance, to make a din, uproar, noise, etc.

P شورَ پوشت *shora-pūsht*, adj. Quarrelsome, encouraging tumult, noisy, etc.; (Fem.) شورَ پوشته *shora pūshta'h*. شور شغب *shor shaghab*, s.m. (9th) Noise, tumult, disturbance, clamour, bustle. Sing. and Pl. شور آچول *shor āchawul* or شور کول *shor kawul*, verb trans. To make a noise, to raise a tumult.

شورت *shorat*, s.m. (6th) The name of a fruit very acid. Sing. and Pl.

شورق *shoraḳ*, s.m. (2nd) The skin of the tongue. Pl. شورقونه *shoraḳ-ūnah*. See شولځ

شوروه *shorwa'h*, s.f. (3rd) Soup, broth. Pl. ۍ *ey*.

شوروک *shorawak* or شوراوک *shorā-wak*, s. prop. The name of a district between Khelāt-i-Balūch and Kandahār. See ښوروک

شوړه *shorra'h*, s.f. (3rd) The beard on the ear of millet or the like grain. 2. The stopper of a *kūza'h* or earthen water-vessel, made of grass. Pl. ۍ *ey*. See لاشه, ګيرټي, and پونړي

شوشۍ *sho-sha'ī*, s.f. (6th) A firebrand, lighted embers. Sing. and Pl.

A شوق *shauḳ*, s.m. (2nd) Desire, avidity, eagerness, fondness, longing, love, inclination. Pl. شوقونه *shauḳūnah*. شوق و ذوق *shauḳ-ow-zauḳ*, Pleasure, delight, gratification. شوق لرل *shauḳ laral*, verb trans. To have desire or inclination for, to incline to, to have a fondness for. شوق کول *shauḳ kawul*, verb trans. To show inclination for, to manifest eagerness or avidity, etc. شوقي shauḳī, adj. Desirous, eager, intent upon, a desirer. (Masc. and Fem.)

A P شوقدر shau-ḳadr, s.m. (9th) The night of power, or شب برات shab-i-barāt, which see. 2. The name of a fortified frontier post in the Peshāwer district, to the north-west. Sing. and Pl.

شوك shūk, adj. Stripped by force, plucked, bare, naked, extracted, wrenched out, rooted up, etc.; (Fem.) شوكه shūka'h. شوك پوك shūk-pūk, adj. Torn, rent, torn to tatters, stripped by force, plucked, bare, naked; (Fem.) شوكه پوكه shūka'h-pūka'h; or شوك مشوك shūk-mashūk; (Fem.) شوكه مشوكه shūka'h mashūka'h.

شوكول shūkawul, verb trans. To extract, to pluck out, to tear out, to wrench, to wring from, to pull out (as hair by the roots), to pluck fruit from a tree, to gather, etc. Pres. شوكوي shūkawī; past و شوكاوه wu-shūkā-wuh or شوكاوو shūkā-wo; fut. و به شوكوي wu bah shūkawī; imp. و شكوه wu-shūkawah; act. part. شوكوونكَي shūkawūnkaey or شوكوونَي shūkawūnaey; past part. شوكولَي shūkawulaey; verb. n. شوكونه shūkawuna'h. See شكول

A شوكت shau-kat, s.m. (2nd) Dignity, state, magnificence, majesty. Pl. شوكتونه shaukatūnah.

شوكور sho-kor, adj. Night-blind, a person afflicted with night-blindness; (Fem.) شوكوره sho-kora'h. شوكوري sho-korī, s.f. (3rd) Night-blindness. Pl. ئي a'ī. See شمكور

شوكه shūka'h, s.f. (3rd) The beak of a bird. Pl. ي ey. See مشوكه

P شوگير sho-gīr, s.m. (5th) Watching or sitting up at night, one who watches by night. 2. A night attack. Pl. شوگيران sho-gīrān.

شوگه shūga'h, s.f. (3rd) A kind of rice. Pl. ي ey.

شول sh'wal, verb intrans. To be, to become, to exist, to accrue, to appear, to arise, to come forth, etc. Pres. شي shī; past و شه wu-shah; fut. و به شي wu bah shī or به و شي bah wu-shī; imp. شه shah or و شه wu-shah; act. part. شوونكَي sh'wūnkaey or شوونَي sh'wūnaey;

past part. شوي shawaey or شولَي sh'walaey; verb. n. شونه sh'wana'h.

شولخ sho-lakh, s.m. (2nd) The skin of the tongue. Pl. شولخونه sho-lakhūnah. See شورق

شل و شول shal-ow-shūl, adj. Paralytic, palsied, one who has lost the use of his limbs; (Fem.) شل و شوله shal-ow-shūla'h. See شل

شولگره sholgara'h, s.f. (3rd) Rice-ground, land in which rice is cultivated, a paddy-field. Pl. ي ey. See شاليزاره

شوله shola'h, s.f. (3rd) Rice in the husk, paddy. 2. (P) Rice and pulse boiled together and given to the sick. Pl. ي ey. See شالي

شوله shwala'h, s.f. (3rd) The colic, a severe pain in the bowels. Pl. ي ey.

شوم shūm, adj. Faint for want of food, hungry. 2. (A) Unfortunate, unlucky, disgraceful. 3. Niggard, stingy, a miser; (Fem.) شومه shūma'h. شوم بخت shūm-bakht or شوم طالع shūm-ṭā-liæ, adj. Unfortunate, unlucky; (Fem.) شوم بخته shūm-bakhta'h or شوم طالعه shūm-ṭā-liæa'h. شوم شغال shūm-shaghāl, adj. Ill-natured, disobliging, ill-disposed, evil-minded, malign, malignant; (Fem.) شوم شغاله shūm-shaghālah. شومي shūmī, s.f. (3rd) Stinginess, Niggardliness. Pl. ئي a'ī; or شوميت shūmi-yat, s.m. (2nd). Pl. شوميتونه shūmi-yatūnah.

شوملي shomley, s.f. (3rd) (Pl.) Butter-milk, sour milk. The singular form is not used. See also شلومبي and شلونبي

شومه shūma'h, s.f. (3rd) Food, victuals. Pl. ي ey.

شومي shūmī, s.f. (3rd) Hunger, Faintness through want of food. 2. Extorting payment of a debt or compliance with any demand by sitting before a person's door and refusing to take food until granted. Pl. ئي a'ī. شومي نيول shūmī nīwal, verb trans. To extort compliance to a request, to starve one's-self. See نهوه

شونټي shūn-tta'ī, s.f. (6th) The wood of a species of the pine, slips of which are used as torches. Sing. and Pl.

شوند shūndd, s.m. (5th) (W.) The lip. Pl. شوندان shūnddān. See سوند

شونډ *s͟hūnḍḍ*, s.m. (6th) Dry ginger. Sing. and Pl. See سونډ

شونډک *s͟hūnḍḍak*, s.m. (5th) The proboscis of an elephant. Pl. شونډکان *s͟hūnḍḍakān*. See سونډک

شونډه *s͟hūnḍḍa'h*, s.f. (3rd) (E.) The lip. Pl. ې *ey*. See شونډ

شوونکي *s͟h'wūnkaey* or شووني *s͟h'wūnaey*, adj. (act. part. of شول) Possible, practicable, feasible, attainable, compatible, etc.; (Fem.) شوونکې *s͟h'wūnki* or شوون *s͟h'wūni*. Pl. (Masc. and Fem.) ي *ī*. Also د شوو *da s͟h'wo* or د شولُ *da s͟hwalo* (noun of fitness). Sing. and Pl.

شوه *s͟hawa'h*, s.f. (3rd) The name of a tree (Dalbergia sisu). 2. A kind of shrub without leaves, highly cathartic. Pl. ې *ey*.

شوي *s͟ho-e*, s.m. (6th) Coarse cotton cloth. Sing. and Pl. 2. A word or exclamation in driving bullocks and cows. Sing. and Pl.

شها *s͟hahā*, s.f. (6th) A mistress, a sweetheart. (E.) Sing. and Pl. (W.) شهاوي *s͟hahā-wī*.

A شهادت *s͟hahādat*, s.m. (2nd) Evidence, testimony, witness. 2. Martyrdom. Pl. شهادتونه *s͟hahādatūnah*.

P شهباز *s͟hah-bāz*, s.m. (5th) A royal falcon. Pl. شهبازان *s͟hah-bāzān*. See شاه باز

P شهپر *s͟hah-par*, s.m. (2nd) The principal feather in a bird's wing. Pl. شهپرونه *s͟hah-parūnah*.

P شهد *s͟hahad*, s.m. (6th) Honey. Sing. and Pl. See گربني and مچمچي

شهر *s͟huhr*, s.m. (2nd) Any desperate, unheard of, or incredible action or matter (bad). Pl. شهرونه *s͟huhrūnah*.

A شهرت *s͟huhrat*, s.m. (2nd) Renown, fame, celebrity, rumor. Pl. شهرتونه *s͟huhratūnah*. شهرت کول *s͟huhrat kawul*, verb trans. To rumor, to celebrate, to make famous.

A شهلا *s͟hahlā*, adj. Having dark grey eyes with a shade of red. شهلا سترګي *s͟hahlā stargey*, s.f. (3rd) Pl. Dark grey eyes.

شهند *s͟hahand*, s.m. (5th) A kind of falcon (Falco christalellus). Pl. شهندان *s͟hahandān*.

A شهوت *s͟hahwat*, s.m. (2nd) Lust, desire, appetite, sensuality, concupiscence. Pl. شهوتونه *s͟hahwatūnah*. شهوت پرست *s͟hahwat parast*, adj. Carnal, sensual, lascivious; (Fem.) شهوت پرسته *s͟hahwat parasta'h*. شهوتي *s͟hahwatī*, adj. Lustful, lascivious (Masc. and Fem.)

A شهيد *s͟hahīd*, s.m. (5th) A witness, a martyr. Pl. شهيدان *s͟hahīdān*. 2. adj. Killed, martyred. 3. Ashamed, abased, disgraced, dishonoured; (Fem.) شهيده *s͟hahīda'h*. شهيد کيدل *s͟hahīd kedal*, verb intrans. To become a martyr. 2. To become disgraced, ashamed, dishonoured. شهيد کول *s͟hahīd kawul*, verb trans. To martyr, to kill. 2. To disgrace, to dishonour.

P شهين *s͟hah-īn*, s.m. (5th) A kind of falcon. 2. The beam of a scale. 3. A gun carried on a camel. Pl. شهينان *s͟hah-īnān*. شهين چي *s͟hah-īn c͟hī*, s.m. (5th) A soldier who fires a camel gun. Pl. شهين چيان *s͟hah-īn c͟hī-ān*.

A شيَ *s͟haey*, s.m. (1st) A thing, an article. Pl. ي *ī*. Also (A) Pl. اشيا *as͟hīā*.

شيبه *s͟hebah*, adj. Heavy, violent, pouring, used with regard to rain only.

شيبره *s͟hebara'h*, s.f. (3rd) A burning fever. Pl. ې *ey*.

A شيخ *s͟haik͟h*, s.m. (5th) A chief, a prelate, a venerable old man. 2. A title taken by descendants of the prophet, and given to Muḥammadan proselytes. Pl. شيخان *s͟hek͟hān*.

P شيدا *s͟haidā*, adj. Mad, deeply in love, a lover, 2. The name of an Afg͟hān poet, Muḥammad Kāẓīm K͟hān, surnamed S͟haidā, a descendant of K͟hūs͟hḥāl K͟hān, the celebrated K͟hattak chief and author, portions of whose writings will be found in my Pus͟hto "Text Book."

شيدي *s͟hīdey*, s.f. (3rd) Pl. Milk. See شوده and پئ

P شير *s͟hīr*, s.m. (9th) Milk, only used in composition, as شيرخوار *s͟hīr-k͟hwār*, adj. A suckling, an infant; (Fem.) شير خواره *s͟hīr k͟hwāra'h*. شير ګرم *s͟hīr garm*, adj. Milk-warm, lukewarm. شير مست *s͟hīr-mast*, adj. A fine plump suckling, a fatling; (Fem.) شير مسته *s͟hīr-masta'h*. See پئ

شيرازه *shīrāza'h*, s.f. (3rd) The stitching of the back of a book. 2. The wall of a fort on the inner face of the ditch. Pl. ئ *ey*.

شيراني *shīrānī*, s.m. (1st) Pl. The name of a tribe of Afghāns. Sing. شيرانيَ *shīrānaey*, A male of the Shīrānī tribe. شيرانۍ *shīrāna'ī*, s.f. (6th) A female of the above tribe. Sing. and Pl.

شير خط *shīr-khaṭ*, s.m. (2nd) Throwing or tossing up money into the air, tossing up for anything. شير *shīr*, Head. خط *khaṭ*, Tail. Pl. شير خطونه *shīr khaṭ-ūnah*. شير خط کول *shīr-khaṭ kawul*, verb trans. To toss up for anything.

P شيرک *shīrak*, s.m. (5th) A hero, a champion (dimin. of شير *shīr*, A lion). Pl. شيرکان *shīrakān*. شيرکه *shīraka'h*, s.f. (3rd) A bold or intrepid woman. Pl. ئ *ey*. شيرکيَ *shīrakaey*, s.m. (1st) A champion, a hero, a warrior (W.) Pl. ي *ī*.

P شيرين *shīrīn*, adj. Sweet, pleasant, gentle, affable (used in composition); (Fem.) شيرينه *shīrīna'h*. شيرين زبان *shīrīn zabān*, adj. Eloquent, sweet-spoken, affable; (Fem.) شيرين زبانه *shīrīn-zabāna'h*. شيرين زباني *shīrīn-zabānī*, s.f. (3rd) Eloquence, affability. Pl. ئي *a'ī*. شيرين گفتار *shīrīn guftār*, adj. Sweet spoken, pleasant in speech; (Fem.) شيرين گفتاره *shīrīn guftāra'h*. شيريني *shīrīnī*, s.f. (3rd) Sweetness, pleasantness. 2. Sweetmeat. Pl. ئي *a'ī*. شيرين کيدل *shīrīn kedal*, verb intrans. To become sweet or pleasant. شيرين کول *shīrīn kawul*, verb. trans. To sweeten, to render sweet, pleasant, etc. See خوږ

شوشک *shūshk*, s.m. (2nd) The curve of an arch. Pl. شوشکونه *shūshkūnah*.

شيشکيَ *sheshkaey*, s.m. (1st) A hedgehog. Pl. ي *ī*. See څزکي

A شيطان *shaiṭān*, s.m. (5th) (from شطن) The devil, Satan. Pl. شيطانان *shaiṭānān*.

A شيطاني *shaiṭānī*, s.f. (3rd) Devil's tricks, devilry, wickedness. Pl. ئي *a'ī*; or شيطانت *shaiṭānat*, s.m. (2nd). Pl. شيطانتونه *shaiṭānatūnah*.

شيطان خطا کول *shai-ṭān khaṭā kawul*, verb trans. Emissio seminis (in sleep).

A شيعه *shī'aeh*, s.m. (5th) (from شاع) A sectary, a follower of the sect of Ælī. Pl. شيعهگان *shī'aehgān*. شيعه واليَ *shī'aeh-wālaey*, s.m. (1st) The customs or rites and doctrines of the Shī'aeh's. Pl. والي *wālī*; or شيعه توب *shī'aeh-tob*, s.m. (2nd). Pl. توبونه *tobūnah*; or شيعه گلوي *shī'aeh-galwī*, s.f. (3rd). Pl. ئي *a'ī*.

شيله *shela'h*, s.f. (3rd) A small water-course or dry bed of a river. Pl. ئ *ey*. See خوړ

شين *shīn*, adj. Green, verdant, fresh, bluish-green. Pl. شنهٔ *shnaeh*; (Fem.) شنه *shna'h*. Pl. شني *shney*. شين واليَ *shīn-wālaey*, s.m. (1st) Greenness, verdancy, freshness. Pl. والي *wālī*. شين گښتي *shin gashtī* (W.) or *gakhtī* (E.), s.f. (3rd) Verdure, herbage, green things. Pl. ئي *a'ī*. شين تغ *shīn-tagh*, s.m. (5th) A blue jay (Coracias Bengalensis). Pl. شين تغ *shīn-taegh*; also written شين تغ *shīn-ttagh* and شين تغ *shīn-ttaegh*. See شين طوطي

شين توپۍ *shīn-topa'ī*, s.f. (6th) The common wagtail. Sing. and Pl. See زيرانکه

شين خورکه *shīn-khwaraka'h*, s.f. (3rd) A large green lizard, the iguana. Pl. ئ *ey*.

شين طوطي *shīn ṭo-ṭī* or *ṭū-ṭī*, s.m. (5th) A blue jay (Coracias Bengalensis). Pl. طوطيان *ṭo-ṭīān* or *ṭū-ṭīān*. See شين تغ

شين غوده *shīn-ghoda'h*, s.f. (3rd) A lapwing. Pl. ئ *ey*.

شين مزريَ *shīn-m'zaraey*, s.m. (1st) The lion. 2. A brave man, a champion, a hero. Pl. ي *ī*. شنه مزرۍ *shna'h-m'zara'ī*, s.f. (6th) A lioness. Sing. and Pl.

شينکيَ *shīnkaey*, adj. Clothed in green. 2. As s.m. (1st) An unripe water melon. Pl. ي *ī*.

شينيَ *shīnaey*, s.m. (1st) A whitlow. 2. A tick, a dog-louse. Pl. ي *ī*. See کنړ and شني.

A شيوخ *sheokh*, (Pl. of شيخ) Old men, elders, chiefs, prelates, etc.

شيوه *shewa'h*, s.f. (3rd) Descent, declivity, inclination, slope. 2. Leaning, sloping, slanting, shelving, inclining. Pl. ي *ey*. See سر and خوره . سر زوره شيوه کيدل *sh̲ewa'h kedal*, verb intrans. To slide down a declivity, to slip down, to descend, to come down. 2. To take an oblique direction. شيوه کول *sh̲ewa'h kawul*, verb trans. To make slide, to make slip, to slide down. 2. To slope, to incline (as the bank of a river, etc.)

P شيوه *sh̲ewa'h*, s.f. (3rd) Business, trade, profession, manner, habit, custom. 2. Amorous looks. Pl. ي *ey*.

شيوه گر *sh̲ewa'h-gar*, s.m. (5th) An artist, a tradesman. Pl. شيوه گرٌ *sh̲ewa'h-gær*. 2. adj. Expert, skilful, clever. شيوه گره *sh̲ewa'h-gara'h*, s.f. (3rd). Pl. ي *ey*.

ښ

ښ *kh̲īn*, the twenty-third letter of the Push̲to alphabet, pronounced *sh̲ey* by the Western Afgh̲āns, with the exception of some similarity to the ک *k'ch* of the Ch̲āldaic, has no equivalent in sound in any of the languages of the old world, and is pronounced by bringing the tip of the tongue to the roof of the mouth. With Persian words adopted into the language it is commonly substituted for ش, and in some instances, particularly in most modern manuscripts, which should never be looked on as authorities in the matter, it is used indiscriminately, according to the ignorance or otherwise of the copyists.

ښاپيرک *sh̲āperak* (W.) or *kh̲āperak* (E.) s.m. (5th) A bat. Pl. ښاپيرکان *sh̲āperakān* or *kh̲āperakān*. ښاپيرکه *sh̲āperaka'h* (W.) or *kh̲āperaka'h* (E.) s.f. (3rd) A female bat. Pl. ي *ey*. See شوبرک

ښاخ *sh̲āk̲h̲* (W.) or *kh̲āk̲h̲* (E.) s.m. (2nd) (from P شاخ), A bough or branch of a tree. 2. The branch or arm of a river. Pl. ښاخونه *sh̲āk̲h̲ūnah* or *kh̲āk̲h̲ūnah*. ښاخ دار *sh̲āk̲h̲* or *kh̲āk̲h̲dār*, adj. Branchy, having numerous boughs or branches; (Fem.) ښاخ داره *sh̲āk̲h̲* or *kh̲āk̲h̲dāra'h*.

ښاد *sh̲ād* (W.) or *kh̲ād* (E.) adj. (from P شاد) Pleased, delighted, exulting, cheerful, happy, gay, joyous; (Fem.) ښاده *sh̲āda'h* or *kh̲āda'h*. ښاد من *sh̲ād man* or *kh̲ād-man* or مند *mand*, adj. Gay, cheerful, merry, glad, delighted, joyful; (Fem.) ښاد منه *sh̲ād-mana'h* or *kh̲ād mana'h* or منده *manda'h*. ښاديدل *sh̲ādedal* (W.) or *kh̲ādedal* (E.) verb intrans. To become glad, pleased, cheerful, happy, gay, delighted, etc. Pres. ښاديږي *sh̲ādejzī* (W.) or ښاديگي *kh̲ādegī* (E.); past ښاد شه *sh̲ād sh̲ah* or *kh̲ād sh̲ah* or وُ شه *wu-sh̲ah*; fut. ښاد به شي *sh̲ād bah sh̲ī* or *kh̲ād bah sh̲ī* or به وُ شي *bah wu-sh̲ī*; imp. ښاد شه *sh̲ād sh̲ah* or *kh̲ād-sh̲ah* or وُ شه *wu-sh̲ah*; act. part. ښاديدونکيَ *sh̲ādedūnkacy* or *kh̲ādedūnkacy* or ښاديدونيَ *sh̲ādedūnaey* or *kh̲ādedūnaey*; past part. ښاد *sh̲ād* or *kh̲ād* or ښاد شويَ *sh̲ād sh̲awaey* or *kh̲ād sh̲awaey*; verb. n. ښاديدنه *sh̲ādedana'h* or *kh̲ādedana'h* or ښاديده *sh̲ādedah* or *kh̲ādedah*. ښادول *sh̲ādawul* (W.) or *kh̲ādawul* (E.) To gladden, to please, to delight, to rejoice, to exhilarate, to make happy, etc. Pres. ښادوي *sh̲ādawī* or *kh̲ādawī*; past ښاد کړ *sh̲ād kaṟṟ* or *kh̲ād kaṟṟ* or وُ کړ *wu-kaṟṟ*; fut. ښاد به کړي *sh̲ād bah kṟṟī* or *kh̲ād bah kṟṟī* or به وُ کړي *bah wu-kṟṟī*; imp. ښاد کړه *sh̲ād-kṟṟah* or *kh̲ād kṟṟah* or وُ کړه *wu-kṟṟah*; act. part. ښادوونکيَ *sh̲ādawūnkaey* or *kh̲ādawūnkacy* or ښادوونيَ *sh̲ādawūnaey* or *kh̲ādawūnaey*; past part. ښاد کړي *sh̲ād kaṟṟaey* or *kh̲ād kaṟṟaey*; verb. n. ښادونه *sh̲ādawuna'h* or *kh̲ādawuna'h*.

ښادان *sh̲ā-dān* (W.) or *kh̲ā-dān* (E.) (P شادان) adj. Pleased, delighted, joyful, cheerful, gay, merry, glad; (Fem.) ښادانه *sh̲ādāna'h* or *kh̲ādāna'h*. ښادان کول *sh̲ādān* or *kh̲ādān kawul*, verb trans. To please, to gladden, to render gay or cheerful.

ښادي *sh̲ādī* (W.) or *kh̲ādī* (E.) s.f. (3rd) Joy, delight, pleasure, happiness, gladness, gaiety, rejoicing. Pl. ي *a'ī*. ښادي کول *sh̲ādī* or *kh̲ādī kawul*, verb trans. To make merry, to rejoice, to manifest gladness or gaiety.

ښاديانه *sh̲ādiyāna'h* or *kh̲ādiyāna'h*, s.f. (3rd)

Music and rejoicings on festive occasions. Pl. ئ *ey*.

ښارک *shārak* (W.) or *khārak* (E.) s.m. (2nd) A piece of wood in the mouth of a mill-stone, into which the iron axle is inserted. Pl. ښارکونه *shārakūnah* or *khārakūnah*.

ښارګ *shā-rag* or *khā-rag*, s.m. (2nd) The jugular vein. Pl. ښارګونه *shā-ragūnah* or *khā-ragūnah*. (P شارګ).

ښارو *shārū* or *khārū*, s.m. (5th) A mainā (Coracias indicus). Pl. ښاروګان *shārūgān* or *khārūgān*.

ښاروڼئ *shārūna'ī* or *khārūna'ī*, s.f. (6th) A starling. Sing. and Pl.

ښاغل *shāghal* or *khāghal*, verb trans. To please, to prefer, to like, to choose, to have satisfaction in, to gratify, to content. Pres. ښاغي *shāghī* or *khāghī*; past وُ ښاغه *wu-shāghah* or *wu-khāghah*; fut. وُ به ښاغي *wu bah shāghī* or *wu bah khāghī*; imp. وُ ښاغه *wu-shāghah* or *wu-khāghah*; act. part. ښاغونکئ *shāghūnkaey* or *khāghūnkaey* or ښاغونئ *shāghūnaey* or *khāghūnaey*; past part. ښاغلئ *shāghalaey* or *khāghalaey* or ښاغئ *shāghaey* or *khāghaey*; verb. n. ښاغنه *shāghana'h* or *khāghana'h*.

ښاغلئ *shāghalaey* or *khāghalaey*, adj. (past part. of ښاغل) Pleased, gratified, contented, satisfied, preferred, liked, chosen; (Fem.) ښاغلِ *shāghali* or *khāghali*. Pl. (Masc. and Fem.) ي *ī*.

ښامار *shā-mār* or *khā-mār*, s.m. (5th) A large serpent, a dragon, the king of serpents. Pl. ښاماران *shā-mārān* or *khā-mārān*.

ښانک *shānak* or *khānak*, s.m. (2nd) A kneading trough of wood. Pl. ښانکونه *shānakūnah* or *khānakūnah*.

ښانګه *shānga'h* or *khānga'h*, s.f. (3rd) The leg including the thigh; the leg and the foot. Pl. ئ *ey*. ښانګهور *shānga'h-war* or *khānga'h-war*, adj. Long-legged, spindle-shanked; (Fem.) ښانګهوره *shānga'h-wara'h* or *khānga'h-wara'h*.

ښايست *shā-īst* or *khā-īst*, s.m. (6th) Beauty, elegance, grace, symmetry, comeliness, loveliness, prettiness, handsomeness. Sing. and Pl. ښايسته *shā-īstah* or *khā-īstah*, adj. Beautiful, elegant, graceful, pretty, comely, handsome. ښايسته کيدل *shā-īstah* or *khā-īstah kedal*, verb intrans. To become beautiful, comely, pretty, elegant, handsome, etc. ښايسته کول *shā-īstah* or *khā-īstah kawul*, verb trans. To beautify, to make comely, pretty, elegant, handsome, etc.

ښائي *shā-yī* or *khā-yī*, adv. May be, perhaps, perchance, probably, possibly. Also ښائيږي *shā-yīzhī* (W.) or ښائيګي *kha-yīgī* (E.) (Pres. of ښائيدل an infinitive now obsolete). See ګوندِ.

ښپه *khpa'h* (E.), s.f. (3rd) The foot. Pl. ئ *ey*; or (W.) پښه *pkha'h* and پښي *pkhey*, which see. ښپه آرتول *khpa'h āratawul*, verb trans. (*lit.* to release the foot) To visit the betrothed at her own house for the first time on the part of the lover. ښپه آرته *khpa'h āratah*, adj. Foot-released; the lover who visits his betrothed for the first time. آرتي ښپي *āratey khpey*, adj. Straddle-footed.

ښتګرئ *shat-garaey* (W.) or *khat-garaey* (E.), s.m. (1st) The ankle joint. Pl. ي *ī*. See بجل.

ښچي *kha-chey* or *sha-chey* (W.) (from ښه چه), Good that! ښچي راغي *kh-chey rā-ghī*, It is well that he is come.

ښڅلئ *shatsulaey*, s.m. (1st) A chisel. Pl. ي *ī*. See سورلي and ښڅرلي

ښخ *shakh* or *khakh*, adj. Buried, interred, inhumed, entombed, concealed, covered; (Fem.) ښخه *shakha'h* or *khakha'h*. ښخيدل *shakhedal* or *khakhedal*, verb intrans. To become buried, interred, entombed, concealed, covered, inserted, etc. Pres. ښخيږي *shakhejzī* (W.) or ښخيګي *khakhegī* (E.); past ښخ شه *shakh shah* or *khakh shah* or وُ شه *wu-shah*; fut. ښخ به شي *shakh bah shī* or *khakh bah shī* or وُ به شي *bah wu-shī*; imp. ښخ شه *shakh* or *khakh shah* or وُ شه *wu-shah*; act. part. ښخيدونکئ *shakhedūnkaey* or *khakhedūnkaey* or ښخيدونئ *shakhedūnaey* or *khakhedūnaey*; past part. ښخ *shakh* or *khakh* or ښخ شوئ *shakh* or *khakh shawaey*; verb. n. ښخيدنه *shakhedana'h* or *khakhedana'h* or ښخيده *shakhedah* or *khakhedah*. ښخول *shakhawul* or *khakhawul*, verb trans. To bury, to inter, to inhume, to entomb, to conceal, to cover, to insert. Pres. ښخوي *shakhawī* or *khakhawī*; past ښخ کړ *shakh* or *khakh karr* or وُ کړ *wu-karr*; fut. ښخ به کړي *shakh* or *khakh bah krrī* or وُ کړي به *bah wu-krrī*; imp. ښخ کړه *shakh* or *khakh krrah* or وُ کړه *wu krrah*; act. part. ښخوونکي *shakh-awūnkaey* or *khakhawūnkaey* or ښخووني *shakh-awūnaey* or *khakhawūnaey*; past part. ښخ کړي *shakh* or *khakh karraey*; verb. n. ښخونه *shakh-awuna'h* or *khakhawuna'h*. See خښل

ښخ *shakh* or *khakh*, adj. Stiff, hard, not easily bent; (Fem.) ښخه *shakha'h* or *khakha'h*. ښخ مخ *shakh-makh* or *khakh-makh*, adj. Stiff in the limbs, rigid; (Fem.) ښخه مخه *shakha'h-makha'h* or *khakha'h-makha'h*. ښخ مخ کيدل *shakh-makh* or *khakh-makh kedal*, verb in-trans. To become stiff or rigid. ښخ مخ کول *shakh makh* or *khakh-makh kawul*, verb trans. To make stiff or rigid.

ښرا *sharā* or *kharā*, s.f. (6th) Imprecation, curse, ill-wish. (E.) Sing. and Pl. (W.) Pl. ښراوي *sharāwī*. ښرا کول *sharā* or *kharā kawul*, verb trans. To curse, to imprecate, to wish ill. See ښيره

ښروه *sharawa'h* or *kharawa'h*, s.f. (3rd) The name of a tree producing a very hard and tough wood. Pl. ي *ey*.

ښره *shara'h* or *khara'h*, s.f. (3rd) Nitre. Pl. ي *ey*. See ښوره

ښره رود *sharah-rūd* or *kharah-rūd*, s. prop. The name of a river containing much nitre, west-ward of Kandahār; hence the name—the Sharah-rūd.

ښزونک *shazū-nak* or *khazū-nak*, s.m. (5th) An hermaphrodite. Pl. ښزونک *shazū-næk* or *khazū-næk*; also ښزونکي *shazū-nakaey*, s.m. (1st). Pl. ي *ī*. See ښځونک, etc. or ښځونکي *khadzū-nakaey*, s.m. (1st). Pl. ي *ī*.

ښځونک *shadzū-nak* (W.) or *khadzū-nak* (E.), s.m. (5th) An hermaphrodite, an effeminate person. Pl. ښځونک *shadzū-næk* or *khadzū-næk*. See ښزونکي

ښځه *shadza'h*, (W.) or *khadza'h* (E.), s.f. (3rd) A woman, a female, a wife. Pl. ي *ey*. 2. adj. Feminine gender, feminine. ښځه خلاصول *shadza'h* or *khadza'h khalāṣawul*, verb trans. To deliver a woman (in childbirth).

ښکار *sh'kār* or *kh'kār*, s.m. (2nd) (from P شکار) Hunting, chase. 2. Prey, game. 3. Plunder. Pl. ښکارونه *sh'kārūnah* or *kh'kārūnah*. ښکار گاه *sh'kār-gāh* or *kh'kār'gāh*, s.m. (2nd) A place for hunting in, a place abounding in game, a chase. Pl. ښکارگاهونه *sh'kār-gāh-ūnah* or *kh'kār-gāhūnah*. ښکار کول *sh'kār* or *kh'kār kawul*, verb trans. To go a hunting, to go in quest of game. ښه ښکار *shah-sh'kār* (W.) or *khah kh'kār* (E.), Good sport. ښکاري *sh'kārī* or *kh'kārī*, s.m. (5th) A huntsman, a sportsman, a fowler. Pl. ښکاريان *sh'kārī-ān* or *kh'kārī-ān*.

ښکاره *sh'kārah* or *kh'kārah*, adj. Evident, ap-parent, manifest, clear, obvious, palpable, ostensible, discernible, visible. (Phr.) Plain as the nose on one's face, etc. ښکاره والي *sh'kā-rah wālaey* or *kh'kārah-wālaey*, s.m. (1st) Appearance, distinctness, conspicuous-ness, visibility, clearness. Pl. والي *wālī*. ښکاره کيدل *sh'kārah* or *kh'kārah kedal*, verb intrans. To become evident, manifest, clear, apparent, obvious, conspicuous; to become exposed, revealed, or made known. ښکاره کول *sh'kārah* or *kh'kārah kawul*, verb trans. To make manifest, to make evident, clear, apparent, discernible, conspicuous, obvious, palpable; to expose, to reveal, etc.

ښکالوه *shkāl-wah* (W.) or *khkāl-wah* (E.), s.m. (6th) Discourse, mention, talk, discussion. 2. The sound of conversation, hum, muttering, chattering, murmur. 3. The sound of foot-steps. Sing. and Pl. ښکالوه لرل *kh'kālwah laral* or کول *kawul*, verb trans. To murmur, chatter, make a humming sound, to sound as footsteps. See سکالوه and کنکوسي

ښکته *kh'katah* (E.), adv. Below, beneath, under, down. 2. adj. Inferior, lower, under. See زير and دلاندِ. ښکته کيدل *kh'katah kedal*, verb intrans. To become lowered or let down.

کښته کول *kh'katah kawul*, verb trans. To lower, to let down. See (W.) کښته and ښکته

ښکر *sh'kar* or *kh'kar*, s.m. (5th) The horn of an animal, an antler, a powder horn. Pl. ښکرُ *sh'kær* or *kh'kær*. ښکرور *sh'kærawar* or *kh'kærawar*, adj. Horned, having horns, as a goat, cow, etc.; (Fem.) ښکروره *sh'kærawara'h* or *kh'kærawara'h*. ښکر لګول *sh'kær lagawul* or *kh'kær lagawul*, verb trans. To cup, to draw blood by cupping, which is done by applying the horn of an animal, by the Afghāns. په ښکر وهل *pah sh'kær* or *pah kh'kær wahal*, verb trans. To strike with the horns, to gore.

ښکرۍ *shkara'ī* or *khkara'ī*, s.f. (6th) A flat basket made in the shape of a tray, of cane, grass, or wood. Sing. and Pl. See شکورۍ and شکرۍ

ښکل *kh'kul*, s.m. (2nd) A kiss, a buss, salute, embrace. Pl. ښکلونه *kh'kulūnah*. ښکل کول *kh'kul kawul*, verb trans. To kiss, to salute.

ښکل *sh'kal* or *kh'kal*, verb trans. To draw, to pull, to tighten, to pull or draw out or along, to flay, to strip off, to remove. 2. To write, to pen, to write out, to transcribe, to scribble. 3. To suffer, to endure, etc. Pres. ښکي *sh'kī* or *kh'kī*; past و ښکه *wu-sh'kah* or *wu-kh'kah*; fut. و به ښکي *wu bah sh'kī* or *wu bah kh'kī*; imp. و ښکه *wu sh'kah* or *wu kh'kah*; act. part. ښکونکَي *sh'kūnkaey* or *kh'kūnkaey* or ښکونَي *sh'kūnaey* or *kh'kūnaey*; past part. ښکلَي *sh'kalaey* or *kh'kalaey*; verb. n. ښکنه *sh'kana'h* or *kh'kana'h*. See کښل

ښکلول *sh'kulawul* or *kh'kulawul*, verb trans. To kiss, to caress, to salute. Pres. ښکلوي *sh'kulawī* or *kh'kulawī*; past ښکل کړ *sh'kul karr* or *kh'kul karr* or و کړ *wu-karr*; fut. ښکل به کړي *sh'kul bah krrī* or *kh'kul bah krrī* or به و کړي *bah wu-krrī*; imp. ښکل کړه *sh'kul krrah* or *kh'kul krrah* or و کړه *wu-krrah*; act. part. ښکلونکَي *sh'kulawūnkaey* or *kh'kulawūnkaey* or ښکلونَي *sh'kulawūnaey* or *kh'kulawūnaey*; past part. ښکلولَي *sh'kulawulaey* or *kh'kulawulaey*; verb. n. ښکلونه *sh'kulawuna'h* or *kh'kulawuna'h*.

ښکلَي *sh'kulaey* or *kh'kulaey*, adj. (past part.) (*lit.* Kissed) pretty, good-looking, handsome, graceful, bonny, well-formed, etc.; (Fem.) ښکلِ *sh'kuli* or *kh'kuli*. Pl. (Masc. and Fem.) ي *ī*. See ښايسته

ښکنځل *sh'kandzal* or *kh'kandzal*, s.m. (6th) Abuse, upbraiding, invective, vituperation, reviling, contumely, execration. Sing. and Pl. ښکنځل کول *sh'kandzal* or *kh'kandzal kawul*, verb trans. to abuse, to upbraid, to revile, to execrate, to call names, to vituperate; or ښکنځل *sh'kandzal* or *kh'kandzal* verb trans. Pres. ښکنځي *sh'kandzī* or *kh'kandzī*; past و ښکانځه *wu-sh'kāndzah* or *kh'kāndzah*, or و ښکانځ *wu-sh'kāndza* or *wu-kh'kāndza*; fut. و به ښکنځي *wu bah sh'kandzī* or *wu bah kh'kandzī*; imp. و ښکنځه *wu-sh'kandzah* or *wu-kh'kandzah*; act. part. ښکنځونکَي *sh'kandzūnkaey* or *kh'kandzūnkaey* or ښکنځونَي *sh'kandzūnaey* or *kh'kandzūnaey*; past part. ښکنځلَي *sh'kandzalaey* or *kh'kandzalaey*; verb. n. ښکنځنه *sh'kandzana'h* or *kh'kandzana'h*.

ښکول *kh'kūl*, verb trans. To write, to pen, to transcribe, to write out. See ښکل

ښکيدل *shakedal* or *khakedal*, verb intrans. To slip, to slide, to glide, to fall, etc. Pres. ښکيږي *shakejzī* (W.) or ښکيګي *khakegī* (E.); past و ښکيده *wu-shakedah* or *wu-khakedah* or و ښکيدَ *wu-shakeda* or *wu-khakeda*; fut. و به ښکيږي *wu bah shakejzī* or ښکيګي *khakegī*; imp. و ښکيږه *wu-shakejzah* or و ښکيګه *wu-khakegah*; act. part. ښکيدونکَي *shakedūnkaey* or *khakedūnkaey* or ښکيدونَي *shakedūnaey* or *khakedūnaey*; past part. ښکيدلَي *shakedalaey* or *khakedalaey*; verb. n. ښکيدنه *shakedana'h* or *khakedana'h* or ښکيده *shakedah* or *khakedah*. ښکول *shakawul* or *khakawul*, verb. trans. To make slip or slide, to thrust along, to thrust by slipping. 2. To pull or push from side to side, as in loosening a peg from the ground to pull it out, shaking a tree to make the fruit fall, etc. Pres. ښکوي *shakawī* or *khakawī*; past و ښکاوه *wu-shakāwuh* or *wu-khakāwuh* or و ښکاوو *wu-shakāwo* or *wu-*

Khakāwo ; fut. وُ به ښکوي *wu bah shakawī* or *Khakawī* ; imp. وُ ښکوه *wu-shakawah* or *wu-Khakawah* ; act. part. ښکوونکيَ *shakawūnkaey* or *khakawūnkaey* or ښکووني *shakawūnaey* or *Khakawūnaey* ; past part. ښکوليَ *shakawulaey* or *khakawulaey* ; verb. n. ښکونه *shakawuna'h* or *khakawuna'h*.

ښکيدنه *shakedana'h* or *Khakedana'h*, s.f. (3rd) (verb. n.) Slipping, sliding, gliding, falling, etc. Pl. يْ *ey* ; or ښکيده *shakedah* or *Khakedah*, s.m. (6th) (verb. n.) Sing. and Pl.

ښکيل *shkel* or *Khkel*, s.m. (2nd) Tying a horse's or other animal's two fore feet, or a fore foot and hind foot together, to prevent its straying. 2. The rope or fastening for the above. 3. Cozenage, a trick to cheat by, fraud, etc. Pl. ښکيلونه *shkelūnah* or *Khkelūnah*. See شکيل . ښکيل کول *shkel* or *Khkel kawul*, verb trans. To fasten the legs of a horse or other animal to prevent straying. 2. To cozen, to trick, to cheat.

ښکيه *sh'keah*, adv. Below, beneath, under, down. 2. adj. Inferior, lower, under. See کته and ښکته

ښلونه *shalūna'h* or *Khalūna'h*, s.f. (3rd) A whitlow, a boil, a sore. Pl. يْ *ey*. See ښنزه and شيني

ښندل *shandal* or *Khandal*, verb trans. To give, to bestow, to accord, to give out, to dispense, to spend, to contribute. Pres. ښندي *shandī* or *Khandī* ; past وُ ښانده *wu-shāndah* or *wu-Khāndah* or وُ ښاندَ *wu-shānda* or *wu-Khānda* ; fut. وُ به ښندي *wu bah shandī* or *wu bah Khandī* ; imp. وُ ښنده *wu-shandah* or *wu-Khandah* ; act. part. ښندونکيَ *shandūnkaey* or *Khandūnkaey* or ښندونيَ *shandūnaey* or *Khandūnaey* ; past part. ښندليَ *shandalaey* or *Khandalaey* ; verb. n. ښندنه *shandana'h* or *Khandana'h*.

ښندنه *shandana'h* or *Khandana'h*, s.f. (3rd) (verb. n.) Giving, bestowing, conferring, granting ; bounty, gift, allowance, contribution, gratuity, etc. Pl. يْ *ey*.

ښنزه *shanza'h* or *Khanza'h*, s.f. (3rd) A boil, a sore, an abscess, a gathering. Pl. يْ *ey*. See ښلونه , نونکی , نانکي , and لوني

ښنگري *shangaraey* or *Khangaraey*, s.m. (1st) A cloven hoof, as of a bullock, sheep, goat, etc. Pl. ي *ī*.

ښنه *sh'na'h* or *Kh'na'h*, s.f. (3rd) The bone which connects the thigh bone to the spine—the os ilium. Pl. يْ *ey*.

ښوڅه *Khūtsa'h*, s.f. (3rd) A kind of rash or eruption which produces a sensation as if a worm or something of the kind was under the skin. Pl. يْ *ey*. ښوڅه ښوڅه *Khūtsa'h-Khūtsa'h*, Uncomfortable, irritating, stinging, tormenting.

ښور *shor* or *Khor*, s.m. (2nd) A bee's, hornet's, or ant's nest. Pl. ښورونه *shorūnah* or *Khorūnah*. See گربني and ميرېتون

ښورنه *shorana'h* or *Khorana'h*, s.f. (3rd) Barren or sterile land, land containing salt or nitre, hence the name. Pl. يْ *ey*. See ښوره

ښوروا *shorwā* or *Khorwā*, s f. (6th) Soup, broth (E.) Sing. and Pl. (W.) Pl. ښورواوي *shorwāwī*. See زومنه

ښوره *shora'h* or *Khora'h*, s.f. (3rd) (from P شوره) Saltpetre, nitre. Pl. يْ *ey*. See ښره

ښوريدل *shoredal* or *Khoredal*, verb intrans. To move, to shake, to wave, to wag, to vibrate, to swing, to undulate, to move backwards and forwards. Pres. ښوريږي *shorejzī* (W.) or ښوريگي *Khoregī* (E.) ; Past وُ ښوريده *wu-shoredah* or *wu-Khoredah* ; fut. وُ به ښوريږي *wu bah shorejzī* or ښوريگي *Khoregī* ; imp. وُ ښوريږه *wu-shorejzah* or وُ ښوريگه *wu-Khoregah* ; act. part. ښوريدونکيَ *shoredūnkaey* or *Khoredūnkaey* or ښوريدونيَ *shoredūnaey* or *Khoredūnaey* ; past part. ښوريدليَ *shoredalaey* or *Khoredalaey* ; verb. n. ښوريدنه *shoredana'h* or *Khoredana'h* or ښ ريده *shoredah* or *Khoredah*. ښورول *shorawul* or *Khorawul*, verb trans. To move to and fro, to move, to shake, to wave, to move from one side to the other, to make swing or undulate, to rock, to wag. Pres. ښوروي *shorawī* or *Khorawī* ; past وُ ښوراوه *wu-shorā-wuh* or *wu-Khorā-wuh* or وُ ښوراوو *wu-shorā-wo* or *wu-Khorā-wo* ; fut. وُ به ښوروي

wu bah shorawī or *Khorawī*; imp. وُ ښوروه *wu-shorawah* or *wu-Khorawah*; act. part. ښوروونکَي *shorawūnkaey* or *Khorawūnkaey* or ښوروونَي *shorawūnaey* or *Khorawūnaey*; past part. ښورولَي *shorawulaey* or *Khorawulaey*; verb. n. ښورونه *shorawuna'h* or *Khorawuna'h*.

ښوريده *shoredah* or *Khoredah*, s.m. (6th) (verb. n.) moving to and fro, waving, shaking, wagging, undulating, rocking. Sing. and Pl.; or ښوريدنه *shoredana'h* or *Khoredana'h*, s.f. (3rd) (verb. n.) Pl. ېَ *ey*.

ښونه *shona'h* or *Khona'h*, s.f. (3rd) The name of a tree, the cow tree. Pl. ېَ *ey*.

ښونګري *shongaraey* or *Khongaraey*, s.m. (1st) A cloven hoof, the hoof of a goat, sheep, or the like animal. Pl. ي *ī*. See ښنګري

ښوول *sho-wul* or *Kho-wul*, verb trans. To show, to point out, to indicate, to manifest, to exhibit, to demonstrate, to teach, to instruct. This infinitive is imperfect, and takes the present and future tenses and imperative from ښيل. Pres. ښيي *sha-yī* or *Kha-yī*; past وُ ښوو *wu-sho-wū* or *wu-Kho-wū*; fut. وُ به ښيي *wu bah sha-yī* or *wu bah Kha-yī*; imp. وُ ښيه *wu-sha-yah* or *wu-Kha-yah*; act. part. ښووونکَي *sho-wūnkaey* or *Kho-wūnkaey* or ښووونَي *sho-wūnaey* or *Kho-wūnaey*; past part. ښوولَي *sho-wulaey* or *Kho-wulaey*; verb. n. ښوونه *sho-wuna'h* or *Kho-wuna'h*. See ښيل

ښوونه *sho-wuna'h* or *Kho-wuna'h*, s.f. (3rd) (verb. n.) Indication, exposition, expression, manifestation, showing. 2. Teaching, instruction, explanation. Pl. ېَ *ey*. ښوونه کول *sho-wuna'h* or *Kho-wuna'h kawul*, verb trans. To teach, to instruct, to explain, to show, to indicate, to point out.

ښوهيدل *shwa-hedal* (W.) verb intrans. To slip, to slide, to fall, to swallow, to slip down, to be slippery. ښوهول *shwa-hawul*, verb trans. To make slip or slide, to cause to fall or stumble, to swallow, to make slippery. See ښوئيدل

ښوي *shwaey* or *Khwaey*, adj. Slippery, lubricous, smooth, glib, soapy, oily, not easily held, apt to slip away, not affording firm footing; (Fem.) ښويه *shwaya'h* or *Khwaya'h*; or ښويندار *shwayandār* or *Khwayandār*; (Fem.) ښوينداره *shwayandārah* or *Khwayandārah*; or ښويند *shwayand* or *Khwayand*; (Fem.) ښوينده *shwayanda'h* or *Khwayanda'h*. ښوينده زمکه *shwayanda'h* or *Khwayanda'h z'maka'h*, s.f. (3rd) Slippery ground. Pl. ېَ *ey*. ښوي والَي *shwaey-wālaey* or *Khwaey-wālaey* or ښويند والَي *shwayand-wālaey* or *Khwayand-wālaey*, s.m. (1st) Smoothness, slipperiness, lubricity, glibness, soapiness, oiliness, etc. Pl. والي *wālī*.

ښوئيدل *shwa-yedal* or *Khwa-yedal*, verb intrans. To slip, to slide, to fall, to slip down, to glide, to move along the surface of anything, to become lubricous, smooth, slippery, etc. Pres. ښوئيږي *shwa-yejzī* (W.) or ښوئيکي *Khwa-yegī* (E.); past وُ ښوئيده *wu-shwa-yedah* or *wu-Khwa-yedah* or وُ ښوئيدِ *wu-shwa-yeda* or *wu-Khwa-yeda*; fut. وُ به ښوئيږي *wu bah shwa-yejzī* or وُ به ښوئيکي *wu bah Khwa-yegī*; imp. وُ ښوئيږه *wu-shwa-yejzah* or وُ ښوئيکه *wu-Khwa-yegah*; act. part. ښوئيدونکَي *shwa-yedūnkaey* or *Khwa-yedūnkaey* or ښوئيدونَي *shwa-yedūnaey* or *Khwa-yedūnaey*; past part. ښوئيدلَي *shwa-yedalaey* or *Khwa-yedalaey*; verb. n. ښوئيدنه *shwa-yedana'h* or *Khwa-yedana'h* or ښوئيده *shwa yedah* or *Khwa-yedah*. ښويول *shwa-yawul* or *Khwa-yawul*, verb trans. To thrust along by slipping, to slide or slip along, to cause to, or make, slip or slide, to glide, to thrust along the surface of anything, to make slippery, smooth, lubricous. Pres. ښويوي *shwa-yawī* or *Khwa-yawī*; past وُ ښوياوه *wu-shwa-yāwuh* or *wu-Khwa-yāwuh* or وُ ښوياوو *wu-shwa-yāwo* or *wu-Khwa-yāwo*; fut. وُ به ښويوي *wu bah shwa-yawī* or *wu bah Khwa-yawī*; imp. وُ ښويوه *wu-shwa-yawah* or *wu-Khwa-yawah*; act. part. ښويوونکَي *shwa-yawūnkaey* or *Khwa-yawūnkaey* or ښويوونَي *shwa-yawūnaey* or *Khwa-yawūnaey*; past part. ښويولَي *shwa-yawulaey* or *Khwa-yawulaey*; verb. n. ښويونه *shwa-yawana'h* or *Khwa-yawana'h*.

ښه *shæh* (W.) or *Khæh* (E.) adj. (Sing. and Pl.) Good, pleasant, well, fair, fit, proper, choice, fine, rare, prime, sound, healthy, beneficial, valuable, advantageous, etc. 2. interj. Good! right! (Fem.) ښه *sha'h* or *Kha'h*. Pl. ښې *shey* or *Khey*, ښه کيدل *shæh kedal* (W.) or *Khæh kedal* (E.) verb intrans. To become good, beneficial, advantageous, precious, valuable, propitious, sound, choice, nice, fine, superior, excellent, serviceable, etc. ښه کول *shæh* or *Khæh kawul*, verb trans. To confer benefit, to render or make beneficial, good, advantageous, valuable, sound, choice, excellent or serviceable, to improve, to repair, to correct, to rectify, etc. ښه آواز *shæh* or *khæh āwāz*, A sweet or pleasant sound. ښه بوي *shæh* or *Khæh bū-e*, A pleasant smell. ښه تيږه *sha'h te-jza'h* or ښه تيګه *Kha'h tega'h*, A good or serviceable stone. ښه تولي *shæh* or *Khæh ttolaey*, Good company. ښه جوړ *shæh* or *Khæh jorr*, Very well, in very good health. ښه خبر *shæh* or *Khæh khabar*, good news, glad tidings. ښه خبره *sha'h* or *Kha'h khabara'h*, A good saying, a fine speech. ښه زړه *shæh* or *khæh-z'rrah*, A good heart. ښه زړي *shæh* or *Khæh-z'rraey*, adj. Good-hearted; (Fem.) ښه زړې *sha'h* or *kha'h-zrri*. Pl. (Masc. and Fem.) ي *ī*. ښه ساعت *shæh* or *Khæh-sā-æat*, Prosperity. ښه سړي *shæh* or *Khæh-sarracy*, A good man. ښه ښځه *sha'h* or *Kha'h shadza'h* or *Khadza'h*, A good or virtuous woman. ښه ښکار *shæh-sh'kār* or *Khæh-Kh'kār*, Good sport, etc.

ښهر *shæhr* or *Khæhr*, s.m. (2nd) (from P شهر) A city, a town. Pl. ښهرونه *shæhrūnah* or *Khæhrūnah*. د ښهر آستوګي *da shæhr* or *Khæhr āstoge-aey*, adj. as s.m. (1st) A townsman, a resident of a town. Pl. ي *ī*. د ښهر آستوګيې *da shæhr* or *Khæhr āstoge-ya'ī*, s.f. (6th) A townswoman, a woman of a town. Sing. and Pl.

ښي *shaey* (W.) or *Khaey* (E.) adj. Right, not left; (Fem.) ښۍ *sha'ī* or *Kha'ī*. ښي لاس *shaey* or *Khaey lās*, The right hand. په ښي لاس *pah shaey* or *Khaey lās*, On the right hand, at the right hand. ښي طرف *shaey* or *Khaey taraf* or ښي لور *shaey* or *Khaey-lor*, The right side or towards the right. په ښي لور *pah shaey* or *Khaey lor*, or په ښي طرف *pah shey* or *Khaey taraf*, At the right side, or on the right side. ښي و کينړ *shaey-ow-kīrrn* or *Khaey-ow-kīrrn*, Right and left, all around, on both, or on all sides.

ښيره *shera'h* or *Khera'h*, s.f. (3rd) Imprecation, curse, ill-wish, execration, denunciation, ban, abuse. Pl. ي *ey*. ښيره کول *shera'h* or *Khera'h kawul*, verb trans. To curse, to accurse, to imprecate, to abuse, to scold, to execrate. See ښرا

ښيښه *shī-sha'h* or *Khī-Kha'h*, s.f. (3rd) A bottle, a phial, glass in general, a glass. Pl. ي *ey* (from P شيشه). ښيښه ګر *shī-sha'h-gar* or *Khī-Kha'h-gar*, s.m. (5th) A glass maker. Pl. ښيښه ګران *shī-sha'h garān* or *Khī-Kha'h-garān*; or s.m. (6th). Pl. ښيښه ګر *shī-sha'h* or *Khī-Kha'h gær*.

ښيګړه *she-garra'h* or *Khe-garra'h*, s.f. (3rd) Goodness, excellence, value, worth, estimation, preciousness, kindness. 2. Profit, advantage, success, etc. Pl. ي *ey*. Also ښګړه *shigarra'h* or *Khigarra'h*, and ښيګړي *she-garracy* or *Khe-garracy*, s.m. (1st). Pl. ي *ī*. ښيګړه کول *she-garra'h* or *Khe-garra'h kawul*, verb trans. To benefit, to produce good, to show kindness towards, to profit.

ښيل *sha-yal* or *Kha-yal*, verb trans. To show, to point out, to indicate, to manifest, to demonstrate, to exhibit, to teach, to instruct, etc. This infinitive is imperfect, and its tenses, as many as there are, are used to complete the infinitive ښوول, which is imperfect also. It is peculiar to the Khattak tribe. Pres. ښيي *sha-yī* or *Kha-yī*; fut. و به ښيي *wu bah sha-yī* or *Kha-yī*; imp. و ښيه *wu-sha-yah* or *wu-Kha-yah*. The other inflections are wanting. See ښوول

ښيل *sha-yal* or *Kha-yal*, verb trans. To reject, to exclude, to repudiate, to black-ball, used with reference to a disobedient child. Pres. ښيي *s͟ha-yī* or *K͟ha-yī*; past وُ ښايه *wu-s͟hāyah* or *wu-K͟hāyah*; fut. وُ به ښيي *wu bah s͟ha-yī* or *K͟ha-yī*; imp. وُ ښيه *wu-s͟hayah* or *wu-K͟hayah*; act. part. ښيونكيَ *s͟ha-yūnkaey* or *K͟ha-yūnkaey* or ښيونيَ *s͟ha-yūnaey* or *K͟ha-yūnaey*; past part. ښيليَ *s͟ha-yalaey* or *K͟ha-yalaey*; verb. n. ښينه *s͟ha-yana'h* or *K͟ha-yana'h*.

ښيليَ *s͟ha-yalaey* or *K͟ha-yalaey*, adj. Rejected, repelled, repudiated, excluded, black-balled, as a son or a daughter for disobedience or misconduct to a parent or a teacher; (Fem.) ښيلِ *s͟ha-yali* or *K͟ha-yali*. Pl. (Masc. and Fem.) ي *ī*.

ښينه *s͟hena'h* or *K͟hena'h*, s.f. (3rd) A wife's sister, a sister-in-law. Pl. ې *ey*; also خوښينه *k͟hūs͟hīna'h* or *k͟hūK͟hīna'h*, s.f. (3rd). Pl. ې *ey*.

ښيوه *s͟hewa'h* or *K͟hewa'h*, s.f. (3rd) Ornament, dress, embellishment, decoration, etc. 2. Amorous looks. Pl. ې *ey*.

ص

ص *ṣad*, called صاد مهمله and صاد غير منقوطه, the fourteenth letter of the Arabic alphabet, does not properly occur in the Pus͟hto more than in the Persian tongue; but as a number of Arabic words have been adopted into the language from time to time, it is now generally considered one of the letters of the Pus͟hto alphabet, in which it stands twenty-fourth. It has no corresponding letter in the Sanskrit. The pronunciation is hardly distinguished from that of س in this language, but by the Arabs it is sounded as *ss* with a mixture of *w*. It also stands for 90 according to the *abjad*.

A صابر *ṣā-bir*, adj. (act. part. of صبر) Patient, long suffering; (Fem.) صابره *ṣā-bira'h*.

A صابون *ṣā-būn*, s.m. (6th) Soap. Sing. and Pl.

A صاحب *ṣā-ḥib*, s.m. (5th) (act. part. of صحبت) A lord, a master, a companion (in composition). A possessor, possessed of, endowed with, etc. Pl. صاحبان *ṣā-ḥibān*. صاحب د اختيار *ṣā-ḥib da ik͟htiyār*, Possessed of authority, free in action, possessing the option. صاحب د اعتبار *ṣā-ḥib da iætibār*, Worthy of confidence, trustworthy, possessed of credit. صاحب خانه *ṣā-ḥib-i-k͟hānah*, Master of the house, the host. صاحب زاده *ṣā-ḥib-zādah*, Genteelly born, a gentleman. صاحب غرض *ṣā-ḥib-i-g͟haraẓ*, Selfish, designing. صاحب عقل *ṣā-ḥib-i-æaḳl*, Intelligent, wise. صاحب كمال *ṣā-ḥib-i-kamāl*, adj. Perfect, excellent. صاحب عزت *ṣā-ḥib-i-æizzat*, adj. Powerful, honorable, possessed of grandeur, power, etc. صاحب ولايت *ṣā-ḥib-i-wilāyat*, A saint, a holy man.

صاحبه *ṣā-ḥiba'h*, s.f. (3rd) A lady, a mistress. Pl. ې *ey*.

A صاخه *ṣā-k͟ha'h*, s.f. (3rd) A sound which grates or stuns the ear, discord. 2. A calamity. 3. The day of judgment. Pl. ې *ey*.

A صادر *ṣā-dir*, adj. (act. part. of صدر) Proceeding, produced, derived, happened, arrived, passed, issued, etc.; (Fem.) صادره *ṣā-dira'h*. صادر كيدل *ṣā-dir kedal*, verb intrans. To proceed, to be produced, to be derived, to issue, to emerge, to happen. صادر كول *ṣā-dir kawul*, verb trans. To make to happen, to make or cause to issue, or arrive.

A صادق *ṣā-diḳ*, adj. (act. part. of صدق) Just, true, sincere; (Fem.) صادقه *ṣā-diḳa'h*.

A صاف *ṣāf*, adj. (act. part. of صفو) Clean, pure, clear, innocent, candid, downright, frank; (Fem.) صافه *ṣā-fa'h*. صافي *ṣā-fī*, s.f. (3rd) Cleanness, purity, clearness, innocency, candor, sincerity. Pl. ئي *a'ī*.

صافي *sā-fī*, s.f. (5th) A strainer, a filter. Pl. صافيگاني *ṣāfī-gāni* or صافيگان *ṣāfī-gānī*.

صافيدل *ṣāfedal*, verb intrans. To become clean, clear, purified, candid. صافول *ṣāfawul*, verb trans. To cleanse, to clean, to purify, to render innocent, candid. See پاك

صالح *ṣā-liḥ*, adj. (act. part. of صلح) Good, apt, fit, proper. 2. A man of honor and probity, a sedate steady person; (Fem.) صالحه *ṣā-liḥa'h*.

A صبا *ṣa-bā*, s.m. (9th) The morning breeze. 2. To-morrow. Sing. and Pl.

A صبحَ *ṣubḥa*, s.f. (3rd) Morning, dawn of day. Pl. ئ *ey*; or (ے) *i*. صبحَ خيز *ṣubḥa k͟hez*, adj. Rising early in the morning, an early riser; (Fem.) صبحَ خيزه *ṣubḥa k͟heza'h*. صبحَ دم *ṣubḥa dam*, The dawn of day; or صبحَ صادق *ṣubḥa ṣādiḳ*. صبح كاذب *ṣubḥ-i-kāẕib*, Just before day-break.

A صبر *ṣabr*, s.m. (9th) Patience, endurance, long-suffering. Sing. and Pl. صبر كول *ṣabr kawul*, verb trans. To wait, to endure, to bear, to have patience, to put up with.

A صحاب *ṣi-ḥāb*, s.m. (Pl. of صاحب), Companions, particularly those of the Prophet.

A صحاف *ṣaḥḥāf*, s.m. (5th) A bookbinder, a bookseller. Pl. صحافان *ṣaḥḥāfān*. صحافي *ṣaḥḥāfī*, s.f. (3rd) The business of a bookbinder. Pl. ئي *a'ī*. صحافي كول *ṣaḥḥāfī kawul*, verb trans. To carry on the business of bookbinding.

A صحبت *ṣuḥbat*, s.m. (2nd) Companionship, society. 2. Coition, cohabitation. Pl. صحبتونه *ṣuḥbat-ūnah*. صحبتي *ṣuḥbatī*, s.m. (5th) A comrade, a companion, an associate. Pl. صحبتيان *ṣuḥbatī-ān*. صحبتئ *ṣuḥbata'ī*, s.f. (6th) A female companion or friend. Sing. and Pl. صحبت كول *ṣuḥbat kawul*, verb trans. To associate, to keep company. 2. To cohabit, to copulate.

A صحت *ṣiḥhat*, s.m. (2nd) (from صح) Health, entireness, soundness, perfection, integrity, correctness. Pl. صحتونه *siḥhatūnah*.

A صحرا *ṣaḥrā*, s.f. (6th) A desert, a wilderness. (E.) Sing. and Pl. (W.) Pl. صحراوي *ṣaḥrā-wī*. صحرا نشين *ṣaḥrā nis͟hīn*, s.m. (5th) or صحرا شين *ṣaḥrā-s͟hīn* (corrup.) An inhabitant of the desert. Pl. نشينان *nis͟hīnān* or شينان *s͟hīnān*. صحرا نشينه *ṣaḥrā-nis͟hīna'h*, s.f. (3rd). Pl. ئ *ey*.

صحي *ṣaḥī*, adj. (corrup. of A صحيح) Accurate, perfect, entire, sound, certain, authentic, correct, genuine, just, pure. صحي كيدل *ṣa-ḥī kedal*, verb intrans. To become accurate, perfect, correct, entire, etc. صحي كول *ṣa-ḥī kawul*, verb trans. To correct, to make accurate, to make perfect, sound, correct, authentic, certain; to inquire, to discover, to make sure of.

صحيح *ṣaḥiḥ*, adj. (from صح) Accurate, perfect, etc.; (Fem.) صحيحه *ṣaḥīḥa'h*. See preceding.

A صداقت *ṣadāḳat*, s.m. (2nd) (from صدق) Sincerity, friendship, candor. 2. Truth, correctness, accuracy, authenticity. Pl. صداقتونه *ṣadāḳat-ūnah*. صداقت لرل *ṣadāḳat laral*, verb trans. To have or possess truth, correctness, accuracy, to have sincerity or candor (to be candid, etc., verb neut. in English).

A صدره *ṣad-ra'h*, s.f. (3rd) A party of faḳīrs or devotees who go about in bodies visiting different shrines. Pl. ئ *ey*.

A صدف *ṣadaf*, s.m. (2nd) A shell, a pearl, mother of pearl. Pl. صدفونه *ṣadaf-ūnah*. See ماهي غوږ or ماهي غوږ

A صدق *ṣidḳ*, s.m. (9th) Truth, veracity, sincerity, candor. Sing. and Pl.

A صدقه *ṣadḳa'h* or *ṣadaḳa'h*, s.f. (3rd) Alms, propitiatory offerings, sacrifice. Pl. ئ *ey*. صدقه وركول *ṣadaḳa'h war-kawul*, verb trans. To give alms.

A صديق *ṣadīḳ*, adj. Just, true, a sincere friend; (Fem.) صديقه *ṣadīḳa'h*.

A صراف *ṣarrāf*, s.m. (5th) A banker, a money-changer. Pl. صرافان *ṣarrāf-ān*. صرافي *ṣarrāfī*, s.f. (3rd) Banking, money-changing. Pl. ئي *a'ī*. صرافي كول *ṣarrāfī kawul*, verb trans. To carry on banking transactions.

A صرصر *ṣar-ṣar*, s.m. (9th) A cold boisterous wind. Sing. and Pl. See سرسر

A صرف *ṣirf*, adv. Merely, purely, only, solely, alone.

A صرف *ṣarf*, s.m. (9th) Expenditure, expense. 2. Increase, gain, excess. Sing. and Pl. صرف كول *ṣarf kawul*, verb trans. To spend, to disburse, to expend, to employ. صرف كيدل *ṣarf kedal*, verb intrans. To be expended, to be disbursed, to be spent.

A صرفه *ṣarfa'h*, s.f. (3rd) Expense, expending.

2. Profusion, profit, utility, surplus, redundancy, addition. Pl. ي *ey.* صرفه كول *ṣarfa'h kawul*, verb trans. To keep one's expenses within bounds, to live within the means.

A صريح *ṣarīḥ*, adj. (from صرح) Evident, apparent, palpable, clear; (Fem.) صريحه *ṣarīḥa'h.*

A صف *ṣaff*, s.m. (2nd) A series, a rank, a line, a file, a row. Pl. صفونه *ṣaff-ūnah.* صف ترنه *ṣaff tarrana'h*, s.f. (3rd) Arraying, marshaling, arraying in order of battle. Pl. ي *ey.* صف ترل *saff tarral*, verb trans. To form a rank, line, row, etc; to array or marshal in order of battle.

A صفا *ṣafā*, adj. Pure, clear, clean. صفائي *ṣafāī*, s.f. (3rd) Purity, cleanness, clearness, perspicuity, innocence. Pl. ي *a'ī.* صفائي لرل *ṣafā-ī laral*, verb trans. To have purity, clearness, cleanness, etc.; (Eng., verb intrans. To be clean). صفائي كول *ṣafā-ī kawul*, verb trans. To clear, to prove innocent of any crime or fault.

A صفت *ṣifat*, s.m. (2nd) (from وصف) Praise, commendation, laud, encomium. 2. Quality, attribute. 3. Manner, description. 4. An adjective. Pl. صفتونه *ṣifatūnah.* صفت كول *ṣifat kawul*, verb trans. To praise, to commend, to laud.

A صفحه *ṣaf-ḥa'h*, s.f. (3rd) The page of a book, face, surface. Pl. ي *ey.*

A صفرا *ṣaf-rā*, s.f. (6th) The gall, bile, yellow. (E.) Sing. and Pl. (W.) Pl. صفراوي *ṣaf-rāwī.* صفرائي *ṣafrā-ī*, adj. Bilious. (Masc. and Fem.)

صفره *ṣafar-a'h*, s.f. (3rd) (from صفر A) The second month of the Muḥammadan year. Pl. ي *ey.*

P صفشكن *ṣaf-shikan*, s.m. (5th) A blunderbuss. Pl. صفشكنان *ṣaf-shikanān.*

صلحه *ṣulha'h*, s.f. (3rd) (from صلح A) Peace, reconciliation, treaty, truce, concord. Pl. ي *ey.* صلحه كول *ṣulḥa'h kawul*, verb trans. To make peace, to reconcile, to make a treaty or truce. صلحه نامه *ṣulḥa'h nāmah*, s.f. (3rd) A bond of peace, a treaty of peace. Pl. ي *ey.*

A صلوة *ṣalāt*, s.m. (2nd) Prayer, benediction. 2. Compassion or mercy of God. Pl. صلوتونه *ṣalātūnah.*

A صندل *ṣandal*, s.m. (6th) Sandal, sanders. Sing. and Pl.

A صندوق *ṣandūḳ*, s.m. (5th) A box, a trunk, a coffer, a coffin, a chest. Pl. صندوقان *ṣandūḳān.* صندوقچه *ṣandūḳcha'h*, s.f. (3rd) A small box or coffer. Pl. ي *ey.*

A صنف *ṣinf*, s.m. (2nd) Species, kind, sort, genus. Pl. صنفونه *ṣinf-ūnah.*

A صنوبر *ṣano-bar*, s.m. (6th) Fir, pine, any cone-bearing tree. Sing. and Pl.

A صواب *ṣawāb*, s.m. (2nd) Rectitude, success, a virtuous action, truth, the right. Pl. صوابونه *ṣawābūnah.* د صواب لوري *da ṣawāb loraey*, The path of rectitude or truth.

صوبه *ṣūba'h*, s.f. (3rd) A province. Pl. ي *ey.* صوبه دار *ṣūba'h-dār*, s.m. (5th) A viceroy, the lieutenant or governor of a province. Pl. صوبه داران *ṣūba'h-dārān.* صوبه داري *ṣūba'h-dārī*, s.f. (3rd) The office of a lieutenant of a province. Pl. ي *a'ī.*

A صورت *ṣūrat*, s.m. (2nd) (inf. II of صار) Form, figure, face, shape, countenance, fashion, appearance, portrait. 2. Manner, condition, state, case, circumstance. Pl. صورتونه *ṣūrat-ūnah.* صورت حال *ṣūrat-i-ḥāl*, s.m. (2nd) A written declaration, a statement. Pl. صورت حالونه *ṣūrat-ḥālūnah.*

A صوفي *ṣūfī*, adj. Wise, pious, devout, spiritual. 2. s.m. (5th) A man of the Ṣūfī order of monks. Pl. صوفيان *ṣūfī-ān.*

A صياد *ṣai-yād*, s.m. (5th) A hunter, a fowler, a fisherman. Pl. صيادان *ṣai-yādān.* صيادي *ṣai-yādī*, s.f. (3rd) Hunting, fowling, shooting. Pl. ي *a'ī.* صيادي كول *ṣai-yādī kawul*, verb trans. To hunt, to fowl, to shoot.

A صيد *ṣaid*, s.m. (2nd) Game, prey, any animal hunted or fished for. Pl. صيدونه *ṣaid-ūnah.* صيد گاه *ṣaid-gāh*, s.m. (2nd) A place for game, a chase, a preserve. Pl. صيد گاهونه *ṣaid-gāh-ūnah.*

A صيقل *ṣai-ḳal*, s.m. (2nd) (from صقل) Polishing, polish, cleaning, furbishing. 2. An instrument for polishing. Pl. صيقلونه *ṣai-ḳalūnah.* صيقل كول *ṣai-ḳal kawul,* verb trans. To polish, to furbish, to burnish. صيقل گر *ṣai-ḳal gar,* s.m. (5th) An armourer, a polisher, a furbisher. Pl. صيقل گرُ *ṣai-ḳal-gær* or صيقل گران *ṣai-ḳal-garān.* صيقل شوَي *ṣai-ḳal shawaey,* adj. (past part.) Polished, bright, burnished; (Fem.) صيقل شو *ṣai-ḳal shawi.* Pl. (Masc. and Fem.) ي *ī.*

ض

ض *ẓad,* called ضاد معجمه and ضاد منقوطه, the fifteenth letter of the Arabic, is only used in Pushto with words adopted into it from the former language. Its pronunciation is hardly distinguished from that of ز, but the correct sound, is composed of *d, th,* and *w,* which is only to be acquired from an Arab mouth. This letter has no corresponding sound in Sanskrit, and stands twenty-fifth letter in the Pushto alphabet. According to the *abjad* system of numerals it denotes 800.

A ضابط *ẓā-biṭ,* s.m. (6th) (act. part. of ضبط), A governor, a master, a possessor, a restrainer. Sing. and Pl. ضابطه *ẓā-biṭa'h,* s.f. (3rd). Pl. ې *ey.* ضابطه *ẓā-biṭa'h,* s.f. (3rd) Canon, ordinance, regulation, rule, law. Pl. ې *ey.* بې ضابطه *bey-ẓā-biṭah,* adj. Illegal, unlawful, against rule or regulation.

A ضامن *ẓā-min,* s.m. (5th) (act. part. of ضمن), A surety, a sponsor, a bondsman, bond, security, bail. Pl. ضامنان *ẓā-minān.* ضامني *ẓā-minī,* s.f. (3rd) Surety, bail. Pl. ئي *a'ī.*

A ضايع *ẓā-īæ,* adj. (act. part. of ضيع), Lost, destroyed, fruitless, abortive, perished, gone to the dogs. ضايع كول *ẓā-īæ kawul,* verb trans. To lose, to destroy, to consume.

A ضبط *ẓabṭ,* s.m. (9th) Confiscation, sequestration, taking possession, seizing. 2. Check, control, possession. Sing. and Pl. 3. adj. Confiscated, sequestered, seized. ضبط كيدل *ẓabṭ kedal,* verb intrans. To be taken possession of, to be confiscated, sequestered. ضبط كول *ẓabṭ kawul,* verb trans. To confiscate, to sequester, to seize, to take possession of. ضبطي *ẓabṭī,* adj. Anything sequestered or confiscated. (Masc. and Fem.)

A ضحا *ẓu-ḥā,* s.m. (6th) That part of the day between sunrise and meridian, the brightest part of the day. 2. A prayer repeated at this time. Sing. and Pl.

A ضد *ẓidd,* s.m. (6th) The contrary, the opposite, contrariety, opposition. Sing. and Pl. 2. adj. Contrary, opposed, at enmity; (Fem.) ضده *ẓidda'h.* ضد كول *ẓidd kawul,* verb trans. To persist, to persevere, to contradict, to spite. ضديت *ẓidd-iyat,* s.m. (2nd) Spite, contrariety, opposition, perversity. Pl. ضديتونه *ẓidd-iyatūnah.* ضدي *ẓiddī,* adj. Perverse, contrary, spiteful. (Masc. and Fem.)

A ضرب *ẓarb,* s.m. (2nd) A blow, beating. 2. Violence. 3. Striking, emphasis. 4. Stamping, coining. Pl. ضربونه *ẓarbūnah.* 5. adj. Struck, coined. ضرب رسول *ẓarb rasawul,* verb trans. To injure, to show violence towards. ضرب وهل *ẓarb wahal,* verb trans. To stamp, to coin. ضرابي *ẓarābī,* s.m. (5th) A coiner. Pl. ضرابيان *ẓarābīān.* ضراب خانه *ẓarāb khāna'h,* s.f. (3rd) A mint. Pl. ې *ey.*

A ضرر *ẓarar,* s.m. (2nd) Injury, damage, detriment, loss, ruin. 2. Anguish, affliction. Pl. ضررونه *ẓarar-ūnah.* ضرر رسول *ẓarar rasawul,* verb trans. To injure, to ruin, to cause detriment or injury to any one. 2. To afflict.

A ضرور *ẓarūr,* adj. (from ضر) Necessary, expedient, unavoidable; (Fem.) ضروره *ẓarūra'h.* جاي ضرور *jā-ey-ẓarūr,* The necessary.

A ضرورت *ẓarūrat,* s.m. (2nd) Necessity, exigence, want, indigence. 2. Force, violence, compulsion, restraint. Pl. ضرورتونه *ẓarūrat-ūnah.* ضروري *ẓarūrī,* adj. Necessary, unavoidable. (Masc. and Fem.)

A ضعف *ẓaæf* or *ẓuæf,* s.m. (9th) Weakness, infirmity, imbecility of body or mind. Sing. and Pl.

A ضعيف *ẓa-æīf,* adj. Weak, feeble, infirm, impotent, emaciated, frail, old; (Fem.) ضعيفه *za-æīfa'h.* ضعيفي *za-æīfi*, s.f. (3rd) Weakness, emaciation, infirmness, inpotency. Pl. ئ *a'ī.*

ضلعه *zil-æa'h*, s.f. (3rd) (corrup. of A ضلع) A district, a division. Pl. ي *ey.*

A ضماد *zamād*, s.m. (2nd) A plaster, a cataplasm, an embrocation, a bandage for a wound. Pl. ضمادونه *zamād-ūnah.* See تكور

A ضمانت *zamānat*, s.m. (2nd) Security, bail, surety. Pl. ضمانتونه *zamānat-ūnah.* ضمانت آخستل *zamānat ākhistal*, verb trans. To take bail or security, to release on bail. ضمانت وركول *zamānat war-kawul*, verb trans. To give security, to furnish bail; or ضامن وركول *zāmin war-kawul*, verb trans. To give a security or surety.

A ضمن *zimn*, s.m. (9th) Contents, anything comprehended, contained or inserted, a subject, an idea, a conception. 2. Suretyship, an obligation. 3. Aid, favour. Sing. and Pl. ضمناً *zimnan*, adv. Comprehensively, by the way, tacitly, by-the-bye.

A ضيافت *zī-āfat*, s.m. (2nd) A feast, a banquet, entertainment, hospitality, invitation. Pl. ضيافتونه *zī-āfatūnah.* ضيافت كول *zī-āfat kawul*, verb trans. To feast, to treat, to entertain.

ط

ط *to-ey*, or in Arabic *tā*, called طاي مهمله or طاي غير منقوطه, the sixteenth letter of the Arabic, stands twenty-sixth in the Pushto alphabet. It is only used with Arabic words introduced into the latter language, and has no equivalent in Sanskrit. Its real sound is much stronger and harsher than that of ت. According to the system of letters for numerals it stands for 9.

A طابوت *tā-būt*, s.m. (2nd) A bier. Pl. طابوتونه *tā-būtūnah.*

A طاعت *tā-æat*, s.m. (2nd) Devotion, obedience, obsequiousness. Pl. طاعتونه *tā-æatūnah.* طاعت كول *tā-æat kawul*, verb trans. To obey, to pay obedience unto, to show devotion.

A طاق *tāk*, s.m. (2nd) A cupola, an arch, an arched building. Pl. طاقونه *tākūnah.* 2. adj. Unique, singular, odd, not even; (Fem.) طاقه *tāka'h.* جفت و طاق *juft-o-tāk*, The game of even and odd. طاقچه *tāk-chah*, s.f. (3rd) A recess in the wall, a niche, a shelf. Pl. ي *ey.* Also (corrup.) طاخچه *tākh-cha'h.*

A طاقت *tā-kat*, s.m. (2nd) Strength, power, ability, force. Pl. طاقتونه *tā-katūnah.* طاقت لرل *tā-kat laral*, verb trans. To have power, strength, force, ability, etc. طاقت كول *tā-kat kawul*, verb trans. To have patience, to endure (fig.), to put up with.

P A طاقي *tā-kī*, adj. Arched, made with an arch or niche.

A طالب *tā-lib*, s.m. (5th) Asking, demanding, interrogating; an inquirer, a seeker, an asker, a candidate, a lover. Pl. طالبان *tā-lib-ān.* طالب دنيا *tā-lib-i-dun-yā*, adj. Worldly minded. طالب العلم *tā-lib-ul-æilm*, adj. Searching after knowledge, a student; (Fem.) طالب العلمه *tā-lib-ul-æilma'h*, A female student.

طالبه *tā-liba'h*, s.f. (3rd) A mare seeking the male. Pl. ي *ey.*

A طالع *tā-liæ*, s.m. (9th) (act. part. of طلع) Rising (as the sun), appearing. Sing. and Pl. طالع مند *tā-liæ mand* or طالع من *tā-liæ-man*, adj. Fortunate, prosperous, wealthy; (Fem.) منده *manda'h* or منه *mana'h.* طالع مندي *tā-liæ-mandī*, s.f. (3rd) Prosperity, fortune, wealth. Pl. ئ *a'ī.*

A طاؤس *tā-ūs*, s.m. (5th) A peacock. Pl. طاؤسان *tā-ūsān.*

A طايفه *tā-īfa'h*, s.f. (3rd) People, tribe, a troop, a band; suit, equipage. Pl. ي *ey.* See طلفه

A طب *tibb*, s.m. (9th) Medicine. 2. Magic. Sing. and Pl. طبابت *tabābat*, s.m. (2nd) The science or practice of medicine. Pl. طبابتونه *tabābat-ūnah.*

A طباشير *tabā-shīr*, s.m. (2nd) The sugar of the bamboo. Sing. and Pl.

طبعه *ṭabæa'h*, s.f. (3rd) (corrup. of A طبع) Nature, genius, temperament, quality, disposition. Pl. ي *ey*. خوش طبعه *khūsh ṭabæa'h*, adj. Good-natured, benevolent. تيز طبعه *tez ṭabæa'h*, adj. Capricious, whimsical, fantastic. 2. Ready-witted, ingenious. طبعي *ṭabæī*, adj. Innate, natural. (Masc. and Fem.)

A طبل *ṭabl*, s.m. (2nd) A drum. Pl. طبلونه *ṭablūnah*. طبله *ṭabla'h*, s.f. (3rd) A small tambourine. 2. A wooden dish, or large platter, generally of painted wood, for fruits, perfumes, etc. Pl. ي *ey*.

A طبيب *ṭabib*, s.m. (5th) (adj. v. from طب), A physician. Pl. طبيبان *ṭabīb-ān*. طبيبي *ṭabībī*, s.f. (3rd) The business of a physician, the practice of physic. Pl. ئي *a'ī*.

A طبيعت *ṭabī-æat*, s.m. (2nd) (from طبع), Genius, nature, disposition, constitution, temperament, essence, property. Pl. طبيعتونه *ṭabī-æatūnah*.

A طبيله *ṭabela'h*, s.f. (3rd) A stable. Pl. ي *ey*.

طرحه *ṭar-ḥa'h*, s.f. (3rd) (A طرح) Manner, mode. 2. Position, establishment. Pl. ي *ey*. طرحه په طرحه *ṭar-ḥa'h pah ṭar-ḥa'h*, Various sorts, different descriptions. (A طرح.)

A طرز *ṭarz*, s.m. (2nd) Manner, mode, form. Pl. طرزونه *ṭarzūnah*.

A طرف *ṭaraf* or *ṭarf*, s.m. (2nd) Side, margin, corner, quarter, extremity, towards. Pl. طرفونه *ṭaraf-ūnah*. See لور and خوا

P طرفدار *ṭaraf-dār*, s.m. (5th) A follower, a partizan, a sectary, an assistant, an aider. Pl. طرفداران *ṭaraf-dārān*. 2. adj. Partial; (Fem.) طرفداره *ṭaraf-dāra'h*. طرفداري *ṭaraf-dārī*, s.f. (3rd) Partiality, favour, assistance, following, etc. Pl. ئي *a'ī*. طرفداري كول *ṭaraf-dārī kawul*, verb trans. To favour, to assist, to show partiality towards.

A طرفين *ṭarafain* or *ṭarfain*, s.m. (6th) (dual of طرف), Both sides, both parties.

A طريقه *ṭarīḳa'h*, s.f. (3rd) Way, path, road. 2. Manner, custom, fashion. 3. Rite, religion. Pl. ي *ey*. Also طريقت *ṭarīḳat*, s.m. (2nd). Pl. طريقتونه *ṭarīḳatūnah*.

طراق طراق *ṭrrāḳ ṭrrāḳ*, A tapping, knocking, rapping, etc. طراق طراق كول *ṭrrāḳ-ṭrrāḳ kawul*, verb trans. To tap, to knock (as at a door, etc.) See تراق

P طشت *ṭasht*, s.m. (2nd) A large basin, a bowl, a cup, an ewer. Pl. طشتونه *ṭashtūnah*.

A طعام *ṭa-æām*, s.m. (2nd) (from طعم) Victuals, food. 2. Eating. Pl. طعامونه *ṭa-æāmūnah*. See خوارۀ and خوراك

A طعنه *ṭa-æna'h*, s.f. (3rd) Taunting, reproach, gibe, scoff, ignominy, disgrace, aspersion. Pl. ي *ey*. طعنه وركول *ṭa-æna'h war-kawul*, verb trans. To taunt, to reproach, to gibe, to asperse.

A طغيان *ṭugh-yān*, s.m. (2nd) (from طغي) Rebellion, sedition, insolence, perverseness. Pl. طغيانونه *ṭugh-yānūnah*. طغياني *ṭugh-yānī*, s.f. (3rd) Excess, deluge, inundation, overflowing. Pl. ئي *a'ī*.

A طفل *ṭifl*, s.m. (5th) An infant, a child, a young animal. Pl. طفلان *ṭiflān*. طفله *ṭifla'h*, s.f. (3rd) A female infant. Pl. ي *ey*. طفوليت *ṭufūliyat*, s.m. (2nd) Infancy, childhood. Pl. طفوليتونه *ṭufūliyat-ūnah*.

طفه *ṭafa'h*, s.f. (3rd) A people, a tribe, a troop, a band, a bevy, a concourse. Pl. ي *ey*. See طايفه

A طفيل *ṭufail*, s.m. (2nd) A parasite, one who accompanies a guest to a feast, although uninvited. Pl. طفيلونه *ṭufailūnah*. 2. adv. By the means, through. طفيلي *ṭufailī*, adj. Parasitical, sponging.

P طلا *ṭilā*, s.f. (6th) Gold, a gold coin brought from Bokhārā, in value about thirteen shillings. (E.) Sing. and Pl. (W.) Pl. طلاوي *ṭilāwī*.

A طلاق *ṭalāḳ*, s.m. (2nd) (from طلق) Divorce, repudiation. Pl. طلاقونه *ṭalāḳūnah*. طلاقيدل *ṭalāḳedal*, verb intrans. To become divorced, or repudiated (as a wife). طلاقول *ṭalāḳawul*, verb trans. To repudiate, to divorce. طلاقه *ṭalāḳa'h*, s.f. (3rd) A divorced woman. Pl. ي *ey*.

A طلب *ṭalab*, s.m. (2nd) Pay, wages, salary.

2. Desire, wish, search, demand, request, inquiry, sending for, summons. 2. Seeking, requiring. Pl. طلبونه *ṭalabūnah.* طلبيدل *ṭalabedal,* verb intrans. To be demanded, requested, wished for, searched after, summoned, etc. Pres. طلبيږي *ṭalabejzī* (W.) or طلبيګي *ṭalabegī* (E.); past طلب شه *ṭalab shah* or وُ شه *wu-shah*; fut. طلب به شي *ṭalab bah shī* or به وُ شي *bah wu-shī*; imp. طلب شه *ṭalab shah* or وُ شه *wu-shah*; act. part. طلبيدونکَي *ṭalabedūnkaey* or طلبيدونَي *ṭalabedūnaey*; past part. طلب شوَي *ṭalab shawaey*; verb. n. طلبيدنه *ṭalabedana'h* or طلبيده *ṭalabedah.* طلبول *ṭalabawul,* verb trans. To demand, to seek, to call, to ask for, to require, to summon. Pres. طلبوي *ṭalabawī*; past طلب کړ *ṭalab karr* or وُ کړ *wu-karr*; fut. طلب به کړي *ṭalab bah krrī* or به وُ کړي *bah wu-krrī*; imp. طلب کړه *ṭalab-krrah* or وُ کړه *wu-krrah*; act. part. طلبوونکَي *ṭalabawūnkaey* or طلبوونَي *ṭalabawūnaey*; past part. طلب کړَي *ṭalab karraey*; verb. n. طلبونه *ṭalabawuna'h.*

P A طلبدار *ṭalab-dār,* s.m. (2nd) One who receives pay, a creditor. 2. Asking, inquiring, demanding, Pl. طلبداران *ṭalab-dārān.* طلبداره *ṭalab-dāra'h,* s.f. (3rd). Pl. ې *ey.*

P طلبګار *ṭalab-gār,* s.m. (5th) A seeker; desirous. Pl. طلبګاران *ṭalab-gārān.* طلبګاره *ṭalab-gāra'h,* s.f. (3rd) Pl. ې *ey.*

A طلسم *ṭilisim,* or *ṭilisam,* s.m. (2nd) A talisman, a charm. Pl. طلسمونه *ṭilisimūnah.*

A طمع *ṭamaæ,* s.f. (1st) Avarice, greediness, avidity, covetousness. Pl. طمع *ṭamaæi.* طمع کول *ṭamaæ kawul,* verb trans. To covet, to desire.

A طناب *ṭanāb,* s.m. (2nd) A line for hanging clothes on, a tent rope. Pl. طنابونه *ṭanābūnah* or طناو *ṭanāow,* s.m. (2nd). Pl. طناوونه *ṭanāow-ūnah.*

A طواف *ṭawāf,* s.m. (2nd) (from طوف) Turning, encompassing, a pilgrimage, making the circuit of Makka or some other holy place. Pl. طوافونه *ṭawāfūnah.* طواف کول *ṭawāf kawul,* verb trans. To go on, or perform a pilgrimage.

A طور *ṭaur,* s.m. (2nd) Mode, manner, way, fashion, state, condition. Pl. طورونه *ṭaurūnah.*

H I طوطا *ṭo-ṭā,* s.m. (5th) A parrot. Pl. طوطاګان *ṭo-ṭāgān.*

P طوطي *ṭū-ṭī,* s.m. (5th) A parrot, a paroquet. Pl. طوطيان *ṭū-ṭīān.*

A طوفان *ṭū-fān,* s.m. (2nd) A deluge, an inundation. 2. The universal deluge. 3. A hurricane, a storm of wind and rain. Pl. طوفانونه *ṭū-fānūnah.* طوفاني *ṭūfānī,* adj. Stormy, tempestuous, boisterous. (Masc. and Fem.)

A طوق *ṭauḳ,* s.m. (2nd) A collar, a yoke. 2. A necklace, a ring, a chain for the neck, either as ornament or punishment. Pl. طوقونه *ṭauḳūnah.*

A طومار *ṭomār,* s.m. (2nd) A roll of paper written on, an account book, a scroll, a book. Pl. طومارونه *ṭomārūnah.*

A طي *ṭai,* s.m. (9th) (from H טוה To spin) Rolling up, folding, travelling. Sing. and Pl. طي کول *ṭai kawul,* verb trans. To constrain, to abridge, to travel.

ظ

ظ *ẓoey,* or in Arabic *ẓā,* called ظاء معجمه or ظاء منقوطه, is the seventeenth letter of the Arabic, and the twenty-seventh of the Pushto; and is only used with Arabic words introduced into the language. It has no equivalent in Sanskrit; and stands for 900 in the system of using letters for numbers.

A ظالم *ẓālim,* s.m. (5th) A tyrant, an oppressor. Pl. ظالمان *ẓālimān.* 2. adj. Tyrannical, unjust; (Fem.) ظالمه *ẓālima'h.* Also, A mistress. Pl. ې *ey.*

A ظاهر *ẓāhir,* adj. Apparent, evident, open, manifest; (Fem.) ظاهره *ẓāhira'h.* ظاهريدل *ẓāhiredal,* verb intrans. To become public or manifest, to be revealed, to be disclosed, to appear, to become evident. Pres. ظاهريږي

ẓāhirejzī (W.) or ظاهريكي ẓāhiregī (E.); past ظاهر شه ẓāhir shah or وُ شه wu-shah; fut. ظاهر به شي ẓāhir bah shī or به وُ شي bah wu-shī; imp. ظاهر شه ẓā-hir shah or وُ شه wu-shah; act. part. ظاهريدونكي ẓāhiredūnkaey or ظاهريدوني ẓāhiredūnaey; past part. ظاهر ẓāhir or ظاهر شوي ẓāhir shawaey; verb. n. ظاهريدنه ẓāhiredana'h or ظاهريده ẓāhiredah. ظاهرول ẓāhirawul, verb trans. To publish, to show, to disclose, to discover, to make known, to reveal, to exhibit, to tell, to manifest, to explain, to pretend. Pres. ظاهروي ẓā-hirawī; past ظاهر كړ ẓā-hir karr or وُ كړ wu-karr; fut. ظاهر به كړي ẓā-hir bah krrī or به وُ كړي bah wu-krrī; imp. ظاهر كړه ẓāhir krrah or وُ كړه wu-krrah; act. part. ظاهروونكي ẓāhirawūnkaey or ظاهرووني ẓā-hirawūnaey; past part. ظاهر كړي ẓā-hir karraey; verb. n. ظاهرونه ẓā-hirawuna'h.

ظاهري ẓā-hirī, adj. Apparent, external. (Masc. and Fem.) ظاهراً ẓā-hiran, adv. Outwardly, apparently, openly, publicly, manifestly, evidently, seemingly, plainly.

A ظرف ẓarf, s.m. (2nd) A vase, a vessel. Pl. ظرفونه ẓarfūnah. See لوښي

A ظفر ẓafar, s.m. (2nd) Victory. Pl. ظفرونه ẓafarūnah. ظفر طراز ẓafar ṭarāz, adj. Victorious, conquering.

A ظلم ẓulm, s.m. (2nd) Injustice, oppression, tyranny, injury, violence. Pl. ظلمونه ẓulm-ūnah. ظلم رسيده ẓulm-rasīdah, adj. Oppressed, injured. ظلم كول ẓulm kawul, verb trans. To oppress, to tyrannize over, to practice injustice or violence.

A ظلمت ẓulmat, s.m. (2nd) Darkness. Pl. ظلمتونه ẓulmat-ūnah.

A ظن ẓann, s.m. (9th) Suspicion, jealousy, opinion. Sing. and Pl.

ع

ع æin, called عين غير منقوطه or عين مهمله, the eighteenth letter of the Arabic, and the twenty-eighth of the Pushto, only occurs in Arabic words adopted into the language, and has no similar sound in the Sanskrit. It is one of the guttural letters, and is formed in the lower part of the throat, by a compression of the fauces, and may be written and sounded as æ in English. It stands for 70 in the Arabic *abjad* system of substituting letters for numbers.

A عابد æābid, s.m. (5th) (act. part. of عبد), An adorer, a worshipper, a votary, a devotee. Pl. عابدان æābidān. عابده æābida'h, s.f. (3rd) Pl. ې ey.

A عاجز æā-jiz, adj. (act. part. of عجز) Exhausted, unable, weak, humble, dejected, hopeless, impotent; (Fem.) عاجزه æā-jiza'h. عاجزي æā-jizī, s.f. (3rd) Weakness, dejection, hopelessness, humility. Pl. ئي a'ī. عاجزي كول æā-jizī kawul, verb trans. To implore, to beseech, to entreat, to supplicate.

A عادت æādat, s.m. (2nd) (from عود), Habit, custom, usage, practice. Pl. عادتونه æādat-ūnah. عادت كول æādat kawul, گرزول garz-awul or نيول nī-wal, verb trans. To adopt a habit or practice, to introduce a custom or usage, to accustom, etc.

عادت لرل æādat laral, verb trans. To hold any habit, custom, or usage, to be wont, to be in the habit of, to be habitual (Eng. verb intrans.)

P A عادتي æādatī, adj. Accustomed, habituated. 2. A catamite. (Masc. and Fem.)

A عادل æā-dil, adj. (act. part. of عدل) Just, equitable, impartial; (Fem.) عادله æā-dila'h.

A عار æār, s.m. (9th) (from عري) Bashfulness, modesty. 2. Ignominy, disgrace, reproach, shame. Sing. and Pl.

A عارف æā-rif, adj. (act. part. of عرف) Wise, ingenious, sagacious, pious, devout. 2. A holy man; (Fem.) عارفه æā-rifa'h.

A عاري æā-rī, adj. Naked, void of, free from.

A عاريت æā-rīyat, s.m. (2nd) (from عور) Borrowing or lending anything which is itself again to be returned. به عاريت آخستل

pah æā-rīyat ākkhistal, verb trans. To borrow. په عاريت وركول *pah æā-rīyat war-kawul*, verb trans. To lend. عاريتي *æā-rīyatī*, adj. Borrowed, lent. 2. Not one's own, factitious, (Masc. and Fem.) عاريتاً *æā-rīyatan*, By way of a loan.

A عازم *æā-zim*, adj. (act. part. of عزم) Applying one's mind or powers to any undertaking, intending, determining, resolved on, bound up in.

A عاشق *æā-shik*, (act. part. of عشق) (used substantively), A lover; (Fem.) عاشقه *æā-shika'h*. عاشق كيدل *æā-shik kedal*, verb intrans. To fall in love, to become a lover. عاشقي *æā-shikī*, s.f. (3rd) Making love, courtship, gallantry, the state of being a lover, love, amour. Pl. ئ *a'ī*. عاشقي كول *æā-shikī kawul*, verb trans. To make love, to court. See مين and مين توب

A عاشوره *æā-shūra'h*, s.f. (3rd) (from عشر) The first ten days of the Muharram. Pl. ئ *ey*.

A عاصي *æā-ṣī*, adj. (act. part. of عصي) Disobedient, criminal, rebellious. 2. A rebel, a sinner.

A عافيت *æā-fiyat*, s.m. (2nd) (from SYR עפיא) Health, safety. Pl. عافيتونه *æā-fiyatūnah*. خير و عافيت *khair-o-æā-fiyat*, Health, safety.

A عاق *æākk*, adj. (act. part. of عق) Disobedient, rebellious (as a child to its parents or teacher); (Fem.) عاقه *æākka'h*. عاق كول *æākk kawul*, verb trans. To rebel, to manifest disobedience.

A عاقبت *æā-kibat*, s.m. (2nd) (from عقب) The end, conclusion, futurity, future state. Pl. عاقبتونه *æā-kibatūnah*. 2. adv. Finally, at the end, at last, after all.

A عاقل *æā-kil*, adj. (act. part. of عقل), Wise, intelligent, sensible, sagacious; (Fem.) عاقله *æā-kila'h*.

A عالم *æā-lam*, s.m. (2nd) The world, the universe, time, regions, state, beauty. Pl. عالمونه *æā-lamūnah*.

A عالم *æālim*, adj. (from علم) Learned, knowing; (Fem.) عالمه *æā-lima'h*. عالم غيب *æā-lim-i-ghaib*, Prescient, knowing what is concealed, the past and future.

A عالي *æā-lī*, adj. (act. part. of علو) High, sublime, grand, eminent. (Masc. and Fem.). عالي جاه *æā-lī-jāh* or عالي شان *æā-lī-shān*, adj. Of high rank, magnificent. عالي قدر *æā-lī-kadr* or عالي مرتبه *æā-lī-martaba'h*, adj. High in rank or dignity. عالي مقام *æā-lī-mukām* or عالي مقدار *æā-lī-mikdār*, adj. Exalted, high dignity. عالي همت *æā-lī-himmat*, adj. High-minded, ambitious.

A عام *æāmm*, adj. (from عم) Common, public, general, plebeian. 2. The vulgar, the common people; (Fem.) عامه *æāmma'h*. خاص و عام *khāṣ-o-æāmm*, adj. High and low, peculiar and popular.

A عامل *æā-mil*, adj. (act. part. of عمل) An intendant of the finances, a collector of the revenue, a governor, a ruler; (Fem.) عامله *æā-mila'h*.

A عامي *æā-mī*, adj. (act. part. of عمي) Blind, ignorant. (Masc. and Fem.)

A عايد *æā-īd*, adj. (act. part. of عود), Happening, reverting, coming back, returning, being restored (as money, etc.)

A عايشه *æā-eysha'h*, s. prop. The name of Muhammad's favourite wife.

A عبادت *æibādat*, s.m. (2nd) (from عبد) Divine worship, adoration, obedience, service. Pl. عبادتونه *æibādatūnah*. عبادت كول *æibādat kawul*, verb trans. To worship, to adore, to pay obedience. عبادت گاه *æibādat-gāh*, s.m. (2nd) A place of worship. Pl. عبادت گاهونه *æibādat-gāhūnah*. عبادتي *æibādatī*, s.m. (5th) A devotee, a religious person. Pl. عبادتيان *æibādatī-ān*.

A عبارت *æibārat*, s.m. (2nd) (from عبر) Style, mode of expression or explanation, signification, import, meaning, phraseology, phrase. Pl. عبارتونه *æibārat-ūnah*.

A عبث *æabas*, adj. Vain, idle, absurd, trifling, profitless. 2. adv. In vain, idly, absurdly; (Fem.) عبثه *æabasa'h*.

A عبرت *æibrat*, s.f. (2nd) (from عبر) An example, a warning. Pl. عبرتونه *æibratūnah.* عبرت ور كول *æibrat war-kawul,* verb trans. To make an example of, to give as an example. عبرت آخستل *æibrat ākhistal,* verb trans. To take as an example.

A عبور *æubūr,* s.m. (9th) (from عبر) Passing, crossing, passing over; a ford, a ferry, a pass. Sing and Pl. عبور كول *æubūr kawul,* verb trans. To cross, to pass over, to ford.

A عتاب *æitāb,* s.m. (2nd) (from عتب) Reproof, reprimand, reproach, rebuke, anger, displeasure. Pl. عتابونه *æitābūnah.* عتاب كول *æitāb kawul,* verb trans. To reprove, to reprimand, to rebuke, to reproach.

A عثمان *æaṣmān,* s. prop. The name of the third Khalīf—Othmān.

A عجايب *æajā-īb,* s.m. (6th) Wonders, curiosities. Sing. and Pl. 2. adj. Wonderful, astonishing; (Fem.) عجايبه *æajā-ība'h.*

A عجايبات *æajā-ībāt.* Sing. and Pl. See عجايب

A عجب *æa-jab,* adj. Wonderful, astonishing, amazing, miraculous, rare, strange, droll, etc.; (Fem.) عجبه *æa-jaba'h.*

A عجز *æajz* or *æijz,* s.m. (9th) Weakness, impotence, submission, wretchedness. Sing. and Pl.

A عجم *æajam,* s.m. (6th) Barbarians, all people not Arabs, Persians; countries not Arabia, Persia. Sing. and Pl.

A عجمي *æajamī,* adj. Persian, barbarian.

A عدالت *æadālat,* s.m. (2nd) A court of justice, an assize. 2. Justice, law, equity. Pl. عدالتونه *æadālat-ūnah.* عدالت كول *æadālat kawul,* verb trans. To administer justice, to hold court or assize. عدالتي *æadālatī,* s.m. (5th) An officer of justice, one who administers justice. Pl. عدالتيان *æadālatīān.* 2. adj. Just, equitable, one who acts justly or administers justice.

A عداوت *æadāwat,* s.m. (2nd) (from عدو) Enmity, hostility, hatred, strife, hate, animosity. Pl. عداوتونه *æadāwatūnah.* عداوت كول *æadāwat kawul,* verb trans. To show enmity or hostility towards, to hate.

A عدد *æadad,* s.m. (2nd) Number. Pl. عددونه *æadadūnah.*

A عدل *æadl,* s.m. (2nd) Justice, equity, rectitude. Pl. عدلونه *æadl-ūnah.* عدل كول *æadl kawul,* verb trans. To do justice, to act with rectitude and equity.

A عدم *æadam,* s.m. (9th) Non-existence, nonentity, nothing, privation, annihilation. Sing. and Pl.

A عدول *æadūl,* s.m. (9th) (from عدل) Declining, refusing, receding, deserting, returning. Sing. and Pl. عدول كول *æadūl kawul,* verb trans. To deviate from, to disobey, to decline, to refuse.

A عده *æada'h* or عدة *æadat,* s.f. (3rd) The period during which it is unlawful to have intercourse with a woman, as when menstruous, when divorced, or when mourning the death of her husband. Pl. ي *ey.*

A عذاب *æazāb,* s.m. (2nd) Pain, misfortune, torment, martyrdom, punishment, anguish. Pl. عذابونه *æazābūnah.* په عذاب كول *pah æazāb kawul,* verb trans. To pain, to torment, to give or cause anguish.

A عذر *æuzr,* s.m. (2nd) Excuse, apology. Pl. عذرونه *æuzrūnah.* عذر خواه *æuzr khwāh,* adj. Apologizing, an apologist. 2. A condoler; (Fem.) عذر خواهه *æuzr khwāha'h.* عذر خواهي *æuzr khwāhī,* s.f. (3rd) Apology, excuse, asking pardon, making apology. 2. Condolence. Pl. ئي *a'ī.* عذر راوړل *æuzr rā-w'ṛral* or عذر كول *æuzr kawul,* verb trans. To apologize, to ask pardon, to make an apology or excuse; or عذر خواهي كول *æuzr khwāhī kawul,* verb trans. 2. To condole with.

A عراق *æirāḳ,* s. prop. A territory divided into two portions; *æirāḳ-i-æarab,* Babylonia or Chaldea; and *æirāḳ-i-æajam,* Media. عراقان *æirāḳān,* The cities of Basrah and Kūfah. عراقي *æirāḳī,* adj. Produced in *æirāḳ* (applied to a breed of horses from that country).

A عرب *æarab,* s. prop. Arabia. 2. s.m. (6th) An Arabian. Sing. and Pl.; (Fem.) عربه *æaraba'h.* عربي *æarabī,* adj. Arabian, Arabic;

the Arabic language, an Arab horse. عربستان *æarabistān*, s. prop. The country of Arabia.

A عرس *æurs*, s.m. (2nd) A concourse of people asembled at a shrine for religious purposes on the anniversary of the saint. 2. Oblations, offerings to a saint. 3. A marriage feast. 4. A day set apart for visiting the shrine of a saint. Pl. عرسونه *æurs-ūnah*.

A عرش *æarsh*, s.m. (9th) A roof. 2. A throne. 3. The ninth heaven where God's throne is. Sing. and Pl.

A عرصه *æarṣa'h*, s.f. (3rd) Area, space, a plain, time, while, interval. Pl. ې *ey*. عرصات *æarṣāt*, or *æaraṣāt*, s.m. (9th) The plain in which all will assemble at the last day. Sing. and Pl.

A عرض *æarẓ*, s.m. (2nd) A petition, a request, a representation. Pl. عرضونه *æarẓūnah*. عرض بيګي *æarẓ-begī*, An officer who presents letters and petitions, an usher. عرضداشت *æarẓ-dāsht*, s.m. (2nd) A written petition or statement. Pl. عرضداشتونه *æaraẓ-dāshtūnah*. عرض كول *æarẓ kawul* or په عرض رسول *pah æarẓ rasawul*, verb trans. To represent, to offer, to propose, to state, to set forth. عرض دار *æarẓ-dār*, s.m. (5th) A petitioner. Pl. عرض داران *æarẓ-dārān*. عرض داره *æarẓ-dārah*, s.f. (3rd). Pl. ې *ey*.

A عرضي *æarẓī*, s.f. (3rd) A petition, a memorial, a letter (from an inferior), a representation. Pl. ئي *a'ī*.

A عرف *æurf*, adj. Known (by name), commonly called, alias. 2. Proper, equitable. 3. Goodness, merit. 4. Confession.

A عرفات *æarafāt*, s. prop. The name of a place 12 miles from Makka, where the pilgrims halt.

P A عرفي *æurfī*, adj. Well-known, notorious, public.

A عرق *æarak*, s.m. (2nd) Juice, essence, spirit, sap, sweat. Pl. عرقونه *æarak-ūnah*. عرق آلوده *æarak-ālūdah*, adj. Sweaty, covered with sweat. See خوله

A عزت *æizzat*, s.m. (2nd) Grandeur, power, honor, glory, respect. Pl. عزتونه *æizzatūnah*. عزت دار *æizzat-dār*, adj. Honorable, powerful, grand; (Fem.) عزت داره *æizzat-dāra'h*. عزت وركول *æizzat war-kawul*, verb trans. To honor, to dignify.

A عزرائيل *æiz-rā'īl*, s. prop. The angel of death.

A عزلت *æuz-lat*, s.m. (2nd) Retirement, retiring. Pl. عزلتونه *æuz-latūnah*. عزلت كول *æuz-lat kawul*, verb trans. To retire from the world, to become a recluse. عزلتي *æuz-latī*, adj. A hermit, a recluse. (Masc. and Fem.)

A عزم *æazm*, s.m. (2nd) Design, intention, purpose, undertaking, resolution, determination. Pl. عزمونه *æazamūnah*. عزم جزم *æazm-jazm*, Fixed intention or purpose.

A عزيز *æazīz*, adj. (from عز) Dear, darling, worthy, respected, beloved, honored, esteemed, excellent, precious, friend. 2. s.m. (5th) A nephew. Pl. عزيزان *æazīzān*; (Fem.) عزيزه *æazīza'h*, and s.f. (3rd) A niece. Pl. ې *ey*. عزيز لرل *æazīz laral*, verb trans. To hold in great esteem, to value highly, to love, to respect, to revere. عزيز والىَ *æazīz-wālaey*, s.m. (1st) Respect, love, esteem, reverence. Pl. والي *wālī*; or عزيز توب *æazīz-tob*, s.m. (2nd). Pl. توبونه *tobūnah*; and عزيز تيا *æazīz-tīā*, s.f. (6th). (E.) Sing. and Pl. (W.) Pl. تياوي *tī'āwī*. عزيزګلوي *æazīz galwī*, s.f. (3rd) The relationship between an uncle and his nephew or niece. Pl. ئي *a'ī*.

A عزيزي *æazīzī*, s.f. (3rd) Friendship, esteem, respect, reverence. Pl. ئي *a'ī*. عزيزي كول *æazīzī kawul*, verb trans. To show friendship to, to love, to esteem, to respect.

A عسل *æasal*, s.m. (6th) Honey. Sing. and Pl.

A عشر *æushr*, s.m. (2nd) The tenth part. Pl. عشرونه *æushr-ūnah*.

A عشرت *æishrat*, s.m. (2nd) (vulg. *æashrat*) Society, pleasant and familiar intercourse or conversation; pleasure, delight, enjoyment, mirth. Pl. عشرتونه *æishratūnah*. عشرت كول *æishrat kawul*, verb trans. To enjoy one's-self.

A عشق *æishk*, s.m. (2nd) Love, affection. Pl. عشقونه *æishkūnah*. عشقباز *æishk-bāz*, adj. Gallant, amorous; (Fem.) عشقبازه *æishk-bāza'h*.

عشقبازي *æishk-bāzī*, s.f. (3rd) Ardour, amorousness, gallantry. Pl. ئي *a'ī*. عشق كول *æishk kawul*, verb trans. To love, to have affection for, to hold dear. See مينه

A عطا *æaṭā*, s.f. (6th) A gift, a present, a favour, giving. (E.) Sing. and Pl. (W.) Pl. عطاوي *æaṭāwī*. عطا كول *æaṭā kawul*, verb trans. To grant, to give, to bestow, to confer.

A عطار *æaṭṭār*, s.m. (5th) (from عطر) A perfumer, a druggist. Pl. عطاران *æaṭṭār-ān*. عطاري *æaṭṭārī*, s.f. (3rd) The business of a perfumer or druggist. Pl. ئي *a'ī*.

A عطر *æaṭr* or *æiṭr*, s.m. (6th) Perfume, fragrance, essence, ottar. Sing. and Pl. عطر دان *æaṭr-dān*, s.m. (2nd) A perfume box, a receptacle for perfume. Pl. عطر دانونه *æaṭr-dānūnah*.

A عظمت *æaẓamat*, s.m. (2nd) Greatness, magnificence, magnitude, aggrandizement. Pl. عظمتونه *æaẓamatūnah*.

A عظيم *æaẓīm*, adj. Great, large, high in dignity; (Fem.) عظيمه *æaẓīma'h*.

A عفريت *æifrīt*, s.m. (5th) A giant, a demon, a spectre. Pl. عفريتان *æifrītān*.

عفوه *æafūa'h*, s.f. (3rd) Absolution, forgiveness, pardon. Pl. ئي *ey*. عفوه كيدل *æafūa'h kedal*, verb trans. To be pardoned or forgiven. عفوه كول *æafūa'h kawul*, verb trans. To forgive, to pardon (A عفو).

A عقايد *æaḳā-īd*, s.m. (6th) (Pl. of عقيده) Articles of religion. Sing. and Pl.

A عقب *æaḳab*, adv. Behind, after, in the rear. See وروست

A عقد *æaḳd*, s.m. (2nd) A knot, the marriage-knot, marriage, a compact, an agreement. 2. A collar, a necklace. Pl. عقدونه *æaḳdūnah*. عقد كول *æaḳd kawul*, verb trans. To make a compact or agreement. عقد ترل *æaḳd taṟṟal*, verb trans. To tie the marriage-knot, to marry, to make a compact.

A عقده *æuḳda'h*, s.f. (3rd) A knot, an excrescence, a node. 2. An impediment in speech. 3. Perplexed affairs, entangled things, confused words. Pl. ئي *ey*.

A عقل *æaḳl*, s.m. (2nd) Wisdom, opinion, sense, understanding, reason, intellect, etc. Pl. عقلونه *æaḳl-ūnah*. عقل مند *æaḳl mand* or من *man*, adj. Wise, intelligent, sagacious; (Fem.) عقل منده *æaḳl manda'h* or منه *mana'h*. عقل مندي *æaḳl-mandī*, s.f. (3rd) Intelligence, wisdom, understanding. Pl. ئي *a'ī*.

A عقوبت *æuḳūbat*, s.m. (2nd) Punishment, torment, chastisement, torture. Pl. عقوبتونه *æuḳūbatūnah*. په عقوبت كول *pah æuḳūbat kawul*, verb trans. To put in torment, to punish, to chastise.

A عقيده *æaḳīda'h*, s.f. (3rd) (from عقد) Faith, belief, tenet, fundamental article of religion. Pl. ئي *ey*.

A عقيق *æaḳīḳ*, s.m. (6th) A cornelian. Sing. and Pl.

A عكس *æaks*, s.m. (2nd) Reflection, inversion. 2. A shadow or reflected image. 3. The contrary, the reverse, opposite. Pl. عكسونه *æaksūnah*.

A علاج *æilāj*, s.m. (2nd) (from علج) A remedy, a medicine, a cure. Pl. علاجونه *æilājūnah*. علاج كول *æilāj kawul*, verb trans. To cure, to remedy. to apply a remedy.

A علاقه *æalāḳa'h*, s.f. (3rd) Dependence, relation, connection, interest. 2. Commerce, intercourse, communication, correspondence. Pl. ئي *ey*. علاقه لرل *æalāḳa'h laral*, verb trans. To concern, to interest, to be connected to, to relate or belong to, to regard, to hold relation or connection.

A علامت *æalāmat*, s.f. (3rd) A mark, a sign, a symptom, coat of arms, emblem, ensign. Pl. علامتونه *æalāmatūnah*. Also علامه *æalāma'h*, s.f. (3rd). Pl. ئي *ey*.

A علاوه *æalāwah*, adv. Besides, moreover.

A علت *æillat*, s.m. (2nd) Disease, defect. 2. cause, pretext. 3. Dirt, filth. Pl. علتونه *æillatūnah*. علتي *æillatī*, adj. Diseased, having some defect. (Masc. and Fem.)

A علم *æilm*, s.m. (2nd) Science, knowledge. Pl. علمونه *æilm-ūnah*.

A علما *æulamā*, s.m. (6th) The learned. Sing. and Pl.

A علمي *æilmī*, adj. Scientific, learned. علميت *æilmi-yat*, s.m. (2nd) Learning in general. Pl. علميتونه *æilmi-yatūnah*.

A علوفه *æulūfa'h*, s.f. (3rd) (Pl. of علف) Stipend, salary, daily pay, subsistence money, provisions. Pl. ې *ey*.

A علي *æalī*, adj. High, eminent, noble; a proper name—Muhammad's son-in-law.

A علي بوبو *æalī bau-bau*, s.m. (9th) A scare-crow, a bugaboo or bogie, etc. to frighten children. Sing. and Pl.

A عليحده *æalaḥidah*, adj. or adv. Separate, apart, distinct. عليحده كول *æalaḥidah kawul*, verb trans. To separate, to part, to make distinct.

A عليم *æalīm*, adj. Wise, learned; (Fem.) عليمه *æalīma'h*.

A عمارت *æimārat*, s.m. (2nd) (from عمر) A public edifice, a building, a structure, cultivation, building. 2. A habitation, a fortification. Pl. عمارتونه *æimāratūnah*.

A عماري *æimārī*, s.f. (3rd) A litter or seat with a canopy placed on the back of a camel or elephant. Pl. ئي *a'ī*.

A عمان *æumān*, s.m. (9th) The sea, the ocean. Sing. and Pl.

A عمده *æumdah*, adj. Great, noble, excellent, prime, good, etc. عمده والي *æumdah wālaey*, s.m. (1st) Greatness, sumptuousness, excellence. Pl. والي *wālī*.

A عمر *æumr*, s.m. (2nd) Lifetime, age, period of life. Pl. عمرونه *æumrūnah*. 2. *æumar*, s. prop. The name of the second Khalīf—Omar.

A عمق *æumuḳ*, s.m. (2nd) Depth, profundity. Pl. عمقونه *æumuḳūnah*. See ژورتيا

A عمل *æaml*, s.m. (2nd) Action, act, operation, work, practice, rule, sway, jurisdiction, effect, etc. Pl. عملونه *æaml-ūnah*. عملدار *æaml-dār*, s.m. (5th) A governor, one who holds command. Pl. عملداران *æaml-dārān*. عملداري *æaml-dārī*, s.f. (3rd) Government, rule. Pl. ئي *a'ī*. عمل كول *æaml kawul*, verb trans. To act, to practice, to proceed.

A عمله *æamala'h*, s.f. (3rd) Operators, executors, parties who carry on any duties in the state. Pl. ې *ey*.

A عملي *æamlī*, adj. Artificial, practical. (Masc. and Fem.)

A عمه *æama'h*, s.f. (3rd) A paternal or maternal aunt. Pl. ې *ey*.

A عميق *æamīk*, adj. Deep, profound; (Fem.) عميقه *æamīka'h*. See ژور

A عناب *æanāb*, The jujube fruit and tree. Sing. and Pl.

A عناد *æinād*, s.m. (2nd) (from عند) Obstinacy, perverseness, resistance, contumacy, stubbornness. Pl. عنادونه *æinādūnah*. عناد كول *æinād kawul*, verb trans. To oppose, to resist, to show stubbornness or contumacy. عناد لرل *æinād laral*, verb trans. To have obstinacy or perverseness. (Eng. verb intrans.) To be contumacious, stubborn. عنادي *æinādī*, adj. Obstinate, perverse, contumacious, stubborn.

A عناصر *æanāṣir*, s.m. (6th) The elements. (Pl. of عنصر).

A عنان *æinān*, s.m. (2nd) A bridle, the reins of a bridle. Pl. عنانونه *æinānūnah*.

A عنايت *æināyat*, s.m. (2nd) Favour, gift, present, bounty, bestowal. Pl. عنايتونه *æināyat-ūnah*. عنايت كول *æināyat kawul*, verb trans. To give, to grant, to bestow, to present, to confer.

A عمبر *æambar*, s.m. (6th) Ambergris. Sing. and Pl. عمبر بوي *æambar-bū-e*, adj. Fragrant; (Fem.) عمبر بويه *æambar-bū-e-a'h*. عمبري *æambarī*, adj. Of the colour or smell of ambergris.

A عندليب *æandalīb*, s.m. (5th) A nightingale. Pl. عندليبان *æandalībān*.

A عنقا *æanḳā*, s.f. (6th) The phœnix, a fabulous bird. (E.) Sing. and Pl. (W.) Pl. عنقاوي *æanḳāwī*. See سيمرغ. 2. adj. Rare, wonderful, curious.

A عنقريب *æanḳarīb*, adv. Near, soon, shortly, nearly, almost.

A عنكبوت *æankabūt*, s.m. (6th) A spider. Sing. and Pl. See غنه

A عنوان *æunwān* or *æinwān*, s.m. (2nd) (from

(عنن) The title of a book, that by which any thing is known. 2. Manner, mode. Pl. عنوانونه *æunwānūnah* or *æinwānūnah*.

A عنين *æinnīn*, adj. (from عن) Impotent; (Fem.) عنينه *æinnīna'h*.

A عوام *æawām*, s.m. (6th) (from عامة) The vulgar, the common people. Sing. and Pl. عوام الناس *æawāmmu-n-nās*, The vulgar, the crowd.

A عود *æūd*, s.m. (6th) Wood, timber. 2. A staff, a stick. 3. The wood aloes. 4. A lute, a harp. Sing. and Pl.

A عورت *æaurat*, s.m. (2nd) The pudenda of a man or woman, that which is concealed. Pl. عورتونه *æauratūnah*.

عورته *æaurata'h*, s.f. (3rd) A woman, a wife. Pl. ې *ey*. عورته كول *æaurata'h kawul*, verb trans. To take a wife, to marry.

A عوض *æiwaẓ*, s.m. (2nd) Reward, retribution, return, retaliation, anything substituted for another, exchange, recompense. Pl. عوضونه *æiwaẓūnah*.

A عهد *æahd*, s.m. (2nd) Contract, compact, obligation, promise, treaty. 2. Time, season, conjuncture. Pl. عهدونه *æahdūnah*. عهد شكن *æahd shikan*, adj. A promise-breaker, faithless to one's word or engagement; (Fem.) عهد شكنه *æahd-shikana'h*. عهد شكني *æahd shikanī*, s.f. (3rd) Breach of faith, promise-breaking. Pl. ئ *a'ī*. عهد كول *æahd kawul*, verb trans. To promise, to vow, to contract. عهد نامه *æahd nāma'h*, s.f. (3rd) A contract or agreement in writing, articles of peace or armistice, etc. Pl. ې *ey*.

A عهده *æuhda'h*, s.f. (3rd) A commission, an obligation, an agreement. 2. Business, office, post, appointment. Pl. ې *ey*. عهده دار *æuhda'h-dār*, s.m. (5th) An officer, employed, holding a commission. Pl. عهده داران *æuhda'h dārān*. عهده داري *æuhda'h dārī*, s.f. (3rd) Employment, office, term of office. Pl. ئ *a'ī*. عهده وركول *æuhda'h war-kawul*, verb trans. To commission, to appoint to any office or duty. عهده داري كول *æuhda'h-dārī kawul*, verb trans. To carry on any employment, to perform any office.

A عيار *æayār*, s.m. (2nd) (from عير) Proof, test, assay, standard, touch, a touchstone. Pl. عيارونه *æayār-ūnah*.

A عياش *æaiyāsh*, adj. (from عيش) Luxurious; (Fem.) عياشه *æaiyāsha'h*. عياشي *æaiyāshī*, s.f. (3rd) Luxury. Pl. ئ *a'ī*.

A عيال *æiyāl*, s.m. (2nd) Family, children, domestics. Pl. عيالونه *æiyālūnah*. عيالدار *æiyāl-dār*, s.m. (5th) Having a family. Pl. عيالداران *æiyāl-dārān*. عيالداره *æiyāl-dāra'h*, s.f. (3rd) A woman having a family. Pl. ې *ey*. عيالداري *æiyāl-dārī*, s.f. (3rd) The having a family. Pl. ئ *a'ī*. عيال و اطفال *æiyāl-ow-aṭ-fāl*, Family, household.

A عيان *æayān*, adj. Clear, manifest, public, conspicuous, visible, apparent, evident; (Fem.) عيانه *æayāna'h*. عيان كيدل *æayān kedal*, verb intrans. To become clear, manifest, visible. عيان كول *æayān kawul*, verb trans. To make visible, clear, conspicuous, apparent.

A عيب *æaib*, s.m. (2nd) Fault, disgrace, vice, blemish, infirmity, sin, disgrace, infamy. Pl. عيبونه *æaib-ūnah*. عيب پوښ *æaib posh* (W.) or *pokh* (E.) adj. Concealer of fault or defect; (Fem.) عيب پوښه *æaib posha'h* or *pokha'h*. عيب پوښي *æaib-poshī* or *pokhī*, s.f. (3rd) Concealment of fault or defect. Pl. ئ *a'ī*. عيب جوي *æaib-jo-e*, adj. Censorious, malevolent, malicious, malignant, caviller, carper; (Fem.) عيب جويه *æaib-jo-ea'h*. عيب جوئي *æaib-jo'ī*, s.f. (3rd) Censoriousness, criticism, cavil. Pl. ئ *a'ī*. عيب گوي *æaib-go-e*, adj. One who finds fault, a slanderer; (Fem.) عيب گويه *æaib-go-ea'h*. عيب گيري *æaib-gīrī*; s.f. (3rd) Finding fault, censuring. Pl. ئ *a'ī*. عيب پوري كول *æaib pūrī kawul*, verb trans. To defame, to censure, to asperse.

PA عيب ناك *æaib-nāk* or عيبي *æaibī*, adj. Faulty, blemished, defective, disgraced; (Fem.) عيب ناكه *æaib-nāka'h*.

A عيد *æīd*, s.m. (9th) A festival, a holy day, a solemnity. 2. Easter. Sing. and Pl. عيدگاه

<u>æīd-gāh</u>, s.m. (2nd) A place where festivals are held or celebrated. Pl. عيد گاهونه *æīd-gāhūnah*.

A عيسي *æīsā*, s. prop. Jesus Christ (from H ישע to save). عيسائي *æīsā'ī*, adj. Of or belonging to Jesus, a Christian. (Masc. and Fem.) Also عيسوي *æīsawī*.

A عيش *æaish*, s.m. (2nd) Pleasure, delight, enjoyment. Pl. عيشونه *æaishūnah*. عيش و عشرت *æaish-ow-æishrat*, Pleasure and delight. عيش كول *æaish kawul*, verb trans. To enjoy one's-self.

عينكه *æainaka'h*, s.f. (3rd) (A عينك) Spectacles, glasses to assist the sight. Pl. ي *ey*.

غ

غ *ghain*, called غين منقوطه or غين مهمله, the nineteenth letter of the Arabic, twenty-second of the Persian, and the twenty-ninth of the Pushto alphabet, has no corresponding character in the Sanskrit, and appears peculiar to the Semitic family of languages. It is one of the guttural letters, its sound being like a *g* uttered with compression deeply in the throat, and bears the same relation to ګ that غ has to ک. According to the system of numbers by letters, it stands for 1,000.

غاب *ghāb*, s.m. (2nd) A dish, a plate, a large dish. Pl. غابونه *ghābūnah* (A قاب).

غاپ *ghāp*, s.m. (5th) The barking of a dog. Pl. غاپهار *ghāpahār*. See غپ

غاتر *ghā-tar*, s.m. (5th) A mule. Pl. غاتران *ghā-tarān*. غاتره *ghā-tara'h*, s.f. (3rd) A mare of the above, a she mule. Pl. ي *ey*. See تاتر

A غار *ghār*, s.m. (2nd) A cavern, a pit, a cave. Pl. غارونه *ghārūnah*. See سمخ and سمست

A غارت *ghārat*, s.m. (2nd) Rapine, plunder, devastation. Pl. غارتونه *ghāratūnah*. غارت كول *ghārat kawul*, verb trans. To plunder, to ravage, to spoil, to devastate. غارت گر *ghārat-gar*, s.m. (5th) A plunderer, an oppressor, a robber. Pl. غارت گر *ghārat-gær*. غارت گره *ghārat-gara'h*, s.f. (3rd). Pl. ي *ey*.

غارمه *ghārmah*, s.m. (6th) The heat of mid-day, noon-day. Sing. and Pl. See غرمه

غارندونه *ghārandūna'h*, s.f. (3rd) A skink, a kind of lizard. Pl. ي *ey*.

غاري *ghāraey*, s.m. (1st) A glutton. Pl. ي *ī*. غارئ *ghāra'ī*, s.f. (3rd). Sing. and Pl.

غاړه *ghārra'h*, s.f. (3rd) The throat. 2. Shore, border, margin, coast. 3. The neck of a bottle or other vessel. 4. A joke, pleasantry. 5. Sore throat, stoppage of the voice from cold. Pl. ي *ey*. سره غاړه *sara'h ghārra'h*, s.f. (3rd) The gullet, the esophagus. Pl. ي *ey*. وچه غاړه *wucha'h ghārra'h*, s.f. (3rd) The windpipe. Pl. ي *ey*. غاړه تازه كول *ghārra'h tāzah kawul*, verb trans. To hem, to clear the throat. غاړه خپه كول *ghārra'h khapah kawul*, verb trans. To seize by the throat, to throttle, to strangle, to choke. غاړه غړئ *ghārra'h gharra'ī*, s.f. (6th) Mixing, intermingling, embracing. Sing. and Pl. 2. adj. Connected, joined together, partner. غاړه غړئ كيدل *ghārra'h gharra'ī kedal*, verb intrans. To become connected, joined (as in trade, etc.) غاړه غړئ كول *ghārra'h gharra'ī kawul*, verb trans. To embrace, to enclose, to encircle, to hug; or تر غاړه وتل *tar ghārra'h watal*, verb intrans. غاړه غړول *ghārra'h gharrawul*, verb trans. To put off, to put aside, to make excuses, to shirk, to fight shy of.

غاز *ghāz*, s.m. (2nd) A small copper coin. 2. Stickiness of dough. Pl. غازونه *ghāzūnah*.

A غازي *ghāzī*, s.m. (5th) (from غزا) A conqueror, a hero, a champion, one who fights against infidels. Pl. غازيان *ghāzī-ān*.

غاښ *ghāsh* (W.) or *ghākh* (E.) s.m. (2nd) A tooth. Pl. غاښونه *ghāshūnah* or *ghākhūnah* غاښ ټنبوني *ghāsh-ttunbūnaey* or *ghākh-ttunbūnaey*, s.m. (1st) A toothpick. Pl. ي *ī*. غاښ زيزيدل *ghāsh zejzedal* (W.) or غاښ زيگيدل *ghākh zegedal* (E.) verb intrans. To teeth. غاښ چيچل *ghāsh* or *ghākh chechal*, verb trans. To gnash the teeth, to grind the teeth. غاښ لګول *ghāsh* or *ghākh lagawul*, verb trans. To seize with the teeth, to bite. غاښي *ghāshaey* or *ghākhaey*, adj. as s.m. (1st) A person having large teeth. 2. The peak or crest of a mountain, a pass. Pl. ي *ī*. غاښئ *ghāsha'ī* or *ghākha'ī*, s.f. (6th) A woman having large teeth. Sing. and Pl. غاښ وتل *ghāsh* or *ghākh watal*, verb intrans. To shed the teeth. د مخ غاښونه *da makh ghāshūnah* or *ghākhūnah*, The fore teeth. د زامي غاښونه *da zāmey ghāshūnah* or *ghākhūnah*, The jaw, or double, teeth.

غاښ برهان *ghāsh* (W.) or *ghākh* (E.) *bur-hān*, adj. Plain, apparent, obvious, evident, palpable, as plain as the nose on one's face, as plain as a pike-staff (*lit.* plain as the teeth in one's mouth).

غاښ سکوي *ghāsh-skoe* (W.) or *ghākh-skoe* (E.) s.m. (2nd) A particle of meat or anything of the kind which gets between the teeth when eating. Pl. غاښ سکويونه *ghāsh* or *ghākh-skoe-ūnah*.

A غافل *ghāfil*, adj. (from غفل) Negligent, neglectful, inattentive, remiss, indolent, careless, thoughtless, imprudent; (Fem.) غافله *ghāfila'h*. غافل کيدل *ghāfil kedal*, verb intrans. To become remiss, negligent, idle, careless, indolent, thoughtless, etc.

A غالب *ghālib*, adj. (act. part. of غلب) Overcoming, overpowering, victorious, predominant, excelling, superior, most likely; (Fem.) غالبه *ghāliba'h*. غالب کيدل *ghālib kedal*, verb intrans. To overcome, to excel, to conquer, to be victorious over.

A غالب *ghālab*, s.m. (2nd) A mould, a model, a form. Pl. غالبونه *ghālabūnah* (A قالب).

غالبوزه *ghāl-būza'h*, s.f. (3rd) A large red wasp or hornet. Pl. ې *ey*. See دنبره and دنداره

غالوبول *ghāl-o-būl*, s.m. (9th) Tumult, disturbance, noise, din, uproar, clamour, sound, etc. Sing. and Pl. غالوبول کول *ghāl-o-būl kawul*, verb trans. To create a tumult, noise, disturbance, etc. See زوږ

غال و غول *ghāl-o-ghūl*, s.m. (9th) Noise, din, outcry, tumult, riot, hullaballoo. Sing. and Pl. غال و غول کول *ghāl-o-ghūl kawul*, verb trans. To raise an outcry, tumult, hullaballoo, etc.

A غالئ *ghāla'ī*, s.f. (6th) A large carpet. Sing. and Pl.

A غاليچه *ghālīcha'h*, s.f. (3rd) A small carpet, a rug. Pl. ې *ey*.

غانده *ghāndah*, adj. Disliked, offensive, loathsome, nauseous, repulsive, revolting, disgusting, disagreeable. 2. A disgusting, stinking person. See غندل

غاو *ghāw*, s.m. (2nd) Noise, disturbance, tumult, brawl, uproar. Pl. غاوونه *ghāwūnah*. غاو کول *ghāw kawul*, verb trans. To create a disturbance, tumult, etc.

غاوچي *ghāw-chī*, s.m. (5th) A door-keeper, a porter. Pl. غاوچيان *ghāw-chīān*.

غاويدل *ghāwedal*, verb intrans. To become noisy, clamorous, to cry out, to squeal, etc. غاوول *ghāwawul*, verb trans. To make or render noisy, clamorous, uproarious, to cause or make to cry out.

غاويده *ghāwedah*, s.m. (6th) (verb. n.) Being noisy or uproarious, crying out, noise, clamour, uproar.

A غايب *ghā-īb*, adj. (act. part. of غيب) Absent, away, concealed, invisible, vanished; (Fem.) غايبه *ghā-ība'h*. غايب والي *ghā-īb-wālaey*, s.m. (1st) Absence, invisibility, concealment, etc. Pl. والي *wālī*. See غيب. غايبانه *ghā-ībānah*, adj. In absence, behind the back, invisibly.

A غايت *ghā-yat*, s.m. (2nd) The end, extremity, extreme. 2. Ordure, filth. Pl. غايتونه *ghā-yatūnah*. 3. adj. Very, extremely, chiefly. غايت کول *ghā-yat kawul*, verb trans. To go to stool. غايت نيول *ghā-yat nī-wal*, verb trans. To want to go to stool, to be taken short (A غايط).

A غبار *ghubār*, s.m. (2nd) Dust, dirt, vapour, clouds of dust, foulness, impurity, Pl. غبارونه *ghubār-ūnah*. غبار آلوده *ghubār ālūdah*, adj. Covered or polluted with dust, dusty.

غبرګ *gh'barg*, adj. Double, duplex, bifarious, two-fold; (Fem.) غبرګه *gh'barga'h*, A woman or animal who brings forth twins. 2. The flat land between two mountains, a valley. 3. The two hands together, as at the time of begging or making supplication. غبرګ والي *gh'barg wālaey*, s.m. (1st) The state of being double, duplication. Pl. والي *wālī*. غبرګونی *gh'bargūnaey*, s.m. (1st) A twin, one of two (male) young ones born together; غبرګون *gh'bargūni*, s.f. (8th). Pl. ي *ī*. غبرګوني زیږیدل *gh'bargūnī zejzedal* (W.) or زیګیدل *zegedal* (E.), To bring forth twins. غبرګ کول *gh'barg kawul*, verb trans. To double, to add one to another.

P غبغب *ghab-ghab*, s.m. (2nd) A double chin, a dewlap. Pl. غبغبونه *ghab-ghabūnah*. See جججوره

غپ *ghap*, s.m. (5th) The barking of a dog, the sound or smack of a blow, a snap, a sudden bite. Pl. غپهار *ghapahār*. غپل *ghapal*, verb trans. To bark at, to yelp at, etc. (peculiar to dogs). Pres. غاپي *ghāpī*; past وُ غپل *wu-ghapal*; fut. وُ به غاپي *wu bah ghāpī*; imp. وُ غاپه *wu-ghāpah*. The other inflections are wanting. غپ وهل *ghap wahal*, verb trans. or غپیدل *ghapedal*, verb intrans. To bark, to yelp. Pres. غپیږي *ghapejzī* (W.) or غپیګي *ghapegī* (E.); past وُ غپیده *wu-ghapedah* or غپیده *ghapeda*; fut. وُ به غپیږي *wu bah ghapejzī* or غپیګي *ghapegī*; imp. وُ غپیږه *wu-ghapejzah* or وُ غپیګه *wu-ghapegah*; act. part. غپیدونکی *ghapedūnkaey* or غپیدونی *ghapedūnaey*; past part. غپیدلی *ghapedalaey*; verb. n. غپیدنه *ghapedana'h* or غپیده *ghapedah*. غپول *ghapawul*, verb trans. To make bark, to cause to yelp or bark. Pres. غپوي *ghapawī*; past وُ غپاوه *wu-ghapāwuh* or غپاوو *ghapāwo*; fut. وُ به غپوي *wu bah ghapawī*; imp. وُ غپوه *wu-ghapawah*; act. part. غپوونکی *ghapawūnkaey* or غپوونی *ghapawūnaey*; past part. غپولی *ghapawulaey*; verb. n. غپونه *ghapawuna'h*.

غپا *ghapā*, s.f. (6th) A bark, a yelp. 2. Snapping (as a dog), bolting food. (W.) Pl. غپاوي *ghapāwī*.

غپه *ghupa'h*, s.f. (3rd) A dip, a dive, a plunge. 2. Immersion, dipping, diving. Pl. ې *ey*. غپه خوړل *ghupa'h khwarral*, verb trans. To dive, to take a dip, to plunge one's-self into the water. غپه کول *ghupa'h kawul*, verb trans. To dip, to plunge into the water, to duck, to baptize; or غپه ورکول *ghupa'h warkawul*. Also written غوپه *ghopa'h* and غیپه *ghue-pa'h*. See غوټه

غټ *ghatt*, adj. Large, stout, great, burly, corpulent, fat, plump, lusty, chubby, full grown, considerable, bulky, big, etc. 2. Great in rank or power; (Fem.) غټه *ghatta'h*. غټیدل *ghattedal*, verb intrans. To become larger, to expand, to grow, to increase, to gather flesh, to become corpulent, etc. Pres. غټیږي *ghattejzī* (W.) or غټیګي *ghattegī* (E.); past غټ شه *ghatt shah* or وُ شه *wu-shah*; fut. غټ به شي *ghatt bah shī* or به وُ شي *bah wu-shī*; imp. غټ شه *ghatt shah* or وُ شه *wu-shah*; act. part. غټیدونکی *ghattedūnkaey* or غټیدونی *ghattedūnaey*; past part. غټ *ghatt* or غټ شوی *ghatt shawaey*; verb. n. غټیدنه *ghattedana'h* or غټیده *ghattedah*. غټول *ghattawul*, verb trans. To render larger, to distend, to expand, to amplify, to render stout, fat, etc. Pres. غټوي *ghattawī*; past غټ کړ *ghatt karr* or وُ کړ *wu-karr*; fut. غټ به کړي *ghatt bah krrī* or به وُ کړي *bah wu-krrī*; imp. غټ کړه *ghatt krrah* or وُ کړه *wu-krrah*; act. part. غټوونکی *ghattawūnkaey* or غټوونی *ghattawūnaey*; past part. غټ کړي *ghatt karraey*; verb. n. غټونه *ghattawuna'h*.

غټ والي *ghatt-wālaey*, s.m. (1st) Corpulence, plumpness, size, magnitude, stoutness, development, distension, expansion, etc. Pl. والي *wālī*.

غټ کتل *ghatt katal*, verb trans. To stare at, to eye, to gaze at, to look intently, to ogle, to gloat over.

غټي *ghattaey*, s.m. (1st) A lump, a block, a mass. Pl. ي *ī*.

غټۍ *ghutta'ī*, s.f. (6th) A rose-bud, a bud, a button, a bubble, a globule. 2. An ornament, a kind of jewellery. Sing. and Pl. See غوټۍ

غټيالَي *ghutt-yālaey*, s.m. (1st) The crop of a bird, a double chin, the dewlap of a goat or cow, etc. Pl. ي *ī*. See ججوره

غجري *ghajarī*, s.f. (3rd) A saddle-cloth, placed over a saddle and reaching to the horse's tail. Pl. ئ *a'ī*. See قجري

غجل *ghujal*, s.f. (1st) A cow-house, shed, or pen. Pl. غجلِ *ghujali*. See غوجل

غڅکَي *ghutskaey*, s.m. (1st) A bullock, an ox or bull in general. Pl. ي *ī*. غڅکۍ *ghutska'ī*, s.f. (6th) A cow. Sing. and Pl. See دنګر , ستور , and غويي

غڅيدل *ghutsedal*, verb intrans. To become severed or cut. غڅول *ghutsawul*, verb trans. To cut, to sever. See غوڅيدل and غوڅول

غچ *ghach*, s.m. (2nd) Malice, spite, rancor, resentment, hatred, grudge, pique. 2. Sound, noise, resonance. Pl. غچونه *ghachūnah*. غچ لرل *ghach laral*, verb intrans. To entertain or nourish malice towards any one, to have a spite or grudge against. غچ کښل *ghach k'shal* (W.) or *ghach k'khal* (E.), verb trans. To vent one's hatred or malice on, to take revenge or vengeance.

غچکه *ghachaka'h*, s.f. (3rd) A kind of violin. Pl. ئ *ey*. See سرنده

غچه *ghuchah* or غچي *ghuchey*, interj. Oh! halloo! indeed!

غچي *ghachī*, s.f. (3rd) A pair of scissors, or shears. Pl. ئ *a'ī*. See بياتي

A غدر *ghadr*, s.m. (2nd) Fraud, deceit, perfidy, ingratitude, villany. Pl. غدرونه *ghadr-ūnah*. غدر کول *ghadr kawul*, verb trans. To defraud, to act perfidiously or villanously.

A غذا *ghazā*, s.f. (6th) Food, provision, diet. aliment, (E.) Sing. and Pl. (W.) غذاوي *ghazāwī*.

غر *ghar*, s.m. (7th) A mountain, a hill, a crag, a mount. Pl. غرونَ *gh'rūna* or غرونه *gh'rūnah*. د غرّ پلوسي *da gh'ra palū-sey*, A species of thorny tree growing in the hills, and only used for fuel. See پلوسي

غر *ghur*, s.m. (2nd) The goiture or bronchocele. Pl. غرونه *ghurūnah*. غرَي *ghuraey*, s.m. (1st) A person afflicted with goiture. Pl. ي *ī*; or غرۍ *ghura'ī*, s.f. (6th). Sing. and Pl.

غړ *ghær*, s.m. (5th) Wind from behind, a fart. 2. The rattle of carriage wheels. Pl. غړهار *ghæra-hār*. غړهار لرل *ghæra-hār laral*, verb trans. To have flatulency, to be troubled with flatulency. غړ آچول *ghær āchawul*, verb trans. To break wind. غړاونړ *ghærā-wurrn*, adj. A farter, a mean cowardly fellow, a dastard, a recreant; (Fem.) غراونړه *ghærā-wurrna'h*. See تيز , etc.

غړ *ghær*, s.m. (9th) A leap, a jump, a bound, a spring. Sing. and Pl. غړ وهل *ghær wahal*, verb trans. To bound, to leap, to spring. See ترپ

غرا *gharā*, s.f. (6th) Thundering, pealing, roaring, resounding. (W.) Pl. غراوي *gharāwī* (E.) Sing. and Pl. غرا کول *gharā kawul*, verb trans. To thunder, to roar, to peal, to resound.

A غراره *gharāra'h*, s.f. (3rd) A large sack. Pl. ئ *ey*.

غرانډه *gharāndda'h*, s.f. (3rd) A flame or blaze with smoke. Pl. ئ *ey*. See دانډئ

A غربت *ghurbat*, s.m. (2nd) Emigration, being far from country and friends, travelling. Pl. غربتونه *ghurbatūnah*.

غربه *gharaba'h*, s.f. (3rd) A cannon, a gun. Pl. ئ *ey*.

غربي *gharabbaey*, s.m. (1st) A buckle, a breast or waist plate, a hook and loop for a belt. 2. The boom or report of a gun. Pl. ي *ī*.

غرپش *ghur-pash* or *ghur-pish*, s.m. (2nd) Disturbance, clamor, tumult, din, noise, etc. Pl. غرپشونه *ghur-pashūnah* or *ghur-pishūnah*.

A غرة *gharat* or *ghurrah*, adj. Proud, haughty, arrogant. (Masc. and Fem.)

غرڅني *ghartsanaey*, s.m. (1st) A mountain goat, sheep, or deer in general. Pl. ي *ī*. s.f. (6th) ئ *a'ī*. Sing. and Pl.

غرڅني پيش *gharts̲anaey pīs̲h*, s.m. (6th) A mountain cat. Sing. and Pl. See پرانګ پيش

غرڅه *gharts̲ah*, adj. Mountain, dwelling in or pertaining to a mountain (as animals, etc.)

غرچيدل *ghurc̲hedal*, verb trans. To roar, to bellow (as a bull, etc.)

P غرزنګ *ghur-zang*, s.m. (2nd) A leap, a jump, a spring, a bound. Pl. غرزنګونه *ghur-zang-ūnah*. See ترپ

غرزي *ghurzaey*, s.m. (1st) A surge, eddy, whirl, gurge, strong current of a river. 2. A drain or water course leading from a river. Pl. ي *ī*. په غرزي تلل *pah ghurzī t'lal*, verb intrans. To go or pass along with a strong current, to flow with a surge or eddy (as a stream).

غرزيدل *ghur-zedal*, verb intrans. To jump, to leap, to bound, to shake, to palpitate, to bob, to surge, to toss about, to flop, to be agitated (as the sea, etc.) Pres. غرزي *ghurzī* ; past وُ غرزيده *wu-ghurzedah* or غرزيد *ghurzeda* ; fut. وُ به غرزي *wu bah ghurzī* ; imp. وُ غرزه *wu-ghurzah* ; act. part. غرزيدونکي *ghurze-dūnkaey* or غرزيدوني *ghurzedūnaey* ; past part. غرزيدلي *ghurzedalaey* ; verb. n. غرزيدنه *ghurzedana'h* or غرزيده *ghurzedah*. غرزول *ghur-zawul*, verb trans. To throw, to propel, to project, to fling, to pitch, to jerk, to toss, to agitate, to tumble, etc. Pres. غرزوي *ghur-zawī* ; past وُ غرزاوه *wu-ghurzāwuh* or غرزاوو *ghurzāwo* ; fut. وُ به غرزوي *wu bah ghur-zawī* ; imp. وُ غرزوه *wu ghurzawah* ; act. part. غرزوونکي *ghurzawūnkaey* or غرزووني *ghur-zawūnaey* ; past part. غرزولي *ghurzawulaey* ; verb. n. غرزونه *ghurzawuna'h*.

غرشين *ghar-s̲hīn*, s.m. (5th) The name of an Afghān tribe of the Sarah-barrn division. Pl. غرشينان *ghar-s̲hīnān*. غرشينه *ghar-s̲hīna'h*, s.f. (3rd) A female of the above tribe. Pl. ې *ey*.

A غرض *gharaẓ*, s.m. (2nd) Design, intention, object, aim, end, purpose, view, wish, meaning, need, occasion, use, want, interest, selfishness, etc. Pl. غرضونه *gharaẓūnah*. 2. adv. In short, in fine, in a word. غرض مند *gharaẓ mand* or من *man*, adj. Selfish, designing, interested, desirous ; (Fem.) غرض منده *gharaẓ manda'h* or منه *mana'h*. غرض لرل *gharaẓ laral*, verb trans. To have an interest, design, aim, or object in anything, to need, to want, to have occasion for. غرض کول *gharaẓ kawul*, verb trans. To design, to aim at, to purpose, to mean, to intend, to want, to require.

غرغره *ghar-gharra'h*, s.f. (3rd) Gurgling. 2. A flame. Pl. ې *ey*. غرغره کول *ghar-gharra'h kawul*, verb trans. To make a gurgling sound in the throat, like an angry camel. وقت د غرغرې *wakt da ghar-gharrey*, The agony of death (the period when the death rattle is in the throat).

غرغشت *ghar-ghus̲ht*, s.m. (2nd) Play, sport, mirth, amusement, a kind of play amongst women. Pl. غرغشتونه *ghar-ghus̲htūnah*.

غرغشت *ghar-ghus̲ht* or *ghar-ghas̲ht*, s. prop. The name of the second son of Æabd-ur-Ras̲hīd, Pattān, from whom one of the great divisions of the Afghān tribes takes its name. غرغشتي *ghar-ghus̲htī*, s.m. (1st) Pl. The name of one of the great divisions of the Afghāns. غرغشتي *ghar-ghus̲htaey*, A man of the above. 2. The name of a village. غرغشتۍ *ghar-ghus̲hta'ī*, s.f. (6th) A female of the above. Sing. and Pl.

A غرق *ghark*, adj. Drowned, immersed, sunk ; (Fem.) غرقه *gharka'h*. غرق کيدل *ghark kedal*, verb intrans. To become immersed, sunk or drowned. غرق کول *ghark kawul*, verb trans. To sink, to drown, to immerse. غرقيدل *ghark-edal*, verb intrans. and غرقول *ghark-awul*, verb trans. See دوب

P غرقاب *ghark-āb*, s.m. (2nd) A vortex, a whirlpool, deep water. Pl. غرقابونه *gharkābūnah*.

غرکمانه *ghur-kamāna'h*, s.f. (3rd) A pellet bow. Pl. ې *ey*.

غرګي *ghar-gaey*, s.m. (1st) A pebble, a small round stone. Pl. ي *ī*. See غنده and قرت کانړي

غرمه *gharma'h*, s.f. (3rd) Noon, the middle of the day. 2. The heat of the sun. Pl. ې *ey*. تکنده غرمه *ttakanda'h gharma'h* or تکنۍ غرمه

ttakana'ī gharma'h, Exactly noon, mid-day, the period when the heat is the greatest. غرمه غو gharma'h gho, Copulation in the day time or about mid-day.

غرندي gharandaey, s.m. (1st) The wind-pipe, the throat. 2. The hollow over the collar bone. Pl. ي ī. See غري and غاړه

غرنګ gharang, s.m. (5th) The creaking sound of a spinning wheel or of a well. Pl. غرنګهار gharangahār. غرنګهار لرل gharangahār laral or غرنګ وهل gharang wahal, verb trans. To creak, to make a sharp grating sound.

غرنيکه ghar-nīkæh, s.m. (5th) A great grandfather. Pl. غرنيکهګان ghar-nīkæhgān. غر له انا ghar lah anā, s.f. (5th) A great grandmother. Pl. غر له اناګانِ ghar lah anāgāni. See ورنيکه

A غروب ghurūb, s.m. (9th) The setting of the sun. 2. The west. Sing. and Pl. غروب کيدل ghurūb kedal, verb intrans. To set as the sun, moon, or stars. See نمر پريوتل

A غرور ghurūr, s.m. (9th) Pride, vanity, vainglory, haughtiness. Sing. and Pl. غرور لرل ghurūr laral, verb trans. To have pride, vanity, haughtiness (Eng. verb intrans.) to be vain, etc.

غروړي ghurūrraey, s.m. (1st) A tumour, a swelling, a lump, an excrescence, a node. Pl. ي ī.

غر و سم ghar-o-sam, Hill and dale, mountain and plain.

غره gharah, adj. Proud, haughty, vain, arrogant. (Masc. and Fem.)

غره ghara'h, s.f. (3rd) The backside, podex. Pl. ئ ey. See کونه

غرئ gharaey, s.m. (1st) The wind-pipe, the throat, the pit or hollow over the collar bone. Pl. ي ī. See غرندي

غرياښي ghar-yākhaey or ghar-yāshaey, s.m. (1st) A button hole, a loop for a button. Pl. ي ī. See غرياشه and غوتي

A غريب gharīb, adj. (from غربت) Poor, humble, meek, mild, foreign, strange, wonderful. 2. A stranger, a foreigner; (Fem.) غريبه gharīb-a'h. غريبي gharībī, s.f. (3rd) Humility. meekness, wretchedness, foreignness. Pl. ئ a'ī.

غريدل gharedal, verb intrans. To jabber, to babble, to chatter, to twaddle. Pres. غريږي gharejzī (W.) or غريګي gharegī (E.); past و غريده wu-gharedah or غريدَ ghareda; fut. و به غريږي wu bah gharejzī or غريګي gharegī; imp. و غريږه wu-gharejzah or و غريګه wu-gharegah; act. part. غريدونکئ gharedūnkaey or غريدونئ gharedūnaey; past part. غريدلئ gharedalaey; verb. n. غريدنه gharedana'h or غريده gharedah.

غريشئ ghar-yasha'ī, s.f. (6th) A loop for a button, a button-hole. Sing. and Pl. See پلواهه and غوتي

غريو gh'rew, s.m. (9th) Grief, sorrow, anxiety, lamentation, groaning, weeping. Sing. and Pl. غريو ناك gh'rew-nāk, adj. About or ready to weep, vexed, anxious, sorrowful; (Fem.) غريو ناکه gh'rew-nāka'h.

غړاشه gharr-āsha'h, s.f. (3rd) A loop hole for a button, a button-hole. Also غرياشه ghurr-yāsha'h, s.f. (3rd). Pl. ئ ey. See پلواهه

غړانګه gharrānga'h, s.f. (3rd) A loud noise, a squall, scream, a screech, outcry, vociferation. 2. A long neck. Pl. ئ ey. غړانګه ور gharrānga'h war, adj. Long-necked, having a long neck; (Fem.) غړانګه وره gharrānga'h-wara'h.

غړپ ghurrap, s.m. (2nd) A draught, a dram, a gulp. Pl. غړپونه ghurrapūna'h. غړپول ghurrapawul, verb trans. To gulp, to take down, to imbibe, to take by mouthfuls, to guzzle, to swill. Pres. غړپوي ghurrapawī; past غړپ کړ ghurrap karr or و کړ wu-karr; fut. غړپ به کړي ghurrap bah krrī or به و کړي bah wu-krrī; imp. غړپ کړه ghurrap krrah or و کړه wu-krrah; act. part. غړپوونکئ ghurrapawūnkaey or غړپوونئ ghurrapawūnaey; past part. غړپ کړئ ghurrap karraey; verb. n. غړپونه ghurrapawuna'h.

غړڅکئ ghurrutskaey, s.m. (1st) Burning straw, etc. anything thrown out by a fire, a spark. 2. An atom, a small quantity. Pl. ي ī. See ښخري and ښکرکي

غړل *gharral*, verb trans. To twist, to spin, to plait. Pres. غړي *gharrī*; fut. وُ به غړي *wu bah gharrī*; imp. وُ غړه *wu-gharrah*. This infinitive is imperfect, and the other tenses are taken from غښتل, which is also imperfect with regard to the inflections in which the former is perfect.

غړنب *ghurrumb* or *ghurrunb*, s.m. (5th) A roar, a peal, a swell, a blast, a boom, thunder, echo. 2. The roar of a wild beast. Pl. غړنبهار *ghurrumbahār* or *ghurrunbahār*. غړنبل *ghurrumbal*, verb trans. To roar, to peal, to boom, to echo, to thunder, to roar as a beast. Pres. غړانبي *ghurr-ānbī*; past وُ غړنبل *wu-ghurrumbal*; fut. وُ به غړانبي *wu bah ghurr-ānbī*; imp. وُ غړنبه *wu-ghurrambah*; act. part. غړنبونکَي *ghurrumbūnkaey* or غړنبونَي *ghurrumbūnaey*; past part. غړنبلي *ghurrumbalī* (Pl.); verb. n. غړنبنه *ghurrumbana'h*.

غړنبيدل *ghurrumbedal*, verb intrans. To roar, to bellow, to cry with a loud noise, to peal, to swell, to boom, to thunder, to echo. Pres. غړنبيږي *ghurrumbejzī* (W.) or غړنبيکي *ghurrumbegī* (E.); past وُ غړنبيده *wu-ghurrumbedah* or غړنبيدَ *ghurrumbeda*; fut. وُ به غړنبيږي *wu bah ghurrumbejzī* or غړنبيکي *ghurrumbegī*; imp. وُ غړنبيږه *wu-ghurrumbejzah* or غړنبيکه *ghurrumbegah*; act. part. غړنبيدونکَي *ghurrumbedūnkaey* or غړنبيدونَي *ghurrumbedūnaey*; past part. غړنبيدلَي *ghurrumbedalaey*; verb. n. غړنبيدنه *ghurrumbedana'h* or غړنبيده *ghurrumbedah*. غړنبول *ghurrumbawul*, verb trans. To make or cause to roar, bellow, peal, swell, boom, to thunder, to echo, etc. Pres. غړنبوي *ghurrumbawī*; past وُ غړنباوه *wu-ghurrumbāwuh*; fut. وُ به غړنبوي *wu bah ghurrumbawī*; imp. وُ غړنبوه *wu-ghurrumbawah*; act. part. غړنبوونکَي *ghurrumbawūnkaey* or غړنبوونَي *ghurrumbawūnaey*; past part. غړنبولَي *ghurrumbawulaey*; verb. n. غړنبونه *ghurrumbawuna'h*. See تنرا

غړند *gharrand*, adj. Loose, lax, relaxed; weak, frail, soft; lazy, negligent, idle, slothful; slow, tardy, inactive, dilatory; languid, feeble (through sickness). 2. Stealthy, sly, sneaking, skulking, feline, close. 3. Cautious, wary, chary; (Fem.) غړنده *gharranda'h*. غړند والَي *gharrand wālaey*, s.m. (1st) Looseness, weakness, laziness, slothfulness; languor, feebleness. 2. Stealth, slyness; caution, weariness. Pl. والي *wālī*. په غړند تلل *pah gharrand t'lal*, verb intrans. To go along stealthily or slyly like a cat, to sneak along like a thief.

غړوندَي *gharrwandaey*, s.m. (1st) A rope for fastening horses, etc. 2. A collar for a dog. 3. A halter. 4. The mark jazm (ـْ). Pl. ي *ī*.

غړَي *gharraey*, s.m. (1st) A kind of bread given to the poor. 2. The calf or fleshy part of the leg. Pl. ي *ī*.

غړيدل *gharredal*, verb intrans. To deviate, to radiate, to swerve, to wander from, to turn aside, to digress, to go astray. 2. To prick, to irritate, to grate, to annoy, to vex, to perplex. Pres. غړيږي *gharrejzī* (W.) or غړيکي *gharregī* (E.); past وُ غړيده *wu-gharredah* or غړيدَ *gharreda*; fut. وُ به غړيږي *wu bah gharrejzī* or غړيکي *gharregī*; imp. وُ غړيږه *wu-gharrejzah* or غړيکه *gharregah*; act. part. غړيدونکَي *gharredūnkaey* or غړيدونَي *gharredūnaey*; past part. غړيدلَي *gharredalaey*; verb. n. غړيدنه *gharredana'h* or غړيده *gharredah*. غړول *gharrawul*, verb trans. To cause to deviate, to make to swerve, to turn aside. 2. To turn, to turn round, to twirl, to trundle, to spin, to revolve. Pres. غړوي *gharrawī*; past وُ غړاوه *wu-gharrāwuh* or غړاوو *gharrāwo*; fut. وُ به غړوي *wu bah gharrawī*; imp. وُ غړوه *wu-gharrawah*; act. part. غړوونکَي *gharrawūnkaey* or غړوونَي *gharrawūnaey*; past part. غړولَي *gharrawulaey*; verb. n. غړونه *gharrawuna'h*.

غړيدل *ghurredal*, verb intrans. To open, to spread, to unclose (as a flower). 2. To become soiled. And غړول *ghurrawul*, verb trans. To unclose, to open, to unfold. 2. To soil, to anoint. See غوړيدل and غوړول

غز *ghaz*, s.m. (2nd) The tamarisk tree (Tamarix Indica). Pl. غزونه *ghazūnah*.

A غزا *ghazā*, s.f. (6th) Making war against infidels. (E.) Sing. and Pl. (W.) Pl. غزاوي *ghazā-wī*. 2. interj. How wonderful! astonishing! غزا كول *ghazā kawul*, verb trans. To make war on infidels.

غزار *ghuzār*, adj. Fallen, overturned, upset, dropped, descended; (Fem.) غزاره *ghuzārah*. غزاريدل *ghuzāredal*, verb intrans. To fall, to tumble, to slip, to plump down, to descend, to drop, to alight, to come down. Pres. غزاريږي *ghuzārejzī* (W.) or غزاريگي *ghuzāregī* (E.); past غزار شه *ghuzār shah* or وُ شه *wu-shah*; fut. غزار به شي *ghuzār bah shī* or به وُ شي *bah wu-shī*; imp. غزار شه *ghuzār shah* or وُ شه *wu-shah*; act. part. غزاريدونكَي *ghuzāredūnkaey* or غزاريدونَي *ghuzāredūnaey*; past part. غزار *ghuzār* or غزار شوَي *ghuzār shawaey*; verb. n. غزاريدنه *ghuzāredana'h* or غزاريده *ghuzāredah*. غزارول *ghuzārawul*, verb trans. To throw, to throw down, to fling down, to overturn, to prostrate in wrestling. Pres. غزاروي *ghuzārawī*; past غزار كړ *ghuzār kurr* or وُ كړ *wu-karr*; fut. غزار به كړي *ghuzār bah krrī* or به وُ كړي *bah wu-krrī*; imp. غزار كړه *ghuzār krrah* or وُ كړه *wu-krrah*; act. part. غزاروونكَي *ghuzārawūnkaey* or غزاروونَي *ghuzārawūnaey*; past part. غزار كړَي *ghuzār karraey*; verb. n. غزارونه *ghuzārawuna'h*.

A غزال *ghazāl*, s.m. (5th) A fawn, a young deer. Pl. غزالان *ghazālān*. غزاله *ghazāla'h*, s.f. (3rd). Pl. ي *ey*. See كبلي

A غزل *ghazal*, s.m. (2nd) An ode, an amatory poem. Pl. غزلونه *ghazalūnah*. غزلي *ghazalī*, s.m. (5th) A reciter of odes, a bard, a minstrel. Pl. غزليان *ghazaliān*.

غزيدل *ghazedal*, verb intrans. To repose, to recline, to stretch out, to lie along, to lie down, to lie flat, to retire to rest. Pres. غزيږي *ghazejzī* (W.) or غزيگي *ghazegī* (E.); past وُ غزيده *wu-ghazedah* or غزيدَ *ghazeda*; fut. وُ به غزيږي *wu bah ghazejzī* or غزيگي *ghazegī*; imp. وُ غزيږه *wu-ghazejzah* or غزيگه *ghazegah*; act. part. غزيدونكَي *ghazedūnkaey* or غزيدونَي *ghazedūnaey*; past part. غزيدلَي *ghazedalaey*; verb. n. غزيدنه *ghazedana'h* or غزيده *ghazedah*. غزول *ghazawul*, verb trans. To level, to lay down, to floor, to prostrate, to lay flat, to make recline. Pres. غزوي *ghazawī*; past وُ غزاوه *wu-ghazāwuh* or غزاوو *ghazāwo*; fut. وُ به غزوي *wu bah ghazawī*; imp. وُ غزوه *wu-ghazawah*; act. part. غزوونكَي *ghazawūnkaey* or غزوونَي *ghazawūnaey*; past part. غزولَي *ghazawulaey*; verb. n. غزونه *ghazawuna'h*.

غږ *ghajz*, s.m. (2nd) (W.) Sound, noise, strain, voice, intonation, resonance, accent. Pl. غږونه *ghajzūnah*. غږيدل *ghajzedal*, verb intrans. To sound, to give out or emit sound, to resound, to intonate. Pres. غږيږي *ghajzejzī*; past وُ غږيده *wu-ghajzedah* or غږيدَ *ghajzeda*; fut. وُ به غږيږي *wu bah ghajzejzī*; imp. وُ غږيږه *wu-ghajzejzah*; act. part. غږيدونكَي *ghajzedūnkaey* or غږيدونَي *ghajzedūnaey*; past part. غږيدلَي *ghajzedalaey*; verb. n. غږيدنه *ghajzedana'h* or غږيده *ghajzedah*. غږول *ghajzawul*, verb trans. To sound, to noise abroad, to make resound, etc. Pres. غږوي *ghajzawī*; past وُ غږاوه *wu-ghajzāwuh* or غږاوو *ghajzāwo*; fut. وُ به غږوي *wu bah ghajzawī*; imp. وُ غږوه *wu-ghajzawah*; act. part. غږوونكَي *ghajzawūnkaey* or غږوونَي *ghajzawūnaey*; past part. غږولَي *ghajzawulaey*; verb. n. غږونه *ghajzawuna'h*. See ږغ and شك

A غسل *ghusl*, s.m. (2nd) Bathing, ablution. Pl. غسلونه *ghuslūnah*. غسل كول *ghusl kawul*, verb trans. To bathe, to wash. غسل خانه *ghusl khāna'h*, s.f. (3rd) A bath, a bagnio. Pl. ي *ey*. غسل وركول *ghusl war-kawul*, verb trans. To wash, to cleanse, to bathe (another person). See لمبيدل

غشايه *ghushāyah*, s.m. (4th) (Pl.) Dung of a cow, buffalo, horse, and the like. Sing. غشوي *ghusho-e*, but rarely used. See پچه

غشو *ghasho*, s.m. (2nd) A curry comb for a horse. Pl. غشوونه *ghasho-ūnah*. غشو كول *ghasho kawul*, verb trans. To curry-comb, to curry, to scrape.

غشيَ *ghashaey*, s.m. (1st) An arrow, the pole of a plough or cart, the spoke of the wheel of a Persian wheel. Pl. يِ *ī*. 2. adj. Swift, straight, direct. غش لاستيَ *ghash-lāstaey* or غشيَ لاستيَ *ghashaey-lāstaey* (corrup. of غش لاسيَ *ghash-lāsaey* or غشيَ لاسيَ *ghashaey-lāsaey*), An archer, a good marksman with an arrow. Pl. يِ *ī*. د غشي خوله *da ghashī khūla'h*, s.f. (3rd) The notch in the end of an arrow to which the bow-string is fitted. Pl. يْ *ey*. د غشي پر خانه *da ghashī par khāna'h*, s.f. (3rd) The place in which the feathers are inserted in an arrow or dart. Pl. يْ *ey*.

غښتل *ghashtal* (W.) or *ghakhtal* (E.) verb intrans. To twist, to spin, to roll up. This infinitive is imperfect with respect to all the present tenses, and the imperative, which are taken from غړل, also defective in the past tenses. Past وُ غښت *wu-ghasht* or *wu-ghakht*; act. part. غښتونكيَ *ghashtūnkaey* or *ghakhtūnkaey* or غښتونيَ *ghashtūnaey* or *ghakhtūnaey*; past part. غښتليَ *ghashtalaey* or *ghakhtalaey*; verb. n. غښتنه *ghashtana'h* or *ghakhtana'h*.

غښتليَ *ghashtalaey* (W.) or *ghakhtalaey* (E.) adj. (past part.) Twisted, spun. 2. Strong, well-knit, powerful, muscular; (Fem.) غښتلې *ghashtali* or *ghakhtali*. Pl. (Masc. and Fem.) يِ *ī*.

غښتل *ghushtal* or *ghukhtal*, verb trans. To desire, to call for, to ask, to request, etc. See غوښتل

A غصب *ghaṣab*, s.m. (2nd) Violence, force, plunder, injustice, oppression, ravishing. Pl. غصبونه *ghaṣabūnah*. غصب كول *ghaṣab kawul*, verb trans. To dispossess by force, to ravish, to show violence.

A غصه *ghuṣṣa'h*, s.f. (3rd) (from غص) Anger, passion, rage. Pl. يْ *ey*. غصه ناك *ghuṣṣa'h nāk*, adj. Angry, passionate; (Fem.) غصه ناكه *ghuṣṣa'h-nāka'h*. غصه كول *ghuṣṣa'h kawul*, verb trans. To rage.

A غضب *ghaẓab*, s.m. (2nd) Violence, compulsion, injustice, oppression, passion, rage, fury, wrath, anger, vengeance, calamity. Pl. غضبونه *ghaẓabūnah*. غضب ناك *ghaẓab-nāk*, adj. Enraged, indignant, wrathful; (Fem.) غضب ناكه *ghaẓab nāka'h*. غضب كول *ghaẓab kawul*, verb trans. To oppress, to tyrannize over.

غفار *ghaffār*, adj. (sup. of غفر) Forgiving, a forgiver (the Deity).

A غفر *ghafr* or غفران *ghufrān*, s.m. (9th) Pardon, remission of sins. Sing. and Pl.

A غفلت *ghaflat*, s.m. (2nd) Carelessness, negligence, neglect, inattention, inadvertency, remissness. Pl. غفلتونه *ghaflat-ūnah*. غفلت كول *ghaflat kawul*, verb trans. To show or act with carelessness, remissness, or inattention.

A غفور *ghafūr*, adj. (sup. of غفر) Clement, forgiving, merciful.

غګ *ghag*, s.m. (2nd) (E.) Sound, noise, strain, voice, intonation, resonance, accent. Pl. غګونه *ghagūnah*. غګيدل *ghagedal*, verb intrans. To sound, to emit sound, to resound, to make a noise. Pres. غګيږي *ghagegī*; past وُ غګيده *wu-ghagedah* or غګيدَ *ghageda*; fut. وُ به غګيږي *wu bah ghagegī*; imp. وُ غګيږه *wu-ghagegah*; act. part. غګيدونكيَ *ghagedūnkaey* or غګيدونيَ *ghagedūnaey*; past part. غګيدليَ *ghagedalaey*; verb. n. غګيدنه *ghagedana'h* or غګيده *ghagedah*. غګول *ghagawul*, verb trans. To sound, to noise abroad, to intonate, to make resound. Pres. غګوي *ghagawī*; past وُ غګاوه *wu-ghagāwuh* or غګاوو *ghagāwo*; fut. وُ به غګوي *wu bah ghagawī*; imp. وُ غګوه *wu-ghagawah*; act. part. غګوونكيَ *ghagawūnkaey* or غګوونيَ *ghagawūnaey*; past part. غګوليَ *ghagawulaey*; verb. n. غګونه *ghagawuna'h*. See غ and غ يدل

غل *ghal*, s.m. (4th) A thief, a robber, a plunderer. Pl. غلُ *gh'læ* or غلهٔ *gh'læh*. غله *gh'la'h*, s.f. (3rd). Pl. يْ *ey*.

غل *ghul*, s.m. (6th) Excrement, alvine discharge (pec. of human beings). Sing. and Pl. غل كول *ghul kawul*, verb trans. To evacuate, to ease one's-self, to go to stool, to void excrement. غلو نيول *ghulo nīwal*, verb trans. To be taken short (*lit.* To seize excrement).

غلا *ghlā*, s.f. (6th) Theft, robbery, stealing, thieving, pilfering, larceny, peculation. (E.) Sing. and Pl. (W.) Pl. غلاوي *ghlāwī*. غلا کول *ghlā kawul*, verb trans. To steal, to rob, to filch, to pilfer, to plunder, to embezzle. په غلا تلل *pah ghlā t'lal*, verb intrans. To become stolen, pilfered, filched, embezzled, etc.

A غلاف *ghilāf*, s.m. (2nd) (from غلف) A case, a cover, a sheath. Pl. غلافونه *ghilāfūnah*. See تیکي and پوښ

A غلام *ghulām*, s.m. (5th) A slave. Pl. غلامان *ghulāmān*. غلامي *ghulāmī*, s.f. (3rd) Slavery, service. Pl. ئي *a'ī*. See مرئي and وينځه

غلانزه *ghulānza'h*, s.f. (3rd) The udder of a cow, goat, etc. Pl. ئي *ey*; or غلانځه *ghulāndza'h*, s.f. (3rd). Pl. ئي *ey*.

غلبله *ghal-bala'h*, s.f. (3rd) Outcry, noise, sound, roaring, screaming, bellowing. Pl. ئي *ey*. غلبلي وهل *ghal-baley wahal*, verb trans. To raise a noise, outcry, disturbance, to scream, to roar, to bellow. (HI غلبلا)

A غلبه *ghalaba'h*, s.f. (3rd) Superiority, prevalence, conquest, overcoming, advantage, assault, strength. Pl. ئي *ey*. غلبه کول *ghalaba'h kawul*, verb trans. To overpower, to conquer, to overcome.

غلبیل *ghalbel*, s.m. (2nd) A sieve, a riddle, a colander, a sifter. 2. Sifting, cleaning, winnowing. Pl. غلبیلونه *ghalbelūnah*. غلبیلول *ghalbelawul*, verb trans. To sift, to part, to separate, to clean, to winnow. Pres. غلبیلوي *ghalbelawī*; past غلبیل کړ *ghalbel karr* or وُ کړ *wu-karr*; fut. غلبیل به کړي *ghalbel bah krrī* or به وُ کړي *bah wu-krrī*; imp. غلبیل کړه *ghalbel krrah* or وُ کړه *wu-krrah*; act. part. غلبیلوونکَي *ghalbelawūnkaey* or غلبیلوونَي *ghalbelawūnaey*; past part. غلبیل کړَي *ghalbel karraey*; verb. n. غلبیلونه *ghalbelawuna'h*. See پیزل

غلت *ghulat*, s.m. (9th) Cheating at play, trick, subterfuge. Sing. and Pl.

غلتي *ghulatī*, s.f. (3rd) Cheating or tricking at play. Pl. ئي *a'ī*. 2. adj. A cheat at play. (Sing. and Pl.; Masc. and Fem.) غلتي کول *ghulatī kawul*, verb trans. To cheat, to play unfairly.

غلتیا *ghulatī'ā*, s.f. (6th) Cheating, unfairness at play. (E.) Sing. and Pl. (W.) Pl. غلتیاوي *ghulatī'āwī*.

غلجي *ghal-jī*, s.m. (1st) Pl. The name of a tribe of Afghāns. Also written غلزي *ghal-zī*, both of which are corruptions of the words غل *ghal*, a thief, and زوي *zoey*, a son, from which the word is derived. See Introduction to Grammar, page 16. غلجي *ghal-jaey* or غلزي *ghal-zaey*, (Sing.) A man of the above tribe. غلجۍ *ghal-ja'ī* or غلزۍ *ghal-za'ī*, s.f. (6th) A female of the above. Sing. and Pl.

A غلط *ghalaṭ*, s.m. (2nd) An error, a mistake, a blunder. Pl. غلطونه *ghalaṭūnah*. 2. adj. Wrong, erroneous, mistaken; (Fem.) غلطه *ghalaṭa'h*. غلطي *ghalaṭī*, s.f. (3rd) An error, a mistake, a blunder. Pl. ئي *a'ī*. غلطي کول *ghalaṭī kawul*, verb trans. To make an error, mistake, blunder, etc. غلط تیا *ghalaṭ-tī'ā*, s.f. (6th) Mistake, error, blunder, etc. (E.) Sing. and Pl.; (W.) Pl. تیاوي *tī'āwī*.

غلطیدل *ghalaṭedal*, verb intrans. To mistake, to commit error, to blunder, to err, to lose one's-self, to miscalculate, to misunderstand. Pres. غلطیږي *ghalaṭejzī* (W.) or غلطیګي *ghalaṭegī* (E.); past غلط شه *ghalaṭ shah* or وُ شه *wu-shah*; fut. غلط به شي *ghalaṭ bah shī* or به وُ شي *bah wu-shī*; imp. غلط شه *ghalaṭ shah* or وُ شه *wu-shah*; act. part. غلطیدونکَي *ghalaṭedūnkaey* or غلطیدونَي *ghal-aṭedūnaey*; past part. غلط *ghalaṭ* or غلط شوَي *ghalaṭ shawaey*; verb. n. غلطیدنه *ghalaṭ-edana'h* or غلطیده *ghalaṭedah*. غلطول *ghal-aṭawul*, verb trans. To mislead, to cause to err, to delude, to lead astray, to beguile, to deceive. Pres. غلطوي *ghalaṭawī*; past غلط کړ *ghalaṭ karr* or وُ کړ *wu-karr*; fut. غلط به کړي *ghalaṭ bah krrī* or به وُ کړي *bah wu-krrī*; imp. غلط کړه *ghalaṭ krrah* or وُ کړه *wu-krrah*; act. part. غلطوونکَي *ghalaṭawūnkaey* or غلطوونَي *ghalaṭawūnaey*; past part. غلط کړَي

<u>gh</u>alaṭ karraey; verb. n. غلطونه <u>gh</u>alaṭa-wuna'h.

P غلغله <u>gh</u>ul<u>gh</u>ula'h, s.f. (3rd) Noise, tumult, disturbance, din, uproar, etc. Pl. ې ey. غلغله كول <u>gh</u>ul<u>gh</u>ula'h kawul, verb trans. To make a noise, to create a tumult or disturbance.

غلوزه <u>gh</u>lawza'h, s.f. (3rd) The honey bee. Pl. ې ey. See لوزه and مچ مچۍ

A غله <u>gh</u>ala'h, s.f. (3rd) (from غل) The produce of the earth, corn, grain. Pl. ې ey.

غلي <u>gh</u>alaey, adj. Silent, concealed, hidden, still, lurking, crouching, lying hid, lying in ambush; (Fem.) غل <u>gh</u>ali. Pl. (Masc. and Fem.) ي ī. غلي توب <u>gh</u>alaey-tob, s.m. (2nd) Concealment, hiding, secrecy, stealth. Pl. توبونه tobūnah. غلي كول <u>gh</u>alaey kawul, verb trans. To place in ambush or concealment, to conceal. غلي كيدل <u>gh</u>alaey kedal, verb intrans. To crouch, to lurk, to lie in wait, to lie in ambush, to conceal one's-self.

غليدل <u>gh</u>uledal, verb intrans. To be deceived, to be misled, to be cheated, to be imposed upon, to be bamboozled, hoaxed, juggled, etc. Pres. غليږي <u>gh</u>ulejzī (W.) or غليكي <u>gh</u>ulegī (E.); past و غليده nu-<u>gh</u>uledah or غليد <u>gh</u>uleda; fut. و به غليږي nu bah <u>gh</u>ulejzī or غليكي <u>gh</u>ulegī; imp. و غليږه nu-<u>gh</u>ulejzah or و غليكه nu-<u>gh</u>ulegah; act. part. غليدونكي <u>gh</u>uledūnkaey or غليدوني <u>gh</u>uledūnaey; past part. غليدلي <u>gh</u>uledalaey; verb. n. غليدنه <u>gh</u>uledana'h or غليده <u>gh</u>uledah. غلول <u>gh</u>ulawul, verb trans. To deceive, to mislead, to cheat, to dupe, to defraud, to take in, to bamboozle, to trick. Pres. غلوي <u>gh</u>ulawī; past و غلاوه nu-<u>gh</u>ulāwuh or غلاوو <u>gh</u>ulāwo; fut. و به غلوي nu bah <u>gh</u>ulawī; imp. و غلوه nu-<u>gh</u>ulawah; act. part. غلوونكي <u>gh</u>ulawūnkaey or غلووني <u>gh</u>ulawūnaey; past part. غلولي <u>gh</u>ulawulaey; verb. n. غلونه <u>gh</u>ulawuna'h.

غليم <u>gh</u>alīm, s.m. (5th) (corrup. of A غنيم) An enemy, an adversary, a foe, a plunderer. Pl. غليمان <u>gh</u>alīmān. غليمه <u>gh</u>alīma'h, s.f. (3rd). Pl. ې ey. غليمي <u>gh</u>alīmī, s.f. (3rd) Enmity, animosity, hostility. Pl. ئ a'ī. غليمي كول <u>gh</u>alīmī kawul, verb trans. To evince enmity, to show hostility or animosity.

A غم <u>gh</u>am, s.m. (2nd) Grief, sorrow, distress, anxiety. Pl. غمونه <u>gh</u>amūnah. غمجن <u>gh</u>am-jan, adj. Grieved, sad, woful, sorrowful; (Fem.) غمجنه <u>gh</u>amjana'h. غم خور <u>gh</u>am-<u>kh</u>or, adj. Afflicted, sad. 2. A condoler, an intimate friend, a comforter; (Fem.) غم خوره <u>gh</u>am-<u>kh</u>ora'h. غم خوري <u>gh</u>am-<u>kh</u>orī, s.f. (3rd) Condolence, comfort, commiseration. 2. Affliction, distress. Pl. ئ a'ī. غم خوري كول <u>gh</u>am-<u>kh</u>orī kawul, verb trans. To console, to comfort, to commiserate. غم خوړل <u>gh</u>am-<u>kh</u>warral, verb trans. To grieve, to mourn. غم ديده <u>gh</u>am-dīdah, غم رسيده <u>gh</u>am-rasedah, or غم زده <u>gh</u>am-zadah, adj. Afflicted, accustomed to grief, distressed. غم غلط <u>gh</u>am-<u>gh</u>alaṭ, adj. A driver away of grief, a consoler, an antidote, a sedative; (Fem.) غم غلطه <u>gh</u>am-<u>gh</u>alaṭa'h. غم گسار <u>gh</u>am-gusār, adj. A remover of grief, a consoler, a confidant, an intimate friend; (Fem.) غم گساره <u>gh</u>am gusāra'h. غم گين <u>gh</u>am-gīn, adj. Sorrowful, grieved, sad, woful; (Fem.) غم گينه <u>gh</u>am-gīna'h. غم گيني <u>gh</u>am-gīnī, s.f. (3rd) Sorrowfulness, sadness, wofulness. Pl. ئ a'ī. غم كول <u>gh</u>am kawul, verb trans. To lament, to grieve. غم ناك <u>gh</u>am-nāk, adj. Sorrowful, sad, woful; (Fem.) غم ناكه <u>gh</u>am-nāka'h. غم نتلي <u>gh</u>am-natalaey, adj. Overwhelmed or overcome by grief, sorrow, etc.; (Fem.) غم نتلِ <u>gh</u>am-natali. Pl. (Masc. and Fem.) ي ī.

A غماز <u>gh</u>amāz, s.m. (5th) (from غمز) An informer, a backbiter, a talebearer. Pl. غمازان <u>gh</u>amāzān. غمازه <u>gh</u>amāza'h, s.f. (3rd). Pl. ې ey. غمازي <u>gh</u>amāzī, s.f. (3rd) Talebearing, backbiting. Pl. ئ a'ī. غمازي كول <u>gh</u>amāzī kawul, verb trans. To carry tales.

غماشه <u>gh</u>umā<u>sh</u>a'h, s.f. (3rd) A gnat, a mosquito. Pl. ې ey. See ماشي

غمبه <u>gh</u>umba'h, s.f. (3rd) A hard swelling, a protuberance, a gland, a knot, a tumour, a bubo, a scirrhus. Pl. ې ey. See غند and بوبكه

A غمزه ghamza'h, s.f. (3rd) A wink, an amorous glance, ogling, cast of the eyes, coquetry. Pl. ي ey. غمزه کول ghamza'h kawul, verb trans. To wink, to cast amorous glances, to ogle.

غمي ghamaey, s.m. (1st) The stone of a ring, on which the name or device is cut. 2. The ferule of a knife-handle, etc. Pl. ي ī.

غميدل ghamedal, verb intrans. To be overcome, to be conquered, subdued, subjugated, overpowered, worsted, etc. Pres. غميږي ghamejzī (W.) or غميگي ghamegī (E.); past وُ غميده wu-ghamedah or غميدَ ghameda; fut. وُ به غميږي wu bah ghamejzī or غميگي ghamegī; imp. وُ غميږه wu-ghamejzah or غميگه ghamegah; act. part. غميدونکي ghamedūnkaey or غميدونَي ghamedūnaey; past part. غميدلَي ghamedalaey; verb. n. غميدنه ghamedana'h or غميده ghamedah.

غمول ghamawul, verb trans. To overcome, to subdue, to conquer, to subjugate, to overpower, to get the upper hand of, to worst, to floor. Pres. غموي ghamawī; past وُ غماوه wu-ghamāwuh or وُ غماوو wu-ghamāwo; fut. وُ به غموي wu bah ghamawī; imp. وُ غموه wu-ghamawah; act. part. غموونکي ghamawūnkaey or غموونَي ghamawūnaey; past part. غمولَي ghamawulaey; verb. n. غمونه ghamawuna'h.

غمونه ghamawuna'h, s.f. (3rd) (verb. n.) Overpowering, overcoming, conquering, getting the upper hand, flooring, subduing. Pl. ي ey.

A غنا ghanā, s.f. (6th) Riches, wealth, opulence, content. (E.) Sing. and Pl. (W.) Pl. غناوي ghanāwī.

P غنچه ghuncha'h, s.f. (3rd) A bud, a sprout, a shoot, a rosebud. 2. A nosegay. Pl. ي ey.

غندِ ghundi, adj. Alike, similar, resembling, like, near, such as. 2. adv. As if, as it were, just as. See غندي and غوندِ.

غندل ghandal, s.f. (1st) A bud, a sprout, a shoot, particularly of the mustard plant, which is cooked and eaten as a vegetable. Pl. غندلِ ghandali.

غندل ghandal, verb trans. To dislike, to disapprove of, to regard with aversion or displeasure, to disrelish, to find fault with, to disparage, to run down, to animadvert upon. Pres. غندي ghandī; past وُ غانده wu-ghāndah or غاندَ ghānda; fut. وُ به غندي wu bah ghandī: imp. وُ غنده wu-ghandah; act. part. غندونکي ghandūnkaey or غندونَي ghandūnaey; past part. غندلَي ghandalaey; verb. n. غندنه ghandana'h.

غندنه ghandana'h, s.f. (3rd) (verb. n.) Disproval, dispraise, detraction, reprobation, animadversion, blame, censure. Pl. ي ey.

غندَي ghundaey, s.m. (1st) A kind of bag or pannier made of goat's hair for carrying loads on camels, asses, etc. Pl. ي ī. See غوندي

غندي ghundaey, adj. Alike, similar, resembling, like, near. 2. adv. As if, as it were, just as, such as. See غوندي

غنډ ghundd, adj. Round, globular, circular, orbicular. 2. Plump, squat. 3. s.m. (5th) A bubo. Pl. غنډان ghunddān; (Fem.) غنډه ghundda'h. غنډي ghunddaey, adj. (dimin. of غنډ) Little, small, low in stature, squat, dumpy, dwarfish. 2. A little fat man, a dwarf. 3. A venomous spider. Pl. ي ī. غنډۍ ghundda'ī, s.f. (6th) A little fat woman, a dwarf. 2. A large black spider, a tarantula, 3. A plant the remedy for its bite. Sing. and Pl.

غنډه ghundda'h, s.f. (3rd) A detached hill, separated from the higher range. 2. A round piece of leaven. 3. A large round stone, a pebble. Pl. ي ey. غنډه مرۍ ghundda'h mara'ī, s.f. (6th) Adam's apple, the prominent part of the throat. Sing. and Pl. غنډ ژبي ghundd-jzabey, adj. Thick-tongued, speaking a difficult dialect; all Afghāns who change the گ gāf for ږ jze, ز ze for څ dze, ج jīm for ژ jze, and ښ khīn for ښ shay—all Western Afghāns.

غنډارَي ghunddāraey or غنډهارَي ghunddhāraey, s.m. (1st) A kind of tumour, a bump, a bubo. 2. A noose, a snare. 3. A tumour which breaks out on the back of the neck, and very dangerous, often causing death. Pl. ي ī.

غنډايه ghunddāyah, s.m. (5th) A clown, a young man, a stripling, a lad, an unformed youth. Pl. غنډايان ghunddāyān.

غنډري ghundduraey, s.m. (1st) A ball, anything round, a circle. 2. A splinter of wood, etc. Pl. ي ī.

غنډكي ghunddaka'ī, s.f. (6th) Anything round; the mons veneris. Sing. and Pl.

غنډۍ ghundda'ī, s.f. (6th) A mound or detached hill separated from the higher range. Sing. and Pl.

غنزاښي ghunzāshaey (W.) or ghunzākhaey (E.), s.m. (1st) A kind of sweetmeat made of flour and sugar fried in butter, generally taken on a journey. Pl. ي ī.

غنم ghanam, s.m. (6th) Wheat. Sing. and Pl. غنم رنګ ghanam rang, adj. Wheat-coloured, brown, russet; (Fem.) غنم رنګه ghanam ranga'h, (P گندم)

غنه ghana'h, s.m. (3rd) The thorny branch of a tree, a bramble. 2. (W.) The branch of a tree. Pl. ې ey. 3. adj. Abashed, humbled.

A غني ghanī, adj. (act. part. of غنا) Independent, rich, opulent, wealthy.

A غنيمت ghanīmat, s.m. (2nd) Plunder, a prize, 2. Abundance, good fortune, a blessing. Pl. غنيمتونه ghanīmatūnah. غنيمت شميرل ghanīmat sh'meral, verb trans. To account as gain or good fortune.

غنړه gharrna'h, s.f. (3rd) A spider. Pl. ې ey. See جولا

غو gho or غوو gho-o, s.m. (9th) Copulation, coition. Sing. and Pl. غو gho or غوو كول gho-o kawul, verb trans. To copulate, to have connection with; or غوول gho-wul, verb trans. To copulate, to have coition. This verb is imperfect, and requires the imperfect infinitive غيل to make the conjugation complete. Pres. غيي gha-yey (from غيل); past وُ غوو wu-gho-wo; fut. وُ به غيي wu bah gha-yey; imp. وُ غيه wu-gha-yah; act. part. غووونكي gho-wūnkaey or غووونى gho-wūnaey; past part. غوولى gho-wulaey; verb. n. غوونه gho-wuna'h.

غوا ghwā, s.f. (6th) A cow in general. (E.) Sing. and Pl. (W.) Pl. غواوي ghwāwī.

غوباړي gho-bārraey, s.m. (1st) A horse-fly, a gad-fly, the breese (Tabanus). Pl. ي ī.

غوبل gho-bal, s.m. (2nd) Treading out corn, threshing, treading under foot. Pl. غوبلونه ghobalūnah. غوبل كول gho-bal kawul, verb trans. To tread out corn, to press or beat out with the feet.

غوبه ghobah, s.m. (4th) A cowherd, a herdsman, Pl. غوبانه ghobāna'h. غوبنه ghobana'h, s.f. (3rd) A herdswoman, a woman who grazes or tends cattle. Pl. ې ey.

غوبني ghobanī, s.f. (3rd) The business of a herdsman, herding or grazing cattle. Pl. ۍ a'ī. غوبني كول ghobanī kawul, verb trans. To herd cattle, to tend flocks.

غوپه ghūpa'h or ghopa'h, s.f. (3rd) (from A غوطه) Dipping, diving, immersion. 2. A dive, a dip, a plunge, an immersion. Pl. ې ey. غوپه خوړل ghūpah khwarral, verb trans. To dive, to dip, to be immersed.

غوټ ghūtt, adj. Close-shaved, docked, ears or nose cut off, clipped, shortened, cut short, curtailed; (Fem.) غوټه ghūtta'h. غوټ كول ghūtt kawul, verb trans, To dock, to cut off, to curtail, to clip, to shorten, to cut off the ears, nose, etc., as a punishment, to cut the ears or tail of a horse, dog, etc. غوټ پريكول ghūtt pre-kawul, verb trans. To cut close, to cut off altogether, as the hair, etc.

غوټه ghotta'h, s.f. (3rd) (from A غوطه) Dipping, diving, immersion. 2. A dip, a dive, a plunge. 3. A spring, a snatch, an assault, a clutch, a swoop, a wrench. 4. A fit, fainting. 5. adj. Overwhelmed in care, grief, etc. Pl. ې ey. غوټه خوړل ghotta'h khwarral, verb trans. To dive, to plunge one's-self into the water. غوټه وركول ghotta'h war-kawul, verb trans. To dip, to plunge under water, to immerse, to baptize. غوټه كول ghotta'h kawul, verb trans. To spring, to make a snatch at anything, to clutch, to make a swoop or assault. 2. To plunge in grief, sorrow, etc.

غوټه ghūtta'h, s.f. (3rd) A knot, a joint, an articulation, a band, a strap, a fastening. 2. A knot, or band of horsemen. Pl. ي *ey*. سخره غوټه *s<u>kh</u>ara'h <u>gh</u>ū<u>tt</u>a'h*, s.f. (3rd) A hard knot, one not easily opened. غوټيدل *<u>gh</u>ū<u>tt</u>edal*, verb intrans. To become knotted, entangled, entwined, ravelled, matted, to form knots or joints (as plants). Pres. غوټيږي *<u>gh</u>ū<u>tt</u>ejzī* (W.) or غوټيګي *<u>gh</u>ū<u>tt</u>egī* (E.); past غوټه شه *<u>gh</u>ū<u>tt</u>a'h <u>sh</u>ah* or وُ شه *wu-<u>sh</u>ah*; fut. غوټه به شي *<u>gh</u>ū<u>tt</u>a'h bah <u>sh</u>ī* or به وُ شي *bah wu-<u>sh</u>ī*; imp. غوټه شه *<u>gh</u>ū<u>tt</u>a'h <u>sh</u>ah* or وُ شه *wu-<u>sh</u>ah*; act.part. غوټيدونکَي *<u>gh</u>ū<u>tt</u>edūnkaey* or غوټيدونَي *<u>gh</u>ū<u>tt</u>edūnaey*; past part. غوټه شوَي *<u>gh</u>ū<u>tt</u>a'h <u>sh</u>awaey*; verb. n. غوټيدنه *<u>gh</u>ū<u>tt</u>edana'h* or غوټيده *<u>gh</u>ū<u>tt</u>eda'h*. غوټول *<u>gh</u>ū<u>tt</u>awul*, verb trans. To knot, to form a knot, to entangle, to plait, to mat or make matted, to entwine. Pres. غوټوي *<u>gh</u>ū<u>tt</u>awī*; past غوټه کړ *<u>gh</u>ū<u>tt</u>a'h karr* or وُ کړ *wu-ka<u>rr</u>*; fut. غوټه به کړي *<u>gh</u>ū<u>tt</u>a'h bah k<u>rr</u>ī* or به وُ کړي *bah wu-k<u>rr</u>ī*; imp. غوټه کړه *<u>gh</u>ū<u>tt</u>a'h k<u>rr</u>ah* or وُ کړه *wu-k<u>rr</u>ah*; act. part. غوټوونکَي *<u>gh</u>ū<u>tt</u>awūnkaey* or غوټوونَي *<u>gh</u>ū<u>tt</u>awūnaey*; past part. غوټه کړَي *<u>gh</u>ū<u>tt</u>a'h ka<u>rr</u>aey*; verb. n. غوټونه *<u>gh</u>ū<u>tt</u>awuna'h*.

غوټَي *<u>gh</u>ū<u>tt</u>aey*, adj. Crop-eared, docked, having the ears cropped, one whose ears, nose, etc. have been cut off; (Fem.) غوټۍ *<u>gh</u>ū<u>tt</u>a'ī*. 2. s.f. (6th) A rose-bud, a bud, a shoot. 3. A bubble, a drop, a globule. 4. A button, a kind of jewel or ornament. غوټَي غوټَي *<u>gh</u>ū<u>tt</u>aey <u>gh</u>ū<u>tt</u>aey*, in drops, in globules, in knots. See غټي , غوټ , and غوټه

غوځ *<u>gh</u>wu<u>ts</u>*, adj. Cut, wounded, separated, cut off, hacked, gashed, ripped, lacerated, chopped up, severed, incised, divided, wounded, etc.; (Fem.) غوځه *<u>gh</u>wu<u>ts</u>a'h*. غوځيدل *<u>gh</u>wu<u>ts</u>edal*, verb intrans. To be cut, cut off, gashed, lacerated, incised, divided, wounded, etc. Pres. غوځيږي *<u>gh</u>wu<u>ts</u>ejzī* (W.) or غوځيګي *<u>gh</u>wu<u>ts</u>egī* (E.); past غوځ شه *<u>gh</u>wu<u>ts</u> <u>sh</u>ah* or وُ شه *wu-<u>sh</u>ah*; fut. غوځ به شي *<u>gh</u>wu<u>ts</u> bah <u>sh</u>ī* or به وُ شي *bah wu-<u>sh</u>ī*; imp. غوځ شه *<u>gh</u>wu<u>ts</u> <u>sh</u>ah* or وُ شه *wu-<u>sh</u>ah*; act. part. غوځيدونکَي *<u>gh</u>wu<u>ts</u>edūnkaey* or غوځيدونَي *<u>gh</u>wu<u>ts</u>edūnaey*; past part. غوځ شوَي *<u>gh</u>wu<u>ts</u>* or غوځ شوَي *<u>gh</u>wu<u>ts</u> <u>sh</u>awaey*; verb. n. غوځيدنه *<u>gh</u>wu<u>ts</u>edana'h* or غوځيده *<u>gh</u>wu<u>ts</u>edah*. غوځول *<u>gh</u>wu<u>ts</u>awul*, verb trans. To cut, to cut off, to sever, to hack, to gash, to incise, to divide, to wound, etc. Pres. غوځوي *<u>gh</u>wu<u>ts</u>awī*; past غوځ کړ *<u>gh</u>wu<u>ts</u> ka<u>rr</u>* or وُ کړ *wu-ka<u>rr</u>*; fut. غوځ به کړي *<u>gh</u>wu<u>ts</u> bah k<u>rr</u>ī* or به وُ کړي *bah wu-k<u>rr</u>ī*; imp. غوځ کړه *<u>gh</u>wu<u>ts</u> k<u>rr</u>ah* or وُ کړه *wu-k<u>rr</u>ah*; act. part. غوځوونکَي *<u>gh</u>wu<u>ts</u>awūnkaey* or غوځوونَي *<u>gh</u>wu<u>ts</u>awūnaey*; past part. غوځ کړَي *<u>gh</u>wu<u>ts</u> ka<u>rr</u>aey*; verb. n. غوځونه *<u>gh</u>wu<u>ts</u>awuna'h*. See غځيدل and غځول

غوجل *<u>gh</u>ūjal*, s.f. (1st) A cow-house, a cow-pen. Pl. غوجل *<u>gh</u>ūjali*. See غجل

غوچ´ *<u>gh</u>ū<u>ch</u>*, s.m. (5th) A fighting ram. Pl. غوچان *<u>gh</u>ū<u>ch</u>ān* (T قوچ). See ګډ

غوچه *<u>gh</u>ū<u>ch</u>a'h*, interj. Oh! halloo! indeed! See غوچي and غچه

A غور *<u>gh</u>aur*, s.m. (2nd) Reflection, consideration, deliberation, thought, meditation. Pl. غورونه *<u>gh</u>aurūnah*. غور کول *<u>gh</u>aur kawul*, verb trans. To consider, to reflect, to investigate, to meditate.

غورزيدل *<u>gh</u>orzedal* or *<u>gh</u>ūrzedal*, verb intrans. To jump, to leap, to shake, to bound, to bob, to palpitate, to flop, to surge, to toss about, to be agitated. غورزول *<u>gh</u>orzawul* or *<u>gh</u>ūrzawul*. verb trans. To throw, to propel, to project, to fling, to pitch, to jerk, to toss, to agitate, to tumble. For tenses see غرزيدل and غرزول

P غوره *<u>gh</u>ūrah*, s.m. (6th) A cotton pod. 2. Unripe grapes or dates. Sing. and Pl. See کالکه and غوزه

غوره *<u>gh</u>warah*, adj. Chosen, picked, selected, preferred, fancied, choice, excellent, good, exquisite. غوره کيدل *<u>gh</u>warah kedal*, verb intrans. To be chosen, selected, preferred, fancied. غوره کول *<u>gh</u>warah kawul*, verb trans. To pick, to choose, to select, to prefer, to fancy.

غوري *<u>gh</u>warī*, s.m. (1st) (Pl.) The name given to the Mohmands of the plain of Pe<u>sh</u>āwer by way of distinguishing them from those of the hills called خښي *<u>kh</u>a<u>kh</u>ī* or *<u>kh</u>a<u>sh</u>ī*. Sing.

غوړي *ghwaraey*, A man of the above tribe. غوړۍ *ghwara'ī*, s.f. (6th) A female of the above tribe. Sing. and Pl.

غوړ *ghwarr*, s.m. (6th) Grease, fat, suet. Sing. and Pl. 2. adj. Greasy, fat, gross, oily, unctuous, adipose, viscous; (Fem.) غوړه *ghwarra'h*. غوړېدل *ghwarredal*, verb intrans. To become greasy, fat, unctuous, to become oiled, greased, etc. Pres. غوړېږي *ghwarrejzī* (W.) or غوړېګي *ghwarregī* (E.); past غوړ شه *ghwarr shah* or وُ شه *wu-shah*; fut. غوړ به شي *ghwarr bah shī* or به وُ شي *bah wu-shī*; imp. غوړ شه *ghwarr shah* or وُ شه *wu-shah*; act. part. غوړېدونکي *ghwarredūnkaey* or غوړېدوني *ghwarredūnaey*; past part. غوړ *ghwarr* or غوړ شوي *ghwarr shawaey*; verb. n. غوړېدنه *ghwarredana'h* or غوړېده *ghwarredah*. غوړول *ghwarrawul*, verb trans. To oil, to grease, to anoint, to make greasy, fat, gross, oily, unctuous, etc. Pres. غوړوي *ghwarrawī*; past غوړ کړ *ghwarr karr* or وُ کړ *wu-karr*; fut. غوړ به کړي *ghwarr bah krrī* or به وُ کړي *bah wu-krrī*; imp. غوړ کړه *ghwarr krrah* or وُ کړه *wu-krrah*; act. part. غوړوونکي *ghwarrawūnkaey* or غوړووني *ghwarrawūnaey*; past part. غوړ کړي *ghwarr karraey*; verb. n. غوړونه *ghwarrawuna'h*.

غوړپکه *ghorr-paka'h*, s.f. (3rd) An accident, incident, occurrence, event, adversity, calamity, misfortune. 2. A blow, a shock, a stroke of fortune. 3. Novelty, adventure. 4. A cry of anger or vexation. Pl. ې *ey*.

غوړي *ghwarrī*, s.m. (1st) (Pl.) Clarified butter, fat, grease, butter, tallow, etc. The singular form of this noun is not used.

غوړېدل *ghwarredal*, verb intrans. To open, to spread, to grow, to expand, to germinate, to blow (as a flower), to swell, to outgrow, to sprout. Pres. غوړېږي *ghwarrejzī* (W.) or غوړېګي *ghwarregī* (E.); past وُ غوړېده *wu-ghwarredah* or غوړېدَ *ghwarreda*; fut. وُ به غوړېږي *wu bah ghwarrejzī* or غوړېګي *ghwarregī*; imp. وُ غوړېږه *wu-ghwarrejzah* or غوړېګه *ghwarregah*; act. part. غوړېدونکي *ghwarredūnkaey* or غوړېدوني *ghwarredūnaey*; past part. غوړېدلي *ghwarredalaey*; verb. n. غوړېدنه *ghwarredana'h* or غوړېده *ghwarredah*. غوړول *ghwarrawul*, verb trans. To render larger, to distend, to develope, to inflate, to rarefy, to blow up, to unclose, to lay open, to spread, to raise. Pres. غوړوي *ghwarrawī*; past وُ غوړاوه *wu-ghwarrāwuh* or غوړاوو *ghwarrāwo*; fut. وُ به غوړوي *wu bah ghwarrawī*; imp. وُ غوړوه *wu-ghwarrawah*; act. part. غوړوونکي *ghwarrawūnkaey* or غوړووني *ghwarrawūnaey*; past part. غوړولي *ghwarrawulaey*; verb. n. غوړونه *ghwarrawuna'h*. See also غړېدل and غړول

غوز *ghoz*, s.m. (2nd) The fat of the kidneys. Pl. غوزونه *ghozūnah*.

غوزکرکي *ghozakarkaey*, s.m. (1st) A kind of beetle (Scarbæus). Pl. ي *ī*; or غوزي *ghozaey*, s.m. (1st). Pl. ي *ī*. See ګونګټ

غوزه *ghoza'h*, s.f. (3rd) A pod, a capsule, a cotton pod, a husk, a shell, a cocoon. Pl. ې *ey*. See کالکه, پلي, and غوره (P غوژه).

غوزي *ghūzaey*, s.m. (1st) The embrace, the arms, the bosom, the space between the bosom and the arms. 2. An armful, as much as can be carried in the arms. Pl. ي *ī*. په غوزي کښې نیول *pah ghūzī kshe* or *kkhey nīwal*, verb trans. To take in the arms, to embrace. See غېږ and غېګ

غوږ *ghwajz*, s.m. (2nd) (W.) The ear, an ear, the screw of a violin. Pl. غوږونه *ghwajzūnah*. غوږ پېچل *ghwajz pechal* or غوږ تاوول *ghwajz tā-wawul* or غوږ مروړل *ghwajz m'rorral*, verb trans. To pull, to twist, to rub the ears, to punish, to chastise. غوږ یستل *ghwajz yastal*, verb trans. To give ear, to attend to, to mark, to notice. غوږ باسه *ghwajz bāsah*, adv. (imp.) Hark! listen! give ear! attend! have a care! beware!

غوږ څارنه *ghwajz tsārna'h*, s.f. (3rd) Eaves-dropping, listening, overhearing. Pl. ې *ey*. غوږ څارل *ghwajz tsāral*, verb trans. To listen secretly, to prick up one's ears, to overhear, to practice eaves-dropping. See غوګ

غورزې *ghwajzaey*, s.m. (1st) A flood-gate, a sluice, a lock, a channel to allow the water of a *band* or reservoir when over full to run out. 2. The sun shining through the clouds—a sign of rain. 3. The horn of a bow. 4. The key of a violin. Pl. ي *ī*. See غوګي

غوشاك *ghoshāk*, s.m. (6th) Cow-dung, or dung of the buffalo. Sing. and Pl.

غوشوي *ghosho-e*, s.m. (4th) Moist cow-dung or horse-dung. Pl. غوشايه *ghoshāyah*. See خوشوي and غشوي

غوښت *ghosht* (W.) or *ghokht* (E.), s.m. (6th) Millet, particles of rice ground and made into bread. Sing. and Pl. See خمچي

غوښت *ghosht* (W.) or *ghokht* (E.), s.m. (6th) Desire, wish, request, hankering, longing, relish, bent, fancy, yearning. Sing. and Pl.; or غوښته *ghoshtah* or *ghokhtah*, s.m. (6th). Sing. and Pl.; and غوښتنه *ghoshtana'h* or *ghokhtana'h*, s.f. (3rd). Pl. ې *ey*. غوښتل *ghoshtal* (W.) or *ghokhtal* (E.), To desire, to wish for, to request, to hanker after, to long for, to solicit, to thirst after. Pres. غواړي *ghwārrī*; past وُ غوښت *wu-ghosht* or *wu-ghokht*; fut. وُ به غواړي *wu bah ghwārrī*; imp. وُ غواړه *wu-ghwārrah*; act. part. غوښتونکي *ghoshtūnkaey* or *ghokhtūnkaey* or غوښتونې *ghoshtūnaey* or *ghokhtūnaey*; past part. غوښتلې *ghoshtalaey* or *ghokhtalaey*; verb. n. غوښتنه *ghoshtana'h* or *ghokhtana'h* or غوښته *ghoshtah* or *ghokhtah*.

غوښي *ghoshaey* (W.) or *ghokhaey* (E.), s.m. (1st) The horn or crooked end of a bow. 2. The peg of a violin, etc. Pl. ي *ī*. See also غوري or غوګي

غوښه *ghwasha'h* (W.) or *ghwakha'h* (E.), s.f. (3rd) Flesh, meat. Pl. ې *ey*. غوښه آخستل *ghwasha'h ākhistal* or *ghwakha'h ākhistal*, verb trans. To take or pick up flesh, to increase in size, to get stout. غوښه تورل *ghwasha'h to-wul*, verb trans. (W.) or غوښه تويول *ghwakha'h toey-awul*, verb trans. (E.) To shed or throw flesh, to make or render thin; or غوښه توئيدل *ghwasha'h* or *ghwakha'h toey-yedal*, verb intrans. To lose flesh, to grow thin or emaciated.

غوښور *ghwashawar* (W.) or *ghwakhawar* (E.), adj. Fleshy, stout, plump, chubby, jolly, bouncing; (Fem.) غوښوره *ghwashawara'h* or *ghwakhawara'h*. غوښور توب *ghwashawar-tob* (W.) or *ghwakhawar-tob* (E.), s.m. (2nd) Stoutness, plumpness, chubbiness, embonpoint. Pl. توبونه *tobūnah*; or غوښور تيا *ghwashawar-tī'ā* or *ghwakhawar-tī'ā* (W.), s.f. (6th). Pl. تياوي *tī'āwī*. (E.) Sing. and Pl.

P غوغا *gho-ghā*, s.f. (6th) Noise, disturbance, uproar, clamor, alarm, brawl. (E.) Sing. and Pl. (W.) Pl. غوغاوي *ghogā-wī*. غوغا كول *ghoghā kawul*, verb trans. To create a noise or tumult. See زوږ

غوګ *ghwag* (E.), s.m. (2nd) The ear, an ear. Pl. غوګونه *ghwagūnah*. For different words used with this, see the Western form of the word, in which the ږ is substituted for ګ

غوګي *ghwagaey*, s.m. (1st) The horn or crooked end of a bow. 2. The key of a violin, etc. 3. A flood-gate, a sluice, a lock, a channel to allow water to escape from a reservoir when over full. 4. The beams of the sun or ray of light appearing through the clouds. Pl. ي *ī*. See غوري

A غول *ghūl* (vul. *ghol*), s.m. (5th) An imaginary sylvan demon, a man-wolf, a loup garou. Pl. غولان *ghūlān*.

غول *ghol*, s.m. (2nd) A corps, a division, a gang, a troop, a company, a crowd, a division, a throng, a flock, a flight of birds. Pl. غولونه *gholūnah*. غول غول *ghol-ghol* or غول په غول *ghol pah ghol*, adj. In crowds, crowd upon crowd, troop by troop, etc. غولئ *ghola'ī*, s.f. (6th) A small crowd, a small party, a knot, a crew, a covey, a bevy. Sing. and Pl. غولئ غولئ *ghola'ī-ghola'ī*, adj. In coveys, in knots, in small parties. غولئ غولئ گرزيدل *ghola'ī-ghola'ī garzedal*, verb intrans. To move about in knots, in swarms, in parties. غولئ غولئ كيدل *ghola'ī-ghola'ī kedal*, verb intrans. To swarm, to collect together in flocks, in knots, or in small parties. غولي غولي کول <u>gh</u>ola'ī <u>gh</u>ola'ī kawul, verb trans. To divide or separate into small parties, or in knots. See تول

غولونکيَ <u>gh</u>olawunkaey, s.m. (1st) A sty on the eyelid. Pl. ي ī.

غوله کمانه <u>gh</u>ola'h-kamāna'h, s.f. (3rd) A pellet bow. Pl. يْ ey. See غرکمانه

غوليَ <u>gh</u>olaey, s.m. (1st) A court-yard, a yard, a close, a court. Pl. ي ī.

غوليدل <u>gh</u>oledal, verb intrans. To be deceived, to be misled, to be cheated or imposed upon, to be juggled, hoaxed, etc. غولول <u>gh</u>olawul, verb trans. To deceive, to mislead, to cheat, to dupe, to trick, to take in. For inflections see غليدل and غلول, the more correct and general spelling of the words.

غونډِ <u>gh</u>ūndi or غونډي <u>gh</u>ūndī, adj. Alike, similar, like, resembling, near. 2. adv. As if, as it were, just as, such as. See غنډِ

غونډيَ <u>gh</u>ūndaey, s.m. (1st) A bag or pannier of goat's hair for camels, donkeys, etc. Pl. ي ī. See غنډي and انډي

غونډ <u>gh</u>ūn<u>dd</u>, adj. Round, globular, circular, orbicular. 2. Squat, plump; (Fem.) غونډه <u>gh</u>ūn<u>dd</u>a'h. For other definitions and compositions of this word see غنډ

غونډهاريَ <u>gh</u>ūn<u>dd</u>hāraey, s.m. (1st) A tumor, a bump, a bubo. Pl. ي ī. See غنډهاريَ

غونډۍ <u>gh</u>ūn<u>dd</u>a'ī, s.f. (6th) A mound or detached hill separated from the higher range. Sing. and Pl. See غنډۍ

غونه <u>gh</u>ūna'h, s.f. (3rd) The hair of the body, the pores of the body. 2. Color, the color of the skin. Pl. يْ ey. غونه زيګيدل <u>gh</u>ūna'h zīgedal, verb intrans. To stand on end (as the hair of the body or head, through fear or cold).

غوو <u>gh</u>o-o, s.m. (9th) Copulation, coition. Sing. and Pl. غوو کول <u>gh</u>o-o kawul or غوول <u>gh</u>o-wul, verb trans. To copulate with, to have coition. See غو for different inflections.

غوولتيا <u>gh</u>o-wul-tī'ā, s.f. Cowardliness, impotency, imbecility. 2. Cheating at play; trickery, subterfuge. (E.) Sing. and Pl. (W.) Pl. غوولتياوي <u>gh</u>o-wul-tī'āwī.

غووليَ <u>gh</u>o-wulaey, adj. (past part.) Impotent, dastard, cowardly. 2. A catamite, a eunuch, a term of abuse; (Fem.) غوول <u>gh</u>o-wuli, A woman who has been copulated with, a strumpet, a whore. Pl. (Masc. and Fem.) ي ī.

غويره <u>gh</u>werah, adj. Chosen, selected, desired, wished for. See غوره

غويلنګ <u>gh</u>waey-lang, s.m. (2nd) The groin. Pl. غويلنګونه <u>gh</u>waey-langūnah. See مغانه

غويمنډ <u>gh</u>oey-man<u>dd</u>, s.m. (2nd) The running of cattle, treading under foot, tumbling one over the other, tumbling head over heels. 2. Making a road through snow by driving cattle over it. 3. Ruining, destroying, treading under foot, etc. Pl. غويمنډونه <u>gh</u>oey-man<u>dd</u>ūnah. غويمنډ کيدل <u>gh</u>oey-man<u>dd</u> kedal, verb intrans. To be trodden under foot, to be destroyed, to tumble head over heels. غويمنډ کول <u>gh</u>oey-man<u>dd</u> kawul, verb trans. To destroy, to trample under foot, to throw head over heels, one over the other.

غويمه <u>gh</u>wayama'h, s.f. (3rd) A cow or female buffalo ready to take, or seeking the male. Pl. يْ ey. غويمتوب <u>gh</u>wayam-tob, s.m. (2nd) Animal heat of a cow or female buffalo when ready for the male. Pl. توبونه tobūnah. غويمه کيدل <u>gh</u>wayama'h kedal, verb intrans. To become desirous for the male.

غوييَ <u>gh</u>wayaey, s.m. (4th) (E.), A bull, a bullock, an ox. Pl. غوايه <u>gh</u>wāyah. غوائيِ <u>gh</u>wāyaey (W.), s.m. (1st). Pl. غوايي <u>gh</u>wāyī. غويي ختل <u>gh</u>wayaey <u>kh</u>atal, verb intrans. To cover, to mount, to copulate with a cow (*lit.* to ascend). verb trans. in English; or غويي دنګل <u>gh</u>wayaey dangal, verb trans.

غه <u>gh</u>ah, for the remote demonstrative pronoun هغه haghah, That, the ه of which is sometimes lost by elision.

A غيب <u>gh</u>aib, s.m. (9th) (from غيب) Mystery, absence, invisibility. Sing. and Pl. 2. adj. Absent, concealed, latent, invisible, mysterious; (Fem.) غيبه <u>gh</u>aiba'h. غيب ويل <u>gh</u>aib wayal, verb trans. To foretell, to predict, to augur, to prophesy. See پت

A غيبت ghaibat, s.m. (2nd) Speaking ill of any one behind his back, backbiting, slander, detraction. 2. Absence. Pl. غيبتونه ghaibat-ūnah. غيبت كول ghaibat kawul, verb trans. To backbite, to slander.

A غير ghair, adj. Foreign, strange, exotic, different, other; (Fem.) غيره ghaira'h. See پرته and پردي

A غيرت ghairat, s.m. (2nd) Modesty, bashfulness, courage, honour. 2. Jealousy, enmity, emulation, a nice sense of honour. Pl. غيرتونه ghairatūnah. غيرت مند ghairat-mand, adj. Jealous, emulous, high-minded; (Fem.) غيرت منده ghairat-manda'h or غيرت ناك ghairat-nāk; (Fem.) غيرت ناكه ghairat-nāka'h, and غيرتي ghairatī. (Masc. and Fem.)

غيره gh'yara'h, s.f. (3rd) The wild ass or onager. Pl. ې ey.

غيږ ghejz (W.), s.f. (1st) The embrace, the arm, the bosom, the space between the bosom and the arms. 2. An armful. 3. A wallet. Pl. غيږ ghejzi په غيږ كښي نيول pah ghejz kshey or kkhey nīwal, verb trans. To embrace, to take in the arms; or (E.) غيګ gheg. Pl. غيګِ ghegi, etc. غيږ or غيګ يستل ghejz or gheg yastal, verb trans. To wrestle, to struggle.

A غيل ghīl, s.m. (2nd) A forest, a wood, a thicket, a copse, a grove, etc. Pl. غيلونه ghīlūnah.

غيل ghayal, verb trans. To copulate, to have sexual intercourse. This infinitive is imperfect, and is used with that of غوول, which see.

غيلي gheley, s.f. (3rd) Pl. Sheep or goats, flocks in general. The singular form of this word is not used. See پسه

غيندئ ghayandaey, adj. (past part.) as s.m. (5th) A catamite, a man addicted to fornication. Pl. ي ī. غيندۍ ghayanda'ī, s.f. (6th) A libidinous woman, a whore, a fornicatress. Sing. and Pl.

غيړن ghīrrn, s.m. (2nd) The penis of a man or beast. Pl. غيړنونه ghīrrnūnah or (W.) s.m. (5th). Pl. غيړنان ghīrrnān.

ف

ف fey, in Arabic fā, the twentieth letter of the Arabic and the twenty-third of the Persian, is the thirtieth letter of the Pushto alphabet. It has no exact equivalent in the Sanskrit, the letter फ being substituted. Its sound is the same as English f. It stands for 80 in the adoption of letters for numbers, and is often interchanged in Pushto with, and substituted for پ.

A فاتحه fā-tiha'h, s.f. (3rd) (from فتح) Commencement, exordium. 2. The first chapter of the Ku'rān, repeated when praying for the souls of the dead, and prayers offered to saints, etc. Pl. ې ey. فاتحه كول fā-tiha'h kawul, verb trans. To offer up prayers, etc. See پاتا

A فاجر fājir, s.m. (5th) (act. part. of فجر) A fornicator, an adulterer. Pl. فاجران fājir-ān. فاجره fājira'h, s.f. (3rd) An adultress, a fornicatress. 2. Sinful, unchaste. Pl. ې ey.

A فاحش fā-hish, adj. (act. part of فحش) Obscene, indecent, shameful, gross; (Fem.) فاحشه fā-hisha'h, A harlot, a whore.

P فارسي fārsī, adj. Persian, relating to Persia. (Masc. and Fem.) فارسي ژبه fārsī jzaba'h, The Persian language. فارسي بان fārsī-bān, A Persian scholar, a person speaking the Persian language; (Fem.) فارسي بانه fārsī-bāna'h.

A فارغ fārigh, adj. (act. part. of فرغ) Free, disengaged, at leisure, ceasing from labour on completing it. 2. Absolved, disengaged. 3. Contented; (Fem.) فارغه fārigha'h. فارغ كيدل fā-righ kedal, verb intrans. To cease work, to become disengaged, to be at leisure. فارغ كول fā-righ kawul, verb trans. To free, to absolve, to disengage.

A فاروق fārūk, adj. (act. part.) A distinguisher, a discoverer; (Fem.) فاروقه fārūka'h.

A فاسد fāsid, adj. (act. part. of فسد) Perverse, vicious, depraved, corrupt, pernicious, bad, noxious; (Fem.) فاسده fāsida'h.

A فاسق *fāsiḳ*, adj. (act. part. of فسق) Impious, sinful. 2. s.m. (5th) A sinner, a fornicator, an adulterer, a worthless fellow. Pl. فاسقان *fāsiḳān*; (Fem.) فاسقه *fāsiḳa'h*, s.f. (3rd). Pl. ي *ey*.

A فاصله *fā-ṣila'h*, s.f. (3rd) Space, interstice, distance, intermediate space. Pl. ي *ey*. See لري والي

A فاضل *fāẓil*, adj. (act. part. of فضل) Excellent, learned, virtuous. 2. Abundant; (Fem.) فاضله *fāẓila'h*.

A فاطمه *fāṭima'h*, s. prop. The name of Muḥammad's daughter, the wife of Æalī. 2. The name of a woman.

A فاعل *fā-æil*, s.m. (5th) (act. part. of فعل) Making, doing, operating. 2. An agent, the actor, the active participle in grammar. Pl. فاعلان *fā-æilān*. فاعله *fā-æila'h*, s.f. (3rd). Pl. ي *ey*. فاعل مختار *fā-æil-i-mukhtār*, A free actor, master of one's own actions.

A فاقه *fāḳa'h*, s.f. (3rd) (from فوق) Poverty, want, necessity. 2. A fast, fasting from want. Pl. ي *ey*. فاقه كول *fāḳa'h kawul*, verb trans. To fast. See لوره or لوكه

A فال *fāl*, s.m. (2nd) Augury, an omen, enchantment, a presage. Pl. فالونه *fālūnah*. فال بين *fāl-bīn*, s.m. (5th) An augur, one who foretells, a fortune-teller. Pl. فال بينان *fāl-bīnān*. فال بينه *fāl-bīna'h*, s.f. (3rd). Pl. ي *ey*. فال نيول *fāl nīwal*, verb trans. To take an omen, to augur. فال بيني *fāl-bīnī*, s.f. (3rd) Augury, fortune-telling. Pl. ي *a'ī*. فال بيني كول *fāl-bīnī kawul*, verb trans. To foretell, to presage.

P فالوده *fālūda'h* or پالوده *pālūda'h*, s.f. (3rd) A kind of flummery. Pl. ي *ey*.

P فانوس *fā-nūs*, s.m. (2nd) A shade, a lantern, a pharos, a lighthouse. Pl. فانوسونه *fā-nūsūnah*.

A فاني *fānī*, adj. (act. part. of فنا) Transitory, frail, inconstant, perishable. (Masc. and Fem.)

A فايده *fā-īda'h*, s.f. (3rd) (from فيد) Profit, gain, advantage, benefit, interest, utility. Pl. ي *ey*. فايده مند *fā-īda'h mand*, adj. Profitable, with gain, advantageous; (Fem.) فايده منده *fā-īda'h manda'h*. فايده آخستل *fā-īda'h ākhistal* or فايده مندل *fā-īda'h mundal*, verb trans. To reap benefit, to derive profit or advantage. فايده كول *fā-īda'h kawul*, verb trans. To benefit, to profit. فايده رسول *fā-īda'h rasawul*, verb trans. To benefit any one, to confer benefit or advantage.

فتحه *fatḥa'h*, s.f. (3rd) (corrup. of A فتح) Victory, conquest. 2. An opening, an aperture. Pl. ي *ey*. فتحه مند *fatḥa'h-mand*, adj. Triumphant, victorious, conqueror; (Fem.) فتحه منده *fatḥa'h-manda'h*. فتحه مندي *fatḥa'h mandī*, s.f. (3rd) Victory, triumph, victoriousness. Pl. ي *a'ī*. فتحه ياب *fatḥa'h-yāb*, adj. Victorious; (Fem.) فتحه يابه *fatḥa'h-yāba'h*. فتحه كيدل *fatḥa'h kedal*, verb intrans. To be conquered, to be overcome. فتحه كول *fatḥa'h kawul*, verb trans. To conquer.

A فتق *fatḳ*, s.m. (2nd) A rupture, hernia. Pl. فتقونه *fatḳūnah*. فتق بند *fatḳ band*, s.m. (2nd) A truss. Pl. فتق بندونه *fatḳ-bandūnah*.

A فتنه *fitna'h*, s.f. (3rd) Sedition, mutiny. 2. Perfidy. 3. Mischief, calamity, evil, sin, pest. 4. Seduction, temptation. Pl. ي *ey*. فتنه انگيز *fitna'h angez*, adj. Turbulent, insurgent, mutinous, seditious, exciting sedition, an incendiary; (Fem.) فتنه انگيزه *fitna'h angeza'h*. فتنه انگيزي *fitna'h angezī*, s.f. (3rd) Causing disturbances, seditiousness. Pl. ي *a'ī*. فتنه انگيزي كول *fitna'h angezī kawul*, verb trans. To cause disturbances, to create or excite sedition. فتنه كول *fitna'h kawul*, verb trans. To injure, to create a mutiny or sedition.

A فتور *futūr*, s.m. (9th) (from فتر) Weakness, infirmity, impotence. 2. (Pushto) Quarrelling, brawling. Sing. and Pl. فتور كول *futūr kawul*, verb trans. To quarrel, to brawl.

A فتوي *fat-wā*, s.f. (6th) (from فتو) A decree, award, sentence, decision, a judgment. (E.) Sing. and Pl. (W.) Pl. فتواوي *fat-wāwī*. فتوي وركول *fatwā war-kawul*, verb trans. To pass sentence, to give a decree or award, to decide.

A فحش *fuḥsh*, s.m. (2nd) Obscenity (in word or deed), bawdry, grossness. Pl. فحشونه *fuḥsh-ūnah*. فحش ويل *fuḥsh wa-yal*, verb trans. To speak obscenely.

A فخر *fakhr*, s.m. (9th) Glory, nobility, grace, ornament. 2. Boasting, ostentation, pride, egotism. Sing. and Pl. فخر كول *fakhr kawul*, verb trans. To boast, to manifest ostentation.

A فدا *fidā*, s.m. (9th) A sacrifice, consecration, redemption, devoting one's-self to save another, ransom, cartel, exchange. Sing. and Pl. فدا كول *fidā kawul*, verb trans. To devote, to sacrifice. See جار

P فراخ *farākh*, adj. Ample, capacious, spacious, wide, large, abundant, plentiful, cheap; (Fem.) فراخه *farākha'h*. فراخي *farākhī*, s.f. (3rd) Abundance, cheapness, largeness, wideness. Pl. ئ *a'ī*.

A فرار *firār*, s.m. (9th) Running away, flight. Sing. and Pl. فرار كيدل *firār kedal*, verb trans. To flee, to take to flight. فرار كول *firār kawul*, verb trans. To put to flight, to run away with, to seduce.

A فراست *farāsat*, s.m. (2nd) Penetration, sagacity. Pl. فراستونه *farāsatūnah*.

A فراش *farāsh*, s.m. (5th) A bedmaker, a chamberlain, one whose business is to spread the carpets, etc. Pl. فراشان *farāshān*. فراشه *farāsha'h*, s.f. (3rd) A chambermaid. Pl. ئ *ey*. فراش خانه *farāsh khāna'h*, s.f. (3rd) A house where carpets are kept. Pl. ئ *ey*. فراشي *farāshī*, s.f. (3rd) The business of a farāsh, spreading carpets, etc. Pl. ئ *a'ī*.

A فراغت *farāghat*, s.m. (2nd) Cessation, disengagement, ease, leisure, repose, freedom from care. Pl. فراغتونه *farāghatūnah*.

A فراق *firāḳ*, s.m. (9th) (from فرق) Separation, absence, distance, departing, distinction. Sing. and Pl.

A فرحت *farḥat*, s.m. (2nd) Delight, pleasure, cheerfulness, joy, amusement. Pl. فرحتونه *farḥatūnah*.

A فردوس *far-daus*, s. prop. A garden, paradise. Sing. and Pl.

P فرزند *farzand*, s.m. (5th) A child, a son or a daughter. Pl. فرزندان *farzandān*. په فرزندي نيول *pah farzandī nīwal*, verb trans. To adopt a child.

P فرسخ *far-sakh*, s.m. (2nd) A farsang, or measure of about 6000 yards, a league. Pl. فرسخونه *far-sakhūnah*.

A فرش *farsh*, s.m. (2nd) Anything for spreading, as carpeting, bedding, a cushion, a mat, a carpet, a pavement, etc. Pl. فرشونه *farsh-ūnah*.

فرښته *firishta'h* (W.) or *firikhta'h* (E.), s.f. (3rd) An angel, an apostle, a messenger. Pl. ئ *ey*. (P فرشته).

A فرصت *fur-ṣat*, s.m. (2nd) (from فرص) Leisure, freedom, ease, convenience, opportunity, occasion, time, rest, relief. Pl. فرصتونه *fur-ṣat-ūnah*. فرصت لرل *fur-ṣat laral*, verb trans. To have leisure, to have time or opportunity. فرصت وركول *fur-ṣat war-kawul*, verb trans. To grant or give leisure.

A فرض *farẓ*, s.m. (6th) A divine command, a duty the omission of which is considered a mortal sin, an obligation. Sing. and Pl. فرض كول *farẓ kawul*, verb trans. To consider as a positive or indispensable duty, to assume, to admit. 2. To obey the divine commands; or فرض ادا كول *farẓ adā kawul*, verb trans.

A فرعون *far-œaun*, s. prop. Pharoah. 2. Any cruel tyrant. Sing. and Pl. فرعوني *far-œaunī*, s.f. (3rd) Haughtiness, arrogance. Pl. ئ *a'ī*.

A فرق *farḳ*, s.m. (2nd) Difference, distance, distinction, separation, dispersion. 2. The head, the top of anything, the summit. 3. adj. Distinct, distant, separate. Pl. فرقونه *farḳ-ūnah*. فرق كول *farḳ kawul*, verb trans. To distinguish, to part, to make difference or distinction. فرق لرل *farḳ laral*, verb trans. To have distinction, distance, difference, or separation. (Eng. verb intrans.) To be different or distinct.

A فرقه *firḳa'h*, s.f. (3rd) A sect, tribe, class, kind, troop, company, society. Pl. ئ *ey*. See خيل

P فرمان *farmān*, s.m. (2nd) A command, a mandate, an order, an edict. 2. A royal patent, a grant. Pl. فرمانونه *farmānūnah.* فرمان بردار *farmān bardār*, adj. Obedient, subject to orders, subject; (Fem.) فرمان برداره *farmān bardāra'h.* فرمان برداري *farmān bardārī*, s.f. (3rd) Obedience, fealty, subjection. Pl. ئي *a'ī.* فرمان برداري كول *farmān bardārī kawul*, verb trans. To obey, to pay fealty unto.

فرمايل *farmāyil*, verb trans. To order, to command, to commission, to will, to direct, to enjoin, to ordain, to bid, to enact. Pres. فرمايي *farmāyī*; past وُ فرمايه *wu-farmāyah*; fut. وُ به فرمايي *wu bah farmāyī*; imp. وُ فرمايه *wu-farmāyah*; act. part. فرمايونكيَ *farmāyūnkaey* or فرمايونيَ *farmāyūnaey*; past part. فرمايليَ *farmāyalaey*; verb. n. فرماينه *farmāyana'h.*

P فرنكي *farangī*, s.m. (5th) A Frank, a European. Pl. فرنگيان *farangīān.* فرنگئي *faranga'ī*, s.f. (6th) A Frank female. Sing. and Pl. فرنگستان *farangistān*, s. prop. Europe. باد فرنگ *bād-i-farang*, The French pox.

P فرهاد *far-hād*, s. prop. A celebrated Persian statuary, the lover of S͟hīrīn.

P فرياد *faryād*, s.m. (2nd) Complaint, exclamation, lamentation, crying out for assistance. Pl. فريادونه *faryādūnah.* فرياد رس *faryād-ras*, A redresser of grievances. فرياد رسي *faryād-rasī*, s.f. (3rd) Redress, succour. Pl. ئي *a'ī.* فرياد كول *faryād kawul*, verb trans. to complain, to cry out for redress. فريادي *faryādī*, adj. A complainant, a plaintiff. (Masc. and Fem.)

P فريب *fareb*, s.m. (2nd) Deceit, trick, deception, fraud, allurement. 2. Cheating, deceiving. Pl. فريبونه *farebūnah.* فريب خورل *fareb k͟hwarral*, verb trans. To swallow deception, (Eng. verb intrans.) to be deceived. فريب وركول *fareb war-kawul*, verb trans. To cheat, to trick, to impose on, to beguile, to cozen; or فريب كول *fareb kawul*, verb trans. فريبي *farebī*, adj. An imposter, a cheat, an artful person. (Masc. and Fem).

P فريفته *fareftah*, adj. (from فريفتن) Deceived, enamoured, charmed, infatuated. See غليدلي.

فريوان *f'rewān*, adj. Much, abundant, copious, sufficient, opulent (corrup. of P فراوان); (Fem.) فريوانه *f'rewāna'h.*

A فساد *fasād*, s.m. (2nd) Mischief, violence, mutiny, sedition, rebellion, wickedness, iniquity, depravity, disturbance. Pl. فسادونه *fasādūnah.* فساد كول *fasād kawul*, verb trans. To create a mutiny, rebellion, disturbance. 2. To make mischief. فسادي *fasādī*, adj. Mutinous, seditious, rebellious, mischievous, vicious, quarrelsome. (Masc. and Fem.)

A فسق *fisḳ*, s.m. (2nd) Adultery, obscenity, impudence, iniquity, sin, impiety. Pl. فسقونه *fisḳūnah.* فسق كول *fisḳ kawul*, verb trans. To commit iniquity, to sin.

فش *fas͟h*, adj. (corrup. of P فاش ?) Apparent, manifest, divulged, made known, notorious; (Fem.) فشه *fas͟ha'h.* فش كول *fas͟h kawul*, verb trans. To divulge, to reveal, to discover, to make notorious.

فصاحت *faṣāḥat*, s.m. (2nd) (from فصح) Eloquence. Pl. فصاحتونه *faṣāḥatūnah.*

فصحا *fuṣaḥā*, (Pl. of A فصيح) adj. Eloquent (men), the eloquent or sweet-tongued.

فصل *faṣl*, s.m. (2nd) Time, season, crop, harvest. Pl. فصلونه *faṣlūnah.*

A فصيح *faṣīḥ*, adj. Eloquent, sweet-tongued; (Fem.) فصيحه *faṣīḥa'h.*

A فصيل *faṣīl*, s.m. (2nd) A parapet, a breastwork, an entrenchment. Pl. فصيلونه *faṣīlūnah.* See مردرو

A فضل *faẓl*, s.m. (9th) Excellence, virtue. 2. Increase, gain. 3. Gift, reward, favour, grace. Sing. and Pl.

A فضول *faẓūl* or *fuẓūl*, adj. Exuberant, excessive, redundant, extravagant; (Fem.) فضوله *faẓūla'h.* فضولي *faẓūlī*, s.f. (3rd) Exuberance, redundance, excess, extravagance. Pl. ئي *a'ī.* فضولي كول *faẓūlī kawul*, verb trans. To commit excess or extravagance.

A فضيحت *faẓī-ḥat*, s.m. (2nd) (from فضح) Disgrace, infamy, ignominy. Pl. فضيحتونه *faẓī-*

ḥatūnah. فضيحت كول fazī-ḥat kawul, verb trans. To defame, to disgrace. فضيحت كيدل fazīḥat kedal, verb intrans. To become infamous, to be disgraced. فضيحتي fazī-ḥatī, adj. Infamous, disgraceful. (Masc. and Fem.)

A فضيلت fazīlat, s.m. (2nd) (from فضل) Excellence, perfection, virtue, learning, knowledge. Pl. فضيلتونه fazīlatūnah.

A فطرت fiṭrat, s.m. (2nd) Wisdom, sagacity, cunning. 2. Trick, deceit. Pl. فطرتونه fiṭratūnah.

A فعل fiʿl, s.m. (2nd) Action, work, operation. 2. Verb. Pl. فعلونه fiʿlūnah.

A فقر faḳr, s.m. (9th) Poverty, beggary. Sing. and Pl. فقر كول faḳr kawul, verb trans. To beg.

A فقط faḳaṭ, adv. Merely, simply, only, solely.

فقهه fiḳha'h, s.f. (3rd) (A فقه) Knowledge of religion and law, theology, jurisprudence. Pl. ي ey.

A فقير faḳīr, s.m. (5th) (from فقر) A beggar, a darwesh, a mendicant. Pl. فقيران faḳīrān. فقيره faḳīra'h, s.f. (3rd). Pl. ي ey. فقيري faḳīrī, s.f. (3rd) Poverty, the life of a darwesh, beggary. Pl. ي a'ī. فقيري كول faḳīrī kawul, verb trans. To beg, to live as a darwesh, to lead a beggar's life.

فقيه faḳīh, s.m. (5th) A theologian. Pl. فقيهان faḳīh-ān.

A فكر fikr, s.m. (2nd) Care, concern, counsel, advice, anxiety, solicitude, idea, conceit, imagination, thought, reflection, notion. Pl. فكرونه fikrūnah. فكر مند fikr mand, adj. Anxious, thoughtful; (Fem.) فكر منده fikr-manda'h. بي فكر bey fikr, adj. Careless, neglectful; (Fem.) بي فكره bey fikra'h.

فلانىَ falānaey, adj. Such a one, so and so, a certain person or thing; (Fem.) فلانۍ falāna'ī. See پلانكي (from P).

A فلك falak, s.m. (9th) The heavens, the sky, the firmament. 2. Fate, fortune, destiny. Sing. and Pl.

A فليته falīta'h, s.f. (3rd) A match, torch, wick, fusee. Pl. ي ey. فليته دار falīta'h-dār, adj. A matchlock, being fired with a match.

فليل fulel, s.m. (2nd) A kind of oil of sweet smell used by women for their hair. Pl. فليلونه fulel-ūnah.

فم fam, s.m. (2nd) The orifice of the stomach. Pl. فمونه fam-ūnah.

A فن fann, s.m. (2nd) Science. 2. Skill, art. Pl. فنونه fann-ūnah.

A فنا fanā, s.f. (6th) (from فني) Mortality, frailty, perdition, death, destruction. (E.) Sing. and Pl. (W.) Pl. فناوي fanāwī. فنا كيدل fanā kedal, verb intrans. To perish, to die. فنا كول fanā kawul, verb trans. To destroy, to blight, to dilapidate.

P A فندق fan-duḳ, s.m. (2nd) A filbert nut (met. The lip of one's beloved). 2. (T) A bud. Pl. فندقونه fan-duḳ-ūnah.

A فواره fawāra'h, s.f. (3rd) A fountain, a jet, a spring, a drain. Pl. ي ey.

A فوج fauj, s.m. (2nd) An army, a multitude. Pl. فوجونه faujūnah. فوج كښي fauj kas͟hī or kak͟hī, s.f. (3rd) The collecting or assembling of an army. Pl. ي a'ī.

فو فنا fū-fanā, adj. Entirely destroyed, gone to perdition, gone to the dogs, gone to wreck, trampled under foot, cut up root and branch. فو فنا كول fū-fanā kawul, verb trans. To destroy, to exterminate, to annihilate. See فنا

فوكي fūkaey, s.m. (1st) A puff, a breath of air, a whiff, a blow, the act of blowing (corrup. of پوكي). Pl. ي ī.

P فولاد folād or fūlād, s.m. (6th) Steel. Sing. and Pl.

P فولادي folādī or fūlādī, adj. Made of steel, steel.

P فهرست fihrist, s.m. (2nd) An inventory, a list, an index, etc. Pl. فهرستونه fihristūnah.

P فهم fahm, s.m. (9th) Understanding, intellect, comprehension, sense. Sing. and Pl. فهم كول fahm kawul, verb trans. To comprehend, to understand, to weigh, to consider. See پوهه

A في الجمله fī-l-jumlah, adv. On the whole, upon the whole. في الحال fī-l-hāl, adv. Immediately, instantly, on the spot, now, directly.

في الحقيقت *fī-l-ḥaḳīḳat*, adv. Indeed, in fact, really, truly.

فيروژه *fīrojza'h*, s.f. (3rd) (corrup. of P فيروزه) The turquoise stone. Pl. ي *ey*. See پيروژه

A فيصله *faiṣala'h*, s.f. (3rd) (from فصل) A decree, a settlement, decision, adjudication, sentence, finding, award. Pl. ي *ey*. فيصله كول *faiṣala'h kawul*, verb trans. To adjudicate, to give a decree, to decide.

A فيض *faiẓ*, s.m. (9th) Plenty, abundance, overflowing, profit. 2. Grace, favour, bounty. Sing. and Pl. فيض رسان *faiẓ-rasān*, adj. Bountiful, beneficent; (Fem.) فيض رسانه *faiẓ-rasāna'h*. فيض رساني *faiẓ rasānī*, s.f. (3rd) Munificence, beneficence. Pl. ي *a'ī*.

P فيل *fīl*, s.m. (5th) An elephant. Pl. فيلان *fīlān*. فيله *fīla'h*, s.f. (3rd) A female elephant. Pl. ي *ey*. فيل وان *fīl-wān*, s.m. (5th) An elephant driver or feeder. Pl. فيل وانان *fīl-wānān*. فيل خانه *fīl-khāna'h*, s.f. (3rd) An elephant house. Pl. ي *ey*. فيل مرغ *fīl-murgh*, s.m. (5th) A turkey-cock. Pl. فيل مرغان *fīl-murghān*. فيل مرغه *fīl-murgha'h*, s.f. (3rd) A hen turkey. Pl. ي *ey*. داء الفيل *dāu-l-fīl*, s.m. (9th) Elephantiasis. Sing. and Pl. See هاتي

ق

ق *ḳāf*, called قاف قرشت *ḳāf-i-ḳarashat*, the twenty-first letter of the Arabic alphabet, occurs but rarely in pure Pushto terms, being merely used with such Arabic words as have been introduced into the language, and has no analogous letter in the Sanskrit. It stands thirty-first in the Pushto alphabet. In sound it differs from ك, inasmuch that it must be uttered by pressing the root of the tongue on the throat. It stands for 100 according to the Arabic system of numbers, and is sometimes used for غ

A قابض *ḳā-biẓ*, (act. part. of قبض) Seizing, holding, grasping, taking. 2. Astringent. 3. A receiver, a possessor; (Fem.) قابضه *ḳā-biẓa'h*.

A قابل *ḳā-bil*, adj. (act. part. of قبل) Receiving, taking. 2. Possible, capable, worthy, fit, skilful, sufficient, able, clever, deserving; (Fem.) قابله *ḳābila'h*; also, A mid-wife, s.f. (3rd). Pl. ي *ey*. قابل كيدل *ḳābil kedal*, verb intrans. To merit, to deserve, to be worthy of.

A قابليت *ḳābil-īyat*, s.m. (2nd) Skill, sufficiency, capacity, capability, accomplishment, possibility. Pl. قابليتونه *ḳābil-īyatūnah*.

A قابو *ḳābū*, s.m. (9th) (from T قابو) Authority, power, command, opportunity, possession, will. Sing. and Pl. قابو موندل *ḳābū mūndal*, verb trans. To get advantage or power over, to find opportunity.

قاتر *ḳātar*, s.m. (5th) A mule. Pl. قاتران *ḳātarān*. قاتره *ḳātara'h*, s.f. (3rd) A female mule. Pl. ي *ey*. See غاتر and خچر or قچر

A قاتل *ḳā-til*, s.m. (5th) (from قتل) Killing, homicide. 2. A murderer, an assassin. Pl. قاتلان *ḳātilān*. 3. adj. Mortal, deadly, fatal. قاتله *ḳātila'h*, s.f. (3rd) A murderess. Pl. ي *ey*.

قاتي *ḳātī*, s.f. (3rd) (corrup. of A قحط) Famine, dearth, scarcity. Pl. ي *a'ī*. See كاختي

A قادر *ḳā-dir*, adj. (act. part. of قدر) Potent, powerful, mighty, capable, skilful; (Fem.) قادره *ḳā-dira'h*.

قادري *ḳādaraey*, adj. Short, docked, curtailed; (Fem.) قادرئ *ḳādara'ī*. 2. s.m. (1st) A long and very full coat or shirt worn by the Yusūfzīs. 2. A short full robe worn by the Western Afghāns. Pl. ي *ī*. See لندي

قار درياب *ḳāri daryāb*, s.m. (2nd) The ocean, the salt sea. Pl. قار دريابونه *ḳāri-daryābūnah*. See قهر درياب and تالي درياب

قارغه *ḳārghah*, s.m. (5th) A crow. Pl. قارغان *ḳārghān* or قارگه *ḳārgah* and قارگان *ḳārgān*.

A قارون *ḳārūn*, s. prop. A person supposed to be the same as Korah, whom the Muḥammadans state to have been the cousin of Moses; a general name for a miser.

A قاري *ḳārī*, s.m. (5th) A reader of the Ḳu'rān, one who reads well. Pl. قاريان *ḳārī-ān*. (Masc. and Fem.)

قاش قاش *ḳā͟sh-ḳā͟sh*, s.m. (6th) Poppy seed, a poppy. Sing. and Pl. See قش قاش

قاشوغه *ḳā͟sho͟gha'h*, s.f. (3rd) A ladle made of wood, iron, brass, etc. Pl. ې *ey*. See خونخي

A قاصد *ḳā-ṣid*, s.m. (5th) A courier, an express, a messenger, an envoy, a postman. Pl. قاصدان *ḳā-ṣidān*. قاصدي *ḳā-ṣidī*, s.f. (3rd) Travelling as courier or messenger. Pl. ئ *a'ī*.

A قاصر *ḳā-ṣir*, adj. (act. part. of قصر) Defective, unable, impotent, deficient, failing; (Fem.) قاصره *ḳā-ṣira'h*.

A قاضي *ḳā-ẓī*, s.m. (5th) act. part. of قضا) A judge, a justice. Pl. قاضيان *ḳā-ẓī-ān*.

A قاعده *ḳā-æida'h*, s.f. (3rd) (from قعد) Rule, custom, institute, system, institution, manners. Pl. ې *ey*.

قاغه *ḳā͟gha'h*, s.f. (3rd) A kind of rook, a jackdaw. Pl. ې *ey*. (s كاګ) قاغي *ḳā͟gha'ī*, s.f. (6th) (W.) A common crow, a rook, a jackdaw. Sing. and Pl.

A قافله *ḳāfila'h*, s.f. (3rd) A caravan, a body of travellers. Pl. ې *ey*. قافله باشي *ḳāfila'h bā͟shī*, s.m. (5th) The leader or chief of a caravan. Pl. باشيان *bā͟shī-ān*. قافله باشي توب *ḳāfila'h bā͟shī-tob*, s.m. (2nd) The business of a caravan leader. Pl. توبونه *tobūnah*.

A قافيه *ḳāfiya'h*, s.f. (3rd) (from قفا) Rhyme, cadence, metre, the last letter in a verse to which the other distichs rhyme. Pl. ې *ey*.

A قالب *ḳālib*, s.m. (2nd) A mould, a model, a form. 2. A bust, a figure. Pl. قالبونه *ḳālibūnah*. See غالب

قام *ḳām*, s.m. (2nd) Tribe, sect, family, people, nation. Pl. قامونه *ḳāmūnah*. See قوم

A قامت *ḳāmat*, s.m. (2nd) Stature, shape, form, figure, body. Pl. قامتونه *ḳāmatūnah*.

A قانع *ḳā-niæ*, adj. (act. part. of قناعت) Contented, satisfied.

G قانون *ḳānūn*, s.m. (9th) Rule, regulation, statute, canon, institute, system. 2. A dulcimer or harp. Sing. and Pl.

A قايم *ḳā-īm*, adj. (act. part. of قوم) Firm, fixed, constant, stable, durable, lasting, continuing. 2. Standing erect, perpendicular; (Fem.) قايمه *ḳā-īma'h*. قايم مقام *ḳā-īm-maḳām*, A viceroy, a lieutenant, a deputy, a vicegerent.

P A قبا *ḳabā*, s.f. (6th) A robe, a dress, a quilted jacket, a mantle, a cover for a book. (E.) Sing. and Pl. (W.) قباوي *ḳabāwī*.

A قباحت *ḳabā-ḥat*, s.m. (2nd) (from قبح) Villany, deformity, turpitude, dishonesty, baseness, a base action, evil, ill. Pl. قباحتونه *ḳabā-ḥatūnah*.

A قبر *ḳabr*, s.m. (2nd) A grave, a tomb. Pl. قبرونه *ḳabr-ūnah*. قبر كند *ḳabr-kand*, s.m. (5th) A grave-digger. Pl. قبر كندان *ḳabr-kandān*. قبر ګاه *ḳabr-gāh* or قبرستان *ḳabr-istān*, s.m. (2nd) A grave-yard, a burying ground. Pl. قبر ګاهونه *ḳabr-gāhūnah* or قبرستانونه *ḳabristānūnah*.

A قبض *ḳabẓ*, s.m. (2nd) A receipt. 2. A tax, a tribute. 3. Contraction. 4. Costiveness. Pl. قبضونه *ḳabẓ-ūnah*. قبض كيدل *ḳabẓ kedal*, verb intrans. To become costive. قبض كول *ḳabẓ kawul*, verb trans. To make costive. قبض وركول *ḳabẓ war-kawul*, verb trans. To give a receipt.

A قبضه *ḳabẓa'h*, s.f. (3rd) (from قبض) Grasp, gripe (of the hand), clutch, possession. 2. A handle, a hilt. Pl. ې *ey*. په قبضه رسيدل *pah ḳabẓa'h rasedal*, verb intrans. To come into one's possession or hands. په قبضه راوړل *pah ḳabẓa'h rā-w'ṟṟal*, To get into one's possession, to seize, to appropriate.

A قبل *ḳabl*, adj. First, the first; (Fem.) قبله *ḳabla'h*. 2. adv. Before, previously. See اول and ړمبي

قبل *ḳabl*, adj. Surrounded, inclosed, invested, blockaded, besieged; (Fem.) قبله *ḳabla'h*. 2. *ḳibal*, s.m. (2nd) Power. Pl. قبلونه *ḳibalūnah*.

A قبله *ḳibla'h*, s.f. (3rd) Anything opposite. 2. That part to which the Faithful turn their faces to pray, hence Makka. Pl. ې *ey*. قبله ګاه *ḳibla'h-gāh*, s.m. (2nd) The place turned to in prayer. Pl. قبله ګاهونه *ḳibla'h-gāhūnah*. 2. s.m. (5th) A father, or one beloved. Pl. قبله ګاهان *ḳibla'h-gāhān*. قبله نماي *ḳibla'h-numāe*, s.m. (5th) A compass to show the direction of Makka. Sing. and Pl.

A قبول *ḳubūl* or *ḳabūl*, s.m. (9th) (from قبل) Consent, favorable reception, concession, approbation, assent. Sing. and Pl. 2. adj. Accepted, approved, consented, agreed; (Fem.) قبوله *ḳabūla'h*. قبول كيدل *ḳabūl kedal*, verb intrans. To be accepted, to be agreed or assented to. قبول كول *ḳabūl kawul*, verb trans. To assent to, to agree to, to allow, etc. قبليدل *ḳab-ledal*, verb trans. To be accepted, to be agreed to, to be assented to, to be favorably received, to be approved, to be consented to. Pres. قبليږي *ḳablejzī* (W.) or قبليكي *ḳablegī* (E.); past قبول شه *ḳabūl shah* or وُ شه *wu-shah*; fut. قبول به شي *ḳabūl bah shī* or به وُ شي *bah wu-shī*; imp. قبول شه *ḳabūl shah* or وُ شه *wu-shah*; act. part. قبليدونكَي *ḳabledūnkaey* or قبليدونَي *ḳable-dūnaey*; past part. قبول *ḳabūl* or قبول شوَي *ḳabūl shawaey*: verb. n. قبليدنه *ḳabledana'h* or قبليده *ḳabledah*. قبلول *ḳablawul*, verb trans. To accept, to receive, to take, to assent, to allow, to confess, to consent, to deign, to agree to, to promise, to own. Pres. قبلوي *ḳablawī*; past قبول كړ *ḳabūl karr* or وُ كړ *wu-karr*; fut. قبول به كړي *ḳabūl bah krrī* or به وُ كړي *bah wu-krrī*; imp. كبول كړه *ḳabūl krrah* or وُ كړه *wu-krrah*; act. part. قبلوونكَي *ḳablawūnkaey* or فبلوونَي *ḳablawūnaey*; past part. قبول كړَي *ḳabūl karraey*; verb. n. قبلونه *ḳablawuna'h*.

A قبه *ḳubba'h*, s.f. (3rd) (from قب) A vault, an arch, a dome, a cupola, an alcove. Pl. ېَ *ey*. See تنبي

A قبيله *ḳabīla'h*, s.f. (3rd) A family, a tribe. 2. A wife. Pl. ېَ *ey*.

قپ *ḳap* and قپا *ḳapā*. See كپ

قت *ḳat*, s.m. (2nd) A fold, a plait, a layer, stratum. Pl. قتونه *ḳatūnah*. قت په قت *ḳat pah ḳat*, adj. Folded, plaited, layer on layer. قت كول *ḳat kawul*, verb trans. To fold, to lay one over the other.

قتار *ḳatār*, s.m. (2nd) (corrup. of A قطار) A line, a rank, a file, order, series, row, range. Pl. قتارونه *ḳatārūnah*. هير قتار *her-ḳatār*, A file or string of camels.

قتارَي *ḳatāraey*, s.m. (1st) Foolish talk, frivolous contention, squabbling. Pl. ي *ī*. ويت قتارَي *wīt-ḳatāraey*, adj. A talker of nonsense. 2. Quarrelsome, a squabbler, a litigious person; (Fem.) ويت قتارِ *wīt-ḳatāri*. Pl. (Masc. and Fem.) ي *ī*. See ويته

قتره *ḳatra'h*, s.f. (3rd) A piece, a morsel, a drop, etc. Pl. ېَ *ey*. Corrup. of قطره, which see. قتره روته *ḳatra'h rota'h*, s.f. (3rd) A collop, a steak, a piece of grilled meat. Pl. ېَ *ey*. See قطره

قتغ *ḳatagh*, s.m. (2nd) Meat, fish, soup, etc., eaten with bread, to give it a savour, a relish. Pl. قتغونه *ḳataghūnah*.

H قتل *ḳatl*, s.m. (2nd) Slaughter, killing, homicide, murder, assassination. Pl. قتلونه *ḳatl-ūnah*. قتل عام *ḳatl-i-ææmm*, A general massacre. قتل گاه *ḳatl-gāh*, s.m. (2nd) A place of slaughter or murder. Pl. قتل گاهونه *ḳatl-gāhūnah*. قتليدل *ḳatledal*, verb intrans. To be killed, murdered, slaughtered assassinated, etc. Pres. قتليږي *ḳatlejzī* (W.) or قتليكي *ḳatlegī* (E.); past قتل شه *ḳatl shah* or وُ شه *wu-shah*; fut. قتل به شي *ḳatl bah shī* or به وُ شي *bah wu-shī*; imp. قتل شه *ḳatl shah* or وُ شه *wu-shah*; act. part. قتليدونكَي *ḳatledūnkaey* or قتليدونَي *ḳatledūnaey*; past part. قتل شوَي *ḳatl shawaey*; verb. n. قتليدنه *ḳatledana'h* or قتليده *ḳatledah*. قتلول *ḳatl-awul*, verb trans. To kill, to murder, to execute, to assassinate. Pres. قتلوي *ḳatlawī*; past قتل كړ *ḳatl karr* or وُ كړ *wu-karr*; fut. قتل به كړي *ḳatl bah krrī* or به وُ كړي *bah wu-krrī*; imp. قتل كړه *ḳatl krrah* or وُ كړه *wu-krrah*; act. part. قتلوونكَي *ḳatlawūnkaey* or قتلوونَي *ḳatlawūnaey*; past part. قتل كړَي *ḳatl karraey*; verb. n. قتلونه *ḳatlawuna'h*.

قتي *ḳutta'ī*, s.f. (6th) A powder horn of wood covered with leather, a flask. Sing. and Pl.

قتَي *ḳutaey*, s.m. (1st) A ball used in a game played by children. Pl. ي *ī*. See گند

قجري *ḳajarī*, s.f. (3rd) A saddle-cloth placed

over the saddle and reaching to the horse's tail. Pl. ئ *a'ī*. See ثجري

قچر *ḳac̲h̲ar*, s.m. (5th) A mule. Pl. قچران *ḳac̲h̲arān*. قچره *ḳac̲h̲ara'h*, s.f. (3rd) A female mule. Pl. ئ *ey*. (H I نچر) See غاتر and قاتر

قچي *ḳic̲h̲aey*, s.m. (1st) A band, a set, a party, a knot, a gang, a small party, a bevy, a flock, etc. Pl. ي *ī*.

قچي قچي *ḳic̲h̲ī-ḳic̲h̲ī*, adj. In knots, in bands, in flocks, in small bodies, etc.

A قد *ḳadd*, s.m. (2nd) Stature, height. Pl. قدونه *ḳaddūnah*. قد و قامت *ḳadd-o-ḳāmat*, Stature, figure (of a person).

A قدر *ḳadr*, s.m. (2nd) Worth, value, price, importance, dignity. 2. Quantity, size, magnitude, bulk, measure, degree. 3. Fate, destiny. Pl. قدرونه *ḳadrūnah*. قدر دان *ḳadr-dān*, adj. A just appreciator, knowing the worth of, a patron; (Fem.) قدر دانه *ḳadr-dāna'h*. قدر داني *ḳadr dānī*, s.f. (3rd) Due regard to worth, appreciation. Pl. ئ *a'ī*.

A قدرت *ḳud-rat*, s.m. (2nd) Power, authority. 2. Omnipotence. Pl. قدرتونه *ḳudratūnah*.

P قدغن *ḳadag̲h̲an*, s.m. (2nd) An injunction, a prohibition. Pl. قدغنونه *ḳadag̲h̲anūnah*. قدغن كول *ḳadag̲h̲an kawul*, verb trans. To prohibit, to forbid, to enjoin.

A قدم *ḳadam*, s.m. (2nd) A pace, a step, a footstep. 2. The foot, the sole of the foot. Pl. قدمونه *ḳadamūnah*. قدم په قدم *ḳadam pah ḳadam*, Step by step, by degrees.

A قديم *ḳadīm*, adj. (from قدم) Old, ancient, aged; (Fem.) قديمه *ḳadīma'h*.

قر *ḳur*, s.m. (5th) Grumbling sound as produced in the bowels, the croak of a frog. Pl. قرهار *ḳurahār*. قرقر *ḳur-ḳur*, Grumbling of the bowels, Borborygmi. 2. The sound of a horse when trotting. قرقر كول *ḳur-ḳur kawul*, verb trans. To grumble, to croak. See تق تق

A قرابت *ḳarābat*, s.m. (2nd) Affinity, propinquity, relationship, kin, vicinity, alliance. Pl. قرابتونه *ḳarābatūnah*. قرابت لرل *ḳarābat laral*, verb trans. To have or hold affinity, to have propinquity (to be related).

قرابين *ḳarābīn*, s.m. (2nd) A carabine, a blunderbuss. Pl. قرابينونه *ḳarābīnūnah*. (French.)

A قرات *ḳir'āt*, s.m. (2nd) (from قرأ) Pronunciation, reading the Ḳu'rān. Pl. قراتونه *ḳir'āt-ūnah*.

A قرار *ḳarār*, s.m. (9th) Rest, residence, tranquility, quietness. 2. Firmness, stability. 3. s.m. (2nd) Agreement, engagement. Pl. قرارونه *ḳarārūnah*. 4. adj. Firm, strong, fixed, established; (Fem.) قراره *ḳarāra'h*. قرار داد *ḳarār dād*, An engagement, a contract, an agreement. قرار قرار *ḳarār-ḳarār* or قلار قلار *ḳalār ḳalār*, Gently, slowly, softly. قراره قراري *ḳarāra'h-ḳarārī*, Rest and tranquility, complete repose. قراريدل *ḳarāredal*, verb intrans. To repose, To be at rest, to be tranquil, to keep quiet. 2. To be firm, settled, to acquire stability. Pres. قراريږي *ḳarārejzī* (W.) or قراريگي *ḳarāregī* (E.); past قرار شه *ḳarār s̲h̲ah* or وُ شه *wu-s̲h̲ah*; fut. قرار به شي *ḳarār bah s̲h̲ī* or به وُ شي *bah wu-s̲h̲ī*; imp. قرار شه *ḳarār s̲h̲ah* or وُ شه *wu-s̲h̲ah*; act. part. قراريدونكي *ḳarāredūnkaey* or قراريدونيَ *ḳar-āredūnaey*; past part. قرار *ḳarār* or قرار شويَ *ḳarār s̲h̲awaey*; verb. n. قراريدنه *ḳarāre-dana'h* or قراريده *ḳarāredah*. قرارول *ḳarār-awul*, verb trans. To tranquilize, to reconcile, to compose, to settle, to arrange, to quiet, to give stability to. Pres. قراروي *ḳarārawī*; past قرار كړ *ḳarār kaṟ* or وُ كړ *wu-kaṟ*; fut. قرار به كړي *ḳarār bah kṟṟī* or به وُ كړي *bah wu-kṟṟī*; imp. قرار كړه *ḳarār kṟṟah* or وُ كړه *wu-kṟṟah*; act. part. قراروونكيَ *ḳarārawūnkaey* or قراروونيَ *ḳarārawūnaey*; past part. قرار كړيَ *ḳarār kaṟṟaey*; verb. n. قرارونه *ḳarārawuna'h*.

A قرآن *ḳur-ān*, s.m. (2nd) The book containing the precepts, etc. of the Prophet Muḥammad, the Alkorān. Pl. قرآنونه *ḳur-ānūnah*. قرآن آخستل *ḳur'ān āk̲h̲istal*, verb trans. To swear, to take an oath on the Ḳur'ān.

T قراول *ḳarāwul*, s.m. (6th) The advanced guard of an army. 2. A sentinel, a picquet. Sing. and Pl. (vulg.) قرول *ḳarawal*.

A قربان *ḳurbān*, s.m. (9th) A sacrifice, a victim,

an offering. Sing. and Pl. قربان کيدل *ḳurbān kedal,* verb intrans. To be sacrificed or devoted. قربان کول *ḳurbān kawul,* verb trans. To sacrifice, to devote, to offer up. قرباني *ḳurbānī,* adj. Devoted, sacrificed, offered up.

قرت *ḳurut,* s.m. (6th) Coagulated milk boiled, a kind of cheese. Sing. and Pl. See بکوره

قرت کانړي *ḳurt ḳārrnī,* s.m. (1st) Pl. Gravel, small stones or fragments of stone or small pebbles. Sing. کانړی *ḳarrnāey,* seldom used.

A قرص *ḳurṣ,* s.m. (2nd) An orb, the disc of the sun or moon. Pl. قرصونه *ḳurṣ-ūnah.* See تکي

A قرض *ḳarẓ,* s.m. (2nd) A loan, a debt, money borrowed at interest. Pl. قرضونه *ḳarẓūnah.* قرض دار *ḳarẓ-dār,* A debtor, a creditor; (Fem.) قرض داره *ḳarẓ-dāra'h.* قرض داري *ḳarẓ dārī,* s.f. (3rd) Being in debt. Pl. ئي *a'ī.* قرض کول *ḳarẓ kawul* or قرض آخستل *ḳarẓ ākhistal,* verb trans. To borrow, to take on loan. قرض ورکول *ḳarẓ war-kawul,* verb trans. To lend.

قرقره *ḳarḳara'h,* s.f. (3rd) An ornament for the turban, a plume, an aigrette. Pl. ئي *ey.*

قرقرى *ḳar-ḳaraey,* s.m. (1st) The gripes in a horse, belly-fretting. Pl. ي *ī.*

قرقيچن *ḳar-ḳechan,* adj. Mumped, chilled with the cold, frost-bitten; (Fem.) قرقيچنه *ḳar-kechana'h.* See قرقيچن.

A قرمز *ḳirmiz,* s.m. (9th) Cochineal, crimson. Sing. and Pl.

P قرمساق *ḳurram-sāḳ,* adj. A pimp, a term of abuse, or قرمساغ *ḳurramsāgh.* See دهوس

A قرن *ḳarn,* s.m. (2nd) A conjunction of the planets. 2. A century, a period of thirty years. Pl. قرنونه *ḳarnūnah.*

قرنا *ḳurnā,* s.f. (6th) A trumpet, a horn, a clarion, a cornet. (E.) Sing. and Pl. (W.) Pl. قرناوي *ḳur-nāwī.* (A H CH قرنائي)

A قريب *ḳarīb,* adv. (from قرب) Near, nigh, almost, about, akin, relative, neighbouring; (Fem.) قريبه *ḳarība'h.*

A قرينه *ḳarīna'h,* s.f. (3rd) Context, conjecture, similarity, analogy, symmetry, order, regularity, connection, correspondence. Pl. ئي *ey.*

قړچ *ḳurrch,* s.m. (2nd) The white rose tree. Pl. قړچونه *ḳurrchūnah.* See پهلواړي

قړقيچن *ḳarr-ḳechan,* adj. Mumped, chilled with the cold, benumbed, frost-bitten; (Fem.) قړقيچنه *ḳarr-kechana'h.*

T قزل باش *ḳazal-bāsh,* s.m. (5th) A kind of Mughal soldier, a tribe of Mughals located at Kabul. Pl. قزل باشان *ḳazal-bāshān.* قزل باشه *ḳazal-bāsha'h,* s.f. (3rd) A female of the above. Pl. ئي *ey.*

قسب *ḳasab,* s.m. (6th) A kind of red silk, a small turban. Sing. and Pl. See سر بسته

A قسط *ḳist,* s.m. (2nd) A tax, an instalment. Pl. قسطونه *ḳistūnah.* قسط تړل *ḳist tarral,* verb trans. To fix instalments, to settle for payment of instalments.

A قسم *ḳism,* s.m. (2nd) Kind, sort, species. 2. Division, part. Pl. قسمونه *ḳismūnah.*

A قسم *ḳasam,* s.m. (2nd) An oath, an affirmation. Pl. قسمونه *ḳasmūnah.* قسم آخستل *ḳasam ākhistal* or قسم خوړل *ḳasam khwarral,* verb trans. To take an oath, to swear. قسم ورکول *ḳasam war-kawul,* verb trans. To administer an oath, to adjure.

A قسمت *ḳismat,* s.m. (2nd) Fortune, fate, destiny, lot. 2. Share, portion, division, distribution. Pl. قسمتونه *ḳismatūnah.* See بخره and ويش

قشقاش *ḳash-ḳāsh,* s.m. (6th) A poppy, bark, rind, poppy-seed. Sing. and Pl.

قشلاق *ḳishlāḳ,* s.m. (2nd) The winter station of the pastoral tribes of the West, in contradistinction to Eilāk—the summer station. Pl. قشلاقونه *ḳishlāḳūnah* (T قيشلاق)

A قصاب *ḳaṣṣāb,* s.m. (5th) (adj. of قصب) A butcher. Pl. قصابان *ḳaṣṣābān.* قصابي *ḳaṣṣābī,* s.f. (3rd) The business of a butcher. Pl. ئي *a'ī.*

A قصاص *ḳiṣāṣ,* s.m. (2nd) The law of retaliation. Pl. قصاصونه *ḳiṣāṣūnah.*

A قصد *ḳaṣd,* s.m. (2nd) Intention, design, aim, desire, wish, inclination, purpose, project, attempt, conspiracy. Pl. قصدونه *ḳaṣdūnah.* قصد کول *ḳaṣd kawul,* verb trans. To intend, to design, to project, to propose, to resolve, to make one's object or aim. قصداً *ḳaṣdan*, adv. Voluntarily, intentionally, purposely, wilfully, expressly.

A قصور *ḳuṣūr*, s.m. (2nd) (from قصر) Defect, fault, want, faultiness, deficiency, omission, failure, blame. Pl. قصورونه *ḳuṣūrūnah*. قصور كول *ḳuṣūr kawul*, verb trans. To fail, to be deficient, to commit a fault, to blunder.

A قصه *ḳiṣṣa'h*, s.f. (3rd) (from قص) A tale, a story, a narration. 2. Quarrel, dispute. Pl. ي *ey*.

A قصيده *ḳaṣīda'h*, s.f. (3rd) A long poem or ode. Pl. ي *ey*.

A قضا *ḳaẓā*, s.f. (6th) (from قضي) Fate, destiny, decree. 2. Death, fatality. 3. Praying at the appointed time. 4. Judgment, decree, administration of justice. (E.) Sing. and Pl. (W.) Pl. قضاوي *ḳaẓā-wī*.

A قضيه *ḳaẓiya'h*, s.f. (3rd) (from قضي) Declaration, determination, proposition. 2. Death. 3. (peculiar to Pus͟hto) A quarrel, wrangling, contention, broil, law-suit, litigation, action at law. Pl. ي *ey*. قضيه كول *ḳaẓiya'h kawul*, verb trans. To quarrel, to wrangle.

A قطار *ḳaṭār* or *ḳiṭār*, s.m. (2nd) A line, a rank, a file, a row, a range, a series. 2. A string of camels. Pl. قطارونه *ḳaṭārūnah*. See قتار. هير قطار *her ḳaṭār*, moving along one after the other as camels.

A قطب *ḳuṭb*, s.m. (2nd) The Polar star, the North Pole. 2. A spindle or axis of a mill-stone. Pl. قطبونه *ḳuṭbūnah*.

A قطره *ḳaṭra'h*, s.f. (3rd) A drop, a sprinkling, an atom. Pl. ي *ey*. قطره قطره *ḳaṭra'h ḳaṭra'h*, adj. In drops, in atoms.

تغالئ *ḳug͟hālaey*, s.m. (1st) A hole made in the centre of a dish of rice, filled with oil or *g͟hī*. Pl. ي *ī*; also pronounced قوغالئ *ḳū-g͟hālaey* and كوغالئ *ko-g͟hālaey*.

A قفس *ḳafas* or قفص *ḳafaṣ*, s.m. (2nd) (from H and CH) A cage, a lattice, a network. Pl. قفسونه *ḳafasūnah* or قفصونه *ḳafaṣūnah*.

A قفل *ḳufl* or قلف *ḳulf*, (W.) s.m. (2nd) A lock, a bolt. Pl. قفلونه *ḳuflūnah* or قلفونه *ḳulf-ūnah*. See جندره

قق قق *ḳuḳ-ḳuḳ*, s.m. (5th) The sound made by a trotting horse. Pl. قق ققهار *ḳuḳ-ḳuḳahār*. See قر

A ققنس *ḳaḳnas* or ققنوس *ḳuḳnūs*, s.m. (6th) The phœnix, a fabulous bird. Sing. and Pl.

قلا *ḳalā*, s.f. (6th) (corrup. of A قلعه) A fort, a castle, a fortress. (E.) Sing. and Pl. (W.) Pl. قلاوي *ḳalāwī*.

قلار *ḳalār*, s.m. (9th) A promise, agreement, promising. Sing. and Pl. See قرار and اقلار

قلار قلار *ḳalār-ḳalār*, adv. Gently, slowly, softly. See قرار قرار

A قلبه *ḳulba'h*, s.f. (3rd) A plough. 2. Quantity of land enough for one plough. Pl. ي *ey*. قلبه كول *ḳulba'h kawul*, verb trans. To plough. See يوي and يويه

قلپ *ḳalp*, adj. (corrup. of قلب) Adulterated, counterfeit (as money); (Fem.) قلپه *ḳalpa'h*.

A قلعه *ḳilaæ'h* or *ḳalaæ'h*, s.f. (3rd) A fort, a castle, a fortress. Pl. ي *ey*. قلعچه *ḳalac͟ha'h*, s.f. (3rd) A redoubt, a small fortress. Pl. ي *ey*.

قلعي *ḳalaæī*, or (vulg.) قليي *ḳalayī*, s.m. (9th) Tin. Sing. and Pl. قلعي گر *ḳalaæī-gar*, s.m. (5th) A tinner of pots. Pl. قلعي گړ *ḳalaæī-gær*.

قلف *ḳulf*, s.m. (2nd) (corrup. of قفل) A lock, a bolt. Pl. قلفونه *ḳulfūnah*. قلف كول *ḳulf kawul*, verb trans. To lock, to bolt.

A قلم *ḳalam*, s.m. (2nd) A reed, a pen. 2. The cutting of a tree or plant. Pl. قلمونه *ḳalam-ūnah*. قلم تراش *ḳalam-tarās͟h*, s.m. (2nd) A pen-knife. Pl. قلم تراشونه *ḳalam-tarās͟hūnah*.

قلم دان *ḳalam-dān*, s.m. (2nd) An inkstand, a writing-case. Pl. قلم دانونه *ḳalam-dānūnah*.

قلم رو *ḳalam-rau*, s.m. (2nd) Empire, dominion, sovereignty. Pl. قلم روونه *ḳalam-rau-ūnah*.

قلم قط *ḳalam-ḳaṭ*, s.m. (2nd) A pin or peg on which the nibs of pens are cut. Pl. قلم قطونه *ḳalam ḳaṭ-ūnah*. قلم ييښول *ḳalam yes͟hawul* or *yek͟hawul* or قلم ييښل *ḳalam yes͟hal* or *yek͟hal*, verb trans. To plant slips or cuttings.

A قلنج *ḳulinj*, s.m. (9th) The colic. Sing. and Pl.

A قلندر *ḳalandar*, s.m. (5th) An order of devotees

or monks, who desert the world, wife, friends, etc. Pl. قلندران *ḳalandarān*.

قلندري *ḳalandarī*, s.f. (3rd) The practice of a kalandar. Pl. ئي *a'ī*.

قلنگ *ḳulang*, s.m. (2nd) Land-tax, revenue, a tax in general. 2. The name of a bird, a fowl of a large breed. Pl. قلنگونه *ḳulangūnah*. See کلنگ

T قمچي *ḳamchī*, s.f. (3rd) A horsewhip, a twig of cane. Pl. ئي *a'ī*; or قمچينه *ḳam-chīna'h*, s.f. (3rd). Pl. ئي *ey*.

A قمر *ḳamar*, s.m. (9th) The moon. Sing. and Pl. See سپوږمي or سپوګمي

A قمري *ḳumrī*, s.f. (3rd) A turtle-dove. Pl. ئي *a'ī*.

A قميص *ḳamīṣ*, s.m. (2nd) A shirt, a chemise. Pl. قميصونه *ḳamīṣūnah*.

قنات *ḳanāt*, s.m. (5th) (A قناد) Sweetmeats, confectionary. Pl. قناتان *ḳanātān*.

A قناعت *ḳanā-æat*, s.m. (2nd) (from قنع) Content, tranquility. 2. Abstinence. Pl. قناعتونه *ḳanā-æatūnah*. قناعت کول *ḳanā-æat kawul*, verb trans. To be contented with, to satisfy the mind.

A قنج *ḳanj*, s.m. (2nd) Dissimulation, deceit, trick, imposture. Pl. قنجونه *ḳanj-ūnah*. قنج کول *ḳanj kawul*, verb trans. To act with dissimulation or deceit.

A قند *ḳand*, s.m. (2nd) Sugar or sugar-candy. Pl. قندونه *ḳandūnah*.

A قنديل *ḳandīl*, s.m. (2nd) A hanging lamp, a chandelier, a shade. Pl. قنديلونه *ḳandīlūnah*.

A قواعد *ḳawā'æid*, s.m. (9th) Rules, regulations. 2. Military evolutions, drill. Sing. and Pl. قواعد کول *ḳawā'æid kawul*, verb trans. To practice military evolutions.

A قوام *ḳiwām*, s.m. (2nd) Syrup, essence. Pl. قوامونه *ḳiwāmūnah*. قوامي *ḳiwāmī*, adj. Syrup-like, syrupy.

A قوت *ḳūt*, s.m. (9th) Food, aliment, victuals, subsistence, livelihood. Sing. and Pl. قوت لايموت *ḳūt-lā-yamūt*, Sufficient to sustain life.

A قوت *ḳūwat*, s.m. (2nd) (from قوي) Power, virtue, authority, faculty, strength, vigour. Pl. قوتونه *ḳūwatūnah*.

T قوچق *ḳo-chaḳ*, adj. Lusty, fat, brawny, in good condition (as a man or beast); (Fem.) قوچقه *ḳo-chaḳa'h*.

قوده *ḳawda'h*, s.f. (3rd) A handful, as much as can be held in, or seized by, the hand. Pl. ئي *ey*. See کوده

A قول *ḳaul*, s.m. (9th) A word, a saying, assertion. 2. Agreement, promise, contract, consent, affirmation. Sing. and Pl. قول و قرار *ḳaul-o-ḳarār*, s.m. (9th) Agreement, compact. Sing. and Pl. قول و قرار کول *ḳaul-o-ḳarār kawul*, verb trans. To stipulate, to covenant, to agree to.

A قوم *ḳaum*, s.m. (2nd) A tribe, a sect, a people, a nation, a family. Pl. قومونه *ḳaumūnah*. See خيل and قام

A قوي *ḳawī*, adj. Strong, solid, powerful, vigorous. (Masc. and Fem.)

A قهر *ḳahr*, s.m. (2nd) Force, severity, chastisement, rage, fury, indignation, vengeance, calamity, judgment. Pl. قهرونه *ḳahrūnah*. قهر جن *ḳahr-jan*, adj. Passionate, angry, irascible; (Fem.) قهر جنه *ḳahr-jana'h*; or قهر ناك *ḳahr-nāk*, and قهر ناكه *ḳahr-nāka'h*. قهر قهر *ḳahr-ḳahr*, adj. Exceedingly enraged, foaming with passion. قهريدل *ḳahredal*, verb intrans. To be furious with anger, to be exasperated, to be violent and tumultuous, to storm, to fret, to chafe, to fume. Pres. قهريږي *ḳahrejzī* (W.) or قهريكي *ḳahregī* (E.); past وُ قهريده *wu-ḳahredah* or قهريدَ *ḳahreda*; fut. وُ به قهريږي *wu bah ḳahrejzī* or قهريكي *ḳahregī*; imp. وُ قهريږه *wu-ḳahrejzah* or قهريكه *ḳahregah*; act. part. قهريدونكي *ḳahredūnkaey* or قهريدونيَ *ḳahredūnaey*; past part. قهريدليَ *ḳahredalaey*; verb. n. قهريدنه *ḳahredana'h* or قهريده *ḳahredah*. قهرول *ḳahrawul*, verb trans. To make furious with anger, to exasperate, to make to storm or fret, to chafe, to irritate, etc. Pres. قهروي *ḳahrawī*; past وُ قهراوه *wu-ḳahrāwuh* or قهراوو *ḳahrāwo*; fut. وُ به قهروي *wu bah ḳahrawī*; imp. وُ قهروه *wu-ḳahrawah*; act. part. قهروونكي *kahrawūnkaey* or قهرووني *ḳahr-*

awūnaey; past part. قهرولىٓ ḳahrawulaey; verb. n. قهرونه ḳahrawuna'h.

قهقهه ḳah-ḳaha'h, s.f. (3rd) Loud laughter, horse-laugh. Pl. يْ ey. قهقهه كول ḳah-ḳaha'h kawul, verb trans. To laugh aloud or heartily, to giggle. (A قهقه).

A قهوه ḳahwa'h, s.f. (3rd) Coffee. Pl. يْ ey.

A قي ḳai, s.m. (9th) Vomiting. Sing. and Pl. قي وهل ḳai wahal or قي كول ḳai kawul, verb trans. To vomit, to evacuate the contents of the stomach, to spew.

A قياس ḳiyās, s.m. (2nd) (from قيس) Measuring or comparing in the mind, judgment, opinion, supposition, thought, guess, theory, a syllogism. Pl. قياسونه ḳiyāsūnah. قياس كول ḳiyās kawul, verb trans. To consider, to suppose, to think, to guess. قياسي ḳiyāsī, adj. Conjectural, theoretical, analogous. (Masc. and Fem.)

A قيامت ḳiyāmat, s.m. (9th) The general resurrection, the last day. Sing. and Pl. قيامت گلىٓ ḳiyāmat-gulaey, s.m. (1st) The name of a yellow flower. Pl. ي ī.

A قيد ḳaid, s.m. (2nd) Imprisonment, bond, bondage. 2. An obstacle. 3. An obligation, a compact. Pl. قيدونه ḳaidūnah. قيد خانه ḳaid khāna'h, s.f. (3rd) A prison, a jail. Pl. يْ ey. قيد كول ḳaid kawul, verb trans. To imprison, to bind, to fetter, to captivate. قيد كيدل ḳaid kedal, verb intrans. To be imprisoned, to be bound.

قيزه ḳaiza'h, s.f. (3rd) A watering-bridle. Pl. يْ ey. See ملونه

A قيل ḳīl, s.m. (9th) A word, a speech, a saying. Sing. and Pl. قيل و قال ḳīl-o-ḳāl, Conversation, confabulation, clack, babble, controversy, altercation.

A قيمت ḳīmat, s.m. (2nd) Price, value. Pl. قيمتونه ḳīmatūnah. قيمتي ḳī-matī, adj. Valuable, high-priced. (Masc. and Fem.)

ك

ك kāf, called كاف كلمن, the twenty-second letter of the Arabic, is the thirty-second letter of the Pus͟hto alphabet. It corresponds to English k, and has the same power as Sanskrit क. According to the system of letters for numbers, it stands for 20. The Eastern Afg͟hāns change it for ږ sometimes.

كَ ka, In poetry is often thus written for كه kah, and وُ كه wu-kah, the imperfect and past tenses of the verb كول kawul, 'to do.' It may also signify the third person of the present tense, both singular and plural, as also the imperative form of the verb. See Grammar, page 148.

كا kā, The third person singular and plural of كول, and used also as the imperfect, and past tense, for explanation of which see Grammar.

P كابل kābul, s. prop. The name of a city in Afg͟hānistān. كابلىٓ kā-bulaey, s.m. (1st) A native of Kābul. Pl. ي ī. كابلۍ kābula'ī, s.f. (6th) A female of Kābul. Sing. and Pl.

P كابين kā-bīn, s.m. (2nd) A marriage portion given to the bride's father, or settled on the bride, a jointure, a dower. Pl. كابينونه kā-bīnūnah.

كاته kātah, s.m. (6th) (verb. n.) Seeing, beholding, viewing, contemplating, surveying. 2. Look, glimpse, glance, gaze, stare, regard, etc. Sing. and Pl. See كتل

A كاتب kā-tib, s.m. (5th) A scribe, a writer, a copier, a clerk, an amanuensis. Pl. كاتبان kā-tibān.

كاچو kā-c͟hū, s.m. (5th) A clasp-knife. Pl. كاچوگان kā-c͟hūgān; or چاكو c͟hā-kū and چاكوگان c͟hākūgān.

كاچوغه kā-c͟hogha'h, s.f. (3rd) A ladle made of wood, iron, or brass. Pl. يْ ey. See خمڅۍ

كاختي kāk͟h-tī, s.f. (3rd) Famine, dearth. Pl. ئي a'ī. د كاختۍ كال da kāk͟h-ta'ī kāl, A famine year, a year of dearth.

A كاذب kā-ẕib, s.m. (5th) (act. part. of كذب) A liar. Pl. كاذبان kā-ẕibān. 2. adj. False, untrue; (Fem.) كاذبه kā-ẕiba'h.

P كار kār, s.m. (2nd) Business, action, affair, work, labor, profession, operation. Pl. كارونه kārūnah. (E.) چار. كار آزموده kār āzmūdah.

adj. Experienced, practised, veteran. کار و بار *kār-o-bār*, s.m. (2nd) Business, affair. Pl. کار و بارونه *kār-o-bārūnah*. کار خانه *kār-khāna'h*, s.f. (3rd) A manufactory, a dock-yard, an arsenal, a workshop. Pl. ې *ey*. کار دیده *kār-dīdah*, adj. Experienced, tried, veteran. کار رواڼي *kār-rawā-ī*, s.f. (3rd) Carrying on a business, management, performance. Pl. ئ *a'ī*. کار زار *kār-zār*, s.m. (2nd) Battle, conflict. Pl. کار زارونه *kār-zārūnah*. کارساز *kār-sāz*, adj. Adroit, clever; (Fem.) کار سازه *kār-sāza'h*. کار ساري *kār-sāzī*, s.f. (3rd) Cleverness, adroitness. Pl. ئ *a'ī*. کار کند *kār-kund* (corrup. of P کار کن) adj. Adroit, clever, experienced. 2. A director, a manager; (Fem.) کار کنده *kār-kunda'h*. کار کول *kār kawul*, verb trans. To work, to labor, to trade. په کار راتلل *pah kār rā-t'lal* or راغلل *rāgh-lal*, verb intrans. To be fit, to come into use, to be of use, to be proper or useful. په کار راوول *pah kār rā-w'rral*, verb trans. To bring to use, to make use of, to expend. په کار دي *pah kār daey*, It is useful. په کار نه دي *pah kār nah daey*, It is useless.

P کارستان *kār-istān*, s.m. (2nd) A place of work, a manufactory, an arsenal. Pl. کارستانونه *kār-istānūnah*.

کارښت *kārisht* (W.) or *kārikht* (E.), s.m. (2nd) A place where the juice is expressed from the grapes in making wine, and made of brick and lime in the shape of a cauldron, a wine-press. Pl. کارښتونه *kārishtūnah* or *kārikht-ūnah*.

کارغه *kār-ghah*, s.m. (5th) A crow, the common crow. Pl. کارغان *kār-ghān*. سیلاټي کارغه *selātaey kār-ghah* or سیلاني کارغه *selānaey kār-ghah*, A rook. د کارغه پسکۍ *da kār-ghah puska'ī*, s.f. (6th) A shell, the shell of a snail (*lit.* a crow's fart). Sing. and Pl. See ګجي and شاپیتي

کارګوټي *kār-gottaey*, s.m. (1st) (dimin. of P کار) A small matter or affair, unimportant business, a trifling matter. Pl. ي *ī*.

P کاروان *kār-wān*, s.m. (2nd) A caravan, a party of travellers. Pl. کاروانونه *kār-wānūnah*. کارواني *kār-wānī*, adj. Belonging to a caravan. کاروان سراي *kār-wān-sarā'e*, s.m. (2nd) A caravansera. Pl. سرایونه *sarā'eūnah*.

کاره *kāra'h*, s.f. (3rd) A large wooden vessel used for covering meat, as a dish cover, also made of cane like a basket. Pl. ې *ey*. See سوده

کارۍ *kāra'ī*, s.f. (6th) A creek, a bay, a small inlet of the sea. Sing. and Pl. (s کهاري)

P کاریز *kār-ez*, s.m. (2nd) A canal for watering ground, a subterranean canal. Pl. کاریزونه *kār-ezūnah*. کاریزي *kār-ezī*, adj. Watered by canals (as land).

P کاریګر *kārī-gar*, s.m. (5th) An artificer, a workman, a manufacturer. Pl. کاریګرٌ *kārī-gær*. کاریګره *kārī-gara'h*, s.f. (3rd). Pl. ې *ey*. کاریګري *kārī-garī*, s.f. (3rd) Masterly work, workmanship. Pl. ئ *a'ī*.

کاړساو *kārr-sāwo*, adj. Having a long face. 2. s.m. (5th) A long-faced person. Pl. کاړساوان *kārr-sāwo-ān*. 3. Sorrowful, anxious, down in the mouth; (Fem.) کاړساوه *kārr-sāwa'h*, adj. and s.f. (3rd). Pl. ې *ey*.

کاړي واړي *kārrī-wārrī*, adj. Infirm, languid, weakly, decrepit; lazy, indolent, slothful.

P کاز *kāz*, s.m. (2nd) Shears, scissors. 2. The den of a wild beast. 3. A cavern in which men or sheep are lodged in the winter. Pl. کازونه *kāzūnah*. See بیاتي and نغم

کاږل *kājzal*, verb trans. (W.) To pull or draw out, to extract, to pluck out, to root up, to remove, to express, to elicit, to extricate. 2. To write, to take down. This infinitive is imperfect and requires the aid of کښل to complete the conjugations. Pres. کاږي *kājzī*; past (from کښل) وُ کیښ *wu-kesh* or وُ کِښ *wu-kish*; fut. وُ به کاږي *wu bah kājzī*; imp. وُ کاږه *wu-kājzah*; act. part. کښونکی *k'shūnkaey* or کښونی *k'shūnaey*; past part. کښلی *k'shal-aey*; verb. n. کاږنه *kājzana'h*. See کاګل

کاږه *kājzah* or کاګه *kā-gah*. See کوږ and کوګ

P کاسب *kā-sib*, s.m. (5th) A tradesman, an artist. Pl. کاسبان *kā-sibān*. کاسبّه *kā-siba'h*, s.f. (3rd) A tradeswoman. Pl. ې *ey*.

P كاسني *kās-nī*, s.m. (6th) Endive (Cichorium endivia). Sing. and Pl.

A كاسه *kā-sa'h*, s.f. (3rd) A cup, a bowl, a plate, a goblet. Pl. ي *ey.* د سر كاسه *da sar kāsa'h*, The skull. شنه كاسه سره كاسه *sh'na'h kāsa'h sara'h kā-sa'h*, A rainbow. See د بودي تال

كاسي *kā-sī*, s.m. (1st) (Pl.) The name of a tribe of Afghāns. كاسيَ *kā-saey*, A man of the Kā-sī tribe. كاسئ *kā-sa'ī*, s.f. (6th) A female of the above. Sing. and Pl.

كاسير *kā-sīr*, s.m. (5th) An adulterer, a whoremonger. Pl. كاسيران *kā-sīrān*. كاسيره *kā-sīra'h*, s.f. (3rd) A whore, a strumpet. 2. The fourth part of a pice. (s كسيره). Pl. ي *ey*. See ككړ and ككړه

كاسيري *kā-sīrī*, s.f. (3rd) Adultery, whoremongering, fornication, etc. Pl. ئ *a'ī*.

كاش *kāsh*, s.m. (2nd) (corrup. of T قاش) The bow or pommel of a saddle. Pl. كاشونه *kāsh-ūnah*.

P كاشكي *kāsh-kī*, interj. Would to God! God send! May it happen! See كشكي *kashkī*.

P كاشي *kā-shī*, s.m. (6th) Glazed tile or brick. Sing. and Pl. كاشي گر *kā-shī-gar*, s.m. (5th) A maker of glazed pottery or tiles, a brick-maker. Pl. كاشي گرُ *kā-shī-gær*.

كاشين *kā-shīn*, s.m. (5th) A kind of rough porcelain, glazed pottery. Pl. كاشينان *kā-shīnān*.

كاغ *kāgh*, (W.) adj. Cunning, clever, acute, knowing; (Fem.) كاغه *kāgha'h*. كاغ واليَ *kāgh wālaey*, s.m. (1st) Cleverness, acuteness, sharpness, cunning. Pl. والي *wālī*.

P كاغذ *kā-ghaz*, s.m. (2nd) Paper. Pl. كاغذونه *kā-ghazūnah*. كاغذي *kā-ghazī*, adj. Delicate, soft, thin. د طلاق كاغذ *da ṭalāk kā-ghaz*, A deed of divorce.

كاغذ باد *kā-ghaz-bād*, s.m. (2nd) A paper kite. Pl. كاغذ بادونه *kā-ghaz-bādūnah*.

كاغه *kā-gha'h*, s.f. (3rd) A raven. Pl. ي *ey*.

A كافر *kā-fir*, s.m. (5th) An infidel. Pl. كافران *kā-firān*. كافره *kāfira'h*, s.f. (3rd). Pl. ي *ey*.

كافري *kā-firī*, s.m. (1st) Pl. The name of a people, consisting of eighteen tribes, inhabiting Kāfiristān, a country of Hindū Kush north of Jelālābād, supposed to be descendants of the Greeks. They are also called Sī'āh-posh. كافريَ *kā-firaey*, A male of the above tribe. كافرئ *kā-fira'ī*, s.f. (6th) A female of the above. Sing. and Pl. See my *Notes on Kāfiristān:* "Bengal Asiatic Journal," No. IV.—1859.

A كافور *kā-fūr*, s.m. (6th) Camphor. Sing. and Pl.

A كافي *kā-fī*, adj. (act part. of كفا) Sufficent, enough; able, competent.

P كاك *kāk*, s.m. (2nd) Biscuit, a bannock, a kind of bread baked on heated stones. Pl. كاكونه *kāk-ūnah*.

HI كاكا *kā-kā*, s.m. (5th) A paternal uncle. Pl. كاكاگان *kā-kā-gān*.

كاكړ *kā-karr*, s.m. (5th) The name of a numerous and simple tribe of Afghāns. 2. A male of the tribe. Pl. كاكړان *kā-karrān*. كاكړه *kā-karra'h*, s.f. (3rd) A female of the above tribe. Pl. ي *ey*.

P كاكل *kā-kul*, s.m. (2nd) A curl, a lock, a ringlet. Pl. كاكلونه *kā-kulūnah*.

كاكنج *kā-kanj*, s.m. (6th) The name of a grain (Arzan), millet. Sing. and Pl. See ږدن

HI كاكي *kā-ka'ī*, s.f. (6th) A paternal uncle's wife. Sing. and Pl.

كاګل *kā-gal*, verb trans. (E.) To pull or draw out, to pluck out, to extract, to root up, to remove, to express, to elicit, to extricate. 2. To write, to take down. For inflections see (W.) كاږل and substitute ګ for ږ and in كښل use *kh* for *sh*.

كاګه ويلني *kā-gah wele-nī*, s.m. (1st) Pl. Large aniseed, fennel. See خواږه ولني

كال *kāl*, s.m. (2nd) A year. Pl. كالونه *kālūnah* or (W.) كلونه *kalūnah*. (s كال, Time, age, etc.) سږ كال *sajz kāl* or سږنيَ كال *sajzanaey kāl* (W.); and سخ كال *sakh kāl* or سخنيَ كال *sakhanaey kāl* (E.), The present year, مخيَ كال *makhaey kāl* or راتلونيَ كال *rā-t'lūnaey kāl*, The next year, the coming year. پروس كال *parr-os kāl* or پرو سږ كال *paro-sajz kāl*

(W.), Last year. ورم كال *warram-kāl*, The year before last. لا ورم كال *lā warram kāl*, Three years ago. كال په كال *kāl-pah-kāl*, Year by year. هر كال *har kāl*, Every year. كال و تلين *kāl-o-t'līn* or وارٔه كال *wārræh kāl* and كال و سر *kāl-o-sar* (E.) The whole year.

كالبوت *kāl-būt*, s.m. (2nd) (corrup. of P كالبد) A model, a figure, a form. 2. The human body, the heart. Pl. كالبوتونه *kāl-būtūnah*.

كالخواهي *kāl-khwāhī*, s.f. (3rd) Choice, will, option, election, authority, power; approval, adoption. Pl. ئي *a'ī*. كالخواهي لرل *kāl-khwāhī laral*, verb trans. To have or possess the choice, to have the option, choice, authority, power. كالخواهي كول *kāl-khwāhī kawul*, verb trans. To act for another, to take authority or power. كالخواهي وركول *kāl-khwāhī war-kawul*, verb trans. To give the option, choice, power, or authority to another.

كالكوچ *kāl-kūch*, s.m. (6th) Distortion, twist, wryness, contortion, malformation. 2. (met.) Cunning, craft, subtlety, archness, deceit, duplicity. Sing. and Pl. كالكوچن *kāl-kūchan*, adj. Distorted, irregular, crooked, twisted, awry. 3. Crafty, artful, cunning, sly, arch, designing, insidious, deep, tricky, cunning as a fox; (Fem.) كالكوچنه *kāl-kūchana'h*; also كالكوچيَ *kāl-kūchaey*; (Fem.) كالكوچِي *kāl-kūchi*. Pl. (Masc. and Fem.) ي *ī*.

كالكنديَ *kāla-kunddaey*, s.m. (1st) A kind of vegetable or melon (Cucumis Madraspatanus). Pl. ي *ī*.

كالكه *kāla-ka'h*, s.f. (3rd) Cotton in the pod, the cotton tree. Pl. ئي *ey*. كالك چو *kā-lak cho*, s.m. (6th) The dry stalks of the cotton tree used for fuel (W.); or پمبي چو *pumbey-cho*, s.m. (6th) (E.). Sing. and Pl.

كاله پانړي *kāla'h pārrnī*, s. prop. The name of a forest in the Khattak country in which there is much game. This term is generally applied to a place where there are hills, rivulets, and a forest.

كاليَ *kā-laey*, s.m. (1st) An article, a thing, an instrument, a tool. 2. A dress, any article of dress. 3. An ornament. Pl. كالي *kālī*. The plural form when used signifies, Apparatus, tools, the furniture of a matchlock, articles of clothing, a barber's instruments, a goldsmith's tools, dress and ornaments. د پريوتو كالي *da pre-wato kālī*, Bed clothes. د لاندِ يستو كالي *da lāndi yesto kālī*, Carpets, etc. د آغستو كالي *da āghusto kālī*, Wearing apparel.

P كام *kām*, s.m. (2nd) The palate. 2. (s) Desire, wish, inclination. Pl. كامونه *kām-ūnah*. كام نا كام *kām-nā-kām*, Willing or unwilling, nolens volens.

A كامل *kā-mil*, adj. (act. part. of كمال) Perfect, complete, accomplished, entire. 2. Learned; (Fem.) كامله *kā-mila'h*.

P كامياب *kām-yāb*, adj. Prosperous, happy, successful, satisfied, obtaining one's object, or all that one desires; (Fem.) كاميابه *kām-yāba'h*. كاميابي *kām-yābī*, s.f. (3rd) Prosperity, happiness, attainment of one's wishes. Pl. ئي *a'ī*.

P كان *kān*, s.m. (2nd) A mine. Pl. كانونه *kān-ūnah*.

كانجړ *kān-jarrn*, s.m. (2nd) The large wooden shaft or axle of a Persian wheel. Pl. كانجړونه *kān-jarrnūnah*.

كاندِ *kāndi*, The third person singular and plural of the present tense of كول 'to do.' Also written كاندي *kāndey*.

كانده *kāndah* (W.) A form of imperative for the second person singular of كول, Do thou. Pl. كاندئ *kānda'ī*, Do you.

كانگه *kān-ga'h*, s.f. (3rd) The gripes or colic, a violent pain in the bowels, acute pain. 2. Vomiting, evacuating the stomach (W.) Pl. ئي *ey*. كانگه وهل *kān-ga'h wahal*, verb trans. To vomit.

كانگيَ *kān-gaey*, s.m. (1st) Echo, reverberation, peal, swell, re-echo, boom, roar, etc. Pl. ي *ī*. The plural form is mostly used. كانگيَ كيدل *kān-gaey kedal*, verb intrans. To resound, to echo, to reflect sound. كانگيَ كول *kān-gaey kawul*, verb trans. To re-echo, to echo, to reverberate, to resound.

کانه *kā-na'h*, s.f. (3rd) A misfortune, a calamity, a disaster. 2. An affair, a matter, an action. 3. One of the principal feathers in a bird's wing. 4. An improper, unbecoming, or inadmissible action or affair; impropriety, unseemliness, indecorum. 5. The upper part of the face. 6. The frame of a mirror or anything similar, edge, margin, side. Pl. ې *ey*.

کانه *kā-nah*, adj. Foolish, ignorant, weak-minded, stupid. 2. Rotten at the kernel. 3. Blind of an eye. (s काना).

کانئ *kā-na'ī*, s.f. (6th) A straw, chaff, anything worthless. 2. The whiskers. Sing. and Pl.

P کاني *kān-ī*, adj. Mineral, of a mine, fossil. (Masc. and Fem.)

کاڼړی *kā<u>rrn</u>-aey*, s.m. (1st) A stone. 2. A stone for grinding condiments, a muller. Pl. ي *ī*.

کاڼريځ *kā<u>rrn</u>-e<u>dz</u>*, adj. Stony, abounding with stones. 2. Hard, cruel, unrelenting, pitiless; (Fem.) کاڼريځه *kā<u>rrn</u>-e<u>dz</u>a'h*. کاڼريځه زمکه *kā<u>rrn</u>-e<u>dz</u>a'h z'maka'h*, Stony ground. کاڼړي زړه *kā<u>rrn</u>-aey z'<u>rr</u>ah*, A hard heart.

کاڼړئ *kā<u>rr</u>na'ī*, The second person plural of the imperative of کول 'to do,' which see.

کاواك *kā-wāk*, adj. Hollow, empty within, empty, void, vacuous, cracked, useless, tending to decay; (Fem.) کاواکه *kā-wāka'h*. Also ميان کاواك *mī-ān kā-wāk*.

کاوه *kāwah*, Imperfect tense of کول, which see.

کاهښت *kā-ha<u>sh</u>t* (W.) or *kā-ha<u>kh</u>t* (E.) s.m. (2nd) The itch, the scab, the mange. 2. Setting the teeth on edge, acrimony, exasperating, acritude, poignancy, harshness, etc. Pl. کاهښتونه *kā-ha<u>sh</u>tūnah* or *kā-ha<u>kh</u>tūnah*.

A کاهل *kā-hil*, adj. (act. part. of کهل) Lazy, indolent, slow, languid, relaxed, tardy, sick; (Fem.) کاهله *kā-hila'h*. کاهلي *kā-hilī*, s.f. (3rd) Indolence, laziness, slowness, tardiness, apathy, sloth, neglect, remissness, languor. Pl. ئ *a'ī*.

A کاهن *kā-hin*, s.m. (5th) A soothsayer, an astrologer, an augur, a magician, a (Jewish) priest. Pl. کاهنان *kā-hinān*. کاهنه *kā-hina'h*, s.f. (3rd) A sorceress. Pl. ې *ey*. کاهني *kā-hinī*, s.f. (3rd) Sorcery, magic, astrology, jugglery. Pl. ئ *a'ī*. کاهني کول *kā-hinī kawul*, verb trans. To practice sorcery, magic, etc.

P کاهو *kā-hū*, s.m. (5th) The name of a vegetable the seed of which is used medicinally, a lettuce. Pl. کاهوګان *kā-hūgān*.

کاهئ *kā-ha'ī*, s.f. (6th) A ditch, a trench, a moat, a ravine. Sing. and Pl. See کهي

A کب *kab*, s.m. (2nd) A fish. Pl. کبونه *kab-ūnah*. See ماهي

P کباب *kab-āb*, s.m. (2nd) Roasted meat, a roast. Pl. کبابونه *kab-ābūnah*. 2. adj. Roasted; (Fem.) کبابه *kab-āba'h*. کباب کيدل *kab-āb kedal*, verb trans. To be roasted, to burn; to be enraged, or afflicted. کباب کول *kab-āb kawul*, verb trans. To roast, to burn; to distress, to afflict.

P کباب چيني *kab-āb <u>ch</u>ī-nī*, s.m. (6th) Cubebs. Sing. and Pl.

کبابي *kab-ābī*, s.m. (5th) A cook, a roaster of meat. Pl. کبابيان *kab-ābīān*.

A کبر *kibr*, s.m. (2nd) Grandeur, arrogance, pride, haughtiness. Pl. کبرونه *kibr-ūnah*. کبر جن *kibr-jan*, adj. Proud, arrogant. 2. Grand; (Fem.) کبرجنه *kibr-jana'h*.

P کبك *kabk*, s.m. (5th) A partridge. Pl. کبکان *kabk-ān*. See زرکه

کبل *kabl*, s.m. (2nd) Reason, cause, motive, principle. Pl. کبلونه *kablūnah*. 2. s.m. (6th) The name of a grass (Agrostis linearis). Sing. and Pl.

کبل ډکي *kabl <u>dd</u>akaey*, s.m. (1st) The name of a kind of grass. Pl. ي *ī*.

کبلی *kab-laey*, s.m. (1st) A fawn, a young gazelle. Pl. ي *ī*. کبلئ *kab-la'ī*, s.f. (6th) A female fawn. Sing. and Pl.

کبي *kabī*, s.f. (3rd) A halter for a horse. Pl. ئ *a'ī*. See باڼي

A کبير *kab-īr*, adj. (from کبر) Great, large, full-grown, senior; (Fem.) کبيره *kab-īra'h*. See لوي

S کپرئ *kup-ra'ī* or *kap-ra'ī*, s.f. (6th) The skull, the pate. Sing. and Pl. (s کهوپري).

کپړئ *kup-<u>rr</u>a'ī*, s.f. (6th) A small leathern bottle, a flask. Sing. and Pl. Also کپئ *kupa'ī*, s.f. (6th). Sing. and Pl.

كپن *kapan* or (P) كفن *kafan*, s.m. (2nd) A shroud, a winding-sheet. Pl. كپنونه *kapan-ūnah* or *kafan-ūnah*. كپن كښ *kapan-kash* (W.) or *kakh* (E.) s.m. (5th) A shroud-stealer, a miscreant, a caitiff. Pl. كښان *kashān* or *kakhān*.

كپه *ka-pa'h*, s.f. (3rd) A powder, a medicine taken dry and unmixed, generally in the palm of the hand. 2. A tray made of grass for holding fruit. Pl. ې *ey*.

كپي *kap-ī*, s.f. (3rd) A halter for a horse. Pl. ئي *a'ī*.

كپئي *ku-pa'ī*, s.f. (6th) A small leathern bottle, a flask. Sing. and Pl.

كت *kat*, s.m. (2nd) A heap, a pile, a store, a supply, a repository, etc. Pl. كتونه *katūnah*. كت په كت *kat pah kat*, In heaps, pile upon pile.

كت *kat*, s.m. (6th) Catechu, terra japonica, an astringent vegetable extract from the Mimosa (Chadria). Sing. and Pl. (HI كتهه).

A كتاب *kitāb*, s.m. (2nd) (from كتب) A book, writing, despatches, a letter, etc. Pl. كتابونه *kitābūnah*. كتاب خانه *kitāb khāna'h*, s.f. (3rd) A library. Pl. ې *ey*. كتاب فروش *kitāb farosh*, s.m. (5th) A bookseller. Pl. فروشان *farosh-ān*.

A كتابت *kitā-bat*, s.m. (2nd) Writing. 2. Motto, an inscription. Pl. كتابتونه *kitā-batūnah*.

A كتان *kat-tān*, s.m. (6th) A kind of cloth or linen. Sing. and Pl.

كتاني *katānī*, s.m. (1st) Pl. The name of a tribe of people said to be Afghāns, about whose descent there are numerous disputes. كتانې *katānaey*, A man or male of the above tribe. كتانئي *katāna'ī*, s.f. (6th) A female of the above. Sing. and Pl.

كتل *kat-al*, verb trans. To see, to behold, to eye, to scan, to look on, to survey, to contemplate, to watch, to bend one's looks upon, to gaze at, to stare, to ogle, to notice, to view, etc. This infinitive is imperfect, and requires the present tenses of ګورل, which has no past tenses, to complete it. Pres. ګوري *go-rī*; past و كوت *wu-kot* or و كاته *wu-kātah*; fut. و به ګوري *wu bah go-rī*; imp. و ګوره *wu-gorah*; act. part. كتونكې *kat-ūnkaey* or كتونې *kat-ūnaey*; past part. كتلې *katalaey*; verb. n. كتنه *katana'h* or كاته *kātah*.

كتنه *katana'h*, s.f. (3rd) (verb. n. of كتل) Seeing, beholding, viewing, contemplating, surveying. 2. Look, glimpse, glance, gaze, stare, regard, etc. Pl. ې *ey*. See also كاته

كته *kata'h*, s.f. (3rd) A pack-saddle, a pad for bullocks, donkeys, etc. Pl. ې *ey*. 2. *katah* prep. Below, beneath, under. See ښكته and كښته

كتي پتي *ki-tī pi-tī*, s.m. (1st) Pl. Absurd talk, nonsense, unmeaning language or words.

كتي لعل *kutī-læal*, s.m. (2nd) The name of a shrub bearing a small red berry. Pl. كتي لعلونه *kutī-lœalūnah*.

كټ *katt*, s.m. (2nd) A bed, a bedstead. Pl. كټونه *katt-ūnah*. (S كهټ).

كټ مټ *katt-matt*, adj. Exact, similar, precise, resembling, twin, analogous, allied to, as like as two peas, a chip of the old block, the very image, the picture of, true to nature; (Fem.) كټه مټه *katta'h matta'h*.

كټر *kattar* or كټړ *kattarr*, s.m. (6th) The name of a numerous tribe dwelling at, and about Kālā-bāgh on the banks of the Indus below Attak. They are designated Hindkis by the Afghāns, a name given to people of Indian descent. They are in all probability a sept of the aboriginals of those parts, the remains of the Indians of the classical authors. 2. A male of the above tribe. Sing. and Pl. كټره *kattar-a'h* or كټړه *kattarra'h*, s.f. (3rd) A female of the above. Pl. ې *ey*.

كټكي *katt-key*, s.m. (1st) A small bed or bedstead, a footstool (dimin. of كټ). Pl. ي *ī*.

كټ وټ *katt-watt*, adj. Mixed, promiscuous, unsorted, confused, involved, scattered, indiscriminate, miscellaneous; (Fem.) كټه وټه *katta'h-watta'h*. كټ وټ كيدل *katt-watt kedal*, verb intrans. To become mixed, confused, involved, etc. كټ وټ كول *katt-watt kawul*, verb trans. To mix, to confuse, to involve, to derange.

كتوري *kat̲toraey*, s.m. (1st) A brass cup, a small bowl or goblet of metal. Pl. ي *ī*. (HI كتورا).

كتوئي *kat̲t-wa'ī*, s.f. (6th) A small caldron, a small earthen pot for cooking. Sing. and Pl.

كتوئي چټ *kat̲t-wa'ī-c̲h̲att*, s.m. (5th) A pot-licker, a parasite, a lick-spittle, a toad-eater. Pl. چټان *c̲h̲at̲t-ān*. كتوئي چټه *kat̲t-wa'ī c̲h̲at̲t-a'h*, s.f. (3rd) A female as above. Pl. ې *ey*.

كټه *kat̲tæh*, adj. Large, great, big, stout, robust; (Fem.) كټه *kat̲ta'h*. See غټ and غټه (HI كتا)

كته *kut̲tah*, s.m. (5th) A dog, other than a grey-hound. Pl. كتهگان *kut̲tah-gān*. (HI كتا)

كټه باز *kat̲tæh bāz*, s.m. (5th) A goshawk, a large species of falcon used in hunting. Pl. كټه بازان *katt-æh bāzān*.

كته چرگه *kut̲ta'h-c̲h̲arga'h*, s.f. (3rd) A hen which has ceased to lay eggs. Pl. ې *ey*.

كته گوته *katta'h gūt-a'h*, s.f. (3rd) The thumb, the great toe. Pl. ې *ey*.

كتي *katt-aey*, s.m. (1st) A male buffalo-calf. Pl. ي *ī*. كتي *kat̲t-a'ī*, s.f. (6th) A female of the above. Sing. and Pl.

كتيل *kat̲te-yal*, verb trans. To cut (with a shears or the like), to shear, to clip (as the hair), to dock. Pres. كتيي *kat̲te-yī*; past وُ كتييه *wu-kat̲te-yah*; fut. وُ به كتيي *wu bah kat̲te-yī*; imp. وُ كتييه *wu-kat̲te-yah*; act. part. كتيونكي *kat̲te-yūnkaey*; past part. كتيلي *kat̲te-yalaey*; verb. n. كتيينه *kat̲te-yana'h*.

A كثرت *kaṣ-rat*, s.m. (2nd) Excess, abundance, multitude, plurality, multiplicity. Pl. كثرتونه *kaṣ-ratūnah*.

A كثير *kaṣ-īr*, adj. (from كثر) Many, much, abundant, fruitful; (Fem.) كثيره *kaṣ-īra'h*.

كڅوړه *kat̲s-or̲ra'h*, s.f. (3rd) A bag, a purse, a cover for a book, a wallet. Pl. ې *ey*. Also written كڅوړي *kat̲s-or̲raey*, s.m. (1st). Pl. ي *ī*.

كڅوك *kat̲s-wak*, s.m. (2nd) A species of small pox in which the pustules are few in number. Pl. كڅوكونه *kat̲s-wakūnah*.

P كج *kaj*, adj. Crooked, curved, awry, askew, distorted; (Fem.) كجه *kaja'h*. كج والي *kaj-wālaey*, s.m. (1st) Crookedness, curvature, wryness, crossness. Pl. والي *wālī*. كج و كول *kaj-o-kol* or كج و كيڼ *kaj-o-kīr̲rn*, very crooked, all manner of ways.

P كجاوه *kajā-wa'h*, s.f. (3rd) A camel litter. Pl. ې *ey*.

كجك *kajak*, s.m. (2nd) The cock of a gun. 2. A lock of hair or curl worn on the forehead by females. Pl. كجكان *kajak-ān*.

S كجل *kaj-jal*, s.m. (6th) Collyrium prepared from soot, soot, lamp-black. Sing. and Pl.

كجولي سترگي *kajūley stargey* or كجلي سترگي *kaj-aley stargey*, eyes anointed or blackened with kajal, a collyrium prepared from lamp-black.

كچ *kac̲h̲*, s.m. (9th) Measurement. Sing. and Pl. كچ كول *kac̲h̲ kawul*, verb trans. To measure.

كچ *kac̲h̲*, s.m. (2nd) A fault, a flaw, an injury. Pl. كچونه *kac̲h̲-ūnah*.

HI كچ *kac̲h̲*, adj. Small, less, little, diminutive; (Fem.) كچه *kac̲h̲a'h*.

كچ *kuc̲h̲*, s.m. (6th) Butter made from sheep's or cow's milk. Sing. and Pl. See كچي

P كچكول *kac̲h̲-kol*, s.m. (2nd) A bowl, a kind of oblong wooden vessel used by darwes̲h̲es, a cup, a wallet. Pl. كچكولونه *kac̲h̲-kolūnah*.

كچماچو *kac̲h̲-māc̲h̲ū*, s.m. (5th) The plant solanum-nigrum, nightshade, fox's grapes. Pl. كچماچوگان *kac̲h̲-māc̲h̲ūgān*.

كچنئي *kac̲h̲ana'ī*, s.f. (6th) (corrup. of S كنچني) A dancing girl, a courtezan, a strumpet. Sing. and Pl. See لولي

كچني *kuc̲h̲inaey*, adj. Small, diminutive, puny; (Fem.) كچنئي *kuc̲h̲-na'ī*.

كچوټوالي *kac̲h̲ut̲t-wālaey*, s.m. (1st) Puniness, smallness, diminutiveness, infancy, babyhood, childhood. Pl. والي *wālī*.

كچوټي *kac̲h̲ūt̲taey*, adj. Small, diminutive, puny, a young child; (Fem.) كچوټِ *kac̲h̲ūt̲ti*. Pl. (Masc. and Fem.) ي *ī*.

HI كچه *kac̲h̲ah* or كچَ *kac̲h̲a*, adj. Raw, crude, immature. 2. Silly, inexperienced.

كچه گوته *kac̲h̲a'h gūt-a'h*, s.f. (3rd) The little finger, the little toe. Pl. ې *ey*.

کچي *ku-chī*, s.m. (1st) (Pl.) Butter (W.) The singular form is not used. See کچ

کدائي *kadā'ī*, s.f. (5th) A garment, a robe, a vest, a long full robe reaching to the ground. Pl. کدائيان *kadā'īāni*.

P کد خدا *kad-khudā*, s.m. (5th) The head man of a village or small clan, the master of a house, the father of a family. Pl. کد خدايان *kad-khudā-yān*.

کدله *kaddala'h*, s.f. (3rd) A hut or cabin made of reeds or grass. Pl. ي *ey*. See منډو

کډه *kadda'h*, s.f. (3rd) Family (such as wife, children, mother, sister, domestics, etc.) the household in general. 2. Migration, march, emigration, flitting, departure. Pl. ي *ey*. کډه کول *kadda'h kawul*, verb trans. To migrate, to emigrate, to rove, to march.

کدهل *kadd-hal*, s.m. (2nd) Land or a portion of land prepared for sowing rice in. Pl. کدهلونه *kadd-halūnah*.

کډئ *kadda'ī*, s.f. (6th) The hole made in the ground under the loom for the weaver's feet. Sing. and Pl.

کر *kar*, s.m. (9th) Ploughing and sowing, husbandry, farming, tillage, agriculture. Sing. and Pl. کرل *kar-al*, verb trans. To till, to cultivate, to prepare the ground by ploughing and sowing. Pres. کري *kar-ī*; past و کاره *wu-kārah* or و کارَ *wu-kāra*; fut. و به کري *wu bah kar-ī*; imp. و کره *wu-karah*; act. part. کرونکي *karūnkaey* or کروني *karūnaey*; past part. کرلي *karalaey* or کري *karaey*; verb. n. کرنه *karana'h*.

کړ *kær*, s.m. (2nd) Thin excrement, looseness of the bowels, diarrhœa or dysentery. Pl. کړونه *kær-ūnah*. کړ وهل *kær wahal*, verb trans. To discharge thin excrement from the bowels.

کرار کرار *kar-ār kar-ār*, adv. Gently, slowly, softly, leisurely. See قلار قلار

کراسته *krāsta'h*, s.f. (3rd) Felt, a kind of cloth made from wool. Pl. ي *ey*.

A کرام *kir-ām*, adj. Great, noble, high in rank or authority, venerable; (Fem.) کرامه *kir-āma'h*. کرامٌ کاتبين *kirāmuṇ kātabīṇ*, The recording angels on the right and left of the throne of God, who record the good and evil deeds of mankind.

A کرامت *kirā-mat*, s.m. (2nd) Generosity, magnificence, nobleness, excellence. 2. A miracle. Pl. کرامتونه *kirā-matūnah*.

A کراهت *karā-hat*, s.m. (2nd) (from کره) Dislike, disgust, aversion. Pl. کراهتونه *karā-hatūnah*. See کرکه

کراهه *kirā-ha'h*, s.f. (3rd) (corrup. of P کرايه) Hire, rent, fare. Pl. ي *ey*. په کراهه آخستل *pah kirā-ha'h ākhistal*, verb trans. To hire, to rent. په کراهه ورکول *pah kirā-ha'h war-kawul*, verb trans. To let on hire, to hire out. کراهه دار *kirā-ha'h dār* or کراهه کښ *kirā-hah kash* (W.) or *kakh* (E.) s.m. (5th) A tenant, a renter, a hirer. Pl. داران *dār-ān* or کښان *kashān* or *kakhān*. کراهه داره *kirā-ha'h dāra'h* or کراهه کښه *kirā-ha'h kasha'h* or *kakha'h*, s.f. (3rd) Pl. ي *ey*.

A کربلا *kar-balā*, s. prop. The name of a place where Ḥusain, son of Æalī, was buried.

کربوري *kar-borraey*, s.m. (1st) A chamelion, a species of lizard. Pl. ي *ī*.

کرپ *krap*, s.m. (5th) Munching, chewing with violence, craunching; a craunch, a munch. Pl. کرپهار *krapa-hār*. کرپيدل *krapedal*, verb intrans. To give forth a craunching noise, as from a biscuit or the like chewed with violence or noise. Pres. کرپيږي *krapejzī* (W.) or کرپيګي *krapegī* (E.); past و کرپيده *wu-krapedah*; fut. و به کرپيږي *wu bah krapejzī* or کرپيګي *krapegī*; imp. و کرپيږه *wu-krapejzah* or کرپيګه *krapegah*; act. part. کرپيدونکي *krapedūnkaey* or کرپيدوني *krapedūnaey*; past part. کرپيدلي *krapedalaey*; verb. n. کرپيدنه *krapedana'h* or کرپيده *krapedah*. کرپول *krapawul*, verb trans. To gnash the teeth, to munch, to craunch. Pres. کرپوي *krapawī*; past و کرپاوه *wu-krapāwuh* or کرپاوو *krapāwo*; fut. و به کرپوي *wu bah krapawī*; imp. و کرپوه *wu-krapawah*; act. part. کرپوونکي *krapawūnkaey* or کرپووني

krapawūnaey; past part. کرپولي *krapawulaey*; verb. n. کرپونه *krapawuna'h*.

کرپندوکي *krapan-dūkaey*, s.m. (1st) Gristle, cartilage. Pl. ي *ī*. See تندوي and کرچوني

کرپندي *krapandaey*, s.m. (1st) Same as preceding. Pl. ي *ī*.

A کرت *karat*, s.m. (2nd) One time, one attack or assault. Pl. کرتونه *karat-ūnah*. کرات مرات *karāt-marāt*, Numbers of times, often.

کرت *kurut*, s.m. (6th) Coagulated milk boiled, a kind of cheese. Sing. and Pl. See قرت and بگوره

S کرتوت *kar-tūt*, s.m. (2nd) Action, business, affair. Pl. کرتوتونه *kar-tūtūnah*.

P کرته *kur-ta'h*, s.f. (3rd) A kind of tunic, a shirt, a waistcoat or jacket. Pl. ې *ey*.

کرټ *krutt*, adv. In the least, at all, by no means, never, not at all.

کرچ *krach*, s.m. (2nd) An old hawk or falcon well taught. Pl. کرچونه *krachūnah*. کرچه *kracha'h*, s.f. (3rd) A hen bird of the above description. Pl. ې *ey*.

کرچ *krach*, s.m. (5th) Craunching or crushing with the teeth, a craunch, a crush with the teeth, munching, craunching. Pl. کرچهار *kracha-hār*. کرچول *krachawul*, verb trans. To craunch, to crush with the teeth (as gristle or bone) to chew with violence and noise. Pres. کرچوي *krachawī*; past وُ کرچاوه *wu-krachāwuh* or کرچاوو *krachāwo*; fut. وُ به کرچوي *wu bah krachawī*; imp. وُ کرچوه *wu-krachawah*; act. part. کرچوونکي *krachawūn-kaey* or کرچووني *krachawūnaey*; past part. کرچولي *krachawulaey*; verb. n. کرچونه *krach-awuna'h*.

کرچوني *krachūnaey*, s.m. (1st) Cartilage, gristle. Pl. ي *ī*.

کرچي *krachaey*, s.m. (1st) Gristle, cartilage. 2. The name of a shrub. Pl. ي *ī*.

P کردار *kir-dār*, s.m. (2nd) Action, deed, art, business, labour, doing, manner, conduct. Pl. کردارونه *kir-dārūnah*. کرداري *kirdārī*, adj. The performer of a good action.

P کردگار *kirda-gār*, s.m. (9th) God the Creator. Sing. and Pl.

P کرده *karda'h*, s.f. (3rd) (from کردن) Act, deed, performance. Pl. ې *ey*.

کرړي *kir-rraey*, s.m. (1st) A cricket. Pl. ي *ī*.

کرړي *karirrī* or *kirarrī*, s.m. (1st) (Pl.) The name of one of the great divisions of the Afghān tribes, in contradistinction to the Sarrabans. کرړي *karirraey* or *kirarraey* (Sing.) A male of the above. کرړۍ *karirra'ī* or *kirarra'ī*, s.f. (6th) A female of the above. Sing. and Pl.

A کرسي *kur-sī*, s.f. (3rd) The crystalline or empyrean heaven, a throne, a seat, a stool. Pl. ۍ *a'ī*. کرسي نامه *kur-sī nāma'h*, s.f. (3rd) A genealogical tree. Pl. ې *ey*.

P کرشمه *karash-ma'h*, s.f. (3rd) An amorous look or gesture, a wink, a glance, ogling, blandishment. Pl. ې *ey*.

کرښنه *karashna'h* (W.) or *karakhna'h* (E.) s.f. (3rd) Painting, drawing, embroidering, picture, engraving, carving, delineation, etc. Pl. ې *ey*.

کرښه *kar-sha'h* (W.) or *kar-kha'h* (E.) s.f. (3rd) A line, a streak, a mark, lineament. 2. Scrawl, scribble, scratch, scribbling. Pl. ې *ey*.

کرغ *kurugh*, s.m. (2nd) A pasture, a meadow, a field, a grazing-ground, a grass-plot. Pl. کرغونه *kurughūnah*.

کرغ *kurugh*, s.m. (2nd) An embargo. 2. Confiscating, a seizure, laying on an embargo. 3. Inclosure, hindrance, prevention of access. Pl. کرغونه *kurughūnah*. کرغ کول *kurugh kawul*, verb trans. To lay an embargo on, to confiscate. 2. To forbid access, to hinder. (A قرق)

کرفس *kar-fas*, s.m. (6th) Dill-seed. Sing. and Pl. See سپيرکي

P کرک *kar-ak*, s.m. (5th) A quail. Pl. کرکان *karak-ān*. See مرز

P کرک *kark*, s.m. (2nd) A rhinoceros. 2. Rhinoceros hide. Pl. کرکونه *kark-ūnah*. د کرک سپر *da kark s'par*, A shield of rhinoceros hide.

کرک *krak*, s.m. (2nd) A mark made by a ploughshare, a furrow, a rut. Pl. کرکونه *krak-ūnah*.

کرکنډه *kar-kandda'h*, s.f. (3rd) A rolling stone from a mountain. 2. A stone thrown from a hill or the battlements of a castle on an enemy. Pl. ي *ey*.

کرکڼ *kar-karrn*, s.m. (2nd) A brake, a copse, a bush, brush-wood, underwood, a thicket. Pl. کرکڼونه *kar-karrnūnah*. See ځنګل

کرکڼه *kar-karrna'h*, s.f. (3rd) The wild jujube and its fruit. 2. A small thorny tree, a brier. Pl. ي *ey*. See بده بیره

کرکه *krak-a'h*, s.f. (3rd) Disgust, repugnance, aversion, loathing, abomination, horror, detestation, antipathy, abhorrence. Pl. ي *ey*. 2. adj. Nauseous, disgusting, odious, hateful, abominable, repulsive.

کرلاڼي *kar-lārrnī*, s.m. (1st) The name of a division of the Afghāns, generally applied to those of the west. کرلاڼی *kar-lārrnaey*, Sing. A male of the above. کرلاڼۍ *kar-lārrna'ī*, s.f. (6th) A female of the above. Sing. and Pl.

A کرم *karam*, s.m. (2nd) Liberality, generosity, kindness, graciousness, bounty, clemency, benignity. Pl. کرمونه *karamūnah*. کرم کول *karam kawul*, verb trans. To act with kindness or liberality, to show clemency or benignity towards.

کرمنګ *kur-mang*, s.m. (5th) A large kind of fowl, a pheasant. Pl. کرمنګان *kur-mangān*.

S کروړ *karorr*, adj. Ten millions; (Fem.) کروړه *karorra'h*.

کروړه *kar-orra'h*, s.f. (3rd) A whip, a scourge. 2. A stroke with a whip, a stripe. Pl. ي *ey*. کروړي خوړل *kar-orrey khwarral*, verb trans. To receive stripes (to be punished with stripes), to receive a flogging. کروړي وهل *kar-orrey wahal*, verb trans. To flog, to punish with stripes, to administer corporal punishment.

کروسند *kro-sand*, s.m. (6th) Any stiff or brittle wood which cannot be bent. Sing. and Pl.

P کروه *kroh*, s.m. (2nd) A land measure equal to about two miles, but varying in different localities. Pl. کروهونه *krohūnah*.

کره *karah*, s.m. (5th) A spade, a kind of hoe. Pl. کرهان *kara-hān*. See یوم

کره *karah*, adj. Pure, prime, first sort, genuine, unadulterated. 2. Honest, sincere, candid. (کهرا s).

کرهد *kur-hadd*, s.m. (6th) A kind of greens or pot-herbs (Chenopodium album). Sing. and Pl. (E.) s.m. (2nd). Pl. کرهدونه *kur-haddūnah*. See سارمه

کرۍ *kar-a'ī*, s.f. (6th) A ring, an ox muzzle, or halter for a horse. Sing. and Pl.

کري *kur-ey*, interj. Begone! get away! Applied to a dog.

کرياب *kar-yāb*, adj. Unemployed, disengaged, idle, neglected, obsolete; (Fem.) کريابه *kar-yāba'h*. کريابيدل *kar-yābedal*, verb intrans. To become idle, disengaged, neglected, to be shelved. کريابول *kar-yābawul*, verb trans. To render idle, neglected, or obsolete, to put out of use or employ, to shelve.

کرياب *kari-yāb*, adj. Hindered, prevented, impeded, retarded, obstructed, interrupted, hampered, clogged, shackled. 2. Distressed, helpless, tired; (Fem.) کريابه *kari-yāba'h*. کريابيدل *kari-yābedal*, verb trans. To be hindered, impeded, retarded, hampered, clogged, obstructed, etc. Pres. کريابيږي *kari-yābejzī* (W.) or کريابيګي *kari-yābegī* (E.); past کرياب شه *kari-yāb shah* or و شه *wu-shah*; fut. کرياب به شي *kari-yāb bah shī* or به و شي *bah wu-shī*; imp. کرياب شه *kari-yāb shah* or و شه *wu-shah*; act. part. کريابيدونکی *kari-yābedūnkaey* or کريابيدونی *kari-yābedūnaey*; past part. کرياب *kari-yāb* or کرياب شوی *kari-yāb shawaey*; verb. n. کريابيدنه *kari-yābedana'h* or کريابيده *kari-yābedah*. کريابول *kari-yābawul*, verb trans. To impede, to hinder, to obstruct, to clog, to cramp, to thwart, to balk, to incommode, to retard, to prevent, etc. Pres. کريابوي *kari-yābawī*; past کرياب کړ *kari-yāb karr* or و کړ *wu-karr*; fut. کرياب به کړي *kari-yāb bah krrī* or به و کړي *bah wu-krrī*; imp. کرياب کړه *kari-yāb krrah* or و کړه *wu-krrah*; act. part. کريابوونکی *kari-yābawūnkaey* or کريابوونی *kari-yābawūnaey*; past part. کرياب

کړيابيدنه kari-yāb kaṟṟaey; verb. n. کړيابيدنه kari-yābedana'h.

کړيابي kari-yābī, s.f. (3rd) Hindrance, impedidition, stoppage, interruption, an impediment, a hindrance, an obstacle, an encumbrance, a clod, a bar, a hitch, etc. Pl. ئي a'ī. Also کړياب والیَ kari-yāb wālaey, s.m. (1st). Pl. والي wālī.

کړئي روځ kara'ī r'wadz, All the day, the whole day, from morning to night.

کرِيړه kir-īṟṟa'h, s.f. (3rd) Weeds, grass, or rubbish collected from a ploughed field. 2. The name of a plant (Capparis aphylla). Pl. ئي ey.

کرِيړیَ kirī-ṟṟaey, s.m. (1st) The name of a tree, the Pīlū (Salvadora persica). Pl. ي ī.

P کريز kur-īz, s.m. (2nd) Moult, the act of changing the feathers, moulting. Pl. کريزونه kur-īz-ūnah. کريز کول kur-īz kawul, verb trans. To moult, to shed or cast the feathers.

کړئي شپه kara'ī shpa'h, The whole night, all the night, from night till morning.

کريهه krey-ha'h, s.f. (3rd) Hire, fare, rent (corrup. of P کرايه). Pl. ئي ey. See کراهه

S کريله karela'h, s.f. (3rd) The name of a vegetable (Momordica charantia). Pl. ئي ey.

A کريم karīm, adj. (from کرم) Bountiful, gracious, an epithet of God.

A کريه karīh, adj. (from کره) Detestable, abominable, disgusting, execrable, filthy, dirty. See کرکه

کريه kar-ya'h, s.f. (3rd) Injunction, charge, command. Pl. ئي ey. کريه کول kar-ya'h kawul, verb trans. To enjoin strictly, to press, to insist, to charge, to command.

کړ kuṟṟ, s.m. (5th) A gurgling, rippling sound, as from a small brook, or from a ḥukka'h. 2. Cluck, cackle (as a laying hen), etc. Pl. کړهار kuṟṟa-hār. کړهار کول kuṟṟa-hār kawul, verb trans. To cluck, to cackle (as a laying hen). (S کڑک) کړ کړ کول kuṟṟ-kuṟṟ kawul, verb trans. To emit a gurgling, rippling sound (as a brook, etc.) 2. To cackle, to cluck.

کړاک kṟṟāk, s.m. (6th) A pea. 2. A small piece of stone inserted in a pestle and mortar to assist in grinding or pulverizing anything, in order to make the inside rough. Sing. and Pl.

کړاونه kaṟṟāw-na'h, s.f. (3rd) A clog, a patten made of wood, a kind of sandal. Pl. کراونی kaṟṟāw-ney, A pair of clogs or pattens. See کنړاوه

کړبيزن kaṟṟ-bezan, s.m. (6th) A sniveller, (lit. a snotty-nose fellow), a mean worthless creature. Pl. کړبيزن kaṟṟ-bezæn. کړبيزنه kaṟṟ-bezana'h, s.f. (3rd) A snivelling, mean, worthless female. Pl. ئي ey. See کړميزه

کړبيزي kaṟṟ-bezey, s.f. (3rd) Pl. Mucus from the nose. See کړميزي

کړپ kṟṟap, s.m. (5th) A slam, a bang, a swap, a rap, a dab, a bump, the sound produced by striking anything hollow or soft. Pl. کړپهار kṟṟapa-hār. کړپيدل kṟṟapedal, verb trans. To slam, to bang, to dab, to rap, to bump. Pres. کړپيږي kṟṟapejzī (W.) or کړپيکي kṟṟapegī (E.); past وُ کړپيده wu-kṟṟapedah; fut. وُ به کړپيږي wu bah kṟṟapejzī or کړپيکي kṟṟapegī; imp. وُ کړپيږه wu-kṟṟapejzah or کړپيکه kṟṟapegah; act. part. کړپيدونکیَ kṟṟapedūnkaey or کړپيدونیَ kṟṟapedūnaey; past part. کړپيدلیَ kṟṟapedalaey; verb. n. کړپيدنه kṟṟapedana'h or کړپيده kṟṟapedah.

کړپول kṟṟapawul, verb trans. To chew with violence, to craunch, to munch, to make a noise as when eating a biscuit or the like, to gnash the teeth. Pres. کړپوي kṟṟapawī; past وُ کړپاوه wu-kṟṟapāwuh or وُ کړپاوو wu-kṟṟapāwo; fut. وُ به کړپوي wu bah kṟṟapawī; imp. وُ کړپوه wu-kṟṟapawah; act. part. کړپوونکیَ kṟṟapawūnkaey or کړپوونیَ kṟṟapawūnaey; past part. کړپولیَ kṟṟapawulaey; کړپونه kṟṟapawuna'h.

کړتیَ kṟṟattaey, s.m. (1st) A wrinkle, a furrow in the face or body, a crease, a crumple, a pucker, a plait, a rumple. Pl. ي ī. کړتیَ کيدل kṟṟattaey kedal, verb intrans. To become or grow wrinkled, creased, furrowed, etc. کړتیَ کول kṟṟattaey kawul, verb trans.

To make wrinkled, to furrow, to crease, to wrinkle.

کړدار *kirr-dār.* See کردار

کړړی *kirr-rraey,* s.m. (1st) A cricket. Pl. ي *ī.* See کرري

کړشپ *karr-shap,* adj. Toothless, old, having no teeth and the lips having shrunk back; (Fem.) کړشپه *karr-shapa'h.*

کړشپي *karr-shapaey,* s.m. (1st) A person having no teeth, and whose mouth has fallen in. Pl. ي *ī.* کړشپۍ *karr-shapa'ī,* s.f. (6th) A toothless old woman. Sing. and Pl.

کړکړۍ *kurr-kurra'ī,* s.f. (6th) A turtle-dove. Sing. and Pl.; or کوتره کړکړۍ *kurr-kurra'ī kaw-tara'h,* s.f. (3rd). Pl. ې *ey.* See ګګشتو

کړکه *kurr-ka'h,* s.f. (3rd) A clucking hen. Pl. ې *ey.* See کړ

کړکۍ *kurr-ka'ī,* s.f. (6th) A kind of snare or trap made from the horn of a buffalo, and catgut. Sing. and Pl.

کړکۍ *karr-ka'ī,* s.f. (6th) A framework or screen made of grass, a screen or shutter for a doorway or window. 2. A window, a sally-port, a casement, a wicket, a loop-hole. Sing. and Pl. (HI کھڑکي)

کړل *krral,* verb trans. To do, act, perform, operate, commit, perpetrate, exercise, inflict, practice; to form, make, set, put in execution, cause, etc. This verb is with کول generally used as an auxiliary. Pres. کړي *krrī*; past ؤ کړ *wu-karr*; fut. به ؤ کړي *bah wu-krrī*; imp. کړه *krrah* or ؤ کړه *wu-krrah*; act. part. کړونکي *karrūnkaey* or کړونی *karrūnaey*; past part. کړی *karraey* or کړلی *krralaey*; verb. n. کړنه *krrana'h* or کړه *krrah.*

کړلاڼي *karr-lārrnī,* s.m. (1st) Pl. See کرلاڼي

کړم *karram,* adj. Helpless from wounds, maimed, mutilated, crippled, lamed; (Fem.) کړمه *karrama'h.* کړم کيدل *karram kedal,* verb intrans. To become maimed, mutilated, crippled, helpless, etc. کړم کول *karram kawul,* verb trans. To mutilate, to maim, to cripple, to lame.

کړميزي *karr-mezey,* s.f. (3rd) Pl. Snot, snivel, mucus from the nose. Sing. not used. کړميزن *karr-mezan,* s.m. (6th) A sniveller, a snotty-nosed fellow, a mean worthless person. Pl. کړميزنه *karr-mezæn.* کړميزه *karr-meza'h,* s.f. (3rd) A snivelling, mean, worthless, good-for-nothing female, a trollop. Pl. ې *ey.*

کړنګ *krring,* adj. Askew, awry, crooked, distorted, twisted, all on one side. 2. Squint-eyed, hump-backed; (Fem.) کړنګه *krringa'h.* See کرينګ

کړنګی *krringaey,* adj. as s.m. (1st) A hump-back, a person having a squint eye or eyes, or deformed in any way. Pl. ي *ī.* کړنګۍ *krringa'ī,* s.f. (6th) A female as above. Sing. and Pl.

کړنګ والی *krring wālaey,* s.m. (1st) Crookedness, distortion, wryness, twist. Pl. والي *wālī.* کړنګيدل *krringedal,* verb intrans. To become or grow crooked, distorted, wry, askew, all on one side, etc. کړنګول *krringawul,* verb trans. To distort, to make crooked, wry, to twist. See کرينګ

کړوسي *karr wasaey,* s.m. (1st) A great grandson. Pl. ي *ī.* کړوسۍ *karr-wasa'ī,* s.f. (6th) A great grand-daughter. Sing. and Pl. See کودي

کړه *krrah,* s.m. (6th) Doing, acting, making, performing, act, action, etc. (verb. n. of کړل) Sing. and Pl.

کړه وړه *krrah wrrah,* s.m. (6th) Beauty, gracefulness, good looks, grace, neatness, comeliness, spruceness. Sing. and Pl. See جوراب

کړهی *karrah-aey,* s.m. (1st) A cauldron, a shallow iron boiler. Pl. ي *ī.* (S کړاها)

کړهي *kurr-haey,* s.m. (1st) The fourth part of an *ao-gaey*—a measure of seven seers. Pl. ي *ī.* See اوګي

کړی *kurraey,* s.m. (1st) A dry measure. Pl. ي *ī.* See preceding.

کړېڅۍ *karretsa'ī* or کړېچۍ *karrecha'ī,* s.f. (6th) A ladle, an iron spoon. Sing. and Pl. (HI کرچها)

کړيدل *karredal,* verb intrans. To be parched, grilled, toasted, scorched, baked, to become reduced or diminished by heat, to waste away through grief, sickness, etc. 2. To be tired, fatigued, oppressed, perplexed. Pres. كړيږي *karrejzī* (W.) or كړيګي *karregī* (E.); past وُ كړيده *wu-karredah* or وُ كړيدَ *wu-karreda*; fut. وُ به كړيږي *wu bah karrejzī* or كړيګي *karregī*; imp. وُ كړيږه *wu-karrejzah* or كړيګه *karregah*; act. part. كړيدونكَي *karredūnkaey* or كړيدونَي *karredūnaey*; past part. كړيدلَي *karredalaey*; verb. n. كړيدنه *karredana'h* or كړيده *karredah*. كړول *karrawul*, verb trans. To roast, to toast, to grill, to simmer, to reduce or diminish by heat, to parch, to scorch, to shrivel, to shrink, to reduce in flesh, to wither (as disease), to waste, to attenuate, etc. 2. To distress, to perplex, to aggrieve. Pres. كړوي *karrawī*; past وُ كړاوه *wu-karrāwuh* or كړاوو *karrāwo*; fut. وُ به كړوي *wu bah karrawī*; imp. وُ كړوه *wu-karrawah*; act. part. كړوونكَي *karrawūnkaey* or كړوونَي *karrawūnaey*; past part. كړولَي *karrawulacy*; verb. n. كړونه *karrawuna'h*.

كړولَي *karra-wulaey*, adj. (past part.) Reduced, wasted, parched, grilled, shrivelled through heat or through sickness, withered. 2. Perplexed, aggrieved, distressed. 3. Soiled, dirty, used. 4. Tired, fatigued, worn out, wearied; (Fem.) كړولِ *karra-wuli*. Pl. (Masc. and Fem.) ي *ī*.

كړيدلَي *karredalaey*, adj. (past part.) Reduced or wasted away through sickness, grief, affliction, diminished or reduced by heat, become parched, grilled, baked, or toasted; fatigued, worn out, perplexed, oppressed, etc.; (Fem.) كړيدلِ *karredali* or كړيدلې *karredaley*. Pl. (Masc. and Fem.) ي *ī*.

كړينګ *krrīng*, adj. Askew, awry, crooked, distorted, twisted, all on one side. 2. Hump-backed, squint-eyed; (Fem.) كړينګه *krrīnga'h*.

كړينګيدل *krrīngedal*, verb intrans. To become contorted, twisted, crooked, to grow askew or awry, to grow all on one side. Pres. كړينګيږي *krrīngejzī* (W.) or كړينګيګي *krrīngegī* (E.); past كړينګ شه *krrīng shah* or وُ شه *wu-shah*; fut. كړينګ به شي *krrīng bah shī* or وُ به شي *bah wu-shī*; imp. كړينګ شه *krrīng-shah* or وُ شه *wu-shah*; act. part. كړينګيدونكَي *krrīngedūnkaey* or كړينګيدونَي *krrīngedūnaey*; past part. كړينګ *krrīng* or كړينګ شوَي *krrīng shawaey*; verb. n. كړينګيدنه *krrīngedana'h* or كړينګيده *krrīngedah*. كړينګول *krrīngawul*, verb trans. To distort or contort, to make crooked or awry, to twist. Pres. كړينګوي *krrīngawī*; past كړينګ كړ *krrīng karr* or وُ كړ *wu-karr*; fut. كړينګ به كړي *krrīng bah krrī* or وُ به كړي *bah wu-krrī*; imp. كړينګ كړه *krrīng krrah* or وُ كړه *wu-krrah*; act. part. كړينګوونكَي *krrīngawūnkaey* or كړينګوونَي *krrīngawūnaey*; past part. كړينګ كړَي *krrīng karraey*; verb. n. كړينګونه *krrīngawuna'h*.

كړينګ والَي *krrīng-wālaey*, s.m. (1st) Wryness, deformity, crookedness, twist. Pl. والي *wālī*.

كځله *kadzala'h*, s.f. (3rd) A dung-heap, a dung-hill, a pile of rubbish, sweepings, etc. Pl. ې *ey*.

كژ *kajz*, s.m. (2nd) The lower part of the jaws, the chin. Pl. كژونه *kajzūnah*. لاس تر كژونه *lās tar kajzūnah*, With hand under the chin, as when contemplating, grieving, down-hearted, etc.

كژ *kajz*, adj. (W.) Crooked, bent. See كوږ

كژدنه *kujz-dana'h*, s.f. (3rd) Betrothing, asking in marriage, affiance, betrothment, promise of marriage. Pl. ې *ey*. كژدنه كول *kujz-dana'h kawul*, verb trans. To affiance, to betroth, to engage.

كژدۍ *kijzda'ī* or *kajzda'ī*, s.f. (6th) A tent made of goat's hair or coarse black camlet in which the Afghān pastoral tribes generally dwell. Sing. and Pl. See ګګدي

كژل *kajzal*, verb trans. To dislike, to disapprove of, to regard with aversion or displeasure, to disrelish, to find fault with, to disparage, to run down, to animadvert upon. Pres. كژي *kajzī*; past وُ كاژه *wu-kājzah*; fut. وُ به كژي *wu bah kajzī*; imp. وُ كژه *wu-kajzah*; act. part. كژونكَي *kajzūnkaey* or كژونَي *kajzūnaey*;

past part. كږلئ *kajẕalaey*; verb. n. كږنه *kajẕana'h*. See غندل

كږلئ *kajẕalaey*, adj. (past part.) Unlucky, untoward, unwelcome, calamitous, woful, dreadful, deplorable; (Fem.) كږلِ *kajẕali*. Pl. (Masc. and Fem.) ي *ī*.

كږ ليچ *kajẕ-lech*, s.m. (2nd) A bend, a turn, an inclination, a turning, a circuit, a detour, meandering, winding. Pl. كږ ليچونه *kajẕ-lechūnah*. كږ ليچ كول *kajẕ lech kawul*, verb trans. To take a bend, to make a bend, turn, or inclination (as a river, road, etc.), to make a detour. كږ ليچ وركول *kajẕ-lech war-kawul*, verb trans. To give a bend to (as a wall), to make a bend in a road or the like.

كږ والئ *kajẕ wālaey*, s.m. (1st) Crookedness, angularity, curvature, distortion, convexity, twist, winding, zig-zag. Pl. والي *wālī*. كږيدل *kajẕedal*, verb intrans. To become crooked, bent, angular, forked, zig-zag, curved, distorted, twisted, etc. Pres. كږيږي *kajẕejzī*; past كوږ شه *kojẕ shah* or وُ شه *wu-shah*; imp. كوږ به شي *kojẕ bah shī* or به وُ شي *bah wu-shī*; imp. كوږ شه *kojẕ shah* or وُ شه *wu-shah*; act. part. كږيدونكئ *kajẕedūnkaey* or كږيدونئ *kajẕedūnaey*; past part. كوږ *kojẕ* or كوږ شوئ *kojẕ shawaey*; verb. n. كږيدنه *kajẕedana'h* or كږيده *kajẕedah*. كږول *kajẕawul*, verb trans. To bend, to curve, to twist, to distort, to crook, to render curved, angular, forked, or zig-zag, to bow, etc. Pres. كږوي *kajẕawī*; past كوږ كړ *kojẕ karr* or وُ كړ *wu-karr*; fut. كوږ به كړي *kojẕ bah krrī* or به وُ كړي *bah wu-krrī*; imp. كوږ كړه *kojẕ krrah* or وُ كړه *wu-krrah*; act. part. كږوونكئ *kajẕawūnkaey* or كږوونئ *kajẕawūnaey*; past part. كوږ كړئ *kojẕ karraey*; verb. n. كږونه *kajẕawuna'h*.

P كس *kus*, s.m. (2nd) The female organ of generation (pudenda femina). Pl. كسونه *kusūnah*. كسئ *kusa'ī*, s.f. (6th) A strumpet, a whore. Sing. and Pl. كس دِ خوار *kus di khwār*, A term of abuse. See چندري

P كس *kas*, s.m. (5th) A person, any one, a man, a human being. Pl. كسان *kasān*.

A كسب *kasb*, s.m. (2nd) Trade, profession, employment. Pl. كسبونه *kasb-ūnah*.

A كسبت *kisbat*, s.m. (2nd) A case or bag for powder, ball, flints, etc.; a case or bag in which barbers, surgeons, workmen, etc. keep their tools. Pl. كسبتونه *kisbatūnah*. See كمر كيسه

كستيج *kus-tīj*, s.m. (2nd) The hole in the hem of a pair of drawers through which the string passes. Pl. كستيجونه *kus-tījūnah*. See نيفه

كسكر *kus-kar*, adj. Burnt up or consumed, burnt black, scorched, frost-bitten, shrivelled, contracted. 2. Scorched or burnt with love, inflamed with desire. كسكر كيدل *kus-kar kedal*, verb intrans. To become burnt or consumed, to become scorched, contracted or shrivelled, etc. كسكر كول *kus-kar kawul*, verb trans. To burn, to scorch, to shrivel up, to contract.

كسل *kasal*, verb trans. To look, to view, to see, to behold, a word almost exclusively used by the Khattak tribe for كتل, which see.

كسورئ *kasūraey*, adj. Broken spirited, unequal to, distressed, humble; (Fem.) كسورِ *kasūri*. Pl. (Masc. and Fem.) ي *ī*.

كسوړه *kusorra'h*, s.f. (3rd) A linen bag, a purse, a wallet, a cover for a book. Pl. ئ *ey*. See كخوري

كسئ *kasaey*, s.m. (1st) The pupil of the eye. Pl. ي *ī*. See ليمه, توري, and باتور

كشاله *kashāla'h*, s.f. (3rd) Pulling or dragging along, trailing along the ground. Pl. ئ *ey*. كشاله كول *kashāla'h kawul*, verb trans. To pull or drag along, to trail on the ground.

كشپ *kashap*, s.m. (5th) A tortoise, a turtle. Pl. كشپان *kashap-ān*. كشپه *kashapa'h*, s.f. (3rd) The female of the above. Pl. ئ *ey* (P كشف). See شمشتئ

كشته *kishta'h*, s.f. (3rd) A dried apricot. Pl. ئ *ey*.

كشر *kashr*, adj. Junior, younger, minor, less, subaltern, cadet. 2. s.m. (5th) A young man. Pl. كشران *kasharān*; (Fem.) كشره *kashra'h*. Also s.f. (3rd) A young woman. Pl. ئ *ey*.

كشرنزي *ka**sh**-ranzī*, s.m. (1st) (Pl.) The name of an Afghān tribe. كشرنزىَ *ka**sh**-ranzaey*, (Sing.) A male of the above tribe. كشرنزۍ *ka**sh**-ranza'ī*, s.f. (6th) A female of the above. Sing. and Pl. See مشرنزي

T كشك *ka**sh**ak*, s.m. (5th) A watchman, a porter, a guard. Pl. كشكان *ka**sh**akān*. كشك گالل *ka**sh**ak gāl-al*, verb trans. To keep watch, to guard.

كشكي *ka**sh**-key*, interj. Would to God! may it happen! God-send! See كاشكي

كشمالو *ka**sh**-mālū*, s.m. (5th) The name of a herb, the holy basil. Pl. كشمالوگان *ka**sh**-mālūgān*.

كشمالىَ *ka**sh**-mālaey*, s.m. (1st) The flower and plant sweet basil. Pl. ي *ī*. See كشمالو

كشو *ka**sh**-aw*, s.m. (5th) A kind of weasel or mongoose which bites, and from the bones of which rings are made as charms to drive away disease. Pl. كشوگان *ka**sh**aw-gān*.

P كشور *ki**sh**-war*, s.m. (2nd) A climate, a clime, a region, a country. Pl. كشورونه *ki**sh**-war-ūnah*.

كشور *ki**sh**or*, s.m. (5th) A polecat. Pl. كشوران *ki**sh**or-ān*.

كشهار *ka**sh**a-hār*, s.m. (5th) (Pl.) The rustling of a silk dress, the noise of footsteps amongst bushes or corn, the sound or rustle of dry leaves (E.) كشهار لرل *ka**sh**a-hār laral*, verb trans. To rustle, to clank, to creak, to jangle.

كشۍ *ka**sh**a'ī*, s.f. (6th) A mattock, a hoe, a bar of iron. Sing. and Pl.

كشىَ *ka**sh**aey*, adj. as s.m. (1st) An only son. كش *ka**sh**i* or كشۍ *ka**sh**ey*, s.f. (8th) An only daughter. Pl. (Masc. and Fem.) ي *ī*.

كښ *ka**sh*** (W.) or *ka**kh*** (E.) s.m. (2nd) A pull, a draw (of a pipe), drawing the breath, a drawer, a puller, etc. Pl. كښونه *ka**sh**ūnah* or *ka**kh**ūnah*.

كښ *ka**sh***, s.m. (5th) (W.) Rustle, noise of the foot, or dry leaves, creak, jangle. Pl. كښهار *ka**sh**a-hār*. كښهار لرل *ka**sh**a-hār laral*, verb trans. To rustle, to creak, to jangle. See كشهار

كښت *ki**sh**t*, s.m. (2nd) (W.) or *ki**kh**t* (E.) A sown field, a field. Pl. كښتونه *ki**sh**tūnah* or *ki**kh**tūnah*. كښت گر *ki**sh**t-gar* or *ki**kh**t-gar*, s.m. (5th) A husbandman, an agriculturist. Pl. كښت گرٌ *ki**sh**t-gær* or *ki**kh**t-gær*. كښت كول *ki**sh**t* or *ki**kh**t kawul*, verb trans. To till, to sow (P كشت).

كښت *ku**sh**t*, s.m. (2nd) (W.) or *ku**kh**t* (E.) An opening between two mountains, a gap, interval, interstice, cleft, a gorge, a defile, an aperture. Pl. كښتونه *ku**sh**tūnah* or *ku**kh**tūnah*.

كښل *k'**sh**al* (W.) or *k'**kh**al* (E.) verb trans. To pull or draw out, to pluck or root out, to remove, to express, to elicit, to extricate. 2. To write, to take down in writing, to record, to register. This infinitive is imperfect, and requires the tenses of the imperfect verb كاږل to complete it. For conjugations see the latter and كاگل

كښول *k'**sh**awul* (W.) or *k'**kh**awul* (E.) verb. trans. (caus.) To cause to pull or draw out, to cause to remove. 2. To cause to write or take down, to depose to, to cause to be registered. Pres. كښوي *k'**sh**awī* or *k'**kh**awī*; past وُ كښاوه *wu-k'**sh**āwuh* or *k'**kh**āwuh* or كښاوو *k'**sh**āwo* or *k'**kh**āwo*; fut. وُ به كښوي *wu bah k'**sh**awī* or *k'**kh**awī*; imp. وُ كښوه *wu-k'**sh**awa'h* or *k'**kh**awah*; act. part. كښوونكىَ *k'**sh**awūnkaey* or *k'**kh**awūnkaey* or كښوونىَ *k'**sh**awūnaey* or *k'**kh**awūnaey*; past part. كښولىَ *k'**sh**awulaey* or *k'**kh**awulaey*; verb. n. كښونه *k'**sh**awuna'h* or *k'**kh**awuna'h*.

كښل *k'**sh**ul* (W.) or *k'**kh**ul* (E.) s.m. (2nd) A kiss, a salute, a caress, a buss. Pl. كښلونه *k'**sh**ulūnah* or *k'**kh**ulūnah*. كښلول *k'**sh**ulawul* (W.) or *k'**kh**ulawul* (E.) verb trans. To kiss, to salute, to caress. Pres. كښلوي *k'**sh**ulawī* or *k'**kh**ulawī*; past وُ كښلاوه *wu-k'**sh**ulāwuh* or *k'**kh**ulāwuh* or وُ كښلاوو *wu-k'**sh**ulāwo* or *k'**kh**ulāwo*; fut. وُ به كښلوي *wu bah k'**sh**ulawī* or *k'**kh**ulawī*; imp. وُ كښلوه *wu-k'**sh**ulawah* or *k'**kh**ulawah*; act. part. كښلوونكىَ *k'**sh**ulawūnkaey* or *k'**kh**ulawūnkaey* or كښلوونىَ *k'**sh**ulawūnaey* or *k'**kh**ulawūnaey*; past part. كښلولىَ

k'shulawulaey or *k'khulawulaey*; verb. n. کښلونه *k'shulawuna'h* or *k'khulawuna'h*. See ښکلول

کښلئ *k'khulaey* (W.) or *k'shulaey* (E.) adj. (past part.) Pretty, handsome, good-looking, bonny, fair, comely (*lit.* kissed); (Fem.) کښلې *k'khuli*. Pl. (Masc. and Fem.) ي *ī*. See کوښلئ and ښکلئ

کښې *kshey* (W.) or *kkhey* (E.) prep. In, within, among, between, at, etc. Also written کښِ *kshi* or *kkhi*. See په کښې

کښئ *kashaey* (W.) or *kakhaey* (E.) s.m. (1st) A watchman, a man employed to keep birds from sown fields. Pl. ي *ī*. کښئ *kasha'ī* or *kakha'ī*, s.f. (6th) A female employed as above. Sing. and Pl.

کښېباسل *k'she-bāsal* (W.) or *k'khe-bāsal* (E.) verb trans. To insert, to introduce, to implant, to thrust in, to thrust, to stick in, to deposit, to locate, to wedge in, etc. For inflections of this infinitive, which is imperfect, see کښېيستل

کښيده *kasheda'h* or *kakheda'h*, s.f. (3rd) A kind of needlework or embroidery, a flower or leaf on silk or other descriptions of cloth. Pl. ئ *ey*. کښيده کول *kasheda'h* or *kakheda'h kawul*, verb trans. To embroider, to make flowers, etc. on cloth or silk.

کښېږدل *kshejz-dal* (W.) verb trans. To place, to put, to set, to arrange, to dispose, to set in order, to range, to rank. This verb is imperfect, and is used to complete the inflections of کښېښول *kshe-shwal*, verb trans. Pres. کښېږدي *kshejz-dī*; past کښېښو *kshe-sho*; fut. وُ به کښې ږدي *wu bah kshejz-dī* or کښې به ږدي *kshe bah jzdī*; imp. کښېږده *kshejz-dah*; act. part. کښېښوونکئ *kshe-shawūnkaey* or کښېښوونئ *kshe-shawūnaey*; past part. کښېښولئ *kshe-shawulaey*; verb. n. کښېښونه *kshe-shawuna'h*. Also written کښېښوول *kshe-showul*. See کېښول

کښېکښل *kshe-kshal* (W.) verb trans. To shampoo, to knead and press the limbs and flesh. Pres. کښېکاږي *kshe-kājzī*; past کښېکښ *kshe-kesh*; fut. کښې به کاږي *kshe bah kājzī* or کښې به وُ کاږي *kshe bah wu-kājzī*; imp. کښېکاږه *kshe-kājzah*; act. part. کښېکښونکئ *kshe-kshūnkaey* or کښېکښونئ *kshe-kshūnaey*; past part. کښېکښلئ *kshe-kshalaey*; verb. n. کښېکښنه *kshe-kshana'h*. See چاپي کول

کښېناستل *kshe-nāstal* (W.) verb trans. To sit, to sit down, to settle (as birds), to squat on the buttocks, to rest on the feet as fowls, etc. Pres. کښېني *kshe-nī*; past کښېناست *kshe-nāst*; fut. کښې به ني *kshe bah nī*; imp. کښېنه *kshe-nah*; act. part. کښېناستونکئ *kshe-nāstūnkaey* or کښېناستونئ *kshe-nāstūnaey*; past part. کښېناستئ *kshe-nāstaey* or کښېناستلئ *kshe-nāstalaey*; verb. n. کښېناستنه *kshe-nāstana'h* or کښېناسته *kshe-nāstah*. کښېنول *kshe-nawul*, verb trans. To seat, to cause to sit, to settle, to fix in a particular place, to instal. Pres. کښېنوي *kshe-nawī*; past کښېناوه *kshe-nāwuh* or کښېناوو *kshe-nāwo*; fut. کښې به نوي *kshe bah nawī*; imp. کښېنوه *kshe-nawah*; act. part. کښېنوونکئ *kshe-nawūnkaey* or کښېنوونئ *kshe-nawūnaey*; past part. کښېنولئ *kshe-nawulaey*; verb. n. کښېنونه *kshe-nawuna'h*. See کېنول

کښېوتل *kshe-watal* (W.) verb intrans. To fall into, to drop into (as birds in a net), to slip or slide into, to go down into, to plump into, to sprawl into, etc. Pres. کښېوزي *kshew-zī*; past کښېوت *kshe-wut* or کښېووت *kshe-wot*; fut. کښې به وزي *kshe bah wuzī*; imp. کښېوزه *kshe-wuzah*; act. part. کښېوتونکئ *kshe-wutūnkaey* or کښېوتونئ *kshe-wutūnaey*; past part. کښېوتلئ *kshe-watalaey*; verb. n. کښېوتنه *kshe-watana'h* or کښېواته *kshe-wātah*.

کښېيستل *kshe-yastal* (W.) verb trans. To insert, to introduce, to implant, to thrust in, to stick in, to deposit, to locate, to wedge in, to fix in, to make enter, etc. Pres. کښېباسي *kshe-bāsī* (from کښېباسل); past کښېيوست *kshe-yost*; fut. کښې به باسي *kshe bah bāsī*; imp. کښېباسه *kshe-bāsah*; act. part. کښېيستونکئ *kshe-yastūnkaey* or کښېيستونئ *kshe-yastūnaey*; past part. کښېيستلئ *kshe-yastalaey*; verb. n. کښېيستنه *kshe-yastana'h* or کښېياسته *kshe-yāstah*. See کېيستل

A كعبه *kaæ-ba'h*, s.f. (3rd) A square building, the temple at Makka. Pl. ې *ey*.

A كف *kuf*, adj. (for كفو) Alike, similar. See سيال

A كفارة *kafārat*, s.m. (2nd) (from كفر) Penitence, penance, atonement, expiation for sin. Pl. كفارتونه *kafārat-ūnah*. كفارت وركول *kafārat war-kawul*, verb trans. To atone for, to expiate.

A كفايت *kifā-yat*, s.m. (2nd) (from كفي) sufficiency, abundance, plenty, surplus, enough, economy, thrift. Pl. كفايتونه *kifā-yatūnah*. كفايت لرل *kifā-yat laral*, verb trans. To have or possess sufficiency, abundance, etc.

P كفتر *kaf-tar*. See كوتر

A كفر *kufr*, s.m. (2nd) Paganism, infidelity, incredulity, ingratitude. Pl. كفرونه *kufrūnah*. كفر كول *kufr kawul*, verb trans. To blaspheme, to scoff, to profane.

A كفن *kaf-an*, s.m. (2nd) A shroud, a winding-sheet, a coffin. Pl. كفنونه *kaf-anūnah*. See كپن

كك *kak*, s.m. (2nd) A straw, a splinter, a piece of grass, any useless straw or rubbish. 2. Treacle, syrup. Pl. ككونه *kakūnah*.

ككرئ *kakar-a'ī*, s.f. (6th) The skull. Sing. and Pl. See كپړي

ككرئ *kakar-aey*, s.m. (1st) A pup, a puppy. Pl. ي *ī*. ككرئ *kakar-a'ī*, s.f. (6th) A female pup. Sing. and Pl. See كنكري

ككړ *kakarr*, adj. Polluted, defiled, contaminated, tainted, stained, soiled, corrupted (in mind or in body). 2. A good tempered man. (Fem.) ككړه *kakarra'h*, Deflowered, polluted. 2. s.f. (3rd) A whore, a strumpet. Pl. ې *ey*.

ككړوالي *kakarr wālaey*, s.m. (1st) Uncleanness, foulness, impurity, pollution, nastiness, defilement. 2. Dirt, filth, ordure, etc. Pl. والي *wālī*. ككړيدل *kakarre-dal*, verb intrans. To become unclean, polluted, defiled, tainted; deflowered, etc. Pres. ككړيږي *kakarre-jzī* (W.) or ككړيګي *kakarre-gī* (E.); past ككړ شه *kakarr shah* or و شه *wu-shah*; fut. ككړ به شي *kakarr bah shī* or به و شي *bah wu-shī*; imp. ككړ شه *kakarr shah* or و شه *wu-shah*; act. part. ككړيدونكي *kakarredūnkaey* or ككړيدونى *kakarredūnaey*; past part. ككړ شوئ *kakarr shawaey*; verb. n. ككړيدنه *kakarredana'h* or ككړيده *kakarredah*. ككړول *kakarrawul*, verb trans. To defile, to pollute, to debase, to taint, to render unclean, to smear, to daub; to deflower. Pres. ككړوي *kakarrawī*; past ككړ كړ *kakarr karr* or و كړ *wu-karr*; fut. ككړ به كړي *kakarr bah krrī* or به و كړي *bah wu-krrī*; imp. ككړ كړه *kakarr krrah* or و كړه *wu-krrah*; act. part. ككړوونكي *kakarrawūnkaey* or ككړوونى *kakarrawūnaey*; past part. ككړ كړي *kakarr karraey*; verb. n. ككړونه *kakarr-awuna'h*.

ككوئ *kakawaey*, s.m. (1st) The name of a bird, about the size of a crow, which cries at night. It dwells on the banks of rivers. Pl. ي *ī*.

ككوړئ *kakorraey*, s.m. (1st) A round cake of bread, a kind of biscuit, bread cooked on the ashes. 2. The orb of the sun or moon. Pl. ي *ī*.

ككيدل *kagedal*, verb intrans. (E.) To become bent, crooked, curved, twisted, distorted, etc. ككول *kagawul*, verb trans. To bend, to curve, to twist, to distort, etc. See (W.) كږيدل and كږول, etc. for inflections under كوږ, and substitute ګ for ږ

ككي ښپي *kagey khpey* (E.) Bandy-legged, knock-kneed.

P كل *kal*, adj. Bald from age, having no hair on the head; (Fem.) كله *kala'h*. كل كول *kal kawul* or كلول *kalawul*, verb trans. To shave the head, to make bald. (P كل scald-headed.)

كل *kal*, s.m. (6th) Oil-cake. Sing. and Pl. (S كهل).

S كل كل *kal-kal*, s.m. (9th) Vain or empty words, wrangling. Sing. and Pl.

A كل *kul*, adj. All, universal, the whole; (Fem.) كله *kula'h*. See تول

P S كلال *kulāl*, s.m. (5th) A potter. Pl. كلالان *kulālān*.

A كلام *kalām*, s.m. (2nd) A word, a speech, a discourse, talk, conversation. Pl. كلامونه *kalām-ūnah*.

كلت *kulat* or *kalut*, s.m. (6th) The name of a

grain (Dolichos biflorus). Sing. and Pl. (s کلتهی).

کلک *klak*, adj. Hard, rigid, firm, stiff, tense, horny, inflexible, unyielding, severe, morose, austere; (Fem.) کلکه *klaka'h*. کلک والي *klak-wālaey*, s.m. (1st) Hardness, firmness, rigidity, stiffness, inflexibility. Pl. والي *wālī*. کلکيدل *klake-dal*, verb trans. To harden, to stiffen, to become rigid, inflexible, or unyielding, austere, morose. Pres. کلکيږي *klake-jzī* (W.) or کلکيګي *klake-gī* (E.); past کلک شه *klak shah* or و شه *wu-shah*; fut. کلک به شي *klak bah shī* or به و شي *bah wu-shī*; imp. کلک شه *klak shah* or و شه *wu-shah*; act. part. کلکيدونکَي *klake-dūnkaey* or کلکيدونَي *klake-dūnaey*; past part. کلک *klak* or کلک شوي *klak shawaey*; verb. n. کلکيدنه *klake-dana'h* or کلکيده *klake-dah*. کلکول *klakawul*, verb trans. To render or make hard, to stiffen or make stiff, to ossify, to petrify, to render rigid or inflexible, to make morose or austere. Pres. کلکوي *klakawī*; past کلک کړ *klak karr* or و کړ *wu-karr*; fut. کلک به کړي *klak bah krrī* or به و کړي *bah wu-krrī*; imp. کلک کړه *klak krrah* or و کړه *wu-krrah*; act. part. کلکوونکَي *klakawūnkaey* or کلکوونَي *klaka-wūnaey*; past part. کلک کړَي *klak karraey*; verb. n. کلکونه *klakawuna'h*.

کلمه *kul-ma'h*, s.f. (3rd) An entrail, a gut. Pl. کلمې *kul-mey*, The entrails, the guts. غټه کلمه *ghatta'h kul-ma'h*, s.f. (3rd) The large gut. Pl. ې *ey*. کلمه وتل *kul-ma'h watal*, verb intrans. To come out, as the intestinum rectum when prolapsed. کلمه وتنه *kul-ma'h watana'h*, s.f. (3rd) Prolapsus ani. Pl. ې *ey*.

A کلمه *kalima'h*, s.f. (3rd) A word, a speech. 2. The Muḥammadan confession of faith, the belief. Pl. ې *ey*. کلمه ويل *kalima'h wa-yal*, verb trans. To repeat the Muḥammadan belief.

کلنګ *kulang*, s.m. (2nd) Furniture of every description which a bride brings to her husband, dower. Pl. کلنګونه *kulangūnah*.

P کلنګ *kulang*, s.m. (5th) A fowl of a large breed, a crane, a heron. 2. A pick or pick-axe. Pl. کلنګان *kulangān*.

کلنګي چرګ *kulangaey chirg*, s.m. (5th) A cock of the kulang breed. Pl. چرګان *chirgān*. کلنګۍ چرګه *kulanga'ī chirga'h*, s.f. (3rd) A hen of the above breed. Pl. ې *ey*.

کلني *kalanaey* (in composition), A termination affixed to numbers to denote so many years old; as شپږ کلني *shpajz-kalanaey* or شپګ کلني *shpag kalanaey*, Six years old. 2. adj. Prior, former, anterior, ancient, previous, antecedent; (Fem.) کلنۍ *kalana'ī*. 3. s.m. (1st) One of the ancients, an ancestor. Pl. ي *ī*. کلنۍ *kalana'ī*, s.f. (6th) An ancestress, etc. Sing. and Pl. See ږونبني and پخواني

کلوټ *kalott*, adj. Dark-complexioned, blackish or darkish; (Fem.) کلوټه *kalotta'h*.

کلوښته *kaloshta'h* (W.) or *kalokhta'h* (E.) s.f. (3rd) A wisp of straw or grass, a fardel, a floss of silk and the like, a curl, a tuft or lock of hair, etc. Pl. ې *ey*.

کله *kalah*, adj. Ever, at any time, sometime, once, one time. کله کله *kalah kalah*, Now and then, sometimes, occasionally, at times. کله شو لا کله *kalah shū lā kalah*, Since when? how long? (*i.e.* for a long time), long since. کله نَي *kalah-naey*, adj. Prior, former, anterior, ancient. Pl. ي *ī*; (Fem.) کله نۍ *kalah-na'ī*. Sing. and Pl. See کلني

P کله *kala'h*, s.f. (3rd) The head. Pl. ې *ey*. کله منار *kala'h-minār*, s.m. (2nd) A tower of skulls erected on a field of battle. Pl. کله منارونه *kala'h-minārūnah*. کله پز *kala'h paz*, s.m. (5th) One who cooks and sells sheeps' heads. Pl. کله پزان *kala'h paz-ān*.

P A کله شرطق *kula'h-shartak*, The name of a game similar to foot-ball, but with a cap in place of the ball.

کلَي *kalaey*, s.m. (1st) A village, a hamlet. Pl. ي *ī*. د کلي سړي *da kalī sarraey*, A villager. د کلي ښځه *da kalī shadza'h* or *khadza'h*, A village female. کلَي کول *kalaey kawul*, verb trans. To take up one's residence in the same village, to live, to reside, to associate with.

کلي *kilī*, s.f. (3rd) A key. Pl. ئي *a'ī*. See کنجي

کلَی *kalaey*, adj. An animal whose horns may not have grown out, short-horned; (Fem.) کلئ *kala'ī*.

کلئ *kala'ī*, s.f. (6th) A corn, a bunion, a gall, a callosity. Sing. and Pl. See بورئ

کم *kam*, interrog. pron. What? which? generally applied to inanimate objects; (Fem.) کمه *kama'h*. See کوم and کومه. (A *kam*, S *kim*).

P کم *kam*, adj. chiefly used in composition, Less, little, deficient, scanty, seldom, etc.; (Fem.) کمه *kama'h*. کم اصل *kam aṣl*, adj. Low-bred, vile; (Fem.) کم اصله *kam-aṣla'h*. کم اصلي *kam aṣlī*, s.f. (3rd) Vileness, lowness or baseness of origin. Pl. ئي *a'ī*. کم بخت *kam bakht*, adj. Unfortunate. 2. Wretch, rascally; (Fem.) کم بخته *kam-bakhta'h*. کم بختي *kam-bakhtī*, s.f. (3rd) Adversity, misfortune, unfortunateness. Pl. ئي *a'ī*. کم و بيښ *kam-o-besh* (W.) *kam-o-bekh* (E.) More or less. کم حوصله *kam-ḥauṣila'h*, adj. Poor-spirited, unaspiring. کم حوصلگي *kam-ḥauṣilagī*, s.f. (3rd) Poor-spiritedness. Pl. ئي *a'ī*. کم خرڅ *kam kharts*, adj. Parsimonious, miserly; (Fem.) کم خرڅه *kam-khartsa'h*. کم خرڅي *kam-khartsī*, s.f. (3rd) Parsimony, stinginess. Pl. ئي *a'ī*. کم خور *kam-khor*, adj. Abstemious, eating little; (Fem.) کم خوره *kam-khora'h*. کم خوري *kam-khorī*, s.f. (3rd) Abstinence, abstemiousness. Pl. ئي *a'ī*. کم ذات *kam-zāt*, adj. Low-bred, of low descent; (Fem.) کم ذاته *kam zāta'h*, کم ذاتي *kam-zātī*, s.f. (3rd) Lowness of origin or descent. Pl. ئي *a'ī*. کم زور *kam-zor*, adj. Weak, powerless, impotent; (Fem.) کم زوره *kam-zora'h*. کم زور تيا *kam-zor tī'ā*, s.f. (6th) Weakness, debility, impotence. (E.) Sing. and Pl. (W.) Pl. تياوي *tī'āwī*; also کم زور والَی *kam-zor wālaey*, s.m. (1st) Pl. والي *wālī*. کم و زيات *kam-o-zī-āt*, More or less. کم عقل *kam-œaḳl*, adj. Stupid, ignorant; (Fem.) کم عقله *kam-œaḳla'h*. کم

عقلي *kam-œaḳlī*, s.f. (3rd) Stupidity, ignorance. Pl. ئي *a'ī*. کم فرصت *kam-furṣat*, adj. Occupied, engaged, having no leisure. کم فرصتي *kam-furṣatī*, s.f. (3rd) Want of leisure or opportunity. Pl. ئي *a'ī*. کم فهم *kam-fahm*, adj. Stupid, doltish; (Fem.) کم فهمه *kam-fahma'h*. کم فهمي *kam-fahmī*, s.f. (3rd) Stupidity, ignorance. Pl. ئي *a'ī*. کم قدر *kam-ḳadr*, adj. Worthless; (Fem.) کم قدره *kam-ḳadra'h*. کم قدري *kam-ḳadrī*, s.f. (3rd) Worthlessness. Pl. ئي *a'ī*. کم قوت *kam-ḳūwat*, adj. Feeble, powerless; (Fem.) کم قوته *kam-ḳūwata'h*. کم قوتي *kam-ḳūwatī*, s.f. (3rd) Feebleness, inability. Pl. ئي *a'ī*; or کم قوت والَی *kam-ḳūwat wālaey*, s.m. (1st) Pl. ي *ī*. کم قيمت *kam-ḳīmat*, adj. Low-priced, cheap; (Fem.) کم قيمته *kam-ḳīmata'h*. کم قيمتي *kam-ḳīmatī*, s.f. (3rd) Cheapness, lowness of price. Pl. ئي *a'ī*. کم کم *kam-kam*, A little, little by little. کم گوي *kam-go-e*, adj. Taciturn; (Fem.) کم گويه *kam-go-ea'h*. کم مايه *kam mā-yah*, adj. Deficient in quantity, wealth, or capital. 2. Poor, scarce. کم محنت *kam-miḥ-nat*, adj. Lazy, indolent; (Fem.) کم محنته *kam-miḥ-nata'h*. کم نصيب *kam-naṣīb*, adj. Unfortunate, luckless; (Fem.) کم نصيبه *kam-naṣība'h*. کم نصيبي *kam-naṣībī*, s.f. (3rd) Misfortune, bad luck. Pl. ئي *a'ī*. کم نظر *kam-nazar*, adj. Dim-sighted, weak sighted. 2. Inattentive, unkind; (Fem.) کم نظره *kam-nazara'h*. کم والَی *kam-wālaey*, s.m. (1st) Deficiency, littleness, paucity. Pl. والي *wālī*. کم همت *kam-himat*, adj. Spiritless, mean-spirited; (Fem.) کم همته *kam-himmata'h*. کم همتي *kam-himmatī*, s.f. (3rd) Meanness, spiritlessness. Pl. ئي *a'ī*. کم ياب *kam-yāb*, adj. Scarce, rare, uncommon; (Fem.) کم يابه *kam-yāba'h*. کم يابي *kam-yābī*, s.f. (3rd) Scarcity, rarity. Pl. ئي *a'ī*. کميدل *kame-dal*, verb intrans. To decrease, to lessen, to diminish, to dwindle. Pres. کميږي *kame-jzī* (W.) or کميگي *kame-gī* (E.); past کم شه *kam shah* or و شه *wu-shah*; fut. کم به شي *kam bah shī* or

به وُ شي *bah wu-shī* ; imp. كم شه *kam shah* or وُ شه *wu-shah* ; act. part. كميدونكَي *kamedūnkaey* or كميدونيَ *kamedūnaey* ; past part. كم *kam* or كم شويَ *kam shawaey* ; verb. n. كميدنه *kamedana'h* or كميده *kamedah*. كمول *kamawul*, verb trans. To decrease, to make less, to diminish, to curtail, to abridge, to reduce, etc. Pres. كموي *kamawī* ; past كم كړ *kam karr* or وُ كړ *wu-karr* ; fut. كم به كړي *kam bah krrī* or به وُ كړي *bah wu-krrī* ; imp. كم كړه *kam krrah* or وُ كړه *wu-krrah* ; act. part. كمونكَي *kamawūnkaey* or كمونيَ *kamawūnaey* ; past part. كم كړيَ *kam karraey* ; verb. n. كمونه *kamawuna'h*. See لږ and لكث

A كمال *kamāl*, s.m. (9th) Perfection, excellence, completion, conclusion. Sing. and Pl. 2. adj. Complete, entire, perfect, finished ; (Fem.) كماله *kamāla'h*. كمال دار *kamāl-dār*, adj. Perfect, excellent, a saint ; (Fem.) كمال داره *kamāl-dāra'h* ; or صاحب كمال *ṣāḥib kamāl* ; (Fem.) صاحب كماله *ṣāḥib kamāla'h*.

كمالزي *kamāl-zī*, s.m. (1st) (Pl.) The name of an Afghān tribe. كمالزيَ *kamāl-zaey* (Sing.) A male of the above tribe. كمالزِئ *kamāl-za'ī*, s.f. (6th) A female of the above. Sing. and Pl.

كمان گر *kamān-gar*, s.m. (5th) A bow maker (from P.) Pl. كمان گرُ *kamān-gær*.

P كمانچه *kamān-cha'h*, s.f. (3rd) The bow of a violin. Pl. ې *ey*.

كمائي *kamā-ī*, s.f. (3rd) Earning, gain, performance, work, wages, money earned. Pl. ئ *a'ī*. كمائي كول *kamā-ī kawul*, verb trans. To gain, to earn, to work, to labour. See گټه and گټنه

كمبلئ *kam-bala'ī*, s.f. (6th) A butterfly. Sing. and Pl.

كمپاره *kam-pāra'h*, s.f. (3rd) The name of a medicine (four-seeds), a remedy for diarrhœa (fleawort ?). Pl. ې *ey*.

كمچه *kam-cha'h*, s.f. (3rd) The little finger, the little toe. Pl. ې *ey*. See چنچه

P كمر *kamar*, s.m. (2nd) The middle of a mountain, a precipice, a cliff, an escarpment, the high bank of a river, a place where a portion has fallen from a mountain. Pl. كمرونه *kamarūnah*. كمر بند *kamar band*, s.m. (2nd) A girdle, a zone, a waist belt. Pl. كمر بندونه *kamar bandūnah*. كمر كيسه *kamar kīsa'h*, s.f. (3rd) A waist-belt with powder horn, and other furniture for a soldier. Pl. ې *ey*. See ملا

P كمري *kamarī*, adj. Weak in the loins (as a horse), respecting the loins. (Masc. and Fem.)

P كمك *kumak*, s.m. (2nd) Aid, help, assistance. 2. The reserve of an army. Pl. كمكونه *kumakūnah*. كمك ور كول *kumak war-kawul*, verb trans. To aid, to assist, to help.

P كمكي *kumakī*, s.m. (5th) A helper, an aider. 2. adj. Auxiliary, ally, aider. Pl. كمكيان *kumakī-ān*. كمكئ *kumaka'ī*, s.f. (6th). Sing. and Pl.

كمكَي *kam-kaey*, adj. (dim. of كم) Little, small, less. 2. A word of endearment to a child ; (Fem.) كمكئ *kam-ka'ī*. See كونكي and كچ

P كمند *kamand*, s.m. (2nd) A lasso, a snare, a noose, a halter, a kind of scaling ladder, a rope to which a line of horses are picketed. 2. The long ringlets of a beautiful woman. Pl. كمندونه *kamandūnah*.

كمنړ *kumarrn*, adj. Faded, withered, dead, decayed ; (Fem.) كمنړه *kumarrna'h*. كمنړ واليَ *kumarrn wālaey*, s.m. (1st) Decay, impairment, wane, decline. Pl. ي *ī*. كمنړيدل *kumarrnedal*, verb trans. To fade, to wither, to die away. كمنړول *kumarrnawul*, verb trans. To cause to fade or decay, to wither up.

كميس *kamīs*, s.m. (2nd) (corrup. of A قميص) A shirt, a chemise. Pl. كميسونه *kamīsūnah*.

A كمين *kamīn*, s.m. (2nd) An ambush, a cover, a hiding or lurking place. Pl. كمينونه *kamīnūnah*. See پټكنئ

P كمينه *kamīnah*, adj. Base, mean, ignoble, abject, defective. 2. Humble, meek. (Masc. and Fem.) ; also كمين *kamīn*.

P كميني *kamīnī*, s.f. (3rd) Humility, meekness. 2. Meanness, baseness. Pl. ئ *a'ī*. كميني لرل *kamīnī laral*, verb trans. To possess humility, meekness. كميني كول *kamīnī kawul*, verb trans. To act with humility.

كميو *kam-yo* or كم يو *kam-yow*, pron. Which

one? which? (Fem.) كمه يوه *kama'h-yona'h.*

كناټی *kunāttaey,* s.m. (1st) The rump, the buttock. Pl. كناټي *kunāttī,* The buttocks. كناټور *kunātta-war,* Having large buttocks; (Fem.) كناټوره *kunātta-wara'h,* A woman with large buttocks.

A كنايت *kinā-yat,* s.m. (2nd) Pl. كنايتونه *kinā-yatūnah.* See following word.

A كنايه *kināyah,* s.m. (9th) (from كنا) Allusion, metaphor, sarcasm, ironical expression. Sing. and Pl.

كنټكين *kantt-kīn,* adj. Made of thread; (Fem.) كنټكينه *kantt-kīna'h.*

P كنج *kunj,*s.m. (2nd) A corner, a confined place, a grove, a bower. Pl. كنجونه *kunjūnah.*

كنجكه *kun-jaka'h,* s.f. (3rd) A small shell used as a coin (Cypræa moneta). Pl. ي *ey.*

كنجوغه *kan-jogha'h,* s.f. (3rd) Saddle straps for fastening anything to a saddle. Pl. ي *ey.*

S كنجۍ *kunja'ī,* s.f. (6th) A key. 2. A small earthern vessel for water. Sing. and Pl. See كلي

كند *kand,* s.m. (2nd) A ravine, a chasm, a cleft, a gorge, a channel made by a mountain torrent. Pl. كندونه *kand-ūnah.*

كند *kind* or *kand,* s.m. (5th) A patched or ragged garment. Pl. كندان *kindān,* or (2nd) كندونه *kindūnah.* See گند

كنداغ *kundāgh,* s.m. (2nd) The stock of a gun or musket. Pl. كنداغونه *kundāghūnah.* كنداغ ور آچول *kundāgh war-āchawul,* verb trans. To stock a gun.

كندري كودري *kandarey kawdarey,* s.m. (1st) A shard, a piece or fragment of a broken vessel, or any brittle substance. Pl. ي *ī.* See كودري and كندي

كندرۍ كودرۍ *kandaraey kawdaraey,* s.f. (3rd) Pl. Rough unbroken ground, ground filled with fissures, ravines, and the like. The Sing. form is not used. See also كندي كودري

كندل *kan-dal,* verb trans. To dig, to delve, to excavate, to sink, to scoop out. This infinitive is imperfect in the present tenses and imperative, and requires the aid of the verb كنل, which is also imperfect in the past tenses, to complete it. Pres. كني *kanī* (from كنل); past وُ كند *wu-kand*; fut. وُ به كني *wu bah kanī*; imp. وُ كنه *wu-kanah*; verb. n. كندونكی *kandūnkaey* or كندونی *kandūnaey*; past part. كندلی *kandalaey*; verb. n. كندنه *kandana'h.*

كندو *kandū,* s.m. (5th) A large earthen vessel for holding grain. Pl. كندوان *kandū-ān.*

A كنده *kunda'h,* s.f. (3rd) A ploughshare on which the iron head is placed, a block or billet of wood, stocks for confining criminals. Pl. ي *ey.*

PLV كنده *kanda'h,* s.f. (3rd) A cavity, a chasm, a cleft, a channel made by a torrent, an abyss, a ravine. 2. A large pit or ditch in which a number of dead bodies are buried after a battle. There are several of these at the top of the Malakand Pass, leading into Suwāt from Peshāwer, and weapons and bones are often found protruding. Pl. ي *ey.* See كند

كندی *kandaey,* s.m. (1st) A fragment of a broken vessel or any brittle substance, a shard. Pl. ي *ī.* See كندري كودري

كندي *kandey,* s.f. (3rd) (the Pl. of كنده) Uneven or broken ground, ground filled with ravines and chasms; or كندي كودري *kandey kawdarey.*

كندی *kandaey,* s.m. (1st) A division, a district, a parish, a ward, a quarter of a town or city. Pl. ي *ī.* (S كهنڈه).

كنډ *kandd,* s.m. (6th) Sugar-candy. 2. Gum-resin. Sing. and Pl. (HI كهنڈ). See كندري

كنډ *kundd,* adj. as s.m. (5th) A widower, a man who has lost a wife. Pl. كنډان *kunddān.*

كنډا *kanddā,* adj. Having a hare-lip, a cow or other animal having a broken horn (Masc. and Fem.). See شوند پاره

كنډاس *kanddās,* adj. as s.m. (6th) A man who has lost his teeth, or whose teeth may have been broken, particularly the front teeth; an old man. Sing. and Pl. كنډاسه *kanddāsa'h,* adj. as s.f. (3rd) A toothless old woman. Pl. ي *ey.*

كنډال *kanddāl,* s.m. (2nd) A cup, a pan, a vessel.

2. A tanner's vessel for steeping skins. Pl. کندالونه *kanddālūnah*. See کندولي and کندول

کندر *kanddar*, s.m. (2nd) A ruinous or broken down building, the ruins of a house, village, etc. 2. A place haunted by demons. Pl. کندرونه *kanddarūnah*. (s کهنڈر).

کندړی *kandduraey*, s.m. (1st) (dimin. of کند) Gum in general. Pl. ي *ī*.

کندك *kanddak*, s.m. (2nd) A flock of sheep, a herd of deer, etc. 2. A piece of bread. Pl. کندکونه *kanddakūnah*. See رمه

کند کپړ *kandd-kaparr*, adj. Broken in bits, cut to pieces, helpless from wounds, severely wounded and completely done up; (Fem.) کند کپړه *kandd-kaparra'h*. کند کپړ کيدل *kandd-kaparr kedal*, verb intrans. To become helpless from wounds, to be severely wounded. کند کپړ کول *kandd-kaparr kawul*, verb trans. To render helpless from wounds, to wound severely.

کندلي *kanddala'ī*, s.f. (6th) A kind of thistle or circular thorn which sticks to the fleece of sheep or to the clothes. Sing. and Pl.

کندو *kanddaw*, s.m. (2nd) A notch, a dent, an opening, hole, or passage made in a wall, hedge, etc. کندوونه *kanddawūna'h*, adj. Notched, dented, crenated, loop-holed; (Fem.) کندوه *kanddawa'h*.

کندولی *kan-ddolaey*, s.m. (1st) An earthen cup or vessel, a darwesh's cup. Pl. ي *ī*.

کنده *kandd-a'h*, s.f. (3rd) The source of a river, a spring. Pl. ي *ey*.

کنده *kundd-a'h*, s.f. (3rd) A widow. 2. A hook for a door, a fish-hook, an instrument for driving an elephant. Pl. ي *ey*. (HI کنڈي).

کندۍ *kun-dda'ī*, s.f. (6th) A wooden cup or bowl. Sing. and Pl. See کنړۍ

کندي کودري *kanddaey kawdarey*, s.f. (3rd) Pl. Broken uneven ground, ground full of ruts, chasms, etc. Sing. not used.

کنزل *kan-zal*, s.m. (6th) Abuse, upbraiding, invective, vituperation, reviling, etc. Sing. and Pl. 2. verb trans. To abuse, to upbraid, to revile, to execrate. Pres. کنزي *kanzī*: past

و کانزه *wu-kānzah* or و کانز *wu-kānza*; fut. و به کنزي *wu bah kanzī*; imp. و کنزه *wu-kanzah*; act. part. کنزونکی *kanzūnkaey* or کنزونی *kanzūnaey*; past part. کنزلي *kanzalaey*; verb. n. کنزنه *kanzana'h*. See ښکنځل

کنزله *kan-zala'h*, s.f. (3rd) The sesamum, from which oil is extracted. Pl. کنزلي *kanzaley*, Sesamum seed.

کنزه گوته *kanza'h gūta'h*, s.f. (3rd) The third finger, the ring-finger. Pl. ي *ey*.

A کنعان *kanæān*, s.prop. The land of Canaan.

A کنف *kanaf*, s.m. (2nd) A side, brink, margin, shore. Pl. کنفونه *kanafūnah*.

کنگخړ *kanga-kharr*, s.m. (6th) Rubbish carried down by a flood or river, rubbish generally found on the banks of rivers. Pl. کنگخړ *kanga-khærr*. See نيز وري

P کنگره *kangara'h* or *kangura'h*, s.f. (3rd) A pinnacle, a turret, a niched battlement of a castle, a porthole, a loophole, a vidette, a parapet wall. Pl. ي *ey*.

کنگری *kungaraey*, s.m. (1st) A pup, a cub, a whelp. Pl. ي *ī*. کنگرۍ *kungara'ī*, s.f. (6th) A bitch pup or whelp. Sing. and Pl.; also کوتری *ku-taraey*. Pl. ي *ī*. کوترۍ *ku-tara'ī*. s.f. (6th) Sing. and Pl.

کنگس *kan-gas*, s.m. (2nd) A trip, a stumble, striking the foot against anything. Pl. کنگسونه *kan-gasūnah*. کنگس خوړل *kangas khwarral*, verb trans. To trip, to stumble.

کنگل *kangal*, s.m. (6th) Ice, anything congealed or frozen by the cold. 2. adj. Dense, solid, compact, close. Sing. and Pl.; (Fem.) کنگله *kangala'h*. کنگل کيدل *kangal kedal*, verb intrans. To freeze, to become frozen, to congeal.

کنگو *kangū* or *kungū*, s.m. (6th) Saffron. Sing. and Pl.

کنودل *kanowdal*, verb trans. To dig, to delve, to excavate, to sink, to scoop out, etc. This infinitive is imperfect with regard to the present tenses, which are taken from کنل which has no past tenses. Pres. کني *kanī*; past و کنود *wu-kanoud*; fut. و به کني *wu bah kanī*; imp. و کنه *wu-kanah*; act. part. کنودونکی *kanoud-*

ūnkaey or كنودوني kanoudūnaey; past part. كنودلي kanoudalaey; verb. n. كنودنه kanoudana'h. See كندل

S كنول kanwal, s.m. (6th) The lotus (Nymphæa nelumbo). Sing. and Pl.

P كنه kana'h, s.f. (3rd) A tick or louse affecting camels, dogs, sheep, etc. 2. The border of a shawl or garment. Pl. ې ey. See كونړ

كنړاوه karrnāwa'h, s.f. (3rd) A clog or patten made of wood, a kind of sandal. Pl. كنړاوې karrnāwey, A pair of clogs or pattens. See كړاونه . (HI كهړنو).

كنړه karrnah, conj. If not, then, otherwise, and if, etc.

كنړي karrnaey, s.m. (1st) The warp, the threads which are extended lengthwise upon a loom. Pl. ي ī.

كنړئي kurrna'ī, s.f. (6th) A wooden cup or bowl. Sing. and Pl. See كندي

كنړيدل karrnedal, verb intrans. To become deaf or hard of hearing.

كنړول karrnawul, verb trans. To make deaf, or hard of hearing. See under كونړ

كواره kawāra'h, s.f. (3rd) A kind of oblong basket narrow at the ends, used for carrying fruit, a kind of pannier. Pl. ې ey.

كوب k'wab, s.m. (2nd) The hump of a cow, ox, camel, hunch of a man, etc. Pl. كوبونه k'wabūnah.

كوبي kū-baey, s.m. (1st) A piece of wood in the horizontal wheel of a Persian wheel, of which there are several, and which catches the cogs (termed بوري) of the smaller one. Pl. ي ī.

كوبي kūbaey, s.m. (1st) A person having a hump-back, a hunch-back. Pl. ي ī. كوبئي kuba'ī, s.f. (6th) A female with a hump-back. Sing. and Pl.

كوت kawt, adj. Contracted, pinched up (as the belly of a horse from exercise, or a person through hunger), drawn in, attenuated, shrunk up, condensed, compact. 2. (P) Gouty, infirm in the feet, unable to rise; (Fem.) كوته kawta'h. كوت كول kawt kawul, verb trans. To contract, to pinch up, to condense, to attenuate, etc.

كوپ kūp, adj. Crooked, bent in the back, a person who stoops through age or weakness. Pl. كوپان kūpān; (Fem.) كوپه kūpa'h. Pl. كوپې kūpey. كوپ كيدل kūp kedal, verb intrans. To become bent from age, etc. كوپ كول kūp kawul, To bend, to cause to stoop. See تيت

كوپله kop-la'h, s.f. (3rd) A kind of lark. Pl. ې ey. See خراړه

كوپي kū-paey, s.m. (1st) A hunch-back. Pl. ي ī. كوپئي kū-pa'ī, s.f. (6th) A female with a hump-back. Sing. and Pl. See كوبي

كوتان ko-tān, s.m. (5th) a wild goose. Pl. كوتانان ko-tānān; s.f. (3rd) كوتانه kotāna'h. Pl. ې ey. See زانړه

P كوتاه ko-tāh, adj. Short, little, small, brief; (Fem.) كوتاهه ko-tāha'h. كوتاه بين ko-tāh bīn, adj. Short-sighted; (Fem.) كوتاه بينه ko-tāh bīna'h. كوتاه بيني ko-tāh bīnī, s.f. (3rd) Short-sightedness. Pl. ئي a'ī. كوتاه فكر ko-tāh fikr, adj. Indiscreet, imprudent, short-sighted; (Fem.) كوتاه فكره ko-tāh fikra'h. كوتاه قد ko-tāh ḳadd, adj. Short in stature; (Fem.) كوتاه قده ko-tāh ḳadda'h, كوتاهي ko-tāhī, s.f. (3rd) Smallness, shortness, brevity. 2. Littleness. 3. Deficiency. Pl. ئي a'ī. كوتاهي كول ko-tāhī kawul, verb trans. To neglect, to slight, to disregard. كوتاه كيدل ko-tāh kedal, verb intrans. To shorten, to become short, small, or brief. كوتاه كول ko-tāh kawul, verb trans. To lessen, to shorten, to decrease, to make brief. لاس كوتاه كول lās ko-tāh kawul, To give over, to give up, to abstain from, to abandon.

كوتر kow-tar, s.m. (5th) A pigeon. Pl. كوتران kow-tarān. كوتره kow-tara'h, s.f. (3rd) A hen pigeon. 2. The whole species of pigeons. Pl. ې ey.

كوتري kūtar-aey, s.m. (1st) A pup, a puppy, a cub, a whelp. Pl. ي ī. كوترئي kūtar-a'ī, s.f. (6th) A bitch pup, cub, etc. Sing. and Pl.

T كوتك kū-tak, s.m. (2nd) A club, a pestle. Pl. كوتكان kū-takān.

HI كوتل ko-tal, s.m. (2nd) A led horse. Pl.

كوتلونه *ko-talūnah* ; s.f. (3rd) كوتله *ko-tala'h*. Pl. ې *ey*.

كوتل *ko-tal*, s.m. (2nd) A pass over a mountain. Pl. كوتلونه *ko-talūnah*.

كوتل *kūtal*, verb trans. To cut up, to divide into joints (as meat). Pres. كوتي *kūtī* ; past وُ كوته *wu-kūtah* ; fut. وُ به كوتي *wu bah kūtī* ; imp. وُ كوته *wu-kūtah* ; act. part. كوتونكې *kūtūnkaey* or كوتونې *kūtūnaey* ; past part. كوتلې *kūtalaey* ; verb. n. كوتنه *kūtana'h*.

كوتلې *kūtalaey*, adj. (past part.) Killed for food, lawfully killed (*lit.* cut up into joints) ; (Fem.) كوتلِ *kūtali*. Pl. (Masc. and Fem.) ي *ī*.

كوتي لال *kūtī-lāl*, s.m. (6th) The name of a plant bearing a red berry, the ranunculus or crow-foot. Sing. and Pl.

s كوټ *kott*, s.m. (2nd) A fort, a castle, a stronghold, a keep (generally applied to small forts on hills or other difficult situations). Pl. كوټونه *kottūnah*.

كوټخه *kottakha'h*, s.f. (3rd) A cap made to cover the forehead and ears. Pl. ې *ey*.

كوټک *ko-ttak*, s.m. (2nd) The back of the head. 2. A bludgeon, a club, a stick, a pestle. Pl. كوټكونه *ko-ttakūnah*. See كوتک

كوټل *kūttal*, verb trans. To pound, to bruise, to macerate, to cudgel, to contuse, to abrade. Pres. كوټي *kūttī* ; past وُ كوټه *wu-kūttah* ; fut. وُ به كوټي *wu bah kūttī* ; imp. وُ كوټه *wu-kūttah* ; act. part. كوټونكې *kūttūnkaey* or كوټونې *kūttūnaey* ; past part. كوټلې *kūttalaey* ; verb. n. كوټنه *kūttana'h*.

كوټلې *kūttalaey*, adj. (past part.) Pounded, bruised, cudgeled, contused, ill-used ; (Fem.) كوټلِ *kūttali*. Pl. (Masc. and Fem.) ي *ī*.

كوټوال *kottwāl*, s.m. (5th) The chief police officer of a city or town. Pl. كوټوالان *kottwālān*. كوټوالي *kottwālī*, s.f. (3rd) The office of a Kottwāl, a police office. Pl. ئ *a'ī*. (s كوټنا)

كوټنه *kūttana'h*, s.f. (3rd) (verb. n.) Pounding, bruising, abrading, macerating. 2. Cudgeling, beating, ill-using. Pl. ې *ey*.

كوټه *kotta'h*, s.f. (3rd) A house with a flat roof, a room, a chamber, an apartment. Pl. ې *ey*. (s كوٹها).

كوته *kūttah*, s.m. (5th) A dog of any breed but a greyhound. Pl. كوتهگان *kūttah-gān*. Used adjectively, as كوته سپي *kūttah-spaey*, A dog of the above breeds. كوته سپۍ *kūtta'h spa'ī*, A bitch of the above.

كوټې *kūttaey*, s.m. (1st) A young donkey. Pl. ي *ī*. كوټ *kūtti*, s.f. (8th) (W.) A young female donkey. Pl. ي *ī*. See كوچي

كوټې *ko-ttaey*, s.m. (1st) The head. Pl. ي *ī*.

A كوثر *kau-ṣar*, s.m. (9th) The name of a river or fountain in Paradise. Sing. and Pl.

كوڅه *kū-tsa'h*, s.f. (3rd) A lane, a narrow street, an alley. Pl. ې *ey* (P كوچه). كوڅه ډب *kū-tsa'h-ddab*, s.m. (6th) A mean or cowardly person, a poltroon, a low fellow. Sing. and Pl. كوڅه ډبه *kū-tsa'h ddaba'h*, s.f. (3rd) A mean low woman. Pl. ې *ey*. كوڅه گرد *kū-tsa'h gard*, s.m. (6th) A street-walker, a vagabond, a stroller, a vagrant. كوڅه گرده *kū-tsa'h garda'h*, s.f. (3rd) A woman of bad character, a whore, a street-walker. Pl. ې *ey*. كوڅه گردي *kū-tsa'h gardī*, s.f. (3rd) Strolling, walking the streets, vagabondism. Pl. ئ *a'ī*.

كوڅي *kū-tsa'ī*, s.f. (6th) The long braided hair of a female which hangs down the back, a plait, a braid. Sing. and Pl. See كونځي

P كوچ *kūch* or *koch*, s.m. (2nd) A march, marching. Pl. كوچونه *kūchūnah* or *kochūnah*. كوچ كول *kūch* or *koch kawul*, verb trans. To march, to depart.

كوچټ والې *kūchutt-wālaey*, s.m. (1st) Childhood, infancy. 2. Smallness, littleness, diminutiveness, etc, Pl. والي *wālī*. See هلكينه

كوچمال *koch-māl*, s.m. (5th) A leader, a conductor, either of troops or a caravan ; a chief, manager, supervisor, inspector, a lictor, a sergeant, a pursuivant. Pl. كوچمالان *koch-mālān*. كوچماله *koch-māla'h*, s.f. (3rd) A conductress, a guide, a governess. Pl. ې *ey*.

كوچې *kū-chaey*, s.m. (1st) The tendon of the foot (Tendo Achillis). Pl. ي *ī*.

كوچي *kū-chaey*, s.m. (1st) (E.) A young donkey.

Pl. ي *ī*. كوچ *kū-chi*, s.f. (8th) A young female donkey. Pl. ي *ī*. See كوتي

كوچئي *ko-cha'ī*, s.f. (6th) A short coat made of felt. Sing. and Pl.

كودالئي *kodāla'ī*, s.f. (6th) A mattock, a hoe. Sing. and Pl. See سېبسوره

كودري *kawdaraey*, s.m. (1st) A shard, a fragment of any brittle substance. Pl. ي *ī*. See كندي

كودن *kaw-dan*, adj. Foolish, silly, shallow, weak; dull, doltish, stupid, addle-headed, imbecile; (Fem.) كودنه *kaw-dana'h*. كودن والئ *kaw-dan wālaey*, s.m. (1st) Incapacity, poverty of intellect, dullness, doltishness. Pl. والي *wālī*.

كودئ *ko-daey*, s.m. (1st) A large pot or vessel made of black earth. 2. A piece of a smutty pot, or of a pot in general, a shard. Pl. ي *ī*.

كوديك *kow-dīk*, s.m. (2nd) A pot or other vessel. Pl. كوديكونه *kow-dīkūnah*.

كوډه *ko-dda'h*, s.f. (3rd) Enchantment, juggling, sorcery, necromancy. Pl. ې *ey*. كوډ گر *kodd-gar*, s.m. (5th) A conjuror, a sorcerer, an enchanter. Pl. كوډ گرُ *kodd-gær*. كوډ گره *kodd-gara'h*, s.f. (3rd) A sorceress, an enchantress. Pl. ې *ey*. كوډې كول *ko-ddey kawul*, verb trans. To practice incantations or sorcery, to enchant, to conjure.

كوډئي *kowdda'ī*, s.f. (6th) A small shell used as a coin (Cypræa moneta). See كانجكه (s كوڙي).

كوډئي *kūdda'ī*, s.f. (6th) A hut, a shed, a temporary shelter of straw, branches of trees, etc. Sing. and Pl.

كور *kor*, s.m. (2nd) A house, a dwelling, a habitation, a residence. Pl. كورونه *korūnah*. كورا كور *korā-kor*, From house to house, from one dwelling to another. كور كول *kor kawul*, verb trans. To live, reside, or associate with. 2. To marry, to take a wife. كوروالئ *kor-wālaey*, s.m. (1st) Household economy, conjugal duty. Pl. ي *ī*. كور والئ كول *kor-wālaey kawul*, verb trans. To carry on housekeeping, to act the husband. كورنئ *koranaey*, s.m. (1st) A male domestic, one of a household, a man-servant. Pl. ي *ī*. كورنئي *korana'ī*, s.f. (6th) A female of a house, a female domestic. Sing. and Pl. كوربه *kor-bah*, s.m. (4th) A male relation or connection. Pl. كوربانه *kor-bānah*, The male relations of a bride. كوربنه *kor-bana'h*, s.f. (3rd) A female relation or member of a family, the female connection of a bride. Pl. ې *ey*.

كور *k'war*, s.m. (6th) (E.) A grape, a wild grape. Sing. and Pl.

كورته *korta'h* or *kūrta'h*, s.f. (3rd) A coat, a short shirt. Pl. ې *ey*. (P كرته)

كور چوړ *kor chawrr* or كور چوړي *kor chawrraey*, adj. House-abandoned or ruined, a term of abuse signifying a base or mean person, a scoundrel; (Fem.) كور چوړِ *kor chawrri*. Pl. (Masc. and Fem.) ي *ī*. كور چوړيه *kor chawrrīah* or چوړيَ *chawrrīa*, interj. Oh rascal! oh base one!

كوركمان *kor-kamān*, s.m. (6th) (E.) Turmeric. Sing. and Pl.; or كور كمن *kor-kaman*, s.m. (6th) (W.) Sing. and Pl.

كورمانه *kor-māna'h*, s.f. (3rd) Domestic economy, household affairs, housewifery. Pl. ې *ey*. See كور والي

كوره *korah*, adj. New, unused, unbleached, unworn (as clothes). (HI كورا)

كورئ *ko-raey*, s.m. (1st) A kind of net for carrying grass or forage. Pl. ي *ī*.

كوري *kūrī*, A word used in driving away donkeys or horses. كوري كول *kūrī kawul*, verb trans. To drive away a donkey or horse.

كوړ *korr*, s.m. (2nd) Leprosy. Pl. كوړونه *korr-ūnah*. (s كوڙهه)

كوړمه *korrma'h*, s.f. (3rd) Family, wife, household, etc. Pl. ې *ey*.

كوړه *korra'h*, s.f. (3rd) A hole or pit made in the ground to fire into in a game at marbles. Pl. ې *ey*.

كوړي *korrī*, adj. Leprous. 2. A leper; (Fem.) كوړئي *korra'ī*.

كوز *kūz*, adv. Below, beneath, under. كوز و پاس *kūz-o-pās*, Under and over, below and above. كوزيدل *kū-zedal*, verb intrans. To descend, to sink, to drop, to come down, to alight, to settle, etc. Pres. كوزيږي *kū-zejzī* (W.) or كوزيږي *kū-zegī* (E.); past كوز شه *kūz shah* or وُ شه *wu-shah*; fut. كوز به شي *kūz bah shī* or به وُ شي *bah wu-shī*; imp. كوز شه *kūz shah* or وُ شه *wu-shah*; act. part. كوزيدونكي *kūze-dūnkaey* or كوزيدوني *kūzedūnaey*; past part كوز *kūz* or كوز شوي *kūz shawaey*; verb. n. كوزيدنه *kūzedana'h*. كوزول *kūzawul*, verb trans. To make or cause to descend, to cause or make come down or alight, etc. Pres. كوزوي *kūzawī*; past كوز كړ *kūz karr* or وُ كړ *wu-karr*; fut. كوز به كړي *kūz bah krrī* or به وُ كړي *bah wu-krrī*; imp. كوز كړه *kūz krrah* or وُ كړه *wu-krrah*; act. part. كوزوونكي *kūza-wūnkaey* or كوزووني *kūzawūnaey*; past part. كوز كړي *kūz karraey*; verb. n. كوزونه *kūza-wunah*.

كوز كتل *kūz katal*, verb trans. To look down; to be sick at stomach, to feel nausea.

په اوږو كوزول *pah aojzo kūzawul*, verb trans. To receive on one's shoulder, or take on the shoulder (as a person from a wall or window) and lower him down.

كوزده *koz-da'h*, s.f. (3rd) Betrothal, affiance, asking in marriage. Pl. ې *ey*. كوزده كول *koz-da'h kawul*, verb trans. To affiance, to betroth. See كوژده and كژدنه

كوزغالي *kūz-ghālaey*, s.m. (1st) A dog's basin or platter. Pl. ي *ī*; or كوزغلي *kūz-ghalaey*. Pl. ي *ī*.

P كوزه *kūza'h*, s.f. (3rd) An earthen vessel for water with a spout, a gugglet. Pl. ې *ey*.

كوژدنه *kojz-dana'h*, s.f. (3rd) (W.) Betrothal, affiance, asking in marriage. Pl. ې *ey*. كوژدنه كول *kojz-dana'h kawul*, verb trans. To betroth, to affiance. See كژدنه and كوزده

كوږ *kojz*, adj. Crooked, bent, angular, twisted, distorted. (Pl.) كاږه *kājzah*; (Fem.) كږه *ka-jza'h*. (Pl.) كږې *kajzey*. See (E) كوك, كريدل, and كږول. كږې سترګې *kajzey stargey*, Crooked or squinting eyes. (W.)

كوږ *kojz*, s.m. (W.) (4th) A hyena. Pl. كاږه *kājzah*. See كوګ

كوږل *k'wajzal* (W.), verb trans. To endeavour, to essay, to make effort or exertion, to strive, to attempt, to show application, to study. Pres. كوږي *k'wajzī*; past وُ كوږل *wu-k'wajzal*; fut. وُ به كوږي *wu bah k'wajzī*; imp. وُ كوږه *wu-k'wajzah*; act. part. كوږونكي *k'wajzūn-kaey* or كوږوني *k'wajzūnaey*; past part. كوږلي *k'wajzalaey*; verb. n. كوږنه *k'wajz-ana'h*.

كوږ ووږ *kojz-wojz*, adj. Very much bent, quite crooked, all manner of ways. Pl. كاږه واږه *kājzah-wājzah*; (Fem.) كږه وږه *kajza'h-wa-jza'h*. Pl. كږې وږې *kajzey-wajzey*. كږې پښې *kajzey pshey* (W.) or ښپې *khpey* (E.) Bandy-legged, bow-legged, knock-kneed.

كوږه *k'wajzah* (W.) or كوګه *k'wagah* (E.) or وُ كوږه *wu-k'wajzah* or وُ كوګه *wu-k'wagah* (imp. of كوږل), Try, endeavour, see what thou canst do, etc.

P كوس *kos*, s.m. (2nd) A large kettle drum or cymbal. Pl. كوسونه *kosūnah*.

كوسي *ko-saey*, s.m. (1st) A coat or robe made of felt, with long sleeves, a felt *choga'h*. Pl. ي *ī*.

P كوشش *ko-shish*, s.m. (2nd) Effort, endeavour. exertion, attempt, application, study. Pl. كوششونه *ko-shishūnah*. كوشش كول *ko-shish kawul*, verb trans. To attempt, to endeavour, to make effort, to study.

كوښښ *ko-shish* (W.), s.m. (2nd) (from P كوشش) Effort, endeavour, exertion, attempt, study, application. Pl. كوښښونه *ko-shishūnah*. كوښښ كول *ko-shish kawul*, verb trans. To strive, to endeavour, make effort, essay.

كوښلي *kūkhalaey*, adj. Pretty, handsome, good-looking, graceful, comely, fair, bonny; (Fem.) كوښلې *kūkhali*. Pl. (Masc. and Fem.) ي *ī*. See ښكلي and كښلي

كوښه *ko-sha'h* (W.) or *ko-kha'h* (E.), s.f. (3rd) A shoe, a slipper (generally of a female). Pl. ې *ey*. See پيزار and پيزره

كوغالي *ko-ghālaey*, s.m. (1st) A hole made in the centre of a dish of rice, etc., filled with oil or melted butter. Pl. ي *ī*. Also كغالي *kaghālaey*. Pl. ي *ī*. See تغالي

S كوك *kūk*, s.m. (5th) A loud noise, outcry.

2. Sobbing, crying, blubbering. Pl. كوكهار *kūka-hār* or كوكار *kū-kār*, etc. كوك وهل *kūk wahal*, verb trans. To sob, to cry, to blubber, to raise an outcry.

كوكړي *kūkuraey*, s.m. (1st) A puppy, a cub, a whelp. Pl. ي *ī*. See كوتري and كنكري

كوكړي *kū-karraey*, s.m. (1st) A large round cake of bread, baked when a child is first able to place its feet to the ground without assistance. It is then trundled along on its edge after the child, that its daily bread may follow it. The cake is afterwards cut up and given to the poor. Pl. ي *ī*.

P كوكنار *kok-nār*, s.m. (6th) The poppy. Sing. and Pl.

كوكه *kūka'h*, s.f. (3rd) Noise, outcry, complaint, lamentation. 2. Report, fame, rumour. Pl. ې *ey*. كوكه وهل *kūka'h wahal*, verb trans. To complain, to lament, to cry out. 2. To report, to speak about.

كوكوړي *kokorraey*, s.m. (1st) A round cake of bread, a bannock, bread baked in the ashes. Pl. ي *ī*. See ككوري

كوږ *kog*, adj. Crooked, bent, distorted, twisted, angular. (E.) Pl. کاګه *kāgah*; (Fem.) کګه *kaga'h*. (Pl.) کګې *kagey*. كوږ ووږ *kog-wog*, Very much bent, quite crooked. (Pl.) کاګه واګه *kāgah-wāgah*; (Fem.) کګه وګه *kaga'h-waga'h*. (Pl.) کګې وګې *kagey wagey*. کګي سترګي *kagey stargey*, Crooked or squinting eyes. کږ والي *kag-wālaey*, s.m. (1st) Crookedness, bend, twist, wryness. Pl. والي *wālī*; or کږ ليچ *kag-lech*, s.m. (2nd). Pl. کږ ليچونه *kag-lech-ūnah*. See کګيدل , کوږ, and کګول

كوږ *kog*, s.m. (4th) (E.) A hyena. Pl. کاګه *kā-gah*. See کوږ

كوګل *k'wagal* (E.), To endeavour, to essay, to make effort or exertion, to strive, to attempt, to show application, to study. See conjugation of کوړل and substitute ګ for ړ

كول *kawul*, verb trans. To do, to act, to perform, to operate, commit, perpetrate, exercise, inflict, practice; to form, make, set, put in execution, etc. This verb is used together with کړل as an auxiliary, and has no past part., but uses that of the latter infinitive. Pres. كوي *kawī*, کا *kā*, کاندِ *kāndi* or كوينَ *kawīna*; past وُ که *wu-kah*, وُ کا *wu-kā*, وُ کَ *wu-ka*, or وُ کې *wu-kaey* (W.); fut. وُ به کي *wu bah kī*, وُ به کا *wu bah kā*, or وُ به کاندِ *wu bah kāndi*; imp. که *kah*, وُ که *wu-kah*, كوه *kawah*, or وُ كوه *wu-kawah*; act. part. كوونكي *kawūnkaey* or كوونې *kawūnaey*; past part. کړي *karraey*; verb. n. كونه *kawuna'h*.

كول *kūl*, adj. Of the same age, a companion, a cotemporary, born in the same year; (Fem.) كوله *kūla'h*. See همزولي

كول *kol*, s.m. (2nd) A family, a house, a race or tribe of people. (corrup. of کهول) Pl. كولونه *kolūnah*.

سر كول *sir-kol*, s.m. (2nd) A mill dam. Pl. سر كولونه *sir-kol-ūnah*.

كولنډ *ko-landd*, s.m. (2nd) A block of wood, fastened to the neck of an ox or cow to prevent their straying. Pl. كولنډونه *ko-landdūnah*.

كوليار *kol-yārr*, s.m. (6th) Name of a tree (Bauhinia variegata). Sing. and Pl.

كوم *kom*, int. pron. What? which? generally applied to objects inanimate. Sing and Pl.; (Fem.) كومه *koma'h*. See کم and کمه

P كومک *kūmak*, s.m. (2nd) Aid, help, assistance. 2. A reserve. Pl. كومكونه *kūmakūnah*. كومكي *kūmakī*, s.m. (5th) An aider, a helper, an assistant. Pl. كومكيان *kūmakīān*. كومكۍ *kūmaka'ī*, s.f. (6th). Sing. and Pl. كومک ورکول *kūmak war-kawul*, verb trans. To aid, to render aid, assistance, help. See کمک

كومي *kūmaey*, s.m. (1st) The palate, the ridge or slit in the roof of the mouth. Pl. ي *ī*. See کام

كونتر *koun-tar*, s.m. (5th) A pigeon, a wood-pigeon. Pl. كونتران *koun-tarān*. كونتره *koun-tara'h*, s.f. (3rd) A hen pigeon. 2. The whole species. Pl. ې *ey*. صحرائي كونتره *ṣaḥ-rāna'ī koun-tara'h* or صحرايي كونتره *ṣaḥ-rāa'ī koun-tara'h*, A wild or wood-pigeon. See كوتر

كونټي *kūnttaey*, s.m. (1st) A stick with a crook

at the end of it, a shepherd's crook. Pl. ي *ī*.

كونځۍ *kon-tsa'ī*, s.f. (6th) The long or braided hair of a woman, a plait, a braid. Sing. and Pl. See كوځۍ

كونډه *kūndda'h*, s.f. (3rd) A widow. 2. A fish hook, a ring or staple for a door. Pl. ئ *ey*. See نوكوښ

كونسټ *kūn-satt*, s.m. (5th) Bread baked under the ashes, bread which has fallen into the ashes. Pl. كونستان *kūnsattān*. 2. adj. Scorched, shrivelled, shrunk up, as from fire or frost-bites; (Fem.) كونسته *kūn-satta'h*.

كونسته *kon-satta'h*, s.f. (3rd) Foundation, basis, root, used only as a term of reproach, as كونسته دِ وُ خيژه *kon-satta'h di wu-khejzah*, Be thy foundation destroyed! may misfortune befal thee! Pl. ئ *ey*. See بونسټ

كون سوي *kūn sawaey*, adj. (past part.) Rubbed from riding, or from riding without a saddle (*lit.* backside rubbed); (Fem.) كون سوِ *kūn sawi*. Pl. (Masc. and Fem.) ي *ī*. كون سوي كيدل *kūn sawaey kedal*, verb intrans. To lose leather, to be rubbed from riding.

كونكَی *kon-kaey*, adj. Small, diminutive, little, less; (Fem.) كونكۍ *konka'ī*. See كمكي

كونګري *kūngraey*, s.m. (1st) A pup, a puppy, a whelp, a cub. Pl. ي *ī*. كونګرۍ *kūngra'ī*, s.f. (6th). Sing. and Pl. See كنكري and كوكري

كونه *kūna'h*, s.f. (3rd) The backside (Podex). Pl. ئ *ey*. كوني *kūnī*, s.m. (5th) A catamite, a eunuch. Pl. كونيګان *kūnīgān*; or كونيكي *kūnī-gaey*, s.m. (1st). Pl. ي *ī*. كونه ستركي *kūna'h-starkaey* or كونستركي *kūna-starkaey*, s.m. (1st) A clout, a child's napkin. Pl. ي *ī*.

كوني *kūnaey*, s.m. (1st) A tick, a dog or sheep louse. Pl. ي *ī*. See ورارِه and كنه

كونَی *kūnaey*, s.m. (1st) Lime, mortar. Pl. ي *ī*. See چونه and اهاك

كوني كبر *kūnī-kabar*, s.m. (5th) A crab. Pl. كوني كبران *kūnī-kabarān*. See كوي كبر

كوڼر *korrn*, s.m. (5th) A large species of tick or louse, infesting dogs and cattle. Pl. كوڼران *korrnān*. See كوني

كوڼر *korrn*, adj. Deaf, hard of hearing. Pl. كاڼره *kārrnah*; (Fem.) كڼره *karrna'h*. Pl. كڼرئ *karrney*. ټپ كوڼر *ttap korrn*, Deaf as a post. كوڼر والَی *korrn-wālaey*, s.m. (1st) Deafness, hardness of hearing, surdity. Pl. والي *wālī*; or كڼروالَی *karrn-wālaey*, etc. ګڼريدل *karrne-dal*, verb trans. To become or grow deaf, to be hard of hearing. Pres. كڼريږي *karrne-jzī* (W.) or كڼريكي *karrne-gī* (E.); past كوڼر شه *korrn shah* or وُ شه *wu-shah*; fut. كوڼر به شي *korrn bah shī* or به وُ شي *bah wu-shī*; imp. كوڼر شه *korrn shah* or وُ شه *wu-shah*; act. part. كڼريدونكَی *karrne-dūnkaey* or كڼريدونَی *karrne-dūnaey*; past part. كوڼر *korrn* or كوڼر شوَی *korrn shawaey*; verb. n. كڼريدنه *karrne-dana'h* or كڼريده *karrnedah*. كڼرول *karrnawul*, verb trans. To make deaf, to cause deafness. Pres. كڼروي *karrnawī*; past كوڼر كړ *korrn karr* or وُ كړ *wu-karr*; fut. كوڼر به كړي *korrn bah krrī* or به وُ كړي *bah wu-krrī*; imp. كوڼر كړه *korrn krrah* or وُ كړه *wu-krrah*; act. part. كڼروونكَی *karrna-wūnkaey* or كڼروونَی *karrna-wūnaey*; past part. كوڼر كړَی *korrn karraey*; verb. n. كڼرونه *karrnawuna'h*.

كوهي *kū-haey*, s.m. (1st) A well. Pl. ي *ī*. See څاه

كوي *ko-e*, s.m. (2nd) Itching, titillation. Pl. كويونه *ko-e-ūnah*. كوي كول *ko-e kawul*, verb trans. To itch, to have a desire to scratch; or كويل *ko-yal*, verb trans. Pres. كويي *ko-yī*; past وُ كويه *wu-ko-yah*; fut. وُ به كويي *wu bah ko-yī*; imp. وُ كويه *wu-ko-yah*; act. part. كويونكَی *ko-yūnkaey* or كويونَی *ko-yūnaey*; past part. كويلَی *ko-yalaey*; verb. n. كوينه *ko-yana'h*. See كهه

كويښل *k'wekhal*, verb trans. To write, to pen, to inscribe, to indite, to put or set down in writing. This verb is peculiar to the Khattak tribe, and is imperfect. Past وُ كويښ *wu-k'wekh*; act. part. كويښونكَی *k'wekhūnkaey* or كويښونَی *k'wekhūnaey*; verb. n. كويښنه *k'wekh-ana'h*. The other inflections are taken from كاږل, which see.

كوي كبر *ko-e-kabar*, s.m. (5th) A crab. Pl. كوي كبران *ko-e-kabarān*. See كوني كبر

كوينَ *kawīna*. See كول

كويني *ko-yinaey*, s.m. (1st) The scrapings of a pot, the burnt part of victuals that sticks at the bottom of the pot. Pl. ي *ī*.

كه *kih*, conj. That, as, because, etc. Also used in Persian.

كهاره *kahāra'h*, s.f. (3rd) A large basket or pannier for carrying fruit. Pl. ئ *ey*. See كواره and كاره

كهاره *kuhārra'h*, s.f. (3rd) A ring made of rope stuck up as a mark for arrows. Pl. ئ *ey*.

كهالي *kahā-lī*, s.f. (3rd) Gaping, yawning, stretching. 2. Indolence, laziness. Pl. ئ *a'ī*. كهالي آچول *kahā-lī ācharwul*, verb trans. To yawn, to gape, to stretch out. كهالي كول *kahā-lī kawul*, verb trans. To do anything in a lazy or indolent manner.

P كهتر *kihtar*, adj. Small, little, less, junior, mean; (Fem.) كهتره *kihtara'h*. كهتري *kihtarī*, s.f. (3rd) Smallness, littleness, meanness, mediocrity, insignificance. Pl. ئ *a'ī*.

P كهربا *kah-rubā*, s.f. (6th) Straw attracting, amber. (E.) Sing. and Pl. (W.) Pl. كهرباوي *kah-rubāwī*.

كهند *kuhand*, adj. Old, ancient, veteran (corrup. of P كهن); (Fem.) كهنده *kuhanda'h*; or (W.) كهنگ *kuhang* and كهنگه *kuhanga'h*.

كهول *ka-hol*, s.m. (2nd) A family, a house, a race or tribe of people. Pres. كهولونه *kahol-ūnah* or كهلونه *khol-ūnah*. كهولي *kahol-aey*, s.m. (1st) Domestic affairs, household matters, family affairs. Pl. ي *ī*; or كهول والي *kahol-wālaey*, s.m. (1st) Pl. ي *ī*. See كول

كهه *kaha'h*, s.f. (3rd) Itching, a desire to scratch, titillation. Pl. ئ *ey*. كهه كول *kaha'h kawul*, verb trans. To itch, to have a desire to scratch. See كوي

كهه *kaha'h*, s.f. (3rd) Nausea, sickness at stomach, qualmishness, a qualm. Pl. ئ *ey*. كهيدل *kahe-dal*, verb intrans. To be sick at stomach, to feel nausea, to become qualmish. Pres. كهيږي *kahejzī* (W.) or كهيګي *kahegī* (E.); past وُ كهيده *wu-kahedah*; fut. وُ به كهيږي *wu bah kahejzī* or كهيګي *kahegī*; imp. وُ كهيږه *wu-kahejzah* or وُ كهيګه *wu-kahegah*; act. part. كهيدونكي *kahedūnkaey* or كهيدوني *kahedūnaey*; past part. كهيدلي *kahedalaey*; verb. n. كهيدنه *kahedana'h* or كهيده *kahedah*.

كهئي *kaha'ī*, s.f. (6th) A hoe or kind of pickaxe. 2. The iron axle-tree of a water-mill. 3. (E.) A ditch, a trench, a moat. Sing. and Pl. See كاهي

كهيدل *kahedal*, verb intrans. To be sick at stomach, to feel qualmish. See كهه

كي *kaey* or (Fem.) كئ *ka'ī*, A particle of diminution applied to nouns; as, ډنډ *ddandd*, A pond; ډنډوكي *ddanddūkaey*, A small pond. See Grammar, page 38.

T كيجم *ke-jam*, s.m. (2nd) A peculiar kind of saddle-cloth made from *pashm* or shawl-wool, dyed of various colours, and brought from Badakhshān and Tūrkestān. Called also جايجم *je-jam* and قجري *kajarī* by the Persians. Pl. كيجمونه *ke-jam-ūnah*. كيجم دار *ke-jam dār*, adj. Covered with a *ke-jam* saddle-cloth (a horse).

كيدل *kedal*, sub. verb, To be, to become, used together with شول in forming the passive voice. The former has but three tenses. Pres. كيږي *kejzī* (W.) or كيګي *kegī* (E.); fut. وُ به كيږي *wu bah kejzī* or وُ به كيګي *wu bah kegī*; imp. كيږه *kejzah* or وُ كيږه *wu-kejzah*, or كيګه *kegah* or وُ كيګه *wu-kegah*; act. part. كيدونكي *kedūnkaey* or كيدوني *kedūnaey*; verb. n. كيدنه *kedana'h* or كيده *kedah*. The other inflections are taken from شول, which see.

كيدنه *kedana'h*, s.f. (3rd) (verb. n.) Being, existing, existence, entity, subsistence. Pl. ئ *ey*; or كيده *kedah*, s.m. (6th) Sing. and Pl.

كير *kīr*, s.m. (6th) Rice and milk. Sing. and Pl. (s كهير).

كيرړي *kīr-rraey*, s.m. (1st) The mole-cricket (Gryllus gryllotalpa). Pl. ي *ī*.

كيرئ *kīra'ī*, s.f. (6th) The felloe of a wheel, the exterior part or rim supported by the spokes. See دراكر

كير *kerr*, s.m. (2nd) A hedge made of the branches of the ghaz, or tamarisk. Pl. كيرونه *kerrūnah*.

كيره *kerra'h*, s.f. (3rd) An iron ring in a plough. 2. A kind of basket work made of saplings of the tamarisk, and used for the ceiling of houses. Pl. ي *ey*.

كيږدل *kejzdal*, verb trans. (W.) To place, to put, to set, to arrange, to dispose, to set in order, to range, to rank. This infinitive is imperfect, and requires the aid of كيښول, which see for inflections of both. (E.) كيګدل

P كيش *kesh*, s.m. (2nd) Faith, religion, manner, quality. 2. A kind of cloth, diaper, damask. (HI كهيس). Pl. كيشونه *keshūnah*. كافر كيش *kā-fir kesh*, Prone to infidelity. روي كيش *rawaey kesh*, The quality of a demon or goblin, diablerie, the black art.

كيښودل *ke-khodal*, verb trans. (E.) To place, to put, to arrange, to set in order, etc. This infinitive is imperfect. Past كيښود *ke-khod*; act.part. كيښودونكي *ke-khodūnkaey* or كيښودوني *ke-khodūnaey*; verb. n. كيښودنه *ke-khodana'h*. The remaining inflections are taken from كيګدل See كښيښول and كښيږدل

كيښول *ke-khwal*, verb trans. (E.) To place, to put, to arrange, to dispose, etc, Pres. كيږدي *kejzdī* (W.) or كيګدي *kegdī* (E.); past كيښو *kekho*; fut. كي به ږدي *ke bah jzdī* or كي به ګدي *ke bah gdī*; imp. كيږده *kejzdah* or كيګده *kegdah*; act. part. كيښوونكي *ke-khwūnkaey* or كيښووني *ke-khwūnaey*; past part. ييښي *yekhaey* (from ييښل); verb. n. كيښونه *ke-khwana'h*. See كښيښول

كيښوول *ke-khowul*, verb trans. (E.) To place, to put, etc. This verb is also imperfect. Past كيښو *kekho*; act. part. كيښووونكي *ke-khowūnkaey* or كيښوووني *ke-khowūnaey*; verb. n. كيښوونه *ke-khowun'ah*. See كښيښول

A كيف *kaif* or كيپ *kaip*, s.m. (2nd) Intoxication, drunkenness. Pl. كيفونه *kaif-ūnah* or كيپونه *kaip-ūnah*. كيپ *kaip* or كيف كول *kaif kawul*, verb trans. To intoxicate, to make drunk. كيفي *kaifī* or كيپي *kaipī*, adj. Intoxicated; a drunken man, a drunkard.

A كيفيت *kaifiyat*, s.m. (2nd) (from كيف) Mode, state, condition, circumstances, account, statement. Pl. كيفيتونه *kaifiyatūnah*.

كيكر *kī-kur*, s.m. (6th) The acacia tree. Sing. and Pl. (HI كيكر).

كيګدل *keg-dal*, verb trans. To place, to put, to set, to arrange, etc. This is the Eastern pronunciation, and the verb is imperfect. The inflections will be found with those of كيښول *ke-khwal*, which see.

كيل *kīl*, s.m. (2nd) The marks of a carriage wheel, a furrow made by a plough, a rut, a path, a track, a trace, etc. Pl. كيلونه *kīlūnah*.

كيلك *kī-lak*, s.m. (2nd) A cord for fastening the scabbard to the hilt of a sword. 2. A fastening for a horse's feet to prevent his straying. Pl. كيلكونه *kī-lak-ūnah*. See هكيل and شكيل

S كيله *kela'h*, s.f. (3rd) The fruit of the plantain or banāna, the name of the tree. Pl. ي *ey*.

كيمخت *kī-mukht*, s.m. (2nd) The leather of a horse or ass, shagreen. Pl. كيمختونه *kī-mukht-ūnah*. Also written كيمخ *kī-mukh*, etc.

G كيميا *kī-miyā*, s.f. (6th) Alchemy, chemistry. (E.) Sing. and Pl. (W.) Pl. كيمياوي *kī-miyāwī*. كيميا كول *kī-miyā kawul*, verb trans. To work miracles, to do anything wonderful.

كيمياګر *kī-miyā-gar*, s.m. (5th) An alchemist, a chymist. Pl. كيمياګر *kī-miyā-gær*. كيميا ګره *kī-miyā-gara'h*, s.f. (3rd). Pl. ي *ey*. كيميا ګري *kī-miyā-garī*, s.f. (3rd) Alchemy, chemistry. Pl. ئ *a'ī*.

كيناستل *ke-nāstal*, verb intrans. (E.) To sit, to sit down, to loll, to recline. Pres. كيني *ke-nī*; past كيناست *ke-nāst*; fut. كي به ني *ke bah nī*; imp. كينه *ke-nah*; act. part. كيناستونكي *ke-nāstūnkaey* or كيناستوني *ke-nāstūnaey*; past part. كيناستلي *ke-nāstalaey* or كيناستي *ke-nāstaey*; verb. n. كيناستنه *ke-nāstana'h*. See (W.) كښيناستل

كيند *kīnd*, s.m. (2nd) A darwesh's habit, a ragged garment. Pl. كيندونه *kīndūnah*. See كند

كينول *ke-nawul*, verb trans. To seat, to make to sit, to locate, to station. Pres. كينوي *ke-*

nawī; past کيناوه *ke-nāwuh* or کيناوو *ke-nāwo*; fut. کي به نوي *ke bah nawī*; imp. کينوه *ke-nawah*; act. part. کينوونکي *ke-nawūnkaey* or کينووني *ke-nawūnaey*; past part. کينولي *ke-nawulaey*; verb. n. کينونه *ke-nawuna'h*. See کښينول

P کينه *kīna'h*, s.f. (3rd) Malice, spite, rancor, resentment, hatred, grudge. Pl. ئ *ey*.

کينه ور *kīna'h-war*, adj. Malicious, spiteful, rancorous; (Fem.) کينه وره *kīna'h-wara'h*. کينه کول *kīna'h kawul*, verb trans. To show spite or resentment towards any one. کينه لرل *kīna'h laral*, verb trans. To bear a grudge, to nourish malice.

کينړ *kīrrn*, adj. Left, the left side, the left hand side; (Fem.) کينړه *kīrrna'h*. کينړ لاس *kīrrn lās*, s.m. (2nd) The left hand. Pl. کينړ لاسونه *kīrrn lāsūnah*. کينړ لور *kīrrn lor*, s.m. (9th) The left side. Sing. and Pl. See کږ and کڼخي

گ

گ *gāf*, called کاف عجمي *kāf-i-ạjamī*, the twenty-sixth letter of the Persian, is the thirty-third of the Pushto alphabet. The corresponding letter of the Sanskrit is ग, and its sound in English is as *g* in 'good.' The Eastern Afghāns use this letter where the Western tribes use ږ *jze*, and vice versâ.

گاټي *gā-ttaey*, s.m. (1st) An earthern ball, used with a sling to frighten away birds, a pellet, a ball. 2. A large round stone. Pl. ي *ī*. See گټ and گټه

گاټئ *gā-tta'ī*, s.f. (6th) A small stone placed at the bottom of a pipe bowl to keep the tobacco or fire from getting into the stem. Sing. and Pl.

گاډي *gāddaey*, s.m. (1st) A cart, a wagon, a wheeled carriage in general. Pl. ي *ī*; or (W.) گاډئ *gādda'ī*, s.f. (6th) Sing. and Pl. گاډي وان *gāddaey-wān*, s.m. (5th) A cart-man, a coach-man, a cart-driver. Pl. گاډي وانان *gāddaey-wānān*. (S گاڙي).

گاډيره *gāddera'h*, s.f. (3rd) Mixed grain. Pl. گاډيري *gādderaey*, A dish composed of various kinds of grain; or گاډيرون *gāddcrūn*.

گازره *gāzara'h*, s.f. (3rd) A carrot (Daucus carota). Pl. ئ *ey*. (S گاجر). See (W.) زردکه

گالل *gāl-al*, verb trans. To keep, to preserve, to guard, to keep guard, to attend to, etc. 2. To terminate, to complete, to bring to an end.

P گام *gām*, s.m. (2nd) Pace. Pl. گامونه *gāmūnah*.

گانده *gāndah*, s.m. (6th) The future, the coming time. Sing. and Pl. 2. adv. To-morrow, the morrow. See صبا

گانډئ *gāndda'ī*, s.f. (6th) The long beam of a Persian wheel, to which the bullocks or camels are fastened. Sing. and Pl.

گانګوړه *gān-gūrra'h*, s.f. (3rd) Speaking indistinctly or through the nose, through weakness, cold, etc. Pl. ئ *ey*. گانګوړه کيدل *gān-gūrra'h kedal*, verb intrans. To lisp, to speak indistinctly or through the nose. گانګوړه کول *gān-gūrra'h kawul*, verb trans. To make to lisp or speak indistinctly.

گاڼره *gārrna'h*, s.f. (3rd) Pledge, pawn. Pl. ئ *ey*. گاڼره کول *gārrna'h kawul*, verb trans. To pawn, to pledge. (S گهنا).

گاڼرئ *gārrna'ī*, s.f. (6th) An oil-press. Sing. and Pl. گاڼرئ وال *gārrna'ī-wāl*, s.m. (5th) An oil-presser. Pl. گاڼرئ والان *gārrna'ī-wālān*.

P گاودم *gāw-dum*, adj. Thick at one end and thin at the other, taper. 2. Sloping, acclivity, descent; (Fem.) گاودمه *gāw-duma'h*.

گاوز *gā-waz*, s.m. (5th) A hill-goat, a chamois. Pl. گاوزان *gā-wazān*. گاوزه *gāwaza'h*, s.f. (3rd) Pl. ئ *ey*.

گاولي *gāw-laey*, s.m. (1st) A kind of sandal made of leather. Pl. ي *ī*.

گاوميښ *gāw-mesh* (W.), s.m. (5th) A male buffalo. Pl. گاوميښان *gāw-meshān*. گاوميښه *gāw-mesha'h*, s.f. (3rd) A female buffalo. Pl. ئ *ey*. (P گاوميش). See ميښه

گاونډ *gā-wandd*, s.m. (5th) A neighbour, a countryman, an associate. Pl. گاونډان *gā-wanddān*. گاونډه *gā-wandda'h*, s.f. (3rd) Feminine of the above. Pl. ئ *ey*; also گاونډي *gā-wanddaey*, s.m. (1st) Pl. ي *ī*; and گاونډئي *gā-wandda'ī*, s.f. (6th) Sing. and Pl. See گواندي

P گاه *gāh*, s.m. (2nd) Time. 2. Place. Pl. گاهونه *gāhūnah*. (In composition) گاه گاه *gāh-gāh*, adv. Now and then, sometimes, again and again. ښکار گاه *sh'kār-gāh* (W.), or ښکار *kh'kār-gāh* (E.), s.m. (2nd) A place for hunting, a park, a chase. Pl. گاهونه *gāhūnah*. عبادت گاه *æibādat-gāh*, s.m. (2nd) A place of worship, a place of prayer. Pl. گاهونه *gāhūnah*.

گاهر *gā-har*, s.f. (1st) A herd of cattle. Pl. گاهرِ *gā-hari*.

گاهو *gā-hū*, s.m. (5th) A herdsman. Pl. گاهوگان *gā-hūgān*.

گاهي *gā-hī*, s.f. (3rd) A deep wound or sore. Pl. ئي *a'ī*. See گايل

P گاهي *gā-hey*, adv. One time, once, at any time, sometime. گاهي گاهي *gā-hey gā-hey*, At times, now and then, sometimes.

گايل *gā-yil*, adj. Wounded, injured; (Fem.) گايله *gā-yila'h*. گايل کيدل *gā-yil kedal*, verb intrans. To become wounded. گايل کول *gā-yil kawul*, verb trans. To wound. (HI گهايل)

P گبر *gabr*, s.m. (5th) A worshipper of fire, a follower of Sapetman Zoroaster, an infidel. Pl. گبران *gabr-ān*. گبره *gabra'h*, s.f. (3rd) A female fire-worshipper, etc. Pl. ئ *ey*.

گبينه *gabīna'h*, s.f. (3rd) Honey-comb, honey. Pl. ئ *ey*. See گربيني and د مچي کور

گپه *gapa'h*, s.f. (3rd) Prattle, talk, clatter. 2. A lump or clod of mud, as much as can be taken in both the hands. Pl. ئ *ey*. گپي کول *gapey kawul*, verb trans. to chatter, to prattle.

گپي *gapī*, s.f. (3rd) A cord used as a bridle, a kind of halter. Pl. ئي *a'ī*. See پائي and خيي

گتمه *gutma'h*, s.f. (3rd) A loop, a ring, a loop in the string of a sling, a button hole, a loop for a button. 2. A thimble generally made of leather. Pl. ئ *ey*. See گټمه and گټمئي

گته *guta'h*, s.f. (3rd) A finger, a toe. 2. A ring. Pl. ئ *ey*. بټه گته *batta'h-guta'h*, s.f. (3rd) The thumb, the great toe. Pl. ئ *ey*. See گوته

گټ *gatt*, s.m. (2nd) A large round stone, a rock. 2. A black or louring cloud. Pl. گټونه *gattūnah*. Also گټه *gatta'h*, s.f. (3rd). Pl. ئ *ey*. See گاټي

گټ *gutt*, s.m. (2nd) A corner, a side. 2. A hole dug in the wall of a house by thieves. Pl. گټونه *guttūnah*. See کوټ

گټل *gattal*, verb trans. To gain, to acquire, to win, to get, to realize, to derive, to come by, to bag, to profit, to turn to profit. 2. To worst, to beat, to check-mate, to nonsuit, etc. Pres. گټي *gattī*; past وُ گاټه *wu-gāttah*; fut. وُ به گټي *wu bah gattī*; imp. وُ گټه *wu-gattah*; act. part. گټونکئ *gattūnkaey* or گټونئ *gattūnaey*; past part. گټلئ *gattalaey*; verb. n. گټنه *gattana'h* or گټه *gattah*.

گټمه *guttma'h*, s.f. (3rd) A loop for a rope or for a button, a noose, a ring. 2. A thimble. Pl. ئ *ey*. See گتمه and گته

گټمئي *guttma'ī*, s.f. (6th) A thimble. Sing. and Pl. See گتمه

گټنه *gattana'h*, s.f. (3rd) (verb. n. of گټل) Profit, advantage, gain, emolument, produce, earning, gaining, winning, etc. Pl. ئ *ey*.

گټه *gatta'h*, s.f. (3rd) A large round stone or pebble. 2. Profit, gain, advantage, earning. Pl. ئ *ey*. گټه وټه *gatta'h watta'h*, s.f. (3rd) Profit, winnings, produce, gain. Pl. گټي وټي *gattey-wattey*. گټه کول *gatta'h kawul*, verb trans. To gain, to win, to earn, to acquire.

گټئي *gitta'ī*, s.f. (6th) A small piece of broken flat stone, a potsherd, a shard. 2. The gravel. Sing. and Pl.

گټي *gittaey*, s.m. (1st) A pebble, a small round stone. Pl. ي *ī*. (W.) See گاټي

گټين *gittīn*, adj. Stony, gravelly, pebbly; (Fem.) گټينه *gittīna'h*.

گڅ *gats*, adj. Left, the left side,; (Fem.) گڅه *gatsa'h*. گڅ لاس *gats lās*, The left hand.

گڅي *gatsaey*, s.m. (1st) A left-handed person. 2. adj. Left-handed, having the left hand stronger than the right. Pl. ي *ī*. گڅئي *gatsa'ī*, s.f. (6th) A left-handed female. 2. adj. Left-handed. Sing. and Pl.

HI گچ *gach*, s.m. (6th) Mortar, lime, cement. Sing. and Pl.

P گدا *gadā* or گداي *gadā-e*, s.m. (5th) A beggar, a mendicant. Pl. گدايان *gadā-yān* or *gadā-e-ān*. گدائي *gadā'ī*, s.f. (3rd) Begging, beggary, poverty, mendicity. Pl. ئي *a'ī*. گدائي کول *gadā'ī kawul*, verb trans. To beg.

گدل *g'dal*, verb trans. (E.) To place, to put, to lodge, to post, to fix, to establish, to plant, to lay, to set. Pres. گدي *g'dī*; past کيښو *ke-kho* (from کيښول); fut. و به گدي *wu bah g'dī*; imp. گده *g'dah*; act. part. کيښونکي *ke-khūnkaey* or کيښوني *ke-khūnaey*; past part. يښلي *yekhalaey* (from ييښل); verb. n. ييښنه *yekhana'h*. See ږدل

گدر *gudar*, s.m. (2nd) A ferry, a ford. 2. A place made on the banks of a river in order that cattle may be able to come and drink. Pl. گدرونه *gudarūnah*. گدر پوري وتل *gudar pūrī watal*, verb intrans. To ford a river, to cross over. (P گذر)

گډ *gædd*, s.m. (5th) A ram, the male of the sheep. 2. The mountain sheep. Pl. گډان *gæddān*. گډه *gædda'h*, s.f. (3rd) An ewe. 2. A woman, a female (in a contemptible sense). Pl. ئي *ey*. See مږ

گډ *gadd*, adj. Mixed, mingled, intermixed, commingled, hashed up, imbued, infused, compounded, blended, amalgamated; (Fem.) گډه *gadda'h*. گډ وډ *gadd wadd*, adv. (Masc.) Topsy-turvy, higgledy-piggledy, in confusion; (Fem.) گډه وډه *gadda'h wadda'h*. گډه وډه ږيره *gadda'h wadda'h jzīra'h* (W.) or گيره *gīra'h* (E.) A grisly beard. گډ وډ گيري or ږيري *gadd wadd gīraey* or *jzīraey*, s.m. (1st) A grey-beard, a middle aged man. Pl. ي *ī*. See کروينبته.

گډي وروځي *gaddey wrūdzey*, Eyebrows meeting over the nose. گډيده د بازار *gaddedah da bāzār*, The bustle of a market. گډيدل *gaddedal*, verb intrans. To become united, to mix, to mingle, to become entangled with, to be jumbled together, to be huddled together. 2. To dance. 3. To become acquainted or intimate. Pres. گډيږي *gaddejzī* (W.) or گډيگي *gaddegī* (E.); past گډ شه *gadd shah* or و شه *wu-shah*; fut. گډ به شي *gadd bah shī* or به و شي *bah wu-shī*; imp. گډ شه *gadd shah* or و شه *wu-shah*; act. part. گډيدونکي *gaddedūnkaey* or گډيدوني *gaddedūnaey*; past part. گډ or گډ شوي *gadd* or *gadd shawaey*; verb. n. گډون *gaddūn*, گډيدنه *gaddedana'h* or گډيده *gaddedah*. گډول *gaddawul*, verb trans. To join, to mix, to mingle, to unite, to associate, to blend, to amalgamate, to infuse, to jumble together, etc. Pres. گډوي *gaddawī*; past گډ کړ *gadd karr* or و کړ *wu-karr*; fut. گډ به کړي *gadd bah krrī* or به و کړي *bah wu-krrī*; imp. گډ کړه *gadd krrah* or و کړه *wu-krrah*; act. part. گډوونکي *gaddawūnkaey* or گډووني *gaddawūnaey*; past part. گډ کړي *gadd karraey*; verb. n. گډونه *gaddawuna'h*.

گډ *gudd*, adj. Lame, crippled, hobbling, injured in the limbs; (Fem.) گډه *gudda'h*. گډ والي *gudd wālaey*, s.m. (1st) Lameness, impaired strength of the body. Pl. والي *wālī*. Also گډ توب *gudd tob*, s.m. (2nd). Pl. توبونه *tobūnah*; and گډ تيا *gudd tīā*, s.f. (6th). (E.) Sing. and Pl.; (W.) Pl. تياوي *tī'āwī*. گډيدل *guddedal*, verb trans. To become lame, crippled. Pres. گډيږي *guddejzī* (W.) or گډيگي *guddegī* (E.); past گډ شه *gudd shah* or و شه *wu-shah*; fut. گډ به شي *gudd bah shī* or به و شي *bah wu-shī*; imp. گډ شه *gudd shah* or و شه *wu-shah*; act. part. گډيدونکي *guddedūnkaey* or گډيدوني *guddedūnaey*; past part. گډ or گډ شوي *gudd* or *gudd shawaey*; verb. n. گډيدنه *guddedana'h* or گډيده *guddedah*. گډول *guddawul*, verb trans. To lame, to cripple in the limbs, to injure. Pres. گډوي *guddawī*; past گډ کړ *gudd karr* or و کړ *wu-karr*; fut. گډ به کړي *gudd bah krrī* or به و کړي *bah wu-krrī*; imp. گډ کړه *gudd krrah* or و کړه *wu-krrah*; act. part. گډوونکي *guddawūnkaey* or گډووني *guddawūnaey*; past part. گډ کړي *gudd karraey*; verb. n. گډونه *guddawuna'h*. گډي ښپي *guddey khpey* (E.) adj. Lame of both legs, lame-legs; or گډي پښي *guddey pshey* (W.) See شل

گدړ *giddarr* or گدر *giddar*, s.m. (5th) A jackal. Pl. گدړان *giddarrān* or گدران *giddarān*.

گدړه *giddarra'h* or گدره *giddara'h*, s.f. (3rd) A female jackal. Pl. ې *ey*. (HI گدڙ).

گدندي *gaddandaey*, s.m. (1st) A dancer. Pl. ي *ī*. گدندۍ *gaddanda'ī*, s.f. (6th) A dancing girl, a female dancer. Sing. and Pl.

گډوري *gæddo-raey*, s.m. (1st) A lamb. Pl. ي *ī*. گډورۍ *gæddo-ra'ī*, s.f. (6th) An ewe lamb. Sing. and Pl. See گډ and وري

گدوزي *guddozaey*, s.m. (1st) A span, the space between the thumb and fore finger. Pl. ي *ī*. See لويشت

گدون *gaddūn*, s.m. (9th) (verb. n.) Mixture, intermixture, intercourse, association. Sing. and Pl. See گديدنه and گديده

گدون *gaddūn*, s.m. (4th) The name of a tribe of Afghāns. 2. A male of the tribe. Pl. گدانه *gaddānah*. گدونه *gaddūna'h*, s.f. (3rd) A female of the above. Pl. ې *ey*.

گدونکي *gaddūnkaey* or گدوني *gaddūnaey*, adj. (act. part.) A dancer; (Fem.) گدونکې *gaddūnki* or گدونې *gaddūni*, A dancing girl, a female dancer. Pl. (Masc. and Fem.) ي *ī*.

گدهل *gadd-hal*, s.m. (2nd) A trough, a tub, a bucket, a pail. Pl. گدهلونه *gadd-halūnah*. See تغار

گدي *guddaey*, s.m. (1st) A lame person, one injured in a limb. Pl. ي *ī*. گدۍ *gudda'ī*, s.f. (6th) A lame female. 2. A doll, a puppet. Sing. and Pl. See ناوکي

گديدنه *gaddedana'h*, s.f. (3rd) (verb. n.) Mixture, mixing, intercourse, association, blending, intermixing. Pl. ې *ey*. Also گديده *gaddedah*, s.m. (6th). Sing. and Pl. See گد

گديره *gadderah*, adj. Mixed, adulterated, alloyed. گديره کيدل *gadderah kedal*, verb intrans. To become mixed, alloyed, adulterated. گديره کول *gadderah kawul*, verb trans. To mix to alloy. See گديدل *gaddedal*, etc.

گديکه *gaddeka'h*, s.f. (3rd) A stilt, a crutch, the support of a spinning wheel. Pl. گديکي *gaddekaey*, A pair of stilts, crutches.

گذار *guzār*, s.m. (2nd) A blow, a stroke, a tap, a knock, a pass, a lunge, a swap, a thrust, a shove, a jog, a shock, a crash, an encounter. Pl. گذارونه *guzārūnah*. گذار کول *guzār kawul*, verb trans. To make a blow, strike, pass, etc.

گذارل *guzāral*, verb trans. To do, to perform (devotions) to complete, to finish. Pres. گذاري *guzārī*; past وگذاره *wu-guzārah*; fut. و به گذاري *wu bah guzārī*; imp. و گذاره *wu-guzārah*; act. part. گذارونکي *guzārūnkaey* or گذاروني *guzārūnaey*; past part. گذارلي *guzāralaey*; verb. n. گذارنه *guzārana'h*. گذاريدل *guzāredal*, verb intrans.; and گذارول *guzārawul*, verb trans. See غزاريدل and غزارول

P گذر *guzar*, s.m. (2nd) A ford, a ferry, a passage. Pl. گذرونه *guzarūnah*. گذر کول *guzar kawul*, verb trans. To ford, to pass a river; or گذر پوري وتل *guzar pūrī watal*, verb intrans.

P گذران *guz-rān*, s.m. (2nd) Life, living, employment, livelihood. Pl. گذرانونه *guz-rānūnah*. گذران کول *guz-rān kawul*, verb trans. To live, to subsist, to spend time or life.

P گر *gar* (In composition), A maker, doer, worker. Pl. گر *gær*; (Fem.) گره *gara'h*.

گر *gar*, s.m. (5th) The sound produced by the wheels of a cart or carriage, rattle or clatter of wheels. Pl. گرهار *gara-hār*.

گران *grān*, adj. (corrup. of گران) Precious, dear. 2. Heavy, important, momentous; (Fem.) گرانه *grāna'h*. گراني *grānī*, s.f. (3rd) Scarcity, dearth, dearness. 2. Weight, importance. Pl. ۍ *a'ī*. گران مايه *grān-māya'h*, adj. Valuable, of great price. گرانيدل *grānedal*, verb intrans. To become dear, valuable, or of high price. Pres. گرانيږي *grānejzī* (W.) or گرانيږي *grānegī* (E.); past گران شه *grān shah* or و شه *wu-shah*; fut. گران به شي *grān bah shī* or و به شي *bah wu-shī*; imp. گران شه *grān shah* or و شه *wu-shah*; act. part. گرانيدونکي *grānedūnkaey* or گرانيدوني *grānedūnaey*; past part. گران *grān* or گران شوي *grān shawaey*; verb. n. گرانيدنه *grānedana'h* or گرانيده *grānedah*. گرانول *grānawul*, verb trans. To make or render dear, or high priced. Pres. گرانوي *grānawī*; past گران کړ *grān karr* or و کړ *wu-karr*; fut. گران به کړي *grān bah* *k<u>rr</u>ī* or به وُ کړي *bah wu-k<u>rr</u>ī*; imp. گران کړه *grān k<u>rr</u>ah* or وُ کړه *wu-k<u>rr</u>ah*; act. part. گرانوونکَي *grānawūnkaey* or گرانوونَي *grānawūnaey*; past part. گران کړَي *grān-ka<u>rr</u>aey*; verb. n. گرانونه *grānawuna'h*.

گربينَي *garbīnaey*, s.m. (1st) Honey-comb. Pl. ي *ī*. See گبينه

گرت *grut*, s.m. (2nd) The space between the fingers and the toes. 2. The angle between the trunk and branch of a tree. 3. Taking between the finger and thumb (as an arrow). Pl. گرتونه *grutūnah*.

گرد *gird*, adj. Round, circular (W.). 2. All, the whole; (Fem.) گرده *girda'h*. (P گرد)

P گرداب *girdāb*, s.m. (2nd) A whirlpool, a gulf, a vortex, an abyss. Pl. گردابونه *girdābūnah*; or گرداو *girdāo*, s.m. (2nd). Pl. گرداوونه *girdāo-ūnah*.

P گردا گرد *gird-ā-gird*, All round, round about, on all sides.

P گردني *gardanī*, s.f. (3rd) A head covering for a horse. Pl. ئ *a'ī*.

P گردون *gardūn*, s.m. (9th) A wheel, a chariot. 2. The heavens, the firmament. 3. Fortune, destiny, chance. Sing. and Pl.

گردي ليچي *gardaey le<u>ch</u>aey*, s.m. (1st) The upper part of the arm above the elbow. Pl. ي *ī*.

گرز *garz*, s.m. (2nd) Dirt, dust, sand, etc. Pl. گرزونه *garzūnah*. گرز وهلي *garz-wahalaey*, adj. Dusty, dirty, covered with dust; (Fem.) گرزوهلِ *garz-wahali*. Pl. (Masc. and Fem.) ي *ī*.

P گرز *gurz*, s.m. (2nd) A mace, a pointed iron club, a battle axe. Pl. گرزونه *gurzūnah*.

گرزندي *gærzandaey*, s.m. (1st) A whirligig, a kind of swing. Pl. ي *ī*. See بنړيچغ and بامبوره

گرزنَي *gær-zanāey*, s.m. (1st) A reel, a spindle. Pl. ي *ī*. See جلك

گرزيدل *gærzedal*, verb intrans. To turn, to turn back, to wheel, to go round, to circumvolve, to spin, to revolve, to walk up and down, etc. Pres. گرزي *gærzī*; past وُ گرزيده *wu-gærzedah*; fut. وُ به گرزي *wu bah gærzī*; imp. وُ گرزه *wu-gærzah*; act. part. گرزيدونكَي *gærzedūnkaey* or گرزيدونَي *gærzedūnaey*; past part. گرزيدلَي *gærzedalaey*; verb. n. گرزيدنه *gærzedana'h* or گرزيده *gærzedah*. گرزول *gærzawul*, verb trans. To turn, to change, to make to turn or gyrate, to wheel, to twirl, to put round or about, to turn back, etc. Pres. گرزوي *gærzawī*; past وُ گرزاوه *wu-gærzāwuh* or گرزاوو *gærzāwo*; fut. وُ به گرزوي *wu bah gærzawī*; imp. وُ گرزوه *wu-gærzawah*; act. part. گرزوونكَي *gærzawūnkaey* or گرزوونَي *gærzawūnaey*; past part. گرزولَي *gærzawulaey*; verb. n. گرزونه *gærzawuna'h*.

گرږل *gar-<u>jz</u>al*, verb trans. To scratch, to tear with the nails, to scrape. (W.) Pres. گرږي *gar-<u>jz</u>ī*; past وُ گرږه *wu-gar-<u>jz</u>ah*; fut. وُ به گرږي *wu bah gar-<u>jz</u>ī*; imp. وُ گرږه *wu-gar-<u>jz</u>ah*; act. part. گرږونكَي *gar-<u>jz</u>ūnkaey* or گرږونَي *gar-<u>jz</u>ūnaey*; past part. گرږلَي *gar-<u>jz</u>alaey*; verb. n. گرږنه *gar-<u>jz</u>ana'h*.

گركنډه *gar-kan<u>dd</u>a'h*, s.f. (3rd) A rolling stone from a mountain. 2. A stone thrown from a hill or the battlements of a castle. Pl. ئ *ey*. See كركنده

گركَي *gar-kaey*, s.m. (1st) The rattle of carriage wheels, or of a cart, or chariot. Pl. ي *ī*. See گر

گرگ *garg*, s.m. (2nd) The scab, the mange. Pl. گرگونه *gargūnah*. گرگَي *gar-gaey*, adj. Scabby, mangy, a mean low fellow. Pl. ي *ī*; (Fem.) گرگئ *gar-ga'ī*. Sing. and Pl. گرگ نيول *garg nīwal*, verb trans. To take the mange or scab (to become mangy).

گرگره *gur-gura'h*, s.f. (3rd) The sloe. Pl. ئ *ey*. See گرنده

گرگس *gar-gas*, s.m. (5th) A vulture. Pl. گرگسان *gar-gasān*. See گنجي

گرگس *gar-gas*, s.m. (2nd) The cavity or interior of the chest, the breast. Pl. گرگسونه *gar-gasūnah*. See كوكل, گوگل, and تټر

گرگه *gar-ga'h*, s.f. (3rd) A log of wood, a piece of unhewn timber. 2. The trunk or stem of a tree or shrub, the stalk of a plant. Pl. ئ *ey*.

P گرم *garm*, adj. Hot, warm. 2. Ardent, active, eager, zealous, choleric, virulent, fiery, passionate, intent on. 2. Thronged or crowded (as a market or assembly); (Fem.). گرمه *garma'h.* گرم کيدل *garm kedal,* verb intrans. To become hot, warm, ardent, angry, etc.; to become thronged (as a market). گرم کول *garm kawul,* verb trans. To make hot, warm, eager, angry, passionate; to throng, to crowd. See تود and تودکي

گرم *guram,* s.m. (2nd) Internal perturbation from grief, anxiety, and the like. 2. A clump of trees. Pl. گرمونه *guramūnah.* See بنړ

گرم *gram,* adj. Confuted, convicted, convinced. 2. Censured, reproached, rebuked, blamed; (Fem.) گرمه *grama'h.* گرم والَي *gram-wālaey,* s.m. (1st) Reproach, blame, rebuke, censure. 2. Confutation, conviction. Pl. والي *wālī.* گرم کيدل *gram kedal,* verb intrans. To be rebuked, blamed, censured. گرم کول *gram kawul,* verb trans. To rebuke, to censure.

گرمکه *gar-maka'h,* s.f. (3rd) A small pustule. Pl. گرمکۍ *gar-makey,* The prickly heat.

گرمه *garmah,* s.m. (6th) A water-melon. Sing. and Pl. See سرده

P گرمي *garmī,* s.f. (3rd) Warmth, heat, fieriness, eagerness, choler, zeal. 2. Throng of a market. 3. Venereal disease. Pl. ئ *a'ī.* د گرمۍ موسم *da garma'ī mosam* or وخت *wakht,* The hot season, the summer. See تود والي and تودونه

گرنډه *garandda'h,* s.f. (3rd) A aloe. Pl. ۍ *ey.* See ګرګره

گرو *grau,* s.m. (2nd) (from P *girau*) A pledge, a pawn, a gage. 2. A bet, a wager. Pl. گروونه *grau-ūnah.* گرو کيدل *grau kedal,* verb intrans. To become pledged or pawned, to be mortgaged. گرو کول *grau kawul,* verb trans. To pawn, to pledge, to mortgage.

گروليَ *grol-baey,* s.m. (1st) Phlegm, mucus from the chest. Pl. ي *ī.*

گرول *garawul,* verb trans. To scratch, to scrape, to rub slightly with the nails. Also written گرهول *garah-wul.* Pres. گروي *garawī;* past وُ گراوه *wu-garāwuh* or گراوو *garāwo;* fut. وُ به گروي *wu bah garawī;* imp. وُ گروه *wu-garawah;* act. part. گروونکَي *garawūnkaey* or گرووني *garawūnaey;* past part. گروليَ *garawulaey;* verb. n. گروونه *garawuna'h.*

گروه *g'rawa'h,* s.f. (3rd) The collar-bone, the collar of a dress. 2. A loop, a button loop. Pl. ۍ *ey.* See گريوه (s گريوا, The neck).

P گروه *guroh,* s.m. (2nd) A band, a troop, a gang, a company, a crew, a people, a tribe, etc. Pl. گروهونه *gurohūnah.*

گروهيدل *grohedal,* verb intrans. To follow, to admire, to adore, to believe, to place confidence in, to be attracted, captivated. Pres. گروهيږي *grohejzī* (W.) or گروهيگي *grohegī* (E.); past وُ گروهيده *wu-grohedah;* fut. وُ به گروهيږي *wu bah grohejzī* or گروهيگي *grohegī;* imp. وُ گروهيږه *wu-grohejzah* or گروهيگه *grohegah;* act. part. گروهيدونکَي *grohedūnkaey* or گروهيدونَي *grohedūnaey;* past part. گروهيدليَ *grohedalaey;* verb. n. گروهيدنه *grohedana'h.*

P گريوان *gire-wān,* s.m. (2nd) The collar or cape of a garment. 2. The neck (fig.). Pl. گريوانونه *gire-wānūnah.*

گريوه *grewa'h,* s.f. (3rd) A collar or cape of a dress. 2. The collar bone. 3. A button-hole, a loop. Pl. ۍ *ey.* See گروه and گريوان

گړ *garr,* s.m. (2nd) A fort, a castle, a tower. Pl. گړونه *garrūnah.* (s گڑھ).

گړدۍ *garr-da'ī,* s.f. (6th) The leather whisp of a spindle, the whirl of a spindle. Sing. and Pl.

گړنج *g'rranj,* s.m. (5th) The tinkling of a bell, the ring of money, chime, jingle, clink. Pl. گړنجهار *g'rranjahār.* گړنجاوو *g'rranjāwū,* s.m. (5th) A child's rattle. Pl. گړنجاووگان *g'rranjāwūgān.* See چنچڼري

گړنج *gurranj,* s.m. (2nd) A low sound or voice, a whisper of anything, speaking with suspicion or timorous caution, breathing. Pl. گړنجونه *gurranjūnah.* گړنج آچول *gurranj āchawul,* verb trans. To whisper, to speak with caution and suspicion.

گړنجيدل *g'rranje-dal,* verb intrans. To tinkle, to chime, to ring, to jingle, to chink. Pres. گړنجيږي *g'rranje-jzī* (W.) or گړنجيگي *g'rranje-gī* (E.); past وُ گړنجيده *wu-g'rranje-dah;* fut.

گرنجيږي و به wu bah g'rranje-jzī or گرنجيګي g'rranje-gī; imp. و گرنجيږه wu-g'rranjejzah or گرنجيګه g'rranjegah; act. part. گرنجيدونکي g'rranjedūnkaey or گرنجيدوني g'rranjedūnaey; past part. گرنجيدلي g'rranjedalaey; verb. n. گرنجيدنه g'rranjedana'h or گرنجيده g'rranjedah. گرنجول g'rranjawul, verb trans. To make to tinkle or jingle, to ring, to clink. Pres. گرنجوي g'rranjawī; past و گرنجاوه wu-g'rranjāwuh or و گرنجاوو wu-g'rranjāwo; fut. و به گرنجوي wu bah g'rranjawī; imp. و گرنجوه wu-g'rranjawah; act. part. گرنجوونکي g'rranjawūnkaey or گرنجووني g'rranjawūnaey; past part. گرنجولي g'rranjawulaey; verb. n. گرنجونه g'rranjawuna'h.

گرندي garrandaey, adj. Swift, fleet, nimble, fast, speedy, rapid, brisk; (Fem.) گرندۍ garranda'ī. گرندي توب garrandaey tob, s.m. (2nd) Velocity, speed, celerity, swiftness, fleetness, quickness. Pl. توبونه tobūnah. گرندي کول garrandaey kawul, verb trans. To make haste to speed, to press forward, to hie, to hasten.

گرنګ garrang, s.m. (2nd) An abyss, a deep hollow, a shaft, a gulf, a crater, a cavity. Pl. گرنګونه garrangūnah.

گرنګ g'rrang, s.m. (6th) Mucus from the nose. Sing. and Pl. گرنګان g'rrangān, adj. A person from whose nose mucus is always running (as a child), snotty-nosed; (Fem.) گرنګنه g'rrangana'h.

گروبي gurrobaey, s.m. (1st) Sherbet, sugar and water, eau sucré, lemonade, etc. Pl. ي ī. See گره

گرونج garr-wanj, s.m. (2nd) (W.) A stand for water vessels, a kind of wooden stool. Pl. گرونجونه garr-wanjūnah. (s گهڙونچا)

گرونجۍ garr-wanja'ī, s.f. (6th) See preceding. Sing. and Pl.

گره gurra'h, s.f. (3rd) Raw sugar, molasses, treacle. Pl. ې ey. (s گڙ).

گرۍ garra'ī, s.f. (6th) A space of twenty-four minutes. 2. A large pool of rain water, a mere. Sing. and Pl. (P گري, s گهڙي).

P گز gaz, s.m. (2nd) A measure, a yard, an ell. Pl. گزونه gazūnah. گزيدل gazedal, verb intrans. To be measured. گزول gazawul, verb trans. To measure.

گزاري gazārī, s.m. (1st) Pl. Chaff, refuse from sifting, worthless matter. Sing. not used; or (W.) گزاري gazāraey, s.f. (3rd) Pl. See دروزه

گزک gazak, adj. Festered, purulent, frost-bitten, etc. 2. s.m. (2nd) Corruption, decay, putrefaction. Pl. گزکونه gazakūnah. گزک آخستل gazak ākhistal, verb trans. To fester.

گزن guzan, s.m. (2nd) The palsy, paralysis. Pl. گزنونه guzanūnah. گزن وهلي guzan wahalaey, adj. Palsied, struck with the palsy; (Fem.) گزن وهلې guzan wahali. Pl. (Masc. and Fem.) ي ī. گزن وهل guzan wahal, verb trans. To palsy, to paralyze. See افليج

گڅاري gadzārey, s.f. (3rd) Pl. Chaff, refuse, siftings, any worthless thing, heads of corn left after threshing. Sing. not used. See also دروزه and گزاري

گږ gajz, adj. Piebald, party-coloured, motley, mottled, dappled, tattooed, spotted with the leprosy. 2. A mixed breed, hybrid, a person whose descent is unknown; (Fem.) گږه gajza'h; گږ ويښتي gajz weshtey, Grizzled or grizzly hair, a person with grizzly hair. گږ کيدل gajz kedal, verb intrans. To become grizzly, mottled, spotted, etc. گږ کول gajz kawul, verb trans. To make grizzly (as the hair by age), to spot, to make mottled. See برګ

گس gas, adj. Left, the left, the left-hand side; (Fem.) گسه gasa'h. گس لاس gas lās, The left-hand, on the left.

P گستاخ gus-tākh, adj. Saucy, pert, uncivil, insolent, arrogant, impertinent, presumptuous, rude, cruel, abrupt; (Fem.) گستاخه gus-tākha'h.

P گستاخي gus-tākhī, s.f. (3rd) Sauciness, impertinence, insolence, assurance, rudeness, pertness, impudence, presumption, arrogance, cruelty. Pl. ئ a'i. گستاخي کول gus-tākhī kawul, verb trans. To act saucily, impudently, etc.; to presume.

ګسه *gasa'h*, s.f. (3rd) Recoil, rebound, ricochet, repercussion, blow, stroke, bump. Pl, ې *ey*. ګسه ورکول *gasa'h war-kawul*, verb trans. To recoil, to rebound, to ricochet. ګسه وهل *gasa'h wahal*, verb trans. To send home, as in thrusting anything in. لغته

ګسي *gasaey*, adj. Left-handed, having the left hand stronger than the right. 2. s.m. (1st) A left-handed person. Pl. ي *ī*. ګسئي *gasa'ī*, s.f. (6th) Sing. and Pl. See ګڅي

ګسيا *gasīā*, adj. Rubbed, abraded, worn, grated, ground, rubbed down, etc. (Masc. and Fem.) ګسيا کيدل *gasīā kedal*, verb intrans. To become rubbed, abraded, worn, frayed, pared, etc. ګسيا کول *gasīā kawul*, verb trans. To abrade, to rub, to bray, to rasp, to wear away, to file. ګسيا والي *gasīā wālaey*, s.m. (1st) Abrasion, rasping, grating, wearing away. Pl. والي *wālī*.

ګښت *gas͟ht* (W.) or *gak͟ht* (E.) s.m. (2nd) Patrolling, walking about, strolling, going round, a walk, a stroll, a tour. Pl. ګښتونه *gas͟htūnah* or *gak͟htūnah*. (P ګشت). ګښت کول *gas͟ht kawul* or *gak͟ht kawul*, verb trans. To go rounds, to patrol, to stroll, to walk about.

P ګفتار *guftār*, s.m. (2nd) Speech, discourse, dialogue, chit-chat. Pl. ګفتارونه *guftārūnah*.

P ګفتګوي *guft-o-go-e*, s.m. (2nd) Speech, talk, discourse, conversation. Pl. ګفتګويونه *guft-o-go-eūnah*. ګفتګوي کول *guft-o-go-e kawul*, verb trans. To speak, to talk, to enter into conversation.

ګګر *gagar*, adj. Strong, muscular, stout, brawny; (Fem.) ګګره *gagara'h*. ګګر والي *gagar wālaey*, s.m. (1st) Sturdiness, stoutness, energy, strength, lustiness. Pl. والي *wālī*.

ګګروځه *gagarrodza'h*, s.f. (3rd) Shivering or trembling from cold or fever, quaking, shaking. Pl. ې *ey*. ګګروځه نيول *gagarrodza'h nīwal*, verb trans. To tremble, to shiver, as from cold or ague.

ګګوشتو *gugūs͟htū*, s.m. (5th) A ring-dove. Pl. ګګوشتوګان *gugūs͟htūgān* or ګګوشتوان *gugūs͟htūān*. See ګرګري , تتوه and سپلمه

P ګل *gul*, s.m. (2nd) A rose, a flower in general, 2. A disorder of the eyes—the albugo. 3. Monday. Pl. ګلونه *gulūnah*. Used in composition; as ګل انار *gul-anār*, adj. Scarlet-coloured; (Fem.) ګل اناره *gul-anāra'h*. ګل اندام *gul-andām*, adj. Slender, delicate, of a pleasing nature; (Fem.) ګل اندامه *gul-andāma'h*. ګل بدن *gul-badan*, s.m. (2nd) A kind of red silk with narrow white stripes. Pl. ګل بدنونه *gul-badanūnah*. 2. adj. Rosy-bodied; (Fem.) ګل بدنه *gul-badana'h*. ګل جعفري *gul-i-jaæafarī*, Tagetes patula. ګل خيرو *gul-i-k͟hairū*, s.m. (9th) The Chinese and Persian hollyhock. Sing. and Pl. ګل داودي *gul-i-dā'ūdī*, s.m. (9th) Chrysanthemum indicum. Sing. and Pl. ګل دسته *gul-dasta'h*, s.f. (3rd) A nosegay. Pl. ې *ey*. ګل رخ *gul-ruk͟h* or ګل رخسار *gul-ruk͟hsār*, adj. Rosy-cheeked; (Fem.) ګل رخه *gul-ruk͟ha'h* or ګل رخساره *gul-ruk͟hsāra'h*. ګل رعنا *gul-i-raænā*, s.f. (6th) A beautiful delicate scented rose. (E.) Sing. and Pl.; (W.) Pl. ګل رعناوي *gul-raænāwī*. ګل رنګ *gul-rang*, adj. Rose-coloured, red; (Fem.) ګل رنګه *gul-ranga'h*. ګل ريز *gul-rez*, s.m. (2nd) A kind of firework. Pl. ګل ريزونه *gul-rezūnah*. ګل زار *gul-zār*, s.m. (2nd) A bed or garden of roses. Pl. ګل زارونه *gul-zārūnah*. ګل ستبر *gul-i-sat-bar*, s.m. (6th) The name of a yellow flower—ox-eye, a species of chamomile. Sing. and Pl. ګل سرنجان *gul-i-saranjān*, s.m. (9th) Flowers of the hermodactyl plant (Colchicum Illyricum). Sing. and Pl. ګل سوسن *gul-i-sosan*, s.m. (9th) The lily. Sing. and Pl. ګل شبوي *gul-i-s͟haboey*, s.m. (9th) The tuberose (Polianthes tuberosa). Sing. and Pl. ګل عباسي *gul-i-aæbbāsī*, s.m. (9th) Name of a plant—marvel of Peru (Mirabilis jalapa). Sing. and Pl. ګل عذار *gul-æiz̤ār*, adj. Rosy-cheeked; (Fem.) ګل عذاره *gul-æiz̤āra'h*. ګل فام *gul-fām*, adj. Rose-coloured; (Fem.) ګل فامه *gul-fāma'h*. ګل فرنګ *gul-i-farang*, s.m. (9th) The name of a flower (Vinca rosea). Sing. and Pl. ګل قند *gul-ḳand*, s.m. (6th) Conserve of roses. Sing. and Pl. گل گلاب *gul-i-gulāb*, s.m. (6th) The rose, the rose tree. Sing. and Pl. گل ميخ *gul-mekh*, s.m. (2nd) A stud, a tack, a nail. Pl. گل ميخونه *gul-mekhūnah*.

P گلاب *gul-āb*, s.m. (6th) Rose-water. Sing. and Pl.

گلابي *gulābī*, s.m. (5th) (E.) A hair-dresser, a perfumer, a barber. Pl. گلابيان *gulābīān*. 2. adj. Rose-coloured.

P گلخن *gul-khan*, s.m. (2nd) A stone for a bath, a stone in general. Pl. گلخنونه *gul-khanūnah*.

P گلستان *gulistān*, s.m. (2nd) A rose garden, a delightful spot. 2. The celebrated work of Shaikh Sæadī, of which there is a good translation in Pushto. See my Pushto "Text-Book." Pl. گلستانونه *gulistānūnah*.

P گلشن *gul-shan*, s.m. (2nd) A rose-garden. Pl. گلشنونه *gulshan-ūnah*.

P گله *gila'h*, s.f. (3rd) Complaint, lamentation, reproach, blame. Pl. ي *ey*. گله من *gila'h-man*, adj. Complaining, a complainant, one who grieves or laments; (Fem.) گله منه *gila'h-mana'h*. گله کول *gila'h kawul*, verb trans. To complain, to lament, to blame, to reproach.

گلي *gala'ī*, s.f. (6th) A hailstone, hail. (E.) Sing. and Pl. See ږلي. گلي لويدل *gala'ī l'wedal*, or گلي وو ريدل *gala'ī wo-redal* or اوريدل *ao-redal*, verb intrans. To hail.

گمارل *gumāral*, verb trans. To consign, to intrust, to commit, to make over, to give in charge. Pres. گماري *gumārī*; past وُ گماره *wu-gumārah*; fut. وُ به گماري *wu bah gumārī*; imp. وُ گماره *wu-gumārah*; act. part. گمارونکي *gumārūnkaey* or گماروني *gumārūnaey*; past part. گمارلي *gumāralaey*; verb. n. گمارنه *gumārana'h*.

P گماشته *gumāshtah*, s.m. (5th) An agent, a factor. Pl. گماشتگان *gumāshtagān*.

P گمان *gumān*, s.m. (2nd) Doubt, distrust, suspicion, imagination, supposition, fancy, opinion. Pl. گمانونه *gumān-ūnah*. گمان کول *gumān kawul*, verb trans. To doubt, to suspect, to imagine, to fancy. گماني *gumānī*, adj. Imaginary, suspicious (person), doubting. (Masc. and Fem.)

P گم راه *gum-rāh* or گم ره *gum-rah*, adj. Astray, wandering, erring, depraved, abandoned. (Masc. and Fem.) گم راهي *gum-rāhī* or گم رهي *gum-rahī*, s.f. (3rd) Error, depravity. Pl. ي *a'ī*. گم راه کيدل *gum-rāh kedal*, verb intrans. To be led astray, to become depraved. گم راه کول *gum-rāh kawul*, verb trans. To lead astray, to make depraved or abandoned.

گمنز *gumanz*, s.f. (1st) A comb. Pl. گمنزِ *gumanzi*. See منز, منگز and مگنز

P گناه *gunāh*, s.m. (2nd) A fault, a crime, a sin. Pl. گناهونه *gunāh-ūnah*. گناه کول *gunāh kawul*, verb trans. To sin, to offend. گناه گار *gunāh-gār*, s.m. (5th) A sinner, a culprit, an offender, a criminal. Pl. گناه گاران *gunāh-gārān*. گناه گاره *gunāh-gāra'h*, s.f. (3rd) A female offender or sinner. Pl. ي *ey*. گناه گاري *gunāh-gārī*, s.f. (3rd) Criminality, guiltiness. Pl. ي *a'ī*.

گنبت *gunbat*, s.m. (2nd) A jump, a leap, a vault, a bound, a caper, a caracole, a spring, a skip, a hop. Pl. گنبتونه *gunbatūnah*. گنبت وهل *gunbat wahal*, verb trans. To leap, to hop, to jump, to bound, to vault. See ترپ

گنبته *gunbata'h*, s.f. (3rd) A vault, an arch, a dome, a cupola. Pl. ي *ey*. (P گنبذ). See قبه and تنبي

P S گنج *ganj*, s.m. (2nd) A granary, a market, a mart; a treasure, a hoard. Pl. گنجونه *ganjūnah*.

گنجه *gunja'h*, s.f. (3rd) A wrinkle on the face, a furrow, a crease, a crumple, a rumple, a pucker, a plait. Pl. ي *ey*. See کرتي, گنزه, جوهره, and چيچرم. گنجي کيدل *gunjaey kedal*, verb intrans. To become wrinkled or furrowed. گنجي کول *gunjaey kawul*, verb trans. To wrinkle, to frown.

گنجي *ganjaey*, adj. Scald-headed, bald. 2. s.m. (1st) A person with a scald head, or bald from Tinea capatis. Pl. ي *ī*; (Fem.) گنجۍ *ganja'ī*. Sing. and Pl. See سدر and لينده. (HI گنج).

گنجي *ganjaey*, s.m. (1st) A vulture. Pl. ي *ī*.

گنجۍ *ganja'ī*, s.f. (6th) A hen vulture. Sing.

and Pl. ميرګنج mīr-ganj, The king of the vultures. See ګرګس

P ګنجيفه gan-jīfa'h, s.f. (3rd) A pack of cards, a game of cards. Pl. ې ey.

ګند gand, s.m. (5th) A patched garment worn by devotees. Pl. ګندان gandān.

ګند gind, s.m. (5th) A ball of wood or of leather, Pl. ګندان gindān. (s ګيند).

ګند gund, adj. Equal, even, level, on a par with, on a level with, co-equal. 2. A match, a peer, an equal, a compeer; (Fem.) ګنده gunda'h.

ګندي gundī, s.f. (3rd) Parity, equality, level, sameness of quality or degree. Pl. ۍ a'ī. ګندي کول gundī kawul, verb trans. To equal, to match, to come up to, to cope with. See سيال

ګندِ gundi, adv. Perhaps, by chance. See ګندي

ګندنه gandana'h, s.f. (3rd) A leek (Allium porrum). Pl. ې ey. Also ګندنا gandanā, s.f. (6th). (E.) Sing. and Pl. (W.) Pl. ګندناوي gandanāwī (s ګند).

ګندولَي gando-laey, s.m. (1st) A kind of smock-frock or tunic worn by women, a shift without sleeves. Pl. ي ī. See پيپني

ګنډ gandd, s.m. (2nd) A kind of garment. 2. A kind of ornamental collar worn by women, the edging of a garment. 3. An edge of clay round a mill stone. Pl. ګنډونه ganddūnah.

ګنډپور ganddapūr, s.m. (6th) The name of a tribe of Afghāns. 2. A male of the tribe. Sing. and Pl. ګنډپوره ganddapūra'h, s.f. (3rd) A female of the above. Pl. ې ey.

ګنډل ganddal, verb trans. To sew, to stitch, to cobble, to fasten. Pres. ګنډي ganddī; past وګانډه wu-gānddah; fut. وبه ګنډي wu bah ganddī; imp. وګنډه wu-ganddah; act. part. ګنډونکَي ganddūnkaey or ګنډونَي ganddūnaey; past part. ګنډلَي ganddalaey; verb. n. ګنډنه ganddana'h. ګنډول ganddawul, verb trans. (caus.) To cause to sew.

ګنډولي ganddolaey, s.m. (1st) A kind of short tunic, a sort of jacket with short sleeves worn by women. Pl. ي ī. See ګنډولي

ګنډهير gandd-her, s.m. (6th) The name of a poisonous plant, wild raddish (Aristoloch rododaphne). Sing. and Pl.

H I ګنډهيري gandd-herī, s.f. (3rd) A portion or segment of sugar-cane. Pl. ۍ a'ī.

ګنډي gunddī, s.m. (1st) Pl. The ears of corn remaining on the threshing floor after threshing. See ګزاري

ګنډيري gandderaey, s.m. (1st) The name of a poisonous plant and flower (Nerium odorium). Pl. ي ī.

ګنز gunz, s.f. (1st) A comb. Pl. ګنزِ gunzi. See ګونز

ګنزه gunza'h, s.f. (3rd) A wrinkle, a furrow, a crease, a pucker, a crumple. 2. A comb. Pl. ې ey. ګنزي کيدل gunzaey kedal, verb intrans. To become wrinkled or furrowed, creased, puckered, etc. ګنزي کول gunzaey kawul, verb trans. To furrow, to wrinkle, to pucker, to crease. 2. To frown. See ګنجه

ګنس gans, adj. Stunned, deafened from sounds, as of cannon, etc.; (Fem.) ګنسه gansa'h. ګنس کيدل gans kedal, verb intrans. To become stunned, deafened, confounded. ګنس کول gans kawul, verb trans. To deafen, to stun, to confound. ګنس والَي gans wālaey, s.m. (1st) Deafening, stunning, making deaf, rendering impervious to sound, confounding with noise. Pl. والي wālī; or ګنس توب gans-tob, s.m. (2nd) Pl. توبونه tobūnah.

P ګنګ gung, adj. Dumb; (Fem.) ګنګه gunga'h. ګنګي gungaey, s.m. (1st) A dumb person. Pl. ي ī. ګنګۍ gunga'ī, s.f. (6th) A dumb female. Sing. and Pl. ګنګ کيدل gung kedal, verb intrans. To become dumb. ګنګ کول gung kawul, verb trans. To make or render dumb. See چاړا. ټپ ګنګ ttap-gung, adj. Very deaf, deaf as a post; (Fem.) ټپه ګنګه ttapa'h-gunga'h.

ګنګړَي gin-garraey, s.m. (1st) A small bell, a hawk's bell. Pl. ي ī.

ګنګري gungrī, s.m. (1st) (Pl.) Boiled grain, saturated or steeped in water.

ګنګس gangas, s.m. (6th) The narcissus, which grows spontaneously in Suwāt. Sing. and Pl. See ګنګس

گنگوسی *gungosaey*, s.m. (1st) Discourse, mention, talk, report, talking over past events. 2. Sound of conversation, muttering, hum, chattering. 3. The sound of footsteps, etc. Pl. ي *ī*. See ښکالوه and سکالوه

P گنه *gunah*, s.m. (2nd) Sin, crime, fault. Pl. گنهونه *gunahūnah*. گنهګار *gunah-gār*, s.m. (5th) A criminal, a culprit, a sinner. Pl. گنهګاران *gunah-gārān*. گنهګاره *gunah-gāra'h*, s.f. (3rd) Feminine of the above. Pl. ې *ey*. گنهګاري *gunah-gārī*, s.f. (3rd) Criminality, guiltiness. Pl. ئي *a'ī*. گنه کول *gunah kawul*, verb trans. To sin, to commit a crime, or fault. See گناه

گنهر *gun-har*, s.m. (6th) A kind of vegetable (Aramanthus polygamus). Sing. and Pl. See also سور گوګي

گنړ *garrn*, adj. Dense, thick, compact, crowded, assembled, teeming, clustered, packed, grouped, swarming, etc. 2. Shady, umbrageous. 3. Lurid, cloudy, muggy; (Fem.) گنړه *garrna'h*, used in composition as گنړ باران *garrn bārān*, Heavy rain. گنړ پصل or فصل *garrn paṣl* or *faṣl*, A good or teeming crop. گنړه اوريځ *garrna'h aor-yedz*, Thick or dense clouds. گنړه ږيره *garrna'h jzīra'h* (W.) or گنړه ګيره *garrna'h gīra'h* (E.) A thick or bushy beard. گنړ وېښته *garrn weshtah* (W.) or *wekhtah* (E.) A thick head of hair. گنړ بنړ *garrn barrn*, A thick grove, etc. گنړ والَي *garrn wālaey*, s.m. (1st) Density, compactness, thickness, impenetrability. 2. Shadiness, umbrageousness. 3. Luridness, cloudiness. Pl. والي *wālī*. گنړ کيدل *garrn kedal*, verb intrans. To become or grow thick, dense, compact, to teem, to swarm. 2. To become cloudy, lurid. گنړ کول *garrn kawul*, verb trans. To make dense, thick, compact, to crowd. 2. To render cloudy, lurid. See گور

گنړل *garrnal*, verb trans. To consider, to conclude, to deduce, to infer, to estimate, to distinguish, to know, to perceive, to ascertain, to comprehend, to be aware of, to ken. Pres. گنړي *garrnī*; past وُ ګانړه *wu-gārrnah*; fut. وُ به گنړي *wu bah garrnī*; imp. وُ گنړه *wu-garrnah*; act. part. گنړونکَي *garrnūnkaey* or گنړونَي *garrnūnaey*; past part. گنړلَي *garrnalaey*; verb. n. گنړنه *garrnana'h*.

گنړه *garrnah*, adv. As though, as if, as it were.

گوار *go-ār*, s.f. (1st) A flock, a herd, a drove. Pl. گوارِ *go-āri*. See گوهار and ګاهر

گواښ *gwāsh* (W.) or *gwākh* (E.) s.m. (2nd) Peace, settlement, mediation, intervention, parley, negociation, making up a quarrel. Pl. گواښونه *gwāshūnah* or *gwākhūnah*. گواښ گرندَي *gwāsh-grandaey* (W.) or *gwākh-grandaey* (E.), adj. as s.m. (1st) A mediator, a negociator, an intercessor, a peace-maker, an arbitrator. Pl. ي *ī*. گواښ گرندِ *gwāsh grandi* or *gwākh-grandi*, s.f. (8th). Pl. ي *ī*. گواښل *gwāshal* (W.) or *gwākhal* (E.) verb trans. To mediate, to settle, to make peace, to parley, to compromise, to interfere, to interpose, to make up a quarrel. Pres. گواښي *gwāshī* or *gwākhī*; past وُ گواښه *wu-gwāshah* or *wu-gwākhah*; fut. وُ به گواښي *wu bah gwāshī* or *gwākhī*; imp. وُ گواښه *wu-gwāshah* or *wu-gwākhah*; act. part. گواښونکَي *gwāshūnkaey* or *gwākhūnkaey* or گواښونَي *gwāshūnaey* or *gwākhūnaey*; past part. گواښلَي *gwāshalaey* or *gwākhalaey*; verb. n. گواښنه *gwāshana'h* or *gwākhana'h*.

گواندَي *gawānddaey*, s.m. (1st) A neighbour. Pl. ي *ī*. گواندئي *gawāndda'ī*, s.f. (6th) A female neighbour. Sing. and Pl.

P گواه *gawāh*, s.m. (5th) A witness, an evidence. Pl. گواهان *gawāhān*. گواهي *gawāhī*, s.f. (3rd) Evidence, testimony. Pl. ئي *a'ī*. گواهي ادا کول *gawāhī adā kawul* or گواهي ورکول *gawāhī-war kawul* or گواهي لل *gawāhī lal*, verb trans. To give evidence, to testify. Pres. گواهي لي *gawāhī lī*; past گواهي وُ له *gawahī wu-lah*; fut. گواهي به لي *gawāhī bah lī* or به وُ لي *bah wu-lī*; imp. گواهي وُ له *gawāhī wu-lah*; act. part. گواهي لونکَي *gawāhī lūnkaey* or گواهي لونَي *gawāhī lūnaey*; past part. گواهي للَي *gawāhī lalaey*; verb. n. گواهي لنه *gawāhī lana'h*. This latter infinitive is almost peculiar to the

West, and لل is seldom used apart from گواهي and a few other words.

گوپ *gūp*, s.m. (9th) The planet Venus, the evening star. Sing. and Pl. See د ميلمانه ستركه

گوته *gūta'h*, s.f. (3rd) A finger, a toe. Pl. ئ *ey*. بټه گوته *batta'h gūta'h* or غټه گوته *ghatta'h gūta'h* (W.); and كټه گوته *katta'h gūta'h*, s.f. (3rd) The thumb or great toe. شين غټه گوته *shīn-ghatta'h gūta'h* (W.) or مسواك گوته *miswāk* (tooth-brush) *gūta'h* (E.) The fore finger, the first toe. مينځه گوته *mīandza'h-gūta'h*, The middle finger or toe. خمته گوته *khamta'h gūta'h* (E.) The third finger or toe. كيچه گوته *kīcha'h gūta'h* (E.) or خمچه گوته *khamacha'h gūta'h* (W.) The little finger or toe. Pl. ئ *ey*. Also written گته, which see.

گوټ *gott* or *gūtt*, s.m. (2nd) A corner, a nook. Pl. گوټونه *gottūnah* or *gūttūnah*. See گټ

گوجر *gūjar*, s.m. (5th) A cowherd, a herdsman. 2. The name of a tribe in the Panjāb. Pl. گوجران *gūjar-ān*. گوجره *gūjara'h*, s.f. (3rd) A female of the above. Pl. ئ *ey*.

گوجئ *gūjaey*, s.m. (1st) A snail-shell, a small fresh water shell. Pl. ي *ī*. See پسكي and شاپيتي

گودا *godā*, s.m. (5th) A doll, a puppet, an image. Pl. گوداگان *godā-gān*. گوډئ *goda'ī*, s.f. (6th) A female doll or puppet. Sing. and Pl. See گډئ and ناوكئ

گودر *gūdar*, s.m. (2nd) A landing-place, a ford, a ferry, a watering-place for cattle, a sloping place made on the banks of a river for washing and bathing. Pl. گودرونه *gūdarūnah*. See گدر

گوډئ *gūddaey*, s.m. (1st) A pouch, a scrip, a wallet. Pl. ي *ī*.

P گور *gor*, s.m. (2nd) A grave, a tomb, a sepulchre. Pl. گورونه *gorūnah*. گور كن *gor-kan*, s.m. (5th) A grave-digger, a sexton. Pl. گور كنان *gor-kanān*.

گور *gūr*, adj. Thick, close, compact, thickset, swarming, teeming, well-laden, well stocked (as fruit on a tree). 2. Shady, umbrageous (as a tree). 3. Misty, muggy, lurid, cloudy; (Fem.) گوره *gūrah*. گور كيدل *gūr kedal*, verb intrans. To teem, to abound, etc.

گورا گور *gorā-gor*, adj. Swift, nimble, fast, fleet; (Fem.) گورا گوره *gorā-gora'h*. See گرندي

P گورستان *goristān*, s.m. (2nd) A grave-yard, a burying-ground. Pl. گورستانونه *goristānūnah*.

گور كښ *gor-kash* (W.) or *gor-kakh* (E.) s.m. (5th) The name of an animal that feeds on carcasses—the Indian badger (Ursus Indicus). Pl. گور كښان *gor-kashān* or *gor-kakhān*.

گورل *go-ral*, verb trans. To see, to behold, to descry, to perceive, to espy, to look, to view, to eye, to scan, to glance on, to regard, to inspect, to survey, to contemplate, to watch, to gaze, to stare, to pore over, to bend one's looks upon, etc. This verb is imperfect, and requires the past tenses of the imperfect verb كتل to complete it. Pres. گوري *gorī*; past وُ كاته *wu-kātah* or وُ كوت *wu-kot*; fut. وُ به گوري *wu bah gorī*; imp. وُ گوره *wu-gorah*; act. part. كتونكئ *katūnkaey* or كتونئ *katūnaey*; past part. كتلئ *katalaey*; verb. n. كتنه *katana'h* or كاته *kātah*. See كتل

گورم *goram*, s.m. (2nd) A herd of cattle, a drove, Pl. گورمونه *goramūnah*. See گاهر and گوار

گور والئ *gūr-wālaey*, s.m. (1st) Thickness, closeness, compactness. 2. Plenty, abundance. 3. Shade, umbrageousness. 4. Luridness, cloudiness. Pl. والي *wālī*.

گوروان *gor-wān*, s.m. (5th) A herdsman, a grazier, a drover. Pl. گوروانان *gor-wānān*. See گاهو

گوره خر *gorah-khar*, s.m. (6th) The wild ass or onager. Sing. and Pl. (P گورخر).

گورهنده *gor-handa'h*, s.f. (3rd) Rough or uneven ground with roots of trees in it. 2. A ravine, a chasm, a pit, a grave. Pl. ئ *ey*.

گوړئ *gūrra'ī*, s.f. (6th) The juice or sap of trees, vegetables, etc. Sing. and Pl. د ځوز گوړئ *da dzoz gūrra'ī*, s.f. (6th) Manna. Sing. and Pl. See ځوز

گوزار *gūzār*. See گزار

P گوزن *gavazn*, s.m. (6th) An elk. Sing. and Pl.

گوزن *gūzan* (E.) s.m. (2nd) Palsy, paralysis. Pl. گوزنونه *gūzanūnah*. گوزن وهلئ *gūzan wahalaey*, adj. Palsied, paralyzed; (Fem.) گوزن وهلِ *gūzan wahali*. Pl. (Masc. and Fem.) ي *ī*. گوزن وهل *gūzan wahal*, verb trans. To palsy, to paralyze. See گزن and افليج

گوشي *go-shī*, s.f. (3rd) A capitation tax on cattle. Pl. ۍ *a'ī*. گوشي آخستل *goshī ākhistal*, verb trans. To collect a tax on cattle.

گوښه *go-sha'h* (W.) or *go-kha'h* (E.) s.f. (3rd) A corner, a nook, an angle, a closet, a cell, a retired place, privacy, retirement. Pl. ې *ey*. گوښه نشين *go-sha'h-nishīn* (W.) or *go-kha'h-nishīn* (E.) s.m. (5th) A hermit, a recluse, sitting in retirement. 2. adj. Solitary, private, retired. گوښه نشينه *go-sha'h-nishīna'h* or *go-kha'h-nishīna'h*, s.f. (3rd) A female hermit. Pl. ې *ey*. گوښه نشيني *go-sha'h* or *go-kha'h-nishīnī*, s.f. (3rd) Retirement, the life of a recluse. Pl. ۍ *a'ī*. گوښه گوښه *go-sha'h-go-sha'h* or *go-kha'h-go-kha'h*, adj. Retired, separate, one by one, by separate bodies; or گوښي گوښي *go-shey-go-shey* or *go-khey-go-khey*; and گوښي گوښي *goshī-goshī* or *gokhī-gokhī* (P گوشه)

گوگړ *go-garr*, s.m. (6th) Brimstone, sulphur. Sing. and Pl. (P گوگرد).

گوگل *go-gal*, s.m. (2nd) The cavity or interior of the chest, the breast. Pl. گوگلونه *gogalūnah*. See تټر and سينه

گوگل *go-gil*, s.m. (6th) Brimstone, sulphur. 2. (s) The name of a gum—Bdellium. Sing. and Pl.

P S گولۍ *go-la'ī*, s.f. (6th) A ball, a bullet, a globule. Sing. and Pl. See مردک

گوله *go-la'h*, s.f. (3rd) A mouthful. Pl. ې *ey*.

گونز *gūnz*, s.f. (1st) A comb. Pl. گونز *gūnzi*.

گونزه *gūnza'h*, s.f. (3rd) A wrinkle, a furrow, a crease. Pl. ې *ey*. گونزه کيدل *gūnza'h kedal*, verb intrans. To grow or become wrinkled, creased, furrowed. گونزه کول *gūnza'h kawul*, verb trans. To furrow, to crease, to wrinkle. See گنزه, گنجه, and جوهره

گونځه *gūndza'h*, s.f. (3rd) A wrinkle, a pucker, a crease, a furrow. Pl. ې *ey*. See preceding. گونځي کيدل *gūndzey kedal*, verb intrans. To become wrinkled, furrowed, creased, puckered. گونځي کول *gūndzey kawul*, verb trans. To wrinkle, to furrow, to pucker. 2. To look angry, to wrinkle the forehead. گونځي گونځي *gūndzey-gūndzey*, adj. Wrinkled, furrowed, creased.

گونګټ *gūn-gatt*, s.m. (5th) The dung beetle (Scarabæus). Pl. گونګټان *gūn-gattān*. See غوزکرکي

گونګو *gūngū*, s.m. (9th) The name of a shrub of a bright yellow colour, hence the face is compared as more yellow or sallow than the gūngū, through sorrow or sickness. 2. Bastard saffron. Sing. and Pl.

گونګي *gūngaey*, s.m. (1st) An owl. Pl. ي *ī*.

گوهاټه *go-hātta'h*, s.f. (3rd) A stack of dried cow-dung for fuel. Pl. ې *ey*. See توپ and تپي

گوهار *go-hār*, s.f. (1st) A herd, a drove. Pl. گوهارِ *go-hāri*. See گوهر and گورم

P گوهر *gau-har*, s.m. (2nd) A gem, a pearl, a jewel. 2. Essence, nature, substance. Pl. گوهرونه *gau-harūnah*.

P گوي *go-e*, s.m. (2nd) A ball for play, of wood or leather. Pl. گويونه *go-e-ūnah*. See گند

گوي *go-e*, s.m. (6th) The dry dung of animals. Sing. and Pl.

P گويا *go-yā*, adv. (act. part. of گفتن) As you would say, as if, one would say, thus, etc. See گنړه

P گه گه *gah-gah*, adv. Now and then, sometimes, occasionally, again and again; or گهي گهي *gah-e-gah-e*. See گاه

P گهواره *gah-wāra'h*, s.f. (3rd) A swing, a cradle. Pl. ې *ey*. See زانګو

گهور *guhūr*, adj. Thick, close, compact, thickset, teeming, well-laden. 2. Shady, umbrageous. 3. Cloudy, lurid, muggy; (Fem.) گهوره *guhūra'h*. گهور کيدل *guhūr kedal*, verb intrans. To teem, to abound, etc. See گور and گڼړ

گهيځ *ga-hīdz*, s.m. (2nd) The morning, dawn of day. Pl. گهيځونه *ga-hīdzūnah*.

P گياه *gi-yāh*, s.m. (2nd) grass, green herbage, straw. Pl. گياهونه *gi-yāhūnah*.

گيدي *ge-daey*, s.m. (1st) A donkey. Pl. ي *ī*. گيدۍ *ge-da'ī*, s.f. (6th) A female donkey. Sing. and Pl.

گيډه *gedda'h*, s.f. (3rd) The belly. Pl. ې *ey*. گيډه ور *gedda'h-war*, s.m. (5th) A glutton, a gormandizer. 2. A pot-belly. Pl. گيډه وَر *gedda'h-wær*. گيډه وره *gedda'h wara'h*, s.f. (3rd) Pl. ې *ey*. See خيټه

گيډي *geddaey*, s.m. (1st) A load of grass or fire-wood, a load for the head, or small enough to be carried on the head. Pl. ي *ī*. See بنډه

گيډۍ *gedda'ī*, s.f. (6th) A small bundle of grass, a small sheaf of corn, a truss of straw. Sing. and Pl.

P گير *gīr*, adj. (part. of گرفتن) in compos. Taking, seizing; a taker, a seizer, a holder, a conqueror; taken, seized; (Fem.) گيره *gīra'h*. گيريدل *gīredal*, verb intrans. To become seized, taken, held, etc. گيرول *gīrawul*, verb trans. To seize, to take, to hold, etc.

گيره *gīra'h*, s.f. (3rd) (E.) The beard. Pl. ې *ey*. See ږيره

گيږکه *gījzaka'h*, s.f. (3rd) A magpie. Pl. ې *ey*.

P گيسو *gesū*, s.m. (9th) A side-lock, a ringlet, a curl. Sing and Pl.

گينډي *genddaey*, s.m. (1st) A rhinoceros. 2. A shield made of a rhinoceros' hide. Pl. ي *ī*. گينډۍ *gendda'ī*, s.f. (6th) The female of the above. Sing. and Pl. (s گينڈا).

ل

ل *lam*, The twenty-third letter of the Arabic, and the twenty-seventh of the Persian, is the thirty-fourth letter of the Pu<u>sh</u>to alphabet, and corresponds to Sanskrit ल. It is one of the dental letters, and is equivalent to English *l*. It stands for 30 according to the Arabic system of letters for numbers.

ل A letter the sign of the infinitive of many Pu<u>sh</u>to verbs, which are for the most part pure, and not deducible from any noun or adjective. The other infinitive affixes are يدل and ول. See my Grammar, page 62.

لا *lā*, adv. Yet, still, hitherto, to this very time. 2. Otherwise, unless. 3. Also used in an affirmative sense, Surely, certainly. لا به ښه وي *lā bah <u>sh</u>æh we* (W.) or *lā bah <u>kh</u>æh we* (E.) It would have been well. لا به کله *lā bah kalah*, adv. Till when, how long. لا تر کومَ *lā tar koma* or کمَ *kama*, adv. How much longer? as yet how long? لا بل صبا *lā bal ṣabā*, adv. After three days, three days hence. لا ورمه ورځ *lā warrma'h wradz*, adv. Three days since. لا لا ورمه روځ *lā lā warr-ma'h rwadz*, Four days since, etc. لا د پاس *lā da pāsa*, adv. Besides, moreover, also, likewise.

A لا *lā*, A negative or privative particle, No, not, by no means, without; or similar to English *un, in, ir, im*, etc. Used in composition, as, لا جواب *lā-jawāb* or لا ځواب *lā-<u>dz</u>awāb*, adj. Speechless, silenced, confuted, disconcerted. لا چار *lā-<u>ch</u>ār*, adj. Helpless, destitute, without remedy. 2. Certainly, without help. لا چاري *lā-<u>ch</u>ārī*, s.f. (3rd) Forlornness, helplessness. Pl. ې *a'ī*. لا وارث *lā-wāriṣ*, adj. Heirless; (Fem.) لا وارثه *lā-wāriṣa'h*.

لاپه *lāpa'h*, s.f. (3rd) (corrup. of P لاف) Boasting, bragging, self-praise, vanity. Pl. ې *cy*. لاپ شاپ *lāp-<u>sh</u>āp*, s.f. (1st) Boasting, vanity, pride, arrogance, bombast, gasconade. Pl. لاپِ شاپِ *lāpi-<u>sh</u>āpi*; or لاپې شاپې *lāpey-<u>sh</u>āpey*, s.f. (3rd) Pl. لاپې وهل *lāpey wahal*, or لاپې شاپې وهل *lāpey-<u>sh</u>āpey wahal*, verb trans. To boast, to brag, to vaunt, to strut, to swagger, to talk big. لاپک *lāpuk*, adj. as s.m. (6th) A boaster, a braggart, a pretender, a gascon, a puppy. Pl. لاپکان *lāpukān*. لاپکه *lāpuka'h*, s.f. (3rd) Pl. ې *ey*. See لقه

لات *lāt*, s.m. (9th) The name of an idol of the ancient Arabians. Sing. and Pl. See منات

لاټو *lāṭṭū*, s.m. (5th) A shrike, the butcher bird. Pl. لاټوګان *lāṭṭū-gān*.

لاجبر *lāj-bar*, s.m. (6th) Azure, lapis-lazuli. (corrup. of P لاجورد) Sing. and Pl.

P لاجورد *lāja-ward*, s.m. (6th) Lapis-lazuli. Sing. and Pl.

لاچي *lā-chī*, s.f. (3rd) Cardamom seed. Pl. ئي *a'ī*. See الاچي

لاډو *lāḍḍū*, s.m. (5th) A humming top. Pl. لاډوګان *lāḍḍū-gān*.

لار *lār*, s.f. (1st) A road, a track, a path, a way, a footpath, a highway, a path way, a thoroughfare. Pl. لارِ *lāri*. بي لارِ *be-lāri*, adj. Lost, astray, depraved, erring, wandering. (Masc. and Fem.) بي لارِ کيدل *be-lāri kedal*, verb intrans. To go astray, to err, to wander. بي لارِ کول *be-lāri kawul*, verb trans. To lead astray, to cause to err, to make depraved. لار پريښوول *lār pre-sho-wul* (W.) or *lār pre-kho-wul* (E.), verb trans. To give way, to admit. لار پريکول *lār pre-kawul*, verb trans. To travel along or on a road. لار ترل *lār tarral*, verb trans. To refuse admittance, to cease all intercourse. د لارِ خرڅ *da lāri kharts*, Travelling expenses, way-charges, transit duties. لار ښوول *lār showul* (W.) or *lār kho-wul* (E.), verb trans. To show or point out a road, to set on the right path. لار کتل *lār katal*, verb trans. To expect, to await, to look out or wait for. لار کول *lār kawul*, verb trans. To contract friendship, to make acquaintance, to introduce or intercede. لارِ په لارِ *lāri-pah-lāri*, adj. Following different customs, at variance, at odds, disagreeing. لارِ په لارِ کيدل *lāri-pah-lāri kedal*, verb intrans. To be at variance, to be at odds, to be disunited. لارِ په لارِ کول *lāri-pah-lāri kawul*, verb trans. To set at odds, to cause disunion or clashing. لار نيول *lār nīwal*, verb trans. To go or take one's way (to go, to depart). 2. To agree, to make up a dispute. لار وهل *lār wahal*, verb trans. To waylay, to rob, to commit highway robbery. لار وهونکي *lār-wahūnkaey* or لار وهوني *lār-wahūnaey*, s.m. (1st) (act. part.) A highwayman. Pl. ي *ī*.

لارغه *lārghah*, s.m. (6th) Delay, tardiness, slowness, lateness, dallying. Sing. and Pl. 2. adv. Formerly, whilom, long ago, before now, long since, lang syne. لري لارغه *lirey lārghah*, In days of yore, long long ago. See درنګ

لاړل *lārral*, verb intrans. To go, to depart, to set out, to begone, to go forth, to set forward. This verb is imperfect, having only a past tense, and is used to complete the conjugation of تلل, which is also imperfect. See تلل

لاړه *lārra'h*, s.f. (3rd) Spittle, saliva, slaver. Pl. ئي *ey*. The plural form is generally used. لاړي توکل *lārraey tūkal*, verb trans. To spit, to eject saliva from the mouth; or لاړي غورزول *lārraey ghor-zawul*, verb trans. (s لار) See لاړي

A لازم *lāzim*, adj. (act. part. of لزم) Incumbent, necessary, requisite, urgent, indispensable, suitable, proper, important, inseparable; (Fem.) لازمه *lāzima'h*. لازميدل *lāzimedal*, verb intrans. To be incumbent, necessary, requisite, proper, or inseparable. Pres. لازميږي *lāzimejzī* (W.) or لازميګي *lāzimegī* (E.); past لازم شه *lāzim shah* or وُ شه *wu-shah*; fut. لازم به شي *lāzim bah shī* or به وُ شي *bah wu-shī*; imp. لازم شه *lāzim shah* or وُ شه *wu-shah*; act. part. لازميدونکي *lāzimedūnkaey* or لازميدوني *lāzimedūnaey*; past part. لازم *lāzim* or لازم شوي *lāzim shawaey*; verb. n. لازميدنه *lāzimedana'h* or لازميده *lāzimedah*. لازمول *lāzimawul*, verb trans. To render or make incumbent, necessary, inseparable. Pres. لازموي *lāzimawī*; past لازم کړ *lāzim karr* or وُ کړ *wu-karr*; fut. لازم به کړي *lāzim bah krrī* or به وُ کړي *bah wu-krrī*; imp. لازم کړه *lāzim krrah* or وُ کړه *wu-krrah*; act. part. لازموونکي *lāzimawūnkaey* or لازمووني *lāzimawūnaey*; past part. لازم کړي *lāzim karraey*; verb. n. لازمونه *lāzimawuna'h*.

لاس *lās*, s.m. (2nd) The hand. Pl. لاسونه *lās-ūnah*. لاس ولوني *lās-wulūnaey*, s.m. (1st) A wash-hand basin of brass, copper, etc. Pl. ي *ī*. See سلمچي. لاس آچول *lās āchawul*, verb trans. To encroach, to meddle, to interfere. لاس آخستل *lās ākhistal*, verb trans. To relinquish, to refrain from, to abstain from. لاس پر سينه دريدل *lās par sīna'h daredal*, verb intrans. To stand with hands folded on the breast. لاس پر له مښول *lās par lah mas͟h-awul* (W.) or *mak͟hawul* (E.) verb trans. To wring the hands, to lament, to regret. لاس پريکړی *lās pre-karraey*, adj. (past part.) Hand-severed, with the hand cut off, handless; (Fem.) لاس پريکړه *lās pre-karri*. Pl. (Masc. and Fem.) ي *ī*. لاس پريکول *lās pre-kawul*, verb trans. To cut off the hand, a punishment for theft. لاس په لاس *lās pah lās*, adv. Speedily, with celerity, hand over hand, out of or off-hand, expeditiously. لاس په لاس کول *lās pah lās kawul*, verb trans. To pass from hand to hand, or from one to another. لاس په ډوډي کول *lās pah ddūddī kawul*, verb trans. To place the hand on the hip (to be very feeble). لاس ټکول *lās ttakawul*, verb trans. To clap the hands, to praise. لاس څنډل *lās tsanddal*, verb trans. To wash the hands of, to give up any affair. لاس کوته کول *lās kotah kawul*, verb trans. To abstain from, to refrain from. لاس لګول *lās lagawul*, verb trans. To punish, to fight with, to reprove, to handle. لاس مچول *lās machawul*, verb trans. To kiss the hand. لاس نيول *lās nīwal*, verb trans. To take by the hand, to aid, to assist. 2. To follow, to become a disciple. لاس ورکول *lās war-kawul*, verb trans. To make a bargain by seizing the hand of another under a cloth; to aid, to help or assist. لاس ور وړل *lās war-w'rral*, verb trans. To put or thrust the hand in, to meddle, to handle, to interfere, to feel. 2. To injure a female's character (met.) لاس وندي *lās wandaey*, s.m. (1st) A bracelet, an ornament for the wrists. Pl. ي *ī*.

لاسته *lāsta'h*, s.f. (3rd) Side, margin, quarter, extremity, towards. Pl. ې *ey*. Also written لاستَ *lāsta* and لاستِ *lāsti*.

لاستَي *lāstaey*, s.m. (1st) A handle, a hilt, a haft, a shaft, a pestle. 2. The handle of a mill. Pl. ي *ī*.

لاشوره *lā-shorra'h*, s.f. (3rd) The name of a glutinous plant (Cordea mysea). Pl. ې *ey*.

لاشه *lāsha'h*, s.f. (3rd) The sting of a scorpion, wasp, etc., a splinter, a spike of barley or some kinds of grasses. Pl. ې *ey*. See لشه

لاش *lās͟h* (W.) or *lāk͟h* (E.) s.m. (2nd) A dead body, a corpse, a carcass. 2. A steep or scarped place in a mountain inaccessible. Pl. لاشونه *lās͟hūnah* or *lāk͟hūnah*. (P لاش).

لافه *lāfa'h*, s.f. (3rd) Boasting, gasconade, bragging, vanity, self-praise (corrup. of P لاف). Pl. ې *ey*. لافې کول *lāfey kawul* or لافې وهل *lāfey wahal*, verb trans. To boast, to brag.

لافک *lāfuk*, s.m. (5th) A boaster, a gascon, a braggart, a pretender, a puppy. Pl. لافکان *lāfuk-ān*. لافکه *lāfuka'h*, s.f. (3rd). Pl. ې *ey*. See لاپه

لاک *lāk*, s.m. (6th) Sealing-wax. 2. Gum lac. Sing. and Pl.

لاکن *lākin*, adj. Filled or covered with wax; (Fem.) لاکنه *lākina'h*.

P لال *lāl*, s.m. (2nd) (corrup. of لعل) A ruby. Pl. لالونه *lālūnah*.

لا لره *lā larah*, To me or to us, used in poetry occasionally for را لره *rā larah*.

S لالن *lā-lan*, s.m. (6th) A sweetheart, a lover. Pl. لالَن *lā-læn*. لالنه *lā-lana'h*, s.f. (3rd) A mistress, a sweetheart. Pl. ې *ey*.

P لاله *lāla'h*, s.f. (3rd) A tulip. Pl. ې *ey*. لاله رخ *lāla'h rukh*, adj. Tulip-cheeked, red-cheeked; (Fem.) لاله رخه *lāla'h rukha'h*. لاله زار *lāla'h-zār*, s.m. (2nd) A bed or garden of tulips. Pl. لاله زارونه *lāla'h-zārūnah*.

لالي *lā-ley*, adj. Dear, beloved, darling, a word of endearment. 2. s.m. (1st) A darling, a favorite. Pl. ي *ī*. adj. and s.f. (6th). لالئ *lā-la'ī*, Sing. and Pl.

لانبو *lān-bo*, s.f. (9th) Swimming, floating on the water. Sing. and Pl. لانبو زن *lān-bo-zan*, s.m. (5th) A swimmer. Pl. لانبو زَن *lān-bo-zæn*. لانبو زنه *lān-bo-zana'h*, s.f. (3rd). Pl. ې *ey*. لانبو کول *lān-bo kawul*, verb trans. To swim, to float.

لاندِ *lāndi*, adv. Below, beneath, down, under. لاندِ باندِ *lāndi-bāndi*, Topsy-turvy, higgledy-piggledy, upside down, in confusion. 2. adj. Confused, over-turned. See لاندي

لانده *lāndah*, adj. Pl. of لوند, which see.

لانديس *lān-<u>dd</u>es*, s.m. (6th) The cassia fistula. 2. A kind of cucumber. Sing. and Pl. See جرانكو

لاندي *lāndey*, adv. Below, under, beneath, down. لاندي باندي *lāndey-bāndey*, Topsy-turvy, upside down, in confusion. See لاندِ

لانديَ *lāndaey*, s.m. (1st) A sheep or bullock fattened in the summer to be slaughtered and dried in the winter. Pl. ي *ī*. د لاندي غوښي *da lāndī <u>gh</u>wa<u>sh</u>ey* (W.) or *<u>gh</u>wa<u>kh</u>ey* (E.) Mutton or goat's flesh salted and dried in the sun.

لانګه *lānga'h*, s.f. (3rd) A lace or rope at the bottom of a bedstead used for tightening the lacing. 2. The name of a tree from the wood of which arrows are made. 3. The name of a village. Pl. ې *ey*. See پيارمه

لانوده *lānw-dah*, adj. (Pl. of لوند) Wet, damp, moist, etc. 2. The name given to that portion of the Suwāt valley lying on the right or northern bank of the river of that name, the Suastus of the Greeks. The other side is termed وچه, which see.

لاړي *lā<u>rr</u>ney*, s.f. (3rd) (Pl.) Spittle, saliva, slaver. لاړي توكل *lā<u>rr</u>ney tūkal*, verb trans. To spit, to eject saliva from the mouth.

لاهو *lāhū*, adj. Flooded, carried away by a flood as the banks of a river or land in the vicinity of a river. (Masc. and Fem.) لاهو كيدل *lā-hū kedal*, verb intrans. To become flooded or carried away by a flood, to be launched (as a boat). لاهو كول *lā-hū kawul*, verb trans. To flood, to carry away (as land or river banks); to launch (as a boat).

لاي *lā-e*, s.m. (2nd) Mud, mire. 2. A fold, a plait. Pl. لايونه *lā-e-ūnah*. See لي

A لايق *lā-īḳ*, adj. (act. part. of ليق) Worthy, suitable, fit, adapted, proper, becoming, expedient, able, capable, qualified, deserving; (Fem.) لايقه *lā-īḳa'h*. لايق والي *lā-īḳ-wālaey*, s.m. (1st) Propriety, aptitude, capacity, fitness, expediency, capability, worth, merit, ability. Pl. ي *ī*. لايق كيدل *lā-īḳ kedal*, verb intrans. To deserve, to merit, to be fit for, to be worthy of.

A لباس *libās*, s.m. (2nd) Dress, attire, clothes, habit. 2. Flattery, cajolery. 3. Forgery, deception. Pl. لباسونه *libāsūnah*. لباسي *libāsī*, adj. A flatterer, a cajoler. 2. False, counterfeit. (Masc. and Fem.) ژبه د لباس *<u>jz</u>aba'h da libās*, Flattery, fawning, adulation, toad-eating, sycophancy, deception. لباس آغستل *libās ā<u>gh</u>ustal*, verb trans. To dress one's-self, to put on clothes. لباس واغستول *libās wā<u>gh</u>ustawul*, verb trans. To dress, to clothe, to dress another. See پوښاك and جوړه

لپ څټ *lap-<u>ts</u>a<u>t</u>t*, adj. Fertile, fruitful (as land); (Fem.) لپه څټه *lapa'h-<u>ts</u>a<u>tt</u>a'h*.

لپړ *lapa<u>rr</u>*, s.m. (2nd) The name of a kind of game of pitch and toss. 2. A round stone or pebble used in the game. Pl. لپړونه *lapa<u>rr</u>ūnah*.

لپكيَ *lapakaey*, s.m. (1st) (dimin. of لپه) The quantity containable in both hands held together. Pl. ي *ī*. See لپه

لپه *lapa'h*, s.f. (3rd) The space in the palm of the hand, closed so as to hold anything, a handful. Pl. ې *ey*; also written لپَ *lapa*.

لت پت *lat-pat*, adj. Smeared, stained, besmeared, splashed, daubed. 2. Soiled, polluted; (Fem.) لته پته *lata'h-pata'h*. لت پت كيدل *lat-pat kedal*, verb intrans. To become smeared, soiled, etc. لت پت كول *lat-pat kawul*, verb trans. To daub, to smear, to pollute.

لتاړه *latā<u>rr</u>ah*, adj. Trodden under foot, ruined, devastated, desolated, ravaged. (Masc. and Fem.) لتاړيدل *latā<u>rr</u>edal*, verb intrans. To become ruined, desolated, ravaged. Pres. لتاړيږي *latā<u>rr</u>ejzī* (W.) or لتاړيګي *latā<u>rr</u>egī* (E.); past لتاړ شه *latā<u>rr</u> <u>sh</u>ah* or وُ شه *wu-<u>sh</u>ah*; fut. لتاړ به شي *latā<u>rr</u> bah <u>sh</u>ī* or به وُ شي *bah wu-<u>sh</u>ī*; imp. لتاړ شه *latā<u>rr</u> <u>sh</u>ah* or وُ شه *wu-<u>sh</u>ah*; act. part. لتاړيدونكيَ *latā<u>rr</u>edūnkaey* or لتاړيدونيَ *latā<u>rr</u>edūnaey*; past part. لتاړ *latā<u>rr</u>* or لتاړ شويَ *latā<u>rr</u> <u>sh</u>awaey*; verb. n. لتاړيدنه *latā<u>rr</u>edana'h* or لتاړيده *latā<u>rr</u>edah*. لتاړول *latā<u>rr</u>awul*, verb trans. To desolate, to ravage, to tread under foot, to devastate. Pres. لتاړوي *latā<u>rr</u>awī*; past لتاړ كړ *latā<u>rr</u> ka<u>rr</u>* or وُ كړ *wu-ka<u>rr</u>*; fut. لتاړ به كړي *latā<u>rr</u> bah k<u>rr</u>ī* or

به وُ كړي *bah wu-kṟṟī*; imp. لتاړ كړه *latāṟṟ kṟṟah* or وُ كړه *wu-kṟṟah*; act. part. لتاړوونكي *latāṟṟawūnkaey* or لتاړووني *latāṟṟawūnaey*; past part. لتاړولي *latāṟṟawulaey*; verb. n. لتاړونه *latāṟṟawuna'h*.

لته *lata'h*, s.f. (3rd) A kick, a blow with the foot. Pl. ي *ey*. لته وهل *lata'h wahal*, verb trans. To kick, to launch out; or په لته وهل *pah lata'h wahal*. (HI لات or لت).

لټ *latt*, s.m. (2nd) The axle of a Persian wheel, or an axle in general. 2. A fishing stake. Pl. لټونه *laṯṯūnah*.

لټ *laṯṯ*, adj. Lazy, stubborn (as a bullock which will not work in a plough). (Fem.) لټه *laṯṯa'h*.

لټ پټ *laṯṯ-paṯṯ* or لټ په لټ *laṯṯ pah laṯṯ*, adj. Trampled on, beaten down, trodden under foot. 2. (HI) Tangled, folded, entangled, clotted (as hair); (Fem.) لټه پټه *laṯṯa'h-paṯṯa'h*. لټ پټ كيدل *laṯṯ-paṯṯ kedal*, verb intrans. To be trampled on, entangled, clotted, etc. لټ پټ كول *laṯṯ-paṯṯ kawul*, verb trans. To trample under foot, to entangle, to clot or mat (as the hair, etc.)

لټول *laṯṯawul*, verb trans. To search, to seek, to look for, to pursue, to examine, to institute. Pres. لټوي *laṯṯawī*; past وُ لټاوه *wu-laṯṯāwuh* or وُ لټاوو *wu-laṯṯāwo*; fut. وُ به لټوي *wu bah laṯṯawī*; imp. وُ لټوه *wu-laṯṯawah*; act. part. لټوونكي *laṯṯawūnkaey* or لټووني *laṯṯawūnaey*; past part. لټولي *laṯṯawulaey*; verb. n. لټونه *laṯṯawuna'h*.

لټ *laṯṯ*, adj. Lazy, indolent, idle, remiss, slack, inert, heavy, dull, listless, dawdling, laggard, dilatory; (Fem.) لټه *laṯṯah*.

لټه پير *laṯṯah-per*, s.m. (2nd) Romping, fun, frolic, prank, antic, caper. Pl. لټه پيرونه *laṯṯah-perūnah*. لټه پير كول *laṯṯah-per kawul*, verb trans. To romp, to play pranks, to cut capers. See تيل تال

ليچ *læch*, s.m. (2nd) A disease of the eyes, ophthalmia. Pl. ليچونه *læchūnah*. ليچن *læchan*, adj. Afflicted with sore eyes; (Fem.) ليچنه *læchana'h*. See ليچ

لڅ *luts*, adj. Naked, bare, stark, nude, denuded, exposed. 2. Poor, destitute; (Fem.) لڅه *lutsa'h*. لڅ لپړ *luts-laparr* or لڅ پڅ *luts-puts*, adj. Stark-naked, in a state of nature, (Fem.) لڅه لپړه *lutsa'h-laparra'h* or لڅه پڅه *lutsa'h putsa'h*. لڅي پښي *lutsey-pshey* (W.) or لڅي پخي *lutsey-pkhey* (E.) or لڅي خپي *lutsey khpey*, adj. Bare-footed. لڅ سر *luts sar*, adj. Bare-headed. لڅ والي *luts-wālaey*, s.m. (1st) Nakedness, bareness, nudeness, nudity, denudation. Pl. والي *wālī*; or لڅ توب *luts-tob*, s.m. (2nd). Pl. توبونه *tobūnah*; and لڅ تيا *luts-tī'ā*. (E.) Sing. and Pl. (W.) Pl. تياوي *tī'āwī*. و لڅه ته وتل *wa lutsah tah watal*, verb intrans. To become exposed, bare, or known (as a secret, etc.) لڅيدل *lutsedal*, verb intrans. To become naked, nude, denuded, stripped, ragged, roofless, destitute, exposed, etc. Pres. لڅيږي *lutsejzī* (W.) or لڅيكي *lutsegī* (E.); past لڅ شه *luts shah* or وُ شه *wu-shah*; fut. لڅ به شي *luts bah shī* or به وُ شي *bah wu-shī*; imp. لڅ شه *luts shah* or وُ شه *wu-shah*; act. part. لڅيدونكي *lutsedūnkaey* or لڅيدوني *lutsedūnaey*; past part. لڅ *luts* or لڅ شوي *luts shawaey*; verb. n. لڅيدنه *lutsedana'h* or لڅيده *lutsedah*.

لڅول *lutsawul*, verb trans. To strip, to divest, to uncover, to lay bare, to denude, to unroof, to rob, to plunder, to deprive, to bereave, to unrig, to make bare by cutting, grazing, etc. Pres. لڅوي *lutsawī*; past لڅ كړ *luts karr* or وُ كړ *wu-karr*; fut. لڅ به كړي *luts bah kṟṟī* or به وُ كړي *bah wu-kṟṟī*; imp. لڅ كړه *luts kṟṟah* or وُ كړه *wu-kṟṟah*; act. part. لڅوونكي *lutsawūnkaey* or لڅووني *lutsawūnaey*; past part. لڅ كړي *luts karraey*; verb. n. لڅونه *lutsawuna'h*. (HI لچ)

A لحد *lahad*, s.m. (2nd) A niche in the side of a sepulchre in which dead bodies are deposited. Pl. لحدونه *lahadūnah*.

A لحظه *lahza'h*, s.f. (3rd) A moment, the twinkling of the eye. 2. A glance, a look. Pl. ي *ey*.

لد *lid*, s.m. (2nd) Dung, excrement. Pl. لدونه *lidūnah*. (HI ليد)

A لدن *ladun* or لدون *ladūn* or علم لدن *æilm-i-ladun* or علم لدون *æilm-i-ladūn*, s.m. (9th) Inspired or inherent wisdom or knowledge. Sing. and Pl. علم لدني *æilm-i-laduney* or لدوني *ladūney*, Inspiration, inspired knowledge.

لدر *laddar*, s.m. (5th) A dealer in old clothes, etc. Pl. لدران *laddarān*. 2. adj. Stupid, foolish, dull, wanting intellect; (Fem.) لدره *laddara'h*.

A لذت *lazzat*, s.m. (2nd) Pleasure, enjoyment, delight, flavour, taste, savour, sweetness, deliciousness. Pl. لذتونه *lazzatūnah*. لذت آخستل *lazzat ākhistal*, verb trans. To taste, to savour, to enjoy.

A لذيذ *lazīz*, adj. Delicious, pleasant, savoury, luscious, delightful, pleasant, nice; (Fem.) لذيذه *lazīza'h*.

لر *lar*, adj. Lower, minor, inferior, subordinate, lesser. 2. Vanquished; (Fem.) لره *lara'h*. 3. prep. Beneath, below, in a less degree. لر پښتون *lar-pushtūn* (W.) or *lar-pukhtūn* (E.) The Lower Afghāns, the tribes nearest to Hindūstān and Kashmīr, the Eastern Afghāns, whose language contains a number of Sanskrit words, and who pronounce four letters differently to their Western brethren, viz., ښ *khīn* (E.) for *shay* (W.), ګ *gāf* (E.) ږ *jzay* (W.), ز *zay* (E.) ځ *dzay* (W.), ج *jīm* (E.) ژ *jzay* (W.). The Western Afghāns are those about Kandahār, Shorāwak, Pishīn, and Kābul, and are called بر پښتون *bar-pushtūn* or *bar-pukhtūn*, or Upper Afghāns. لر طرف *lar-taraf*, The losing side, the south, the lower side. لر بر کتل *lar-bar katal*, verb trans. To look about on all sides, to labor under embarrassment or perplexity. لره خوا *lara'h-khwā* or لري خوا *larey-khwā*, The lower side or part.

لرِ *liri*, adj. Distant, far, remote. 2. adv. Far away, afar off. See لري

لرغون *lar-ghūn*, adv. Before, previously, ere now, ere while, before now, already, yet. See لارغه

لرغوني *lar-ghūnaey*, adj. Previous, former, preceding, anterior, antecedent, introductory, prefatory. 2. adv. Before, prior, sooner, heretofore, ago, long since. See لري لارغه

لرګي *largaey*, s.m. (1st) Wood, timber, a stick, a staff, a piece of wood. Pl. ي *ī*.

لرګي *liragaey*, s.m. (1st) The lobe of the ear. Pl. ي *ī*. See نرمي

لرل *laral*, verb trans. To have, to possess, to hold, to own, to inherit, to be worth, etc. Pres. لري *larī*; past و لاره *wu-lārah*; fut. و به لري *wu bah larī*; imp. و لره *wu-larah*; act. part. لرونکي *larūnkaey* or لروني *larūnaey*; past part. لرلي *laralaey*; verb. n. لرنه *larana'h*. See درلول

لره *larah*, post. governing the dative case, To, unto. It is also construable, For, for the sake of, on account of, towards, near, before, at hand, etc. The other postpositions governing this case are ته and له. See Grammar, page 7.

لري *laraey*, s.m. (1st) The bowels, the intestines. 2. (from لر) Discomfiture, defeat, loss, forfeiture. Pl. ي *ī*. See اوژري and اوجري

لري *lirī*, adj. Distant, far, remote, far off. 2. adv. Far away, afar off, a great way off, yonder, abroad, beyond. لري کيدل *liri kedal*, verb intrans. To be distant, far, remote, to extend to. لري کول *lirī kawul*, verb trans. To put to a distance, to keep at a distance, to remove, to reject, to repel, to dispel. See لر and بيرته

HI لړ *larr*, s.m. (2nd) A string (of pearls, beads, etc.), a thread, a row, Pl. لړونه *larrūnah*. لړ لړ *larr-larr*, s.m. (2nd) An ornament worn by females, consisting of a string of pearls passing over the head and supporting the *ttika'ī* on the forehead. Pl. لړ لړونه *larr-larr-ūnah*.

لړزه *larrza'h*, s.f. (3rd) (P لرزه) Shivering, quaking, trembling, tremor, quivering. 2. An earthquake. Pl. ې *ey*. لړزيدل *larrzedal*, verb intrans. To shiver, to quake, to tremble, to be in a tremor. Pres. لړزيږي *larrzejzī*

(W.) or لړزيگي *la<u>rr</u>zegī* (E.); past وُ لړزيدهٔ *wu-la<u>rr</u>ze-dah*; fut. وُ به لړزيږي *wu bah la<u>rr</u>zejzī* or لړزيگي *la<u>rr</u>zegī*; imp. وُ لړزيږه *wu-la<u>rr</u>zejzah* or وُ لړزيگه *wu-la<u>rr</u>zegah*; act. part. لړزيدونكَي *la<u>rr</u>zedūnkaey* or لړزيدونيَ *la<u>rr</u>zedūnaey*; past part. لړزيدليَ *la<u>rr</u>zedalaey*; verb. n. لړزيدنه *la<u>rr</u>zedana'h* or لړزيدهٔ *la<u>rr</u>zedah*.

لړزول *la<u>rr</u>zawul*, verb trans. To agitate, to cause to quiver, to make tremble, to put in a tremor. Pres. لړزوي *la<u>rr</u>zawī*; past وُ لړزاوهٔ *wu-la<u>rr</u>zāwuh* or وُ لړزاوو *wu-la<u>rr</u>zāwo*; fut. وُ به لړزوي *wu bah la<u>rr</u>zawī*; imp. وُ لړزوه *wu-la<u>rr</u>zawah*; act. part. لړزوونكَي *la<u>rr</u>zawūnkaey* or لړزووني *la<u>rr</u>zawūnaey*; past part. لړزوليَ *la<u>rr</u>zawulaey*; verb. n. لړزونه *la<u>rr</u>zawuna'h*. See ريږدول, ريږديدل and ګګروشه

لړل *la<u>rr</u>al*, verb trans. To stir, to mix, to combine, to blend, to move, to put into action. 2. To smear, to anoint, to dip. Pres. لړي *la<u>rr</u>ī*; past وُ لاړه *wu-lā<u>rr</u>ah*; fut. وُ به لړي *wu bah la<u>rr</u>ī*; imp. وُ لړه *wu-la<u>rr</u>ah*; act. part. لړونكَي *la<u>rr</u>ūnkaey* or لړونيَ *la<u>rr</u>ūnaey*; past part. لړليَ *la<u>rr</u>alaey*; verb. n. لړنه *la<u>rr</u>ana'h*.

لړليَ *la<u>rr</u>alaey* or لړه‌ليَ *la<u>rr</u>ah-laey*, adj. (past part.) Combined, mixed, blended, mixed up; hybrid, mongrel. 2. Stained, polluted, smeared, dirtied, dipped. 3. A person who lives an iniquitous life, a rascal, a blackguard; (Fem.) لړلِ *la<u>rr</u>ali*. Pl. (Masc. and Fem.) ي *ī*.

لړم *la<u>rr</u>am*, s.m. (5th) A scorpion. Pl. لړمان *la<u>rr</u>amān*. لړمه *la<u>rr</u>ama'h*, s.f. (3rd) The female of the above. Pl. يْ *ey*. د لړم باليښت *da la<u>rr</u>am bāli<u>kh</u>t* (E.) A species of milleped or wood-louse, called also a grammer-sow (*lit.* a scorpion's pillow).

لړمون *larr-mūn*, s m. (4th) The intestines, heart, liver, bowels, etc. Pl. لړمانه *la<u>rr</u>mānah*.

لړمه *la<u>rr</u>ama'h*, s.f. (3rd) The erysipelas, an eruption of the body. Pl. يْ *ey*. The plural form is generally used.

لړوڅټو *la<u>rr</u>o-tsa<u>tt</u>o*, adj. A rascal, a low or mean person. (Masc. and Fem.)

لړه *la<u>rr</u>a'h*, s.f. (3rd) A mist, a fog, a vapor. 2. Twilight, the dusk, the grey of the morning. 3. Battle, fighting, quarrel (s बाद). Pl. يْ *ey*.

لږ *la<u>jz</u>*, adj. (W.) Little, small, scarce, few, scanty, seldom, less; (Fem.) لږه *la<u>jz</u>a'h*. 2. adv. A little, slightly, not much, in some degree; so-so, pretty well, tolerably. لږ لږ *la<u>jz</u>-la<u>jz</u>*, A little, little by little, a small quantity. لږكوټيَ *la<u>jz</u>-ko<u>tt</u>aey*, Very little; (Fem.) لږ كوټِ *la<u>jz</u>-ko<u>tt</u>i*. Pl. (Masc. and Fem.) ي *ī*. لږيدل *la<u>jz</u>edal*, verb intrans. (W.) To be small, little, less, few, scanty, trivial, etc. 2. To lessen, to diminish. Pres. لږيږي *la<u>jz</u>ejzī*; past لږ شه *la<u>jz</u> <u>sh</u>ah* or وُ شه *wu-<u>sh</u>ah*; fut. لږ به شي *la<u>jz</u> bah <u>sh</u>ī* or وُ به شي *bah wu-<u>sh</u>ī*; imp. لږ شه *la<u>jz</u> <u>sh</u>ah* or وُ شه *wu-<u>sh</u>ah*; act. part. لږيدونكَي *la<u>jz</u>edūnkaey* or لږيدونيَ *la<u>jz</u>edūnaey*; past part. لږ *la<u>jz</u>* or لږ شويَ *la<u>jz</u> <u>sh</u>awaey*; verb. n. لږيدنه *la<u>jz</u>edana'h* or لږيدهٔ *la<u>jz</u>edah*. لږول *la<u>jz</u>awul*, verb trans. To make small, less, few, scanty, trivial, etc. Pres. لږوي *la<u>jz</u>awī*; past لږ كړ *la<u>jz</u> ka<u>rr</u>* or وُ كړ *wu-ka<u>rr</u>*; fut. لږ به كړي *la<u>jz</u> bah k<u>rr</u>ī* or وُ به كړي *bah wu-k<u>rr</u>ī*; imp. لږ كړه *la<u>jz</u> k<u>rr</u>ah* or وُ كړه *wu-k<u>rr</u>ah*; act. part. لږوونكَي *la<u>jz</u>awūnkaey* or لږووني *la<u>jz</u>awūnaey*; past part. لږ كړيَ *la<u>jz</u> ka<u>rr</u>aey*; verb. n. لږونه *la<u>jz</u>awuna'h*. See لك

لږ ډير *la<u>jz</u> <u>dd</u>er*, adj. More or less, somewhat.

لږواليَ *la<u>jz</u>-wālaey*, s.m. (1st) Smallness, littleness, scantiness, paltriness, meagreness, triflingness. Pl. والي *wālī*.

لس *las*, adj. Ten. لسم *lasam*, The tenth; (Fem.) لسمه *lasama'h*.

لستوڼيَ *lastū<u>rr</u>naey*, s.m. (1st) The sleeve of a garment. Pl. ي *ī*.

لسته *lasta'h*, s.f. (3rd) Side, margin, quarter, extremity, towards. Pl. يْ *ey*. See لاسته and لاستَ

لسره *lasarah*, adv. Never, at no time, ever, at any time, on no occasion, never more. See هيڅري

لشمكي *la<u>sh</u>-maka'ī*, s.f. (6th) A deceitful, insidious, artful woman. Sing. and Pl. See شتاهه and نشمي

لشه *lasha'h*, s.f. (3rd) The spike or beard of wheat or barley, and some kinds of grasses. 2. The sting of a wasp, scorpion, etc. 3. A splinter. Pl. ي *ey*. See لاشه

لښ *lash* (W.) or *lakh* (E.) s.m. (2nd) A corpse, a dead body, a carcass. Pl. لښونه *lashūnah* or *lakhūnah*. See لاښ

لښته *lashta'h* (W.) or *lakhta'h* (E.) s.f. (3rd) A rod, a switch, a wand, a stick, a cane, a ratan, the small branch of a tree. Pl. ي *ey*. په لښته وهل *pah lashta'h* or *lakhta'h wahal*, verb trans. To cane, to scourge, to thrash, to flag, to castigate.

لښتئ *lashta'ī* (W.) or *lakhta'ī* (E.) s.f. (6th) The name of a plant which, if a person eat a little of it, and afterwards breathe in the ear of a wounded person, the wounds of the latter will never heal until the spittle of the former is applied to them. (Æajā'ib-ul-Lughat). 2. A kind of ornament for the ear. 3. A dancing-girl. Sing. and Pl.

لښتئ *lashtaey* (W.) or *lakhtaey* (E.) s.m. (1st) A brook, a spring, a rivulet, a small stream. Pl. ي *ī*.

لښکر *lashkar* (W.) or *lakhkar* (E.) s.m. (2nd) An army. Pl. لښکرونه *lashkarūnah* or *lakhkarūnah*; or s.f. (1st) Pl. لښکر *lashkari* or *lakhkari*. لښکري *lashkarī* or *lākhkarī*, adj. A soldier, a camp-follower, belonging to an army. (Masc. and Fem.) لښکر گاه *lashkar-gāh* (W.) or *lakhkar-gāh* (E.) s.m. (2nd) A camp or cantonment. Pl. لښکر گاهونه *lashkar-gāhūnah* or *lakhkar-gāhūnah*. لښکري عدالت *lashkarī* or *lakhkarī æadālat*, A court-martial. لښکر کښي *lashkar-kashī* (W.) or *lakhkar-kakhī* (E.) s.f. (3rd) Levying troops, assembling or sending forth an army. Pl. ي *a'ī*. (P لشکر).

لښکي *lashkī* (W.) or *lakhkī* (E.) adv. Ever so little, very little, a very small quantity. See لږکوټي and لکوټي

A لطافت *laṭāfat*, s.m. (2nd) Fineness, thinness, delicacy, elegance, neatness, deliciousness. Pl. لطافتونه *laṭāfatūnah*. لطافت لرل *laṭāfat laral*, verb trans. To have or be possessed of delicacy, fineness, etc.

A لطيف *laṭīf*, adj. Elegant, agreeable, delicate, delicious, exquisite; (Fem.) لطيفه *laṭīfa'h*.

A لطيفه *laṭīfa'h*, s.f. (3rd) A jest, a joke, raillery, pleasantry. Pl. ي *ey*. لطيفه ويل *laṭīfa'h wa-yal*, verb trans. To crack a joke.

P لعل *laæl*, s.m. (2nd) A ruby. Pl. لعلونه *laæl-ūnah*. See also لال

A لعن *laæn*, s.m. (2nd) Cursing, imprecating. Pl. لعنونه *laæn-ūnah*.

A لعنت *laænat*, s.m. (2nd) A curse, an anathema, an execration, an imprecation. Pl. لعنتونه *laænatūnah*. لعن *laæn* or لعنت ويل *laænat wa-yal*, verb trans. To curse, to execrate.

P A لعنتي *laænatī*, adj. Accursed, execrated. (Masc. and Fem.); also لعين *laæ'īn*; (Fem.) لعينه *laæ'īna'h*.

A لغت *lughat*, s.m. (2nd) (from لغو) Dialect, language. 2. A dictionary. 3. A word. Pl. لغتونه *lughatūnah*.

لغته *laghata'h*, s.f. (3rd) A kick, a blow with the foot. Pl. ي *ey*. لغتي وهل *laghatey wahal*, verb trans. To kick, to launch out. په لغتي وهل *pah laghatey wahal*, verb trans. To kick, to strike with the foot or feet, to recoil (as a gun). (P لگد). See لته

لغړ *laghaṟṟ*, adj. Naked, bare, stark, nude, denuded, exposed. 2. Poor, destitute, roofless; (Fem.) لغړه *laghaṟṟa'h*. لڅ لغړ *luts-laghaṟṟ*, adj. Stark-naked, bare as a coot. لغړ والئ *laghaṟṟ-wālaey*, s.m. (1st) Nakedness, bareness, rudeness, nudity, denudation. 2. Poverty. Pl. والي *wālī*. لغړه توره *laghaṟṟa'h-tūra'h*, s.f. (3rd) A naked sword. Pl. ي *ey*. لغړيدل *laghaṟṟedal*, verb intrans. To become naked, bare, nude, exposed, poor, destitute, etc. Pres. لغړيږي *laghaṟṟejzī* (W.) or لغړيگي *laghaṟṟegī* (E.); past لغړ شه *laghaṟṟ shah* or و شه *wu-shah*; fut. لغړ به شي *laghaṟṟ bah shī* or به و شي *bah wu-shī*; imp. لغړ شه *laghaṟṟ shah* or و شه *wu-shah*; act. part. لغړيدونکي

lagharredūnkaey or لغړيدونې *lagharredūnacy*; past part. لغړ *lagharr* or لغړ شوئ *lagharr shawaey*; verb. n. لغړيدنه *lagharredana'h* or لغړيده *lagharredah*. لغړول *lagharrawul*, verb trans. To strip, to denude, to lay or make bare, to divest, to uncover. Pres. لغړوي *lagharrawī*; past لغړ کړ *lagharr karr* or وُ کړ *wu-karr*; fut. لغړ به کړي *lagharr bah krrī* or به وُ کړي *bah wu-krrī*; imp. لغړ کړه *lagharr krrah* or وُ کړه *wu-krrah*; act. part. لغړوونکئ *lagharrawūnkaey* or لغړوونئ *lagharrawūnaey*; past part. لغړولئ *lagharrawulaey*; verb.n. لغړونه *lagharrawuna'h*. See لغ

لغړن *lagharran*, adj. Smoked black, smoky, unclean, dirty, untidy, slovenly. 2. Inflamed, scorched (with love), charred; (Fem.) لغړنه *lagharrana'h*. لغړن کيدل *lagharran kedal*, verb intrans. To become smoked, charred, scorched, untidy, dirty, etc. لغړن کول *lagharran kawul*, verb trans. To smoke, to char, to scorch, to inflame, to soil, to dirty.

A لغز *laghz*, s.m. (2nd) A slip, a trip, slipping. Pl. لغزونه *laghzūnah*. لغزيدل *laghzedal*, verb intrans. To slip, to trip, to slide, to stumble. لغزول *laghzawul*, verb trans. To cause to slip, trip or stumble. See ښوييدل

A لفظ *lafz*, s.m. (2nd) A word, a saying. Pl. لفظونه *lafzūnah*.

A لقب *lakab*, s.m. (2nd) A title, a surname, a byename. Pl. لقبونه *lakabūnah*. لقب ورکول *lakab war-kawul*, verb trans. To grant a title, to give a surname or nickname to any one.

A لقمه *lukma'h*, s.f. (3rd) A mouthful, a morsel. Pl. ې *ey*. See ګوله

A لقوه *lakwa'h*, s.f. (3rd) (from لقا) A disease, a spasmodic distortion of the face. Pl. ې *ey*.

لقه *lukah*, adj. A bully, a bragger, a braggadocio, an empty fellow. (Masc. and Fem.) See لاپک

لکت *lak*, adj. Stiff, standing, rigid, unbending, tense, standing upright. 2. Pierced, perforated, bored, punctured; (Fem.) لکه *laka'h*. لکيدل *lakedal*, verb intrans. To stand, to stand upright, to become rigid, unbending, tense. 2. To be perforated, bored, punctured. Pres. لکيږي *lakejzī* (W.) or لکيګي *lakegī* (E.); past لکت شه *lak shah* or وُ شه *wu-shah*; fut. لکت به شي *lak bah shī* or به وُ شي *bah wu-shī*; imp. لکت شه *lak shah* or وُ شه *wu-shah*; act. part. لکيدونکئ *lakedūnkaey* or لکيدونئ *lakedūnaey*; past part. لکت *lak* or لکت شوئ *lak shawaey*; verb. n. لکيدنه *lakedana'h* or لکيده *lakedah*. لکول *lakawul*, verb trans. To stiffen, to harden, to render hard, stiff, tense, rigid. 2. To perforate, to pierce, to bore, to stab, to impale, to transfix. 3. To erect, to fix in the ground (as a spear). Pres. لکوي *lakawī*; past لکت کړ *lak karr* or وُ کړ *wu-karr*; fut. لکت به کړي *lak bah krrī* or به وُ کړي *bah wu-krrī*; imp. لکت کړه *lak krrah* or وُ کړه *wu-krrah*; act. part. لکوونکئ *lakawūnkaey* or لکوونئ *lakawūnaey*; past part. لکت کړئ *lak karraey*; verb. n. لکونه *lakawuna'h*.

PS لکت *lak*, s.m. (2nd) A hundred thousand. Pl. لکونه *lakūnah*.

لکټي *lakuttey*, adv. A little, slightly, not much, in some degree. See لږ and بڅاني

لکړه *lakarra'h*, s.f. (3rd) A staff, a crutch, a beam of wood. Pl. لکړي *lakarrey*. (HI لکڑ wood) See امسا and همسا

لکوټي *lakottey*, adv. A little, etc. See لکټي

لکوړي *lakorraey*, s.m. (1st) The name of a fruit. Pl. ي *ī*.

لکه *lakah*, adv. So, as, in like manner, to that degree, thus, in this manner. Also written لکَ *laka*. This word is, with but few exceptions, generally followed by هسي. See Grammar, page 26.

لکه *laka'h*, s.f. (3rd) A spot, a blot, a stain, a brand, a blemish. Pl. ې *ey*.

لکه لمي *lakah-lamaey* or لکهلمي *lakah-lamaey*, s.m. (1st) The rump bone. Pl. ي *ī*.

لکئ *laka'ī*, s.f. (6th) The tail of an animal or bird. Sing. and Pl. لکئ ښورول *laka'ī shorawul* (W.) or *khorawul* (E.) verb trans. To wag the tail, as a dog. 2. To flatter, to wheedle, to cajole (met.) لکي په کونه ننيستل *laka'ī pah kūna'h nana-yastal*, verb trans. To put the tail between the legs (as a dog when cowed or frightened).

لگ *lag* (E.) adj. A little, small, scarce, few, scanty, seldom, less. 2. adv. A little, slightly, not much, in some degree; (Fem.) لگه *lagah*. لگ‌لگ *lag-lag*, A small quantity, very little, little by little. لگيدل *lagedal*, verb intrans. To become small, to grow less, to diminish, to be little, less, few, scanty, trivial. لگول *lagawul*, verb trans. To make small, to diminish, to lessen, to make few or scanty. For inflections of the above see the Western form لږيدل and لږول and substitute the E. لگ for لږ. لگ والَي *lag-wālaey*, s.m. (1st) Littleness, smallness, scantiness, thinness, scarceness, scarcity, fewness. Pl. والي *wālī*.

HI لگړ *lagaṛr*, s.m. (5th) A falcon. Pl. لگړان *lagaṛrān*. لگړه *lagaṛra'h*, s.f. (3rd) The hen bird. Pl. ئ *ey*.

لگيا *lagī'ā*, adj. Applied, attached, planted, placed, inflicted, connected, fastened, engaged, employed, spread. (Masc. and Fem.) لگيا کيدل *lagī'ā kedal*, verb intrans. To become attached, applied, planted, employed, etc. لگيا کول *lagī'ā kawul*, verb trans. To attach, to apply, to plant, to employ; or لگيدل *lagedal*, verb intrans. To be applied, to apply, begin, to be fixed, attached, close; to adjoin, touch, be employed; to attain, to reach, to join; to befal, to happen, etc. Pres. لگيږي *lagejzī* (W.) or لگيگي *lagegī* (E.); past وُ لگيده *wu-lagedah*; fut. وُ به لگيږي *wu bah lagejzī* or لگيگي *lagegī*; imp. وُ لگيږه *wu-lagejzah* or لگيگه *lagegah*; act. part. لگيدونکَي *lagedūnkaey* or لگيدونَي *lagedūnaey*; past part. لگيدلَي *lagedalaey*; verb. n. لگيدنه *lagedana'h* or لگيده *lagedah*. لگول *lagawul*, verb trans. To apply, attach, close, join, affix, ascribe, impose, lay, add, place, put, plant, set, inflict, spread, fasten, connect, put to work, employ, engage, use, report (as malice), etc. Pres. لگوي *lagawī*; past وُ لگاوه *wu-lagāwuh* or لگاوو *lagāwo*; fut.

وُ به لگوي *wu bah lagawī*; imp. وُ لگوه *wu-lagawah*; act. part. لگوونکَي *lagawūnkaey* or لگوونَي *lagawūnaey*; past part. لگولَي *lagawulaey*; verb. n. لگونه *lagawuna'h*. (s लग)

لل *lal*, verb trans. To perform, pronounce, utter, express, give, etc. (particularly and peculiarly applied to giving evidence, paying respects, etc.) Pres. لي *lī*; past وُ له *wu-lah* or وُ لَ *wu-la*; fut. وُ به لي *wu bah lī*; imp. وُ له *wu-lah*; act. part. لونکَي *lūnkaey* or لونَي *lūnaey*; past part. للَي *lalaey*; verb. n. لنه *lana'h*. شاهدي لل *shāhidī lal*, verb trans. To give evidence, to depose to. سلام لل *salām lal*, verb trans. To pay one's respects, to express veneration. See لودل

لل *lal*, adj. Dumb, speechless, tongue-tied (corrup. of P لال); (Fem.) لله *lala'h*. لل والَي *lal wālaey*, s.m. (1st) Dumbness, muteness, aphony. Pl. والي *wālī*.

للمي *lalmī*, s.m. (1st) Pl. Growing spontaneously, applied particularly to crops wholly dependent on rain for irrigation, or spring crops. The singular form is not used. See آبي

للو للو *lalo-lalo*, s.m. (9th) A lullaby, a song to soothe a child, solace. Sing. and Pl. للو للو کول *lalo-lalo kawul*, verb trans. To soothe, to cheer, to comfort (a child). See تاتي

للون *lalūn*, s.m. (4th) Weeding a field or garden. Pl. للانه *lalānah*. للون کول *lalūn kawul*, verb trans. To weed, to separate, to thin. See پوجي and للان

لم *lam*, s.m. (2nd) The tail of an animal, the fat tail of an Afghān sheep. 2. End, extremity, termination, tag, tip, nib, butt-end, etc. Pl. لمونه *lamūnah*. لمور *lamawar*, adj. Large tailed, a fat-tail sheep (*dumbah*); (Fem.) لموره *lamawara'h*; or لمه ور *lamah-war* and لمه وره *lamah-wara'h*. See لکي

لمبر *lumbaṛr*, s.m. (2nd) The front, the fore-part, the face, front-rank, the van, the bow, the prow. Pl. لمبرونه *lumbaṛrūnah*. لمبرَي *lumbaṛraey*, adj. Fore, front, anterior, frontal; adv. Before, in the front, ahead, in advance; (Fem.) لمبرئ *lumbaṛra'ī*. لمبرَي کيدل *lum-*

barṟaey kedal, verb intrans. To be advanced or placed in front or the van. لمبرَي كول *lumbarṟaey kawul*, verb trans. To advance to the front, to place in front or the van. See وړاندِ

لمبر *lambaṟr*, s.m. (5th) A male fox. Pl. لمبران *lambaṟrān*. لمبره *lambaṟra'h*, s.f. (3rd) A bitch or female fox, and also applied to the species generally when the gender is not actually specified. Pl. ي *ey*. (HI لمبر). See ترورْي

لمبل *lambal*, verb trans. To bathe, to wash, to lave, to duck, to dip, to cleanse, to purify, to sponge, to clean, to rinse, etc. Pres. لامبي *lāmbī*; past وُ لمبل *wu-lambal*; fut. وُ به لامبي *wu bah lāmbī*; imp. وُ لامبه *wu-lāmbah*; act. part. لمبونكَي *lambūnkaey* or لمبونَي *lambūnaey*; past part. لمبلَي *lambalaey*; verb. n. لمبنه *lambana'h*. See لمبيدل

لمبه *lamba'h*, s.f. (3rd) Flame, blaze. Pl. ي *ey*. See لنبه

لمبيدل *lambedal*, verb intrans. To wash, to bathe, to perform the act of ablution, to soak. Pres. لمبيږي *lambejẕī* (W.) or لمبيكي *lambegī* (E.); past وُ لمبيده *wu-lambedah*; fut. وُ به لمبيږي *wu bah lambejẕī* or لمبيكي *lambegī*; imp. وُ لمبيږه *wu-lambejẕah* or لمبيكه *lambegah*; act. part. لمبيدونكَي *lambedūnkaey* or لمبيدونَي *lambedūnaey*; past part. لمبيدلَي *lambedalaey*; verb. n. لمبيدنه *lambedana'h* or لمبيده *lambedah*. لمبول *lambawul*, verb trans. To render clean, to bathe, to wash, to cleanse, to dip, to immerse, to absterge. Pres. لمبوي *lambawī*; past وُ لمباوه *wu-lambāwuh* or لمباوو *lambāwo*; fut. وُ به لمبوي *wu bah lambawī*; imp. وُ لمبوه *wu-lambawah*; act. part. لمبوونكَي *lambawūnkaey* or لمبوونَي *lambawūnaey*; past part. لمبولَي *lambawulaey*; verb. n. لمبونه *lambawuna'h*. See لمبل and لنبل

لمڅي *lamtsaey*, s.m. (1st) Felt, a kind of cloth made from wool by rolling. Pl. ي *ī*. See لمسي, كوسي, كراسته, and

لمسول *lamsawul*, verb trans. To incite, to stimulate, to instigate, to impel, to encourage, to prompt, to animate, to urge, to rouse, to sway, to bias. Pres. لمسوي *lamsawī*; past وُ لمساوه *wu-lamsāwuh* or لمساوو *lamsāwo*; fut. وُ به لمسوي *wu bah lamsawī*; imp. وُ لمسوه *wu-lamsawah*; act. part. لمسوونكَي *lamsawūnkaey* or لمسوونَي *lamsawūnaey*; past part. لمسولَي *lamsawulaey*; verb. n. لمسونه *lamsawuna'h*.

لمسونه *lamsawuna'h*, s.f. (3rd) (verb. n.) Inciting, incitement, stimulating, prompting, stimulus, provocation. Pl. ي *ey*.

لمسي *lamsaey*, s.m. (1st) Felt, a kind of woollen cloth. Pl. ي *ī*. See لمڅي

لمغرۍ *lamgharra'ī*, s.f. (6th) Stratagem, trick, device, manœuvre, wile, dodge, ruse, finesse. Sing. and Pl. لمغرۍ كول *lamgharra'ī kawul*, verb trans. To intrigue, to manœuvre, to practice stratagem or artifice. 2. To play the old soldier.

لمن *laman*, s.f. (1st) The skirt of a dress, margin, hem, border. Pl. لمن *lamani*. د غرَ لمن *da ghra laman*, The skirt, foot, or declivity of a mountain. لمن نيول *laman nīwal*, verb trans. To beg, to petition, to desire (*lit.* to seize the skirt of one's own dress and hold it out.) تر لمن نيول *tar laman nīwal*, verb trans. To seize by the skirt, to seize the hem of another's garment, to take refuge or protection. په لمن كښي آچول *pah laman kshey* (W.) or *k'khey* (E.) *āchawul*, verb trans. To throw one's-self on another's protection.

لمور *lamawar*, adj. Large or long-tailed. 2. The fat-tailed sheep; (Fem.) لموره *lamawara'h*. See لم

لنبل *lanbal*, verb trans. To wash, to bathe, etc. See لمبل

لنبه *lanba'h*, s.f. (3rd) Flame, blaze. Pl. ي *ey*. See لمبه

لنبيدل *lanbedal*, verb intrans, to bathe, to perform ablution; and لنبول *lanbawul*, verb trans. To clean, to bathe. See لمبيدل and لمبول

لنده *linda'h*, s.f. (3rd) A bow. Pl. ي *ey*. See لينده

لندي *lin-daey*, s.m. (1st) An archer. Pl. ي *ī*.

لندۍ *linda'ī*, s.f. (6th) A bow used by stonecutters and carpenters, the bow of a fiddle. 2. One of the bones of the lower part of the arm below the elbow. 3. A piece of wood bent over the head of a cradle and covered with a cloth as a canopy. 4. The tendons under the knees. 5. A gush, a jet, a squirt, a spirt, a rush (of water, blood, etc.) 6. The motion made by boiling water, ebullition. 7. The guard of a sword. Sing. and Pl.

لنډ *landd*, adj. Short, brief, curt, stumpy, small, little; (Fem.) لنډه *landda'h*. لنډ لغړ *landd-lagharr*, adj. Stark naked, bare as a coot, as naked as when born; (Fem.) لنډه لغړه *landda'h-lagharra'h*. لنډ والې *landd-wālaey*, s.m. (1st) Shortness, brevity, smallness, stumpiness. Pl. والي *wālī*. لنډې *landdaey*, adj. (dimin. of لنډ) An animal with a short tail, docktailed, curtailed, short, dumpy. 2. The name of a river to the north of Peshāwer. Pl. ي *ī*; (Fem.) لنډۍ *landda'ī*. لنډيدل *landdedal*, verb intrans. To be short, shortened, contracted, abridged, to grow short, dumpy, or curt, to be brief, small, etc. Pres. لنډيږي *landdejzī* (W.) or لنډيگي *landdegī* (E.); past لنډ شه *landd shah* or ؤ شه *wu-shah*; fut. لنډ به شي *landd bah shī* or به ؤ شي *bah wu-shī*; imp. لنډ شه *landd shah* or ؤ شه *wu-shah*; act. part. لنډيدونکې *landdedūnkaey* or لنډيدونې *landdedūnaey*; past part. لنډ *landd* or لنډ شوې *landd shawaey*; verb. n. لنډيدنه *landdedana'h* or لنډيده *landdedah*. لنډول *landdawul*, verb trans. To shorten, to abridge, to contract, to curtail, to clip, to dock, to crop, to cut short. Pres. لنډوي *landdawī*; past لنډ کړ *landd karr* or ؤ کړ *wu-karr*; fut. لنډ به کړي *landd bah krrī* or به ؤ کړي *bah wu-krrī*; imp. لنډ کړه *landd krrah* or ؤ کړه *wu-krrah*; act. part. لنډوونکې *landdawūnkaey* or لنډوونې *landdawūnaey*; past part. لنډ کړې *landd karraey*; verb. n. لنډونه *landdawuna'h*.

لنډه *landda'h*, s.f. (3rd) The spine at the waist. Pl. ې *ey*.

لنډۍ *landda'ī*, s.f. (6th) A broad-headed snake, a small poisonous reptile found in Afghānistān, like a snake with a nob at the tail. 2. A description of poetry consisting of seven or eight syllables to the line. Sing. and Pl. See لنډه

P لنگ *lung*, s.m. (2nd) A cloth worn round the loins when bathing. Pl. لنگونه *lungūnah*.

HI لنگر *langar*, s.m. (2nd) An anchor. 2. An almshouse. Pl. لنگرونه *langarūnah*. لنگر آچول *langar āchawul*, verb trans. To cast anchor. لنگر کول *langar kawul*, verb trans. To anchor. لنگر آخستل *langar ākhistal*, verb trans. To weigh anchor. لنگر چلول *langar chalawul*, verb trans. To keep up an almshouse.

HI لنگرې *langaraey*, s.m. (1st) A large shallow pan or dish in which bread is kneaded. Pl. ي *ī*.

لنگور *langor*, s.f. (1st) The space between the end of the thumb and the fore-finger, a space or measure of the above length. Pl. لنگورِ *langori*.

لنگه *langa'h*, adj. Puerperal, a woman for forty days after child-birth, any animal who has just given birth. لنگ والې *lang-wālaey*, s.m. (1st) Lying-in, bringing forth offspring. Pl. والي *wālī*. لنگيدل *langedal*, verb intrans. To bring forth young, to lie in, to bear a child. Pres. لنگيږي *langejzī* (W) or لنگيگي *langegī* (E.); past لنگه شوه *langa'h shwah* or ؤ شوه *wu-shwah*; fut. لنگه به شي *langa'h bah shī* or به ؤ شي *bah wu shī*; imp. لنگه شه *langa'h shah* or ؤ شه *wu-shah*; act. part. لنگيدونکِ *langedūnki* or لنگيدونِ *langedūni*; past part. لنگه *langa'h* or لنگه شوِ *langa'h shawi*; verb. n. لنگيدنه *langedana'h*. لنگول *langawul*, verb trans. To cause to lie in or bring forth, to bring in the family way, to make pregnant. Pres. لنگوي *langawī*; past لنگه کړه *langa'h krrah* or و کړه *wu-krrah*; fut. لنگه به کړي *langa'h bah krrī* or به ؤ کړي *bah wu-krrī*; imp. لنگه کړه *langa'h krrah* or ؤ کړه *wu-krrah*; act. part. لنگوونکې *langawūnkaey* or لنگوونې *langawūnaey*; past part. لنگه کړِ *langa'h karri*; verb. n. لنگونه *langawuna'h*.

P لنګئي *lunga'ī*, s.f. (6th) A cloth worn round the waist, a scarf, a kind of striped cloth. Sing. and Pl.

لو *lau*, s.m. (2nd) Reaping, gathering, crop, harvest. Pl. لوونه *lau-ūnah*. لو ګرَي *lau-garaey*, s.m. (1st) A reaper. Pl. ي *ī*. لوګرئي *lau-gara'ī*, s.f. (6th) A female reaper. Sing. and Pl. لو کول *lau kawul*, verb trans. To reap, to cut a field of corn, to gather in. (s ꝗ cut.)

لو *lo*, adj. (contract. of لوي) Large, big, great, bulky, immense, huge, enormous.

لو *lū*, s.m. (9th) Smoke, vapor, fume, fumigation, scent raised by fire. Sing. and Pl. لو کول *lū-kawul*, verb trans. To raise a smoke or fume, to fumigate, to fume, to perfume. See لوکي

لوار *l'wārr*, adj. Coarse, thick, rough, not fine, coarsely ground grain. 2. Rude, unpolished (as a man), gruff, blunt, churlish, uncivil, ungracious, bearish, austere, boorish. 3. Gross, inelegant, unrefined; (Fem.) لواره *l'wārra'h*. لوار والَي *l'wārr wālaey*, s.m. (1st) Coarseness of grain, roughness, largeness of size, unrefined state. 2. Rudeness, want of polish, grossness. Pl. والي *wālī*. لواريدل *l'wārredal*, verb intrans. To become or grow coarse, rough, etc. لوارول *l'wārrawul*, verb trans. To make or render rough, coarse, etc. لواري خبري *l'wārrey khabarey*, s.f. (3rd) Pl. Rough, uncourteous words. لواري خبري کول *l'wārrey khabarey kawul*, verb trans. To speak in a rough or churlish manner.

لواره *l'wārra'h*, adj. All, the whole, every one, total.

A لواطة *lawāṭat*, s.m. (2nd) An unnatural crime, sodomy. Pl. لواطتونه *lawāṭatūnah*. لواطة کول *lawāṭat kawul*, verb trans. To commit sodomy.

لوال *liwāl*, adj. Peckish, inclined to eat, hungry, craving, desirous, inclined, eager, hankering after; (Fem.) لواله *liwāla'h*. See وري or وکي and ليوال

لواور *lawa-āor*, s.m. (2nd) A sickle, a scythe. Pl. لواورونه *lawa-āorūnah*. See لور

A لوبان *lobān*, s.m. (6th) Incense, benzoin (resin), a kind of gum. Sing. and Pl.

لوبه *luwaba'h*, s.f. (3rd) Play, sport, amusement, fun, frolic, pleasantry. Pl. ي *ey*. Also (E.) *loba'h* and *lobey*. لوبه کول *luwaba'h kawul* or *loba'h kawul*, verb trans. To play, to sport, to frolic.

لوبيا *lobiyā*, s.f. (6th) A kind of bean (Dolichos sinensis.) (E.) Sing. and Pl. (W.) Pl. لوبياوي *lobiyāwī*.

S لوټ *lūṯṯ*, s.m. (2nd) Plunder, spoil, booty, prey. Pl. لوټونه *lūṯṯūnah*. لوټ پوټ *lūṯṯ-pūṯṯ*, adj. Spoiled, plundered, sacked; (Fem.) لوټه پوټه *lūṯṯa'h pūṯṯa'h*. لوټ مار *lūṯṯ-mār*, s.m. (5th) A plunderer, a spoiler, a robber. Pl. ماران *mārān*. لوټيدل *lūṯṯedal*, verb intrans. To be plundered, sacked, robbed, stripped, rifled, pillaged, fleeced. Pres. لوټيږي *lūṯṯejzī* (W.) or لوټيګي *lūṯṯegī* (E.); past لوټ شه *lūṯṯ shah* or وُ شه *wu-shah*; fut. لوټ به شي *lūṯṯ bah shī* or به وُ شي *bah wu-shī*; imp. لوټ شه *lūṯṯ shah* or وُ شه *wu-shah*; act. part. لوټيدونکَي *lūṯṯedūnkaey* or لوټيدونَي *lūṯṯedūnaey*; past part. لوټ شوَي *lūṯṯ shawaey*; verb. n. لوټيدنه *lūṯṯedana'h* or لوټيده *lūṯṯedah*. لوټول *lūṯṯawul*, verb trans. To plunder, to rob, to strip, to rifle, to pillage, to fleece, etc. Pres. لوټوي *lūṯṯawī*; past لوټ کړ *lūṯṯ karr* or وُ کړ *wu-karr*; fut. لوټ به کړي *lūṯṯ bah krrī* or به وُ کړي *bah wu-krrī*; imp. لوټ کړه *lūṯṯ krrah* or وُ کړه *wu-krrah*; act. part. لوټوونکَي *lūṯṯawūnkaey* or لوټوونَي *lūṯṯawūnaey*; past part. لوټ کړَي *lūṯṯ karraey*; verb. n. لوټونه *lūṯṯawuna'h*. Also لوټل *lūṯṯal*, verb trans. To rob, to plunder, to pillage, to fleece, to strip. Pres. لوټي *lūṯṯī*; past وُ لوټه *wu-lūṯṯah*; fut. وُ به لوټي *wu bah lūṯṯī*; imp. وُ لوټه *wu-lūṯṯah*; act. part. لوټونکَي *lūṯṯūnkaey* or لوټونَي *lūṯṯūnaey*; past part. لوټلَي *lūṯṯalaey*; verb. n. لوټنه *lūṯṯana'h*.

لوټونه *lūṯṯawuna'h* or لوټنه *lūṯṯana'h*, s.f. (3rd) (verb. n.) Spoliation, plunder, pillage, rapine, sack, marauding. Pl. ي *ey*.

لوټه *lūṯṯa'h*, s.f. (3rd) A clod of earth, a clod, a clot. Pl. ي *ey*. لوټه مار *lūṯṯa'h-mār* or لوټ

مار lūṯṯ-mār, s.m. (2nd) A piece of wood for breaking clods. Pl. مارونه mārūnah.

لوتكي loṯṯkaey, s.m. (1st) An earthen pot, of the kind used for Persian wheels. 2. A piece of baked earth in the shape of a small pillar, on three of which the iron pan for baking cakes is placed. Pl. ي ī.

لوڅ lūts, adj. Naked, bare, nude; (Fem.) لوڅه lūtsa'h. See لڅ, and use in the same manner.

لوڅك lūtsak, adj. Alone, sole, solitary, without relation or friend, lonesome, desolate. 2. Vagabond; (Fem.) لوڅكه lūtsaka'h. See لوچك

لوڅي پوڅي lūtsey-pūtsey, s.m. (6th) Playing, as a child by rolling and throwing its hands and feet about on a bed or on the floor; rolling on the ground, as a horse, donkey, dogs, etc. 2. The agonies of death. Sing. and Pl.

لوچك lūchak, adj. Having little hair on the body (a dog). 2. Lonesome, desolate, without relation or friend. 3. Vagabond, libertine; (Fem.) لوچكه lūchaka'h. See لوڅك

A لوح lauḥ, s.m. (9th) A black board used as a slate for writing on, a tablet. Sing. and Pl. لوح محفوظ lauḥ-i-maḥ-fūẓ, The guarded table in Paradise, on which the destinies of mankind are written. لوح و قلم lauḥ-o-kalam, The tablet and pen with which the decrees of the Deity are written.

لوحه loha'h, s.f. (3rd) A ruler or scale of iron for drawing lines with. Pl. ئ ey.

لوخړه lūkharra'h, s.f. (3rd) A great flame with smoke, a blaze. Pl. ئ ey.

لوخه lūkha'h, s.f. (3rd) Gorse, reed, long-grass, papyrus. Pl. ئ ey. نرلوخ nar-lūkh, The flowery top of the gorse, etc. See بدګال. (P لوخ).

لودل law-dal, verb trans. To perform, to pronounce, to utter, to express, to give, etc. (particularly applied to giving evidence, paying respects, etc.) Pres. لوي lawī; past وُ لوده wu-lawdah; fut. وُ به لوي wu bah lawī; imp. وُ لوه wu-lawah; act. part. لودونكي law-dūnkaey or لودوني law-dūnaey; past part. لودلي law-dalaey or لودي law-daey; verb. n. لودنه lawdana'h. See لل

لودي lūdī, s.m. (1st) Pl. The name of a tribe of Afghāns from whom Sūltān Bāhlol and his son Sikandar, Emperors of Hindūstān, descended. لودي lūdaey (Sing.), A man of the Lūdī tribe. لودۍ lūda'ī, s.f. (6th) A female of the above tribe. Sing. and Pl.

لور lor, s.m. (2nd) A sickle, a scythe. Pl. لرونه larūnah. See لواور

لور lor, s.m. (9th) Side, part, quarter, flank, direction, extremity, margin; towards. Sing. and Pl. لور په لور lor-pah-lor, adv. From side to side, side by side, abreast, cheek by jowl. لور د لورَ lor da lora, adv. On all sides, in all directions, everywhere. ښي لور shaey (W.) or khaey (E.) lor, The right side, on the right hand. كيڼ لور kīṛṛn lor, The left side, on the left. See لوري

لور lūr, s.f. (5th) A daughter, Pl. لوڼړ lūṛṛni or لوڼړي lūṛṛnī. مشره لور mash-ra'h lūr, An elder daughter. كشره لور kash-ra'h lūr, A younger daughter. منځوۍ لور mandz-wa'ī lūr, A middle daughter.

لورايه la-warāyah or la-w'rāyah, adv. From afar, from a distance, a long way off; or لورا la-w'rā.

لورشا lor-shā, s. prop. The name of a mountain in the country of the Upper Mohmands, or Mohmands of the hills.

لوري loraey, s.m. (1st) Side, part, quarter, flank, direction, extremity, margin; towards. Pl. ي ī. لري لوري lirī-lorey, adv. A long way off, at a long distance, afar off. له كمَ لوري lah kama lorī, From whence? from where? ښي لوري shaey loraey (W.) or khaey loraey (E.) On the right hand, to the right. كيڼ لوري kīṛṛn loraey, On the left hand, to the left. See لور

لوړ lawaṛṛ, s.m. (2nd) A wooden pestle, a club, a staff, a bludgeon. Pl. لوړونه lawaṛṛūnah.

لوړ l'waṛṛ, adj. High, lofty, elevated, tall, towering, beetling, elevated, raised, upland, hilly, alpine; (Fem.) لوړه l'waṛṛa'h. لوړه l'waṛṛa'h, s.f. (3rd) Rising ground, a hill, hilly ground, highland. Pl. ئي *ey*. لوړ والئ *l'warr-wālaey*, s.m. (1st) Height, altitude, elevation, eminence, tallness. Pl. والي *wālī*; or لوړ توب *l'warr-tob*, s.m. (2nd) Pl. توبونه *tobūnah*; and لوړ تیا *l'warr tīā*, s.f. (6th). (E.) Sing. and Pl. (W.) Pl. تیاوي *tīāwī*. لوړه ژوره *l'warrah jzawarah* (W.); or لوړه جوره *l'warrah-jawarah*, adj. High and low, broken or uneven (ground).

لوړیدل *l'warredal*, verb intrans. To be or become high, lofty, towering, to tower, to soar, to overtop, to impend, to rise, etc. Pres. لوړیږي *l'warrejzī* (W.) or لوړیګي *l'warregī* (E.); past لوړ شه *l'warr shah* or وُ شه *wu-shah*; fut. لوړ به شي *l'warr bah shī* or به وُ شي *bah wu-shī*; imp. لوړ شه *l'warr shah* or وُ شه *wu-shah*; act. part. لوړیدونکئ *l'warredūnkaey* or لوړیدونئ *l'warredūnaey*; past part. لوړ *l'warr* or لوړ شوئ *l'warr shawaey*; verb. n. لوړیدنه *l'warredana'h* or لوړیده *l'warredah*. لوړول *l'warrawul*, verb trans. To render or make high, to raise, to elevate, to perch up, to upraise, to upheave, to erect, to set up, etc. Pres. لوړوي *l'warrawī*; past لوړ کړ *l'warr karr* or وُ کړ *wu-karr*; fut. لوړ به کړي *l'warr bah krrī* or به وُ کړي *bah wu-krrī*; imp. لوړ کړه *l'warr krrah* or وُ کړه *wu-krrah*; act. part. لوړوونکئ *l'warrawūnkaey* or لوړوونئ *l'warrawūnaey*; past part. لوړ کړئ *l'warr karraey*; verb. n. لوړونه *l'warrawuna'h*.

لوړیدل *l'warredal*, verb intrans. To become disjoined, detached, parted, riven, cleft; to part, to divide, to be disconnected, etc. Pres. لوړي *l'warrī*; past وُ لوړیده *wu-l'warredah*; fut. وُ به لوړي *wu bah l'warrī*; imp. وُ لوړه *wu-l'warrah*; act. part. لوړیدونکئ *l'warredūnkaey* or لوړیدونئ *l'warredūnaey*; past part. لوړیدلئ *l'warredalaey*; verb. n. لوړیدنه *l'warredana'h* or لوړیده *l'warredah*. See لوښتل لوړول *l'warrawul*, verb trans. To disjoin, detach, part, sunder, divide, sever, cleave, rive, separate, disconnect, etc. Pres. لوړوي *l'warrawī*; past ولوړاوه *wal'warrāwuh* or ولوړاوو *wal'warrāwo*; fut. وُ به لوړوي *wu bah l'warrawī*; imp. ولوړوه *wal'warrawah*; act. part. لوړوونکئ *l'warrawūnkaey* or لوړوونئ *l'warrawūnaey*; past part. لوړولئ *l'warrawulaey*; verb. n. لوړونه *l'warrawuna'h*. See لوستل

لوږه *lwajza'h*, s.f. (3rd) (W.) Hunger, craving, appetite, voracity, longing, yearning. Pl. ئي *ey*. See لوګه and وږي or وګی

لوستل *l'wastal*, verb trans. To read, to learn or acquire by reading, to peruse, to spell. Pres. لولي *l'walī*; past وُ لوست *wu-l'wust* or *wu-l'wast*; fut. وُ به لولي *wu bah l'walī*; imp. وُ لوله *wu-l'walah*; act. part. لوستونکئ *l'wastūnkaey* or لوستونئ *l'wastūnaey*; past part. لوستلئ *l'wastalaey* or لوستئ *l'wastaey*; verb. n. لوستنه *l'wastana'h*. لولول *l'walawul*, verb trans. (caus.) To cause to read, to teach, to cause to acquire. Pres. لولوي *l'walawī*; past وُ لولاوه *wu-l'walāwuh* or وُ لولاوو *wu-l'walāwo*; fut. و به لولوي *wu bah l'walawī*; imp. وُ لولوه *wu-l'walawah*; act. part. لولوونکئ *l'walawūnkaey* or لولوونئ *l'walawūnaey*; past part. لولولئ *l'walawulaey*; verb. n. لولونه *l'walawuna'h*.

لوستل *lawastal*, verb trans. To disperse, to diffuse, to scatter, to strew, to sprinkle, to sow, to scatter to the winds, etc. Pres. لوني *lawanī*; past وُ لوست *wu-lawast*; fut. وُ به لوني *wu bah lawanī*; imp. وُ لونه *wu-lawanah*; act. part. لوستونکئ *lawastūnkaey* or لوستونئ *lawastūnaey*; past part. لوستلئ *lawastalaey* or لوستئ *lawastaey*; verb. n. لوستنه *lawastana'h*.

لوشل *l'washal*, verb trans. To milk. Pres. لوشي *l'washī*; past وُ لوشله *wu-l'washalah*; fut. وُ به لوشي *wu bah l'washī*; imp. وُ لوشه *wu-l'washah*; act. part. لوشونکئ *l'washūnkaey* or لوشونئ *l'washūnaey*; past part. لوشلِ *l'washali*; verb. n. لوشنه *l'washana'h*.

لوښتل *l'wushtal* (W.) or *l'wukhtal* (E.), verb intrans. To become disjoined, detached, parted, sundered, severed; to part, to divide, to be severed, to be riven, cleaved, disconnected, etc. Pres. لوړي *l'warrī*; past وُ لوښت *wu-l'washt* or *wu-l'wukht*; fut. وُ به لوړي *wu bah l'warrī*; imp. وُ لوړه *wu-l'warrah*; act. part.

لوښتونکيَ *l'wu<u>sh</u>tūnkaey* or *l'wu<u>kh</u>tūnkaey*, or لوښتونيَ *l'wu<u>sh</u>tūnaey* or *l'wu<u>kh</u>tūnaey*; past part. لوښتليَ *l'wu<u>sh</u>talaey* or *l'wu<u>kh</u>talaey*, and لوښتيَ *l'wu<u>sh</u>taey* or *l'wu<u>kh</u>taey*; verb. n. لوښتنه *l'wu<u>sh</u>tana'h* or *l'wu<u>kh</u>tana'h.*

لوښي *lo-<u>sh</u>aey* (W.) or *lo-<u>kh</u>aey* (E.) s.m. (1st) A vessel in general, a basin, a pot, a pan, a dish. Pl. ي *ī*.

لوښي *lo-<u>kh</u>aey* (E.), s.m. (1st) Quality, nature, custom, temperament. Pl. ي *ī*.

لوغزه *lwag<u>h</u>-za'h*, adj. as s.f. (3rd) A goat, ewe, cow, or female buffalo when in milk, sent to one's friends to retain for a time. Pl. ې *ey*.

لوغړن *lū-g<u>h</u>a<u>rr</u>an*, adj. Charred, scorched, smoky, smoked black, inflamed. 2. Dirty, untidy, slovenly; (Fem.) لوغړنه *lū-g<u>h</u>a<u>rr</u>ana'h.* لوغړن كيدل *lū-g<u>h</u>a<u>rr</u>an kedal*, verb intrans. To become charred, scorched, smoked. لوغړن كول *lū-g<u>h</u>a<u>rr</u>an kawul*, verb trans. To char, to scorch, to smoke black. See لغړن

لوغه *l'wag<u>h</u>a'h*, s.f. (3rd) (E.) Hunger, appetite, craving, longing, yearning. Pl. ې *ey*. See لوږه and وكي

لوگي *lū-gaey*, s.m. (1st) Smoke, vapour, fume, fumigation, scent raised by fire. Pl. ي *ī*. لوگي كول *lū-gaey kawul*, verb trans. To raise a smoke or fume, to fumigate, to perfume. See لو

لولپه *lū-lapah*, adj. Burnt to ashes, entirely burnt or consumed. (Masc. and Fem.) لولپه كيدل *lū-lapah kedal*, verb intrans. To be entirely consumed or burnt to ashes. لولپه كول *lū-lapah kawul*, verb trans. To burn to ashes.

لولو *lo-lo*, s.m. (6th) An ornament worn round the upper part of the arm, and also, at times, in a turban. Sing. and Pl.

لولول *l'walawul*, verb trans. (caus.) To cause to read or peruse, to teach, to cause to acquire by reading. See لوستل

P لوله *lo-la'h*, s.f. (3rd) A skein or ball of silk or cotton. 2. A roll of cloth, paper, etc. Pl. ې *ey*.

P لولي *lo-la'ī*, s.f. (6th) A whore, a courtezan. Sing. and Pl.

لومكه *lūmaka'h*, s.f. (3rd) A noose, a snare, a net, a hair trap for catching birds. Pl. ې *ey*; or لومه *lūma'h*. Pl. لومې *lūmey*.

A لون *laun*, s.m. (2nd) Colour, hue, species, kind, genus, external form or appearance. Pl. لونونه *launūnah*. لون لون *laun-laun*, adj. Various, of different kinds or species. څو څو لونَ *<u>ts</u>o-<u>ts</u>o launa*, Of various kinds and species.

لونبړ *lūnba<u>rr</u>*, s.m. (5th) A male fox. Pl. لونبړان *lūnba<u>rr</u>ān*. لونبړه *lūnba<u>rr</u>a'h*, s.f. (3rd) A female fox. Pl. ې *ey*. See لمبړ

لونبړ *lūn-ba<u>rr</u>*, s.m. (2nd) The front, the forepart, the face, the front rank, van, prow, bow, etc. Pl. لونبړونه *lūn-ba<u>rr</u>ūnah*. See لمبړ for other forms of this word.

لوند *lūnd*, adj. Damp, moist, humid, wet, watery, dank, muggy, dewy, juicy. Pl. (Masc.) لانده *lāndah* or لاونده *lāwn-dah*; (Fem.) لنده *landa'h*. Pl. لندې *landey*. لوند خوشت *lūnd-<u>kh</u>ū<u>sh</u>t* (E.) or لوند خشت *lūnd-<u>kh</u>i<u>sh</u>t* (W.), adj. Reeking, wringing wet, wet through, soaked; (Fem.) لنده خوشته *landa'h <u>kh</u>ū<u>sh</u>ta'h* or خشته *<u>kh</u>i<u>sh</u>ta'h.* لوند والي *lūnd-wālaey*, s.m. (1st) Moisture, moistness, humidity, dampness, wetness, dew. Pl. والي *wālī*. لونديدل *lūndedal*, verb intrans. To become moist, wet, damp, humid, etc. Pres. لونديږي *lūndejzī* (W.) or لونديگي *lūndegī* (E.); past لوند شه *lūnd <u>sh</u>ah* or وُ شه *wu-<u>sh</u>ah*; fut. لوند به شي *lūnd bah <u>sh</u>ī* or به وُ شي *bah wu-<u>sh</u>ī*; imp. لوند شه *lūnd <u>sh</u>ah* or وُ شه *wu-<u>sh</u>ah*; act. part. لونديدونكيَ *lūndedūnkaey* or لونديدونيَ *lūndedūnaey*; past part. لوند *lūnd* or لوند شويَ *lūnd <u>sh</u>awaey*; verb. n. لونديدنه *lūndedana'h* or لونديده *lūndedah*. لوندول *lūndawul*, verb trans. To moisten, to damp, to bedew, to wet, to humectate. Pres. لوندوي *lūndawī*; past لوند كړ *lūnd ka<u>rr</u>* or وُ كړ *wu-ka<u>rr</u>*; fut. لوند به كړي *lūnd bah k<u>rr</u>ī* or به وُ كړي *bah wu-k<u>rr</u>ī*; imp. لوند كړه *lūnd k<u>rr</u>ah* or وُ كړه *wu-k<u>rr</u>ah*; act. part. لوندوونكيَ *lūndawūnkaey* or لوندوونيَ *lūndawūnaey*; past part. لوند كړيَ *lūnd ka<u>rr</u>aey*; verb. n. لوندونه *lūndawuna'h*.

P لوند *lawand*, s.m. (5th) An adventurer, a rake,

a volunteer. 2. adj. Free, independent, having no fixed residence. Pl. لوندان *lawandān*. لونده *lawanda'h*, s.f. (3rd) and adj. A loose female, etc. Pl. ې *ey*.

لونډ *lawandd*, adj. as s.m. (5th) A rake, a debauchee, a wild dissolute fellow, an adventurer. 2. A bachelor, a widower. Pl. لونډان *lawanddān*; (Fem.) لونډه *lawandda'h*, as s.f. (3rd) A loose woman. Pl. ې *ey*. لونډ والی *lawandd-wālaey*, s.m. (1st) Dissipation, debauchery, licentiousness, rakishness, sensuality. Pl. والي *wālī*; or لونډ توب *lawandd-tob*, s.m. (2nd). Pl. توبونه *tobūnah*. (P لوند).

s لونګ *lawang*, s.m. (6th) A clove, cloves. Sing. and Pl. لونګين هار *lawangīn-hār*, s.m. (2nd) A kind of necklace made of cloves, sent by the bridegroom to a bride. Pl. لونګين هارونه *lawangīn-hārūnah*.

لونه *lūna'h*, s.f. (3rd) A boil, a sore, an ulcer, an abscess. Pl. ې *ey*. See بهلونه , نونكي and بهنزه

s لوهار *lo-hār*, s.m. (5th) A blacksmith. Pl. لوهاران *lo-hārān*.

لوهاني *lo-hānī*, s.m. (1st) Pl. The name of a tribe of Afghāns who are chiefly carriers between Afghānistān, Hindūstān, and the Panjāb. لوهانی *lo-hānaey* (Sing.) A man of the Lohānī tribe. لوهانۍ *lo-hāna'ī*, s.f. (6th) A female of the above. Sing. and Pl.; also (W.) لوهاړني *lo-hārrnī*, etc.

لوهټ *lo-hatt*, s.m. (5th) A kind of pheasant. Pl. لوهټان *lo-hattān*.

لوغونه *lawa-ghūna'h*, s.f. (3rd) A milk pail, an earthen vessel for holding milk. Pl. ې *ey*. See دونړي

لوي *lo-e*, adj. Great, large, big, bulky, massy, huge, immense, vast, mighty. 2. Corpulent, stout, lusty. 3. Grown up, arrived at years of maturity. 4. Great in rank or office, honorable, respectable, venerable. 5. as s.m. (5th) An elder, a chief, a superior. Pl. لويان *lo-e-ān*; (Fem.) لويه *lo-e-a'h*, s.f. (3rd) Pl. ې *ey*. لوي والی *lo-e-wālaey*, s.m. (1st) Bulk, magnitude, degree in rank, or size. Pl. والي *wālī*. لوي اختر *lo-e-akhtar*, The great festival held on the 10th of Ẕu-l-ḥijja, in commemoration of Abraham's offering up Isaac. لويه خوله *lo-e-a'h khūla'h*, A large mouth, wide-mouthed.

لوييدل *lo-e-edal*, verb intrans. To grow or become large, great, big, mighty; to increase in years or age, to become great in rank or degree, etc. Pres. لوييږي *lo-e-ejzī* (W.) or لوييګي *lo-e-egī* (E.); past لوي شه *lo-e shah* or وُ شه *wu-shah*; fut. لوي به شي *lo-e bah shī* or به وُ شي *bah wu-shī*; imp. لوي شه *lo-e shah* or وُ شه *wu-shah*; act. part. لوييدونکی *lo-e-edūnkaey* or لوييدونی *lo-e-edūnaey*; past part. لوي *lo-e* or لوي شوی *lo-e shawaey*; verb. n. لوييدنه *lo-e-edana'h* or لوييده *lo-e-edah*.

لويول *lo-e-awul*, verb trans. To render large, big, great, mighty, to increase in years, rank, or dignity. Pres. لويوي *lo-e-awī*; past لوي کړ *lo-e karr* or وُ کړ *wu-karr*; fut. لوي به کړي *lo-e bah krrī* or به وُ کړي *bah wu-krrī*; imp. لوي کړه *lo-e-krrah* or وُ کړه *wu-krrah*; act. part. لويونکی *lo-e-awūnkaey* or لويونی *lo-e-awūnaey*; past part. لوي کړی *lo-e karraey*; verb. n. لويونه *lo-e-awuna'h*.

لويټ *lo-yatt*, s.m. (2nd) Greatness, largeness, magnitude, size; grandeur, eminence. Pl. لويټونه *lo-yatt-ūnah*. Also لويټه *lo-yatta'h*, s.f. (3rd). Pl. ې *ey*.

لويدل *lwe-dal*, verb intrans. To fall, to descend, to fall or drop down, to come down, to plump down from a high place. Pres. لويږي *lwe-jzī* (W.) or لويګي *lwe-gī* (E.); past وُ لويده *wu-lwe-dah*; fut. وُ به لويږي *wu bah lwe-jzī* or لويګي *lwe-gī*; imp. وُ لويږه *wu-lwe-jzah* or وُ لويګه *wu-lwe-gah*; act. part. لويدونکی *lwe-dūnkaey* or لويدونی *lwe-dūnaey*; past part. لويدلی *lwe-dalaey*; verb. n. لويدنه *lwe-dana'h* or لويده *lwe-dah*. See آچول

لويشت *lwesht*, s.f. (1st) A span, the distance between the tip of the thumb and little finger. Pl. لويشتې *lweshti*.

لويشتينک *lweshtīnak*, adj. (dimin. of above), A dwarf, a pigmy. 2. A precocious child; (Fem.) لويشتينکه *lweshtīnaka'h*.

لويګنده *lwey-ganda'h*, s.f. (3rd) The temple of

the head, the fissure in the head of a new born child. Pl. ئ *ey*. See شير دانه

لوينه *l'wīna'h*, s.f. (3rd) A net or snare for catching birds. Pl. ئ *ey*.

لوېږند *l'we-jzand* (W.) or لويگند *l'we-gand* (E.) adj. as s.m. (6th) A sponger, a hanger on, one who comes when dinner is ready, a parasite. Sing. and Pl. (Fem.) لوېږنده *lwe-jzanda'h*; or لويگنده *lwe-ganda'h*, s.f. (3rd). Pl. ئ *ey*.

لويي *lo-e-ī*, s.f. (3rd) Greatness, magnitude, dimension, largeness, greatness in age, rank, or degree. Pl. ئي *a'ī*. لويي ويل *lo-e-ī-wa-yal*, verb trans. To praise, to speak well of. See لوي

له *lah*, prep. From, governing the ablative case. له نه *lah nah* is also used for this case as preposition and postposition respectively, the له preceding and نه following the substantive. 2. A postposition governing the dative case. See ته , لره, and Grammar, pages 7 and 10.

لهړی *laharraey*, s.m. (1st) A ridge-pole, a straight beam. Pl. ي *ī*.

له سره *lah sarah* or له سرَ *lah sara*, adv. Entirely, wholly, fully, perfectly, altogether, utterly, outright.

لهلپاند *lah-lapānd*, adj. Burnt to ashes or to a cinder, entirely burnt or consumed; (Fem.) لهلپانده *lah-lapānda'h*. See لولپه

A لياقت *lī-ākat*, s.m. (2nd) (from ليق) Fitness, expediency, propriety, capability, capacity, aptitude, worth, merit, skill, abilities. Pl. لياقتونه *lī-ākatūnah*. لياقت لرل *lī-ākat laral*, verb trans. To have or possess fitness, ability, aptitude, etc.

ليټئي *letta'ī*, s.f. (6th) Paste, batter, a kind of caudle given after childbirth, and after burials. Sing. and Pl.

ليټي *lettaey*, s.m. (1st) Hard clay. Pl. ي *ī*. See خوري and خاوري

لېڅ *lets*, adj. Naked, bare, stark, exposed; (Fem.) لېڅه *letsa'h*. لېڅ لغړ *lets-lagharr*, adj. Stark-naked, as bare as a coot; (Fem.) لېڅه لغړه *letsa'h-lagharra'h*. لېڅېدل *letsedal*, verb intrans. To become naked, bare, nude, denuded, etc. لېڅول *letsawul*, verb trans. To strip, to divest, to denude, to lay bare. For inflections see لڅ and بربند

لېڅه *letsa'h*, s.f. (3rd) (W.) The fore-arm, the arm from the wrist to the elbow. Pl. ئ *ey*. See لېچه and سنګل

لېچ *lech*, s.m. (2nd) Ophthalmia, a disease of the eyes, rheum. Pl. لېچونه *lechūnah*.

لېچن *lechan*, adj. Rheumy-eyed, having sore eyes, afflicted with ophthalmia; (Fem.) لېچنه *lechana'h*. See لېچ

لېچه *lecha'h*, s.f. (3rd) (E.) The arm from wrist to elbow. Pl. ئ *ey*. See لېڅه

لېچی *lechaey*, s.m. (1st) See preceding. Pl. ي *ī*.

لېچئي *lecha'ī*, s.f. (6th) The trotters of a sheep, goat, etc.

ليدل *līdal*, verb trans. To see, to behold, to discern, to perceive, to descry, to spy, to espy, etc. Pres. ويني *wīnī*; past و ليده *wu-līdah* or و ليد *wu-līd*; fut. و به ويني *wu bah wīnī*; imp. وينه *wīnah* or و وينه *wu-wīnah*; act. part. ليدونکی *līdūnkaey* or ليدونی *līdūnaey*; past part. ليدلی *līdalaey*; verb. n. ليدنه *līdana'h* or ليده *līdah*. The present tenses appear to be derived from some unknown or obsolete root.

ليده *līdah*, s.m. (6th) (verb. n.) Seeing, beholding, perceiving, vision, sight, survey. Sing. and Pl.; or ليدنه *līdana'h*, s.f. (3rd). Pl. ئ *ey*.

ليري *līrī*, adj. Far, distant, remote, far off. adv. Far away, at a long distance. See لري

ليرئي *lera'ī*, s.f. (6th) The narrow ridge of a mountain. Sing. and Pl.

لېږدل *lejzdal*, verb trans. (W.) To march, to set out, to depart, to go from one stage to another (applied to a number of persons such as an army, caravan, etc.) Pres. لېږدي *lejzdī*; past و لېږده *wu-lejzdah*; fut و به لېږدي *wu bah lejzdī*; imp. و لېږده *wu-lejzdah*; act. part. لېږدونکی *lejzdūnkaey* or لېږدونی *lejzdūnaey*; past part. لېږدلی *lejzdalaey*; verb. n. لېږدنه *lejzdana'h*. لېږدول *lejzdawul*, verb trans. (caus.) To cause to march, depart, set out, etc. Pres. لېږدوي *lejzdawī*; past و لېږداوه

wu-lejzdāwuh or وُ ليږداوو *wu-lejzdāwo*; fut. وُ به ليږدوي *wu bah lejzdawī*; imp. وُ ليږدوه *wu-lejzdawah*; act. part. ليږدوونکي *lejzdawūnkaey* or ليږدووني *lejzdawūnaey*; past part. ليږدولي *lejzdawulaey*; verb. n. ليږدونه *lejzdawunah*. See ليګدل and ليګدول

ليږدل *lejzdal*, verb trans. (W.) To send, to dispatch, to transmit, to send out. Pres. ليږي *lejzī*; past وُ ليږه *wu-lejzah*; fut. وُ به ليږي *wu bah lejzī*; imp. وُ ليږه *wu-lejzah*; act. part. ليږونکي *lejzūnkaey* or ليږوني *lejzūnaey*; past part. ليږلي *lejzalaey*; verb. n. ليږنه *lejzana'h*. See ليګل and آستول

ليښل *leshal* (W.) or *lekhal* (E.), verb trans. To load, to lay on a burden. 2. To march, to set out on a journey (as a caravan, etc.); past وُ ليښ *wu-lesh* or *wu-lekh*; act. part. ليښونکي *leshūnkaey* or *lekhūnkaey* or ليښوني *leshūnaey* or *lekhūnaey*; past part. ليښلي *leshalaey* or *lekhalaey*; verb. n. ليښنه *leshana'h* or *lekhana'h*. The other inflections are wanting, and are taken from the verb trans. ليږدل which see.

S ليک *līk*, s.m. (2nd) A line, a mark, a ruled line, a rut, a trace, a track (as of wheels, etc.) Pl. ليکونه *līkūnah*.

ليکل *līkal*, verb trans. To write, to pen, to transcribe. Pres. ليکي *līkī*; past وُ ليکه *wu-līkah*; fut. وُ به ليکي *wu bah līkī*; imp. وُ ليکه *wu-līkah*; act. part. ليکونکي *līkūnkaey* or ليکوني *līkūnaey*; past part. ليکلي *līkalaey*; verb. n. ليکنه *līkana'h*. See also ښکل and کښل

A ليکن *lekin*, conj. But, yet, moreover. See ولي

ليکه *līka'h*, s.f. (3rd) Marks of a wheel, rut, path, track, trace; a ruled line, a line, a mark. Pl. ئ *ey*. See ليک

ليګدل *leg-dal*, verb trans. (E.) To march, to set out on a journey. ليګدول *leg-dawul*, verb trans. (caus.) To cause to march. For inflections see (W.) ليږدل and ليږدول, and change the ږ into ګ

ليګل *leg-al*, verb trans. (E.) To send, to transmit, to send out, to dispatch. For inflections see (W.) ليږل and substitute ګ for ږ

A ليلي *lailā*, s. prop. Name of the celebrated mistress of Majnūn. 2. A mistress in general.

ليمه *lemah*, s.m. (6th) The pupil or apple of the eye; the eye. Sing. and Pl.

ليندۀ *lenda'h*, s.f. (3rd) A bow. Pl. ئ *ey*. See لندۀ

ليندئ *lenda'ī*, s.f. (6th) A bow. 2. A jet of water, etc. For various meanings see لندئ. Sing. and Pl.

ليندۀ *lenddah*, adj. Bald, scald-headed. (Masc. and Fem.) See ګنجي and سدر

لينګي *len-gaey*, s.m. (1st) The leg from the knee to the ankle. Pl. ي *ī*.

S ليو *lew*, s.m. (2nd) Plaster, mud ground and used to plaster walls. Pl. ليوونه *lew-ūnah*. See کل

ليوال *lewāl*, adj. Peckish, inclined to eat, hungry, craving, hankering after, inclined; (Fem.) ليواله *lewālah*. 2. s.f. (3rd) Hunger, appetite, hankering, longing after food, etc. Pl. ئ *ey*.

ليور *lewar*, s.m. (2nd) A husband's brother. Pl. ليورونه *lewarūnah*.

ليوني *lewanaey*, adj. Mad, insane, crazy, lunatic, touched, cracked, demented, daft, moon-struck, wandering, frantic, raving, out of one's mind or wits. Pl. ي *ī*; (Fem.) ليونئ *lewana'ī*. 2. as s.m. (1st) A madman, a maniac. Pl. ي *ī*. ليونئ *lewana'ī*, s.f. (6th) A mad woman, etc. Sing. and Pl. ليون توب *lewan-tob*, s.m. (2nd) Madness, insanity, lunacy, phrensy, raving, wandering, disordered intellect. Pl. توبونه *tobūnah*. ليوني کيدل *lewanaey kedal*, verb intrans. To become or grow mad, frantic, demented, crazy, etc. ليوني کول *lewanaey kawul*, verb trans. To drive mad, crazy, insane, to madden, to infatuate, to addle the wits, to turn the brain.

ليوه *lewah*, s.m. (5th) A wolf. Pl. ليوان *lewān* and ليوهګان *lewah-gān*. See شرمښ

م

م *mīm*, the twenty-fourth letter of the Arabic and twenty-eighth of the Persian, is the thirty-fifth of the Pushto alphabet, and corresponds to Sanskrit म. It is one of the labial letters, and is similar in sound to the English *m*. In the numerical arrangement of the Arabic alphabet it stands for 40.

It is sometimes changed into ن, as لنبه for لمبه 'a flame.'

This letter is also one of the affixed personal pronouns (ضماير متصله) used in forming the tenses of intransitive and substantive verbs, and, with the exception of the six past tenses, for those of transitives also. They are inseparable from the verbs, and have no independent signification. 2. This letter with a (ـِ) or written مي is also used as the agent in a sentence for the first person singular, and with any other than active or transitive verbs points out the object or possessive case. See my Grammar, pages 44 and 47, on the pronouns. 3. This letter is also prefixed to the imperative of a verb in place of the particle مه to indicate prohibition, and occasionally in a deprecative sense. See Grammar, page 162.

ما *mā*, To me, etc., the inflected form of the personal pronoun of the 1st person. (Masc. and Fem.) See Grammar, page 30.

مابوب *mā-būb*, s.m. (5th) (corrup. of A محبوب) A beloved friend. Pl. مابوبان *mā-būbān*. مابوبه *mā-būba'h*, s.f. (3rd) A sweetheart, a mistress. Pl. ې *ey*.

ماپښين *mā-p'shīn* (W.) or *mā-p'khīn* (E.) (corrup. of P پيشين), s.m. (2nd) The afternoon. 2. Afternoon prayers. Pl. ماپښينونه *mā-p'shīnūnah* or *mā-p'khīnūnah*.

مات *māt*, adj. Broken, cracked, smashed, shivered, shattered, torn, broken up, disjoined, detached, sundered, split, splintered, cracked, rent, dispersed, etc.; (Fem.) ماته *māta'h*. مات والي *māt-wālaey*, s.m. (1st) Demolition, destruction, breaking or falling to pieces, fracture, rupture, etc. Pl. والي *wālī*. مات مات *māt-māt*, adj. Broken or smashed to bits; (Fem.) ماته ماته *māta'h-māta'h*. زړه ماتي *z'rrah-mātaey*, adj. Broken hearted; (Fem.) زړه ماتې *z'rrah-māti*. Pl. (Masc. and Fem.) ي *ī*. ماتيدل *mātedal*, verb intrans. To become broken, smashed, torn, shivered, cracked, rent, etc.; to fall to pieces, to crumble away, to break up. Pres. ماتيږي *mātejzī* (W.) or ماتيګي *mātegī* (E.); past مات شه *māt shah* or وُ شه *wu-shah*; fut. مات به شي *māt bah shī* or به وُ شي *bah wu-shī*; imp. مات شه *māt shah* or وُ شه *wu-shah*; act. part. ماتيدونکي *mātedūnkaey* or ماتيدوني *mātedūnaey*; past part. مات *māt* or مات شوي *māt shawaey*; verb. n. ماتيدنه *mātedana'h* or ماتيده *mātedah*. ماتول *mātawul*, verb trans. To break, to smash, to shiver, to crack, to rend, to demolish, to destroy, to crush, to squash, to tear or shake to pieces, to dilapidate, to dismantle, etc. Pres. ماتوي *mātawī*; past مات کړ *māt karr* or وُ کړ *wu-karr*; fut. مات به کړي *māt bah krrī* or به وُ کړي *bah wu-krrī*; imp. مات کړه *māt krrah* or وُ کړه *wu-krrah*; act. part. ماتوونکي *mātawūnkaey* or ماتووني *mātawūnaey*; past part. مات کړي *māt karraey*; verb. n. ماتونه *mātawuna'h*.

ماته *mā-ta'h*, s.f. (3rd) Prey (of wild beasts), quarry. Pl. ې *ey*. ماته کول *mā-ta'h kawul*, verb trans. To seize (as prey), to hunt for food (as a beast or bird of prey).

ماتيدونکي *mātedūnkaey* or ماتيدوني *mātedūnaey*, adj. (act. part. of ماتيدل), Brittle, liable to be broken or cracked (as glass); (Fem.) ماتيدونکې *mātedūnki* and ماتيدونې *mātedūni*. Pl. (Masc. and Fem.) ي *ī*.

ماڅوڅکي *ma-tsotskaey*, s.m. (1st) The name of a plant which grows in low ground, and is used by alchemists on account of its yellow colour. Pl. ي *ī*. مچچکي

ماټس *māttus*, s.m. (5th) A bump or swelling occasioned by the blow of a stone, club, or the bite of a wasp, etc. Pl. ماټسان *māttusān*. See پوپکه

ماچي *mā-chey*, s.f. (1st) Pl. (W.) Vermicelli. The Sing. form not used. See مايچي

ماخستن *mā-khustan*, s.m. (9th) (W.) The first watch of the night, the period between evening and going to rest. Sing. and Pl. د ماخستن

خوراک *da mā-khustan khwarāk*, Supper. د ماخستن نمونځ *da mā-khustan n'mūndz*, The prayer said before retiring to rest.

مادہ *māda'h*, s.f. (3rd) A matter, a subject, an article, an affair, a clause. Pl. ي *ey*. (A مادّہ).

P مار *mār*, s.m. (5th) A snake, a serpent, a viper. Pl. ماران *mārān* or (2nd) مارونه *mārūnah*. مار بچړي *mār-bachrraey* or مار بچوړي *mār-bachorraey*, s.m. (1st) A young snake. Pl. ي *ī*. مار پيچ *mār-pech*, adj. Crooked, winding, snaky, serpentine, twisting and turning; (Fem.) مار پيچه *mār-pecha'h*. مار پيچه لار *mār-pecha'h lār*, s.f. (1st) A crooked or winding path. Pl. لار *lāri*. مار گير *mār-gīr*, s.m. (5th) A snake catcher. Pl. مار گيران *mār-gīrān*. مارمهي *mār-mahaey*, s.m. (1st) An eel. Pl. ي *ī*. د مار هگۍ *da mār haga'ī*, s.f. (6th) The egg of a snake. Sing. and Pl.

A مارج *mārij*, s.f. (1st) A flame of fire, a tongue-shaped flame of fire. Pl. مارج *māriji*. مارجي *mārijaey*, adj. Infernal, belonging to the flames; (Fem.) مارجۍ *mārija'ī*.

مارجرۍ *mār-jara'ī* or مارجړۍ *mār-jarra'ī*, s.f. (6th) A bulbous root a remedy for snake bites, and from which pickles are made. Sing. and Pl.

ماردندان *mār-dandān*, s.m. (6th) Tares growing amongst wheat. Sing. and Pl. See جودر

مارړي هارړي *mārraey-hārraey*, interj. An exclamation of lamentation, complaint or supplication.

ماز دگر *'māz-digar* or ماز ديگر *'māz-dīgar*, s.m. (9th) (corrup. of P نماز ديگر), Time of evening prayer. 2. Evening. Sing. and Pl.

P مازو *mā-zū*, s.m. (6th) The gall-nut or oak-apple. Sing. and Pl.

ماس پښين *mās-p'shīn* (W.) or *mās-p'khīn* (E.) s.m. (2nd) Afternoon. 2. Afternoon prayers. Pl. ماس پښينونه *mās p'shīnūnah* or *p'khīnūnah*. See ماپښين

ماسته *māstah*, s.m. (6th) Coagulated milk, butter milk. Sing. and Pl.

ماسختن *mās-khutan*, s.m. (9th) The time of prayer before going to rest. Sing. and Pl. د ماسختن نمونځ *da mās-khutan n'mūndz*, The prayer said before going to rest. See ماخستن

A ماسوا *mā-siwā*, adv. Besides, moreover, save, over and above.

ماسه *māsa'h*, s.f. (3rd) The name of a small weight used by goldsmiths. Pl. ي *ey*. (S ماشه).

P ماش *māsh*, s.m. (6th) The name of a kind of pulse (Phaseolus mungo). Sing. and Pl. گرگره ماش *gir-girah māsh*, Ground pulse.

ماشله *māshila'h*, s.f. (3rd) A skein of silk or thread. Pl. ي *ey*.

ماشوړه *mā-shorra'h*, s.f. (3rd) Same as preceding. Pl. ي *ey*.

ماشوق *mā-shūk*, s.m. (5th) A beloved friend. Pl. ماشوقان *mā-shūkān*. ماشوقه *māshūka'h*, s.f. (3rd) A mistress, a sweetheart. Pl. ي *ey* (corrup. of A معشوق).

ماشي *māshaey*, s.m. (1st) A gnat, a musquito. Pl. ي *ī*. See غماشه

ماښام *mā-shām* (W.) or *mā-khām* (E.) s.m. (9th) Evening, twilight. Sing. and Pl.

ماغزه *māgh-zah*, s.m. (6th) Marrow, kernel, core, heart. Sing. and Pl. د سر ماغزه *da sar māgh-zah*, The brain.

ماکو *mākū*, s.m. (5th) A weaver's shuttle. Pl. ماکوگان *mākū-gān*. 2. s.m. (6th) The name of a tribe of Afghāns. Sing. and Pl.

A مال *māl*, s m. (2nd) Property, wealth, goods, effects, merchandize, cattle, etc. Pl. مالونه *mālūnah*. مال دار *māl-dār*, adj. Wealthy, rich, possessed of much cattle, etc.; (Fem.) مال داره *māl-dāra'h*. مال داري *māl-dārī*, s.f. (3rd) Wealthiness, opulence. Pl. ئ *a'ī*.

مالت *mālat*, s.m. (2nd) A division, a district, a ward, a parish, a quarter. Pl. مالتونه *mālatūnah*. See خم and کندي

A مالک *mālik*, s.m. (5th) (from ملک) Master, lord, possessor, proprietor, owner. Pl. مالکان *mālikān*. مالکه *mālika'h*, s.f. (3rd) A mistress, lady, proprietress. Pl. ي *ey*. See څښتن

مال کنړۍ *māl-kurrna'ī*, s.f. (6th) The name of a thorny plant. Sing. and Pl.

مالگه *māl-ga'h*, s.f. (3rd) Salt. Pl. ي *ey*. مالگبه *mālg-bah*, s.m. (4th) A man who collects and sells salt. Pl. مالگبانه *mālg-bānah*.

د مالګي ګل *da māl-gī gul*, The fine portion of salt which rises to the top in the preparation of it (*lit.* The flower of salt).

مالګين *mālgīn*, adj. Salt, saline; (Fem.) مالګينه *mālgīna'h*. مالګين والي *mālgīn-wālaey*, s.m. (1st) Saltness. Pl. والي *wālī*.

مالګيړي *māl-gīrrney*, s.f. (3rd) Pl. A children's game, one side standing in the shade and the other in the moonlight. Also مارګړني *mār-gir-rrney*.

مالوچ *mā-lūch*, s.m. (6th) Cleaned cotton. Sing. and Pl. Also written مالوج *mā-lūj*.

ماله *māla'h*, s.f. (3rd) A weaver's brush. 2. A large flat piece of board drawn over a field after ploughing to smoothe the earth, a sort of harrow. Pl. ي *ey*.

s ماما *mā-mā*, s.m. (5th) A maternal uncle. Pl. ماماګان *mā-mā-gān*. See کاکا

مامن کوټ *mā-man-kott*, A place of safety, a dwelling, a home.

A مامور *mā-mūr*, adj. (past. part. of امر) Ordered, determined, fixed, commanded, established, usage; (Fem.) ماموره *mā-mūra'h*. مامور کول *mā-mūr kawul*, verb trans. To order, to fix, to determine, to establish.

مامولکه *māmū-laka'h*, s.f. (3rd) The birds of the wag-tail (Motacilla) species, applied generally. 2. The hen bird. Pl. ي *ey*. مامولک *māmū-lak*, s.m. (5th) The cock wagtail. Pl. مامولکان *māmū-lakān*.

ماموي *māmū-ī*, s.f. (3rd) A kind of dried apricot with the kernel inserted. Pl. ئي *a'ī*. See کشته

مانجي *mānjī*, s.m. (5th) The marriage guest of the bridegroom. Pl. مانجيان *mānjīān*. See جانجي

ماندره *mān-dara'h*, s.f. (3rd) A tent-rope. 2. A heart-string. Pl. ي *ey*. See مانده and مرانده

مانده *mān-da'h*, s.f. (3rd) A heart-string. Pl. ي *ey*. See preceding.

مانده *māndah*, s.m. (2nd) The dry bed of a river, or the bed of a torrent. Pl. ماندونه *māndūnah*. See خوړ

ماندينه *mān-dīna'h*, s.f. (3rd) A female in general, a wife, a married woman. Pl. ي *ey*.

A مانع *māniæ*, adj. (act. part. of منع), A forbidder, a preventer, a hinderer, an obstacle or impediment; (Fem.) مانعه *māniæa'h*.

مانګي *mān-gacy*, s.m. (1st) A boatman, a sailor, a steersman. Pl. ي *ī*. مانګي *mānga'ī*, s.f. (6th) A boatman's wife, etc. Sing. and Pl. (HI مانجهي)

مانموله *mān-mola'h*, s.f. (3rd) A kind of vegetable. Pl. ي *ey*.

مانه *māna'h*, s.f. (3rd) Complaint, blame, murmur, mutter, plaint, lamentation, complaining. Pl. ي *ey*. مانه کول *māna'h kawul*, verb trans. To complain, to murmur, to blame, to lament.

مانړګي *mārrn-gacy*, s.m. (1st) A boatman. Pl. ي *ī*. مانړګي *mārrn-ga'ī*, s.f. (6th) A boatman's wife, etc. Sing. and Pl. See مانګي

مانړو *mārrnū*, s.m. (5th) The name of a wild fruit, something like a sloe. 2. A species of herb or grass like wild rue. Pl. مانړوګان *mārrnūgān*.

مانړئي *mārrna'ī*, s.f. (6th) A building, a fabric, a dwelling, a house, a residence, an edifice, a pile, a tenement, etc. Sing. and Pl.

مانړي *mārrnacy*, s.m. (1st) Misunderstanding amongst friends, mutual coolness between two persons; pique, umbrage, estrangement. Pl. ي *ī*. مانړي کول *mārrnacy kawul*, verb trans. To stir up discord or dissension, to create misunderstanding.

ماولي *māw-la'ī*, s.f. (6th) A piece of wood inserted in the hollow part of the upper stone of a mill as an axle on which it revolves. Sing. and Pl. See کمي

P ماه *māh*, s.m. (9th) The moon. 2. A month. Sing. and Pl. Used in composition; as ماه پيکر *māh-paikar*, A face like the moon, a sweetheart; (Fem.) ماه پيکره *māh-paikara'h*. ماه جبين *māh-jabīn*, adj. Having a forehead beautiful as the moon; (Fem.) ماه جبينه *māh-jabīna'h*. ماه روي *māh-rū'e*, adj. Having a face beautiful as the moon; (Fem.) ماه رويه *māh-rū'e-a'h*. ماه به ماه *māh-bah-māh*, adv. Monthly, every month. See سپوږمي and مياشت

P ماهي *mā-haey*, s.m. (1st) A fish in general. Pl. ي *ī*; or s.m. (5th) Pl. ماهيان *mā-haeyān*. غوګ or د ماهي غوږ *da mā-hī ghwajz* (W.) or *ghwag* (E.) s.m. (2nd) A shell, an oyster shell. Pl. غوږونه *ghwajzūnah* or غوګونه *ghwagūnah*. ماهي ګير *mā-haey-gīr*, s.m. (5th) A fisherman. Pl. ماهي ګيران *mā-haey gīrān*.

مايچي *māe-chey*, s.f. (3rd) (Pl.) Vermicelli. See ماچي

A مايل *mā'īl*, adj. (act. part. of ميل) Inclined, bent, inclined towards, desirous, fond, taking delight in, having a propensity, inclination, or partiality, addicted, apt; (Fem.) مايله *mā'īla'h*. مايل کيدل *mā'īl kedal*, verb intrans. To incline towards, to become partial or addicted. مايل کول *mā'īl kawul*, verb trans. to incline towards, to bias, to render desirous, addicted, partial.

مايوپ *mā-yūp*, adj. (from A معيوب ?), Short-sighted, near-sighted; (Fem.) مايوپه *mā-yūpa'h*. مايوپ والې *mā-yūp wālaey*, s.m. (1st) Short-sightedness, near-sightedness. Pl. والي *wālī*.

P مايه *mā-ya'h*, s.f. (3rd) Stock, capital, fund, wealth, means. 2. Leaven, ferment. Pl. ې *ey*. See تومنه or تومه

P مايه *mā-yah*, adj. as s.m. (5th) A camel with two humps. Pl. مايهګان *mā-yahgān*.

A مباح *mubāḥ*, adj. (past part. of بوح) Any indifferent action or lawful pleasure. مباحي *mubā-ḥī*, s.m. (9th) Freewill, whatever may be done or left alone, and to which no punishment is attached. Sing. and Pl.

P مبادا *mubādā* or *mabādā*; interj. (from بودن) Be it not! God forbid! by no means! lest!

A مبارک *mubārak*, adj. (past part. III of برک) Blessed, happy, fortunate, august, auspicious, holy. 2. interj. Welcome! hail! may you be happy! etc; (Fem.) مبارکه *mubāraka'h*.

A مبارکي *mubārakī*, s.f. (3rd) Congratulation, benediction, happiness, auspiciousness. Pl. ئ *a'ī*. مبارکي ورکول *mubārakī war-kawul*, verb trans. To congratulate, to wish success, to hail, to welcome, to felicitate.

A مبالغه *mabālagha'h*, s.f. (3rd) (inf. III of بلغ) Exaggeration, hyperbole, bombast, amplification. Pl. ې *ey*. مبالغه کول *mabālagha'h kawul*, verb trans. To exaggerate.

A مبتدا *mubtadā*, s.f. (6th) (past part. of بدأ) Commencement, principle, or subject of a proposition. 2. A substantive noun in nominative case. Pl. (W.) مبتداوي *mubtadāwī*; (E.) Sing. and Pl.

A مبتدي *mubtadī*, s.m. (5th) A young scholar, a tyro, a disciple just commencing to learn. 2. Beginning. 3. A founder. Pl. مبتديان *mubtadī-ān*; s.f. (6th) مبتدئ *mubtada'ī*. Sing. and Pl.

A مبتلا *mubtalā*, adj. (past part. VIII of بلا) Afflicted, distressed, distracted, enamoured, fascinated, captivated. (Masc. and Fem.) مبتلا کيدل *mubtalā kedal*, verb intrans. To become afflicted, distressed, fascinated. مبتلا کول *mub-talā kawul*, verb trans. To distress, to perplex, to fascinate, to captivate, to make enamoured.

A مبلغ *mablagh*, s.m. (2nd) (from بلغ) A sum, ready money. Pl. مبلغونه *mablaghūnah*.

مبهم *mub-ham*, adj. (past part. of بهم) Occult, unknown, ambiguous, equivocal; (Fem.) مبهمه *mub-hama'h*.

مپت *mupt*, adv. (corrup. of P مفت) Gratis, for nothing, gratuitously, given away without return or benefit. See وبريا and وريا

A متابعت *mutā-baæat*, s.m. (2nd) (inf. III of تبع) Obsequiousness. 2. Submitting, obeying, following. Pl. متابعتونه *mutā-baæatūnah*. متابعت کول *mutā-baæat kawul*, verb trans. To follow, to obey, to submit to.

متر *matar* or *matr*, s.m. (2nd) A kind of coagulated milk eaten fresh. 2. Sediment, refuse. 3. A kind of syllabub given to lying-in women. Pl. مترونه *matarūnah* or *matrūnah*.

A مترجم *mutarjim*, s.m. (5th) (act. part. of ترجم) A translator, an interpreter. Pl. مترجمان *mutarjimān*.

A متردد *mutaraddid*, adj. (past part. of رد) Rejected. 2. Irresolute, perplexed, hesitating, wavering. 3. Adverse. 4. Wandering; (Fem.) متردده *mutaraddida'h*.

مترة *matr-a'h*, s.f. (3rd) Coagulated milk. 2. Dregs, dross, refuse, sediment. Pl. ې *ey*.

مترة *matra'h*, adj. Rare, scarce, not procurable. 2. s.f. (3rd) Scarcity, dearth, rareness. Pl. ې *ey*. مترة كيدل *matra'h kedal*, verb intrans. To become scarce, rare, dear. مترة كول *matra'h kawul*, verb trans. To make or render rare, scarce, dear, etc.

متر *mutarr*, adj. A foolish doltish man, a piss-a-bed; (Fem.) مترة *mutarra'h*. (s मूत्र urine.)

A متصل *muttaṣil*, adj. (act. part. VIII of وصل) Joined, near, contiguous, adjoining, successive, continual, continually; (Fem.) متصلة *muttaṣila'h*.

A متعلق *mutaæ-liḳ*, adj. (act. part. of علق), Belonging to, appendant, concerning, relative to. 2. Connected with, attached to, addicted, occupied or engaged in; (Fem.) متعلقة *mutaæ-liḳa'h*. متعلقان *mutaæ-liḳān*, s.m. (5th) Pl. Domestics, children, family, possessions.

A متغير *muta-ghaiyir*, adj. (act. part. V of غير) Inconsistent, changed, disturbed, perplexed; (Fem.) متغيرة *muta-ghaiyira'h*.

A متفق *muttafiḳ*, adj. (act. part. VIII. of وفق), Agreeing, consenting, conspiring, according, united. 2. s.m. (9th) An accomplice, a co-operator; (Fem.) متفقة *muttafiḳa'h*. Sing. and Pl.

متل *matal*, s.m. (2nd) A saying, a proverb, an adage. Pl. متلونة *matalūnah*. (A مثل).

A متن *matan*, s.m. (2nd) The text in a book, the middle. Pl. متونة *matanūnah*.

A متولي *mutawallī*, s.m. (5th) (act. part. V of ولي), A superintendent or treasurer of a mosque. Pl. متوليان *mutawallīān*.

مته *matæh*, s.m. (6th) A wild boar. Sing. and Pl. See سدر and سركوزي

متيازي *miti-yāzey*, s.f. (3rd) Pl. Urine. Sing. form not used. متيازي كول *miti-yāzey kawul*, verb trans. To pass urine, to piss.

مُټ *mætt*, s.m. (2nd) The arm above the elbow. Pl. مټونة *mættūnah*.

مټ *matt*, s.m. (2nd) Quickness, celerity, despatch. 2. Deep dust in a road. 3. A large earthen vessel. (HI مټكا). Pl. مټونة *mattūnah*. مټ كول *matt kawul*, verb trans. To act with celerity and quickness.

مټ *mutt*, s.m. (2nd) The fist, the hand doubled up. Pl. مټونة *mutt-ūnah*. مټ كول *mutt kawul*, verb trans. To fist, to strike with the fist. (s مٹھ).

مټاك *mattāk*, s.f. (1st) A kind of walnut. Pl. مټاكِ *mattāki*. See چغزي

مټاكه *mattāka'h*, s.f. (3rd) A bump or swelling from the bite of any insect, a blister, a pimple. 2. A kind of walnut with a hard skin. 3. The ball of a pellet bow. Pl. ې *ey*.

HI مټائي *mittā'ī* or مټيائي *mittī-ā'ī*, s.f. (3rd) A sweetmeat, a confection. Pl. ئ *a'ī*.

مټكي *matt-kaey*, s.m. (1st) A large earthen vessel or jar. Pl. ي *ī*. (HI مټكا)

مټه *matta'h*, s.f. (3rd) Stickiness, adhesiveness, cohesiveness. Pl. ې *ey*. مټه خاورة *matta'h khāwra'h* or مټينه خاورة *mattīna'h khāwra'h*, s.f. (3rd) Sticky or glutinous earth, clay. Pl. ې *ey*. مټه *matta'h* or مټينه زمكه *mattīna'h z'maka'h*, s.f. (3rd) Clay-soil, marl. Pl. ې *ey*. مټين *mattīn*, adj. Clayey, glutinous, adhesive, sticky; (Fem.) مټينه *mattīna'h*.

مټه *mattah*, adj. Lazy, applied to a horse, etc. (Masc. and Fem.)

مټئي *mutta'ī*, s.f. (6th) An instrument for cleaning cotton, also the club with which the cleaner strikes the string of the instrument. 2. The handle of a plough. 3. The part of anything which is held in the hand, as a haft, shaft, etc. Sing. and Pl. See مشته and هروي

مټي *muttaey*, s.m. (1st) (W.) A handle, a hilt, a haft, a shaft, etc. Pl. ي *ī*. (s مٹھي).

مټيائي *mittī-ā'ī*, s.f. (3rd) Sweetmeat. Pl. ئ *a'ī*. See مټائي

مټيز *mattīz*, s.m.(5th) A man who may have eloped with a female of his own village and taken shelter with another clan, or in another village, Pl. مټيزان *mattīzān*. مټيز كيدل *mattīz kedal*, verb intrans. To elope, to bolt, to abscond, to elude, to escape, to give one the slip, to cut and run, to take French leave.

متيز کول *mattīz kawul*, verb trans. To run away with, to carry off (as a woman).

متيزه *mattī-za'h*, s f. (3rd) Elopement, running away (as a female with her paramour). Pl. ي *ey*. See نتواني . متيزه کيدل *mattī-za'h kedal*, verb intrans. To elope, to run away (as a woman with her lover).

A مثال *miṣāl*, s.m. (2nd) (from مثل) Simile, parable, saying, example. Pl. مثالونه *miṣālūnah*. See متل

A مثقال *miṣḳāl*, s.m. (2nd) (from ثقل) A weight containing 4 māshas and 3½ rattīs (Indian weight). Pl. مثقالونه *miṣḳālūnah*. See توله

A مثل *miṣal*, s.m. (2nd) Allegory, fable, simile, parable, metaphor, proverb, similitude, likeness. Pl. مثلونه *miṣalūnah*. See متل

A مثلاً *maṣalan*, adv. For example, namely.

A مجاور *majāwir*, s.m. (5th) (act. part. III of جور) A sweeper at a mosque, or attendant at a shrine. Pl. مجاوران *majāwirān*; or by some مينجور *mīn-jawar*, s.m. (5th). Pl. مينجور *mīn-jawær*.

A مجرا *muj-rā*, s.f. (6th) (past part. IV of جري) Allowance, premium, deduction. (E.) Sing. and Pl.; (W.) Pl. مجراوي *muj-rāwī*. مجرا ورکول *mujrā war-kawul*, verb trans. To deduct, to make an allowance, or take off something on account, to give a premium.

A مجرب *mujarrab*, adj. (inf. III of جرب) Tried, proved; expert, skilful; (Fem.) مجربه *mujarraba'h*.

A مجرد *mujarrad*, adj. (past part. II of جرد) Alone, solitary, single, unmarried, incorporeal, immaterial; (Fem.) مجرده *mujarrada'h*.

A مجرم *mujrim*, adj. (act. part. IV of جرم) Criminal. 2. s.m. (5th) A criminal, a sinner. Pl. مجرمان *mujrimān*; (Fem.) مجرمه *mujrima'h*. Pl. ي *ey*.

A مجلس *maj-lis*, s.m. (2nd) (from جلس) An assembly, a company, a congregation, a party, a conventicle. Pl. مجلسونه *maj-lisūnah*. مجلس کول *maj-lis kawul*, verb trans. To assemble together for conversation or consultation.

A مجمر *maj-mir*, s.m. (2nd) A chafing-dish, a censer for incense. 2. Perfume. Pl. مجمرونه *maj-mir-ūnah*.

A مجمل *muj-mal*, s.m. (2nd) (past part. IV of جمل), An abstract, a summary, an abridgement. Pl. مجملونه *muj-malūnah*.

P مجنون *maj-nūn*, s. prop. The name of the celebrated lover of Lailā.

مچ *mach*, s.m. (5th) A fly. 2. The sight of a gun. Pl. مچان *machān*. د سپي مچ *da spaey mach*, A tick, a dog-louse. مچ شړونی *mach-sharrūnaey*, s.m. (1st) A fly-flapper of leather or horse hair. Pl. ي *ī*.

مچچکي *machuchkaey*, s.m. (1st) The name of a plant which grows in low ground, used in alchemy. Pl. ي *ī*. See مچوچکي

مچک *machak*, s.m. (5th) A shepherd's crook, a stick with a crook at the end of it. Pl. مچکان *machakān*.

مچلوغزه *mach-loghza'h*, s.f. (3rd) A sling. Pl. ي *ey*. See مچوغنه

مچمچي *mach-macha'ī*, s.f. (6th) (W) The honey-bee. Sing. and Pl. See مچي

مچوغنه *machoghna'h*, s.f. (3rd) A sling. Pl. ي *ey*. See مچلوغزه

مچوقنه *machokna'h*, s.f. (3rd) Corrup. of the preceding. Pl. ي *ey*.

مچه *macha'h*, s.f. (3rd) (W.) A kiss. Pl. ي *ey*. مچه آخستل *macha'h ākhistal*, verb trans. To take a kiss, to salute. مچه ورکول *macha'h war-kawul*, verb trans. To give a kiss. مچول *machawul*, verb trans. To kiss, to salute, to caress. Pres. مچوي *machawī*; past مچه کړ *macha'h karr* or وُ کړ *wu-karr*; fut. مچه به کړي *macha'h bah krrī* or به وُ کړي *bah wu-krrī*; imp. مچه کړه *macha'h krrah* or وُ کړه *wu-krrah*; act. part. مچوونکي *machawūnkaey* or مچووني *machawūnaey*; past part. مچه کړي *macha'h karraey*; verb. n. مچونه *machawuna'h*. See ښکل

مچي *macha'ī*, s.f. (6th) A bee in general. Sing. and Pl. سره مچي *sara'h-macha'ī*, s.f. (6th). Sing. and Pl.; or دنداره *ddanddāra'h*, s.f. (3rd) A hornet, a wasp. Pl. ي *ey*. See دنبره

A محافظت *mahāfazat*, s.m. (2nd) (inf. III of

حفظ), Preservation, protection, guardianship, care, custody. Pl. محافظتونه *maḥāfaẓatūnah.* See ساتل

A محال *muḥāl,* adj. (past part. IV of حول), Impossible, absurd; (Fem.) محاله *muḥāla'h.*

A محبت *muḥabbat,* s.m. (2nd) (from حب), Love, affection, friendship. Pl. محبتونه *muḥabbatūnah.* محبت كول *muḥabbat kawul,* verb trans. To manifest love or affection for, to act friendly towards.

A محبوب *maḥ-būb,* adj. (past part. of حب), Beloved, loved, lovely; (Fem.) محبوبه *maḥbūba'h.* See مابوب

A محتاج *muḥtāj,* adj. (past part. VIII of حوج), Necessitous, indigent, in want; (Fem.) محتاجه *muḥtāja'h.*

A محتسب *muḥtasib,* s.m. (5th) (act. part. VIII of حسب), A censor, a superintendent of weights and measures. Pl. محتسبان *muḥtasibān.*

A محراب *miḥrāb,* s.m. (2nd) (from حرب), The principal place in a mosque where the priest prays before the people with his face towards Makka. Pl. محرابونه *miḥrābūnah.*

محرمه *muharramah,* adj. (from A محرم), Sacred, venerable, forbidden, excluded. 2. s.f. (3rd) The name of the first Muḥammadan month, held sacred on account of the death of Ḥasan, son of Æalī, killed near Kūfah, by Yazīd. Pl. ې *ey.*

A محروم *maḥ-rūm,* adj. (past part. of حرم) Prohibited, excluded, unfortunate, wretched, disappointed, deprived; (Fem.) محرومه *maḥrūma'h.* محروم راز *maḥ-rūm-i-rāz,* A confidant, a confidential person; (Fem.) محروم رازه *maḥrūm-i-rāza'h.* محروم كول *maḥ-rūm kawul,* verb trans. To exclude, to prohibit, to disappoint.

A محصل *muḥaṣṣil,* s.m. (5th) (act. part. II of حصل) A tax-gatherer, a bailiff, a dun. 2. Collecting, gathering, acquiring. Pl. محصلان *muḥaṣṣilān.*

محصول *maḥ-ṣūl,* s.m. (2nd) (past part. of حصل) Tax, duty, excise, custom, income, revenue. Pl. محصولونه *maḥ-ṣūlūnah.*

A محض *maḥẓ,* adj. Pure, unmixed. 2. adv. Merely, solely, entirely, wholly, purely.

A محظور *maḥ-ẓūr,* adj. (past part. of حظر) Forbidden, unlawful; (Fem.) محظوره *maḥẓūra'h.*

A محفوظ *maḥ-fūẓ,* adj. (past part. of حفظ) Protected, guarded, preserved, secure; (Fem.) محفوظه *maḥ-fūẓa'h.* See ساتل

A محكم *muḥ-kam,* adj. (past part. IV of حكم) Firm, strong, fortified, strengthened. 2. adv. Firmly, strongly; (Fem.) محكمه *muḥ-kama'h.* محكمي *muḥ-kamī,* s.f. (3rd) Firmness, strength. Pl. ئ *a'ī.*

A محكمه *maḥkama'h,* s.f. (3rd) (from حكم) A tribunal, a court of justice, assize. Pl. ې *ey.*

محله *maḥalla'h,* s.f. (3rd) from حل) A district, a quarter, a ward, a parish, a place, a building, etc. Pl. ې *ey.* محله دار *maḥalla'h-dār,* s.m. (5th) The head man of a ward or quarter. Pl. داران *dārān.*

A محمد *muḥammad,* adj. (past part. II of حمد) Praised, blessed. 2. s. prop. The name of the Arabian prophet.

محمدزي *muḥammad-zī,* s.m. (1st) Pl. The name of an Afghān tribe dwelling to the north of the Kābul river. محمدزی *muḥammad-zaey,* Sing. A male of the above tribe. محمدزئ *muḥammad-za'ī,* s.f. (6th) A female of the above. Sing. and Pl.

A محنت *miḥnat,* s.m. (2nd) Labour, toil, industry, exercise, trouble, misfortune, difficulty, calamity, trial, affliction, sorrow, perplexity. Pl. محنتونه *miḥnatūnah.* محنت كول *miḥnat kawul,* verb trans. To toil, to labor, to work hard. محنتي *miḥnatī,* adj. Laborious, industrious, laboring, hard-working, difficult, unfortunate. (Masc. and Fem.)

مخ *makh,* s.m. (2nd) The face, front, fore part, exterior, the outside, the surface, the disc, the skin, the outer part of a garment in opposition to the lining, the upper leather of a shoe or boot. 2. Civility, courtesy, kindness. Pl. مخونه *makhūnah.* مخا مخ *makhā-makh,* adv. Face to face, before, in front, opposite. مخ پټي *makh puttaey,* adj. Hiding the face, concealed,

2. A kind of rice. 3. s.m. (1st) A veil, a sheet for covering the face. Pl. ي *ī*; (Fem.) مخ پټ *makh putti*. Pl. (Masc. and Fem.) ي *ī*. مخ پټول *makh puttawul*, verb trans. To hide the face, to veil the face. مخ توري *makh toraey*, adj. Disgraced, criminal, sinner, unfortunate; (Fem.) مخ تورِ *makh tori*. Pl. (Masc. and Fem.) ي *ī*. مخ توري *makh torī*, s.f. (3rd) Disgrace, dishonour, criminal conduct. Pl. ئي *a'ī*. تور مخي *tor makhaey*, adj. Disgraced, criminal; (Fem.) تور مخيِ *tor makhey* or تور مخِ *tor makhi*. Pl. (Masc. and Fem.) ي *ī*. مخ د توري *makh da tūrey*, The edge of a sword. مخ رونړي *makh rūrrnaey*, adj. Unblamable, honest, respectable, of enlightened understanding; (Fem.) مخ رونړِ *makh rūrrni*; or مخ سپيني *makh spīnaey*; (Fem.) مخ سپينِ *makh spīni*. Pl. (Masc. and Fem.) ي *ī*. مخ سپيني *makh spīnī*, s.f. (3rd) Innocence, blamelessness, guiltlessness. Pl. ئي *a'ī*. مخ ور کول *makh war-kawul*, verb trans. To attend to, to regard. مخ گرزول *makh gærzawul*, verb trans. To turn the face from, to abandon, to dislike, to frown, to contract the face into wrinkles, to scowl at, to look angry or enraged.

A مخالف *mukhālif*, adj. (past part. III of خلف), Opposite, adverse, contrary, dissentient. 2. s.m. (5th) A foe, an opponent, an adversary. Pl. مخالفان *mukhālifān*; (Fem.) مخالفه *mukhālifa'h*; and s.f. (3rd). Pl. ي *ey*. مخالفت *mukhālifat*, s.m. (2nd) Opposition, dissension, enmity, variance. Pl. مخالفتونه *mukhālifatūnah*.

A مخبر *mukhbir*, s.m. (5th) (act. part. IV of خبر), An informer, a reporter; announcing news, certifying. Pl. مخبران *mukhbirān*. مخبره *mukhbira'h*, s.f. (3rd). Pl. ي *ey*.

A مختار *mukhtār*, s.m. (5th) (past part. VIII of خير), An agent, a free agent. Pl. مختاران *mukhtārān*. 2. adj. Chosen, selected. مختاره *mukhtāra'h*, s.f. (3rd). Pl. ي *ey*. مختاري *mukhtārī*, s.f. (3rd) Free-will, independence, authority. Pl. ئي *a'ī*.

A مختصر *mukhtaṣar*, adj. (past part. VIII of خصر), Abbreviated, abridged, small; (Fem.) مختصره *mukhtaṣara'h*. See كوتاه

A مختلف *mukhtalif*, adj. (act. part. VIII of خلف), Diverse, discordant, different, various; (Fem.) مختلفه *mukhtalifa'h*.

مختورن *makh-toran*, adj. Disgraced, criminal, guilty, unfortunate; (Fem.) مختورنه *makh-torana'h*. See مخ

مخسره *makhsara'h*, s.f. (3rd) Ridicule, joke, fun, pleasantry. Pl. ي *ey*. See مسخره and توكه

A مخفي *makhfī*, adj. (past part. of خفي), Concealed, secret, clandestine, occult, private. See پټ

A مخلص *mukhliṣ*, adj. (act. part. IV of خلص), Sincere, a sincere friend; (Fem.) مخلصه *mukhliṣa'h*.

A مخلوق *makh-lūḳ*, adj. (past part. of خلق), Created, formed. 2. s.m. (2nd) Created creature, a human being. Pl. مخلوقونه *makh-lūḳūnah*. (A Pl. مخلوقات *makhlūḳāt* generally used.)

A مخمل *makhmal*, s.m. (6th) (from خمل), Velvet. Sing. and Pl. See بخمل

مخوكه *makhūka'h*, s.f. (3rd) The beak of a bird. Pl. ي *ey*. See مښوكه

مخه *mukha'h*, s.f. (3rd) A butt for archery. 2. A mark for arrows. Pl. ي *ey*.

مخه *makha'h*, s.f. (3rd) Side, direction, way, course, inclination, range, path. Pl. ي *ey*.

مخي *makhaey* or *mukhaey* (W.) adj. Even, equal, level in rank or degree, on a par with, up to the mark, equivalent, tantamount. 2. Of the same tribe or clan. 3. An equal; (Fem.) مخيِ *makha'ī*. مخي توب *makhaey-tob*, s.m. (1st) Equality, parity, sameness in quality or degree. Pl. توبونه *tobūnah*. See سيال

A مدام *mudām*, adv. or adj. (from دوم), Continually, eternally, perpetual, lasting, eternal; (Fem.) مدامه *mudāma'h*. مدامي *mudāmī*, adj. Continuing, ceaseless, eternal.

A مدت *muddat*, s.m. (2nd) (from مد) A space or length of time, a long time, antiquity. Pl. مدتونه *muddatūnah*.

A مدد *madad*, s.m. (2nd) (from مد) Aid, assistance, help, succour. Pl. مددونه *madadūnah*. مدد وركول *madad war-kawul*, verb trans. To aid, to succour, to assist. مدد خواه *madad khwāh*, s.m. (5th) one who asks assistance. Pl. مدد خواهان *madad-khwāhān*. مدد خواهه *madad-khwāha'h*, s.f. (3rd). Pl. ي *ey*. مدد گار *madad-gār*, s.m. (5th) An assister, an aider, a protector, an ally, an auxiliary, a helper. Pl. مدد گاران *madad-gārān*. مدد گاره *madad-gāra'h*, s.f. (3rd). Pl. ي *ey*. مدد گاري *madad-gārī*, s.f. (3rd) Assistance, aid, help. Pl. ئ *a'ī*.

A مدعا *mudda-ææā*, s.f. (6th) (past part. VIII of دعا) Desire, wish, meaning, suit, view, object, scope. (E.) Sing. and Pl. (W.) Pl. مدعاوي *mudda-æāwī*.

A مدعي *mudda-æī*, s.m. (5th) A plaintiff, a suitor, a claimant, a prosecutor, an accuser. Pl. مدعيان *mudda-æīān*. مدعي *mudda-æī*, s.f. (5th). Pl. مدعيانِ *mudda-æīāni*. مدعي عليه *mudda-æī-æalaihi*, s.m. (9th) A defendant, a criminal. Sing. and Pl. (Masc. and Fem.) Sometimes written مديان

A مدفون *mad-fūn*, adj. (from دفن) Buried, interred, concealed; (Fem.) مدفونه *mad-fūna'h*. See بت

A مدلل *muddallal* (past part. of دلالت) Indicated, demonstrated, proved, shown.

A مدينه *madīnah*, s. prop. The name of a city in Arabia.

A مذكور *maz-kūr*, adj. (past part. of ذكر) Before-mentioned, aforesaid, said, mentioned. 2. s.m. (2nd) Mention, discourse. Pl. مذكورونه *maz-kūrūnah*; (Fem.) مذكوره *maz-kūra'h*. مذكور كول *maz-kūr kawul*, verb trans. To mention, to relate, to discourse about.

A مذمت *mazamat*, s.m. (2nd) (from ذم) Blame, abuse, scorn, contempt. Pl. مذمتونه *maz-amat-ūnah*.

A مذهب *maz-hab*, s.m. (2nd) (from ذهب) Sect, religion, way, mode. Pl. مذهبونه *maz-hab-ūnah*.

A مراد *murād*, s.m. (2nd) (past part. of رود) Desire, wish, intention, design, purport, inclination. Pl. مرادونه *murādūnah*. مراد من *murād-man* or مند *mand*, adj. One who has attained his desires or wishes; (Fem.) مراد منه *murād-mana'h* or منده *manda'h*.

مراوه *m'rā-wa'h*, s.f. (3rd) A part of a Persian wheel which supports one of the troughs. Pl. ي *ey*.

A مربي *murabbī*, s.m. and f. (5th) (act. part. II of ربو) A tutor, a guardian, a patron, a protector. Pl. مربيان *murabbīān*; f. Pl. مربيانِ *murabbī-āni*.

مرت *murt*, s.m. (6th) A kind of worm-wood. 2. A powder applied to the private parts of young children. Sing. and Pl.

A مرتبه *martaba'h*, s.f. (3rd) (from رتب) Dignity, degree, office, employment, rank, order, class, time, turn. Pl. ي *ey*.

مرتد *mur-tadd*, s.m. (5th) (past part. VII of رد) An apostate, a renegade. Pl. مرتدان *mur-taddān*. مرتده *mur-tadda'h*, s.f. (3rd) A female renegade or apostate. Pl. ي *ey*. مرتد كيدل *mur-tadd kedal*, verb intrans. To apostatize, to leave one's faith, to turn renegade. مرتد كول *mur-tadd kawul*, verb trans. To make an apostate of, to cause one to leave his faith. مرتد والئ *mur-tadd wālaey*, s.m. (1st) Apostasy, total abandonment of one's religious faith. Pl. والي *wālī*.

P مرجان *mar-jān*, s.m. (6th) Coral. Sing. and Pl.

مرجيونړه *mar-jīwarrnah*, s.m. (5th) A diver, a pearl diver (s मज्जक). Pl. مرجيونړه گان *mar-jīwarrnah-gān*.

S مرچ *mrich* or *mirch*, s.m. (6th) Pepper. Sing. and Pl. سره مرچ *sarah-mrich* or *mirch*, Red pepper, capsicum.

P مرد *mard*, s.m. (5th) A male, a man, a brave man. Pl. مردان *mardān*. مرد آزماي *mard-āzmā-e*, s.m. (5th) A goblin, a demon. Pl. مرد آزمايان *mard-āzmā-e-ān*.

P مردار *murdār*, adj. Polluted, impure, squalid, ugly, profane. 2. Carrion; (Fem.) مرداره *murdāra'h*. مرداري *murdārī*, s.f. (3rd) Pollution, impurity, profanity. Pl. ئ *a'ī*. مرداري كول *murdārī kawul*, verb trans. To act profanely. مرداريدل *murdāredal*, verb intrans. To become polluted, impure, or profane. مردارول *murdārawul*, verb trans. To make or render impure, to pollute, to profane.

P مردانه *mardānah*, adj. Manly, brave, man-like. 2. adv. Manfully, like a man. See ميړه

مردرو *marad-rau* or *mard-rau*, s.m. (2nd) A parapet, a breastwork, an entrenchment. Pl. مردرونه *marad-rau-ūnah* or *mard-rau-ūnah*.

مردک *mardak*, s.m. (5th) A bullet, a ball, a marble. Pl. مرډك *mardæk*.

مردكه *mardaka'h*, s.f. (3rd) A marble. Pl. ئ *ey*. مردكي كول *mardakaey kawul*, verb trans. To play at marbles.

مردكي *mardakaey*, s.m. (1st) A ball, a bullet, a pellet, a marble, etc. Pl. ي *ī*. See preceding.

P مرده *murdah*, adj. Dead. 2. s.m. (5th) A corpse, a dead body. Pl. مردگان *murdagān*. Also s.f. (5th). Pl. مردگانِ *murdagānī*. See مړي.

مرده رنگ *murdah-rang*, adj. Deadly pale, pale as death; (Fem.) مرده رنگه *murdah ranga'h*.

مردي *mardī*, s.f. (3rd) Seed, semen. Pl. ئ *a'ī*; or مردوي *mardwī*. Pl. ئ *a'ī*.

مرسته *marasta'h* or مرستَ *marasta*, s.f. (3rd) Partiality, favor, favoritism, aid, help, assistance. Pl. ئ *ey*. مرسته كول *marasta'h kawul*, verb trans. To act with partiality, to favor, to lean towards, to aid, to help.

A مرشد *mur-shid*, s.m. (5th) (act. part. IV of رشد) An instructor, a director, a spiritual guide, a monitor, a teacher. Pl. مرشدان *mur-shidān*. مرشده *murshida'h*, s.f. (3rd). Pl. ئ *ey*.

P A مرشدي *murshidī*, s.f. (3rd) Instruction in religious matters, guidance. Pl. ئ *a'ī*.

A مرض *maraz* or *marz*, s.m. (2nd) Sickness, disease, infirmity. Pl. مرضونه *marazūnah*. مرضي *marazī*, adj. Sick, diseased, infirm, ailing. (Masc. and Fem.) مرض نيول *maraz nīwal*, verb trans. To catch a disease, to fall sick.

A مرضي *mar-zī*, s.f. (3rd) (from رضو) Will, pleasure, assent, consent. Pl. ئ *a'ī*.

مرغ *m'ragh*, s.m. (2nd) A large stone just the weight to be lifted by a man, and used in the game or exercise of putting the stone. Pl. مرغونه *m'raghūnah*.

مرغچچي *mar-ghachichaey*, s.m. (1st) A kind of grain about the size of a pea made into necklaces and other ornaments for women. Pl. ي *ī*. See شل دانه

مرغړي *mar-gharraey*, s.m. (1st) A hard lump formed in the flesh, a glandulous swelling. Pl. ي *ī*.

مرغلره *mar-ghalara'h*, s.f. (3rd) A pearl. Pl. ئ *ey*. See در

مرغمي *mar-ghamaey*, s.m. (1st) A male kid. Pl. ي *ī*. مرغمۍ *marghamey* or مرغم *mar-ghami*, s.f. (8th) A female kid. Pl. ي *ī*. See ورغمي

A مرغوب *mar-ghūb*, adj. Desired, desirable, amiable, beautiful, estimable, etc.; (Fem.) مرغوبه *mar-ghūba'h*.

مرغه *mar-gha'h*, s.f. (3rd) A description of grass given to horses. Pl. ئ *ey*.

مرغه *murghah*, s.m. (5th) (P مرغ) A fowl or bird in general. Pl. مرغان *murghān*. د مرغه چيچي *da murghah chīchaey*, s.m. (1st) A young bird, a chicken until the feathers have come out. Pl. ي *ī*. د مرغه چيچۍ *da murghah-chīcha'ī*, s.f. (6th) A young hen bird. Sing. and Pl. 2. مرغۍ *murgha'ī*. s.f. (6th) A sparrow in general, cock or hen, a small bird. 2. Any eatable bird or game, in distinction to مرغه *murghah*, a bird of prey. Sing. and Pl. بنده كړي مرغي *banda'h karrey murgha'ī*, s.f. (6th) A decoy bird, a decoy duck. Sing. and Pl.

مرغ باز *murgh-bāz*, s.m. (5th) A cock-fighter. Pl. مرغ بازان *murgh-bāzān*. See چرگ باز

مرغېچي *murghechaey*, s.m. (1st) A man or boy who drives away or frightens the birds from a corn field. Pl. ي *ī*.

مركنډۍ *mar-kandda'ī*, s.f. (6th) The throat, the windpipe, the gullet. 2. The end of the backbone where the neck joins. Sing. and Pl. See مرۍ

P مرگ *marg*, s.m. (2nd) Death. Pl. مرگونه *mar-*

gūnah. Also مرگي margacy, s.m.(1st). Pl. ي ī. مرگ و ژواك marg-o-jzwāk or مرگ ژواك marg jzwāk, Life and death, living and dying. مرگ ماهي marg-i-māhī, s.m. (6th) The name of a seed for killing fish. Sing. and Pl. مرگ مفاجات marg-i-mafājāt. Sudden death. مرگ موش marg-i-mūsh, s.m. (6th) Arsenic. Sing. and Pl.

مرگټ margaṯṯ, s.m. (2nd) (corrup. of s مرگهټ) A place where Hindūs burn their dead. Pl. مرگټونه margaṯṯūnah. See هندو سوز

مرگوټي margoṯṯaey, s.m. (1st) (dimin. of P مرگ) Death, demise, decease, dissolution. Pl. ي ī.

G مرمر mar-mar or سنگ مرمر sang-i-mar-mar, s.m. (6th) Marble. Sing. and Pl.

A مروت murūwat, s.m. (2nd) (from مرا) Affection, kindness, humanity, generosity, affability, urbanity. 2. Fortitude, manliness. Pl. مروتونه murūwatūnah. مروت کول murūwat kawul, verb trans. To show kindness or affection, to act with generosity or urbanity.

مروت murwat, s.m. (6th) The name of a district of Afghānistān—Derah Ismāæl Khān, as far as the Sūlīmān Range. 2. The people inhabiting it. Sing. and Pl.

مروت mar-wat, s.m. (2nd) Twist, coil, plait, fold, a revolution. 2. A screw. Pl. مروتونه mar-watūnah. See پيچ

مرور marawur, adj. Vexed, displeased, angry, offended; (Fem.) مروره marawura'h. مرور کيدل marawur kedal, verb intrans. To become vexed, displeased, offended, مرور کول marawur kawul, verb trans. To offend, to displease, to vex. مرور والَي marawur-wālaey, s.m. (1st) Vexation, displeasure, umbrage, pique. 2. Huff, pet, a passion. Pl. والي wālī. Also مرور توب marawur-tob, s.m. (2nd). Pl. توبونه tobūnah; and مرور تيا marawur-tī'ā, s.f. (6th). (E.) Sing. and Pl. (W.) Pl. تياوي tī'āwī.

مرونډۍ marwanḏḏa'ī, s.f. (6th) The name of a shrub. Sing. and Pl.

مروري marorī, s.m. (1st) Pl. Camomile.

HI مروړ marorr, s.m. (2nd) Twist, turn, writhe, contortion, convolution. Pl. مروړونه marorrūnah. مروړ ور کول marorr war-kawul, verb trans. To twist, to contort, to distort, to gripe.

A مرهم mar-ham, s.m. (2nd) A plaster, a salve. Pl. مرهمونه mar-hamūnah. See ملهم

مرۍ mara'ī, s.f. (6th) A bone joining the spine to the neck, the gullet, the windpipe. 2. A bead, a shell. 3. A charm, an antidote. Sing. and Pl. See مرکنډۍ

A مريد murīd, s.m. (5th) (act. part. IV of رود) A disciple, a scholar, a follower. Pl. مريدان murīdān. مريده murīda'h, s.f. (3rd). Pl. ې ey.

A مريدي murīdī, s.f. (3rd) Scholarship, the state of being a disciple, tuition, instruction. Pl. ۍ a'ī. مريدي کول murīdī kawul, verb trans. To act the disciple, to follow.

A مريض marīẓ, adj. (from مرض) Sick, diseased, afflicted; (Fem.) مريضه marīẓa'h.

مرينړه marīrrna'h, s.f. (3rd) A patch or part of a field of corn, etc., left uncut. Pl. ې ey.

مريي m'rayaey, s.m. (1st) (E.) A slave. Pl. ي ī; or (W.) s.m. (5th). Pl. مريان m'rayān.

مړ marr, adj. Dead, defunct, lifeless, inanimate, demised. Pl. مړه m'rræh; (Fem.) مړه m'rra'h. Pl. مړې m'rrey. مړ ژواندي marr-jzwāndaey, adj. Half-dead, near death, at death's door, being on one's last legs; (Fem.) مړ ژواندِ marr-jzwāndi. Pl. (Masc. and Fem.) ي ī. مړ کيدل marr kedal, verb intrans. To die, to expire, to perish. مړ کول marr kawul, verb trans. To kill. مړل m'rral, verb intrans. To die, to expire, to perish. Pres. مري m'rī; past وُ مړ wu-marr or مړ شه marr shah or وُ شه wu-shah; fut. وُ به مري wu bah m'rī; imp. وُ مره wu-m'rah; act. part. مړونکَي m'rrūnkaey or مړونَي m'rrūnaey; past part. مړ marr or مړَي marraey or مړ شوَي marr shawaey; verb. n. مړنه m'rrana'h.

مړام m'rrām, adj. Dead, withered, decayed, faded; (Fem.) مړامه m'rrāma'h. مړاميدل m'rrāmedal, verb intrans. To wither, to die, to decay, to fade. Pres. مړاميږي m'rrāmejzī (W.) or مړاميگي m'rrāmegī (E.); past مړام شه m'rrām shah or وُ شه wu-shah; fut. مړام به شي m'rrām -

bah shī or به وُ شي bah wu-shī; imp. مړام شه m'rrām shah or وُ شه wu-shah; act. part. مړاميدونكَي m'rrāmedūnkaey or مړاميدونَي m'rrāmedūnaey; past part. مړام m'rrām or مړام شوَي m'rrām shawaey; verb. n. مړاميدنه m'rrāmedana'h or مړاميده m'rrāmedah. مړامول m'rrāmawul, verb trans. To wither, to destroy, to dry up, to spoil. Pres. مړاموي m'rrāmawī; past مړام كړ m'rrām karr or وُ كړ wu-karr; fut. مړام به كړي m'rrām bah krrī or به وُ كړي bah wu-krrī; imp. مړام كړه m'rrām krrah or وُ كړه wu-krrah; act. part. مړاموونكَي m'rrāmawūnkaey or مړاموونَي m'rrāmawūnaey; past part. مړام كړَي m'rrām karraey; verb. n. مړامونه m'rrāmawuna'h.

مړانه marrāna'h, s.f. (3rd) Bravery, heroism, intrepidity, gallantry. Pl. ې ey.

مړاو m'rrāw, adj. Dead, withered, faded, decayed, destroyed; (Fem.) مړاوه m'rrāwa'h. مړاوې سترګې m'rrāwey stargey, Sleepy eyes. مړاو كيدل m'rrāw kedal, verb intrans. To wither, to fade, to die, to decay. مړاو كول m'rrāw kawul, verb trans. To destroy, to wither, to make fade or decay; also مړاويدل m'rrāwedal, verb intrans., and مړاوول m'rrāwawul, verb trans. the inflections of which are the same as مړاميدل m'rrāmedal, etc., by substituting و for م.

مړڅپن marr-tsapan, adj. Withered, faded, decayed, drooping, dead; (Fem.) مړڅپنه marr-tsapana'h. See مړام and مړاو

مړد marrd, s.m. (5th) A saint, a religious instructor. Pl. مړدان marrdān. See مرد and بزرګ

مړدكي marr-dakaey, s.m. (1st) A ball, a pellet, a bullet, a marble. Pl. ي ī. See مردكي

مړشومه marr-shūma'h, s.f. (3rd) Food sent to the house of a deceased person on the day of the death and funeral, by friends or acquaintances. Pl. ې ey.

مړز marraz, s.m. (5th) A quail. Pl. مړزان marrazān. مړزه marraza'h, s.f. (3rd) The hen bird. Pl. ې ey. See نورز

مړغوني marraghūnaey, s.f. (3rd) (Pl.) The bitter apple, colocynth. The singular form is not often used. See ترخه ككوړه and ترخه هندوانه

مړغېچن marr-ghechan, adj. Half-dead, faded, withered; (Fem.) مړغېچنه marr-ghechana'h. See مړام and مړاو

مړل m'rral, verb intrans. To die, etc. For inflections see under مړ

مړني marranaey, s.m. (1st) A brave man, a hero, a daring fellow, a Hector. Pl. ي ī. مړنۍ marrana'ī, s.f. (6th) A brave-hearted or courageous female. Sing. and Pl.

مړوالَي marr-wālaey, s.m. (1st) Satiety, satiating, quenching (as hunger, etc.) Pl. والي wālī. See موړ والي

مړوښه marro-sha'h (W.) or marro-kha'h (E.) s.f. (3rd) A married woman, a wife, a woman whose husband is alive, in opposition to a widow. Pl. ې ey.

مړول marrawul, verb trans. To satiate, to satisfy, to cloy, to glut, to surfeit. 2. To quench, to extinguish, to kill, to destroy. See under موړ

مړوند marrwand, s.m. (2nd) The wrist. Pl. مړوندونه marrwandūnah.

مړوندۍ marrwanda'ī, s.f. (6th) A kind of shrub used in dyeing. Sing. and Pl.

مړه marrah, adj. (Fem. of موړ), which see.

مړه marrah, s.m. (only applied in a vocative sense between friends or relations, to a man) Oh friend! oh man! Pl. مړو marro.

مړه خواه marrah khwāh, adj. Satisfied, satiated, cloyed, glutted.

مړه خوږ m'rrah khwajz (W.) مړه خوګ m'rrah khwag (E.) s.m. (6th) The dropsy. Sing. and Pl.

مړَي m'rraey, adj. (past part. of مړل) Dead, lifeless, defunct. 2. As s.m. (1st) A dead body, a dead man. Pl. ي ī. مړي m'rrey or مړ m'rri, s.f. (8th) A dead female. Pl. ي ī.

مړېدل marredal, verb intrans. To become satiated, satisfied, glutted, surfeited, quenched, etc. See under موړ

مړېدنه marredana'h, s.f. (3rd) (verb. n.) Satiety, satisfaction, contentment, repletion, plenty, fulness. Pl. ي ey; or مريده marredah, s.m. (6th). Sing. and Pl. See under مور

A مزاج miz-āj, s.m. (2nd) (from مزج) Constitution, temperament, complexion, habit of body. 2. Disposition, temper, humor. Pl. مزاجونه miz-ājūnah. مزاجي miz-ājī, adj. Constitutional, habitual. (Masc. and Fem.)

A مزاخ mazākh, s.m. (2nd) A jest, a joke, pleasantry. Pl. مزاخونه mazākhūnah. See توكه

P مزد muzd or mazd, s.m. (2nd) Wages, hire, reward, salary, premium. 2. The corn taken by a miller as price for grinding corn at the rate of so many pounds per load. Pl. مزدونه muzdūnah.

مزدگري mazd-garaey, s.m. (1st) A miller, a laborer at a mill. Pl. ي ī; or مزده mazdah or muz-dah, s.m. (6th). Sing. and Pl. See also آسيوان

P مزدور maz-dūr, s.m. (5th) A laborer, a porter, a carrier, a workman. Pl. مزدوران maz-dūrān. مزدوره maz-dūra'h, s.f. (3rd) A female laborer, a char-woman. Pl. ي ey.

P مزدوري maz-dūrī, s.f. (3rd) Labor, laboring, wages, price of labor, hire. Pl. ئي a'ī. مزدوري كول maz-dūrī kawul, verb trans. To work, to labor.

مزري m'zaraey, s.m. (1st) A tiger, a panther. 2. A lion. Pl. ي ī. مزرئ m'zara'ī, s.f. (6th) A tigress, a lioness. Sing. and Pl. شين مزري shīn m'zaraey, adj. A very bold or ravenous tiger or lion.

مزري mazaraey, s.m. (1st) A kind of grass or reed from which sandals (څپلي) or mats are manufactured. Pl. ي ī.

مزكه m'zaka'h, s.f. (3rd) Ground, land, soil, earth. Pl. ي ey. See زمكه

مزل mazal, s.m. (2nd) (corrup. of P منزل) A stage, a march, a day's journey. Pl. مزلونه mazalūnah. مزل كول mazal kawul, or مزل وهل mazal wahal, verb trans. To go a journey, to go a stage or march, to travel.

P مزه maza'h, s.f. (3rd) Taste, relish, flavor, delight, pleasure, enjoyment, anything agreeable to the mind or body. Pl. ي ey. مزه دار maza'h-dār, adj. Delicious, tasteful, palatable; (Fem.) مزه داره maza'h-dāra'h. مزه لرل maza'h laral, verb trans. To possess or be endowed with taste, pleasure, flavor, relish. (Eng. verb intrans. To be delicious). مزه كول maza'h kawul, verb trans. To give pleasure, delight, flavour, relish. مزه آخستل maza'h ākhistal, verb trans. To feel, experience, receive, take pleasure, to enjoy, to revel or riot in. See خوند

مزی mazaey, s.m. (1st) A thread, twist, cord of silk, cotton, flax, etc. 2. The piping round the edge of a dress, a ribbon, a thread, a border, etc. 3. A tent rope. Pl. ي ī.

مزی mazaey, adj. Strong, powerful, brawny, stalwart, well knit; (Fem.) مزِ mazi. Pl. (Masc. and Fem.) ي ī.

مږ majz (W.) s.m. (2nd) A ram. Pl. مږونه majzūnah. See گډ and مير

مږك majzak, s.m. (5th) A mouse in general. Pl. مږكان majzakān. مږك وهونكي majzak-wahūnkaey, s.m. (1st) A mousing hawk. Pl. ي ī. مږك وهونكِ majzak-wahūnki, s.f (8th) The hen bird. Pl. ي ī. See مكك and منگه كوري

مږه majza'h, s.f. (3rd) A rat. Pl. ي ey. See مكه

A مس mis (W.) or mas (E.) s.m. (6th) Copper. 2. A cup for catching lamp black. Sing. and Pl.

A مسافر musāfir, s.m. (5th) (act. part. III of سفر) A traveller, a stranger, a passenger. Pl. مسافران musāfirān. مسافره musāfira'h, s.f. (3rd). Pl. ي ey. مسافري musāfirī, s.f. (3rd) Travelling, journeying, going a journey. Pl. ئي a'ī. مسافري كول musāfirī kawul, verb trans. To travel, to set out on a journey.

P مست mast, adj. Drunk, intoxicated, proud, lustful, lascivious, wanton, sensual; (Fem.) مسته masta'h. مستيدل mastedal, verb intrans. To become drunk, to grow lustful or wanton. مستول mastawul, verb trans. To make drunk, proud, wanton, lascivious, etc. The inflections are according to the common form for verbs derived from adjectives.

مستک *mas-tak*, s.m. (6th) (E.) A weed that grows among corn, tares, the name of certain leguminous plants, the *vicia sativa*, considered to be the darnel (Matt. xiii.) Sing. and Pl.

P مستي *mastī*, s.f. (3rd) Drunkenness, intoxication. 2. Lust, wantonness. 3. Pride. Pl. ئي *a'ī*. مستي کول *mastī kawul*, verb trans. To play pranks, to jump and dance about, to act with pride, wantonness, etc.

A مسجد *mas-jid*, s.m. (2nd) (from سجد) A mosque, a Muḥammadan church. Pl. مسجدونه *mas-jidūnah*.

مسحه *mas'ḥa'h*, s.f. (3rd) (corrup. of A مسح) Wiping, washing, cleaning, anointing, a part of the purification before prayer. Pl. ئي *ey*. مسحه کول *mas'ḥa'h kawul*, verb trans. To wash, to purify, etc.

A مسخره *mas<u>kh</u>ara'h*, s.f. (3rd) Drollery, buffoonery, a jest, a saying. Pl. ئي *ey*. مسخره کول *mas<u>kh</u>ara'h kawul*, verb trans. To joke, to jest, to play the buffoon. مسخراچي *mas<u>kh</u>a-rā<u>ch</u>ī*, s.m. (5th) A buffoon, a jester, a droll. Pl. مسخراچيان *mas<u>kh</u>a-rā<u>ch</u>īān*.

A مسرف *mus-rif*, adj. Extravagant, prodigal (act. part. IV of سرف); (Fem.) مسرفه *mus-rifa'h*.

A مسکن *mas-kan*, s.m. (2nd) (from سکن) An abode, a dwelling, a place of residence, a habitation. Pl. مسکنونه *mas-kanūnah*. See آستوګه

مسکي *muskaey*, s.m. (1st) Smiling, laughing. Pl. يي *ī*. مسکي کول *muskaey kawul*, verb trans. To smile, to laugh. See مسيدل and مسول

مسل *masal*, s.m. (6th) Smiling, laughing, a smile, a grin, a smirk, a simper. Sing. and Pl.

A مسلمان *musalmān*, s.m. (5th) (from سلم) A believer, a follower of Muḥammad. Pl. مسلمانان *musalmānān*. مسلمانه *musal-māna'h*, s.f. (3rd) A female follower of Muḥammad. Pl. ئي *ey*. مسلماني *musal-mānī*, s.f. (3rd) The Muḥammadan religion, circumcision, the tenets of the faith. Pl. ئي *a'ī*.

A مسله *masala'h*, s.f. (3rd) (from سال) Question, problem, proposition, generally a precept of Muḥammad. Pl. ئي *ey*.

A مسند *masnad*, s.m. (2nd) (from سند) A throne, a large cushion, a chair, a prop. Pl. مسندونه *masnadūnah*.

مسواك *miswāk*, s.m. (2nd) (from سوک) A stick used to clean the teeth with, a tooth-brush. Pl. مسواکونه *miswākūnah*.

مسئ *masa'ī*, s.f. (6th) An ornament for the head. Sing. and Pl.

مسيدل *masedal*, verb intrans. To smile, to smirk, to simper, to grin. Pres. مسيږي *mase-<u>jz</u>ī* (W.) or مسيګي *mase-gī* (E.); past ؤ مسيده *wu-masedah*; fut. ؤ به مسيږي *wu bah mase-<u>jz</u>ī* or مسيګي *mase-gī*; imp. ؤ مسيږه *wu-mase<u>jz</u>ah* or مسيګه *masegah*; act. part. مسيدونکي *mase-dūnkaey* or مسيدونی *mase-dūnaey*; past part. مسيدلي *masedalaey*; verb. n. مسيدنه *masedana'h*.

مسين *misīn* or *masīn*, adj. Brazen, made of brass; (Fem.) مسينه *misīna'h* or *masīna'h*.

مسينه *masīna'h* or *misīna'h*, s.f. (3rd) A set of brass pots and pans for household purposes. Pl. ئي *ey*.

A مشابه *mu<u>sh</u>ābih*, adj. (act. part. III of شبه) Like, resembling, analogous. (Masc. and Fem.)

مشابهت *mu<u>sh</u>ā-bahat*, s.m. (2nd) (inf. III of شبه) Resemblance, similitude, agreement, conformity. Pl. مشابهتونه *mu<u>sh</u>ā-bahatūnah*. مشابهت لرل *mu<u>sh</u>ā-bahat laral*, verb trans. To have or hold resemblance or similarity.

مشاته *ma<u>sh</u>āta'h*, s.f. (3rd) The face; an ugly or sour looking face. Pl. ئي *ey*. See مشاد

مشاد *ma<u>sh</u>ād*, adj. Ugly, sour looking, ill-tempered, cross looking; (Fem.) مشاده *ma<u>sh</u>-āda'h*.

مشال *ma<u>sh</u>āl*, s.m. (2nd) (corrup. of A مشعل) A torch, a flambeau. Pl. مشلونه *ma<u>sh</u>alūnah*.

P مشت *mu<u>sh</u>t*, s.m. (2nd) The fist, a blow with the fist, a handful. Pl. مشتونه *mu<u>sh</u>t-ūnah*. مشت و ګريبان *mu<u>sh</u>t-ow-girebān*, Fist and collar, fighting, struggling.

مشته *mu<u>sh</u>ta'h*, s.f. (3rd) A kind of club which

a cotton cleaner uses in striking the string of the cleaning instrument. Pl. ي *ey*. See متي

مشر *mashar*, adj. Elder, senior, aged, old, venerable. 2. A patriarch, the elder of a tribe, a chief; (Fem.) مشره *mashra'h*, An elderly female, etc. كشر مشر *kashar mashar*, Young and old, junior and senior, small and great; (Fem.) كشره مشره *kashra'h mashra'h*. مشرنزي *mash-ranzī* or مشر رانړيزي *mashar-rāṛṛnīzī*, s.m. (1st) (Pl.) The name of a tribe of Afghāns, a sept of the Kamālzīs. مشرنزي *mashran-zaey* or مشر رانړيزي *mashar rāṛṛnīzaey* (Sing.) A man or male of the above tribe. s.f. (6th) Sing. and Pl. ي *a'ī*.

A مشرف *musharraf*, adj. (past part. II of شرف) Exalted, ennobled, honored; (Fem.) مشرفه *musharrafa'h*. مشرف كول *musharraf kawul*, verb trans. To exalt, to ennoble.

A مشرق *mashriḳ*, s.m. (9th) (from شرق) The east. Sing. and Pl.

A مشرك *mush-rik*, s.m. (5th) (act. part. IV of شرك) An infidel, an idolater, a polytheist. Pl. مشركان *mush-rikān*. مشركه *mush-rika'h*, s.f. (3rd) An idolatress. Pl. ي *ey*.

A مشغول *mash-ghūl*, adj. (past part. of شغل) Occupied, employed, diligent, anxious, busy; (Fem.) مشغوله *mash-ghūla'h*. مشغوليدل *mash-ghūledal*, verb intrans. To become busied, employed, occupied. مشغولول *mash-ghūlawul*, verb trans. To employ, to occupy, to make busy.

مشغولا *mash-ghūlā*, s.f. (6th) Business, employment, occupation. 2. Pastime, discourse, conversation. (E.) Sing. and Pl. (W.) Pl. مشغولاوي *mash-ghūlāwī*.

A مشفق *mushfiḳ*, adj. (act. part. IV of شفق) Kind, shewing favor, condoling, merciful. 2. A friend, a companion; (Fem.) مشفقه *mushfiḳa'h*.

A مشق *mashḳ*, s.m. (2nd) An example, a copy to write from, an exercise, practice, usage, use. Pl. مشقونه *mashḳūnah*.

A مشقت *mashaḳḳat*, s.m. (2nd) (inf. of شق) Trouble, labour, pains, toil, assiduity. Pl. مشقتونه *mashaḳḳatūnah*. مشقت كول *mashaḳḳat kawul*, verb trans. To labour, to toil, to take pains, to be assiduous.

P مشك *mashk*, s.m. (2nd) A leather bag for carrying water, a water bag. Pl. مشكونه *mashkūnah*.

P مشك *mushk*, s.m. (6th) Musk. Sing. and Pl. مشكنډۍ *mush-kunḍḍa'ī*, s.f. (6th) A pod of musk. Sing. and Pl. مشكين *mush-kīn*, adj. Musky, emitting musk. مشكين مږك *mushkīn-majzak* (W.) or مګك *magak* (E.), A musk-rat.

مشكار *mash-kār*, s.m. (5th) (corrup. of P ميرشكار) A falconer, a trainer of hawks, a bird-catcher, a huntsman. Pl. مشكاران *mash-kārān*.

A مشكل *mush-kil*, adj. (act. part. IV of شكل) Difficult, intricate, hard, painful; (Fem.) مشكله *mush-kila'h*.

مشكنړه *mash-karṛna'h*, s.f. (3rd) A glass bead. Pl. ي *ey*.

P̄ مشكي *mushkaey*, adj. Dark bay approaching to black, musk coloured; (Fem.) مشكۍ *mushka'ī*.

مشل *mashal*, s.m. (2nd) A torch, a flambeau. Pl. مشلونه *mashalūnah*. See مشال

مشوانړۍ *mashwāṛṛna'ī*, s.f. (6th) An inkstand. Sing. and Pl.

مشوانړي *mash-wāṛṛnī*, s.m. (1st) Pl. The name of an Afghān tribe dwelling in the vicinity of Shurrah-rūd. مشوانړي *mash-wāṛṛnaey* (Sing.) A male of the above tribe. مشوانړۍ *mash-wāṛṛna'ī*, s.f. (6th) A female of the above. Sing. and Pl.

A مشورت *mashwarat*, s.m. (2nd) (from شور) Counsel, consultation, advice. Pl. مشورتونه *mashwaratūnah*. مشورت كول *mashwarat kawul*, verb trans. To consult, to advise.

مشوكه *mashūka'h*, s.f. (3rd) The beak of a bird. Pl. ي *ey*. See مښوكه

A مشهور *mash-hūr*, adj. (past part. of شهر) Celebrated, published, conspicuous, famous, divulged, well-known, notorious; (Fem.) مشهوره *mash-hūra'h*. مشهور كيدل *mash-hūr kedal*, verb intrans. To become famous, notorious, conspicuous. مشهور كول *mash-hūr kawul*, verb trans. To render famous, to publish, to celebrate, to proclaim.

مښک mu*kh*k (E.) or mu*sh*k (W.) s.m. (6th) Musk. Sing. and Pl. مښکين *mu*kh*kīn* or *mu*sh*kīn*, adj. Musky, emitting musk; (Fem.) مښکينه *mu*kh*kīna'h* or *mu*sh*kīna'h*. See مشک

مښکي *ma*sh*kaey* (W.) or *ma*kh*kaey* (E.) s.m. (1st) A musk rat, a mole. Pl. ي *ī*. See مشکين مږک

مښکۍ *ma*kh*ka'ī* (E.) or *ma*sh*ka'ī* (W.) s.f. (6th) A kind of sweet-scented grass. Sing. and Pl.

مښکيرک *mu*sh*-gīrak* or *mu*kh*-gīrak*, s.m. (5th) A mousing hawk. Pl. مښکيرکان *mu*sh*-gīrakān* or *mu*kh*-gīrakān*. See مږک وهونکي

مښل *mu*sh*al* (W.) or *mu*kh*al* (E.) verb trans. To rub, to anoint, to lubricate, to grease, to rub up, to clean, to burnish, to polish. 2. To arouse, to awaken, to excite by friction. Pres. مږي *mujzī* or مګي *mugī*; past وُ مښه *wu-mu*sh*ah* or *mu*kh*ah*; fut. وُ به مږي *wu bah mujzī* or مګي *mugī*; imp. وُ مږه *wu-mujzah* or وُ مګه *wu-mugah*; act. part. مښونکي *mu*sh*ūnkaey* or *mu*kh*ūnkaey* or مښونَي *mu*sh*ūnaey* or *mu*kh*ūnaey*; past part. مښلَي *mu*sh*alaey* or *mu*kh*alaey*; verb. n. مښنه *mu*sh*ana'h* or *mu*kh*ana'h*.

جهان مښل *jahān mu*sh*al* or *mu*kh*al*, verb trans. To scour the world in search of a thing, to make a great search, to travel all over the world.

مښنه *mu*sh*ana'h* (W.) or *mu*kh*ana'h* (E.) s.f. (3rd) (verb. n.) Rubbing, anointing, coating with grease, cleaning, exciting by friction. Pl. ئ *ey*. Also مښود *mu*sh*od* or *mu*kh*od*, s.m. (6th). Sing. and Pl.

مښوکه *ma*kh*ūka'h* (E.) or *ma*sh*ūka'h* (W.) s.f. (3rd) The beak or bill of a bird. Pl. ئ *ey*. See مشوکه

A مصر *miṣr*, s. prop. Egypt, a large city.

A مصرف *maṣ-raf*, s.m. (2nd) (from صرف) Expenditure, expense, disbursement, cost. Pl. مصرفونه *maṣ-rafūnah*. په مصرف خرڅول *pah maṣ-raf* *kh*ar*ts*awul*, verb trans. To expend in a proper manner. بي مصرفَ خرڅول *bey maṣ-rafa* *kh*ar*ts*awul*, verb trans. To expend improperly, not to apply to a proper purpose.

A مصرف *muṣrif*, adj. (act. part. of صرف) Prodigal; (Fem.) مصرفه *muṣrifa'h*.

A مصروف *maṣrūf*, adj. (past part. of صرف) Expended, employed. 2. Occupied, busy; (Fem.) مصروفه *maṣrūfa'h*.

A مصرۍ *miṣ-ra'ī*, s.f. (6th) A good sword, an Egyptian cimetar. Sing. and Pl.

A مصلحت *maṣlaḥat*, s.m. (2nd) (from صلح) The what is right, fit, convenient; convenience, expedience, counsel, advice. Pl. مصلحتونه *maṣlaḥatūnah*. مصلحت کول *maṣlaḥat kawul*, verb trans. To consult, to advise, to conspire, to counsel.

مصله *muṣalla'h*, s.f. (3rd) (corrup. of A مصلا) A place of prayer, a carpet to pray on. Pl. ئ *ey*.

A مصور *maṣauwir*, s.m. (5th) (act. part. II of صور) A painter, a limner, a drawer, a sculptor. Pl. مصوران *maṣauwirān*. مصوره *maṣauwira'h*, s.f. (3rd) A female artist, etc. Pl. ئ *ey*.

A مصيبت *muṣībat*, s.m. (2nd) (from صوب) Misfortune, disaster, affliction, calamity, adversity, evil, ill, misery. Pl. مصيبتونه *muṣībatūnah*.

A مضبوط *maẓ-būṭ*, adj. (past part. of ضبط) Strong, fast, firm, fixed. 2. Possessed, occupied, restrained; (Fem.) مضبوطه *maẓ-būṭa'h*. مضبوط کول *maẓ-būṭ kawul*, verb trans. To strengthen, to render firm, fixed. 2. To strengthen in possession.

A مضبوطي *maẓ-būṭī*, s.f. (3rd) Strength, firmness, durability. Pl. ئ *a'ī*.

A مضطرب *muẓ-ṭarib*, adj. (act. part. VIII of ضرر) Agitated, distracted, disturbed in mind; (Fem.) مضطربه *muẓ-ṭariba'h*.

A مضمون *maẓ-mūn*, s.m. (2nd) (past part. of ضمن) Purport, meaning, sense, signification. Pl. مضمونونه *maẓ-mūnūnah*.

A مطابق *muṭābiḳ*, adj. (act. part. III of طبق) Suitable, conformable, equal, identical, answering, agreeable to, corresponding; (Fem.) مطابقه *muṭābiḳa'h*.

A مطابقت *muṭābaḳat*, s.m. (2nd) Conformity,

equality, identity, analogy, correspondence. Pl. مطابقتونه *muṭābaḳatūnah.*

A مطالعه *muṭā-liæa'h,* s.f. (3rd) (act. part. III of صلع) Contemplation, consideration, reading, study, perusal. Pl. ې *ey.* مطالعه کول *muṭā-liæa'h kawul,* verb trans. To read, to study, to peruse.

A مطلب *maṭ-lab,* s.m. (2nd) (from طلب) Intention, wish, desire, object, aim, purpose, purport, meaning, demand. Pl. مطلبونه *maṭ-labūnah.* مطلب لرل *maṭ-lab laral,* verb trans. To have or possess an object, wish, desire, aim. مطلب کول *maṭ-lab kawul,* verb trans. To effect one's object, aim, purpose.

A مطلق *muṭ-laḳ,* adj. (past part. IV of طلق) Absolute, altogether, universal, principal, supreme. 2. adv. Wholly, at all, not in the least, entirely, altogether; (Fem.) مطلقه *muṭ-laḳa'h.*

A مطلوب *maṭ-lūb,* adj. (past part. of طلب) Required, demanded, wanted, desired, necessary; (Fem.) مطلوبه *maṭ-lūba'h.*

A مظلوم *maẓ-lūm,* adj. (past part. of ظلم) Injured, oppressed. 2. Mild, gentle, modest; (Fem.) مظلومه *maẓ-lūma'h.*

A معاش *ma-æāsh,* s.m. (2nd) (from عيش) Means or place of living, livelihood, subsistence, living. Pl. معاشونه *ma-æāshūnah.*

A معاف *mu-æāf,* adj. (act. part. III of عفو) Pardoned, excused, absolved, exempted, forgiven; (Fem.) معافه *mu-æāfa'h.* معاف کيدل *mu-æāf kedal,* verb intrans. To become forgiven, pardoned, absolved. معاف کول *mu-æāf kawul,* verb trans. To pardon, to forgive, to absolve, to exempt.

A معافي *mu-æāfī,* s.f. (3rd) (act. part. III of عفو) Exempt from tax and rent. 2. A grant of land from a sovereign, free of tax, immunity, exemption, remission, pardon, absolution. Pl. ئ *a'ī.*

A معالجه *mu-æālaja'h,* s.f. (3rd) (inf. III of علج) Curing, healing, treatment. 2. A cure, a remedy. Pl. ې *ey.* معالجه کول *mu-æālaja'h kawul,* verb trans. To heal, to cure, to attend.

A معاملت *mu-æāmalat,* s.m. (2nd) (inf. III of عمل), Affair, treaty, transaction, business, negotiation, procedure, concern, cause or suit in law. Pl. معاملتونه *mu-æāmalatūnah*; or معامله *mu-æāmala'h,* s.f. (3rd). Pl. ې *ey.* معامله کول *mu-æāmala'h kawul,* verb trans. To treat with, to negotiate, to deal with.

A معتبر *muæ-tabar,* adj. (past part. VIII of عبر) Confidential, respectable, worthy of confidence, credible, creditable, trustworthy, reputable; (Fem.) معتبره *muæ-tabara'h.*

A معتقد *muæ-taḳid,* s.m. (5th) (act. part. of عقد) A believer, a faithful friend, a servant, an adherent. Pl. معتقدان *muæ-taḳidān.* معتقده *muæ-taḳida'h,* s.f. (3rd). Pl. ې *ey.*

A معذور *maæ-ẕūr,* adj. (past part. of عذر) Excusable, excused. 2. Disappointed; (Fem.) معذوره *maæ-ẕūra'h.* معذور گڼل *maæ-ẕūr gaṛṇal,* verb trans. To consider excusable, to hold excused.

A معرفت *maæ-rifat,* s.m. (2nd) (from عرف) Account, cause, (by) reason, (by) means, (through) the means. 2. Knowledge, understanding. Pl. معرفتونه *maæ-rifatūnah.*

A معرکه *maæ-rika'h,* s.f. (3rd) A party of arbitrators or persons sent to make peace between two tribes, etc. 2. The business of making peace or any arrangement between two parties. Pl. ې *ey.* See جرگه

A معشوق *maæ-shūḳ,* s.m. (5th) (past part. of عشق) A beloved object, a very dear friend or companion. Pl. معشوقان *maæ-shūḳān.* معشوقه *maæ-shūḳa'h,* s.f. (3rd) A sweetheart, a mistress. Pl. ې *ey.*

P A معشوقي *maæ-shūḳī,* s.f. (3rd) Loveliness, the state of being loved, love. Pl. ئ *a'ī.*

A معطل *muæaṭṭal,* adj. (past part. II of عطل) Unemployed, vacant, disengaged, neglected, idle, suspended from office; (Fem.) معطله *muæaṭṭala'h.* معطل کول *muæaṭṭal kawul,* verb trans. To suspend, to neglect, to render unemployed.

A معقول *maæ-ḳūl,* adj. (past part. of عقل) Pertinent, proper, fair, just, reasonable, probable, intelligible; (Fem.) معقوله *maæ-ḳūla'h.*

A معلوم *maæ-lūm*, adj. (past part. of علم) Known, notorious, distinguished, evident, apparent, obvious; (Fem.) معلومه *maæ-lūma'h.* معلوميدل *maæ-lūmedal*, verb intrans. To appear, to seem, to become evident, apparent, obvious, distinguished. 2. To become known. Pres. معلوميږي *maæ-lūmejzī* (W.) or معلوميګي *maæ-lūmegī* (E.); past معلوم شه *maæ-lūm shah* or و شه *wu-shah*; fut. معلوم به شي *maæ-lūm bah shī* or به و شي *bah wu-shī*; imp. معلوم شه *maæ-lūm shah* or و شه *wu-shah*; act. part. معلوميدونکي *maæ-lūmedūnkaey* or معلوميدونې *maæ-lūmedūnaey*; past part. معلوم *maæ-lūm* or معلوم شوې *maæ-lūm shawaey*; verb. n. معلوميدنه *maæ-lūmedana'h* or معلوميده *maæ-lūmedah.* معلومول *maæ-lūmawul*, verb trans. To find out, to discover, to know, to understand, to suppose, to deem. Pres. معلوموي *maæ-lūmawī*; past معلوم کړ *maæ-lūm karr* or و کړ *wu-karr*; fut. معلوم به کړي *maæ-lūm bah krrī* or به و کړي *bah wu krrī*; imp. معلوم کړه *maæ-lūm krrah* or و کړه *wu-krrah*; act. part. معلومونکي *maæ-lūmawūnkaey* or معلومونې *maæ-lūmawūnaey*; past part. معلوم کړې *maæ-lūm karraey*; verb. n. معلومونه *maæ-lūmawuna'h.*

A معني *maæ-nī* or معنا *maæ-nā*, s.f. (6th) (from عني) Meaning, signification, sense, acceptation, reality. (E.) Sing. and Pl. (W.) Pl. معناوي *maæ-nāwī.*

A معين *mu-æaiyan*, adj. (past part. II of عين) Fixed, established, appointed, certified, ascertained; (Fem.) معينه *mu-æaiyana'h.*

مغار *mughār*, s.m. (2nd) A cavern, a pit, an abyss. Pl. مغارونه *mughārūnah.*

A مغالطه *mughālaṭa'h*, s.f. (3rd) (inf. III of غلط) Leading into ambiguity, error, or delusion. Pl. ې *ey.*

مغانه *m'ghāna'h*, s.f. (3rd) The groin. Pl. ې *ey.* See غويلنګ

A مغرب *maghrab* or *maghrib*, s.m. (9th) The west, the place where the sun sets, sunset. Sing. and Pl.

A مغرور *magh-rūr*, adj. (past part. of غرّ) Proud, arrogant, haughty, fastidious; (Fem.) مغروره *magh-rūra'h.* مغروري *magh-rūrī*, s.f. (3rd). Pride, arrogance. Pl. ئ *a'ī.*

مغزن *magh-zan*, adj. Strong, powerful, sturdy, stalwart; (Fem.) مغزنه *magh-zana'h.*

مغزې *maghzaey*, s.m. (1st) The hem, border or edging of a garment, etc. 2. The brain, the marrow, a kernel. 3. The neck. Pl. ي *ī.* (P مغز).

P مغل *mughal*, s.m. (6th) A Mughal. Sing. and Pl. مغله *mughala'h*, s.f. (3rd) A Mughal female. Pl. ې *ey.* مغل والې *mughal-wālaey*, s.m. (1st) Tyranny, oppression, the custom of Mughals. Pl. والي *wālī.* Sometimes written مغل واره *mughal-wāra'h*, s.f. (3rd). Pl. ې *ey.*

A مغلوب *magh-lūb*, adj. (past part. of غلب) Overcome, conquered, discomfited; (Fem.) مغلوبه *magh-lūba'h.* مغلوب کول *magh-lūb kawul*, verb trans. To conquer, to overcome.

A مفاجات *mafūjāt*, s.m. (9th) (inf. III. of فجأ) Sudden death. Sing. and Pl.

A مفارقت *mufāraḳat*, s.m. (2nd) (inf. III of فرق) Separation, absence, alienation. Pl. مفارقتونه *mufāraḳatūnah.*

P مفت *muft*, adv. Gratuitously, gratis, for nothing, acquired without cost or labour, without return or benefit. See مېت and ويريا

A مفتي *muftī*, s.m. (5th) (act. part. IV of فتو) A superior officer among Muḥammadans whose decrees are regarded as law, a Muftī. Pl. مفتيان *muftīān.* مفتي ګري *muftī-garī*, s.f. (3rd) The business of a Muftī. Pl. ئ *a'ī.*

A مفسد *mufsid*, s.m. (5th) (act. part. IV of فسد) A seditious person, author of evil, mischief-maker, mischievous, noxious, incendiary. Pl. مفسدان *mufsidān.* مفسده *mufsida'h*, s.f. (3rd). Pl. ې *ey.*

مفسدي *mufsidī*, s.f. (3rd) Seditiousness, mischievousness. Pl. ئ *a'ī.* مفسدي کول *mufsidī kawul*, verb trans. To create or cause mischief or sedition.

A مفلس *muflis*, adj. (act. part. IV of فلس) Wretched, poor, beggarly, bankrupt; (Fem.) مفلسه *muflisa'h.*

A مفلسي *muflisī*, s.f. (3rd) Poverty, indigence, bankruptcy. Pl. ي *a'ī*.

A مفيد *mufīd*, adj. (act. part. IV of فيد) Profitable, useful, beneficial, salutary, advantageous; (Fem.) مفيده *mufīda'h*.

A مقابل *muḳābil*, adj. (act. part. III of قبل) Opposite, confronting, opposing, matching, resembling, equal, comparing; (Fem.) مقابله *muḳābila'h*. See مخامخ

A مقابله *muḳābala'h*, s.f. (3rd) (inf. III of قبل) Comparison, collation, opposition, confronting, contest, contending, presence. Pl. ي *ey*. مقابله كيدل *muḳābala'h kedal*, verb intrans. To confront, to meet, to be in front. مقابله كول *muḳābala'h kawul*, verb trans. To contend, to confront, to oppose, to compare, to emulate.

A مقام *muḳām* or *maḳām*, s.m. (3rd) (from قوم) Dwelling, mansion, station, abode, place, place of residence or encamping. 2. A halting place. Pl. مقامونه *muḳāmūnah* or *maḳāmūnah*. مقام كول *muḳām kawul*, verb trans. To halt, to encamp, to take up residence.

A مقبول *maḳ-būl*, adj. (past part. of قبل) Acceptable, agreeable, accepted, grateful, taken in good part, agreed on; (Fem.) مقبوله *maḳ-būla'h*.

A مقتدي *muḳtadī*, s.m. (5th) (act. part. VIII of قدو) A follower, an imitator. Pl. مقتديان *muḳtadī-ān*.

A مقتول *maḳ-tūl*, adj. (past part. of قتل) Killed, slain; (Fem.) مقتوله *maḳ-tūla'h*.

A مقدم *muḳaddam*, adj. (past part. II of قدم) Antecedent, prior, preceding. 2. A chief, a leader; (Fem.) مقدمه *muḳaddama'h*.

A مقدمه *muḳaddama'h*, s.f. (3rd) (past part. II of قدم) Preamble, preface, preliminary. 2. Affair, business, matter, subject, thesis. 3. A cause in law. Pl. ي *ey*. مقدمه كول *muḳaddama'h kawul*, verb trans. To litigate, to squabble, to quarrel, to split, to declare war.

A مقدور *maḳ-dūr*, s.m. (2nd) (past part. of قدر) Power, possibility, ability, authority. Pl. مقدورونه *maḳ-dūrūnah*.

A مقرر *muḳarrar*, adj. (past part. II of قر) Fixed, ascertained, established, certain, infallible, unquestionable, appointed, employed. 2. adv. Certainly, assuredly, positively; (Fem.) مقرره *muḳarrara'h*. مقرر كول *muḳarrar kawul*, verb trans. To fix, to appoint, to establish, to ascertain, to settle, to assign. مقرر كيدل *muḳarrar kedal*, verb intrans. To be settled, established, assigned.

A مقصد *maḳ-ṣad*, s.m. (2nd) (from قصد) Design, intention, meaning, purpose, object, aim, purport, desire, wish, scope. Pl. مقصدونه *maḳ-ṣadūnah*; or مقصود *maḳ-ṣūd* (past part. of قصد). Pl. مقصودونه *maḳ-ṣūdūnah*.

A مقل *muḳl*, s.m. (6th) The fruit of the dwarf palm. The name of a tree or gum (Amyris agallocha). Sing. and Pl.

A مقيش *maḳḳaish*, s.m. (6th) Brocade (gold or silver thread); brocade (a garment), ornamented with gold or silver thread.

A مكار *makkār*, s.m. (5th) (adj.sup. of مكر) A cheat, a knave, an impostor. 2. adj. Deceitful, insidious, artful. Pl. مكاران *makkārān*. مكاره *makkāra'h*, s.f. (3rd). Pl. ي *ey*.

A مكاري *makkārī*, s.f. (3rd) Fraud, deceitfulness, imposture, cheating, artifice, roguery. Pl. ي *a'ī*. مكاري كول *makkārī kawul*, verb trans. To cheat, to impose, to deceive.

A مكتب *maktab*, s.m. (2nd) (from كتب) A school, an academy. Pl. مكتبونه *maktab-ūnah*.

A مكر *makr*, s.m. (2nd) Fraud, deceit, imposture, artifice, evasion. Pl. مكرونه *makrūnah*. مكر كول *makr kawul*, verb trans. To deceive, to impose on, to evade. مكر جن *makr-jan*, s.m. (5th) A deceiver, an evader. Pl. مكرجن *makr-jæn*. مكر جنه *makr-jana'h*, s.f. (3rd). Pl. ي *ey*.

A مكرر *mukarrar*, adj. (past part. II of كر) Repeated, again; (Fem.) مكرره *mukarrara'h*. مكرر ويل *mukarrar wayal*, verb trans. To repeat.

A مكروه *mak-rūh*, adj. (past part. of كره) Hated, odious, abominable, detestable, execrable, disgusting, obscene, abhorred; (Fem.) مكروهه *mak-rūha'h*.

مکنړا *mak-ṟṟnā*, s.f. (6th) A kind of spoke in the cross piece of a Persian wheel in which the upright cylinder turns, and to which the bullock or camel is yoked. (E.) Sing. and Pl. (W.) Pl. مکنړاوي *mak-ṟṟnāwī*.

A مکه *makkah*, s. prop. The name of a city in Arabia, the birth-place of Muḥammad.

مکیز *makez*, s.m. (2nd) Coquetry, amorousness, pretence, blandishment. Pl. مکیزونه *makez-ūnah*. مکیز کول *makez kawul*, verb trans. To coquet, to feign.

مګ *mag*, s.m. (2nd) A ram. Pl. مګونه *mag-ūnah*. مګه *maga'h*, s.f. (3rd) An ewe. Pl. ئ *ey*. See میږ and میګ

P مګر *magar*, conj. Unless, perhaps, only, except, but, however. See ولي

مګک *magak*, s.m. (5th) (E.) A mouse, a rat. Pl. مګکان *magakān*. See مږک and مګه or منګه

مګنز *maganz*, s.f. (1st) or منګز *mangaz*, A comb for the hair. Pl. مګنزِ *maganzi* or منګزِ *man-gazi*.

مګنځ *magandz*, s.f. (1st) A comb. Pl. مګنځِ *magandzi*. See ګنز and ږمنز

مګه *maga'h*, s.f. (3rd) (E.) A rat, a bandicoot rat. Pl. ئ *ey*. See مږه

مګهر *maghar*, s.m. (2nd) A peg or stone used in playing a game like pitch and toss. Pl. مګهرونه *magharūnah*. See موسي

مګه کوري *maga'h-kūraey* (E.) or مږه کوري *majza'h-kūraey* (W.) s.m. (1st) A young rat, a mouse. Pl. ي *ī*. See منګه کوري

مل *mal*, s.m. (4th) A companion, an associate, a compeer, a comrade, a chum, a crony, a messmate, a fellow-traveller. 2. adj. Crony, boon, intimate, sociable, companion. Pl. مَل *m'la* or مله *m'lah*. مله *m'la'h*, adj. and s.f. (3rd) A female companion, associate, etc. Pl. ملئ *m'ley*. مل ګیري *mal-gīrī*, s.f. (3rd) Friendship, companionship, association, intercourse, consortship, acquaintanceship, fellowship. Pl. ئي *a'ī*; or ملګر تیا *mal-gar-tī'ā*, s.f. (6th). (E.) Sing. and Pl. (W.) Pl. تیاوي *tī'āwī*. مل ګیري کول *mal-gīrī kawul*, verb trans. To consort, to associate with, to pick or scrape acquaintance, to fraternize.

ملا *m'lā*, s.f. (6th) The waist, the loins. (W.) Pl. ملاوي *m'lāwī*. (E.) Sing. and Pl. ملا تړل *m'lā taṟṟal*, verb trans. To gird the loins, to prepare for action, etc. ملا وستني *m'lā-was-tanaey*, s.m. (1st) A girdle, a waist-band. Pl. ي *ī*. دوه بغرګه ملا *dwah b'gharga'h m'lā*, Double, bent, crooked (as the waist, from age, toil, etc.)

A ملا *mullā*, s.m. (5th) (corrup. of مولي) A doctor, a schoolmaster. 2. Learned in Arabic. Pl. ملایان *mullā-yān*.

ملا تړ *m'lā-taṟṟ*, s.m. (6th) (*lit.* loins-binder) Assistance, aid, support, succour. 2. A feudal retainer. 3. A reserve. Sing. and Pl.

ملا چرګک *mullā-chargak*, s.m. (5th) A huddud, the hoopoe. 2. The penis (met.) Pl. ملا چرګکان *mullā-chargakān*.

A ملاح *mallāḥ*, s.m. (5th) (adj. sup. of ملح) A sailor, a boatman, a mariner, a waterman. Pl. ملاحان *mallāḥān*. See مانګي and مهانه

A ملاحظه *mulā-ḥiẓa'h*, s.f. (3rd) (inf. III of لحظ) Contemplating, looking at, consideration, view, notice, regard. Pl. ئ *ey*. ملاحظه کول *mulā-ḥiẓa'h kawul*, verb trans. To view, to look at, to contemplate, to regard, to notice.

ملاست *m'lāst*, adj. Recumbent, reclining, lying down, sitting, reposing, resting, unrestrained, going to sleep, etc.; (Fem.) ملاسته *m'lāsta'h*. ملاست کول *m'lāst kawul*, verb trans. To sleep with, to lie down or go to bed with. ملاستل *m'lāstal*, verb intrans. To recline, to lie down, to sit, to repose, to rest, to go to sleep, etc. This infinitive is imperfect, and requires the aid of څملل to complete it, which is also imperfect with regard to the inflections which the other has. Pres. څملي *tsamlī*; past وُ ملاست *wu-m'lāst*; fut. وُ به څملي *wu bah tsamlī*; imp. څمله *tsamlah* or وُ څمله *wu-tsamlah*; act. part. ملاستونکي *m'lāstūnkaey* or ملاستوني *m'lāstūnaey*; past part. ملاست *m'lāst* or ملاستلي *m'lāstalaey*; verb. n. ملاستنه *m'lāstana'h* or ملاسته *m'lāsta'h*. See څملاستل

ملاسته *m'lāsta'h* or ملاستنه *m'lāstana'h*, s.f. (3rd) (verb. n.) Recumbency, lying down, prostration, reposing, reclining, resting, etc. Pl. ې *ey*. See خملاستل

A ملاقات *mulāḳāt*, s.m. (2nd) (inf. III of لقي) Interview, meeting, visiting, encountering, conversation. Pl. ملاقاتونه *mulāḳātūnah*. ملاقات کول *mulāḳāt kawul*, verb trans. To meet, to visit, to encounter.

A ملال *malāl*, s.m. (6th) Sadness, grief, anguish, dejection, languor. 2. Sad, dejected. Sing. and Pl.; (Fem.) ملاله *malāla'h*. ملالي سترګي *malāley stargey*, Languishing eyes.

A ملامت *malāmat*, s.m. (2nd) (from لوم) Reproach, blame, rebuke, censure. Pl. ملامتونه *malāmatūnah*. ملامت کول *malāmat kawul*, verb trans. To blame, to reproach, to censure, to rebuke.

A ملامتي *malāmatī*, adj. Reproached, blamable, reprehensible. (Masc. and Fem.)

ملامتتيا *malāmat-tī'ā*, s.f. (6th) Accusation, criminality, disgrace, censure. (E.) Sing. and Pl. (W.) Pl. تياوي *tī'āwī*.

ملامتيدل *malāmatedal*, verb intrans. To become censured, rebuked, blamed, reproached. Pres. ملامتيږي *malāmatejzī* (W.) or ملامتيګي *malāmategī* (E.); past ملامت شه *malāmat shah* or و شه *wu-shah*; fut. ملامت به شي *malāmat bah shī* or به و شي *bah wu-shī*; imp. ملامت شه *malāmat shah* or و شه *wu-shah*; act. part. ملامتيدونکی *malāmatedūnkaey* or ملامتيدونې *malāmatedūnaey*; past part. ملامت *malāmat* or ملامت شوی *malāmat shawaey*; verb. n. ملامتيدنه *malāmatedana'h* or ملامتيده *malāmatedah*. ملامتول *malāmatawul*, verb trans. To blame, to reproach, to censure, to rebuke. Pres. ملامتوي *malāmatawī*; past ملامت کړ *malāmat karr* or و کړ *wu-karr*; fut. ملامت به کړي *malāmat bah krrī* or به و کړي *bah wu-krrī*; imp. ملامت کړه *malāmat krrah* or و کړه *wu-krrah*; act. part. ملامتوونکی *malāmatawūnkaey* or ملامتوونې *malāmatawūnaey*; past part. ملامت کړی *malāmat karraey*; verb. n. ملامتونه *malāmatawuna'h*.

ملا وستنې *m'lā-wastanaey*, s.m. (1st) A girdle, a waistband. Pl. ي *ī*.

A ملتوي *multawī*, adj. (act. part. VIII of لوي) Delayed, postponed, protracted, spinning out. 2. Bent, crooked. (Masc. and Fem.) ملتوي کول *multawī kawul*, verb trans. To postpone, to delay, to protract.

ملخ *malakh*, s.m. (5th) A locust. Pl. ملخان *malakhān* or sometimes ملک *malak*. Pl. ملکان *malakān*.

ملخوزې *malkhozey*, s.f. (3rd) Fenugreek seed. The singular form ملخوزه *malkhoza'h* is used only as the name of the plant.

A ملک *mulk*, s.m. (2nd) A country, a kingdom, a realm, a region. Pl. ملکونه *mulkūnah*. ملک نيول *mulk nīwal*, verb trans. To conquer a country.

A ملک *malik*, s.m. (5th) A king, a chief, a master, the head man of a village. Pl. ملکان *malikān*. ملکه *malika'h*, s.f. (3rd) A queen, a mistress. ملک زاده *malik-zādah*, s.m. (5th) A king's son, the son of a chief. Pl. ملک زادګان *malik-zādagān*. ملکي *malakī*, adj. Relating to government. ملکي کول *malikī kawul*, verb trans. To govern, to rule.

A ملک *milk*, s.m. (2nd) Possession, property, right, dominion. Pl. ملکونه *milkūnah*.

ملکه *malaka'h*, s.f. (3rd) An angel (corrup. of A ملک). Pl. ې *ey*. ملک الموت *malaku-l-maut*, The angel of death.

ملګری *mal-garaey*, s.m. (1st) A companion, an associate, a compeer, a comrade, a chum, a crony, a messmate, a fellow-traveller; (Fem.) ملګر *mal-gari*. Pl. (Masc. and Fem.) ي *ī*. See مل

HI ململ *mal-mal*, s.m. (6th) Muslin. Sing. and Pl.

ملنډه *malandda'h*, s.f. (3rd) A joke, a jest, drollery, jesting, buffoonery. Pl. ې *ey*. ملنډي کول *malanddey kawul*, verb trans. To joke, to jest, to play the fool. See ټوکه

ملنډې *malanddaey*, s.m. (1st) A droll, a jester, a buffoon. Pl. ي *ī*. ملنډي *malandda'ī*, s.f. (6th) A female as above. Sing. and Pl. See ټوکي

HI ملنګ *malang,* s.m. (5th) A kind of darwesh. Pl. ملنګان *malangān.* ملنګه *malanga'h,* s.f. (3rd) A female darwesh. Pl. ې *ey.*

ملنګيان *malangiān,* s.m. (6th) The name of a drug given as a stomachic. Sing. and Pl.

ملو *malaw,* s.m. (2nd) A sort of sack or bag, in which articles are packed previous to being loaded on camels, etc. Pl. ملوونه *malaw-ūnah.*

ملوب *mal-ob,* s.m. (2nd) Blood and water, or blood and matter. Pl. ملوبونه *mal-obūnah.*

ملوک *malūk,* adj. Delicate, handsome; (Fem.) ملوکه *malūka'h.* Pl. ملوکي *malūkey*; also used to signify 'the fair.'

A ملول *malūl,* adj. (past part. of ملل) Sad, dejected, grieved, languid, fatigued, melancholy; (Fem.) ملوله *malūla'h.*

ملونه *m'lūna'h,* s.f. (3rd) A bridle for a horse, reins, bit, etc., complete. Pl. ې *ey.*

مله *mala'h,* s.f. (3rd) A kind of grass. Pl. ې *ey.*

P ملهم *mal-ham,* s.m. (2nd) (corrup. of مرهم) Salve, plaster, ointment. Pl. ملهمونه *mal-ham-ūnah.*

مليا *milī-ā,* adj. Encountering, meeting, joining, coming into contact. مليا کيدل *milī-ā kedal.* verb intrans. To encounter, to meet, to fall in with, to happen. مليا کول *milī-ā kawul,* verb trans. To cause to or make meet, to bring about a meeting or encounter. See ميليا. (s ملن).

مليزي *malle-zī,* s.m. (1st) Pl. The name of a tribe of Afghāns. مليزی *malle-zaey* (Sing.) A male of the above tribe. مليزئ *malle-za'ī,* s.f. (6th) A female of the above. Sing. and Pl.

ممانړنه *mamāṛṛn-na'h* or ممانړه *mamāṛṛna'h,* s.f. (3rd) A wild fruit tree bearing a red berry, also the fruit. Pl. ې *ey.*

A ممتاز *mum-tāz,* adj. (past part. VIII of ميز) Chosen, exalted, eminent, distinguished; (Fem.) ممتازه *mum-tāza'h.*

P مه يز *mam-rez,* s.m. (2nd) A spur. Pl. ممريزونه *mam-rezūnah.*

A ممکن *mum-kin,* adj. (act. part. IV of مکن) Possible, contingent; (Fem.) ممکنه *mum-kina'h.*

A مملکت *mumlakat* or *mamlukat,* s.m. (2nd) (inf. of ملک) Dominion, sovereignty, country, region, kingdom. Pl. مملکتونه *mumlakatūnah* or *mamlukatūnah.*

A مملوک *mam-lūk,* adj. (past part. of ملک) In one's power, possessed. 2. A Mamlūk—a purchased slave or captive; (Fem.) مملوکه *mamlūka'h.*

A من *mann,* s.m. (4th) The name of a weight which varies considerably, the Ḳandahār or Tabrīz *mann* being only 8lbs. whilst that of Peshāwer is 80lbs. Pl. منونه *m'nnūnah.*

منا *manā,* s.f. (6th) (E.) A raised stage for watching a field from. Sing. and Pl. See منه

A منات *manāt,* s. prop. An idol of the Arabs before they embraced Islāmism. لات و منات *lāt-o-manāt,* Two idols worshipped by the ancient Arabs.

A مناجات *manājāt,* s.m. (2nd) (inf. III of نجو) Supplication, prayer. Pl. مناجاتونه *manājāt-ūnah.* مناجاتي *manājātī,* One who prays. See نمونځ

A منادي *manādī,* s.f. (3rd) (from ندا) A proclamation. Pl. ئ *a'ī.* See جار and جارچي

A مناره *manāra'h,* s.f. (3rd) (from نور) A turret, a minaret. Pl. ې *ey*; also منار *manār,* s.m. (5th). Pl. مناران *manārān.* کله منار *kala'h-manār,* A tower of heads or skulls erected on a field of battle.

A مناسب *munāsib,* adj. (act. part. III of نسب) Fit, proper, meet, suitable, becoming, expedient, pertinent, apposite, congruous; (Fem.) مناسبه *munāsiba'h.*

A مناسبت *munāsabat,* s.m. (2nd) (inf. III of نسب) Suitableness, fitness, meetness, connection, relation, consistency, expediency, analogy, comparison, accordance. Pl. مناسبتونه *munāsabatūnah.* مناسبت لرل *munāsabat laral,* verb trans. To have or possess fitness, suitableness, relation, consistency, analogy.

منافق *manāfiḳ,* s.m. (5th) (act. part. III of نفق) A hypocrite, an atheist, an enemy. Pl. منافقان *manāfiḳān.* منافقي *manāfiḳī,* s.f. (3rd) Hypocrisy, atheism, enmity. Pl. ئ *a'ī.*

A ممبر *mimbar*, s.m. (2nd) (from نبر) A pulpit. Pl. ممبرونه *mimbar-ūnah*.

A منت *minnat*, s.m. (2nd) An obligation, a favour, an entreaty, a supplication. Pl. منتونه *minnat-ūnah*. منت بار *minnat-bār*, adj. Obliged, favoured, under obligation; (Fem.) منت باره *minnat-bāra'h*. منت كول *minnat kawul*, verb trans. To supplicate, to entreat. 2. To oblige.

S منتر *mantar*, s.m. (2nd) A charm, a spell, an incantation, a philter. Pl. منترونه *mantar-ūnah*. منترويل *mantar wayal*, verb trans. To exorcise, to charm, to bewitch. See پاړ

A منتظر *mun-taẓir*, adj. (act. part. VIII of نظر) Expecting with impatience, looking out for, waiting or tarrying for; (Fem.) منتظره *mun-taẓira'h*. منتظر كيدل *mun-taẓir kedal*, verb intrans. To be expectant, to be looking out for.

منج *manj*, s.m. (2nd) A bed, a bedstead. Pl. منجونه *manjūnah* (S منجا)

منج *munj*, s.m. (6th) A kind of grass from which ropes are made (Saccharum munja). Sing. and Pl. (S مونج)

منجقي *manjaḳaey*, s.m. (1st) The clitoris. Pl. ي ī.

منجقيه *manjaḳaeyah*, A term of abuse; also منجقو *manjaḳū*.

منجله *manjala'h*, s.f. (3rd) A kind of ring of grass, rope, or wood, used to support a vessel with a round bottom, or placed on the head as a pad to support a load in general. Pl. ې *ey*.

منجيله *manjīla'h*, s.f. (5th) Same as preceding. Pl. ې *ey*.

منډ *mand*, A particle adopted from the Persian, which, added to nouns, implies possession or having; (Fem.) منده *manda'h*. At times corrupted into من *man* and منه *mana'h*.

منداړو *mandārrno*, s.m. (5th) The name of a plant. Pl. منداړوګان *mandārrno-gān*.

منداړو *mandārrno*, s.m. (5th) A churning stick. 2. A rolling pin. Also written منډاړو *manddārrnū*. Pl. منداړوګان *mandārrnogān*, etc. See وړي

منداو *mandāow*, s.m. (2nd) The withers of a horse. Pl. منداوونه *mandāow-ūnah*.

مندري *mandaraey*, adj. Small, little, short in stature. 2. s.m. (1st) A little man. Pl. ي ī. 3. (Fem.) مندرئ *mandara'ī*, and s.f. (6th) A little woman. 4. An ornament for the ears. 5. A pearl. Sing. and Pl. (HI مندرا).

موندل *mundal*, verb trans. To find, to find out, to get, to meet with, to fall upon, to trace, to get at, to stumble upon, to detect. See موندل

مندنه *mundana'h*, s.f. (3rd) (verb. n.) Finding, discovering, acquiring, detecting, obtaining. Pl. ې *ey*. See موندنه

مندو *mandow*, s.m. (2nd) The withers of a horse. Pl. مندوونه *mandow-ūnah*. See منداو

مندو *mandaw*, s.m. (6th) (W.) The seed of the mustard plant, from which oil is extracted. Sing. and Pl.

منډ *mandd*, s.m. (2nd) A footmark, a footprint of man or beast. 2. A pathway made in the snow from one village to another. 3. The stump or trunk of a tree. Pl. منډونه *mandd-ūnah*. See also غويمنډ

منډر *munddar*, s.m. (2nd) The stump or trunk of a tree. Pl. منډرونه *munddarūnah*. See منډ and مونډ

منډر *manddar*, s.m. (6th) The name of one of the two great divisions of the Yūsufzīs. Sing. and Pl. See منډر

منډل *manddal*, verb trans. To thrust, to stuff, to cram, to force or run in, to foist, to insinuate. 2. To knead the limbs, to shampoo. Pres. منډي *manddī*; past و ماندده *wu-mānddah*; fut. و به منډي *wu bah manddī*; imp. و منډه *wu-manddah*; act. part. منډونكي *manddūnkaey* or منډوني *manddūnaey*; past part. منډلي *manddalaey*; verb. n. منډنه *manddana'h*.

منډو *manddaw*, s.m. (2nd) A hut of grass or wood, a shed, a porch. Pl. منډوونه *manddaw-ūnah*. (S منډوا).

منډوس *manddūs*, s.m. (2nd) A ball of cloth or leather used in play. 2. A cloth tied over the turban and under the chin. Pl. مندوسونه *manddūsūnah*. See پندوس

مندده *mandda'h*, s.f. (3rd) A run, a course, a rush, a step, a pace, a race, a spurt, etc. Pl. ي *ey*. مندي وهل *manddey wahal*, verb trans. To run a course, to rush, to bound, to dash on, to gallop, to bolt, to trot, etc. خر مندي *khar manddey*, Cutting capers or antics (*lit.* the capers of an ass).

مندي *munddaey*, s.m. (1st) The innermost of the two bullocks in treading out corn or working a well or Persian wheel. 2. A tree with its branches cut off. 3. A person who has lost an arm or leg. 4. A squat, dapper person. Pl. ي *ī*. مندئ *mandda'ī*, s.f. (6th) A short dumpy woman, etc. Sing. and Pl. See موندي and نوي

A منزل *manzil*, s.m. (2nd) (from نزل) A day's journey, a stage, a march. Pl. منزلونه *manzilūnah*. منزل كول *manzil kawul*, verb trans. To camp, to halt, to make a stage of or halting place. منزل وهل *manzil wahal*, verb trans. To finish a journey, to travel.

A منزلت *manzilat*, s.m. (2nd) Dignity, station, rank, condition, post of honour. Pl. منزلتونه *manzilatūnah*.

منځ *mandz*, adv. and prep. Between, betwixt, among, amongst, midst. په منځ *pah mandz* or په منځ كښه *pah mandz kshey* or *kkhey*, In between, in the midst. منځ گري *mandz-garaey*, s.m. (1st) A mediator, a peacemaker, an intercessor. Pl. ي *ī*. منځ گرئ *mandz-garey* or منځ گرِ *mandz-gari*, s.f. (8th). A mediatrix. Pl. ي *ī*. منځ گري كوَل *mandz-garaey kawul*, verb trans. To mediate, to intercede, to compromise, to make peace. See گوابس

A منصب *manṣab*, s.m. (2nd) (from نصب) Dignity, office, ministry, rank. Pl. منصبونه *manṣabūnah*. منصب دار *manṣab-dār*, s.m. (5th) A person holding a government appointment. Pl. منصب داران *manṣab-dārān*.

A منصف *munṣif*, s.m. (5th) (act. part. IV of نصف) A judge, an arbitrator, a dispenser of justice. 2. adj. Equitable, just, fair. Pl. منصفان *munṣifān*. (Fem.) منصفه *munṣifa'h*, adj. and s.f. (3rd). Pl. ي *ey*.

A منصفي *munṣifī*, s.f. (3rd) Arbitration, judgment, justice, decision. Pl. ي *a'ī*. منصفي كول *munṣifī kawul*, verb trans. To judge, to arbitrate, to decide.

A منظور *man-ẓūr*, adj. (past part. of نظر) Approved of, agreeable, chosen, acceptable, admissible, admired; (Fem.) منظوره *man-ẓūra'h*. منظور كول *man-ẓūr kawul*, verb trans. To approve of, to accept, to admire.

منعه *manæa'h*, s.f. (3rd) (from A منع) Prohibition, forbidding, refusal, hindrance. Pl. ي *ey*. منعه كول *manæa'h kawul*, verb trans. To forbid, to prohibit, to hinder, to dissuade.

A منكر *munkir*, s.m. (5th) (act. part. IV of نكر) Denying, rejecting, a denier, a rejecter. Pl. منكران *munkirān*. منكره *munkira'h*, s.f. (3rd). Pl. ي *ey*. منكريدل *munkiredal*, verb intrans. To deny, to reject (*lit.* to become a rejecter). Pres. منكريږي *munkirejzī* (W.) or منكريگي *munkiregī* (E.); past منكر شه *munkir shah* or ؤ شه *wu-shah*; fut. منكر به شي *munkir bah shī* or به ؤ شي *bah wu-shī*; imp. منكر شه *munkir shah* or ؤ شه *wu-shah*; act. part. منكريدونكَي *munkiredūnkaey* or منكريدونَي *munkiredūnaey*; past part. منكر *munkir* or منكر شوَي *munkir shawaey*; verb. n. منكريدنه *munkiredana'h* or منكريده *munkiredah*. منكرول *munkirawul*, verb trans. To make another reject or deny, or make a rejecter. Pres. منكروي *munkirawī*; past منكر كړ *munkir karr* or ؤ كړ *wu-karr*; fut. منكر به كړي *munkir bah krrī* or به ؤ كړي *bah wu-krrī*; imp. منكر كړه *munkir krrah* or ؤ كړه *wu-krrah*; act. part. منكروونكَي *munkirawūnkaey* or منكروونَي *munkirawūnaey*; past part. منكر كړَي *munkir karraey*; verb. n. منكرونه *munkirawuna'h*.

منكر نكير *munkar nakīr*, s. prop. The names of two angels who, agreeably to the Muḥammadan creed, examine the spirits of departed persons in the tomb.

منگار *mangār*, s.m. (2nd) A kind of viper exceedingly venomous. Pl. منگارونه *mangārūnah.* See منگور

منگاره *mangāra'h,* s.f. (3rd) A scratch, scratching, wounding with the nails. Pl. ې *ey.* منگارې کول *mangārey kawul,* verb trans. To scratch, to wound with the nails.

منگر *mangar,* conj. (corrup. of P مگر) But, if, although, otherwise, unless, by chance, perhaps.

منگر *mangar,* s.m. (9th) The name of the eighth month of the Hindū calendar, used by the Eastern Afg͟hāns in agricultural matters. Sing. and Pl.

منگري *mangaraey,* s.m. (1st) A kind of viper, a small snake. Pl. ي *ī.*

منگړ *mangurr,* s.m. (5th) A bug. Pl. منگړان *mangurrān.* See منگنړ

منگز *mangaz,* s.f. (1st) A comb for the hair. Pl. منگزِ *mangazi.* See گمنز and گونز

منگل *mangul,* s.f. (1st) A paw, a hand, a talon, a grasp, the five fingers. Pl. منگلِ *manguli.* See منگول and خپړ

منگنړ *mungarrn,* s.m. (5th) A bug. Pl. منگنړان *mungarrnān.* See منگړ

منگوټي *mangottaey,* s.m. (1st) A small earthen pot. Pl. ې *ey.* See منگي

منگور *mangor,* s.m. (2nd) A kind of viper, very venomous. Pl. منگورونه *mangorūnah.* See منگري and منگار

منگول *mangūl,* s.f. (1st) The hand including the five fingers, the paw of a beast, the talon of a bird. Pl. منگولِ *mangūli.*

منگه *mungah,* One of the plural forms of the first personal pronoun, We. See موږ and "Grammar," page 31. Also written منگَ *munga* and مونگه *mūngah.*

منگَي *mangaey,* s.m. (1st) An earthen pot, a pitcher. Pl. ي *ī.* منگوټَي *mangottaey,* s.m. (1st) (dimin. of منگي) A small earthen pot. Pl. ي *ī.*

منل *manal,* verb trans. To obey, to submit to, to serve, to succumb to, to comply, to follow, to attend, to comply with the commands of another, to be ruled by, to yield, to cringe, to bend to. Pres. مني *manī*; past وُ منل *wu-manal* (W.) or وُ مانه *wu-mānah* (E.); fut. وُ به مني *wu bah manī*; imp. وُ منه *wu-manah*; act. part. منونکَي *manūnkaey* or منونَي *manūnaey*; past. part. منلَي *manalaey*; verb n. مننه *manana'h.*

A منور *munauwur,* adj. (past part. II of نور) Illuminated, explained, illustrated, enlightened, clear, splendid, brilliant, elucidated; (Fem.) منوره *munauwara'h.*

منه *manah,* s.m. (2nd) A hut of grass or branches, a temporary residence, a shed. Pl. منهونه *manahūnah.*

منه *mina'h,* s.f. (3rd) A house, a dwelling, a place of residence, a mansion. Pl. ې *ey.* See مينه

منَي *munaey,* s.m. (1st) (S मुनि) A pious, God-fearing person. 2. A sage. 3. adj. Pious, godly, devout, religious. 4. Sage, wise. Pl. ي *ī.* منۍ *muna'ī,* s.f. (6th) A pious, devout, or wise female. 2. adj. Pious, devout. 3. Wise, sage. Sing. and Pl.

منَي *manaey,* s.m. (1st) Autumn, the autumnal harvest. Pl. ي *ī.*

A مني *manī,* s.f. (3rd) Sperma genitale viri aut mulieres. 2. (P) Egotism, boasting, presumption. 3. Pride, grandeur. Pl. ئ *a'ī.*

منړه *marrnah,* s.f. (3rd) An apple. Pl. ې *ey.*

مو *mo,* The second person plural of a form of pronoun used with all past tenses of verbs in the active voice, and in other than the active voice of transitives, points out the object or the possessive case. It has but one inflection, and signifies, You, yours, or to you. See Grammar, page 44.

مو *mū,* The plural form for the first person of the pronouns mentioned above, and signifying We, ours, or to us.

مو *mū,* s.m. (6th) Fat, grease, tallow. Sing. and Pl.

A مواجب *ma-wājib,* s.m. (2nd) Salary, pension, wages. Pl. مواجبونه *ma-wājibūnah.*

موړه *muwarra'h,* s.f. (3rd) An instrument for cleaning cotton. Pl. ې *ey.* See منتَي

مواس *ma-wās,* s.m. (5th) A tell-tale, a tale-bearer, a backbiter, a spy, an informer. 2. A mischief-maker, a fomenter of sedition, an insurgent, a turbulent person. 3. The devil (met.) Pl. مواسان *ma-wās-ān*. مواسه *ma-wāsa'h*, s.f. (3rd) A tell-tale or mischief-making female, etc. Pl. ي *ey*.

HI مواس *ma-wās*, s.m. (2nd) Protection, refuge, asylum, retreat. Pl. مواسونه *ma-wās-ūnah*. مواس نيول *ma-wās nī-wal*, verb trans. To take refuge, to seek a retreat or asylum with anyone.

A موافق *muwāfiḳ*, adj. (act. part. III of وفق) Conformable, consonant, congruous, apt, like, fit, analogous, agreeing, according, concordant, suitable, favorable, propitious; (Fem.) موافقه *muwāfiḳa'h*.

A موافقت *muwāfaḳat*, s.m. (2nd) Conformity, analogy, agreement, accordance, affinity, concord. Pl. موافقتونه *muwāfaḳatūnah*. موافقت کول *muwāfaḳat kawul*, verb trans. To conform with, to agree, to enter into friendship.

A موت *maut*, s.m. (9th) Death, annihilation. Sing. and Pl.

موټ *mott*, s.m. (6th) A kind of lentil vetch, also the grain (Phaseolus max, or radiatus). Sing. and Pl. See مي

موټ *mūtt*, s.m. (2nd) A handle, a hilt; fist, hand, handful. Pl. موټونه *mūttūnah*. (S موٹھ). موټک وهل *mūttak wahal*, verb trans. (from موټ) To practice self-pollution or onanism.

موټي *mūttaey*, s.m. (1st) The hilt of a sword, a haft, a handle, etc. Pl. ي *ī*. (S موٹها).

A موج *mauj*, s.m. (2nd) A wave, a billow, a surge. Pl. موجونه *maujūnah*. موج وهل *mauj wahal*, verb trans. To billow, to wave, to surge.

A موجب *mūjib*, s.m. (2nd) (act. part. IV of وجب) Cause, reason, motive, object. Pl. موجبونه *mūjibūnah*.

A موجود *mo-jūd* or *maujūd*, adj. (past part. IV of وجد) Present, existing, existent, standing before, at hand, ready; (Fem.) موجوده *mo-jūda'h*. موجود کول *mo-jūd* or *maujūd kawul*, verb trans. To bring, to cause to be or make present.

موچړنه *mocharrna'h*, s.f. (3rd) A shoe. Pl. ي *ey*.

موخه *mūkha'h*, s.f. (3rd) A target or mark for arrows. Pl. ي *ey*. موخي کول *mūkhey kawul*, verb trans. To practice shooting at a mark.

موده *mūda'h*, s.f. (3rd) Appointed time, season, or period. Pl. ي *ey*.

A موذن *mū-azzin*, s.m. (5th) (act. part. II of اذن) A public crier to prayers. Pl. موذنان *mū-azzinān*.

A موذي *mū-zī*, adj. (act. part. IV of اذي) Importunate, troublesome; pesterer, troubler, vexer, tormenter, botherer, hurter; pernicious, noxious.

مور *mor*, s.f. (5th) A mother. Pl. ميندي *mendey* or *maindey* or ميند *mendi* or *maindi*; (W.) مندي *mandey*. مور زاده *mor-zādah*, adj. Innate, as born of the mother (Masc. and Fem.) مورګنۍ *mor-gana'ī*, s.f. (6th) A mother's relations or connections. Sing. and Pl. مورنی *moranaey*, adj. Born of one mother and by two fathers; (Fem.) مورنۍ *morana'ī*. مور والی *mor-wālaey*, s.m. (1st) Maternity, motherhood. Pl. والي *wālī*. See پلار

S مور *mor*, s.m. (1st) A peacock. Pl. موران *morān*.

مورانۍ *mūrāna'ī*, s.f. (6th) The ferrule of a knife handle. Sing. and Pl. See غمي

P مورچه *morcha'h*, s.f. (3rd) A battery. Pl. ي *ey*.

مورګه *morga'h*, s.f. (3rd) The lip or edge of a vessel, cup, etc.; brim, edge, verge, brink, margin, border, rim, side, etc. Pl. ي *ey*. See غاړه

A موروث *mau-rūṣ*, adj. (past part. of ورث) Hereditary, heritage; (Fem.) موروثه *mau-rūṣa'h* or موروثي *mau-rūṣī* (Masc. and Fem.).

P مورۍ *mora'ī*, s.f. (6th) A pipe or subterranean passage for water. Sing. and Pl.

موړ *morr*, adj. Satisfied, satiated, glutted, surfeited, sated, contented, filled, snug, comfortable, well off, well to do in the world. Pl. ماړه *mārrah*; (Fem.) موړه *marra'h*. Pl. موړي *marrey*. موړ تيا *morr-tiā*, s.f. (6th) Satiety, repletion, gratification, content, contentment, snugness, comfort, peace of mind, well being. (E.) Sing. and Pl. (W.) Pl. تياوي *tī'āwī*.

مړيدل *marredal*, verb intrans. To become satisfied, satiated, glutted, contented, filled, snug, comfortable, well off, etc. Pres. مړيږي *marrejzī* (W.) or مړيګي *marregī* (E.); past موړ شه *morr shah* or وُ شه *wu-shah*; fut. موړ به شي *morr bah shī* or به وُ شي *bah wu-shī*; imp. موړ شه *morr shah* or وُ شه *wu-shah*; act. part. مړيدونکَي *marredūnkaey* or مړيدونَي *marredūnaey*; past part. موړ *morr* or موړ شوَي *morr shawaey*; verb. n. مړيدنه *marredana'h* or مړيده *marredah*. مړول *marrawul*, verb trans. To satiate, to satisfy, to glut, to gratify, to slake, to quench, to fill, to make snug or comfortable, to render content. Pres. مړوي *marrawī*; past موړ کړ *morr karr* or وُ کړ *wu-karr*; fut. موړ به کړي *morr bah krrī* or به وُ کړي *bah wu-krrī*; imp. موړ کړه *morr krrah* or وُ کړه *wu-krrah*; act. part. مړوونکَي *marrawūnkaey* or مړوونَي *marrawūnaey*; past part. موړ کړَي *morr karraey*; verb. n. مړونه *marrawuna'h*.

موړه *morra'h*, s.f. (3rd) A sort of padded saddle, a pad or cushion put upon the back of an animal, and on which the load is placed. 2. A stool. Pl. ي *ey*.

موز *moz*, s.m. (6th) A plantain. Sing. and Pl.

P موزه *moza'h*, s.f. (3rd) A stocking, a boot, a covering for the legs, a long boot. Pl. ي *ey*.

موزي *mo-zī*, adj. (corrup. of A موذي) Noxious, pernicious, troublesome, importunate, vexatious. 2. Hurter, vexer, tormenter, teaser, pesterer.

موږ *mujz*, We. The plural form of the first personal pronoun. Masc. and Fem. See مونږ and مونکه

موږري *mojzaey*, s.m. (1st) (W.) A wooden peg or stake. Pl. ي *ey*. See موګي

A موسىٰ *mūsā*, s. prop. Moses, the patriarch Moses.

A موسم *mausim*, s.m. (2nd) (from وسم) Season, time, period. Pl. موسمونه *mausimūnah*.

موسئي *mosa'ī*, s.f. (6th) A round counter of stone or mud used by children in a game similar to pitch-and-toss. Sing. and Pl. See مکهر

موسيدل *mūsedal*, verb intrans. To smile, to simper, to smirk, to grin. For inflections see مسيدل and add an extra و.

P موسيقار *mūsīkār*, s.m. (5th) A musician. 2. The Pandean-pipes. 3. A fabulous bird supposed to have various holes in its beak from which sounds issue. Pl. موسيقاران *mūsīkārān*.

G موسيقي *mūsīkī*, s.f. (3rd) Music, musical sounds in general. Pl. ئي *a'ī*.

P موشګير *mūsh-gīr*, s.m. (5th) A sparrow-hawk. Pl. موشګيران *mūsh-gīrān*. Also موش ګيرک *mūsh-gīrak*, s.m. (5th). Pl. موش ګيرکان *mūsh-gīrakān* (from P موش *mūsh*, A rat).

A موقوف *maukūf*, adj. (past part. of وقف) Stopped, settled, rested, bound, fixed or dependent on, deferred, postponed, abolished, relinquished; (Fem.) موقوفه *maukūfa'h*. موقوف کيدل *maukūf kedal*, verb intrans. To be stopped, to cease, to be dependent on. موقوف کول *maukūf kawul*, verb trans. To stop, to cease, to leave off, to abolish, to abrogate, to annul.

موک *mok*, s.m. (2nd) A bribe, a gift. Pl. موکونه *mokūnah*. موک آخستل *mok ākhistal*, verb trans. To take or receive a bribe; or موک خوړل *mok khwarral*, verb trans. موک ور کول *mok war-kawul*, verb trans. To give a bribe. See بډه

موګي *mo-gaey*, s.m. (1st) A wooden stake or peg. Pl. ي *ī*. See موږري

A مولا *maulā*, s.m. (5th) (from ولي) God. 2. A judge, master, lord, the Lord. Pl. مولايان *maulāyān*. See خښتن

مولَي *molaey*, s.m. (1st) A large wooden pestle for beating or pounding grain. 2. The stump of a tree left standing in the ground. Pl. ي *ī*. See بغري

مولئي *mūla'ī*, s.f. (6th) A radish. Sing. and Pl. (s مولي).

P موم *mūm*, s.m. (6th) Wax. Sing. and Pl. موم جامه *mūm-jāma'h*, s.f. (3rd) Waxed-cloth, cerecloth. Pl. ي *ey*.

A مومن *mūmin*, adj. (act. part. IV of أمن)

Orthodox, faithful, believing. 2. s.m. (5th) A believer, an orthodox Muhammadan. Pl. مومنان *mūminān*. مومنه *mūmina'h*, s.f. (3rd). Pl. ې *ey*.

s مونج *mūnj*, s.m. (6th) The name of a grass from which ropes are made (Saccharum munja). Sing. and Pl. See منج

موندره *mūnd-ra'h*, s.f. (3rd) A ring, an ear-ring. Pl. ې *ey*. (s موندري).

موندل *mūndal*, verb trans. To find, to obtain, to acquire, to derive, to procure, to gain, to win, to receive, to reap, to come by, to come in for, to bag, to net, to get at, to find out, to trace, to detect, to meet with, etc. Pres. مومي *mumī*; past وُ موند *wu-mūnd*; fut. وُ به مومي *wu bah mumī*; imp. وُ مومه *wu-mūmah*; act. part. موندونکَي *mūndūnkaey* or موندوني *mūndūnaey*; past part. موندلَي *mūndalaey*; verb. n. موندنه *mūndana'h*. See مندل

موندلَي *mūndalaey*, adj. (past part.) Found, discovered, obtained, acquired, met with, detected; (Fem.) موندلِ *mūndali*. Pl. (Masc. and Fem.) ي *ī*.

موندنه *mūndana'h*, s.f. (3rd) (verb. n. of موندل) Finding, discovering, meeting with, recovering, acquiring, detecting, obtaining, etc. Pl. ې *ey*. See مندنه

مونډَي *mūndaey*, s.m. (1st) A he-goat or ram having small ears. Pl. ي *ī*. مونډئ *mūnda'ī*, s.f. (6th) An ewe or goat with small ears. Sing. and Pl.

مونډ *mūndd*, s.m. (2nd) The root of a tree, the germ or radix of a plant. 2. Cause, source, nucleus, stem, stock. Pl. مونډونه *mūnddūnah*. See وله and وبخ

مونډهي *mūnddhaey*, s.m. (1st) The inside bullock of a pair in treading out corn, or in working a well. Pl. ې *ey*. See نوي and منډي

مونډي *mūnddaey*, s.m. (1st) The inner bullock of a pair or row in working a wheel, or treading out corn. 2. The trunk of a tree having all its branches cut off, a stump. 3. A man who has lost a leg or an arm. 4. A squat, dumpy, dapper person. مونډئ *mūndda'ī*, s.f. (6th) A short, dumpy female. 2. A female who has lost a limb. See منډي and نوي

مونز *mūnz*, s.m. (4th) Prayer. Pl. مانزه *mānzah* or مانزَ *mānza*. See نمونځ

مونګَ *mūn-ga* or مونګه *mūngah*, We. The plural form of the personal pronoun of the 1st person. (Masc. and Fem.) See موږ and منګه and Grammar, page 31.

مونړَي *mūrrnaey*, s.m. (1st) A plug made of cloth or rags for stopping the hole of a water tank or cistern. Pl. ي *ī*.

مويښي *maweshey* (W.) or *mawekhey* (E.) s.f. (3rd) Pl. Hemorrhoids, the piles. See بواسير

مه *mah*, adv. of prohibition, Do not, prefixed to the imperatives of verbs.

P مهار *muhār*, s.m. (2nd) A bridle or rein for a camel fastened to the نته. Pl. مهارونه *muhārūnah*.

A مهال *mahāl*, s.m. (2nd) Delay, pause, respite. Pl. مهالونه *mahālūnah*.

مهتابئ *mah-tāba'ī*, s.f. (6th) A description of firework (from P مهتاب). Sing. and Pl.

A مهتر *mihtar*, s.m. (5th) A prince; the title given to the Ban-i-Israel by some historians. 2. A groom, a horsekeeper. Pl. مهتران *mihtarān*. مهتري *mihtarī*, s.f. (3rd) The business of a horsekeeper or groom. Pl. ئ *a'ī*.

A مهجور *mah-jūr*, adj. (past part of هجر) Separated, cut off, left, forsaken; (Fem.) مهجوره *mahjūra'h*.

A مهر *mahr*, s.m. (2nd) A marriage portion or gift settled upon a wife before marriage, a jointure, alimony. Pl. مهرونه *mahrūnah*.

P مهر *muhr*, s.m. (2nd) A seal. 2. A gold coin. Pl. مهرونه *muhrūnah*. مهر دار *muhr-dār*, s.m. (5th) A keeper of the seal, an officer of state. Pl. مهرداران *muhr-dārān*. مهر کول *muhr kawul*, verb trans. To seal, to close up.

P مهر *mihr*, s.m. (2nd) Love, friendship, kindness, affection. Pl. مهرونه *mihrūnah*. مهربان *mihr-bān*, adj. Friendly, kind, affectionate, indulgent, gracious; (Fem.) مهربانه *mihr-bāna'h*. مهرباني *mihr-bānī*, s.f. (3rd) Kindness, favor, friendship, affection, graciousness. Pl. ئ *a'ī*; or

مهربانگي *mihr-bāngī* and مهربانگئ *mihr-bānga'ī*. مهرباني کول *mihr-bānī kawul*, verb trans. To favor, to befriend, to show kindness to, or friendship for.

P مهر کن *muhr-kan*, s.m. (5th) A seal-engraver. Pl. مهر کنان *muhr-kanān*. مهر کني *muhr-kanī*, s.f. (3rd) The business of a seal-engraver. Pl. ئ *a'ī*; also مهر کند *muhr-kand* and مهر کندي *muhr-kandī*.

P مهره *muhra'h*, s.f. (3rd) A shell. 2. A rubber for smoothing paper. Pl. ې *ey*.

A مهلت *muhlat*, s.m. (2nd) (from مهل) Retarding, deferring. 2. Delay, laziness, indolence, time, respite, leisure, intermission, cessation, armistice. Pl. مهلتونه *muhlatūnah*. مهلت ورکول *muhlat war-kawul*, verb trans. To grant a respite, to make or enter into an armistice.

مهلک *muhlik*, adj. (act. part. IV of هلک) Deadly, mortal, killing, destroying, fatal, destructive; (Fem.) مهلکه *muhlika'h*.

A مهم *muhim*, adj. (act. part. IV of هم) Important, serious. 2. s.m. (2nd) An important affair, urgent business, affair of consequence, exigence, exploit, enterprise. Pl. مهمونه *muhimūnah*.

P مهمان *mihmān*, s.m. (5th) A guest, a stranger. Pl. مهمانان *mihmānān*. مهمانه *mihmāna'h*, s.f. (3rd) A female guest, etc. Pl. ې *ey*. مهمان خانه *mihmān-khāna'h*, s.f. (3rd) A dining-room, a place for the reception of strangers or guests. Pl. ې *ey*. مهمان دار *mihmān-dār*, s.m. (5th) A host or entertainer. 2. An officer appointed to receive an ambassador. Pl. مهمان داران *mihmān-dārān*. مهمان داري *mihmān-dārī*, s.f. (3rd) Entertainment, hospitality. Pl. ئ *a'ī*. مهمان دوست *mihmān-dost*, adj. Hospitable; (Fem.) دوسته *dosta'h*.

P مهماني *mihmānī*, s.f. (3rd) Entertainment, hospitality, a feast, a banquet. Pl. ئ *a'ī*. مهماني کول *mihmānī kawul*, verb trans. To feast, to entertain, to give a feast or banquet.

مهمند *mohmand* or *mahmand*, s.m. (6th) The name of an Afghān tribe inhabiting the plain of Peshāwer to the north-west; those in the plain are called Lower, and those in the hills to the west, Upper Mohmands. مهمنده *mohmanda'h*, s.f. (3rd) A female of the above tribe. Pl. ې *ey*.

مهڼړه *maharrnah*, s.m. (5th) A boatman, a sailor, a mariner. Pl. مهڼړګان *maharrna-gān*. (Panjābī).

مهوت *mahawat*, s.m. (5th) An elephant-keeper. Pl. مهوتيان *mahawat-yān* (from s مهاوت).

مهئ *mahaey*, s.m. (1st) A fish. Pl. ي *ī*. مهئ گير *mahaey-gīr*, s.m. (5th) A fisherman. Pl. مهئ گيران *mahaey-gīrān*. مهئخورک *mahaey-khwarak*, s.m. (5th) A king-fisher. Pl. مهئخورکان *mahaey-khwarakān*. See ماهي

مهئ *mahey*, s.f. (3rd) Pl. A kind of pulse. 2. Bread made of pulse and other similar grain. See زاره

مهيرګه *maher-ga'h*, s.f. (3rd) The epilepsy. Pl. ې *ey*. (HI مرگي). See پتو مهيرګه

P مهين *mihīn*, adj. Fine, subtile, thin, not coarse; (Fem.) مهينه *mihīna'h*.

مهينه *mahīnah*, adj. Prior, preceding, antecedent, former, ancient, foregoing. 2. The elder born or first-born. 3. Early sown (as a field). 4. adv. Before, prior to, already, erewhile, before now, previously, See پسينه and زاري

مهينه *mahīna'h*, s.f. (3rd) Monthly wages, salary, pay. Pl. ې *ey*.

P مي *mai*, s.m. (6th) Wine, spirituous liquor. Sing. and Pl. مي پرست *mai-parast*, s.m. (5th) A lover of wine, a wine-bibber, a sot, a drunkard. Pl. مي پرستان *mai-parastān*, or مي خور *mai-khor*, s.m. (5th). Pl. مي خوران *mai-khorān*. مي پرستي *mai-parastī* or مي خورگي *mai-khwaragī*, s.f. (3rd) Love of wine, wine-drinking, drunkenness. Pl. ئ *a'ī*. ميِ ناب *mai-i-nāb*, Pure wine.

ميا *mī'ā*, s.m. (5th) (corrup. of HI ميان) A title given to holy men, master, sir. Pl. مياگان *mī'ā-gān*.

مي *mī*, I, mine, of me—one of a class of personal pronouns used with all past tenses of the active voice, to denote the agent in a sentence. With other than transitive verbs, they point out the object or possessive case. Pl.

مو *mū*, We, ours, of us. See Grammar, p. 44.

مياشت *mī-ā*s*h*t*, s.f. (1st) A month, the new moon, the first and last two or three days of the moon. Pl. مياشتِ *mī-ā*s*h*ti*. مياشت په مياشت *mī-ā*s*h*t-pah-mī-ā*s*h*t*, Month by month, monthly, every month.

P ميان *mī'ān*, s.m. (2nd) The middle, the waist, the loins. 2. The scabbard of a sword, etc. Pl. ميانونه *mī'ānūnah*. 3. prep. Between, betwixt, in, etc. See مينځ and منز

P ميانه *mī'ānah*, adj. Middling, moderate (Masc. and Fem.) Used in composition, as ميانه حال *mī'ānah ḥāl*, Middling, moderate. ميانه قد *mī'ānah ḳadd*, Of middling stature.

ميانه *mī'āna'h*, s.f. (3rd) The eleventh month of the Af*gh*ān year, so called as being between the festival of the Ramaẓān and Ḳurbān. Pl. ئ *ey*; or ميني *mi-yanī* (W.) s.f. (3rd). Pl. ئِ *a'ī*.

ميتل *mītal*, verb trans. To piss, to pass urine. Pres. ميژي *mī*z*zī*; past وُ ميتل *wu-mītal*; fut. وُ به ميژي *wu bah mī*z*zī*; imp. وُ ميژه *wu-mī*z*zah*; act. part. ميتونكي *mītūnkaey* or ميتوني *mītūnaey*; past part. ميتلي *mītalaey*; verb. n. ميتنه *mītana'h*.

ميچ *mec*h*, s.m. (9th) Measurement, measure, extent, scale, estimation, reckoning. Sing. and Pl. ميچ كړي *mec*h* karraey*, adj. (past part.) Measured, estimated, reckoned, appraised; (Fem.) ميچ كړ *mec*h*-karri*. Pl. (Masc. and Fem.) ي *ī*. ميچ كول *mec*h* kawul* or ميچول *mec*h*awul*, verb trans. To measure, to estimate, to survey, to gauge, to graduate, to appraise. Pres. ميچوي *mec*h*awī*; past ميچ كړ *mec*h* karr* or وُ كړ *wu-karr*; fut. ميچ به كړي *mec*h* bah krrī* or وُ به كړي *bah wu-krrī*; imp. ميچ كړه *mec*h* krrah* or وُ كړه *wu-krrah*; act. part. ميچوونكي *mec*h*a-wūnkaey* or ميچووني *mec*h*a-wūnaey*; past part. ميچ كړي *mec*h* karraey*; verb. n. ميچونه *mec*h*awuna'h*.

ميچن *mīc*h*an*, s.f. (1st) A hand-mill. Pl. ميچنِ *mīc*h*ani*. د ميچنِ خوله *da mīc*h*ani* *kh*ūla'h*, The mouth of a mill or place where the grain is poured in.

P ميخ *me*kh**, s.m. (2nd) A nail, a brad, a pin, a tent pin, a tenter, a bolt. Pl. ميخونه *me*kh*ūnah*.

P ميخانه *mai-*kh*āna'h*, s.f. (3rd) A wine shop, a tavern. Pl. ئ *ey*.

ميخورك *mai-*kh*varak*. See مهخورك

P ميدان *mai-dān*, s.m. (2nd) A plain, a field, an area. 2. A field of battle, a parade ground. Pl. ميدانونه *mai-dānūnah*.

P ميده *maidah*, s.m. (9th) Flour of the purest sort sifted, anything like flour, or finely pulverized. Sing. and Pl. See وړو

P مير *mīr*, s.m. (5th) A chief, a leader. 2. A title given to Suyeds. Pl. ميران *mīrān*. مير آخور *mīr-ā*kh*or*, The master of the horse. مير مجلس *mīr-majlis*, A president or chairman. ميره *mīra'h*, s.f. (3rd) A female of a *mīr* or Suyed. Pl. ئ *ey*.

A ميراث *mīrāṣ*, s.m. (2nd) (from ورث) Heritage, patrimony, hereditary, a bequest. Pl. ميراثونه *mīrāṣ-ūnah*. ميراثي *mīrāṣī*, adj. Inherited, hereditary. (Masc. and Fem.) ميراث خور *mīrāṣ-*kh*or*, s.m. (5th) The holder of a heritage or hereditary estate. Pl. خوران *kh*orān*. ميراث خوره *mīrāṣ-*kh*ora'h*, s.f. (3rd). Pl. ئ *ey*.

ميرڅمن *mīr-*ts*aman*, adj. Deceitful, false, lying; odious, hateful, abominable, vile; (Fem.) ميرڅمنه *mīr-*ts*amana'h*.

ميرڅي *mīr-*ts*ī*, s.f. (3rd) Distress, trouble, sorrow, affliction, woe. 2. Enmity, umbrage, grudge, bitterness. Pl. ئِ *a'ī*.

ميرخاني *mīr-*kh*āna'ī*, s.f. (6th) A kind of turban of fine cloth. 2. A kind of fine muslin used in making turbans. 3. A turban of large dimensions. Sing. and Pl.

ميرخيل *mīr-*kh*el*, s.m. (6th) A class of religious beggars. Sing. and Pl.

ميرزا *mīr-zā*, s.m. (5th) A prince, a title of some noble Persians. 2. A title given to a secretary or mun*sh*ī. Pl. ميرزايان *mīr-zā-yān*. (P مرزا).

ميرځري *mīr-*dz*araey*, s.m. (1st) The name of a tree resembling the date. Pl. ي *ī*. See ميزري

P مير سنگ *mīr-sang*, s.m. (2nd) A large shell,

a conch which, amongst the Hindūs, is blown before the temples, and, in Afghānistān, by the people of the *ḥammāms*, or hot-baths, to announce when they are open. Pl. سنګونه *sang-ūnah.*

میرګاټی *mīr-gāṭṭaey*, s.m. (1st) A kind of gravel which children use in play. 2. The name of a game played by children. Pl. ي *ī.*

میرګنج *mīr-ganj*, s.m. (5th) The king of the vultures. Pl. میرګنجان *mīr-ganjān.* See ګنجي

میرګی *mer-gaey*, s.m. (1st) (W.) The epilepsy. Pl. ي *ī.* (HI مرګي). See مهیرګي

میرمن *mer-man*, s.f. (1st) A lady, madam, a princess, a hostess, a matron. Pl. میرمنِ *mer-mani.* Also میرمنه *mer-mana'h*, s.f. (3rd). Pl. ې *ey.*

میره *maira'h*, s.f. (3rd) A mother-in-law, a step-mother. 2. A desert, an open plain, the name of a desert tract of land to the north and east of Noh-shairah, between Attak and Peshāwer. Pl. ې *ey.* A mother-in-law is also called by some tribes مره *mara'h.*

میره *merrah*, s.m. (2nd) A husband, a master, a lord. Pl. میرونه *merrūnah* or مرونه *marrūnah.*

P میزان *mīzān*, s.m. (2nd) A balance, a pair of scales. 2. Measure, metre. 3. Addition (in arithmetic). Pl. میزانونه *mīzānūnah.*

میزر *mai-zar*, s.m. (2nd) A veil worn by women of very fine muslin, etc. Pl. میزرونه *mai-zarūnah.*

میزری *mai-zaraey*, s.m. (1st) A tree like the date-palm, from which mats, sandals or *tsap-la'īs*, and the like are made. Pl. ي *ī.* See مزري and مېځري

میږ *mejz*, s.f. (1st) An ewe. Pl. میږِ *mejzi.* See مږ, ګډ, and ګډه. (s میکھ).

میږي *mejzaey*, s.m. (1st) An ant in general. Pl. ي *ī.* ښانګور میږي *shāngawar-mejzaey* (W.), The large long-legged black ant. سور میږي *sor-mejzaey*, The small red ant. اوینه *aoey-nah*, The white ant. Sing. and Pl. See میګي

میږتون *mejza-tūn*, s.m. (4th) An ant's nest. Pl. میږتانه *mejza-tānah.*

A میسر *muyassar*, adj. (past part. of یسر) Attained, attainable, procurable, obtainable, easy, favorable, facilitated; (Fem.) میسره *muyassara'h.*

میشته *mīshta'h*, s.f. (3rd) A dwelling, a residence, abode, quarters, domicile. Pl. ې *ey.* میشته کول *mīshta'h kawul*, verb trans. To dwell, to take up one's abode, to reside.

میښ *mesh* (W.) or *mekh* (E.) s.m. (5th) A male buffalo. Pl. میښان *meshān* or *mekhān*, or ګاو میښ *gā'o-mesh* or *gā'o-mekh.* Pl. ګاو میښان *gāo-meshān* or *gāo-mekhān.* میښه *mesha'h* or *mekha'h*, s.f. (3rd) A female buffalo. Pl. ې *ey.* See ګاومیښ and سنډه

میښ میښ *mīsh-mīsh* (W.) or *mīkh-mīkh* (E.) adj. Sick in the stomach, feeling nausea. 2. Disappointed.

A میعاد *mī-ææd*, s.m. (2nd) The time or place for the fulfilment of a promise or agreement. Pl. میعادونه *mī-ææd ūnah.*

میګی *megaey*, s.m. (1st) (E.) The ant, an ant in general. Pl. ي *ī.* ښانګور میګي *khāngawar-megaey*, The large long-legged black ant. سور میګي *sor-megaey*, The small red ant. See میږي

میګتون *mega-tūn*, s.m. (4th) An ant's nest. Pl. میګتانه *mega-tānah.*

P میل *mīl*, s.m. (2nd) A needle, a bodkin, a skewer, an instrument used to apply a collyrium to the eyes, and when heated, to blind people by drawing it hot over the eyes. 2. The barrel of a gun. Pl. میلونه *mīlūnah.* 3. adj. A horse which rears and stands on its hind legs.

میلمستیا *melmastī'ā*, s.f. (6th) Hospitality, entertainment, heartiness, conviviality. (E.) Sing. and Pl. (W.) Pl. میلمستیاوي *mel-mastī'āwī.* میلمستیا ورکول *mel-mastī'ā war-kawul*, verb trans. To show or practice hospitality, to entertain.

میلمه *mel-mah*, s.m. (4th) A guest, a visitor. Pl. میلمانه *mel-mānah.* میلمنه *melmana'h*, s.f. (3rd) A female guest or visitor. Pl. ې *ey.* د میلمانهٔ ستږګه *da melmānah starga'h*, s.f. (3rd) The evening star, Venus or Hesperus, so called because it rises about the time that wayfarers or guests drop in of an evening. Pl. ې *ey.*

ميلو *mīlū*, s.m. (5th) A bear. Pl. ميلوګان *mīlū-gān*. سپين ميلو *spīn-mīlū*, The white or brown bear. تور ميلو *tor-mīlū*, The black bear. ميلو *mīlū*, s.f. (5th) A female bear. Pl. ميلوګانې *mīlūgāney* or ميلوګانِ *mīlūgāni*. See يږ

ميله *mela'h*, s.f. (3rd) A fair, a concourse of people for religious or commercial purposes, an assemblage of faḳīrs. Pl. ې *ey*. (s ميلا). ميله كول *mela'h kawul*, verb trans. To assemble together for religious purposes, etc.

ميليا *mīlī'ā*, adj. Encountering, meeting, joining, coming into contact. See مليا

مي مي *mey-mey*, The bleating of a sheep, lamb, kid, etc. مي مي كول *mey-mey kawul*, verb trans. To bleat, as a sheep, lamb, or kid.

مين *ma-yan*, adj. In love, loving, fond of, attached to, distracted, tender, spoony. 2. s.m. (5th) A lover, an adorer. Pl. مئِين *ma-yæn*; (Fem.) مينه *ma-yana'h*, adj. and s.f. (3rd). Pl. ې *ey*. مين توب *ma-yan-tob*, s.m. (2nd) Love, fondness, affection, tenderness, attachment, passion, adoration. Pl. توبونه *tobūnah*. مين كيدل *ma-yan kedal*, verb intrans. To love, to like, to dote on. 2. To fall in love, to become attached to, to become enamoured, to lose one's heart. مين كول *ma-yan kawul*, verb trans. To love, to regard with affection, to esteem, to adore.

HI مينا *mai-nā*, s.f. (6th) The name of a bird (Coracias indica). (E.) Sing. and Pl. (W.) Pl. ميناوي *mai-nāwī*.

مينجور *mīn-jawar*, s.m. (5th) An attendant at a mosque, one who sweeps at a mosque or shrine. Pl. مينجوُر *mīn-jawær*. مينجوره *mīn-jawara'h*, s.f. (3rd) A female attendant at a mosque. Pl. ې *ey*. See مجاور

مينده *mīn-dah*, s.m. (5th) A male kept for breeding purposes, generally applied to a male buffalo, a bull, a he-goat, or a ram. Pl. ميندان *mīn-dān*. See ترم and هينده

مينز *mi-yanz*, s.m. (2nd). Pl. مينزونه *mi-yanzūnah*. See following.

مينځ *mi-yandz*, s.m. (2nd) The middle of anything, the centre. Pl. مينځونه *mi-yandzūnah*. 2. adv. and prep. In, between, in the midst, among, betwixt, during. مينځ غالیَ *mi-yandz-ghālaey*, s.m. (1st) An interstice, opening, chasm, gap, a gorge. Pl. ي *ī*. په مينځ *pah mi-yandz*, or په مينځ کښي *pah mi-yandz kshey* (W.) or *kkhey* (E.) In the midst, in the middle, in between. د مينځ ګوته *da mi-yandz gūta'h*, s.f. (3rd) The middle finger. Pl. ې *ey*. مينځميَ *mi-yandzmaey*, مينځنيَ *mi-yandz-naey*, or مينځويَ *mi-yandzwaey* (W.) adj. Middle, mid, middlemost, intermediate, central. 2. A middle brother. Pl. ي *ī*. (Fem.) ې *a'ī*. Sing. and Pl. See منځ

مينځل *mīn-dzal*, verb trans. (W.) To wash, to cleanse, to purify, to clean, to lave, to absterge. Pres. مينځي *mīn-dzī*; past و مينځه *wu-mīn-dzah*; fut. و به مينځي *wu bah mīn-dzī*; imp. و مينځه *wu-mīn-dzah*; act. part. مينځونكيَ *mīn-dzūn-kaey* or مينځونيَ *mīn-dzūnaey*; past part. مينځليَ *mīn-dzalaey*; verb. n. مينځنه *mīn-dzana'h*. See (E.) وينځل and ولل

مينځه *mīn-dza'h*, s.f. (3rd) A slave-girl, a handmaid, a female slave. Pl. ې *ey*. See وينځه

مينه *mīna'h*, s.f. (3rd) Love, affection, liking, inclination, regard, partiality, attachment, devotion, friendship. Pl. ې *ey*. مينه كول *mīna'h kawul*, verb trans. To make love to, to show love for or attachment to, to manifest regard or partiality, etc. 2. To fondle, to caress.

مينه *me-na'h*, s.f. (3rd) A dwelling, a habitation, a residence. Pl. ې *ey*. See منه

ميو *mi-yaw*, s.m. (5th) The mewing of a cat. Pl. ميوهار *mi-yaw-hār*. ميو كول *mi-yaw kawul*, verb trans. To mew, as a cat, or ميوهار لرل *mi-yaw-hār laral*, verb trans.

ميور *m'yawr*, s.m. (5th) A peacock. Pl. ميوران *m'yawrān*. ميوره *m'yawra'h*, s.f. (3rd) A peahen. Pl. ې *ey*. (s मयुर).

P ميوه *mewa'h*, s.f. (3rd) Fruit in general. Pl. ې *ey*. ميوه دار *mewah-dār*, adj. Fruitful, bearing fruit; (Fem.) ميوه داره *mewah-dāra'h*. ميوه نيول *mewah nī-wal*, verb trans. To bear fruit.

مئي *ma'yī*, s.m. (1st) The name of a kind of pulse (Phaseolus mungo).

ن

ن **nūn**, the twenty-fifth letter of the Arabic, and twenty-ninth of the Persian, is the thirty-sixth letter of the Pushto alphabet, and corresponds to Sanskrit न. It is one of the dental letters, and has the sound of English *n*; and in the application of the Arabic letters to denote numbers, it stands for 50.

It is often substituted before ب for م, as in لنبه 'a flame,' for لمبه; هونبره 'so much,' for هومبره; عنبر 'ambergris,' for عمبر, etc.

It is also used as an adverb of negation, joined to a word instead of نه, and affixed to some nouns forms an adjective; as پم *pam*, scab, پمن *paman*, scabby. See Grammar, page 177.

P S نا *nā*, adv. No, not, a negative prefix to nouns or particles having the same meaning as English *un, in, dis, non*, etc. نا آشنا *nā-āshnā*, adj. Unacquainted, stranger. (Masc. and Fem.) نا آشنائي *nā-āshnā'ī*, s.f. (3rd) Friendlessness, being without acquaintance. Pl. ئي *a'ī*. نا اميد *nā-umīd*, adj. Hopeless, despairing; (Fem.) نا اميده *nā-umīda'h*. نا اميدي *nā-umīdī*, s.f. (3rd) Despair, hopelessness. Pl. ئي *a'ī*. نا انصاف *nā-inṣāf*, adj. Unjust; (Fem.) نا انصافه *nā-inṣāfa'h*. نا اهل *nā-ahl*, adj. Unworthy, unfit, incapable; (Fem.) نا اهله *nā-ahla'h*. نا بالغ *nā-bāligh*, adj. Not arrived at puberty; (Fem.) نا بالغه *nā-bāligha'h*. نا پکار *nā-pakār*, adj. Useless, vile, worthless, good for nothing; (Fem.) نا پکاره *nā-pakāra'h*. نا پکاري *nā-pakārī*, s.f. (3rd) Uselessness, worthlessness. Pl. ئي *a'ī*. نا بلد *nā-balad*, adj. Without a country, a foreigner, an alien; (Fem.) نا بلده *nā-balada'h*. نا بود *nā-būd*, adj. Annihilated, non-existent, vanished. 2. Fallow (land), unproductive, waste; (Fem.) نا بوده *nā-būda'h*. نا بوده زمکه *nā-būda'h z'maka'h*, s.f. (3rd) Fallow or waste land. Pl. ئي *ey*. نا بودي *nā-būdī*, s.f. (3rd) Annihilation, non-existence. Pl. ئي *a'ī*. نا بيان *nā-biyān*, adj. Unspeakable, unexplainable; (Fem.) نا بيانه *nā-biyāna'h*. نا بينا *nā-bīnā*, adj. Blind. (Masc. and Fem.) See نا روند. نا پاك *nā-pāk*, adj. Impure, defiled, polluted, unclean, filthy, dirty; (Fem.) نا پاکه *nā-pāka'h*. نا پاك كيدل *nā-pāk kedal*, verb intrans. To become impure, polluted, unclean. نا پاك كول *nā pāk kawul*, verb trans. To pollute, to render impure or unclean. نا پاكي *nā-pākī*, s.f. (3rd) Defilement, impurity, pollutedness, uncleanness. Pl. ئي *a'ī*. نا پايان *na-pā'e-ān*, adj. Endless, immense, deep, bottomless, unfathomable; (Fem.) نا پايانه *nā-pā'e-āna'h*; or نا پاياو *nā-pā'e-āw*; (Fem.) نا پاياوه *nā-pā'e-āwa'h*. نا پايدار *nā-pā'e-dār*, adj. Unstable, unsteady, frail, fickle, transitory; (Fem.) نا پايداره *nā-pā'e dāra'h*. نا پروا *nā-parwā*, adj. Independent, fearless, free from concern or care. (Masc. and Fem.) نا پسند *nā-pasand*, adj. Disagreeable, disapproved of, unacceptable; (Fem.) نا پسنده *nā-pasanda'h*. نا پيدا *nā-paidā*, adj. Unborn, inexistent, that has never existed. (Masc. and Fem.) نا پوه *nā-poh*, adj. Ignorant, foolish, simple; (Fem.) نا پوهه *nā-poha'h*. نا پوهي *nā-pohī*, s.f. (3rd) Ignorance, simplicity, foolishness. Pl. ئي *a'ī*. نا تاب *nā-tāb*, adj. Weak, infirm; (Fem.) نا تابه *nā-tāba'h*. نا تجربه *nā-tajribah*, adj. Inexperienced, untried. (Masc. and Fem.) نا ترس *nā-tars*, adj. Fearless, pitiless, severe, hard-hearted; (Fem.) نا ترسه *nā-tarsa'h*. نا تمام *nā-tamām*, adj. Unfinished, imperfect, deficient; (Fem.) نا تمامه *nā-tamāma'h*. نا تمامي *nā-tamāmī*, s.f. (3rd) Deficiency, imperfection. Pl. ئي *a'ī*. نا توان *nā-tawān*, adj. Powerless, weak, infirm, impotent; (Fem.) نا توانه *nā-tawāna'h*. نا تواني *nā-tawānī*, s.f. (3rd) Impotence, weakness. Pl. ئي *a'ī*. نا څار *na-tsār*, adj. Helpless, forlorn, distressed, constrained, remediless; (Fem.) نا څاري *nā-tsārī*, s.f. (3rd) Helplessness, constraint, distress. Pl. ئي *a'ī*. نا څيزه *nā-tsīzah*, adj. Of no consequence, insignificant, worthless, contemptible. (Masc. and

Fem.) نا څيزي *nā-tsīzī*, s.f. (3rd) Insignificance, worthlessness. Pl. ئ *a'ī*. نا جنس *nā-jins*, adj. Strange in kind, of another species or race; (Fem.) نا جنسه *nā-jinsa'h*. نا جنسي *nā-jinsī*, s.f. (3rd) Being of a different race or kind, want of gentility. Pl. ئ *a'ī*. نا جوړ *nā-joṛṛ*, adj. Indisposed, unwell, sick, ailing; (Fem.) نا جوړه *nā-joṛṛa'h*. نا جوړ تيا *nā-joṛṛ-tī'ā*, s.f. (6th) Indisposition, sickness. (E.) Sing. and Pl. (W.) Pl. تياوي *tī'āwī*. نا حق *nā-ḥaḳḳ*, adj. Unjust, improper, illegal, undeserved; (Fem.) نا حقه *nā-ḥaḳḳa'h*. نا حقي *nā-ḥaḳḳī*, s.f. (3rd) Injustice, illegality, impropriety. Pl. ئ *a'ī*. نا خوال *nā-khwāl*, adj. Improper, unbecoming; (Fem.) نا خواله *nā-khwāla'h*. نا خدا ترس *nā-khudā-tars*, adj. Ungodly, not fearing God; (Fem.) نا خدا ترسه *nā-khudā-tarsa'h*. نا خوانده *nā-khwāndah*. adj. Unread, unlearned, illiterate. (Masc. and Fem.) نا خواه *nā-khwāh*, adj. Unwilling, constrained. 2. adv. Constrainedly, unwillingly. خواه نا خواه *khwāh nā-khwāh*, adj. Nolens volens, willingly or unwillingly. نا خوښ *nā-khwash* (W.) or *nā-khwakh* (E.) adj. Displeased, disgusted, unpleasant, unhappy; (Fem.) نا خوښه *nā-khwasha'h* or *nā-khwakha'h*. نا خوښي *nā-khwashī* or *nā-khwakhī*, s.f. (3rd) Displeasure, unpleasantness, disagreeableness. Pl. ئ *a'ī*. نا دار *nā-dār*, adj. Poor, insolvent, helpless; (Fem.) نا داره *nā-dāra'h*. نا داري *nā-dārī*, s.f. (3rd) Insolvency, distress, poverty. Pl. ئ *a'ī*. نا ديده *nā-dīdah*, adj. Unseen, a person who has seen little, inexperienced. (Masc. and Fem.) نا راست *nā-rāst*, adj. Untrue, wrong, unjust, false; (Fem.) نا راسته *nā-rāsta'h*. نا راستي *nā-rāstī*, s.f. (3rd) Injustice, dishonesty, falseness. Pl. ئ *a'ī*. نا راض *nā-rāẓ*, adj. Discontented, dissatisfied; (Fem.) نا راضه *nā-rāẓa'h*. نا روا *nā-rawā*, adj. Unworthy, unlawful, illegal. (Masc. and Fem.) نا روغ *nā-rogh*, adj. Unwell, indisposed, not well, ailing; (Fem.) نا روغه *nā-rogha'h*. نا زو کړي *nā-zū-karraey*, adj. Not brought forth, unborn. نا زور *nā-zor*, adj. Weak, infirm; (Fem.) نا زوره *nā-zora'h*. نا شدني *nā-shudanī*, adj. Impossible, improbable. نا شکر *nā-shukr*, adj. Ungrateful; (Fem.) نا شکره *nā-shukra'h*. نا شکري *nā-shukrī*, s.f. (3rd) Ingratitude. Pl. ئ *a'ī*. نا شکري کول *nā-shukrī kawul*, verb trans. To act with ingratitude. نا شناس *nā-shinās*, adj. Ignorant, foolish; (Fem.) نا شناسه *nā-shināsa'h*. نا ښاد *na-shād* (W.) or *nā-khād* (E.) adj. Cheerless, low-spirited, dull, dissatisfied; (Fem.) نا ښاده *nā-shāda'h* or *nā-khāda'h*. نا ښايسته *nā-shā-īstah* (W.) or *nā-khā-īstah* (E.), adj. Ugly, bad-looking, sour. (Masc. and Fem.) نا صاف *nā-ṣāf*, adj. Impure, unclean; (Fem.) نا صافه *nā-ṣāfa'h*. نا صواب *nā-ṣawāb*, adj. Not right, sinful, bad; (Fem.) نا صوابه *nā-ṣawāba'h*. نا طاقت *nā-ṭāḳat*, adj. Infirm, weak, powerless; (Fem.) نا طاقته *nā-ṭāḳata'h*. نا غوره *nā-ghwarah*, adj. Not chosen, unselected, not picked out. (Masc. and Fem.) نا فرمان *nā-farmān*, adj. Disobedient, stubborn; (Fem.) نا فرمانه *nā-farmāna'h*. نا فرماني *nā-farmānī*, s.f. (3rd) Disobedience, stubbornness. Pl. ئ *a'ī*. نا فهم *nā-fahm*, adj. Stupid, ignorant, unintelligent; (Fem.) نا فهمه *nā-fahma'h*. نا فهمي *nā-fahmī*, s.f. (3rd) Stupidity, folly, ignorance. Pl. ئ *a'ī*. نا قابل *nā-ḳābil*, adj. Unfit, incapable, worthless; (Fem). نا قابله *nā-ḳābila'h*. نا قبول *nā-ḳabūl*, adj. Unacceptable, refusing, rejecting; (Fem.) نا قبوله *nā-ḳabūla'h*. نا قرار *nā-ḳarār*, adj. Unstable, uneasy; (Fem.) نا قراره *nā-ḳarāra'h*. نا کار *nā-kār*, adj. Useless, of no use, worthless; (Fem.) نا کاره *nā-kāra'h*. نا کاري *nā-kārī*, s.f. (3rd) Uselessness, worthlessness. Pl. ئ *a'ī*. نا کام *nā-kām*, adj. Disappointed, useless; (Fem.) نا کامي *nā-kāmī*, s.f. (3rd) Discontent, disappointment. Pl. ئ *a'ī*. نا کردي *nā-kardaey*, adj. Improper, unfit to be done. نا کس *nā-kas*, adj. A person of light character or no consequence; (Fem.) نا کسه *nā-kasa'h*. نا گومان *nā-gūmān*, adj. Unexpected, unsuspected; (Fem.) نا گومانه *nā-gūmāna'h*. نا لايق *nā-lā-īḳ*, adj. Unfit, unworthy, improper; (Fem.) نا لايقه *nā-lā-īḳa'h*. نا مبارک *nā-*

mubārak, adj. Unfortunate, unblessed; (Fem.) نا مباركه *nā-mubāraka'h*. نا محرم *nā-maḥram*, adj. A stranger, not a confidant, one not permitted to enter the women's apartment; (Fem.) نا محرمه *nā-maḥrama'h*. نا مراد *nā-murād*, adj. Dissatisfied, disappointed in one's hopes or wishes; (Fem.) نا مراده *nā-murāda'h*. نا مرادي *nā-murādī*, s.f. (3rd) Dissatisfaction, disappointment of one's hopes. Pl. ئي *a'ī*. نا مرد *nā-mard*, adj. Unmanly, a coward, impotent; (Fem.) نا مرده *nā-marda'h*. نا مردي *nā-mardī*, s.f. (3rd) Unmanliness, impotence, cowardliness. Pl. ئي *a'ī*. نا معلوم *nā-maæ-lūm*, adj. Unknown, undiscovered; (Fem.) نا معلومه *nā-maæ-lūma'h*. نا ممكن *nā-mumkin*, adj. Impossible, not to be done; (Fem.) نا ممكنه *nā-mumkina'h*. نا مناسب *nā-munāsib*, adj. Inconsistent, unbecoming, improper, unfit; (Fem.) نا مناسبه *nā-munāsiba'h*. نا موافق *nā-mūā-fiḳ*, adj. Disagreeing, dissimilar, adverse, unwholesome; (Fem.) نا موافقه *nā-mūā-fiḳa'h*. نا موافق كيدل *nā-mūā-fiḳ kedal*, verb intrans. To disagree, to become unwholesome. نا مهربان *nā-mihrbān*, adj. Unkind, unfriendly; (Fem.) نا مهربانه *nā-mihrbāna'h*. نا مهرباني *nā-mihrbānī*, s.f. (3rd) Unkindness, unfriendliness. Pl. ئي *a'ī*. نا وارث *nā-wāriṣ*, adj. Friendless, patronless, without friend or protector; (Fem.) نا وارثه *nā-wāriṣa'h*. نا واقف *nā-wāḳif*, adj. Unskilled, unacquainted, ignorant, inexperienced; (Fem.) نا واقفه *nā-wāḳifa'h*. نا واقفيت *nā-wāḳfiyat*, s.m. (2nd) Inexperience, ignorance. Pl. نا واقفيتونه *nā-wāḳfiyatūnah*. نا وقت *nā-waḳt*, adj. Out of time, unseasonable; (Fem.) نا وقته *nā-waḳta'h*. نا ولي *nā-wulaey*, adj. Unwashed, unclean. نا ياب *nā-yāb*, adj. Rare, scarce, difficult to be found out; (Fem.) نا يابه *nā-yāba'h*. نا يابي *nā-yābī*, s.f. (3rd) Scarcity, rareness. Pl. ئي *a'ī*.

P ناب *nāb*, adj. Pure, clear, genuine; (Fem.) نابه *nāba'h*.

نابړ *nā-baṟṟ*, adj. Robust, sturdy, bluff, clumsy; (Fem.) نابړه *nā-baṟṟa'h*.

ناپړ *nā-paṟṟ*, adj. (Fem.) ناپړه *nā-paṟṟa'h*. See preceding.

نا تار *nā-tār*, s.m. (2nd) Plunder, robbery. 2. Injury, destruction. Pl. ناتارونه *nā-tārūnah*. نا تار كول *nā-tār kawul*, verb trans. To plunder, to destroy.

ناتكي *nāt-ka'ī*, s.f. (6th) Unity (in number) singleness, oneness, individuality. Sing. and Pl. See وتر

نا څاپه *nā-tsāpah*, adv. Suddenly, all at once, all of a sudden.

ناجو *nā-jū*, s.m. (5th) A fir-tree, a pine. Pl. ناجوګان *nā-jūgān*. See سراسر

P نادان *nā-dān*, adj. Ignorant, simple, silly; (Fem.) نادانه *nā-dāna'h*.

P ناداني *nā-dānī*, s.f. (3rd) Ignorance, folly, foolishness, stupidity, simplicity. Pl. ئي *a'ī*. ناداني كول *nā-dānī kawul*, verb trans. To act foolishly, stupidly, to manifest ignorance, stupidity, etc.

A نادر *nā-dir*, adj. (act. part. of ندر) Rare, wonderful, exquisite, choice; (Fem.) نادره *nā-dira'h*. نادري *nā-dirī*, s.f. (3rd) A rarity, rarity, choiceness. Pl. ئي *a'ī*.

نار *nār*, s.m. (2nd) A sprout, a shoot. Pl. نارونه *nārūnah*.

P نارنج *nā-ranj*, s.m. (6th) An orange. Sing. and Pl.

نارو *nā-rū*, s.m. (5th) A Guinea-worm. 2. A disease known as the guinea-worm (Filaria medinensis). Pl. ناروګان *nā-rūgān*. (HI نهاروا)

ناره *nāra'h*, s.f. (3rd) (corrup. of A نعره) A sound, a noise, shout, crying, clamor. Pl. ئي *ey*. ناري سوري *nārey sūrey*, s.f. (3rd) (Pl.) Loud noise, shouts, bawling, clamor, hullaballoo, hubbub. ناره كول *nāra'h kawul*, verb trans. To call or cry out, to shout, to raise a clamor; or ناري وهل *nārey wahal*, verb trans.

S ناريل *nāriyal*, s.m. (6th) A cocoa-nut, the cocoa-nut tree. Sing. and Pl.

نارينه *nārīnah*, s.m. (6th) A male, a man, a husband, a brave man. 2. Mankind. Sing. and Pl. 3. adj. Masculine, male. See سري

ناري *nāraey*, s.m. (1st) Food eaten at breakfast, breakfast. Pl. ي *ī*. See نهاري

نار *nā<u>rr</u>*, s.m. (9th) The stalks of barley, wheat, or other description of grain left in the ground after reaping, stubble. Sing. and Pl. نارگوره *nā<u>rr</u>-gora'h*, s.f. (3rd) Stubble land. Pl. ې *ey*. See خريز

نارہ *nā<u>rr</u>a'h*, s.f. (3rd) The stem or main axis of a plant, such as the stalk of a tulip, etc. Pl. ې *ey*. See موند

P ناز *nāz*, s.m. (2nd) Fondling, blandishment, coquetry, playfulness, gracefulness, elegance, soothing, amorous playfulness. 2. Pride, consequential airs. Pl. نازونه *nāzūnah*. ناز پرور *nāz-parwar*, adj. Delicately brought up, pampered, spoiled (as a child); (Fem.) ناز پروره *nāz-parwara'h* or نازولَي *nāzawulaey*; (past part.) (Fem.) نازولِ *nāzawuli*. ناز کول *nāz kawul*, To fondle, to play, to coquet, to show consequential airs. ناز وړل *nāz-w'<u>rr</u>al*, verb trans. To bear or put up with the airs or whims of another. ناز و نخره *nāz-o-na<u>kh</u>ra'h*, s.f. (3rd) Coquetry, dalliance, toying, blandishment. Pl. ې *ey*. Also ناز و نياز *nāz-o-nī-āz*, s.m. (2nd). Pl. ناز و نيازونه *nāz-o-nī-āzūnah*. نازيدل *nāzedal*, verb intrans. To coquet, to assume graceful or amorous airs. Pres. نازيږي *nāze<u>jz</u>ī* (W.) or نازيگي *nāzegī* (E.); past وُ نازيده *wu-nāzedah*; fut. وُ به نازيږي *wu bah nāze<u>jz</u>ī* or نازيگي *nāzegī*; imp. وُ نازيږه *wu-nāze<u>jz</u>ah* or وُ نازيگه *wu-nāzegah*; act. part. نازيدونکَي *nāze-dūnkaey* or نازيدونَي *nāze-dūnaey*; past part. نازيدلَي *nāze-dalaey*; verb n. نازيدنه *nāzedana'h* or نازيده *nāzedah*. نازول *nāzawul*, verb trans. To treat with an appearance of tenderness or regard, to coquet, to pamper, to spoil as a child, to soothe, to fondle. Pres. نازوي *nāzawī*; past وُ نازاوه *wu-nāzāwuh* or نازاوو *nāzāwo*; fut. وُ به نازوي *wu bah nāzawī*; imp. وُ نازوه *wu-nāzawah*; act. part. نازوونکَي *nāzawūnkaey* or نازوونَي *nāza-wūnaey*; past part. نازولَي *nāzawulaey*; verb. n. نازونه *nāzawuna'h*.

P نازک *nā-zuk*, adj. Thin, light, subtile, delicate, tender, nice, fragile, elegant; (Fem.) نازکه *nā-zuka'h*. نازک بدن *nā-zuk-badan*, adj. Thin, delicate (in the limbs); (Fem.) نازک بدنه *nā-zuk-badana'h*.

نازکه *nāzaka'h*, s.f. (3rd) A doll, a puppet. Pl. ې *ey*. See نينزکه and گودا

P نازکي *nāzukī*, s.f. (3rd) Delicacy, nicety, tenderness, delicateness. Pl. ې *a'ī*.

نازل *nāzil*, s.m. (9th) (act. part. نزل) Descending, dismounting, alighting (as a calamity). نازليدل *nāziledal*, verb intrans. To descend, to alight, to come down. Pres. نازليږي *nāzile<u>jz</u>ī* (W.) or نازليگي *nāzilegī* (E.); past نازل شه *nāzil <u>sh</u>ah* or وُ شه *wu-<u>sh</u>ah*; fut. نازل به شي *nāzil bah <u>sh</u>ī* or به وُ شي *bah wu-<u>sh</u>ī*; imp. نازل شه *nāzil <u>sh</u>ah* or وُ شه *wu-<u>sh</u>ah*; act. part. نازليدونکَي *nāziledūnkaey* or نازليدونَي *nāziledūnaey*; past part. نازل شوَي *nāzil <u>sh</u>awaey*; verb. n. نازليدنه *nāziledana'h* or نازليده *nāziledah*. نازلول *nāzilawul*, verb trans. To make descend, to cause to alight. Pres. نازلوي *nāzilawī*; past نازل کړ *nāzil ka<u>rr</u>* or وُ کړ *wu-ka<u>rr</u>*; fut. نازل به کړي *nāzil bah k<u>rr</u>ī* or به وُ کړي *bah wu-k<u>rr</u>ī*; imp. نازل کړه *nāzil k<u>rr</u>ah* or وُ کړه *wu-k<u>rr</u>ah*; act. part. نازلوونکَي *nāzilawūnkaey* or نازلوونَي *nāzila-wūnaey*; past part. نازل کړَي *nāzil ka<u>rr</u>aey*; verb. n. نازلونه *nāzilawuna'h*.

A نازله *nāzila'h*, s.f. (3rd) A calamity, a misfortune, disorder. Pl. ې *ey*.

P نازنين *nāznīn*, adj. Delicate, lovely; (Fem.) نازنينه *nāznīna'h*, as s.f. (3rd) A delicate female, a belle, a sweetheart. Pl. ې *ey*.

ناست *nāst*, adj. Seated, sitting, reclining, lolling, squatting; (Fem.) ناسته *nāsta'h*. ناست ولاړ *nāst-walā<u>rr</u>*, Sitting and standing, distracted, restless.

په پښو ناستل *pah p<u>sh</u>o* (W.) or *p<u>kh</u>o* (E.) *nāstal*, verb intrans. To sit on the feet (ready to rise up), to be ready prepared for any matter, to expect, to anticipate anything.

ناسته *nāsta'h*, s.f. (3rd) (verb. n. of ناستل *nāstal*, To sit, etc. It is conjugated with a prefix. See کښيناستل), Sitting, lolling, the act of sitting down, incubation, perching, alighting. Pl. ي *ey*. ناسته ولاړه *nāsta'h-walāṟṟa'h*, Sitting and standing, restlessness. د ناستي ځاي *da nāstey dzā-e*, s.m. (2nd) A seat, a place for sitting on. Pl ځايونه *dzā-e-ūnah*.

ناسره *nā-sarah*, adj. Bad, counterfeit, alloyed, impure, not current.

ناسوار *nāswār*, s.m. (6th) Snuff. Sing. and Pl. See نسوار

A ناسوت *nā-sūt*, s.m. (9th) Humanity, human, kind, human nature. Sing. and Pl.

A ناسور *nāsūr*, s.m. (9th) (from نسر) A disease in the corner of the eye or in the gums, a disease in the podex attended by constant defluxion. Sing. and Pl.

ناسولت *nā-solaṯṯ*, adj. Uncircumcised, a term of abuse. See شوپا

ناشپاتي *nāsh-pātaey*, s.m. (1st) A pear. Pl. ي *ī*.

P ناشته *nāshta'h*, s.f. (3rd) A morning repast, breakfast. Pl. ي *ey*. See نهاري

نا ښنده *nā-khanda'h*, (E.) s.f. (3rd) Impropriety, wrong, etc. Pl. ي *ey*. See ناښني and نښنده

ناښني *nā-khaney*, (E.) s.f. (3rd). (Pl.) Impropriety, inconsistency, wrong, what ought not to be done, unlawfulness.

A ناصح *nā-ṣiḥ*, s.m. (5th) (act. part. of نصح) An adviser, a monitor, a sincere friend or counsellor. Pl. ناصحان *nā-ṣiḥān*. ناصحه *nā-ṣiḥa'h*, s.f. (3rd). Pl. ي *ey*.

ناصر *nāṣar*, s.m. (6th) The name of a powerful tribe of Afghāns. 2. A man or male of the Nāṣar tribe. Sing. and Pl. ناصره *nāṣara'h*, s.f. (3rd) A female of the above. Pl. ي *ey*.

A ناظر *nā-ẓir*, s.m. (5th) (act. part. of نظر) Seeing, looking, inspecting, beholding. 2. An inspector, a superintendent, a keeper. 3. An officer in judicial courts, a sort of sheriff. Pl. ناظران *nāẓirān*. ناظره *nāẓira'h*, s.f. (3rd). Pl. ي *ey*.

A ناظم *nā-ẓim*, s.m. (5th) (from نظم) A governor, a ruler. 2. A composer, an arranger, an adjuster. Pl. ناظمان *nā-ẓimān*.

T ناغه *nā-gha'h*, s.f. (3rd) Adjournment, respite, putting off. 2. A fine, a mulct. Pl. ي *ey*. 3. adj. Vacant, void, unemployed. 4. Sunk in (as the eyes from sickness). (Masc. and Fem.) ناغه وهل *nā-gha'h wahal*, verb trans. To sink into the forehead (as the eye).

A نافع *nā-fiæ*, adj. (act. part. of نفع) Salutary, useful, profitable, advantageous; (Fem.) نافعه *nā-fiæa'h*.

P نافه *nāfa'h*, s.f. (3rd) A pod of musk. Pl. ي *ey*.

A ناقص *nā-ḳiṣ*, adj. (act. part. of نقص) Defective, imperfect, deficient, mutilated, inexpert; (Fem.) ناقصه *nā-ḳiṣa'h*. ناقص عقل *nā-ḳiṣ æaḳl*, adj. Deficient in understanding, foolish, ignorant; (Fem.) ناقص عقله *nā-ḳiṣ æaḳla'h*. ناقص كيدل *nā-ḳiṣ kedal*, verb intrans. To want, to fail. ناقص كول *nā-ḳiṣ kawul*, verb trans. To mutilate, to render or make deficient.

A ناقل *nā-ḳil*, s.m. (5th) (act. part. of نقل) A reciter, a reporter, a narrator, a relater. Pl. ناقلان *nā-ḳilān*. ناقله *nā-ḳila'h*, s.f. (3rd). Pl. ي *ey*.

ناك *nāk*, s.m. (6th) A pear. Sing. and Pl. See ناشپاتي

ناكه *nā-ka'h*, s.f. (3rd) An alligator. Pl. ي *ey*. (s ناكا)

P ناگاه *nā-gāh*, adv. Suddenly, unexpectedly, all at once, unawares, abruptly.

ناگدون *nāg-dūn*, s.m. (6th) Worm-wood. Sing. and Pl. (s ناگدونا)

P ناگمان *nā-gumān*, adj. Unsuspected, sudden, unexpected, all at once; (Fem.) ناگمانه *nā-gumāna'h*. 2. adv. Suddenly, unexpectedly.

P ناگه *nā-gah*. See ناگاه

P ناگهان *nā-gahān*, adj. Sudden. 2. adv. Suddenly, unawares; and ناگهاني *nā-gahānī*.

نال *nāl*, s.m. (2nd) (corrup. of A نعل) A horseshoe, the iron portion of a horse-shoe. Pl. نالونه *nālūnah*. نالول *nālawul*, verb trans. To shoe a horse. نال آچول *nāl āchawul*, verb trans. To cast a shoe (as a horse).

ناله *nāla'h*, s.f. (3rd) A rivulet, a brook, a canal, a gutter, a furrow, a ravine. Pl. ي *ey*. (HI نالا)

نالي *nālī*, s.f. (3rd) A kind of quilt, a cushion,

a small carpet. Pl. ئي a'ī. (Corrup. of P نهالي which see.)

P نام nām, s.m. (2nd) Name, appellation (used in Pushto composition only), as نام خدا nām-i-khudā, interj. In God's name! bravo! نام دار nām-dār, adj. Famous, celebrated, notorious; (Fem.) نام داره nām-dāra'h. نام داري nām-dārī, s.f. (3rd) Celebrity, fame. Pl. ئي a'ī. نام و ننگ nām-o-nang, Honour, reputation; shame, disgrace. نام ور nām-war, adj. Celebrated, renowned; (Fem.) نام وره nām-wara'h. نام وري nām-warī, s.f. (3rd) Renown, celebrity. Pl. ئي a'ī. See نوم

A ناموس nāmūs, s.m. (2nd) (from نمس) Reputation, fame, renown. 2. Disgrace. 3. The female part of a family. Pl. ناموسونه nāmūs-ūnah.

نامه nāma'h, s.f. (3rd) A letter, a writing, a history, a work, a treatise, a book. Pl. ئي ey.

نامي نامي nāmī-nāmaey, adj. Unknown, mean, poor, humble; (Fem.) نامي نام nāmī-nāmi. Pl. (Masc. and Fem.) ي ī.

نامير nāmer, adj. Renowned, celebrated, famous (for beauty), etc. 2. Lovely; (Fem.) ناميره nāmera'h.

نان واي nān-wā-e, s.m. (5th) (from P) A baker. Pl. نان وايان nān-wā-e-ān. نان وائي nān-wā'ī, s.f. (3rd) The business of a baker, bakery. Pl. ئي a'ī. نان وائي كول nān-wā'ī kawul, verb trans. To carry on the business of a baker; also written نان بائي nān-bā'ī, etc.

نانگه nān-gah, s.m. (5th) A blackberry. 2. The name of a tree. Pl. نانگان nān-gān or نانگه گان nān-gah-gān.

ناور nāwar, s.m. (2nd) A small pond in which rain water is collected, a tank. Pl. ناورونه nāwarūnah.

ناوك nāwak, s.m. (6th) A sort of arrow. 2. A bee's sting. 3. The tube through which arrows are pointed. Sing. and Pl.

ناوكۍ nāwaka'ī, s.f. (6th) A doll, a puppet, a plaything. Sing. and Pl. See گودا

ناوكي nāwakaey, s.m. (1st) (from P ناوك) A sort of arrow or dart. Pl. ي ī.

ناونده nāwn-dah, adj. (Pl. of نوند) Damp, wet, moist, etc. See لونده

ناوه nāwa'h, s.f. (3rd) A gutter, a canal, a launder, a tube for carrying off water. 2. A long barrelled musket. Pl. ئي ey. ناوه گۍ nāwa'h-ga'ī, s.f. (6th) (dimin. of ناوه) A small tube or gutter; the leaves of some kinds of grain tube-shaped.

ناوي nā-wey, s.f. (5th) A bride. Pl. ناويانِ nā-weyāni.

ناويات nā-wiyāt, adj. Rare, peerless, nonesuch, crack, matchless, tip-top, admirable, choice; (Fem.) ناوياته nā-wiyāta'h.

S نائي na'ī, s.m. (5th) A barber, a hairdresser. Pl. نائيان nā'ī-ān or نائيگان nā'ī-gān. نايته nā-yana'h or نايڑه nā-yarrna'h, s.f. (3rd) A barber's wife, female of the above. Pl. ئي ey.

A نا ويسا nā-waisā, adj. Of no credit or estimation, not to be trusted or relied on.

A نايب nā-īb, s.m. (5th) (act. part. of نوب) A deputy, a delegate, a vicegerent, an attorney, a lieutenant. Pl. نايبان nā-īb-ān. نايبي nā-ībī, s.f. (3rd) The business of a deputy, agency, delegation. Pl. ئي a'ī.

P نبات nabāt, s.m. (6th) Sugar, sweetmeat. Sing. and Pl.

A نبض nabẓ, s.m. (2nd) The pulse. Pl. نبضونه nabẓūnah. نبض كتل nabẓ katal, verb trans. To feel the pulse (lit. 'to see the pulse').

A نبوت nubūwat, s.m. (2nd) (from نبأ) Prophecy. Pl. نبوتونه nubūwat-ūnah.

A نبي nabī, s.m. (5th) A prophet. Pl. نبيان nabīān (or A Pl. انبيا anbī'ā).

نتكۍ nat-ka'ī, s.f. (6th) A small ring worn in the nose by females. Sing. and Pl.

نتل natal, verb trans. To carry off or away, to lay violent hands on, to pillage, to rifle, to sack, to despoil, to strip. Pres. نتي natī; past وُ ناته wu-nātah; fut. وُ به نتي wu bah natī; imp. وُ نته wu-natah; act. part. نتونكي natūnkaey or نتوني natūnaey; past part. نتلي natalaey; verb. n. نتنه natana'h.

نتلي natalaey, adj. Pillaged, rifled, ransacked,

despoiled, carried off, stripped; (Fem.) نتلِ *natali*. Pl. (Masc. and Fem.) ي *ī*.

نته *nata'h*, s.f. (3rd) A ring worn by females in the left nostril. 2. The piece of wood in a camel's nose. Pl. ي *ey*. See نتكي (s نتهِ)

A نتيجه *natīja'h*, s.f. (3rd) (from نتج) Result, consequence, deduction, inference, issue, conclusion. 2. Fœtus, birth, offspring. Pl. ي *ey*.

S نټ *natt*, s.m. (5th) The name of a tribe who are generally jugglers, rope-dancers, tumblers, etc. 2. A cheat, a knave, a deceiver. Pl. نټان *nattān*. نټه *natta'h*, s.f. (3rd) A female of the above tribe, a courtezan. Pl. ي *ey*.

A نثار *nisār*, s.m. (2nd) (from نثر) Scattering, strewing, throwing. 2. Money thrown among the people or to the bride on festive occasions. Pl. نثارونه *nisār-ūnah*. نثاركول *nisār kawul*, verb trans. To throw, to scatter (as money or flowers).

نڅا *natsā*, s.f. (6th) Dancing, waving or shaking (as the branches of trees by the wind). (E.) Sing. and Pl. (W.) Pl. نڅاوي *natsāwī*. نڅيدل *natsedal*, verb intrans. To dance. 2. To wave, to shake (as the branches of a tree by wind). نڅول *natsawul*, verb trans. To make or cause to dance. 2. To make to shake or wave. See ګډيدل

نڅا *nitsā*, s.f. (6th) Agitation (as of a tree from the wind), stir, shake, tremor, trepidation, quiver, commotion, turmoil, etc. (E.) Sing. and Pl. (W.) Pl. نڅاوي *nitsāwī*. په نڅا ګډول *pah nitsā gaddawul*, verb trans. To shake, to agitate, to toss, to disturb, to shake up, to buffet, to make the sport of the winds, to shake like an aspen-leaf.

نڅئي *natsa'ī*, s.f. (6th) Thread or string made from wool, camel's hair, etc. Sing. and Pl. See انڅئي

A نجا *najā*, s.f. (6th) Liberating, escaping, being set free. (E.) Sing. and Pl. (W.) Pl. نجاوي *najāwī*.

A نجات *najāt*, s.m. (2nd) Freedom, liberation, deliverance, salvation, escape, pardon, absolution. Pl. نجاتونه *najātūnah*. نجات موندل *najāt mūndal*, verb trans. To obtain freedom, deliverance, salvation, absolution.

A نجار *najjār*, s.m. (5th) (W.) A carpenter. Pl. نجاران *najjārān*. See تركاڼ

نجاري *najjārī*, s.f. (3rd) The business of a carpenter, carpentry. Pl. ي *a'ī*. نجاري كول *najjārī kawul*, verb trans. To carry on the business of a carpenter.

A نجاست *najāsat*, s.m. (2nd) (from نجس), Filth, nastiness, dirtiness, impurity. Pl. نجاستونه *najāsatūnah*.

نجتل *'n'jatal*, verb trans. To plant in the ground (as a spear), to stick in, to erect in the ground by sticking in, to plant, to thrust in, to ingraft, to insert. Pres. نجتي *'n'janī*; past وُ نجت *wu-'n'jat*; fut. وُ به نجني *wu bah 'n'janī*; imp. وُ نجته *wu-'n'janah*; act. part. نجتونكي *'n'jatūnkaey* or نجتوني *'n'jatūnaey*; past part. نجتلي *'n'jatalaey* or نجتي *'n'jataey*; verb. n. نجتنه *'n'jatana'h* or نجته *'n'jata'h*.

نجته *'n'jata'h* or نجتنه *'n'jatana'h*, s.f. (3rd) (verb. n.) Planting in the ground, sticking in, inserting, implanting, erecting. Pl. ي *ey*.

نجل *'n'jal*, s.f. (1st) A young woman, a damsel, a girl betrothed, but living in the house of her parents. Pl. نجلِ *'n'jali*. See جل

A نجوم *najūm*, s.m. (9th) Astrology, astronomy. Sing. and Pl.

نجومي *najūmī*, s.m. (5th) An astrologer, a fortune-teller. Pl. نجوميان *najūmī-ān*.

نچا *nachā*, نچيدل *nachedal*, and نچول *nachawul*. See نڅا, etc.

نچورول *nichorawul*, verb trans. (E.) To wring, to squeeze, to press, to strain, to express, to extort, to exact. Pres. نچوروي *nichorawī*; past نچور كړ *nichor karr* or وُ كړ *wu-karr*; fut. وُ به نچوروي *wu bah nichorawī*; imp. نچور كړه *nichor krrah* or وُ كړه *wu-krrah*; act. part. نچوروونكي *nichorawūnkaey* or نچوروني *nichorawūnaey*; past part. نچور كړي *nichor karraey*; verb. n. نچورونه *nichorawuna'h*. See نبښيخل

نچه *nicha'h*, s.f. (3rd) A weaver's reel. 2. The

stem of a *ḥukka* or *kalliān*. Pl. ې *ey*. See نيچه

A نحس *naḥs*, adj. Bad, unlucky, inauspicious. 2. Unlucky planet; (Fem.) نحسه *naḥsa'h*.

A نحسيت *naḥsīat*, s.m. (2nd) (from نحس) Unluckiness, inauspiciousness, abomination. Pl. نحسيتونه *naḥsīat-ūnah*.

نخالس *na-khālus*, adj. Pure, unmixed, unadulterated; (Fem.) نخالسه *na-khālusa'h*.

نخچ *na-khach*, s.m. (6th) A kind of grass. Sing. and Pl.

نخره *nakhra'h*, s.f. (3rd) Trick, artifice, joke, waggery, pleasantry, fun, deceit, pretence, sham. 2. A fracture, a hole, a cleft, a crevice (corrup. of P رخنه). Pl. ې *ey*. نخره باز *nakhra'h-bāz*, s.m. (5th) An affected person; adj. Affected. Pl. بازان *bāzān*. نخره بازه *nakhra'h-bāza'h*, s.f. (3rd). Pl. ې *ey*. نخره كول *nakhra'h kawul*, verb intrans. To practice or play tricks, to pretend, to practice deceit. 2. To fracture, to rend, to make a cleft or crevice in anything.

نخبن *nu-khash* (W.) or *nu-khakh* (E.) s.m. (2nd) An iron hook used for drawing meat out of a pot. Pl. نخبنونه *nu-khashūnah* or *nu-khakh-ūnah*.

نخښه *nakhsha'h* (W.) or *nakhkha'h* (E.) s.f. (3rd) A sign, a mark, a token, a cipher, an emblem, a device, a countersign, a pass-word. Pl. ې *ey*.

A نخل *nakhl*, s.f. (1st) A date tree, a palm tree, a young plant. Pl. نخل *nakhli*.

A نخلستان *nakhlistān*, s.m. (5th) A date grove. Pl. نخلستانان *nakhlistānān*.

A نخوت *nakhwat*, s.m. (2nd) Pride, arrogance, haughtiness, pomp, magnificence. Pl. نخوتونه *nakhwatūnah*.

P نخود *nukhūd*, s.m. (6th) A kind of pulse (Cicer arietinum). Sing. and Pl. See چنره

A ندا *nidā*, s.f. (6th) Sound, voice, calling, call to prayer, proclamation, vocative. (E.) Sing. and Pl. (W.) Pl. نداوي *nidāwī*. ندا كول *nidā kawul*, verb trans. To call out, to exclaim.

نداپ *naddāp* or (P) نداف *naddāf*, s.m. (5th) A cleaner of cotton, a cotton dresser. Pl. نداپان *naddāpān* or ندافان *naddāfān*. نداپه *naddāpa'h* or ندافه *naddāfa'h*, s.f. (3rd) The feminine of the above. Pl. ې *ey*.

نداپي *nadāpī* or (P) ندافي *nadāfī*, s.f. (3rd) The business of a cotton dresser, cotton cleaning. Pl. ئي *a'ī*.

A ندامت *nadāmat*, s.m. (2nd) (from ندم) Repentance, penitence, regret, contrition. Pl. ندامتونه *nadāmatūnah*. See پښيماني

ندرور *'n'dror*, s.f. (5th) A husband's sister. Pl. ندرندې *'n'drandey* or ندرندِ *'n'drandi*.

A نذر *nazr*, s.m. (2nd) A gift, a present, an offering. Pl. نذرونه *nazrūnah*. نذر كول *nazr-kawul* or نذر ور كول *nazr war-kawul*, verb trans. To make a present, to present a gift.

A نذرانه *nazrāna'h*, s.f. (3rd) A gift, a present offered or received when people of rank meet. Pl. ې *ey*.

P S نر *nar*, s.m. (5th) A male, a man. Pl. نر *nær*. 2. adj. Masculine, male.

P نرخ *nirkh*, s.m. (2nd) Price current, tariff, rate, Pl. نرخونه *nirkhūnah*. نرخ نامه *nirkh-nāma'h*, s.f. (3rd) A paper containing the price current. Pl. ې *ey*.

نرسوی *nar-sawaey*, s.m. (1st) A kind of pomegranate. 2. The rind of the fruit. Pl. ي *ī*.

نرغټ *nar-ghutt*, s.m. (5th) A he-cat. Pl. نرغټان *nar-ghuttān*. See برغټ

نركښ *nar-kash* (W.) or *nar-kakh* (E.) s.m. (5th) A mountain ram, the leader of the flock. Pl. نركښان *nar-kashān* or *nar-kakhān*.

نركوښ *nar-kosh* (W.) or *nar-kokh* (E.) s.m. (2nd) A fish-hook, a hook used in gathering fruit. Pl. نركوښونه *nar-koshūnah* or *nar-kokhūnah*.

P نرگس *nar-gis*, (s.m.) 6th The narcissus, (met.) the eye of a mistress. Sing. and Pl.

نرلوخ *nar-lūkh*, s.m. (6th) The flowery top of the gorse. Sing. and Pl.

P نرم *narm*, adj. Soft, tender, mild. 2. Easy, gentle, ductile, silly; (Fem.) نرمه *narma'h*.

P نرمي *narmī*, s.f. (3rd) Softness, tenderness, mildness. 2. Easiness, gentleness, ductileness, silliness. Pl. ئي *a'ī*; also نرم والي *narm-*

wālaey, s.m. (1st). Pl. والي *wālī*. نرم زړه *narm z'rrah*, adj. Soft-heart. نرم زړي *narm z'rraey*, adj. A soft or tender hearted person; (Fem.) نرم زړِ *narm z'rri*. Pl. (Masc. and Fem.) ي *ī*.

نرميدل *narmedal*, verb intrans. To soften, to grow soft, tender, mild, to mollify; to become gentle. Pres. نرميږي *narmejzī* (W.) or نرميگي *narmegī* (E.); past نرم شه *narm shah* or وُ شه *wu-shah*; fut. نرم به شي *narm bah shī* or به وُ شي *bah wu-shī*; imp. نرم شه *narm shah* or وُ شه *wu-shah*; act. part. نرميدونکي *narmedūnkaey* or نرميدوني *narmedūnaey*; past. part. نرم *narm* or نرم شوي *narm shawaey*; verb. n. نرميدنه *narmedana'h* or نرميده *narmedah*. نرمول *narmawul*, verb trans. To make or render soft, to soften, to mollify, to relax. Pres. نرموي *narmawī*; past نرم کړ *narm karr* or وُ کړ *wu-karr*; fut. نرم به کړي *narm bah krrī* or به وُ کړي *bah wu-krrī*; imp. نرم کړه *narm krrah* or وُ کړه *wu-krrah*; act. part. نرموونکي *narmawūnkaey* or نرمووني *narmawūnaey*; past part. نرم کړي *narm karraey*; verb. n. نرمونه *narmawuna'h*.

نرمۍ *nar-ma'ī*, s.f. (6th) The lobe of the ear. Sing. and Pl.; or نرمه *nar-ma'h*, s.f. (3rd). Pl. ۍ *cy*.

نر ناحق *nar-nā-hakk*, adj. Totally unjust, entirely illegal, improper, wrong, undeserved, etc.

نري *naraey*, adj. Thin, slender, fine, narrow, slim, taper, spare, delicate, scant; (Fem.) نرۍ *nara'ī*. نري نري *naraey-naraey*, Very thin, exceedingly slender, thin as a lath, very slim or spare; (Fem.) نرۍ نرۍ *nara'ī-nara'ī*.

نري والي *naraey-wālaey*, s.m. (1st) Slenderness, thinness, fineness, spareness, narrowness, tenuity. Pl. والي *wālī*. نري رنز *naraey ranz*, Slight fever, slight indisposition, slightly unwell, so-so. نري کيدل *naraey kedal*, verb intrans. To become or grow thin, small, narrow, slim, scant, emaciated, attenuated. نري کول *naraey kawul*, verb trans. To render thin, small, slight, etc.; to emaciate, to attenuate.

نرۍ اوبه *nara'ī aobah*, s. prop. The name of a river in Afghānistān in the Kohātt district.

نړا *narrā*, s.f. (6th) The cry, bellow, bell, bray, etc. of animals. (E.) Sing. and Pl. (W.) Pl. نړاوي *narrāwī*.

نړل *narral*, verb trans. To bawl, to cry out. 2. To bray. Pres. ناړي *nārrī*; past وُ نړل *wu-narral*; fut. وُ به نړي *wu bah narrī*; imp. وُ ناړه *wu-nārrah*; act. part. نړونکي *narrūnkaey*; past part. نړلي *narralaey*; verb. n. نړنه *narrana'h*.

نړۍ *narra'ī*, s.f. (6th) The world, the universe, the earth, the globe. Sing. and Pl.

نړيدل *narredal*, verb intrans. To be razed, demolished, levelled, overthrown, upset, prostrated, turned over, subverted, knocked down, etc. Pres. نړيږي *narrejzī* (W.) or نړيگي *narregī* (E.); past وُ نړيده *wu-narredah*; fut. وُ به نړيږي *wu bah narrejzī* or نړيگي *narregī*; imp. وُ نړيږه *wu-narrejzah* or وُ نړيگه *wu-narregah*; act. part. نړيدونکي *narredūnkaey* or نړيدوني *narredūnaey*; past part. نړيدلي *narredalaey*; verb. n. نړيدنه *narredana'h* or نړيده *narredah*. نړول *narrawul*, verb trans. To raze, to demolish, to level, to overthrow, to upset, to prostrate, to subvert, to knock down, etc. Pres. نړوي *narrawī*; past وُ نړاوه *wu-narrāwuh* or وُ نړاوو *wu-narrāwo*; fut. وُ به نړوي *wu bah narrawī*; imp. وُ نړوه *wu-narrawah*; act. part. نړوونکي *narrawūnkaey* or نړووني *narrawūnaey*; past part. نړولي *narrawulaey*; verb. n. نړونه *narrawuna'h*.

نړيدلي *narredalaey*, adj. (past part.) Become demolished, razed, levelled; (Fem.) نړيدلِ *narredali*. Pl. (Masc. and Fem.) ي *ī*. نړولي *narrawulaey*, adj. Destroyed, razed, turned over, demolished, knocked down; (Fem.) نړولِ *narrawuli*. Pl. (Masc. and Fem.) ي *ī*.

P نزاکت *nazākat*, s.m. (2nd) Delicacy, delicateness, elegance, neatness, softness. Pl. نزاکتونه *nazākatūnah*.

P نزد *nazd*, adj. Near, close to, hard by, contiguous, neighbouring, adjacent. 2. adv. Almost, about, near, within a little. See نژدې

A نزله *nazla'h*, s.f. (3rd) (from نزل) A defluxion of humours, rheum, a catarrh. Pl. ې *ey*.

نژتې *n'jzataey*, adj. Erect, standing or sticking out (as the fingers when raised to the ears at the commencement of prayer); (Fem.) نژتِ *n'jzati*. Pl. (Masc. and Fem.) ي *ī*. See نجتل

نژدې *najzdey*, adj. Near, close to, hard by, contiguous, neighbouring. adjacent. 2. adv. Almost, near, within a short distance.

نژديکي *najzde-kī*, s.f. (3rd) Nearness, closeness, propinquity, proximity, vicinity, contiguity. Pl. ئ *a'ī*. Also (W.) نژديکت *najzdekat*, s.m. (2nd). Pl. نژديکتونه *najzdekat-ūnah*.

P نژدې کيدل *najzdey kedal*, verb intrans. To draw near, to approach. نژدې کول *najzdey kawul*, verb trans. To come near to, to cause or make to approach.

نږې *n'jzaey*, s.m. (1st) (W.) A sneeze. Pl. ي *ī*. نږې کول *n'jzaey kawul* or نږل *n'jzal*, verb trans. To sneeze. Pres. نږي *n'jzī*; past وُ نږه *wu-n'jzah* or وُ نږل *wu-n'jzal*; fut. وُ به نږي *wu bah n'jzī*; imp. وُ نږه *wu-n'jzah*; act. part. نږونکې *n'jzūnkaey* or نږونې *n'jzūnaey*; past part. نږلې *n'jzalaey*; verb. n. نږنه *n'jzana'h*. See نګل and پرچ

نږور *n'jzor*, s.f. (5th) A son's wife, a daughter-in-law. Pl. نږيندې *n'jzendey*. See نګور

نږول *n'jzawul*, verb trans. (caus.) To make or cause to sneeze (as snuff, etc.). See نګول

نس *nas*, s.m. (2nd) The belly, the lower part of the stomach. 2. Concupiscence, sensuality, desire, envy (corrup. of A نفس). Pl. نسونه *nasūnah*. نس خوږي *nas-khūjzī*, s.f. (3rd) Flux, diarrhœa, purging, loosening. Pl. ئ *a'ī*. لوې نسې *lo-e nasaey*, adj. Gluttonous, greedy, gormandizing; (Fem.) لوې نسِ *lo-e nasi*. Pl. (Masc. and Fem.) ي *ī*. نسور *nasa-war*, adj. Big-bellied, pot-bellied, a big belly; (Fem.) نسوره *nasa-wara'h*. See ګيډه

A نسب *nasab*, s.m. (2nd) Genealogy, lineage, family, descent. Pl. نسبونه *nasabūnah*.

نسب نامه *nasab-nāma'h*, s.f. (3rd) Pedigree, a genealogical tree. Pl. ې *ey*.

A نسبت *nis-bat*, s.m. (2nd) Relation, affinity, respecting, regarding, attribute, reference. Pl. نسبتونه *nisbatūnah*. نسبت لرل *nisbat laral*, verb trans. To have or bear affinity, relation or reference to. نسبت کول *nisbat kawul*, verb trans. To attribute, to refer.

A نسخ *naskh*, s.m. (9th) A kind of Arabic character, in which Pushto is written. Sing. and Pl.

A نسخه *nuskha'h*, s.f. (3rd) (from نسخ) A recipe, a prescription of ingredients. 2. A copy, a model, a prototype. 3. A writing book. Pl. ې *ey*.

P نسرين *nas-rīn*, s.m. (9th) A wild rose. Sing. and Pl.

نسغ کول *nasagh kawul*, verb trans. To pierce the nose with a spike or large needle as a punishment, after which a piece of wood with reins attached (as to the nose of a camel) is inserted, and the criminal is led about as an example to others.

نسکور *nas-kor*, adj. Inverted, upside down, reverse, inverse, antipodal; (Fem.) نسکوره *nas-kora'h*. نسکور والې *nas-kor wālaey*, s.m. (1st) Inversion, contraposition, reversion, anteposition, opposition, antipodes. Pl. والي *wālī*. نسکوريدل *nas-koredal*, verb intrans. To become inverted, reversed, capsized, upturned, upside down. Pres. نسکوريږي *nas-korejzī* (W.) or نسکوريګي *nas-koregī* (E.); past نسکور شه *nas-kor shah* or وُ شه *wu-shah*; fut. نسکور به شي *nas-kor bah shī* or به وُ شي *bah wu-shī*; imp. نسکور شه *nas-kor shah* or وُ شه *wu-shah*; act. part. نسکوريدونکې *nas-koredūnkaey* or نسکوريدونې *nas-koredūnaey*; past part. نسکور *nas-kor* or نسکور شوې *nas-kor shawaey*; verb.n. نسکوريدنه *nas-koredana'h* or نسکوريده *nas-koredah*.

نسکورول *nas-korawul*, verb trans. To invert, to reverse, to overturn, to upset, to turn topsy-turvy, to tilt over, to capsize. Pres. نسکوروي *nas-korawī*; past نسکور کړ *nas-kor karr* or وُ کړ *wu-karr*; fut. نسکور به کړي *nas-kor bah krrī* or

کړي بهٔ وُ *bah wu-krrī*; imp. نسکور کړه *nas-kor krrah* or وُ کړه *wu-krrah*; act. part. نسکوروونکَي *nas-korawūnkaey* or نسکوروونَي *nas-korawūnaey*; past part. نسکور کړَي *nas-kor karraey*; verb. n. نسکورونه *nas-korawuna'h*.

A نسل *nasl*, s.m. (2nd) Race, pedigree, descent, breed, cast, origin, family, offspring, lineage. Pl. نسلونه *naslūnah*. نسلي *naslī*, adj. Of or relating to a family. (Masc. and Fem.)

نسوار *naswār*, s.m. (6th) Snuff. Sing. and Pl. See ناسوار

A نسيم *nasīm*, s.m. (9th) (from نسم) A fragrant air, a gentle zephyr. Sing. and Pl.

A نسيه *nasīah* or *nasiyah*, s.m. (9th) Credit, delay allowed for the payment of money. Sing. and Pl. په نسيه آخستل *pah nasīah ākhistal*, verb trans. To buy on credit.

P نشتر *nashtar*, s.m. (2nd) A lancet, a fleam. Pl. نشترونه *nashtarūnah*. په نشتر وهل *pah nashtar wahal*, verb trans. To bleed, to phlebotomize.

نشته *na-shta'h*, Is not, the negative form of شته

نشم *nashm*, s.m. (2nd) Deceit, artfulness, craft, insidiousness. Pl. نشمونه *nashmūnah*. نشم کول *nashm kawul*, verb trans. To act with artfulness or deceit. See لشمکي

نشمي *nashmī*, adj. Deceitful, insidious, artful; (Fem.) نشمۍ *nashma'ī*. See شتاهه

A نشه *nasha'h*, s.f. (3rd) (from نشو or نشي) Intoxication, intoxicating liquor. Pl. ې *ey*. نشه خور *nasha'h khor*, s.m. (5th) A person who takes intoxicating drinks. Pl. خوران *khorān*. نشه خوره *nasha'h khora'h*, s.f. (3rd) A drunken female. Pl. ې *ey*.

نښان *nishān* (W.) or *nikhān* (E.) s.m. (2nd) A mark, sign, signal, proof, type, emblem, device, impression, scar, badge, flag, standard, colours. 2. A butt for arrows. Pl. نښانونه *nishānūnah* or *nikhānūnah*. نښان ورکول *nishān* or *nikhān war-kawul*, verb trans. To give a sign, signal, emblem, etc. نښانه *nishāna'h* or *nikhāna'h*, s.f. (3rd) A mark for arrows, a target, a butt, aim. Pl. ې *ey*. نښان ويشتل *nishān* or *nikhān-wīshtal*, or نښانه ويشتل *nishāna'h* or *nikhāna'h wīshtal*, verb trans. To hit the mark or butt. (P نشان)

نښاني *nishānī* or *nikhānī*, s.f. (3rd) A mark, a sign, a token, a model. 2. A keepsake, a token of remembrance. Pl. ۍ *a'ī*.

نښتر *nashtar* (W.) or *nakhtar* (E.) s.m. (5th) The mountain pine. Pl. نښتړ *nashtær* or *nakhtær*.

نښتل *n'shatal* (W.) or *n'khatal* (E.), verb intrans. To stick, to cling, to cleave, to hold, to grow or hang together, to become suspended, hitched, fastened, entrapped, as a bird in a net, etc. Pres. نښلي *n'shalī* (W.) or *n'khalī* (E.), past وُ نښت *wu-n'shat* or *wu-n'khat*; fut. وُ به نښلي *wu bah n'shalī* or *n'khalī*; imp. وُ نښله *wu-n'shalah* or *wu-n'khalah*; act. part. نښتونکَي *n'shatūnkaey* or *n'khatūnkaey* or نښتونَي *n'shatūnaey* or *n'khatūnaey*; past part. نښتلَي *n'shatalaey* or *n'khatalaey* or نښتَي *n'shataey* or *n'khataey*; verb. n. نښتنه *n'shatana'h* or *n'khatana'h* or نښته *n'shata'h* or *n'khata'h*.

نښته *n'shata'h* (W.) or *n'khata'h* (E.), s.f. (3rd) (verb. n.) Sticking, clinging, adhering. 2. Confusion, struggling, fighting, clinging, holding fast. 3. Catching, dangling, flapping (as a bird in a net). Pl. ې *ey*; or نښتنه *n'shatana'h* or *n'khatana'h*. Pl. ې *ey*.

نښتَي *n'shataey* (W.) or *n'khataey* (E.), adj. (past part.) Caught, entrapped, stuck, suspended, adhering; (Fem.) نښتِ *n'shati* or *n'khati*. Pl. (Masc. and Fem.) ي *ī*.

نښتِ ژبه *n'shati* or *n'khati jzaba'h*, Stammering-tongue, having an impediment in the speech. ژبه نښتل *jzaba'h n'shatal*, or *n'khatal*, verb trans. To stammer in speaking.

نښتېځل *nashtedzal* (W.) or *nakhtedzal* (E.) To wring, to squeeze out, to press, to strain, to express, to extort, to exact, to extract, etc. Pres. نښتېځي *nashtedzī* or *nakhtedzī*; past وُ نښتېځه *wu-nashtedzah* or *nakhtedzah*; fut. وُ به نښتېځي *wu bah nashtedzī* or *nakhtedzī*; imp. وُ نښتېځه *wu-nashtedzah* or *nakhtedzah*; act. part. نښتېځونکَي *nashtedzūnkaey* or *nakhtedzūnkaey* or نښتيدونى *nashtedzūnaey* or *nakhtedzūnaey*; past part. نښتيدلى *nashtedzalaey* or *nakhtedzalaey*; verb. n. نښتيدنه *nashtedzana'h* or *nakhtedzana'h*. See نچورول

نښليدل *n'shaledal* (W.) or *n'khaledal* (E.) To stick, to cling, to cleave, to grow or hang together, to become suspended, hitched, fastened, entrapped (as a bird in a net), etc. Pres. نښليږي *n'shalejzī* (W.) or نښليګي *n'khalegī* (E.); past وُ نښليده *wu-n'shaledah* or *wu-n'khaledah*; fut. وُ به نښليږي *wu bah n'shalejzī* or نښليګي *n'khalegī*; imp. وُ نښليږه *wu-n'shalejzah* or وُ نښليګه *wu-n'khalegah*; act. part. نښليدونکى *n'shaledūnkaey* or *n'khaledūnkaey* or نښليدونى *n'shaledūnaey* or *n'khaledūnaey*; past part. نښليدلى *n'shaledalaey* or *n'khaledalaey*; verb. n. نښليدنه *n'shaledana'h* or *n'khaledana'h* or نښليده *n'shaledah* or *n'khaledah*. نښلول *n'shalawul* or *n'khalawul*, verb trans. To catch, to hitch, to suspend, to entrap, to embroil, to cause confusion. Pres. نښلوي *n'shalawī* or *n'khalawī*; past وُ نښلاوه *wu-n'shalāwuh* or *wu-n'khalāwuh* or وُ نښلاوو *wu-n'shalāwo* or *wu-n'khalāwo*; fut. وُ به نښلوي *wu bah n'shalawī* or *n'khalawī*; imp. وُ نښلوه *wu-n'shalawah* or *wu-n'khalawah*; act. part. نښلوونکى *n'shalawūnkaey* or *n'khalawūnkaey* or نښلوونى *n'shalawūnaey* or *n'khalawūnaey*; past part. نښلولى *n'shalawulaey* or *n'khalawulaey*; verb. n. نښلونه *n'shalawuna'h* or *n'khalawuna'h*. See نښتل

نښني *na-khaney*, s.f. (3rd) (Pl.) Wrong, impropriety, etc. See ناښني

نښه *nasha'h* (W.) or *nakha'h* (E.) s.f. (3rd) A sign, a mark, a token, an emblem, a countersign, a pass-word. 2. A butt, a target. Pl. ي *ey*. See نخښه

A نصيب *naṣīb*, s.m. (2nd) (from نصب) Fortune, lot, luck, chance, portion, fate, destiny. Pl. نصيبونه *naṣībūnah*.

A نصيحت *naṣī-ḥat*, s.m. (2nd) (from نصح) Advice, counsel, admonition, precept. Pl. نصيحتونه *naṣī-ḥatūnah*. نصيحت كول *naṣī-ḥat kawul*, verb trans. To advise, to counsel, to admonish, to exhort. 2. To reprove, to reprimand; or نصيحت وركول *naṣī-ḥat war-kawul*.

A نظر *naẓar*, s.m. (2nd) Sight, vision, look, regard, a glance, a view, inspection, observation. Pl. نظرونه *naẓarūnah*. نظر كول *naẓar kawul*, verb trans. To look, to see, to behold. نظر بند *naẓar-band*, adj. Strictly watched without being imprisoned, under arrest; (Fem.) نظر بنده *naẓar-banda'h*. نظر بند كول *naẓar-band kawul*, verb trans. To watch closely, to place under arrest. نظر بندي *naẓar bandī*, s.f. (3rd) Confinement, arrest. 2. Fascination, juggle. Pl. ئي *a'ī*.

A نظم *naẓm*, s.m. (2nd) Poetry, verse. 2. Order, arrangement. 3. A string. Pl. نظمونه *naẓmūnah*.

A نعره *naæra'h*, s.f. (3rd) Clamor, noise, shout, crying out. Pl. ي *ey*. نعره زن *naæra'h-zan*, adj. Crying out, shouting, exclaiming; (Fem.) نعره زنه *naæra'h-zana'h*. نعره كول *naæra'h kawul*, verb trans. To shout out, to exclaim. See ناره

A نعل *naæl*, s.m. (2nd) The shoe of a horse, the ferrule of a scabbard. Pl. نعلونه *naælūnah*. نعل بند *naæl-band*, s.m. (5th) A farrier, a blacksmith who shoes horses. Pl. نعلبندان *naæl-bandān*. نعلول *naælawul*, verb trans. To shoe a horse or bullock. See نال and نالول

A نعمت *niæmat*, s.m. (2nd) Favor, graciousness, benefit. 2. Delight, joy. 3. Affluence, ease, wealth, comforts of life. Pl. نعمتونه *niæmatūnah*. نعمت لرل *niæmat laral*, verb trans. To have or possess the comforts of life, ease, or affluence. نعمت وركول *niæmat war-kawul*, verb trans. To grant a favor, benefit, etc.

A نعوذ بالله *na'æūẕu-bi-l-lāhi*, interj. Let us flee to God for protection (from anything wicked).

نغاره *naghāra'h*, s.f. (3rd) A kettle drum. Pl. ي *ey*. نغارچي *naghārchī*, s.m. (5th) One who beats the kettle drum. Pl. نغارچيان *naghārchīān*. See A نقاره

نغاړل *n'ghāṛral*, verb trans. To twist, to roll up, or fold up, as a cloth or mat; to coil up, to wrap up, to pack, etc. Pres. نغاړي *n'ghārrī*; past وُ نغاړه *wu-n'ghārrah*; fut. وُ به نغاړي *wu bah n'ghārrī*; imp. وُ نغاړه *wu-n'ghārrah*; act. part. نغاړونکَي *n'ghārrūnkaey* or نغاړونَي *n'ghārrūnaey*; past part. نغاړلَي *n'ghārralaey*; verb. n. نغاړنه *n'ghārrana'h*.

نغتل *n'ghutal*, verb trans. To obey, to attend to, to listen to, to hearken to, to attend, to regard, to give heed to. See نغوتل

نغري *n'gharaey*, s.m. (1st) A fire-place. Pl. ي *ī*.

نغړدل *n'gharrdal*, verb trans. To swallow, to bolt, to take down, to gulp. Pres. نغړي *n'gharrī*; past وُ نغړد *wu-n'gharrd*; fut. وُ به نغړي *wu bah n'gharrī*; imp. وُ نغړه *wu-n'gharra'h*; act. part. نغړدونکَي *n'gharrdūnkaey* or نغړدونَي *n'gharrdūnaey*; past part. نغړدلَي *n'gharrdalaey* or نغړدَي *n'gharrdaey*; verb. n. نغړدنه *n'gharrdana'h*.

نغښتل *n'ghashtal* (W.) or *n'ghakhtal* (E.) verb trans. To wrap up, to roll up, to fold, to pack. Past وُ نغښت *wu-n'ghasht* or *wu-n'ghakht*; act. part. نغښتونکَي *n'ghashtūnkaey* or *n'ghakhtūnkaey* or نغښتونَي *n'ghashtūnaey* or *n'ghakhtūnaey*; past part. نغښتلَي *n'ghashtalaey* or *n'ghakhtalaey*; verb. n. نغښته *n'ghashta'h* or *n'ghakhta'h*. The other inflections are wanting, and are taken from نغاړل, which see.

نغلاند *nagh-lānd*, adj. Hungry, craving, sharp-set, voracious, desirous; (Fem.) نغلانده *nagh-lānda'h*. نغلاندَي *nagh-lāndaey*, s.m. (1st) A hungry, peckish person. Pl. ي *ī*. نغلاندِ *nagh-lāndi*, s.f. (8th). Pl. ي *ī*. نغلاند سترگي *nagh-lānd stargey*, adj. A greedy, rapacious, insatiable, or covetous person, hungry-eyed; (Fem.) نغلاند سترگِ *nagh-lānd stargi*. Pl. (Masc. and Fem.) نغلاند سترگي *nagh-lānd stargī*.

P نغم *nagham*, s.m. (2nd) A mine, a subterranean passage. Pl. نغمونه *naghamūnah*.

A نغمه *naghma'h*, s.f. (3rd) Melody, song, modulation. 2. A musical note. Pl. ې *ey*.

نغوتان *n'ghwatān*, s.m. (9th) (verb. n.) Hearing, listening, attending, giving ear to, obeying, etc. Sing. and Pl. See نغوتل

نغوتل *n'ghwatal*, verb trans. To give ear to, to attend, to listen, to obey, to regard, etc. Pres. نغوږي *n'ghwajzī* (W.) or نغوگي *n'ghwagī* (E.); past وُ نغوت *wu-n'ghwat*; fut. وُ به نغوږي *wu bah n'ghwajzī* or نغوگي *n'ghwagī*; imp. وُ نغوږه *wu-n'ghwajzah* or وُ نغوگه *wu-n'ghwagah*; act. part. نغوتونکَي *n'ghwatūnkaey* or نغوتونَي *n'ghwatūnaey*; past part. نغوتلَي *n'ghwatalaey*; verb. n. نغوتنه *n'ghwatana'h* or نغوته *n'ghwata'h*.

نغوتنه *n'ghwatana'h* or نغوته *n'ghwata'h*, s.f. (3rd) (verb. n.) Attending, giving ear to; regard, attention, obedience. Pl. ې *ey*.

نغَي *nughaey*, s.m. (1st) A scar, a cicatrix, a brand, a mark made by burning with a hot iron, cutting off the nose, ears, etc., a mark of infamy. Pl. ي *ī*. نغنَي *nughanaey*, adj. Branded, marked, stigmatized; (Fem.) نغنِ *nughani*. Pl. (Masc. and Fem.) ي *ī*. نغَي ايښول *nughaey aeshawul* (W.) or *aekhawul* (E.) verb trans. To brand, to impress a mark with a hot iron as a sign of infamy.

A نفاق *nifāk*, s.m. (9th) (from نفق) Hypocrisy, fallacy, prevarication. 2. Disagreement, enmity. Sing. and Pl.

A نفر *nafr* or *nafar*, s.m. (5th) A groom, a servant, a person, an individual. Pl. نفران *nafarān*. نفره *nafra'h* or *nafara'h*, s.f. (3rd). Pl. ې *ey*.

A نفرت *nafrat*, s.m. (2nd) Abomination, disgust, aversion, abhorrence, detestation. Pl. نفرتونه *nafratūnah*.

P نفرين *nafrīn*, s.m. (2nd) A curse, an imprecation. Pl. نفرينونه *nafrīnūnah*. See ښرا

A نفس *nafas*, s.m. (2nd) The breath, respiration, the voice or sound from the breast. Pl. نفسونه *nafasūnah*. نفس کښل *nafas k'shal* or ښکل *kh'kal*, verb trans. To breathe, to draw breath. نفس وهل *nafas wahal* or شړل *sharral*, verb trans. To pant, to breathe heavily. See شاخ

A نفس *nafs*, s.m. (2nd) The soul, spirit, essence, self. 2. Sensuality, concupiscence. 3. Desire. 4. Sperm. 5. Gravity, pride. 6. Envy. 7. Vice. Pl. نفسونه *nafsūnah*. نفس وجلل *nafs waj-lal* or نفس وژل *nafs wajzal* (W.), verb trans. To mortify the sensual desires.

A P نفساني *nafsānī*, adj. Sensual, carnal, lustful, luxurious. (Masc. and Fem.)

نفعه *nafæa'h*, s.f. (3rd) (corrup. of A نفع) Gain, profit, advantage, interest. Pl. ي *ey*. نفعه لرل *nafæa'h laral*, verb trans. To have or possess advantage or profit (Eng. To be profitable or advantageous). نفعه کول *nafæa'h kawul*, verb trans. To profit, to benefit.

A نفقه *nafaḳa'h*, s.f. (3rd) Necessary expenses of living. Pl. ي *ey*.

A نفل *nafl*, s.m. (2nd) A voluntary act of devotion which may be omitted, a work of supererogation. Pl. نفلونه *nafl-ūnah*.

نفيه *nafia'h*, s.f. (3rd) (corrup. of A نفي) Forbidding, prohibition. 2. Rejecting, refusing. 3. Negation. 4. Nonexistence, refuse. Pl. ي *ey*.

A نقاب *niḳāb*, s.m. (2nd) (from نقب) A veil. Pl. نقابونه *niḳābūnah*. See پروني

A نقاره *naḳāra'h*, s.f. (3rd) A kettle drum. Pl. ي *ey*. See نغاره

A نقد *naḳd*, s.m. (6th) Ready money, cash. Sing. and Pl.

A نقدي *naḳdī*, adj. Relating to cash, in cash, possessing ready money, moneyed. (Masc. and Fem.)

A نقره *nuḳra'h*, s.f. (3rd) (from نقر) Silver. Pl. ي *ey*. See سپين زر

نقرائي *nuḳ-rā'ī*, adj. Made of silver, silver. (Masc. and Fem.)

A نقش *naḳsh*, s.m. (2nd) Painting, embroidering, carving, engraving, delineation, plan, drawing, impression, etc. Pl. نقشونه *naḳshūnah*. نقاش *naḳāsh*, s.m. (5th) An engraver, a carver, painter, etc. Pl. نقاشان *naḳāshān*. نقاشه *naḳāsha'h*, Feminine of the preceding. Pl. ي *ey*.

A نقشه *naḳsha'h*, s.f. (3rd) A model, a pattern, a map, a chart, a delineation, a drawing. Pl. ي *ey*. نقشي *naḳshī*, adj. Painted, drawn, delineated.

A نقصان *nuḳṣān*, s.m. (2nd) (from نقص) Loss, defect, deficiency, detriment, damage, injury, blemish, prejudice, mischief. Pl. نقصانونه *nuḳṣānūnah*. نقصان لرل *nuḳṣān laral*, verb trans. To possess or bear injury, detriment, loss (*i.e.*, 'to be injurious or detrimental'). نقصان کول *nuḳṣān kawul*, verb trans. To make or cause loss, deficiency, detriment, injury.

A P نقصاني *nuḳṣānī*, adj. Detrimental, injurious, prejudicial. (Masc. and Fem.)

A نقطه *nuḳ-ṭa'h*, s.f. (3rd) A point, a dot, a spot, a stain, a vowel. 2. (met.) A fault, a flaw. Pl. ي *ey*. نقطه يښول *nuḳ-ṭa'h yeshawul* or *yeKhawul*, verb trans. To criticise, to impute a fault to.

A نقل *naḳl*, s.m. (2nd) A history, narrative, tale, story, anecdote, fable. 2. Copying, mimicing, acting. 3. Transcript, copy, counterpart. 4. Removing, translation from one place to another. Pl. نقلونه *naḳlūnah*. نقل کول *naḳl kawul*, verb trans. To copy, to transcribe. 2. To relate, to narrate. نقلي *naḳlī*, adj. Copied, traditional, fictitious. 2. s.m. (5th) A narrator, a story-teller. Pl. نقليان *naḳlī-ān*.

نکاح *nikāḥ*, s.m. (2nd) Matrimony, marriage. 2. Copulation. Pl. نکاحونه *nikāḥ-ūnah*. نکاح ترل *nikāḥ tarral*, verb trans. To marry (to perform the ceremony as a priest). نکاح کول *nikāḥ kawul*, verb trans. To marry, to take a wife.

A نکته *nukta'h*, s.m. (3rd) (from نکت) A point of wit, a wise or pithy saying. Pl. ي *ey*. نکته ويل *nukta'h wa-yal*, verb trans. To make a witty speech. نکته گير *nukta'h-gīr*, s.m. (5th) Subtle, sagacious person. 2. adj. Subtle, nice. Pl. نکته گيران *nukta'h-gīrān*. نکته گيره *nukta'h-gīra'h*, adj. and s.f. (3rd). Pl. ي *ey*. نکته گيري *nukta'h-gīrī*, s.f. (3rd) Criticism, sagacity, captiousness, cavil. Pl. ي *a'ī*. نکته گيري کول *nukta'h gīrī kawul*, verb trans. To criticise, to cavil at.

نکريزي *nukrezey* or *nakrezey*, s.f. (3rd) Pl. The name of a dye, Eastern privet, ḥinnā. The Sing. form not used.

A نکهت *nuk-hat*, s.m. (2nd) Perfume, anything odoriferous. Pl. نکهتونه *nuk-hat-ūnah*.

A نكير *nakīr*, s. prop. The name of an angel. See منكر

P نگار *nigār*, s.m. (6th) A picture, an idol, an effigy. Sing. and Pl. نگاره *nigāra'h*, s.f. (3rd) A beautiful woman, a mistress. Pl. ې *ey*. نقش و نگار *naḳsh-o-nigār*, Portraits, paintings, etc.

P نگاه *nigāh*, s.m. (2nd) A look, a glance, a sight, a view, aspect. 2. Watching, observation. 3. Care, custody. Pl. نگاهونه *nigāh-ūnah*. نگاه کول *nigāh kawul*, verb trans. To observe, to regard, to view, to oversee.

P نگاهبان *nigāh-bān*, s.m. (5th) A guard, a keeper, an observer. Pl. نگاهبانان *nigāh-bānān*. نگاهبانه *nigāh-bāna'h*, s.f. (3rd) Feminine of the preceding. Pl. ې *ey*.

P نگاهباني *nigāh-bānī*, s.f. (3rd) Watching, guarding, taking care of, guardianship. Pl. ئي *a'ī*. نگاهباني کول *nigāh-bānī kawul*, verb trans. To guard, to protect.

نګبي *n'gubaey*, s.m. (1st) The pommel of a saddle. Pl. ي *ī*. See کاش and انه

نګښي *n'gas̲h̲aey* (W.) or *n'gak̲h̲aey* (E.), s.m. (1st) The hair plaited on the temples or foreheads of young women. Pl. ي *ī*.

نګوبي *n'gūbaey*, s.m. (1st) The pommel of a saddle. Pl. ي *ī*. See نګبي

نګور *n'gor*, s.f. (5th) A son's wife. Pl. نګیندې *n'gendey* or نګینډِ *n'gendi*. See نرور

نګولئ *n'golaey*, s.m. (1st) Meat or fish, etc., eaten with bread and rice. Pl. ي *ī*. See قتغ

نګون *nigūn*, adj. Hanging downwards, upside down; (Fem.) نګونه *nigūna'h*. نګون بخت *nigūn bak̲h̲t*, adj. Helpless, unfortunate; (Fem.) نګون بخته *nigūn bak̲h̲ta'h*. See نسکور

نګه *nigah*, contract. of نګاه which see.

نګهبان *nigah-bān* and نګهباني *nigahbānī*. See نګاهبان, etc.

نګئ *n'gaey*, s.m. (1st) (E.) A sneeze. Pl. ي *ī*. نګئ کول *n'gaey kawul*, verb trans. To sneeze; or نګل *n'gal*, verb trans. For inflections see (W.) نږل *n'jzal*, substituting ګ for ږ. See پرچ

نګول *n'gawul*, verb trans. (caus.) To cause or make to sneeze (as snuff, etc.)

S نل *nal*, s.m. (5th) A cane, a tube, the stalk of a tree, a reed, a shepherd's pipe. Pl. نلان *nalān*. نل وهل *nal wahal*, verb trans. To play on the pipe. See شپیلۍ and درمه

نل پیچ *nal-pec̲h̲*, s.m. (2nd) The tube of a ḥukkah or tobacco pipe. Pl. نل پیچونه *nal-pec̲h̲ūnah*.

نله *nula'h*, s.f. (3rd) A ureter, a urinary duct. Pl. ې *ey*.

نم *nam*, adj. The ninth; (Fem.) نمه *nama'h*. See نهم

P نم *nam*, adj. Moist, damp, wet, humid; (Fem.) نمه *nama'h*. 2. s.m. (2nd) Moistness, dampness, humidity. Pl. نمونه *namūnah*. نم دار *nam-dār* or نم ناك *nam-nāk*, adj. Moist, damp, wet; (Fem.) نم داره *nam-dāra'h* or نم ناکه *nam-nāka'h*. نم ناکي *nam nākī*, s.f. (3rd) Dampness, moistness, moisture, humidity. Pl. ئي *a'ī*. نم کیدل *nam kedal*, verb intrans. To become moist, damp, wet. نم کول *nam kawul*, verb trans. To make wet or damp, to moisten. See نو and لوند

نمازل *n'māzal*, verb trans. To nourish, to support, to maintain, to foster, to sustain, to rear, to bring up, to patronize, to protect, to educate, to nurse. Pres. نمازي *n'māzī*; past وُ نمازه *wu-n'māzah*; fut. وُ به نمازي *wu bah n'māzī*; imp. وُ نمازه *wu-n'māzah*; act. part. نمازونکئ *n'māzūnkaey* or نمازونئ *n'māzūn-aey*; past part. نمازلئ *n'māzalaey*; verb. n. نمازنه *n'māzana'h*. See نمانځل

نمازنه *n'māzana'h*, s.f. (3rd) (verb. n.) Nourishment, support, maintenance, protection; sustaining, rearing, fostering, etc. Pl. ې *ey*.

نماست *n'māst*, adj. Sitting, lying down, reclining, stretched out at full length; (Fem.) نماسته *n'māsta'h*. See خملاست and ملاست

نماښام *n'mā s̲h̲ām* (W.) or *n'mā-k̲h̲ām* (E.), s.m. (9th) Early evening, the time of evening prayer (corrup. of P نماز شام).

نمایه *nimāyah*, adj. See نیم

نمانځل *n'mān̲d̲z̲al*, verb trans. To nourish, to support, to sustain, to foster, to rear, to nurse, to bring up, to protect, to patronize, to educate, etc. Pres. نمانځي *n'mān̲d̲z̲ī*; past وُ نمانځه

wu-n'mān<u>dz</u>ah ; fut. وُ به نمانځي *wu bah n'mān<u>dz</u>ī* ; imp. وُ نمانځه *wu-n'mān<u>dz</u>ah* ; act. part. نمانځونکي *n'mān<u>dz</u>ūnkaey* or نمانځونَي *n'mān<u>dz</u>ūnaey*; past part. نمانځلي *n'mān<u>dz</u>al-aey* ; verb. n. نمانځنه *n'mān<u>dz</u>ana'h.*

نمانځنه *n'mān<u>dz</u>ana'h,* s.f. (3rd) (verb. n.) Nourishment, protection, sustenance, protection, support; rearing, nursing, bringing up, patronizing, educating, etc. Pl. ي *ey.*

نمد *numd,* adj. Wet, damp, moist; (Fem.) نمده *numda'h.* نمد والي *numd-wālaey,* s.m. (1st) Dampness, wetness, humidity. Pl. والي *wālī.* See لوند

نمر *n'mar,* s.m. (2nd) The sun, sunshine. Pl. نمرونه *n'marūnah.* د نمر روښنائي *da n'mar ro<u>sh</u>nā'ī* (W.) or *ro<u>kh</u>nā'ī* (E.), s.f. (3rd) The light of the sun, sunshine. Pl. ئي *a'ī.* نمر پريوتل *n'mar pre-watal,* verb intrans. To set, to go down (as the sun); or نمر لويدل *n'mar l'wedal* (W.) verb intrans. or نمر ختل *n'mar <u>kh</u>atal* (E.), verb intrans. To rise (as the sun). نمر پريواته *n'mar pre-wātah,* s.m. (6th) Sunset, the going down of the sun. 2. The west. Sing. and Pl. نمر خاته *n'mar <u>kh</u>ātah,* s.m. (6th) The rising of the sun, sunrise. 2. The east. Sing. and Pl. نمر تندر نيول *n'mar tandar nī-wal,* verb trans. To eclipse (*lit.* The sun to take an eclipse). See نور

A نمرود *nimrūd,* s. prop. Nimrod.

نمري *n'marī,* s.m. (1st) Pl. Clothes, dress, habiliments.

نمړ *numarr,* adv. Before, previously, ere now, formerly, prior, etc. 2. adj. Fixed, determined, appointed, pledged. 3. Betrothed, promised, engaged; (Fem.) نمړه *numa<u>rr</u>a'h.* نمړ کول *numa<u>rr</u> kawul,* verb trans, To determine, to fix, to engage, to betroth.

نمړي *numa<u>rr</u>aey,* adj. Previous, former, before, preceding, antecedent, anterior; (Fem.) نمړئي *numa<u>rr</u>a'ī.*

نمړئي *n'ma<u>rr</u>a'ī,* s.f. (6th) A mouthful. 2. Bread. Sing. and Pl.

نمسي *n'masaey,* s.m. (1st) A grandson. Pl. ي *ī.* نمسئي *n'masa'ī,* s.f. (6th) A grand-daughter. Sing. and Pl.

P نمک *namak,* s.m. (9th) Salt; used only in composition, as نمک حرام *namak ḥarām,* adj. Disloyal, wicked, perfidious, traitor, ungrateful; (Fem.) نمک حرامه *namak ḥarāma'h.* نمک حرامي *namak ḥarāmī,* s.f. (3rd) Disloyalty, perfidy, treachery, ingratitude. Pl. ئي *a'ī.* نمک حرامي کول *namak ḥarāmī kawul,* verb trans. To act perfidiously, disloyally, or traitorously. نمک حلال *namak ḥalāl,* adj. Loyal, faithful, grateful; (Fem.) نمک حلاله *namak ḥalāla'h.* نمک حلالي *namak ḥalālī,* s.f. (3rd) Fidelity, loyalty, gratitude. Pl. ئي *a'ī.* نمک حلالي کول *namak ḥalālī kawul,* verb trans. To show fidelity, loyalty, gratitude.

نمله *namla'h,* s.f. (3rd) A pad for a horse, or for a saddle. Pl. ي *ey.*

P نمود *namūd,* s.m. (2nd) (from P نمودن) Index, guide, show, display, appearance. Pl. نمودونه *namūdūnah.* نمود کول *namūd kawul,* verb trans. To display, to exhibit, to show, to expose.

P نمودار *namūdār,* s.m. (5th) An exemplar, a proof, a symbol, specimen, model. Pl. نموداران *namūdārān.* 2. adj. Famed, noted, conspicuous, manifest, showy, gaudy; (Fem.) نموداره *namūdāra'h.*

نمونځ *n'mūn<u>dz</u>,* s.m. (4th) (E.) Prayer, supplication. Pl. نمانځَ *n'mān<u>dz</u>a* or نمانځه *n'mān<u>dz</u>ah*; (W.), s.m. (2nd). Pl. نمونځونه *n'mūn<u>dz</u>ūnah.* نمونځ کول *n'mūn<u>dz</u> kawul,* verb trans. To pray, to offer up a prayer. نمانځي *n'mān<u>dz</u>ī,* adj. One who prays, pious, religious; or نمانځ گذار *n'mān<u>dz</u>-gu<u>z</u>ār*; (Fem.) نمانځ گذاره *n'mān<u>dz</u> gu<u>z</u>āra'h.*

P نمونه *namūna'h,* s.f. (3rd) A pattern, example, sample, model, type, specimen, muster. Pl. ي *ey.*

P نمي *namī,* s.f. (3rd) Dampness, humidity. Pl. ئي *a'ī.* See لونه and نو

نن *nan,* adv. To-day, this day. نن روځ *nan-rwa<u>dz</u>* or ننئي روځ *nanana'ī-rwa<u>dz</u>,* To-day, this very day. نن شپه nan-<u>sh</u>pa'h, To-night; or ننني شپه nanana'ī-<u>sh</u>pa'h. نن و صبا nan-o-ṣabā, Now-a-days, to-day or to-morrow, in a day or two.

ننداره nandāra'h, s.f. (3rd) A spectacle, sight, show, entertainment, amusement, fun, etc. Pl. نندارې nan-dārey. نندارچي nandār<u>ch</u>ī, s.m. (5th) A spectator, a beholder, an observer, a looker on, a witness, a bystander. Pl. نندارچيان nandār<u>ch</u>īān. نندارچي nandār-<u>ch</u>ī, s.f. (5th). Pl. نندارچيانِ nandār<u>ch</u>īāni. ننداره كول nandāra'h kawul, verb trans. To make a show, display, pageant, spectacle, parade, etc.; to get up an entertainment.

ننزړه nanzaṛrah, s.m. (6th) Tar, a resinous substance obtained from the pine. Sing. and Pl. See زرنړه and رانځره

P ننګ nang, s.m. (2nd) Honor, reputation, good name, esteem. 2. Disgrace, infamy. Pl. ننګونه nangūnah. ننګ و ناموس nang-o-nāmūs, Honor, reputation. 2. Disgrace, ignominy. ننګ يالَي nang-yālaey, adj. Honorable, reputable, esteemed. 2. s.m. (1st) An esteemed or respected person. Pl. ننګ يالي nang-yālī. ننګ يالۍ nang-yāla'ī, s.f. (6th) A female as above. Sing. and Pl. ننګ كول nang kawul, verb trans. To act honorably.

نننَي nananey, adj. Hodiernal, of to-day, of this day; (Fem.) ننني nanana'ī. See نن

ننوتل nana-watal, verb intrans. To enter, to go in, to come into, to introduce one's-self, to find one's way into. 2. To take refuge with a person, to throw one's-self on the protection of another. Pres. ننوزي nanawuzī; past ننووت nanawot; fut. نن به وزي nana bah wuzī; imp. ننوزه nanawuzah; act. part. ننوتونكَي nanawatūnkaey or ننوتونَي nanawatūnaey; past part. ننوتلَي nanawatalaey; verb. n. ننوتنه nanawatana'h or ننواته nanawāta'h.

ننواته nanawātah, s.m. (6th) (verb. n.) Entrance, ingress, admission, introduction. 2. Taking refuge or sanctuary in the house of another and refusing to eat or drink until one's request be complied with, and which it is considered a point of honor to accede to; asking assistance. 3. Shelter, refuge, asylum. Sing. and Pl. ننواتَي nanawātaey, (past part.) as s.m. (1st) A person who has taken refuge in the house of another. ننواتِ nanawāti, s.f. (8th) A female who has taken refuge, a refugee. Pl. (Masc. and Fem.) ي ī.

ننه nanah, adv. Inside, in, within. See دننه

ننيستل nana-yastal, verb trans. To insert, to introduce, to make or cause to enter, to lead or bring in, to conduct and make known, to import, to insinuate, etc. This infinitive, like يستل, from which it is taken, is imperfect, using the present tenses of باسل to complete it. Pres. ننباسي nana-bāsī; past ننيوست nana-yost; fut. نن به باسي nana bah bāsī; imp. ننباسه nana-bāsah; act. part. ننيستونكَي nana-yastūnkaey or ننيستونَي nana-yastūnaey; past part. ننيستلَي nana-yastalaey; verb. n. ننيستنه nana-yastana'h.

نو naw, s.m. (2nd) (W.) Moisture, humidity, dampness, wetness. Pl. نوونه naw-ūnah. See لوند. نون nawan (W.) adj. Damp, moist, humid; (Fem.) نونه nawana'h; or نون nau-an, and نونه nau-ana'h; also نوجن. nau-jan and نوجنه nau-jana'h.

نو nū, s.m. (9th) The navel. Sing. and Pl. See نوم

A نواب nuwwāb, s.m. (5th) A nābob, a governor, a chief. Pl. نوابان nuwwābān. نوابه nuwwāba'h, s.f. (3rd) The wife of a nābob or chief. Pl. ې ey.

A نواحي nawāḥī, s.f. (3rd) (Pl. of ناحيه) Territories, environs, parts, suburbs. Pl. ئې a'ī.

HI نوار niwār or nawār, s.m. (6th) Tape of a coarse kind, used for fastenings or strings of drawers, lacings of beds, etc. Sing. and Pl.

نواره nawāra'h, s.f. (3rd) A habitation, an inhabited, pleasant, or cultivated place; cultivation, population, prosperity. Pl. ې ey. نواره كول nawāra'h kawul, verb trans. To people, to populate, to bring under cultivation, etc.

نواړ niwāṛr or nawāṛr, s.m. (6th). Sing. and Pl. See نوار

نواړي nawāṛraey, s.m. (1st) The belt of a pair

of drawers or breeches, the part of the drawers through which the string runs. 3. A kind of double seam, a fell. Pl. ي *ī*. See سروزنه

P نواز *nawāz*, act. part. (in composition) Cherishing, caressing, soothing; (Fem.) نوازه *nawāza'h*.

P نوازش *nawāzi<u>sh</u>*, s.m. (2nd) Caress, blandishment, kindness, favor, patronage. Pl. نوازشونه *nawāzi<u>sh</u>ūnah*. نوازش کول *nawāzi<u>sh</u> kawul*, verb trans. To patronize, to favor, to cherish.

P نوبهار *no-bahār*, s.m. (9th) The spring. Sing. and Pl. See پسرلي

A نوبت *naubat* or *nobat*, s.m. (2nd) (from نوب) Time, period, turn, access (of fever), a fit. 2. Relieving guard, keeping watch. 3. An accident. 4. Opportunity, occasion, vicissitude. 5. Instruments of music sounded at the gate of a great man. 6. (fig.) Death. Pl. نوبتونه *naubatūnah* or *nobatūnah*. نوبت خانه *naubat-<u>kh</u>āna'h*, s.f. (3rd) A guard or watchhouse. Pl. ې *ey*. نوبت ږغول *naubat <u>jz</u>a<u>gh</u>awul* (W.) or غږول *<u>gh</u>agawul* (E.) or وهل *wahal*, verb trans. To beat the *naubat*. See وار

نور *nūr*, adj. Other, another, not the same, quite another thing, different, more. 2. adv. Moreover, likewise, furthermore, besides; (Fem.) نوره *nūra'h*. نور څوک *nūr <u>ts</u>ok*, Another or a different person. نور کله *nūr kalah*, A different time, another time. نور نور *nūr-nūr*, Various, different, diverse, heterogeneous, multifarious; (Fem.) نوري نوري *nūrey-nūrey*. نوریدل *nūredal*, verb intrans. To be different, to be other, to differ, to vary, to change, to be variable. Pres. نورېږي *nūre<u>jz</u>ī* (W.) or نوریگي *nūregī* (E.); past نور شه *nūr <u>sh</u>ah* or وُ شه *wu-<u>sh</u>ah*; fut. نور به شي *nūr bah <u>sh</u>ī* or به وُ شي *bah wu-<u>sh</u>ī*; imp. نور شه *nūr-<u>sh</u>ah* or وُ شه *wu-<u>sh</u>ah*; act. part. نوریدونکي *nūredūnkaey* or نوریدوني *nūredūnaey*; past part. نور *nūr* or نور شوي *nūr <u>sh</u>awaey*; verb. n. نوریدنه *nūredana'h* or نوریده *nūredah*. نورول *nūrawul*, verb trans. To vary, to change, to alter, to render different, to modify, to transform. Pres. نوروي *nūrawī*; past نور کړ *nūr ka<u>rr</u>* or وُ کړ *wu-ka<u>rr</u>*; fut. نور به کړي *nūr bah k<u>rr</u>ī* or به وُ کړي *bah wu-k<u>rr</u>ī*; imp. نور کړه *nūr k<u>rr</u>ah* or وُ کړه *wu-k<u>rr</u>ah*; act. part. نوروونکي *nūrawūnkaey* or نوروونې *nūrawūnaey*; past part. نور کړي *nūr-ka<u>rr</u>aey*; verb. n. نوروونه *nūrawuna'h*.

نور *n'war*, s.m. (2nd) The sun, sunshine. Pl. نورونه *n'warūnah*. نور پريوتل *n'war pre-watal*, verb intrans. To set, to go down (as the sun), or نور لويدل *n'war l'wedal* (W.) verb intrans. نور ختل *n'war-<u>kh</u>atal*, verb intrans. To rise as the sun. نور پريواته *n'war pre-wātah*, s.m. (6th) Sunset, the going down of the sun. 2. The west. Sing. and Pl. نور خاته *n'war <u>kh</u>ātah*, s.m. (6th) The rising of the sun, sunrise. 2. The east. Sing. and Pl. نور تندر نيول *n'war tandar nī-wal*, verb trans. To eclipse (*lit.* The sun to take an eclipse). د نور روښنائي *da n'war ro<u>sh</u>nā'ī*, or *ro<u>kh</u>nā'ī*, s.f. (3rd) Sunlight, sunshine. Pl. ئي *a'ī*. See نمر

A نور *nūr*, s.m. (2nd) Light, splendor. Pl. نورونه *nūrūnah*. د سترگو نور *da sturgo nūr*, s.m. (2nd) The light of the eyes. 2. A son. Pl. نورونه *nūrūnah*. See رڼا

A P نوراني *nūrānī*, adj. Serene, bright, light, clear. (Masc. and Fem.)

نورز *n'waraz*, s.f. (1st) A sandpiper or titmouse. 2. A quail. (?) Pl. نورزِ *n'warazi*. See چتي

نورزي *nūr-zī*, s.m. (1st) Pl. The name of a powerful tribe of the Af<u>gh</u>āns. نورزي *nūr-zaey* (Sing.) A male of the Nūr-zī tribe. نورزئي *nūr-za'ī*, s.f. (6th) A female of the above. Sing. and Pl.

P نوروز *nau-roz*, s.m. (2nd) New year's day of the Persian calendar. Pl. نوروزونه *nau-rozūnah*.

نوري *n'waraey*, s.m. (1st) A garment, a dress, a vestment. Pl. ي *ī*. نوري آغوستل *n'warī ā<u>gh</u>ūstal*, verb trans. To put on one's clothes, to dress one's-self, to array, to apparel.

نوړز *n'wa<u>rr</u>z*, s.f. (1st) A quail. Pl. نوړزِ *n'wa<u>rr</u>azi*. See نورز and مړز

نوړزه *n'wa<u>rr</u>aza'h*, s.f. (3rd) A quail. Pl. ې *ey*. See preceding.

نوړئي *n'wa<u>rr</u>a'ī*, s.f. (6th) A morsel, a mouthful. 2. Bread. Sing. and Pl. See مړئي and نمړئي

نوړيدل *n'warredal*, verb intrans. To peel off, to become stripped, pared, excoriated. نوړول *n'warrawul*, verb trans. To peel, to strip off, to excoriate. See لوړيدل and لوړول and substitute ن for ل

نوږ *nojz* (W.) or نوګ *nog* (E.) adj. Pure, clean, genuine, unmixed, unadulterated; unsullied, spotless, taintless, immaculate. Pl. (Masc.) نارږه *nājzah* or ناګه *nāgah*; (Fem.) نوږه *nojza'h* or نوګه *noga'h*. Pl. نوږي *nojzey* or نوګي *nogey*.

نوس *nos*, s.m. (2nd) The soul, spirit, essence, substance, self. 2. Lust, sensuality, inordinate desire (corrup. of A نفس which see). Pl. نوسونه *nos-ūnah*.

نوسي *n'wasaey*, s.m. (1st) A grandson. Pl. ي *ī*.

نوسۍ *n'wasa'ī*, s.f. (6th) A grand-daughter. Sing. and Pl. See نمسي

نوعه *nauæ'h*, s.f. (3rd) (corrup. of A نوع) Species, kind, sort, manner, mode. Pl. ې *ey*.

نوک *nūk*, s.m. (2nd) The nail of a finger or toe, the claw of an animal or bird. Pl. نوکونه *nūkūna'h*. (W.) s.m. (5th). Pl. نوکان *nūkān*. (P *nok*).

نوکاره *nūkāra'h*, s.f. (3rd) Scratching, scraping with the nails, clawing, tearing with the nails. 2. A scratch, a slight wound. Pl. ې *ey*. نوکاري کول *nūkārey kawul*, verb trans. To scratch, to claw, to rend or tear with the nails or talons.

P نوکر *nau-kar*, s.m. (5th) A servant, an attendant, a servitor, a vassal. Pl. نوکران *nau-karān*. نوکره *nau-kara'h*, s.f. (3rd) A female servant. Pl. ې *ey*.

P نوکري *nau-karī*, s.f. (3rd) Service, dependence, servitude, vassalage, attendance. Pl. ۍ *a'ī*. نوکري کول *nau-karī kawul*, verb trans. To perform service, to serve, to attend on. نوکر پيشه *nau-kar pesha'h*, One who lives on servitude or attendance.

نوګ *nog* (E.) adj. Pure, genuine, unadulterated; clean, unsullied, spotless, taintless, immaculate. Pl. ناګه *nāgah*; (Fem.) نوګه *noga'h*. Pl. ې *ey*. See نوږ

نول *nūl*, s.m. (2nd) Grief, sorrow, affliction, concern, distress of mind. Pl. نولونه *nūlūnah*. See نوليدل etc.

نولس *naw-las*, adj. Nineteen. نو لسم *naw-lasam*, The nineteenth; (Fem.) نو لسمه *naw-lasama'h*.

نولئ *no-lacy*, s.m. (1st) A mongoose, a ferret, a weasel. Pl. ي *ī*.

نوليدل *nūledal*, verb intrans. To waste away, to pine (through sorrow), to grieve, to fret, to mourn, to worry one's-self, to droop, to despair. Pres. نوليږي *nūlejzī* (W.) or نوليګي *nūlegī* (E.) past وُ نوليده *wu-nūledah*; fut. وُ به نوليږي *wu bah nūlejzī* or نوليګي *nūlegī*; imp. وُ نوليږه *wu-nūlejzah* or وُ نوليګه *wu-nūlegah*; act. part. نوليدونکئ *nūledūnkaey* or نوليدونئ *nūledūnaey*; past part. نوليدلئ *nūledalaey*; verb. n. نوليدنه *nūledana'h*. نولول *nūlawul*, verb trans. To make or cause to pine, to fret, to aggrieve, to worry, to make to droop or despair, to make thin or emaciated (as grief). Pres. نولوي *nūlawī*; past وُ نولاوه *wu-nūlāwuh* or وُ نولاوو *wu-nūlāwo*; fut. وُ به نولوي *wu bah nūlawī*; imp. وُ نولوه *wu-nūlawah*; act. part. نولوونکي *nūlawūnkaey* or نولوونئ *nūlawūnaey*; past part. نولولئ *nūlawulaey*; verb. n. نولونه *nūlawuna'h*.

نوم *nūm*, s.m. (2nd) Name, appellation, reputation, character, honor, fame. 2. The navel. Pl. نومونه *nūmūnah*. نوم ور *nūm-war*, adj. Famous, renowned, celebrated; (Fem.) نومه وره *nūma'h-wara'h*. نوم وري *nūm warī*, s.f. (3rd) Fame, renown, celebrity. Pl. ۍ *a'ī*. نوم يښول *nūm yeshawul* or *yekhawul*, verb trans. To name, to give a name unto.

نوماندئ *nūmāndaey*, adj. Named, yclept, called, denominated, designated by name; (Fem.) نوماندِ *nūmāndi*. Pl. (Masc. and Fem.) ي *ī*. نوماندي کول *nūmāndaey kawul*, verb trans. To name, to call, to yclep, to designate, to style. See نمري

نومد *nūmd*, adj. Damp, moist, humid; (Fem.) نومده *nūmda'h*. See لوند

نومړئ *nūmarraey*, adj. Named, called, designated, yclept, known as. 2. Ordained, determined, named, nominated. 3. Celebrated, eminent, great, honorable; (Fem.) نومړِ *nūm-*

a<u>rr</u>i. نومري كول *nūma<u>rr</u>aey kawul*, verb trans. To name, to designate, to yclep, to style. See نمر

P نوميد *naumīd*, adj. Hopeless, despairing; (Fem.) نوميده *naumīda'h*. نوميدي *naumīdī*, s.f. (3rd) Hopelessness, despair. Pl. ئ *a'ī*. See نا اميد

نوند *nūnd*, adj. Damp, wet, moist, humid; (Fem.) نونده *nūnda'h*. نوند والي *nūnd-wālaey*, s.m. (1st) Dampness, moisture, humidity. Pl. والي *wālī*. نونديدل *nūndedal*, verb intrans. To grow or become damp, moist, etc. نوندول *nūndawul*, verb trans. To make damp, moist, humid. For inflections see لونديدل *lūndedal*, etc. and substitute ن for ل

نونكۍ *nonaka'ī*, s.f. (6th) A sore, a pimple, a pustule, a blister, etc. Sing. and Pl. See also لوني , خلوني , and بهنزه

نويشت *na-wī<u>sh</u>t* or نوويشت *naw-wī<u>sh</u>t* or نه ويشت *noh-wī<u>sh</u>t*, adj. (W.) Twenty-nine. نوويشتم *naw-wī<u>sh</u>tam* or نه ويشتم *noh-wī<u>sh</u>tam*, The twenty-ninth; (Fem.) نوويشتمه *naw-wī<u>sh</u>tama'h* or نه ويشتمه *noh-wī<u>sh</u>tama'h*.

نوی *nawaey*, adj. New, fresh, unused, modern, late; (Fem.) نوِ *nawi*. نوي والي *nawaey-wālaey*, s.m. (1st) Newness, freshness, lateness. Pl. والي *wālī*. نوي كيدل *nawaey kedal*, verb intrans. To become new, renewed, restored. نوي كول *nawaey kawul*, verb trans. To make new, to renovate, to restore. (P نو, S नव)

نوي *nū-e*, s.m. (2nd) A mother's brother, a maternal uncle. Pl. نويونه *nū-e-ūnah*.

نوی *nawaey*, s.m. (1st) The inside bullock of a pair in treading out corn or in working a well. Pl. ي *ī*.

نوي *nawey* or نوِ *nawi*, adj. Ninety. نويم *naweyam*, The ninetieth; (Fem.) نويمه *naweyama'h*.

نه *nah*, neg. part. No, not, nay, neither, nor. نه نه *nah-nah*, No no, by no means.

نه *noh*, adj. Nine. نهم *naham*, The ninth; (Fem.) نهمه *nahama'h*. نه لس *noh-las*, Nineteen. نه لسم *noh-lasam*, The nineteenth. نه ويشت *noh-wī<u>sh</u>t*, Twenty-nine. نه ويشتم *noh-wī<u>sh</u>tam*, The twenty-ninth. نه ديرش *noh-der<u>sh</u>*, Thirty-nine. نه ديرشم *noh-der<u>sh</u>am*, The thirty-ninth. نه څلويښت *noh-<u>ts</u>alwe<u>sh</u>t* or *noh-<u>ts</u>alwe<u>kh</u>t*, Forty-nine. نه څلويښتم *noh-<u>ts</u>alwe<u>sh</u>tam* or *noh-<u>ts</u>alwe<u>kh</u>tam*, The forty-ninth. نه پنځوس *noh-pin<u>dz</u>os*, Fifty-nine. نه پنځوسم *noh-pin<u>dz</u>osam*, The fifty-ninth. نه شپيته *noh-<u>sh</u>petah*, Sixty-nine. نه شپيتم *noh-<u>sh</u>petam*, The sixty-ninth. نه اويا *noh-awyā*, Seventy-nine. نه اويايم *noh-awyāam* or *awyāyam*, The seventy-ninth. نه اتيا *noh-atī'ā*, Eighty-nine. نه اتيايم *noh-atī'āyam*. The eighty-ninth. نه نوي *noh-nawey* or نه نوِ *noh-nawi*, Ninety-nine. نه نويم *noh-naweyam* or نه نوم *noh-nawyam*, The ninety-ninth. The feminines are formed by fixing ه to the final م

P نهاري *nihāraey*, s.m. (1st) Breakfast, food taken in the morning. Pl. ي *ī*. ناري كول *nā-raey kawul* or نهاري كول *nahāraey kawul*, verb trans. To breakfast, to take breakfast. نهاري ور كول *nahāraey war-kawul*, verb trans. To give a breakfast.

P نهال *nihāl*, s.m. (2nd) A young plant, a shoot, a sapling, a sucker. Pl. نهالونه *nihālūnah*.

P نهالي *nihālī*, s.f. (3rd) A quilt, a wrapper, a coverlet, a mattress, a cushion. Pl. ئ *a'ī*. See تولائي

P نهايت *nihāyat*, s.m. (2nd) (from نهي) The extreme, extremity, end, bound, limit, boundary. 2. Excess. Pl. نهايتونه *nihāyatūnah*. 3. adj. Very much, extreme, excessive, remarkable; (Fem.) نهايته *nihāyata'h*. 4. adv. At the utmost, at last, at the furthest, at the end.

A نهر *nahr*, s.m. (2nd) A stream, a rivulet, a brook, a canal. Pl. نهرونه *nahrūnah*. See لښتي , واله , and خور

نهر *nahar*, adj. Fasting, lenten, unfed, famished; (Fem.) نهره *nahara'h*.

نهری *nharaey*, s.m. (1st) (W.) Breakfast. Pl. ي *ī*. See نهاري and ناري

P نهنګ *nahang*, s.m. (5th) A crocodile, alligator,

or shark. 2. A water-dragon or other such like monster. Pl. نهنگان *nahangān.*

نهوه *nahwa'h,* s.f. (3rd) Refusing to take food, starving one's-self, fasting. Pl. ي *ey.* نهوه نيول *nahwa'h nī-wal,* verb trans. To fast, to refuse to take food. See شومي

نهه *naha'h,* s.f. (3rd) Tuesday. Pl. ي *ey*; or نهي *naha'ī,* s.f. (6th). Sing. and Pl.

نه يرزن *nah-yar-zan,* adj. Unworthy, unfit, improper, unsuitable, incapable, unqualified, unbecoming; (Fem.) نه يرزنه *nah-yar-zana'h.* See يرز

نهيه *nahīa'h,* s.f. (3rd) Prohibition, interdiction. 2. An interdict. Pl. ي *ey.* نهيه كول *nahīa'h kawul,* verb trans. To prohibit, to interdict. (A نهي).

نهيل *nahīl,* adj. Meagre, weak, slender; (Fem.) نهيله *nahīla'h.* (A نحيل).

ني *nai,* s.m. (5th) A reed, a tube, a pipe, a flute, a cane. Pl. نيان *nai-ān.*

P ني *ne,* neg. part. No, not, neither, nor. See نه

نيا *nī'ā,* s.f. (5th) A grandmother, either paternal or maternal. Pl. نياگان *nī'ā-gāni.* د نيا مور *da nī'ā mor,* s.f. (5th) A great-grandmother. Pl. د نيا ميندِ *da nī'ā mendi.* د نيا نيا مور *da nī'ā nī'ā mor,* s.f. (5th) A great-great-grandmother. Pl. د نيا نيا ميندِ *da nī'ā nī'ā mendi.* نياگانه *nī-ā-gāna'h,* s.f. (3rd) A mother's family or relations. Pl. ي *ey.* See مورگنۍ and under انا

P نياز *niyāz,* s.m. (2nd) Petition, supplication, prayer. 2. Indigence, poverty. 3. Anything dedicated, an offering. Pl. نيازونه *niyāzūnah.* نياز كول *niyāz kawul,* verb trans. To petition, to supplicate. نياز ييښول *niyāz yeshawul* or *yekhawul,* verb trans, To dedicate, to devote, to consecrate anything. نياز مند *niyāz-mand* or نياز من *niyāz-man,* adj. Indigent, necessitous, suppliant; (Fem.) نياز منده *niyāz-manda'h* or نياز منه *niyāz-mana'h.* نياز مندي *niyāz-mandī,* s.f. (3rd) Necessitousness, supplication. Pl. ي *a'ī.*

S نياو *nyāw,* s.m. (2nd) Justice, equity, right. Pl. نياوونه *nyāwūnah.* نياو كول *nyāw kawul,* verb trans. To administer justice, to judge.

نيايه *niyā-yah,* s.m. (2nd) A maternal uncle. Pl. نييونه *nia-yūnah.* See نوي

A نيت *nī-yat,* s.m. (3rd) (from نوي) Intention, design, will, purpose, desire, wish, aim. Pl. نيتونه *nī-yatūnah.* نيت لرل *nī-yat laral,* verb trans. To have or hold an intention, design, purpose, to intend, to mean. نيت كول *nī-yat kawul,* verb trans. To purpose, to design, to intend, to will.

نيته *netta'h,* s.f. (3rd) A promise, a contract, an engagement, an agreement, a bargain. Pl. ي *ey.* نيته كول *netta'h kawul,* verb trans. To make or give a promise, to engage, to agree, to bargain, to stipulate. نيته ماتول *netta'h mātawul,* verb trans. To break an engagement, to break one's word or promise.

P نيرنگ *nairang,* s.m. (2nd) Deceit, trick, pretence, evasion, incantation, magic, sorcery. Pl. نيرنگونه *nairangūnah.* نيرنگ ساز *nairang sāz,* s.m. (5th) A magician, a sorcerer. Pl. سازان *sāzān.* نيرنگ سازه *nairang sāza'h,* s.f. (3rd) A sorceress. Pl. ي *ey.* نيرنگ سازي *nairang sāzī,* s.f. (3rd) Magic, sorcery, incantation. Pl. ي *a'ī.*

نيره *nīra'h,* s.f. (3rd) A shoemaker's awl. Pl. ي *ey.* See رينه

نيز *nīz,* s.m. (4th) An inundation, a flood, a torrent, a deluge. Pl. نيازه *nī-āzah.* نيازه وړی *nī-āzah warraey,* s.m. (1st) Rubbish or the like carried along by a flood. Pl. ي *ī.* 2. adj. Carried or floated away (by a flood or inundation); (Fem.) نيازه وړ *nī-āzah warri.* Pl. (Masc. and Fem.) نيازه وړي *nī-āzah warrī.* See نيوز

P نيزه *neza'h,* s.f. (3rd) A spear, a lance, a javelin, a dart, a pike. 2. A piece of reed from which pens are made. Pl. ي *ey.* نيزه باز *neza'h-bāz,* s.m. (5th) A spearman, a player with the spear. Pl. نيزه بازان *neza'h bāzān.* نيزه بازي *neza'h bāzī,* s.f. (3rd) Throwing the spear. Pl. ي *a'ī.* د نيزو بند *da nezo band,* s.m. (2nd) A sort of litter or stretcher made by fastening several spears together, and used for carrying wounded persons. Pl. بندونه *band-ūnah*.

A نیستي *nestī*, s.f. (3rd) Non-existence, nullity, annihilation. Pl. ۍ *a'ī*. نیستي کول *nestī kawul*, verb trans. To annihilate, to destroy.

P نیشتر *nesh-tar*, s.m. (2nd) A lancet. Pl. نیشترونه *nesh-tarūnah*.

نیښ *nesh* (W.) or *nekh* (E.) s.m. (2nd) The sting of any venomous animal. 2. A puncture. 3. A lancet. 4. The tusk of a camel or dog, etc. Pl. نیښونه *neshūnah* or *nekhūnah*. نیښ زن *nesh-zan* or *nekh-zan*, adj. A stinger, an animal that stings; (Fem.) نیښ زنه *nesh-zana'h* or *nekh-zana'h*. نیښ وهل *nesh wahal* or *nekh wahal*, verb trans. To sting, to puncture. (P نیش).

نیغ *negh*, adj. Rigid, hard, strait, stiff, tense, firm, unbending, unyielding; (Fem.) نیغه *negha'h*. نیغ والیَ *negh-wālaey*, s.m. (1st) Hardness, rigidity, stiffness, tenseness, firmness, etc. Pl. والي *wālī*. نیغ کتل *negh katal*, verb trans. To look fixedly on, to stare at, to gaze, to gloat on. نیغ کیدل *negh kedal*, verb intrans. To become stiff, rigid, tense, etc. نیغ کول *negh kawul*, verb trans. To render hard, stiff, rigid, tense.

نیغيَ *neghaey*, s.m. (1st) The clitoris. Pl. ي *ī*. See منجقيَ

P نیک *nek*, adj. Good, lucky. 2. s.m. (5th) Anything good, a pious or good man. Pl. نیکان *nekān*; (Fem.) نیکه *neka'h*. Pl. ې *ey*. نیک اختر *nek-akhtar*, adj. Fortunate, auspicious; (Fem.) نیک اختره *nek-akhtara'h*. نیک اندیش *nek-andesh*, Well-disposed, meaning well; (Fem.) نیک اندیشه *nek-andesha'h*. نیک بخت *nek-bakht*, Fortunate, of good disposition; (Fem.) نیک بخته *nek-bakhta'h*. نیک بختي *nek-bakhtī*, s.f. (3rd) Virtue, good fortune. Pl. ۍ *a'ī*. نیک خواه *nek-khwāh*, Well-wishing, faithful, grateful; (Fem.) نیک خواهه *nek-khwāha'h*. نیک خوي *nek-kho-e*, Of good disposition, good-hearted; (Fem.) نیک خویه *nek-kho-e-a'h*. نیک ذات *nek-zāt*, Of good family, of good disposition; (Fem.) نیک ذاته *nek-zāta'h*. نیک ذاتي *nek-zātī*, s.f. (3rd) Goodness of family, goodness of disposition. Pl. ۍ *a'ī*. نیک عهد *nek-æahd*, Good to one's engagements; (Fem.) نیک عهده *nek-æahda'h*. نیک کردار *nek-kirdār*, Of good habits; (Fem.) نیک کرداره *nek-kirdāra'h*. نیک مرد *nek-mard*, A good man. نیک نام *nek-nām*, Of good repute, of good name, respectable; (Fem.) نیک نامه *nek-nāma'h*. نیک نامي *nek-nāmī*, s.f. (3rd) Good character, renown. Pl. ۍ *a'ī*. نیک نیتيَ *nek-nīyataey*, Of good intentions, meaning well; (Fem.) نیک نیتِ *nek-nīyati*.

نیکهٔ *nīkæh*, s.m. (5th) A paternal grandfather. 2. The name given to the chief of the Wazīrī tribe. Pl. نیکگان *nīkæ-gān*; or s.m. (2nd) Pl. نیکونه *nīkūnah*. ور نیکه *wær nīkæh*, A great-grandfather on the father's side. غرٌ نیکهٔ *ghær nīkæh* or لا وٌر نیکهٔ *lā wær nīkæh*, A great-great-grandfather. ټر نیکهٔ *ṯær nīkæh* or لا لا وٌر نیکهٔ *lā lā wær nīkæh*, A great-great-great-grandfather.

P نیکي *nekī*, s.f. (3rd) Goodness, good, virtue, piety, beauty, probity. Pl. ۍ *a'ī*. نیکي کول *nekī kawul*, verb trans. To manifest goodness or virtue, to act uprightly.

PS نیل *nīl*, s.m. (6th) Indigo, blue. Sing. and Pl.

P نیلاب *nīl-āb*, s. prop. The name given to the river Indus, Sindhu, or Aṯṯak by the Persians, and نیلاو *nīl-āow* by the Afghāns, both of which words mean the "Blue water." See ابا سیند and سین or سیند

S نیلم *nīlam* or نیلمني *nīl-manī*, s.m. (6th) A gem, a sapphire. Sing. and Pl.

P نیلوفر *nīlofar*, s.m. (6th) The lotus nilofer, the water-lily (Nymphæa lotus). Sing. and Pl.

نیله *nīlah*, adj. Of a blue color, indigo colored. (Masc. and Fem.) See سرمائي

نیليَ *nīlaey*, s.m. (1st) A white horse or donkey. Pl. ي *ī*. نیلۍ *nīla'ī*, s.f. (5th) A white mare, etc. Sing. and Pl.

P نیم *nīm*, adj. Half, the middle; (Fem.) نیمه *nīma'h*. نیم بسمل *nīm-bismil*, adj. Half dead; (Fem.) نیم بسمله *nīm-bismila'h*.

HI نيم بولي *nīm-boley*, s.f. (3rd) Pl. A necklace of gold and glass beads, an ornament worn in the nose and which lies on the lips.

نيمه خوا *nīma'h-khwā*, adj. Mutable, erratic, variable, ever changing, unstable, fluctuating. 2. Unfinished, incomplete, embryonic, raw, immature, crude. 3. Unavailing, bootless, unattained, baffled. (Masc. and Fem.)

نيم زال *nīm-zāl*, adj. Middle-aged man ; (Fem.) نيم زاله *nīm-zāla'h*, A middle-aged female.

نيم سرَي *nīm-siraey*, s.m. (1st) A pain affecting a half of the head, a species of headache. Pl. ي *ī*.

نيم سڑي *nīm-sarraey*, adj. Half a man, a thing, an ass, a coward, a poltroon. Pl. ي *ī*.

نيمه شپه *nīma'h-shpa'h*, s.f. (3rd) Midnight, the middle of the night, the dead of night. Pl. ې *ey*. 2. adj. and adv. Midnight, at midnight.

نيم كوره *nīm-korah*, adj. A person having two houses and residing in each occasionally. 2. A house only occupied occasionally.

نيمگڑي *nīm-garraey*, adj. Incomplete, unfinished, imperfect, deficient, unaccomplished. 2. Embryo, immature, crude, incipient, inchoative ; (Fem.) نيمگڑ *nīm-garri*. Pl. (Masc. and Fem.) ي *ī*.

نيمايه *nīmāyah*, s.m. (6th) Half, one of two equal parts. Sing. and Pl.

نيمچه *nīmcha'h*, s.f. (3rd) A kind of pelisse with short sleeves, made of prepared sheep or kid skin, with the hair inside. Pl. ې *ey*.

نيمچه *nīmchah*, s.m. (6th) The name applied to some Seāh-posh Kāfirs and other tribes to the north of the Kābul river, between Kābul and Jelālābad, who are not Afghāns, but have embraced Islāmism. Sing and Pl.

نيمَي *nemaey*, s.m. (1st) A half, a part of anything, a moiety. Pl. ي *ī*.

نينزكه *nenzaka'h*, s.f. (3rd) A doll, a puppet, a plaything. Pl. ې *ey*. See نازكه , گودا and ناوكي

نيني *nīney*, s.f. (3rd) Pl. Roasted grain (taken on a journey generally). نيني كول *nīney kawul*, verb trans. To roast grain.

نيوز *nī-ūz*, s.m. (2nd) A torrent, an inundation, a flood. Pl. نيوزونه *nī-ūzūnah*. See نيز

نيول *nī-wal*, verb trans. To take, to get, to lay, to catch, to take or catch hold of, to possess one's-self of, to resume, to appropriate, etc. This infinitive is imperfect, and takes some of its inflections from the obsolete infinitive نسل . Pres. نسي *nasī* or *nisī* ; past وَ نيوه *wu-nī-wah* ; fut. وَ به نسي *wu bah nasī* or *nisī* ; imp. وَ نسه *wu-nasah* or *nisah* ; act. part. نيوونكَي *nī-wūn-kaey* or نيوونَي *nī-wūnaey* ; past part. نيولَي *nī-walaey* ; verb. n. نيونه *nī-wana'h* or نيوه *nī-wah*.

نيوه *nī-wah*, s.m. (6th) (verb. n.) Taking, appropriation, sequestration. Sing. and Pl. ; or نيونه *nī-wana'h*, s.f. (3rd). Pl. ې *ey*.

و

و *wāw*, the twenty-sixth letter of the Arabic and thirtieth of the Persian, is the thirty-eighth letter of the Pushto alphabet, and corresponds to Sanskrit व. It stands for six according to the Arabic system of substituting letters for numbers.

This letter is variously sounded according to the several vowel points, and may be either *w*, *ū*, *o*, *ow*, or *au*. Thus it is one of the labial letters having the sound of English *w*. With *ẓamma'h* (ـُ) it is called *wāw-i-maæ-rūf*, or known, from its occurring in Arabic and exhibiting the full sound of *ẓamma'h*, and is equivalent to *oo* or *ū* in English. It is called *wāw-i-maj'hūl*, unknown or concealed, when it bears the sound of *o*, because it does not occur in Arabic, and because the sound of *ẓamma'h* (ـُ) is here obscured by an admixture of that of *fat'ḥa'h* (ـَ). It is also called *wāw-i-œajamī* or *wāw-i-fārsī*. When a quiescent و follows a letter having *fat'ḥa'h* (ـَ), the diphthong *au* is formed, and the و is then called *wāw-i-sākin* or *wāw-i-mā-ḳabl-i-maftūḥ*. The و never occurs after *kasra'h* (ـِ).

Its other uses are—1. It may be used as the

conjunction 'and,' as in Persian and Arabic. 2. As a prefix to the particles marking the dative case of nouns and pronouns. 3. As the particle governing the vocative case. 4. It is affixed to all nouns capable of inflection to mark the plural oblique cases, and also to the personal pronoun of the third person. 5. As the affixed personal pronoun added to verbs to mark the first person plural. 6. It is prefixed to the simple past, aorist, and the imperative mood, in the same manner as Persian ب, and like that prefix is often rejected as redundant. 7. With (ـُ) it is often used for وُه, the third person singular of the masculine form of the past tense of the verb 'To be,' and with (ـَ) for the third person feminine plural of the same tense. 8. It is used with the particle به to mark the masculine singular and feminine plural forms of the conditional or optative tense of the same verb. 9. It is used with (ـَ) for وي, the third person plural of the imperfect tense of the infinitive ويل 'To say.' 10. It is often used in the place of (ـُ) and *vice versâ*. When used with Arabic and Persian words, it is subject to the rules of those languages. See "Grammar."

P وابسته *wā-bastah*, s.m. (5th) An adherent, a dependent. Pl. وابستگان *wā-bastagān*. 2. Bound, related, connected. (Masc. and Fem.)

واته *wātah*, s.m. (6th) (verb. n. of وتل) Coming forth, going out, departure, exit, egress, issue. Sing. and Pl. واته نتواته *wātah-nana-wātah*, Exit and entrance, going and coming.

H واټ *wāṯṯ*, s.f. (1st) A road, a path. Pl. واټِ *wāṯṯi*.

واټن *wāṯṯan*, s.m. (2nd) Distance, space, interval, extent, scope, range, remoteness. Pl. واټنونه *wāṯṯanūnah*.

واج *wāj*, s.m. (2nd) Exchange, trading in kind, giving goods in exchange for others without payment of money. Pl. واجونه *wājūnah*. په واج سودا كول *pah wāj saudā kawul*, verb trans. To trade in kind, to exchange.

A واجب *wā-jib*, adj. (past part. of وجب) Necessary, incumbent, obligatory, expedient, proper, worthy, fit, meet, convenient, just, reasonable; (Fem.) واجبه *wā-jiba'h*. واجب كول *wā-jib kawul*, verb trans. To render or make necessary, incumbent, obligatory, etc.

A واجبي *wā-jibī*, adj. Necessary, expedient.

A واحد *wā-ḥid*, adj. (past part. of وحد) Sole, single, one, singular, individual; (Fem.) واحده *wā-ḥida'h*.

واخ *wā<u>kh</u>*, interj. Alas! sorrow! well-a-day! See آخ

واده *wādah*, s.m. (2nd) A marriage, a wedding, a marriage festival. Pl. ودونه *wadūnah* or وادونه *wādūnah*. واده كيدل *wādah kedal*, verb intrans. To be married. 2. To marry and reside with the parents of the bride. واده كول *wādah kawul*, verb trans. To marry, to take a wife. واده كړي *wādah karraey*, adj. (past part.) Married (a man). واده شوِ *wādah <u>sh</u>awi*, Married (a woman). وديدل *wadedal*, verb intrans. To marry, to enter into the conjugal state, to unite, as husband or wife, to take a husband or wife. Pres. وديږي *wadejzī* (W.) or وديګي *wadegī* (E.); past واده شه *wādah <u>sh</u>ah* or وُ شه *wu-<u>sh</u>ah*; fut. واده به شي *wādah bah <u>sh</u>ī* or به وُ شي *bah wu-<u>sh</u>ī*; imp. واده شه *wādah <u>sh</u>ah* or وُ شه *wu-<u>sh</u>ah*; act. part. وديدونكيَ *wadedūnkaey* or وديدونيَ *wadedūnaey*; past part. واده شويَ *wādah <u>sh</u>awaey*; verb. n. وديدنه *wadedana'h* or وديده *wadedah*. ودول *wadawul*, verb trans. To marry, to unite in wedlock, to join a man or woman for life, to dispose of in marriage, to take for husband or wife. Pres. ودوي *wadawī*; past واده كړ *wādah karr* or وُ كړ *wu-karr*; fut. واده به كړي *wādah bah krrī* or به وُ كړي *bah wu-krrī*; imp. واده كړه *wādah krrah* or وُ كړه *wu-krrah*; act. part. ودوونكيَ *wadawūnkaey* or ودوونيَ *wadawūnaey*; past part. واده كړيَ *wādah karraey*; verb. n. ودونه *wadawuna'h*.

واده *wāda'h*, s.f. (3rd) (corrup. of A وعده) A promise, vow, agreement, bargain, assignation, appointment. Pl. ئ ey. واده ترل wāda'h tarral or واده كول wāda'h kawul, verb trans. To enter into an agreement, to bargain, to agree, to promise.

وار wār, s.m. (2nd) Time, period, turn (for duty, etc.), season, opportunity, occasion, vicissitude. 2. (HI) A blow with a sword, an attack, assault, a lunge, a pass, a charge, an onset. 3. (s) Leisure, spare time. Pl. وارونه wārūnah; or واري wāraey, s.m. (1st). Pl. ي ī. واري كول wāraey kawul, verb trans. To make a lunge or blow with a sword, to pass, to charge, to attack, to assault. وار په وار wār pah wār, adv. Frequently, often, always, continually. وار و پار wār-o-pār, Through and through, right through, on both sides. وار خطا wār khaṭā, A lost opportunity, a person who has lost an opportunity for performing any affair, missed, lost, gone by. يو وار yow wār, Once. دوه واره dwah wārah, Twice, etc.

P وار wār, A particle affixed to words signifying like, resembling, having, possessed, endowed with; as اميد وار umīd-wār, Hopeful. شاه وار shāh-wār, Worthy of a king.

A وارث wāris, s.m. (5th) (act. part. of ورث) An heir, a master, lord, owner. Pl. وارثان wārisān. وارثه wārisa'h, s.f. (3rd) A female heir. Pl. ئ ey.

وارى wārey. See وار

واريزه wāreza'h, s.f. (3rd) Fever, intermittent. Pl. ئ ey.

واړه wārrah, adj. All, the whole, every, total, entire, integral. 2. adv. Wholly, entirely, totally, altogether, all in all.

واړه wārrah, adj. Pl. of ووړ, which see.

P واز wāz, adj. Open, unclosed, not fastened; (Fem.) وازه wāza'h. واز خولي wāz-khūley, adj. Open-mouthed, astonished, gaping with astonishment; (Fem.) واز خولِ wāz-khuli. وازي سترگي wāzey-stargey, Immodest eyes. واز سترگئ wāz-stargaey, adj. Having immodest eyes, impudent, immodest; (Fem.) واز سترگې wāz-stargi. وازيدل wāze-dal, verb intrans. To unclose, to open, to unfold, to unclose itself, to gape, to begin to appear. وازول wāzawul, verb trans. To unclose, to lay open, to reveal, to disclose, to make gape, etc. See پرانتل

وازده wāz-da'h, s.f. (3rd) Fat, blubber, grease. suet. Pl. ئ ey. See وازگه

وازگه wāz-ga'h, s.f. (3rd). Pl. ئ ey. See preceding.

P واژگون wājz-gūn, adj. Inverted, upside down, contrary, preposterous; (Fem.) واژگونه wājz-gūna'h. See نسكور

وازه wāzah, s.m. (2nd) A fathom, the space from the ends of the fingers with the arms stretched out, stretch of a horse from the fore to the hind feet. Pl. وازونه wāz-ūnah or وزونه waz-ūnah.

A واسطه wās-ṭa'h, s.f. (3rd) Account, sake, cause, reason. 2. wāsiṭa'h, Means, medium, motive, cause, the thing intermediate. Pl. ئ ey.

واسيكه wāsī-kah, adj. Now, immediately, just now.

واښ wāsh, s.m. (2nd) (W.) or wākh (E.) Rope made from the hair of goats, camels, wool of sheep, etc. Pl. واښونه wāshūnah or wākhūnah.

واښكي wāsh-kaey (W.) or wākh-kaey (E.) s.m. (1st) Rope made of the hair of goats, camels, wool of sheep, etc. Pl. ي ī.

واښه wāshah (W.) or wākhah (E.) s.m. (6th) Grass, hay, fodder, straw. Sing. and Pl. سابه واښه sā-bah wāshah or wākhah, s.m. (5th) A superior kind of grass, produced in the spring months, and very nourishing. Sing. and Pl. وچ واښه wuch-wākhah or wāshah, Dry grass, hay. لامده واښه lāmdah wāshah or wākhah, Green grass. واښه ريبل wāshah or wākhah rebal, verb trans. To mow, cut, or reap grass.

A واصل wā-ṣil, adj. (past part. of وصل) Joined, connected, coupled, arrived; one who meets and enjoys the society of his beloved; (Fem.) واصله wā-ṣila'h. واصل كيدل wā-ṣil kedal, verb intrans. To become joined, coupled, connected, to meet one's beloved. واصل كول wā-ṣil kawul, verb trans. To join, to couple, to connect, to make or cause to meet.

A واعظ *wā-œiz̤*, s.m. (5th) (act. part. of وعظ) A preacher, a monitor, an admonisher, an adviser. Pl. واعظان *wā-œiz̤ān*. واعظه *wā-œiz̤a'h*, s.f. (3rd) A female monitor. Pl. ې *ey*.

واغوز *wā-ghoz*. See under سنګ پاره

P واف *wāf*, s.m. (2nd) A nightingale, a songster, a singer. Pl. وافونه *wāf-ūnah*.

A واقع *wāḳiœ* (act. part. of وقع) Befalling, happening, occurring, arriving, appearing; situate; (Fem.) واقعه *wāḳiœa'h*.

A واقعه *wāḳiœa'h*, s.f. (3rd) (from وقع) Event, occurrence, incident, intelligence, news. 2. Death. Pl. ې *ey*. واقعه کيدل *wāḳiœa'h kedal*, verb intrans. To happen, to come about, to occur, to befal, etc. واقعه کول *wāḳiœa'h kawul*, verb trans. To bring about, to make or cause to happen or befal.

A واقعي *wāḳiœī*, adj. True, real. 2. adv. Really, truly, verily, in fact, certainly, actually.

A واقف *wā-ḳif*, adj. (act. part. of وقف) Acquainted, experienced, conversant, intelligent, knowing, learned, sensible; (Fem.) واقفه *wā-ḳifa'h*. واقف حال *wāḳif-i-ḥāl*, adj. Experienced, expert, intelligent. واقف کيدل *wā-ḳif kedal*, verb intrans. To become or grow conversant, experienced, acquainted, etc. واقف کول *wā-ḳif kawul*, verb trans. To make acquainted, conversant, to acquaint, to teach.

واقفيت *wāḳif-īyat*, s.m. (2nd) Experience, knowledge, intelligence, acquaintance. Pl. واقفيتونه *wāḳif-īyatūnah*. واقفيت لرل *wāḳif-īyat laral*, verb trans. To have or possess experience, acquaintance or knowledge.

P واك *wāk*, s.m. (2nd) Will, choice, authority, command, sway, control, influence. 2. Power, might, force, capability, capacity, ableness. Pl. واکونه *wākūnah*. واك رسيدل *wāk rasedal*, verb intrans. To be or become capable, able, to be qualified, efficient, strong, competent, etc.; to be able to reach. واك لرل *wāk laral*, verb trans. To have or hold authority, will, choice, command, influence. واك ورکول *wāk war-kawul*, verb trans. To give or grant authority, will, or control (to another).

واګه *wāga'h*, s.f. (3rd) A rein, a bridle. Pl. ې *ey*. See ملونه and جلب

وال *wāl*, An affix applied to nouns in forming patronymical adjectives, as بنير *buner*, The district of Buner. بنير وال *buner-wāl*, An inhabitant of Buner, etc.

P والا *wālā*, s.f. (6th) A kind of silk or sarcenet. (E.) Sing. and Pl. (W.) Pl. والاوي *wālā-wī*.

H I والا *wālā*, s.m. (6th) (in composition) Agent, doer, keeper, man, possessor, owner, etc., as آس والا *ās-wālā*, The owner of a horse. ډوډۍ والا *ḏdoḏda'ī wālā*, A bread-man, a baker or seller of bread. (Masc. and Fem.)

واله *wāla'h*, s.f. (3rd) A canal, a water-course, a stream. Pl. ې *ey*; or وله, which see. Also لښتي

A والي *wālī*, s.m. (5th) A prince, a chief, a superior, a sovereign, a master, a ruler. Pl. واليان *wālīān*.

والۍ *wālacy*, s.m. (1st) An ear-ring passing through the centre of the ear. Pl. ي *ī*. (s بالي).

وانړه *wārrna'h*, s.f. (3rd) A large heap of uncleaned grain which has been trodden out, but not yet separated from the husk. Pl. ې *ey*.

واوره *wāwra'h*, s.f. (3rd) A fall of snow, a flake of snow. Pl. ې *ey*. واوره اوريدل *wāwra'h aoredal* or پريوتل *prewatal*, verb intrans. To fall (as snow), to snow.

A وا ويلا *wā-wailā*, s.f. (6th) Lamentation, bewailing. (W.) Pl. وا ويلاوي *wā-wailāwī*. (E.) Sing. and Pl. وا ويلا کول *wā-wailā kawul*, verb trans. To bewail, to lament.

P واه *wāh*, interj. Bravo! well done! excellent! fie! alas! واه واه *wāh-wāh*, Excellent! very good indeed!

A واهمه *wāhima'h*, s.f. (3rd) (act. part. Fem. of وهم) Imagination, fancy. 2. Fear, apprehension. Pl. ې *ey*. واهمه لويدل *wāhima'h l'wedal* or واهمه پريوتل *wāhima'h prewatal*, verb intrans. To fear, to apprehend, to fancy, to fall into doubt or apprehension, etc.

A واي *wā-e*, interj. Alas! woe! fie! or واي واي

wā-e-wā-e. واي په تا باندِ *wā-e pah tā bāndi,* Woe unto thee!

A وبا *wabā,* s.f. (6th) Pestilence, plague, great sickness. (E.) Sing. and Pl. (W.) Pl. وباوي *wabāwī.* وبا لويدل *wabā l'wedal* or گډيدل *gaḏḏedal,* verb intrans. To break out, as a plague or pestilence. وبا وهل *wabā wahal,* verb trans. To be stricken with a plague or pestilence.

A وبال *wabāl,* s.m. (2nd) (from وبل) An unhealthy climate. 2. A crime, fault, punishment. 3. Pest, plague, vexation, misfortune, ruin, curse. Pl. وبالونه *wabālūnah.* See اوبال

وبله *wab-lah* or وبلته *wab-latah* or وبله ته *wab-lah tah,* adv. One with another, together, one on another, in concert, in company.

وبله باندِ *wab-lah bāndi,* Together, in folds, scattered, in strata. 2. Behind and before, above and below, one on another; or زبله باندِ *zab-lah bāndi.* See بل

وپار *wapār,* s.m. (2nd) Trade, commerce, traffic. Pl. وپارونه *wapārūnah.* وپار کول *wapār kawul,* verb trans. To trade, to carry on trade, to traffic (peculiar to Hindūs). See also سوداگر

وپاري *wapārī,* s.m. (5th) A trader, a merchant. Pl. وپاريان *wapārīān.* (S بيپار, etc.)

وت *wat,* s.m. (2nd) Interval, break, gap, interstice, chasm, hiatus, a cleft, a crevice, a cranny, a fissure, a fracture. 2. A gorge, a defile, a ravine, a pass. Pl. وتونه *watūnah.*

وت *wit,* adj. Wide open, gaping, ajar, yawning. 2. Pert, saucy, wanton, impudent, mischievous, hurtful; (Fem.) وته *wita'h.* وت کيدل *wit kedal,* verb intrans. To gape, to yawn, to become ajar or gaping. وت کول *wit-kawul,* verb trans. To make or cause to gape, open wide, etc. See وته

و تا وته *wa tā wa-tah,* To, *or* unto thee. See "Grammar," page 32, par. 108.

وتر *watar,* adj. A field or portion of land ready for the plough or for sowing, after it has been watered; (Fem.) وتره *watara'h.*

وتر *witar,* s.m. (6th) The prayer repeated before retiring to rest. Sing. and Pl. 2. Singleness, unity. 3. adj. Single, sole, individual. (Masc. and Fem.)

وتراوي *watr-āwī,* adj. Without harmony, unaccented (peculiarly applied to verse).

وتل *watal,* verb intrans. To go out, to come out or come forth, to emerge, issue or move out; to exude, to run through, to percolate, to ooze, to trickle, to drop, to gush, to spout, run, or flow out. Pres. وزي *wuzī*; past ؤ ووت *wu-wot*; fut ؤ به وزي *wu bah wuzī*; imp. ؤ وزه *wu-wuzah*; act. part. وتونکی *watūnkaey* or وتونی *watūnaey*; past part. وتلی *watalaey*; verb. n. وتنه *watana'h* or واته *wātah.*

وته *wita'h,* s.f. (3rd) Forwardness, wantonness, assurance, pertness, impudence. 2. Mischief, harm, hurt. Pl. ي *ey.* وت خولی *wit khūlaey,* adj. Open-mouthed, agape, flabbergasted, all agog, struck all of a heap, amazed, astonished, inquisitive, gaping, on the tip-toe of expectation, over curious; (Fem.) وت خولِ *wit khūli.* Pl. (Masc. and Fem.) ي *ī.* See ويته and ويتکي

وټه *waṭṭa'h,* s.f. (3rd) Deficiency, defect, blemish, injury. 2. Discount, exchange. Pl. ي *ey.* وټه لرل *waṭṭa'h laral,* verb trans. To bear discount or deficiency. (HI بٹا).

وڅکه *watska'h,* s.f. (3rd) A kind of raisin with a stone, a raisin or currant. Pl. ي *ey.*

وجاړ *wijāṛṛ,* adj. Desolate, dilapidated, destroyed, demolished, devastated; (Fem.) وجاړه *wijāṛṛa'h.* وجاړ والی *wijāṛṛ-wālaey,* s.m. (1st) Destruction, desolation, dilapidation, demolition. Pl. والي *wālī.* وجاړيدل *wijāṛṛedal,* verb intrans. To become desolate, laid waste, devastated, to go to the dogs, etc. Pres. وجاړيږي *wijāṛṛejzī* (W.) or وجاړيګي *wijāṛṛegī* (E.); past وجاړ شه *wijāṛṛ shah* or ؤ شه *wu-shah*; fut. وجاړ به شي *wijāṛṛ bah shī* or به ؤ شي *bah wu-shī*; imp. وجاړ شه *wijāṛṛ shah* or ؤ شه *wu-shah*; act. part. وجاړيدونکی *wijāṛṛedūnkaey* or وجاړيدونی *wijāṛṛedūnaey*; past part. وجاړ *wijāṛṛ* or وجاړ شوی *wijāṛṛ shawaey*; verb. n. وجاړيدنه *wijāṛṛedana'h* or وجاړيده *wijāṛṛedah.* وجاړول *wijāṛṛawul,* verb trans. To desolate, to destroy, to lay waste, to devastate, to demolish. Pres. وجاړوي *wijārrawī*; past وجاړ کړ *wi-jārr karr* or وُ کړ *wu-karr*; fut. وجاړ به کړي *wijārr bah krrī* or به وُ کړي *bah wu-krrī*; imp. وجاړ کړه *wijārr krrah* or وُ کړه *wu-krrah*; act. part. وجاړوونکي *wijārrawūnkaey* or وجاړووني *wijārrawūnaey*; past part. وجاړ کړي *wijārr karraey*; verb.n. وجاړونه *wijārrawuna'h*.

وجاړي *wijārraey*, adj. Desolated, devastated, destroyed; (Fem.) وجاړ *wijārri*. Pl. (Masc. and Fem.) ي *ī*. See preceding.

وجلل *waj-lal*, verb trans. To kill, to slay, to murder, to put to death, to slaughter, to deprive of life, to despatch, to put an end to. Pres. وجني *wajnī*; past وُ واجه *wu-wājah*; fut. وُ به وجني *wu bah wajnī*; imp. وُ وجنه *wu-wajnah*; act. part. وجلونکي *wajlūnkaey* or وجلوني *wajlūnaey*; past part. وجلي *waj-laey* or وجللي *wajlalaey*; verb. n. وجلنه *wajlana'h* or وجله *wajlah*. See وژل

A وجود *wujūd*, s.m. (9th) (from وجد) Intention. 2. Existence, essence, being, substance, body. 3. Penis. Sing. and Pl.

وجه *wuja'h*, s.f. (3rd) (W.) A nerve, a tendon. Pl. ې *ey*. See وژه

وجه *waja'h*, s.f. (3rd) (E.) The hollow part of the back of the neck where the head joins the spine between the tendons. Pl. ې *ey*.

A وجهه *wajha'h*, s.f. (3rd) Cause, reason. 2. Manner, mode, way. 3. Face, visage, semblance, appearance. Pl. ې *ey*. په څه وجهه *pah tsah wajha'h* or په کمه وجهه *pah kama'h wajha'h* or په کومه وجهه *pah koma'h wajha'h*, How? in what manner or way? why? wherefore? په هيڅ وجهه *pah hets wajha'h*, By no means.

وچ *wuch*, adj. Dry, not wet, arid, dried up, parched, undamped, sapless; (Fem.) وچه *wucha'h*. تپ وچ *ttap-wuch*, Dry as a bone, dry as a stick; (Fem.) تپه وچه *ttapa'h-wucha'h*. وچ دکي *wuch ddakaey*, s.m. (1st) A piece of dry straw or stick, or any useless herb, etc. Pl. ي *ī*. وچ ککر *wuch kakar*, adj. Dry as a bone, dry as a biscuit, dry as a stick, dry

as dust; (Fem.) وچه ککره *wucha'h kakara'h*. وچ واښه *wuch wāshah* (W.) or *wuch wākhah* (E.), s.m. (6th) Dry grass or straw. Sing. and Pl. وچ والي *wuch wālaey*, s.m. (1st) Dryness, aridity, drought, siccity. Pl. والي *wālī*. وچيدل *wuchedal*, verb intrans. To become dry, to dry up, to become parched or arid. Pres. وچيږي *wuchejzī* (W.) or وچيګي *wuchegī* (E.); past وچ شه *wuch shah* or وُ شه *wu-shah*; fut. وچ به شي *wuch bah shī* or به وُ شي *bah wu-shī*; imp. وچ شه *wuch shah* or وُ شه *wu-shah*; act. part. وچيدونکي *wuche-dūnkaey* or وچيدوني *wuchedūnaey*; past part. وچ *wuch* or وچ شوي *wuch shawaey*; verb. n. وچيدنه *wuchedana'h* or وچيده *wuchedah*.

وچول *wuchawul*, verb trans. To dry, to make dry, to dry up, to parch. Pres. وچوي *wuchawī*; past وچ کړ *wuch karr* or وُ کړ *wu-karr*; fut. وچ به کړي *wuch bah krrī* or به وُ کړي *bah wu-krrī*; imp. وچ کړه *wuch krrah* or وُ کړه *wu-krrah*; act. part. وچوونکي *wuchawūnkaey* or وچووني *wuchawūnaey*; past part. وچ کړي *wuch karraey*; verb. n. وچونه *wuchawuna'h*.

وچکول *wuch-kūl*, s.m. (5th) (W.) A castrated ram. Pl. وچکولان *wuch-kūlān*.

وچکولي *wuch-kūlaey*, s.m. (1st) (E.) See preceding. Pl. ي *ī*.

وچکۍ *wuchaka'ī*, s.f. (6th) Burning fever. Sing. and Pl.

وچولي *wuch-wulaey*, s.m. (1st) The forehead. Pl. ي *ī*. See اچولي

وچه *wucha'h*, adj. (Fem. of وچ *wuch*), The name given to all that part of the Suwāt valley lying on the left or southern bank of the river. See وچ

وچه غاړه *wucha'h-ghārra'h*, s.f. (3rd) The windpipe. Pl. ې *ey*.

وچ موري *wuch-moraey*, adj. as s.m. (1st) A weanling, a child stinted in milk (*lit.* mother dried up), a child or animal newly weaned before its time; (Fem.) وچ مور *wuch-mori* or وچ مورې *wuch-morey*. Pl. (Masc. and Fem.) ي *ī*. See بهاري

A وحش *waḥsh*, s.m. (5th) A wild beast. Pl. وحشان *waḥshān*. وحشه *waḥsha'h*, s.f. (3rd) A female wild beast. Pl. ې *ey*.

A وحشت *waḥshat*, s.m. (2nd) Fright, fear, dread, loneliness, solitariness. 2. A desert, a wild, a solitude, a dreary place. 3. Wildness, ferocity, savageness. Pl. وحشتونه *waḥshatūnah*. وحشت ناك *waḥshat-nāk*, adj. Horrible, frightful; (Fem.) وحشت ناكه *waḥshat-nāka'h*.

A وحشي *waḥshī*, adj. Wild, savage, ferocious. 2. s.m. and f. (5th) A wild beast, a savage, a brute. Pl. وحشيان *waḥshīān*; (Fem.) وحشيانِ *waḥshīāni*.

وخ *ūkh*, An exclamation of sorrow, distress, or pain.

وخت *wakht*, s.m. (2nd) (corrup. of A وقت) Time, season, opportunity, turn. Pl. وختونه *wakhtūnah*. وخت په وخت *wakht-pah-wakht*, From time to time, frequently, occasionally; or وخت نا وخت *wakht-nā-wakht*. بي وخت *bey wakht*, Out of season, at an unstated time. په خپل وخت *pah khpul wakht*, At a stated time, seasonably. وختي *wakhtī*, Betimes, early, in one's own season, seasonably. وخت تيرول *wakht terawul*, verb trans. To pass away the time. هر وخت *har wakht*, Always, ever, at all times, whenever. څو وختَ *tso-wakhta*. How often? how many times? كم *kam* or كوم وخت *kom wakht*, When? at what time? وخت كتل *wakht katal*, verb trans. To look out for an opportunity, to bide one's time.

A وداع *widāæ*, s.m. (9th) Farewell, adieu, bidding farewell. Sing. and Pl. وداع كول *widāæ kawul*, verb trans. To bid farewell or adieu, to say good bye.

ودان *wadān*, adj. Cultivated, peopled, inhabited, populous, prosperous; (Fem.) ودانه *wadāna'h*.

وداني *wadānī*, s.f. (3rd) Cultivation, population, prosperity. Pl. ې *a'ī*.

ودانيدل *wadānedal*, verb intrans. To become peopled, cultivated, inhabited, prosperous. ودانول *wadānawul*, verb trans. To people, to inhabit, to cultivate, to improve, to render populous.

ودريدل *wudredal*, verb intrans. To stand, to stand up, to stand erect, to be upon the feet, not to sit, kneel, or lie, to stop, to halt, to lie fixed or steady, to maintain one's ground. 2. To persist, to abide, to make delay. Pres. ودريږي *wudrejzī* (W.) or ودريګي *wudregī* (E.); past ودريده *wudredah*; fut. وُ به دريږي *wu bah drejzī* or دريګي *dregī*; imp. ودريږه *wudrejzah* or ودريګه *wudregah*; act. part. ودريدونکَي *wudredūnkaey* or ودريدونَي *wudredūnaey*; past part. ودريدلَي *wudredalaey*; verb, n. ودريدنه *wudredana'h*. ودرول *wudrawul*, verb trans. To cause or make to stand, to make abide, to cause to halt, stay, or remain, to pitch (as a tent), to support, to prop, to uphold, to fix. Pres. ودروي *wudrawī*; past ودراوه *wudrāwuh* or ودراوو *wudrāwo*; fut. وُ به دروي *wu bah drawī*; imp. ودروه *wudrawah*; act. part. ودروونکَي *wudrawūnkaey* or ودروونَي *wudrawūnaey*; past part. ودرولَي *wudrawulaey*; verb. n. ودرونه *wudrawuna'h*.

ودل *o-dal*, verb. trans. To weave. See اودل and وودل

وده *ū-da'h*, s.f. (3rd) Breath, respiration, breathing on a wound or snake bite, as a charm. Pl. ې *ey*. وده كول *ū-da'h kawul*, verb trans. To breathe, to breathe on, to charm. See اوده and هوده

واديدل *wadedal*, verb intrans. To marry, to be married. ودول *wadawul*, verb trans. To marry, to give in marriage. See under واده

ود *wadd*, s.m. (2nd) Land lying fallow, or from which the crop has been cut. Pl. ودونه *waddūnah*.

P ور *war*, particle applied to nouns in composition, implying possession, enjoying, having; as, ګيډه ور *gedda'h-war*, Pot-belly. جان ور *jān-war*, An animal, a beast. ژبه وره *jzaba'h-wara'h*, A long-tongued woman, etc.

ور *war*, s.m. (2nd) A door, a gate. Pl. ورونه *warūnah*. ور پوري كول *war pūrī-kawul*, verb trans. To shut a door or gate. ور ترل *war-*

tarral, verb trans. To fasten a door. ور خلاصول *war khalāṣawul* or ور پرانتل *war prā-natal*, verb trans. To open or unfasten a door.

ور *war*, One of the pronominal dative affixes or second form of pronouns used in the Pushto language for the third person singular and plural, signifying To him, her, it, or them, and is not liable to change for gender. It may be also inflected; as, ور ته , لره or له *war-tah*, *larah* or *lah*. See Grammar, page 46.

ورهسته *war histah*, adv. Towards him, her, it, or them, that side, yonder, across.

ورا *w'rā*, s.f. (6th) A party of women who accompany the bride in procession to the house of the bridegroom, a marriage procession. (E.) Sing. and Pl. (W.) Pl. وراوي *w'rāwī*. See جانجي

ور *w'ra* or وره *w'rah* for ووړه *w'rrah*, imp. of وړل, which see.

A ورا *warā*, adv. Far, far off, far away, beyond, yonder, at a great distance off. 2. Besides, except. له ورا *lah warā*, From a distance. See ورايه

وراباړنى *w'rābārrnaey*, s.m. (1st) (W.) A man who forms one of a *w'rā* or marriage procession. Pl. ي *ī*. وراباړنړ *w'rābārrni*, s.f. (8th) A female as above. Pl. ي *ī*. See جانجي

A وراثت *wirāṣat*, s.m. (2nd); (from ورث) Heritage, heirship. Pl. وراثتونه *wirāṣatūnah*.

وراره *w'rārah*, s.m. (2nd) A nephew, a brother's son. Pl. ورارونه *w'rārūnah* or وررونه *w'rarūnah*. See خورئي

وراره *w'rāra'h*, s.f. (3rd) A woman who may have lost her brother by death. Pl. ئ *ey*.

وراڅه *w'rādza'h*, s.f. (3rd) A small red insect or species of tick infesting dogs, sheep, and camels in particular. Pl. ئ *ey*.

وراشه *w'rāsha'h*, s.f. (3rd) Speech, language, parlance, talk, locution, say, oral communication. Pl. ئ *ey*.

وران *warān*, adj. Ruined, desolated, deserted, destroyed, razed, sacked; (Fem.) ورانه *warāna'h*. ورانيدل *warānedal*, verb intrans. To be or become ruined, desolated, destroyed, sacked; to go to the dogs. ورانول *warānawul*, verb trans. To ruin, to destroy, to desolate, to sack. (P ويران). See روان

وراني *warānī*, s.f. (3rd) Ruin, desertion, desolation, destruction, devastation. Pl. ئي *a'ī*.

ورايه *warāyah* or *w'rāyah*, adv. Far, far away, a-far off, a long way off, beyond, yonder; or له ورايه *lah warāyah* or *lah w'rāyah*, From a-far, etc. ډير له ورايه *dder lah w'rāyah*, A very great distance off, very very far away.

وربوز *wurbūz*, s.m. (2nd) The lower part of the face (particularly applied to the lips and nostrils of a horse and other animals. Pl. وربوزونه *wurbūzūnah*. په وربوز خبري کول *pah wurbūz khabarey kawul*, verb trans. To speak to a person with the head turned aside, as when forced to answer against one's wish, or when angry or disgusted. See تمبوزک

ورتګ *war-tag*, s.m. (9th) (from ورتلل) Departure, outset, exit, removal. Sing. and Pl.

ورتيدل *wuratedal*, verb intrans. To be fried, cooked, roasted, grilled, etc. Pres. ورتيږي *wuratejzī* (W.) or ورتيګي *wurategī* (E.); past ورت شه *wurat shah* or وُ شه *wu-shah*; fut. وُ به ورتيږي *wu bah wuratejzī* or ورتيګي *wurategī*; imp. ورت شه *wurat shah* or وُ شه *wu-shah*; act. part. ورتيدونکي *wuratedūnkaey* or ورتيدوني *wuratedūnaey*; past part. ورت *wurat* or ورت شوي *wurat shawaey*; verb. n. ورتيدنه *wuratedana'h* or ورتيده *wuratedah*.

ورتول *wuratawul*, verb trans. To roast, to fry, to grill, to cook. Pres. ورتوي *wuratawī*; past ورت کړ *wurat karr* or وُ کړ *wu-karr*; fut. ورت به کړي *wurat bah krrī* or به وُ کړي *bah wu krrī*; imp. ورت کړه *wurat krrah* or وُ کړه *wu krrah*; act. part. ورتوونکي *wuratawūnkaey* or ورتووني *wuratawūnaey*; past part. ورت کړي *wurat karraey*; verb. n. ورتونه *wuratawuna'h*. See وريت *wurīt*, etc.

ورټ *wratt*, s.m. (9th) A flood or outburst of tears, a gush of tears. Sing. and Pl. په ورټ ورټ ژړل *pah wratt-wratt jzarral*, verb trans. To cry violently, to burst into tears, to cry one's eyes out. See رټ

ورجي *w'rijey*, s.f. (3rd) (Pl.) Rice. The singular form is rarely used, except to signify a single grain. See ورژي

ورچني *war-chiney*, adj. Without, outside, exterior. See ورچيني and ورځني

ورچيني *war-chiney*, adv. See preceding.

ورخ *warkh*, s.m. (2nd) A small passage to allow water for irrigation purposes to pass from one bed to another, or from one portion of ground to another. Pl. ورخونه *warkhūnah*.

ورخاړي *war-khārraey*, s.m. (1st) The herb purslain (Portulaca oleracea). 2. (W.) A disease amongst sheep and goats, a murrain. Pl. ي *ī*.

ورخته *war-khatah*, adv. First, in the first place, in the beginning. له ورخته *lah war-khatah*, From the first, from the beginning. ورختني *war-khatanaey*, s.m. (1st) A precursor, predecessor, the leader, the first person. Pl. ي *ī*.

ورختني *war-khatana'ī*, s.f. (6th) A female as above. Sing. and Pl.

ورخړه *war-kharra'h*, s.f. (3rd) Rubbish, sweepings, litter of any kind. Pl. ې *ey*. See خزله

ورخه *war-kha'h*, s.f. (3rd) A small channel in a field for irrigation purposes. Pl. ې *ey*. See ورخ

A ورد *wird*, s.m. (2nd) Daily use, practice, task, a portion of the Ḳur'ān fixed for reading at a certain time. Pl. وردونه *wirdūnah*.

ورريدل *w'raredal*, verb intrans. To become lacerated, to become torn away or broken (as the nose of a camel, the soft part of the ear, etc.), to be torn asunder, separated, to be rent away. Pres. ورريږي *w'rarejzī* (W.) or ورريګي *w'raregī* (E.); past ؤ ورريده *wu-w'raredah*; fut. ؤ به ورريږي *wu bah w'rarejzī* or ورريګي *w'raregī*; imp. ؤ ورريږه *wu-w'rarejzah* or ؤ ورريګه *wu-w'raregah*; act. part. ورريدونکي *w'raredūnkaey* or ورريدونې *w'raredūnaey*; past part. ورريدلي *w'raredalaey*; verb. n. ورريدنه *w'raredana'h* or ورريده *w'raredah*. وررول *w'rarawul*, verb trans. To tear away or asunder, to rend, to lacerate, to forcibly detach or separate. Pres. وررووي *w'rarawī*; past ؤ وررواه *wu-w'rarāwuh* or ؤ وررراوو *wu-w'rarāwo*; fut. ؤ به وررووي *wu bah w'rarawī*; imp. ؤ وررووه *wu-w'rarawah*; act. part. ورروونکي *w'rarawūnkaey* or وررووني *w'rarawūnaey*; past part. وررولي *w'rarawulaey*; verb. n. وررونه *w'rarawuna'h*.

ورز *w'raz*. See ورځ

ورزيدل *wur-zedal*, verb intrans. To fly, to take wing, to move through the air. Pres. ورزي *wur-zī*; past ؤ ورزه *wu-wur-zah*; fut. ؤ به ورزي *wu bah wur-zī*; imp. ؤ ورزيده *wu-wur-zedah*; act. part. ورزيدونکي *wur-zedūnkaey* or ورزيدوني *wur-zedūnaey*; past part. ورزيدلي *wur-zedalaey*; verb. n. ورزيدنه *wur-zedana'h*.

ورزول *wur-zawul*, verb trans. To make or cause to fly, to put to flight. Pres. ورزوي *wur-zawī*; past ؤ ورزاوه *wu-wur-zāwuh*; fut. ؤ به ورزوي *wu bah wur-zawī*; imp. ؤ ورزوه *wu-wur-zawah*; act. part. ورزوونکي *wur-zawūnkaey* or ورزووني *wur-zawūnaey*; past part. ورزولي *wur-zawulaey*; verb. n. ورزونه *wur-zawuna'h*.

ورځ *wradz*, s.f. (1st) Day, a day, the day-time. Pl. ورځ *wradzi*. ورځ به ورځ *wradz pah wrádz* or ورځا ورځ *wradzā-wradz*, adv. Daily, every day, constantly. د ميعاد ورځ *da mīʿād wradz*, The last day, or judgment-day. شپه و ورځ *shpa'h-o-wradz*, Night and day, constantly. هره ورځ *hara'h wradz*, Every day, always. ښه ورځ *sha'h* (W.) or *kha'h* (E.) *wradz*, A great or solemn day, a feast, a sabbath. نن ورځ *nan wradz*, To-day, this very day. پرون ورځ *parūn wradz*, Yesterday. ورمه ورځ *warrma'h wradz*, The day before yesterday. لا ورمه ورځ *lā warrma'h wradz*, Four days since. See روځ

ورځني *war-dzaney*, adj. Outside, without, exterior. See ورچني

ورځه *w'radza'h*, s.f. (3rd) The eye-brow. Pl. ې *ey*. ګډي ورځي *gaddey-w'radzey*, Eyebrows meeting over the nose. تونډي ورځي *tūndey w'radzey*, Full and long eyebrows. کږي ورځي *kajzey w'radzey* (W.) or کګي ورځي *kagey w'radzey* (E.) Arched eyebrows.

ورژل *war-jzal*, verb trans. To chop, to mince, to cut up, to make mince-meat of. Pres. ورژني *warjzanī*; past ؤ ورژه *wu-warjzah*; fut. ؤ به

ورژني *wu bah warjzanī*; imp. وُ ورژه *wu-warjzah*; act. part. ورژونکي *war-jzūnkaey* or ورژوني *war-jzūnaey*; past part. ورژلي *war-jzalaey*; verb. n. ورژنه *war-jzana'h.*

ورژنه *war-jzana'h*, s.f. (3rd) (verb. n.) Hacking, lacerating, cutting up, mincing, cutting into small pieces (as meat). Pl. ې *ey.*

ورژون *w'ra-jzūn*, s.m. (9th) Dispersion, scattering, dissipation; casting forth, dispelling, etc. Sing. and Pl. د گناه ورژون *da gunāh w'rajzūn*, An atonement or expiation for sin. See رژيدل

ورژې *w'rijzey*, s.f. (3rd) Pl. Rice. ورژه *w'rijza'h*, A grain of rice. See ورجي

ورږ *w'rajz* (W.) s.m. (6th) The mane of a horse, ass, or mule, etc. Sing. and Pl. See ورکث

ورږه *wur-jzah*, s.m. (6th) The first milk given by a cow, goat, etc., after calving, biestings. Sing. and Pl. See ورگه

ورستو *w'rusto*, adv. and prep. In the rear, after, behind, astern, ago, afterwards, in the absence. 2. Remaining behind after another's departure (being left behind). په ورستو لويدل *pah w'rusto l'wedal*, verb intrans. To run after, to importune, to dun, to persecute, to torment. ورستو آستول *w'rusto āstawul*, verb trans. To send after or in the rear of another. ورستو پاتکيدل *w'rusto pātakedal* or پاتيدل *pātedal*, verb intrans. To be in the rear, to lag or remain behind, to drop astern. په ورستو *pah w'rusto* or ورستو تلل *w'rusto t'lal*, verb intrans. To follow, to follow or go after, to set out after, to bring up the rear, to be in the wake of, to come after. 2. To obey, to follow the ways or customs of another. د *da* or په *pah w'rusto z'ghāstal* or ورستو زغاستل زغاښتل *z'ghākhtal*, verb intrans. To run after, to follow, to pursue, to chase, to hunt. ورستو کول *w'rusto kawul*, verb trans. To send after, to dispatch after another. ورستو کيدل *w'rusto kedal*, verb intrans. To lag behind, to follow in the rear. ورستو وتل *w'rusto watal*, verb intrans. To follow, to set out after another has departed, to follow in the rear. ورستو راتلل *w'rusto rā-t'lal*, verb intrans. To come after, to follow after, to come up in the rear. ورستو وړاندِ *w'rusto w'rrāndi*, Behind and before, past and present.

ورستول *war-stawul*, verb trans. To send, to transmit, to impel; to utter, to ejaculate. See آستول

ورسته *w'rustah*, s.m. (6th) The rear, the stern, the poop, the croup, the after part, the background, the heels, the breech. Sing. and Pl.

ورستي *w'rustaey*, adj. Hinder, postern, the rearmost, rear, back, posterior, hindermost; (Fem.) ورستئ *w'rusta'ī*. ورستي کال *w'rustaey kāl*, Last year. ورستئ مياشت *w'rusta'ī mī'āsht*, Last month. ورستئ ورځ *w'rusta'ī wradz* or روځ *rwadz*, The last day of the month, year, life, etc.

ورستيدل *w'rastedal*, verb intrans. To decay, to stink, to become putrid, rotten, offensive. ورستول *w'rastawul*, verb trans. To make rotten, to make putrid, to cause to decay. For inflections see ووست

ور سر کول *war sar kawul*, verb trans. To give freely, liberally, bounteously, or largely, to bestow without scruple or reserve, to act liberally.

ورشو *wur-sho*, s.f. (9th) A meadow, a place for grazing, a field. Sing. and Pl.

ورشه *war-shah*, imp. second person singular of the infinitive تلل 'To go,' Go thou. Pl. ور شئ *war-sha'aī*, Go you.

A ورطه *war-ṭa'h*, s.f. (3rd) (from ورط) A maze, a labyrinth, a whirlpool, embarrassment, difficulty. Pl. ې *ey.*

ورغالي *orghālaey*, s.m. (1st) A fire-place, a hole dug in the ground to light a fire in or for cooking. Pl. ي *ī*. See اورغالي

ورغاړي *war-ghārrnaey*, s.m. (1st) Rubbing a new born child, or woman after childbirth, with wheat flour and clarified butter, also the butter and flour so used. Pl. ي *ī.*

ورغلل *wu-raghlal*, verb intrans. To go, to depart, or set out (towards him, her, it, or them). It appears to be a corruption of ور *war*, To him, etc., and راغلل *rāgh-lal*, 'To go,' but without the former غلل has no meaning. For inflections see راغلل and leave out the را and add ور

ورغومي *wur-ghūmaey*, s.m. (1st) A young male kid. Pl. ي *ī*. ورغوم *wur-ghūmi*, s.f. (8th) A female kid. Pl. ي *ī*.

ورغوي *war-ghowaey*, s.m. (1st) The palm of the hand, the sole of the foot. When distinction is required, the word 'hand' or 'foot' is used. Pl. ي *ī*.

A ورق *waraḳ*, s.m. (2nd) The leaf of a book, a card, a slice. Pl. ورقونه *waraḳūnah*. Also ورقه *waraḳa'h*, s.f. (3rd) (W.) Pl. ې *ey*.

ورك *wuruk*, adj. Lost, mislaid, missed, wasted, lapsed, alienated, minus, bereaved of, forfeited, irrecoverable; (Fem.) وركه *wuruka'h*. ورك كيدل *wuruk kedal* or وركيدل *wurukedal*, verb intrans. To be or become lost, missed, mislaid, wasted, lapsed, bereaved of, alienated. ورك كول *wuruk kawul* or وركول *wurukawul*, verb trans. To lose, to mislay, to miss, to alienate, to forfeit.

وركړل *war-kṟral*, verb trans. To give, to bestow, to grant. See وركول

وركړونې *war-kṟrūnaey*, s.m. (1st) (act. part. of the preceding), A giver, a bestower, a granter; وركړونِ *war-kṟrūni*, s.f. (8th). Pl. (Masc. and Fem.) ي *ī*. See وركونكي

وركړه *war-kṟrah*, s.m. (6th) Giving, bestowing, donation, offering, presentment, endowment, charity, bounty. Sing. and Pl.

وركړه راكړه *war-kṟrah-rā-kṟrah*, Giving and receiving, trade and commerce, barter, traffic.

وركول *war-kawul*, To give, to bestow, to accord, to confer, to grant, to concede, to present, to give away, to assign, to allow, to endow, to invest, to contribute, to consign, etc. In the conjugation of this infinitive, that of كول must be adopted, and را, در or ور prefixed, according as to whether the meaning be intended for 'me' or 'us,' 'thee' or 'you', and 'him', 'her', 'it,' or 'them.'

وركوونكې *war-kawūnkaey*, s.m. (1st) (act. part. of the preceding). وركوونِ *war-kawūni*, s.f. (8th) Pl. (Masc. and Fem.) ي *ī*. This form signifies the giver, bestower, etc., to 'him,' 'her,' 'it' or 'them;' thus را and در must be used instead, if the receiver be either in the first person or the second. See Grammar, page 46. This word may also be written in the same manner as the second form of act. part. of verbs.

وركه *wuruka'h*, s.f. (3rd) Loss, lapse, deprivation, losing, mislaying, etc. Pl. ې *ey*. See ورك

ورگ *warg*, s.m. (2nd) The fleece of a sheep. Pl. ورگونه *wargūnah*.

ورگ *w'rag* (E.) s.m. (6th) The mane of a horse, ass, etc. See ورږ , يال and اوشي

ورگه *w'raga'h*, s.f. (3rd) A flea. Pl. ې *ey*. See روگه

ورگه *wur-gah*, s.m. (6th) The first milk given by a cow, goat, etc., after calving, biestings. Sing. and Pl. See ورږه

وړله *war-la'h*, adj. Pregnant, big, breeding, with young, in the family way. 2. s.f. (3rd) A pregnant woman, etc. Pl. ې *ey*. وړله توب *wār-la'h-tob*, s.m. (1st) Pregnancy, fecundity, fertility, pullulation, propagation, procreation. Pl. توبونه *tobūnah*; or وړله تيا *war-la'h-tīā*, s.f. (6th) (E.) Sing. and Pl. (W.) Pl. تياوي *tīāwī*. وړله كيدل *war-la'h kedal*, verb intrans. To become pregnant, to get in the family way, to become big with young. وړله كول *war-la'h kawul*, verb trans. To make pregnant, to get or bring in the family way, or with young. See بلاربه

A ورم *waram*, s.m. (2nd) A swelling, a tumour. 2. Inflation, conceit, vanity; comfortable circumstances, happiness, independence; good condition, fatness. Pl. ورمونه *waramūnah*. 3. adj. Swelled, inflated; (Fem.) ورمه *warama'h*. ورم كيدل *waram kedal*, verb intrans. To swell up, to become inflated. ورم كول *waram kawul*, verb trans. To cause or make to swell, to inflate. See پاړسوب

ورماگه *war-māgah*, s.m. (9th) A disease in children, in which boils break out on the face. Sing. and Pl.

ورمارگه *war-mārgah*, s.m. (9th) (W.). See preceding. Sing. and Pl.

ور ميږ *war-mejz*, s.m. (2nd) (W.) The neck, the

back of the neck. Pl. ورميږونه *war-mejzūnah.*

ورميګ *war-meg*, s.m. (2nd) (E.) The neck, the throat. Pl. ورميګونه *war-megūnah.* See preceding.

وندار *warandār*, s.f. (1st) A brother's wife. Pl. ورندارِ *warandāri.* See وندیار

ورنيکه *wær-nīkæh*, s.m. (5th) A great-grandfather on the father's side, an ancestor. Pl. ورنيکه ګان *wær-nīkæh-gān.* See نيکه

ورو *w'ro*, adv. Slowly, gently, gradually, leisurely, deliberately. په ورو ورو *pah w'ro-w'ro*, By degrees, gradually. See رو and رورو

ورور *w'ror*, s.m. (2nd) A brother. Pl. وروڼرَ *w'rūrrna* or وروڼړه *w'rūrrnah.* ديني ورور *dīnī w'ror*, A brother in faith, a friend. کشر ورور *kashar w'ror*, A younger brother. مشر ورور *mashar w'ror*, An elder brother. منځوي ورور *mandz-waey w'ror* or منزوي ورور *manz-waey w'ror*, A middle brother, between the elder and younger brother. ناسکه ورور *nā-sakah w'ror*, A half-brother, either by a different father or by a different mother. د تي ورور *da tī w'ror*, A foster-brother. ورور ګلوي *w'ror galwī*, s.f. (3rd) Brotherhood, brotherliness. Pl. ئي *a'ī*; also ورور والَي *w'ror-wālaey*, s.m. (1st). Pl. والي *wālī*; and ورور ولي *w'ror-walī*, s.f. (3rd). Pl. ئي *a'ī*.

وروري *w'rorī*, s.f. (3rd) Brotherhood, fraternity, relationship, company. Pl. ئي *a'ī.* وروري کول *w'rorī kawul*, verb trans. To show fraternity, to act in a brotherly manner; also to show enmity (Afghān brotherliness).

وروزه *w'rūza'h*, s.f. (3rd) (E.) The eyebrow. Pl. ئي *ey.* See ورځه

وروځه *w'rūdza'h*, s.f. (3rd) See preceding. Pl. ئي *ey.* For different combinations with this word, see ورځه

وروست *w'rost*, adj. Rotten, decayed, putrid, rank, stinking, offensive. Pl. وراسته *w'rāstah*; (Fem.) ورسته *w'rasta'h.* Pl. ورستي *w'rastey.* وروست والَي *w'rost-wālaey*, s.m. (1st) Rottenness, decay, rankness, offensiveness. Pl. والي *wālī.*

ورستيدل *w'rastedal*, verb intrans. To rot, to stink, to decay, to become rotten, putrid, offensive. Pres. ورستيږي *w'rastejzī* (W.) or ورستيګي *w'rastegī* (E.); past وروست شه *w'rost shah* or وُ شه *wu-shah*; fut. وروست به شي *w'rost bah shī* or به وُ شي *bah wu-shī*; imp. وروست شه *w'rost shah* or وُ شه *wu-shah*; act. part. ورستيدونکَي *w'rastedūnkaey* or ورستيدونَي *w'rastedūnaey*; past part. وروست *w'rost* or وروست شوَي *w'rost shawaey*; verb. n. ورستيدنه *w'rastedana'h* or ورستيده *w'rastedah.* ورستول *w'rastawul*, verb trans. To make rotten, to cause to stink, to make putrid. Pres. ورستوي *w'rastawī*; past وروست کړ *w'rost karr* or وُ کړ *wu-karr*; fut. وروست به کړي *w'rost bah krrī* or به وُ کړي *bah wu-krrī*; imp. وروست کړه *w'rost-krrah* or وُ کړه *wu-krrah*; act. part. ورستونکَي *w'rastawūnkaey* or ورستوونَي *w'rastawūnaey*; past part. وروست کړَي *w'rost karraey*; verb.n. ورستونه *w'rastawana'h.* See سخا

ورون *w'rūn*, s.m. (2nd) The thigh. Pl. ورنونه *w'ranūna'h.* په ورنو کښي نيول *pah w'rano kshe* or *kkhe nī-wal*, To take or press between the thighs (as a horseman pressing the flanks of his horse, etc.)

ورهيدل *wur-hedal*, verb intrans. To become free or liberated, to escape, to be delivered, acquitted, discharged, relieved, saved, manumitted. Pres. ورهيږي *wur-hejzī* (W.) or ورهيګي *wur-hegī* (E.); past وُ ورهيده *wu-wur-hedah*; fut. وُ به ورهيږي *wu bah wur-hejzī* or ورهيګي *wur-hegī*; imp. وُ ورهيږه *wu-wur-hejzah* or وُ ورهيګه *wu-wur-hegah*; act. part. ورهيدونکَي *wur-hedūnkaey* or ورهيدونَي *wur-hedūnaey*; past part. ورهيدلَي *wur-hedalaey*; verb. n. ورهيدنه *wur-hedana'h.* ورهول *wur-hawul*, verb trans. To free, to liberate, to acquit, to release, to deliver, to save, to manumit. Pres. ورهوي *wur-hawī*; past وُ ورهاوه *wu-wur-hāwuh*; fut. ر به ورهوي *wuh bah wur-hawī*; imp. وُ ورهوه *wu-wur-hawah*; act. part. ورهونکَي *wur-hawūnkaey* or ورهوونَي *wur-hawūnaey*; past part. ورهولَي *wur-hawulaey*; verb. n. ورهونه *wur-hawuna'h.*

وري *w'raey*, s.m. (1st) A lamb. Pl. ئي *ī.* ورئي

w'ra'ī, s.f. (6th) The feminine of the above. Sing. and Pl.

وړی *waraey* or *wuraey*, s.m. (1st) A load for the head, one of the packs placed on the back of a camel, pony, etc., a load. Pl. ي *ī*.

وريت *w'rīt*, adj. Fried, cooked, roasted, grilled, broiled, toasted, parched; (Fem.) وريته *w'rīta'h*. وريتيدل *w'rītedal*, verb intrans. To become fried, cooked, broiled, grilled, toasted, etc. وريتول *w'rītawul*, verb trans. To grill, to toast, to fry, to parch, to broil, to roast. For inflections see ورتيدل and add an extra ي

وريدل *ore-dal* or وويدل *wore-dal*, verb intrans. To rain, to fall, as snow or hail, to drizzle, to mizzle, to drop, to trickle, to distil. Pres. وري *orī* or وريږي *orejzī* or وورېږي *wo-rejzī* (W.) or وريګي *oregī* or ووري *wo-rī* or ووريګي *wo-regī* (E.); past وُ وريده *wu-oredah* or وُ ووريده *wu-wo-redah*; fut. وُ به وري *wu bah orī* or ووري *wo-rī*; imp. وُ وره *wu-orah* or وُ وريږه *wu-orejzah* or وُ وريګه *wu-oregah* or وُ وورِه *wu-wo-rah* or وُ ووريږه *wu-wo-rejzah* or وُ ووريګه *wu-wo-regah*; act. part. وريدونکي *oredūnkaey* or ووريدونکي *wo-redūnkaey* or وريدوني *ore-dūnaey* or ووريدوني *wo-redūnaey*; past part. وريدلي *oredalaey* or ووريدلي *wo-redalaey*; verb. n. وريدنه *oredana'h* or ووريده *wo-redah*. ورول *orawul* or وورول *worawul*, verb trans. To pour, to drop, to discharge, to pour out, to shower down, to cause to fall (as rain, snow, hail, etc.) Pres. وروي *orawī* or ووروي *wo-rawī*; past وُ وراوه *wu-orāwuh* or وُ ووراوه *wu-wo-rāwuh* and وُ وراوو *wu-orāwo* or وُ ووراوو *wu-wo-rāwo*; fut. وُ به وروي *wu bah orawī* or وُ به ووروي *wu bah wo-rawī*; imp. وُ وروه *wu-orawah* or وُ ووروه *wu-wo-rawah*; act. part. وروونکي *orawūnkaey* or ووروونکي *wo-rawūnkaey* and وروونی *ora-wūnaey* or ووروونی *wo-rawūnaey*; past part. ورولي *orawulaey* or ووروليَ *wo-rawulaey*; verb. n. ورونه *orawuna'h* or ووورونه *wo-rawuna'h*. See اوريدل and اورول

وريره *warera'h*, s.f. (3rd) A brother's daughter, a niece. Pl. ې *ey*.

وريز *war-yaz*, s.f. (1st) A cloud, mist. Pl. وريزِ *war-yazi*. See اوريزه

وريزه *war-yaza'h*, s.f. (3rd). See preceding. Pl. ې *ey*.

وريځ *war-yadz*, s.f. (1st) (W.) A cloud, a mist. Pl. وريځ *war-yadzi*. Also وريځه *war-yadza'h*, s.f. (3rd) Pl. ې *ey*. See اوريځ and اوريځه

وريشل *w'reshal*, verb trans. To spin, to twist. For inflections see ريشل and add the و

وريښم *w'reshm* (W.) or *w'rekhm* (E.) s.m. (6th) Silk, silk-cloth. Sing. and Pl. وريښمين *w'reshmīn* or *w'rekhmīn*, adj. Silken, made of silk; (Fem.) وريښمينه *w'reshmīna'h* or *w'rekhmīna'h*. د وريښمُ غوزه *da w'reshmo* or *w'rekhmo ghoza'h*, s.f. (3rd) The silk cocoon. Pl. ې *ey*. د وريښمُ چينجي *da w'reshmo* or *w'rekhmo chīnjaey*, s.m. (1st) The silkworm. Pl. ي *ī*. See ريښم

ورئيزه *w'reyza'h*, s.f. (3rd) A female member of a bridal procession summoned by the bride-groom. Pl. ې *ey*. See ورا and جانجي

وړ *wurr*, adj. Small, diminutive, less, little, minute, inconsiderable, puny, wee, petty, undersized. Pl. واړه *wārrah*; (Fem.) وړه *wurra'h*. Pl. وړې *wurrey*. وړوکي *wurrūkey*, adj. A little one, a wee thing, a little child (dimin. of وړ); (Fem.) وړوکۍ *wurrūki*. وړ والي *wurr wālaey*, s.m. (1st) Littleness, smallness, minuteness, diminutiveness, puniness, undersize. Pl. والي *wālī*. وړيدل *wurredal*, verb intrans. To become or grow small, minute, little, puny, diminutive. 2. To become or grow humble, meek, humbled, lessened, humiliated. Pres. وړيږي *wurrejzī* (W.) or وړيګي *wurregī* (E.); past وړ شه *wurr shah* or وُ شه *wu-shah*; fut. وړ به شي *wurr bah shī* or به وُ شي *bah wu-shī*; imp. وړ شه *wurr shah* or وُ شه *wu-shah*; act. part. وړيدونکي *wurredūnkaey* or وړيدوني *wurredūnaey*; past part. وړ *wurr* or وړ شوي *wurr shawaey*; verb n. وړيدنه *wurredana'h* or وړيده *wurredah*. وړول *wurrawul*, verb trans. To make small, little, puny, minute, diminutive, etc. 2. To humble, to humiliate. Pres. وروي *wurrawī*; past ور کړ *wurr-karr* or وُ کړ *wu-karr*; fut. ور به کړي *wurr bah krrī* or وُ به کړي *wu-bah krrī*; imp. ور کړه *wurr krrah* or وُ کړه *wu-krrah*; act. part. ورووںکَي *wurrawūnkaey* or ورووںيَ *wurrawūnaey*; past part. ور کړيَ *wurr karraey*; verb. n. وروںه *wurrawuna'h*. See وور

ور *wærr*, adj. Successful, winning, triumphant, conquering, victorious, beating, gaining a suit at law, attaining, etc.; (Fem.) وړه *wærra'h*. ور واليَ *wærr wālaey*, s.m. (1st) Success, prize, successfulness, triumph. Pl. والي *wālī*. ور طرف *wærr taraf*, The winning side. ور کيدل *wærr kedal*, verb intrans. To become successful, to become the winner in a race, match, or suit, etc. ور کول *wærr kawul*, verb trans. To make or cause to win, to cause to succeed, to make the winner or conqueror, to give the victory unto. See ورانه and پر

ور *warr*, s.m. (2nd) The scab of a wound. 2. Small pieces of gold and silver collected together, a kind of miscellany, a mass. Pl. وروںه *warrūnah*. See خير

وړَ *wurra* or وړه *wurrah*. Imp. of ورل which see.

وړاندِ *w'rrāndi* or وړاندي *w'rrāndī*, s.m. (9th) Bow, prow, van, fore, front, vanguard, face, front-rank. Sing. and Pl. 2. adj. Preceding, prior, previous, anterior, before. (Masc. and Fem.) 3. adv. Before, in the front, ahead, in advance, foremost, headmost. 2. Long before, some time previously. وړاندني *w'rrāndinaey* or وړانديني *w'rrāndīnaey*, adj. Former, prior, preceding, anterior, antecedent, previous, before. 2. Preliminary, preparatory, introductory. 3. Fore, front, frontal; (Fem.) وړاندنۍ *w'rrāndina'ī* or وړانديںۍ *w'rrāndīna'ī*. وړاندني کال *w'rrāndinaey-kāl*, The prior or previous year. وړاندنۍ مياشت *w'rrāndina'ī miāsht*, The preceding or previous month. وړاندنۍ ورځ *w'rrāndina'ī wradz* or روځ *rwadz*, The preceding or prior day. وړاندنۍ شپه *w'rrāndina'ī shpa'h*, The prior or preceding night. وړاندِ آستول *w'rrāndi āstawul*, verb trans. To send on or despatch before, to send on in advance. وړاندِ تلل *w'rrāndi t'lal*, verb intrans. To go on in advance, to get the lead, to get before, to get the start. وړاندِ راتلل *w'rrāndi rā-t'lal*, verb intrans. To precede, to come on before. وړاندِ زغاستل *w'rrāndi z'ghāstal* or زغاښتل *z'ghākhtal*, verb intrans. To run on before, to take the lead. وړاندِ کول *w'rrāndi kawul*, verb trans. To place in the front or van, to place before, to prefix, to send on before. وړاندِ کيدل *w'rrāndi kedal*, verb intrans. To be before, to come to the front. وړاندِ وتل *w'rrāndi watal*, verb intrans. To come out before, to pass out or issue before another (as in leaving a house). وړاندِ ورستو *w'rrāndi w'rusto*, Before and behind, in front and rear, before and after. وړاندِ ورستو کتل *w'rrāndi w'rusto katal*, verb trans. To have a care, to consider, to look both before and behind, to have one's wits about one. وړاندِ واليَ *w'rrāndi-wālaey*, s.m. (1st) Getting the start in anything, anticipating, anticipation, being beforehand, surpassing, excelling. Pl. والي *wālī*. See also دوړاندِ which may be used indiscriminately with وړاندِ

ورانه *warr-āna'h*, s.f. (3rd) Winning, gaining, succeeding in anything, success, luck, prize, emolument. Pl. ۍ *ey*. ورانه پرانه *warrāna'h-parrāna'h*, Winning and losing, gain and loss. See ور and پر

وړکَي *w'rrukaey*, adj. Little, small, wee. 2. A wee thing, a little one, a term of endearment to a child; (Fem.) وړکۍ *w'rrukey* or وړکِ *w'rruki* (dimin. of ور which see). Pl. (Masc. and Fem.) ي *ī*. See وور and کچني

ورل *w'rral*, verb trans. To bear, to carry, to remove, to transport, to carry over, to convey, to waft, etc. (particularly applied to inanimate things, in distinction to بيول which see.) Pres. وړي *w'rrī*; past يو ور *yo-wurr*; fut. وُ به وړي *wu bah w'rrī*; imp. وړه *w'rrah*; act. part. وړونکَي *w'rrūnkaey* or وړونَي *w'rrūnaey*; past part. وړيَ *warraey*; verb. n. وړنه *w'rrana'h*.

پناه وړل *panāh w'rral*, verb trans. To take refuge or shelter.

وړم كال *warrm kāl*, adv. The year before last, two years since. وړمه ورځ *warrma'h wradz*, or روځ *rwadz*, The day before yesterday. لا وړمه ورځ *lā warrma'h wradz* or روځ *rwadz*, Three days since. وړمه شپه *warrma'h shpa'h*, The night before last. وړمه مياشت *warrma'h miāsht*, The month before last.

وړمبئ *w'rrumbaey*, adj. First, the first, primary, original, primitive, chief, principal; (Fem.) وړمبۍ *w'rrumba'ī*. 2. adv. First, in the first place. See also رمبي and رنبي

وړن *warran*, adj. Shaggy, having a long or shaggy fleece or coat, as a sheep or camel; hairy; (Fem.) وړنه *narrana'h*. وړينه *warrīnah*, adj. Of wool, woollen, made of wool or camel's hair. See وړۍ

وړنبلئ *w'rrum-balaey*, adj. First, etc.; (Fem.) ۍ *a'ī*. See preceding and following.

وړنبئ *w'rrunbaey*. See وړمبي and امړي

وړوکئ *nurrūkaey*. See وړکي

وړه *warrah*, s.m. (6th) Flour, meal. Sing. and Pl. See اوړه

وړه پړه *w'rra'h-p'rra'h*, s.f. (3rd) Winning and losing, gain and loss. Pl. ې *ey*. See وړ and وړانه پړانه

وړۍ *warra'ī*, s.f. (6th) Wool. Sing. and Pl.

وړينه *warrīnah*, adj. Woollen, made of wool.

وړئ *worraey*, s.m. (1st) Summer. Pl. ي *ī*. See اوړي

وړي *ūrraey*, A particle of diminution applied to nouns; as, چرګ *chirg*, A cock; چرګوړي *chirgūrraey*, A little or young cock, etc.

وړيا *wirrī-ā* or *narrī-ā*, adv. Gratis, for nothing, given away without return or benefit, freely, gratuitously, without recompense. See ويړيا

وړيدل *warredal*, verb intrans. To become ground, triturated, rubbed, scoured, etc. وړول *warrawul*, verb trans. To grind, to triturate, to pulverize, to rub, to scour, to polish, etc. See اوړيدل and اوړول

وز *wuz*, s.m. (7th) A he-goat. Pl. وزونه *w'zūnah*. وزه *wuza'h*, s.f. (3rd) A she-goat. Pl. ې *ey*. (P بز). وزګړئ *wuz-garaey*, s.m. (1st) A young he-goat (dim. of وز). Pl. ي *ī*. وزګړۍ *wuz-gari*, s.f. (8th) A young she-goat. Pl. ي *ī*.

وزبك *wuz-bak*, s.m. (5th) The name of a tribe residing about Balkh, an Uzbek. Pl. وزبكان *wuz-bakān*. وزبكه *wuz-baka'h*, s.f. (3rd) A female of the above tribe. Pl. ې *ey*.

وزر *wazr*, s.m. (2nd) The wing of a bird, the largest feather in a bird's wing. Pl. وزرونه *wazrūnah*. See بڼره

وزر سست كول *wazar sust kawul*, verb trans. To lower or flap the wings before alighting, as a bird.

وزګار *waz-gār*, adj. Unemployed, out of work, idle, unoccupied, doing nothing, set aside; (Fem.) وزګاره *waz-gāra'h*. وزګار توب *waz-gār-tob*, s.m. (2nd) Inactivity, inaction, being out of work or employment. Pl. توبونه *tob-ūnah*.

وزګاريدل *waz-gāredal*, verb intrans. To be out of work or employment, idle, doing nothing, laid on the shelf, set aside, to be laid up in ordinary, etc. Pres. وزګاريږي *waz-gārejzī* (W.) or وزګاريګي *waz-gāregī* (E.); past وزګار شه *waz-gār shah* or وُ شه *wu-shah*; fut. وزګار به شي *waz-gār bah shī* or به وُ شي *bah wu-shī*; imp. وزګار شه *waz-gār-shah* or وُ شه *wu-shah*; act. part. وزګاريدونكئ *waz-gāredūnkaey* or وزګاريدونئ *waz-gāredūnaey*; past part. وزګار *waz-gār* or وزګار شوئ *waz-gār shawaey*; verb. n. وزګاريدنه *waz-gāredana'h* or وزګاريده *waz-gāredah*. وزګارول *waz-gārawul*, verb trans. To render inactive, to set aside, to put out of work, to shelve, to supersede, to discard, to dismiss. Pres. وزګاروي *waz-gārawī*; past وزګار كړ *waz-gār karr* or وُ كړ *wu-karr*; fut. وزګار به كړي *waz-gār bah krrī* or به وُ كړي *bah wu-krrī*; imp. وزګار كړه *waz-gār krrah* or وُ كړه *wu-krrah*; act. part. وزګارونكئ *waz-gārawūnkaey* or وزګارونئ *waz-gārawūnaey*; past part. وزګار كړئ *waz-gār karraey*; verb. n. وزګارونه *waz-gārawuna'h*.

وزګړئ *wuz-garaey*, s.m. (1st) A young he-goat. Pl. ي *ī*. See وز

A وزير *wazīr*, s.m. (5th) A Minister of State. Pl. وزيران *wazīrān*.

P A وزيري *wazīrī*, s.f. (3rd) The office of a Minister of State. Pl. ئ *a'ī*.

وزيري *wazīrī*, s.m. (1st) (Pl.) The name of a tribe of Afghāns, notorious robbers, dwelling round about the mountain known as Soloman's Throne. وزيرئ *wazīraey* (Sing.) A male of the above tribe. وزيرئ *wazīra'ī*, s.f. (6th) A female of the above. Sing. and Pl.

وزيمه *wazema'h*, s.f. (3rd) A she-goat or ewe ready for the male. Pl. ې *ey*. وزيمه توب *wazema'h-tob*, s.m. (2nd) The state of being ready for the male, the animal heat. Pl. توبونه *tobūnah*.

وُ ژگوره *wu-jzghorah*, adv. (imp. of ژغورل) Keep, preserve, shield (us), etc.

وژل *wajzal* (W.) verb trans. To kill, to slay, to deprive of life, to put an end to, to murder, to put to death, to slaughter. Pres. وژني *wajznī*; past وُ وژي *wu-wajzī*; fut. وُ به وژني *wu bah wajznī*; imp. وُ وژنه *wu-wajznah*; act. part. وژلونکئ *wajz-lūnkaey* or وژلونئ *wajz-lūnaey* or وژونکئ *wajzūnkaey* or وژونئ *wajzūnaey*; past part. وژلئ *wajzalaey*; verb. n. وژنه *wajzana'h*. See وژلل and وجلل

وژلل *wajz-lal*, verb trans. To kill, etc. For inflections see وجلل and substitute ژ for ج

وژه *wujza'h*, s.f. (3rd) A vein, a nerve, a tendon. Pl. ې *ey*.

وژه *wajza'h*, s.f. (3rd) The hollow of the back part of the neck where the head joins the spine. Pl. ې *ey*.

وږد *ūjzd*, adj. Long, longsome, lengthy, outstretched, lengthened, elongated, prolonged. 2. Tall, a tall man, etc. Pl. وږده *ūjzdæh*; (Fem.) وږده *ūjzda'h*; also a tall woman. وږد والئ *ūjzd-wālaey*, s.m. (1st) Length, longitude, span, elongation, prolongation. Pl. والي *wālī*. وږديدل *ūjzdedal*, verb intrans. To become or grow long, longsome, lengthy, elongated, tall, to shoot out, to sprout. وږدول *ūjzdawul*, verb trans. To make or render long, to elongate, to extend, to prolong, to stretch, to spin or draw out. See اوږد and اوگد

وږم *wajzm* (W.) s.m. (2nd) Steam, glowing heat, vapor, exhalation, effluvium, scent. Pl. وږمونه *wajzmūnah*. وږم کول *wajzm kawul* or وږم لرل *wajzm laral*, verb trans. To steam, to throw out steam, vapor, etc.

وږمکئ *wajz-maka'ī*, s.f. (6th) The moon, moonlight. Sing. and Pl. See also سپوږمئ

وږمه *wajz-ma'h*, (E.) s.f. (3rd) Breath, respiration; steam, vapor, exhalation. 2. A light air or breeze, a cat's paw. Pl. ې *ey*. See وگمه

وږمئ *wajz-ma'ī*, s.f. (6th) The moon, moonlight. Sing. and Pl. See وږمکئ

وږئ *wajzaey*, adj. Hungry, pinched with hunger, craving, peckish, voracious, ravenous; (Fem.) وږې *wajzi*. Pl. (Masc. and Fem.) ي *ī*. وږئ کيدل *wajzaey kedal*, verb intrans. To hunger, to crave, to become peckish, voracious, ravenous. وږئ کول *wajzaey kawul*, verb trans. To make hungry, to pinch with hunger, to make voracious or ravenous. See لوږه and لوگه

وږي *wajzaey*, s.m. (1st) An ear of corn. Pl. ي *ī*. See وگي. وږي چي *wajzaey-chaey*, s.m. (1st) A male gleaner. Pl. ي *ī*. وږي چئ *wajzaey-cha'ī*, s.f. (6th) A female gleaner. Sing. and Pl.

وس *was*, s.m. (2nd) Endeavour, attempt, essay, trial. 2. Power, energy, force, ability, control, ableness, competency, etc. Pl. وسونه *wasūnah*. وس کول *was kawul*, verb trans. To endeavour, to attempt, to essay, to try. وس لرل *was laral*, verb trans. To have or possess power, energy, competency, ability.

وس *was*, s.m. (2nd) (s वस, Dwell) Abundance, prosperity; cultivation, population. Pl. وسونه *was-ūnah*.

وساه *wisā'h*, s.f. (9th) Belief, trust, credit, confidence, dependence on, reliance, assurance. Sing. and Pl. وساه کول *wisā'h kawul*, verb trans. To place faith on, to trust, to credit, to confide in, to rely upon. وساه لرل *wisā'h laral*, verb trans. To have faith or reliance on, to have dependence or confidence in. See ساويسا and ويساد

وسپنه *wuspina'h*, s.f. (3rd) Iron. Pl. ي *ey*.

وسپنخرئ *wuspin-kharraey*, s.m. (1st) The dross of iron remaining after smelting. Pl. ي *ī*.

وسته *wasta'h*, s.f. (3rd) A small pond or lake, a pool of water. Pl. ي *ey*.

وسکَ *was-ka* or وسکه *waskah*, adv. Then, therefore, moreover, finally. 2. As if, as, as it were. See سکه

وسله *wasla'h*, s.f. (3rd) Arms, tools, weapons, implements, accoutrements, etc. Pl. ي *ey*. See درسته

A وسمه *was-ma'h*, s.f. (3rd) (from وسم) The leaves of the woad or indigo plant, from which an extract is made, and used for dyeing hair, clothes, etc. Pl. ي *ey*.

A وسواس *was-wās*, s.m. (2nd) (from وسوس) The temptations of the Devil, distraction of the mind. 2. Doubt, suspense, hesitation, apprehension, suspicion, dread, perplexity, superstition, fluctuation of mind, scrupulousness. Pl. وسواسونه *was-wāsūnah*. وسواس کول *was-wās kawul*, verb trans. To doubt, to hesitate; to make suspicious or apprehensive; to perplex.

A وسواسي *was-wāsī*, adj. Doubtful, causing suspense, distracting, scrupulous, apprehensive.

A وسوسه *was-wasa'h*, s.f. (3rd) Temptation, evil suggestion. Pl. ي *ey*. وسوسه آچول *was-wasa'h āchawul*, verb trans. To tempt, to endeavour to lead astray, to incite to evil.

وسه *wasa'h*, s.f. (3rd) Summer rain, a summer shower. Pl. ي *ey*. See د ووري باران

A وسيله *wasīla'h*, s.f. (3rd) Affinity, propinquity. 2. Cause, occasion, conjuncture. 3. Support, prop. 4. Means, mediation, intervention, patronage. Pl. ي *ey*. وسيله دار *wasīla'h-dār*, s.m. (5th) A client, a dependent. Pl. وسيله داران *wasīla'h-dārān*. وسيله داره *wasīla'h-dāra'h*, s.f. (3rd). Pl. ي *ey*. وسيله داري *wasīla'h dārī*, s.f. (3rd) Clientship, patronage, dependence. Pl. ئي *a'ī*. وسيله لرل *wasīla'h laral*, verb trans. To have or possess patronage, mediation, intervention. وسيله کول *wasīla'h kawul*, verb trans. To make or obtain patronage or mediation.

وشته *washta'h* or *wushta'h*, s.f. (3rd) Joking, jesting, pleasantry, mirth, drollery, jocularity. 2. A joke, a jest, a sally, a retort. Pl. ي *ey*. وشته کول *washta'h kawul*, verb trans. To jest, to crack a joke; also وشتي کول *washtey kawul*. See توقه

وښتي *washtey* (W.) or *wakhtey* (E.), s.f. (3rd) Pl. A kind of rice grown in the hills, which is of a brown colour when cooked. وښته *washta'h* or *wakhta'h*, A grain of rice of the above species.

وښخور *wash-khor* (W.) or *wakh-khor* (E.) adj. An eater of grass (animal) in opposition to a beast of prey; (Fem.) وښخوره *wash-khora'h* or *wakh-khora'h*.

وښکل *wu-sh'kul* or *wu-kh'kul*, verb trans. To draw out. See ښکل

وښئ *washaey* (W.) or *wakhaey* (E.), s.m. (1st) A bracelet. Pl. ي *ī*.

A وصال *wiṣāl*, s.m. (9th) (from وصل) Meeting, interview, connection. 2. Death. 3. Society, confederacy. 4. Fruition, enjoyment. Sing. and Pl.

A وصف *waṣf*, s.m. (2nd) Praise, encomium, description of qualities, merits, virtue, worth, attributes, etc. Pl. وصفونه *waṣf-ūnah*. وصف کول *waṣf kawul*, verb trans. To describe, to praise.

A وصل *waṣl*, s.m. (9th) Meeting, union, conjunction, connection. Sing. and Pl. وصل کول *waṣl kawul*, verb trans. To unite, to attach, to cement, to conjoin, to annex. وصل کيدل *waṣl kedal*, verb intrans. To become united, joined.

A وصلت *waṣlat*, s.m. (2nd) Conjunction, joining, meeting, connection. Pl. وصلتونه *waṣlat-ūnah*. وصلت کول *waṣlat kawul*, verb trans. To attach, to join, to cause to meet.

A وصول *wuṣūl*, s.m. (9th) (from وصل) Arrival, conjunction, acquisition, or enjoyment. Sing. and Pl. وصول کول *wuṣūl kawul*, verb trans. To collect, to acquire. وصول کيدل *wuṣūl kedal*, verb intrans. To get, to obtain, to derive.

A وصي *waṣī*, s.m. (5th) (from وصي) An executor, an administrator, a preceptor. Pl. وصيان *waṣīān*.

A وصيت *waṣī-yat*, s.m. (2nd) A last will and testament, a legacy, a bequest. 2. A precept, a mandate. 3. Making a will. Pl. وصيتونه *waṣī-yatūnah*. وصيت نامه *waṣī-yat nāma'h*, s.f. (3rd) A testament, a will. Pl. ئ *ey*. وصيت كول *waṣī-yat kawul*, verb trans. To bequeath, to devise, to leave by will.

وضبك *waẓ-bak*. See وزبك

A وضو *waẓū*, s.m. (9th) (from وضأ or وضو) Ablution before prayer. وضو كول *waẓū kawul*, verb trans. To perform the required ablutions before prayer. Sing. and Pl. See اودس

A وطن *waṭan*, s.m. (2nd) Native country, home, country, abode, residence. Pl. وطنونه *waṭanūnah*. جلاوطن *jalā-waṭan*, Emigration, leaving one's country. جلا وطني *jalā-waṭanī*, Banishment, expulsion from one's native land. جلا وطن كيدل *jalā waṭan kedal*, verb intrans. To be exiled, to emigrate or abandon one's country. جلا وطن كول *jalā waṭan kawul*, verb trans. To banish, to exile.

P A وطني *waṭanī*, adj. Belonging to one's country.

A وطواط *waṭ-wāṭ*, s.m. (2nd) A mountain swallow, a martinet. 2. A man having a voice like a swallow. 3. A bat, a rere mouse. 4. A timid or languid man. Pl. وطواطونه *waṭ-wāṭūnah*. وطواطه *waṭ-wāṭa'h*, s.f. (3rd). Pl. ئ *ey*.

A وظيفه *waẓīfa'h*, s.f. (3rd) (from وظف) A pension, a stipend, a salary, stipulated allowance, a daily performance or task, land bestowed in gift for past services. Pl. ئ *ey*.

A وعده *waæda'h*, s.f. (3rd) (from وعد) A promise, a vow, agreement, bargain, appointment, assignation. Pl. ئ *ey*. وعده خلاف *waæda'h khilāf*, A false contract, a person who does not keep his promise; (Fem.) وعده خلافه *waæda'h khilāfa'h*, A female who does not keep a promise. وعده خلافي *waæda'h khilāfī*, s.f. (3rd) Breach of promise, breaking a contract. Pl. ئ *a'ī*. وعده كول *waæda'h kawul*, verb trans. To make an agreement or bargain, to promise, to appoint, to make an appointment. وعده وفا *waæda'h wafā*, adj. True to one's word or promise.

A وعظ *waæẓ*, s.m. (9th) Advice, admonition, exhortation, sermon. Sing. and Pl. وعظ كول *waæẓ kawul*, verb trans. To preach, to exhort.

وغه *wagha'h*, s.f. (3rd) A large red worm, particularly the species infesting children. Pl. ئ *ey*. See جنجي

A وغيره *wa-ghaira'h*, Et cætera, and so forth.

A وفا *wafā*, adj. (from وفي) Performing a promise, fulfilment, sincerity, fidelity, faithfulness. (E.) Sing. and Pl. (W.) Pl. وفاوي *wafāwī*. وفا دار *wafā-dār*, adj. Faithful, sincere, constant; (Fem.) وفا داره *wafā-dāra'h*. وفا داري *wafā-dārī*, s.f. (3rd) Faithfulness, constancy, sincerity. Pl. ئ *a'ī*. وفا كول *wafā kawul*, verb trans. To perform a promise. وفاداري كول *wafā-dārī kawul*, verb trans. To act with faithfulness, constancy, or sincerity.

A وقار *wiḳār*, s.m. (2nd) (from وقر) Dignity, estimation. 2. Steadiness, constancy. 3. Majesty, authority, dignity. 4. Mildness, gravity, modesty; honor, reputation. Pl. وقارونه *wiḳārūnah*.

A وقت *waḳt*, s.m. (2nd) Time, season, opportunity. Pl. وقتونه *waḳtūnah*. For the different combinations of this word see under وخت

A وقف *waḳf*, s.m. (2nd) A legacy for pious uses, an endowment, dedication, or foundation for pious purposes. Pl. وقفونه *waḳfūnah*. وقف كول *waḳf kawul*, verb trans. To dedicate to pious uses.

A وقوف *wuḳūf*, s.m. (9th) (from وقف) Understanding, information, sense, experience, wisdom. Sing. and Pl. وقوف دار *wuḳūf-dār*, adj. Informed of, experienced; (Fem.) وقوف داره *wuḳūf-dāra'h*.

A وكالت *wakālat*, s.m. (2nd) (from وكل) Embassy, agency, deputation, delegation, commission. Pl. وكالتونه *wakālatūnah*. وكالت

کول *wakālat kawul*, verb trans. To act as agent, or delegate.

وُ کړه *wu-kṟrah*, s.m. (6th) (past tense of کړل) Action, act, deed, doing, proceeding. 2. Labour, art, business, manner, conduct, etc. Sing. and Pl.

وکښل *wu-k'khal*, verb trans. To pull or draw out, to remove, to elicit, to express, to extricate. See کښل and prefix و

A وکيل *wakīl*, s.m. (5th) (from وکل) An agent, ambassador, representative, counsellor (at law), attorney, deputy, delegate, commissioner. Pl. وکيلان *wakīlān*.

وګد *ūgd* or ووګد *wūgd*, adj. (E.) Long, lengthened, lengthy. Pl. وګډه *ūgdæh* or ووګډه *wūgdæh*. (Fem.) وګده *ūgda'h*. Pl. وګدې *ūgdey*. وګد والي *ūgd-wālaey*, s.m. (1st) Length, elongation, span, longitude, prolongation. Pl. والي *wālī*. وګديدل *ūgdedal*, verb intrans. To become or grow long, lengthy, to shoot out, to grow apace. وګدول *ūgdawul*, verb trans. To make long, to prolong, to extend, to spin out. For other combinations see اوږد, اوګد, and ورد

وګړي *wagaṟraey* or *wugaṟraey*, s.m. (1st) A person, a human being, a living creature. Pl. وګړي *wagaṟrī* or *wugaṟrī*, People, human beings, persons.

وګم *wagm*, s.m. (2nd) (E.) Steam, vapor, exhalation, glowing heat. 2. Effluvium, scent. Pl. وګمونه *wagmūnah*. وګم لرل *wagm laral* or وګم کول *wagm kawul*, verb trans. To steam, to exhale, to throw out or have or contain effluvium or smell. See ورم

وګمه *wag-ma'h*, s.f. (3rd) Breath, respiration, steam, vapor, effluvium. 2. A light air, a gentle breeze, a cat's paw. Pl. ې *ey*. See وګم and ورمه

وګي *wagaey*, s.m. (1st) (E.) An ear of corn. Pl. ي *ī*. وګي چاڼړي *wagaey chāṟrnaey*, adj. as s.m. (1st) A gleaner; (Fem.) وګي چاڼړ *wagaey chāṟrni*. Pl. (Masc. and Fem.) ي *ī*. See وري

وګي *wagaey* or *wugaey*, adj. Hungry, peckish, voracious, pinched with hunger, craving, ravenous; (Fem.) وګې *wagi* or *wugi*. وګي کيدل *wagaey kedal*, verb intrans. To hunger, to crave, to become peckish, ravenous, voracious. وګي کول *wagaey kawul*, verb trans. To make hungry or peckish, to pinch with hunger, to render ravenous or voracious. See لوږه, وږي and لوګه

ول *wal*, s.m. (7th) Cheapness, low price. Pl. ولونه *w'lūnah*. وَل or په وله *pah w'lah* or *w'la*, adj. Cheap, moderate, reasonable, low in price. See ويل

ول *wal*, s.m. (2nd) A twist, a curl, a turn, a coil, a bend, a wind, a wrench, a tangle. 2. Entanglement, winding, turning, twisting. Pl. ولونه *walūnah*. ول کيدل *wal kedal*, verb intrans. To become twisted, curled, tangled, bent, etc. ول کول *wal kawul*, verb trans. To bend, turn, tangle, coil, twist, etc. ول دار *wal-dār*, adj. Bent, twisted, curled, coiled, tangled, turned, etc.; (Fem.) ول داره *wal-dāra'h*.

ول *wul*, A particle affixed to adjectives and other words in forming the infinitives of transitive verbs, together with ل. See Grammar, page 49.

ولاړ *walāṟr*, adj. Standing, erect, on the feet (in opposition to sitting or lying down), remaining erect, upright (generally applied to animate objects); (Fem.) ولاړه *walāṟra'h*. ولاړ کيدل *walāṟr kedal* or ولاړيدل *walāṟredal*, verb intrans. To rise up, to stand, to stand erect, to be on the feet, to be erect, to become erect, to stop, to halt, not to proceed. Pres. ولاړيږي *walāṟrejẕī* (W.) or ولاړيګي *walāṟregī* (E.); past ولاړ شه *walāṟr shah* or وُ شه *wu-shah*; fut. ولاړ به شي *walāṟr bah shī* or به وُ شي *bah wu-shī*; imp. ولاړ شه *walāṟr shah* or وُ شه *wu-shah*; act. part. ولاړيدونکي *walāṟredūnkaey* or ولاړيدونې *walāṟredūnaey*; past part. ولاړيدلي *walāṟredalaey*; verb. n. ولاړيدنه *walāṟredana'h* or ولاړيده *walāṟredah*, and ولاړه *walāṟra'h*. ولاړول *walāṟrawul*, verb trans. To cause or make to stand, to raise up, to erect, to place on the feet, to make to halt, stop, etc. Pres. ولاړوي *walāṟrawī*; past ولاړ کړ *walāṟr kaṟr* or وُ کړ

wu-karr; fut. ولاړ به کړي *walārr. bah krrī* or به وُ کړي *bah wu-krrī*; imp. ولاړ کړه *walārr krrah* or وُ کړه *wu-krrah*; act. part. ولاړوونکيَ *walārrawūnkaey* or ولاړووني *walārrawūnaey*; past part. ولاړ کړيَ *walārr karraey*; verb. n. ولاړونه *walārranuna'h.*

ولاړه *walārra'h*, s.f. (3rd) Rising up, standing on the feet, the act of being erect, halting, stopping. Pl. ي *ey*; also ولاړيده *wa-larredah*, s.m. (6th). Sing. and Pl.; and ولاړيدنه *walārredana'h*, s.f. (3rd). Pl, ي *ey*; (verb. ns. of ولاړيدل), ناسته ولاړه *nāsta'h walārra'h*, Sitting down and rising up, visiting, acquaintance.

ولاړي *walārrey* or ولاړ *walārr*, adv. A short time, a little, somewhat, a small quantity, slightly, a few minutes or moments.

A ولايت *wilāyat*, s.m. (2nd) An inhabited country, dominion, district, a foreign country, abroad. Pl. ولايتونه *wilāyatūnah*.

ولايتي *wilāyatī*, adj. Foreign, of a foreign country, a foreigner.

ولل *w'lal*, verb trans. To wash, to cleanse, to purify, to lave, to absterge, to clean. Pres. ولي *w'lī*; past وُ ولل *wu-w'lal* or وُ وله *wu-w'lah*; fut. وُ به ولي *wu bah w'lī*; imp. وُ وله *wu-w'lah*; act. part. ولونکيَ *w'lūnkaey* or ولونيَ *w'lūnaey*; past part. وللي *w'lalaey* or وليَ *w'laey*; verb. n. وله *w'la'h* or ولنه *w'lana'h*. See وينځل and مينځل

وله *w'lah*, s.m. (6th) (verb. n. of ولل) Cleaning, washing, laving, ablution. Sing. and Pl.; or ولنه *w'lana'h*, s.f. (3rd). Pl. ي *ey*.

وله *wula'h* or *wala'h*, s.f. (3rd) The root of a tree, particularly the smaller parts, a fibre. 2. *wala'h*, A canal, a small stream, a watercourse. 3. A willow. a sort of cane. Pl. ي *ey*. See واله

و له *wa-lah*, prep. or post. 'Unto' or 'to,' one of the signs of the dative case. See Grammar, page 30.

A ولي *walī*, s.m. (5th) A prince, a lord, a master, a friend of God, a saint. 2. A slave, a servant. Pl. وليان *waliān*.

ولي *waley* or ولِ *wali*, adv. Why, wherefore, on what account or reason. (W.) ولي *walī*.

P ولي *wal-e*, adv. But, yet, however, besides, also, likewise.

وليَ *walaey*, s.m. (1st) The shoulder-blade of an animal used in augury. Pl. ي *ī*.

ولي *wili*, adj. Melted, liquified (as snow, etc.). See ويلي

وليشت *w'lesht*, s.f. (1st) A span, the distance between the tip of the thumb and the little finger when stretched out. Pl. وليشتِ *w'leshti*.

وليشتينک *w'leshtīnak*, adj. (dimin. of the above) A dwarf, a pigmy; a precocious child; (Fem.) وليشتينکه *w'leshtīnaka'h*.

ولينبت *w'lekht* or *w'lesht*, s.f. (1st). Pl. ولينبتِ *w'lekhti* or *w'leshti*. See preceding.

ومړي *wum-rrey*, adv. Before, previously, in time past, erewhile, before now.

ونَ *wana*, s.f. (3rd) A tree. Pl. ونِ *wani*. See ونه

وند *wand*, s.m. (2nd) A dike, a bank of earth raised to restrain a river or the like. Pl. وندونه *wandūnah*.

وندر *wandar*, s.f. (1st) A rope having several nooses to which the feet of cows and the like are fastened, and the heads of sheep and other small animals when pent up at night. Pl. وندر *wandari*.

وندنَي *wandanaey*, s.m. (1st) The band of a sheaf of corn, a rope made of grass or straw. Pl. ي *ī*.

ونديار *wand-yār*, s.f. (1st) A brother's wife, a sister-in-law. Pl. ونديار *wand-yāri*. See ورندار

ونډ *wandd*, s.m. (2nd) A share, a lot, an allotment, a portion, a division, a quota, a meed, a dividend, a distribution. 2. The land of a ward of a town, an estate, or farm. Pl. ونډونه *wanddūnah*. ونډ کول *wandd kawul*, verb trans. To portion, to divide, to allot, to share, to dole or parcel out.

ونډه *wandda'h*, s.f. (3rd) (W.) A share, a lot, a portion, etc. Pl. ي *ey*. ونډه کول *wandda'h kawul*, verb trans. To allot, to share. See preceding.

ونزل *winzal*, verb trans. To wash. See وينځل

ونزه *winza'h*, s.f. (3rd) A female slave, a handmaid. Pl. ې *ey*. See وينځه and وينزه

ونګره *wangara'h*, s.f. (3rd) A pool, a pond, a lake, a small reservoir of water. Pl. ې *ey*. See ناور and وسته

ونه *wana'h*, s.f. (3rd) A tree in general. Pl. ې *ey*. آغزنه ونه *āgh-zana'h wana'h*, s.f. (3rd) A thorny tree. Pl. ې *ey*. ګنړي وني *garrney waney*, Trees thick or close together, a thicket.

وُ *wū*, The plural form of the past tense of 'To be,' for the first and third persons, which are distinguishable by their prefixed personal pronouns. See Grammar, page 52.

وو *wo*, s.m. (9th) Wind, draught, stream, or breath of air. 2. Pains in the limbs, rheumatism. Sing. and Pl. وو آلوتل *wo-ālwatal*, verb intrans. To blow (as the wind). وو وړی *wo-warraey*, adj. Carried away by the wind, the sport of the winds (met.) a traveller. 2. A gossamer; (Fem.) وو وړِ *wo-warri*. Pl. (Masc. and Fem.) ي *ī*.

وودل *wo-dal*, verb trans. To weave, to plait, to mat, to braid. Pres. وويي *wo-yī*; past وُ وود *wu-wod*; fut. وُ به وويي *wu bah wo-yī*; imp. وُ وويه *wu-woyah*; act. part. وودونکی *wo-dūnkaey* or وودونی *wo-dūnaey*; past part. وودلی *wo-dalaey*; verb. n. وودنه *wo-dana'h*. See اودل

وده *wūdah*, adj. Asleep, sleeping, fast asleep, sound asleep, napping. (Masc. and Fem.) وده کیدل *wūdah kedal*, verb intrans. To fall or go to sleep, to slumber, to drop to sleep, to take a nap. وده کول *wūdah kawul*, verb trans. To put to sleep, to make sleep, to put to bed. See بیده and خوب. کلک وده *klak wūdah* or اوده *ū-dah*, adj. Fast asleep, in a sound sleep, sleeping like a top.

ووږږه *wūrjzah*, s.m. (6th) The first milk given by a cow, goat, etc. after calving, biestings. Sing. and Pl. See وږږه and وږګه

ووریدل *wo-redal*, verb intrans. To rain, to drizzle, to drop, to trickle, to fall as snow or hail. ووروّل *wo-rawul*, verb trans. To pour, to drop, to discharge, to shower, to shower down, to cause to fall, or drop as rain, hail, snow, etc. For inflections see وریدل and اوریدل

ووړ *worr*, adj. (W.) Small, minute, puny, diminutive, less, petty, undersized. 2. Humble, humiliated, mean. Pl. واړه *wārrah*. (Fem.) ووړه *warra'h*. Pl. ووړې *warrey*. For other combinations of this word see وړ

ووړکی *worr-kaey*, adj. as s.m. (1st) A little one, a child, a term of affection. ووړکِ *worr-ki* or ووړکې *worr-key*, s.f. (8th) A little girl, etc. Pl. (Masc. and Fem.) ي *ī*. See وړکي

ووړه *worrah*, s.m. (6th) Flour, meal. Sing. and Pl. See اوړه or اوړَ

ووړی *worraey*, s.m. (1st) Summer, the hot season. Pl. ي *ī*. See اوړي

ووږد *wūjzd*. See وږد and اوږد

ووږی *wojzaey*, s.m. (1st) A measure for corn and other dry goods, holding four pounds or two *sīrs* (Indian weight). Pl. ي *ī*. See ووکي

ووسِۍ *wo-sa'ī*, s.f. (6th) Deer, gazelle, applied to the species in general. Sing. and Pl. ووسی *wo-saey*, s.m. (1st) A male deer or gazelle, a stag. Pl. ي *ī*. ووسِۍ *wo-sa'ī*, s.f. (6th) A hind, a female deer or gazelle. See اوسي

ووګد *wūgd*. See وګد and اوګد

ووګی *wo-gaey*, s.m. (1st) (E.) A corn measure containing four pounds. Pl. ي *ī*. See ووږي

وونه *wū-na'h*, s.f. (3rd) A description of sword with black or dark damascene on it. Pl. ې *ey*.

وو وړی *wo-warraey*, s.m. (1st) Gossamer, a seed with a light filmy substance outside, many of which are carried about by the wind in summer. Pl. ي *ī*.

وُ وینه *wu-wīnah*, adv. (imp. of لیدل) Look out! take care!

وه *wuh*, He *or* it is. The past tense, third person singular masculine of the substantive verb 'To be'; (Fem.) وَه *wah*, She is.

وهل *wahal*, verb trans. To strike, to beat, to smite, to hit, to thump, to whack, to cuff, to punch, to pummel, to thrash, to whip, to scourge, to lash, etc. 2. To give impetus, to propel or discharge. Pres. وهي *wahī*; past وُ واهه *wu-wāhah*; fut. وُ به وهي *wu bah wahī*;

imp. وُ وهه *wu-wahah*; act. part. وهونكَي *wah-ūnkaey* or وهونيَ *wahūnaey*; past part. وهلي *wahalaey*; verb. n. وهنه *wahana'h*.

وهلندي *wah-landaey*, adj. Winding (as a road or river), meandering, waving (curls), undulating, snaky, serpentine, tortuous, sinuous, wreathed, frizzled, twisted, dishevelled; coiled, spiral. Pl. ي *ī*. (Fem.) وهلندۍ *wah-landa'ī*. وهلندي توب *wah-landaey-tob*, s.m. (2nd) Winding, wave, undulation, meandering, sinuosity, involution. Pl. توبونه *tobūnah*. See اولندي

A وهم *wahm*, s.m. (2nd) Fancy, idea, imagination, conjecture, apprehension, anxiety, opinion, dread. Pl. وهمونه *wahmūnah*. وهم لرل *wahm laral*, verb trans. To have or possess fancy, imagination, anxiety, dread. وهم كول *wahm kawul*, verb trans. To fancy, to imagine, to apprehend, to conjecture, to fear, to dread.

A P وهمي *wahmī*, adj. Imaginary, conjectural, visionary, ideal, fanciful, fidgetty.

وهنه *wahana'h*, s.f. (3rd) Beating, thrashing, striking, hitting; castigation, discipline, punishment. 2. Highway robbery. Pl. ې *ey*.

وهوه *wah-wah*, interj. Well done! bravo! See also واه واه

وهويله *wah-wela'h*, s.f. (3rd) Complaint, lamentation, wailing, wail. Pl. ې *ey*. وهويلي كول *wah-weley kawul*, verb trans. To complain, to lament, to wail. See وا ويله

وهير *wa-her*, adj. Forgotten, unremembered; (Fem.) وهيره *wa-hera'h*. وهير غاړي *wa-her-ghārraey*, adj. A forgetter, a forgetful, heedless person; (Fem.) وهير غاړِ *wa-her-ghārri*. Pl. (Masc. and Fem.) ي *ī*. وهيريدل *wa-heredal*, verb intrans. To slip from the memory, to be forgotten. وهير كول *wa-her kawul*, verb trans. To forget, to lose. See هير etc.

وي *waey*, Thou wast. وۍ *waa'ī*, You were. See 'To be,' Grammar, page 52.

ويار *wi-yār* or *wī-ār*, s.m. (9th) Jealousy, envy. Sing. and Pl. ويار كول *wi-yār kawul*, verb trans. To envy, to entertain jealousy.

ويارړ *wī-ārr*, s.m. (9th) Vanity, vain-glory, conceit, pride, self-confidence, self-gratulation. Sing. and Pl.

ويارل *wī-ārral*, verb trans. To boast of, to plume one's-self on, to exult, to crow, to chuckle, to hug one's-self, to laugh in one's sleeve, to grin, to simper, to smirk. Pres. وياري *wī-ārrī*; past وُ ويارل *wu-wī-ārral*; fut. وُ به وياري *wu bah wī-ārrī*; imp. وُ وياره *wu-wī-ārrah*; act. part. ويارونكي *wī-ārrūnkaey* or وياروني *wī-ārrūnaey*; past part. ويارلي *wī-ārralaey*; verb. n. ويارنه *wī-ārrana'h*.

ويارنه *wī-ārrana'h*, s.f. (3rd) (verb. n.) Exultation, rejoicing, triumph, gratulation, laughing in one's sleeve, chuckling, pluming one's-self, being in high glee, simpering, smirking, coquetting, etc. Pl. ې *ey*.

ويت *wīt*, adj. Wide open, gaping, ajar, yawning. 2. Pert, saucy, wanton, impudent, mischievous, hurtful; (Fem.) ويته *wīta'h*. ويت كيدل *wīt kedal*, verb intrans. To gape, to yawn, to become ajar or gaping. ويت كول *wīt kawul*, verb trans. To make or cause to gape, to open wide, etc. ويت خولي *wīt-khūlaey*, adj. Open-mouthed, agape, all agog, flabbergasted, struck all of a heap, amazed, astonished; inquisitive, over-curious, on tip-toe of expectation; (Fem.) ويت خولِ *wīt-khūli*. Pl. (Masc. and Fem.) ي *ī*. See وت

ويتكي *wītakaey*, s.m. (1st) A child who is forward and talks much, a precocious, forward, talkative child. Pl. ي *ī*. ويتكۍ *wītaka'ī*, s.f. (6th) A girl as above. Sing. and Pl.

ويته *wīta'h*, s.f. (3rd) Forwardness, wantonness, assurance, pertness, impudence, precociousness. 2. Mischief, harm, hurt. Pl. ې *ey*. See وته

ويجاړ *wījārr*, adj. Uncultivated, desolated, desolate, destroyed, depopulated, demolished; (Fem.) ويجاړه *wījārra'h*. ويجاړ والي *wījārr-wālaey*, s.m. (1st) Desolation, destruction, depopulation. Pl. والي *wālī*. ويجاړيدل *wījārr-edal*, verb trans. To become desolate, or depopulated. ويجاړول *wījārrawul*, verb trans. To depopulate, to desolate. See under وجاړ for inflections, and add an extra ي

ويجاړه *wijarra'h*, s.f. (3rd) Uncultivated land, waste or fallow land. Pl. ئ *ey*.

ويخ *wekh*, s.m. (2nd) The root of a tree, root, origin, foundation. Pl. ويخونه *wekhūnah*. (P بيخ).

وير *wīr*, s.m. (2nd) Grief, sorrow, lamentation, mourning, beating the breast. Pl. ويرونه *wīrūnah*. وير کول *wīr kawul*, verb trans. To mourn, to lament, to beat the breast. ويره ژلئ *wīrah-jzalaey*, adj. (as s.m.) One who beats his breast, a mourner, a lamenter; (Fem.) ويره ژلِ *wīrah-jzali*. Pl. (Masc. and Fem.) ي *ī*. Also written ويره جلي

P ويران *wairān*, adj. Ruined, laid waste, depopulated, desolated; (Fem.) ويرانه *wairāna'h*.

P ويرانه *wairāna'h*, s.f. (3rd) A solitude, a desolate or desolated place. Pl. ئ *ey*.

P ويراني *wairānī*, s.f. (3rd) Desolation, depopulation, destruction, desert place. Pl. ئ *a'ī*. See وجاړ and ويجاړ or وران

ويران کيدل *wairān kedal*, verb intrans. To become ruined, depopulated or desolated. ويران کول *wairān kawul*, verb trans. To desolate, to depopulate, to ruin.

ويره *wera'h*, s.f. (3rd) Fear, timidity, fright, dread, terror, apprehension, awe, alarm, trepidation, nervousness, hesitation, qualm, want of confidence. Pl. ئ *ey*.

ويروونکئ *werawūnkaey* or ويروونئ *werawūnaey*, adj. (act. part. of verb trans.) Inspiring fear, fearful, alarming, horrid, dreadful, formidable; (Fem.) ويروونکِ *werawūnki* or ويروونِ *werawūni*. Pl. (Masc. and Fem.) ي *ī*.

ويريدل *weredal*, verb intrans. To fear, to be afraid, to apprehend, to take alarm, to quail, to funk, to tremble, to shake, to cower. Pres. ويريږي *werejzī* (W.) or ويريګي *weregī* (E.); past وُ ويريده *wu-weredah*; fut. وُ به ويريږي *wu bah werejzī* or ويريګي *weregī*; imp. وُ ويريږه *wu-werejzah* or وُ ويريګه *wu-weregah*; act. part. ويريدونکئ *weredūnkaey* or ويريدونئ *weredūnaey*; past part. ويريدلئ *weredalaey*; verb. n. ويريدنه *weredana'h* or ويريده *weredah*. ويرول *werawul*, verb trans. To terrify, to frighten, to alarm, to scare, to dismay, to appal, to intimidate, to startle, to cow. Pres. ويروي *werawī*; past وُ ويراوه *wu-werāwuh* or وُ ويراوو *wu-werāwo*, fut. وُ به ويروي *wu bah werawī*; imp. وُ ويروه *wu-werawah*; act. part. ويروونکئ *werawūnkaey* or ويروونئ *werawūnaey*; past. part. ويرولئ *werawulaey*; verb. n. ويرونه *werawuna'h*.

ويريدونکئ *weredūnkaey* or ويريدونئ *weredūnaey*, adj. (past part. of verb intrans.) Fearful, timid, timorous, nervous, frightened, alarmed, terrified, cowed, panic-struck. 2. A coward; (Fem.) ويريدونکِ *weredūnki* or ويريدونِ *weredūni*. Pl. (Masc. and Fem.) ي *ī*.

وير *wirr*, adj. Spread, expanded, enlarged, distended, opened out, unrolled; (Fem.) ويره *wirra'h*. ويره خوله *wirra'h-khula'h*, adj. Open-mouthed, grinning, laughing. ويره خولئ *wirra'h-khūlaey*, adj. A person always laughing or grinning; (Fem.) ويره خول *wirra'h-khūli*. وير والئ *wirr-wālaey*, s.m. (1st) Expansion, extension, spread, enlargement. Pl. والي *wālī*. ويريدل *wirredal*, verb intrans. To become or grow larger, to enlarge, to unroll, to expand, to open, to extend, to deploy, etc. Pres. ويريږي *wirrejzī* (W.) or ويريګي *wirregī* (E.); past وير شه *wirr shah* or وُ شه *wu-shah*; fut. وير به شي *wirr bah shī* or به وُ شي *bah wu-shī*; imp. وير شه *wirr shah* or وُ شه *wu-shah*; act. part. ويريدونکئ *wirredūnkaey* or ويريدونئ *wirredūnaey*; past part. ويريدلئ *wirredalaey*; verb. n. ويريدنه *wirredana'h* or ويريده *wirredah*. ويرول *wirrawul*, verb trans. To render larger, to expand, to open out, to distend, to unroll. Pres. ويروي *wirrawī*; past وير کړ *wirr-karr* or وُ کړ *wu-karr*; fut. وير به کړي *wirr bah krrī* or به وُ کړي *bah wu-krrī*; imp. وير کړ *wirr-karr* or وُ کړ *wu-karr*; act. part. ويروونکئ *wirrawūnkaey* or ويروونئ *wirrawūnaey*; past part. ويرولئ *wirrawulaey*; verb. n. ويرونه *wirrawuna'h*.

ويريده *wirredah*, s.m. (6th) (verb. n.) Expanding, unrolling, dispansion, spread, extension. Sing. and Pl.; or ويريدنه *wirredana'h*, s.f.

(3rd). Pl. ئ *ey*. ويرونه *wīrrawuna'h*, s.f. (3rd) (verb. n. of verb. trans.) Causing to or making expand or unroll, increasing, spreading out. Pl. ئ *ey*.

ويريا *werrīā*, adv. Gratis, free, gratuitous, free of cost, without charge. See وريا

ويزار *wezār*, adj. Vexed, angry, disgusted, out of humour, displeased; (Fem.) ويزاره *wezāra'h*. ويزاريدل *wezāredal*, verb intrans. To become vexed, angry, displeased, out of humour. ويزارول *wezārawul*, verb trans. To vex, to displease, to disgust, to put out of humour. See بيزار

ويزاري *wezārī*, s.f. (3rd) Anger, bad humour, displeasure, disgust. Pl. ئ *a'ī*.

ويسا *wīsā*, s.f. (6th) Faith, belief, trust, credit, confidence, dependence, reliance, assurance. (W.) Pl. ويساوي *wīsāwī*. (E.) Sing. and Pl. ويسا لرل *wīsā laral*, verb trans. To place, or have faith in, to have confidence in, or dependence upon. ويسا كول *wīsā kawul*, verb trans. To rely on, to place faith in, to trust, to depend on. See ساويسا and وساه

ويساك *waisāk*, s.m. (9th) (corrup. of بيساكه) The first solar month of the Hindū year—April-May. Sing. and Pl.

ويش *wesh*, s.m. (2nd) Division, share, distribution, portion. 2. A division or interchange of lands peculiar to Yūsufzīs and a few other clans, a kind of agrarian law. Pl. ويشونه *weshūnah*. ويشل *weshal*, verb trans. To divide, to share, to distribute, to portion, to apportion, to distribute. Pres. ويشي *weshī*; past وُ ويشه *wu-weshah*; fut. وُ به ويشي *wu bah weshī*; imp. وُ ويشه *wu-weshah*; act. part. ويشونكي *weshūnkaey* or ويشوني *weshūnaey*; past part. ويشلي *weshalaey*; verb. n. ويشنه *weshana'h*.

ويشتل *wīshtal*, verb trans. To throw, to project, to propel, to cast, to lance, to hurl, to dart, to let off, to discharge, to shoot, to launch, to let fly, etc. Pres. ولي *wulī*; past وُ ويشت *wu-wīsht*; fut. وُ به ولي *wu bah wulī*; imp. وُ وله *wu-wulah*; act. part. ويشتونكي *wīshtūnkaey* or ويشتوني *wīshtūnaey*; past part. ويشتلي *wīshtalaey*; verb. n. ويشتنه *wīshtana'h*.

ويشتلي *wīsh-talaey*, adj. (past part. of ويشتل) Struck, hurted, hit, wounded, injured, bruised, mauled, scotched, etc.; (Fem.) ويشتل *wīshtali*. Pl. (Masc. and Fem.) ي *ī*.

ويشتنه *wīshtana'h*, s.f. (3rd) (verb. n.) Propulsion, pushing, discharging, shooting, launching, etc. Pl. ئ *ey*.

ويشله *weshala'h*, s.f. (3rd) A kind of unleavened bread. Pl. ئ *ey*.

ويښ *wīsh* (W.) or *wīkh* (E.) adj. Awake, watchful, aroused, vigilant, active; (Fem.) ويښه *wīsha'h* or *wīkha'h*. ويښيدل *wīshedal* (W.) or *wīkhedal* (E.) verb intrans. To awake, to become aroused, to be vigilant, active, or watchful. Pres. ويښيږي *wīshejzī* or ويښيګي *wīkhegī*; past ويښ شه *wīsh* or *wīkh shah* or وُ شه *wu-shah*; fut. ويښ به شي *wīsh* or *wīkh bah shī* or به وُ شي *bah wu-shī*; imp. ويښ شه *wish* or *wīkh shah* or وُ شه *wu-shah*; act. part. ويښيدونكي or *wīshedūnkaey* or *wīkhedūnkaey* or ويښيدوني *wīshedūnaey* or *wīkhedūnaey*; past part. ويښيدلي *wīshedalaey* or *wīkhedalaey*; verb. n. ويښيدنه *wīshedana'h* or *wīkhedana'h* or ويښيده *wīshedah* or *wīkhedah*. ويښول *wīshawul* (W.) or *wīkhawul* (E.) To awaken, to arouse, to make active, vigilant, or watchful. Pres. ويښوي *wīshawī* or *wīkhawī*; past ويښ كړ *wīsh* or *wīkh karr* or وُ كړ *wu-karr*; fut. ويښ به كړي *wīsh* or *wīkh bah krrī* or به وُ كړي *bah wu-krrī*; imp. ويښ كړه *wīsh* or *wīkh krrah* or وُ كړه *wu-krrah*; act. part. ويښوونكي *wīshawūnkaey* or *wīkhawūnkaey* or ويښووني *wīshawūnaey* or *wīkhawūnaey*; past part. ويښولي *wīshawulaey* or *wīkhawulaey*; verb. n. ويښونه *wīshawuna'h* or *wīkhawuna'h*.

ويښته *weshtah* (W.) or *wekhtah* (E.) s.m. (6th) Hair, the hair of a human being or animal. Sing. and Pl. ويښته په ويښته *weshtah pah weshtah* or *wekhtah pah wekhtah*, Hair by hair. تور ويښته *tor weshtah* or *wekhtah*, Black hair.

سور *sūr* or ساره ويښته *sārah weshtah* or *wekhtah*, Red hair. سپين ويښته *spīn weshtah* or *wekhtah*, White hair. گږ ويښته *gajz weshtah* (W.) or برگ ويښته *brag wekhtah* (E.) Grey hair.

ويل *wa-yal*, verb trans. To speak, to say, to tell, to talk, to discourse, to declaim, to hold forth, to speechify, to harangue, to lecture, etc. Pres. وايي *wā-yī*; past وُ وايه *wu-wā-yah* or وُ وي *wu-wey* or وُ و *wu-wi* or وُ ويل *wu-wa-yal*; fut. وُ به وايي *wu bah wā-yī*; imp. وُ وايه *wu-wā-yah*; act. part. ويونكَي *wa-yūnkaey* or ويونَي *wa-yūnaey*; past part. ويلَي *wa-yalaey*; verb. n. وينه *wa-yana'h*.

ويل *wel*, s.m. (2nd) Cheapness, low price. Pl. ويلونه *wel-ūnah*. په ويل *pah wel* or په ويل کښي *pah wel kshey*, or *kkhey*, adj. At a low rate, cheap, moderate in price.

ويلني *wīlanī* or *welanī*, s.m. (1st) (Pl.) The herb mint. خوارږه ويلني *khwājza'h wīlanī* or کاگه ويلني *kāga'h wīlanī*, Large aniseed, fennel.

ويله *we-la'h*, s.f. (3rd) A small stream, a brook, a rivulet, a small river or canal. Pl. ي *ey*. See وله

ويلي *wī-lī*, adj. Melted, molten, liquefied, unfrozen, melted or fused by heat, thawed, heated. ويلي والَي *wī-lī-wālaey*, s.m. (1st) Fusion, melting, liquefaction, thaw, dissolving, deliquation. Pl. والِي *wālī*. ويلي کيدل *wī-lī kedal*, verb intrans. To melt, to run, to dissolve, to thaw, to fuse, to become liquefied. ويلي کول *wī-lī kawul*, verb trans. To heat, to melt, to make or render liquid or molten, to fuse, to dissolve, to liquefy, to thaw.

ويلي وچولَي *wī-lī wuchwulaey*, adj. Of an open countenance, gay, cheerful, blithe. په ويلي وچولَي *pah wī-lī wuchwulaey*, Cheerfully, blithely, openly.

وينا *wai-nā*, s.f. (6th) Speech, prattle, palaver, recitation, delivery, harangue, sermon, tirade, soliloquy, etc. (E.) Sing. and Pl. (W.) Pl.ويناوي *wai-nāwī*. وينا ويل *wai-nā wa-yal*, verb trans. To discourse, to make a speech, to recite, to harangue, to soliloquize, to say, to speechify, to preach, to hold forth.

وينزل *wīn-zal*, verb trans. To wash, to lave, to clean. See وينځل

وينزه *wīnza'h*, s.f. (3rd) A slave girl, a handmaid, a female slave. Pl. ي *ey*. See وينځه

وينځل *wīn-dzal*, verb trans. To wash, to cleanse, to purify, to lave, to absterge, to clean. Pres. وينځي *wīn-dzī*; past وُ وينځه *wu-wīn-dzah*; fut. وُ به وينځي *wu bah wīn-dzī*; imp. وُ وينځه *wu-wīn-dzah*; act. part. وينځونكَي *wīn-dzūnkaey* or وينځونَي *wīn-dzūnaey*; past part. وينځلَي *wīn-dzalaey*; verb. n. وينځنه *wīn-dzana'h*. See also مينځل and ولل

وينځه *wīn-dza'h*, s.f. (3rd) A slave-girl, a handmaid, a female slave. Pl. ي *ey*. Also ونځه, ونزه, and وينزه

وينه *o-ena'h*, s.m. (6th) A white ant. Sing. and Pl. Also اوينه, which see.

وينه *wī-na'h*, s.f. (3rd) Blood, gore. Pl. ي *ey*. The plural form is generally used. په وينو لړلَي *pah wī-no larralaey*, adj. Bloody, covered with blood. سره په وينو *s'rah pah wī-no*, Red with blood, bloody.ويني تووِل *wī-ney to-wal*, or تويول *to-yawul*, verb trans. To shed blood, to slaughter, to butcher, to assassinate, to put to the sword. ويني ښكل *wī-ney kh'kal* (E.) or كښل *k'shal* (W.), verb trans. To bleed, to let blood, to phlebotomize. وينيدل *wīnedal*, verb intrans. To bleed, to run with blood (by whatever means), to lose blood. وينول *wī-na-wul*, verb trans. To bleed, to let blood, to take blood from by opening a vein, etc.

وينه *wa-yana'h*, s.f. (3rd) Speaking, saying, discoursing, breaking silence. 2. Speech, talk, parlance, palaver, prattle, oration, recitation. 3. Elocution, eloquence, oratory, declamation. Pl. ي *ey*. See وينا

ويونكَي *wa-yūnkaey* or ويونَي *wa-yūnaey*, s.m. (1st) (act. part.) An orator, a speaker, a spokesman, a mouth-piece, a speechmaker, a spouter. ويونكِ *wa-yūnki* or ويونِ *wa-yūni*, s.f. (8th) An oratress, etc. Pl. (Masc. and Fem.) ي *ī*.

ويي *wa-yaey*, s.m. (1st) A saying, speech, word, talk, conversation, chatter, gab, nonsense, prattle, cackle, loquacity, garrulity, talkativeness, twaddle, volubility. Pl. ي *ī*. ويىدل *wa-yedal*, verb trans. To talk, to prate, to chatter, to be loquacious, to twaddle, to jabber, to spin a long yarn. Pres. ويىږي *wa-yejzī* (W.) or ويىگي *wa-yegī* (E.); past وُ ويىده *wu-wa-yedah*; fut. وُ به ويىږي *wu-bah wa-yejzī* or ويىگي *wa-yegī*; imp. وُ ويىږه *wu-wa-yejzah*; or وُ ويىگه *wu-wa-yegah*; act. part. ويىدونکي *wa-yedūnkaey* or ويىدوني *wa-yedūnaey*; past part. ويىدلي *wa-yedalaey*; verb. n. ويىدنه *wa-yedana'h*. ويول *wa-yawul*, verb trans. To cause or make to chatter, prate, or gabble, to make loquacious or garrulous. Pres. ويوي *wa-yawī*; past وُ وياوه *wu-wa-yāwuh* or وُ وياوو *wu-wa-yāwo*; fut. وُ به ويوي *wu bah wa-yawī*; imp. وُ ويوه *wu-wa-yawah*; act. part. ويوونکي *wa-yawūnkaey* or ويووني *wa-yawūnaey*; past part. ويولي *wa-yawulaey*; verb. n. ويونه *wa-yawuna'h*.

ه

ه *hā*, called هاي هوز *hā-i-hawaz* or هاي مدوره *hā-i-mudawwara'h*, the twenty-seventh of the Arabic and thirty-first of the Persian, is the thirty-ninth letter of the Pushto alphabet, and corresponds to Sanskrit ह. It is one of the guttural letters, and has the sound of English *h*.

When it occurs at the end of a word it is either 'perceptible or apparent,' called هاي ظاهر *hā-i-ẓāhir*, as in ويښته *weshtah* or *wekhtah*, Hair, or قارگه *ḳār-gah*, A crow; or هاي خفي *hā-i-khafī*, 'imperceptible, secret, or concealed,' as in ښځه *khadza'h* or *shadza'h*, A woman, a female, or وينه *wī-na'h*, Blood. All words ending in the former are masculine, and all those ending in the latter are feminine.

When it occurs at the end of Arabic words it is generally written with two points over it, thus ة, and is pronounced as *t*. When used for a number it denotes five; and in words ending with *hā-i-ẓāhir*, it is sometimes lost or suffers apocope in the plural, as مرغه *mur-ghah*, A bird; مرغان *mur-ghān*, Birds; and at times retained as آه *āh*, A sigh; آهونه *āhūnah*, Sighs.

The *hā-i-khafī* is also prefixed to all masculine nouns terminating in any other letter than ي (with the exception of some nouns terminating in *yā-i-moḳūf* or silent ي) in the formation of their feminines; as اوښ *ūsh* or *ūkh*, A male camel; اوښه *ūsha'h* or *ūkha'h*, A female camel. سوي *so-e*, A hare; سويه *so-ea'h*, The female. لوي *lo-e*, Great (male); لويه *lo-ea'h*, Great (female). In the uninflected nominative plural the ه is changed to ې.

This letter, it must also be remembered, is often dropped for (ـَ), particularly at the end of a line in poetry. It also occurs as the termination of the imperative mood of the second person singular; in the past tense, etc.; the whole of which will be found explained in the Grammar.

ها *hā*, s.f. (6th) The egg of a bird. (E.) Sing. and Pl. (W.) Pl. هاوي *hā-wī*. See هگي

ها *hā*, adv. A word which expresses affirmation or consent, Yes, very good, very well. 2. Of astonishment or surprise, as Lo! behold! see! just look!

هاتي *hātī*, s.m. (5th) (corrup. of S هاتهي) An elephant. Pl. هاتيان *hātī-ān*. هاتړه *hātarra'h*, s.f. (3rd). Pl. ې *ey*. د هاتي غاښ *da hātī ghāsh* or *ghākh*, Ivory, elephant's tooth.

هاجي *hā-jī*. See حاجي

A هادي *hā-dī*, s.m. and f. (5th) (act. part. of هدي) A leader, a director, a guide (spiritual). Pl. هاديان *hā-dīān*; (Fem.) Pl. هادياني *hā-dīāney* or هاديان *hā-dīāni*.

P S هار *hār*, s.m. (2nd) A necklace of pearls, etc., a wreath, a chaplet. Pl. هارونه *hārūnah*.

هار *hār*, A particle affixed to nouns signifying sound of any kind, in forming the plural, as گرنگ *grrang*, Ring, jingle, clatter. Pl. گرنگهار *grranga-hār*, Clatterings, jingles, etc.

هاړه هوړه *hārra'h-hūrra'h*, s.f. (3rd) Noise, din, confusion, tumult, disturbance, commotion, turmoil, riot, rumpus. Pl. هاړې هوړې

hāṟṟey-hūṟṟey. هاړي هوړي كول *hāṟṟey-hūṟṟey kawul,* verb trans. To create a noise, tumult or uproar, to raise a disturbance or riot.

هاړي هاړي *hāṟṟey-hāṟṟey,* s.f. (3rd) Pl. Coaxing, wheedling, supplicating, entreating. 2. An exclamation of surprise or pleasure. هاړي هاړي كول *hāṟṟey-hāṟṟey kawul,* verb trans. To wheedle, to coax, to entreat.

A هاله *hā-la'h,* s.f. (3rd) A halo or circle of mist round the moon. Pl. ي *ey.*

هاله *hā-lah,* adv. Then, at that time. See هله

هاها *hā-hā,* The sound produced when laughing heartily. هاها كول *hā-hā kawul,* verb trans. To laugh, to laugh heartily.

هاهو *hā-hū,* s.m. (9th) Noise, clamor, tumult, disturbance, row, din, riot. Sing. and Pl. هاهو آچول *hā-hū āchawul* or كول *kawul,* verb trans. To create a tumult or disturbance, to get up a row or riot. See هاړه هوړه

S هاي *hā-e,* interj. Alas! ah! sorrow! هاي هاي *hā-e hā-e,* Oh dear! alas, alas! alack-a-day! dear me! هاي هاي كول *hā-e hā-e kawul,* verb trans. To lament, to wail, to cry out. هاي هوي *hā-e hū-e* (P) interj. Ah me! woe, woe! well-a-day! alas the day! etc. 2. A confused noise (as of combatants). هاي هوي كول *hā-e hū-e kawul,* verb trans. To wail, to bewail, to lament, to sigh, to grieve. 2. To make a great noise, to create confusion.

هايه *hā-yah,* A prox. dem. pron. somewhat emphatic in its meaning, 'This,' 'this very,' etc. (Masc. and Fem. and Sing. and Pl.)

هبته *haba-tah,* adj. (corrup. of A حبطه) Useless, futile, bootless, inefficient, unavailing, unprofitable, fruitless, vain, worthless, valueless, nugatory, ill-spent, good for nothing. (Masc. and Fem.) هبته كيدل *haba-tah kedal,* verb intrans. To become useless, futile, worthless, nugatory, good for nothing. هبته كول *haba-tah kawul,* verb trans. To render nugatory, futile, vain or valueless, to make unavailing or good for nothing. هبته والي *haba-tah wālaey,* s.m. (1st) Inutility, uselessness, inefficacy, futility, vanity, unprofitableness. 2. Trash. Pl. والي *wālī.*

A هبه *hiba'h,* s.f. (3rd) A gift, a bequest. Pl. ي *ey.* هبه كول *hiba'h kawul,* verb trans. To devise, to bequeath. هبه نامه *hiba'h nāma'h,* s.f. (3rd) A deed of gift.

هبه ډبه *haba'h-ḏḏaba'h,* s.f. (3rd) A disease to which children are liable, the hooping cough. Pl. ي *ey.*

هپ دپ *hap-dap,* adj. Quick, hasty, unexpected, all at once. 2. Lost unexpectedly; (Fem.) هپه دپه *hapa'h-dapa'h.* 2. adv. Hastily, quickly, unexpectedly, all of a sudden.

هپه *hapa'h,* s.f. (3rd) Assistance, aid, help, succour; rescuing property from thieves or from the men of another clan who may have made a foray. 3. The people who set out in pursuit. 4. An attack or assault on a village, a foray by day. Pl. ي *ey.* هپه كول *hapa'h kawul,* verb trans. To render assistance, to aid, to help. 2. To attack, to make a foray. په هپه وتل *pah hapa'h watal,* verb intrans. To set out in pursuit of plunderers, to sally forth to the rescue.

هته *hata'h,* s.f. (3rd) A part of a weaver's loom, the yarn beam. 2. A cubit, the distance between the elbow and the tips of the fingers. Pl. ي *ey.* See اته (HI هتها).

هتيات *hatī-āt,* s.m. (2nd) (corrup. of A احتياط) Caution, foresight, circumspection, scrupulousness, care. Pl. هتياتونه *hatī-ātūnah.* په هتيات سره *pah hatī-āt sarah,* With care, carefully, cautiously. هتيات لرل *hatī-āt laral,* verb trans. To have or be endowed with caution, circumspection, or foresight. هتيات كول *hatī-āt kawul,* verb trans. To act with care and caution, to manifest foresight and circumspection, to take care or precaution.

هتياتي *hatī-ātī,* adj. Careful, circumspect, thoughtful, cautious, wary, discreet, steady. 2. s.f. (3rd) Discretion, caution, circumspection, wariness, steadiness, foresight. Pl. ئ *a'ī.* هتياتي لرل *hatī-ātī laral,* verb trans. See under هتيات. هتياتي كول *hatī-ātī kawul,* verb trans. To act with caution and circumspection, to manifest caution, discretion, steadiness, etc. په هتياتي ييښول *pah hatī-ātī ye<u>sh</u>-awul* (W.) or *ye<u>kh</u>awul* (E.) verb trans. To place or put down carefully (as anything brittle).

s هتيار **hati-yār**, s.m. (2nd) A tool, an implement, a weapon, apparatus. Pl. هتيارونه *hati-yārūnah*. هتيار ترل *hati-yār tarral*, verb trans. To arm, to prepare for action or work.

هټ **ha<u>tt</u>**, s.m. (2nd) Obstinacy, perverseness, resistance, crossness, disobedience, unpersuadableness. Pl. هټونه *ha<u>tt</u>ūnah*. (s हठ). See زد

هټ **ha<u>tt</u>**, adj. Standing up, erect, risen up (from a sitting posture), standing still (in a road), rooted, stopping, stationary, etc.; (Fem.) هټه *ha<u>tt</u>a'h*. هټيدل *ha<u>tt</u>edal*, verb intrans. To stand up, to stand erect, to rise up, to stand still, to stop, to stay, to become stationary, rooted, etc. هټول *ha<u>tt</u>awul*, verb trans. To cause or make to stand up, stand still, to make to stay, to raise up, to station, etc. See هتال

هتال **hi<u>tt</u>āl**, adj. Stopped, prevented, repelled, driven backwards, foiled. 2. Distressed, reduced to difficulties, rendered desperate; (Fem.) هتاله *hi<u>tt</u>āla'h*. هتال والئ *hi<u>tt</u>āl-wālaey*, s.m. (1st) Prevention, repulsion, stopping, foiling. 2. Distress, desperation, difficulty. Pl. والي *wālī*. هتاليدل *hi<u>tt</u>āl-edal*, verb intrans. To be stopped, prevented, foiled, repelled, to be driven back, to retreat, to boggle. 2. To become desperate or reduced by difficulties, or distressed. Pres. هتاليږي *hi<u>tt</u>āl-ejzī* (W.) or هتاليګي *hi<u>tt</u>āl-egī* (E.); past هتال شه *hi<u>tt</u>āl <u>sh</u>ah* or و شه *wu-<u>sh</u>ah*; fut. هتال به شي *hi<u>tt</u>āl bah <u>sh</u>ī* or به و شي *bah wu-<u>sh</u>ī*; imp. هتال شه *hi<u>tt</u>āl <u>sh</u>ah* or و شه *wu-<u>sh</u>ah*; act. part. هتاليدونکئ *hi<u>tt</u>āledūnkaey* or هتاليدونئ *hi<u>tt</u>āledūnaey*; past part. هتال *hi<u>tt</u>āl* or هتال شوئ *hi<u>tt</u>āl <u>sh</u>awaey*; verb. n. هتاليدنه *hi<u>tt</u>āledana'h* or هتاليده *hi<u>tt</u>āledah*. هتالول *hi<u>tt</u>ālawul*, verb trans. To stop, to prevent, to repel, to foil, to drive back. 2. To reduce to extremities, to distress, to render desperate. Pres. هتالوي *hi<u>tt</u>āl-awī*; past هتال کړ *hi<u>tt</u>āl ka<u>rr</u>* or و کړ *wu-ka<u>rr</u>*; fut. هتال به کړي *hi<u>tt</u>āl bah k<u>rr</u>ī* or به و کړي *bah wu-k<u>rr</u>ī*; imp. هتال کړه *hi<u>tt</u>āl k<u>rr</u>ah* or و کړه *wu-k<u>rr</u>ah*; act. part. هتالوونکئ *hi<u>tt</u>ālawūnkaey* or هتالوونئ *hi<u>tt</u>ālawūnaey*; past part. هتال کړئ *hi<u>tt</u>āl ka<u>rr</u>aey*; verb. n. هتالونه *hi<u>tt</u>ālawuna'h*.

هټکئ **ha<u>tt</u>-kaey** (E.) s.m. (1st) The hiccough, a hiccough. Pl. ي *ī*. هټکي لګيدل *ha<u>tt</u>-kī lagedal*, verb intrans. To hiccough, to have convulsive catches of the respiratory muscles before death, to be in the agonies of death. هټکي وهل *ha<u>tt</u>-kī wahal*, verb trans. To hiccough. See هکلي (W.)

هټه **ha<u>tt</u>ah** or هټ **ha<u>tt</u>a**, adj. Stout, active, robust, vigorous. (s हट्टा).

هټئ **ha<u>tt</u>a'ī**, s.f. (6th) A chandler's shop. Sing. and Pl. (s هټي).

هڅ **hu<u>ts</u>**, adj. Infatuated, mad, perplexed, confused, through grief or distress; (Fem.) هڅه *hu<u>ts</u>a'h*. هڅ والئ *hu<u>ts</u> wālaey*, s.m. (1st) Infatuation, perplexity, confusion. Pl. والي *wālī*. هڅ کيدل *hu<u>ts</u> kedal*, verb intrans. To become perplexed, troubled in mind, distressed, or infatuated. هڅ کول *hu<u>ts</u> kawul*, verb trans. To distress, to perplex, to render infatuated. (HI هچ)

هڅه **ha<u>ts</u>a'h**, s.f. (3rd) Fatigue, labour, endeavour, trouble, bustle, toil, running about on business or in search of employment, great exertion. 2. Desire, wish, inclination. Pl. ې *ey*. هڅه کول *ha<u>ts</u>a'h kawul*, verb trans. To toil, to bustle, to endeavour, to take great trouble in any matter. Also written هڅڅه *ha<u>ts</u>-<u>ts</u>a'h*. See هنده

A هجر **hajr** or **hijr**, s.m. (9th) Separation, disjunction, desertion of country and friends, absence. Sing. and Pl.

A هجران **hijrān**, s.m. (9th) Separation, etc. See preceding. Sing. and Pl. د هجران شپه *da hijrān <u>sh</u>pa'h*, The night of separation and absence.

A هجرت **hij-rat**, s.m. (9th) Flight, the flight of

Muḥammad from Makka to Madīnah. Sing. and Pl.

هجري *hijrī*, adj. Of or belonging to the *hij-rat* or flight, the name given to the Muḥammadan era.

هجره *huj-ra'h*, s.f. (3rd) (corrup. of A حجره) A chamber, a closet, a pavilion. Amongst the Afghāns, the public room of a village, where the people meet on public occasions, and where travellers are lodged. Pl. ې *ey*. See my "Account of Peshāwer," *Bombay Geographical Transactions*, 1851-52.

هجړي *hij-ṛraey*, s.m. (1st) An hermaphrodite, an eunuch. Pl. ي *ī*. (HI هجڑا).

هجګي *hij-gī*, s.f. (3rd) Spelling as children when learning their lessons. Pl. ئ *a'ī*. (A هجا). په هجګي ويل *pah hij-gī wa-yal*, verb trans. To spell, to tell or name the letters of a word, with division into syllables. See پيزي and هيرګي

هيچ *hich*, adj. (corrup. of P هيچ) Nothing. 2. adv. Never, at no time, on no account.

A هدايت *hidā-yat*, s.m. (2nd) (from هدي) Direction, guidance, direction in the right way, in the road to salvation, righteousness. Pl. هدايتونه *hidā-yatunah*. هدايت كول *hidā-yat kawul*, verb trans. To guide, to direct, to set on the right path.

هديره *hade-ra'h*, s.f. (3rd) An enclosure, a yard, a fold. 2. A burying-ground or grave-yard. Pl. ې *ey*.

A هديه *hadī-ya'h*, s.f. (3rd) A present to a Mullā or schoolmaster after spelling through the Ḳur'ān. 2. (A) A present. Pl. ې *ey*.

هډ *hadd*, s.m. (2nd) A bone, bone. 2. Nobility, greatness, grandeur. 3. Ancestry, lineage. Pl. هډونه *haddūnah*. د هډو درد *da haddo dard*, Pain in the bones, rheumatism. هډ ماتول *hadd mātawul*, verb trans. To show great kindness or favour to any one. 2. To cause enmity between two parties (*lit.* to break a bone between, a bone of contention). (S هڈّ a bone). See هډوكي

هډ والي *hadd-wālaey*, s.m. (1st) Strength, sturdiness, having large bones, boniness. Pl. والي *wālī*.

هډور *haddawar*, adj. Bony, having long and large bones, full of bones, stout, strong; (Fem.) هډوره *haddawara'h*.

هډو *haddo*, A word of endearment. 2. adv. Never, by no means.

هډوكي *haddūkaey*, s.m. (1st) A bone, a small bone (dimin. of هډ). Pl. ي *ī*.

هډي *haddaey*, s.m. (1st) The bone-spavin in horses. 2. One of the small bones at the back of the tongue, one of the tonsils. Pl. ي *ī*.

S هر *har*, s.m. (5th) A rogue, a wag. Pl. هران *har-ān*. هره *hara'h*, s.f. (3rd) A roguish female, a wag. Pl. ې *ey*.

هُر *hær*, s.m. (5th) The bray of an ass. Pl. هُرهار *hæra-hār*. هُرهار لرل *hæra-hār laral* or كول *kawul*, verb trans. To bray, as an ass.

P هر *har*, adj. Every, any. Used in composition prefixed to words, as هر څو *har tso*, adv. How many, how much soever, how much, so much, so many. هر څوك *har tsok*, Whoever or whomever. هر څومره *har tsombrah*, As much as. هر چا *har chā*, By whomever. هر چرته *har chirtah* or هر يو ځاي *har yow dzā-e*, Every where, in all places. په هر حال *pah har ḥāl* or په هر حال كښي *pah har ḥāl kshey* or *kkhey*, Under any circumstances, by hook or by crook, by all means, howsoever. هر دم *har dam*, Every moment. هر رنګ *har rang*, Every color, every way, mode, or method. هر ځاي *har dzā-e*, Everywhere, every place. هر ځله *har dzalah*, Every time, as often as, whenever. هر طرف *har ṭaraf*, Every side, on all sides. هر طور *har ṭaur*, Every mode or fashion, by every means, under every circumstance. هر كار *har kār*, All sorts of work, every sort of business. هر كال *har kāl*, Every year, yearly. هر كله *har kalah*, Always, ever, constantly, frequently. هر كله چه *har kalah chih*, Whenever. هرګاه *har gāh*, Whenever, always. 2. Wherever, everywhere. هرګز *har-giz*, Ever. هر هر *har har*, Every one, all, the whole. Pl. هرو هرو

haro haro. هر وار *har wār*, Every time, each time. هر وخت *har wakht*, Always, at all times, each time. هر يو *har yow* or *yo*, Every one, each, each one; (Fem.) هره يوه *hara'h yowa'h.* هره پلا *hara'h plā*, Every time, always, ever, each time. هره شپه *hara'h shpa'h*, Every night, nightly. هره روځ *hara'h rwadz* or ورځ *wradz*, Every day, daily. هره مياشت *hara'h mī-āsht*, Every month, monthly.

هراول *harāwal*, s.m. (6th) The advanced guard of an army, an advanced picquet. Pl. هراوّل *harāwæl.* هراولي *harāwalī*, s.f. (3rd) Skirmishing, the business of an advanced guard or picquet. Pl. ئي *a'ī.* See قراول

هراند *har-ānd*, adj. Timid, timorous, fearful, frightened, abashed, alarmed, cowed, overawed; (Fem.) هرانده *har-ānda'h.* هراند والي *har-ānd wālaey*, s.m. (1st) Timidity, fear, nervousness, fright, dread, awe, dismay, panic. Pl. والي *wālī.* هرانديدل *har-āndedal*, verb intrans. To fear, to be afraid, to take alarm, to distrust, to quake, to apprehend, to stand aghast, to grow pale. هراندول *har-āndawul*, verb trans. To alarm, to excite fear, to terrify, to frighten, to scare, to daunt, to awe.

هرړئي *hara-rra'ī*, s.f. (6th) The handle of a plough. Sing. and Pl. See منتي

هرړی *hir-rraey*, s.m. (1st) A common long-tailed sheep (a ram). Pl. ي *ī.* هرړئي *hir-rra'ī*, s.f. (6th) An ewe. Sing. and Pl. See هيري and كدوري (s بهيړ).

هرځائي *har-dzā'ī*, s.m. and f. (5th) A vagabond, a stroller, a rascal. Pl. هرځائيان *har-dzā-ī-ān.* Pl. (Fem.) هرځائيانې *har-dzā-ī-āni.*

هرزه *har-zah*, adj. Absurd, nonsensical, frivolous, trifling. (Masc. and Fem.)

P هركاره *har-kārah*, s.m. (5th) (from هر Every, and كار Business) A running footman, a courier. 2. A spy or emissary. 3. A messenger. 4. One who does all sorts of work. A man of all work. Pl. هركارګان *har-kāragān.* 5. adj. Doing all sorts of work. (Masc. and Fem.)

هركاره *har-kāra'h*, s.f. (3rd) A large iron spoon or ladle. Pl. ئي *ey.*

هرګوره *har-gorah*, adv. Altogether, wholly, entirely, thoroughly.

هرئي *hira'ī*, s.f. (6th) Pretence, excuse, plea, pretext, shift. Sing. and Pl. هرئي كول *hira'ī kawul*, verb trans. To pretend, to make shift or excuse.

هريړه *hare-rra'h*, s.f. (3rd) A dried fruit given in medicine, myrobalan. Pl. ئي *ey.* (HI هڙ).

هريز *hur-yez*, s.f. (1st) A cloud, a mist, mist. Pl. هريز *hur-yezi.* See اوريځ

هرپئي *harr-pa'ī*, s.f. (6th) A small box or casket. Sing. and Pl.

هزاره *hazārah*, s.m. and f. (5th) The name of a tribe of Mughals or Tārtars, dwelling in the hills between Kābul and Hirāt. Pl. هزارګان *hazāra-gān*; Fem. Pl. هزارګانې *hazāra-gāni.*

هزم *hazm*, s.m. (2nd) Digestion. Pl. هزمونه *hazm-ūnah.* هزميدل *hazmedal*, verb intrans. To become digested. هزمول *hazmawul*, verb trans. To digest. See هضم

هژدات *hajz-dāt*, s.m. (6th) (corrup. of s اژدهات) The name of a mixed metal, bell-metal, brass. Sing. and Pl. د هژداتو غر *da hajz-dāto ghar*, A mountain of brass, a brazen mountain.

هسار *hisār*, s.m. (2nd) (corrup. of A حصار) A fort, a fortress, a fortification. Pl. هسارونه *hisārūnah.*

هساريدل *hisāredal*, verb intrans. To become a prisoner or captive. هسارول *hisārawul*, verb trans. To confine, to make captive (corrup. from A حصار A fortress, which see).

هسپه *has-pa'h*, s.f. (3rd) A kind of rupture breaking out on the face and body, particularly the former, a kind of erysipelas. Pl. ئي *ey.*

هسپه بوټی *has-pa'h būtaey*, s.m. (1st) The name of a plant used in medicine, a remedy for erysipelas. Pl. ي *ī.*

P هستي *hastī*, s.f. (3rd) Existence, entity, world. Pl. ئي *a'ī.* هستي نيستي *hastī-nīstī*, Existence and non-existence, entity and non-entity. هستي لرل *hastī laral*, verb trans. To have or possess entity or existence.

هسک *hask*, adj. High, tall, lofty, uppermost. 2. prep. Up, above, aloft; (Fem.) هسکه *haska'h*. هسک کول *hask kawul*, verb trans. To raise aloft, above, or on high. هسک کیدل *hask kedal*, verb intrans. To become high, tall or lofty, to shoot up as a plant, tree, etc.; to be raised aloft or on high.

هسک *hisk*, s.f. (1st) (W.) Lot, chance, lottery, toss up, hazard. 2. Drawing lots by placing pieces of paper in a bag with the names of the drawers written on them, or with the dung of sheep, camels, etc. placed in a turban or skirt, or by pieces of wood differently marked. Pl. هسکِ *hiski*. هسک *hisk* (E.) s.m. (2nd). Pl. هسکونه *hisk-ūnah*. هسک کول *hisk kawul* or آچول *āchawul*, verb trans. to cast or draw lots, to raffle, to toss up. See بچه and خسنړي

هسي *hasey* or هس *hasi*, adv. As, in like manner, thus, therefore, for this reason, denoting similarity or resemblance. It is generally preceded or followed by لکَ *laka* or لکه *lakah* or شان *shān*, as *as* and *so* in English. See Grammar, page 26. 2. دا هسي *dā hasey* or داسي *dā-sey* or دغه سي *daghah-sey*, Thus, so, in this manner.

هښمه *hashma'h* (W.) or *hakhma'h* (E.) s.f. (3rd) A shower of rain, a spring shower lasting for a short time, but falling heavily. Pl. ې *ey*.

هښيار *hush-yār* (W.) or *hukh-yār* (E.) adj. (P هوشيار) Intelligent, prudent, cautious, acquainted; alert, watchful, awake, in senses, abstinent, sober. 2. adv. Be cautious! take care! (Fem.) هښياره *hush-yāra'h* or *hukh-yāra'h*. هښياريدل *hush-yāredal* or *hukh-yāredal*, verb intrans. and هښيارول *hush-yārawul* or *hukh-yārawul*, verb trans. See under هوښيار

هښياري *hush-yārī* or *hukh-yārī*, s.f. (3rd) Understanding, care, attention, study. Pl. ئِي *a'ī*. See هوښياري

A هضم *hazm*, s.m. (2nd) Digestion. Pl. هضمونه *hazmūnah*. هضميدل *hazmedal*, verb intrans. To become digested, to digest. Pres. هضميږي *hazmejzī* (W.) or هضميګي *hazmegī* (E.); past هضم شه *hazm shah* or وُ شه *wu-shah*; fut. هضم به شي *hazm bah shī* or به وُ شي *bah wu-shī*; imp. هضم شه *hazm shah* or وُ شه *wu-shah*; act. part. هضميدونکيَ *hazmedūnkaey* or هضميدونيَ *hazmedūnaey*; past part. هضم شويَ *hazmshawaey*; verb n. هضميدنه *hazmedana'h* or هضميده *hazmedah*. هضمول *hazmawul*, verb trans. To digest, to embezzle. Pres. هضموي *hazmawī*; past هضم کړ *hazm karr* or وُ کړ *wu-karr*; fut. هضم به کړي *hazm bah krrī* or به وُ کړي *bah wu-krrī*; imp. هضم کړه *hazm krrah* or وُ کړه *wu-krrah*; act. part. هضموونکيَ *hazmawūnkaey* or هضمووني *hazmawūnaey*; past part. هضم کړيَ *hazm karraey*; verb. n. هضمونه *hazmawuna'h*. See also هزم, etc.

هغومبره *haghom-bra'h*, adv. So much; or هغونبره *haghon-bra'h*, and هغونمبره *haghonm-bra'h*. هغومبره قدر *haghom-bra'h kadr*, etc. That much. See هومبره and دهومبره

هغه *haghah*, The personal pronoun of the 3rd person Sing. and Pl., 'He, she, it, they,' and also used as the remote demonstrative pronoun 'that.' When inflected it becomes هِغِه *highih* or هغې *highey* for the feminine Sing. and هغو *hugho* and هغوې *hughoey* for the Masc. and Fem. Pl.; but the latter forms are not so common as the former. See Grammar, page 35. هغه پلو *haghah pal-aw* or *pal-o* or هغه خوا *haghah khwā*, Beyond, on that side, there, thither. هغه جهان *haghah jahān*, That world, the world to come. هغه دغه *haghah-daghah*, This and that, these and those; and هغو دغو *hagho dagho*. هغه شان *haghah shān*, هغه رنګ *haghah rang*, or هغه طور *haghah ṭaur*, So, in that way or manner. هغه ځاي *haghah dzā-e*, That place, there, thither. له هغه ځايه *lah haghah dzā-e-a'h* or ځايَ *dzā-ea*, From thence or from thither. هغه وخت *haghah wakht*, Then, at that time. له هغه سببَ *lah haghah sababa*, For that reason, on that account, therefore. تر هغه پور *tar haghah pūri* or پوري *pūrī*, So far, to that degree.

P هفته *haf-ta'h*, s.f. (3rd) A week. Pl. ې *ey*.

هره هفته *hara'h haf-ta'h*, Every week, weekly.

هک پک *hak-pak*, adj. Confused, confounded, aghast; (Fem.) هکه پکه *haka'h-paka'h*. هک پک کیدل *hak-pak kedal*, verb intrans. To become confused or confounded. هک پک کول *hak-pak kawul*, verb trans. To confound, to confuse. See حلق دلق and هاړه هوړه

هګئ *haga'ī*, s.f. (6th) An egg. Sing. and Pl. See ها

S هل *hal*, s.m. (2nd) The handle of a plough, a plough. Pl. هلونه *halūnah*. See يويه

A هلاك *halāk*, s.m. (6th) (from هلك) Perdition, destruction, ruin, slaughter, death. Sing. and Pl. 2. adj. Lost, destroyed, ruined, fatigued; (Fem.) هلاكه *halāka'h*. هلاك والئ *halāk-wālaey*, s.m. (1st) Perdition, ruin, destruction, annihilation. Pl. والي *wālī*; or هلاك توب *halāk-tob*, s.m. (2nd). Pl. توبونه *tobūnah*; and هلاك تيا *halāk-tī'ā*, s.f. (6th). (E.) Sing. and Pl. (W.) Pl. تياوي *tī'āwī*. هلاكيدل *halākedal*, verb intrans. To become destroyed, ruined, slaughtered, annihilated. Pres. هلاكيږي *halākejzī* (W.) or هلاكيګي *halākegī* (E.); past هلاك شه *halāk shah* or وُ شه *wu-shah*; fut. هلاك به شي *halāk bah shī* or به وُ شي *bah wu-shī*; imp. هلاك شه *halāk shah* or وُ شه *wu-shah*; act. part. هلاكيدونكئ *halākedūnkaey* or هلاكيدونئ *halāk-edūnaey*; past part. هلاك شوئ *halāk* or *halāk shawaey*; verb. n. هلاكيدنه *halākedana'h* or هلاكيده *halākedah*. هلاكول *halākawul*, verb trans. To destroy, to drive to destruction, to kill, to annihilate. Pres. هلاكوي *halākawī*; past هلاك كړ *halāk karr* or وُ كړ *wu-karr*; fut. هلاك به كړي *halāk bah krrī* or به وُ كړي *bah wu-krrī*; imp. هلاك كړه *halāk krrah* or وُ كړه *wu-krrah*; act. part. هلاكوونكئ *halākawūn-kaey* or هلاكوونئ *halākawūnaey*; past part. هلاك كړئ *halāk karraey*; verb. n. هلاكونه *halākawuna'h*.

A هلاكت *halākat*, s.m. (2nd) (from هلك) Death, destruction, perdition, annihilation. Pl. هلاكتونه *halākat-ūnah*; or

A هلاكي *halākī*, s.f. (3rd) Death, destruction, perdition, ruin. Pl. ئ *a'ī*. See هلاك والئ, etc.

A هلال *hilāl*, s.m. (9th) The new moon, the first and last two or three days of the moon. Sing. and Pl.

هلال *halāl*, adj. Lawful (corrup. of A حلال, which see).

S P هلاهل *halā-hal* or *halā-hil*, s.m. (6th) Poison. Sing. and Pl. 2. adj. Deadly, mortal (as poison).

هلته *hal-tah*, adv. There, thither, in that place, yonder; as in the proverb, چرته ډب هلته ادب *chartah ddab hal-tah adab*, 'Where there is chastisement, there is respect.'

هلته كي *haltah-kī*. See preceding.

هلك *halak*, s.m. (5th) A boy, a youth, a lad until the age of puberty. Pl. هلكان *halak-ān*. 2. adj. Small, little, diminutive, young, youthful; (Fem.) هلكه *halaka'h*. هلك والئ *halak-wālaey*, s.m. (1st) Boyhood, youth, the time of boyhood, school-boy days. Pl. والي *wālī*. See الك

هلكت *halakat* or *halkat*, s.m. (2nd) Boyhood, youth. Pl. هلكتونه *halakatūnah*. See preceding.

هلكينه *hal-kīna'h*, s.f. (3rd) Infancy, childhood, youth, boyhood, girlhood. Pl. ئ *ey*.

هلم *halam*, s.m. (6th) Cresses, a kind of greens, asparagus (?). Sing. and Pl.

هلواك *hal-wāk*, adj. Fast, swift, rapid, fleet, agile, nimble-footed, eagle-winged; (Fem.) هلواكه *hal-wāka'h*. هلواك كول *hal-wāk kawul*, verb trans. To make haste, to hie, to hasten, to push on. په هلواك تلل *pah hal-wāk t'lal*, verb intrans. To walk or move briskly or with speed, to cut along. هلواك والئ *hal-wāk wālaey*, s.m. (1st) Velocity, speed, haste, fleetness. Pl. والي *wālī*.

هله *halah*, adv. Then, at that time.

هله *hala'h*, s.f. (3rd) An attack, assault, tumult, uproar (corrup. of A حمله). Pl. ئ *ey*. هله كول *hala'h kawul*, verb trans. To assault, to attack, to storm. 2. To raise an uproar or tumult.

هلي *haley*, adv. Here, hither, in this place.

هم *hum*, conj. Also, even, same, likewise, in the same manner, equally (P هم *ham*). In composition, Together, with, same, etc.; as هم اصل *hum aṣal*, adj. Of the same origin or descent. هم پیاله *hum piyāla'h*, adj. Pot companion. هم پیشه *hum pesha'h*, adj. Of the same trade, similar in occupation. هم جنس *hum jins*, adj. Of the same species, of a feather, homogeneous, fellow creature. هم چشم *hum chashm*, adj. An equal, a fellow, an enemy. هم چشمي *hum chashmī*, s.f. (3rd) Equality, strife, contention. Pl. ئي *a'ī*. هم چسمي کول *hum chashmī kawul*, verb trans. To contend, to strive against. هم خواب *hum khwāb*, adj. A bed-fellow; or هم خوابه *hum khwāba'h*, A spouse, a wife. هم درد *hum dard*, adj. A condoler, a partner in adversity, a fellow-sufferer. هم دم *hum dam*, adj. Intimate, friendly. هم ذات *hum ẕāt*, adj. Of the same nature or kind. هم راز *hum rāz*, Acquainted with each other's secrets, a confidant. هم رنګ *hum rang*, adj. Of the same color or disposition. هم ژبه or زبان *hum jzaba'h* or *zabān*, Speaking the same language. هم زولي *hum-zolaey*, adj. Cotemporary, of the same age; (Fem.) هم زولِ *hum-zoli*. Pl. (Masc. and Fem.) ي *ī*. هم سایه *hum-sā-yah*, A neighbour, neighbouring. هم سایه توب *hum-sā-yah-tob*, s.m. (2nd) Neighbourliness, kindness. Pl. توبونه *tobūnah*; or هم سایه ګلوي *hum-sā-yah galwī*, s.f. (3rd). Pl. ئي *a'ī*. هم سبق *hum sabaḳ*, A class-fellow. هم شکل *hum shakl*, adj. Alike, of the same appearance, resembling. هم صحبت *hum ṣuḥ-bat*, Associating, of the same society. هم عمر *hum œumr*, adj. Coeval of the same age. هم قد *hum ḳadd*, adj. Of equal stature. هم کوم *hum kaum*, adj. Of the same clan or tribe; also هم خیل *hum khel* or هم قام *hum ḳām*. هم کار *hum kār*, adj. Of the same business, fellow-workman. هم کلي *hum kalaey*, Of the same village or hamlet. هم کور *hum kor*, A fellow-lodger, an inmate, a companion. هم مذهب *hum maẕ-hab*, Of the same religion. هم نام *hum nām*, Of the same name, a namesake. هم نسل *hum nasl*, Of the same breed. هم نشین *hum nishīn*, A companion. هم وزن *hum wazn*, Of the same weight. هم وطن *hum waṭan*, A fellow-countryman, a compatriot, etc. The feminines may be formed by adding ه, as explained in Grammar.

A هم *hamm*, s.m. (2nd) Grief, care, solicitude, turning over a thing anxiously in the mind. Pl. همونه *hammūnah*.

P هما *humā*. See همای

P همای *humā-e*, s.m. (9th) A bird of happy omen, an eagle or phœnix, and it is supposed that every head it overshadows will wear a crown. Sing. and Pl. See عنقا

همبره *humbra'h*, adv. That much. See هومبره

A همت *him-mat*, s.m. (2nd) (from هم) Spirit, mind, resolution, inclination, bravery, liberality, courage, magnanimity, design, purpose. Pl. همتونه *him-matūnah*. همت لرل *him-mat laral*, verb trans. To possess or have spirit, courage, resolution, etc. همت کول *him-mat kawul*, verb trans. To manifest or show spirit, resolution, bravery, or inclination.

A P همتي *him-matī*, adj. Bold, daring, resolute. (Masc. and Fem.)

P هم راه *ham-rāh*, s.m. (5th) A fellow traveller, a comrade, an acquaintance. Pl. همراهان *ham-rāhān*. همراهه *ham-rāha'h*, s.f. (3rd. Pl. ئي *ey*. See ملګري

همره *hum-ra'h*. See هومبره

همسا *ham-sā*, s.f. (6th) A staff, a crutch, a stick, a bludgeon. (E.) Sing. and Pl. (W.) Pl. همساوي *ham-sāwī*. See امسا

P همګي *hama-gī*, adj. All, the whole. See تول

A هموث *ham-oṣ*, s.m. (9th) A lion tearing his prey (in composition). Sing. and Pl. Also written هموس *ham-os*.

P همه *hamah*, adj. All, the whole. See تول

P همياني *ham-yānī*, s.f. (3rd) A purse. Pl. ئي *a'ī*.

P هميشه *hamesha'h* or هميش *hamesh*, adv. Always, ever, at all times, continually. See هر کله and مدام

هنبره *hun-bra'h*. See هومبره

هنج *hanj*, s.m. (6th) (W.) Assafœtida. Sing. and Pl. See under.

هنجه *hanja'h*, s.f. (3rd) Assafœtida or devil's

dung. 2. The business of collecting and preparing the gum. Pl. ي ey. هنجه كول *hanja'h kawul*, verb trans. To manufacture assafœtida. (s هينګ).

هند *hind*, s. prop. India, Hindūstān.

هنداره *hindāra'h*, s.f. (3rd) A mirror, a looking-glass. Pl. ي ey. See اهنه

هندكو *hind-ko*, s.f. (9th) The language of India. Sing. and Pl. See هندي

هندكي *hind-kī*, s.m. (1st) Pl. The name of a tribe, not Afghāns, supposed to be of Indian descent. They are numerous about Peshāwer and in Bajawarr or Bājourr, and some are found in the Yūsufzī country. 2. A name given to the people of India. هندكي *hind-kaey* (Sing.) A male of the above class, a Hindūstānī. هندكۍ *hind-ka'ī*, s.f. (6th) A female of the above. Sing. and Pl.

A P هندو *hindū*, s.m. (5th) A Hindū, a Gentū, a worshipper of idols. Pl. هندوان *hinduān*.

هندوبار *hindū-bār*, s.m. (9th) A place where Hindūs meet or dwell. Sing. and Pl.

هندوستان *hindūstān*, s. prop. India or Hindūstān, chiefly applied to the upper provinces.

هندوګي *hindū-gaey*, s.m. (1st) (dimin. of هندو) A chandler, a grain-dealer. 2. A designation of vileness or meanness applied to Hindūs in general. Pl. ي ī. هندوګۍ *hindūga'ī*, s.f. (3rd) A Hindū female. Sing. and Pl.

P هندوانه *hinduwāna'h*, s.f. (3rd) A water-melon. Pl. ي ey. Also هندوانه *hind-wāna'h*.

هندوانړۍ *hind-wārrna'ī*, s.f. (6th) A Hindū female in general. Sing. and Pl.

هنده *han-da'h*, s.f. (3rd) Wish, desire. Pl. ي ey. See هنډه

A P هندي *hindī*, adj. Relating to India, Indian, the Hindī language. See هندكو

هنډ *hindd*, s.m. (9th) The name of a village in the Yūsufzī country situated in the Sudhum valley. 2. The name of a ferry on the Sindhu, Attak, or Indus. Sing. and Pl.

هنډه *handda'h*, s.f. (3rd) Desire, wish, want, inclination, leaning, bent, fancy, partiality, longing, yearning, ambition. Pl. ي ey. هنډه لرل *handda'h laral*, verb trans. To desire, to want, to have a bent or inclination for, to long for. په or و هنډه رسيدل *pah* or *wa handda'h rasedal*, verb intrans. To attain one's desires or wants. See هڅه

هنډه *hinddah*, s.m. (5th) A bull, a stallion, or male animal kept for breeding purposes. Pl. هنډان *hinddān*. See مينده

S هنډۍ *hundda'ī*, s.f. (6th) A bill of exchange. Sing. and Pl.

P هنر *hunr*, s.m. (2nd) Art, skill, excellence in any art, attainment, ingenuity, cleverness, virtue. Pl. هنرونه *hunrūnah*. هنر مند *hunr-mand* or هنرور *hunr-war*, adj. Skilful, clever, ingenious; (Fem.) هنر منده *hunr-mandah* or هنر وره *hunr-wara'h*. هنر مندي *hunr-mandī*, s.f. (3rd) Skilfulness, ingeniousness. Pl. ي a'ī. هنر لرل *hunr laral*, verb trans. To have or be possessed of skill in any art or trade.

هنبره *hun-bra'h* or هنمره *hunm-bra'h*. See هومبره

هنكهار *hanka-hār* or هنګهار *hanga-hār*, s.m. (5th) Pl. Groaning, moaning, as a sick person. هنكهار *hanka-hār* or هنګهار كول *hanga-hār kawul*, or هنكهار *hanka-hār* or هنګهار لرل *hanga-hār laral*, verb trans. To groan, to moan, to cry out. See هينګ

S هنس *hans*, s.m. (5th) A goose. 2. A bird that, the Afghāns say, lives on pearls, which are its only food. Pl. هنسان *hansān*. هنسه *hansa'h*, s.f. (3rd) The hen bird. Pl. ي ey.

هنړ *harrn*, s.m. (5th) The neigh of a horse, or bray of an ass when requiring grain or water. Pl. هنړهار *harrna-hār*. هنړيدل *harrnedal*, verb intrans. To neigh, to bray. Pres. هنړيږي *harrnejzī* (W.) or هنړيګي *harrnegī* (E.); past وُ هنړيده *wu-harrnedah*; fut. وُ به هنړيږي *wu bah harrnejzī* or هنړيګي *harrnegī*; imp. وُ هنړيږه *wu-harrnejzah* or وُ هنړيګه *wu-harrnegah*; act. part. هنړيدونكي *harrnedūnkaey* or هنړيدوني *harrnedūnaey*; past part. هنړيدلي *harrnedalaey*; verb. n. هنړيدنه *harrnedana'h* or هنړيده *harrnedah*.

هو *ho*, adv. Yes, ay, be it so. 2. vocative part.

Ho! halloo! 3. Hurrah, or word used in an attack. هو كول *ho kawul*, verb trans. To say yes to, to agree to, to answer in the affirmative. 2. To halloo, to call out, to cheer. (هو s).

هوا *hawā*, interj. Alas! ah! ah me! sorrow! dear me! See هاي

A هوا *hawā*, s.f. (6th) (from هوي) Lust, desire. 2. Love, affection. 3. Air, atmosphere, wind. (E.) Sing. and Pl. (W.) Pl. هواوي *hawāwī*. هوا دار *hawā-dār*, adj. Airy, well ventilated. 2. A vain or proud person. 3. A lover; (Fem.) هوا داره *hawā-dāra'h*. هوا ور كول *hawā war-kawul*, verb trans. To air, to put anything out for an airing. هوا و هوس *hawā-o-hawas*, Lust, concupiscence, sensuality, vanity, ambition, luxury.

هواد *hiwād*, s.m. (2nd) A country, a region, a tract of country, a distant land. Pl. هوادونه *hiwādūnah*. See هيواد

هوار *hawār*, adj. Even, smooth, level, flat; (Fem.) هواره *hawāra'h*. هوار توب *hawār-tob*, s.m. (2nd) Evenness, levelness, flatness, smoothness. Pl. توبونه *tobūnah*; or هوار والي *hawār-wālaey*, s.m. (1st). Pl. والي *wālī*; and هوار تيا *hawār-tī'ā*, s.f. (6th). (E.) Sing. and Pl. (W.) Pl. تياوي *tī'āwī*. هواريدل *hawāre-dal*, verb intrans. To become level, smooth, flat. Pres. هواريږي *hawārejzī* (W.) or هواريگي *hawāregī* (E.); past هوار شه *hawār shah* or وُ شه *wu-shah*; fut. هوار به شي *hawār bah shī* or به وُ شي *bah wu-shī*; imp. هوار شه *hawār shah* or وُ شه *wu-shah*; act. part. هواريدونكي *hawāredūnkaey* or هواريدوني *hawāredūnaey*; past part. هوار *hawār* or هوار شوي *hawār shawaey*; verb. n. هواريدنه *hawāredana'h* or هواريده *hawāredah*. هوارول *hawārawul*, verb trans. To level, to make level, flat, smooth. Pres. هواروي *hawārawī*; past هوار كړ *hawār karr* or وُ كړ *wu-karr*; fut. هوار به كړي *hawār bah krrī* or به وُ كړي *bah wu-krrī*; imp. هوار كړه *hawār krrah* or وُ كړه *wu-krrah*; act. part. هواروونكي *hawārrawūnkaey* or هواروونې *hawārrawūnaey*; past part. هوار كړي *hawār karraey*; verb. n. هوارونه *hawārawuna'h*.

A هوبهو *hū-ba-hū*, adv. Quite, exactly, perfectly, the very same and no other.

A هود *hūd*, s. prop. A prophet—the patriarch Heber, so called by the Arabs.

هوده *hūda'h*, s.f. (3rd) Blowing or breathing on anything (as old women when charming, and conjurers and jugglers when exorcising or juggling). 2. Business, office, post, commission, appointment. (A عهده) Pl. ې *ey*. هوده كول *hūda'h kawul*, verb trans. To breathe on, to charm, to exorcise. هوده دار *hūda'h-dār*, adj. An exorcist, a juggler, one who charms. 2. Intrusted with any office, employed, an officer; (Fem.) هوده داره *hūda'h-dāra'h*.

هودج *haw-da'h*, s.f. (3rd) A litter used by eastern females when they travel, the open seat on an elephant. Pl. ې *ey*.

هوډ *hodd*, s.m. (2nd) The contrary, the opposite, contrariety, obstinacy, opposition, perverseness. Pl. هوډونه *hoddūnah*. هوډ كول *hodd kawul*, verb trans. To persist, to spite, to persevere, to contradict, to act with obstinacy and contrariety. هوډ لرل *hodd laral*, verb trans. To be possessed of or affected with obstinacy, spite, perversity (English verb intrans. To be obstinate or perverse). هوډي *hoddī*, adj. Obstinate, perverse, contrary, a perverse or obstinate person. (Masc. and Fem.)

هوډه *hodda'h*, s.f. (3rd) Obstinacy, etc. Pl. ې *ey*. See preceding.

هوډی *hoddaey*, s.m. (1st) A perverse, stubborn, captious, wayward person. 2. The name of the high mountain facing Attak on the Indus. Pl. ي *ī*. هوډۍ *hodda'ī*, s.f. (3rd) A perverse, wayward female. Sing. and Pl.

هور *hor*, s.m. (2nd) Fire. (H אור). 2. Time, period, season. Pl. هورونه *horūnah*. See اور

هور *hor*, s.m. (5th) A deer. Pl. هوران *hor-ān*. هوره *hora'h*, s.f. (3rd) The female of the above. Pl. هورې *horey*. This word is almost obsolete.

هور *hūri* or هوري *hūrey*, adv. There, thither, in

that place; also هور ته *hūri tah* and هوري ته *hūrey tah* or هور ته *hor tah*.

هوره *hūṟra'h*. See هاره

هوږه *hūjza'h*, s.f. (3rd) (W.) Garlic. Pl. ې *ey*. See هوګه

A هوس *hawas*, s.m. (2nd) Desire, lust, sensuality, concupiscence. 2. Ambition. 3. Inordinate desire. 4. Curiosity. Pl. هوسونه *hawasūnah*. هوس ناك *hawas-nāk*, adj. Desirous, sensual, ambitious, full of desire; (Fem.) هوس ناكه *hawas-nāka'h*. هوس كول *hawas kawul*, verb trans. To show great desire, ambition, or curiosity, to desire, to wish or long for. هوسيدل *hawasedal*, verb intrans. To be desirous, to become or grow desirous, curious, ambitious of, to become eager, anxious, covetous, sensual, etc. هوسول *hawasawul*, verb trans. To make eager, desirous, curious, anxious, covetous, to create, excite, or provoke desire, to render sensual, to fill with ambition.

هوسا *hosā*, adj. Refreshed, untired, unwearied, restored, recruited, renewed in strength. (Masc. and Fem.) هوسا كيدل *hosā kedal*, verb intrans. To become refreshed, recruited, repaired, refitted, regaled. هوسا كول *hosā kawul*, verb trans. To recruit, to refresh (as a commander his troops before action), to repair, to refit, to give tone to.

هوسي *ho-saey*, s.m. (1st) An antelope, a deer. Pl. ي *ī*. هوسئ *ho-sa'ī*, s.f. (6th) The feminine of the above, a hind. Sing. and Pl. See اوسي and كبلي

P هوشنګ *ho-shang*, s. prop. The name of the second Persian monarch of the Peshdadian dynasty.

هوښ *hosh* (W.) or *hokh* (E.) s.m. (9th) (from P هوش) Understanding, sense, judgment, capacity, instinct, intelligence, recollection. 2. Mind, soul. Sing. and Pl. هوښ كول *hosh* or *hokh kawul*, verb trans. To use judgment (in any matter or work), to show capacity or understanding, to act with sense and intelligence. هوښ لرل *hosh* or *hokh laral*, verb trans. To have or be endowed with understanding, capacity, or intelligence. په *pah* or پر هوښ كيدل *par hosh* or *hokh kedal*, verb intrans. To come to one's-self, to recover one's senses or recollection. په *pah* or پر هوښ كول *par hosh* or *hokh kawul*, verb trans. To bring another to his senses or intellect, to recover.

هوښيار *hosh-yār* (W.) or *hokh-yār* (E.) adj. Intelligent, clever, sensible, wise, endowed with judgment or capacity, careful, prudent, discreet, cautious, attentive, alert, awake, watchful, accurate, sober, etc.; (Fem.) هوښياره *hosh-yāra'h* or *hokh-yāra'h*. هوښيار كيدل *hosh-yār* or *hokh-yār kedal*, verb intrans. To become sensible, intelligent, attentive, alert, etc. هوښيار كول *hosh-yār* or *hokh-yār kawul*, verb trans. To make or render sensible, intelligent, alert, active, etc.

هوښيار تيا *hokh-yār tī'ā* (E.) or *hosh-yār tī'ā* (W.) s.f. (6th) Prudence, sobriety, caution, foresight, intelligence, watchfulness. (E.) Sing. and Pl. (W.) Pl. تياوي *tī'āwī*.

هوښياري *hosh-yārī* or *hokh-yārī*, s.f. (3rd) Intelligence, prudence, caution, care, discretion, watchfulness, carefulness, sobriety, activity, alertness. Pl. ئي *a'ī*. هوښياري كول *hosh-yārī* or *hokh-yārī kawul*, verb trans. To show intelligence, to act with caution and prudence.

هوك *hūk*, adj. Sunk, overwhelmed (in water or grief), flooded, inundated, overflowed; (Fem.) هوكه *hūka'h*. هوك كيدل *hūk kedal*, verb intrans. To become flooded, inundated, overwhelmed. هوك كول *hūk kawul*, verb trans. To flood, to inundate, to overflow. See لاهو

هوكلي *hok-la'ī*, s.f. (6th) A large wooden pestle. Sing. and Pl. See بغرئ

هوكه *hau-kah*, adj. Fatigued, tired, weary, jaded, knocked up, foot-sore, worn out, spent, unrefreshed. (Masc. and Fem.) هوكه كيدل *hau-kah kedal*, verb intrans. To become tired, fatigued, jaded, knocked up. هوكه كول *hau-kah kawul*, verb trans. To tire, to jade, to knock up. See ستړي

هوكي *ho-kaey*, s.m. (1st) Consent of parents or

friends of a girl to her marriage, agreement, (from هو *ho*, Yes). Pl. ي *ī*. هوکي راوړل *ho-kaey rā-w'rral*, verb trans. To bring consent of parents to a betrothal or marriage. هوکي ورکول *ho-kaey war-kawul*, verb trans. To give consent.

هوګه *hū-ga'h* (E.) s.f. (3rd) Garlic. Pl. ې *ey*. See هوږه

هول *hūl*, s.m. (2nd) A bar or bolt for a door, a prop to a matted shutter. Pl. هولونه *hūlūnah*. See تنبه (W.)

A هول *haul*, s.m. (2nd) Fear, terror, horror, dismay. Pl. هولونه *haul-ūnah*. هول ناك *haul-nāk*, adj. Terrific, horrible, dismal, horrid, terror-striking; (Fem.) هول ناکه *haul-nāka'h*. هولي *haulī*, adj. Terrified, horrified, terror-struck, dismayed. (Masc. and Fem.) هول آخستل *haul ākhistal*, verb trans. To take fright. (Eng. verb intrans.) To become horrified at, to become dismayed; or هول کول *haul kawul*, verb trans.

هول آخستونې *haul ākhistūnaey* or آخستونکې *ākhistūnkaey*, adj. Fearful, timid; (Fem.) آخستونې *ākhistūni* or آخستونکې *ākhistūnki*. Pl. (Masc. and Fem.) ي *ī*. هول آخستلې *haul ākhistalaey*, adj. Horrified, terror-stricken; (Fem.) آخستلې *ākhistali*. Pl. (Masc. and Fem.) ي *ī*.

P A هولناکي *haul-nākī*, s.f. (3rd) Frightfulness, dreadfulness, terror. Pl. ئي *a'ī*.

هومره *hom-ra'h*, adv. So much. May also be written هونبره *hon-bra'h* and د هومبره *da hom-bra'h* or د هونبره *da hon-bra'h*. هومره قدر *hom-ra'h ḳadr*, etc. That much. See also هغومبره

هونبره *hon-bra'h*. See preceding. Also د هونبره *da hon-bra'h*.

هونړا *horrnā*, s.m. (5th) A snare or net for catching birds. 2. A sort of perch placed over the snare for the bird to alight upon. Pl. هونړاګان *horrnā-gān*.

هوي *hū-e*, An exclamation of sorrow or distress. See هاي هوي

P هويدا *huwaidā*, adj. Clear, manifest, plain, evident, open. See ښکند

سويه *ho-ya'h*. s.f. (3rd) An egg. Pl. ې *ey*.

هه *hah*, interj. Indeed! really! 2. A sound made use of in rousing a person from sleep—ho! halloo! ahoy! etc.

هي هي *hai hai*, interj. Alas, alas! dear, dear! 2. Wonderful! strange! هي هي کول *hai hai kawul*, verb trans. To cry out, to lament, to bewail. See هاي

A هيات *hai-āt*, s.m. (2nd) (from هي) Aspect, face, outward form, figure, countenance, manner. Pl. هياتونه *hai-ātūnah*.

A هيبت *hai-bat*, s.m. (2nd) (from هيب) Fright, panic, horror, dread, awe, perturbation. Pl. هيبتونه *hai-batūnah*. هيبت ناك *hai-bat nāk*, adj. Frightful, terrible, terrific, awful, tremendous, dreadful; (Fem.) هيبت ناکه *hai-bat-nāka'h*. هيبت آخستل *hai-bat ākhistal*, verb trans. To become panic-struck, to take fright, to be seized with horror, awe, perturbation, or dismay. هيبت لرل *hai-bat laral*, verb trans. To be possessed with horror, dread, or panic. هيبت کول *hai-bat kawul*, verb trans. To awe, to daunt, to alarm, to appal, to dismay. هيبت وهل *hai-bat wahal*, verb trans. To terrify, to strike with horror or dismay, to petrify, to make one's hair stand on end. هيبت وهلې *hai-bat wahalaey*, adj. (past part.) Horror-struck, panic-stricken, petrified; (Fem.) هيبت وهلې *haibat wahali*. Pl. (Masc. and Fem.) ي *ī*.

هيڅ *hīts*, adv. In no degree, none, naught, nothing whatever. هيڅ څوك *hīts-tsok* or هيڅ کس *hīts-kas*, Nobody, no one. هيڅ کله *hīts kalah*, هيڅ کله نه *hīts kalah nah*, or هيڅ وخت *hīts wakht*, Never, at no time. په هيڅ رنګ *pah hīts rang*, or په هيڅ طور *pah hīts ṭaur* or صورت *ṣūrat*, By no means, by no means whatever.

هيچري *hīchari* or هيچري *hīcharey*, adv. Never, at no time.

هيچرته *hīchartah*, adv. Nowhere.

هير *her*, adj. Forgotten, unremembered, slipped from the memory, lost, effaced, bygone, buried or sunk in oblivion; (Fem.) هيره *hera'h*.

هيريدل *heredal*, verb intrans. To slip, to escape or fade from the memory, to sink into oblivion, to be forgotten or unremembered. Pres. هيريږي *herejzī* (W.) or هيريگي *heregī* (E.); past هير شه *her shah* or وُ شه *wu-shah*; fut. هير به شي *her bah shī* or به وُ شي *bah wu-shī*; imp. هير شه *her shah* or وُ شه *wu-shah*; act. part. هيريدونكَي *heredūnkaey* or هيريدونيَ *heredūnaey*; past part. هير *her* or هير شوَيَ *her shawaey*; verb. n. هيريدنه *heredana'h* or هيريده *heredah*. هيرول *herawul*, verb trans. To forget, to lose, to unlearn, to efface, to discharge from the memory, to mistake, to err. Pres. هيروي *herawī*; past هير كړ *her karr* or وُ كړ *wu-karr*; fut. هير به كړي *her bah krrī* or به وُ كړي *bah wu-krrī*; imp. هير كړه *her krrah* or وُ كړه *wu-krrah*; act. part. هيروونكَي *herawūnkaey* or هيروونيَ *herawūnaey*; past part. هير كړيَ *her karraey*; verb. n. هيرونه *herawuna'h*. هير واليَ *her-wālaey*, s.m. (1st) Forgetfulness, want of memory, oblivion, error, mistake. Pl. والي *wālī*; or هير تيا *her-tī'ā*, s.f. (6th). (E.) Sing. and Pl. (W.) Pl. تياوي *tī'āwī*.

هيړيَ *her-rraey*, s.m. (1st) A short-tailed or common sheep. Pl. ي *ī*. هيړئِي *her-rra'ī*, s.f. (6th) An ewe. Sing. and Pl. See هړيَ, هړ, and بري and ايري (s بيزۀ).

هير قطار *hīr kaṭār*, s.m. (2nd) Filing along, going one after the other in single file like camels. Pl. قطارونه *kaṭār-ūnah*. See پره

هيړ *herr*, s.m. (6th) Time, period, season. Sing. and Pl. يو هيړ *yo* or *yow herr*, adv. Once, one time, etc. بل هيړه *bal-herrah* or هيړَ *herra*, Again, another time. See هيړه

هيړه *herra'h*, s.f. (3rd) Time, occasion, a period of time. Pl. ي *ey*. يوه هيړه *yawa'h herra'h*, adv. Once, one time, on one occasion.

هيړيَ *herraey*, s.m. (1st) A long-tailed sheep, the common sheep, a ram. Pl. ي *ī*. هيړئِي *herra'ī*, s.f. (6th) An ewe. Sing. and Pl. See بري, ايري, هيړيَ, هړ, and بري

P هيز *hīz*, s.m. (5th) An hermaphrodite. Pl. هيزان *hīz-ān*. See هجړي

هيزگي *hez-gī*, s.f. (3rd) Spelling words by naming the letters and syllables (as children when learning to read). Pl. ي *a'ī*. هيزگي كول *hez-gī kawul*, verb trans. To spell, to name the letters and syllables of words. See هجكي and پيزي

هيځگي *hedz-gī*, s.f. (3rd). See preceding. Pl. ي *a'ī*.

هيسته *hīs-tah*, adv. Here, hither, in this place. هيسته شه *hīs-tah shah*, Get out, be off, get hence, etc. را هيسته *rā-hīs-tah*, Near me or us. در هيسته *dar-hīs-tah*, Near thee or you. ور هيسته *war-hīs-tah*, Near him, her, it, or them.

هي شه *hai shah*, interj. Alas! well-a-day! alack! dear me! ah me! heigh ho!

هيښ *hesh* (W.) or *hekh* (E.), adj. Perplexed, astonished, confounded, amazed, disturbed; (Fem.) هيښه *hesha'h* or *hekha'h*. هيښ كيدل *hesh* or *hekh kedal*, verb intrans. To become perplexed, amazed, confounded astonished. هيښ كول *hesh* or *hekh kawul*, verb trans. To perplex, to confound, to astonish.

هيغ *hegh*, adj. Straight, unbent, rigid, stiff, firm, unyielding, tense; (Fem.) هيغه *hegha'h*. هيغ نيغ *hegh-negh*, adj. Unable to move from sickness, such as rheumatism, etc.; cramped, stiff; (Fem.) هيغه نيغه *hegha'h-negha'h*. هيغ واليَ *hegh-wālaey*, s.m. (1st) Erectness, uprightness, straightness. 2. Stiffness, rigidity, tenseness. 3. Cramping. Pl. والي *wālī*. هيغ كول *hegh kawul*, verb trans. To make straight or upright, to cramp, to stiffen, to harden.

هيكل *hai-kal*, s.m. (2nd) An ornament worn round the neck in the figure of a man or beast. 2. Figure, face, form, appearance, person, stature, shape. Pl. هيكلونه *hai-kalūnah*.

هيل *hel*, s.m. (6th) Cardamoms. Sing. and Pl.

هيله *hīla'h*, s.f. (3rd) Pretence, etc. (corrup. of A حيله, which see). 2. Hope, expectation, trust, dependence. Pl. ي *ey*. هيله لرل *hīla'h laral*, verb trans. To have hope or expectation from anyone, to trust to; also هيله كول *hīla'h kawul*. See اميد

هيلۍ *helaʼī*, s.f. (6th) A water-fowl, a duck, a teal. 2. The name of a village. Sing. and Pl. توره هيلۍ *toraʼh helaʼī*, A dip-chick, a black water-fowl which is in the continual habit of diving. خراړه هيلۍ *khrārraʼh helaʼī*, A grey water-fowl. پرانګه هيلۍ *prāngaʼh helaʼī*, A spotted wild fowl.

هينګ *heng*, s.m. (5th) A groan, a sigh, a moan. Pl. هينګهار *hengahār*, Moaning, groaning, groans or moans. هينګهار لرل *hengahār laral*, verb trans. To groan, to moan, to sigh, to cry out through sickness or pain; or هينګهار کول *hengahār kawul*, verb trans. See زګيروي and انګهار

هيواد *hewād*, s.m. (2nd) A country, a region, a tract of country, a distant land. Pl. هيوادونه *hewādūnah*. 2. Lamenting, bewailing, grieving. See هواد

P هيون *ha-yūn*, s.m. (5th) A horse. 2. A camel of burden. Pl. هيونان *ha-yūnān*. هيونه *ha-yūnaʼh*, s.f. (3rd) A mare. 2. A female camel. Pl. ې *ey*.

A هيهات *hai-hāt*, interj. (from هيه) Alas! alack-a-day! begone! Part. Bewailing, lamenting.

ي

ي *yā*, called ياي حطي *yā-i ḥuṭṭī* or ياي تحتاني *yā-i taḥ-tānī*, The twenty-eighth letter of the Arabic and thirty-second of the Persian, is the fortieth and last letter of the Pushto alphabet. It corresponds to Sanskrit य; and when appropriated to denote a number, it stands for 10.

There are several modifications and sounds of which this letter is capable, and which are of great importance and require explanation, as the corresponding letter of whatever language, introduced into Pushto, is subject to these rules.

1. *Yā-i taḥ-tānī mā-ḳabl-i-maf-tūḥ*, i.e. ي with (َ) *fat-haʼh* preceding it, being a compound of *fat-ḥaʼh* and *yā* quiescent, is used as the singular termination of a number of nouns, and by which their gender may be known. In the plural it is changed into *yā-i-maæ-rūf* or ي preceded by (ِ) *kasraʼh*; as سړی *sarraey*, A man; سړي *sarrī*, Men. These letters and combinations are also used for the Pushto masculine *yā-i-nisbat*, to express relation or connection; as قندهار *ḳanda-hār*, The city of Ḳandahār; قندهاری *ḳanda-hāraey*, A man or male of Ḳandahār; قندهاري *ḳanda-hārī*, Men of Ḳandahār, etc.

2. Feminine nouns ending in ه (*hā-i-khafī*) take *yā-i-maj-hūl* (ې) in the plural; as, ښځه *shadzaʼh* (W.) or *khadzaʼh* (E.) A woman; ښځې *shadzey* or *khadzey*, Women.

3. *Yā-i-maæ-rūf mā-ḳabl-i-hamzaʼh-i-khafī-i-maksūr, i.e.* ي with (ِٔ) preceding it, ۍ *aʼī*, is the termination of a number of feminine nouns, which are both singular and plural; as جينۍ *jīnaʼī*, A girl or girls. This termination is also used as the *yā-i-nisbat* for the feminine gender, to denote relation or connection; as قندهارۍ *ḳanda-hāraʼī*, A female or females of Ḳandahār.

4. The letter ې is used as the affixed personal pronouns of the second person, as in the Semitic, Persian, and Sindian languages; thus, *yā-i-maj-hūl* denotes or stands for the termination of the second person singular; as, آخلې *ākhal-ey*, Thou takest, and is changed in the plural to *hamzaʼh-i-malaiyinah-i-maksūr wo yā-i-taḥ-tānī-i-maæ-rūf*, i.e., softened *hamzaʼh* and ي with *kasraʼh* (ِ); as, آخلئ *ākhal-aʼaī*, You take. This is often written by way of distinction by some of the oldest authors with (ْ) *jazmaʼh* over ي, but I have generally adopted the former as being the more correct method. The Western Afghāns, however, do not usually make any difference between the pronunciation of this termination and that of the third person singular and plural hereafter noticed.

5. *Yā-i-maæ-rūf mā-ḳabl-i-mak-sūr* is used as the pronominal termination or affixed personal pronoun of the third person, both singular and

plural; as, آخلي *ākhal-ī*, He, she, it, or they take, which sound the Western Afghāns give to the termination of the second person plural also.

6. *Yā-i taḥ-tānī-i-sākin mā-ḳabl-i-maf-tūḥ* is (as in No. 1) affixed to the infinitives, and sometimes to the roots of verbs in forming the past participle for the masculine singular; as, آخستلي *ākhistalaey* or آخستي *ākhistaey*; which is changed into *yā-i-maj-hūl* for the singular feminine. This latter, however, by way of distinction, I have written with simple (ـِ) *kasra'h*, which also gives the pronunciation, and more particularly as the vowel points (ـَ) (ـِ) and (ـُ) are commonly used in Pushto for, and indiscriminately with ا, ي, and و. The plurals of both genders take *yā-i-maæ-rūf mā-ḳabl-i-maksūr*, يِ *ī*. The terminations وَنكي and وَني added to the roots of verbs in forming the active participle are subject to precisely the same changes as for the past participles already described.

7. Numerous words in the language terminate in *yā-i maæ-rūf mā-ḳabl-i-maksūr*, and are for the most part feminine. Amongst them will be found a number of foreign words adopted from the Persian and other languages. They take *yā-i-maæ-rūf mā-ḳabl-i hamza'h-i-khafi-i-maksūr* in the plural; as, ميرځي *mīr-tsī*, Distress, ميرځئي *mīr-tsa'ī*, Distresses. This latter termination, as warranted by the system of ancient Eastern Afghān writers, may also be written with (ـٔ) over it—ميرځئي, which conveys the same sound.

8. A number of foreign words have been adopted from Persian, Sanskrit, and other languages, which may be either masculine or feminine, terminating in *yā-i-maæ-rūf mā-ḳabl-i-maksūr*, as in No. 7; but they all take either ان, گان, or يان for the masculine, and انِ, گانِ, or يانِ for the feminine, plurals; or اني, گاني, or ياني for the feminine, plurals; as, هاتِي *hā-tī*, An elephant, هاتيان *hā-tīān*, elephants; دائي *dā'ī*, A nurse, دائيگانِ *dā'ī-gāni*, Nurses.

As in Arabic, ي is like ا and و, is one of the *ḥurūf i-æillat*, or weak letters; and is, like the English *y*, sometimes a consonant and sometimes a vowel.

P يا *yā*, conj. Or. 2. A vocative particle, O! or Oh! as يا خداي *yā khudā-e-a*, Oh God!

HI يابو *yā-bū*, s.m. and f. (5th) A pony, a galloway. Pl. يابوگان *yā-bū-gān*. Pl. (Fem.) يابوگانِ *yābū-gāni*.

A ياجوج ماجوج *yā-jūj mā-jūj*, s. prop. Gog and Magog.

P ياد *yād*, s.m. (2nd) Memory, recollection, remembrance, retentiveness. Pl. يادونه *yādūnah*. ياد داشت *yād-dāsht*, s.m. (2nd) A memorandum, a keepsake. Pl. ياد داشتونه *yād-dāshtūnah*. ياد دهي *yād-dih-ī*, s.f. (3rd) Putting in mind, reminiscence. Pl. ئي *a'ī*. ياد دهي كول *yād-dih-ī kawul*, verb trans. To put one in mind of anything. ياد گار *yād-gār*, s.m. (2nd) A memorial, a valuable present, a monument, a souvenir, a keepsake, a token. Pl. ياد گارونه *yād-gārūnah*. په ياد راغلل *pah yād rā-ghlal*, verb intrans. To recur, to come to mind, to come to one's recollection. په ياد وركول *pah yād war-kawul*, verb trans. To remind, to bring to one's recollection. يادېدل *yādedal*, verb intrans. To recur, to return to the recollection, to come to mind. Pres. يادېږي *yādejzī* (W.) or يادېگي *yādegī* (E.); past ياد شه *yād shah* or وُ شه *wu-shah*; fut. ياد به شي *yād bah shī* or به وُ شي *bah wu-shī*; imp. ياد شه *yād shah* or وُ شه *wu-shah*; act. part. يادېدونكي *yādedūnkaey* or يادېدوني *yādedūnaey*; past part. ياد شوي *yād shawaey*; verb. n. يادېدنه *yādedana'h* or يادېده *yādedah*. يادول *yādawul*, verb trans, To recollect, to call to mind, to remember, to keep in mind, to carry in the memory, to know by heart, to learn, to get by heart. Pres. يادوي *yādawī*; past ياد كړ *yād karr* or وُ كړ *wu-karr*; fut. ياد به وُ كړي *yād bah krrī* or به وُ كړي *bah wu-krrī*; imp. ياد كړه *yād krrah* or وُ كړه *wu-krrah*; act. part. يادوونكي *yādawūnkaey* or يادووني *yād-*

awūnaey; past part. ياد كړى *yād karracy*; verb. n. يادونه *yādawuna'h*.

P يار *yār*, s.m. (5th) A friend, a lover, a gallant, a paramour. 2. An assistant, a companion, a comrade. Pl. ياران *yārān*. ياره *yāra'h*, s.f. (3rd) A mistress, a sweetheart. Pl. ې *ey*. يار بازي *yār-bāzī*, s.f. (3rd) Fornication, wantonness. Pl. ئ *a'ī*. ياري *yārī*, s.f. (3rd) Friendship, love, gallantry, intriguing. Pl. ئ *a'ī*. ياري كول *yārī kawul*, verb trans. To intrigue, to show friendship, to manifest love or affection. يار غار *yār-i-ghār*, A sincere friend; (Fem.) يار غاره *yār-i-ghāra'h*. وفادار يار *wafādār yār*, A faithful friend; (Fem.) وفاداره ياره *wafādāra'h yāra'h*.

ياره *yāra'h*, s.f. (3rd) A female friend, a sweetheart, a mistress, a paramour. Pl. ې *ey*.

ياسته *yās-tah*, s.m. (6th) (verb. n. of يستل) Putting out, ejecting, expelling, expulsion, ejection, exclusion, extraction, hatching, putting forth, etc. Sing. and Pl. See يستل

ياستئ *yāsta'aī*, You are, a word derived from an obsolete infinitive. See Grammar, page 52.

P ياسمين *yās-mīn* or *yāsa-mīn*, s.m. (6th) Jasmine. Sing. and Pl.

T ياغي *yāghī*, adj. Rebel, rebellious, mutinous. (Masc. and Fem.) 2. as s.m. (5th) A rebel, a mutineer. Pl. ياغيان *yāghīān*; Fem. Sing. the same. Pl. ياغيانې *yāghīāni*. ياغي كيدل *yāghī kedal*, verb intrans. To become rebellious or mutinous, to rebel, to mutiny, to revolt. ياغي كول *yāghī kawul*, verb trans. To make rebellious or mutinous, to cause to rebel, to incite to rebellion. (A باغي).

ياغيگر *yāghī-gar*, s.m. (5th) A mutineer, a rebel, Pl. ياغيگران *yāghī-garān*. ياغيگره *yāghī-gara'h*, s.f. (3rd). Pl. ې *ey*.

ياغيگري *yāghī-garī*, s.f. (3rd) Mutiny, rebellion, revolt, sedition. Pl. ئ *a'ī*. ياغيگري كول *yāghī-garī kawul*, verb trans. To rebel, to mutiny, to revolt, to rise.

A ياقوت *yākūt*, s.m. (6th) A ruby. Sing. and Pl. ياقوتي *yākūtī*, adj. Of or relating to a ruby.

P T يال *yāl*, s.m. (2nd) The mane of a horse. Pl. يالونه *yālūnah*. See ورږ and ورګ

يانه *yānah*. See يون

P ياور *yā-war*, adj. Friendly, aiding. 2. s.m. (5th) An assistant, a friend, a coadjutor, a comrade, a companion. Pl. ياوران *yāwarān*; ياوره *yāwara'h*, s.f. (3rd) A female friend. Pl. ې *ey*.

ياوره *yā-wara'h*, adj. Big-bellied (applied to horses, mares, and females in general).

ياوري *yāwarī*, s.f. (3rd) Aid, assistance, favour, friendship. Pl. ئ *a'ī*.

A ياهو *yā-hū*, s. prop. Jehovah.

يبل *yabl*, adj. Barefooted, unshod; (Fem.) يبله *yabla'h*. ښپه يبله *khpa'h yabla'h* (E.) or پښه يبله *psha'h yabla'h* (W.) Barefoot; or يبله ښپه *yabla'h khpa'h* or پښه *pshah*. See ابل

A يتيم *yat-īm*, s.m. (5th) (from H and A يتم) An orphan, a fatherless boy, a ward. Pl. يتيمان *yat-īmān*. يتيمه *yat-īma'h*, s.f. (3rd) A fatherless or orphan girl. Pl. ې *ey*; also پلار مړى *plār-marracy*, etc., which see.

P يخ *yakh*, s.m. (9th) Cold. Sing. and Pl. 2. adj. Cold, chill, bleak, raw, inclement, nipping, piercing, torpid, cool. 3. Satiated, glutted, satisfied, slacked, damped, cooled; (Fem.) يخه *yakha'h*. See سوړ and ساړه.

يخيدل *yakhedal*, verb intrans. To freeze, to congeal, to benumb, to become cold or torpid. 2. To become satiated or glutted (as in one's passions), to become slacked or quenched.

يخول *yakhawul*, verb trans. To make or cause to freeze or congeal, to make or render cool, to damp, to slack, to quench, to satiate. See سړيدل, etc.

يخني *yakhnī*, s.f. (3rd) Cold, coldness, frigidity, chilliness, chill. 2. (P) Gravy used in dressing *pulā'o*, sauce, stew, hash. Pl. ئ *a'ī*. يخني لرل *yakhnī laral*, verb trans. To have coldness, chilliness, or frigidity. (Eng. verb intrans. To be cold as a country or a bleak day). يخني پخول *yakhnī pakhawul* or جوړول *jorrawul*, verb trans. To prepare gravy, stew, etc.

P يخ *ya<u>kh</u>*, s.m. (1st) Ice, cold, gelidness. Pl. يخونه *yak<u>kh</u>ūnah.* يخي *yak<u>kh</u>aey*, s.m. (1st) Ice, cold, frigidity. Pl. ي *ī*.

يرړي *yer-<u>rr</u>aey*, s.m. (1st) A long-tailed sheep. Pl. ي *ī*. s.f. (6th) ئي *a'ī*. Sing. and Pl. See هيرړي, etc.

يرز *yarz*, s.m. (2nd) Fitness, capacity, worth, merit, skill, ability; congruity, consistency, expediency, propriety, etc. Pl. يرزونه *yarz-ūnah.* يرزن *yarz-an*, adj. Worthy, suitable, fit, capable, qualified, expedient, consistent, adapted, apposite; (Fem.) يرزنه *yarz-ana'h.* يرز لرل *yarz laral*, verb trans. To hold or possess merit, fitness, worth. (Eng.) To merit, to deserve, to be worthy of, etc.

P يرغمال *yar-<u>gh</u>amāl*, s.m. (2nd) A hostage, a surety, a sponsor. Pl. يرغمالونه *yar-<u>gh</u>amāl-ūnah.* يرغماله *yar-<u>gh</u>amāla'h*, s.f. (3rd). Pl. ئي *ey*. See يرغمل

P يرغه *yar<u>gh</u>ah*, adj. An ambling horse, ass, etc. (Masc. and Fem.) يرغه تلل *yar<u>gh</u>ah t'lal* or وهل *wahal*, verb trans. To amble.

يره *yera'h* or *era'h*, s.f. (3rd) Fear, timidity, fright, apprehension, dread, alarm, trepidation, qualm, nervousness, awe, want of confidence, etc. Pl. ئي *ey*. يريدل *yeredal* or *eredal*, verb intrans. To fear, to be afraid, to take alarm, etc. يرول *yerawul* or *erawul*, verb trans. To alarm, to frighten, to scare, etc. See ويره and ويريدل, etc.

P يزدان *yaz-dān*, s. prop. God. يزداني *yaz-dānī*, adj. Divine, of or from God.

يزيد *yazīd*, s. prop. The name of an arch heretic amongst the Muḥammadans, who caused the murder of Ḥasan and Ḥusain, sons of Æali (hence) wicked, cruel, accursed.

يږ *yajz*, s.m. (5th) A bear. Pl. يږان *yajzān.* يږه *yajza'h*, s.f. (3rd) A she bear. Pl. ئي *ey*. تور يږ *tor yajz*, A black bear. سپين يږ *spīn yajz*, A white or brown bear. See يك and ميلو

يستل *yas-tal*, verb trans. To put out, to eject, to take out, turn out, or expel, to cause to issue, to exclude, to extract, to perform, to accomplish, to discover, to produce, to hatch, to put forth, to extricate, to exhibit, to pick, to clean, to sift, to clear off, etc. This infinitive is imperfect in all the present tenses, which are taken from باسل *bāsal*, which also is imperfect in the past tenses. Pres. باسي *bāsī*; past و يوست *wu-yost*; fut. و به باسي *wu bah bāsī*; imp. و باسه *wu-bāsah*; act. part. يستونكي *yastūnkaey* or يستوني *yastūnaey*; past part. يستلي *yastalaey* or يستي *yastaey*; verb. n. يستنه *yastana'h* or ياسته *yāstah*.

يستنه *yastana'h*, s.f. (3rd) Putting out, ejecting, ejection, expulsion, etc. Pl. ئي *ey*.

P يشم *ya<u>sh</u>m* or يشب *ya<u>sh</u>ab*, s.m. (6th) Agate. Sing. and Pl.

يشند *ya<u>sh</u>and*, adj. Boiling, bubbling through heat, scalding hot, seething, etc.; (Fem.) يشنده *ya<u>sh</u>anda'h.* يشندي اوبه *ya<u>sh</u>andey ao'bah*, Boiling water.

يشنا *ya<u>sh</u>nā*, s.f. (6th) Ebullition, boiling, effervescence, coction. (E.) Sing. and Pl. (W.) Pl. يشناوي *ya<u>sh</u>nāwī*; or يشيدنه *ya<u>sh</u>edana'h*, s.f. (3rd). Pl. ئي *ey*. See ايشنا

يشيدل *ya<u>sh</u>edal*, verb intrans. To boil, to bubble by the action of heat, to boil over, to chafe, to be agitated, to be agitated by the action of heat, etc. Pres. يشي *ya<u>sh</u>ī*; past و يشيده *wu-ya<u>sh</u>edah*; fut. و به يشي *wu bah ya<u>sh</u>ī*; imp. و يشه *wu-ya<u>sh</u>ah*; act. part. يشيدونكي *ya<u>sh</u>e-dūnkaey* or يشيدوني *ya<u>sh</u>edūnaey*; past part. يشيدلي *ya<u>sh</u>edalaey*; verb. n. يشيده *ya<u>sh</u>e-da'h* or يشنه *ya<u>sh</u>na'h.* يشول *ya<u>sh</u>awul*, verb trans. To boil, to make to boil, to stew, to cook, to seethe, to scald, to parboil. Pres. يشوي *ya<u>sh</u>awī*; past و يشاوه *wu-ya<u>sh</u>āwuh* or و يشاوو *wu-ya<u>sh</u>āwo*; fut. و به يشوي *wu bah ya<u>sh</u>awī*; imp. و يشوه *wu-ya<u>sh</u>awah*; act. part. يشوونكي *ya<u>sh</u>awūnkaey* or يشووني *ya<u>sh</u>-awūnaey*; past part. يشولي *ya<u>sh</u>awulaey*; verb. n. يشونه *ya<u>sh</u>awuna'h*.

يهل *ye<u>sh</u>al* (W.) or *ye<u>kh</u>al* (E.) verb trans. To place, to put, to locate, to lay, to set, to seat, to deposit, to stow, to fix, to root, to plant, etc. Applied to inanimate things. This infinitive is imperfect, and takes some of its inflections from ږدل or ګدل and کيښول . Pres. ږدي *jz'dī* (W.) or ګدي *g'dī* (E.); past کيښو *ke-sho* or *ke-kho*; fut. وُ به ږدي *wu bah jz'dī* or ګدي *g'dī*; imp. ږده *jz'dah* or ګده *g'dah*; act. part. يښونکيَ *yeshūnkaey* or *yekhūnkaey* or يښونيَ *yeshūnaey* or *yekhūnaey*; past part. يښيَ *yekhaey* or *yeshaey*; verb. n. يښنه *yeshana'h* or *yekhana'h*. See also ږدل or ګدل, کيږدل or کيګدل and کيښول

يښودل *yekhodal* (E.) or *yeshodal* (W.) verb trans. To place, to put, to locate, etc. See preceding, and اېښودل

يښوده *yeshoda'h* (W.) or *yekhoda'h* (E.), s.f. (3rd) (verb. n.) Placing, putting, locating. 2. Arranging or sorting the threads of the warp in a loom for the woof. Pl. يْ *ey*.

يښول *yesharwul* (W.) verb trans. To place, to put, to locate, to arrange, etc. See preceding.

يښيَ *yashaey* (W.) or *yakhaey* (E.) adj. (past part.) Arranged, located, placed, distributed, put, set, ranged, grouped, assorted, etc.; (Fem.) يښِ *yashi* or *yakhi*. Pl. (Masc. and Fem.) ي *ī*.

A يعني *yaænī*, adv. (aorist of عني H) To wit, namely, for, because, that is to say, videlicit, i.e., etc.

A يقين *yaḳīn*, adj. (from يقن) Certain, true, sure, real, indisputable. 2. adv. Certainly, truly, assuredly, infallibly. يقين واليَ *yaḳīn wālaey*, s.m. (1st) Certainty, reality, infallibility, truth. Pl. والي *wālī*. يقين راوړل *yaḳīn rā-w'rral*, verb trans. To believe, to credit, to place faith in. يقين کول *yaḳīn kawul*, verb trans. To ascertain, to believe, to make certain, to discover.

A يقيناً *yaḳīn-an*, adv. Certainly, assuredly, indisputably, infallibly.

A يقيني *yaḳīnī*, s.f. (3rd) Certainty, truth, reality. Pl. ئي *a'ī*. 2. adj. Certain, real, indisputable. (Masc. and Fem.)

P يک *yek* or *yak*, adj. One, a, an. Only used in Pushto composition; as, يکايک *yekā-yek*, All at once, immediately; يکبارګي *yek-bārgī*, All at once, suddenly, immediately, at once; يک تا *yek-tā*, Single, unique; يکتائي *yek-tā'ī*, s.f. (3rd) Unity, singleness, uniqueness. Pl. ئي *a'ī*. يک جهت *yek-jihat*, Of one accord, unanimous. 2. A friend. يکجهتي *yek-jihatī*, s.f. (3rd) Unanimity, friendship, agreement. Pl. ئي *a'ī*. يک دل *yek-dil*, adj. Of one heart or mind, unanimous; (Fem.) يک دله *yek-dila'h*. يک دلي *yek-dilī*, s.f. (3rd) Accord, unanimity, agreement. Pl. ئي *a'ī*. يک سان *yek-sān*, adj. Equal, alike, even, in the same manner, the same, ditto, uniform, conformable, level, parallel, plain; (Fem.) يک سانه *yek-sāna'h*. يک ساني *yek-sānī*, s.f. (3rd) Uniformity, parity, sameness, identity. Pl. ئي *a'ī*. يک لخت *yek-lakht*, All at once. 2. Entirely, wholly, totally, suddenly, all of a sudden; or يک لخته *yek-lakhtah*.

P يک لنګه *yek-linga'h*, s.f. (3rd) A lever supported on a post, with a bucket suspended at one end and a weight of stone or earth at the other, used in drawing water from a well, etc. Pl. يْ *ey*. See ډنګرۍ

يکشنبه *yek-shamba'h*, s.f. (3rd) Sunday. Pl. يْ *ey*.

P يکلائي *yek-lā'ī*, s.f. (3rd) A veil or cloak worn over the head and shoulders, a coat or upper dress of single cloth. Pl. ئي *a'ī*.

يکه *yekah*, adj. Single, solitary, unique, unequalled. (Masc. and Fem.) 2. A single child, an only child. 3. The ace (at cards). 4. A soldier who serves alone. يک همان *yek-hamān*, adj. Alike, similar.

يکهمان *yekah-mān*, adj. (P يک One; S मन Mind, heart) Alone, by itself, all alone, single; (Fem.) يکهمانه *yekah-māna'h*.

P يکهمان *yek-hamān*, adj. Alike, similar, uniform, identical, parallel; (Fem.) يکهمانه *yek-hamāna'h*.

يکي *yekī*, s.f. (3rd) The name of a small coin, a copper coin. Pl. ئي *a'ī*.

يګ *yag*, s.m. (5th) A bear. (E.) Pl. يګان *yagān*. يګه *yaga'h*, s.f. (3rd) A she-bear. Pl. يْ *ey*. تور يګ *tor-yag*, A black bear. سپين يګ

spīn-yag, A white or brown bear. See يږ and ميلو

P يگانگي *yagāna-gī*, s.f. (3rd) Concord, union, unity, unanimity. 2. Singularity, excellence, Pl. ئ *a'ī*. يگانگي لرل *yagāna-gī laral*, verb trans. To have unanimity in any matter (Eng. verb intrans. To be unanimous). يگانگي كول *yagāna-gī kawul*, verb trans. To act with unity or unanimity, to act in union. دم د يگانگي وهل *dam da yagāna-ga'ī wahal*, verb trans. To contract friendship.

P يگانه *yagānah*, adj. Single, sole, singular, unique, unequalled. 2. Agreed, unanimous. (Masc. and Fem.)

يگه *yaga'h*, s.f. (3rd) A she-bear. 2. A kind of tumour on the back, a boil. 3. A disease affecting the tail of a horse and causing the hair to fall off. Pl. ئ *ey*.

T يلغر *yal-ghar*, s.m. (2nd) A sudden incursion, a foray, a raid, the forced march of an army. Pl. يلغرونه *yal-gharūnah*. Also يلغار *yal-ghār* and يلغارونه *yal-ghārūnah*. يلغر *yal-ghar* or يلغار كول *yal-ghār kawul*, verb trans. To make a sudden incursion, raid, foray, etc. Also written ايلغار

يله *yalah*, adj. Free, liberated, at large, unrestrained, uncontrolled, unbridled, unrestricted, disengaged, free and easy, irresponsible, etc. 2. Wandering, vagabond, dissolute. (Masc. and Fem.) يله كيدل *yalah kedal*, verb intrans. To wander, to be or become free, liberated, at large, or unrestrained. يله كول *yalah kawul*, verb trans. To release, to free, to set at large, to wander about, to make a wanderer or vagabond of, to render dissolute. سر يله *sar yalah*, A bad or dissolute man or woman. يله گرد *yalah gard*, s.m. (5th) A wanderer, a vagrant. Pl. گرد *gærd* or گردان *gardān*. يله گرده *yalah garda'h*, s.f. (3rd) A vagabond female. Pl. ئ *ey*. يله گري *yalah garī*, s.f. (3rd) Vagabondism, wandering about, vagrancy. Pl. ئ *a'ī*. Also يله والي *yalah-wālaey*, s.m. (1st). Pl. ي *ī*.

يله دار *yalah-dār*, s.m. (5th) A scout, a sentinel, a vedette. Pl. يله داران *yalah dārān*. See څار and ايله

يله *yala'h*, s.f. (3rd) A bog, a morass, a slough, a quagmire, a marsh. Pl. ئ *ey*.

يله داري *yalah dārī*, s.f. (3rd) The business of a scout. Pl. ئ *a'ī*. يله داري كول *yalah dārī kawul*, verb intrans. To act the scout. See څار كول

H يم *yam*, s.m. (2nd) The ocean, the sea. Pl. يمونه *yamūnah*.

ينده *yenda'h* or *enda'h*, s.f. (3rd) A gulp, swallowing eagerly or by large draughts, a draught, a quaff, a swig, etc. Pl. ئ *ey*. ينده كول *yenda'h* or *enda'h kawul*, verb trans. To gulp up, to toss off, to swallow eagerly. See انده and اينده

ينگ *yang*, s.m. (2nd) Manner, conduct, state, condition, way, mode, method. Pl. ينگونه *yangūnah*. See شان

ينه *yina'h*, s.f. (3rd) The liver, the heart, the vitals. Pl. ئ *ey*. See اينه

يو *yow* or *yo*, adj. One, once, one time. May also be used as an article, *a*, *an*; (Fem.) يوه *yawa'h*. See ړنبي. يو په يو *yow-pah-yow*, One by one, successively, all at once. 2. Singly, individually; (Fem.) يو په يوه *yow pah-yowa'h*. يو تر بلَ *yow tar bala* or بله *balah*, One from another, diverse, opposed to another. يو څو *yow-tso*, Some, several, a few, somewhat. يو دم *yow dam* or په يوَ دم *pah yawa dam*, One moment, in a moment. يو رنگ *yow rang*, Of one colour, uniform, similar, corresponding; (Fem.) يو رنگه *yow ranga'h*. يو زړه *yow-z'rrah*, Unanimous, of one mind, of one heart. يو ځاي *yow dzā-e*, One place, somewhere or other, together. يو ځل *yow dzal*, Once, one time; or يو ځلَ *yow dzala* or ځله *dzalah*. يو ساعت *yow sā-æat*, An hour, a short time. يو شان *yow shān*, Alike, equal, similar, corresponding, uniform, the same, parallel. يو طرف *yow taraf*, On one side, aside. يو طور *yow taur*, One state or condition, of one sort, fashion, or kind. يو قلم *yow kalam*, All, total, entirely, altogether, positively. يو له بلَ *yow lah bala* or بله *balah*, One another, one with another, together, in company, in concert. یو موټ *yow-mutt*, Prompt payment, all at once, at once, immediately. یو نفس *yow nafas*, In a breath, in a moment. یو نه بل *yow nah bal*, One or the other. یو نیم *yow-nīm* or یو و نیم *yow-o-nīm*, One and half. یو نیم *yow-nīm*, adj. A few, some, a small number, not many; (Fem.) یوه نیمه *yowa'h nīma'h*. یو و بل *yow-o-bal*, One and another, one with the other. یو وار *yow-wār* or یوه پلا *yowa'h plā* or یو ځله *yow dzalah*, Once, one time. یوه خوا *yowa'h khwā*, On one side, aside. یوه مرتبه *yowa'h martaba'h*, One time or turn, on one occasion. یو یو *yow yow*, Singly, separately, apart. یو یا دواړه *yow-yā-dwārrah*, One or both.

یواد *yawād*, s.m. (2nd) (W.) A far country. Pl. یوادونه *yawādūnah*. 2. adj. Far, afar off. See هیواد

یو اتیا *yow-at-yā*, adj. Eighty-one. یو اتیایم *yow-at-yāyam*, The eighty-first; (Fem.) یو اتیایمه *yow-at-yāyama'h*.

یوادین *yawādīn*, s.m. (2nd) A distant land, a far country. Pl. یوادینونه *yawādīnūnah*.

یوازي *yawāzaey*, adj. Alone, solitary, single, unique, singular. 2. Apart, private, without company. 3. adv. Separately, alone, by itself; (Fem.) یوازِ *yawāzi*. Pl. (Masc. and Fem.) ي *ī*. یوازي کیدل *yawāzaey kedal*, verb intrans. To become solitary, single, private. یوازي کول *yawāzaey kawul*, verb trans. To isolate, to seclude, to shut up. یوازي توب *yawāzaey-tob*, s.m. (2nd) Solitude, singleness, loneliness, seclusion, privacy, retirement, isolation. Pl. توبونه *tobūnah*; or یوازي والي *yawāzaey-wālaey*, s.m. (1st). Pl. والي *wālī*. See بیل

یواځي *yawādzaey*, adj. See preceding; (Fem.) یواځِ *yawādzi*. Pl. (Masc. and Fem.) ي *ī*.

یو اویا *yow-ow-yā*, adj. Seventy-one. یو اویایم *yow-ow-yāyam*, adj. The seventy-first; (Fem.) یو اویایمه *yow-ow-yāyama'h*.

یو پنځوس *yow-pindzos*, adj. Fifty-one. یو پنځوسم *yow-pindzosam*, The fifty-first; (Fem.) یو پنځوسمه *yow-pindzosama'h*.

یو څلوېښت *yow-tsal-wesht* (W.) or *yow-tsal-wekht* (E.) adj. Forty-one. یو څلوېښتم *yow-tsal-weshtam* or *yow-tsal-wekhtam*, The forty-first; (Fem.) یو څلوېښتمه *yow-tsal-weshtama'h* or *yow-tsal-wekhtama'h*.

یو دیرش *yow-dersh*, adj. Thirty-one. یو دیرشم *yow-dersham*, The thirty-first; (Fem.) یو دیرشمه *yow-dershama'h*.

یور *yor*, s.f. (5th) A husband's brother's wife. Pl. یوړنې *yūrrney*.

یور *yor*, s.m. (2nd) Fire. Pl. یورونه *yorūnah*. (corrup. of اور which see.)

P یوز *yūz*, s.m. (5th) A lynx, a panther. Pl. یوزان *yūzān*. یوزه *yūza'h*, s.f. (3rd) A female lynx or panther. Pl. ي *ey*.

یوسپ *yūsup*, s. prop. (corrup. of A یوسف) The patriarch Joseph.

یوسپزي *yūsup-zī*, s.m. (1st) Pl. The name of one of the most numerous, most powerful, and most pugnacious of the Afghān tribes, who hold the whole of the country to the north of the Kābul river, and immediately west of the Indus, including the Sama'h, Buner, Suwāt, and Panjkorah. یوسپزی *yūsup-zaey*, (Sing.) A male of the above tribe. یوسپزئ *yūsup-za'ī*, s.f. (6th) A female of the above. Sing. and Pl. See یوسف

یوستوی *yawas-tawaey*, adj. Single, simple, of one fold, without a lining (as a garment); (Fem.) یوستوې *yawas-tawey* or یوستوِ *yawas-tawi*. Pl. (Masc. and Fem.) ي *ī*.

A یوسف *yūsuf*, s. prop. The patriarch Joseph.

یوسفزي *yūsuf-zī*, s.m. (1st) Pl. The name of an Afghān tribe. یوسفزی *yūsuf-zaey* (Sing.) A male of the above tribe. یوسفزئ *yūsuf-za'ī*, s.f. (6th) A female of the above. Sing. and Pl. See also یوسپزي

یوسل *yo-sal*, verb trans. To bear, to carry, to remove, to transport, to carry over, to convey, to waft, etc. (applied particularly to inanimate objects, in distinction to بیول). It is also imperfect, and takes its past tenses, etc. from وړل, which see. Pres. یوسي *yo-sī*; past یووړ *yo-warr*; fut. یو به سي *yo bah sī*; imp. یوسه *yo-*

sah; act. part. وروونکې *w'rrūnkaey* or وروونې *w'rrūnaey*; past part. وړې *warraey*; verb. n. وړنه *w'rrana'h* or وړه *w'rrah*.

يو شپېته *yow-shpetah*, adj. Sixty-one. يو شپېتم *yow-shpetam*, The sixty-first; (Fem.) يو شپېتمه *yow-shpetama'h*.

يو لس *yow-las* (E.) or *yaw-o-las* (W.) adj. Eleven. يولسم *yow-lasam* or *yow-o-lasam*, The eleventh; (Fem.) يو لسمه *yow-lasama'h* or *yow-o-lasama'h*.

يوم *yūm*, s.m. (2nd) A spade, a shovel, a kind of hoe. Pl. يومونه *yūmūnah*, or (5th) يومان *yūmān*. See کره

يون *yūn*, s.m. (4th) Gait, movement, carriage, step, motion in walking. 2. Habit, custom, method, practice, way. 3. Moving, passing, gliding along, rolling on (as time), sweeping along (as a river). Pl. يانه *yānah* or يانَ *yāna*. يون کول *yūn kawul*, verb trans. To move along, to pass or glide along, to make to roll, pass, or sweep along.

A يونان *yūnān*, s. prop. Greece, Ionia. يوناني *yūnānī*, s.m. and f. (5th) A Greek, a Grecian. Pl. يونانيان *yūnānīān*; (Fem.) Pl. يونانيانِ *yūnānīāni*.

يو نوي *yow-nawī*, adj. Ninety-one. يو نويم *yow-nawī-am*, The ninety-first; (Fem.) يو نويمه *yow-nawī-ama'h*.

يو والې *yo* or *yow-wālaey*, s.m. (1st) Singularity, excellence. 2. Concord, unanimity, unity, union. Pl. والي *wālī*.

يو ويشت *yow-wīsht*, adj. Twenty-one. يو ويشتم *yow-wīshtam*, The twenty-first; (Fem.) يو ويشتمه *yow-wīshtama'h*.

يوې *yawey*, s.f. (3rd) Pl. (E.) Ploughing, etc. يوې کول *yawey kawul*, verb trans. To plough. See following.

يويه *yow-ya'h*, s.f. (3rd) (W.) A plough. 2. Ploughing, preparing the ground for sowing. Pl. ئې *ey*. يويه کول *yow-ya'h kawul*, verb trans. To plough, to prepare the ground.

ييښل *yeshal* (W.) or *yekhal* (E.) To place, to put, to locate. See يښل and يښول

يه *yah*, adv. No, not.

ئي *yey*, The affixed personal pronoun of the third person. Sing. and Pl., He, she, it, or them; and may also signify, His, hers, its, theirs, or to his, etc. (W.) يه *yah*. 2. The 2nd pers. sing. of the sub. verb 'To be.' See Grammar, pages 44 and 51.

ADDITIONAL WORDS AND IDIOMS,

COLLECTED SINCE THE FIRST EDITION WAS PUBLISHED, AND WHILST THE FOREGOING SHEETS PASSED THROUGH THE PRESS.

ا

په اتفاق سره *pah itta-fāḳ sarah*, By mutual consent, in harmony. 2. Accidently, by chance, incidentally.

P اختر *a<u>kh</u>-tar*, s.m. (2nd) A festival, a feast-day, Pl. اخترونه *a<u>kh</u>-tarūnah*. لوي اختر *lo-e a<u>kh</u>-tar*, The Æīdu-l-ḳurbān, a festival held in commemoration of Abraham's offering up Isaac.

آخستل *ā<u>kh</u>istal*, verb trans. To drive off cattle (as thieves); ex. مويشي ؤ نيوه را و ئي خستله "They seized the cattle and drove them off." See this word at p. 14.

آخوند جيو *ā<u>kh</u>ūnd-jī'o*, s. prop. The name of a poet, inhabitant of Noh-<u>sh</u>airah. 2. A title bestowed on Mullās of celebrity, such as Ā<u>kh</u>ūnd Darwezah. See آخوند

آرت زړه *ārat-z'ṟrah*, s.m. (2nd) An open, frank, or sincere heart. Pl. آرت زړونه *ārat-z'ṟrūnah*. آرت زړي *ārat-z'ṟraey*, adj. Open-hearted, frank, honest, straightforward (person); (Fem.) آرت زړِ *ārat-z'ṟri*. Pl. (M. and F.) ي *ī*.

ارتي *arataey*, s.m. (1st) Wind from behind. Pl. ي *ī*. See ارتل

آرويده *ār-wedah*, s.m. (6th) (verb. n. of آرويدل) Hearing, hearkening, attending. S. and Pl.

اره څکول *ara'h ts'kawul*, verb trans. To saw asunder (as wood).

آړاند *āṟrānd*, adj. Hampered, impeded, hindered, clogged, encumbered, incommoded, saddled with, thwarted, balked, frustrated; (Fem.) آړانده *āṟrānda'h*. آړاند کيدل *āṟrānd kedal*, verb intrans. To be hindered, detained, impeded. آړاند کول *āṟrānd kawul*, verb trans. To hinder, to impede. See آړ

ارړخ لګول *arṟ<u>kh</u>* or *arṟa<u>kh</u> lagawul*, verb trans. To lean on one's elbow, also to lie down.

آزاد وتل *āzād watal*, verb intrans. To pass right through anything, to go in one side and come out the other.

آزميښت *āz-meyi<u>sh</u>t* (W.) or *āz-meyi<u>kh</u>t* (E.), s.m. (2nd) Trial, proof, examination, essay, experiment. 2. Temptation. Pl. آزميښتونه *āz-meyi<u>sh</u>tūnah* or *āz-meyi<u>kh</u>tūnah*. See آزمايښت

اژدهام *i<u>zh</u>dihām*, s.m. (2nd) (corrup. of A ازدحام) A concourse, a crowd of people, press, throng, mob, gathering together of people. Pl. اژدهامونه *i<u>zh</u>dihāmūnah*.

P آس *ās*, s.m. (2nd) A mill-stone. 2. Ground corn; a grinding of wheat, barley, etc. 3. (A) Cinders or ashes remaining in a grate. Ruins or remains of a dwelling. Pl. آسونه *āsūnah*.

آستاندار *āstāna-dār*, s.m. (5th) The member of a holy family, the descendants of the pious men among the Afg<u>h</u>āns of bygone times, who, according to the histories and traditions of that people, were Suyeds, who came and settled among them, and took Afg<u>h</u>ān wives. Pl. آستانداران *āstāna-dārān*. آستنداره *āstāna-dāra'k*, s.f. (3rd) A female as above. Pl. ې *ey*. See ستان

A استقلال *istiḳ-lāl*, s.m. (2nd) Absolute power or authority, sovereignty, independence, absoluteness. 2. Resolution, intrepidity, vigour.

Pl. استیقلالونه *istiḳ-lāl-ūnah.* بالستقلال *bi-l-istiḳ-lāl,* With absolute power, etc. (as a king or ruler), with full power (as a governor) etc.

آستوګیه *āstog-ya'h,* s.f. (3rd) Residence, etc. Pl. ي *ey.* See استوګنه

آستوګیَ *āstọg-yaey,* s.m. (1st) A resident, a dweller, an inhabitant, a sojourner, a denizen, etc. Pl. ي *ī.* آستوګیِي *āstog-ya'ī,* s.f. (6th) The feminine of the above. S. and Pl.

A اعتماد *iæ-timād,* s.m. (2nd) (inf. VIII of عمد) Confidence, trust, dependence, faith, reliance. Pl. اعتمادونه *iæ-timādūnah.* اعتماد کول *iæ-timād kawul* or لرل *laral,* verb trans. To place faith in, to rely on, to depend upon.

A اعیان *aæyān,* s.m. (Pl. of عین) Eyes. 2. Headmen, notables, grandees, nobles, chiefs.

الا *a-lā,* s.f. (6th) (W.) A run. 2. Running. Pl. الاوي *a-lāwī.* الا کول *a-lā kawul,* verb trans. To run, to take a run.

الاج ګر *a-lāj-gar,* s.m. (5th) A comber or carder of cotton. Pl. ګران *garān.* الاج ګره *a-lāj-gara'h,* s.f. (3rd) A female as above. Pl. ي *ey.* See الاج

آلا بلا کول *alā balā kawul,* verb trans. To show or feel inquietude, solicitude, alarm, apprehension, despondency, etc.

P الکه *ul-ka'h,* s.f. (3rd) A province, a district. 2. Dominion, possession. Pl. ي *ey.*

الګه *a-laga'h,* adj. as s.f. (3rd) A female or animal which has had offspring, but has ceased bearing young for a time, or altogether.

A الم *alam,* s.m. (2nd) Grief, affliction, anguish, pain. Pl. المونه *alamūnah.*

آلوتک *āl-watak* or *āl-wutak,* adj. Fledged, feathered, ready or able to fly; (Fem.) آلوتکه *āl-wataka'h* or *āl-wutaka'h.*

الوي *al-wo-e,* s.m. (9th) An unripe head of corn roasted on the fire and eaten. S. and Pl. See داده

امرل *a-maral,* verb. trans. To part, to separate, to detach, to disunite, to segregate, etc. Pres. امري *a-marī*; past و امره *wu-amarah*; fut. و به امري *wu bah a-marī*; imp. و امره *wu-amarah*; act. part. امرونکيَ *a-marūnkaey*; past part. امرليَ *a-maralaey*; verb. n. امرنه *a-marana'h.*

املیل *am-le-yal,* verb trans. To conceal, to hide away, to secrete, to keep back, etc.

انبوهٔ لښکر *an-boh-i-lakhkar* or *lashkar,* The main body of an army. See انبوه

اندت *an-ddat,* s.m. (2nd) Wind from behind. Pl. اندتونه *an-ddat-ūnah.*

انځر *andzar,* s.m. (6th) A fig. Pl. انځرُ *andzær.* See انځیر

انګار *in-gār,* s.m. (2nd) Relinquishment, discontinuance, dropping, leaving off, giving over, etc. Pl. انګارونه *in-gārūnah.* انګار کول *in-gār kawul,* verb trans. To relinquish, to leave off, to discontinue, to give over, to drop.

انګه *an-ga'h,* s.f. (3rd) Way, manner, wise, etc. Pl. ي *ey.* په څه انګه *pah tsah an-ga'h,* How? in what manner?

انه *ana'h,* s.f. (3rd) The pommel of a saddle. Pl. ي *ey.* See کاش and نکبي

اوبول *ao-bawul,* verb trans. To water (as cattle), to give water, to irrigate, to overflow with water, etc. اوبیدل *ao-bedal,* verb intrans. To become satiated with water (as cattle), to grow moist. See اوبه

اوتاك *ao-tāk,* s.m. (2nd) A temporary residence, a lodging. Pl. اوتاکونه *ao-tākūnah.* See اوطاك

اوچار *a-chār,* adj. Apparent, manifest, clear, etc.; (Fem.) اوچاره *a-chāra'h.* See اوڅار

اورجل *aor-jal,* adj. Scorched, burnt; (Fem.) اورجله *aor-jala'h.*

اورغاليَ *aor-ghālaey,* s.m. (1st) A fireplace, a hole dug in the ground for kindling a fire. Pl. ي *ī.* See ورغالي

آوریدل *ā-wurredal,* verb trans. To change, to deviate, to turn, to change about, to alter. 2. To abandon a bad habit or the like. 3. To cross or pass over a mountain, hill, etc. This verb is defective, and has only a few tenses, which are taken to complete another defective verb of the same signification—آوښتل which see.

اوز *aoz,* ind. pro. Some, certain, some one, more than one, etc. See څوک

اورده رجا *aojz-da'h rijā*, Hope of long life, a lengthened hope, hope for the future.

اورمكه *aojz-maka'h*, s.f. (3rd) The new moon, the moon on the wane, particularly the last two or three days. Pl. ي *ey*.

ترخه اوسپينه *tarkha'h aospīna'h*, s.f. (3rd) Bar-iron (particularly the iron brought into Afghānistān from Bombay, considered very inferior). Pl. ي *ey*. خوره اوسپينه *khvajza'h aospīna'h*, The iron of Khurāsān, used in making steel and for all fine work.

اوښكي *aoshkey* or اوښي *aoshey* (W.) or *aokhkey* or *aokhey* (E.) s.f. (3rd) Pl. Tears.

اوښكي *ūshkaey*, s.m. (1st) A sigh, a sob. Pl. ي *ī*. لوي اوښكي *lo-e ūshkaey*, A deep sigh, a convulsive sob. See اسويلي

s اول *ol*, adj. Hostage, subject, enthralled, constrained, subjected; (Fem.) اوله *ola'h*.

اوي *aoe*, int. Alas! sorrow! well-a-day! ah me! etc. See هاي

اهاك *a-hāk*, s.m. (6th) Lime used for building purposes. S. and Pl.

ايرغ *ey-ragh*, s.m. (2nd) A weapon, apparatus, etc. Pl. ايرغونه *ey-raghūnah*. See يرغ

ايشنه *`aeshnah*. See ايشنا and يشنا

ايښ *aesh* (W.) or *aekh* (E.) adj. Poor, distressed, friendless, wretched, contemptible, abject, miserable, etc.; (Fem.) ايښه *aesha'h* or *aekha'h*. See هيښ

ايمنيدل *aem-nedal*, verb intrans. To become or grow calm, quiet, gentle; to become appeased, softened, etc. ايمنول *aem-nawul*, verb trans. To quiet, to appease, to mollify, to soothe, to tranquilize, to pacify. See ايمن

ايسته *īs-ta'h*, s.f. (3rd) (from P استادن) Stand, persistence, endurance, resistance, making a stand (against an enemy). Pl. ي *ey*.

ب

باخملي *bākh-mala'ī* or بخملي *bakh-mala'ī*, s.f. (6th) A sort of palmer worm. S. and Pl. See p. 79.

بادار *bād-ār*, s.m. (5th) A master, an employer, a superior. Pl. باداران *bād-ārān*. باداره *bād-āra'h*, s.f. (3rd) The mistress of a house, etc. Pl. ي *ey*.

P بادشاه *bād-shāh*, s.m. (5th) 2. A Saiyid or Suyed, a descendant of Ḥusain, the grandson of Muḥammad. 3. The queen bee of a hive. Pl. بادشاهان *bād-shāhān*.

P بارگير *bār-gīr*, adj. A bearer of loads, a baggage horse, a camel, a beast of burden. 2. A horse-soldier who does not find his own horse. (Fem.) بارگيره *bār-gīra'h*. See باركښ

s باړئ *bāṟṟa'ī*, s.f. (6th) An inclosed piece of ground, a kitchen garden, a garden; a house with a garden, orchard, etc., attached to it. 2. A hedge of thorns round a village and the space inclosed therein. 3. A breastwork, a palisade, a fortification, etc. See باړه and سنگر S. and Pl.

P باغ باغ *bāgh bāgh*, adj. Delighted, charmed, gladdened, rejoiced, transported. باغ باغ كول *bāgh bāgh kawul*, verb trans. To delight, to gladden, to charm.

بامبوره *bām-būra'h*, s.f. (3rd) A whirligig. Pl. ي *ey*. See بنربچغ

بانگي *bāngī*, s.m. (5th) The *mu'azzin* or crier who calls the people to prayer. Pl. بانگيان *bāngī-ān*. See بانگ

بتكي *batakaey*, s.m. (1st) A small earthen or leathern vessel, the diminutive of بتك (which see). Pl. ي *ī*.

بخت *ba-khut*, adj. Busy, employed, diligent, occupied, etc.; (Fem.) بخته *ba-khuta'h*, بخت كيدل *ba-khut kedal*, verb intrans. To be employed, busy, occupied. بخت كول *ba-khut kawul*, verb trans. To employ, to occupy, to devote one's-self to.

بخله *ba-khula'h*, s.f. (3rd) The agony of death, the signs of dissolution, giving up the ghost. Pl. ي *ey*.

A بدرقه *bad-raḳa'h*, s.f. (3rd) An escort, a convoy, a guide, a guard. Pl. ي *ey*. بدرقاني *bad-raḳānī* or بدرگاني *bad-ragānī*, s.f. (3rd) Hire paid to an escort by merchants and traders for protection, escort money. Pl. ئ *a'ī*. See بدرگه

H I بر *bar*, s.m. (2nd) Breadth, width, amplitude, expanse, extent, only applied to cloth, and the like. Pl. برونه *bar-ūnah*. بردار *bar-dār*, adj. Broad, wide, etc. (Fem.) برداره *bar-dāra'h*. See سور , پسور , and پلن

بربندِ سور *bar-bandd sor*, A light-horseman, a horseman lightly armed. See under بربندِ and سور

P برده *bar-dah*, s.m. (5th) A male slave, a captive, a servant. Pl. بردهگان *bar-dah-gān*, or بردگان *barda-gān*. See other significations at p. 98.

برغنډ برغنډ *bar-ghandd bar-ghandd*, adj. In bits, in pieces, in atoms, etc. (Fem.) برغنډه برغنډه *bar-ghandda'h bar-ghandda'h*.

برګ يالئ *brag-yālaey*, adj. Variegated, varied, motley, mottled, iridescent; (Fem.) برګ يالۍ *brag-yāla'ī*.

بريد *burīd*, s.m. (2nd) A boundary between lands, a small embankment of earth for a boundary. Pl. بريدونه *burīdūnah*. See پوله

بريښيدل *brekhedal* (E) or *breshedal* (W.) verb intrans. To be overpowered by light, to waver (as the sight from intense light). بريښول *brekhawul* or *breshawul*, verb trans. To dazzle (as the sight), to overpower with light.

S بړ *barr*, s.m. (2nd) The name of a tree (Ficus Bengalensis or Indica). Pl. بړونه *barr-ūnah*.

برڅلګه *b'jzalga'h*, s.f. (3rd) A scream, a shriek, outcry, etc. Pl. ې *ey*. برڅلګه کول or وهل *b'jzalga'h kawul* or *wahal*, verb trans. To scream, to shriek, to cry out.

برڅئ *bajzaey*, s.m. (1st) The cramp, convulsion, spasm. Pl. ي *ī*. برڅي نيول *bajzī nī-wal*, verb trans. To cramp, to affect with cramp, to convulse. برڅي نيولئ *bajzī-nī-walaey*, adj. (past p.) Affected with cramp, convulsed.

بسيره *basera'h*, s.f. (3rd) (from S बस Dwell) The time before evening when birds return to their nests. 2. A bird's roost or nest. 3. The remaining of a bird on its roost. 4. A night's lodging. This word is applied more particularly to the falcon tribe by the Afghāns. Pl. ې *ey*. بسيره کول *basera'h kawul*, verb trans. To roost.

بښل *bakhal*, verb trans. To forgive, to pardon, to absolve. See other signification at p. 107.

بګړ *bagarr*, s. prop. The name of a portion of the Yūsufzī district, in which the mountain of Bihī and village of Jalālā are situated.

A بلغا *bulaghā*, adj. Eloquent, poetic.

بلګ *balg*, s.m. (2nd) A leaf. Pl. بلګونه *balgūnah*. See برګ.

بلوسيدل *b'losedal*, verb intrans. To clash, come in contact (as enemies), *fig.* to cross the path of another, to interfere with, to antagonize, etc. See other significations under same word at p. 114, and read "verb intrans." instead of "verb trans."

بلوسيدنه *b'losedana'h*, s.f. (3rd) Antagonism, clashing, crossing one's path, interference, etc. Pl. ې *ey*. See significations at p. 114.

P بند خانه *band-khāna'h*, s.f. (3rd) A prison. Pl. ې *ey*.

بنړيدل *burrnedal*, verb intrans. and بنړکئ *burrnkaey*, s.m. (1st). See بونړيدل and بونړکئ

بندکئ *bandakaey*, s.m. (1st) A mode of plaiting or tracing the hair on the forehead by unmarried females of cities and towns, and different to that called توتکئ which see. Pl. ي *ī*.

A بوتراب *bū-tarāb*, adj. Covered with dust; (Fem.) بوترابه *bū-tarāba'h*.

بوډه *būddah*, s.m. (5th) (S بڈھا An old man. Pl. بوډهګان *būddah-gān* or بوډګان *būddagān*. بوډۍ *būdd-a'ī*, s.f. (3rd) An old woman. S. and Pl. Such words as these, to be found in this book, are, for the most part, used only in Peshāwar and its neighbourhood, where, from proximity to the Panjāb and Hindūstān, such words have crept into the Pushto of that district.

بوراګئ *bawrā-gaey*, s.m. (1st) A black bee. Pl. ي *ī*. See بورا

بورجل *bor-jal*, s.f. (1st) 2. A trysting place, a place where lovers meet. Pl. بورجلِ *bor-jali*. See p. 120.

بهارئ *bahāraey* or *bihāraey*, s.f. (1st) A weanling, a child stinted in milk, a child or animal weaned before its time. بهارِ *bahāri* or *bihāri*, s.f. (8th) A female child as above. Pl. (M. and F.) ي *ī*. See وچ موري

A بهايم *bahāym*, s. (Pl. of A بهيمه) Beasts, brutes, wild beasts.

بهسوت *bih-sūt*, s. prop. The name of a small and weak tribe of Afghāns. 2. A male of the tribe. S. and Pl. بهسوته *bih-sūta'h*, s.f. (3rd) A female of the above. Pl. ې *ey*.

S بهو *bha'o*, s.m. (2nd) Existence, life; living, being. Pl. بهوونه *bha'o-ūnah*.

بهه *baha'h*, s.f. (3rd) Course, stream, current, flow of a river, etc. Pl. ې *ey*.

بي آړکيدو *bey ārr-kedo*, adj. Without prevention, stop, or hindrance. بي نورَ *bey nūra*, adj. Stupid, ignorant; (Fem.) بي نوره *bey-nūra'h*. بي تللئ *bey-talalaey*, adj. Unweighed, unsearched, not examined, etc.; (Fem.) بي تللِ *bey-talali*. Pl. (M. and F.) بي تللي *bey-talalī*, بي وسي *bey-wasī*, s.f. (3rd) Powerlessness, the being without authority, power, means, etc. Pl. ئ *a'ī*. بي وسَ *bey-wasa*, adj. Powerless, helpless, of no authority; (Fem.) بي وسه *bey-wasa'h*. (S बश).

بيا *bī-ā*, adv. 2. Already, erewhile, just now. 3. Then, at that time. See other meanings at p. 138.

بيله *bela'h*, s.f. (3rd) 2. A trough, a gutter, a scupper, a launder, and the like. Pl. ې *ey*. See ترناو

پ

پاټکئ *pāṯṯkaey*, s.m. (1st) A little, a small space, a little way, a scrap. Pl. ي *ī*.

پاړ *pāṟṟ*, s.m. (2nd) A charm, a spell, an incantation. Pl. پاړونه *pāṟṟūnah*. See پاړو

پاسته *pāsta'h*, s.f. (3rd) A thin cake of unleavened bread baked on a girdle, large or small. Pl. ې *ey*. See چپتي

پاسنئ *pāsnaey*, adj. Upper, higher, etc. At Peshāwar, and east of the Khaibar, this term is applied to the people, animals, etc. of Kābul, Kandahār, Ghaznī, etc., whilst at Kandahār it is applied to the people and animals, etc. of the north, such as Ghaznī, Kābul, etc. 2. A male as above. Pl. ي *ī*. (Fem.) پاسنۍ *pāsna'ī*, as s.f. (3rd) A female as above. S. and Pl. See کښيني

پاسول *pāsawul*, verb trans. To anoint a camel or other animal with lime and oil, or the like, as a remedy for the mange. پاسولئ *pāsawulaey*, adj. Anointed as above. (Fem.) پاسولِ *pāsawuli*. Pl. (M. and F.) ي *ī*.

پاشل *pā-shal*, verb trans. To sprinkle, to scatter, to diffuse, to pour out, to dissipate.

پاړ *pāṟṟn*, s.m. (2nd) A cliff, a precipice. See under same word p. 151.

پپلي *piplī*, s.m. (1st) Pl. Long pepper (piper longum). The singular form of the word is only used for a single grain.

پټ پيچان *puṯṯ-pechān*, adj. Armed cap-a-pie (a soldier).

پټان *paṯṯān*, s. prop. The name said to have been bestowed on Æabd-ur-Rashīd, the great ancestor of the Afghāns, and the first Afghān convert to the faith, by Muḥammad. The word is said to signify the keel or keelson of a vessel. 2. s.m. (5th) A name by which the Afghāns are known in India, an Afghān. Pl. پټانان *paṯṯānān*. پټانه *paṯṯāna'h*, s.f. (3rd) An Afghān female. Pl. ې *ey*. Also written بتان

پټکه *paṯṯaka'h*, s.f. (3rd) A razor strap. Pl. ې *ey*.

پټګونۍ *paṯṯ-gona'ī*, s.f. (6th) An ambush, an ambuscade, a cover, a lurking-place. S. and Pl. See پټ ګنئ

پټيل *paṯṯe-yal*, verb trans. To conceal, to hide, to secrete, to cover, to screen, to shroud, to ensconce, to muffle up, etc. Pres. پټيي *paṯṯe-yī*; past وُ پټيه *wu-paṯṯe-yah*; fut. وُ به پټيي *wu-bah paṯṯe-yī*; imp. وُ پټيه *wu-paṯṯe-yah*; act. part. پټيونکئ *paṯṯe-yūnkaey*; past part. پټيلئ *paṯṯe-yalaey*; verb n. پټينه *paṯṯe-yana'h*. See پټول etc.

پښونئ *patsūnaey*, s.m. (1st) An ambush, an ambuscade, a lurking place, cover, a place of concealment. Pl. ي *ī*. په پښوني کښني کښيناستل

pah patsūnī k'shey or k'khey k'shenāstal or k'khenāstal, verb intrans. To lie in ambush, to lurk, etc. See پسوني

پچه paja'h, s.f. (3rd) A furnace, a place for the manufacture of glass, a glass-house, a place where glass is made. Pl. ې ey.

پچه آچول pacha'h āchawul, verb trans. To dung, as goats, sheep, etc. پچه کول pacha'h kawul, verb trans. To cast lots by means of the orbicular dung of animals put into a cap, or the like, shaken, and drawn out (vulgar). پچه وړل pacha'h w'rral, verb trans. To win, to draw the lot, by the method above alluded to. See پچه at p. 156.

پدل padl, s.m. (2nd) Fear, dread, awe, terror. Pl. پدلونه padlūnah.

پدول pudūl, s.m. (5th) A betrayer, a blabber, a tale-bearer. Pl. پدولان pudūlān. پدوله pudūla'h, s.f. (3rd) A female as above. Pl. ې ey.

پدولي pudūlī, s.f. (3rd) Disclosure, betrayal, exposé, revealment. Pl. ۍ a'ī. پدولي کول pudūlī kawul, verb trans. To betray, to divulge, to blab, to peach, to let the cat out of the bag.

پروهل par wahal, verb trans. To fly, to stretch the wings (applied to animals), to stretch one's legs, to go, to walk, to enter.

P پرتاب par-tāb, s.m. (2nd) Shining, brilliancy, brightness. Pl. پرتابونه par-tābūnah.

پرخی par-khaey, s.m. (1st) Augmentation, increase, surplus, addition, excess. Pl. ي ī. 2. adj. More, excessive, too much, too many, etc.; (Fem.) ۍ a'ī. S. and Pl.

پرښه par-sha'h (W.) or par-kha'h (E.) s.f. (3rd) Rock, a rock, a ledge of rock. Pl. ې ey.

P پرمهره par-mukra'h, s.f. (3rd) A cud of feathers, etc., which birds of prey discharge from their crops. Pl. ې ey. پرمهره آچول par muhra'h āchawul or غرزول ghurzawul, verb trans. To discharge the cud of feathers, etc.

پروښول pro-shawul (W.) or pro-khawul (E.) verb trans. To twist, to contort, to writhe, to distort, to wrest. Pres. پروښوي pro-shawī or pro-kharī, or پروښئي pro-shayī or pro-khayī; past و پروښاوه wu-proshāwuh or wu-prokhāwuh; fut. و به پروښوي wu bah pro-shawī or pro-khawī, or و به پروښئي wu bah pro-shayī or pro-khayī; imp. و پروښوه wu-pro-shawah or pro-khawah; act. part. پروښوونکي pro-shawūnkaey or pro-khawūnkaey; past part. پروښولي pro-shawulaey or pro-khawulaey; verb n. پروښونه pro-shawuna'h or pro-khawuna'h.

پرهار ژلي par-hār-jzalaey, adj. Wounded, hurt, etc.; (Fem.) پرهار ژلِ par-hār-jzali. Pl. (M. and F.) ي ī. See under پرهار

پري prey, prep. On him, her, it, etc. It is sometimes used adverbially, and means, thereby, by the means of, by, through, by which, by means of which, whereby, etc. Also written پرِ pri. See پر, and Grammar, p. 48.

پريباسل pre-bāsal, verb trans. To throw, to propel, to fling, to dart, to cast, to project, to discharge, to hurl, to chuck, etc. Pres. پريباسي pre-bāsī; past پريست pre-yast; fut. پري به باسي pre bah bāsī; imp. پريباسه pre-bāsah. The other forms are wanting, and are taken from پريستل, which is also imperfect, the incomplete forms of the two verbs making the conjugation complete.

پريږدل prejz-dal (W.) or پريگدل preg-dal (E.), verb trans. 2. To allow, permit, admit, give leave or permission, concede, tolerate, etc. See other meanings at p. 168.

پريوتل pre-watal, verb intrans. 2. To encamp, to halt, to take up one's residence. 3. To go down (as to go down from Kabul to Peshawar). See other significations at p. 170.

پريوته pre-wata'h, s.f. (3rd) A species of creeper with a white flower, sort of bind-weed. Pl. ې ey.

پړيس prrīs or پړس prrīs, adj. Round, fat, stout, broad, corpulent, obese. (Fem.) پړيسه prrīsa'h or پړسه prrīsa'h. پړس والي or پړيس prrīs or prrīs-wālaey, s.m. (1st) Roundness, stoutness, fatness, rotundity, obesity, corpulence, etc. Pl. والي wālī. See لند

لنډه پزه landda'h paza'h, A long nose. لند پزه

landdd paza'h, A long-nosed person. پزه وتل *paza'h watal,* verb intrans. To break out about the nose in small pimples (as after fever). See پوزه and پزه

پږ *pujz,* s.m. (2nd) A puff, a blast, etc. 2. Squirting or sprinkling water, or the like. Pl. پږونه *pujzūnah.* پږ وهل *pujz wahal,* verb trans. To squirt or sprinkle water. See پور

پستنه لاړل *pastanah-lāṛral,* verb intrans. To retire, to return, to go back, etc. See پستنه

پسولل *p'solal,* verb trans. To put on, to wear, to dress in, to deck or trick one's-self out in jewels, fine clothes, etc. Pres. پسولي *p'solī;* past وُ پسوله *wu-p'solah;* fut. وُ به پسولي *wu bah p'solī;* imp. وُ پسوله *wu-p'solah;* act. part. پسولونکئ *p'solūnkaey;* past part. پسوللئ *p'solalaey;* verb n. پسولنه *p'solana'h.* See پوسلل and پسولول

پسوللئ *p'solalaey,* past part. Decked out, dressed; (Fem.) پسولِل *p'solali.* Pl. (M. and F.) ي *ī.*

پسي *pasey* or پسِ *pasi,* These words when used in a sentence like the following—محمد دا کار وُ کړ پسي دا کار وُ کړ the ي denoting the agent is included in, or rather absorbed into it, but only in the 3rd person. See پس at p. 175.

پسه *pusa'h,* s.f. (3rd) Bread made from the seeds of the mastic tree. Pl. ئ *ey.*

پشقاب *pish-kāb,* s.m. (2nd) A small plate or saucer. Pl. پشقابونه *pish-kābūnah.* See رغي

پښئ *pusha'ī* (W.) or *pukha'ī* (E.), s.f. (6th) A sort of edible rhubarb. S. and Pl. See رواش

ټک *pæk,* adj. Bald, bald-headed; (Fem.) ټکه *pæka'h.* ټک والئ *pæk wālaey,* s.m. (1st) Baldness. Pl. والي *wālī.*

پلانکئ *plānkaey,* adj. Such a one, so and so, what's his name, a certain person or thing; (Fem.) پلانکئ *plānka'ī.* See فلاني

پلس *pils,* s.m. (2nd) (corrup. of P فلس) The scale (of a fish), a scale or anything similar. Pl. پلسونه *pils-ūnah.*

پلوس *palūs,* s.m. (6th) (W.) The cassia fistula. S. and Pl. See جرانګو

پليشه *plesha'h,* s.f. (3rd) A flame of fire. Pl. ئ *ey.*

پن *pun,* s.m. (2nd) (W.) The scab in sheep, the itch. Pl. پنونه *punūnah.* پن آخستل *pun ākhistal,* verb trans. To catch the scab or itch. See پم , پون , and خارښت

پنجک *panj-ak,* s.m. (2nd) A fifth, a tax on land, consisting of a fifth of the produce. Pl. پنجکونه *panj-akūnah.* پنجک آخستل *panj-ak ākhistal* or پنجک ټولول *panj-ak ttolawul,* verb trans. To collect the land-tax or *panj-ak.*

پنجکوره *panj-kora'h,* s.f. (3rd) The name of a mountainous district lying to the north of Peshāwer. Pl. ئ *ey.*

پنډئ *pandda'ī,* s.f. (6th). 2. A socket, a haft. S. and Pl.

پنګئ فروش *panga'ī-farosh,* s.m. (5th) A pedlar, a cadger, a hawker. Pl. فروشان *faroshān.*

S پوټئ *pota'ī,* s.f. (6th) Face, visage, countenance, 2. An unbound book. S. and Pl.

پوڅونئ *potsūnaey,* s.m. (1st) An ambush, a lurking place. Pl. ي *ī.* See پڅونه

پوشا پوش *poshā-posh,* Continual or repeated warnings (from پوشه, 'Take care!').

پوګر *pū-gar,* s.m. (6th) A bellows. 2. A blow-pipe used by goldsmiths. 3. The blower of a bellows. Pl. پوګړ *pū-gær.* پوګره *pū-gara'h,* s.f. (3rd) A female who blows the bellows. Pl. ئ *ey.*

پونده *pūnda'h,* s.f. (3rd) A socket, a haft. Pl. ئ *ey.* Also پونډئ *pūndda'ī,* s.f. (6th). S. and Pl.

پونده *po-wandah,* s.m. (6th) (P v. پويدن) The name given to the nomad tribes of Afghāns who move about with their flocks and herds, and act as carriers between their own country and India. S. and Pl. پونده *po-wanda'h,* s.f. (3rd) A female nomad. Pl. ئ *ey.* See سر ترلي and کوچي

پونړيول *pūrrn-yawul,* verb trans. (W.) To nibble, to munch, to mumble, to gnaw. Ex. وږي مږک وُ پونړياوه *wajzī majzak wu-pūrrn-yāwuh,* "The mouse gnawed or nibbled the corn." (E.) وږي مږک وُ وهل *wajzī majzak wu-wahal.*

پوهوينه *pohawīnah,* pres. tense of پوهول with the

نه affixed, for explanation of which see Grammar, p. 103.

پوهيدل *pohedal*, verb intrans. To comprehend, to have cognizance of, to conceive. See p. 200.

په بريتو غلط شول *pah breto ghalaṭ sh'wal*, verb intrans. To grow or become proud or arrogant, to give one's-self airs, to become vain or conceited, to assume, to presume, strut, etc.

په كار راغلل *pah kār rāghlal*, verb intrans. To become of use. په كار راوول *pah kār rāw'rral*, verb trans. To use, to make use of, to employ, to turn to account, to make the most of.

په څه *pah tso*, Why, wherefore, for what reason. See under څه

په دا *pah dā*, adv. Then, on this, etc.

پيايل *pīā-yal*, verb trans. To make or cause to browse, to graze. This verb is imperfect, and is used to complete the tenses of پوول which is imperfect also. See p. 199.

پيټک *pe-ṯṯak*, s.m. (2nd) A present given to a child soon after birth by relations and connections of the parents. Pl. پيټكونه *pe-ṯṯakūnah.*

پيچمه *pech-ma'h*, s.f. (3rd) Derision, jesting, jest. 2. A laugh, laughter. 3. A laughing-stock. Pl. ې *ey.*

پيڅوني *petsūnaey*, s.m. (1st) An ambush, etc. Pl. ي *ī.* See پڅوني and پوڅوني for other meanings.

پير *per*, s.m. (2nd) Change, revolution, alternation, vicissitude, mutablility, etc. 2. Turning about and facing an enemy when retreating before him, facing about, etc. See under same word, p. 205. Pl. پيرونه *per-ūnah.*

پيرزو لرل *per-zo laral*, verb trans. To be suitable (*lit.* To have or hold what is suitable). See پيرزو

پيرودل *pīrawdal*, verb trans. 2. Occasionally signifies, To seize, to take by force. See p. 206.

پيروي *perawaey*, s.m. (1st) Cream from warm milk, sort of clouted cream. Pl. ي *ī.*

پيږل *pe-jzal*, verb trans. (W.) To notch, as a piece of wood, in order to divide it easily, to cut across with a knife, (as a surgeon when amputating, or the like). Pres. پيږي *pe-jzī*; past وُ پيږه *wu-pe-jzah*; fut. وُ به پيږي *wu bah pe-jzī*; imp. وُ پيږه *wu-pe-jzah*; act. part. پيږونكي *pe-jzūnkaey*; past part. پيږلي *pe-jzalaey*; verb. n. پيږنه *pe-jzana'h.*

پيس *pīs*, s.m. (2nd) Coxcombry, vanity, conceit, swagger, puppyism, pertness, assumption, etc. Pl. پيسونه *pīs-ūnah.* پيس كول *pīs kawul*, verb trans. To show off, to swagger, to act the puppy.

پيسي *pīsaey*, s.m. (1st) A puppy, a coxcomb, a dandy, a fop, etc. Pl. ي *ī.* پيسۍ *pīsa'ī*, s.f. (6th) A vain conceited female. S. and Pl.

پيشك *peshak*, s.m. (2nd) The leprosy. Pl. پيشكونه *peshak-ūnah.* See پيس

پيشكي *pesh-kaey*, s.m. (1st) A leper. Pl. ي *ī.* پيشكۍ *pesh-ka'ī*, s.f. (6th) A female leper. S. and Pl.

P پيشين *peshīn*, s.m. (2nd) The afternoon, the time of afternoon prayer. Pl. پيشينونه *peshīn-ūnah.*

پيل ومټ *pīl-o-maṯṯ*, Great or utmost endeavour, making every attempt or essay possible. پيل is probably corrup. of A فعل. See مټ.

پيمل *p'yamal*, verb trans. To measure (as liquids, or as grain, etc.). Pres. پيمي *p'yamī*; past وُ پيمه *wu p'yamah*; fut. وُ به پيمي *wu bah p'yamī*; imp. وُ پيمه *wu-p'yamah*; act. part. پيمونكي *p'yamūnkaey*; past part. پيملي *p'yamalaey*; verb. n. پيمنه *p'yamana'h.*

پيوستيدل *paiwastedal*, verb intrans. To be bound, become fastened, tied, etc. See other significations of the same word, p. 214.

پييل or پيُل *pe-yal*, verb trans. To thread (as a needle), to string (as beads or pearls), to pass through, to spit, to stick, to empale, to pierce, to spear, etc. Pres. پيبي *pe-yi*; past وُ پييه *wu-pe-yah*; fut. وُ به پيبي *wu bah pe-yī*; imp. وُ پييه *wu-pe-yah*; act. part. پييونكي *pe-yūnkaey*; past part. پييلي *pe-yalaey*; verb. n. پيينه *pe-yana'h.*

ت

تارول *tārawul*, verb trans. To shake or ruffle the feathers, as a bird when pleased. Pres. تاروي

tārawī; past تارول وُ *wu tārawul*; fut. وُ به تاروي *wu bah tārawī*; imp. وُ تاروه *wu-tārawah*; act. part. تاروونکي *tārawūnkaey*; past part. تارولي *tārawulaey*; verb n. تارونه *tārawuna'h*.

تاړ *tāṟṟ*, s.m. (2nd) A band of raiders. 2. A raid, a foray. Pl. تاړونه *tāṟṟūnah*. See p. 217.

تاقي *tā-ḳī*, adj. Clasped, having a collar, ring, or clasp round the neck (corrup. of A طوق, A collar, a yoke).

P تانسته *tānista'h*, s.f. (3rd) A spider's web. Pl. ې *ey*.

تپتي *tap-ta'ī*, s.f. (6th) Adversity, difficulty, distress, calamity, misfortune. S. and Pl.

A تجلا *tajallā*, s.f. (6th) (A تجلي) Brilliancy, brightness, lustre, splendour, clearness, etc. (E.) S. and Pl. (W.) Pl. تجلاوي *tajallāwī*. تجلا کول *tajallā kawul*, verb trans. To shine, to glisten, to gleam, to give forth lustre, brightness, etc. See تجله

تراره *tarāra'h*, s.f. (3rd) Confusion, disorder, perturbation. 2. Fear, terror, alarm, panic. Pl. ې *ey*.

تربت *tar-bat*, adj. Choked, obstructed, interrupted, hampered, hindered, etc.; (Fem.) تربته *tar-bata'h*. تربت کیدل *tar-bat kedal*, verb intrans. To become choked or obstructed. تربت کول *tar-bat kawul*, verb trans. To choke, obstruct, impede.

تربوزک *tar-būzak*, s.m. (2nd) The muzzle, the mouth and nose of an animal, also the muzzle or fastening for the mouth of an animal. Pl. تربوزکونه *tar-būzakūnah*. See تمبوزک.

S ترت *turt*, adv. Instantly, immediately, quickly, directly, hastily.

ترڅ *trats*, s.m. (2nd) Side, margin, border, edge, shore, etc. Pl. ترڅونه *tratsūnah*. په ترڅ کښې ویل *pah trats kshey* or *kkhey wa-yal*, verb trans. To speak secretly, or say aside, or by stealth.

ترږمي *tarajzma'ī*, s.f. (6th) (W.) Darkness, murkiness, gloom. S. and Pl. See تورګمي

ترکي *taraka'ī*, s.f. (6th) A pile of rocks separated from a mountain range, or jutting out into a plain. S. and Pl. See غونډي and راغه

ترمه *trama'h*, s.f. (3rd) A bog, a quagmire, a swamp. 2. Sediment, dregs, lees, etc. Pl. ې *ey*. See ترمنه

P ترنج *turanj*, adj. Wrinkled, drawn together. 2. Hard, dry, rough; (Fem.) ترنجه *turanjah*.

A تزویج *taz-wīj*, s.m. (2nd) Joining, associating, marrying. Pl. تزویجونه *taz-wījūnah*.

تلاوه *talāwa'h*, s.f. (3rd) (from P. تلایه ?) Watching, keeping guard, keeping watch and ward. Pl. ې *ey*. Ex. څو سړي ئې د تلاوي د ها هو دپاره واستول "He sent some men to patrol, and to keep watch and ward." See هاي هوي

تلنه *til-nah*, s.m. (6th) A complete or full year. S. and Pl.

تلول *tal-wal*, adj. Abundant, abounding, plenteous, replete, plentiful; (Fem.) تلوله *talwala'h*.

تلول *talawul*, verb trans. To slide, to slip, to thrust along, or thrust by slipping. 2. To make to slip, to cause to err, etc. For conjugation see تلول 'To fry,' at p. 256. تلیدل *taledal*, verb intrans. To slide, to slip, to slide along (as on ice, etc.) Pres. تلیږي *tale-jzī*; past وُ تلیده *wu-taledah*; fut. وُ به تلیږي *wu bah tale-jzī*; imp. وُ تلیږه *wu-tale-jzah*; act. part. تلیدونکي *tale-dūnkaey*; past part. تلیدلي *tale-dalaey*; verb. n. تلیدنه *tale-dana'h*. See ښوهیدل and ښکیدل

تمبوګي *tambūgaey*, s.m. (1st) A small tent. (from HI تمبو). 2. A spider's web or dwelling. Pl. ي *ī*. See تانسته

تمندار *tuman-dār*, s.m. (5th) The leader of a brotherhood, the chief or head man of a clan. Pl. تمنداران *tuman-dārān*. See تومن

تن توش *tan-tosh*, s.m. (2nd) Provision for a journey. Pl. تن توشونه *tan-toshūnah*. See خوري

تنځرَي *tandzaraey*, s.m. (1st) The common grey partridge. Pl. ي *ī*. Some of the mongrel Peshawarīs not being able to pronounce the Afghan letter څ, use Arabic ذ or ز, which is alike common to Persian and Afghan, instead. See p. 262.

تړاکه چاودل *tarrnā-ka'h chāwdal*, verb trans. To lay (*fig.*), to allay, to cool, sober down, restrain, curb, bring down, tame.

توپ *top*, s.m. (1st) (E.) A cannon. Pl. توپِ *topi*. See under p. 266.

توتکي *to-takaey*, s.m. (2nd) A knot of hair worn in front, on the forehead, by virgins. This refers to a strange custom prevalent some hundred years since amongst the whole of the Afghāns, and still observed by the Ghalzīs, and other tribes of central Afghānistān, of plaiting the front hair of young girls, from about eight years of age, until their marriage, in a large round plait, often the size of a saucer, in front of the forehead, and sometimes reaching to the tip of the nose, covering the eyes, and acting, in fact, the part of a mask. It may be raised or put aside to enable the wearer to eat. On the morning of the marriage it is opened, and not plaited again. See "Character and Costume of Afghānistān," a series of drawings by the late Capt. L. W. Hart, of the former Bombay Army, where there is a drawing of a female with one. Pl. ي *ī*. See غونه

توده *tūda'h*, s.f. (3rd) A heap, a pile, a sheaf or bundle of arrows, a hillock, a tumulus. 2. A little heap of sand or earth, as a target for arrows. Pl. ئ *ey*.

تورخيل *tor-khel*, s.m. (2nd) A slave (*lit.* the black clan or khel), first applied to negro slaves probably, but now used as a general term for slave. Pl. تورخيلونه *tor-khelūnah*. تورخيله *tor-kheld'h*, s.f. (3rd) A female slave. Pl. ئ *ey*.

توره *tora'h*, s.f. (3rd) A collection of *kijzda'īs* or black tents, an encampment of the wandering or pastoral tribes. 2. A village, a hamlet. Pl. ئ *ey*.

توري *toraey*, s.m. (1st) The milt of animals and fish. Pl. ي *ī*. See p. 270.

تورئ *tora'ī*, s.f. (6th) A sort of small trumpet with a shrill sound. S. and Pl.

توزن *tū-zan*, adj. Poor-spirited, base, craven, dastard, cowardly; (Fem.) توزنه *tū-zana'h*. See تزن

توسند *tosand*, adj. Greedy, ravenous, esurient, lustful; (Fem.) توسنده *tosanda'h*.

توشل *taw-shal*, adj. Flat, shallow (as a dish, boat, etc.); (Fem.) توشله *taw-shala'h*. توشل والي *taw-shal-wālaey*, s.m. (1st) Flatness, shallowness, etc. Pl. والي *wālī*. See پلن.

پرځان ته توکل *dzān tah tū-kal* or پرځان توکل *par dzān tū-kal* or پر ږیره توکل *par-jzīra'h tū-kal*, verb trans. To debase one's self, to make a fool of one's self, to lower one's self, to spit upon one's own beard.

توګ *tog*, s.m. (2nd) Method, way, mode, fashion, etc. Pl. توګونه *tog-ūnah*. See توکه

تومن *tūman*, s.m. (2nd) A brotherhood, a clan, a party, a troop, etc. Pl. تومنونه *tūmanūnah*. See تمن

تون *tūn*, s.m. (2nd) A native country, a birthplace, hence the Afghāns are called Pushtūn and Pushtanah, from پاښت *pāsht* or *pākht* or پښت *pasht* or *pakht*, the name of their first locality near the Takht-i-Sūlīmān, west of the Indus. See Introduction to Grammar, p. 8. Pl. تانه *tānah*. بي ځايَ تونَ *bey dzā'ea tūna*, Without a country or home, with no place to lay one's head, homeless.

تهداي *tah-dā-e*, s.m. (2nd) Foundation, basis, basement, plinth, etc. Pl. تهدايونه *tah-dā-e-ūnah*. تهداي آچول *tah-dā-e āchawul* or وهل *wahal*, verb trans. To lay a foundation, to found. See داي

تهنه *tahana'h*, s.f. (3rd) Descent, slope, declivity, a slope or hollow. Pl. ئ *ey*.

تيپ *tīp*, s.m. (2nd) A row, a rank, a squadron, etc. Pl. تيپونه *tīpūnah*. تيپ ترل *tīp tarral*, verb trans. To form in a row, to form ranks, etc.

کاني تيرانداز *kānī tīrandāz*, A skilful bowman or archer, an unerring shot with the bow and arrow. See p. 278, and کاني

تيغون *teghūn*, adj. Golden-winged (as a bird), bright, shining. 2. Wavy (as a sword); (Fem.) تيغونه *teghūna'h*. (P تيغ).

P تيمار *tīmār*, s.m. (2nd) 5. Grooming a horse with a coarse woollen cloth, also the cloth used. Pl. تيمارونه *tīmārūnah*. تيمار کول *tīmār kawul*, verb trans. 2. To groom a horse with a coarse woollen cloth. See p. 281.

ټ

ټال *ṯṯāl*, s.m. (2nd) A lasso, a noose. Pl. ټالونه *ṯṯālūnah*.

ټپريدل *ṯṯapar-edal*, verb intrans. To feel about for (as for anything in the dark), to feel one's way (as a blind person), to grope for. 2. To trudge, to hobble along, to grope. See p. 285.

ټپول *ṯṯapawul*, verb trans. To close (peculiar to books and the like). Pres. ټپوي *ṯṯapawī*; past ټپ کړ *ṯṯap karr* or ټپ وُ کړ *ṯṯap wu-karr*; fut. ټپ به کړي *ṯṯap bah krrī*; imp. ټپ کړه *ṯṯap krrah*; act. part. ټپوونکي *ṯṯapawūnkaey*; past part. ټپ کړي *ṯṯap karraey*; verb. n. ټپونه *ṯṯapawuna'h*. See ټپ

ټکي *ṯṯikaey*, s.m. (1st) The name of an ornament worn by women on the forehead. Pl. ي *ī*.

ټوپ *ṯṯop*, s.m. (2nd) 4. A round tower such as that of Manakīālah in the Panjāb, and those in various parts of Afghānistān, supposed to be Buddhist monuments. 5. A cap wadded with cotton, with flaps for the ears. Pl. ټوپونه *ṯṯopūnah*. See خورجينه

د ويښتانو ټوپۍ *da weshtāno* or *wekhtāno ṯṯopa'ī*, s.f. (6th) A wig, a periwig. S. and Pl.

ټونګرئيل *ṯṯongreyil*, verb trans. To excite, to insult, to provoke, etc. See ټونګاره

ټونګول *ṯṯongawul*, verb trans. To excite, to set on, to irritate, to provoke. See ټونګ

ټيري *ṯṯeraey*, s. prop. The name of a place, south-west of Kohāṯṯ, belonging to the Khaṯṯaks.

ټيک *ṯṯīk*, adj. (HI ٹهيک) Exact, even, accurate, complete, true, just, right, meet, proper, etc.; (Fem.) ټيکه *ṯṯīka'h*.

ټينګول *ṯṯīngawul*, verb trans. 3. To strengthen (as a fortress), to make or render strong. See p. 299.

څ

څارل *tsā-ral*, verb trans. To watch, to mark, to set the eye upon, to peep at, to reconnoitre, to explore, etc. See under څار

څاښي *tsāshaey* (W.) or *tsākhaey* (E.), An axis. Pl. ي *ī*. See p. 302.

څپڅپاڼري *tsap-tsapārrnī*, adj. Agitated, disturbed, distracted, afflicted, chagrined, etc. څپڅپاڼري کيدل *tsap-tsapārrnī kedal*, verb intrans. To become agitated or disturbed. څپڅپاڼري کول *tsap-tsapārrnī kawul*, verb trans. To agitate, to disturb.

څپه *tsapa'h*, s.f. (3rd) Swoop, clutch, carrying off, pouncing upon. Pl. ې *ey*. څپه وهل *tsapa'h wahal*, verb trans. To pounce upon, to carry off, to seize (as a bird of prey does its quarry), to snap at, to clutch. See p. 304.

څرخ *tsarkh*, s.m. (2nd) (P. چرخ). 2. A wheeled-carriage, a gun-carriage, a cart. Pl. څرخونه *tsarkhūnah*. See p. 308.

څرګند *tsargand*, adj. 2. Eminent, distinguished, illustrious, famous, renowned, celebrated. See p. 309.

څره *tsara'h*, s.f. (3rd) A deep pit or well in which grain is stored. Pl. ې *ey*. See کډهل

څړ *tsarr*, s.m. (2nd) (W.) Pasture, forage, pasturing, grazing, etc. Pl. څړونه *tsarrūnah*. څړيدل *tsarredal*, verb intrans. To graze, to browse. څړول *tsarrawul*, verb trans. To graze (supply with food or cause to feed). See (E.) څر

څړه سپاهي *tsarrah s'pāhī*, s.m. (5th) A light armed soldier; also one without baggage. Pl. سپاهيان *s'pāhīān*. See under څړه

څښتن والي *tsashtan* (W.) or *tsakhtan-wālaey* (E.) s.m. (1st) or څښتن توب *tsashtan* or *tsakhtan-tob*, s.m. (2nd) or څښتن تيا *tsashtan* or *tsakhtan-tīā*, s.f. (6th) The business, right, duty, or power of a master, possessor, etc. See څښتن

څک *tsak*, adj. Shapely, well-set, symmetrical; (Fem.) څکه *tsaka'h*. څک والي *tsak-wālaey*, s.m. (1st) Straightness, erectness, uprightness, perpendicularity. Pl. والي *wālī*.

د آسمان څکلي *da āsmān tsakalaey*, s.m. (1st) The common bat. Pl. ي *ī*.

څکول *ts'kawul*, verb trans. To draw or drag along, to extract, to unsheath, etc. See ښکول

څکيدل *tsakedal*, verb intrans. To turn or grow straight, symmetrical, regular, shapely, etc. څکول *tsakawul*, verb trans. To make regular, straight, symmetrical, shapely, etc.

څلي *tsalaey*, s.m. (1st). 5. A heap of stones to mark the scene of a battle, murder, or any remarkable event. Pl. ي *ī*. See p. 314.

څم See under جم and چم

څمڅ *tsmats*, s.f. (1st) A cavern, a cave, a grotto, a cavity. Pl. څمڅې *tsmatsi*. See سمڅ

څنډول *tsanddawul*, verb trans. To shake, to agitate, to clean by shaking. See څنډل and څډوهل

څو *tsaw* or *tsao*, s.m. (2nd) An ambush, an ambuscade, a place of ambush, retreat, cover, lurking place, etc. Pl. څوونه *tsaw-ūnah* or *tsao-ūnah*. څو کول *tsaw* or *tsao kawul*, or په څو or څوي کښيناستل or ناستل *pah tsaw* or *tsawaey k'shenāstal* (W.) or *k'khenāstal* (E.) or *nāstal*, verb intrans. To lie in ambush, to lurk or lie in wait for. څو or څوي کول *tsaw* or *tsawaey kawul*, verb trans. To lay an ambush or ambuscade. See څوي

څور *tsūrr*, adj. Irregular, distorted, twisted, awry, wry, askew, crooked, all manner of ways; (Fem.) څوره *tsūrra'h*. څور والي *tsūrr wālaey*, s.m. (1st) Distortion, wryness, twist, contortion, malformation. Pl. والي *wālī*. څوريدل *tsūrredal*, verb intrans. To turn or grow awry, distorted or twisted, to become or grow crooked. څورول *tsūrrawul*, verb trans. To make or render crooked, to distort, to twist, to contort, to make wry.

څورنګ *tsowrrang*, s.m. (9th) The members or parts of an animal or bird. S. and Pl. (From s चतुरंग).

څور *tsawarr*, s.m. (2nd) (W.) A block of wood bound or fastened round a bullock's neck to keep him from straying. 2. A sort of covering for the loins of horses and asses. Pl. څوورونه *tsawarrūnah*. See کولند

څوکري *tsūk-raey*, s.m. (1st) A stalk of the edible rhubarb plant in its natural state, with greenish red stalks, different to رواش, which has white stalks. Pl. ي *ī*. The plural form is used to indicate the plant generally.

څيره *tsera'h*, s.f. (3rd) A garland or crown of flowers worn by a bridegroom on the night of his marriage. Pl. ې *ey*.

د سر څيري خلق *da sar-tsīrrey khalk*, Troops sent on in advance of the main body, advance of an army, or the advance guard.

ج

جاله *jā-la'h*, s.f. (3rd). 5. A bee-hive. The mode of making a hive among the Afghāns is by inserting an earthen pot in the wall of the house, or a wooden-bowl, and just leaving a hole for the bees to enter. This orifice is then smeared with coarse sugar to attract the bees. The earthen pot used is called منګي *mangaey*, and the wooden bowl is called ډهولکي *ddholkaey* or ډولکي *ddolkaey*, being in shape like a drum. The whole when made and fixed is termed جاله. Pl. ې *ey*. See my "Account of Suwāt," Journal Bengal Asiatic Society for 1862.

A جذبه *jazba'h*, s.f. (3rd). 2. Ecstacy, inspiration, trance, second-sight. Pl. ې *ey*. په جذبه راغلل *pah jazba'h rāghlal*, verb intrans. To fall into (religious) ecstacy, to become inspired, to become gifted with second-sight.

جرأت لرل *jur'āt laral* or جرأت کول *jur'āt kawul*, verb trans. To show courage, to act with courage or temerity, to dare. See جرأت p. 330.

A جريده *jar-īdah*, adj. Alone, unattended, separate, unencumbered, solitary. 2. Light armed (as troops).

جګ *jig*, adj. Stuck up, erected, set up, upreared, elevated, standing erect, uplifted. 2.

High, elevated, tall, lofty, crowning, soaring, etc.; (Fem.) جگه *jiga'h*. Also written جيگ *jīg* and جيگه *jīga'h*, and چگ *chig* and چگه *chiga'h*.

جل *jal*, s.m. (9th) The midst of the sea. 2. (s) Restraint, durance, hiding, concealment, inclosure, limitation, circumscription.

يک جلو *yek-jalaw*, All at once, in a body, altogether, also يک جلبه *yek-jalabah*. See p. 337.

جواب ده *jawāb-dih*, adj. 2. Amenable, accountable, answerable, liable, responsible.

جواب دهي *jawāb-dihī*, s.f. (3rd) Amenability, responsibility, onus, liability, etc. S. and Pl. See جواب p. 342, and correct the misprint.

جوانه *juwānah*, s.m. and s.f. (5th) A young bullock or bull that has not yet been worked. Pl. جوانه گان *juwānah-gān*. Fem. Pl. جوانه گانِ *juwānah-gāni*.

جوړه *jorra'h*, s.f. (3rd) 3. A description of verses or poetry, in singing which two persons take part and answer each other, a sort of part-song. Pl. ې *ey*.

جوړئ *jorra'ī*, s.f. (6th) A kind of cloth made of cotton and very narrow, generally worn by the Afghāns and Sindīans. S. and Pl.

جوگي رنگ *jogī-rang*, A kind of dirty orange color, the color of the clothes worn by Hindū Jogīs or devotees. See under رنگ

د جولا جاله or جالئ *da jolā jā-lah* or *jāla'ī*, A spider's web, a cobweb. See جالئ جولا and تانسه.

جويړ *jo-eyrr*, s.m. (2nd) A hollow or ditch in which the rain accumulates, and the bottom of which is muddy. Pl. جويړونه *jo-eyrrūnah*. Also written جوير

جه *jah*, adj. Inflexible, unyielding, determined, resolute. See p. 348.

جيلاني *jīlānī*, s. prop. The name of a celebrated Pīr or saint of the Musalmāns, so called from Jīlān, in Persia, the province in which he was born. His tomb or shrine is at Baghdād.

چ

چاپلوس *chāp-lūs*, adj. 2. Flattering, sycophantic, fulsome, etc. (Fem.) چاپلوسه *chāp-lūsa'h*. See p. 350.

چار تاره *chār-tāra'h*, s.f. (3rd) A kind of rebeck or four-stringed violin. Pl. ې *ey*.

چار ښاخه *chār-shākha'h* (W.) or *khākha'h* (E.), s.f. (3rd) A kind of pitchfork, an instrument used in winnowing corn. Pl. ې *ey*. See ښانگې

چارياك *chār-yāk*, s.m. (2nd) A quarter, a fourth part. Pl. چارياكونه *chār-yākūnah*. See چاريک

P چاشني *chāshnī*, s.f. (3rd) Taste, trial, tasting a thing by way of sample. Pl. ئ *a'ī*. چاشني كول *chāshnī kawul*, verb trans. To taste, to try, to sample.

چا و چا *chā-o-chā*, Some people, some folks, etc., as چا و چا هسي وُ ويل *chā-o-chā hasī wu-wayal*, "Some people said so."

چپ *chup*, s.m. (2nd) (P چف) A breath, a puff, charming by breathing on a person or a wound, etc. Pl. چپونه *chupūnah*. چپ كول *chup kawul*, verb trans. To breathe, to breathe on by charming. See دم.

چپړوس *chap-rrūs*, adj. Flattering, wheedling, sycophantic, fulsome. Also s.m. (5th) A flatterer, a sycophant, a toad-eater, a parasite. Pl. چپړوسان *chap-rrūsān*. (Fem.) چپړوسه *chap-rrūsa'h*. Also s.f. (3rd). Pl. ې *ey*.

چپښ *chapash* (W.) or *chapakh* (E.), adj. Flat-footed (person), having the sole of the foot flat and the heel very prominent, as in negroes; (Fem.) چپښه *chapasha'h* or *chapakha'h*.

چپلاخه *chapalākha'h*, s.f. (3rd) The flat of the hand, a slap, striking with the flat of the hand. Pl. ې *ey*. په چپلاخه وهل *pah chapalākha'h wahal*, verb trans. To strike with the flat of the hand, to slap, to box (as the ears). See څپيړه

چر *char* (corrup. of چار), which see.

چراتئ *charāta'ī*, s.f. (6th) A kind of gravel or some heavy mineral substance of a dark brown color, found in the passes leading into Suwāt, and in the upper parts of that valley. It is used for shot in shooting small birds, etc. S. and Pl. Also termed کیتي which see.

چراسپه *charāspa'h*, s.f. (3rd) A thick rope or cable made of goat's hair, used for picketing a line of horses, the head-ropes being attached to a *charāspa'h* in front, and the heel-ropes to another behind, a cable used in drawing artillery. 2. A rope made of leather twisted or plaited, used as traces or harness, etc. Pl. ې *ey*.

چرپ *chrrap*, s.m. (5th) The sound produced by the lips meeting, as when kissing with violence, or the splashing of water, making a noise whilst eating, smack. Pl. چرپهار *chrrapahār*. چرپيدل *chrrapedal*, verb intrans. To emit a sound as above. چرپ چرپ کول *chrrap-chrrap kawul*, or چرپول *chrrapawul*, verb trans. To make such a sound with the lips, to splash, to smack.

P شب چراغ *shab-chirāgh*, s.m. (2nd) A carbuncle. 2. A glow-worm. Pl. شب چراغونه *shab-chirāghūnah*.

چغر *chaghar*, adj. Anything dark in which there may be a spot or stye, wall-eyed (as a horse); (Fem.) چغره *chaghara'h*. چغر سترګي *chaghar-starghaey*, adj. Wall-eyed (as a horse, etc.); (Fem.) چغر سترګِ *chaghar-stargi*. Pl. (M. and F.) ي *ī*.

چغله *chughula'h*, s.f. (3rd) A beetle. Pl. ې *ey*. See ګونګټ

چغليدل *chughaledal*, verb intrans. To be traduced, maligned, or calumniated. چغلول *chughalawul*, verb trans. To backbite, to traduce, to slander, to malign, to defame, to blow upon, to be informed against, to tell tales.

چغ و بغ *chagh-o-bagh*, Clamor, noise, din, tumult, hullaballoo. See under چغ

چک *chak*, s.m. (2nd) A band, a party, a concourse, a drove, a gang, etc. 2. (W.) The hand. Pl. چکونه *chakūnah*. چک په چک *chak-pah-chak*, In droves, in bands, in troops, in knots, etc. 2. (W.) Hand in hand.

چکي چکي *chikī-chikī*, Words used in calling goats. See چکر

چمچوړي *chamchura'ī*, s.f. (6th) A young frog, a tadpole. S. and Pl.

چمکلي *chamkala'ī*, s.f. (6th) A kind of ornament worn on the forehead by females. S. and Pl.

چندخ *chindakh*, s.m. (5th) A toad. Pl. چندخان *chindakhān*. See چندخه and چنګهه

چندري *chandaraey*, s.m. (1st) Pudendum muliebre. Pl. ي *ī*.

چنګ *chungh*, s.m. (2nd) A handful, as much as the hand will contain. Pl. چنګونه *chunghūnah*.

چنګوټي *changottaey*, s.m. (1st) A cub, a pup, a kitten, etc. Pl. ي *ī*. چنګوټۍ *changotta'ī*, s.f. (6th) A female cub, etc. S. and Pl.

چنغاله *changhāla'h*, s.f. (3rd) A betrothed girl, but still dwelling in her father's house. Pl. ې *ey*.

چنه *chana'h*, s.f. (3rd) The corner of a wall. Pl. ې *ey*. See other meanings under چنه

چنړ *charrn*, s.m. (2nd) The bottom part of a door which revolves in a socket in the lintel and serves in place of a hinge. Pl. چنړونه *charrnūnah*. See چونړ.

چوپړ *cho-parr*, s.m. (2nd) A sort of beetle or mallet used by washermen and dyers instead of an ironing-box. 2. Drudgery, toil, particularly on foot. Pl. چوپړونه *cho-parrūnah*.

چورلټه *chūr-latta'h*, s.f. (3rd) (from چورليدل) Whirling about, spinning round, twirling, turning, gyrating. Pl. ې *ey*.

په چوغي چوغي تلل *pah chūghī chūghī t'lal*, verb intrans. To crawl or creep along. See چوغي

چونړيا *chūrrnīā*, adj. Purple.

چه *chih*, 2. The relative pronoun. See p. 378, and Grammar, p. 127.

چيچونکي or خوړونکي سپي *chīchūnkaey* or *khwarrūnkaey spaey*, A savage or snarling dog. چيچونکِ or خوړونکِ سپۍ *chīchūnki* or *khwarrūnki spa'ī*, A bitch as above. See سپي and خروړي

چيخل *chī-khal*, verb trans. 2. To cram (fill), to stuff in, to over-eat one's self, etc. See p. 379.

چيشن *che-shan*, adj. Hairy, over-grown with hair, shaggy, bushy, hirsute, rough. (Fem.)

چيشنه che-shana'h. چيشن توب che-shan-tob, s.m. (2nd). Pl. توبونه tobūnah, or چيشن والي che-shan-wālaey, s.m. (1st) Hairiness, roughness, shagginess, shag. Pl. والي wālī.

چيشنيدل che-shanedal, verb intrans. To grow or turn shaggy, hairy, bushy, etc. چيشنول che-shanawul, verb trans. To make hairy, rough, bushy, etc.

ح

حبيبه ḥabība'h, s.f. (3rd) A beloved one, a sweetheart, a mistress. Pl. ې ey. See حبيب p. 383.

A مستور الحديد mastūr-l-ḥadīd, adj. Armed cap-a-pie. See پټ پنهم

حقپليت ḥakk-pul-yat, s.m. (2nd) Saying adieu, bidding farewell, taking leave (lit. asking forgiveness, one friend of another). Pl. حقپليتونه ḥakk-pul-yatūnah. حقپلول ḥakk-pulawul, verb trans. To bid adieu, to say farewell, to take leave, etc. (from A حق, and پلول), which see.

حمايت ḥimā-yat, s.m. (2nd) 2. Assistance, aid, help. Pl. حمايتونه ḥimā-yatūnah. حمايت كول ḥimā-yat kawul, verb trans. To aid, to assist, to help, etc. See p. 392.

خ

خار خوړئ khār-khwarra'ī, s.f. (6th) Broken or uneven ground, ground interspersed with jungle or brushwood, and ravines, good for lying in ambush. S. and Pl. See خوړ

خارښت آخستل khārisht or khārikht ākhistal, verb trans. To catch the itch or scab. See خارښت

خاصي خيل khāṣī khel, s. prop. The name of a small clan amongst the Yūsufzī tribe.

خاك ليوه khāk-lewa'h, s.f. (3rd) The first few days of spring, so called from sheep, etc. eating the young grass, which from its shortness they eat with the earth also, and which causes a disease among them. Pl. ې ey.

خبره khabara'h, s.f. (3rd) 3. Prediction, prophesy. Pl. ې ey. See p. 403.

خبره غبرگول khabara'h gh'bargawul, verb trans. To answer (impertinently), to retort.

خټ khaṭ, s.f. (1st) A shirt, a garment, a vest, a robe, a mantle, etc. Pl. خټې khaṭi.

ختل khatal, verb intrans. 2. To go up (as from Peshāwar to Kābul, or the like). See p. 405.

ختمه khatma'h, s.f. (3rd) A dinner given in the name of a defunct, either on the third or seventh day, the fortieth day, or at the completion of a year, from the decease of the person. Pl. ې ey.

خټكي khaṭṭkaey, s.m. (1st) Ebullition, bubbling, agitation, effervescence. 2. Paroxysm, convulsion, vehemence, rage, wildness, etc. Pl. ي ī. See خوټكي

خټه khuṭṭa'h, s.f. (3rd) 2. A testicle. Pl. ې ey. See خوټه

خرڅيدل khartsedal, verb intrans. To become sold, to sell. خرڅول khartsawul, verb trans. To sell, etc. See p. 410.

خرچله khar-chila'h, s.f. (3rd) Jumping about, cutting capers, caper, kicking out the heels, as a horse, ass, etc. Pl. ې ey. خرچلي وهل khar-chiley wahal, verb trans. To caper about, to cut capers, to kick out with the heels, etc.

خرگي khar-gaey, s.m. (1st) 4. A stand for a lamp, generally made of mud or wood. Pl. ي ī. See p. 412.

خرندل khranddal, verb trans. To importunate, to bore, to pester, to plague, to bother, to worry. Pres. خرندي khranddī; past وُ خرندل wu-khranddal; fut. و به خرندي wu bah khranddī; imp. وُ خرنده wu-khranddah; act. part. خرندونكي khranddūnkaey; past part. خرندلي khranddalaey; verb. n. خرندنه khranddana'h.

خروه kharawa'h, s.f. (1st) The oak tree. Pl. ې ey. دَ خروي داني da kharawey dāney, An acorn. See بلوط

خري kharraey, s.m. (1st) Dross, scum, residue, refuse, scoriæ. 2. Excrement. Pl. ي ī.

خسک *khasak*, s.m. (2nd) A species of bug or wood-louse. Pl. خسکونه *khasak-ūnah*.

خفاف *khaffāf*, s.m. (5th) (W.) A shoemaker, a seller of shoes. Pl. خفافان *khaffāfān*.

خلفه *khulfa'h*, s.f. (3rd) Purslain. Pl. ي *ey*. See خرفه

خوله or خله پرانتل *khula'h* or *khūla'h prā-natal*, verb trans. To open the mouth, to speak, to lift up one's voice, to say, etc. خوله or خله ختل *khula'h* or *khūla'h khatal*, verb intrans. To get rid of one, or one's importunities, to get out of a person's clutches, or become freed from his annoyances or importunites. خوله or خله وتل *khula'h* or *khūla'h watal*, verb intrans. To break out in pimples about the mouth after fever.

T خميازه *khamiyāza'h*, s.f. (3rd) Gaping, yawning, stretching. Pl. ي *ey*. خميازه کول *khamiyāza'h kawul*, verb trans. To gape, to yawn, to stretch.

خميز والي *khamez wālaey*, s.m. (1st) Crookedness, obliquity, bend, curvature. Pl. والي *wālī*.

خوا يخول *khwā yakhawul*, or خوا سړول *khwā sarrawul*, verb trans. To satiate one's rage, revenge, etc., to avenge, to wreak one's anger on. خوا يخيدل *khwā yakhedal* or خوا سړيدل *khwā sarredal*, verb intrans. To become avenged, etc. بده خوا *bada'h khwā*, s.f. (6th) Affront, huff, umbrage, pique, etc. (E.) S. and Pl. (W.) Pl. خواوي *khwāwī*. See خوا

خواجه خدري *khwāja'h khidrī*, s.f. (3rd) The small quantity of bread collected in the evenings by a herdsman, to which he is entitled, after bringing home the village cattle, from each person having cattle in the place. Pl. ئي *a'ī*. The village shepherd gets his food daily according to the number of sheep belonging to each inhabitant, staying in the house of each a certain number of days, according to the number fixed by the Malik or head-man of the town or village. The shepherd is likewise entitled to a certain quantity of grain at each harvest, and to one sheep out of every hundred yearly, by which means he in time obtains a flock of his own. He then retires to his native village, if a stranger, or continues to dwell where he has served. خواجه خدري کول *khwājah khidrī kawul*, verb trans. To collect the bread as already referred to above.

خوباني *khūbāna'ī*, s.f. (6th) Dried apricots. S. and Pl. See کشته.

خوڅ *khūts*, s.m. (5th) Bubbling of water, etc. when boiling. Pl. خوڅهار *khūtsa-hār*. Also خوڅکي *khūts-kaey*, s.m. (1st). Pl. ي *ī*. خوڅيدل *khūtsedal*, verb intrans. To bubble (as water when subjected to heat). خوڅول *khūtsawul*, verb trans. To make to bubble.

خور *khor*, s.m. (2nd) Manner, fashion, mode, way, method. 2. Condition, state. Pl. خورونه *khorūnah*.

خور *khor*, adj. 3. Flourishing, improved, prosperous, etc. خوريدل *khwaredal*, verb intrans. To scatter, to disband. 2. To flourish, to prosper, to improve. خورول *khwarawul*, verb trans. 2. To cause to flourish, to improve. See under خور p. 434.

خورا *khwarā*, adv. of emphasis used with adjectives to denote intensity or emphasis, as خورا زوړ *khwarā zorr*, Very old.

خوړي *khaw-raey*, s.m. (1st) A clay-pit. Pl. ي *ī*.

خوځيدل *khwadzedal*, verb intrans. 2. To be arranged in order of battle, to be put in array. 3. To move, to make a movement (as troops in the field). خوځول *khwadzawul*, verb trans. To array, to move. See p. 437.

خوسي *khosaey*, s.m. (1st) The name of a game in which the players on both sides hold up the left leg with the right hand, and try to upset each other. Pl. ي *ī*. خوسي کول *khosaey kawul*, verb trans. To play at *khosaey*.

بد خوښول *bad khwashawul* or *khwakhawul*, verb trans. To delight in evil, or in doing wrong. نيک خوښول *nek khwashawul* or *khwakhawul*, verb trans. To delight in doing good.

خوګ لن *khūg-lan*, s.m. (2nd) Hot ashes, live coals, cinders. Pl. خوګ لنونه *khūg-lanūnah*.

خوله *khūla'h*, s.f. (3rd) The mouth, mouth, orifice, etc. Pl. ي *ey*. See خله

خونئ *khwanaey*, s.m. (1st) Scattering money, or dried dates, raisins, etc. on marriages or other festive occasions. Pl. ي *ī*.

خوشئ *khūshaey*, s.m. (1st) (W.) A marriage-feast or supper. Pl. ي *ī*.

خونړئ *khūnarraey*, s.m. (2nd) A murderer, a slayer, a homicide, a sanguinary person. Pl. ي *ī*. خونړۍ *khūnarra'ī*, s.f. (6th) A murderess. the feminine of the above. S. and Pl.

خوون *kho-wūn*, s.m. (4th) The olive tree. Pl. خوانه *khwānah*.

خويښ *kh'esh* (W.) or *kh'ekh* (E.) s.m. (5th) (P خويش) A kinsman, a relation or kinsman of one's wife. Pl. خويښان *kh'eshān* or *kh'ekhān*. خويښه *kh'esha'h* or *kh'ekha'h*, s.f. (3rd) A female relation, a kinswoman by marriage. Pl. ي *ey*. خويښي *kh'eshī* or *kh'ekhī*, s.f. (3rd) Relationship by marriage. Pl. ۍ *a'ī*. خويښي كول *kh'ekhī* or *kh'eshī kawul*, verb trans. To contract relationship by marriage. See خپښ

خير *khīr*, adj. 3. Headstrong, obdurate, dogged, stubborn. (Fem.) خيره *khīra'h*. See p. 445.

د

دار درول *dār-darawul*, verb trans. To hang up or suspend a mark for archers to fire at, or men on horseback to tilt at. It is sometimes a stuffed skin, but at times rings of gold, or cups are suspended as prizes. See دري وهل

دار مدار *dār-o-madār* or *dār-madār*, Courtesy, politeness. See p. 450.

دارباز *dār-bāz*, s.m. (5th) A mountebank, a rope-dancer. Pl. دارباز ان *dār-bāzān*. داربازه *dār-bāza'h*, s.f. (3rd) A female mountebank. Pl. ي *ey*. داربازي *dār-bāzī*, s.f. (3rd) The business of a mountebank, rope dancing. Pl. ۍ *a'ī*.

داړه بريوتل *dārra'h prewatal*, verb intrans. To fall upon (as raiders), to attack, داړه كول *dārra'h kawul*, verb trans. To make an irruption or raid. See داړه

P دامن or دامان *dāman* or *dāmān*, s.m. (2nd) The skirt of a garment, the sheet of a sail. Pl. دامنونه or دامانونه *dāmanūnah* or *dāmānūnah*. See p. 451. دامن گير *dāman-gīr*, adj. Affected, impressed, inspired, enkindled, excited, touched. 2. Seizing the skirts, attached to. (Fem.) دامن گيره *dāman-gīra'h*.

P داو *dā'o*, s.m. (2nd) Opportunity, turn, juncture. Pl. داونه *dā'o-ūnah*.

P داي *dā-e*, s.m. (2nd) A layer, a stratum of brick, stone, mud, etc. of a building or wall. Pl. دايونه *dā-e-ūnah*.

دپ *dæp*, adj. Stunned, deafened, rendered deaf (as from noise, etc.); stupefied, overcome, paralyzed, deadened, etc.; (Fem.) دپه *dæpa'h*. دپ كيدل *dæp kedal*, verb intrans. To become stunned or deafened. دپ كول *dæp kawul*, verb trans. To stun, to deafen, to confound. See گنس

دجاجه *dujāja'h*, s.f. (3rd) A hen. Pl. ي *ey*. See دجاج

S دراكړ *drākarr*, s.f. (1st) The felloe of a wheel. Pl. دراكړ *drākarri*.

P درد *durd*, s.m. (2nd) Sediment, lees, dross. Pl. دردونه *durdūnah*.

درغل *dar-ghal*, adj. Deceived, misled, imposed upon, led astray, deluded; wrong, erroneous; (Fem.) درغله *dar-ghala'h*. درغل والئ *dar-ghal-wālaey*, s.m. (1st) Error, mistake, misconception, inaccuracy, blunder, delusion, etc. Pl. ي *ī*. درغل كيدل *dar-ghal kedal*, verb intrans. To become deceived, led astray, drawn into error, misled, to err, to commit error. درغل كول *dar-ghal kawul*, verb trans. To mislead, to lead astray, to make to err or blunder, to delude, to beguile.

درغلل *dar-ghlal*, verb intrans. To come or go to or towards thee or you. This requires some further explanation. راغلل *rā-ghlal*, is used generally to signify To come, to arrive, etc.; but *lit*. means, To come to or towards me or us, whilst درغلل *dar-ghlal* means To come or go to or towards thee or you; and ورغلل *war-ghlal*, To go to or towards him, her, it or them. For explanation of را, در, and ور, see Grammar, p. 46. غلل has no meaning apart from or without those pronominal dative prefixes.

درک *darak*, s.m. (2nd) Entrance, a passage, a place of entrance. 2. Beginning, commencement. Pl. درکونه *darak-ūnah*.

درگه *darga'h*, s.f. (3rd). 2. An impenetrable jungle, a dense forest, a wilderness (particularly of canes, etc.). Pl. ئ *ey*. See p. 458.

درگي *dragaey*, s.m. (1st) Stamping, trampling, trotting, run, trot, etc. Pl. ي *ī*. په درگي تلل *pah dragī t'lal*, verb intrans. To trot, to go at a trot, to run, to double march (as soldiers). درگي کول *dragaey kawul*, verb trans. To make trot or run, to put to the double, etc.

درلل *dar-lal*, verb trans. To have, to hold, to possess, to own, to be master of, to be worth, to have in hand, etc. Pres. درلي *dar-lī*; past ؤ درله *wu-dar-lah*; fut. ؤ به درلي *wu bah dar-lī*; imp. ؤ درله *wu-dar-lah*; act. part. درلونکي *dar-lūnkaey* or درلوني *dar-lūnaey*; past part. درللي *dar-lalaey*; verb. n. درلنه *dar-lana'h*.

درم *darim*, s.m. (6th) (P) The name of a tree. S. and Pl. *daram*, s.m. (2nd) A reed, a cane. Pl. درمونه *daramūnah*.

درمه *darma'h*, s.f. (3rd) A species of cane or reed growing in marshy places. Pl. ئ *ey*.

درنښت *dranæsht* or *dranækht*, s.m. (2nd) Heaviness, weight, gravity, ponderousness. Pl. درنښتونه *dranæsht-ūnah* or *dranækht-ūnah*.

درنگ په درنگ *drang pah drang*, adv. Again and again, every now and again, continually, etc.

دروهول *drohawul*, verb trans. To decoy, to beguile, to deceive. See p. 461.

دروي *darwaey*, s.m. (1st) A species of cane or reed growing in marshy places. Pl. ي *ī*. See درمه

اخوند درويزه *Akhūnd Darweza'h*, s. prop. A celebrated teacher or divine, who lived in the reign of the Mughal Emperor Akbar, and was venerated as a saint by the Afghāns. He was a Tājik by birth, the name applied to inhabitants of Afghānistān, who are not Afghāns, but of Persian descent, or rather descendants of the ancient Irānīāns or Persians. See p. 462, where by an oversight he is called "An Afghān Akhūnd," instead of "An Akhūnd of the Afghāns."

دري ښاخه *drey-shākha'h* or *khākha'h*, s.f. (3rd) A kind of pitchfork with three prongs, made of wood. Pl. ئ *ey*. See ښاخه and چار ښاخه

دريغ کول *daregh kawul*, verb trans. To withhold, to grudge, to hold back, to show dislike or disinclination towards any work, duty, or the like. See دريغ

دريمه *dreyama'h*, s.f. (3rd) Victuals cooked on the third day after the death of a person, and partaken of by all who visit the house of the deceased. Pl. ئ *ey*.

دړه *darra'h*, s.f. (3rd) A piece, a fragment, a portion, a shred, a splinter, etc. Pl. ئ *ey*. دړه کول *darra'h kawul*, verb trans. To split, to reduce to shreds or fragments, to splinter. دړه کيدل *darra'h kedal*, verb intrans. To splinter, to be split or rent into long pieces. دړي دړي *darrey darrey*, adj. Broken to bits, in bits, in shreds, in atoms. دړي دړي کول *darrey darrey kawul*, verb trans. To break to bits, to shiver to atoms, etc. دړي دړي کيدل *darrey darrey kedal*, verb intrans. To become broken, to become shivered to bits. See دړ دړ

دړه *darra'h*, s.f. (3rd) 5. The form, the figure, the body, also a dead body, a corpse, a carcass. Pl. ئ *ey*. دړي وهل *darrey wahal*, verb trans. To tilt at a dead body for practise. It was the custom in ancient times among the Afghāns and other nations, to set up, or hang up a carcass, generally of a cow, sheep, or the like, but at times a corpse was hung up for the same purpose. At these, horsemen tilted with spears, swords, and lances to perfect themselves.

دړۍ *darra'ī*, s.f. (6th) A weight containing about ten pounds. S. and Pl. (HI دهړي)

دست اندازي *dast-andāzī*, s.f. (3rd) 2. Annoyance, molestation. Pl. ئ *a'ī*. See p. 464.

په دست او بازو پوري وتل *pah dast aw bāzū porī*

watal, verb intrans. To cross (a river) by swimming.

دستک *dastak*, s.m. (2nd) 2. A knocker of a door. 3. A small pole. Pl. دستکونه *dastakūnah*. See دستکي and p. 465.

دغه *dagha'h*, s.f. (3rd) (from P. دغا) Deceit, imposture, cheating, fraud. Pl. ي *ey*. دغه باز *dagha'h-bāz*, adj. Deceitful, knavish, fraudulent, treacherous, etc. 2. A knave, a cheat, an impostor, a traitor, a betrayer. (Fem.) دغه بازه *dagha'h-bāza'h*. دغه بازي *dagha'h-bāzī*, s.f. (3rd) Cheating, knavery, imposture, foul play, treason. Pl. ئي *a'ī*.

دل *dal*, s.m. (9th) 2. A small portion, a piece or fragment of anything. S. and Pl. See p. 468.

دلاسه *dilāsa'h*, s.f. (3rd) Corrup. of P. دلاسا which see. Pl. ي *ey*.

دم دَ انا و لا غيري وهل *dam da anā o lā-ghairī wahal*, verb trans. To account others as nothing and self as all, to consider one's self superior to all besides.

دمل *damal*, verb trans. To blow (with the breath, as in breathing or charming, or as the wind), to appear as (the dawn). Pres. دمي *damī*; past وُ دمل *wu damal*; fut. وُ به دمي *wu bah damī*; imp. وُ دمه *wu-damah*; act. part. دمونکَي *damūnkaey*; past part. دملَي *damalaey*; verb. n. دمنه *damana'h*.

دو دله *do-dilah*, adj. Wavering, doubtful, in suspense, irresolute, hesitating, faltering, absent in mind. دو دله کيدل *do-dilah kedal*, verb intrans. To waver, to hesitate, to be irresolute, to falter, to vacillate. دو دله کول *do-dilah kawul*, verb trans. To cause another to hesitate, falter, etc., to make irresolute or undetermined.

دو لړه or لړَ or دو لاړه or لاړَ *do-larrah* or *larra*, or *do-lārrah* or *lārra*, adj. Two-stringed, double.

دورمه *dūrma'h*, s.f. (3rd) A species of reed or cane from which mats are made, a cane growing in marshy ground. Pl. ي *ey*. See درمه

S دوړ *daurr*, s.m. (2nd) Attack, assault, incursion, run, military expedition. Pl. دوړونه *daurrūnah*. دوړ کول *daurr kawul*, verb trans. To attack, to assault, to make an incursion or expedition.

دوهان *do-hān* (corrup. of S. دهوان). See دوهي

دهاړه *dhārra'h*, s.f. (3rd) An attack made on a village by day or night, with violence, a raid, foray, etc. 2. A gang of robbers, raiders, or forayers. Pl. ي *ey*. See داړه, داړ, and هپه

P ديدوان *dīd-wān*, s.m. (2nd) The sight of a gun or matchlock. Pl. ديدوانونه *dīd-wānūnah*. 2. s.m. (5th) A place for looking out, a person on the look out, a watch, an observer. 3. A seer. Pl. ديدوانان *dīd-wānān*. See زري

ديراوت *derā-wat*, s. prop. The name of a district in the Kandahār country.

P ديگر *dīgar*, adj. The time of afternoon prayers. See نماز ديگر.

ډ

دَ زړه ډاډ *da z'rrah ddādd* (*lit.* The heart's consolation), Comfort, solace, consolation. See ډاډ

ډار *ddār*, s.m. (2nd) 2. Threat, menace, intimidation. Pl. ډارونه *ddār-ūnah*. ډارول *ddārawul*, verb trans. To threaten, to menace, to intimidate. See p. 483.

ډال غاړَي *ddāl-ghārraey*, s.m. (1st) A sword and buckler man (*lit.* with buckler round the neck or throat). Pl. ي *ī*.

ډډ *ddadd*, s.m. (2nd) The trunk or hollow of a tree. 2. The bass in music. Pl. ډډونه *ddaddūnah*. 3. adj. Empty, hollow (as a tree, etc.); (Fem.) ډډه *ddadda'h*.

ډډ *ddadd* or ډډو *ddaddū*, s.m. (5th) The large tree toad. Pl. ډډان *ddaddān* or ډډوان *ddaddūān*. See چنگښه

ډډه *ddadda'h*, s.f. (3rd) The hollow over the hip-bone, the hip, the side, the hypochondria. Pl. ي *ey*.

ډره *ddara'h*, s.f. (3rd) A shred, a piece, a fragment, a portion, a splinter, etc. Pl. ي *ey*. ډره کول *ddara'h kawul*, verb trans. To split, reduce to shreds or fragments, to splinter. ډره کيدل *ddara'h kedal*, verb intrans. To splinter, to become split or rent, to fall to shreds, etc.

ډغره *ddaghara'h*, s.f. (3rd) 2. Lashing or beating

of waves. دغره وهل *dd<u>agh</u>ara'h wahal*, verb trans. To lash (as waves).

HI دکه *<u>dd</u>aka'h*, s.f. (3rd) The swoop of a falcon, or such like bird of prey. Pl. ي *ey*. په دکه آخستل *pah <u>dd</u>aka'h ā<u>kh</u>istal*, verb trans. To carry off anything by a swoop (as a bird of prey). دکه وهل *<u>dd</u>aka'h wahal*, verb trans. To make a swoop on. 2. To push, to jolt, to jog. See under دکه, p. 486.

د ماښام دودئ *da mā-<u>kh</u>ām, <u>dd</u>odda'ī*, The Pe<u>sh</u>āwarī term for supper. See شومه

دوزي بلل *<u>dd</u>ūzey balal*, verb trans, To boast, to brag, to strut, to swagger. See دوزه

S دولئ *<u>dd</u>ūla'ī*, s.f. (6th) A kind of sedan for females. 2. A sort of palankeen in which the sick and wounded are carried. S. and Pl.

ر

را مه اوسه *rā mah aosah* or را مه گوره *rā mah gorah*, Come quickly, make haste, be sharp, etc.

راتګ *rā-tag*, s.m. (9th) Arrival, advent, return. S. and Pl.

P راستي *rāstī*, s.f. (3rd) Truth, veracity, etc. Pl. ئ *a'ī*. See راست گوي

راشه *rā-<u>sh</u>ah*, imp. of راغلل, Come, come now, draw near.

راقي *rā-ḳī*, s.f. (3rd) Cornelian, a red gem. Pl. ئ *a'ī*.

راميده *rāmedah*, s.m. (6th) Obedience, tameness, calmness, submission. S. and Pl. راميدل *rāmedal*, verb intrans. To grow tame or domestic, to become obedient or submissive. رامول *rāmawul*, verb trans. To tame, to reduce to submission or obedience, to calm, (P رام)

ربيه خيل *rabīah-<u>kh</u>el*, s. prop. The name of an Af<u>gh</u>ān clan, a sept of the Ismā-ǣlzīs, dwelling in Wā<u>gh</u>oz-gærr. S. and Pl.

رټ *ra<u>tt</u>*, adj. Open, expanded, uncovered, unloosed, ample, extensive, capacious, etc.; (Fem.) رټه *ra<u>tt</u>a'h*. See under ارت p. 18.

رچه *ri<u>ch</u>a'h*, s.f. (3rd) A fragment, a shred, a bit, an atom, etc. Pl. ي *ey*.

P رخنه *ra<u>kh</u>na'h*, s.f. (3rd) A gap, a crevice. 2. Means of entry. 3. Opening, occasion, opportunity, crisis, turn, course, etc. Pl. ي *ey*.

رډ *ra<u>dd</u>*, adj. Open, expanded, dilated, ajar, wide open; amazed, struck, electrified, stunned, confounded, petrified, flabbergasted, struck all of a heap. 2. An animal that stands stock still (as a donkey, etc.); (Fem.) رډه *ra<u>dd</u>a'h*, رډيدل *ra<u>dd</u>edal*, verb intrans. To open, to expand, to dilate. 2. To be struck, electrified, amazed, stunned, flabbergasted. رډول *ra<u>dd</u>-awul*, verb trans. To open, to expand, to dilate. 2. To stun, to amaze, to electrify, to petrify.

رسا ليندي *rasā līndaey*, s.m. (1st) An archer, a bowman. Pl. ي *ī*.

رسئ *rasa'ī*, s.f. (6th) A cable, a hawser, rope. S. and Pl. دَ ميزرو رسئ *da mai-zaro rasa'ī*, Rope or cord made from the *maizarey* tree. See ميزري and p. 505.

رشمه *ra<u>sh</u>ma'h*, s.f. (3rd) Small rope made from *pa<u>sh</u>m* or camel's hair or wool, but less in thickness than رسئ Pl. ي *ey*.

رغدي *ra<u>gh</u>daey*, adj. Pure, simple, true, unadulterated, unmixed, genuine, etc. (Fem.) رغدئ *ra<u>gh</u>da'ī*. رغد والي *ra<u>gh</u>d-wālaey*, s.m. (1st) Purity, clearness, simpleness, reality. Pl. والي *wālī*.

رمنډ *raman<u>dd</u>*, adj. Naked, nude, uncovered, bare, stripped, undressed; (Fem.) رمنډه *raman<u>dd</u>a'h*. See برمنډ

رواش *rawā<u>sh</u>* or *riwā<u>sh</u>*, s.m. (6th) The rhubarb plant. S. and Pl. See شوکري

رودنګ *ro-dang*, s.m. (6th) The name of a vegetable dye of a red or brick color (Rubia manjith. *Roxb.*). S. and Pl. See لورم

روي داري *rū'e-dārī*, s.f. (3rd) 2. Flattery, complaisance, compliment. 3. Regard, countenance, protection. Pl. ئ *a'ī*. See p. 521.

ريچه *rī<u>ch</u>a'h*, s.f. (3rd) A tick, a nit, the egg of a louse. 2. A fragment, a filing, an atom, a bit. Pl. ي *ey*. ريچي ريچي *rī<u>ch</u>ey-rī<u>ch</u>ey*, adj. In bits, in atoms, in fragments. ريچي ريچي کول *rī<u>ch</u>ey-rī<u>ch</u>ey kawul*, verb trans. To reduce to fragments, to break to bits. See خشيرل and رچه

ريد كول *red kawul*, verb trans. To sprout, to germinate, to pullulate, to bud, to open.

ريل *ra-yal*, verb trans. To bray (as an ass). For conjugation see under ريا p. 522.

ړ

ړت ږيرئ *rrat jzīraey* or ړتي ږيرئ *rrataey jzīraey*, s.m. (1st) A coward, a dastard, a poltroon, a milksop. Pl. ي *ī*. See ږيري

ړنده مږه *rranda'h majza'h*, s.f. (3rd) The mole (*lit.* A blind rat). Pl. ۍ *ey*. See مږه

ز

زار و نزار *zār-o-nizār*, adj. Emaciated, weak, thin, etc.; (Fem.) زار و نزاره *zār-o-nizāra'h*.

زامي زني كړپيدل *zāmey zaney krrapedal*, verb intrans. To chatter, as the teeth through excessive fear, or from cold. See زنه

زده كول *z'dah kawul*, verb trans. 2. To get up, to acquire (as knowledge, or the contents of a book, task, etc.). زده كه *z'dah kah*, imp. of the above, Know! mind! recollect!

زدويل *z'do-yal*, verb trans. 2. To chafe. 3. To shape, etc. See p. 532 for other significations.

زر تر زرَ or زره *zar tar zara* or *zarah*, adv. Very quick, quickly, instantaneously.

زړ خوږي *zarr-khūjzī*, s.f. (3rd) (W.) The name of a sickness in which the afflicted person longs after meat, clarified butter, or any greasy food. Pl. ۍ *a'ī*.

زړه خسته *z'rrah khastah* or خسته زړه *khastah z'rrah*, adj. Afflicted in mind, sorrowful, woebegone, unhappy, etc.

زږوالئ *zijz-wālaey*, s.m. (1st) (W.) Roughness, rigidity, stiffness, sternness, harshness, etc. Pl. والي *wālī*.

زلمئ توب *zalmaey-tob*, s.m. (2nd) Youth, juvenescence, the state of youth. 2. Dandyism, foppery, etc. Pl. توبونه *tobūnah*.

زموخ والئ *z'mokh-wālaey*, s.m. (1st) Astringency, dryness (to the taste). Pl. والي *wālī*.

زنبک *zunbak*, s.m. (5th) 2. A peaked beard. 3. A mole with hair on it. 4. A flower, worked or made, on a dress. S. and Pl.

P زور *zor*, s.m. (2nd) 2. Energy, spirit, animation. Pl. زورونه *zor-ūnah*. زور آور *zor-āwar*, adj. Energetic, spirited, animated. 2. Populous (as a town or village). (Fem.) زور آوره *zor-āwara'h*.

په زوري سره روانيدل *pah zorī sarah rawānedal*, verb intrans. To set out in great force or numbers (as an army).

زوړئ *zawarraey*, s.m. (1st) A steep place, the face of a hill or ascent. Pl. ي *ī*. See زور

زوږ *zwajz*, adj. Lost, wanting, missing, mislaid. 2. Distracted, perturbed; (Fem.) زوږه *zwajza'h*, زوږ كيدل *zwajz kedal*, verb intrans. To become lost or mislaid, to become or grow distracted. زوږ كول *zwajz kawul*, verb trans. To lose, to mislay. 2. To distract, to disturb.

زوګ *zwag*, adj. (E.) Same as preceding word, both of which are chiefly used by the Eastern Afghāns, زوږ by the Khattaks, and زوګ by the Tīrāhīs and Banghashīs; (Fem.) زوګه *zwaga'h*. زوګ كيدل *zwag kedal*, verb intrans. زوګ كول *zwag kawul*, verb trans.

زوي مړيَ *zo-e-marrīa*, Oh unfortunate! Poor fellow! Poor creature! Pl. زوي مړيو *zo-e-marrīo*, Poor creatures! See زوي

زوي والئ *zo-e-wālaey*, s.m. (1st) Sonship, filiation, the character of a son. Pl. والي *wālī*; also زوي ګلوي *zo-e-galwī*, s.f. (3rd). Pl. ۍ *a'ī*.

زهر خنډئ *zahr-khanddaey*, s.m. (1st) A week of dark cold weather, just before the vernal equinox, such as cold easterly winds and frosty weather in England in the spring. Pl. ي *ī*. See ژمي

زيرئ *zeraey*, s.m. (1st) A gossamer. Pl. ي *ī*. See وو وري

زيړۍ *z'yarra'ī*, s.f. (6th) Ignominy, infamy, dishonor, disgrace, disrepute. S. and Pl.

زيړۍ كول *z'yarra'ī kawul*, verb trans. To cry out, to sing out, to scream, to cry out before one is hurt.

زيږندي *zejzandaey*, adj. (act. part.) A producer,

bringer forth. 2. Prolific, fecund, productive, generative, procreant; (Fem.) زيږندئي *zejzanda'ī*. See زيږيدل

P زيست *zīst*, s.m. (9th) Life, living, existence. 2. Employment, occupation, etc. S. and Pl.

زيست کول *zīst kawul*, verb trans. To live, to exist. See زست and ژوندون

زيګ والئ *zīg-wālaey*, s.m. (1st) (E.) Roughness, hardness, stiffness, rigidity, sternness. Pl. والي *wālī*. See زږوالئ

زيګګئ *zīgga'ī*, s.f. (6th) The female porcupine or hedge-hog. S. and Pl. See p. 523.

څ

څار و جار *dzār-o-jar*, An expression equivalent to 'thy sins be upon me' of Scripture, sacrifice, propitiatory offering. څار و جار کول *dzār-o-jār kawul*, verb trans. To bid adieu (*lit.*, to say 'thy sacrifice,' etc.), to say 'God bless you,' to bid farewell. See څار

تر سر څارول *tar sar dzārawul*, verb trans. To wave over the head, as a flag or cap, to raise up and cast down, as in wrestling. See سر

په څان *pah dzān* or په څان سره *pah dzān sarah*, In person, personally. څان څاني *dzān-dzānī*, Every one for himself. See p. 555.

په څاي کيدل *pah dzā'e kedal*, verb intrans. To be at rest, to be in tranquillity or repose. په څاي کول *pah dzā'e kawul*, verb trans. To give rest or repose, to tranquillize.

څړول *dzarrawul*, verb trans. To lower, to lower down. See p. 557.

څڅيرل *dzadzeral*, verb trans. To reduce to bits, to break to pieces, etc. See رچه

څژه *dzajza'h*, s.f. (3rd) A slight pain in the stomach, the stomach ache, the first pains of childbirth. Pl. ئ *ey*.

څګر ګوش *dzigar-gosh*, adj. Dearly beloved (person); (Fem.) څګر ګوشه *dzigar-gosha'h*. Also جګر, which see.

څلاند *dzlānd*, adj. (pres. part.) Shining, glittering, refulgent, lucid, sparkling, scintillating; (Fem.) څلانده *dzlānda'h*. See څليدل

څلبلاند *dzal-balānd*, adj. Agitated, distracted, disordered, lost; affected, troubled, chagrined; (Fem.) څلبلانده *dzal-balānda'h*.

څنخول *dzan-khwal*, s.m. (2nd) The pericardium or veil covering the heart. Pl. څنخولونه *dzan-khwalūnah*.

څنل *dzanal*, verb trans. To run through (as with a spear), to pierce through, to perforate, to transpierce, to transfix, to spear, to empale, etc. Pres. څني *dzanī*; past و څانه *wu-dzānah*; fut. و به څني *wu bah dzanī*; imp. و څنه *wu-dzana'h*; act. part. څنونکئ *dzanūnkaey*; past part. څنلئ *dzanalaey*; verb. n. څننه *dzanana'h*.

څواب *dzawāb*, s.m. (2nd) (P. جواب) An answer, a reply, a rejoinder. Pl. څوابونه *dzawābūnah*. See under جواب for various terms and idioms, and substitute څ for ج

څور *dzaur*, s.m. (2nd) (corrup. of A جور) Violence, oppression, tyranny. Pl. څورونه *dzaurūnah*.

څور *dzūr*, adj. Apt, acute, sharp, quick, astute, keen, keen-witted, sagacious, long-headed, intelligent, etc.; (Fem.) څوره *dzūra'h*. څور تيا *dzūr-tī'ā*, s.f. (6th). (E.) S. and Pl.; (W.) Pl. تياوي *tī'āwī*; or څور والئ *dzūr-wālaey*, s.m. (1st) Acuteness, aptitude, quickness, shrewdness, acumen, cleverness, etc. Pl. والي *wālī*.

څوړ *dzwarr*, adj. Low, flat, level with the ground, depressed, below, etc. (Fem.) څوړه *dzwarra'h*; څوړ والئ *dzwarr-wālaey*, s.m. (1st) Lowness, depression, flatness, etc. Pl. والي *wālī*. څوړ لوړ *dzwarr l'warr*, adj. Uneven (as ground), rough, unequal, etc. (Fem.) څوړه لوړه *dzwarra'h l'warra'h*. See لوړ

څوي *dzo-e*, s.m. (5th) A son. Pl. څامن *dzāman*. څوي والئ *dzo-e-wālaey*, s m. (1st) Sonship, the state of being a son, filiation. Pl. والي *wālī*; also څوي ګلوي *dzo-e-galwī*, s.f. (3rd) Pl. ئ *a'ī*. څوي مړئ *dzo-e-marraey* or څو مړئ *dzo-marraey*, A person who has lost a son. (Fem.) څوي مړ *dzo-e-marri* or څو مړ *dzo-marri*. Pl. (M. and F.) ي *ī*. See زوي

څير *dzīr*, s.m. (9th) See p. 561. Also used as

an adjective with شول or کيدل, as ولي موږ ته خير شې *walī mūjz tah dzīr shaey*, Why dost thou gaze or stare thus at me?

ويش خداي دِ په خيرمه شه *wish-khudā-e di pah dzerma'h shah!* The Almighty comfort thee! The Lord have pity on thee! See خيرمه

ژ

ژبه تکول *jzaba'h ttakawul*, verb trans. To smack the lips.

ژبه تلول *jzabah talawul*, verb trans. To loll the tongue, to talk like a fool.

ژر *jzær*, adj. Quick, speedy, nimble, soon, with celerity. ژر تيا *jzær-tī-ā*, s.f. (6th) Speed, celerity, haste, nimbleness, swiftness, etc. (E.) S. and Pl. (W.) Pl. تياوي *tī'āwī*. ژر کول *jzær kawul*, verb trans. To make haste, to be quick, to act with celerity.

ژمي *jzamaey*, s.m. (1st) The winter. See p. 563. The three months of winter are sub-divided thus—The first twenty-five days are called تور ژمي *tor jzamaey*, (*lit.* Black winter), the next forty days are called چله *chila'h*, and the next twenty-five days سپين ژمي *spīn-jzamaey* (*lit.* White winter). This last portion is again sub-divided into four periods, the first twelve days are termed سيهه *sīaha'h*, the six following امني بمني *amanī-bamanī*, the next seven زهر خنډي *zahr khunddaey*, at which time cold winds and frost set in, and the next five days are termed پنج و گنج *panj-o-ganj*, when the buds shoot forth, and spring commences. These periods vary in length at different times.

P ژوليده *jzolīda'h*, adj. Intricate, entangled, difficult. See خپولي

ژوي *jzawaey*, s.m. (1st) A person, an individual, a body, a creature, a mortal, a party, etc. (Fem.) ژو *jzawi*, s.f. (8th) Pl. M. and F. ي *ī*. See وگړي

ژيړه *jz'yarra'h*, s.f. (3rd) Abuse, taunt, reproach, gibe, scoff, aspersion; disgrace, ignominy. Pl. ې *ey*. ژيړي کول *jz'yarrey kawul*, verb trans. To abuse, to taunt, to reproach, to gibe at, to scoff at, to asperse, to disgrace.

س

P ساغري *sāgharī*, s.f. (3rd) The hind quarters of a horse or other animal. Pl. ئې *a'ī*. See p. 572.

ساير *sā-īr*, adj. 2. The remainder, the remaining part or portion, or when applied to persons or people, generally signifies, the crowd, the populace. See p. 574.

سپارلي *spārlī*, s.f. (3rd) 2. Train, cavalcade, retinue. Pl. ئې *a'ī*. See p. 579.

پټ سپاهي *putt sipāh-ī*, s.m. (5th) A soldier armed from head to foot, cap-à-pie. Pl. سپاهيان *sipah-ī-ān*. See p. 574.

سپرمغ *spar-magh*, s.m. (9th) The grease which floats on soup or oil, such as rises to the surface of coffee or cocoa, etc. S. and Pl. بي سپرمغَ شوروا *bey spar-magha shorwā*, or *khorwā*. Poor or thin soup or broth.

سپرول *sparawal*, verb trans. 2. To mount another, to give, or provide another with, a horse. See p. 577.

سپکه *spuka'h*, s.f. (3rd) Nonentity, nothing. 2. A trifle, a small matter, a straw, a rush, a pin, a fig. 3. Trash, stuff, fiddlestick. Pl. ې *ey*; also سپکاوي *spukāwaey*, s.m. (1st). Pl. ي *ī*.

دَ سپلني or سپيلني ملخ *da spalanī* or *spelanī malakh*, s.m. (5th) A grasshopper in contra-distinction to a locust. Pl. ملخان *malakhān*. See p. 934.

سپور والي *spor-wālaey*, s.m. (1st) Dryness, plainness, simplicity, roughness, etc. Pl. والي *wālī*. See سپور

سپيدار *s'pedār*, s.m. (5th) (P. سفيدار) The white poplar, also the wood. Pl. سپيداران *s'pedārān*. See p. 580.

سپيدي دم *sapedey-dam*, s.m. (2nd) The dawn, the time of dawn. Pl. دمونه *damūnah*. See سپيدي داغ

سپيرلم *sper-lam*, s.m. (5th) A fox. Pl. سپيرلمان

sper-lamān. سپيرلمه *sper-lama'h*, s.f. (3rd) A bitch fox. Pl. ي *ey*. See سپلم

سپيغوک *spe-ghok*, s.m. (5th) The name of a small yellow flower. Pl. سپيغوکان *spe-ghokān*.

سپين سره *spīn-sara'h*, s.f. (3rd) An old woman (*lit.*) a white head or grey head. Pl. ي *ey*.

ستاندار *stānadār*, s.m. (2th) A holy family—the descendants of pious men who dwelt among the Afghāns of by-gone times, who, according to the histories and traditions of that people were Suyads, who came and settled among them, and took Afghān wives. Pl. ستانداران *stānadārān*. ستانداره *stānadāra'h*, s.f. (3rd) A female as above. Pl. ي *ey*. See آستاندار and Grammar, Introduction, pp. 9-10.

ستري وتري پريوتل *satrey watrey prewatal*, verb intrans. To fall or lie in heaps, or piled one over another, as fruit on the ground, or the dead and wounded on a battle field, etc. ستري وتري کول *satrey watrey kawul*, verb trans. To lay in heaps or piles, or strew in heaps, etc.

ستړئ *sat-ra'ī*, s.f. (6th) A small stack of corn, a number of sheaves piled up in a field, a cock of hay, etc. S. and Pl. See ستري وتري

ستو کهل *sato-kahl*, adj. Worthless or malicious (person); (Fem.) ستو کهله *sato-kahla'h*. (S खल)

سټ کول *satt kawul*, verb trans. To overthrow, to upset, to knock over or tumble over, to kill, to vanquish, to level (as a wall), to fell (as a tree). سټ ور کول *satt war-kawul*, verb trans. To vanquish, to give a defeat unto. سټ کيدل *satt kedal*, verb intrans. To become overthrown, felled, overturned, killed, knocked over, vanquished, etc.

A سحار *sahār*, s.m. (9th) The early part of the morning from dawn to sunrise. S. and Pl. لوي سحار *lo-e sahār*, s.m. (9th) The dawn of day, day-break. S. and Pl. See سپيدي داغ

سحرگري *sihr-garī*, s.f. (3rd) Enchantment, magic, sorcery, etc. Pl. ئ *a'ī*. See p. 590.

سدوزي *sado-zī*, s.m. (1st) Pl. The name of a tribe of Afghāns, a branch of the Abdālīs, and from which the Afghān sovereigns were chosen, and of whom the unfortunate Shāh Shujāæ

was the last. 2. The name of a clan of the Utmānzī Mandarrs, but in no way connected with the former. See p. 594.

سر *sar*, s.m. (2nd) Anything given to boot in a bargain, boot, profit, advantage. Pl. سرونه *sar-ūnah*. سر ور کول *sar war-kawul*, verb trans. To give to boot. سرڅوري *sar-tsūraey*, s.m. (1st) Good weight, a small quantity added in weighing articles, above the exact weight. Pl. ي *ī*.

سر *sur*, s.m. (5th) The sound produced when swallowing soup, water, or any other liquid greedily. Pl. سرهار *surahār*.

سر پرستي *sar-parastī*, s.f. (3rd) 2. Seeing that all is safe, going round by day or night to see that all is safe. Pl. ئ *a'ī*. سر پرستي کول *sar-parastī kawul*, verb trans. To go round to see that all is safe. 2. To aid, to protect.

سر سره لگيدل *sar sarah lagedal*, verb intrans. To join, to meet (as two hills or mountains), to approach each other, to approximate, to converge. سر سره لگول *sar sarah lagawul*, verb trans. To make peace, to come to terms.

سر تړلي *sar-tarralaey*, s.m. (1st) A man of the pastoral or nomad tribes of Afghāns (*lit.* head-bound), so called from merely wearing a turban without a cap under it. Pl. سر تړلي *sar-tarralī*, Those tribes generally.

سر ټيټي *sar-ttittaey*, s.m. (1st) A hog, a pig. Pl. ي *ī*. سر ټيټ *sar-ttitti*, s.f. (8th) A sow. Pl. ي *ī*. See سرکوزي

سرده *sardah*, s.m. (6th) A melon peculiar to Afghānistān. S. and Pl.

سرغ کول *sargh kawul*, verb trans. To saddle (a horse, etc.) See سرغ

P سرغنه *sar-ghanah*, s.m. (5th) A chief, a great person, one without equal. Pl. سرغنگان *sar-ghanagān*.

سرغونډ *sar-ghūndd*, s.m. (9th) The mumps. S. and Pl.

سرکل *sar-kul*, adj. (W.) Standing on one's head, hanging with the heels in the air and head undermost. See p. 602.

سر کنډئ *sar-kundda'ī*, s.f. (6th) Allowing the hair to grow of its own accord, when naturally short. S. and Pl. سر كنډۍ كول *sar-kunḏḏaey kawul*, verb trans. 2. To crop or cut short the hair of the head. See p. 601-2.

P سرفراز *sur-farāz*, adj. Distinguished, exalted, eminent, promoted. (Fem.) سرفرازه *sar-farāza'h*. سرفراز كول *sar-fārāz kawul*, verb trans. To exalt, to ennoble, to promote, to dignify, to honour.

P سرفرازي *sar-farāzī*, s.f. (3rd) Distinction, exaltation, honour, promotion. Pl. ئي *a'ī*.

A سرور *surūr*, s.m. (2nd) Pleasure, gladness, joy, cheerfulness, delight. Pl. سرورونه *surūrūnah*.

سروځنه *sar-wadzana'h*, s.f. (3rd) The part of the drawers through which the string runs, etc. Pl. ئ *ey*. See سروزنه p. 603.

سر له دي *sarah lah dey*, adv. Although, nevertheless, howbeit, for all that, etc.

سريش *sar-īsh*, s.m. (2nd) The name of a tree (Seris mimosa) Pl. سريشونه *sar-īshūnah* (s सिरीष) See سريخ

سړز *sarrz*, adj. Cold, frigid, cool, chill, frosty. (Fem.) سړزه *sarrza'h*.

يو نيم سړي *yow nīm sarraey*, A few persons (*lit.* one or one and a half).

سږه *sijza'h*, s.f. (3rd) A species of deer, much larger than the antelope of the plains, and inhabiting the hilly parts, at the skirts of hills, and rocky places. It is also called the mountain goat, and considered to be of the same species as the musk-deer. Pl. ئ *ey*. See سرژه or more correctly سرږه and راموسي

سفيدي *s'fedey*, s.f. (3rd) Pl. The dawn. سفيدي داغ *s'fedey dāgh*, The morning's dawn, the time at which the horizon begins to show a little light, the break of day, day-break. سفيدي چاودل *s'fedey chāwdal*, verb trans. To break (as the day), to dawn (from P سفيده).

سكندري *s'kandarī*, s.f. (3rd) Tripping, striking the foot against anything, stumbling, a stumble. Pl. ئ *a'ī*. سكندري خوړل *s'kandarī khwarral*, verb trans. To stumble, to trip.

سكولئ *skwalaey*, s.m. (1st) A sheep-shearer. Pl. ي *ī*.

سل *sal*, s.m. (2nd) A raft made by laying pieces of wood over bundles of canes, and covering the whole with coarse grass or reeds. Used in crossing rivers. Pl. سلونه *salūnah*.

سلائي *salā'ī*, s.m. (5th) 2. A sort of wedge used in lifting a mill-stone. Pl. سلائيگان *salā'ī-gān*. See p. 613.

سلګيدل *sal-gedal*, verb intrans. To force the air with violence through the nostrils (as a horse or a bull when angry), to snort.

سمس *s'mas*, s.f. (1st) (E.) A cave, or cavern. Pl. سمسِ *s'masi*. See سمځ

سَم سيال *sam-sī-āl*, adj. Equal in every way, perfectly equal, on an equality; (Fem.) سمه سياله *sama'h-sī-āla'h*. See سم and سيال

سمور *samūr*, adj. In ear (as grain) but not yet set. (Fem.) سموره *samūra'h*.

سنا *sanā*, s.f. Senna. (E.) S and Pl. (W.) Pl. سناوي *sanāwī*. See سنه مكي

سنجاغ *san-jāgh*, s.m. (2nd) A pin (as used by women). Pl. سنجاغونه *san-jāghūnah*.

سو *so* and په سو *pah so*. See څو

سوباړي *so-bārraey*, s.m. (1st) A wooden instrument with which washermen beat clothes. Pl. ي *ī*. See p. 620.

سوټ *sūtt*, adj. Angry, enraged, vexed. 2. Dry, harsh, withered. 3. Avaricious, ill-natured. 4. Pure, simple, unadulterated; (Fem.) سوټه *sūtta'h*. See سوټ بوټ

سوټه *sūtta'h*, s.f. (3rd) Bread (by the Kākarr Afghāns). Pl. ئ *ey*. See p. 621.

سوران *sūrān*, s.m. (1st) Outcry, noise, clamor, din, uproar, tumult, disturbance, brawl, etc. Pl. سورانونه *sūrānūnah*. سوران كول *sūrān kawul*, verb trans. To make a noise, din, or uproar, to raise a tumult or outcry, to create a disturbance. See سوري

سورلنئ *swar-lanaey*, s.m. (1st) A horseman, a mounted man, a trooper, a horse jockey or breaker. Pl. ي *ī*. 2. Adj. Mounted, riding, on horseback; (Fem.) سورلني *swar-lana'ī*. See سور

سورول *swarawul*, verb trans. 2. To mount another (provide a horse for riding). See p. 622.

سوري سوري *sūrī-sūrī*, adj. Perforated, riddled,

etc. سوري سوري كول sūrī-sūrī kawul, verb trans. To perforate with holes, to riddle.

سوړي كول siw-raey or sor-aey kawul, verb trans. To shadow, to overshadow, to shade, etc.

سولند swaland, adj. Greedy, desirous, inclined, craving, eager, bent on, impetuous, rampant (particularly applied to sensual desires); (Fem.) سولنده swalanda'h.

سولۍ sū-la'ī, s.f. (6th) A cold or high wind with dust. S. and Pl. See p. 627.

سوهانگی so-hāngaey, s.m. (1st) A small file. Pl. ي ī. See سوهان

A P سهيل suhail, s.m. (9th) The south, also the south-west, (the direction of the star Canopus). S. and Pl.

سياه لنگي sī-āh-langī, s.f. (3rd) The scurvy. Pl. ئي a'ī. سياه لنگي نيول or وهل sī-āh langī nī-wal or wahal, verb trans. To become afflicted with scurvy. سياه لنگي نيولیَ or وهلیَ sī-āh-langī nī-walaey or wahalaey, adj. (past part.) Affected with scurvy. (Fem.) سياه لنگي نيولِ or وهلِ sī-āh langī nī-wali or wahali. Pl. (M. and F.) ي ī.

سياهه siyāha'h, s.f. (3rd) Account, list, inventory, written accounts. Pl. ئ ey. (HI. سياها).

سيب s'yab, s.m. (2nd) A roof, a covering, a house, a home, a place of shelter, where one may lay one's head. Pl. سيبونه s'yabūnah.

A P سيلابي sailābī, adj. Relating to a flood or torrent, depending on a flood or torrent (as land). سيلابي زمکه sailābī z'maka'h, s.f. (3rd) Land liable to be flooded, land irrigated only by floods. Pl. ئ ey.

سيلاوه selā-wa'h, s.f. (3rd) A large and long knife, a formidable weapon about two feet long or more, used by the Afghāns. Pl. ئ ey.

سيمک sīmak, s.m. (5th) A plant from which brooms are made (common rush). Pl. سيمکان sīmakān.

ش

شاخ See under نفس

شالشوي shāl-sho-e, s.m. (5th) A fuller, a cleaner of shawls, silks, etc. Pl. شالشويان shāl-sho-e-ān.

شاه باسي shāh-bāsaey, s.m. (1st) (corrup. of P. شاه باشي which see) Applause, praise, laudation. Pl. ي ī. Used chiefly by the people about the city of Peshāwar, who may not be pure Afghāns, who are in the constant habit of vitiating correct words. See p. 641.

شبه shabah, adj. (W.) Heavy, violent, pouring, used with reference to rain, or to volleys of arrows, and the like. See شيبه

پخه شپه pakha'h shpa'h, s.f. (3rd) Midnight. Pl. ئ ey.

شخول shkhol, s.m. (2nd) A kind of wallet, a scrip, or knapsack, made of leather, and carried on the back by a strap. Pl. شخولونه shkholūnah; also شخوليَ shkholaey, s.m. (1st). Pl. ي ī. See جولۍ , څولۍ , بنيَ and گوديَ, and p. 646.

P شرم sharm, s.m. (2nd) 2. Scandal, dishonour, disgrace. 3. Honour. Pl. شرمونه sharmūnah. See p. 649.

شست shast, s.m. (2nd) A ring worn on the thumb of young women with a small mirror or looking-glass inserted, in which they view themselves. 2. (P) The space between the forefinger and thumb, also a thumbstall. Pl. شستونه shastūnah.

شکرانه shukr-āna'h, s.f. (3rd) 2. Money or goods given to Mullās or Faḳīrs in return for any benefit, supposed to have been caused by their prayers, by way of thank-offering. Pl. ئ ey. See p. 655.

P شگون shugūn, s.m. (2nd) Augury, omen, divination. Pl. شگونونه shugūnūnah. See فال

شنالغه shnāl-ghah, s.f. (3rd) Syrup made from the fruit of the mastic tree. Pl. ئ ey. See شني

شنځکۍ shindzaka'ī, s.f. (6th) A pimple, a boil, an abscess. S. and Pl. Also written (W.) شنجکۍ shinjaka'ī.

شنه shna'h, adj. (Fem.) of شين, which see.

شومه shū-ma'h, s.f. (3rd) Evening, the time between sunset and about an hour after, twilight. 2. Supper, the meal taken after sunset. Pl. ئ ey ورمئ شومه or ورنبئ w'rrun-

bana'ī or *w'ṟṟumba'ī shū-ma'h*, Early evening, soon after sunset, twilight. The Peshāwarīs call supper د ما ښام ډوډئ, which see.

شونګړ *shūngarrn*, s.m. (6th) Augury, omen. (P شګون) Pl. شونګړ *shūngærrn*.

A شهاب *shihāb*, s.m. (2nd) A bright or falling star, a meteor, flame. 2. *shahāb*, Milk diluted with water (*fig*. tears). Pl. شهابونه *shihābūnah* or *shahābūnah*.

شیبه *shebah*, adj. Heavy (as rain, volleys of arrows, and the like). See p. 666.

P شیرازي *shīrāzī*, s.f. (3rd) Happiness, felicity, comfort, pleasure, gladness, cheer. Pl. ئ *a'ī* (from P شیراز).

ښ

ښاخله *shākhla'h* or *khākhla'h*, s.f. (3rd) The bough or branch of a tree. Pl. ئ *ey*. ښاخله دار *shākhla'h*, or *khākhla'h dār*, adj. Branchy, having numerous boughs. (Fem.) ښاخله داره *shākhla'h* or *khākhla'h-dāra'h*. See ښاخ

ښاغلَی *shāghalaey* or *khāghalaey*, adj. 2. Excellent, favourite, capital, admirable, etc. 3. Distinguished, honoured, noted, respected, etc. See p. 671.

ښانګئ *shānga'ī* or *khānga'ī*, s.f. (6th) A kind of pitchfork, an instrument used for winnowing corn. S. and Pl. See دري ښاخه and چار ښاخه

ص

صاحب کار *ṣāhib-kār*, s.m. (5th) A steward, a bailiff, a factor, an overseer. Pl. صاحب کاران *ṣāhib-kārān*; also صاف کار *ṣāf-kār*. Pl. صاف کاران *ṣāf-kārān*.

A صرفه *ṣarfa'h*, s.f. (3rd) 3. Neglect, laches, omitting to do anything, failing, passing over, remissness, etc. Pl. ئ *ey*. صرفه کول *ṣarfa'h kawul*, verb trans. 2. To omit, to neglect, to pass over, to be guilty of any neglect, imprudence, or remissness. صرفه نه کول *ṣarfa'h nah kawul*, verb trans. Not to omit to do, not to neglect or pass over, not to let slip an opportunity, not to overlook or disregard.

A صلب *ṣulb*, s.m. (2nd) The loins. 2. Offspring, 3. Race, family. Pl. صلبونه *ṣulb-ūnah*. صلبي *ṣulbī*, adj. Proceeding from the loins, true (as offspring).

ض

ضايفه *ẓā-īfa'h*, s.f. (3rd) A woman, a female in general, as the weaker vessel. (A ضعيف). Pl. ئ *ey*.

P ضميران *ẓamīrān*, s.m. (6th) The herb sweet basil. S. and Pl.

ط

طغ *ṭugh*, s.m. (2nd) (corrup.? A طوغ) An emblem of rank attached to a spear, a standard, a flag. Pl. طغونه *ṭughūnah*. See توغ

A طمع *ṭamaæ*, s.f. (1st) 2. Hope, desire, appetite, cupidity. Pl. طمعِ *ṭamaæi*. See p. 695.

ع

د سر عالم *da sar æā-lam*, s.m. (2nd) The advance of an army, the vanguard. Pl. عالمونه *æā-lamūnah*. See p. 699.

عقل خوځيدلَی *æaḳl khwadzedalaey*, adj. Brainless, foolish, brain-turned, lost; (Fem.) عقل خوځيدلِ *æaḳl khwadzedali*. Pl. (M. and F.) ي *ī*.

A علي الانفراد *æal-ul-infirād*, adj. Separately, exclusively.

غ

غارګه *ghārgah*, s.m. (5th) A crow, the common crow. Pl. غارګان *ghārgān*. Not commonly used. See کارغه and کارګه

غاړه غرونه *ghārrah-gh'rūnah*, Hill and dale, mountain and plain.

غاړه څکول *ghārra'h ts'kawul*, verb trans. To sing, to modulate.

تر غاړه وتل *tar ghārra'h watal*, verb intrans. To fall upon one's neck (embrace). غاړه نيول *ghārra'h nī-wal*, verb trans. To take or catch cold. See غاړه

غبرګولَی *gh'bargolaey*, s.m. (1st) A male twin. Pl. ي *ī*. غبرګولئ *gh'bargola'ī*, s.f. (6th) A female twin. S. and Pl. See غبرګونَي

غراوسمه ghar aw sama'h, Highland and lowland, hill and dale, mountain and plain. See غر

غرړۍ gharjzaey, s.m. (1st) The growl of a dog. Pl. ي ī. غرړيدل gharjzedal, verb intrans. To growl (as a dog). This infinitive is imperfect, and takes its present and future tenses from غرول. غرړول gharjzawul, verb trans. To cause to bark.

A غره ghara'h, adj. (from مغرور) Proud, haughty, arrogant. 2. Cross.

غريبي gharībī, s.f. (3rd) A description of poetry, in which the war-songs of the Afghāns are composed. Pl. ئي a'ī.

P غريز gharīz, s.m. (2nd) Clemency, forbearance. Pl. غريزونه gharīzūnah.

غړيدل gharredal, verb intrans. To go out of the way, to go astray. See p. 724. غړول gharrawul, verb trans. To disobey, to transgress. See p. 724.

غښتلي ghashtalaey or ghakhtalaey, adj. as s.m. (1st) A strong athletic man, a wrestler. Pl. ي ī. See p. 727.

غل غدوي ghal ghadoe, Arrant thieves, freebooters, depredators, robbers, etc. See غل

A غليظ ghalīẓ, adj. (from غلظ) Cruel, severe, stubborn, rude, ragged. 2. Dirty, foul, soiled, etc.; (Fem.) غليظه ghalīẓa'h. غليظ قسم ghalīẓ ḳasam, A binding, severe, or stringent oath.

غنډه ghundda'h, s.f. (3rd) 4. A clod of earth or mud. Pl. ې ey. See p. 734.

غنډول ghunddawul, verb trans. To collect in a heap, to pile up, to amass, to convene, draw together, group, convoke, etc. See غونډول and غونډه

غنه ghana'h, s.f. (3rd) 2. The stout branch of a tree in general, used in making fences, a rail, a pile. Pl. غني ghaney; also used to signify a hedge of thorny branches, a fence round fields or small villages. غني درول ghaney darawul, verb trans. To fence, fix fences, or pales, to rail off, to enclose by railings as above.

غوټه ghūtta'h, s.f. (3rd) A plait or knot of hair worn on the forehead by virgins of the Ghalzī tribe, which is opened on the day of marriage, and not plaited again. Pl. ې ey. See under توتکۍ and غوټه p. 736.

غوړولی ghwarrawulaey, adj. (past part.) Spread (as a carpet), expanded, opened, etc.; (Fem.) غوړولي ghwarrawuli. Pl. (M. and F.) ي ī.

غوزه ghoza'h, s.f. (3rd) A pine cone. Pl. ې ey. See p. 740.

غوزي ghozaey, s.m. (1st) 3. A faggot. Pl. ي ī. See p. 740.

غومبه ghūmba'h, s.f. (3rd) A wen. Pl. ې ey.

غونډه ghūndda'h, s.f. (3rd) A detached hill separated from the higher range, a bluff, a height, a rising ground. 2. A round piece of leaven. 3. A large round stone, a pebble. 4. A clod of earth or mud. Pl. ې ey. غونډول ghūnddawul, verb trans. To collect in a heap, to pile up, to amass, to convene, to draw together, to group, to convoke, etc. See غنډه

غونځيدل ghūndzedal, verb intrans. To creep, to crawl (as a worm, etc.), to move slowly. 2. To move secretly, to move so as to escape detection, or prevent suspicion. 3. To steal in, to move forward unheard and unseen. Pres. غونځيږي ghūndzejzī; past وُ غونځيده wu-ghūndzedah; fut. وُ به غونځيږي wu bah ghūndzejzī; imp. وُ غونځيږه wu-ghūndzejzah; act. part. غونځيدونكی ghūndzedūnkaey; past part. غونځيدلی ghūndzedalaey; verb. n. غونځيدنه ghūndzedana'h.

ف

P فاخته fākhta'h, s.f. (3rd) A ringdove, also the genus. Pl. ې ey. فاختي رنك fākhta-ī rang, Dove colour. See تتوه

فوج د سرعالم fowj da sar ææā-lam, s.m. (2nd) The advance or vanguard of an army. Pl. عالمونه ææā-lamūnah.

ق

A قبل ḳabl, s.m. (2nd) Siege, blockade, obstruction, closing up. Pl. قبلونه ḳablūnah.

T قراولي ḳarāwulī, s.f. (3rd) A picket, a patrol, a guard. Pl. ئي a'ī. قراولي كول ḳarāwulī *kawul*, verb trans. To patrol, to go rounds (as troops), to skirmish.

P قروشج *ḳarūshaj*, s.m. (5th) The male elk. Pl. قروشجان *ḳarūshajān*. قروشجه *ḳarūshaja'h*, s.f. (3rd) The female elk. Pl. ې *ey*.

A قصبه *ḳaṣaba'h*, s.f. (3rd) A small town. Pl. ې *ey*. زوروره قصبه *zor-awara'h ḳaṣaba'h*, A powerful or populous town.

P قلاش *ḳalāsh*, adj. Cunning, crafty, shrewd, malicious. 2. A needy, worthless fellow; (Fem.) قلاشه *ḳalāsha'h*.

A قلب *ḳalb*, adj. Difficult (as a country for military purposes), broken (as ground full of pits and ravines, etc.); (Fem.) قلبه *ḳalba'h*. See کلب

T قلماغ *ḳal-māgh* or قلماق *ḳal-māḳ*, s.m. (5th) A Calmuck Tārtar. Pl. قلماغان *ḳal-māghān* or قلماقان *ḳal-māḳān*. قلماغه *kal-māgha'h* or قلماقه *ḳal-māḳa'h*, s.f. (3rd) A female of the Calmuck tribe. Pl. ې *ey*.

قنديل آخستل *ḳandīl ākhistal*, verb trans. To seize by a swoop (as a hawk his quarry).

تول See under کول next page.

ک

کارګه *kār-gah*, s.m. (5th) A crow, the common crow. Pl. کارګان *kār-gān*. د کارګه or کارغه تکۍ *da kār-gah* or *kār-ghah ttika'ī*, s.f. (6th) The mallow plant. See کارغه

کاړ *kārr*, s.m. (2nd) (W.) A desert, a wilderness, a desolate tract of country. Pl. کاړونه *kārrūnah*.

کاغۍ *kā-gha'ī*, s.f. (6th) A rook, a jackdaw. S. and P. See تاغۍ and تاغه

کافرکی *kā-fir-kaey*, s.m. (1st) A poor, mean, or despicable *kā-fir* or infidel. Pl. ي *ī*. کافرکۍ *kā-fir-ka'ī*, s.f. (6th) A female as above. S. and Pl.

کاني *kānī*, adj. Skilful, clever, a good marksman, etc. (probably from P کان a mine), *i.e.* a 'real' marksman. See تیرانداز

د کاړو ټوپ *da kārrno ttop*, A heap or pile of stones. See کاړي

P کاهبر *kāh-bar*, s.m. (2nd) A packing needle. Pl. کاهبرونه *kāh-barūnah*.

کبۍ *kuba'ī*, s.f, (6th) A bubble. S. and Pl. See کوبۍ

A کتب *katab*, s.m. (2nd) The upright pieces of wood used in making a camel's saddle. Pl. کتبونه *katabūnah*.

کټ *katt*, adj. Large, big, stout, dense, firm. 2. Strong, athletic, muscular; (Fem.) کټه *katta'h*. کټه ګوته *katta'h gūta'h*, The thumb or great toe. See ګوته

P کچکول *kach-kol*, s.m. (2nd) A gourd. Pl. کچکولونه *kach-kol-ūnah*. See p. 782.

کډل *kaddal* or *kuddal*, s.f. (1st) A hut or cabin made of reeds or grass. Pl. کډلِ *kaddali* or *kuddali*; or کډله which see.

کډغالی *kadd-ghālaey* or *kudd-ghālaey*, s.m. (1st) A small hut or cabin made of reeds or grass. 2. A house of grass for fowls, etc. Pl. ي *ī*.

کډهل *kadd-hal*, s.m. (2nd) 2. A pit in general, a ditch where water collects. Pl. کډهلونه *kadd-halūnah*.

کراړه *k'rārra'h*, s.f. (3rd) A kind of *ḳurut* or coagulated milk. Pl. ې *ey*. See قرت or کرت and بګوړه

کراړۍ *kararra'i*, s.f. (6th) A mushroom. S. and Pl.

کرکڼه *karkarrna'h*, s.f. (3rd) Brushwood, low jungle, thicket, and the like. Pl. ې *ey*. See p. 787.

کروړه *kar-warra'h*, s.f. (3rd) A thorny creeper. Pl. ې *ey*.

کروړه *kar-orra'h*, s.f. (3rd) 3. (met.) Cause, occasion, subject, inducement, motive, etc.; ex. پري کروړه شه *prey kar-orra'h shah*, "He was urged to (buy) it, or he was stimulated to do so." See p. 787.

کړس *krras*, s.m. (5th) The sound produced as by volleys of arrows meeting in the air, or the like, crash, crack, snap, etc. Applied to sounds from wood chiefly. Pl. کړسهار *krrasa-hār*. کړسيدل *krrasedal*, verb intrans. To crack, snap, make a crash, etc. کړسول *krras-awul*, verb trans. To crack, clash, snap.

کړم *karram*, adj. Defective, imperfect, deficient, inexpert. 2. Mutilated, docked, tail-cut, etc.;

(Fem.) کرمه *karrama'h.* کرم کول *karram kawul,* verb trans. To mutilate, to dock, to render imperfect or defective. 2. To speak against one, to put a spoke in one's wheel, to render abortive, etc.

کرم *kurram,* s.m. (2nd) A pool of standing water, standing water, a mere. Pl. کرمونه *kurram-ūnah.* See ډنډ

کرنچ *krrunch,* s.m. (5th) The yelping of a dog, a howl. Pl. کرنچهار *krrunchahār*; also کرنچي *krrunchaey,* s.m. (1st) Pl. ي ī; and کرنچوره *krrunchūrah,* s.f. (3rd) Pl. ې *ey.*

کروپ *krrūp,* adj. Bulged, dented; (Fem.) کروپه *krrūpa'h.* کروپيدل *krrūpedal,* verb intrans. To become dented or bulged. کروپول *krrūp-awul,* verb trans. To dent, to bulge.

کروپ والي *krrūp-wālaey,* s.m. (1st) Indentation, dent, hollowness, cavity. Pl. والي *wālī.*

کروه *karrwa'h,* s.f. (3rd) A bullock or buffalo hide stuffed with hay or straw and rolled along before troops to defend the men in advance from the arrows of their opponents. In the battles between the Yūsufzī and Dilazāk Afghāns, in the 15th century, the Utmān-khel (one of the lesser independent Afghān tribes who accompanied the Yūsufzīs when the latter first appeared east of the Khaibar Pass) on one occasion formed the advance, and used these stuffed hides as above mentioned; and it appears they were clever in making them. Pl. ې *ey.*

کسۍ *kisa'ī,* s.f. (6th) An enigma, a riddle. S. and Pl. کسۍ آچول *kisa'ī āchawul,* verb trans. To give a riddle or enigma to another to solve. کسۍ خلاصول *kisa'ī khalāṣawul,* verb trans. To solve or read a riddle.

P کشمکش *kash-ma-kash,* s.m. (2nd) Pulling backwards and forwards; struggle, scuffle, set to, etc. 2. Difficulty, want, distraction, dilemma. Pl. کشمکشونه *kash-ma-kashūnah.* کشمکش کول *kash-ma-kash kawul,* verb trans. To struggle, to scuffle, to have a set to, to fight.

کښته *kshata'h,* adv. (W.) Below, beneath, under. 2. Inferior, lower, under, etc. See (E.) ښکته

P کښتۍ *kishta'ī* (W.) *kikhta'ī* (E.) s.f. (6th) A boat, a bark, a small vessel. S. and Pl. See (P کشتي) بيړۍ.

کښيني *kshenaey,* adj. Lower. Applied by people dwelling on higher elevations or more elevated tracts of country to people dwelling lower; for example, at Kābul, the people of the Peshāwar and neighbouring districts and the people of Ghaznī and Kāndahār are so called. Pl. ي ī. (Fem.) کښينۍ *kshena'ī.* S. and Pl. See پاسني

کلپ *kalp,* adj. Difficult (as a country for military purposes), broken (as ground full of pits, ravines, etc.; (Fem.) کلپه *kalpa'h.* See قلب

کلپي *kalpī,* s.f. (3rd) Falseness, duplicity, dissimulation, evasion, etc. Pl. ۍ *a'ī.* (From A قلب probably).

کلي وهل *kalaey wahal,* verb trans. To plunder or burn a village.

کماله *kumā-la'h,* s.f. (3rd) The name of a description of grass famous for fattening animals, probably the "prangos." Pl. ې *ey.*

کمين توګ *kamīn-tog* or کمينه توګ *kamīnah-tog,* adj. Mean, base, ignoble, vulgar; (Fem.) کمين توګه *kamīn toga'h* or کمينه توګه *kamīna'h toga'h.* See توګه

کمول *kamol,* s.m. (5th) A crane. Pl. کمولان *kamolān.* کموله *kamola'h,* s.f. (3rd) The hen bird. Pl. ې *ey.*

P کنج و کاو *kunj-o-kāw* (from کنج A subterranean excavation, and کاو Hollowing out, digging, etc.) used to signify a cavern, cave, or den.

کندي *kundaey,* s.m. (1st) Traced rope made from hair of animals, but not so thick as واهکي which see. Pl. ي ī.

P کنګاش *kan-gāsh* or *kin-gāsh,* s.m. (6th) Deliberation, counsel, advice. S. and Pl.

کنګس *kangas,* s.m. (6th) The narcissus. S. and Pl. See ګنګس

کوبۍ *kūba'ī,* s.f. (6th) A bubble. S. and Pl. See حباب

کوتان *kotān,* s.m. (5th) A pelican. Pl. کوتانان *kotānān.* See p. 814. کوتانه *kotāna'h,* s.f. (3rd) The hen bird. Pl. ې *ey.*

كوتل *kū-tal*, verb trans. To kill, to slay, to slaughter. See p. 815.

كوټه *kot̲t̲a'h*, s.f. (3rd) A fort, a fortification. Pl. ې *ey*.

كوټه *kwat̲t̲a'h*, s.f. (3rd) A mound, a heap, a pile of earth, stones, etc. 2. The town of S̲h̲āwl in Balūc̲h̲istān is also called *Kwat̲t̲ah* from its being situated on a mound. English writers erroneously call the town Quetta. Pl. ې *ey*.

كوټنۍ *kwat̲t̲ana'ī*, s.f. (6th) A small pile, heap, etc., the diminutive of the preceding. كوټه كول *kwat̲t̲a'h kawul*, verb trans. To heap or pile up, to collect together in a heap, etc. كوټنۍ كول *kwat̲t̲ana'ī kawul*, verb trans. To play a game so called by hopping on one leg on a number of small heaps of earth; or كوټنۍ وهل *kwat̲t̲ana'ī wahal*, verb trans. See خسي

كوچنې *kūc̲h̲ut̲t̲aey*, adj. Small, diminutive, little, minute, tiny, wee, etc.; (Fem.) كوچټې *kūc̲h̲ut̲t̲i*. Pl. (M. and F.) ي *ī*.

كوچيَ *koc̲h̲aey*, s.m. (1st) (P كوچ march, decampment) A nomad, a male of the nomadic or pastoral tribes of the Afg̲h̲āns, not the proper name of a tribe, as some who have written about the Afg̲h̲āns and their country have stated, from not knowing any better. Also used as adj. Nomadic, wandering, etc. Pl. ي *ī*. كوچۍ *ko-c̲h̲a'ī*, s.f. (6th) A female of the nomadic tribes. S. and Pl. كوچيدل *koc̲h̲edal*, verb intrans. To march, to decamp, to set out, to depart.

P كوته مانده *kotah-māndah*, adj. Tired, weary, languid. 2. Broken down (as cattle), infirm, worn out.

كور خوري *kor k̲h̲oraey*, Oh unfortunate! May thy house become desolate (originally كور خور شي, but now used or expressed as above).

د مچۍ كور *da macha'ī kor*, s.m. (2nd) The cell of a honey comb. Pl. كورونه *kor-ūnah*. See كبينه

كور ديده *kor-dīdah*, adj. Foolish, idiotic, simple, soft, a natural, gone in the upper works. (From P.)

P كول *kol*, s.m. (2nd) (for قول) A pond or reservoir. 2. A ford, shallow water, or place where it stagnates. Pl. كولونه *kolūnah*.

كولك *ko-lak*, s.m. (2nd) A hole in the roof of a house to let the smoke out. 2. The brow above the forehead. Pl. كولكونه *ko-lakūnah*.

كويَ *kowaey*, s.m. (1st) The small-pox. Pl. ي *ī*. كويَ نيول *kowaey nī-wal*, verb trans. To catch the small-pox. كوي ټكول *kowī t̲t̲akawul*, verb trans. To mark (as the small-pox) with pock marks.

كهال *kahāl*, adj. Lazy, indolent, slow, slothful, dull, heavy, listless, supine, inert. (Fem.) كهاله *kahāla'h*.

كهل واليَ *kahal-wālaey*, s.m. (1st) Household affairs, care of house and family. 2. Connubial duty. Pl. والي *wālī*; also كهوله *kahola'h*, s.f. (3rd) Pl. ې *ey*.

كهوټ *khot̲t̲*, s.m. (2nd) A fort. Pl. كهوټونه *khot̲t̲ūnah*. See كوټ

كهول *kahol*, s.m. (2nd) 2. Household, wife, family, servant. Pl. كهولونه *kaholūnah*.

ګ

ګاټه *gāt̲t̲a'h* or بده ګاټه *bada'h gāt̲t̲a'h*, s.f. (3rd) A large stone, a boulder. Pl. ې *ey*.

بدي ګاټي *badey gāt̲t̲ey*, s.f. (3rd) Pl. Loose stones and boulders, as found in the dry beds of rivers, ravines, and the passes in Afg̲h̲ānistān.

ګارو *gārū*, s.m. (5th). A boat-builder. Pl. ګاروګان *gārū-gān*.

په ګاندو كښې *pah gāndo ks̲h̲ey* or *kk̲h̲ey*, adv. In future, hereafter, anon, by and by. See په مخ كښې

ګاوۍ *gā-wa'ī*, s.f. (6th) A side lock or curl. S. and Pl. See كجك

ګټ *gutt* or ګوټ *gūtt*, s.m. (2nd) A turn, a bend, as in a range of hills or a river's bank. Pl. ګټونه *gut̲t̲ūnah* or ګوټونه *gūt̲t̲ūnah*. See p. 832.

ګدر *gudar*, s.m. (2nd) 2. A road, a pathway. Pl. ګدرونه *gudarūnah*. See p. 833.

ګډ *gadd*, adj. 2. Launched (as a boat). ګډيدل *gad̲d̲edal*, verb intrans. To become launched. ګډول *gad̲d̲awul*, verb trans. 2. To launch (as a boat, etc.). 3. To attack, to charge. په درياب گد کړل *pah dar-yāb gadd krral*, verb trans. To launch (as a boat or vessel).

گدوه *gadd-wa'h*, s.f. (3rd) An ewer. Pl. ې *ey*.

گذار *guzār*, s.m. (3nd) Attack, onset, assault, cut, charge. 2. Time, period, turn, tour (of duty). Pl. گذارونه *guzār-ūnah*. See p. 835.

P گذر *guzar*, s.m. (2nd) 2. A road, a pathway, a road between two hills, a defile. Pl. گذرونه *guzar-ūnah*.

گربته *gur-bata'h*, s.f. (3rd) A large species of the falcon tribe. Pl. ې *ey*.

گردله *gardala'h*, s.f. (3rd) Snow falling in flakes or eddies, and whirled about by the wind. Pl. ې *ey*.

گردنه *gar-dana'h*, s.f. (3rd) (P گردن) A gorge, a defile. Pl. ې *ey*.

گرميدل *garmedal*, verb intrans. To become or grow hot, warm, etc. گرمول *garmawul*, verb trans. To make hot or warm. See گرم

گرم *gram*, adj. 2. At fault, blameable, censurable, deserving of blame or censure; (Fem.) گرمه *grama'h*. See p. 839.

گريبان *gire-bān*, s.m. (2nd). Pl. گريبانونه *gire-bānūnah*. See گريوان

گربوزی *gurr-būzaey*, s.m. (1st) The space, in length, between the tip of the thumb and the forefinger. Pl. ي *ī*. See لويشت

P گله *gala'h*, s.f. (3rd) A herd, a drove, a flock. 2. A stud of horses. Pl. ې *ey*.

گم گام *gum-gām*, adv. Secretly, underhand, closely, by stealth.

گوال *g'wāl*, s.m. (2nd) A turn or bend in a river or a range of mountains. Pl. گوالونه *g'wālūnah*.

گوتول *gūtawul*, verb trans. To copulate with, to have connection with. See غوول and غيل

گودر *gūdar*, s.m. (2nd) 2. A road, a pathway. Pl. گودرونه *gūdarūnah*. See گدر and گذر

گوسره *gos-rra'h*, s.f. (3rd) A blow with the clenched fist, a punch. Pl. ې *ey*. گوسره وهل *gos-rra'h wahal*, verb trans. To strike with the clenched fist, to punch (HI ?).

گوگ *gog*, s.m. (2nd) A hollow, a cavity, a concavity; a dale, a dell, a glen, a grotto, a cave, a cavern. Pl. گوگونه *gogūnah*.

گوگړ *gūgarr*, adj. Old, aged, weak, worn out (as a man or beast); (Fem.) گوگړه *gūgarra'h*.

گوگن *gogan*, adj. Hollow, concave, cavernous, etc.; (Fem.) گوگنه *gogana'h*. گوگن والی *gogan-wālaey*, s.m. (1st) Hollowness, concavity, etc. Pl. والي *wālī*.

P گولو *gūlū*, The throat, the gullet (rarely used in Pushto). See غاړه

گوندي *gūndī* or گندي *gundī*, adv. Perhaps, by chance, probably; also گوندي چه or گندي or گندِ *gundi*, or *gundī*, or *gūndī chih*. See گندِ and گوندِ

گيدۍ *gedda'ī*, s.f. (6th) 2. A small bundle of sticks. S. and Pl. See p. 855.

گونگوسی *gūngosaey*, s.m. (1st) Muttering, hum, etc. Pl. ي *ī*. See گنگوسي

گهر *guhar*, s.m. (2nd) A pearl, a gem, a jewel. 2. Lustre of a gem or sword. See گوهر

گهڼه *gharrna'h*, s.f. (3rd) Pledge, pawn. 2. Ornaments, jewellery. Pl. ې *ey*. گهڼه کول *gharrna'h kawul*, verb trans. To pawn, to pledge, to mortgage. (S گهنا)

گيلاس *gī-lās*, s.m. (6th) A large description of cherry growing in N. Afghānistān. S. and Pl.

ل

لړ *lārr*, s.m. (2nd) A string (as of beads, pearls, etc.), a thread, a row, a series. Pl. لړونه *lārr-ūnah*. دوه لړه *dwah lārrah*, Two-stringed, double. See لړ and هميل

لاس دورستو تړل *lās da-wrusto tarral* or لاسونه مشکث تړل *lās-ūnah mushk tarral*, verb trans. To bind the hands behind one's back, to pinion (as a criminal).

لاسَ or دَ لاسه *da lāsah* or *lāsa*, adv. Besides, moreover, likewise, too, else, and eke, to boot, withal, with, etc.

لاندی *lāndaey*, s.m. (1st) 2. Any meat salted and dried in the autumn for winter use. Pl. ي *ī*.

لاندي کيدل *lāndey kedal*, verb intrans. To become conquered, to be overcome. 2. To be overtaken. لاندي کول *lāndey kawul*, verb trans. To conquer, to overcome; to overtake, to come up with. See p. 861.

لاه *lāh*, (corrup. of A لا). adv. No, not, not at all, لاه کول *lāh kawul*, verb trans. To give up, to abandon (*lit.* to say no unto).

A لبان *lubān*, s.m. (6th) Frankincense, olibanum, benzoin (resin). S. and P. See لوبان

لتکه *latt-ka'h*, s.f. (3rd) A small snake with a broad head. Pl. ي *ey*. See لندڼ

تر لرغويه *tar larghoeah* or تر لرغويَ *tar larghoea*, adv. Henceforth, for ever, henceforward, from this time, evermore.

دَ ګدڼ لړ *da gada'ī larr*, s.m. (2nd) A strap or handle for a shield. Pl. لړونه *larrūnah*.

لړزاند *larr-zānd*, adj. Trembling, quivering, tremulous; (Fem.) لړزانده *larr-zānda'h*. See لړزيدل

لغت *laghat*, s.m. (2nd) A kick, a blow with the foot. Pl. لغتونه *laghatūnah*. لغت کول *laghat-kawul*, verb trans. To kick, to urge on with the foot (as a horse). See لغته

لغړ پغړ *lagharr-pagharr* or لڅ لغړ *luts-lagharr*, adj. Stark naked, completely nude; (Fem.) لغړه پغړه *lagharra'h-pagharra'h* or لڅه لغړه *lutsa'h-lagharra'h*. See لغړ, p. 870.

لګاو *lagā-o*, s.m. (2nd) Contact, application, adherence, place of attainment, or a place that can be reached or attacked. (S. लग).

لنګتون *lang-tūn*, s.m. (9th) Lying in, bringing forth offspring. S. and Pl. See لنګيدل

لو *law*, s.m. (2nd) The stem or branch of a vine, creeper, or the like. Pl. لوونه *law-ūnah*.

لورم *l'waram*, s.m. (6th) The name of a vegetable dye of a red colour. S. and Pl. See رودنګ

لوړه *lorra'h*, s.f. (3rd) An oath, a vow, swearing. Pl. ي *ey*. لوړه کول *lorra'h kawul*, verb trans. To take oath, to vow, to swear, etc. See ږو

لوړيَ *loarraey*, adj. as s.m. (1st) A holy person, a person by whom one swears. Pl. ي *ī*.; (Fem.) لوړ *loarri*, as s.f. (8th). Pl. ي *ī*.

له بيخَ لوړول *lah bekha l'warrawul*, verb trans. To root up, to take up by the roots.

زاړ لوغزه *zārri l'wagh-za'h*, s.f. (3rd) An animal whose milk has run short, or become less. Pl. ي *ey*. See لوغزه and زاړ

ليزم *le-zam*, adj. Confuted, abashed, ashamed; (Fem.) ليزمه *le-zama'h*. ليزم کيدل *le-zam kedal*, verb intrans. To be confuted, abashed, or ashamed. ليزم کول *le-zam kawul*, verb trans. To confute, to abash, to make ashamed.

ليه *li-yah*, adj. Useless, inutile, unavailing, worthless, good-for-nothing. 2. Unrestrained, unchecked, uncontrolled, unbridled, wanton, 3. (A) Covered, veiled, concealed. 4. High, noble, exalted. 5. adv. Merely, simply, only. ليه کيدل *li-yah kedal*, verb intrans. To grow worthless or useless. 2. To become uncontrolled, wanton, etc., to be let loose, set at large. ليه کول *li-yah kawul*, verb trans. To render worthless, good-for-nothing. 2. To let loose, to set at large, to let one have his own way.

ليه *li-ya'h*, s.f. (3rd) The name of a tree, the tamarisk. Pl. ي *ey*.

م

مات *māt*, adj. 2. Taken, carried by assault, captured. (Fem.) ماته *māta'h*. See p. 893.

ماتيه *māt-ya'h*, s.f. (3rd) Defeat, repulse, discomfiture, rout, overthrow, downfall, wreck. 2. A defeated body of troops. Pl. ي *ey*.

A ماتم *mātam*, s.m. (2nd) Grief, mourning, lament. Pl. ماتمونه *mātamūnah*. ماتم کول *mātam kawul*, verb trans. To mourn, to grieve, to lament. ماتم دار *mātam-dār*, s.m. (5th) A mourner. Pl. داران *dārān*. ماتم داره *mātam-dārah*, s.f. (3rd). Pl. ي *ey*. ماتمي لباس *mātamī libās*, Mourning dress.

مار داړ *mār-dārr*, s.m. (2nd) Conflict, scuffle, conflict and pillage, sack, etc. Pl. مار داړونه *mār-dārrūnah*. مار داړ کول *mār-dārr kawul*, verb trans. To attack and plunder, to pillage, to sack.

ماشه *māsha'h*, s.f. (3rd) The pan of a gun or matchlock where the priming is placed. Pl. ي *ey*. See تشخانه

مالګوانړيَ *mālg-wārrnaey*, s.m. (1st) A man who collects or sells salt. Pl. ي *ī*. See مالګه

مامته *mā-mata'h*, s.f. (3rd) (corrup. of A محوطه) An enclosure, an area, a wall, etc. forming an enclosure. Pl. ې *ey*. See بارې

مانړه *mārrna'h* s.f. (3rd) Complaint, murmur, lamentation. Pl. ې *ey*. See مانه

A مايوس *mā-yūs*, adj. Desperate, hopeless. (Fem.) مايوسه *mā-yūsa'h*. مايوسي *mā-yūsī*, s.f. (3rd) Hopelessness, despair. Pl. ۍ *a'ī*.

مايه *mā-yah*, s.f. (3rd) A cell, the socket of a bone, a small hollow in anything. Pl. ې *ey*. دَ ښني مايه *da shney* or *Khney mā-yah*, One of the sockets of the *os ilium* which receives the bone of the thigh.

متټ کول *matt kawul*, verb trans. 2. To endeavour, to essay, to try hard. See p. 902, and پيل و متټ

متټه *mattah*, adj. Lazy, indolent. Applied to human beings as well as animals. متټه والَي *mattah-wālaey*, s.m. (1st) Laziness, indolence, slothfulness. Pl. والي *wālī*.

مخ *makh*, s.m. (2nd) 3. Honour, glory, celebrity, repute, credit, fame. See p. 906.

په مخ *pah makh* or په مخ کښي *pah makh kshey* or *kKhey*, adv. In future, hereafter, anon, by and by. See ګانده

مرجونړا *mar-jūrrnā*, s.m. (5th) A species of sea bird, probably a species of diver. Pl. مرجونړاګان *mar-jūrrnāgān*. See مرجيونړه

مده *muda'h*, s.f. (3rd) Appointed time, season, period. Pl. ې *ey*. See موده

P مرچه or مورچه *mūrcha'h* or *murcha'h*, s.f. (3d) A battery, a place made or raised to shoot from. Pl. ې *ey*.

مرغ *m'ragh*, s.m. (2nd) 2. Taking omens, or auguring by means of three round stones or pebbles, by throwing them or putting them in a cap, or the like. مرغ نيول *m'ragh nī-wal*, verb trans. To augur by putting the stones in a cap, and marking them. مرغ آچول *m'ragh āchawul*, verb trans. To augur by throwing or pitching the stones.

مزرَي *mazaraey*, s.m. (1st). 2. The dwarf palm, a species of Chamærops. Pl. ي *ī*. See p. 917.

مرړي *marra'ī*, s.f. (6th) Bread. 2. A morsel. S. and Pl. See نمرړي

مقيش دوزي A kind of brocade. See مقيش

مږ *majz* (W.) s.m. (7th) A ram. Pl. مږونه *m'jzūnah*. Sometimes s.m. (2d). See p. 918 and ميږ

مږګوړَي *majz-gorraey*, s.m. (1st) A mouse, a field-mouse. Pl. ي *ī*.

A مسطور *mastūr*, adj. (p. part. of سطر) Written, expressed, aforesaid, specified; (Fem.) مسطوره *mastūra'h*. Peshāwarīs, who are constantly in the habit of corrupting words, write this مستور

A معاملت *mu-æāmalat*, s.m. (2nd) 2. Controversy, brawl, dispute, disagreement. Pl. معاملتونه *mu-æāmalatūnah*. See p. 926.

A معجزه *muæjiza'h*, s.f. (3rd) A miracle. Pl. ې *ey*.

A معصوم *maæ-ṣūm*, s.m. (5th, an infant, a child, an innocent. 2. adj. Simple, innocent, pure. Pl. معصومان *maæ-ṣūmān*. معصومه *maæ-ṣūma'h*, s.f. (3rd) A female infant, etc. Pl. ې *ey*.

A مفصل *mufaṣṣal*, adj. (act. part. II. of فصل) Distinct, detailed, full, ample, etc. 2. adv. Distinctly, fully, in detail; (Fem.) مفصله *mufaṣṣala'h*.

A مقبره *makbara'h*, s.f. (3rd) A burying-place, a tomb, a mausoleum. Pl. ې *ey*.

A مقدس *mukaddas*, adj. (past part. II. of قدس) Consecrated, holy; (Fem.) مقدسه *mukaddasa'h*. بيت المقدس *baitu-l-mukaddas*, Jerusalem.

دَ ملا تړ سړَي *da m'lā tarr sarraey*, A man capable of bearing arms. Pl. ي *ī*.

A ملازمت *mulāzamat*, s.m. (2nd) (inf. III. of لزم) Assiduity, diligence. 2. Service (paying respects to a superior), attendance. Pl. ملازمتونه *mulāzamatūnah*.

مليدل *m'ledal*, verb intrans. To live, to dwell, to remain, to reside, to take up one's abode, to occupy, etc. Pres. ملي *m'lī*; past وُ مليده *wu-m'ledah*; fut. وُ به ملي *wu bah m'lī*; imp. مليده *m'leda'h*; act. part. مليدونکَي *m'ledūnkaey*, or مليدونَي *m'ledūnaey*; past part. مليدلَي *m'ledalaey*; verb. n. مليدنه *m'ledana'h*.

منعه کيدل *manæa'h kedal*, verb intrans. To be forbidden, prohibited, debarred, etc. See منعه

A منفعل *mun-faæil*, adj. (part. act. of فعل) Disturbed, afflicted, affected. 2. Bashful, abashed, ashamed; (Fem.) منفعله *mun-faæila'h*.

منګنی *manganaey*, adj. as s.m. (1st) A term applied to the young of sheep or goats born early in the season. Pl. ي *ī*; (Fem.) as s.f. (6th) منګنۍ *mangana'ī*. S. and Pl. See زاري

P مني *manī*, Egoism, or that sufficiency in himself and independence of other beings, which is peculiar to the Deity.

منړه *marrna'h*, s.f. (3rd) A species of ornament worn round the neck in former times by the Afghān females, consisting of beads in the shape of small apples, hence the word. 2. A bead made of Kāmbay stones, or from the sinews of a camel's feet. Pl. منړي *marrney*, a necklace. See p. 942.

په موږه موږ سره *pah mūjzah mūjz sarah*, Amongst ourselves, between us or ourselves.

موليزي *mo-lezī*, s.m. (1st) Pl. The name of a clan of the Akozī Yūsufzīs. موليزی *mo-lezaey*, S. A male of the above clan. موليزۍ *mo-leza'ī*, s.f. (6th) A female of the above. S. and Pl.

A مهلک *muhlik*, adj. 2. A place of danger. See p. 949.

مهرباش *mihr-bāsh*, adj. Friendly, affectionate, kind, loving; (Fem.) مهرباشه *mihr-bāsha'h*.

A مهم *muhim*, s.m. (2nd) 2. A warlike expedition, a campaign. Pl. مهمونه *muhimūnah*. See p. 949.

P مهماني *mihmānī*, s.f. (3rd) 2. Ministration, accommodation, etc. 3. Supplies, supports, succour. Pl. ۍ *a'ī*.

په دا ميان *pah dā mī'ān* or په دا ميان کښي *pah dā mī'ān kshey* or *kkhey*, adv. Meanwhile, in the mean time, ad interim, etc.

پاسنۍ ميږ *pāsana'ī mejz* (W.) A Kābul sheep. See p. 953.

ميځری *mai-dzaraey*, s.m. (1st) A species of date palm. Pl. ي *ī*. See ميرخري and ميزري

ميلمه *mel-mah*, s.m. (2nd) (E.) A guest, a visitor. Pl. ميلمانه *mel-mānah*. See p. 954.

ن

نار *nār*, s.m. (2nd) A sprout, a shoot. Pl. نارونه *nār-ūnah*.

نا ويسا *nā-wisā*, adj. Unworthy of trust, not to be trusted or relied upon. See p. 968.

نانګه *nānga'h*, s.m. (5th) A species of cherry (small), also a cherry in general, whether wild or otherwise. Pl. نانګان *nāngān*.

نڅۍ *natsa'ī*, s.f. (6th) Yarn, worsted. S. and Pl. See p. 969.

دَ نس خوږ *da nas khūjz*, Flux, diarrhœa, etc. (خوږ a wound, see). See p. 975.

نسکورول *nas-korawul*, verb trans. To unhorse, to dismount. See p. 972.

نسيا *nasī-ā*, s.f. (6th) Credit, trust, tick (E.) S. and Pl. (W.) Pl. نسياوي *nasī-āwī*. See نسيه

نښتر *nashtar* or *nakhtar*, s.m. (5th) 2. The cedar tree and its wood. Pl. نښتر *nashtær* or *nakhtær*. See p. 978.

ځان نښلول *dzān n'shalawul* or *n'khalawul*, verb trans. To entangle one's self in any affair, to embroil one's self, to take to anything, to employ one's self in any difficult matter.

A نعره *naæra'h*, s.f. (3rd) 2. Address, appeal. 3. Exclamation, invocation. Pl. ې *ey*. See p. 980.

A نقلي *nakl-ī*, s.m. (5th) A story-teller, a narrator. Pl. نقليان *nakl-īān*.

P نماز ديګر *namāz-i-dīgar*, The time of afternoon prayers, also the prayers repeated at that time. See نماز

نمرۍ *n'mara'ī*, s.f. (6th) (W.) Clothes, dress, etc. S. and P. See p. 987.

د صحار نمونځ *da ṣahār n'mūndz*, Morning prayer before sunrise, matins. د نما پښين نمونځ *da n'mā-pishīn* or *pikhīn n'mūndz*, The mid-day prayer. د نماز ديګر نمونځ *da n'māz-dīgar n'mūndz*, The prayer before sunset, afternoon prayer. د نما ښام نمونځ *da n'mā-shām* or *n'mā-khām n'mūndz*, Prayer after sunset, early evening prayer. د نما خستن نمونځ *da n'mā-khustan n'mūndz*, The prayer before sleep, repeated about an hour after sunset.

P نمودارې *namūdārī*, s.f. (3rd) Display, show, parade. Pl. ئ *a'ī*. نمودارې کول *namūdārī kawul*, verb trans. To display, exhibit, parade in battle array (applied chiefly to troops).

S نیاو *nyāw*, s.f. (1st) Justice, equity, etc. Pl. (E.) نیاوِ *nyāwi*. This word is used in the same way as لښکر sometimes s.m. (2nd), and sometimes as s.f. (1st). See p. 997.

نیت ترل *nī-yat tarral*, verb trans. To purpose, intend, determine, will, etc. See نیت کول

نیو *n'yaw* or نیاو *n'yāw*, s.m. (2nd) Stay, pause, waiting a little for a person to overtake another. Pl. نیوونه *n'yaw-ūnah* or نیاوونه *n'yāw-ūnah*.

S نیولئ *nī-wala'ī*, s.f. (6th) A weasel, a ferret, a mongoose. S. and Pl.

و

A واقعه *wākiœa'h*, s.f. (3rd) A vision in sleep, a dream. Pl. ئ *ey*. See p. 1007.

ودان *wadān*, adj. 2. Saved, preserved, flourishing; (Fem.) ودانه *wadāna'h*.

ورځ په ورځ or ورځي *wradz pah wradzi* or *wradzī*, adv. Daily, constantly. See ورځ

ورژلي *warjzalaey*, adj. (past part. of ورژل) Chopped, minced, cut up, hacked, lacerated, etc. 2. Ornamented by cross cuts or marks, as trinkets; (Fem.) ورژلِ *warjzali*. Pl. (M. and F.) ي *ī*.

له ورستو *lah w'rusto*, From behind, in the rear, in the wake of. 2. Afterwards, subsequently, at a subsequent or later period, thereafter, etc. See ورستو

ورسک *war-sak*, s.m. (2nd) The spur or ridge of a mountain, a cape, a hummock, an elevation, a peak, a crag. 2. An angle, a bend, etc., in a mountain. Pl. ورسکونه *war-sakūnah*.

ورسکئ *war-sakaey*, s.m. (1st) The diminutive of the above—a little spur or ridge, a small elevation or peak. 2. A small bend or angle in a mountain. Pl. ي *ī*.

ورگ *warg*, adj. 2. A three-year old (ram or goat); (Fem.) ورگه *warga'h*, A three-year old (ewe or she-goat). Sheep and goats above this age are termed خر ورگ *khar-warg* and خر ورگه *khar-warga'h*. See پسرلئ and دوشرل

وسله *wasla'h*, s.f. (3rd) A set or stand of arms. Pl. ئ *ey*. See p. 1033.

وظیفه *wazīfa'h*, s.f. (3rd) A certain portion of the Ḳur'ān appointed to be read daily. Pl. ئ *ey*. See p. 1035.

ولگه *wulga'h*, s.f. (3rd) Appetite, desire. Pl. ئ *ey*. See لیوال

ولمه *wul-ma'h*, s.f. (3rd) Food, victuals, daily food, eatables. This word is used by the Kakarr tribe more particularly. Pl. ئ *ey*.

ولمه *wul-mah*, s.m. (4th) A guest, a visitor. Pl. ولمانه *wul-mānah*. ولمنه *wul-mana'h*, s.f. (3rd) A female guest. Pl. ئ *ey*. See میلمه

ونکه *wanaka'h*, s.f. (3rd) A species of rhubarb (not edible) from which the medicinal root is obtained, Pl. ئ *ey*. See ببئ

ونه *wana'h*, s.f. (3rd) (W.) The mastic tree. د ونې ژاوله *da waney jzāwla'h*, s.f. (3rd) Gum mastic. Pl. ئ *ey*. د ونې تیل *da waney tel*, s.m. (6th) Oil made from the fruit of the mastic tree. S. and Pl.

پسته وور *pas-tah wor*, s.m. (2nd) Light or drizzling rain. Pl. پسته وورونه *pas-tah worūnah*. See باران

ویره *wera'h*, s.f. (3rd) Awe through fear or respect. Pl. ئ *ey*. ویریدل *weredal*, verb intrans. To be filled with awe through fear or respect. ویرول *werawul*, verb trans. To awe, to fill with awe. See 1045.

ویش خداې دِ په زیرمه or خیرمه شه *wīsh, khudāe di pah zerma'h* or *dzerma'h shah*. God bless thee! God be good to thee! God be merciful to thee! The Lord comfort thee!

هاې هوې کول *hā-e hū-e kawul*, verb trans. 3. To call out "all's well" when on sentry (as a soldier or watchman), to patrol at night. 4. To shout or cheer when making an attack. See p. 1053.

هد ماتول *hadd mātawul*, verb trans. 2. To cause

enmity between two parties (*lit.* to break the bone of contention), either by killing a person of a tribe, or carrying off a damsel, or property of a member of another tribe, and causing a feud. See p, 1057.

هر هر څوک *har har tsok*, Every one soever. See څوک

A هكذا *hakazā*, adv. In this manner, thus. See هسي

هلواك *halwāk*, adj, Amazed, completely astonished, at a loss what to do; (Fem.) هلواكه *hal-wāka'h.*

هميل *hamel*, s.m. (2nd) A necklace, an ornament for the neck. Pl. هميلونه *hamelūnah.*

هوسا كيدل *hosā kedal*, verb intrans. To take rest. هوسا كول *hosā kawul*, verb trans. To give rest to.

هو هو *hū-hū*, Calling out, as soldiers when on sentry, such as "all's well," etc. See هاي هوي كول

هيزه *hejza'h*, s.f. (3rd) A bubo. Pl. ي *ey.* See يزه

A هيئت *hai'at*, s.m. (2nd) Outward form or appearance. 2. Astronomy. Pl. هيئتونه *hai'atūnah.* په هيئت عظيم *pah hai'at-i-a'zīm*, In great force, making a great figure, massed together, as troops.

ي

A يحيي *yahyā*, s. prop. The name by which St. John the Baptist is known among Muhammadans; also a common name among Afghāns. The Evangelist John is called يوحنا *yohanā.*

يرغ *y'ragh*, s.m. (2nd) A weapon, arms, apparatus, etc. Pl. يرغونه *y'raghūnah.* See ايرغ (From T يراق ?)

يزه *yajza'h*, s.f. (3rd) A bubo, a tumour. Pl. ي *ey.* See هيزه

يک لخت *yek-lakht*, Of one accord. See p. 1086.

A يمن *yumn*, s.m. (2nd) Felicity, prosperity, good luck. Pl. يمنونه *yumnūnah.*

THE END.

The following New Editions of the Author's Works have just been issued.

I.

In One Volume, Imperial 8vo., Cloth Boards. Price £2 2s.

GULSHAN-I-ROH:

BEING SELECTIONS, PROSE AND POETICAL, IN

THE PUS'HTO, OR AFGHĀN LANGUAGE.

SECOND EDITION.

II.

In One Volume, Imperial 8vo., Cloth Boards. Price £1 1s.

A GRAMMAR OF THE PUK'HTO, PUS'HTO,

OR

LANGUAGE OF THE AFGHĀNS.

THIRD EDITION.

III.

New and Cheaper Edition. In One Volume, Square Crown 8vo., Cloth. Price 14s.

SELECTIONS

FROM

THE POETRY OF THE AFGHĀNS,

FROM THE SIXTEENTH TO THE NINETEENTH CENTURY,

TRANSLATED FROM THE ORIGINAL PUS'HTO,

WITH MEMOIRS OF THE DIFFERENT AUTHORS.

IV.

New and Cheaper Edition. In One Volume, Imperial 16mo., Cloth Boards. Price 5s.

A THESAURUS

OF

ENGLISH AND HINDŪSTĀNĪ TECHNICAL TERMS

USED IN BUILDING AND OTHER USEFUL ARTS; AND

SCIENTIFIC MANUAL

OF WORDS AND PHRASES IN THE HIGHER BRANCHES OF KNOWLEDGE.

From the Secretary to the Civil and Military Examination Committee in the Native Languages, Bombay.—"The undersigned is directed to report that the work is doubtless very useful."—*Bombay Castle, 27th July*, 1859.

ATHENÆUM, *February 11th*, 1860.—"Captain Raverty is already well known in the literary world, by his excellent Pus'hto works. He has here done for one department of Hindūstānī—that is, for technical phraseology—what Mr. Fallon has done for law terms. We have read enough of it to testify that it is a very useful contribution in aid of the Hindūstānī student."

From M. GARÇIN DE TASSY, *Professor of Oriental Languages in the Institute de Paris.*—"The most valuable and useful 'Thesaurus of English and Hindūstānī Technical Terms.' . . . It was forsooth a desideratum for Hindūstānī studies. . . . I shall not fail to speak of it in due time."—*Paris, 26th September*, 1859.

From Lieut. (now Major) J. T. VERTUE, *Madras Engineers, District Engineer, Vizagapatam.*—"I shall, with pleasure, make known the work, which, without flattery is, I may truly say, both very valuable and much required."—*Camp, Waltair, 30th August*, 1859.

From J. NEVILLE WARREN, Esq., *Agent Scinde Railway Company.*—"Your little book is found to be so very useful, that I should be obliged if you would direct 20 more copies to be sent to me."—*Kurrachee, 19th November*, 1859.

From P. P. GORDON, Esq., *Agent Eastern Bengal Railway Company.*—"I believe the work will be found a very useful one."—*Calcutta, 21st January*, 1860.

V.

8vo., Gratis.

THE GOSPEL FOR THE AFGHĀNS,

Being a short critical examination of a portion of a version in the Afghān Language.

LONDON: WILLIAMS AND NORGATE,

HENRIETTA STREET, COVENT GARDEN, AND 20, SOUTH FREDERICK STREET, EDINBURGH.

CALCUTTA: W. NEWMAN AND CO.